Platter's
SOUTH AFRICAN
WINES
2012

THE GUIDE TO CELLARS, VINEYARDS

WINEMAKERS, RESTAURANTS

AND ACCOMMODATION

Innovation ☀ Focus

John Platter SA Wine Guide (Pty) Ltd
www.wineonaplatter.com

PUBLISHER
Andrew McDowall

EDITOR
Philip van Zyl

ASSOCIATE EDITORS
Jos Baker, Tim James, Cathy van Zyl

TASTERS
Michael Fridjhon, Angela Lloyd; Master of Wine Cathy van Zyl; Cape Wine Masters Winnie Bowman, Greg de Bruyn, Tim James, Christine Rudman, Meryl Weaver; David Biggs, Christian Eedes, Fiona McDonald, Ingrid Motteux, Jörg Pfützner, James Pietersen & Dave Swingler.

CONTRIBUTORS
Bob Chappell, Christian Eedes, Tony Jackman, Lynne Kloot, Cathy Marston, Lindsaye McGregor, Joanne Gibson & Wendy Toerien

COORDINATORS
Christina Harvett (wine), Ina Smith (tasting), Ina de Villiers (information)

DATABASE, WEB & GPS
Sean de Kock, Alex Maughan (Digital Energy Media)

MAPS & TYPESETTING
Gawie du Toit, Ryk Taljaard, Heinrich Schloms (VinPro)

PHOTOGRAPHY
Dennis Gordon

ADVERTISING
Linda Ransome · T +27 (0)82-412-3048 · lindar@wineonaplatter.com

SALES
Linda Butler · T +27 (0)83-462-8172 · lindab@wineonaplatter.com

© John Platter SA Wine Guide (Pty) Ltd 2012
PO Box 1466 Hermanus 7200
Tel: +27 (0)28-316-3210/+27 (0)82-490-1820 · Fax: +27 (0)86-513-3908
andrew@wineonaplatter.com

🌐 www.wineonaplatter.com

❑ Facebook: http://www.facebook.com/platterswineguide

❑ Twitter: @wineonaplatter

ISBN 978-0-9870046-0-4

CONTENTS

PHOTO GALLERY:

Our theme this year is Thinking Out Of The Box, and in the full-colour section we feature individuals and organisations who innovatively employ ideas, techniques and technologies to make our experience of wine richer and more rewarding. Whether in the arenas of viticulture, winemaking, packaging, wine tourism, social media, conservation, sustainability, wine-and-food matching or creating new wine styles, we showcase the best of unconventional thinking and thereby reflect some of the dynamism of South African wine today.

FOREWORD

Recently, I sat at a dinner with friends in South Africa and enjoyed a glass of local chardonnay, a profound wine if there ever was one, with deep fruit, silky and rich but not heavy, and with great length on the palate. At the same time, a woman across from me was enjoying the wine and saying that she preferred unoaked chardonnays. I asked her if she thought this wine had been in oak or not, and she said not. As it happened, I knew this was the top-of-the line chardonnay of a top producer and spends a year in new oak, and yet I understood what she was saying. The fruit was so rich it had absorbed the oak like a sponge and transformed it into the complex aromas we were both enjoying. This wine was but one of many luscious South African chardonnays I have tasted recently that can go head-to-head with the best in the world.

From my first visit to South Africa in 1990, through to our investment in land with subsequent planting starting in 1998, followed by my regular three-times-a-year Cape visits to work with our Vilafonté wines, I have watched South African wines, wineries and vineyards fulfil the promise I believed they had on that first visit.

Having watched the Napa Valley transform over three decades from producing wines considered 'an amusing curiosity' internationally, to those considered 'world class', I felt from the beginning that South Africa could do the same. With extraordinarily ancient and diverse soils, a coastal climate, and the varied topography formed by coastal hills, inland valleys and the Cape mountains, coupled with the Cape's visual beauty, sophistication, history and diversity, it seemed inevitable to me that South African wines would be 'discovered', as visitors from around the world began to flock to the Cape.

Given South Africa's rich 350-year winemaking history, its wines were set to blossom forth, like the grasses and flowers after a desert rain, after Apartheid's end in 1994. From the outside, it seems that changes have come fast and furiously: new wineries, new appellations, new vineyard sites, new vine plantings, new industry structures and new varieties. Hordes of young South African winemakers from all backgrounds have done harvests in New Zealand, California, Burgundy and Australia. They have experienced the wine world, brought home knowledge and insights, mixed these with local conditions, and produced astounding wines.

But all is not glorious when a wine industry grows up. New locations, new styles, new varieties and new techniques are tested, and some do not work. Critics criticise. Some wineries succeed and grow. Others weaken and fail. Gold medals are won and lost. Global wine competition is fierce. In what other category are there so many choices for the consumer? Global economics have an impact, for better or for worse. Needed research may be funded, or may not. The way forward is choppy.

But it is also forward. Statistics can measure the progress locally and internationally, but I know the progress from tasting the wines. South Africa is one of few countries in the world with the variety of conditions to allow a broad diversity of fine wine varieties to be grown with great success. And they are. More fine sparkling wines are emerging. Great old vineyards that produce bright and lively chenin blancs have been protected. Refreshing, juicy sauvignon blancs are numerous. Of the reds, the blends have arrived: Bordeaux-style blends, Cape blends (with pinotage) and Rhône-style blends. Top-quality plant material has gone into the ground, and leafroll virus is being controlled. More solid pinot noirs are appearing - it took Sonoma three decades to excel with pinot noir.

With the Napa Valley and Sonoma as my reference points, I know there is much more to accomplish when it comes to South African wines. They will grow more consistent. They will become more profound. Technical issues will disappear. They will continue to become more diverse. They will gain greater acclaim (look at the number of four- and five-star wines in the Platter guides, for example). Wait another 15 years. 'Yesterday' was promising; 'today' is rich indeed; 'tomorrow' can be spectacular, as long as quality is pursued and is the foundation of the South African wine industry.

In 2001, as the Nederburg Auction's guest speaker, I listed what I hoped to see for the future. Much of this has come to pass. Now I will add one hope to the list: that the South African wine industry develops strong organisations and leaders, to lobby the South African government for support and promotion. Wines of South Africa (WOSA) is promoting exports, but I see no comparable organisations developing local marketing and interfacing with government. The wine industry is a major employer, a major exporter and a major taxpayer. Government needs to see this; wine industry leaders need to develop strong relationships with those civic leaders who can impact on their business. Strong industry leadership is essential to drive South Africa forward in this competitive world of wine.

Zelma Long

Vilafonté Winemaking Partner & Zelma Long Wines, International Consultancy

'The guide is getting thicker and thicker' is a comment we hear all the time, and, given that the size of the industry as measured by the number of producers, merchants and brands has doubled in the past decade, it may appear inevitable that the book's waistline would expand accordingly. That's not the case, however, and in fact the total number of pages has remained static — at 608 — since the 2006 edition. This has been the result of a conscious effort, and — among other benefits — it has helped to contain cost increases and thereby aided the affordability of the book.

Among the disadvantages have been ever-tighter limits on word counts for the overview paragraphs and the wine descriptions in the A–Z directory. (The folk on Twitter who fancy they invented the 140-character wine review clearly never looked over the shoulder of Platter tasters as they shoehorned their notes into the allocated spaces!) The quest for brevity also led us into the realm of extreme abbreviation. For example 'barrel' became 'brl', 'fermented' became 'ferm', and 'viognier', a perfumed and charming grape, was reduced to the rather unlovely 'viog'.

Recognising this as unideal, for the current edition we have increased the pagination slightly to reduce some of the pressure on available space, and combined this with an attempt, firstly, to reduce the use of abbreviations in overview paragraphs and wine descriptions to the absolute minimum and, secondly, to mention details of a technical nature (oaking, acidity, residual sugar etc) only when these are essential to understanding the character of a particular wine. We would like to believe that the measures above have resulted in copy that is cleaner, clearer and more readable, and would welcome readers' comments on the new format (to feedback@wineonaplatter.com) as well as their suggestions on how to further improve the guide.

Following on from the successful 'Sustainability' theming of the previous book, we've chosen 'Innovation' as the motif for the current edition. Wineries, organisations and individuals who 'think out of the box' are highlighted in the Photo Gallery (see the various colour sections) and in the introductory paragraphs to the entries in the A–Z. Innovators and innovations will also be featured on our website and social media channels in the coming year.

Regarding the tastings for this edition, our aim and approach have remained unchanged, namely to taste, rate and describe as many South African-made wines available during the currency of the book, both locally and overseas, as possible.

Much as we'd like to, the number of individual wines precludes us from re-tasting/rating vintages

which have been submitted previously yet will still be available for sale during the book's currency. Only wines which last year were reviewed as tank or barrel samples, and thus rated provisionally (or considered too young and unformed to rate), or wines we believe we may have miscalled last time, are revisited for the current book. New and previously untasted vintages are, of course, reviewed as normal.

It bears repeating that the rankings reflected in the book are the result of a process beginning towards the end of June, when we mobilise our team of tasters. The results of their work are reflected in the A–Z section, along with news about the wineries and winemakers, general information about products, vinification facilities, vineyards, amenities available to visitors and more. (Scores for all wines in the A–Z are also listed separately for convenience in the section named 'This Year's Ratings Summarised'.)

For visitors in search of wine-route information, we've incorporated GPS coordinates for as many as possible of the wineries open to the public at set hours or by appointment. The maps have again been fully updated, along with the quick-lookup tables which furnish key visitor information about the wineries of a particular area, such as whether or not they are open on weekends and public holidays, offer meals or refreshments, specifically cater for children, or are friendly to individuals with reduced mobility.

On which subject, our initiative to provide professionally conducted audits of winetasting areas, cellar tours and other visitor facilities in the winelands continues in conjunction with accessibility specialist Guy Davies. See page 100 for details.

Also of interest to tourists and wine-ramblers are the Restaurants and Accommodation sections, featuring hotels, B&Bs, restaurants, delis and a plethora of other dining and unwinding venues among the vines. Well-qualified Jos Baker edits the (sponsored) entries.

Our wine ranking system remains the same as last year. We cover the full spectrum, from wines we consider 'somewhat less than ordinary' (and award 0 stars) to 'superlative Cape classics', worthy of a full 5 stars. Wines rated ★★★★ or higher are usually listed first in each entry, and set in red type. However, wines debuting as barrel/tank previews and therefore provisionally rated 4 or more stars remain in black type. Vintages deviating from the general rating are individually starred in the text. Very good/promising wines and more modest examples (★★★☆ or fewer) are included in the 'run-on' listings at the end of entries. For easy identification, the quaffing best-buys are boxed together and individually labelled with the wallet-cordial 😊 sign. See also the section 'How to Use the Guide' on page 139.

Because of deadlines, many wines in the guide are tasted freshly bottled or as works-in-progress; any considered unrateable as a result are noted as such in the text. It's worth mentioning that we taste from the end of June to mid-August. Except for the bottlings assessed for five stars (see the preamble to the Wines of the Year), all wines are tasted 'sighted' (with labels exposed) and the name of the producer known. As a control, we also double-blind taste hundreds of wines in the course of our assessments. In these corroborative reviews, tasters have no information about the wine save what's in the glass. Because of the subjective element associated with wine assessment, we strongly recommend you view our rankings as adjuncts to the tasting notes rather than as oracular pronouncements. And we continue to urge you, in the words of a local winery's marketing slogan, to 'trust your taste'.

Wines featured in this edition were assessed by a team whose professionalism and unflagging enthusiasm we gratefully acknowledge. Their initials appear below the wines they tasted, as follows: Michael Fridjhon (MF), Angela Lloyd (AL); Master of Wine Cathy van Zyl (CvZ); Cape Wine Masters Winnie Bowman (WB), Greg de Bruyn (GdB), Tim James (TJ), Christine Rudman (CR), Meryl Weaver (MW); David Biggs (DB), Christian Eedes (CE), Fiona McDonald (FM), Ingrid Motteux (IM), Jörg Pfützner (JPf), James Pietersen (JP) and Dave Swingler (DS). For potted biographies of the tasters, see the next section.

In a further endeavour to ensure the fairest possible ratings for wines debuting this edition, or returning after a gap, we've again assembled small panels of tasters to carry out the reviews. The results of their assessments are credited in the text as 'Panel'. Wines reviewed onsite, in Worcester,

Robertson, Olifants River, Klein Karoo and the southern Cape (Elim), are also flagged as 'Panel'.

Warm thanks to the rest of the splendid team, specially to associate editors Tim James (also proof-reader), Cathy van Zyl and Jos Baker; contributors Bob Chappell, Christian Eedes, Tony Jackman, Lynne Kloot, Cathy Marston, Lindsaye McGregor, Joanne Gibson and Wendy Toerien; information coordinator Ina de Villiers, tasting coordinator Ina Smith, wine coordinator Christina Harvett and assistants Alex Reichle, Anche Krige, Bettina Botha, Deon Boonzaier, Duncan Thokoane, Rene Barnard, Ryan Megar, Stephan Steyn, Wilbe Myburgh and Wilhelm Schultz; map and typesetting guru Gawie du Toit; photographer Dennis Gordon; the two Lindas (Ransome and Butler) for advertising and sales; Lara Philp and Johan Rademan of Vineyard Connection for the use of their excellent facilities; Lauren de Kock for fact-checking; Mark Whyte and XtraSmile Couriers; Ryk Taljaard (Geo-Logic Mapping) and Heinrich Schloms (VinPro) for the Wine of Origin maps; the ever-helpful SAWIS; and Michael Bucholz for the calibration samples. Special thanks to Sean de Kock for 24 x 7 help with the database, intranet and website.

Most of all, loving thanks to wife, associate editor and regional tasting coordinator Cathy, astoundingly capable, efficient and tireless, a wonderful source of strength and encouragement; and to son Luke, now 14 and still aiming to take to the skies in the pilot's seat (when not playing computer war games).

Certainly not least, sincere thanks to South Africa's wine producers and negociants, without whose support the book could not be produced.

Finally, an invitation to join us on the web, Facebook and Twitter (see page 2 for details), and to check out the seriously cool iPhone/Pad/Pod version of the guide — see the display advertisement on page 619 for details.

Philip van Zyl

David Biggs

David has been writing about wine for more than 30 years, since attending two Gilbeys courses in 1979, before the establishment of the Cape Wine Academy. He has been a judge in every Veritas competition since its inception, and is a founder member of the Wine-of-the-Month tasting panel. He qualified officially as a wine judge in 2000. For 30 years he wrote a weekly wine column for the Cape Argus newspaper and is a regular contributor to Good Taste magazine. His books on cocktails have been translated into 14 languages.

Winifred Bowman

A qualified physiotherapist and biomedical scientist, and holder of a PhD in Education, Winnie developed an interest in wine during her student days at Stellenbosch and later through frequent travels to international winegrowing areas. Her wine studies, begun at the Cape Wine Academy in 2002, culminated in the Cape Wine Master qualification with the thesis title of An Accreditation Programme for a South African Wine Education Institute. Winnie tastes for Wine-of-the-Month, presents regular corporate and private wine tastings, and writes about wine and food.

Greg de Bruyn

Greg is an architect by profession, practicing in and around the Cape wine industry. He allowed wine to beguile him into leaving Johannesburg in 1999 to seek his future amongst the vines, first to establish and run a wine estate, and later as a specialist consultant in winery construction. He qualified as a wine judge in 1996 and a Cape Wine Master in 2000. Greg has sat on many of the major South African competitions and assessment panels, and has contributed to several publications and websites.

Christian Eedes

After graduating from Stellenbosch University with an Honours degree in Philosophy, Christian joined Wine magazine in 2000 and was editor of the publication from May 2008 until December 2009. He has completed a wine evaluation course as well as a small-scale winemaking programme at Stellenbosch University. He occasionally chairs Wine's tasting panel and has also judged at the Trophy Wine Show since 2007. To accommodate better his predilection for long lunches, he recently embarked on a freelance career.

Michael Fridjhon

Widely consulted liquor industry authority and leading wine writer, Michael is chair of the Trophy Wine Show and has judged in wine competitions in several countries. Visiting professor at the University of Cape Town Graduate School of Business, he is a Chevalier of the French Ordre du Mérite Agricole, and writes for Business Day, Wine, Fine Wine, Decanter and Wine Business International. He has also authored or contributed to over 30 books and has been a taster for the guide since the early 1980s.

Tim James

Tim has a PhD in English Literature but 'no proper ambitions' or full-time job — leaving more time for wine matters. He writes for local and international publications (regularly for World of Fine Wine), including a wine column for the national weekly Mail & Guardian, and writes and tastes for the Grape website. Related activities have included lecturing on wine and studying it (he is a Cape Wine Master). Tim has tasted for this guide for several years now.

Angela Lloyd

Angela's professional involvement with wine spans nearly 30 years. Her enthusiasm and enjoyment for any aspect of the fruit of the grape remain undimmed. Her experience covers lecturing and broadcasting, and even making wine. She's pursued her love of travel, exploring the world's winelands, on occasions as a judge, a role also regularly fulfilled in South Africa. As a wine writer, commissions come from local and international publications; she's also a columnist for Grape.

Fiona McDonald

Fiona trained as a journalist and worked for The Mercury newspaper in Durban before being headhunted to move to the Cape as editor of Wine magazine, a position she held for nearly 8 years. Her interest in wine came about as a result of being press ganged into helping to organise The Mercury Wine Week in the 1990s and having to write about the various exhibitors and their wines. Fiona has served as a judge and jury president at various international wine competitions, among them the International Wine Challenge, Decanter World Wine Awards and Concours Mondial.

Ingrid Motteux

Love of wine and a growing aversion to hospital basements led Ingrid to give up a successful career in nuclear medicine to work first as a vineyard labourer, then as a lecturer and wine writer. Her wine interest took formal shape during more than a decade abroad, where she attained the UK WSET Diploma and, soon after, the Cape WSET Wine Judge certification. An associate of the Institute of Wines & Spirits, Ingrid judges for the International Wine Challenge and runs an independent wine consultancy, advising some of Africa's top game lodges.

Jörg Pfützner

German-born Jörg is an internationally trained and certified sommelier living in South Africa. Apart from being the consulting wine editor for G&W magazine, he's completing his Master in Wine Business Management and runs The Riesling Club, whose members have access to top European bottlings. More recently he founded Fine Wine Events, which celebrates wine and the lifestyle by hosting unique and specifically themed tastings and festivals. He continues to manage a group of private cellars, and travels widely to learn and lecture about wine.

James Pietersen

As a Stellenbosch University student, James helped organise his law professor's cellar. 'In exchange, he opened a few great bottles and I fell in love with wine.' He's since pursued his passion, first as Vineyard Connection's wine buyer, consultant to Singita Game Lodge and lately as the head sommelier for Belthazar in Cape Town, also responsible for the wine program at Balducci's restaurant. Further experience was gained as Trophy Wine Show judge and as a panelist for Wine magazine.

Christine Rudman

Christine started out in FMCG marketing in Johannesburg. Accepting a job at the then Stellenbosch Farmers' Winery and needing to learn about wine, she enrolled with the Cape Wine Academy. Her Cape Wine Masters qualification was earned in 1986; she ran the CWA for seven years, and has since been occupied with consultancy work, professional tastings, wine judging, lecturing and writing. She has travelled widely, tasted on international panels; written A Guide to the Winelands of the Cape; and says there's no retirement in sight, she's having too much fun.

Dave Swingler

Dave earns his keep outside the drinks trade: indulging his hobbies of wine and words for the guide is his pleasure. Having travelled the winelands of the world, he remains misguided enough to continue a pursuit of the vinous Holy Grail — affordable great red Burgundy. Dave is co-author of One Hundred Wines — An Insiders' Guide, drinks contributor to Posh Nosh and an occasional columnist for print and other media. He brings a hearty consumer perspective to the guide.

Cathy van Zyl

South Africa's only resident Master of Wine, Cathy is a regular judge for the Trophy Wine Show and Wine magazine, occasional panellist for several other local competitions and, increasingly, overseas. Co-founder of Grape, she contributes to international magazines and websites, and lectures for the Cape Wine Academy on Tasting and World of Wine Theory. She is currently a member of the Institute of Masters of Wine's education committee responsible for organising its seminar for second-year students.

Meryl Weaver

The Cape winelands lured Meryl away from her legal career and she remains happily under their spell. She is a Cape Wine Master, and recently further honed her skills by graduating from the Wine Judging Academy with distinction. She lectures for the Cape Wine Academy, conducts local wine tours for foreign journalists and presentations abroad on SA wine on behalf of Wines of South Africa. Meryl also judges at local competitions and for wine magazines, and runs a small consultancy business.

WINES OF THE YEAR

In the course of tasting and rating more than 6,000 wines for this edition, the members of our team individually identified a limited number of bottlings showing exceptional quality. These were entered into a second round of tasting, open only to finished/bottled wines, available during the currency of the book. The short-listed wines were retasted 'blind' (without sight of the label) by an assembled panel, and those regarded as superlative in an SA context were awarded the guide's highest grading — five stars. These stand-outs are listed below under the heading 'Five Stars'. The highest scoring five-star wines were subjected to a further evaluation to determine the overall top scorer. The two wines which emerged this year from the stringent selection represent the pinnacle of SA winemaking and are the joint recipients of the guide's highest accolade: Wines of the Year.

Wines which did not make the five-star selection, but which are extremely fine and collectible in their own right, are listed immediately below the Five Stars under the heading 'Highly Recommended'. Implicit in wines of this calibre is the potential to improve with further bottle-maturation — say 8–10 years, perhaps more, in the case of the reds and fortifieds, and around 4–6 years for the whites. (Proper storage is, of course, vital for sound maturation.) During the cycle of tasting, our team identified a number of bottlings, over and above the candidate five-stars, which show particular potential for cellaring. These ageworthy wines are listed separately under the heading 'Buy Now, Drink Later'.

Also listed is a selection of entry-level wines offering exceptional drinkability at budget prices. The 'Superquaffer of the Year' provides the best overall value and quaffability in this category.

There is, too, the prestigious 'super award', Winery of the Year, in recognition of a winegrowing team who, in the opinion of the editor, are ambassadors par excellence for South African wine.

Further details about all releases listed in this section will be found under the names of the relevant producers in the A–Z directory. The five-star tasting is audited by PKF (Cpt) Inc.

Winery of the Year

Boekenhoutskloof Winery
For their remarkable 14 five star ratings stretching back to our 2000 edition - which featured the Syrah 1997, a stylistic window opener for the local industry and one of the most important wines of the modern South African era - and for their understated but highly influential role in placing South Africa on the international fine-fine map, we name Boekenhoutskloof our 2012 Winery of the Year. While some top achievers shy away from the entry level, Boekenhoutskloof co-founder and cellarmaster Marc Kent and his partners almost from the outset embraced the popular palate, first with their Porcupine Ridge label and latterly with another exceptionally drinkable and well-priced range, The Wolftrap. The White version of this budget offering is this edition's Superquaffer of the Year - yet another reason for us to honour and congratulate this consistently exceptional Franschhoek team.

Wines of the Year

FIVE STARS & RED WINE OF THE YEAR
Pinot Noir
- Cape Chamonix Reserve 2010

FIVE STARS & WHITE WINE OF THE YEAR
Natural Sweet
- Badsberg Badslese 2009

Five Stars

Cabernet Franc
- Warwick 2008

Cabernet Sauvignon
- Boekenhoutskloof 2009

- Graham Beck Chalkboard #3 2007

Five Stars *(continued)*
- Stark-Condé Three Pines 2009

Pinot Noir
- Cape Chamonix Reserve 2010
- Newton Johnson Domaine 2010
- Oak Valley 2009

Shiraz
- Boekenhoutskloof 2009
- Fairview The Beacon 2008
- Mont Destin Destiny 2007
- Mullineux Family 2009
- Saxenburg Select 2007

Red Blends
- Bouchard Finlayson Hannibal 2010
- De Toren Fusion V 2009
- Glenelly Lady May 2009
- La Motte Pierneef Shiraz-Viognier 2009
- Meerlust Rubicon 2007
- Miles Mossop Max 2008
- Sadie Family Columella 2009

Chardonnay
- De Wetshof The Site 2009
- Jordan CWG Auction Reserve 2010

Chenin Blanc
- Beaumont Hope Marguerite 2010
- Diemersfontein Carpe Diem 2010
- Vins d'Orrance Kama 2010

Grenache Blanc
- KWV Mentors 2010

Sauvignon Blanc
- Graham Beck Pheasants' Run 2011
- Hermanuspietersfontein No 5 2010
- Kleine Zalze Family Reserve 2010
- Strandveld 2010

White Blends
- Fable Jackal Bird 2010
- Flagstone CWG Auction Reserve Happy Hour 2009
- Mullineux Family White Blend 2010
- Nederburg Ingenuity 2010
- Steenberg CWG Auction Reserve The Magus 2010
- Tokara Director's Reserve 2010

Méthode Cap Classique
- Colmant Brut Chardonnay NV
- Topiary Blanc de Blancs Brut 2009

Natural Sweet
- Badsberg Badslese 2009

Dessert Wine Unfortified
- Boekenhoutskloof Noble Late Harvest 2008
- Fleur du Cap Noble Late Harvest 2010
- Mullineux Family Straw Wine 2010
- Nederburg Edelkeur 2010
- Nederburg Eminence 2010

Port
- Boplaas Cape Vintage Reserve 2009
- De Krans Cape Vintage Reserve 2009

Highly Recommended

Cabernet Sauvignon
- Delaire Graff Reserve 2009
- Meerlust 2009
- Teddy Hall Hercùles van Loon 2008

Merlot
- Hillcrest Quarry 2009
- Shannon Mount Bullet 2009
- Thelema Reserve 2009
- Vergelegen Reserve 2008

Pinotage
- Beyerskloof Diesel 2009
- Chateau Naudé Le Vin de François 2009
- Diemersfontein Carpe Diem 2009
- Kaapzicht Steytler 2008
- Kanonkop 2009
- Spioenkop '1900' 2010

Pinot Noir
- Botanica 2010
- Crystallum Cuvée Cinéma 2010
- Meerlust 2010
- Paul Cluver Seven Flags 2009
- Paul Cluver CWG Auction Reserve 2010

Shiraz
- Bon Courage Inkará 2009
- Boschendal Cecil John Reserve 2009
- Delheim Vera Cruz 2008
- De Trafford '393' 2009
- Graham Beck The Ridge 2008
- Hartenberg Gravel Hill 2007
- Robertson Winery No. 1 Constitution Road 2008
- Rudi Schultz Reserve 2009
- Rustenberg 2009
- Scali 2008
- Stark-Condé Three Pines 2009

Red Blends
- Anwilka 2009
- Beyerskloof Faith 2008
- Constantia Glen Five 2008
- Diemersdal Private Collection 2009
- Ernie Els CWG Auction Reserve 2009
- Groot Constantia Gouverneurs Reserve 2009
- Haskell Haskell II 2009
- Jean Daneel Signature 2008

Highly Recommended (continued)

- Jordan Sophia 2008
- Keets First Verse 2009
- Kronendal Mirari 2008
- Lynx The Lynx 2009
- Mulderbosch Faithful Hound 2009
- Nederburg Ingenuity 2008
- Reyneke Reserve 2009
- Saronsberg Seismic 2008
- Spier Frans K. Smit 2007
- Vergelegen V 2007

Chardonnay

- Cape Chamonix Reserve 2010
- Hamilton Russell 2010
- Haskell Anvil 2010
- Mulderbosch Barrel Fermented 2009
- Rustenberg Five Soldiers 2009
- StellenRust Barrel Fermented 2010
- Vergelegen Reserve 2010
- Waterford Reserve 2010

Chenin Blanc

- Botanica 2010
- Ken Forrester The FMC 2009
- Remhoogte Honeybunch 2010
- Rijk's Reserve 2008
- StellenRust '46' 2010
- The Winery of Good Hope Renaissance 2010

Sauvignon Blanc

- Cape Point Vineyards Reserve 2010
- De Grendel Koetshuis 2011
- Diemersdal 8 Rows 2011
- Reyneke Reserve White 2010
- Vergelegen Reserve 2011
- Woolworths Limited Release (Cape Point Vineyards) 2010

Semillon

- Stellenzicht Reserve 2009

Viognier

- De Grendel 2011

White Blends

- Bizoe Henriëtta 2010
- Black Oystercatcher White Pearl 2009
- Cape Point Vineyards Isliedh 2010
- Graham Beck Chalkboard #1 Sauvignon Blanc-Chenin Blanc-Viognier 2009
- Groot Constantia Gouverneurs Reserve 2010
- Hermit on the Hill The White Knight 2009
- Lammershoek Roulette Blanc 2010
- Nederburg Sauvignon Blanc-Chardonnay Private Bin D253 2010
- Nitida Coronata Integration 2010
- Rall White 2010
- Sadie Family Palladius 2010
- Scali Blanc 2009
- Solms-Delta Amalie 2010
- Steenberg Magna Carta 2010
- Vergelegen White 2010

Méthode Cap Classique

- Colmant Brut Reserve NV

Natural Sweet

- Perdeberg Weisser Riesling 2010

Dessert Wine Unfortified

- Ken Forrester 'T' Noble Late Harvest 2009
- Nederburg Winemaster's Reserve Noble Late Harvest 2010
- Paul Cluver Weisser Riesling Noble Late Harvest 2010
- Rustenberg Straw Wine 2010

Buy Now, Drink Later

Barbera

- Hofstraat 2010

Cabernet Franc

- Rainbow's End Limited Release 2010
- Zorgvliet 2009

Cabernet Sauvignon

- Bergsig Reserve 2008
- Journey's End Cape Doctor 2007
- Klein Constantia 2009
- Landskroon Paul de Villiers 2009
- Le Riche Reserve 2008
- Le Riche CWG Auction Reserve 2008
- Louis 2008
- Nuy Barrel Selection 2008
- Rudera 2009
- Saxenburg Private Collection 2008

- Waterford 2008

Malbec

- Maison de Teijger 2009

Merlot

- Journey's End 2007
- La Petite Ferme 2009
- Rainbow's End Estate 2010
- Yonder Hill 2009

Mourvèdre

- Raka 2009

Pinotage

- Bellevue PK Morkel 2008
- Beyerskloof Reserve 2008
- Clos Malverne Reserve 2009

Platter's
SOUTH AFRICAN
WINE GUIDE
BUY NOW,
DRINK LATER

Buy Now, Drink Later *(continued)*

- Croydon Covenant 2009
- Flagstone Writer's Block 2009
- Lanzerac Pionier 2008
- Maastricht 2010
- Meerendal 2009
- Southern Right 2010
- Stellenzicht Golden Triangle 2009
- Super Single Vineyards Thomas Se Dolland 2008

Pinot Noir

- Bouchard Finlayson Tête de Cuvée Galpin Peak 2010
- Creation Reserve 2010
- Shannon Rockview Ridge 2009

Shiraz

- Andreas 2009
- Avondale Samsara 2006
- Axe Hill 2010
- Bizoe Estalet 2009
- Black Pearl 2009
- Boschendal Reserve 2009
- Dispore Kamma Reserve 2009
- Fable Bobbejaan 2009
- Lord's Wines 2009
- Metzer 2009
- Muratie 2009
- Raka Biography 2009
- Schalk Burger & Sons Welbedacht 2008
- Simonsig Merindol 2008
- Super Single Vineyards Mount Sutherland 2009
- The Bernard Series Basket Press 2009
- The Three Foxes Castillo 2009
- Van Loveren Christina Van Loveren 2009

Touriga Nacional

- De Krans 2010

Red Blends

- Amani Jordan Myers 2009
- Anthonij Rupert Wines Optima 2007
- BABISA Valerie Reserve 2009
- Beau Joubert Reserve 2009
- Beaumont Vitruvian 2008
- Black Oystercatcher Triton 2008
- Camberley Charisma 2008
- Claime d'Or Cabernet Sauvignon-Cabernet Franc 2009
- De Grendel Rubáiyát 2008
- Delheim Grand Reserve 2008
- Dornier Donatus 2009
- Ernie Els Proprietor's Blend 2009
- Grande Provence The Grande Provence 2006
- Hillcrest Estate Hornfels 2009
- Kanonkop Paul Sauer 2008
- Landskroon Paul de Villiers Reserve 2009
- Lourensford Shiraz-Mourvèdre-Viognier 2009
- Mont Destin Passioné 2009

- Morgenster 2009
- Muratie Ansela van de Caab 2008
- Neethlingshof The Caracal 2009
- Noble Hill 1674 Signature Blend 2008
- Post House Penny Black 2008
- Rustenberg John X Merriman 2009
- Saronsberg Full Circle 2009
- Stellenbosch Ridge 2009
- StellenRust Timeless 2008
- Solo CWG Auction Reserve The Guildsman 2009
- The Natalie 2009
- The Wine Fusion The First Chapter 2010
- Uva Mira 2007
- Veenwouden Classic 2007
- Warwick Trilogy 2008

Chardonnay

- De Wetshof Bateleur 2009
- De Wetshof D'Honneur 2007
- Lanzerac 2010
- Mont Rochelle Miko Sur Lie 2009
- Restless River 2008
- Zandvliet Kalkveld 2010

Chenin Blanc

- Allée Bleue 2010
- De Heuvel Barrel Fermented 2010
- De Trafford 2010
- Dewaldt Heyns Family Weathered Hands 2009
- Fort Simon 2010
- Jean Daneel Signature Series 2010
- Teddy Hall Dr Jan Cats Reserve 2010

Sauvignon Blanc

- Benguela Cove 2011
- Jordan The Outlier 2010
- Nitida Club Select 2011
- Southern Right 2011
- Wedderwill 2010

Semillon

- GlenWood Vigneron's Selection 2009

White Blends

- Anatu Fugue 2010
- David Aristargos 2010
- Lourensford '1700' 2010
- Reginald James Sublime 2011
- Strandveld Adamastor 2010
- The Berrio The Weathergirl 2010
- Trizanne Signature Sauvignon Blanc-Semillon 2010

Méthode Cap Classique

- Francois La Garde String of Pearls Blanc de Blancs 2005
- Graham Beck Brut Rosé 2009

Dessert Wine, Unfortified

- Darling Cellars Noble Late Harvest 2010
- Rudera Chenin Blanc Noble Late Harvest 2008

Superquaffer of the Year

White Blends
- Boekenhoutskloof The Wolftrap White 2010

Exceptionally Drinkable & Well Priced

Merlot
- Havana Hills 2008

Pinotage
- Swartland 2010

Shiraz
- False Bay 2010

Red Blends
- Bonnievale Cabernet Sauvignon-Shiraz 2009
- Villiera Down to Earth 2010

Rosé
- Woolworths Pinotage-Shiraz 2011 (Delheim)

Chardonnay
- Durbanville Hills 2010
- Glenelly The Glass Collection 2010
- Pulpit Rock Brink Family 2011

Sauvignon Blanc
- Klawer Birdfield 2011

White Blend
- Post House Blueish White 2010

Platter's SOUTH AFRICAN WINE GUIDE SUPERQUAFFERS ☺

Here we summarise the wines featured in the A–Z section, with their ratings, sorted first by wine style, in alphabetical order, and then by producer or brand. New wines in **bolder type. NS** = no star; **NT** = not tasted; **NR** = tasted but not rated; **D** = discontinued. Where wineries produce more than one version of a particular style, the number of versions is indicated in brackets after the name. A number of wines were tasted as pre-bottling barrel or tank samples, and therefore ratings are provisional. Refer to the A–Z for details.

Barbera

★★★★ Hidden Valley, Hofstraat

★★★☆ Altydgedacht, Fairview, Idiom, Merwida

Blanc de noir

★★★☆ Asara, Mellasat ★★★ Blaauwklippen, Boschendal, Groot Constantia, **Lemberg**, Lynx, Van Loveren, Zandberg ★★☆ Aan de Doorns, Culemborg, Klawer (Light & low-alcohol), **Lovane**, Nieuwedrift, Oude Kaap, Swartland, Van Loveren, Woolworths ★★ Landskroon (2) ★☆ Arra **NT** Buitenverwachting, Lovane, Oudtshoorn, Peter Falke, **Tempel D** Boplaas, Goudini, Hazendal, Lovane, Oude Wellington

Bukettraube

★★★ Cederberg ★★★ Seven Sisters, Simonsvlei, Swartland

Cabernet franc

★★★★★ Warwick

★★★★☆ Nelson, Plaisir, Raats

★★★★ Alluvia, Anthonij Rupert, Buitenverwachting, Claime d'Or, **Druk My Niet**, Hermanuspietersfontein, Knorhoek, **La Petite Ferme**, Longridge, Lynx, Rainbow's End (2), Raka, Ridgeback, Woolworths, Zorgvliet

★★★☆ Avontuur, Eikendal, High Constantia, **Hillcrest, Leopard Frog**, Lovane; **Maison de Teijger** (2), Mooiplaas, Môreson, Oldenburg, Ormonde, Philip Jordaan, Spookfontein , **Vergenoegd** ★★★ Idiom, Signal Hill, Whalehaven ★★★☆ Bushmanspad, Ridgemor **NT** My Wyn **NR** Benguela Cove **D** L'Avenir, Woolworths

Cabernet sauvignon

★★★★★ Boekenhoutskloof, **Graham Beck**, Stark-Condé

★★★★☆ Bilton, De Trafford, Delaire, Edgebaston, Fleur du Cap, Glen Carlou, Grangehurst, Hoopenburg, House of Mandela, **Journey's End**, Kanonkop, La Motte, Le Riche, Louis, Meerlust, Neil Ellis, Nuy, Rickety Bridge, Rudera, Rustenberg, Saxenburg, South Hill, Springfield, Super Single, **Teddy Hall**, The Winery of Good Hope, Thelema (2), Waterford, Woolworths

★★★★ African Pride, Akkerdraai, Alluvia, Alto, **Altydgedacht**, AntHill, Arra (2), Asara, **Bartinney**, Belfield, **Bergsig**, Bilton, Blue Creek, Bon Courage, Bon Terroir, Bonfoi, Boschendal, **Botanica**, Brampton, Buitenverwachting, Cape Chamonix, Cape Hutton, Cathedral Cellar, Cederberg (2), Chateau Naudé, Clovelly, Conviction, Dalla Cia, Darling Cellars, De Meye, De Wetshof, Delheim, DeWaal, Dombeya, Dornier, **Druk My Niet**, Edgebaston, Eikendal (2), Ernie Els, Excelsior, Fairview, Flagstone, Glen Carlou, Goedverwacht, Graceland, Graham Beck (3), Groot Constantia, Guardian Peak, Hartenberg, Hathersage, Idiom, Jordan, Journey's End, Katbakkies, Klein Constantia, Klein Roosboom , Kleine Zalze (2), Knorhoek, Kumkani, L'Avenir, Laibach, Landskroon, Lanzerac, Le Bonheur, Le Riche (2), Linton Park, Lourensford, Lovane, Lynx, **MAN Vintners**, Marianne, Marklew, **MC Square**, Meinert, Mimosa, MolenVliet, Mont du Toit, Namaqua, Nederburg (3), Neil Ellis, Niel Joubert, Nitida Cellars, Noble Hill, Oldenburg, Overgaauw, Pick's Pick, Plaisir, Post House, Rainbow's End, Raka, Rickety Bridge, Robertson, Rudera, Savanha, Schalk Burger, **Springfontein**, Stark-Condé (2), Sterhuis, The Township Winery, The Winery of Good Hope, Tokara, Topiary, Vergelegen, Vergenoegd (2), Villiera, Vriesenhof , Warwick, Webersburg, Windmeul, Woolworths, Zorgvliet

★★★☆ Amares, Annandale, Anthonij Rupert (2), Anura, Arra, Beau Joubert, Bergsig, Bernheim, **Birkenhead**, Blaauwklippen, Bloemendal, Blue Crane, Boekenhoutskloof, Boland (2), Bon Courage, Boplaas, Boschheim (2), Boschkloof, Bosman, Botha (2), Bushmanspad, Calitzdorp, Callender, **Christian Kuun**, Constantia de Tulbagh, Darling Cellars, **De Vallei**, Devon Hill, Devonair (2), Doolhof, Dormershire (2), Eaglevlei, Eerste Hoop, Fairvalley, Feiteiras, Fleur du Cap, Fort Simon, Glenelly, Grande Provence, Groenland, Haut Espoir, Het Vlock, Hildenbrand, Hofstraat, Holden Manz, Hoopenburg, Jacques Smit, Jakob's Vineyards, Joubert-Tradauw, **Juno**, Kaapzicht, **Kanu**, Kloovenburg, KWV, Kyburg, La Capra, La Kavayan, **La Petite Ferme**, Laborie, Landskroon, Leopard's Leap, Linton Park, Longridge, Lovane, **Maastricht**, MAN Vintners, Manley, McGregor, Middelvlei, Miravel (2), Mischa, Mitre's Edge, Mooiplaas, Morgenhof, Mount Rozier, Mount Vernon, Mountain Ridge, Muratie, Nederburg, Neil Ellis Meyer-Näkel, Onderkloof , Opstal, Ormonde, Oude Compagnies Post, Perdeberg, **Pick's Pick**, Pulpit Rock, **Restless River**, Ridgeback, Roodezandt, Rooiberg, Ross Gower, Rust en Vrede, Schalkenbosch, Seidelberg, Simonsvlei, Spookfontein , Stellekaya, StellenRust, Stonewall, Swartland, SylvanVale, The Berrio, **The Wine Fusion**, Tokara, Trajan, Uitkyk, Ultra Liquors, Usana, Van Loveren, Viljoensdrift, Waterkloof,

Wamakersvallei, Wildekrans, Woolworths, Zandberg, Zonnebloem, Zorgvliet ★★★ Abbottshill, African Pride, Agterplaas, Allesverloren, Ashton, Avontuur, Backsberg, Bernheim, Blaauwklippen, Bonnievale, Bovlei (2), Calais Wine, Cape Gable, **Carisbrooke**, Chanteclair, **Cloof**, Conradie, Cranefields, Crows Nest, De Heuvel, De Meye, De Vallei, Devonvale, Diemersfontein, Domaine Brahms, Douglas Green, Durbanville Hills, Eagle's Cliff, Elgin Vintners, Excelsior, Franschhoek Cellar, Galleon, Goede Hoop, Groenland, Havana Hills, High Constantia, Hout Bay, Jacobsdal, Klawer, **Klein Dauphine**, Kleine Zalze, KWV, L'Olivier, La Bri, La Petite Provence, La Petite Vigne, Le Pommier, Lindhorst, Lyngrove, **Maison de Teijger** (2), Meerendal, Merwida, **Mon Rêve**, Mont Rochelle, Montagu Wine & Spirits, Montagu Wine Cellar, Montpellier, Mostertsdrift, Napier, Nederburg, New Beginnings, Niel Joubert, Nwanedi, Obikwa, Oewerzicht, Olifantsberg, Ormonde, Painted Wolf, Perdeberg, Peter Falke, **Phizante**, **Pick 'n Pay**, **Pulpit Rock**, Remhoogte, Retief, **Revelation**, Rico Suter, Riebeek, Robertson (2), Ruitersvlei, Saam, Seidelberg, Seven Sisters, Simonsig, Simonsvlei, Slaley, Slanghoek, **Spier** (Organic), Springfield, Stellar (Organic), Stellenbosch Hills, Stellendrift, Swartland, Thandi, Tukulu, Tulbagh Winery, Ultra Liquors (2), Upland (Organic), Vukani, Waterstone, Waverley Hills (Organic), Welmoed, Woolworths, Zanddrift, Zevenwacht ★★★ African Terroir (4) (Organic, Organic), AlexKia, Alvi's Drift, Arniston Bay, Ayama, Belbon Hills, Blomendahl, Brandvlei, **Breëland**, Bushmanspad, De Doorns, De Krans, De Villiers, **Desert Rose**, Douglas Green, Du Preez, Du Toitskloof, DuVon, Eikehof, Escapade, Goedvertrouw, Goudini, Helderberg, Jacob's Quest, Klein Parys, Kleine Draken (Kosher), Koopmanskloof, Kranskop, **Ladismith**, Long Mountain (2), **Lord Somerset**, Louisvale, Moordenaarskop, Neethlingshof, Nietvoorbij, Orange River, Org de Rac (Organic), Oude Kaap, Overhex (2), **Place in the Sun**, Pulpit Rock, Re'Mogo, Riebeek, Rietvallei, **Rosendal**, Simonsvlei, **Six Hats**, Slowine, Somerbosch, Spier, Tanagra, uniWines, **Valley Vineyards**, Van Loveren, **Vriesenhof**, Vruchtbaar, Wandsbeck, Waterstone, **Wamakersvallei**, **Welvanpas**, **William Everson**, Wines of Cape Town (2), Wineways (3), Woolworths (2), Zidela ★★ **Barrydale**, Beau Joubert, Bergwater, Boplaas, Cape Dreams, Cape Rock, Culemborg, De Wet, Du Preez, Golden Kaan, Imbuko, Jonkheer, Kleinfontein, Libby's Pride, Maske, Mountain River, Namaqua, Nuy, Origin, Oudtshoorn, Quest, Rooiberg, **Simonsvlei**, Stellenzicht, Tulbagh Winery, Waterstone (4), Windfall, Windmeul, Wineways, Woolworths, Zandvliet ★★ Groupe LFE, Langverwacht, Roodezandt, Stellar (Organic), Tulbagh Winery, United Nations, Woolworths ★ Clairvaux **NS Withoek NT** Abingdon, Allée Bleue, Arniston Bay, Benguela Cove, Black Pearl,

Camberley, Drostdy-Hof, Du'SwaRoo, Galleon, Hartswater, Hildenbrand, JP Bredell, Keisseskraal, Kleinbosch, Koningsrivier, Laibach, Landzicht (2), Le Grand, Matuba, Mont Rochelle, Mooi Bly, Moordenaarskop, Mountain River, Org de Rac (Organic), Oude Wellington, Prospect1870, Robertson, Savanha (3), Spier (2), **Steenberg**, Stellendrift (2), **Teubes**, Yonder Hill **NR** Lutzville (2), Seal Breeze, Stoumann's **D** African Pride, Arniston Bay, Ashton, Audacia, Avondale, BABISA, Carisbrooke, Diemersfontein, Du Preez, Golden Kaan (2), Groupe LFE (2), Jacques Smit, La Petite Ferme, Linton Park, Malanot, MAN Vintners, Môreson, Mount Rozier, Natte Valleij, Nederburg, Nelson, Peter Falke, Rijk's Pvt Cellar, Rusticus, Sijnn, Steenberg, Stellenzicht, Stettyn, Stonehill, TTT Cellar, Tulbagh Winery, Van Loveren, Vredenheim

Cape Riesling

★★★ Theuniskraal ★★★ Nederburg ★★ Calais Wine, Goudini **NT** Van Loveren **D** Bon Courage, De Villiers

Carignan

★★★★ Fairview

★★★★ BLANKbottle (2) ★★★ Withington ★★ Le Roux & Fourie

Chardonnay unwooded

★★★★ Constantia Uitsig, Diemersdal, GlenWood, Groote Post, Springfield, Van Zylshof, Woolworths ★★★★ Arniston Bay, Bon Courage, Bouchard Finlayson, Cloverfield, Dalla Cia, De Wetshof (3), Eikendal, Jordan, McGregor (Organic), Rustenberg, **Sterhuis**, Wines of Cape Town, Woolworths (2) ★★★ Brampton, De Meye, **Elgin Ridge**, False Bay, Glenelly, Graham Beck, **Groot Parys** (Organic), Hildenbrand, Juno, **Karusa**, Kleine Zalze, Kloovenburg, Landskroon, Langverwacht, Libby's Pride, Long Mountain, Lord's, Louisvale, Middelvlei, Mont Rochelle, Neethlingshof, New Beginnings, Pick's Pick, Rietvallei, **Seven Springs**, Stellar (Organic), **Stellenzicht**, The Winery of Good Hope, Vriesenhof ★★★ African Terroir (3) (Organic), AlexKia, Asara, Ashton, Ayama, **Birkenhead**, Blomendahl, Brandvlei, De Krans, Doolhof, Douglas Green, **Esona**, Franschhoek Cellar, Groupe LFE, **Leeuwenberg**, Long Mountain, Louiesenhof, Lourensford, Morgenhof, Mostertsdrift, Nederburg, Ormonde, Somerbosch, Tulbagh Winery, **Wamakersvallei**, Wine Village-Hermanus ★★ African Terroir (Organic), Bellpost, Boplaas, Bovlei, Eerste Hoop, **Highgate**, **Koopmanskloof**, Leopard's Leap, Lutzville, Overhex, Schalkenbosch, **Valley Vineyards** (2), **Waterstone**, Weltevrede, Woolworths (2) ★★ **Die Mas**, **Groupe LFE**, Jonkheer, Ladismith, United Nations, uniWines, Zandvliet ★ **Woolworths NT** Calais Wine, Du Preez,

Eagle's Cliff, Goudini, La Petite Ferme, Meerendal, Olsen, Oude Wellington, Oudtshoorn (2), Savanha **NR Le Roux & Fourie D** Barry Gould, Botha, De Villiers, Le Pommier, Linton Park, Mount Rozier, Thelema, Ultra Liquors, Wine4Us

Chardonnay wooded

★★★★★ De Wetshof, Jordan

★★★★☆ Ataraxia, Bouchard Finlayson (2), Cape Chamonix, Crystallum, Glen Carlou, Groot Constantia, Groote Post, Hamilton Russell, Hartenberg, **Haskell**, Hoopenburg, Iona, Jordan, Julien Schaal, Koelfontein, Longridge, Mulderbosch, Oak Valley, Paul Cluver (2), Rijk's Pvt Cellar, Rustenberg, Saxenburg, Springfield, StellenRust, The Winery of Good Hope, Uva Mira, Vergelegen, Waterford, Woolworths

★★★★ Alvi's Drift, Amani (2), Bartinney, **Boschendal**, Boschkloof , Bouchard Finlayson, Buitenverwachting, Callender, Cape Chamonix, Cape Point, Creation, Crystallum, De Wetshof (2), DeMorgenzon, Diemersdal, Dombeya, Durbanville Hills, Edgebaston, Eikendal, Elgin Vintners, Fleur du Cap, Glen Carlou, **Glenelly**, GlenWood, Graham Beck (2), Grande Provence, Hartenberg, Haut Espoir, Havana Hills, House of Mandela, Jordan, Journey's End (2), Kleine Zalze, **KWV**, La Motte, La Petite Ferme, Lanzerac, Le Riche, Linton Park, Lourensford, Marklew, MC Square, Meerlust, Merwida, Mimosa, Mont Rochelle (2), Môreson, Morgenhof, Mulderbosch, Muratie, Napier, Nederburg, Neil Ellis, Newton Johnson (2), Ormonde, Plaisir, Pulpit Rock (2), Quoin Rock, **Restless River**, Rijk's Pvt Cellar, Robertson, Rupert & Rothschild, Rustenberg, Simonsig, Sterhuis, Sumaridge, Thelema (2), Tokara (2), Vergelegen, Vins d'Orrance, Von Ortloff, Vriesenhof , Warwick, Waterford, Waterkloof, Weltevrede, William Everson, Windmeul, Woolworths (3), **Zandvliet**

★★★☆ **Almenkerk**, Anura, Asara, Avontuur, Badsberg, Bergsig, Boland, Bon Courage, Boschendal, Cape of Good Hope, Cathedral Cellar, **Chateau Naudé**, Clos Malverne, Cloverfield, De Heuvel, Delaire, Delheim, Domaine des Dieux, Doolhof, Eerste Hoop, Elemental Bob, Ernst Gouws, Fairview, Fat Bastard, Felicité, Fort Simon, **Four Paws**, Goedverwacht, Groot Parys, Hildenbrand, Hoopenburg, Joubert-Tradauw, Kaapzicht, Kloovenburg, KWV, L'Avenir, La Bri, La Capra, **La Vierge**, Lazanou (Organic), Le Bonheur, Lord's, Lorraine, Louisvale (2), Lyngrove, **Mellasat**, Mountain Oaks (Organic), Nabygelegen, Nederburg, Nelson, Niel Joubert, Nitida Cellars, **Oldenburg**, Ormonde, **Passages**, Rhebokskloof, Riebeek, Rietvallei, Savanha, Schalk Burger, Seidelberg, **Seven Springs** , Slaley, Steenberg, Stellenbosch Hills, StellenRust, Stellenzicht, Stonewall, Teubes,

Thandi, Thelema, Tokara, Tukulu (Organic), Uitkyk, Van Loveren, Vondeling, Vruchtbaar, Waterstone, Weltevrede, **Winters Drift**, Woolworths (2), Zandvliet ★★★ African Pride, Alkmaar, Anura, Backsberg, Beau Joubert, **Bloemendal**, Cape Classics, Cape Dreams, Darling Cellars, **De Wet**, De Wetshof, Douglas Green, Drostdy-Hof, Durbanville Hills, Flagstone, Fleur du Cap, Fort Simon, Galleon, Goede Hoop, Goedvertrouw, Hill & Dale, **Imbuko**, Journey's End, Klawer, Klein Parys, Kumala, KWV, Laborie, Lutzville, MAN Vintners, Meerendal, **Montpellier**, Mount Vernon, Nuy, Obikwa, **Olifantsberg**, **Origin** (Organic), Oude Kaap, Overgaauw, **Overhex**, **Pick 'n Pay**, Pulpit Rock, **Revelation**, Rhebokskloof, Rickety Bridge, Riebeek, Robertson (2), Rooiberg, Simonsig, Simonsvlei, **Six Hats**, Spier, Springfontein, Swartland, Two Oceans, **Val de Vie**, Van Loveren, Viljoensdrift, Woolworths (3) (Organic), Zonnebloem ★★★ Anthonij Rupert, Anthony Smook, Birkenhead, Boland, Buffalo Creek, Calitzdorp, Clovelly, Conradie, Douglas Green, Excelsior, Fairvalley, Goedverwacht, Jonkheer, Kranskop, Laborie, Mooi Bly, Namaqua, Nietvoorbij, Orange River, **Org de Rac**, Origin, Slanghoek, United Nations, Van Zylshof, Welmoed, Weltevrede (2), Whalehaven, Withington, Zidela ★★ Backsberg (Kosher), Bonnievale, **Burgershof**, De Zoete Inval, Du Toitskloof , Eikehof, Golden Kaan, **Hathersage**, **Kingsriver**, Niel Joubert, Rooiberg, Simonsvlei, Stanford Hills, Windmeul ★★ Clairvaux, Kleine Draken (Kosher), Waterstone ★ Four Fields **NT** Abingdon, Amani, Bayede!, Bergsig, Bergwater, Bonfoi, Clos Malverne, Crows Nest, Lourensford, Montagu Wine & Spirits, Onderkloof , Robertson, Savanha, Spier, **Stoep**, Stoumann's, Veenwouden, Waterstone, Welvanpas, Wolfkloof **NR Aaldering**, Delaire, Delheim, Neil Ellis, Topaz **D** Arniston Bay, Avondale, Buitenverwachting, Clos Malverne, Culemborg, Goats do Roam, Golden Kaan, Hillcrest, Klein Constantia (2), Lyngrove, Neethlingshof, Oude Wellington, Tanagra, Van Loveren, Wolvendrift

Chenin blanc off-dry/semi-sweet (w & u/w)

★★★★★ Diemersfontein

★★★★☆ Botanica, Ken Forrester, Rijk's Pvt Cellar, **Spier**, StellenRust

★★★★ DeMorgenzon, Glen Carlou, Kanu, Longridge, Mont Destin, Perdeberg, Rudera, Saam, Stark-Condé, The Winery of Good Hope, Tierhoek ★★★☆ Boschendal, **Dagbreek**, Final Cut, Graham Beck, Kanu, Katbakkies, Knorhoek, La Chataigne, **MAN Vintners**, Mulderbosch, **Painted Wolf**, Remhoogte, Secateurs, Springfontein, StellenRust, **Trajan**, Virgin Earth, Woolworths ★★★ KWV, Landskroon (2), Painted Wolf, Robertson (2), Simonsig, Summerhill ★★★ Bottelary, Brandvlei, Cape Classics, **Cloverfield**, Long Mountain,

Nederburg, Nelson, **Nuweland**, Obikwa, Seven Oaks, **Valley Vineyards** ★★ Drostdy-Hof, Du Toitskloof, Franschhoek Cellar, Golden Kaan (2), Goudini, Leopard's Leap, Robertson (Light & low-alcohol), **Simonsvlei**, Slanghoek, **Zidela** ★★ Goudini, Simonsvlei, **Waboomsrivier**, Zandvliet ★ Woolworths **NT** Botha, Hartswater, Landzicht, Waterstone **D** Juno, Wandsbeck, Zidela

Chenin blanc unwooded dry

★★★★★ Beaumont

★★★★ Babylon's Peak, Groote Post, L'Avenir, Laibach, Mooiplaas, Old Vines, The Winery of Good Hope

★★★★ Alvi's Drift, Anthonij Rupert, Bosman, Catch Of The Day, Cederberg, **Chateau Naudé**, Dornier, **Ernie Els**, Hazendal, Le Pommier, Mooi Bly, Nederburg, Raats, Saam, Simonsvlei, The Winery of Good Hope ★★★ Aan de Doorns, Ayama, Backsberg, Darling Cellars, De Heuvel, De Meye, De Wet, **Diners Club Bartho Eksteen** , Dornier, DuVon, Ernst Gouws, Fairview, False Bay, Halala/Lula, Juno, Ken Forrester, Kleine Zalze (2), L'Avenir, La Capra, **Leopard's Leap**, Lyngrove, MAN Vintners, Montagu Wine & Spirits, Nieuwedrift, Olsen, Opstal, Ormonde (2), Oude Denneboom, Overgaauw, Re'Mogo, Rhebokskloof, Seven Sisters, Slowine, Spier, Stellekaya, Swartland, Teddy Hall, The Mason's, **Tread Lightly**, **TTT Cellar**, Tukulu, Tulbagh Winery, Ultra Liquors, uniWines, Van Zylshof, Veenwouden, Waterstone, Wedgewood, Wildekrans, **Woolworths** ★★★ Badsberg, Bergsig (2), **Blaauwklippen**, Blomendahl, Boland, Bottelary, Brandvlei, **Cloof**, David Frost Signature, De Krans, Delheim, Domaine Brahms, **Douglas Green**, Dragonridge, Fairvalley, Fish Hoek, Glenview, Groenland, Groot Parys (2) (Organic, Organic), Groupe LFE, Hawksmoor, Landskroon, **Lord Somerset**, McGregor, Mellasat, Millstream, Montagu Wine Cellar, Monterosso, Montpellier, Mountain River, Niel Joubert, Nuy, Oude Kaap, **Overhex**, Perdeberg, **Pick 'n Pay**, Pulpit Rock, Riebeek, Rooiberg, Ruitersvlei, Schalk Burger, Ses'Fikile, Seven Oaks, **Six Hats**, Sizanani, Stettyn, Thembi & Co, Tulbagh Winery, Ultra Liquors, United Nations, **Valley Vineyards** (3), Van Loveren, Vaughan Johnson, **Vruchtbaar**, **Wamakersvallei**, Windmeul, Woolworths (4) ★★ **African Pride**, Boland, **Calais Wine**, Cape Dreams, Eagle's Cliff, Groupe LFE, **Jacaranda**, Jason's Hill, Klawer, Kleine Zalze, Koopmanskloof, Langverwacht, Long Mountain, **Napier**, **Oude Kaap**, Rietvallei, Simonsvlei (2), Skilpadvlei, Stellar (Organic), Stellenbosch Hills, United Nations, uniWines, Vaughan Johnson, Versailles, Waterstone, Welmoed, Wines of Cape Town, Wineways, Zidela (2) ★★ Ashton, Culemborg, Groupe LFE (2), Ladismith, Maske,

Orange River, Waterstone ★ Drostdy-Hof **NT** Belbon Hills (2), Botha, Bovlei, Jacques Smit, Lazanou (Organic), Môreson, Napier, Nuy, Nwanedi, Old Vines, Somersbosch, Stoumann's, Viljoensdrift, Westbridge, Wines of Cape Town, Zonnebloem **NR** Lutzville, Rickety Bridge **D** African Pride, Bonnievale, Calitzdorp, Conradie, De Villiers, Groupe LFE (2), Mount Rozier, Oudtshoorn, Ridgemor

Chenin blanc wooded, dry

★★★★★ Beaumont

★★★★☆ Cederberg, Jean Daneel, L'Avenir, Lammershoek, Lazanou (Organic), Post House, **Remhoogte**, Spice Route, Stone Ridge, Teddy Hall, **The Winery of Good Hope**, Woolworths (2)

★★★★ Allée Bleue, Cape of Good Hope, De Heuvel, De Trafford, **Delaire**, **DewaldtHeyns**, Fort Simon, Graham Beck, Groot Parys (Organic), Ken Forrester, Kleine Zalze, KWV, Leopard Frog, **MAN Vintners**, **Mooiplaas**, Morgenhof, Mullineux (Light & low-alcohol), **Oldenburg**, Perdeberg, Reyneke (Organic), **Ridgeback**, Rijk's Pvt Cellar (2), **Robert Stanford**, Rudera, Simonsig, Super Single, Villiera, **Wildehurst**, Windmeul, Woolworths

★★★★ Andy Mitchell, Anura, Arniston Bay, **Avondale** (Organic), Awendland, Barton, **BLANKbottle**, Crios Bride, Fleur du Cap, Fort Simon, Hazendal, Jordan, Klein Parys (2), Kumkani, Maison, Meerendal, Mountain Oaks (Organic), Mulderbosch, Raka, Rickety Bridge, Rudera, Saltaré, Springfontein, **Star Hill**, Sterhuis, **Teddy Hall**, The Bernard, Vruchtbaar, Waterkloof, Wildekrans ★★★ 5 Mountains, **Agterplaas**, DeWaal, Hildenbrand, Kaapzicht, KWV, M'hudi, **Malanot**, Nabygelegen, Schalk Burger, Swartland, Vukani, Waterford, Zevenwacht ★★★ Douglas Green, **Orange River**, **Origin**, Ridgemor, Schonenberg, Villiera ★★ Koelenhof , Origin ★★ Hawksmoor **NT** Barry Gould, Domaine Brahms, Jean Daneel, Lateganskop, Môreson, Mountain Oaks (Organic), Onderkloof , Raats, Spier, SylvanVale **NR** Old Vines **D** Arniston Bay, Avondale (2) (Organic), Bon Courage, Damarakloof, Domaine Brahms, Malanot, Môreson, Mountain Ridge, Riebeek, Stoep, Val du Charron

Cinsaut

★★★★ Howard Booysen, Revelation ★★★ BLANKbottle ★★ Landskroon **D** Culemborg

Colombard

★★★ Van Loveren ★★★ Bon Courage, Clairvaux, McGregor, Nuy (2) ★★ Goedverwacht, Hartswater, Langverwacht, Montagu Wine Cellar, Orange River, Rooiberg ★★ Aan de Doorns, Hartswater **D** Conradie, Wandsbeck

Gamay noir

★★★ Altydgedacht, Kleine Zalze

Gewürztraminer

★★★★☆ Zevenwacht

★★★★ Buitenverwachting, Paul Cluver, Woolworths

★★★★ Neethlingshof, Weltevrede ★★★ Altydgedacht, Bergsig, Simonsig ★★★ Bovlei, Villiera NT Belbon Hills, Groupe LFE NR Delheim

Grenache blanc

★★★★★ KWV

★★★★☆ The Foundry

★★★★ Signal Hill

Grenache noir

★★★★★ Neil Ellis, Tierhoek, Vriesenhof

★★★★ Anura, BLANKbottle, Diemersdal, Lynx, Signal Hill, Six Hats ★★★ Franki's, Nuweland

Hanepoot fortified

★★★★★☆ Boplaas, Constantia Uitsig

★★★★★ Aan de Doorns, Calitzdorp, Ladismith, Nuweland, Opstal, TTT Cellar

★★★★ Badsberg, Boplaas, De Wet, Die Mas, Du Preez, Eaglevlei, Klawer, Mon Rêve, Muratie, Slanghoek, Swartland, Villiersdorp ★★★ Bovlei, Calitzdorp, Clairvaux, Du Toitskloof , Kaapzicht, Orange River, Simonsvlei, Vriesenhof ★★☆ Bergwater, Goudini, SoetKaroo, Waboomsrivier NT Belbon Hills, Landzicht, Montagu Wine Cellar, Oudtshoorn, Stoumann's, Tulbagh Winery D Koelenhof , Seal Breeze

Hanepoot unfortified

★★★ Culemborg ★★ Origin (2) (Light & low-alcohol, Light & low-alcohol), Overhex ★★ Zidela D De Heuvel, Groupe LFE, Wineways

Jerepigo red

★★★★☆ Blaauwklippen

★★★★ Badsberg, Grundheim, Laborie, Swartland ★★★★ Catherine Marshall, Feiteiras, Slanghoek ★★★ Camberley, Pulpit Rock, Simonsvlei, Stonewall ★★★ Botha, Hartswater, Orange River, Tulbagh Winery ★★ Montagu Wine & Spirits NT Landzicht, Oudtshoorn, Solms-Delta, Stoumann's D Boplaas, Lammershoek

Jerepigo white

★★★★ Botha

★★★★ Feiteiras, Niel Joubert, Opstal ★★★ Backsberg, Calitzdorp ★★★ Brandvlei, Chateau Naudé, Orange River, Swartland ★★ Hartswater, Montagu Wine & Spirits, Sedgwick's Old Brown Sherry, Ship Sherry ★★ Lateganskop NT Dellrust, Oudtshoorn, Wamakersvallei

Kosher

★★★ Backsberg ★★★ Backsberg (Pinotage), Kleine Draken ★★ Backsberg (2) (Merlot, Chardonnay wooded), Kleine Draken (2) (Red blends, Cape Bordeaux, Sacramental wine) ★★☆ Kleine Draken (6) (Pinotage, Rosé off-dry/semi-sweet, Chardonnay wooded, Sauvignon blanc unwooded, Sparkling, Non-MCC, white, off-dry/semi-sweet, Natural Sweet, red) ★ Kleine Draken ★ Kleine Draken NT Hill & Dale (2) (Red blends, shiraz/syrah-based, White blends, unwooded, dry)

Late Harvest

★★★★ Delheim

★★★★ Thelema (2) ★★★ Pick 'n Pay ★★ Jonkheer, KWV, Overmeer Cellars, Pick 'n Pay, Robertson ★★ Drostdy-Hof, Kellerprinz ★ Montagu Wine Cellar, Orange River NT Simonsvlei D Riebeek

Light & low-alcohol

★★★★☆ Nederburg

★★★★ Blaauwklippen (Noble Late Harvest), Boschendal (Natural Sweet, white), Lammershoek (Vin de paille), Mullineux (Chenin blanc wooded, dry), Neethlingshof (Noble Late Harvest), Paul Cluver (Riesling (sometimes labelled Rhine/Weisser)), Ridgeback

★★★★ Meerendal ★★★ Solms-Delta ★★★ Alvi's Drift (Sparkling, Non-MCC, rosé, off-dry/semi-sweet), Bottelary (Rosé off-dry/semi-sweet), Flat Roof Manor (Sauvignon blanc unwooded), Groupe LFE (Natural Sweet, white), Klawer (2) (Blanc de noir, Sparkling, Non-MCC, rosé, off-dry/semi-sweet), Lutzville (Natural Sweet, white), Obikwa (2) (Natural Sweet, white, White blends, off-dry/semi-sweet (w & u/w)), Robertson (3) (Sparkling, Non-MCC, white, off-dry/semi-sweet, Sparkling, Non-MCC, rosé, off-dry/semi-sweet, Sparkling, Non-MCC, red), Van Loveren (2) (Natural Sweet, rosé, Sparkling, Non-MCC, rosé, off-dry/semi-sweet) ★★ Botha (White blends, off-dry/semi-sweet (w & u/w)), Conradie (Perlé wines), Darling Cellars (Natural Sweet, white), Douglas Green (2) (Natural Sweet, white, Perlé wines), Drostdy-Hof (Natural Sweet, rosé), Eve (Sparkling, Non-MCC, white, off-dry/semi-sweet), Fleur du Cap (White blends, off-dry/semi-sweet (w & u/w)), Grünberger (2) (Natural Sweet, rosé, Natural Sweet, white), Lutzville (Natural Sweet, rosé), Orange River (Rosé off-dry/semi-sweet), Origin (3) (Sweet red, Hanepoot unfortified, Hanepoot unfortified), Overhex (2) (Sparkling, Non-MCC, white, off-dry/semi-sweet, Sparkling, Non-MCC, rosé, off-dry/semi-sweet), Pearly Bay (2) (Rosé off-dry/semi-sweet, White blends, off-dry/semi-sweet (w & u/w)), Riebeek (2) (Perlé wines, Perlé wines), Robertson (2) (Natural Sweet, white, Chenin blanc off-dry/semi-sweet (w & u/w)), Simonsvlei (Natural Sweet, rosé), JC le Roux (2) (Sparkling, Non-MCC, white, off-dry/semi-sweet, Sparkling, Non-MCC, red), The Saints (2) (Natural Sweet, rosé, Natural Sweet, white), Van Loveren (6) (White blends, unwooded, dry, Natural Sweet, red,

Natural Sweet, rosé, Natural Sweet, white, Sparkling, Non-MCC, white, off-dry/semi-sweet, Sparkling, Non-MCC, rosé), Versus (Natural Sweet, white), Woolworths (3) (Sauvignon blanc unwooded, Natural Sweet, red, Merlot) **★★** Bergsig (Perlé wines), Cold Duck (5th Avenue) (Sparkling, Non-MCC, rosé, off-dry/semi-sweet), Darling Cellars (2) (Natural Sweet, rosé, Natural Sweet, white), De Wet (Perlé wines), **Douglas Green** (Natural Sweet, rosé), Drostdy-Hof (2) (Natural Sweet, red, Natural Sweet, white), Obikwa (Natural Sweet, red), **Origin** (Rosé off-dry/semi-sweet), Pearly Bay (2) (Sparkling, Non-MCC, white, off-dry/semi-sweet, Sparkling, Non-MCC, rosé, off-dry/semi-sweet), Pick 'n Pay (Rosé off-dry/semi-sweet), Robertson (4) (Natural Sweet, rosé, Natural Sweet, rosé, Natural Sweet, rosé, Natural Sweet, white), Slanghoek (Rosé off-dry/semi-sweet), JC le Roux (Sparkling, Non-MCC, white, off-dry/semi-sweet), Woolworths (3) (White blends, off-dry/semi-sweet (w & u/w), Natural Sweet, rosé, Rosé off-dry/semi-sweet) **★** Drostdy-Hof (Chenin blanc unwooded dry), **Jonkheer** (Perlé wines), Orange River (Late Harvest), Pick 'n Pay (White blends, unwooded, dry), Robertson (9) (Natural Sweet, rosé, Natural Sweet, red, Sauvignon blanc unwooded, White blends, unwooded, dry, Natural Sweet, red, White blends, off-dry/semi-sweet (w & u/w), Rosé off-dry/semi-sweet, Sauvignon blanc unwooded, Merlot), Versus (Natural Sweet, red), Woolworths (4) (Shiraz/syrah, Chenin blanc off-dry/semi-sweet (w & u/w), White blends, unwooded, dry, Chardonnay unwooded) **NT** Lutzville **NR** Orange River **D** De Wet (Natural Sweet, white), Groupe LFE (3) (Sparkling, Non-MCC, white, off-dry/semi-sweet, Sparkling, Non-MCC, rosé, off-dry/semi-sweet, White blends, off-dry/semi-sweet (w & u/w)), Overhex (2) (Rosé off-dry/semi-sweet, White blends, off-dry/semi-sweet (w & u/w)), Simonsvlei (Sparkling, Non-MCC, rosé off-dry/semi-sweet), Tulbagh Winery (White blends, unwooded, dry), Twee Jonge/Krone

Malbec

★★★★ Annex Kloof, Anura, Diemersfontein, High Constantia, Le Pommier, **Maison de Teijger**, Mooi Bly, Mount Vernon, Paul Wallace, Plaisir, Raka, Signal Hill
★★★★ Audacia, Blaauwklippen, Doolhof, **Druk My Niet**, Hildenbrand, **Maison de Teijger**, Neethlingshof, Umkhulu **★★★** Flagstone, **Hillcrest**, La Capra, **Maison de Teijger** **★★** Bellevue, Woolworths **NT** Haut Espoir **D** Juno

Merlot

★★★★☆ Amani, Bein (2), Creation, Dombeya, Hillcrest, Meerlust, **Red Tape**, Remhoogte, Saxenburg, Shannon, The Winery of Good Hope, Thelema, Vergelegen, Yonder Hill

★★★★ Akkerdal, Anthonij Rupert, Anura, Bein, Callender, Cape of Good Hope, Cathedral Cellar, De Meye, De Trafford, DeWaal, Durbanville Hills (2), Eikendal, Fleur du Cap, GlenWood, Groot Constantia, Hartenberg, Hathersage, Hazendal, Hofstraat, Jordan, Journey's End, Kaapzicht, Klein Roosboom , La Petite Ferme, Laibach (2), Lanzerac, Linton Park, Marianne, Marklew, Nederburg, Nico van der Merwe, Noble Hill, Org de Rac, Post House, Rainbow's End, Rust en Vrede, **Rustenberg**, Savanha, Schalk Burger, Spier, Steenberg, Stellekaya, Sumaridge, Veenwouden, Vergenoegd, Woolworths (2)

★★★☆ Annandale, Asara, Backsberg, **Barton**, Belfield, Bilton, Blueberry Hill, Boland, Buitenverwachting, Calais Wine, Catherine Marshall, **Clos Malverne**, D'Aria, **De Breede**, **Delaire**, Devon Hill, Diemersdal, Dornier, Du Preez, Elberti, Elgin Vintners, Ernie Els, Ernst Gouws, Fairview, Fleur du Cap, Fort Simon, Fraai Uitzicht 1798 (2), Glenelly, Graceland, Graham Beck, Guardian Peak, Hout Bay, Ken Forrester, Kling, Koelfontein, Kranskop, Kyburg, La Bri, Linton Park, Lourensford, Lynx, M'hudi, **Maison de Teijger**, Meerendal (2), Meinert, Miravel, Mont du Toit, Mooiplaas, Morgenhof, Mount Rozier, Muratie, Niel Joubert, Oude Compagnies Post, Overgaauw, Pick's Pick (2), Plaisir, Quoin Rock, Remhoogte, Rickety Bridge, Ridgeback, Rosendal (2), **Seidelberg**, Slaley, Sterhuis, Thelema, Tread Lightly, Vergenoegd, Viljoensdrift, Villiera, Waterkloof (2), Wines of Cape Town, Woolworths (4) (Organic), Zevenwacht **★★★** AlexKia, **Altydgedacht**, Anura, Arra, Audacia, Ayama, Beau Joubert, **Bellingham**, Blue Crane, Boekenhoutskloof, Boland, **Boschendal**, **Boschkloof**, Boschkloof , Botha, Bovlei (2), Cape Classics, Darling Cellars, De Grendel, De Villiers, Delheim, Doolhof, Du Preez, Dunstone, Excelsior (2), Fish Hoek, Flat Roof Manor, Fort Simon, **Groenland**, Groote Post, Havana Hills, Het Vlock, High Constantia, Hoopenburg, **Kanu**, Klein Parys, Kleine Zalze, Kleinfontein, Kloovenburg, KWV, L'Avenir, La Capra, La Petite Provence, Leopard's Leap, Lindhorst, Longridge, Lyngrove, MAN Vintners, Manley, **Mon Rêve**, Morgenhof, Nabygelegen, Nederburg (2), Niel Joubert, **Old Vines**, Ormonde (2), Oudtshoorn, **Overhex**, Painted Wolf, **Passages**, Perdeberg, **Pulpit Rock**, Quest, Raka, Retief, Rooiberg, Seal Breeze, Spier, Stellenbosch Hills, **StellenRust**, Stony Brook, Thembi & Co, Tulbagh Winery, uniWines, Van Loveren, Wildekrans, Woolworths, Yonder Hill, Zonnebloem, **Zorgvliet** **★★★** African Pride, Badsberg, Bayede!, Bellpost, Blaauwklippen, Bloemendal, Blomendahl, **Boland**, Boplaas, Bottelary, Dellrust, DeWaal, Domaine Brahms, Douglas Green (2), Drostdy-Hof, Du Toitskloof , Durbanville Hills, Eikehof, Escapade, Franschhoek Cellar, Golden Kaan, Hill & Dale, Hoopenburg,

Hornbill , Klawer, Koelenhof , Laborie, **Ladismith**, Landskroon, Libby's Pride, Lomond, Louisvale, **Maison de Teijger**, Maske, Mischa, Mont Rochelle, Namaqua, Neethlingshof, Obikwa, Riebeek (2), Rooiberg, Simonsvlei, Slanghoek, Slowine, Spookfontein , Stellar (2) (Organic, Organic), Stellenzicht, Ultra Liquors, uniWines, **Valley Vineyards** (2), Vredenheim, **Wandsbeck**, Waterstone (2), Welmoed, Whalehaven, Windmeul, Wonderfontein (2), Woolworths (3) (Organic) ★★ African Terroir (2) (Organic), Arniston Bay, Backsberg (Kosher), Barrydale, **Burgershof**, Calitzdorp, Glenview, Goedverwacht, Goudini, Groupe LFE (2), Helderberg, Holden Manz, Jason's Hill, **Kleine Draken**, KWV, **Maison de Teijger**, Mzoli's, **Origin** (Organic), **Place in the Sun**, Robertson (2), Seven Sisters, Somersbosch, Tulbagh Winery, United Nations, Wine Village-Hermanus, Wineways (3), Withington, **Woolworths** (Light & low-alcohol), Zidela ★★ African Terroir (Organic), Bergwater, Buffalo Creek, **Cape Dreams**, **Die Mas**, Klein Parys, **Pick 'n Pay**, Pulpit Rock, Swartland, Wineways (3), Woolworths ★ Jonkheer, Lutzville, Robertson (2) (Light & low-alcohol) **NT** Bonfoi, Camberley, Cranefields, Hartenberg, High Constantia, Kleinbosch, Mitre's Edge, Montagu Wine & Spirits, My Wyn, Nietvoorbij, Org de Rac (Organic), Ross Gower, Rusticus, Savanha (3), Spier, Stellendrift (2), Stoep, Tanagra, The Township Winery, Von Ortloff, Westbridge, Wolfkloof **NR** Anthonij Rupert, Bergwater **D** Culemborg, De Krans, Du Preez, Hornbill , JP Bredell, Linton Park, Môreson, Nelson, Pulpit Rock, Rijk's Pvt Cellar, Stettyn, Wine4Us

Mourvèdre
★★★★☆ Beaumont, Signal Hill

★★★★ Raka

★★★☆ BLANKbottle, Fairview, Hawksmoor, **MAN Vintners**, Spice Route, **Stony Brook** ★★★ Oude Compagnies Post ★★ **Idiom D** Sijnn, Val de Vie

Muscadel, red, fortified
★★★★☆ Boplaas, Rietvallei

★★★★ Badsberg, **Calitzdorp**, De Wet, Nuweland, Van Loveren, Wonderfontein

★★★☆ Bon Courage, Du Toitskloof , Klawer, Nuy, Roodezandt, Seidelberg, Slanghoek, Weltevrede ★★★ Aan de Doorns, Boland, Klein Parys, KWV, McGregor, Orange River, Rietvallei ★★☆ BurCon, Grundheim, Janeza, Montagu Wine & Spirits, Rooiberg, Wandsbeck, Wolvendrift ★★ Ashton, Montagu Wine Cellar, Oudtshoorn, **TTT Cellar NT** Excelsior Vlakteplaas, Jonkheer, Montagu Wine & Spirits, Overhex **NR** Landzicht **D** Alvi's Drift, Avondale, Withoek

Muscadel, white, fortified
★★★★☆ Alvi's Drift, Boplaas, Monis

★★★★ Bon Courage, De Krans (2), De Wet, Graham Beck, KWV, Ladismith, Lutzville, Merwida, Nuy, Orange River

★★★☆ Boplaas, Jonkheer, Klawer, Montagu Wine & Spirits ★★★ Ashton, Calitzdorp (2), De Wetshof, Excelsior Vlakteplaas, McGregor, Montagu Wine Cellar, Oudtshoorn, Weltevrede, Withoek ★★★ Clairvaux, Grundheim ★★ Montagu Wine & Spirits **NT** Jonkheer, Landzicht, Montagu Wine & Spirits, Mostertsdrift, Overhex, Robertson **D** Avondale, Grundheim, KWV, Thelema

Muscadel, white, unfortified
★★★ Karusa, Thelema **D** De Heuvel

Muscat de Hambourg fortified
★★ Stellenbosch Hills

Muscat Ottonel unfortified
★★ Zidela

Natural Sweet, red
★★★★☆ Groot Constantia

★★★★ **Adoro** ★★★ Blomendahl (2), Bosman, Rooiberg ★★ Cape Hutton, Van Loveren (Light & low-alcohol), Wineways (3), Woolworths ★★☆ Drostdy-Hof (Light & low-alcohol), Kleine Draken (Kosher), Obikwa ★ Robertson (2) (Light & low-alcohol), Versus ★ The Saints **NT** Lutzville **D** Allée Bleue

Natural Sweet, rosé
★★★ Seven Sisters, Villiersdorp ★★★ Fort Simon, Jacob's Quest, Van Loveren ★★ Drostdy-Hof (Light & low-alcohol), Grünberger (Light & low-alcohol), Lutzville (Light & low-alcohol), Rooiberg, Simonsvlei (Light & low-alcohol), The Saints (Light & low-alcohol), Van Loveren (Light & low-alcohol), Versus ★★ Clairvaux, Darling Cellars (Light & low-alcohol), **Douglas Green** (Light & low-alcohol), Oudtshoorn, Robertson (3) (Light & low-alcohol, Light & low-alcohol), Woolworths ★ Robertson **NT** Kleinbosch, Landzicht, Oudtshoorn, Simonsvlei **D** Tulbagh Winery

Natural Sweet, white
★★★★★ Badsberg

★★★★☆ Buitenverwachting, Klein Constantia, **Perdeberg**, Quoin Rock, Stony Brook

★★★★ **Boschendal** (Light & low-alcohol), Dornier, Ridgeback (Light & low-alcohol), Stellar ★★★★ **Arra**, Cloof, Meerendal ★★★ Kaapzicht, Lord's, Rickety Bridge ★★★ Groupe LFE (Light & low-alcohol), Lutzville (Light & low-alcohol), Obikwa (Light & low-alcohol), Theuniskraal ★★ Boland, Darling Cellars (Light & low-alcohol), Douglas Green (Light & low-alcohol), Goudini, Grünberger (Light & low-alcohol), Robertson (Light

& low-alcohol), The Saints (Light & low-alcohol), Van Loveren (Light & low-alcohol), Versus (Light & low-alcohol), Woolworths ★★ **Darling Cellars** (Light & low-alcohol), Drostdy-Hof (Light & low-alcohol), Oude Wellington, Robertson (Light & low-alcohol), Rooiberg, Vredenheim ★ Kleine Draken **NT** Bottelary Hills, Landzicht **NR** Orange River **D** De Wet (Light & low-alcohol), Somerbosch, Usana

Nebbiolo

★★★★☆ Steenberg

★★★★ Idiom

★★★ Du Toitskloof ★★★ Dagbreek **NT** Awendland

Noble Late Harvest

★★★★★ Boekenhoutskloof, Fleur du Cap, Nederburg (2), Signal Hill

★★★★☆ Bon Courage, De Wetshof, Joostenberg, Jordan, Ken Forrester, L'illa, Lourensford, Miles Mossop, Mount Rozier, Nederburg (Light & low-alcohol), Paul Cluver, Post House, Rudera, Tokara, Villiera, Woolworths

★★★★ Badsberg (2), Beaumont, Blaauwklippen (2) (Light & low-alcohol), Darling Cellars, Delheim, Eikendal, Kanu, Mulderbosch, Neethlingshof (Light & low-alcohol), Nelson, Signal Hill (3), Simonsig, Slaley, Slanghoek, StellenRust, **Van Loveren**, Villiera, Virgin Earth, Waterford

★★★★ Du Toitskloof ★★★ Altydgedacht, Hildenbrand ★★★ Avontuur **NT** Asara, Delaire, Fort Simon, Groote Post, Morgenhof, Nitida Cellars, Savanha, Springfontein, Tokara, Vruchtbaar **NR** Shannon **D** Blaauwklippen, Cape Point, Iona, Robertson, Van Loveren, Vergelegen

Non-muscat, red, fortified

★★★ uniWines ★★ SoetKaroo **NT** SoetKaroo **D** SoetKaroo

Non-muscat, white, fortified

★★★★ Haute Cabrière, uniWines

Organic

★★★★☆ Lazanou (Chenin blanc wooded, dry), Reyneke (2) (Sauvignon blanc wooded, Sauvignon blanc unwooded), Woolworths

★★★★ Avondale (White blends, wooded, dry), Bon Cap (Red blends, shiraz/syrah-based), Groot Parys (2) (Chenin blanc wooded, dry, Vin de paille), La Motte (Sauvignon blanc unwooded), Laibach (Red blends, Cape Bordeaux), Mountain Oaks (2) (Pinotage, Red blends, Cape Bordeaux), **Porseleinberg** (Shiraz/syrah), Reyneke (4) (Pinotage, Red blends, other, Chenin blanc wooded, dry, White blends, wooded, dry), Stellar (Natural Sweet, white), **Woolworths**

★★★★ Avondale (Chenin blanc wooded, dry), Bon Cap (2) (Red blends, with pinotage, White blends,

unwooded, dry), Lazanou (2) (Shiraz/syrah, Chardonnay wooded), McGregor (Chardonnay unwooded), Mountain Oaks (3) (Red blends, Cape Bordeaux, Chardonnay wooded, Chenin blanc wooded, dry), **Reyneke** (Shiraz/syrah), Stellar (2) (Shiraz/syrah, Sauvignon blanc unwooded), Tukulu (Chardonnay wooded), Van Loveren (Port, red), Waverley Hills (2) (Shiraz/syrah, Red blends, shiraz/syrah-based), Woolworths (3) (Red blends, White blends, wooded, dry, Merlot)

★★★ African Terroir (Viognier), Bon Cap (Sauvignon blanc unwooded), De Breede (Red blends, Cape Bordeaux), **Groot Parys** (Chardonnay unwooded), Lazanou (Red blends, shiraz/syrah-based), Org de Rac (Shiraz/syrah), **Origin** (2) (Chardonnay wooded, White blends, wooded, dry), Seven Oaks (Red blends, Cape Bordeaux), **Spier** (2) (Sauvignon blanc unwooded, Cabernet sauvignon), Stellar (3) (Cabernet sauvignon, Rosé dry, Chardonnay unwooded), Upland (2) (Cabernet sauvignon, Port, red), Waverley Hills (3) (Cabernet sauvignon, Red blends, other, White blends, wooded, dry), Woolworths (2) (Rosé dry, Chardonnay wooded) ★★★ African Terroir (6) (Cabernet sauvignon, Shiraz/syrah, Chardonnay unwooded, Cabernet sauvignon, Shiraz/syrah, Red blends, with pinotage), Bergwater (Shiraz/syrah), Bon Cap (2) (Pinotage, Rosé dry), Groot Parys (2) (Chenin blanc unwooded dry, Chenin blanc unwooded dry), Mountain Oaks (2) (Rosé dry, White blends, unwooded, dry), Org de Rac (Cabernet sauvignon), Origin (3) (Red blends, shiraz/syrah-based, Red blends, with pinotage, Red blends, shiraz/syrah-based), Stellar (6) (Merlot, Pinotage, Sauvignon blanc unwooded, White blends, unwooded, dry, Merlot, Rosé dry), Waverley Hills (Red blends, Cape Bordeaux), **Woolworths** (4) (Pinotage, Merlot, Shiraz/syrah, Sauvignon blanc unwooded) ★★ African Terroir (7) (Pinotage, Sauvignon blanc unwooded, Merlot, Pinotage, Chardonnay unwooded, Sauvignon blanc unwooded, Sparkling, Non-MCC, rosé, dry), Bon Cap (Sparkling, Non-MCC, white, off-dry/semi-sweet), **Origin** (Merlot), Stellar (3) (Chenin blanc unwooded dry, White blends, unwooded, dry, White blends, unwooded, dry), Waverley Hills ★★ African Terroir (Merlot), Stellar (4) (Cabernet sauvignon, Shiraz/syrah, Shiraz/syrah, White blends, off-dry/semi-sweet (w & u/w)), Woolworths (2) (Cabernet sauvignon, White blends, off-dry/semi-sweet (w & u/w)) ★ African Terroir (2) (White blends, unwooded, dry, Rosé dry) **NT** Lazanou (Chenin blanc unwooded dry), Mountain Oaks (Chenin blanc wooded, dry), Org de Rac (3) (Cabernet sauvignon, Merlot, Shiraz/syrah), Waverley Hills **D** Avondale (4) (Chenin blanc wooded, dry, White blends, wooded, dry, Shiraz/syrah, Rosé dry), Tukulu (Sangiovese), Waverley Hills

Perlé wines

★★★ Jacob's Quest ★★ Capenheimer, Conradie (Light & low-alcohol), **Douglas Green** (Light & low-alcohol), Grünberger (2), Riebeek (2) (Light & low-alcohol, Light & low-alcohol) ★★ **Ashton**, Autumn Harvest Crackling (Light & low-alcohol), Bergsig (Light & low-alcohol), De Wet ★ Jonkheer (2) (Light & low-alcohol) **D** Ashton

Petit verdot

★★★★ Bellevue, KWV, Nederburg, Raka, Zorgvliet
★★★☆ Anura, Darling Cellars, **Hillcrest**, Lovane, Nabygelegen, Rico Suter, Signal Hill ★★★ **Calais Wine**, **Maison de Teijger** (2), **Stellenzicht** ★★☆ Doolhof ★★ TTT Cellar **NT** Asara, Du Preez, Haut Espoir, Môreson, My Wyn **D** Fairview

Petite sirah

★★★☆ Fairview

Pinot blanc

D Flagstone

Pinot gris/grigio

★★★☆ Nederburg, The Township Winery ★★★ Anthonij Rupert, Flat Roof Manor, Origin, **Robertson** ★★★ De Grendel, Obikwa, **Usana** ★★ **La Capra**, Two Oceans, Van Loveren, Woolworths **NT** Mount Rozier

Pinot noir

★★★★★ Cape Chamonix, Newton Johnson, Oak Valley

★★★★☆ **Botanica**, Bouchard Finlayson (2), **Creation**, Crystallum, Meerlust, Paul Cluver (2), Shannon, The Winery of Good Hope, Vriesenhof , Woolworths (2)

★★★★ Callender, Catherine Marshall (2), Creation, Crystallum, De Grendel, Domaine des Dieux, Flagstone, **Grande Provence**, Groote Post, Hamilton Russell, Herold, La Vierge, Muratie, Newton Johnson, Paul Cluver, **Spier**, **Strandveld**, Sumaridge, Topaz, Virgin Earth, Woolworths, **Yardstick**

★★★☆ Anura, Avontuur, De Wetshof, Elgin Vintners, Fryer's Cove, Glen Carlou, Haute Cabrière, Herold, Hoopenburg, Kleine Zalze, Signal Hill, Springfield, **Stark-Condé**, Strandveld, Thandi, The Winery of Good Hope, Two Oceans, Waterford, **Woolworths** ★★★ Andy Mitchell, Barrydale, **Beau Joubert**, Ernst Gouws, Felicité, **Haute Cabrière**, Longbarn, Lord's, Robertson, Thelema, Vriesenhof , Whalehaven, **William Everson**, Windfall ★★☆ Nabygelegen, Spookfontein ★★ Goedvertrouw, Quando **NT** Bon Courage, Bouchard Finlayson, Klein Optenhorst, Rusticus **NR** Highlands Road, **Meerendal D** De Trafford, Keisseskraal, Ridgemor, Woolworths

Pinotage

★★★★☆ Beyerskloof (2), Cape Chamonix, Chateau Naudé, DeWaal, Diemersfontein, Fairview, Flagstone, Grangehurst, Kaapzicht, Kanonkop, L'Avenir, Nederburg, Pick's Pick, Southern Right, **Spioenkop**, Stellenzicht, Umkhulu

★★★★ Allée Bleue, Altydgedacht, Anura, **Arra**, **Ashton**, **Bayede!**, Beaumont, Bellevue, Clos Malverne, Croydon, De Zoete Inval, DeWaal, Diemersdal, Diemersfontein, Dornier, Freedom Hill, Hazendal, Hidden Valley, Kaapzicht, **Kleine Zalze**, KWV, L'Avenir, Laibach, **Lammershoek**, Lanzerac (2), Longridge, Maastricht, Meerendal (2), Môreson, Mountain Oaks (Organic), Namaqua, Neethlingshof, Neil Ellis, Painted Wolf, Perdeberg, **Pulpit Rock**, Reyneke (Organic), Rijk's Pvt Cellar (3), Robertson, Rooiberg, Scali, Simonsig, Slaley, Spice Route, **Spier** (2), Springfontein, Stanford Hills, **Super Single**, SylvanVale, Warwick, Welgegund, Wamakersvallei, Wildekrans, Windmeul, Woolworths

★★★☆ Anura, **Badsberg**, Beyerskloof, Bilton, Boland, Boplaas (2), Bosman, Camberley, Cape of Good Hope, Cathedral Cellar, Cloof (2), Conradie, Darling Cellars (2), Delheim, Devon Hill, Devon Rocks, DeWaal, **Diemersdal**, Doolhof, Durbanville Hills, Eaglevlei, Eikendal, Fairview, Fleur du Cap, Fort Simon, Graham Beck, **Hofstraat**, Jonkheer, Kleine Zalze, **Lemberg**, Lindhorst, Lyngrove, M'hudi, **MAN Vintners**, Marklew, Meinert, Middelvlei, Misty Mountains, Mooiplaas, Neethlingshof, Onderkloof , Overhex, Raka, Rhebokskloof, Rico Suter, Riebeek, Romond, Savanha, Saxenburg, Schalk Burger, Schonenberg, Simonsvlei, **Six Hats**, Slaley, Springfontein, **Stellekaya**, Stellenbosch University , **StellenRust**, Swartland, **The Wine Fusion**, The Winery of Good Hope, Tukulu, Tulbagh Winery, **Vriesenhof** , Welgevallen, **Whalehaven**, Woolworths, Zonnebloem ★★★ **Aaldering**, Allée Bleue, Anura, Arniston Bay, Arra, Avontuur, Ayama, Backsberg, Barista, Bellevue, Bergsig (2), Boer & Brit, Boland, Bon Courage, Botha, Bovlei, **Clos Malverne**, De Heuvel, De Krans, De Villiers, Domaine Brahms, Doolhof, Douglas Green, Durbanville Hills, Eagle's Cliff, Escapade, Fairvalley, Fish Hoek, Four Paws, Goede Hoop, Graham Beck, Hawksmoor, Hill & Dale, Imbuko, Jacobsdal, **Klein Parys**, Knorhoek, Koelenhof , Kumkani, KWV, L'Auberge, La Capra, Landskroon, Long Mountain, Lutzville, Lyngrove, MAN Vintners, Manley, **Merwida**, Mountain River, Nederburg, New Beginnings, Nitida Cellars, Obikwa, Olsen, Origin, Oude Compagnies Post, Painted Wolf (2), Perdeberg, **Pick 'n Pay**, Pulpit Rock, Re'Mogo, Remhoogte, Rhebokskloof, Rickety Bridge, Riebeek, Ruitersvlei, Saam, Seidelberg, Ses'Fikile, Simonsvlei, Slanghoek, Stellenbosch Hills, Stellendrift, Swartland, The Bernard, The Township Winery,

Trajan, uniWines (2), Van Loveren (2), Viljoensdrift, Villiera, Vriesenhof , Vruchtbaar, **Wamakersvallei**, Wildekrans, Windmeul, Woolworths (2) ★★★ Aan de Doorns, Backsberg (Kosher), Bergheim, Bernheim, **Bloemendal**, Boland, Bon Cap (Organic), Bovlei, **Breëland**, **Burgershof**, Calais Wine, Calitzdorp, Cape Dreams, De Wet, Drostdy-Hof, Du Toitskloof , False Bay, **Groupe LFE**, Hawksmoor, Ken Forrester, Klawer, Kleine Zalze, L'Avenir, **Ladismith**, Long Mountain (2), **Malanot**, Marianne, McGregor, Morgenhof, Mountain River (2), Nederburg, Niel Joubert, **Origin**, Oude Kaap, **Overhex**, Rooiberg, Schalk Burger, Schalkenbosch, Seidelberg, Simonsig, Simonsvlei, Somerbosch, Spier, Stellar (Organic), StellenRust, **The Grape Grinder**, Tulbagh Winery (2), **Valley Vineyards**, Vukani, **Withington**, **Woolworths** (3) (Organic) ★★ African Pride, African Terroir (4) (Organic, Organic), Alvi's Drift, Ashton, Blomendahl, Culemborg, Goudini, Groupe LFE, Karusa, Klein Parys, Koopmanskloof, Louiesenhof, Montagu Wine & Spirits, **Mount Vernon**, Namaqua, **Nuweland**, Robertson, Sizanani, Two Oceans, Virgin Earth, Vredenheim, **Waboomsrivier**, Waterstone, Welmoed, Wineways, Withington, Zevenwacht ★★ Blomendahl, Bovlei, Buffalo Creek, Café Culture, Cape Gable, Golden Kaan, Jason's Hill, Kleine Draken (Kosher), United Nations, Zidela ★ De Zoete Inval, Wineways **NT** Bottelary Hills, Groot Constantia, **Groupe LFE**, Hawksmoor, Hazendal, Jonkheer, Le Grand, Nietvoorbij, Oude Compagnies Post, Oudtshoorn (2), Savanha, Spier (2), Stellenbosch University , SylvanVale, Tempel, Teubes, Tokara, Westbridge (2), Zonnebloem **D** Arniston Bay, Fort Simon, Graham Beck, Groupe LFE, Hartenberg, Lammershoek, Malanot, Mount Rozier, Nelson, Pulpit Rock, Riebeek (2), Rusticus, Saam, Stellenzicht, Tempel, Tulbagh Winery

Port, pink
★★★ Boplaas **NR** De Krans

Port, red
★★★★★ Boplaas (2), De Krans, JP Bredell
★★★★☆ Allesverloren, Boplaas (2), De Krans (2), Delaire, JP Bredell
★★★★ Axe Hill (2), Bergsig (2), Boplaas (4), De Krans, Grundheim, Jonkheer, JP Bredell, Landskroon, Monis, Morgenhof, Muratie (2), Overgaauw, Peter Bayly, Pick's Pick, Quinta, Swartland
★★★★ Alto, Annandale, Backsberg, Badsberg, Bergsig, Beyerskloof, De Wet, Dellrust, Douglas Green, Du'SwaRoo, Flagstone, **Goede Hoop**, Graham Beck, Groot Constantia, Grundheim, **Hout Bay**, Jacques Smit, Kaapzicht, Louiesenhof, Monis, Riebeek, Rooiberg, Van Loveren (Organic), Vergenoegd, Villiera ★★★ Aan de Doorns, Anura, Beau Joubert, Beaumont, Boland, Bon Courage,

Calitzdorp, Clairvaux, De Wet, De Zoete Inval (2), **Die Mas**, Du Toitskloof , **Holden Manz**, Jean Daneel, Koelenhof , KWV (2), **Louiesenhof**, McGregor, Montagu Wine & Spirits, Ridgeback, Riebeek, TTT Cellar, Tulbagh Winery, **Ultra Liquors**, Upland (Organic), **Vergenoegd**, Windmeul ★★★ Bernheim, Calitzdorp, Goudini, Grundheim, **Montagu Wine & Spirits**, Somerbosch, Swartland, **Withoek** ★★ Bovlei, Montpellier, TTT Cellar, Viljoensdrift, Villiersdorp, Withoek (2) ★★ Oudtshoorn, Tulbagh Winery ★ Du'SwaRoo, Nietvoorbij, Orange River **NT** Allée Bleue, Bonnievale, Botha, JP Bredell, Landzicht, Montagu Wine & Spirits, My Wyn (2), Oudtshoorn, Robertson, Thabani, Wamakersvallei **NR** Muratie, Slanghoek **D** Ashton, Goudini, Hofstraat, Linton Park, Withoek (2)

Port, white
★★★★ Asara
★★★ Axe Hill, Boplaas ★★ Peter Bayly **NS** TTT Cellar **NT** My Wyn **NR** De Krans

Red blends, Cape Bordeaux
★★★★★ De Toren, Glenelly, Meerlust, Miles Mossop
★★★★☆ Beaumont, Beyerskloof, Bilton, Buitenverwachting, Camberley, Cape Chamonix, Constantia Glen (2), Constantia Uitsig, Dalla Cia, Darling Cellars, Delheim, Diemersdal (2), Eikendal, Ernie Els, **Gabriëlskloof**, **Grande Provence**, Grangehurst, Groot Constantia, Hartenberg, Havana Hills, Hidden Valley, Hillcrest, Jordan (2), Kanonkop, **Keets**, Laibach, Lovane, Lynx, Morgenster (2), Mulderbosch, Muratie, Mvemve Raats, Nabygelegen, Neethlingshof, Nick & Forti's, Nitida Cellars, Robert Stanford, Rupert & Rothschild, Rustenberg, Saronsberg, Springfield, Steenberg, **Stellenbosch Ridge**, Thelema, Tokara, Vergelegen (2), Vergenoegd, Vilafonté (2), Von Ortloff, Warwick, **Windmeul**, Woolworths, Yonder Hill
★★★★ Amani, Anthonij Rupert, Asara, **Avondale**, Backsberg, Belfield, Blaauwklippen, Boer & Brit, Bonfoi, Boschkloof , Camberley, Claime d'Or, Cloof (2), Clos Malverne, Damarakloof, De Grendel, De Toren, DeWaal, Dombeya, Dornier, **Druk My Niet**, Durbanville Hills, Eagles' Nest, Epicurean, **Equitania**, **Flagstone**, Glen Carlou, Goats do Roam, Goede Hoop, Grangehurst, Groote Post, Haskell, Hermanuspietersfontein (2), Hout Bay, Iona, JP Bredell, Kaapzicht, Klein Constantia, Kleinfontein, Knorhoek, KWV, L'Avenir, La Bri, La Motte, Laibach (Organic), Le Bonheur, Le Riche, Leopard Frog, Louis, Lourensford, Lyngrove, Lynx, Manley, Meerhof, Meinert, MolenVliet, Mooiplaas, **Môreson**, Morgenhof, Mountain Oaks (Organic), Napier, Nederburg, Neil Ellis (2), Nelson, Nico van der Merwe, Noble Hill, Noble Savage, Oak Valley,

Ormonde, Overgaauw, Peter Falke, Ridgeback, Rietvallei, Romond, Rupert & Rothschild, Russo, Saronsberg, Schalk Burger, Simonsig, Spier, Stellekaya, StellenRust, Stony Brook (2), **The Drift**, **The High Road**, **The Natalie**, **Topaz**, Veenwouden, Vergelegen (2), Vergenoegd, Villiera, Von Ortloff, Vondeling, Vriesenhof , **Waterford**, Webersburg, Woolworths (3), Yonder Hill, Zevenwacht, Zorgvliet ★★★★ **Aaldering**, Alkmaar, Allée Bleue, Anura, Ashton, Avontuur, Beau Joubert, Bellingham, **Bernheim**, Boschendal, Boschkloof , Buitenverwachting, Cape Chamonix, Creation, D'Aria, Doolhof (3), **Dornier**, **Druk My Niet**, Eagles' Nest, Elemental Bob, Elgin Vintners, Emineo, Feiteiras, **Flagstone**, Fundi (2), Hathersage, High Constantia, Holden Manz, Jakob's Vineyards, Jean Daneel, Kanu, Klein Constantia, Kleine Zalze, Kloovenburg, La Vigne, Laborie, Le Joubert, Leopard's Leap, Lindhorst, **Louiesenhof**, **Maison de Teijger**, Mea Culpa, Meerendal, Monterosso, Mountain Oaks (Organic), Namaqua, Nederburg, Neethlingshof, Nelson, Raka, Rosendal, Schalkenbosch, Spookfontein , **Steenberg**, Sterhuis, Stonewall, Stony Brook, The High Road (2), The Winery of Good Hope, **Thunderchild**, Umkhulu (2), Uva Mira, Vendôme, Vredevol, Vuurberg, Wedderwill, Welgemeend (2), Welmoed, Woolworths, **Yardstick**, Zonnebloem ★★★ Agterplaas, Akkerdal, Alluvia, **Appollis Fairtrade**, Ariston Bay, **Arra**, Asara, Avontuur, **Badgerberg**, Bayede!, **Bellevue**, Bellingham, Black Oyster-catcher, BLANKbottle (2), Blomendahl, Bon Courage, Clos Malverne, Crows Nest, De Breede (Organic), **Diemersfontein** (2), Douglas Green (2), **Druk My Niet**, Eagle's Cliff, **Eikendal**, Equitania, Four Fields, Gabriëlskloof, Havana Hills, Hermanuspietersfontein, Hillcrest, Hornbill , Idiom , Jordan (2), Ken Forrester, Klein Dauphine, Klein Parys, Knorhoek, Kronendal, La Petite Ferme, La Petite Provence, **La Vierge**, La Vigne, Landskroon, Louiesenhof, **Maison de Teijger**, **Malanot**, McGregor, MolenVliet, **Morgenhof**, Mostertsdrift, **Napier**, Nico Vermeulen, **Oak Valley**, **Opstal**, Origin, Oude Kaap, Overgaauw, **Passages**, Raats, Ridgeback, Rusticus, Schalkenbosch, Seidelberg, Seven Oaks (Organic), Skilpadvlei, Slaley, Slanghoek, Stellendrift, Thandi, Thelema, Two Oceans, Ultra Liquors, Van Zylshof, Vendôme, Vondeling, Wedgewood, Woolworths ★★★ **Almenkerk**, Anura, Ashton, Bernheim, Beyerskloof, Bottelary, Cape Promise, Craighall, Darling Cellars, Diemersdal, Elemental Bob, **Jacaranda**, KWV, **Lord Somerset**, Nietvoorbij (2), Nomada, Perdeberg, Rhebokskloof, Riebeek, Saxenburg, **Sterhuis**, Tanagra, **uniWines**, **Van Loveren**, Versailles, Waverley Hills (Organic), Welgevallen, Wildekrans, Wineways, Wolvendrift, Woolworths, Zidela ★★

Angels Tears, Blouvlei, Bonnievale, Bottelary Hills, David Frost Signature, Douglas Green, Kleine Draken (Kosher), Main Street, Morgenhof, Origin, Overhex, Rooiberg, Simonsig, Simonsvlei, **Swartland**, Windmeul, **Wineways** (3) ★★ Goedverwacht, **Golden Kaan**, Wineways ★ Lathithá **NT** Alto, Awendland (2), Buitenverwachting, **Equitania**, Hoopenburg, Koningsrivier, **Mimosa**, Mont du Toit, Môreson (2), Noble Hill, Old Vines, Rico Suter, Ruitersvlei, Saltaré, Ses'Fikile, Stellendrift, Tanagra, Ultra Liquors, Viljoensdrift, Welgemeend, Wines of Cape Town, Wolfkloof **NR** Birkenhead **D** Constantia Mist, Fort Simon, Graham Beck, Hout Bay, Klein Gustrouw, Lievland, Mount Rozier, Napier, Orange River, Overhex, Rijk's Pvt Cellar, Virgin Earth, Vriesenhof , Waterstone, Woolworths

Red blends, other

★★★★★ Bouchard Finlayson, Graham Beck

★★★★☆ Anatu, Ataraxia, De Meye, De Trafford, Delaire, Ernie Els (2), Fairview, Fleur du Cap, Jean Daneel, Ken Forrester, Lingen, Mary Le Bow, Mont du Toit (2), Nederburg, Uva Mira, Val de Vie, Waterford, Zorgvliet

★★★★ Akkerdal, Allée Bleue, Amani, **Annandale**, Anthonij Rupert, Backsberg (2), **Beau Joubert**, Bergsig, BLANKbottle (2), Boplaas, Boschendal, Brampton, Bushmanspad, Camberley, Capaia, **Cape Rock**, Cathedral Cellar, Clovelly, De Krans, **Druk My Niet**, Elemental Bob, Faraway House, Fundi, Graceland, Guardian Peak (2), Jean Daneel, Joostenberg, Keermont, **Ken Forrester**, Marianne, MC Square, Micu Narunsky, Mont du Toit, Nederburg, Neil Ellis Meyer-Näkel, **Newton Johnson**, Pick's Pick, Plaisir, Quoin Rock, Reyneke (Organic), Rico Suter (2), Rust en Vrede, Rustenberg, Rusticus, Solo, Somerbosch, Stony Brook, Swartland, **Tierhoek**, TMV, Virgin Earth, **Waterford**, Waterkloof, Woolworths, Zoetendal

★★★★ Adoro, Alto, Annandale, Anura, Audacia, Bilton, Blaauwklippen, Bon Courage, Boplaas, Calais Wine, Capaia, Casa Mori, Cederberg, Cloof, De Vallei, Delheim, **Desert Rose**, Dormershire, Elemental Bob, Four Paws, Fundi, Goats do Roam, Hartenberg, Haut Espoir, Hornbill , Jacques Smit, Juno, **Klein Gustrouw**, Knorhoek, Kumala, Kyburg, La Kavayan, **La Vierge**, Micu Narunsky, Morgenster (2), Mount Rozier, Nederburg, Overgaauw, **Pick's Pick**, Rhebokskloof, Roodeberg, Saxenburg, Signal Hill, Slaley, **Sophie**, Steclkaya, StellenRust, Topiary, Uitkyk, Val de Vie, Veenwouden, Vergenoegd, **Welvanpas**, Woolworths (2) ★★★ Arumdale, **Axe Hill**, Badsberg, Bellingham, Blomendahl, Blue Crane, Boschheim, Calais Wine, Cloof, Cranefields, Darling Cellars, Doolhof, Douglas Green, Du Toitskloof , Franki's, Glen Carlou, Goede Hoop, Graham Beck, Hazendal, Idiom, Janeza, Journey's End, Kumala (3),

La Petite Ferme, **Longridge**, Louisvale, Lynx, **Mon Rêve**, Mont du Toit, Nabygelegen, Prospect1870, Raka, Retief, Robertson, Schalkenbosch, Seven Oaks, Stonehill, TCB Wines, The Township Winery, **The Wine Fusion**, Van Loveren (2), Vaughan Johnson, Vergenoegd (2), Villiera, Waverley Hills (Organic), Zevenwacht ★★★ Aan de Doorns, Arniston Bay, Avontuur, Backsberg, Bayede!, Bergsig, Blouvlei, Boland (2), Bonnievale, Botha, Bottelary Hills, Chateau Libertas, Clos Malverne, **Crows Nest**, De Zoete Inval, Douglas Green, Drostdy-Hof, Durbanville Hills, Hill & Dale, Idiom, Jason's Hill, Landskroon (2), Leopard's Leap, Long Mountain, **Lord Somerset**, Millstream, Mountain Range, Muratie, Nuy, Peter Bayly, Rietvallei, Ruitersvlei, Simonsig, Skilpadvlei, Stettyn, Swartland, Tassenberg, Theuniskraal, TTT Cellar, Two Oceans, **uniWines**, Van Loveren, Vaughan Johnson, Versus, Villiersdorp, Wandsbeck, Waterstone, Weltevrede, Woolworths ★★ Arniston Bay, Ashton, Beaumont, Bergwater, **Burgershof**, Cloverfield, Culemborg, Du Toitskloof , Eikendal, **Eve**, Goudini, Landskroon, Malan Family, Mooiplaas, Mountain River, Mzoli's, **Orange River**, Oude Kaap (2), Retief, Stellenbosch University , Swartland, Taverna Rouge, The Saints, Waterstone (3), **Wineways**, Withington, Woolworths (2), Zandvliet ★★ Abbottshill, Barrydale, Bonnievale, Brandvlei, Clairvaux, Du Preez, Pick 'n Pay, Robertson (2), Roodezandt ★ **Groupe LFE**, Oude Wellington ★ **Tanagra NT** Barry Gould, Bartinney, Bergwater, **Buffalo Creek**, Cape Rock, Groupe LFE, Lemberg, Lourensford, Matuba, Nederburg, Onderkloof , Opstal, Oudtshoorn, Ridgemor, Seven Oaks, Simonsvlei, Stoumann's, Waterstone, Welvanpas, Westbridge **NR** Delaire, Montagu Wine Cellar, **Rosendal**, Wildekrans **D** African Pride, Avondale (3), BABISA, Calitzdorp, Cameradi, Carisbrooke, De Meye, Diemersfontein, Du'SwaRoo, Flat Roof Manor, Golden Kaan, Groupe LFE (2), Haute Cabrière, Lammershoek, Montagu Wine Cellar, Opstal, Schalkenbosch, Tierhoek, Tulbagh Winery, Vredenheim, Waterstone, Withoek

Red blends, shiraz/syrah-based

★★★★★ La Motte, Sadie

★★★★☆ Amani, Anwilka, Creation, **Fable**, **Haskell**, Hoopenburg, Kronendal, Lammershoek, Mont Destin, Newton Johnson, Nico van der Merwe, Post House, Reyneke, Rust en Vrede, Saronsberg, Schalk Burger, Sequillo, The Winery of Good Hope, Woolworths

★★★★ Anwilka, **Avondale**, Ayama, BABISA, **Babylon's Peak**, Badenhorst, Barton, Black Knight, Black Oystercatcher, BLANKbottle, Boekenhoutskloof, Bon Cap (Organic), Bosman, Bovlei, Cape Rock, Catherine Marshall, Cecilia, Crios

Bríde, DeMorgenzon, Diemersfontein, **Domaine des Dieux**, **Eagle's Cliff**, Emineo, Glenelly, Graceland, Grangehurst, Groenland, **Havana Hills**, Hawksmoor (2), Hermanuspietersfontein, **Hermit on the Hill**, Hidden Valley, Hughes Family, Kaapzicht, La Motte, Landskroon, Lindhorst, Lourensford (2), **Malanot**, **MAN Vintners**, Meerhof, **Migliarina**, MolenVliet (2), Mullineux, Nico Vermeulen (Shiraz/syrah), **Noble Hill**, Orangerie, Oude Denneboom, Rall, Rijk's Pvt Cellar (2), Rosendal, Rusticus, Schalkenbosch, Sijnn, Solms-Delta, Spier, Stony Brook, Sumaridge, The Bernard, The Goose, **The Wine Fusion**, The Winery of Good Hope (2), **Val de Vie**, **Wildehurst**, Woolworths (2), Zevenwacht

★★★★ Akkerdal, Annex Kloof, **Anthonij Rupert**, Anura (2), Arra (2), Beaumont, Bellingham (2), Black Pearl, Boekenhoutskloof, Boschendal, Boutros, Cape Rock, D'Aria, Darling Cellars, Edgebaston (2), Ernie Els, Excelsior, Flagstone, Flat Roof Manor, Goats do Roam (2), Groenland, Guardian Peak, Hazendal, Herold, Heron Ridge, Hex River Crossing, Idiom, Joostenberg, Ken Forrester, Kleine Zalze, Koelenhof , Kumkani (2), La Ferme Derik, **La Vierge**, Le Joubert (2), Leopard's Leap, Lievland, Lynx, Mellasat, Mont Destin, Mount Babylon, Naughton's, Nico van der Merwe, **Origin**, Ormonde, Painted Wolf (2), Pick's Pick, Rickety Bridge, Ridgeback, Rietvallei, Schalkenbosch, Schonenberg, Secateurs, Simonsvlei (2), Solms-Delta, Spice Route (2), Springfontein, Stellenbosch Hills, Stettyn, The Winery of Good Hope, Thokozani, Trajan, uniWines, **Val du Charron**, **Vredenheim**, **Waterford**, Waverley Hills (Organic), Welgegund, Woolworths (Organic), Yonder Hill, Zevenwacht, Zonnebloem ★★★ African Pride, Akkerdal, Allée Bleue, **Amani**, Asara, Babylon's Peak, Beau Joubert, Bernheim, **Blue Crane**, Boekenhoutskloof, Boer & Brit, Boschendal, Boschheim, Cape Point, D'Aria, De Heuvel, Dellrust, Dornier, **Du'SwaRoo**, Freedom Hill (2), **GlenWood**, Groot Constantia, **Hermit on the Hill**, Highlands Road, Idiom, Karusa, Kleine Zalze, Kumala, Lazanou (Organic), Leopard Frog, Lyngrove, Manley, Mellasat, Retief, **Revelation**, Ridgeback, Rooiberg, Simonsig, Tanagra, Teddy Hall, Thandi, Thelema, Two Oceans, **Valley Vineyards**, Waterford, Withington ★★★ **Appollis Fairtrade**, Arniston Bay, Audacia, Bellingham, Blaauwklippen, Blue Crane, **Camberley**, Douglas Green, Eagle's Cliff, Groupe LFE, **Hazendal**, Joostenberg, Kanu, Kleine Zalze, Koelenhof , **Le Roux & Fourie**, Long Mountain, Nederburg (2), Origin (2) (Organic, Organic), Overhex, Simonsvlei, **Teddy Hall**, **Valley Vineyards**, **Waka Waka**, Whalehaven, Wine Village-Hermanus, Woolworths (2) ★★ Arniston Bay, **Bellingham**, De Wet, Drostdy-Hof, Du Preez, Karusa, KWV, Libby's Pride, Orange River, Origin, Riebeek, Somerbosch, Summerhill, Tulbagh Winery, Vleiland, **Windfall**,

Zidela (2) ★★ **Keisseskraal**, Simonsvlei, Ultra Liquors **NT** Abbottshill, Croydon, Graham Beck (2), Hill & Dale (Kosher), Juno, Klawer, KWV, Matuba, Noble Hill, Old Vines, Oude Compagnies Post, Prospect1870, Ridgemor, Saam, The Winery of Good Hope **NR** Beaumont, KWV **D** Boschkloof, Gilga, Goats do Roam, Juno, Kumala, Lievland, Long Mountain, Nietvoorbij, Rijk's Pvt Cellar, Secateurs, Sijnn, Swartland, Tulbagh Winery, Val de Vie, Woolworths (2)

Red blends, with pinotage

★★★★☆ Beaumont, Beyerskloof, Graham Beck, Kaapzicht, Lanzerac, Middelvlei, Spier

★★★★ Altydgedacht, Alvi's Drift, Asara, Ashbourne, Beyerskloof, BLANKbottle, Clos Malverne (2), Croydon, Devon Hill, Emineo, Flagstone (2), Grangehurst, Idiom, Kaapzicht, Klein Parys, Marklew, Meinert, Post House, Raka, Rijk's Estate, Schalk Burger, Simonsig, Springfontein, Stellenzicht, SylvanVale, Warwick, Wildekrans, Windmeul

★★★★ Babylon's Peak, Bellingham, Bon Cap (2) (Organic), Cloof, Domaine Brahms (2), Doolhof, Eaglevlei, Fairview, Faraway House, Kaapzicht, Kanonkop, La Chataigne, **Lindhorst**, **Lutzville**, Middelvlei, Mount Vernon, **Nuweland**, Post House, Remhoogte (2), **Spier**, Stellekaya, Stellenbosch University , **StellenRust**, Umkhulu, **Val du Charron** ★★★ Anura, Arra, Bellevue, **Bernheim**, Cloof, Conradie, Douglas Green, Du Toitskloof , Freedom Hill, Fundi, Kaapzicht, Kumala, Kumkani, Lateganskop, **Leeuwenberg**, **Leopard Frog**, Lorraine, Marianne, **Maske**, Mont Rochelle, **Mostertsdrift**, Natte Valleij, Oude Compagnies Post, Schalk Burger, Stellekaya, The Parlotones, **The Wine Fusion**, Umkhulu, Viljoensdrift, **Waterstone**, **Wedderwill**, Wedgewood, Welgemeend ★★★ African Terroir (Organic), Cloof, De Krans, Du Preez, Koopmanskloof, Kumala (2), **Orange River**, **Origin** (Organic), Overmeer Cellars, Slaley, Springfontein, Stellendrift, StellenRust, Vruchtbaar ★★ African Pride, Bellingham, BurCon, De Doorns, Douglas Green, Dragonridge, Drostdy-Hof, Groupe LFE, Jonkheer, Louiesenhof, Overhex, Seven Sisters, Stellenbosch Hills, **Stellendrift**, Two Oceans ★★ Pearly Bay, Slanghoek, Whalehaven, **Wildekrans**, Woolworths (3) ★ Skilpadvlei **NT** African Terroir, Ayama, Belbon Hills, Bernheim, Bottelary Hills, Clos Malverne (2), Grangehurst, Mountain River, Obikwa, Rosendal, Sizanani, SylvanVale **D** African Pride, Alvi's Drift, Beyerskloof, Bonnievale, Devon Hill, Elberti, Kumala, Leopard's Leap, Mount Rozier, Mountain Ridge, Mountain River, Remhoogte, Saam, Tulbagh Winery (2), Vriesenhof

Riesling (sometimes labelled Rhine/Weisser)

★★★★☆ Howard Booysen

★★★★ De Wetshof, Groote Post, Hartenberg, Nitida Cellars, Paul Cluver (2) (Light & low-alcohol), **The Drift**, Woolworths

★★★★ Fairview, Jordan, Klein Constantia, La Vierge, Ross Gower, Thelema, Villiera ★★★ Nederburg, Revelation, Thelema ★★★ Rietvallei **NT** Woolworths **NR** Spioenkop **D** Buitenverwachting

Rosé dry

★★★★ **Akkerdal**, La Petite Ferme, Grangehurst, Solms-Delta

★★★☆ Anatu, Blouvlei, Clouds, Hermanuspietersfontein, Highlands Road, Jordan, Kanonkop, Klein Dauphine, **Lammershoek**, Lanzerac, Nabygelegen, Opstal, Romond, Signal Hill, Sijnn, **Sophie**, **The Drift**, Wildehurst ★★★ Altydgedacht, Andy Mitchell, Anura, Asara, **Avondale**, Barton, Bein, Beyerskloof, Black Oystercatcher, Blomendahl, Boschendal, Brampton, Cederberg, Darling Cellars, De Grendel, De Meye, De Vallei, De Wetshof, Delaire, DeMorgenzon, Diemersdal, Dunstone, Eikendal, Elgin Vintners, Feiteiras, Fort Simon, Hawksmoor, High Constantia, Holden Manz, Hout Bay, **Ken Forrester**, Klein Dauphine, **Le Pommier**, **Lord's**, Meinert, Morgenster, **Oak Valley**, Painted Wolf, **Pick's Pick**, Raka, Rickety Bridge, Ross Gower, Secateurs, Simonsvlei, Sizanani, Spier, Stellar (Organic), Stonehill, Stony Brook, Sumaridge, SylvanVale, Tokara, Vergenoegd, Waterford, Waterkloof, Woolworths ★★★ **Abbottshill**, Backsberg, Beaumont, Bon Cap (Organic), **Bosman**, **Claime d'Or**, Cloof, De Krans, Doolhof, Dornier, Douglas Green, Dragonridge, **Durbanville Hills**, Eerste Hoop, **Escapade**, Felicité, Fish Hoek, Flat Roof Manor, Goats do Roam, Graham Beck, Hildenbrand, Hill & Dale, Hillcrest, **Holden Manz**, **Hoopenburg**, Joostenberg, Juno, Kaapzicht, Klein Constantia, Kleine Zalze, Kleinfontein, Kumala (2), L'Avenir, La Capra, Lynx, MAN Vintners, Mont Rochelle, **Mount Vernon**, Mountain Oaks (Organic), Niel Joubert, Org de Rac, Origin, Oude Compagnies Post, Overgaauw, Overhex, Perdeberg, Saronsberg, Schalk Burger, Schalkenbosch, Slaley, Slowine, Spookfontein , **Springfontein**, Stellar (Organic), **The Parlotones**, Versus, Vukani, Welgegund, **Winters Drift**, Woolworths, Zandvliet, Zorgvliet ★★ African Pride, Ayama, Beau Joubert, Bellingham, Birkenhead, Cape Dreams, De Heuvel, Du'SwaRoo, False Bay, **Groot Parys**, Groupe LFE (3), Haut Espoir, **Jacaranda**, Kloovenburg, Koopmanskloof, **Longridge**, Mellasat, Muratie, New Beginnings, Re'Mogo, Ridgeback, Rietvallei (2), Thandi, Waterstone, Welmoed, **Whalehaven**, Wolfkloof ★★ Groupe LFE (2), Marianne, **Pick 'n Pay** ★ African Terroir (Organic), **Koelenhof** **NT** Abingdon, African Terroir, Avontuur, Blomendahl, Calitzdorp, Cape Hutton, Devonair, Dormershire, **Groupe LFE**, Hawksmoor, Hidden

Valley, High Constantia, Mitre's Edge, Mountain River, Nederburg, Nelson, Onderkloof , Savanha, South Hill, TTT Cellar, Waverley Hills **NR** Eaglevlei **D** African Pride, Allée Bleue, Almenkerk, Avondale (Organic), De Villiers, Fairview, Groupe LFE (2), Longridge, Nederburg, Ridgemor, Steenberg, Zandberg

Rosé off-dry/semi-sweet

★★★★ Stony Brook

★★★★ Lourensford, Mulderbosch, Topiary ★★★ **Allée Bleue**, Backsberg, Devon Rocks, Goedverwacht, Kleine Zalze, Lindhorst, Nelson, **Noble Savage**, **Robert Stanford**, Saxenburg, Seidelberg, Stettyn, **uniWines**, Woolworths (2) ★★★ Arniston Bay, **Badsberg**, Bellingham, Bernheim, Blomendahl, Bottelary (Light & low-alcohol), Brandvlei, Delheim, Drostdy-Hof, Du Toitskloof , Eagle's Cliff, Graça, **Hazendal**, **Kanu**, **Karusa**, KWV, Ladismith, Lorraine, Lutzville, McGregor, Meerendal, **Merwida**, Mooiplaas, Morgenhof, **Mountain Ridge**, Mzoli's, Obikwa, Rooiberg, Seven Oaks, StellenRust, Thokozani, Two Oceans, Van Loveren, **Van Zylshof**, Viljoensdrift, **Welvanpas**, Wonderfontein, Zevenwacht ★★ Angels Tears, Arniston Bay, Bellingham, Bergsig, **Blaauwklippen**, Boland (2), Bon Courage, **Botha**, **Bushmanspad**, D'Aria, Douglas Green, **Eve**, Golden Kaan, Hartswater, Havana Hills (2), Imbuko, Knorhoek, Lathithá, Leopard's Leap, Louiesenhof, Millstream, Mostertsdrift, Nederburg, Nelson, Orange River (Light & low-alcohol), Origin, Pearly Bay (2) (Light & low-alcohol), Rhebokskloof, Riebeek, **Six Hats**, Theuniskraal, Tulbagh Winery, Wandsbeck, **Wildekrans**, Woolworths (2) ★★ **Ashton**, Cellar Cask, **Du Toitskloof** , **Goudini**, Jonkheer, Kleine Draken (Kosher), Koelenhof , **Origin** (Light & low-alcohol), Pick 'n Pay (Light & low-alcohol), **Pulpit Rock**, Slanghoek (Light & low-alcohol), Swartland, Vredenheim, Woolworths (Light & low-alcohol), Zidela ★ Robertson (Light & low-alcohol), **Zidela** ★ Bergwater **NT** Arniston Bay, Benguela Cove, Bovlei (2), **Buffalo Creek**, Drostdy-Hof, Nietvoorbij, Simonsvlei, Stoumann's, Wildekrans **D** Blaauwklippen, Dellrust, Karusa, La Chataigne, Mountain Ridge, Overhex (Light & low-alcohol), Skilpadvlei, Tulbagh Winery, Viljoensdrift, Wineways

Roussanne

★★★★ Mischa, Rustenberg
★★★★ The Bernard, **The Foundry** ★★★ Painted Wolf

Ruby cabernet

★★★ Bellpost ★★★ Langverwacht, Long Mountain, Orange River (2), Robertson (2) ★★ Ladismith, McGregor ★★ **Barrydale**, Hartswater, **Kingsriver**,

Robertson ★ Oude Wellington **NT** Oudtshoorn **D** Goudini, Lutzville

Sacramental wine

★★ Kleine Draken

Sangiovese

★★★★ The Three Foxes
★★★★ Anthonij Rupert, Anura ★★★ Dragonridge, Fairview, Raka ★★★ Koelenhof , Monterosso ★★ Idiom **D** Tukulu

Sauvignon blanc unwooded

★★★★★ Graham Beck, Kleine Zalze, Strandveld
★★★★☆ Ataraxia, Boschendal, Buitenverwachting, De Grendel, Diemersdal (3), Fleur du Cap (2), Groot Constantia, High Constantia, Iona, Nederburg, **Noble Hill**, Quoin Rock, Reyneke (Organic), Saxenburg, Southern Right, Steenberg, Tierhoek, Tokara, Vergelegen, Warwick, Waterford, Wedderwill, Woolworths

★★★★ African Pride, Allée Bleue, Alluvia, Almenkerk, Anura, Bartinney, Bellevue, Benguela Cove, Black Oystercatcher, Boplaas, Bouchard Finlayson, Buitenverwachting, Cape Chamonix, Cape Point, Cathedral Cellar, Catherine Marshall, Cederberg (2), Clouds, Constantia Glen, Constantia Mist, Constantia Uitsig, Creation, Darling Cellars, De Grendel, De Heuvel, Delaire (2), DeMorgenzon, Diemersdal, Domaine des Dieux, Driehoek, Durbanville Hills, Elgin Heights, Flagstone (2), Fort Simon, Fryer's Cove, Graham Beck, Groot Constantia, Groote Post (2), Hermanuspietersfontein (2), Herold, Hidden Valley, Jordan, Klein Gustrouw, Kumkani (2), KWV, La Motte (Organic), La Vierge, **Lanner Hill**, Lomond, Long Mountain, Longridge, Lourensford (2), Lutzville, Nederburg (2), Nitida Cellars (2), Noble Hill, Origin, Paul Cluver, Perdeberg, **Phizante**, Plaisir, Rickety Bridge, Robert Stanford, Robertson, Rustenberg, Sir Lambert, **Sizanani**, Spice Route, Springfield, Steenberg, Sterhuis, The Berrio, Thelema (2), **Tierhoek**, Tokara (2), Usana, Uva Mira, Van Loveren, Vergelegen, Vondeling, **Weßersburg**, Woolworths (3) (Organic), Zevenwacht, Zorgvliet

★★★★ Adoro, Altydgedacht, Amani, **Annandale**, Anthonij Rupert, Avontuur, Bergwater, Bilton, Bloemendal, Blomendahl, Bon Courage, Bonnievale, Boschendal (2), Bottelary Hills, Brampton, Brunia, Bushmanspad, Claime d'Or, Clos Malverne, **COAV**, Conradie, Crios Bríde, D'Aria, Darling Cellars, DeWaal, Durbanville Hills, Eagles' Nest, Elberti, Elgin Ridge, Ernst Gouws, Escapade, Fryer's Cove, Garden Route, Glen Erskine, Grande Provence, Hartenberg, Hathersage, Havana Hills, Hazendal, Hermanuspietersfontein, Hidden Valley, Hillcrest, Hoopenburg (2), Hout Bay, Izak van der Vyver, Joubert-Tradauw, Karusa, Ken Forrester, Klein Constantia (2), Klein Roosboom, Kling, L'Avenir,

L'Olivier, La Chataigne, La Motte, La Petite Ferme, Lanzerac, Le Bonheur, Lindhorst, Lomond, Longbarn, M'hudi, Maastricht, Meerendal, Meinert, Misty Mountains, Mont Rochelle, Mount Rozier, Nederburg, Nico Vermeulen, Nomada, Oak Valley, Ormonde (2), Overhex, Packwood, Pick's Pick, Post House, Raka, Rietvallei, **Rivendell**, Rosendal, Saronsberg, **Seven Springs** , Seven Steps, Signal Gun, Simonsig, **Simonsvlei**, **Sophie**, South Hill, Spring Grove, Springfield, Stellar (Organic), Stellendrift, Strandveld, Sumaridge, Swartland, **Teubes**, Thandi, The Goose, The Township Winery, Trajan, Ultra Liquors, Villiera, Virgin Earth, Von Ortloff, Waterford, Waterkloof, Waterstone, Weltevrede, Wines of Cape Town, Wonderfontein, Zorgvliet ★★★ Aan de Doorns, Alvi's Drift, Ayama, Backsberg, Bergsig, Birkenhead, Blouvlei, Blue Crane, Boekenhoutskloof, Bon Cap (Organic), Botha, Bramon, **Camberley** , Cape Hutton, Cape Promise, Catch Of The Day, **Cloof**, **Dâbar**, Dalla Cia, De Vallei, De Wetshof, Devon Hill, Diemersdal, Doolhof, Dormershire, Du Preez, Du Toitskloof , Durbanville Hills, Eagle's Cliff, Elgin Grove, Elgin Valley, Elgin Vintners, **Ernie Els**, **Esona**, Excelsior, Fairvalley, Fairview, False Bay, Fat Bastard, Fish Hoek, Flag- stone, Fleur du Cap, Fort Simon, Four Paws, Free- dom Hill, Galleon, Glen Carlou, GlenWood, Goede Hoop, Groenland, Helderberg, Het Vlock, High Constantia, Imbuko, Kaapzicht, Klawer, Klein Roosboom , Kleine Zalze, Knorhoek, Kranskop, KWV, Laborie, Langverwacht, Le Pommier, Lemberg, Lomond, Long Beach, Lord's, Louisvale, **LuKa**, Lutzville, Lyngrove, MAN Vintners, **Mimosa**, Mooiplaas, Morgenhof, Mount Vernon, Mountain Ridge, Mulderbosch, Nederburg, Neethlingshof, Niel Joubert, Nuweland, Overgaauw, Peter Falke, Philip Jordaan, Quando, Ridgeback, **Ridgemor**, Robertson (2), Sauvignon.Com, Schalk Burger, Seal Breeze, Seidelberg, Seven Oaks, Seven Sisters, Simonsvlei (2), **Six Hats**, Spier (2) (Organic), **Springfontein**, Stanford Hills, StellenRust, The Goose, Tread Lightly, Uitkyk, uniWines, **Valley Green**, Van Zylshof, Viljoensdrift, Villiera, Welgevallen, **Winters Drift**, Woolworths (6), Yonder Hill, Zandfontein, Zoetendal, Zonnebloem ★★★ African Pride, Angels Tears, Anura (2), Arniston Bay, Asara, Ashton, Avontuur, **Badgerberg**, Badsberg, Blaauwklippen, Boer & Brit, Boland, Boplaas (2), Bovlei, Buffalo Creek, **Burgershof**, **Calais Wine**, Cape Classics, Cape Gable, Cape Point, Clairvaux, Cloverfield, Craighall, De Villiers, De Wet, De Wetshof, Devon Rocks, DeWaal, Doolhof, Dornier, Du Preez, **Flat Roof Manor** (Light & low-alcohol), Franschhoek Cellar, Goedvertrouw, Goudini, Haut Espoir, Havana Hills, Highlands Road, **Kanu**, **Kingsriver**, Kloovenburg, Kumala, La Capra, Landskroon, Leop- ard's Leap, Linton Park, Long Mountain, **Lord**

Somerset, Lorraine, Louiesenhof, Lourensford, Merwida, Miravel, Mischa, Misty Mountains, Muratie, Nabygelegen, Namaqua, Neethlingshof, Nelson, Nuy, **Oak Valley**, Obikwa, Opstal, Origin (2), **Oude Kaap**, **Overhex**, Perdeberg, **Pick 'n Pay**, **Place in the Sun**, Re'Mogo, Rhebokskloof, Rickety Bridge, Riebeek, Rietvallei, Roodezandt, Rosendal, Ruitersvlei, Schalkenbosch, Slaley, Slanghoek, Slowine, Somerbosch, Steenberg, Stellar (Organic), Stellenbosch Hills, Stellenzicht, Stettyn, Stony Brook, Swartland, **TCB Wines**, The Township Winery, Thembi & Co, Tukulu, Tulbagh Winery, Two Oceans, uniWines, **Vaalvlei**, Van Loveren, Versailles, Vredenheim, Vukani, Wandsbeck, Waterford, Waterstone (2), Welmoed, Wildekrans, Windmeul, Wolvendrift, Woolworths (2) (Organic), Zonnebloem ★★ African Terroir (3) (Organic, Organic), Akkerdal, Bayede!, Beau Joubert, **Boland**, Brandvlei, Cape Dreams, Culemborg, **Die Mas**, Douglas Green, Drostdy-Hof, Du Toitskloof , Elgin Valley, **Glenview**, Goedverwacht, Golden Kaan, Hill & Dale, Imbuko, Juno, Klein Parys, Koelenhof , KWV, Ladismith, Libby's Pride, Lievland, McGregor, Monterosso, Morgenhof, Namaqua, Onderkloof , Oudtshoorn, Robertson, Rooiberg, Saam, Skilpadvlei, **Sumsaré**, Tulbagh Winery, United Nations, **Valley Vineyards** (2), **Waboomsrivier**, **Wildekrans**, Wine Village-Hermanus, Wineways, Withoek, Woolworths (Light & low-alcohol), Zandvliet, Zidela ★★ Barrydale, Calitzdorp, Goudini, Jason's Hill, Jonkheer, Kleine Draken (Kosher), Koelenhof , Koopmanskloof, Lateganskop, Mountain River, Weltevrede ★ African Terroir, Robertson (2) (Light & low-alcohol, Light & low-alcohol), Wineways (2) ★ United Nations **NT** Alluvia, Amani, AntHill, Arniston Bay, **Barry Gould**, Belbon Hills, Bonfoi, Crystallum, Dellrust, **Diners Club Bartho Eksteen** , Durbanville Hills (2), DuVon, Freedom Hill, Highlands Road, Jonkheer, Kleinbosch, Louis, Matuba, Montagu Wine & Spirits, Môreson (2), Mountain River, Rico Suter, Ross Gower, Saam, Savanha (2), Spier (2), Stoep, Stoumann's, Welvanpas, Whalehaven, William Everson, Woolworths **NR** Awendland, Delheim, **Le Roux & Fourie**, Montpellier, Neil Ellis, Spioenkop (2) **D** African Pride, Almenkerk, Arniston Bay, Avondale, Bergwater, Boplaas, Crows Nest, Golden Kaan, Groupe LFE, Leopard's Leap, Linton Park, Malanot, Nederburg, Nelson, Nico van der Merwe, Nietvoorbij, Ormonde, Overhex (2), Pulpit Rock, Rijk's Pvt Cellar, Wildekrans, Wine4Us

Sauvignon blanc wooded

★★★★★ Hermanuspietersfontein

★★★★☆ Cape Chamonix, **Cape Point** (2), Klein Constantia, Neil Ellis, Quoin Rock, Reyneke (Organic), Shannon, Waterkloof, Zorgvliet

★★★★ Backsberg, Bouchard Finlayson, Capaia, D'Aria, **De Vallei**, Dombeya, **Hermit on the Hill** (2), Jordan, Meerendal, **Nederburg**, Newton Johnson, Pick's Pick, **Spioenkop**, Stony Brook, Waterkloof, Zevenwacht

★★★★ Edgebaston, Misty Mountains, Peter Falke, Stark-Condé, Steenberg, Stone Ridge ★★★ Barton, Eikendal, **Gabriëlskloof**, Marianne, **Wildekrans**, Windfall **NT** Abingdon **D** La Petite Ferme, My Wyn, Perdeberg

Semillon unwooded

★★★★ KWV, Stellar

★★★★ Bloemendal, **Lutzville**, Ormonde ★★★ Withington **NT** Nederburg, Zonnebloem

Semillon wooded

★★★★☆ Landau du Val, Nitida Cellars, Steenberg, Stellenzicht, Stony Brook

★★★★ Boekenhoutskloof, Cape of Good Hope, Fleur du Cap, GlenWood, Vergelegen, Woolworths
★★★★ Cederberg, Constantia Uitsig, **Escapade**, Fairview, Franschhoek Cellar, Hathersage, Hildenbrand, Rickety Bridge ★★★ Haut Espoir ★★★ La Bourgogne **NT** Creation **D** Bergheim, Eikendal, La Petite Vigne, Rijk's Pvt Cellar

Shiraz/syrah

★★★★★ Boekenhoutskloof, Eagles' Nest, Fairview, Haskell, Mont Destin, Mullineux, Saxenburg, Signal Hill

★★★★☆ Bon Courage, Boschendal (2), Cederberg, Cheviot, De Trafford, Delheim, Driehoek, **Fable**, Fairview (3), GlenWood (2), Graham Beck (2), Groote Post, Hartenberg (2), Haskell, Hawksmoor, **Hermit on the Hill**, Iona, Keermont, KWV, La Motte, Lomond, Lourensford (2), Luddite, Metzer, Muratie, Nederburg, Neil Ellis, Nico van der Merwe, Quoin Rock, Raka, Robertson, Rudi Schultz, Rustenberg, Sanctum, Saxenburg, Scali, Simonsig, Solms-Delta, Stark-Condé, Steenberg, Stellenzicht, Strandveld, Tamboerskloof, The Foundry, The Winery of Good Hope, TMV, Vins d'Orrance, Waterford, Waterkloof.

★★★★ **Aaldering**, Akkerdal, Allesverloren, Amani, Anatu, Andreas, Andy Mitchell, Annandale, Anura, Arra, **Avondale**, Avontuur, **Axe Hill**, Bilton, Bizoe, Blaauwklippen (2), Black Pearl, Boland, Bonfoi, Boplaas, Boschkloof, Boschrivier, Brunia, Camberley, Cameradi, Cederberg, Cirrus, Cloof, Creation, D'Aria, Darling Cellars, De Grendel, De Trafford, DeanDavid, Delaire, Delheim, **DeMorgenzon**, Dispore Kamma, Dombeya, Dunstone, Edgebaston, Flagstone, Fort Simon, **Gabriëlskloof**, Gilga, **Graham Beck**, Grande Provence, Groot Constantia, Hartenberg, Haut Espoir, Hawksmoor, Heron Ridge, Hidden Valley, Hildenbrand, **Holden Manz**, House of Mandela,

Joostenberg, Joubert-Tradauw, Journey's End, JP Bredell, Julien Schaal (2), Kaapzicht, Katbakkies, Kleine Zalze, Kloovenburg, Kumkani, KWV, La Vigne, Laborie, **Ladera**, Lammershoek (2), Linton Park, Longridge, Lord's, Lynx, Maastricht, Meerendal, Meerhof, Metzer, Middelvlei, Migliarina, Mimosa, **Mischa**, MolenVliet, Montagu Wine & Spirits, **Mooiplaas**, Mount Rozier, Mountain Ridge, Muratie, Nabygelegen, Nederburg, Neil Ellis, Nico Vermeulen (Red blends, shiraz/syrah-based), Nuy, Oude Denneboom, Painted Wolf, Pax Verbatim, Plaisir, **Porseleinberg** (Organic), Post House, **Quoin Rock**, Rainbow's End, Rhebokskloof, Rickety Bridge, Ridgeback, Rijk's Estate, Rijk's Pvt Cellar, Rooiberg, Rudera, Rudi Schultz, Rust en Vrede, Saronsberg (2), Schalk Burger, Schonenberg, Signal Gun, Slaley, Spice Route (2), Star Hill, Stark-Condé, Stellekaya, StoneyCroft, Stony Brook, Super Single, Swartland, Teddy Hall, The Bernard, The Three Foxes, Thelema, Tokara, Topaz, Topiary, **Trizanne**, Uva Mira, Val de Vie, Van Loveren, Veenwouden, Vergelegen (2), Vergenoegd (2), Villiera, Von Ortloff, Vondeling, Warwick, **Wildekrans**, Windmeul, Woolworths
★★★★ Aeternitas, African Pride, Allée Bleue, Alto, Altydgedacht, Amani, Amares, Andy Mitchell, AntHill, Anthonij Rupert, Asara, Ayama (2), Babylon's Peak, Bellpost, Benguela Cove, Bergheim (2), Bernheim, Blue Crane, Boekenhoutskloof, Boland, Bon Courage, Bonnievale, Boplaas, Bovlei, Brampton, Cathedral Cellar, Cloof, Clovelly, De Meye, Devon Hill, **Devonvale**, **DewaldtHeyns**, Diemersdal, Diemersfontein, Dispore Kamma, Domaine Brahms, Doolhof, Dormershire, Du Preez, **Du'SwaRoo**, Durbanville Hills, DuVon, Eerste Hoop, Eikendal, **Elgin Heights**, Elgin Vintners, Ernst Gouws, Excelsior, Fairview, Faraway House, Fleur du Cap, Freedom Hill, **Gabriëlskloof**, Garden Route, Glen Carlou, Glenelly, Goede Hoop, Graceland, **Graham Beck**, Groenland (2), Guardian Peak, Halala/Lula, Hazendal, Helpmekaar, **Hermit on the Hill**, Hoopenburg (2), **Hout Bay**, Jacques Smit, Jordan, Juno, Katbakkies, Kleine Zalze, Kling, Knorhoek, Kranskop, KWV, Kyburg, La Capra, La Petite Ferme, Laborie (2), Landskroon, Lazanou (Organic), Leopard Frog, Lievland, Lindhorst, Linton Park, Lomond, Lorraine, Lovane, Lutzville, Lyngrove, Maison, **Malanot**, MAN Vintners, MC Square, Meerendal, Mont du Toit, Mooiplaas, Morton, Namaqua, Naughton's, Nederburg, Nelson, Nick & Forti's, Nico van der Merwe, Niel Joubert, Nieuwedrift, Nwanedi, Obikwa, Oude Compagnies Post, Perdeberg (2), Peter Falke, **Phizante**, Pick's Pick, **Reyneke** (Organic), Riebeek, Robertson (3), Ross Gower, Rust en Vrede, Saltaré, Seven Steps, Signal Hill, Simonsvlei (3), Sir Lambert, Slaley, Solo, Spier, Spring Grove, Stellar (Organic), StellenRust, Stellenzicht, **Stone Ridge**, Stony Brook, Strandveld,

The Winery of Good Hope, Umkhulu, Waverley Hills (Organic), Wedderwill, Wamakersvallei, Wildekrans, William Everson, Wines of Cape Town, Woolworths (2), Zandvliet, Zevenwacht, Zoetendal, Zonnebloem ★★★ Abbottshill, AntHill, Anthonij Rupert, Arra, Ashton (2), Avontuur, Backsberg, Beau Joubert, Blaauwklippen, Black Pearl, Bonnievale, **Boplaas**, Boschendal, Botha, Bottelary Hills, Bovlei, Bushmanspad, Cape Classics, Cape to Cairo, Catch Of The Day, Cloverfield, Darling Cellars, David Frost Signature, De Heuvel, De Meye, De Villiers, **Desert Rose**, Devonvale, Dormershire (2), Douglas Green, Du Toitskloof , Durbanville Hills, Eagle's Cliff, Eaglevlei, Escapade, **Esona**, Excelsior, **Fairvalley**, False Bay, Fat Bastard, Fish Hoek, Fort Simon, **Franschhoek Cellar**, Freedom Hill, Graham Beck, Groupe LFE, Havana Hills, Het Vlock, Hofstraat, Holden Manz, Jordan, Kanu, Karusa, Koelenhof , Koelfontein, Kumkani, La Bri, Ladismith, Le Fût, Le Pommier, Leopard's Leap, Long Mountain, **Lord Somerset**, Manley, Marianne, Mischa, Misty Mountains, Mont Rochelle, Namaqua, Nederburg, Nelson, **New Beginnings**, Niel Joubert, Noble Hill, Nwanedi, Oldenburg, Olifantsberg, Org de Rac (Organic), **Origin**, Ormonde (2), Oude Kaap, Overhex, Perdeberg, Pfeifer's, **Pick's Pick**, Rhebokskloof, **Rijk's Pvt Cellar**, **Rosendal**, Saam, Schalkenbosch, Seidelberg, Signal Hill, Simonsig, Simonsvlei, **Six Hats**, Slanghoek, Slowine, Stellendrift, Stellenzicht, Stone Ridge, Sumsaré, The Goose, Thelema, Thembi & Co, Tukulu, Tulbagh Winery (2), Two Oceans, Ultra Liquors (3), Viljoensdrift, Virgin Earth, Vondeling, Waterstone, Wederom Boutique, **Wamakersvallei**, Weltevrede, Welvanpas, William Everson, Windmeul, Wonderfontein, Woolworths, Yonder Hill, Zanddrift, Zandfontein ★★★ African Terroir (2) (Organic, Organic), Alvi's Drift, Arniston Bay, Audacia, Belbon Hills, Bergwater (2) (Organic), Blomendahl, Calais Wine, Cape Dreams, Crows Nest, DeWaal, Douglas Green, Drostdy-Hof, Du Preez, Du'SwaRoo, Eikehof, Franschhoek Cellar, Galleon, Goedverwacht, Golden Kaan, Haut Espoir, Havana Hills, Imbuko, Jason's Hill, Journey's End, Keissekraal (2), **Kingsriver**, Klawer, Klein Moerbei, KWV, Landskroon, Libby's Pride, Lyngrove, McGregor, Mellasat, Mitre's Edge, Neethlingshof, Orange River, **Overhex**, **Pick 'n Pay**, **Place in the Sun**, Pulpit Rock (2), Ridgemor, Rietvallei, Roodezandt, Rooiberg, Seal Breeze, Somersbosch, StellenRust, Swartland, The Mason's, Tulbagh Winery, Ultra Liquors, **United Nations**, uniWines, **Vaalvlei** (2), Versailles, Vredenheim, Waterstone, Wederom Boutique, Windfall, Wine Village-Hermanus, Woolworths (3) (Organic), Zandvliet, Zidela (2) ★★ African Pride (2), African Terroir (3), Barrydale, **Bellevue**, Calitzdorp, Cape Classics, De Wet, Dellrust, Eerste Hoop, Helderberg, **Idiom**, Joubert-Tradauw, Klein Parys, Koopmanskloof, **La Terre La Mer**, Langverwacht, Lutzville, Montpellier, Mountain River, **Remhoogte**, Rhebokskloof, Riebeek, Ruitersvlei, United Nations (2), Waterstone, Welmoed, **Wineways** ★★ Clairvaux, **Die Mas**, **Elgin Valley**, Jonkheer, **Simonsvlei**, Stellar (2) (Organic, Organic), United Nations, Waterstone, Wineways, Withoek ★ Woolworths ☆ **Burgershof**, Kleine Draken **NT** Abingdon, Anthony de Jager, Anthony Smook (2), Awendland, Bayede!, Bergwater, Cranefields, De Vallei, Eagle's Cliff, Eaglevlei, Elgin Valley, Ernie Els, Final Cut, Goudini, Groot Constantia, Hawksmoor, Jonkheer, Kleinbosch, Koningsrivier, Le Grand, Lomrid, Mooi Bly, Mountain River, My Wyn, Nietvoorbij, Nitida Cellars, Nuy, Onderkloof , Org de Rac (Organic), Oude Wellington, Oudtshoorn (2), Rico Suter, Robertson, Saam, Savanha (3), Ses'Fikile, Simonsvlei, Spier (2), Stellenbosch Hills, Stoep, Stoumann's, SylvanVale, Tanagra, **Teubes**, The Township Winery, The Winery of Good Hope, TTT Cellar, Wandsbeck, Weltevrede, Westbridge, Zandvliet, Zonnebloem **NR** Camanga, **Chateau Naudé**, **Seven Springs** , Uitkyk **D** African Pride, Arniston Bay, Avondale (3) (Organic), BABISA, Bottelary, Catherine Marshall, Clos Malverne, Culemborg, Diemersfontein, Du Preez, Golden Kaan, Jean Daneel, Linton Park, Malanot, MAN Vintners, Mitre's Edge, Overhex, Pfeifer's, Pulpit Rock, Riebeek, Rusticus (2), Stettyn, Tierhoek, Tukulu, Tulbagh Winery, Van Loveren, Wine4Us, Woolworths (2)

Sparkling, Méthode cap classique, red

★★★ Camberley, Nitida Cellars

Sparkling, Méthode cap classique, rosé

★★★★☆ Ambeloui, Villiera, Woolworths

★★★★ Colmant, Domaine des Dieux, **Du Preez**, Graham Beck (2), L'Avenir, Mount Babylon, Silverthorn, Steenberg, Tanzanite, Twee Jonge/Krone ★★★★ Boschendal, Haute Cabrière, Karusa, Klein Optenhorst, Laborie, Ross Gower, Simonsig, JC le Roux, Villiera, Weltevrede, Woolworths ★★★ **Allée Bleue**, Groote Post, Pongrácz, JC le Roux ★★☆ Namaqua **NT** Môreson **D** Woolworths

Sparkling, Méthode cap classique, white

★★★★★ Colmant, Topiary

★★★★☆ Ambeloui, Bon Courage, Boschendal, Colmant, Graham Beck, High Constantia, MC Square, Simonsig, Twee Jonge/Krone, Villiera, Woolworths

★★★★ **Altydgedacht**, Anura, Avontuur, Bon Courage, Cape Chamonix, **Cathedral Cellar**, **Cederberg**, Constantia Uitsig, **Darling Cellars**, Domaine des Dieux, Du Preez, Eikendal, **Francois La Garde** (2), Graham Beck (4), Groot Constantia, Haute Cabrière (2), **Hoopenburg**, Jean Daneel, Kumkani, La Motte, Laborie, Long Mountain, Lourensford,

Meerendal, Môreson, Morgenhof, Muratie, Old Vines, **Perdeberg**, Pongrácz, Quoin Rock, Roodezandt, Signal Hill, Silverthorn, Simonsig, **Spier**, Steenberg, Sterhuis, Stony Brook, Tanzanite, JC le Roux, Twee Jonge/Krone, Villiera, Weltevrede, Woolworths (3)

★★★☆ **Avondale**, Backsberg, **Bon Cap**, **Boplaas**, Buitenverwachting, Crios Bríde, De Grendel, **De Wet**, **De Wetshof**, **Elgin Heights**, Haute Cabrière, Hazendal, Hout Bay, **Kanu**, Karusa (2), Klein Constantia, **Klein Roosboom**, **KWV**, Laborie, Longridge, Lovane, Mooiplaas, Nico van der Merwe, Niel Joubert, Rhebokskloof, Saltaré, **Saronsberg**, Saxenburg, **Schalkenbosch**, Simonsig, Teddy Hall, JC le Roux (2), Ultra Liquors, Van Loveren, Villiera (2), Weltevrede, Woolworths, Zorgvliet ★★★ Backsberg (Kosher), **Boer & Brit**, Haute Cabrière, **Highlands Road**, **Klein Parys**, Montpellier, **Nitida Cellars**, Pongrácz, Riebeek, Saltaré, Viljoensdrift, Virgin Earth, Weltevrede ★★☆ Bramon, De Zoete Inval, JC le Roux, Wildekrans ★★ Nieuwedrift, Waverley Hills **NT** Le Grand, Môreson (3), My Wyn, Somerbosch **D** Avondale, Bergsig, Jean Daneel, Van Loveren

Sparkling, Non-MCC, red
★★★ Solms-Delta ★★★ Robertson (Light & low-alcohol), **Tulbagh Winery** ★★ JC le Roux (Light & low-alcohol), Van Loveren (2) (Light & low-alcohol) **NT** Le Grand

Sparkling, Non-MCC, rosé, dry
★★★ Beyerskloof ★★★ Kloovenburg ★★ African Terroir (Organic), Boplaas, Goedverwacht, Origin, uniWines **NT** African Terroir, Bayede!

Sparkling, Non-MCC, rosé, off-dry/semi-sweet
★★★ Aan de Doorns, Alvi's Drift (Light & low-alcohol), Bon Courage, **Eve**, Klawer (Light & low-alcohol), Koelenhof , Rhebokskloof, Robertson (Light & low-alcohol), Van Loveren ★★ Arniston Bay, De Wet, KWV, Orange River, **Overhex** (Light & low-alcohol), Rooiberg, Stellenbosch Hills, **Thandi**, Woolworths ★★ **Bergwater**, Bovlei, Cold Duck (5th Avenue) (Light & low-alcohol), **Origin**, Pearly Bay **NS** Ashton **D** Groupe LFE (Light & low-alcohol), Simonsvlei

Sparkling, Non-MCC, white, dry
★★★ Du Toitskloof , Eikendal, Merwida, Orange River, JC le Roux ★★★ Botha, **Eve**, Klein Parys, Nederburg, Overhex, Riebeek, Robertson, Swartland, Van Loveren (2) ★★ Arniston Bay, Bergsig, Goedverwacht, Goudini, KWV, Obikwa, Slanghoek, Welmoed, Wines of Cape Town, Woolworths ★★ Bonnievale, Origin, Rooiberg, Woolworths **NT** African Terroir, Drostdy-Hof **D** Ashton, uniWines

Sparkling, Non-MCC, white, off-dry/semi-sweet
★★★ Badsberg, Koelenhof , Nuy, Opstal, Robertson (Light & low-alcohol), Slanghoek, Vredenheim ★★ Bon Cap (Organic), **Eve** (Light & low-alcohol), Grand Mousseux, KWV (2), Orange River, Overhex (Light & low-alcohol), Rhebokskloof, Rooiberg, JC le Roux (Light & low-alcohol), Van Loveren (2) (Light & low-alcohol), Wines of Cape Town, Woolworths ★★ Kleine Draken (Kosher), Pearly Bay (Light & low-alcohol), Swartland, JC le Roux **NT** African Terroir, Montagu Wine Cellar, Oudtshoorn **D** Groupe LFE (Light & low-alcohol), Simonsvlei

Special Late Harvest
★★★★ Nederburg
★★★★ Bon Courage, Robertson ★★★ Badsberg, Bergsig, Fairview, Roodezandt, Slanghoek ★★★ Bovlei, Drostdy-Hof, Van Loveren **NT** Backsberg **D** Ashton

Sweet red
★★★★☆ Signal Hill
★★★★ Dormershire, Herold ★★★ Fairview ★★★ Arra, Bottelary, David Frost Signature, Lynx, Perdeberg ★★ Louiesenhof, **Origin** (Light & low-alcohol), Woolworths ★★ BerRaz, **Culemborg**, Hartswater, **Tulbagh Winery** ★ Cellar Cask, Pick 'n Pay, Robertson (2) **D** Goudini

Sylvaner
★★★ Overgaauw

Tannat
★★★★ Zorgvliet
★★★★ Mooi Bly **D** Fairview

Tempranillo
★★★ De Krans

Tinta barocca
★★★★ De Krans, **Nuweland** ★★★ Allesverloren, Boplaas ★★★ Boplaas, Swartland **D** Lammershoek

Touriga nacional
★★★★ De Krans
★★★★ Boplaas, Dagbreek ★★★ Allesverloren ★★★ Du'SwaRoo ★★ Calitzdorp, **Ladismith**

Trincadeira
D Sijnn

Verdelho
★★★★ Feiteiras ★★★ Boschheim

Vin de paille
★★★★★ Mullineux
★★★★☆ Alluvia, De Trafford, Fairview, Hazendal, Rustenberg, The Winery of Good Hope, TMV, Vondeling
★★★★ Goede Hoop, Groot Parys (Organic), Keermont, Lammershoek (Light & low-alcohol), Nuweland, **Orange River**, Saronsberg, Tierhoek

★★★★ La Capra, Signal Hill, **Simonsig** ★★★ Fairview, Mellasat, Naughton's, Zevenwacht **NT** La Bourgogne

Viognier

★★★★☆ **De Grendel**, Eagles' Nest

★★★★ Alvi's Drift, Arra, Babylon's Peak, Backsberg, **Beau Constantia**, Bilton, Creation, Diemersfontein, Flagstone, Fleur du Cap, Fort Simon, **Iona**, Katbakkies, La Petite Ferme, Louresford, Lynx, Nick & Forti's, Noble Hill, Pax Verbatim, Saronsberg, Tamboerskloof, The Foundry, The Winery of Good Hope, Topaz, Waterkloof

★★★★ African Pride, **Arra**, **Blaauwklippen**, DeWaal, Elgin Vintners, Fairview, Gabriëlskloof, Idiom, Karusa, KWV, **Lemberg**, **Leopard Frog**, Lorraine, Naughton's, Niel Joubert, Painted Wolf, Ridgeback, Riebeek, Rusticus, Solo, Star Hill, Sterhuis ★★★ African Terroir (Organic), Anura, Brampton, Cloof, Eaglevlei, Elgin Valley, Flagstone, Graham Beck, Haut Espoir, Hex River Crossing, **Kanu**, **Katbakkies**, Klawer, Kumkani, La Capra, La Ferme Derik, Le Joubert, **Lynx**, Mischa, Rhebokskloof, Robertson, Schalkenbosch, **Six Hats**, Spice Route, Stellenbosch University , Stonehill, The Bernard, Zonnebloem ★★★ Arra, Bon Cap, Boplaas, Boschheim, Excelsior, Kling, La Bri, Niel Joubert ★★ Eerste Hoop, Riebeek, Wine Village-Hermanus ★☆ Spring Grove **NT** Abingdon, Ayama, High Constantia (2), Ladismith, Lindhorst, Montagu Wine & Spirits, My Wyn, Rudi Schultz **NR** Kranskop **D** Goats do Roam, Rietvallei, Simonsig, Thelema, Tukulu, Van Loveren, Woolworths

White blends, off-dry/semi-sweet (w & u/w)

★★★★★ Fable

★★★★☆ Woolworths

★★★★ Bellingham, Hughes Family, **Muratie**, Painted Wolf, Perdeberg, Pick's Pick, Solms-Delta, Virgin Earth, Waterkloof

★★★☆ Buitenverwachting (3), D'Aria, **Edgebaston**, Slanghoek, Vergelegen ★★★ Allée Bleue, Altydgedacht, Arniston Bay, Boschendal, Drostdy-Hof, Haute Cabrière, Knorhoek, Nederburg, Robertson, Saxenburg, **Wandsbeck**, Zevenwacht ★★★ Angels Tears, Arniston Bay, Bayede!, Bergwater, Bon Courage, Bovlei, Douglas Green, Graça, Groupe LFE, Koelenhof , KWV, **Limelight**, Montpellier, **Obikwa** (Light & low-alcohol), Overhex, Rooiberg, Schalk Burger, Seidelberg, Slanghoek, StellenRust (2), Wines of Cape Town ★★ Barrydale, Blaauwklippen (2), Boland, **Botha** (Light & low-alcohol), Culemborg, De Krans, Douglas Green, Drostdy-Hof, Du Toitskloof , Fleur du Cap (Light & low-alcohol), Haute Cabrière, Jonkheer, Kupferberger Auslese, **KWV**, Legacy, Long Mountain, Malan Family, Morgenhof, Oude Kaap,

Overhex, Pearly Bay (Light & low-alcohol), Pick 'n Pay, Robertson (2), Ruitersvlei, Simonsvlei, **Swartland**, Tulbagh Winery, Two Oceans, Versus, Woolworths ★★ Bonnievale, **Du Toitskloof** , Ladismith, Morgenhof, Overmeer Cellars, Pick 'n Pay, Robertson, Stellar (Organic), The Saints, Virginia, Woolworths (5) (Light & low-alcohol, Organic) ★ Cellar Cask, Robertson **NT** Clairvaux, Du Preez, Landzicht, Manley, Onderkloof , Simonsvlei **NR** TTT Cellar **D** Alvi's Drift, Groupe LFE (Light & low-alcohol), Lutzville, Overhex (Light & low-alcohol), Simonsig, Tulbagh Winery, Twee Jonge/Krone (Light & low-alcohol), Wineways

White blends, other, unwooded, dry

★★★ Boschendal

White blends, unwooded, dry

★★★★☆ Ashbourne, Nederburg, The Berrio

★★★★ Groote Post, KWV, Quando, Rustenberg, Spier, Thokozani, **Truter Family**, Vendôme

★★★★ Ayama, Bellingham, Bon Cap (Organic), Bouchard Finlayson, Cape Chamonix, **Creation**, Groot Constantia, Jean Daneel, Joostenberg, **Lammershoek**, Lazanou, Oude Denneboom, Raka, Seidelberg, The Parlotones, **The Wine Fusion** ★★★ Akkerdal, Altydgedacht, Bellingham, Bloemendal, Bon Courage, Boschendal, Bottelary Hills, Cloof, Flagstone, Glen Carlou, Goats do Roam, Goede Hoop, Highlands Road, Jordan, Kumala, La Petite Ferme, Ladismith, Lateganskop, Mooiplaas, Nabygelegen, Old Vines, **Opstal**, Post House, Saxenburg, Simonsig, Slowine, Springfontein, **Teddy Hall**, Theuniskraal, Villiera, Villiersdorp, Vondeling, **Waka Waka**, Woolworths ★★★ Akkerdal, Arniston Bay, Asara, Beau Joubert, Beaumont, Bellingham (2), Beyerskloof, Bonnievale, Delheim, **Doolhof**, Eikendal, Four Paws, Hathersage, **Hazendal**, Joostenberg, Jordan, Kaapzicht, Karusa, Kumala (5), Landskroon, Mountain Oaks (Organic), Mountain Range, **Napier**, Nuweland, Origin, Rietvallei, Stellar (Organic), Thandi, The Saints, Two Oceans, **uniWines** (2), **Val de Vie**, **Vergenoegd**, Waterstone, Weltevrede, **Welvanpas**, Woolworths (4), Zonnebloem ★★ African Pride, Barrydale, **Breëland**, Darling Cellars, Douglas Green (2), Hartswater, Kumala, Leopard's Leap, Mountain River, Nederburg, Obikwa, Oude Kaap, Overgaauw, Overmeer Cellars, Schalkenbosch (2), Stellar (2) (Organic, Organic), Stellenbosch Hills, Van Loveren (4) (Light & low-alcohol), **Wedderwill**, Whalehaven, Withington, Woolworths ★★ African Terroir, Ashton, Bovlei, Douglas Green, Drostdy-Hof, **Eve**, Groupe LFE, Nuy, **Orange River**, **Overhex**, Pearly Bay, Pick 'n Pay, Robertson (3), Woolworths (3), Zandvliet (2) ★ African Terroir (Organic), Oom Tas, Pick 'n Pay (Light & low-alcohol), Robertson (Light & low-alcohol), Wineways, Woolworths ★ African Terroir **NT** African Terroir, Ayama, Backsberg, **Barton**, Bottelary Hills, **Buffalo**

There's a bottle for
Mediterranean
Lamb shank...

...and just about anything else.

Pɪck n Pay
Inspired by you

Enjoy all your favourite
combinations with
Pick and Pay's wide range of wines

Pick n **P**ay

Inspired by you

Creek, Buitenverwachting, Groupe LFE, Hildenbrand, Hill & Dale (Kosher), Klein Parys, Nico van der Merwe, Nico Vermeulen, Opstal, Oudtshoorn, Rico Suter, Ridgemor, Roodezandt, Simonsvlei, Somerbosch **NR** Stellendrift **D** African Pride, D'Aria, De Villiers, Juno, McGregor, Mountain Ridge, Napier, Skilpadvlei, Swartland, Tulbagh Winery (3) (Light & low-alcohol), Van Loveren, Waterstone, Waverley Hills

White blends, wooded, dry

★★★★★ Flagstone, Mullineux, Nederburg, Steenberg, Tokara, Vins d'Orrance

★★★★☆ Adoro, **Anatu**, Badenhorst, Bizoe, Black Oystercatcher, Cape Point, Darling Cellars, **David**, Fleur du Cap, **Graham Beck**, Groot Constantia, Hermanuspietersfontein, **Hermit on the Hill**, Lammershoek, Miles Mossop, Nederburg, Nitida Cellars, Oak Valley, Rall, Sadie, Scali, Sequillo, Solms-Delta, Steenberg (2), Sterhuis, Stony Brook, Strandveld, TMV, Vergelegen, **Waterford**, Welgegund, Woolworths, Zevenwacht, Zorgvliet

★★★★ Allée Bleue, Altydgedacht, Alvi's Drift, Amani, **Avondale** (Organic), Backsberg, **Badenhorst**, **Bergheim**, BLANKbottle (2), **Bosman**, Constantia Uitsig, Delaire, Dornier, Escapade, Flagstone (2), **Grande Provence**, Hoopenburg, Joostenberg, **Keermont**, Klein Constantia, Kumkani, La Ferme Derik (2), La Vierge, Lanner Hill, Lourensford, Newton Johnson, Orangerie, Ormonde, Quoin Rock, **Reginald James**, Reyneke (Organic), Rijk's Pvt Cellar, Schalk Burger,

Sijnn, The Winery of Good Hope, Thelema, Trizanne, Val de Vie, Vondeling, **Waterford**

★★★★ Aeternitas, Annex Kloof, Anura, Bellingham, **Boekenhoutskloof**, Boschendal, De Grendel, **De Heuvel**, Dragonridge, Du Toitskloof, Gabriëlskloof, **Glen Erskine**, Herold, La Ferme Derik, La Vigne, Laibach, Lomond, **Longridge**, **Malanot**, Mountain Oaks, Springfontein, Stellenbosch Hills, Sumaridge, **The Bernard**, Tierhoek, **Val du Charron**, Vuurberg, Wamakersvallei, Woolworths ★★★ **Bellingham**, **Boekenhoutskloof**, Craighall, **Doolhof**, **Druk My Niet**, Graham Beck, **Hermit on the Hill**, Karusa, Klein Moerbei, Kumala, Kumkani, La Vigne, Nederburg, **Origin** (Organic), Ridgeback, Roodeberg, Solms-Delta, Sterhuis, Thandi, Waverley Hills (Organic), Welmoed, **Wildekrans**, **William Everson**, Woolworths ★★★ **Appollis Fairtrade**, **Bergheim**, Douglas Green, Drostdy-Hof, **Druk My Niet**, Kumala, **Manley**, Nederburg, **Nomada**, Van Loveren, Woolworths ★★ Bellpost, Origin, Two Oceans, Zevenwacht ★★ Withington **NT Abingdon**, Alvi's Drift, Benguela Cove, Hildenbrand, KWV, My Wyn **NR Morgenster D** Avondale (2) (Organic), Bon Cap, De Zoete Inval, Juno, Laborie, Leopard's Leap, Nederburg, Nietvoorbij, Nitida Cellars, Perdeberg, Rijk's Pvt Cellar, Strandveld, The Winery of Good Hope, Tulbagh Winery, Val de Vie, Woolworths (2)

Zinfandel/Primitivo

★★★★ Blaauwklippen, Idiom

★★★☆ Blaauwklippen, Zevenwacht **D** Glen Carlou

Overview

South Africa

According to the latest available data (2010), South Africa has been nudged down a notch — by New World rival Chile — to 8th position on the top wine-producing nations list by volume. Italy, with 17.9% of global production, is the leader, followed by France (17.1%) and Spain (12.2%). South Africa, with ±979m litres, currently contributes 3.7% of global volume but this is set to shrink further if the ±20% average annual reduction in the number of grape growers, and the overall number of wine cellars crushing grapes — currently 3,596 and 573 respectively — are any indicators. Also declining, after extended growth, are private cellars crushing grapes, from 524 in 2009 down to 493. (Producing wholesalers crushing grapes are slightly up, to 26, while co-operatives — 'producer cellars' in officialese — dropped further, to 54). Demonstrating, in some cases, the power of passion over economics, microcellars vinifying fewer than 100 tonnes still constitute ±46% of all producers and remain a potent force in the industry.

Vineyards

After a steady decline, the extent of new vineyard establishment rose very slightly in 2010, to 2,453 ha (equally, uprooting of vines accelerated, to 3,717 ha). Planting for white wine continues to outstrip that for red (1,646 ha vs 807), with chenin retaining its entrenched position as most-planted variety (575 ha added). Second most-planted white-wine variety is colombard, with 425 ha, followed consumer favourite sauvignon with a

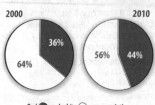

Red ● and white ○ grape varieties
as % of total area

relatively modest 214 ha added; chardonnay is 4th with 205 ha. Pinotage, with 215 ha, turned the tables on shiraz (172 ha) as most-planted red-wine variety, followed by cab and pinot noir (129 and 98 ha). As ever, much more chenin is uprooted than planted, but the variety still leads the overall hectareage table, with 18% of the total 101,016 ha under vine. Cab, with 12%, remains the leading red. The proportion of very young vines continues to decline: only 7.7% is under 4 years, while 33% is 4–10 years and 17.9% older than 20.

Exports

Exports declined for the second consecutive year in 2010, to 378,5 m litres or 48.5% of SA's total wine production, reflecting the troubled global economy and the strength of the rand. Chenin and chardonnay once again topped the list of most-exported varietal wines, with in-vogue pink wines, sauvignon blanc, cab, shiraz, pinotage and merlot also in

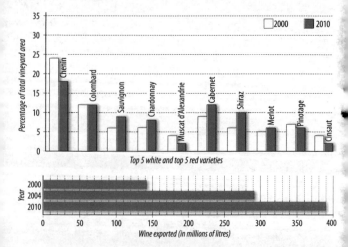

Top 5 white and top 5 red varieties

Wine exported (in millions of litres)

South African Wine Industry — Ten-Year Overview

	2001	2002	2003	2004	2005	2006	2007	2008	2009	2010
Number of wineries	388	428	505	561	581	576	560	585	604	573
Total vine area (excl sultana) (hectares)	94 412	96 233	98 605	100 207	101 607	102 146	101 957	101 325	101 259	101 016
Producing area 4 yrs & older (excl sultana) (hectares)	76 071	79 073	82 719	85 331	87 284	89 426	91 326	92 503	93 285	93 198
Avg yield (tons/hectare)	12.85	13.66	14.91	15.38	13.42	14.55	14.80	15.41	14.45	13.53
Avg grape price — producer cellars/co-ops (R/ton) (2008/2009 est)	1 136	1 333	1 624	1 458	1 387	1 362	1 434	1 522	1 899	1 728
Avg grape price — excl producer cellars/co-ops (R/ton)	3 640	3 953	4 041	4 133	3 593	3 128	2 971	3 173	3 917	3 949
Grapes crushed (millions of tons)	0.98	1.08	1.23	1.31	1.17	1.30	1.35	1.43	1.35	1.26
Total production (millions of litres)	746.5	834.2	956.0	1 015.7	905.2	1 013.0	1 043.5	1 089.0	1 033.41	985.0
Domestic sales (millions of litres)	390.2	387.4	345.5	347.7	340.0	340.4	355.5	355.8	338.4	346.4
Consumption per capita (litres SA wine)	9.0	8.9	7.9	7.7	7.4	7.1	7.4	7.3	6.9	7.0
Export volume (millions of litres)	177.3	217.4	238.5	267.7	281.8	271.7	312.5	411.7	389.1	370.9
Stock (millions of litres)	242.3	209.3	336.8	363.7	339.4	403.1	425.2	357.2	361.7	351.0
Stock : sales ratio	0.43:1	0.35:1	0.57:1	0.59:1	0.54:1	0.65:1	0.64:1	0.47:1	0.49:1	0.48:1

demand. The top five markets for SA wine (both packaged and bulk) remain, in descending order, the UK, Germany, Sweden, Netherlands and Denmark. When it comes to packaged wine only, the UK, Sweden, Netherlands, Germany and Denmark still top the list, followed by the holy grail of many exporters: the US.

Local wine consumption

Estimated South African domestic per-capita wine consumption increased last year for the first time since 2007, to 7.03L, but wine's market share of ±12% remained substantially lower than beer (±46%). Brandy's ±6% share was stable while whisky jumped nearly a point to ±4%. Of natural wine sold in SA during 2010 (including imports), a

steady 48% was in glass, of which about half was in the standard 750ml bottle. Wine in bag-in-box accounted for ±26% of total sales, plastic containers ±23% and Tetra packs ±2%. Foil bags — the notorious *papsakke*, now carefully regulated — represent only 1% .

Note

Statistical data provided by SA Wine Industry Information & Systems (see below).

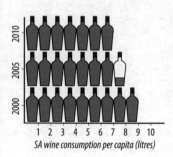

SA wine consumption per capita (litres)

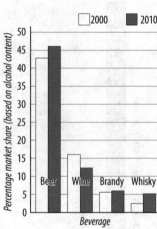

Percentage market share (based on alcohol content) / *Beverage* — Beer, Wine, Brandy, Whisky (2000, 2010)

Wine Industry Organisations

African Vintners Alliance Marketing: Vivian Kleynhans ▪ **T +27 (0)82-764-0503** ▪ ava@africanrootswines.com
Established to create an enabling environment for emerging black-owned wineries.

Agricultural Ethical Trade Initiative of SA (WIETA) CEO: Linda Lipparoni **T +27 (0)21-880-0580** ▪ F +27 (0)21-880-0580 ▪ linda@wieta.org.za; info@wieta.org.za ▪ www.wieta.org.za
Multi-stakeholder, non-profit, voluntary organisation established in 2002 to promote ethical trade in wine, fruit, cut flowers and general agriculture. WIETA has adopted a code of labour standards for the industry, and its main task is to support, enhance and promote members' ethical performance and best practice through training, technical assessments and ethical inspections to assess members' compliance with the code.

ARC Infruitec-Nietvoorbij Research Institute Manager: Dr Johan van Zyl ▪ Acting PR: Odette Beukes ▪ **T +27 (0)21-809-3100** ▪ F +27

(0)21-809-3400 ▪ beukeso@arc.agric.za ▪ www.arc.agric.za
Internationally-regarded one-stop research institute, generating advanced technology for deciduous fruit- and grape-growers and related processors.

Biodiversity & Wine Initiative (BWI) See WWF Biodiversity & Wine Initiative.

Cape Estate Wine Producers' Association (CEWPA) Chair: Braam van Velden ▪ **T +27 (0)21-881-3815** ▪ F +27 (0)21-881-3436 ▪ info@overgaauw.co.za

Cape Port Producers' Association (previously South African Port Producers' Association) Chair: Carel Nel ▪ **T +27 (0)44-213-3326** ▪ F +27 (0)44-213-3750 ▪ boplaas@mweb.co.za

Cape Winemakers Guild (CWG) Chair: Louis Strydom ▪ General Manager: Kate Jonker ▪ **T +27 (0)21-852-0408** ▪ F +27 (0)21-852-0409 ▪ info@capewinemakersguild.com ▪ www.capewinemakersguild.com

Independent, invitation-only association, founded in 1982 to promote winemaking excellence among its members. Since 1985, the CWG has held a highly regarded annual public auction. Established in 1999, the Nedbank CWG Development Trust provides social development investment for school children in the wineland areas, further education trough the Protégé Programme Bursary Fund and the mentorship of just-graduated winemakers through the Protégé Programme.

Chardonnay Forum of South Africa Chair: Matthew van Heerden ▪ matthew@uvamira.co.za ▪ **T +27 (0)21-880-1682 / +27 (0)82-520-9338** ▪ F +27 (0)21-880-1682

Chenin Blanc Association (CBA) Chair: Ken Forrester ▪ **T +27 (0)21-855-2374 / +27 (0)82-783-7203** ▪ F +27 (0)21-855-2373 ▪ ken@kenforresterwines.com ▪ www.chenin.co.za ▪ Manager: Ina Smith ▪ T +27 (0)82-467-4331 ▪ F +27 (0)86-672-8549 ▪ ina.smith@iafrica.com

Fairtrade Label South Africa (FLSA) Executive Director: Boudewijn Goossens ▪ **T +27 (0)21-448-8911** ▪ info@fairtrade.org.za ▪ www.fairtradesa.org.za
The local marketing organisation for Fairtrade. FLSA was established in 2009 as an associate member of FLO and is the first organisation that promotes the Fairtrade label in a producing country, thus being a pioneer in the marketing of Fairtrade in the South. See also Southern Africa Fairtrade Network

Garagiste Movement Coordinator: Tanja Beutler ▪ **T +27 (0)21-855-4275** ▪ F +27 (0)86-612-6118 ▪ tanja@topazwines.co.za

Institute of Cape Wine Masters Chair: Andy Roediger ▪ **T +27 (0)83-250-9821** ▪ Secretary: Margaret Fry ▪ T +27 (0)83-628-6511 ▪ F +27 (0)86-611-7150 ▪ capewinemasters@gmail.com ▪ www.capewinemasters.co.za
Successful completion of examinations set since 1983 by the Cape Wine & Spirit Education Trust and, latterly, the Cape Wine Academy, have qualified 78 Cape Wine Masters. Their Institute holds seminars, runs tasting workshops, charts trends and names a Wine Personality of the Year

Integrated Production of Wine (IPW) Manager: Daniël Schietekat ▪ **T +27 (0)21-889-6555** ▪ F +27 (0)866-903-224 ▪ daniel@ipw.co.za ▪ www.ipw.co.za
Innovative, widely supported initiative aimed at producing wine in an environmentally sustainable, profitable way by means of guidelines for both farm and cellar, embracing all aspects of grape production, winemaking and, now, biodiversity conservation. See also WWF Biodiversity & Wine Initiative and Sustainable Wine South Africa.

Méthode Cap Classique Producers' Association Chair: Peter Ferreira ▪ **T +27(0)21-807-3704 /**

+27 (0)83-309-7621 ▪ F +27 (0)86-600-6393 ▪ els_fer@hotmail.com

Muscadel SA (previously Muscadel Association) Chair: Henri Swiegers ▪ **T +27 (0)23-344-3021** ▪ F +27 (0)86-617-9443 ▪ winemaker@badsberg.co.za ▪ Vice-chair: Nico Grundling ▪ **T +27 (0)23-344-3026** ▪ nico@slanghoek.co.za

Pinotage Association Chair: Beyers Truter ▪ **T +27 (0)21-865-1235** ▪ F +27 ()21-865-2683 ▪ reception@beyerskloof.co.za ▪ Manager: Wendy Burridge ▪ **T +27 (0)21-709-0933** ▪ F +27 (0)86-532-2726 ▪ admin@pinotage.co.za ▪ www.pinotage.co.za

Sauvignon Blanc Interest Group of South Africa (SBIG) Chair: Erika Obermeyer ▪ **T +27 (0)21-874-1258 / +27 (0)82-940-3499** ▪ F 021-874-1712 erika@grahambeckwines.co.za ▪ Secretary: Pieter de Waal ▪ **T +27 (0)83-357-3864** ▪ F +27 (0)21-948-3441 ▪ sbig@dw.co.za

Shiraz South Africa Chair: Edmund Terblanche ▪ **T +27 (0)82-770-2929** ▪ F +27 (0)21-863-4883 ▪ F +27 (0)21-863-4883 ▪ et.cellar@la-motte.co.za ▪ Secretary: Sandra Lotz ▪ **T +27 (0)21-807-3103 / +27 (0)82-924-7254** ▪ F +27 (0)21-863-2079 ▪ info@shirazsa.co.za

South African Port Producers' Association (SAPPA) See Cape Port Producers' Association

South African Black Vintners Alliance See African Vintners Alliance

South African Wine Industry Information & Systems (SAWIS) Executive Manager: Yvette van der Merwe ▪ **T +27 (0)21-807-5703** ▪ F +27 (0)21-807-6000 ▪ info@sawis.co.za
Responsible for the collection, processing and dissemination of industry information. Administers the Wine of Origin (WO) system and manages the Information Centre, a comprehensive information resource base for the South African wine and brandy industry.

South African Wine Industry Trust (SAWIT) Chair: Sharron Marco-Thyse ▪ CEO: Charles Erasmus ▪ **T +27(0)21-889-8101** ▪ F +27 (0)21-889-5900 ▪ sawit@live.co.za ▪ www.sawit.co.za
The vision of SAWIT is the creation of a transformed wine industry that is sustainable and vibrant, populated by an empowered worker community that shares equitably in growth and prosperity.

Southern Africa Fairtrade Network (SAFN) Regional Coordinator: Mkhululi Silandela ▪ T +27 (0)21-448-8911 ▪ m.silandela@fairtradeafrica.net ▪ www.fairtradeafrica.net
SAFN represents regional Fairtrade producers on issues related to standards – campaigning for new prices, revising existing standards or making standards more relevant to local farming practices.

Sustainable Wine South Africa www.swsa.co.za ▪ Contact details as for individual organisations.

Alliance between the Wine & Spirit Board (WSB), Integrated Production of Wine (IPW), Biodiversity & Wine Initiative (BWI) and Wines of South Africa (WOSA), driving the industry's commitment to sustainable, eco-friendly production.

Wine & Spirit Board Chair: Sibongile Nkomo ▪ Secretary: Hugo van der Merwe ▪ **T +27 (0)21-889-6555** ▪ F +27 (0)21-889-5823 ▪ hugo@wsb.org.za

Mainly administers the Wine of Origin, Estate Brandy and Integrated Production of Wine (IPW) schemes.

Wine & Agricultural Ethical Trade Association (WIETA) See Agricultural Ethical Trade Initiative.

Wines of South Africa (WOSA) Chair: Johann Krige ▪ **T/F +27 (0)21-884-4656** ▪ wine@kanonkop.co.za ▪ CEO: Su Birch **T +27 (0)21-883-3860** ▪ F +27 (0)21-883-3861 ▪ info@wosa.co.za ▪ www.wosa.co.za, www.varietyisinournature.com, www.fundiwine.co.za Generic marketing organisation, responsible for raising the profile of SA wine in key export markets. See also WWF Biodiversity & Wine Initiative and Sustainable Wine South Africa.

Wine Industry Development Association (WIDA) Executive Manager: Denver Williams ▪ **T +27 (0)21-872-9181** ▪ F +27 (0)2-872-4560 ▪ denver@wida.co.za ▪ www.wida.co.za Promotes transformation through social development, human resource development and training, economic empowerment, and industrial relations,

and protects the interests of vulnerable communities in the industry.

Wine Industry Network of Expertise & Technology (WINETECH) Executive Manager: Jan Booysen ▪ **T +27 (0)21-807-3324** ▪ F +27 (0)21-807-3385 ▪ booysenj@winetech.co.za Coordinates the research, training and technology transfer programmes of participating institutions and individuals, to improve the competitiveness of the wine industry.

WWF Biodiversity & Wine Initiative (BWI) Extension Officers: Joan Isham (senior officer), Gareth Hardres-Williams, Dale Wright ▪ jisham@wwf.org.za, ghardres-williams@wwf.org.za, dwright@wwf.org.za ▪ www.bwi.co.za Pioneering conservation partnership between the wine industry and conservation sector, aiming to protect places of outstanding conservation value and iconic species, and to maintain living and productive landscapes. This is achieved by steering expansion away from threatened natural vegetation and fostering a culture of sustainable production through wise land use practices. Demonstrating laudable commitment and buy-in, producers have set aside highly threatened natural areas well in excess of the industry's 102,000 ha vineyard footprint. Consumers can support accredited BWI members by buying wines displaying the colourful 'conservation in action' logo, depicting a sugarbird and a protea. See also Integrated Production of Wine & Sustainable Wine South Africa.

Regions, Districts & Wards

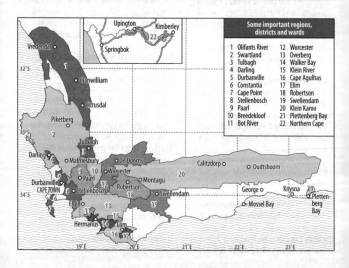

Some important regions, districts and wards	
1 Olifants River	12 Worcester
2 Swartland	13 Overberg
3 Tulbagh	14 Walker Bay
4 Darling	15 Klein River
5 Durbanville	16 Cape Agulhas
6 Constantia	17 Elim
7 Cape Point	18 Robertson
8 Stellenbosch	19 Swellendam
9 Paarl	20 Klein Karoo
10 Breedekloof	21 Plettenberg Bay
11 Bot River	22 Northern Cape

Winegrowing Areas

1 Hout Bay   **2** Constantia   **3** Cape Point

From modest beginnings in the Dutch East India Company's 17th-century gardens below Table Mountain, South Africa's vineyards now cover 101,016 ha and close to 100 official appellations. Changes to the Wine of Origin (WO) scheme of 1972/3 saw 'geographical units' incorporated into the WO classification alongside 'regions', 'districts' and 'wards' (the latter have the smallest footprint of the WO areas, following earlier

amendments to the 'estate' legislation). Below are brief notes on the most important grape cultivation zones. Information supplied by Wines of South Africa (WOSA) and SA Wine Industry Information & Systems (SAWIS), and reflect 2010 data for the WO areas. *Note:* Area maps are not to the same scale.

Breedekloof Large (±12,500 ha) Breede River Valley district producing mainly for brandy industry and merchant trade, but also featuring some quality-focused boutiques and family estates with reputations for pinotage, chardonnay and semillon. Major varieties (ha): chenin (2,811), colombard (1,868), chardonnay (1,061), sauvignon (960), cab (799). See under Robertson for climate, geology etc.

Cape Point Small (32 ha), cool district on mainly western slopes of the Cape Peninsula. Recognised for sauvignon and semillon. Sauvignon (19), cab (5), shiraz (4), semillon (2), chardonnay (1). See also Constantia below.

Cape South Coast Newly 'umbrella' region (2,712 ha) for Cape Agulhas, Overberg, Plettenberg Bay, Swellendam and Walker Bay districts, and Herbertsdale and new Stilbaai East wards.

Central Orange River
Previously 'Lower Orange', this ward along the Orange River (Gariep) is a production zone within the Northern Cape Geographical Unit. Altitude: 500-1,000 m; temp 25.3°C; rain: 250/208 mm; geology: granite, dolorite, shale, alluvial. Overwhelmingly a white-grape area but red plantings are increasing. Sultana (7,841), colombard (2,509), chenin (1,021), muscat d'Alexandrie (183), villard blanc (145).

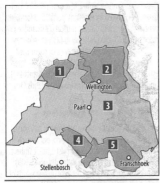

1 Voor Paardeberg   **4** Simonsberg-Paarl
2 Wellington   **5** Franschhoek
3 Paarl

1 Polkadraai Hills   **5** Stellenbosch
2 Bottelary   **6** Simonsberg-Stellenbosch
3 Devon Valley   **7** Jonkershoek Valley
4 Papegaaiberg   **8** Banghoek

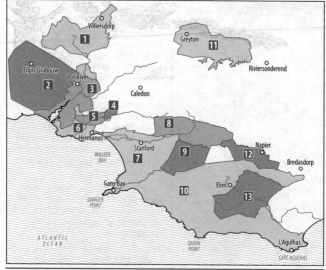

1 Theewater
2 Elgin
3 Bot River
4 Hemel-en-Aarde Ridge
5 Upper Hemel-en-Aarde
6 Hemel-en-Aarde Valley
7 Walker Bay
8 Klein River
9 Sunday's Glen
10 Cape Agulhas
11 Greyton
12 Napier
13 Elim

Constantia Premier viticultural ward on the eastern flank of the Cape Peninsula, cooled by south-easterly sea breezes. Recognised for whites generally, notably sauvignon, semillon and muscat. Altitude: 100–300m; temp (Mean February Temperature, MFT) 20.6℃; rain: total/summer 1,056/335mm; geology: granite (sandstone). Major varieties: sauvignon (173), cab (53), merlot (48), chardonnay (27), cab franc (25).

Darling District encircling the eponymous West Coast town, best known for the wines from its higher-lying ward, Groenekloof, long the source of top sauvignon; growing reputation for reds, especially shiraz. Groenekloof: cab (499), shiraz (355), sauvignon (311), pinotage (215), chenin (204).

Durbanville Ward within the Tygerberg district, with solid reputation for striking merlot and sauvignon. The latter (407) is the dominant variety, followed by cab (288), merlot (233), shiraz (220) and chardonnay (99). Altitude: 150–350m; temp 22.4℃; rain: 481/140mm; geology: shale.

Elgin Cool upland ward within the Overberg district, yielding aromatic whites and elegant reds. Altitude: 200–250m; temp 19.7℃; rain: 1,011/366mm; geology: shale (sandstone). Sauvignon (349), chardonnay (95), pinot (91), shiraz (78), cab (66).

Elim Maritime ward within the Cape Agulhas district, its 146 ha of vineyards are arrayed around the old

mission village of Elim near Africa's most southerly point. Sauvignon (80), shiraz (28), semillon (12), pinot noir (10), cab (7).

Franschhoek Valley A district with 1,395 ha under vine, recognised for cab and semillon. Cab (213), sauvignon (205), shiraz (202), chardonnay (190), merlot (141).

Hemel-en-Aarde See Walker Bay

Klein Karoo Scrubby semi-arid region, reliant on irrigation. Recognised for excellent 'ports', and fortifieds generally. Calitzdorp district: muscat d'Alexandrie (97), colombard (69), cab (24), chenin (23), chardonnay (16). Tradouw ward: chardonnay (21), colombard (17), sauvignon (11), merlot (11), shiraz (10). Interesting stirrings in tiny Langeberg-Garcia district (41), Upper Langkloof (50) and Tradouw Highlands (10) wards.

Northern Cape See Central Orange River.

Olifants River Quality moves are afoot in this northwesterly Cape grape-growing region, particularly in the Bamboes Bay 'micro-ward' (just 5 ha), Lamberts Bay ward (22), and Lutzville Valley district (2,989) nearer the coast, as well as the cool upland wards of Cederberg (70) and Piekenierskloof (483). Further inland, a climate conducive to organic cultivation is being exploited to that end. Altitude: 20–100 m; temp 23℃; rain: 139/47 mm; geology: mainly schist and

1 Montagu	5 Malgas	9 Langeberg-Garcia	12 Calitzdorp	15 Outeniqua
2 Stormsvlei	6 Buffeljags	10 Still Bay East	13 Prince Albert Valley	16 Upper Langkloof
3 Swellendam	7 Tradouw	11 Herbertsdale	14 Swartberg	17 Plettenberg Bay
4 Tradouw Highlands	8 Klein Karoo			

alluvial deposits. Koekenaap ward (Lutzville Valley): chenin (277), colombard (207), sauvignon (167), cab (69), muscat d'Alexandrie (42). Cederberg: shiraz (14), sauvignon (11), chenin (9), chardonnay (8), cab (7). Piekenierskloof: pinotage (74), palomino (53), chenin (51), grenache noir (47), cab (45).

Orange River See Central Orange River

Paarl This district has many mesoclimates, soils and aspects, and thus succeeds with a variety of styles and grapes. Altitude: 100-300m; temp 23.2°C; rain: 945/273mm; geology: granite and shale. Paarl proper is recognised for shiraz and, more recently, viognier and mourvèdre grown on warmer slopes. Chenin (1,563), cab (1,074), shiraz (922), pinotage (514), cinsaut (416). The following are all wards: Wellington increasingly reputed for shiraz and gutsy red blends generally. Chenin (957), cab (752), shiraz (531), pinotage (351), merlot (311). Simonsberg-Paarl, on the warmer slopes of the Simonsberg, recognised for red blends, shiraz and chardonnay. Cab (307), chardonnay (206), sauvignon (185), shiraz (177), chenin (135). Voor Paardeberg, long an uncredited source of top-quality grapes, now becoming a star in own right. Cab (400), shiraz (286), chenin (218), merlot (204), pinotage (164).

Philadelphia A ward of Tygerberg, cooled by the Atlantic air and noted for cab, merlot and Bordeaux-style reds. Cab (225), sauvignon (117), shiraz (65), merlot (65), cab franc (32). See under Durbanville for climate, geology etc.

Robertson Traditionally a white-wine district, increasingly recognised for shiraz and cab. Chardonnay, sauvignon and sparkling remain stand-outs. Altitude: 150-250m; temp 23°C; rain: 280/116mm; geology: shale and alluvial. Chardonnay (2,177), colombard (2,172), chenin (1,667), sauvignon (1,480), cab (1,418).

Stellenbosch To many, this intensively farmed district is the wine capital of South Africa. Key contributors to quality are the cooler mountain slopes, varied soil types and breezes off False Bay which moderate summer temperatures. Altitude: 200-400m; temp 21.5°C;

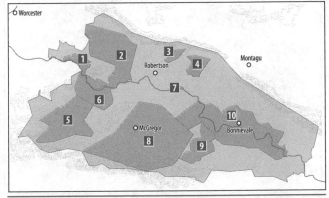

1 Eilandia	3 Hoopsrivier	5 Agterkliphoogte	7 Robertson	9 Boesmansrivier
2 Vinkrivier	4 Klaasvoogds	6 Le Chasseur	8 McGregor	10 Bonnievale

1 Swartland	4 Durbanville	7 Tulbagh
2 Darling	5 Malmesbury	
3 Philadelphia	6 Riebeekberg	

1 Lutzville Valley	6 Olifants River
2 Bamboes Bay	7 Citrusdal Mountain
3 Lamberts Bay	8 Citrusdal Valley
4 Vredendal	9 Piekenierskloof
5 Spruitdrift	10 Cederberg

rain: 713/229mm; geology: granite (sandstone). Jonkershoek Valley, a ward east of Stellenbosch town, is recognised for cab and cab blends. Cab (66), merlot (24), chardonnay (22), shiraz (19), sauvignon (15). Simonsberg-Stellenbosch, in the south-western foothills of the Simonsberg Mountain, is especially recognised for cab, cab blends and pinotage, and reds generally. Cab (326), sauvignon (196), merlot (172), shiraz (151), chardonnay (127). North-west of

Stellenbosch town are four adjoining wards: Papegaaiberg — chardonnay (28), sauvignon (23), chenin (21), pinotage (13), pinot gris (12); Devon Valley, recognised mainly for red blends — merlot (181), cab (160), sauvignon (116), shiraz (86), pinotage (65); Bottelary, noted for pinotage, shiraz and warm-blooded blends — chenin (468), cab (371), sauvignon (341), shiraz (276), pinotage (247); the most westerly ward, Polkadraai Hills — sauvignon (166), cab (161),

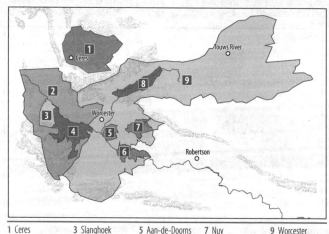

1 Ceres	3 Slanghoek	5 Aan-de-Doorns	7 Nuy	9 Worcester
2 Breedekloof	4 Goudini	6 Scherpenheuvel	8 Hex River Valley	

shiraz (128), merlot (92), chenin (81); and Banghoek, the mountain amphitheatre above the village of Pniel — cab (75), shiraz (44), merlot (30), sauvignon (30), chardonnay (22). The remainder of the district, as yet officially undemarcated, includes Stellenboschberg, Helderberg and Faure, recognised for red blends, chenin and sauvignon. Cab (1,801), shiraz (1,256), sauvignon (1,148), merlot (1,019), chenin (711).

Swartland Traditionally associated with full-bodied reds, but latterly also with chenin and Mediterranean-style red and white blends, this sunny district north of Cape Town has two wards, Malmesbury and Riebeekberg, plus a large unappellated area. Riebeekberg: chenin (233), chardonnay (183), shiraz (176), pinotage (169), cab (134). Malmesbury: cab (743), shiraz (545), chenin (507), pinotage (440), sauvignon (318). 'Swartland': chenin (2,010), cab (837), shiraz (777), pinotage (748), chardonnay (428). Altitude: 100-300m; temp 23.3°C; rain: 523/154mm; geology: granite and shale.

Tulbagh Inland district, traditionally known for sparkling and lightish whites, acquiring reputation for quality reds. Altitude: 160-400m; temp 24°C; rain: 551/175mm; geology: sandstone boulderbeds and shale. Chenin (266), colombard (195), cab (146), shiraz (137), chardonnay (91).

Walker Bay Highly regarded maritime district southeast of Cape Town, recognised for pinot noir, pinotage, sauvignon and chardonnay. Altitude: 100-250m; temp 20.3°C; rain: 722/322mm; geology: shale, granite and sandstone. Sauvignon (267), shiraz (131), pinot (107), chardonnay (92), cab (84). Bot River, Hemel-en-Aarde Ridge, Hemel-en-Aarde Valley, Sunday's Glen and Upper Hemel-en-Aarde Valley are wards.

Worcester District producing chiefly for the brandy industry and merchant trade, but small quantities bottled under own labels often represent good quality/value. Recognised for everyday reds/whites and fortifieds. Chenin (1,865), colombard (1,109), chardonnay (627), shiraz (375), sauvignon (363). See under Robertson for climate, geology etc.

Wine of Origin-defined production areas
(New appellation/s in bold.)

Geographical Unit	Region	District	Ward
Eastern Cape	—	—	**St Francis Bay**
KwaZulu-Natal	—	—	—
Limpopo	—	—	—
Northern Cape	—	Douglas	—
	—	—	Central Orange River
	—	—	Hartswater
	—	—	Rietrivier (Free State)
	—	**Sutherland-Karoo**	
Western Cape	Breede River Valley	Breedekloof	Goudini
			Slanghoek
		Robertson	Agterkliphoogte
			Boesmansrivier
			Bonnievale
			Eilandia
			Hoopsrivier
			Klaasvoogds
			Le Chasseur
			McGregor
			Vinkrivier
		Worcester	Aan-de-Doorns
			Hex River Valley
			Nuy
			Scherpenheuvel
	Cape South Coast	Cape Agulhas	Elim
		Overberg	Elgin
			Greyton
			Klein River
			Theewater

Geographical Unit	Region	District	Ward
Western Cape *(continued)*	**Cape South Coast** *(continued)*	Plettenberg Bay	—
		Swellendam	Buffeljags
			Malgas
			Stormsvlei
		Walker Bay	Bot River
			Hemel-en-Aarde Ridge
			Hemel-en-Aarde Valley
			Sunday's Glen
			Upper Hemel-en-Aarde Valley
	Coastal	Cape Point	—
		Darling	Groenekloof
		Franschhoek Valley	—
		Paarl	Simonsberg-Paarl
			Voor Paardeberg
			Wellington
		Stellenbosch	Banghoek
			Bottelary
			Devon Valley
			Jonkershoek Valley
			Papegaaiberg
			Polkadraai Hills
			Simonsberg–Stellenbosch
		Swartland	Malmesbury
			Riebeekberg
		Tulbagh	—
		Tygerberg	Durbanville
			Philadelphia
		—	Constantia
		—	Hout Bay
	Klein Karoo	Calitzdorp	—
		Langeberg-Garcia	—
		—	Montagu
		—	Outeniqua
		—	Tradouw
		—	Tradouw Highlands
		—	Upper Langkloof
	Olifants River	Citrusdal Mountain	Piekenierskloof
		Citrusdal Valley	—
		Lutzville Valley	Koekenaap
		—	Bamboes Bay
		—	Spruitdrift
		—	Vredendal
	—	—	Cederberg
	—	—	Ceres
	—	—	Herbertsdale
	—	—	Lamberts Bay
	—	—	**Napier**
	—	—	Prince Albert Valley
	—	—	Stilbaai East
	—	—	Swartberg

Boberg (fortified wines from Franschhoek, Paarl and Tulbagh). Source: SAWIS

Grape Varieties

Below are brief notes on some of the grape varieties mentioned in the guide, and their contribution to the national vineyard (statistics from SA Wine Industry Information & Systems — SAWIS). See under Winegrowing Areas for details of the most widely planted and best-performing varieties in the major vine cultivation zones.

Red-wine varieties

Cabernet sauvignon Adaptable and internationally planted black grape making some of the world's finest and longest-lasting wines. And retaining some of its inherent qualities even when overcropped in less suitable soils and climates. Can stand alone triumphantly, but frequently blended with a wide range of other varieties: traditionally, as in Bordeaux, with cab franc, merlot and a few minor others, but also in SA sometimes partnering varieties such as shiraz and pinotage. Number of different clones, with differing characteristics. ±12% of total vineyard area.

Cabernet franc Like its descendant cabernet sauvignon, with which it is often partnered, a classic part of the Bordeaux blend, but in SA and elsewhere — particularly in the Loire — also used for varietal wines. Tiny, stable vineyard area (1%).

Carignan Hugely planted in the south of France, where it is not much respected. But there, as in SA, older, low-yielding vines can produce pleasant surprises. Insignificant vineyard area.

Cinsaut (noir) 'Cinsault' in France. Another of the mass, undistinguished plantings of southern France, which only occasionally comes up trumps. Used to be known locally as hermitage, the name reflected in its offspring (with pinot noir), pinotage. About 2% of vineyard area.

Gamay noir Although it produces some serious long-lived wines in Beaujolais, its use for (mainly) early-and-easy-drinking 'nouveau' wines there, often using carbonic maceration, is the model mostly copied in SA. Insignificant vineyard area.

Grenache (noir) The international (ie French) name for the Spanish grape garnacha. Widespread in Spain and southern France, generally used in blends (as in Rioja and Châteauneuf), but occasionally solo. A favourite for rosés. When vigour restrained, capable of greatness, but this is rare. Tiny plantings here. (White/pink versions also occur.)

Malbec Once a significant part of Bordeaux's blend, now most important in Cahors in western France (where it is known as cot), and as Argentina's signature variety. In SA a few varietal and blended examples; very small plantings.

Merlot Classic blending partner (as in Bordeaux) for cabernet, fashionable around the world, where it tends to be seen as an 'easier' version of cab — although this is perhaps because it is often made in a less ambitious manner. Merlot varietal wines increasingly common in SA too. 6.4% of vineyard area.

Mourvèdre Internationally known by its French name, though originally Spanish (monastrell). In Australia and California also called mataro. Particularly successful in some serious southern French blends, and increasingly modish internationally. Minuscule plantings here.

Nebbiolo Perhaps the greatest red grape to have scarcely ventured from its home — Piedmont in this case, where it makes massive, tannic, long-lived wines. Minute plantings here.

Petit verdot Use of this excellent variety in the Médoc limited by its late ripening. Now appearing in some local blends, and a few varietals. 0.6% of vineyard area.

Pinotage A 1920s cross between pinot noir and cinsaut ('hermitage'). Made in a range of styles, from simply fruity to ambitious, well-oaked examples. 6% of vineyard area.

Pinot noir Notoriously difficult grape to succeed with outside its native Burgundy, but South Africa, along with the rest of the New World, now produces some excellent examples. Slightly increasing 0.9% of the vineyard.

Ruby cabernet US cross between cabernet sauvignon and carignan, designed for heat tolerance. Rather rustic, used mostly in cheaper blends. 2.2% of vineyard area.

Shiraz Better known as syrah outside South Africa and Australia (and on some local labels too). Internationally increasing in popularity, with northern Rhône and now also Australia as its major domiciles. Made here in a variety of styles — generally wooded. 10% of vineyard area.

Tinta barocca Elsewhere spelt 'barroca'. One of the important Portuguese port-making grapes, which is now its primary role in SA, usually blended. Also used for some varietal unfortified wines, and namelessly in some 'dry reds'. 0.2% of vineyard area.

Touriga nacional Important Portuguese port-making grape, now usefully grown here for similar ends, along with tinta franca, tinta roriz (tempranillo) and souzão. Tiny plantings.

Zinfandel The quintessential Californian grape (of European origin, and the same as Italy's primitivo), used here in a small way for some big wines. Tiny plantings.

White-wine varieties

Chardonnay In SA, as elsewhere, many new vineyards of this grape have come on-stream, with wines showing a wide range of styles, quality and price. Generally used varietally, but also in blends, and for sparkling. (Heavily) wooded in more ambitious wines. Steady 8% of vineyard area.

Chenin blanc SA has more chenin (locally also called steen) than even France's Loire Valley, the variety's home. Used here for everything from generic 'dry white' to ambitious sweet wines, to brandy. Increasing numbers of table-wine successes in recent years, as well as inexpensive but flavoursome easy-drinkers. ±18% of vineyard area.

Colombar(d) One of the mainstays of brandy production in South Africa, colombard (usually without the 'd' in SA) is also used for numerous varietal and blended wines, ranging from dry to sweet — seldom wooded. Steady ±11% of vineyard area.

Gewürztraminer Readily identifiable from its rose-petal fragrance, best known in its Alsatian guise. In South Africa usually made off-dry. Insignificant vineyard area.

Hanepoot Traditional Afrikaans name for muscat d'Alexandrie, South Africa's most planted muscat variety (see also muscadel below). 2.1% of vineyard area (some for raisins and table grapes), slowly declining.

Muscadel Name used here for both muscat de Frontignan and muscat blanc à petits grains (both red and white versions). The grape associated with the famous Constantia dessert wines of the 18th century today is used chiefly for dessert and fortified wines and for touching up blends. Red and white versions total less than 1% of vineyard area.

Muscat See Hanepoot and Muscadel.

Riesling New rules apply, and the name by itself now refers to the great German grape (as it does in this guide). Previously, the grape had to carry the prefix 'Rhine' or 'weisser', and the 'riesling' was an official SA synonym for the inferior crouchen blanc, also known as Cape riesling and mostly used anonymously in blends, occasionally varietally. Rhine riesling often off-dry here, in blends or varietally, some excellent botrytised dessert examples. Crouchen: 0.6% of vineyard area, declining; Rhine: small but steady 0.2%.

Sauvignon blanc Prestigious vine most associated with eastern Loire regions, Bordeaux and New Zealand — whose wines have helped restore fashionability to the grape. The SA version no longer a poor relation of these. Usually dry, but some sweet wines; sometimes wooded, more often not (former sometimes called fumé blanc/blanc fumé). 9.5% of vineyard area, still growing.

Semillon

Spelt sémillon in French. Sometimes heavily wooded, sometimes sweet, more often in blends. ±1% of vineyard area. Recent boutique vinifications of rare red version causing excitement.

Viognier Increasingly fashionable variety internationally, spreading out from its home in the northern Rhône, now showing promise here. Usually wooded. Still tiny plantings.

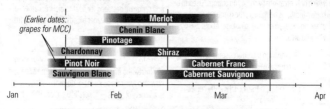

Approximate ripening dates in the Stellenbosch area for some important grape varieties

Competitions, Challenges & Awards

An increasing number of wine competitions, awards and challenges are run by liquor industry bodies, independent companies, publishing houses and individuals. Below are the main national events:

Absa Top Ten Pinotage Competition Run annually by the Pinotage Association and a major financial institution to help set international quality targets for growers of pinotage. Local/overseas judges. See under Industry Organisations for contact details.

Absa Perold Cape Blend Competition New event aimed at creating a signature style for Cape Blends (see SA Wine Styles section). Judges and contacts as for Absa Top Ten Pinotage.

Cape Port Challenge Organised by the Cape Port Producers' Association (previously South African Port Producers' Association) to select the best bottling in each of the various port categories, and an overall winner. Local judges. ▪ info@boplaas.co.za ▪ www.sappa.co.za ▪ T +27 (0)44-213-3326 ▪ F +27 (0)44-213-3750

Classic Wine Trophy Established in 1998 to recognise ageworthy, classic SA wines. Staged under rules of the Office Internationale de la Vigne et du Vin (OIV) in partnership with La Revue du Vin de France. Overseas judges. ▪ info@classicwinetrophy.co.za ▪ www.classicwinetrophy.co.za ▪ T +27 (0)21-683-7479 ▪ F +27 (0)86-588-2989

Diners Club Winemaker of the Year Inaugurated in 1981, this prestigious competition features a different category each year. Local panel with some overseas representation. ▪ winemaker@dinersclub.co.za ▪ www.dinersclub.co.za ▪ T +27 (0)21- 795-5400 ▪ F +27 (0)21-794-8185

Juliet Cullinan Wine Connoisseur's Award National competition organised by local wine-entrepreneur Juliet Cullinan independently of the Juliet Cullinan Standard Bank Wine Festival. ▪ juliet@julietcullinan.co.za ▪ T +27 (0)74-185-0050

Landbouweekblad Woman Winemaker of the Year Skipped in 2011, this competition acknowledges the role and skills of women winemakers, and highlights the special qualities they bring to their craft. Final decisions about the event's future will be made in early 2012. ▪ lorman@yebo.co.za ▪ www.sawinewoman.co.za ▪ T +27 (0)21-856 3194 / +27 (0)82-556-8679 ▪ F 086-555-8061 ▪ Stellenbosch office: T +27 (0)21-865-2815/2440

Old Mutual Trophy Wine Show See Trophy Wine Show.

Michelangelo International Wine Awards Well-established event (1997) featuring a hand-picked international panel and one local judge. Run under international OIV rules. Aims to identify SA wines which will appeal to foreign palates. ▪ lorman@yebo.co.za ▪ www.michelangeloawards.com ▪ T +27 (0)21-856-3194 / +27 (0)82-556-8679 ▪ F 27 (0)86-555-8061 ▪ Stellenbosch office: T +27 (0)21-865-2815 / +27 (0)21-865-2440

Muscadel Award for Excellence Annual competition aimed at raising consumer awareness and recognising quality in the creation, packaging and promotion of SA's muscadel wines. Local judges. ▪ winemaker@badsberg.co.za ▪ T +27 (0)23-344-3021 ▪ F +27 (0)23-344-3023

SAPPA Port Challenge See Cape Port Challenge

South African Airways (SAA) Wine Awards Annual selection of wines to fly with the national carrier (drinkability in flight conditions an important consideration). The top red, white, bubbly and port each receive a trophy. Local and overseas palates. ▪ BongiSodladla@flysaa.com, YolandeSchutte@flysaa.com ▪ T +27 (0)11-978-9304 / +27 (0)11-978-5835; +27 (0))11-978-3982 / +27 (0)11-978-3115 ▪ F +27 (0)11-978-3115

South African Terroir Wine Awards Only wines that truly portray a specific terroir can enter, making this a highly exclusive competition. The best wines certified as from single vineyards, units registered for the production of estate wine or wards in SA's officially recognised winegrowing areas, are awarded. Seven local judges. ▪ mlab@iafrica.com ▪ www.terroirwineawards.co.za ▪ T +27 (0)21-975-8166

South African Young Wine Show Inaugurated 1975 to gauge the quality of embryo wines, prior to finishing and bottling, thereby also recognising wineries which sell their products in bulk. The grand champion receives the General Smuts Trophy. Local judges. ▪ information@veritas.co.za ▪ www.youngwineshow.co.za ▪ T +27 (0)21-807-3104 ▪ F +27 (0)21-863-2079

Top 100 SA Wines New national fine-wine challenge that aims to identify the best 100 wines of South Africa. The winning wines are presented in an annual consumer guide, showcased on the website and made available for tasting by the public. Local/overseas judges. ▪ info@top100sawines.co.za ▪ www.top100sawines.co.za ▪ T +27 (0)21-787-9880 ▪ F +27 (0)86-627-5588

Trophy Wine Show Convened by Michael Fridjhon, sponsored by Old Mutual. Seeks to identify the best wines in SA and award trophies to the top gold medal winner in the major classes, as well as the top producer overall. Local and international judges. ▪ mf@reciprocal.co.za ▪ www.trophywineshow.co.za ▪ T +27 (0)1-482-9178 ▪ F +27 (0)11-482-9168

Veritas SA's biggest competition for market-ready wines, awarding double-gold, gold, silver and bronze medals across a wide range of categories. Local palates with some overseas input. ▪ information@veritas.co.za ▪ www.veritas.co.za ▪ T +27 (0)21-807-3104 ▪ F +27 (0)21-863-2079

Wine Magazine Amorim Cork Cap Classique Challenge Annual competition to anoint SA's top bottle-fermented sparkling wines. Mostly local judges. ▪ celiag@ramsaymedia.co.za ▪ www.winemag.co.za ▪ T +27 (0)21-530-3145 ▪ F +27 (0)21-530-3288

Wine Magazine Nedbank Green Wine Awards A two-part competition, recognising the best wine made from certified organically grown grapes, and the producer with the best environmental practices. A booklet of these results is produced. Local judges. ▪ celiag@ramsaymedia.co.za ▪ www.winemag.co.za ▪ T +27 (0)21-530-3145 ▪ F +27 (0)21-530-3288

Wine Magazine Brenn-O-Kem Shiraz Challenge Uncovering benchmark SA wines made from shiraz/syrah, with a best overall and a best value winner. Local judges. ▪ celiag@ramsaymedia. co.za ▪ www.winemag.co.za ▪ T +27 (0)21-530-3145 ▪ F +27 (0)21-530-3288

Wine Magazine Ultra Liquors Best Value Wine Awards SA judges gather annually to select the best value wines under R60 based on quality. Sponsored by Ultra Liquors, results are published in *Wine*'s Best Value Wine Guide. ▪ celiag@ramsaymedia.co.za ▪ www.winemag.co.za ▪ T +27 (0)21-530-3145 ▪ F +27 (0)21-530-3288

Winemakers' Choice Awards Gives winemakers from all wine regions the opportunity to judge the products of their peers. A Diamond Award is given to all winning wines; trophies and a cash prize are also awarded to the best white and red on show. ▪ richard@ winemakerschoice.co.za, nan@winemakerschoice.co. za ▪ www.winemakerschoice.co.za ▪ T +27 (0)21-887-2377 / +27(0)82-716-7269

Wine Education

Cape Wine Academy Long-established general wine education body. Based in Stellenbosch and Johannesburg with satellites in Durban, Pretoria, Bloemfontein, Namibia and Harare. Runs wine theory and tasting courses with examinations at several levels, and skills workshops for front-of-house sales staff and sommeliers. Also presents corporate tastings. ▪ www.capewineacademy.co.za ▪ Stellenbosch: **T +27 (0)21-889-8844** ▪ F +27 (0)21-889-7391 ▪ michelle@capewineacademy.co.za ▪ Johannesburg: T +27 (0)11- 024-3616 ▪ F +27 (0)11- 440 2157 ▪ marilyn@capewineacademy.co.za

Stellenbosch University Wine Evaluation Course Presented nationally with GetSmarter through online learning and face-to-face contact sessions in Cape Town and Johannesburg. Certifies students to be selected for the Veritas and Wine & Spirit Board tasting panels. ▪ info@getsmarter.co.za ▪ **T +27 (0)21-447-7565** ▪ F +27 (0)21-447-8344 ▪ www.getsmarter.co.za

University of Stellenbosch Garagiste Winemaking Course The premium short course for people interested in producing quality small-scale wines at home or simply expanding their wine knowledge. Attendees receive a set of notes; observe the use of garagiste winemaking equipment; taste different vinifications; bottle their own wine; and receive a certificate from Stellenbosch University. ▪ wdutoit@sun. ac.za ▪ **T +27 (0)21-808-2022** ▪ F 021-808-4781

Wine Tasting Academy Run by Michael Fridjhon and the University of Cape Town's Graduate School of Business, this intensive 3-day tasting and wine judging course aims to increase the number of competent wine judges at work in the local industry. ▪ mf@recip-rocal.co.za

Service Excellence Training Runs wine courses for staff in the licensed restaurant trade to improve their knowledge of viticulture and wine service. ▪ mfine@ icon.co.za ▪ www.bevtrainsa.co.za ▪ **T +27 (0)82-932-9430 / +27 (0)21-782-5472**

Selected Wine Shops

The following retail outlets, on-line emporia and specialist shippers stock a wide range of fine-wines and/or provide specialised services to the wine-consuming public. See our website, www.platteronline.com, for an expanded listing, including special facilities and programmes such as regular tastings, wine clubs and special offers.

Eastern Cape

Makro Port Elizabeth ▪ www.makro.co.za ▪ T +27 (0)41-397-8000 ▪ F +27 (0)41-397-8001

Metro Liquor Mataliele ▪ T +27 (0)39-737-3050 ▪ +27 (0)39-737-3374

Metro Liquor Port Elizabeth ▪ T +27 (0)41-451-2293 ▪ +27 (0)41-451-2391

Picardi Rebel Fig Tree Park (Port Elizabeth) ▪ fig-tree@picardirebel.co.za ▪ www.picardirebel.co.za ▪ T +27 (0)41-368-2840 ▪ F +27 (0)41-368-2420

Spargs Liquor Mart (East London) ▪ T +27 (0)43-711-7700 ▪ F +27 (0)43-748-4707

Ultra Liquors Grahamstown ▪ grahamstown@ ultraliquors.co.za ▪ T +27 (0)46-622-2353 ▪ F +27 (0)46-622-2355

Ultra Liquors East London ▪ eastlondon@ ultraliquors.co.za ▪ T +27 (0)43-743-5174/722-3476 ▪ F +27 (0)43-743-4283

Ultra Liquors Newton Park ▪ newtonpark@ ultraliquors.co.za ▪ T +27 (0)41-364-1103/46 ▪ F +27 (0)41-364-2277

Ultra Liquors Westbourne Road (Port Elizabeth) ▪ westbourne@ultraliquors.co.za ▪ T +27 (0)41-373-1245/6 ▪ F +27 (0)41-374-2203

Ultra Liquors Queenstown ▪ queenstown@sollykramers.co.za ▪ T +27 (0)45-839-3826 ▪ F +27 (0)45-839-7667

Ultra Liquors Joubert Str (Queenstown) ▪ joubert@ultraliquors.co.za ▪ T +27 (0)45-838-2319 ▪ F +27 (0)45-839-2666

Free State

Metro Liquor Bloemfontein ▪ T +27 (0)51-434-1315 ▪ F +27 (0)51-434-3074

Metro Liquor Welkom ▪ T +27 (0)57-355-7741 ▪ F +27 (0)57-355-5047

Ultra Liquors Bedelia (Welkom) ▪ bedelia@ultraliquors.co.za ▪ T +27 (0)57-352-1086 ▪ F +27 (0)57-352-3536

Ultra Liquors Bloemfontein ▪ bloem@ultraliquors.co.za ▪ T +27 (0)51-447-3328 ▪ F +27 (0)51-447-3600

Garden Route

Picardi Rebel Beacon Isle (Plettenberg Bay) ▪ www.picardirebel.co.za ▪ T/F +27 (0)44-533-1225

Picardi Rebel George ▪ george@picardirebel.co.za ▪ www.picardirebel.co.za ▪ T +27 (0)44-887-0053 ▪ F +27 (0)44-887-0054

Picardi Rebel Lagoon Fine Wine & Liquors (Market Square, Plettenberg Bay) ▪ www.picardirebel.co.za ▪ T +27 (0)44-533-2440 ▪ F +27 (0)44-533-2442

Picardi Rebel Liquor Guys Knysna ▪ www.picardirebel.co.za ▪ T +27 (0)44-382-1614 ▪ F +27 (0)382-3307

Picardi Rebel Square (The Square, Plettenberg Bay) ▪ www.picardirebel.co.za ▪ T +27 (0)44-533-1340 ▪ F +27 (0)44-533-0574

Picardi Rebel Waterfront Drive (Knysna) ▪ waterfrontdrive@picardirebel.co.za ▪ www.picardirebel.co.za ▪ T/F +27 (0)44-382-3318

The Oak Barrel (Wilderness) ▪ T +27 (0)44-882-1201 / +27 (0)82-924-6196

34° South (Knysna) ▪ info@34south.biz, keith@34south.biz ▪ www.34south.biz ▪ T +27 (0)44-382-7331/302-5818 ▪ F +27 (0)866-328-454

Ultra Liquors Blanco (George) ▪ blanco@ultraliquors.co.za ▪ T +27 (0)44-870-0917/ 9 ▪ F +27 (0)44-870-0914

Ultra Liquors George ▪ george@ultraliquors.co.za ▪ T +27 (0)44-874-5514 /10 ▪ F +27 (0)44-874-5511

Gauteng

Alpha Liquor Store (Roodepoort) ▪ T +27 (0)11-766-1086 ▪ F +27 (0)11-763-8741 ▪ michael@jumbomeats.com

Bamboo-Love Books See Love Books

Bootleggers Liquor Specialist ▪ Booysens: T +27 (0)11-493-2536 ▪ Fourways Crossing: T +27 (0)11-465-9777 ▪ Glenanda: T +27 (0)11-432-3570 ▪ Glenvista: T +27 (0)11-432-3093 ▪ Lombardy: T +27 (0)11-882-6252

Boulevard Cellars ▪ andrewpanayiotou7@gmail.com ▪ T +27 (0)11-803-6808/6121 ▪ F +27 (0)118-070-675

Central Liquors @ The Square (Boksburg) ▪ kartsounis@telkomsa.net ▪ T +27 (0)11-826-5070 ▪ F +27 (0)11-826-7151

Love Books (Melville) ▪ info@lovebooks.co.za ▪ www.lovebooks.co.za ▪ T +27 (0)11-726-7408 ▪ F +27 (0)866-395-375

Louisiana Liquor (Lynnridge Mall) ▪ T/F +27 (0)12-348-3456

Metro Liquor Boksburg ▪ T +27 (0)11-826-1420 ▪ F +27 (0)11-826-1462

Metro Liquor Devland ▪ T +27 (0)11-933-1667/8/9

Metro Liquor Hillfox (Weltevreden Park) ▪ T +27 (0)11-679-5690/4076 ▪ F +27 (0)11-679-3778

Metro Liquor Pretoria ▪ T +27 (0)12-379-6050 ▪ F +27 (0)12-379-7388

Metro Liquor Pretoria East ▪ T +27 (0)12-809-0800 ▪ F +27 (0)12-809-0786

Metro Liquor Springs ▪ T +27 (0)11-817-1133 ▪ F +27 (0)11-817-1607

Makro Centurion ▪ www.makro.co.za ▪ T +27 (0)860-305-999 ▪ F +27 (0)860-405-999

Makro Crown Mines ▪ www.makro.co.za ▪ T +27 (0)11-309-1100 ▪ F +27 (0)11-309-1089

Makro Germiston ▪ www.makro.co.za ▪ T +27 (0)860-308-999 ▪ F +27 (0)860-408-999

Makro Silver Lakes ▪ www.makro.co.za ▪ T +27 (0)860-307-999 ▪ F +27 (0)860-407-999

Makro Strubens Valley (Roodepoort) ▪ www.makro.co.za ▪ T +27 (0)860-302-999 ▪ F +27 (0)860-402-999

Makro Vaal (Vanderbijlpark) ▪ www.makro.co.za ▪ T +27 (0)860-303-999 ▪ F +27 (0)860-403-999

Makro Wonderboom ▪ www.makro.co.za ▪ T +27 (0)860-306-999 ▪ F +27 (0)860-406-999

Makro Woodmead ▪ www.makro.co.za ▪ T +27 (0)860-301-999 ▪ F +27 (0)860-401-999

Morara Wines & Spirits Emporium (Soweto) ▪ T +27 (0)11-982-2290 ▪ F +27 (0)11-982-3734

Norman Goodfellow's ▪ www.ngf.co.za ▪ Illovo: erick@ngf.co.za ▪ T +27 (0)11-788-4814 ▪ F +27

(0)86-628-8029 ▪ Hyde Park: jeffg@ngf.co.za ▪ T +27 (0)11-325-6462 /-5217 ▪ F +27 (0)86-624-4434 ▪ Melrose Arch: clinton@ngf.co.za ▪ T +27 (0)11-684-2756/7 ▪ F +27 (0)86-582-3273

Picardi Rebel Bedfordview ▪ www.picardirebel. co.za ▪ T +27 (0)11-615-9160 ▪ F +27 (0)11-622-2475

Picardi Rebel Eco Boulevard (Centurion) ▪ www. picardirebel.co.za ▪ T +27 (0)12-661-1529 ▪ F +27 (0)12-661-1516

Picardi Rebel Honeydew (Glen Dayson) ▪ www. picardirebel.co.za ▪ T +27 (0)11-475-4658 ▪ F +27 (0)11-675-6404

Picardi Rebel Moreleta Park ▪ www.picardirebel. co.za ▪ T +27 (0)12-997-4250 ▪ F +27 (0)12-997-4332

Picardi Rebel Morning Glen (Gallo Manor) ▪ www.picardirebel.co.za ▪ T +27 (0)11-802-0964 ▪ F +27 (0)11-802-0965

Picardi Rebel Northmead ▪ www.picardirebel.co. za ▪ T +27 (0)11-849-5392 ▪ F +27 (0)11-849-7332

Picardi Rebel Norwood ▪ www.picardirebel.co.za ▪ T +27 (0)11-728-6709 ▪ F +27 (0)11-728-1632

Picardi Rebel Sandton ▪ sandton@picardirebel.co. za ▪ www.picardirebel.co.za ▪ T +27 (0)11-884-2151 ▪ F +27 (0)11- 884-1067

Solly Kramers Parkview ▪ T +27 (0)11-486-2584 ▪ F +27 (0)11-646-3663 ▪ parkview@ sollykramers.co.za ▪ www.ultraliquors.co.za

Ultra Liquors Blairgowrie ▪ blairgowrie@ ultraliquors.co.za ▪ T/F +27 (0)11-888-6251

Ultra Liquors Church Str West (Pretoria) ▪ churchstreet@ultraliquors.co.za ▪ T +27 (0)11-327-4613 ▪ F +27 (0)12-327-2150

Ultra Liquors Corlett ▪ corlett@ultraliquors.co.za ▪ T +27 (0)11-887-1001/2/3 ▪ F +27 (0)11-887-4947

Ultra Liquors Hazelwood ▪ hazelwood@ ulrtraliquors.co.za ▪ T +27 (0)12-460-6012/4896 ▪ F +27(0)12-460-6831

Ultra Liquors Jules Str (Johannesburg) ▪ jules@ ultraliquors.co.za ▪ T +27 (0)11-615-7371 ▪ F +27 (0)11-616-1322

Ultra Liquors Meyerspark ▪ meyerspark@ ultraliquors.co.za ▪ T +27 (0)12-803-4292 ▪ F +27 (0)12-803-6953

Ultra Liquors Paul Kruger St (Eloffsdal) ▪ paulkruger@ultraliquors.co.za ▪ T +27 (0)12-335-2780/1 ▪ F +27 (0)12-335-5820

Ultra Liquors Parkview ▪ parkview@sollykramers. co.za ▪ T +27 (0)11-486-2584 ▪ F +27 (0)11-646-3663

Ultra Liquors Voortrekker Road (Pretoria) ▪ voortrekker@ultraliquors.co.za ▪ T +27 (0)12-335-0946/7 /0939 ▪ F +27 (0)12-335-6226

Vintages-The Wine Seller (Sandton) ▪ T +27 (0)11-784-8676/7 ▪ F +27 (0)11-784-8674 ▪ thebutchershop@mweb.co.za ▪ www. thebutchershop.co.za

WineDirect (Midrand) ▪ T +27 (0)11-312-4684 ▪ F +27 (0)11-887-4553 ▪ sales@winedirectonline. co.za ▪ www.winedirectonline.co.za

Winesense Melrose Arch ▪ T +27 (0)11-684-1487 ▪ F +27 (0)11-684-2160

KwaZulu-Natal

Broadway Liquors (Durban) ▪ marlynne1@iburst. co.za, dreddy858@gmail.com ▪ T +27 (0)31-564-5044 / +27 (0)82-926-0389 ▪ F +27 (0)31 5645044

Buxtons La Cave Liquors ▪ F +27 (0)31-572-2619 ▪ Umhlanga: T +27 (0)31-561-6792 ▪ La Lucia Mall: T +27 (0)31-572-6073

Liberty Liquors (Durban) ▪ T +27 (0)31-303-9857 ▪ F +27 (0)31-303-9864

Metro Liquor Empangeni ▪ T +27 (0)35-787-2604/6/8 ▪ F +27 (0)35-787-2605

Metro Liquor Newcastle ▪ T +27 (0)34-312-3654 ▪ F +27 (0)34-312-9493

Metro Liquor Pietermaritzburg ▪ T +27 (0)33-398-8900 ▪ F +27 (0)33-398-7980

Metro Liquor Pongola ▪ T +27 (0)34-413-1245 ▪ F +27 (0)34-413-2126

Makro Pietermaritzburg ▪ www.makro.co.za ▪ T +27 (0)33-846-3600 ▪ F +27 (0)33-346-0247

Makro Rossburgh ▪ www.makro.co.za ▪ T +27 (0)31-480-7000 ▪ F +27 (0)31-480-7060

Makro Springfield ▪ www.makro.co.za ▪ T +27 (0)31-203-2800 ▪ F +27 (0)860-409-999

Marriott Gardens Liquor Store (Greyville) ▪ herveallen@hotmail.com ▪ T +27 (0)31-309-2079 ▪ F +27 (0)31-309-2097

Meander Fine Wines (Lions River) ▪ meanderfinewines@yahoo.com ▪ www. meanderfinewines.co.za ▪ T +27 (0)33-234-2913 / +27 (0)83-452-3350

Picardi Rebel Cascade Centre (Pietermaritzburg) ▪ www.picardirebel.co.za ▪ T +27 (0)33-347-3852 ▪ F +27 (0)33-347-1019

Picardi Rebel Emapangeni ▪ www.picardirebel.co. za ▪ T +27 (0)35-772-5537 ▪ F +27 (0)35-772-5543

Picardi Rebel Glenwood (Durban) ▪ www. picardirebel.co.za ▪ T +27 (0)31-201-5487 ▪ F +27 (0)31-201-5488

Picardi Rebel Howick ▪ www.picardirebel.co.za ▪ T +27 (0)33-330-6636 ▪ F +27 (0)33-330-6638

Picardi Rebel Midlands Mall (Pietermaritzburg) ▪ www.picardirebel.co.za ▪ T +27 (0)33-342-1698 ▪ F +27 (0)33-342-1699

Picardi Rebel Shelly Beach ▪ www.picardirebel. co.za ▪ T +27 (0)39-315-1277 ▪ F +27 (0)39-315-1278

Parklane Cellars (Pietermaritzburg) ▪ cameron@ parklane.co.za, parklane@parklane.co.za, wineou@vodamail.co.za ▪ T +27 (0)33-342-3487 / +27 (0)83-628-1575 ▪ F +27 (0)33-342-6413

The Wine Cellar (Rosetta) ▪ info@thewinecellar co. za ▪ www.thewinecellar.co.za ▪ T/F +27 (0)33-267-7044

Tops Village Vineyard (Kloof) ▪ vineyard1@retail. spar.co.za, vineyard2@retail.spar.co.za, villagemall8@retail.spar.co.za ▪ T +27 (0)31-764-6679/5112 ▪ F 031-764-7196

Ultra Liquors New Germany ▪ newgermany@ ultraliquors.co.za ▪ T +27 (0)31-705-3777/3993 ▪ F +27 (0)31-705-6640

Ultra Liquors Tollgate (Mayville) ▪ tollgate@ ultraliquors.co.za ▪ T +27 (0)31-261-2233/67 ▪ F +27 (0)31-261-7980

Ultra Liquors Umbilo Road (Durban) ▪ umbilo@ ultraliquors.co.za ▪ T +27 (0)31-201-0886/2412 ▪ F +27 (0)31-202-3318

Ultra Liquors Westville ▪ westville@ultraliquors. co.za ▪ T +27 (0)31-266-4364/60 ▪ F +27 (0)31-266-4300

Limpopo

Makro Polokwane ▪ www.makro.co.za ▪ T +27 (0)860-009-550

Metro Liquor Brits ▪ T +27 (0)12-252-7318 ▪ F +27 (0)12-252-4777

Metro Liquor Polokwane (Magnesiet Str) ▪ T +27 (0)15-298-8800 ▪ F +27 (0)15-298-8666

Metro Liquor Tzaneen ▪ T +27 (0)15-307-1254 ▪ F +27 (0)15-307-1767

Ultra Liquors Polokwane ▪ polokwane@ ultraliquors.co.za ▪ T +27 (0)15-297-6808/6851 ▪ F +27 (0)15-297-6809

Mpumalanga

Makro Nelspruit ▪ www.makro.co.za ▪ T +27 (0)860-009-548

Metro Liquor Burgersfort ▪ T +27 (0)13-231-7891/2 ▪ F +27 (0)13-231-7018

Metro Liquor Bushbuckridge ▪ T +27 (0)13 799 0448/9 ▪ F +27 (0)13-799-0401

Metro Liquor Ermelo ▪ T +27 (0)17-819-7402 ▪ F +27 (0)17-811-6582

Metro Liquor Hazyview ▪ T +27 (0)13-737-6314 ▪ T +27 (0)13-737-6315

Metro Liquor Nelspruit ▪ T +27 (0)13-753-2146 ▪ T +27 (0)13-752-2915

Metro Liquor Witbank ▪ T +27 (0)13-656-2497 ▪ F +27 (0)13-656-6109

Picardi Rebel Witbank ▪ www.picardirebel.co.za ▪ T +27 (0)13-656-6697 ▪ F +27 (0)13-656-6692

Ultra Liquors Ermelo ▪ ermelo@ultraliquors.co.za ▪ T +27 (0)17-811-4750 ▪ F +27 (0)17-819-4762

Windmill Wine Shop & Cottages (R536 between Hazyview & Sabie) ▪ info@thewindmill.co.za ▪ www.thewindmill.co.za ▪ T +27 (0)13-737-8175 / +27(0)82-930-6289 ▪ F +27 (0)13-737-8966

Northern Cape

Metro Liquor Kimberley ▪ T +27 (0)53-833-4340 ▪ T +27 (0)53-832-0902

Zebrani Liquor City (Upington) ▪ T +27 (0)54-331-2831 ▪ F +27 (0)54-3311-2831

North West

De Wijnwinkel (Wolmaransstad) ▪ gert@pop.co.za ▪ T +27 (0)83-262-0387 / +27 (0)18-596-1606 ▪ F +27 (0)18-596-2890

Picardi Rebel Rustenburg ▪ www.picardirebel.co. za ▪ T +27 (0)14-537-3414 ▪ F +27 (0)14-537-3410

Sharbel Wine (Broederstroom) ▪ phillip@ sharbelwine.co.za, sales@sharbelwine.co.za ▪ www.sharbelwine.co.za ▪ T +27 (0)71-608-8415 / +27 (0)12-333-7921 ▪ F +27 (0)86-272-1314

Ultra Liquors Rustenburg ▪ rustenburg@ ultraliquors.co.za ▪ T +27 (0)14-592-9093 ▪ F +27 (0)14-594-0195

Western Cape

Aroma Fine Wine Centres Constantia (Aroma Liquors Alphen): ▪ alphen@aroma.co.za ▪ T +27 (0)21-794-8693 ▪ F +27 (0)21-794-8694 ▪ Canal Walk (Century City): aromacwa@aroma.co.za ▪ T +27 (0)21-551-7511 ▪ F +27 (0)21-981-5411

Bergkelder Vinoteque Wine Bank See Die Bergkelder Vinoteque Wine Bank

Bottelary Hills Wine Centre (Stellenbosch) ▪ bhwc@telkomsa.net ▪ www.bhwc.co.za ▪ T +27 (0)21-865-2955 ▪ F +27 (0)21-865-2885

Caroline's Fine Wine Cellar (Cape Town) ▪ carowine@mweb.co.za, carowine3@mweb.co.za ▪ www.carolineswine.com ▪ Strand Str: T +27 (0)21-419-8984 ▪ F +27 (0)21-419-8985 ▪ V&A Waterfront: T +27 (0)21-425-5701 ▪ F +27 (0)21-425-5702

Chapmans Peak Wine & Spirits (Hout Bay, Cape Town) ▪ wine@cpws.co.za, lidia@cpws.co.za ▪ T +27 (0)21-790-1088 ▪ F +27 (0)21-790-1089

De Wijngarten Wine Boutique (Bonnievale) ▪ dewijngarten1@telkomsa.net ▪ www.

dewijngarten.co.za ▪ T +27 (0)23-616-2367 ▪ F +27 (0)23-616-3160

Die Bergkelder Vinoteque Wine Bank (Stellenbosch) ▪ info@bergkelder.co.za ▪ www.bergkelder.co.za ▪ T +27 (0)21-809-8280 ▪ F +27 (0)21-883-9533 ▪ See also under Die Bergkelder Wine Centre in the A-Z section

La Cotte Inn Wine Sales/Fromages de France (Franschhoek) ▪ info@lacotte.co.za ▪ www.lacotte.co.za ▪ T +27 (0)21-876-3775 ▪ F +27 (0)21-876-3036

La Verne Wine Boutique (Robertson) ▪ T +27 (0)23-626-4314 ▪ F +27 (0)23-626-1916 ▪ lavernewines@lando.co.za ▪ www.lavernewines.co.za

Metro Liquor George ▪ T +27 (0)44-874-1370 ▪ F +27 (0)44-874-1377

Metro Liquor Oudtshoorn ▪ T +27 (0)44-272-0602 ▪ F +27 (0)44-279-1568

Metro Liquor Vuyani ▪ T +27 (0)21-364-4901 ▪ F +27 (0)21-364-4906

Makro Montagu Gardens ▪ www.makro.co.za ▪ T +27 (0)860-308-999 ▪ F (0)860-408-999

Makro Ottery ▪ www.makro.co.za ▪ T +27 (0)21-704-7400 ▪ F +27 (0)21-703-6348

Manuka Wine Boutique (Somerset West) ▪ T +27 (0)21-851-6060 ▪ F +27 (0)21-851-9145

Mooiberge (Stellenbosch) ▪ **T +27 (0)21-881-3222** ▪ +27 (0)21 8813017 ▪ winery@zetler.co.za ▪ www.zetler.co.za

Old Cape Wine Shop Imhoff Farm (Kommetjie) ▪ info@ocws.co.za ▪ www.ocws.co.za ▪ T +27 (0)21-783-5054

Picardi Rebel Claremont (Main Rd) ▪ claremont@picardirebel.co.za ▪ www.picardirebel.co.za ▪ T +27 (0)21-671-9611 ▪ F +27 (0)21-683-9025

Picardi Rebel Mainstream Centre (Hout Bay) ▪ houtbaycellars@picardirebel.co.za ▪ www.picardirebel.co.za ▪ T +27 (0)21-790-7273 ▪ F +27 (0)21-791-3211

Picardi Rebel Longbeach Mall (Noordhoek) ▪ www.picardirebel.co.za ▪ T +27 (0)21-785-3323 ▪ F +27 (0)21-785-3318

Picardi Rebel Parklands Junction (Parklands) ▪ parklandsjunction@picardirebel.co.za ▪ www.picardirebel.co.za ▪ T +27 (0)21-556-1877 ▪ F +27 (0)21-556-8556

Picardi Rebel Rosmead Ave (Claremont) ▪ www.picardirebel.co.za ▪ T +27 (0)21-683-1406 ▪ F +27 (0)21-674-2094

Picardi Rebel Spearhead (Cape Town Foreshore) ▪ spearhead@picardirebel.co.za ▪ www.picardirebel.co.za ▪ T +27 (0)21-425-1664 ▪ F +27 (0)21-425-9443

Picardi Rebel Sun Valley ▪ www.picardirebel.co.za ▪ T +27 (0)21-785-2149 ▪ F +27 (0)21-785-2942

Picardi Rebel Tygervalley ▪ www.picardirebel.co.za ▪ T +27 (0)21-914-1649 ▪ F +27 (0)21-914-2420

Picardi Rebel Victoria Ave (Hout Bay) ▪ winebarrel@picardirebel.co.za ▪ www.picardirebel.co.za ▪ T +27 (0)21-790-0039 ▪ F +27 (0)21-790-0552

Picardi Rebel Willowbridge ▪ willowbridge@picardirebel.co.za ▪ www.picardirebel.co.za ▪ T +27 (0)21-914-3506 ▪ F +27 (0)21-914-3508

Rubin's Liquor Store (Cape Town) ▪ ian@rubins.co.za, orders@rubins.co.za ▪ T +27 (0)21-425-4692/3 ▪ F +27 (0)21-419-9405

Simon's Town Bottle Store (Cape Town) ▪ T +27 (0)21-786-1438 ▪ F +27(0)21-786-1440

Something To Wine About (Rawsonville) ▪ nell.karlien@gmail.com ▪ +27 (0)23-349-1882 / +27 (0)82-461-3127 ▪ +27 (0)86-514-7893

Spier Wine Shop (Stellenbosch) ▪ info@spier.co.za ▪ www.spier.co.za ▪ T +27 (0)21-809-1143/6 ▪ F +27 (0)21-809-1144

Stellenbosch Wine Export Centre ▪ T/F +27 (0)21-883-3814

Steven Rom Wine Merchants & Exporters (Cape Town) ▪ www.stevenrom.co.za, www.thewinemerchant.co.za ▪ mario@stevenrom.co.za ▪ Sea Point: T +27 (0)21-439-6043 ▪ F +27 (0)21-434-0401 ▪ Three Anchor Bay: T +27 (0)21-439-1112 ▪ F +27 (0)21-434-0401 ▪ Kloof Street: T +27 (0)21-424-8476 ▪ F +27 (0)21-426-0546

The Vineyard Connection (Stellenbosch/Muldersvlei) ▪ info@vineyardconnection.co.za, wine@vineyardconnection.co.za, lara@vineyardconnection.co.za ▪ www.vineyardconnection.co.za ▪ T +27 (0)21-884-4360 ▪ F +27 (0)21-884-4361

The Wine Kollective (Riebeek Kasteel) ▪ espost@telkomsa.net ▪ T +27 (0)22-448-1008 / +27 (0)82-776-9366

The Wine Shop at Constantia Uitsig (Constantia) ▪ T +27 (0)21-794-1810 ▪ F +27 (0)21-794-1812

Ultra Liquors Goodwood ▪ goodwood@ultraliquors.co.za ▪ T +27 (0)21-591-5581 / +27 (0)21-592-5812 ▪ F +27 (0)21-591-8492

Ultra Liquors Greenpoint ▪ greenpoint@ultraliquors.co.za ▪ T +27 (0)21-434-4847/38/4302 ▪ F +27 (0)21-434-7548

Ultra Liquors Parow ▪ parow@ultraliquors.co.za ▪ T +27 (0)21-930- 2415/6/2453 ▪ F +27 (0)21-930-4007

Ultra Liquors Wynberg ▪ wynburg@ultraliquors.co.za ▪ T +27 (0)21-762-5885/1473 ▪ F +27 (0)21-761-6005

Vaughan Johnson's Wine & Cigar Shop See A-Z section for details

Vino Pronto (Cape Town) ▪ T +27 (0)21-424-5587 ▪ F +27 (0)21-424-5587

Wade Bales Wine Society (Cape Town) ▪ info@thewinesociety.co.za ▪ www.wadebaleswinesociety.co.za ▪ T +27 (0)21-794-2151 ▪ F +27 (0)21-794-2821

Wine & Company (Hermanus) ▪ wineandco@telkomsa.net, winenco@telkomsa.net ▪ www.wineandcompany.co.za ▪ T +27 (0)28-313-2047 / +27 (0)82-355-4346 ▪ F +27 (0)86-697-2594

Wine Cellar (incl insulated/secure maturation cellars; Cape Town) ▪ info@winecellar.co.za ▪ www.winecellar.co.za ▪ T +27 (0)21-448-4105

Wine Concepts (Cape Town) ▪ www.wineconcepts.co.za ▪ Newlands: newlandshop@wineconcepts.co.za, michael@wineconcepts.co.za, corlien@wineconcepts.co.za ▪ T +27 (0)21-671-9030 / +27 (0)87-807-7854 ▪ F +27 (0)21-671-9031 ▪ Kloof Str: kloofst@wineconcepts.co.za ▪ T +27 (0)21-426-4401 ▪ F +27 (0)88-021-426-4401

Wines (Franschhoek) ▪ www.wines-wines.com ▪ info@wines-wines.com, wines@project19.co.za elsa@project19.co.za ▪ T +27 (0)21-876-3185 / +27 (0)83-458-9835 ▪ F +27 (0)21-876-3185

Wine Village Hermanus ▪ wine@hermanus.co.za, winevillage@hermanus.co.za ▪ www.winevillage.co.za ▪ T +27 (0)28-316-3988 ▪ F +27 (0)86-509-4931

Online Wine Shops

Arriba Liquor Merchants ▪ www.arriba.co.za

Cybercellar.com ▪ **www.cybercellar.com**

eWine ▪ www.ewine.co.za

Getwine ▪ www.getwine.co.za

Hermanuspietersfontein Wine Shop ▪ http://hpf1855.co.za

Manuka Wine Exports ▪ www.manuka.co.za

Michelangelo Int. Wine Awards Wine Shop ▪ www.michelangeloawards.com

The WineMerchant.co.za ▪ www.thewinemerchant.co.za

The Wine Registry ▪ www.thewineregistry.co.za

SaleWine.co.za ▪ www.salewine.co.za

SA Wines ▪ www.sawines.com

Wine Cellar ▪ www.winecellar.co.za

Wine-Club ▪ www.wine-club.co.za

Wine Direct ▪ www.winedirectonline.co.za

Wine Village Hermanus ▪ www.wine-village.co.za

WineWeb ▪ www.wineweb.co.za

See also A-Z section for wineries' own online retail facilities.

Specialist Wine Shippers

Cape Grape & Wine Logistics ▪ motti@aspiring.co.za ▪ www.aspiring.co.za ▪ T +27 (0)21-881-3477 ▪ F +27 (0)21-881-3476

The Vineyard Connection ▪ info@vineyardconnection.co.za, wine@vineyardconnection.co.za, lara@vineyardconnection.co.za ▪ www.vineyardconnection.co.za ▪ T +27 (0)21-884-4360 ▪ F +27 (0)21-884-4361

A-Code Numbers & Codes

Many wines appear on the market under brand names, with, at first glance, no reference to their producers or purveyors. However, consumers need not buy 'blind', and may trace a wine's provenance by checking the official 'A-number' which appears on the bottle or pack. This identity code tells you either who produced the wine, or who sourced it for resale. In the latter case, an enquiry to the merchant should elicit the source. The list keeps growing and being revised, and is too lengthy to reproduce in this guide. Via the online SAWIS portal (**www.sawis.co.za**), it is possible however to search the list of A-codes, as well as the certification codes issued for each wine by the Wine & Spirit Board, for details about the production area, variety and vintage.

STYLES & VINTAGES

Recent Cape Vintages

South African wines do not exhibit the major vintage variations seen in some winegrowing areas. There are, nevertheless, perceptible differences from year to year. Dry, hot summers are the norm but a variety of factors make generalisations difficult and possibly misleading.

2011 Yet more variable than last vintage, impossible to generalise. As in 2010, producer's track record should guide the buying/cellaring decision.

2010 A real test of the winegrower's savvy, and one of the toughest recent harvests to call. As in 2002, track record should guide the buying/cellaring decision.

2009 Perhaps one of the greatest Cape vintages. Late and gruelling, but whites and reds both look stellar.

2008 Long, wet, late and challenging but also unusually cool season, favouring elegance in both reds and whites.

2007 Elegant, structured whites; smaller red-grape berries resulted in intense colour and fruit concentration, especially for cab and shiraz.

2006 Perhaps the best white-wine vintage in a decade — particularly expressive sauvignon and chenin. Fleshy, mild-tannined reds, with lower alcohols.

2005 Short, early and particularly challenging. Concentrated if alcoholic reds; mostly average whites, some stellar exceptions.

2004 Cooler dry conditions yielded healthy, elegant, often ageworthy wines with lower alcohols and yielding tannins.

2003 Outstanding, especially for reds — concentrated and structured, and often slow to show their best. Difficulties with late-ripeners in some areas.

2002 Challenging and patchy; generally individual producers' track record rather than variety or terroir should guide the purchase/cellaring decision.

Older Vintages

2001 Some excellent reds — fruity and concentrated, best are long-lived. Flavourful if alcoholic whites. **2000** Powerful and concentrated reds, befitting a hot year; the best have kept very well. Whites generally less impressive and not for long ageing. **1999** Fat, alcoholic reds with ripe fruit for earlier drinking. Generally not too much excitement among the whites. **1998** Excellent red vintage with enough fruit for extended cellaring; whites generally not for keeping. **1997** Among coolest and latest vintages on record. Supple, elegant reds; some excellent and stylish whites. **1996** Generally awkward reds, not for keeping; whites, except for top NLHs, best drunk up. **1995** For many, the vintage of the 90s. Concentrated reds, some still maturing spectacularly. **1994** Hottest, driest vintage in decades; variable quality; new-clone cabs and early ripening reds fared well. **1993** Without serious mishaps; some excellent sauvignons; above-average reds. **1992** Coolish season, favouring whites, especially sauvignon; the reds (notably pinotage) very good; **1991** Dry, warm to hot, favouring early to mid-season ripeners; some long-lasting reds. **1990** Uneven year, alternately cool and warm; average whites and reds; not for further ageing. The **1980s**: even years (82, 84, 86) were usually more favourable for reds; uneven years, marginally cooler, favoured whites, but 'white' years 87 and, especially, 89 produced remarkable reds. The **1970s**: again, even years generally favoured reds. Best was 74; but top wines from some other vintages are still delicious. The **1960s** and earlier yielded some astonishingly long-lived wines, prompting a new look at the traditional 'dikvoet' winemaking style.

South African Wine Styles

Blanc de blancs White wine made from white grapes only; also used for champagne and méthode cap classique.

Blanc fumé or **fumé blanc** Dry white from sauvignon, usually but not necessarily wooded (nor smoked, smoky).

Blanc de noir A pink wine (shades range from off-white through peach to pink) made from red grapes. See also Rosé.

Blend See Varietal wine and Cape blend.

Brut See Sugar or sweetness, and Sparkling wine.

Cap classique See Sparkling wine.

Cape Blend Evolving term, increasingly used to denote a (red) blend with pinotage, the 'local' grape making up a significant part of the assemblage; sometimes simply a blend showing a distinct 'Cape' character; occasionally used for chenin-based blends.

Carbonated See Sparkling wine.

Cultivar Grape variety (a contraction of 'cultivated variety').

Cuvée French term for the blend of a wine.

Demi-sec See Sugar or sweetness.

Dessert wine A sweet wine, often to accompany the dessert but sometimes pleasurably prior, as in the famous Sauternes/foie gras combo.

Dry to sweet See Sugar or sweetness.

Estate wine Term now reserved for wine originating from an officially registered 'unit for the production of estate wine' (see www.sawis.co.za for current list).

Fortified wines Increased in alcoholic strength by the addition of spirit, by SA law to minimum 15% alcohol by volume.

Grand cru See Premier Grand Cru.

Jerepiko or jerepigo Red or white wine, produced without fermentation; grape juice is fortified with grape spirit, preventing fermentation; very sweet, with considerable unfermented grape flavours.

Kosher See Winemaking terms section.

Late Harvest Sweet wine from late-harvested and therefore sweeter grapes. See Sugar or sweetness.

Méthode cap classique (MCC) See Sparkling wine.

Noble Late Harvest (NLH) Sweet dessert wine (still, perlé or sparkling) exhibiting a noble rot (botrytis) character, from grapes infected by the *botrytis cinerea* fungus. This mould, in warm, misty autumn weather, attacks the skins of ripe grapes, causing much of the juice to evaporate. As the berries wither, their sweetness and flavour become powerfully concentrated. SA law dictates that grapes for NLH must be harvested at a minimum of 28° Balling and residual sugar must exceed 50g/L.

Nouveau Term originated in Beaujolais for fruity young and light red, usually from gamay and made by the carbonic maceration method. Bottled soon after vintage to capture the youthful, fresh flavour of fruit and yeasty fermentation.

Perlant, perlé, pétillant Lightly sparkling, usually carbonated wine.

Port Fortified dessert with ever-improving quality record in Cape since late 1980s, partly through efforts of Cape Port Producers' Association which recommends use of word 'Cape' to identify the local product. Following are CPPA-defined styles: **Cape White**: non-muscat grapes, wood-aged min 6 mths, any size vessel; **Cape Ruby**: blended, fruity, components aged min 6 mths, up to 3 years depending on size of vessel. Average age min 1 year. **Cape Vintage**: fruit of one harvest; dark, full-bodied, vat-aged (any size); **Cape Vintage**

Reserve: fruit of one harvest in year of 'recognised quality'. Preferably aged min 1 year, vats of any size, sold only in glass; **Cape Late Bottled Vintage** (LBV): fruit of single 'year of quality', full-bodied, slightly tawny colour, aged 3–6 years (of which min 2 years in oak); **Cape Tawny**: wood-matured, amber-orange (tawny) colour, smooth, slightly nutty taste (white grapes not permitted); **Cape Dated Tawny**: single-vintage tawny.

Premier Grand Cru Unlike in France, not a quality rating in SA — usually an austerely dry white.

Residual sugar See Sugar or sweetness.

Rosé Pink wine, made from red or a blend of red and white grapes. The red grape skins are removed before the wine takes up too much colour.

Single-vineyard wine Classification for wines from officially registered vineyards, no larger than 6ha in size and planted with a single variety.

Sparkling wine Bubbly, or 'champagne', usually white but sometimes rosé and even red, given its effervescence by carbon dioxide — allowed to escape in the normal winemaking process. **Champagne** undergoes its second fermentation in the bottle. Under an agreement with France, SA does not use the term, which describes the sparkling wines from the Champagne area. Instead, **méthode cap classique** (MCC) is the SA term to describe sparkling wines made by the classic method. **Charmat** undergoes its second, bubble-forming fermentation in a tank and is bottled under pressure. **Carbonated** sparklers are made by the injection of carbon dioxide bubbles (as in fizzy soft drinks). See also Sugar or sweetness.

Special Late Harvest (SLH) SA designation for a lighter dessert-style wine. There is no legal stipulation for residual sugar content, but if the RS is below 20g/L, the label must state 'extra dry', 'dry', 'semi-dry' or 'sweet', as the case may be. The minimum alcohol content is 11% by volume.

Stein Semi-sweet white wine, usually a blend and often confused with steen, a grape variety (chenin blanc), though most steins are at least made partly from steen grapes.

Sugar or sweetness In still wines: extra-dry or bone-dry wines have less than 2.5g/L residual sugar, undetectable to the taster. A wine legally is dry up to 5g/L. Taste buds will begin picking up a slight sweetness, or softness, in a wine — depending on its acidity — at about 6g/L, when it is still off-dry. By about 8–9g/L a definite sweetness can usually be noticed. However, an acidity of 8–9g/L can render a sweet wine fairly crisp even with a sugar content of 20g/L plus. Official sweetness levels in SA wine are listed in the table opposite.

Varietal wine From a single variety of grape. Legislation requires the presence in the wine of 85% of the stated variety or vintage. Blends may name component parts only if those components were vinified separately, prior to blending; then they are listed with the larger contributor(s) named first. If any one of the blend partners is less than 20%, percentages for all the varieties must be given. Blends may be vinified separately in any recognised WO area; component areas may be named, as above except the threshold is 30%.

Vintage In SA primarily used to denote year of harvest. Not a quality classification (a 'vintage' port in Europe means one from an officially declared great port-grape year).

Wine	Sugar (g/l)
Still wines	
Extra-dry	≤ 2.5
Dry	≤ 5
Semi-dry	5 ≤ 12
Semi-sweet	> 5 < 30
Late Harvest	≥ 20
Special Late Harvest (SLH)	–
Natural Sweet (or Sweet Natural)	> 20
Noble Late Harvest (NLH)	> 50
Naturally dried grape wine (straw wine)	> 30
Sparkling wines	
Brut nature	< 3
Extra brut	< 6
Brut	< 15
Extra-dry	12–20
Dry	17–35
Semi-sweet	33–50
Sweet	> 50

WORDS & PHRASES

Winetasting Terms

Short of a ready description? Here are a few frequently-used words, phrases and explanations that may be helpful. See also Winemaking terms; SA wine styles.

Accessible, approachable Flavours and feel of the wine are harmonious, easily recognised; it is ready to drink.

Aftertaste The lingering flavours and impressions of a wine; its persistence — the longer, the better.

Alcoholic 'Hot' or, in excess, burning character caused by imbalanced or excessive alcohol. Also simply spirituous.

Astringent Mouth-puckering sensation in the mouth, associated with high tannin (and sometimes acid); also bitter, sharp.

Aroma Smells in the bouquet, or nose, especially the odours associated with the grape rather than the winemaking process.

Attack First sensations on palate/nose — pungent, aggressive, quiet etc.

Austere Usually meaning unyielding, sometimes harsh. Sometimes, more favourably, to imply a notable restraint/refinement.

Backbone The wine is well formed, firm, not flabby or insipid.

Baked 'Hot', earthy quality. Usually from scorched/ shrivelled grapes which have been exposed too long to the sun, or from too warm a barrel fermentation, especially in some whites.

Balance Desirable attribute. The wine's chief constituents — alcohol, acid, tannin, fruit and wood (where used) — are in harmony.

Bead Bubbles in sparkling wine; a fine, long-lasting bead is the most desirable. See also Mousse.

Big Expansive in the mouth, weighty, full-bodied, as a result of high alcohol or fruit concentration.

Bite or **grip** Imparted by tannin, acid and/or alcohol, important in young wines designed for ageing. If overdone can impart undesirable bitterness, harshness or spirity 'glow'.

Bitter Sensation perceived mainly on the back of the tongue, and in the finish of the wine. Usually unpleasant, though an accepted if not immediately admired character of certain Italian wines. Sometimes more positively associated with the taste of a specific fruit or nut, such as cherry-kernel or almond.

Body Fullness on the palate.

Botrytis/ed Exhibits a noble rot/botrytis character, from grapes infected by the *botrytis cinerea* fungus.

Bottle-age Negative or positive, depending on context. Positively describes development of aromas/ flavours (ie complexity) as wine moves from youth to maturity. Much-prized attribute in fine whites and reds. Negatively, bottle age results in a wine with stale, empty or even off odours.

Buttery Flavour and texture associated with barrel-fermented white wines, especially chardonnays; rich, creamy smoothness.

Claret Another name for a dry red Bordeaux or Bordeaux-like red.

Classic Showing characteristics of the classics of Bordeaux, Burgundy etc; usually implying balance, elegance, subtlety.

Coarse Rough, unbalanced tannins, acid, alcohol or oak.

Complexity Strong recommendation. A complex wine has several layers of flavour, usually developing with age/maturation. See Bottle age.

Concentration See Intensity.

Confected Over-elaborately constructed, artificial, forced; sometimes overly sweet.

Corked, corky Wine is faulty; its flavours have been tainted by yeast, fungal or bacterial infections, often but not necessarily from the cork. It smells damp and mouldy in its worst stages — but sometimes it's barely detectable. In a restaurant, a corked wine should be rejected and returned immediately; producers are honour-bound to replace corked wine.

Creamy Not literally creamy, of course; more a silky, buttery feel and texture.

Crisp Refers to acidity. Positively, means fresh, clean; negatively, too tart, sharp.

Deep and **depth** Having many layers; intense; also descriptive of a serious wine.

Dense Well-padded texture, flavour packed.

Deposits (also sediment or crust) Tasteless and harmless tartrates, acid crystals or tannin in older red wines. Evidence that wine has not been harshly fined, filtered or cold-stabilised.

Dried out Bereft of fruit, harder constituents remaining; tired.

Earthy Usually positive, wine showing its origins from soil, minerals, damp leaves, mushrooms etc.

Easy Undemanding (and hopefully inexpensive).

Elegant Stylish, refined, 'classic'.

Esters Scents and smells usually generated by alcohols and acids in wine. A wine may be 'estery' when these characteristics are prominent.

Extract An indication of the 'substance' of a wine, expressed as sugar-free or total extract (which would include some sugars). 18g/L would be low, light; anything much above 23g/L in whites is significant; the corresponding threshold for reds is around 30g/L.

Fat Big, full, ample in the mouth.

Finesse Graceful, polished. Nothing excessive.

Finish The residual sensations — tastes and textures — after swallowing. Should be pleasant (crisp, lively) and enduring, not short, dull or flat. See also Length.

Firm Compact, has good backbone.

Flabby Usually, lacking backbone, especially acid.

Flat Characterless, unexciting, lacks acid. Or bubbly which has lost its fizz.

Fleshy Very positive, meaning a wine is well fleshed out with texture and grape flavours.

Flowery, floral Flower-like (ie the smell of rose, honeysuckle, jasmine etc). Distinct from 'fruity' (ie smell/taste of papaya, cantaloupe, grape! etc).

Forward rather than shy; advancing in age too; mature.

Fresh Lively, youthful, invigorating. Closely related to the amount of acid in the wine and absence of oxidative character: a big, intensely sweet dessert without a backbone of acidity will taste flat and sickly; enough acid and the taste is fresh and uncloying.

Fruity See Flowery.

Full High in alcohol and extract.

Gamey Overripe, decadent, not universally unattractive; also meaty, 'wild'.

Gravel/ly With suggestions of mineral, earthy quality; also firm texture.

Green Usually unripe, sour; also herbaceous; sometimes simply youthful.

Grip Gripping, firm on palate, in finish. Acid, tannin, alcohol are contributors.

Heady Usually refers to the smell of a wine. High in alcohol; intense, high-toned.

Herbaceous Grassy, hay-like, heathery; can also indicate under-ripeness.

Hollow Lacking substance, flavours.

Honey or honeyed Sometimes suggesting literally a honey/beeswax taste or flavour; a sign of developing maturity in some varieties or more generally a sign of bottle-age.

Hot Burning sensation of alcohol in finish.

Intensity No flab, plenty of driving flavour; also deep colour.

Lean Thin, mean, lacking charm of ample fruit; also, more positively, compact, sinewy.

Lees/leesy Taste-imparting dead yeast cells (with grape skins and other solid matter) remaining with wine in tank/barrel (or bottle in the case of *méthode champenoise* sparkling wines) after fermentation. The longer the wine is 'on its lees' (*sur lie*) the more richness and flavour it should absorb.

Light/lite Officially wines under 10% alcohol by volume; also light in body (and often short on taste); a health-conscious trend in both reds and whites.

Lively Bouncy, fresh flavours.

Long or length Enduring; wine's flavours reverberate on the palate long after swallowing.

Maderised Oxidised and flat; colour is often brownish. Over-mature.

Meaty Sometimes suggesting a general savouriness; but also literally the aroma of meat — raw, smoked etc.

Mousse Fizz in sparkling wines; usually refers also to quality, size and effervescence of the bubbles. See also Bead.

Mouthfeel, mouthfilling Texture; feel; racy, crispness (fine with appropriate dishes) or generous, supple, smooth.

Neutral What it says, neither here nor there.

New World Generally implies accessible, bold, often extrovert (in terms of fruit and use of oak). **Old World** embraces terms like subtle, complex, less oaky, more varied and generally more vinous (than fruity). See also Classic.

Oaky Having exaggerated oak aromas/flavours (vanilla, spice, char, woodsmoke etc). Oak balanced by fruit in young wines may lessen with age, but over-oaked young wines (where fruit is not in balance) will become over-oaked old wines.

Palate Combination of flavour, taste and texture of a wine.

Pebbly See Gravelly.

Perfumed or scented Strong fragrances (fruity, flowery, animal etc)

Plump Well fleshed in a charming, cherubic way.

Porty Heavy, over-ripe, stewed; a negative in unfortified wine.

Rich Flavourful, intense, generous. Not necessarily sweet.

Robust Strapping, full-bodied (but not aggressive).

Rough Bull-in-a-china-shop wine, or throat sandpapering quality.

Round Well balanced, without gawkiness or jagged edges.

Sharp or tart All about acid, usually unbalanced. But occasionally sharpish, fresh wine is right for the occasion.

Short or quick Insubstantial wine, leaving little impression.

Simple One-dimensional or no flavour excitement.

Stalky Unripe, bitter, stemmy.

Stewed Over-ripe, cooked, soft, soggy fruit.

Structure Vague word, usually refers to the wine's make up (acid, tannin, alcohol) in relation to its ageing ability; if a wine is deemed to have 'the structure to age' it suggests these principal preservatives are in place.

Stylish Classy, distinguished; also voguish.

Supple Very desirable (not necessarily subtle), yielding, refined texture and flavours. See also Mouthfeel.

Tannic Tannins are prominent in the wine, impart-
ing, positively, a mouth-puckering, grippy, tangy
quality; negatively, a harsh, unyielding character.

Tension Racy, nervous fruity-acid play on the palate.

Terpene(s)/terpenoid Strong, floral compounds
influencing the aromas of especially riesling,
gewürztraminer and the muscats; with bottle-age,
terpenes often develop a pungent resinous oiliness.

Texture Tactile 'feel' in the mouth: hard, acidic,
coarse and alcoholic; or, smooth, velvety, 'warm'.

Toasty Often used for barrel-fermented or -aged
wines showing a pleasant biscuity, charry character.

Vegetal Grassy, leafy, herby — in contrast to fruity,
flowery, oaky. Overdone, a no-no.

Yeasty Warm bakery smells, often evident in barrel-
fermented whites and *méthode champenoise* sparkling wines, where yeasts stay in contact with the
wine after fermentation.

Winemaking Terms

A few brief reference explanations. See also sections
Winetasting Terms, SA Wine Styles.

Acid and **acidity** The fresh — or, in excess, sharp or
tart — taste of wine. Too little acid and the wine
tastes dull and flat. In SA, winemakers are permitted to adjust acidity either by adding acid — at any
stage before bottling — or by lowering the acid
level with a de-acidifier. See also Volatile acid and
Malolactic.

Alcohol Essential component of wine, providing fullness, richness and, at higher levels, sometimes an
impression of sweetness. Also a preservative, helping keep wines in good condition. Produced by
yeasts fermenting the sugars in the grape. Measured by volume of the total liquid. Most unfortified table wines in SA have between 11% and 14.
5% alc by vol; fortifieds range from ±16% to
21%. A variation of up to 1% between the
strength stated on the label and the laboratory
analysis is permitted by local law. Various techniques (such as reverse osmosis and 'spinning
cone', also the addition of water) exist to address
the increasingly important issue of high alcohol
levels in wine, and some are legal in SA (though
not for export to, eg, Europe).

Barrels (**barrel-aged**; **barrel-fermented**) Wines
are transferred into barrels to age, pick up oaky flavours etc. When must or fermenting wine is put
into barrels, the resulting wine is called barrel-fermented. A barrel or cask is generally a 225–500L
oak container; *barrique* is a French word for a 225L
barrel; a pipe, adapted from the Portuguese *pipa*,
usually indicates a vessel of 530–630L; vat is a
term generally used for larger (2,000–5,000L)
wooden vessels.

Batonnage See Lees.

Biodynamic See Organic.

Blend A wine made from two or more different
grape varieties, vintages, vineyards or containers.
Some of the world's finest wines are blends.

Bottles While the 750ml (75cl) bottle is now the
most widely used size of container for wine, it is by
no means the only one. Smaller bottles (375 &
500ml) are popular with restaurants and airlines,
and larger sizes are prized by collectors because of
their novelty value and/or their tendency to promote
slower wine ageing. The following are the larger
bottle sizes (note: some no longer in production):

Capacity		Bordeaux	Champagne/Burgundy
litres	bottles		
1.5	2	Magnum	Magnum
3	4	Double magnum	Jéroboam
4.5	6	Jéroboam	Rehoboam
6	8	Impériale	Methuselah
9	12	—	Salmanazar
12	16	—	Balthazar
15	20	—	Nebuchadnezzar

Brettanomyces or **'brett'** Naturally occurring yeast,
usually associated with red wine and regarded as a
spoilage factor, because its growth triggers the formation of volatile acids, phenols and other compounds which, in sufficient concentration, impart a
range of unpleasant characters, from barnyard to
sweat to cheese. At low concentrations, can
enhance complexity and character.

Carbonic maceration or **maceration carbonique**
Method of fermenting wine without first crushing
the grapes. Whole clusters with stalks etc are put
into closed vat; intracellular fermentation occurs
within the grape berries, which then burst.

Chaptalisation Originally French term for the addition of sugar to grape must to raise the alcohol of a
wine. Selectively legal in northern Europe, where
acid adjustments are not allowed as they are in SA.
Winemakers in both hemispheres bend the rules.

Charmat Method of making sparkling wine in a sealed tank (*cuvée close*) under pressure. Easier, cheaper than *méthode champenoise*.

Chips See Oak chips.

Cold ferment 'Cold' is a relative term; applied to fermentation of mainly white wines in temperature-controlled tanks, it refers to a temperature around usually 13–16°C. The benefits, especially important in a warm country, include conserving the primary fruit aromas and ensuring fermentation is carried out steadily and thoroughly.

Cold soak or **cold maceration**. Red winemaking method carried out prior to fermentation. Skins and juice are held, usually for a few days, at a sufficiently cool temperature to prevent fermentation. The theory is that this extracts more favourable colour and aromas than after fermentation.

Cold stabilisation Keeping a wine at about −4°C for a week or more to precipitate tartaric acid and 'clean up' the wine, preventing later formation of (harmless) tartrate crystals in bottle. Some winemakers believe this process damages flavour and prefer to avoid it.

Disgorgement (*dégorgement* in French) Important stage in the production of traditionally fermented sparkling where accumulated sediment (or lees), which could cloud the finished wine, is removed from the neck of the bottle.

Dosage The sugar added to sparkling wine after the second fermentation.

Fermentation The conversion of sugar in grapes into alcohol and carbon dioxide, a function of enzymes secreted by yeasts. Wild yeasts occur in vineyards and wineries, but in modern Cape winemaking cultured yeasts are normally added to secure the process. Beyond about 15% of alcohol, yeasts are overwhelmed and fermentation ceases, although it usually is stopped (for instance by cooling, filtration or the addition of alcohol) before this stage. See also Malolactic.

Filtration Removes last impurities including **yeast** cells. Done excessively, can thin a wine. Some traditionalists bottle without cold- or protein-stabilisation or filtration.

Fining and **protein stabilisation** Fining is ridding wine of suspended particles by adding substances that attract and draw the particles from the wine.

Flash-pasteurisation See Kosher.

Free run After grapes have been de-stalked and crushed, juice runs freely.

Garage wine Generic term for wine made in minuscule quantities, sometimes literally in a garage; a grower of such wine is sometimes called a *garagiste*.

Glycerol Minor product of alcoholic fermentation; from the Greek for sweet. Has an apparent sweetening effect on even dry wines and also gives a viscous, mouthfilling character.

Icewine Sweet, concentrated wine from grapes picked and pressed while frozen. Not a recognised category for SA wine production.

Kosher Wine made 'correctly', i.e. under rabbinical supervision, to be suitable for use by religious Jews. Vinification and any initial movement of the wine must be done by an observant Jew. Flash-pasteurisation, increasingly by means of new flavour-preserving processes such as Thermoflash, renders the resulting *meshuval* wine (literally 'boiled' or 'cooked') fit for handling by non-Jews.

Leafroll virus Virus (or complex of viruses), widespread throughout the winegrowing world, which causes the vine to perform below its potential and thereby produce wine which is lower in colour, body and flavour than that derived from virus-free or 'cleaned-up' plants.

Lees Spent yeast cells and other matter which collect at the bottom of any container in winemaking. Yeast autolysis, or decomposition, can impart richness and flavour to a wine, sometimes referred to as leesy. Lees stirring or *batonnage* involves mixing the bed of lees in a barrel or tank through the wine, which is said to be *sur lie*; it is employed primarily on barrel-fermented white wines. The main effects of mixing lees and wine are to prevent off-odours developing from lack of oxygen, to limit the amount of wood tannin and oak character extracted, and to increase flavour.

Malolactic fermentation (malo) Occurs when bacteria convert malic into lactic acids. This reduces the acidity of a wine, a normal and healthy process, especially in reds — provided, of course, it occurs before bottling.

Maturation Ageing properties are closely related to tannin and/or fixed acid content of a wine. A relatively full red wine with tannin has lasting power. With age, it may develop complexity, subtlety and smooth mellowness. Lighter wines with lower tannins are drinkable sooner but probably will not reach the same level of complexity. A number of Cape whites mature well over several years, but most are best drunk in their fruity youth, up to 18 months.

Méthode champenoise Classic method of making champagne by inducing secondary fermentation in the bottle and producing fine bubbles. Due to French restrictions on terminology, Cape sparkling wines made in this way are called méthode cap classique (MCC).

Micro-oxygenation Technique enabling introduction of precise, controlled doses of oxygen to must/wine. Advocates claim softer tannins, more stable colours and other advantages.

Oak chips, either in older barrels or stainless steel tanks, are used increasingly in SA, as are oak **staves**. Still frowned on by some purists, the 'additives' approximate the flavour effects of a new barrel, far more cheaply, more easily handled.

Oak-matured See Barrels.

Organic viticulture/winemaking Increasingly popular alternative to 'conventional' or 'industrialised' winegrowing, emphasising natural and sustainable farming methods and cellar techniques. A variant is biodynamic viticulture, influenced by anthroposophy, focused on improving wine quality through harmony with nature and its rhythms.

Oxidation Change (usually for the worse) due to exposure to air, in whites often producing dark yellow or yellowish colour (called maderisation), altering, 'ageing' the taste. Controlled aeration is used to introduce acceptable and desirable development in wine.

Pasteurisation See Kosher.

pH A chemical notation, used in winemaking and evaluation. The pH of a wine is its effective, active acidity — not in volume but by strength or degree. The reading provides a guide to a wine's keepability. The optimum pH in a wine is somewhere between 3.1 and 3.4 — which significantly improves a wine's protection from bacterial spoilage, so permitting it to mature and develop if properly stored.

Racking Drawing or pumping wine off from one cask or tank to another, to leave behind the deposit or lees.

Reductive Wine in an unevolved, unoxidised state is said to be 'reductive'; usually with a tight, sometimes unyielding character. The absence of air (in a bottled wine) or the presence of substantial sulphur dioxide (anti-oxidant) levels, will inhibit both oxidation and reduction processes, which are linked and complementary.

Reverse osmosis A specialised filtration technique, now permitted in SA for various purposes, including the removal of water from wine. See also Alcohol.

Skin contact After crushing and de-stemming, white grapes may be left for a period with the juice, remaining in contact with skins (before being moved into the press, from which the grape juice is squeezed). Some winemakers believe the colours and flavours in and under the grape skins should be maximised in this way; others believe extended (or any) contact can lead to coarseness, even bitterness.

Spinning cone See Alcohol.

Sulphur dioxide (SO$_2$) Sterilising agent and preservative, near-ubiquitous in winemaking since antiquity, now strictly controlled. In SA, max total SO$_2$ level for dry wines is 150–160mg/L; for wines with 5+ g/L sugar it is 200mg/L; and botrytis-style wines 300 mg/L. Any wine with more than 10mg/L total SO$_2$ must carry the warning 'Contains sulphites' (or 'sulfites') on the label.

Sur lie See Lees.

Tannin Vital preservative in wine, derives primarily from the grape skins. Necessary for a red wine's longevity. A young wine's raw tannin can give it a harshness, but no red wine matures into a great one without tannin, which itself undergoes change, combines with other substances and mellows. Tannin leaves a mouth-puckering dryness about the gums, gives 'grip' to a wine. A wooded wine will usually also contain some wood tannin.

Tartrates Harmless crystals formed by tartaric acid precipitating in non-cold-stabilised wine. Because of lack of public acceptance, usually avoided through cold stabilisation.

Terroir Important, controversial (and in SA overused) French term embracing soil, climate, topography and other elements which constitute the natural environment of a vineyard site and give it a unique character.

Thermovinification/Thermoflash See Kosher.

Unfiltered See Filtration.

Virus or **virused** See Leafroll.

Volatile acid (VA) The part of the acidity which can become volatile. A high reading indicates a wine is prone to spoilage. Recognised at high levels by a sharp, 'hot', vinegary smell. In SA, most wines must by law be below 1.2g/L of VA; in practice, the majority are well below 1g/L.

Whole-bunch pressing or **cluster pressing** Some SA cellars use this age-old process of placing whole bunches directly in the press and gently squeezing. The more usual method is to de-stem and crush the berries before pressing. Whole-bunch pressing is said to yield fresher, cleaner must, and wine lower in polyphenols which, in excess, tend to age wines faster and render them coarser.

Wood-fermented/matured See Barrels.

Yeasts Micro-organisms that secrete enzymes which convert or ferment sugar into alcohol. See fermentation.

TOURING WINE COUNTRY

Wine Routes, Trusts & Associations

For localised information about regional official wine routes and wineries, contact these organisations:

Breedekloof Wine & Tourism ▪ T +27 (0)23-349-1791 ▪ F +27 (0)23-349-1720 ▪ info@breedekloof.com ▪ www.breedekloof.com

Constantia Valley Wine Route ▪ T +27 (0)21-794-0542 (Jooles Pienaar) ▪ jooles@constantiavalley.com ▪ Chair: Jean Naudé T +27 (0)21-794-5128 ▪ ceo@grootconstantia.co.za ▪ www.constantiavalley.com

The Darling Wine & Art Experience ▪ T +27 (0)22-492-3430 (Shaun McLaughlin) ▪ F +27 (0)22-492-2693 ▪ mclaughlin@worldonline.co.za ▪ www.darlingtourism.co.za

Durbanville Boutique Wine Association ▪ T +27 (0)83-357-3864 ▪ F +27 (0)21-948-3441 info@durbanvilleboutiquewine.co.za ▪ www.durbanvilleboutiquewine.co.za

Durbanville Wine Valley Association ▪ T +27 (0)83-310-1228 ▪ info@durbanvillewine.co.za ▪ www.durbanvillewine.co.za

Elim Winegrowers ▪ T +27 (0)28-482-1880/+27 (0)82-551-2351 (Francis Pratt) ▪ wine@theberrio.co.za

Franschhoek See Vignerons de Franschhoek

Green Mountain Eco Route (Elgin/Bot River) ▪ T +27 (0)21-844-0975 ▪ F +27 (0)21-844-0970 ▪ info@greenmountain.co.za ▪ www.greenmountain. co.za

Helderberg See Stellenbosch

Hermanus Wine Route & Hemel-en-Aarde Winegrowers Association ▪ T +27 (0)83-305-7319, +27 (0)28-316-2761 (Frieda Lloyd) ▪ frieda@hermanuswine.com ▪ +27 (0)72-673-1880, +27 (0)28-212-1127 (Carolyn Martin) ▪ carolyn@creationwines.com ▪ www.hermanuswine.com

Klein Karoo Wine Route ▪ T/F +27 (0)28-572-1284 (Ellen Marais) ▪ info@kleinkaroowines.co.za ▪ www.kleinkaroowines.co.za

Northern Cape Wine Association See Orange River Wine Route

Olifants River Vodacom Wine Route ▪ See West Coast Wine Route

Orange River Wine Route ▪ T +27 (0)54-337-8800 (Karlien Kuhn/Elene Swanepoel) ▪ F +27 (0)54-332-4408 ▪ admin@orangeriverwines.com, info@owk.co.za

Paarl Vintners ▪ T +27 (0)21-863-4886 ▪ F +27 (0)21-863-4883 ▪ info@paarlwine.co.za ▪ www.paarlwine.co.za

Robertson Wine Valley ▪ T +27 (0)23-626-3167 / +27 (0)83-701-5404 ▪ F +27 (0)23-626-1054 ▪ manager@robertsonwinevalley.com ▪ www.robertsonwinevalley.com

Stellenbosch American Express Wine Routes ▪ T +27 (0)21-886-4310 ▪ F +27 (0)21-886-4330 ▪ info@wineroute.co.za ▪ www.wineroute.co.za ▪ Helderberg: T +27 (0)84-551-4759 / +27 (0)21-881-3714 (Margi Hoffe)

Santam Swartland Wine & Olive Route ▪ T +27 (0)22-487-1133 ▪ F +27 (0)22-487-2063 swartlandinfo@westc.co.za ▪ www.swartlandwineroute.co.za

Tulbagh Wine Route ▪ T/F +27 (0)23-230-1348/75 ▪ tulbaghinfo@lando.co.za ▪ www.tulbaghwineroute.com ▪ www.tulbaghtourism.co.za

Vignerons de Franschhoek ▪ T +27 (0)21-876-2861 ▪ F +27 (0)21-876-2768 ▪ marketing@franschhoek.org.za, office@franschhoek.org.za ▪ www.franschhoek.org.za ▪ www.franschhoekwines.co.za

Walker Bay Wine Wander ▪ T +27 (0)28-316-3988 ▪ F +27 (0)28-316-3989 / +27 (0)83-509-4931 ▪ wine@hermanus.co.za

Wellington Wine Route ▪ T +27 (0)21-864-2479 ▪ F +27 (0)21-873-4607 ▪ wine@wellington.co.za ▪ www.wellington.co.za

West Coast Wine Route ▪ T/F +27 (0)27-213-3126 / +27 (0)82-611-3999 ▪ wineroute@vodamail.co.za ▪ www.westcoastwineroute.co.za

Worcester Wine Route ▪ T +27 (0)23-342-8710 ▪ F +27 (0)23-342-2294 ▪ info@worcesterwineroute.co.za ▪ www.worcesterwineroute.co.za

Winelands Tourism Offices

For additional accommodation options, brochures and local advice, contact the information offices and/or publicity associations of the wine areas you plan to visit.

Breedekloof Wine & Tourism ▪ T +27 (0)23-349-1791 ▪ F +27 (0)23-349-1720 ▪ info@breedekloof.com ▪ www.breedekloof.com

Calitzdorp Tourism ▪ T +27 (0)44-213-3775 ▪ F +27 (0)86-569-1447 ▪ calitzdorpinfo@ kannaland.co.za ▪ www.calitzdorp.co.za

Cape Town Tourism ▪ V&A Waterfront Gateway Information Office: T +27 (0)21-405-4500 ▪ F +27 (0)21-405-4524 ▪ info@tourismcapetown. co.za ▪ www.tourismcapetown.co.za

Cape Town Tourism ▪ T +27 (0)21-487-6800 ▪ F +27 (0)21-487-6859 ▪ capetown@capetown. travel

Somerset West: T +27 (0)21-840-1400 ▪ F +27 (0)21-840-1410 ▪ somersetnwest@capetown. travel

Strand: T/F +27 (0)21-853-1688 ▪ strand@cape-town.travel

Elgin Valley Tourism T +27 (0)21-848-9838 ▪ F +27 (0)86-660-0398 ▪ info@elginvalley.co.za ▪ www.elginvalley.co.za

Franschhoek Wine Valley ▪ T +27 (0)21-876-2861/3603 ▪ F +27 (0)21-876-2768 ▪ info@ franschhoek.org.za, office@franschhoek.org.za ▪ www.franschhoek.org.za

Hermanus Tourism Bureau ▪ T +27 (0)28-312-2629 ▪ F +27 (0)28-313-0305 ▪ hermanustourism@hermanus.co.za ▪ www. hermanusaccommodation.co.za, www. hermanusrestaurants.co.za

McGregor Tourism ▪ T +27 (0)23-625-1954 ▪ F +27 (0)86-612-9636 ▪ info@tourismmcgregor. co.za ▪ www.tourismmcgregor.co.za

Northern Cape Tourism ▪ T +27 (0)53-832-2657 ▪ F +27 (0)53-831-2937 ▪ northerncapetourism@ telkomsa.net ▪ www.northerncape.co.za

Paarl Tourism Association ▪ T +27 (0)73-708-2835 ▪ F +27 (0)86-590-871 ▪ info@paarlonline. com ▪ www.paarlonline.com, www.paarltourism. com

Paarl Tourist Information Centre ▪ T +27 (0)21-872 4842 ▪ F +27 (0)21-872-9376 ▪ paarlinfo@ drakenstein.gov.za ▪ www.drakenstein.gov.za

Robertson Tourism Association ▪ T +27 (0)23-626-4437 ▪ F +27 (0)23-626-4290 ▪ info@robert-son.org.za ▪ www.robertsontourism.co.za

Route 62 ▪ T +27 (0)23-616-3563 ▪ F +27 (0)23-616-3422 ▪ info@route62.co.za ▪ www.route62.co.za

Saldanha Bay Tourism Organisation ▪ info@sbto. co.za, marketing@sbto.co.za ▪ www. capewestcoastpeninsula.co.za

Saldanha: T +27 (0)22-714-2088 ▪ F +27 (0)22-714-4240 ▪ saldanha@sbto.co.za

Hopefield: T/F +27 (0)22-723-1720 ▪ hopefield@ sbto.co.za

Langebaan: T +27 (0)22-772-1515 ▪ F +27 (0)22-772-1531 ▪ langebaan@sbto.co.za ▪ www. langebaaninfo.com

Vredenburg: T +27 (0)22-715-1142 ▪ F +27 (0)22-715-1141 ▪ vredenburg@sbto.co.za

Paternoster: T/F +27 (0)22-752-2323 ▪ info@pater-noster.info ▪ www.paternoster.info

St Helena Bay: T +27 (0)76-661-2046 ▪ sthelenabay@sbto.co.za

Stellenbosch Tourism Information Association ▪ T +27 (0)21-883-3584 ▪ F +27 (0)21-882-9550 ▪ info@stellenboschtourism.co.za ▪ www. stellenboschtourism.co.za

Wellington Tourism ▪ T +27 (0)21-873-4604 ▪ F +27 (0)21-873-4607 ▪ info@wellington.co.za ▪ www.wellington.co.za

West Coast Peninsula Tourism Bureau See Saldanha Bay Tourism Organisation

Worcester Tourism Association ▪ T +27 (0)23-348-2795 / +27 (0)23-342-6244 / +27 (0)76-200-8742 ▪ F +27 (0)23-347-4678 ▪ info@ worcestertourism.com ▪ www.worcestertourism. com

Specialist Wine Tours

Adamastor & Bacchus Cape Winelands Tours English, Afrikaans, Dutch, Norwegian, German ▪ johnford@iafrica.com, jarche@iafrica.com ▪ T +27 (0)21-439-3169 / +27 (0)83-229-1172 ▪ F +27 (0)86-604-5169

African Story Wine Tours ▪ English ▪ info@ africanstorytours.com ▪ www.africanstorytours. com ▪ T +27 (0)73-755-0444 / +27 (0)79-694-7915

African Trax Tours ▪ English ▪ info@africantrax.co. za, bookings@africantrax.co.za ▪ www.africantrax. co.za ▪ T +27 (0)83-692-8873

African Wonder Tours ▪ .Afrikaans, English, French, Italian, German ▪ info@africanwonder.co.

za ▪ www.africanwonder.co.za ▪ T +27 (0)82-325-1485 / +27 (0)78-780-4289

Amber Tours ▪ English ▪ lesleyc@wol.co.za ▪ www. ambertours.co.za, www.lesleycox.co.za ▪ T +27 (0)83-448-7016

Bizoe Wine Tours ▪ Afrikaans, English ▪ info@bizoe. co.za ▪ www.bizoe.co.za ▪ T +27 (0)21-843-3307 / +27 (0)83-709-3957 ▪ F +27 (0)86-653-8186

Cape Floral Kingdom Vineyard Tours ▪ sbirch@ iafrica.com ▪ www.CFKvineyardtours.co.za ▪ T +27 (0)76-145-1996

Capefuntours ▪ English ▪ capefuntours@icon.co.za ▪ www.capefuntours.co.za ▪ T +27 (0)21-782-5472 / +27 (0)82-932-9430 ▪ F +27 (0)21-782-5472

Cape Fusion Tours ▪ English ▪ cazcape@mweb.co.za, info@capefusion.co.za ▪ www.capefusiontours.com ▪ T +27 (0)21-461-2437 / +27 (0)83-235-9777 ▪ F +27 (0)86-672-5877

Double Gold Wineland Tours ▪ English ▪ kimdg@cybersmart.co.za, kimdg@absamail.co.za ▪ T +27 (0)21-785-5094 / +27 (0)82-293-3176

D'Vine Wine & Dine ▪ pauline.nel@dvinewinedine.co.za ▪ www.dvinewinedine.co.za ▪ +27 (0)73-972-7830 / +27 (0)21-975-4851 ▪ +27 (0)86-601-1238

Exclusively African Tours ▪ English, Dutch (German, Swedish, French on request) ▪ ian@exclusively-african.com ▪ www.holidaystosouthafrica.co.uk ▪ T +27 (0)21-852-0278 / +27 (0)82-309-9991 ▪ F +27 (0)86-609-0896

Go! Shuttles & Tours ▪ English, German, Afrikaans, French and Italian ▪ info@shuttle.co.za, nic@gotours.co.za ▪ www.gotours.co.za ▪ T +27 (0)72-368-3455 ▪ F +27 (0)86-548-2375

Gourmet Travels ▪ English, German ▪ rainer@gourmettravels.co.za ▪ www.gourmettravels.co.za ▪ T +27 (0)82-449-7666 ▪ F +27 (0)86-542-0542

Gourmet Wine Tours ▪ English ▪ sflesch@iafrica.com ▪ www.gourmetwinetours.co.za ▪ T +27 (0)21-705-4317 / +27 (0)83-229-3581 ▪ F +27 (0)21-706-0766

Grape Wine Encounters ▪ Translator on request ▪ info@grapeencounters.co.za ▪ T +27 (0)83-302-5599 ▪ F +27 (0)86-518-2050

Greatest Cape Wine Tours ▪ English, French ▪ richard@greatestcape.co.za ▪ www.greatestcape.co.za ▪ T +27 (0)21-855-5244 / +27 (0)83-650-5661

Gudrun Grünewald See Happy Holiday

Happy Holiday Wine Tours ▪ German, French, Dutch, English, Afrikaans ▪ gudrun@happyholiday.co.za ▪ www.happyholiday.co.za ▪ T +27 (0)82-699-3098

Janet Malherbe ▪ German, French & Flemish ▪ janetm@mweb.co.za ▪ www.janetmalherbe.webs.com ▪ T +27 (0)82-553-8928 ▪ T/F +27 (0)21-862-1484

Judy Krohn Private & Personal Tours ▪ English, German, Afrikaans ▪ judyk@zsd.co.za ▪ www.judykrohn.co.za ▪ T +27 (0)84-500-1941 / +28 (0)21-851-7009 ▪ F +27 (0)21-851-7009

Klaus Schindler ▪ German, English ▪ schindler@lando.co.za ▪ www.kapstadt.de/schindlers-africa ▪ T +27 (0)83-270-3449

La Route Des Vins ▪ English, French, Spanish ▪ pauline.demartini@gmail.com, info@laroutedesvins.co.za ▪ www.laroutedesvins.co.za ▪ T +27 (0)21-461-1069 / +27 (0)71-499-0768 ▪ F +27 (0)21-461-7689

Ocean & Vine Adventures & Tours ▪ English, translator on request ▪ wayne@wine.co.za, oceanv@netactive.co.za ▪ www.prowinetours.co.za ▪ T +27 (0)21-559-6906 / +27 (0)82-900-6999 ▪ F +27 (0)21-559-6906

Percy Tours ▪ English, Afrikaans & some French, German, Spanish and Italian ▪ travel@percytours.com ▪ www.percytours.com ▪ T +27 (0)72-062-8500 / +27 (0)28-316-4871

Redwood Tours ▪ English, Afrikaans ▪ info@redwoodtours.co.za ▪ www.redwoodtours.co.za ▪ T +27 (0)21-886-8138 / +27 (0)82-443-6480

Southern Destinations ▪ English ▪ info@southerndestinations.com, vanessa@southerndestinations.com ▪ www.southerndestinations.com ▪ T +27 (0)21-671-3090 ▪ F +27 (0)21-674-7481

Taste the Cape Travel & Tours ▪ English ▪ info@tastethecape.co.za ▪ www.tastethecape.co.za ▪ T +27 (0)21-715-3559 / +27 (0)79-812-0220

Tri Active Events Management (Green Mountain Eco Route) ▪ English, Afrikaans ▪ info@triactive.co.za ▪ www.triactive.co.za ▪ T +27 (0)21-844-0975 / +27 (0)83-456-2181 ▪ F +27 (0)21-844-0970

Tsiba Tsiba Wine Tours & Travel ▪ Dutch, English, French, German, Spanish ▪ info@TsibaTsiba.co.za ▪ www.tsibatsiba.co.za ▪ T +27 (0)82-956-8104

Vineyard Ventures English, Afrikaans, German; other languages on request ▪ vinven@iafrica.com ▪ www.vineyardventures.co.za ▪ T +27 (0)21-434-8888 / +27 (0)82-920-2825 ▪ F +27 (0)21-434-9999

Vintage Cape Tours ▪ English, Afrikaans, Dutch, French, German, Italian, Spanish ▪ info@vintagecape.co.za ▪ jade@vintagecape.co.za ▪ www.vintagecape.co.za ▪ T +27 (0) 84-513-3066 ▪ +27(0)21-913-2358 ▪ F +27 (0)86-690-8572

Vintour ▪ German, English, Afrikaans ▪ helmut@vintour.co.za ▪ www.vintour.co.za ▪ T/F +27 (0)21-976-5709 / +27 (0)83-626-0029

Walker Bay Wine Wander ▪ English, Afrikaans, French, German ▪ wine@hermanus.co.za, travel@percytours.com ▪ T +27 (0)28-316-3988 / +27 (0)72-062-8500 ▪ F +27 (0)86-509-4931

Wanderer Wines ▪ English, German, French ▪ wines@wanderer.co.za ▪ www.wanderer.co.za ▪ T +27 (0)21-713-2264 / +27 (0)82-878-1176 ▪ +27 (0)86-648-0352

Wellington Wine Walk ▪ English, Afrikaans ▪ judy@winescapetours.co.za ▪ www.winewalk.co.za

Wine Desk (at V&A Waterfront Information Centre) ▪ Foreign language specialist wine guides available in most languages for private tours ▪ waterfront@winedesk.co.za, info@winedesk.co.za, ligia@winedesk.co.za ▪ www.winedesk.co.za ▪ T +27 (0)21-418-0108 / +27 (0)82-822-6127 ▪ +27 (0)86-661-0545

Wine Escapes ▪ info@wineescapes.co.za ▪ www. wineescapes.co.za ▪ T +27 (0)83-453-2670
Winemaker-led Tasting Tours ▪ English; translators on request with sufficient notice ▪ vitis@

mweb.co.za ▪ www.winetastingtours.co.za ▪ T +27 (0)82-322-3733 ▪ F +27 (0)21-852-6621

Restaurants in the Winelands and Cape Town

Below are some dining out options in Cape Town and the winelands. These are paid entries. The venues supplied information on their cuisine, menus and attractions, which was then edited for consistency of style. For more restaurants among the vines, consult the A–Z section of the guide for wineries which offer light lunches, picnics etc. Look for the 🍽 symbol beside the individual entries. Unless stated to the contrary, all allow you to bring your own (BYO) wine — the corkage fee is indicated at the start of each entry. Should you wish to know about wheelchair access, please discuss with the relevant restaurant.

Index of restaurants
Listed alphabetically, with region.

Camps Bay

Azure Restaurant Twelve Apostles Hotel and Spa, Victoria Road, Camps Bay, Cape Town ▪ SA influenced, modern French cuisine ▪ Open daily: breakfast 7–11, lunch 12.30–2.30 & dinner 6–10.30 ▪ Booking advised ▪ Children welcome ▪ Major credit cards accepted ▪ No BYO ▪ Owner The Tollman Family ▪ azure@12apostles.co.za ▪ www.12apostleshotel.com ▪ S 33° 58' 59.37" E 18° 21'31.43" ▪ **T +27 (0)21-437-9029** ▪ F +27 (0)21-437-9055

A spectacular setting complemented by cuisine that stirs the senses. Sea vistas from cliffside restaurant and balcony are mesmerizing; dishes from executive chef Henrico Grobbelaar divert attention from ocean to plate. Fresh, organic ingredients are from hotel herb garden and local markets, fish is sustainable, and menus mouthwatering. Delight in succulent scallops and deboned springbok shank, ending lightly with rose champagne jelly and berry compote. (See also Accommodation section.)

Cape Town

Aubergine 39 Barnet Street, Gardens, Cape Town ▪ Classical cuisine with innovative twists & Asian influence ▪ Outdoor terrace ▪ Lunch Wed–Fri 12–2; 'Cinq B Sept' Mon–Sat 5–7 & dinner Mon–Sat 7–10 ▪ Closed Sun ▪ Booking advised ▪ Children 5+ welcome ▪ Major credit cards accepted ▪ No BYO ▪ Owner Harald Bresselschmidt ▪ info@aubergine.co.za ▪ www. aubergine.co.za ▪ **T +27 (0)21-465-4909** ▪ F +27 (0)86-671-0835

Warmly sophisticated restaurant revolving round wine-pairing. A 10 000-bottle cellar (selected for food compatibility) allows chef/patron Harald Bresselschmidt's keen palate and culinary skills full scope. Whether fish, seafood, prime aged local meat or tasty vegetarian options, dishes

accent flavor, aroma and texture, while degustation menus offer combinations like zebra with poppyseed polenta and porcini ragout, or crayfish tail with saffron cabbage and star anise bisque. *Eat Out* Top 10, 2010 & 3 stars *Roussouw's Restaurants* 2010 & '11.

Auslese 115 Hope Street, Gardens, Cape Town ▪ Wines paired with tapas-sized dishes in classic yet innovative style ▪ Booking essential, open for pre-booked functions only ▪ Children welcome ▪ Major credit cards accepted ▪ BYO by arrangement ▪ Owner Harald Bresselschmidt ▪ info@auslese.co.za ▪ www. auslese.co.za ▪ **T +27 (0)21-461-9727** ▪ F +27 (0)86-671-0835

Wanting to match gems from your wine collection, but can't cook? Organising anything from corporate events to a private birthday party or wine launch? Aubergine's elegant new venue in a refurbished historic house near the restaurant, is custom-designed for functions. Owner Harald Bresselschmidt will tailor the occasion for you, creating delectable tapas-style dishes to complement wines, either your own or from his 10 000-bottle cellar.

Azure Restaurant see under Camps Bay

Balducci's Ristorante Shop 6162, Victoria Wharf, V&A Waterfront, Cape Town ▪ Italian & Royal Sushi Bar ▪ Open daily 12–late ▪ Booking advised ▪ Children welcome ▪ Major credit cards accepted ▪ No BYO ▪ Owners Ian Halfon & Doron Duveen ▪ info@ slickrestaurants.com ▪ www.balduccis.co.za ▪ S 33° 54' 14" E 18° 25' 16" ▪ **T +27 (0)21-421-6002/3** ▪ F +27 (0)21-421-6010

Trendy venue offering prime waterfront views and generous helpings of 'home-cooked' Italian dishes, backed by slick service. Local ingredients add a fresh twist to tradition (try ostrich lasagna) and best-sellers range from gourmet wood-fired pizzas to export-quality shellfish; grain-fed aged steaks to a signature 180g grain-fed burger. As dessert, Amarula-splashed Tiramisu and classic Malva pudding vie in appeal with cheeseboards parading award-winning Cape cheeses. Diners Club and *Wine Spectator* Winelist Awards 2010. Sushi fans, join the crowd at the award-winning Balducci's Royal Sushi Bar.

Bascule Whisky, Wine and Cocktail Bar Cape Grace, West Quay Road, V&A Waterfront, Cape Town ▪ Bistro ▪ Open daily 10am–close ▪ Major credit cards accepted ▪ No BYO ▪ Owner Meikles Ltd ▪ bascule@ capegrace.com ▪ www.capegrace.com ▪ S 33° 54' 29" E 18° 25' 12" ▪ **T +27 (0)21-410-7082** ▪ F +27 (0)21-419-7622

Over 400 world-wide whiskies and the finest Cape wines – plus a quayside setting in the international yacht marina at Cape Town's Waterfront. By day Bascule is a lively destination, ideal for a cappuccino or light lunch. By night, the space transforms into a glamorous whisky, wine and cocktail bar, where whisky connoisseurs and social butterflies gather to enjoy a shot of Cape Town's social energy. *Eat Out*/V&A Waterfront Restaurant Awards 2009 Best Pub-style & Best Service. (See also Accommodation section.)

Belthazar Restaurant & Wine Bar Shop 153, Victoria Wharf, V&A Waterfront, Cape Town ▪ Steakhouse, seafood, wine bar ▪ Open daily 12–late ▪ Booking advised ▪ Major credit cards accepted ▪ No BYO ▪ Owners Ian Halfon & Doron Duveen ▪ info@slickrestaurants.com ▪ www.belthazar.co.za ▪ S 33° 54′15″ E 18° 25′13″ ▪ **T +27 (0)21-421-3753/6** ▪ F +27 (0)2-421-3748

Explore a palate-pleasing world of wining and dining at this award-winning restaurant and world's biggest wine-by-the-glass bar, where informed sommeliers serve over 200 of the Cape's finest wines by the glass and offer knowledgeable advice on a spoilt-for-choice 600-label winelist. Pair sought-after vintages with specialities ranging from export-quality cuts of butter-tender aged and grain-fed beef to game and the freshest South African and imported shellfish. Amex Platinum Fine Dining Award 2010 and voted one of the best 2010 wine lists by *Wine Spectator*.

Bistro Sixteen82 see under Constantia

Buitenverwachting Restaurant
Buitenverwachting, Klein Constantia Road, Constantia ▪ Modern European ▪ Tue–Sat (Apr–Oct) lunch 12–3, tapas 3–5 & dinner 7–9; Mon–Sat (Nov–March) lunch 12–3, tapas 3–5 & dinner 7–9.30 ▪ Closed Jul/Aug ▪ Booking advised ▪ Children welcome at lunch ▪ Major credit cards accepted ▪ Corkage R25 (from 3rd bottle) ▪ Owner Christine Mueller ▪ restaurant@buitenverwachting.com ▪ www.buitenverwachting.com ▪ S 34° 2′30.4″ E 018° 25′1.5″ ▪ **T +27 (0)21-794-3522** ▪ F +27 (0)21-794-1351

Pamper your palate in elegant surroundings, overlooking vineyards and mountains, or eat more casually in a vine-shaded courtyard. Menus are mouthwatering: chef/patron Edgar Osojnik believes in fresh, organic and local, lifted by superbly flavoured jus. Savour quail saltimbocca with green asparagus in truffled vinaigrette; détour to deconstructed Caesar salad; linger over beef fillet crusted in bone marrow; and allow room for alluring dessert. Flawless service. Tripadvisor Certificate of Excellence (4.5 rating out of 5, best food & service in the Constantia valley) 2011; American Express/Diners Club Platinum Fine Dining Award 2008–11; American Express10 year Achievement Award 2008; honorary member Austrian Food Guide/BOEG since 2006. (See also A–Z section.)

Catharina's at Steenberg see under Constantia

Den Anker Restaurant Pierhead, V&A Waterfront, Cape Town ▪ French/Belgian cuisine ▪ Open daily 11–4 & 6-10.30 (kitchen); 11–late (bar) ▪ Booking advised ▪ Children welcome ▪ Major credit cards accepted ▪ No BYO ▪ Owner E De Visscher ▪ denanker@mweb.co.za ▪ www.denanker.co.za ▪ **T +27 (0)21-419-0249** ▪ F +27 (0)21-419-0251

Watch basking seals from your table. Well into its teens, this buzzing quayside venue updates constantly without losing its charm. The terrace captures picture-postcard mountain views; décor is streamlined and evergreen *moule* & *frites* rubs shoulders with light, contemporary dishes and SA specialties. New is a tapas terrace menu (bitterballen are a must) with a wide selection of wines by the glass or Belgian beers.

Emily's 202 Clock Tower Center, V&A Waterfront ▪ Contemporary South African ▪ Open Mon–Sat for lunch 12–3 & dinner 6.30–closing ▪ Closed Sun, Good Fri & Dec 25 ▪ Children welcome ▪ Booking advised ▪ Private dining area for corporate luncheons ▪ Major credit cards accepted ▪ Corkage R100 ▪ Owner Peter Veldsman ▪ caia@mweb.co.za ▪ www.emily-s.com ▪ **T +27 (0)21-421-1133**

Emily's, celebrating its 10th anniversary at the V&A Waterfront in December, and its 20th since opening, remains reassuringly evergreen. Warmly welcoming, it's ideal for lunch overlooking the harbour and romantic at night. Cuisine updates tradition with innovative touches: try the African-style revamp of bobotie, with curried wild cactus in the custard; or apricots with sea-urchin *vapeur*, *marogo* and pineapple. Vast wine list at very reasonable prices, with many rarities. Now no room on the walls for the accumulated international and local awards.

Nobu One&Only Cape Town, Dock Road, V&A Waterfront, Cape Town ▪ Japanese style with a contemporary South African twist ▪ Dinner 6–11 Mon–Sun (summer) & Tue–Sun (winter) ▪ Booking advised ▪ Children welcome ▪ Major credit cards accepted ▪ No BYO ▪ Owner Kerzner International ▪ restaurant.reservations@oneandonlycapetown.com ▪ www.oneandonlycapetown.com ▪ S 33° 54′30″ E 18° 24′59″ ▪ **T +27 (0)21-431-4511**

Savour signature oriental cuisine in world-renowned Japanese master chef Nobuyuki 'Nobu' Matsuhisa's first restaurant in Africa – there's a unique contemporary South African twist to classic dishes. Enjoy cocktails at the bar, matching made-to-order, tantalising bites to the finest sakes, then move into the minimalist dining room for a sophisticated experience of fine Japanese fare. Don't miss the palate-pleasing speciality: black cod and prawn tempura. 3 stars *Rossouw's Restaurant* 2011; Diners Club Diamond Winelist Award 2010. (See also Accommodation section.)

Pure see under Hout Bay

Reuben's One&Only Cape Town, Dock Road, V&A Waterfront, Cape Town ▪ Wholesome bistro-fare using local flavours ▪ Open Mon–Sun breakfast 6.30-11, lunch 12–3 (Sun 12.30–3) & dinner 6–11 ▪ Booking advised ▪ Children welcome ▪ Major credit cards accepted ▪ No BYO ▪ Owner Kerzner International ▪ restaurant.reservations@oneandonlycapetown.com ▪ www.oneandonlycapetown.com ▪ S 33° 54′ 30″ E 18° 24′ 59″ ▪ **T +27 (0)21-431-4511**

Award-winning chef Reuben Riffel's urban debut is true to his country roots, bringing deceptively simple cuisine to the sophisticated setting of Cape Town's One&Only. His popular, flavour-packed bistro fare showcases the diversity of local ingredients, skillfully re-interpreting traditional recipes for today's spoiled-for-choice taste. Whether West Coast oysters, springbok loin or Namaqua lamb, the tri-level wine loft offers food pairing with some 5,000 local and international wines. (See also Accommodation section.)

Savoy Cabbage Restaurant & Champagne Bar 101 Hout Street, Cape Town ▪ Contemporary cuisine ▪ Lunch Mon–Fri 12–2.30, dinner Mon–Sat 7–10.30 ▪ Closed Sun ▪ Booking essential ▪ Major credit cards accepted ▪ Air-conditioned ▪ Corkage R40 ▪ Owner Caroline Bagley ▪ savoycab@iafrica.com ▪ www.savoycabbage.co.za ▪ S 33° 55′ 12.31″ E 18° 25′ 05.45″ ▪ **T +27 (0)21-424-2626** ▪ F +27 (0)21-424-3366

Heading for 14 years and popular as ever, this city-centre venue boasts a string of accolades, including plaudits from international critics. Expect exposed brick and high ceilings; perennial favourites as menu fixtures; and daily changing dishes offering taste treats like tropical-sauced geelbek ceviche, fennel-dusted warthog loin with red onion marmalade and sour fig syrup, and white chocolate tart crowned with ginger ice-cream. Intelligent boutique winelist.

Signal Restaurant Cape Grace, West Quay Road, V&A Waterfront, Cape Town ▪ Cape contemporary cuisine ▪ Open daily for breakfast 6–11, lunch 12–3 & dinner 6.30–10 ▪ Booking advised ▪ Children welcome ▪ Major credit cards accepted ▪ Corkage R40 ▪ Owner Meikles Ltd ▪ signal@capegrace.com ▪ www.capegrace.com ▪ S 33° 54′ 29″ E 18° 25′ 12″ ▪ **T +27 (0)21-410-7080** ▪ F +27 (0)21-419-7622

Delightfully soothing dining experience, cocooned in soft colours and elegant fabrics under a mirrored, chandelier-studded ceiling. Contemporary, flavour-rich dishes reflect the cultures that shaped Cape Town's culinary heritage, backed by an excellent winelist. Both regular and vegan tasting menus offer fresh, tantalising combos like sweet potato lasagna with espresso reduction, and butter-poached crayfish

with crispy chilli-salted sweetbread. Mouth-melting tea-time treats served in the hotel library. *Eat Out*/V&A Waterfront Awards: Best Deluxe Restaurant 2009. (See also Accommodation section.)

Societi Bistro 50 Orange Street, Gardens, Cape Town ▪ French & Italian influenced bistro ▪ Open for lunch & dinner Mon–Sat 12–11 ▪ Closed Sun ▪ Booking advised ▪ Children welcome ▪ Major credit cards accepted ▪ Corkage R30 ▪ Owners Peter Weetman & Tammy Botbyl ▪ info@societi.co.za ▪ www.societi.co.za ▪ S 33° 55′ 44.78″ E 18° 24′ 47.07″ ▪ **T +27 (0)21-424-2100** ▪ F +27 (0)21-424-1140

Societi is a neighbourhood 'local'; a sanctuary for Capetonians and visitors-in-the-know looking for a home from home. More than cuisine, it's a way of life, where regulars become friends and tasty bistro fare is savoured in good company. Menus change every three months to capture seasonal flavours, but best-sellers are perennial. Favourites are fillet *au poivre*, mushroom risotto, and for dessert, home-made sorbets and ice-cream.

The Square Restaurant Vineyard Hotel & Spa, Colinton Road, Newlands, Cape Town ▪ Eclectic contemporary cuisine ▪ Sushi prepared by skilled Sushi chefs ▪ Breakfast Mon–Sat 7–10.30, Sun & public holidays 7.30–11; lunch daily 12–3 & dinner daily 6–9.30 ▪ Booking advised ▪ Children welcome ▪ Major credit cards accepted ▪ Corkage R60 ▪ eat@vineyard.co.za ▪ www.vineyard.co.za ▪ **T +27 (0)21-657-4500** ▪ F +27 (0)21-657-4501

Dine stylishly in a glass-roofed space softened by indoor trees, soothed by harp or piano. Snack at the super-fresh sushi bar; move to tables to enjoy exec chef Alex Docherty's inventive take on the classics: try pan-roasted beef fillet with veal sweetbreads and wild mushroom ravioli; springbok and porcini suet pudding; or Gorgonzola risotto with apple and pecan salad. Popular fortnightly four/five course wine-pairing evenings. Diners Club Winelist Diamond Award 2009 & '10. (See also Accommodation section.)

The Towers Restaurant African Pride Crystal Towers Hotel & Spa, corner Century Boulevard & Rialto Road, Century City, Cape Town ▪ Original fusion of intercontinental flavours and cooking techniques ▪ Open daily 6.30am–11pm ▪ Booking advised ▪ Children welcome ▪ Major credit cards accepted ▪ Corkage R45 ▪ Owner Protea Hospitality Group (Pty) Ltd ▪ reservations@crystaltowershotel.com ▪ www.africanpridehotels.com/crystaltowers ▪ S 33° 89′ 23.62″ E 18° 51′ 23.06″ ▪ **T +27 (0)21-525-3888** ▪ F +27 (0)21-525-3889

Dining for all tastes and cultures, from halal-friendly to African; carnivorous (savour Chalmar beef) to vegetarian (Norwegian salmon flown in daily). Just alert the chef when booking. Eating options are as versatile, from 24-hour deli (great pastries) and stunning pool deck to Towers restaurant, where choices include the intimate Alice-in-Wonderland room with high-backed chairs, and more casual area looking into the open-plan kitchen. Protea Hotels Food & Beverage Achiever Of The Year Award 2010–2011. (See also Accommodation section.)

Constantia

Bistro Sixteen82 Steenberg Vineyards, Steenberg Estate, Steenberg Road, Tokai ▪ Contemporary bistro ▪ Open Mon–Sun breakfast 9–11, lunch 12–4 & tapas 4.30–8 ▪ Closed 15 Aug–6 Sep ▪ Booking advised ▪ Children welcome ▪ Major credit cards accepted ▪ Corkage R40 ▪ Owner Graham Beck Enterprises ▪ Executive chef Brad Ball ▪ reservations@bistro1682.co.za ▪ www.steenberghotel.com ▪ **T +27 (0)21-713-2211** ▪ F +27 (0)21-713-2201

Flavour-packed vineyard destination, combining bistro fare with award-winning wines in a sophisticated setting with tasting bar and lounge. While tempting desserts fall under the heading 'indulge', this invitation applies to the whole menu, from reviving breakfasts to lunches with treats like braised sweetbreads, jus-glazed veal brisket, and Chalmar beef tataki. From 4pm tuck into tapas indoors or on the terrace overlooking reflection pools and gardens. (See also A–Z section.)

Buitenverwachting Restaurant see under Cape Town

Catharina's at Steenberg Steenberg Estate, Tokai Road, Constantia ▪ Cape contemporary with classic undertones ▪ Open 7–11 daily for breakfast, lunch & dinner ▪ Booking advised ▪ Children welcome ▪ Major credit cards accepted ▪ Corkage R80 ▪ Owner Graham Beck Enterprises ▪ info@steenberghotel.com ▪ www.steenberghotel.com ▪ **T +27 (0)21-713-2222** ▪ F +27 (0)21-713-2251

Cool and classy. That's the mood at Catharina's, where wall-to-wall glass opens up the restaurant to views and vineyards, reflecting the constantly changing contemporary food from exec chef Garth Almazan. Flavour rules: feast on fish and game specialities like caramelised king scallops or kudu fillet; end with indulgent combo brûlée. Zingingly fresh Sunday jazz buffets under oaks or in the new courtyard. Diners Club Winelist Award of Excellence 2006–2008, Diamond Award 2009–2010; American Express Platinum Fine Dining Award 2005–2010. (See also A–Z section.)

Constantia Uitsig Restaurant Constantia Uitsig Wine Estate, Spaanschemat River Road, Constantia, Cape Town ▪ Italian/Mediterranean cuisine with forays into the East & North Africa ▪ Open daily — lunch bookings from 12–2, dinner bookings from 7–9 ▪ Closed eve of Dec 25; Jan 1 ▪ Booking advised ▪

Children welcome ▪ Major credit cards accepted ▪ Corkage wine R50 & sparkling R90 – no BYO for tables of 8 or more ▪ Owner Constantia Uitsig Holdings (Pty) Ltd ▪ restaurant@uitsig.co.za ▪ www.constantia-uitsig.com ▪ S 34° 02′ 45.28″ E 18° 25′ 12.55″ ▪ **T +27 (0)21-794-4480** ▪ F +27 (0)21-794-3105

Housed in the original Cape Dutch Homestead, with beguiling vistas of surrounding mountains and vineyards, this relaxed fine-dining restaurant maintains its popularity among locals and visitors for consistency, warm service and familiar ambience. Best-sellers from head chef Clayton Bell (who has spent 15 years at Constantia Uitsig) include a tasty puff-pastry tomato tart, fresh cumin-crusted linefish, and tender rare springbok loin with caramelised honey/lemon sauce. (See also Accommodation & A–Z sections.)

La Colombe Constantia Uitsig Wine Estate, Spaanschemat River Road, Constantia, Cape Town ▪ Classic and modern French cuisine with Asian influences – Open daily — lunch bookings from 12.30–2, dinner bookings from 7–8.45 ▪ Closed Sun eve (May–Sep); eve of Dec 25; Jan 1 ▪ Winter menu May–Sept annually ▪ Booking advised ▪ Children welcome ▪ Major credit cards accepted ▪ Corkage wine R45 & sparkling R70 – no BYO for tables of 8 or more ▪ Owner Constantia Uitsig Holdings (Pty) Ltd ▪ lacolombe@uitsig.co.za ▪ www.constantia-uitsig.com ▪ S 34° 02′ 45.28″ E 18° 25′ 12.55″ ▪ **T +27 (0)21-794-2390** ▪ F +27 (0)21-794-7914

Head chef Scot Kirton has taken over the La Colombe kitchen seamlessly, delivering the quintessentially elegant cuisine associated with the restaurant. Tempting menus retain their classic base, with innovative touches and inventive combinations of seasonal ingredients: signature veal fillet is a flavour feast of sugar-snap peas and black forest ham, buttered pomme purée, warm ballotine of sweetbreads and morel mushrooms, steamed langoustine and mustard beurre blanc. Restaurant of the Year '08 &'09; 12th place in the Top 50 *San Pellegrino* World's 50 Best Restaurants 2010 & number 82 in the *San Pellegrino* 100 Best Restaurants 2011; 3 stars in *Rossouw's Restaurants 2009 –'11*. (See also Accommodation & A–Z sections.)

Peddlars on the Bend Spaanschemat River Road, Constantia ▪ Country cuisine ▪ Open daily 11am–11pm ▪ Closed Dec 25 & Jan 1 ▪ Booking advised ▪ Children welcome ▪ Major credit cards accepted ▪ Corkage charged from 2nd bottle ▪ Free secure parking ▪ Owners Mike van der Spuy & Ian Wigley ▪ peddlars@mweb.co.za ▪ www.diningout.co.za ▪ **T +27 (0)21-794-7747** ▪ F +27 (0)21-794-2730

Popular with both locals and visitors, this lively restaurant and pub offers warm country charm in a garden setting. Enjoy drinks in the Terraces Pub, which draws an eclectic crowd; order from an extensive menu prepared daily from fresh ingredients: specialities include roast hock of pork, chicken and leek pie and steak tartare. The kitchen is open all day for those wanting lunch or early dinner. Diners Club Wine List of the Year, Platinum Award 2010.

River Café Constantia Uitsig Wine Estate, Spaanschemat River Road, Constantia, Cape Town ▪ Fresh, organic, bistro-style dining ▪ Open daily for breakfast 8.30–11 & lunch 12.30–5 ▪ Closed Jan 1 ▪ Booking advised ▪ Children welcome ▪ Major credit cards accepted ▪ Corkage R30 per bottle for tables of 10 or less ▪ Owner Constantia Uitsig Holdings (Pty) Ltd ▪ rivercafe@uitsig.co.za ▪ www.constantia-uitsig. com ▪ S 34° 02′ 45.28″ E 18° 25′ 12.55″ ▪ **T +27 (0)21-794-3010** ▪ F +27 (0)21-794-1812

Long a popular social destination for sumptuous breakfasts and affordable, café-style lunches. New head chef Dineel Terblanche brings culinary skills, gained while working extensively in Europe, to dishes using the freshest local ingredients and wines from Constantia Valley. Linger over appetising specialities such as crispy battered prawns; tasty fish pie; butter-tender beef fillet with potato fondant, fine beans and herb butter; and decadent open sandwiches. (See also Accommodation & A–Z sections.)

The Conservatory The Cellars-Hohenort Hotel, 93 Brommersvlei Road, Constantia ▪ Inter-continental contemporary classics ▪ Open daily for breakfast 7–10.30, lunch 12–2.30 & dinner 7–9.30 ▪ Booking advised ▪ Children 8+ welcome ▪ Major credit cards accepted ▪ Corkage R60 ▪ Owner Liz McGrath ▪ reservations@collectionmcgrath.com ▪ www. collectionmcgrath.com ▪ S 34° 00′ 07.19″ E 18° 26′ 04.74″ ▪ **T +27 (0)21-794-2137** ▪ F +27 (0)21-794-2149

Stylish restaurant, incorporating a giant 300 year-old oak, with garden vistas from both the airy indoors or sun-drenched terrace. Focus is on modern South African cuisine subtly infused with classic French flavours, but if you're feeling nostalgic, book for Sunday lunch with traditional roast beef and Yorkshire pudding. Before your meal, relax over cocktails in the sophisticated setting of The Martini.

The Greenhouse The Cellars-Hohenort Hotel, 93 Brommersvlei Road, Constantia ▪ Progressive European with South African elements ▪ Dinner Tue–Sat 7–9.30 ▪ Booking advised ▪ Children 12+ welcome ▪ Major credit cards accepted ▪ Corkage R60 ▪ Owner Liz McGrath ▪ reservations@collectionmcgrath.com ▪ www.collectionmcgrath.com ▪ S 34° 00′ 07.19″ E 18° 26′ 04.74″ ▪ **T +27 (0)21-794-2137** ▪ F +27 (0)21-794-2149

Take your tastebuds into new territory in a polished award-winning restaurant, now in a glass 'greenhouse' in the historic Hohenort building, where subtly sophisticated décor, ferns, orchids and urns offset deliciously innovative cuisine from Collection executive chef Peter Tempelhoff. Order dishes like kingklip steamed in nasturtium leaves; or springbok haunch complemented by quince, bitter chocolate, fudged onions and foie gras. Superb winelist and wine-matching choices. Accredited American Express Platinum Fine Dining Restaurant 2008–10; *Eat Out* Top 10 Restaurants in South Africa 2009; Diners Club International Diamond Award for 2008 & '09; *Wine Spectator* Award of Excellence 2009.

Durbanville

Cassia Restaurant, Bar & Function Venue Nitida Wine Estate, Tygervalley Road (M13), Durbanville ▪ Trendy/Continental ▪ Mon–Sat 9–9.30, Sun 9–3 ▪ Closed Sun eve ▪ Booking advised ▪ Children welcome ▪ Major credit cards accepted ▪ Corkage R40 ▪ Owners Warren Swaffield & Bernhard Veller ▪ info@ cassiarestaurant.co.za ▪ www.cassiarestaurant.co.za ▪ **T +27 (0)21-976-0640/975-3825** ▪ F +27 (0)21-976-0645

Welcoming venue on Nitida wine estate, with wrap-round views of Durbanville Wine Valley, against a backdrop of the Drakenstein Mountains. Décor combines comfort with style, while fresh seasonal menus offer a modern take on classic cuisine, inspired by local produce. Order highly rated Nitida wines and enjoy them with sushi, specialities like monkfish saltimbocca with crispy pap and stuffed baby peppers, or popular Sunday roasts. (See also A–Z section.)

Elgin

Gordon Manuel @ The Venue South Hill Vineyards, 113 The Valley Road, Elgin ▪ Gourmet country ▪ Open for lunch Wed–Sun, dinner Sat provided no wedding booked ▪ Closed Mon, Tue and last 3 weeks of August ▪ Booking advised ▪ Children welcome ▪ Major credit cards accepted (excl. American Express) ▪ Corkage R50 ▪ Indoor & outdoor seating, ideal for exclusive weddings and functions ▪ Owner Gordon Manuel ▪ restaurant@southhill.co.za ▪ www.southhill. co.za ▪ S 34° 13′ 59.48″ E 19°06′44.28″ ▪ **T +27 (0)21-844-0033** ▪ F +27 (0)21-844-0959

Hospitable family-run, owner-operated restaurant known for country gourmet meals, set among vineyards and apple orchards. While Gordon's wife Emma handles front of house, he mans the stoves, producing mouth-watering dishes like slow-roasted pork belly. Inspired by produce from the Overberg region, menus change every Saturday to accommodate fresh and new ingredients. Walls are alive with paintings: the restaurant has joined forces with Red! The Gallery. (See also Accommodation & A–Z sections.)

Franschhoek

Babel Restaurant at Babylonstoren see under Paarl

Backsberg Restaurant see under Paarl

Bistro Allée Bleue T-junction R45 & R310, Groot Drakenstein ▪ Bistro style ▪ Open daily 8–5; Fri & Sat dinner by prior arrangement ▪ Booking advised ▪ Children welcome ▪ Major credit cards accepted (excl. Diners Club) ▪ Corkage R40 ▪ Wine Tasting Courtyard for al fresco meals in summer ▪ Both venues available for small private functions ▪ Picnic area ▪ Owners Wilfred & Elke Dauphin ▪ info@alleebleue.com; esther.dewit@alleebleue.com ▪ www.alleebleue.com ▪ S 33° 51' 51.02" E 18° 58' 42.90" ▪ **T +27 (0)21-874-1021** ▪ F +27 (0)21-874-1850

Friendly white-clothed bistro with tempting breakfasts (try the Franschhoek combo) and à la carte lunches, changing weekly to highlight fresh herbs and fruit from the estate. Parma ham-wrapped goats cheese takes persimmon and fig chutney; oven-roasted lamb loin comes wrapped in wild mushrooms. In summer, enjoy *al fresco* fare in the Wine Tasting Courtyard, where dishes range from mixed grills to cheese platters and *flamkuchen*. (See also Accommodation for Kendall Cottage & A–Z sections.)

Bread & Wine Restaurant and Farm Grocer Môreson Farm, Happy Valley Road, Franschhoek ▪ Rustic Mediterranean ▪ Open daily 12–3 ▪ Booking advised ▪ Children welcome ▪ Major credit cards accepted ▪ No BYO ▪ Owner Richard Friedman ▪ Run by chef Neil Jewell & his bread-baking wife Tina ▪ breadandwine@moreson.co.za ▪ www.moreson.co.za ▪ S 33° 53' 228" E 19° 03' 479" ▪ **T +27 (0)21-876-4004** ▪ F +27 (0)21-876-3105

Spilling into a vine-shaded courtyard, this friendly venue offers gourmet flavours in a farm setting, using fresh ingredients with respect and imagination. Neil's pasture pork charcuterie now introduces the menu (try the lamb 'ham'); while Neil's Nosh includes must-sample delights like porcini carpaccio, celery granita and truffle; and mouth-melting potato and fontina cheese gnocchi. Select take-home treats from home-baked bread to pâté at the Farm Grocer. American Express Fine dining 2007 - 2011. (See also The Common Room & The Tasting Room @ Le Quartier Français and A–Z section for Môreson.)

cosecha Restaurant Noble Hill Wine Estate, Simondium-Klapmuts Road, Simondium, Paarl ▪ Latin-inspired, Californian ▪ Open Wed–Mon 10–5 ▪ Closed Tue, 2 weeks in Aug, Dec 24 & 25 ▪ Booking advised ▪ Children welcome ▪ Major credit cards accepted (excl. Diners Club) ▪ Corkage R50 ▪ Pepper and vegetable garden ▪ Owner Noble Hill Trust ▪ info@cosecharestaurant.com ▪ www.

cosecharestaurant.com ▪ S 33° 49' 38.31" E 18° 56' 12.57" ▪ **T +27 (0)21-874-3844** ▪ F +27 (0)21-874-2948

Feast on traditional or contemporary Mexican treats. Bringing the farm-fresh flavors of the family's southwestern roots to Cape Town, cosecha (harvest) reflects the al fresco eatery's location adjoining the crushing and sorting area. For breakfast choose traditional halves rancheros; lunch on Tequila tagliatelle or beef enchiladas. Daily specials are based on freshly picked ingredients from the farm, and tasty bites include *bocaditos*, small-plate morsels to share. (See also A–Z section.)

Dieu Donné Restaurant Dieu Donné Vineyards, Uitkyk Street, Franschhoek ▪ Afro-Franco-Asian & French Huguenot cuisine ▪ Mon–Sat 10–10, Sun 11–5 ▪ Closed for dinner May–Aug ▪ High-tech bistro lunch & dinner daily ▪ Booking advised ▪ Children welcome ▪ Major credit cards accepted ▪ Corkage R25 ▪ First micro-brewery in the Cape winelands ▪ All function venue — dance floor, weddings & corporate events ▪ Owners Robert & Tanya Maingard ▪ Chef Patron/GM Joanne van Staden ▪ info@dieudonnerestaurant.co.za ▪ www.dieudonnerestaurant.co.za, www.dieudonneweddings.co.za ▪ S 33° 53' 48.00" E 19° 07' 45.00" ▪ **T +27 (0)21-876-3384** ▪ F +27 (0)21-876-2935

Indulge in 'Sexy Nosh' (Afro-Franco-Asian and French Huguenot cuisine) in this classy cellar-styled restaurant with glass-walled view over the valley. Whether innovative African Caeser salad, truffled prawn spaghetti, tempting venison, or irresistible desserts, the style is fresh and fun, accenting variety, affordability and quality. Treats like Brewer's and Champagne tapas platters at bistro terrace tables; beer tastings at the first micro-brewery in the Cape Winelands. (See also A–Z section.)

Freedom Hill Country Restaurant Wemmershoek Road, R301, Paarl ▪ Global cuisine ▪ Open from 12pm till late Mon–Sun (in season) & Wed–Sun (off season) ▪ Booking advised ▪ Children welcome ▪ Major credit cards accepted ▪ Corkage R25 ▪ Owners Adrian Buchanan & Ryan Bredenkamp ▪ info@freedomhillrestaurant.co.za ▪ www.freedomhill-live.co.za, www.freedomhillrestaurant.co.za ▪ S 33° 49' 48.35" E 19° 00' 35.57" ▪ **T +27 (0)21-867-0963**

The food's the thing. Cooked with passion, and it shows. Risotto is authentic (chef/patron Adrian learned the secret from his Italian grandmother); pastry mouth-melting, and creamy cheesecake memorable. This largesse, unexpected from an unpretentious country restaurant, is backed by a warm welcome, excellent service and a well-chosen winelist — plus sweeping patio views across the Berg River valley and a brighter, lighter, recently refurbished interior. (See also A–Z section.)

Fyndraai Restaurant Solms-Delta Wine Estate, Delta Road, off R45, Groot Drakenstein, Franschhoek Valley ▪ Traditional Cape cuisine ▪ Open Mon–Sun 9–5 ▪ Closed Dec 25 & Jan 1 ▪ Booking advised ▪ Children welcome ▪ Major credit cards accepted ▪ No BYO ▪ Owner Solms Family Trust, Astor Family Trust & The Wijn de Caab Trust ▪ restaurant@solms-delta.co.za ▪ www.solms-delta.co.za ▪ www.facebook.com/solmsdelta ▪ Twitter @solms_delta ▪ S 33° 51' 13.44" E 18° 59' 12.96" ▪ **T** +27 (0)21-874-3937 ext 115 ▪ F +27 (0)21-874-1852

Walk over history. The glass-floored restaurant on Solms-Delta wine farm is built over the foundations of the original cellar. Then explore the menu: this is 'food of origin', a creative tribute to the diverse cultures that contributed to SA cuisine. Syrups enliven *veldkos; boerekos*, with its strong 'Cape Malay' influences, melds with plants used by Khoi nomads. There's even a tapas selection – and helpful glossary. *Eat Out* 2010 Truly unique South African flavours, & rated one of the 10 best in the country for service (this for serving staff who were originally farm workers). (See also A–Z section.)

Glen Carlou Restaurant see under Paarl

Grande Provence – The Restaurant Grande Provence Heritage Wine Estate, Main Road, Franschhoek ▪ Contemporary, French with Pacific rim influence ▪ Open daily, lunch 12–2.30 & dinner 7–9 ▪ Booking advised ▪ Children welcome for lunch ▪ Major credit cards accepted ▪ No BYO ▪ Owner Grande Provence (Pty) Ltd ▪ reservations@grandeprovence. co.za ▪ www.grandeprovence.co.za ▪ S 33° 53' 57.6" E 19° 06' 10.5" ▪ **T** +27 (0)21-876-8600 ▪ F +27 (0)21-876-8601

Past elegance fuses with contemporary chic in this sophisticated, girder-exposed restaurant where innovative cuisine hits all the high notes. Menus, flavoured with global influences, change weekly to highlight fresh local produce. Treat your tastebuds to specialities like truffled green pea and porcini ravioli; grilled Cape salmon, prawn and green-shell mussel nage; and a global take on Asian braised pork belly with oranges, tatsoi and apple crumble. *Eat Out* Top 10 SA Restaurants 2009. (See also Accommodation & A–Z sections.)

Haute Cabrière Restaurant Haute Cabrière, Lamprechts Street/Franschhoek Pass, Franschhoek ▪ Contemporary cuisine ▪ Lunch daily; Dinner Fri–Sat (May–Sep) & Mon–Sat (Oct–Apr) ▪ Booking advised ▪ Children 12+ welcome ▪ Major credit cards accepted ▪ Corkage R50 (1 bottle per table) ▪ Owner Haute Cabrière ▪ restaurant@cabriere.co.za ▪ www.cabriere. co.za ▪ **T** +27 (0)21-876-3688

Refurbished and revitalised mountainside restaurant above a working cellar, specialising in what owner/cellarmaster Achim von Arnim calls 'the

dance of food and wine'. Innovative contemporary menus are choreographed around Haute Cabrière and Pierre Jourdan wines by passionate new young head chef Ryan Shell, whose experience includes stints at Le Quarter Français, Myoga and as head chef at Ginja. (See also A–Z section.)

La Petite Ferme Restaurant La Petite Ferme, Franschhoek Pass Road, Franschhoek ▪ Continental cuisine ▪ Lunch daily from 12–4 (breakfast served only to stay-over guests) ▪ Friday night live events in summer ▪ Closed Jan 1 ▪ Booking advised ▪ Children welcome ▪ Major credit cards accepted ▪ Corkage R30 ▪ Cellar tours 11am daily ▪ Gift shop ▪ Owner Mark Dendy Young ▪ reception@lapetiteferme.co.za ▪ www.lapetiteferme. co.za ▪ S 33° 55' 13" E 019° 08' 15" ▪ **T** +27 (0)21-876-3016 ▪ F +27 (0)86-720-6284

Evergreen lunch venue on the Franschhoek mountainside, a byword for spectacular views from the covered veranda. Freshness rules menus, rooted in rustic contemporary cuisine, though signature slow-roasted lamb and oak-smoked local trout remain fixtures – remove them and regulars would riot. Try the *plat du jour*, appetisingly described as 'the chef's daily inspiration', and pair your food with hand-crafted wines, made with the restaurant in mind. (See also Accommodation & A–Z sections.)

Mange Tout & The Country Kitchen Mont Rochelle Hotel & Mountain Vineyards, Dassenberg Road, Franschhoek ▪ **Mange Tout** — international cuisine: breakfast daily 7–10.30, lunch Sat–Sun 12.30-2.30 & dinner Wed–Sun 7–9.30 ▪ **Country Kitchen** — rustic bistro style: Mon–Tue 10–9 & Wed–Sun 10–7 ▪ Booking advised ▪ Children welcome ▪ Major credit cards accepted ▪ No BYO ▪ Owners Erwin Schnitzler & Rwayitare family ▪ info@montrochelle.co.za ▪ www. montrochelle.co.za ▪ S 33° 92' 05.20" E 19° 10' 50.53" ▪ **T** +27 (0)21-876-2770 ▪ F +27 (0)21-876-3788

Elegant restaurant with spectacular valley views. Constantly changing menus with a deliciously French slant are inspired by local produce; dishes reflect the kitchen's belief in organic and free range farming, with imaginative vegetarian options. Choices like locally reared French guinea fowl star on the degustation menu; monthly highlights include cured *foie gras*. The rustic Country Kitchen specialises in tasty bistro fare, around the fireplace in winter, and celebrating summer on the terrace or with a Winelands picnic in the garden. *Eat Out* magazine People's Choice awards 2008 Mange Tout: Fab Fifteen, Top 10 Hotel Dining & Top 10 Views; *Eat Out* awards 2010 Mange Tout: Top 10 Tasting menu & Top 10 Best Hotel Restaurant; Great Wine Capitals: Best of Wine Tourism 2008 & 2009, Accommodation & Best Restaurant 2009; Diners Club International winelist Gold award 2009. (See also Accommodation & A–Z sections).

Pierneef à La Motte La Motte Wine Estate, R45 Franschhoek Road, Franschhoek ▪ Traditional Cape Winelands cuisine ▪ Breakfast Sat–Sun, lunch Tue–Sun & dinner Thu–Sat ▪ Closed Mon, winter school holidays & Christian religious holidays ▪ Booking advised ▪ Children welcome ▪ Major credit cards accepted ▪ Corkage R50 ▪ Owner Hanneli Rupert-Koegelenberg ▪ pierneef@la-motte.co.za ▪ www.la-motte.co.za ▪ **T +27 (0)21-876-8800** ▪ F +27 (0)21-876-8855

A seamless blend of history, tradition and cuisine. Innovative menus reflect research into early Dutch recipes, updated and infused with passion by exec chef Chris Erasmus. Match estate wine to almost-forgotten flavours like Cape *bokkom* salad, *sout ribbetjie*, or pumpkin pie with mango sorbet, and dine surrounded by SA artist Pierneef's original linocuts, soothed by replicas of original VOC ceramics, softly chiming from the ceiling. (See also A–Z section).

Reuben's Restaurant & Bar 19 Huguenot Road, Franschhoek ▪ Cosmopolitan cuisine ▪ Open daily for lunch & dinner ▪ Closed Dec 25, Jan 1 & 2 ▪ Booking advised ▪ Children welcome ▪ Major credit cards accepted ▪ Corkage R40 ▪ Owner Reuben Riffel ▪ reubens@mweb.co.za ▪ www.reubens.co.za ▪ **T +27 (0)21-876-3772** ▪ F +27 (0)86-672-1972

Relaxed eateries that has garnered a string of awards since heading *Eat Out's* Top 10 list in its first year (2004). Flavour sizzles in tingling combos from hot and sour tomato soup, coconut sorbet and pineapple, to roasted pork belly with spicy cucumber/ lemongrass salad, chilli and ginger caramel. Extensive winelist with wide choice of wines by the glass and sunny courtyard that beckons in summer. *Eat Out* Johnie Walker Top 20 restaurants in the country 2009 & '10; 3 stars *Rossouw's restaurant guide* 2010.

Rickety Bridge Restaurant in the Vines Rickety Bridge Wine Estate, R45 Main Road, Franschhoek ▪ Gourmet picnic baskets in summer; hearty South African cuisine in winter ▪ Open daily 11-5 ▪ Closed Jan 1 ▪ Booking advised ▪ Children welcome ▪ Jungle gym ▪ Major credit cards accepted ▪ No BYO ▪ Owner Duncan Spence ▪ functions@ricketybridge.com ▪ www.ricketybridge.com ▪ **T +27 (0)21-876-2016** ▪ F +27 (0)21-876-3486

Be hedonistic. Picnic (junior baskets too) at a table on the 'floating' deck among vines, or lazing on the lawn in the heart of the vineyards. Sip estate wine and unpack gourmet treats like fresh asparagus wrapped in smoked springbok carpaccio, or peri-peri prawns, given added zest by the mountain-ringed setting. In winter, hearty home-made soups, curries and casseroles are served in the original cellar. (See also Accommodation & A–Z sections.)

The Common Room @ Le Quartier Français 16 Huguenot Street, Franschhoek ▪ Small plate food ▪ Open daily for breakfast 7.30–10.30, lunch 12–3.30 & dinner 6–10 ▪ Booking advised ▪ Children welcome ▪ Major credit cards accepted ▪ Corkage R60 ▪ Owner Susan Huxter ▪ restaurant@lqf.co.za ▪ www.lqf.co.za ▪ S 33° 912' 580" E 19° 121' 100" ▪ **T +27 (0)21-876-8442** ▪ F +27 (0)21-876-3105

Relaunched as The Common Room (to counterpoint Le Quartier's gourmet Tasting Room) this convivial foodie hangout couldn't be less commonplace. You're encouraged to linger with friends over lip-smacking bites, served as snacks or as building blocks to a more substantial meal. Relax. Order tasty options like avocado/macadamia /grapefruit salad, satay spiced squid, and velvety cheesecake and sit back with a glass or two of wine. Diners Club International Diamond Award for winelist 2008–'10; *Wine Spectator* Award of Excellence 2008. (See also Bread & Wine and The Tasting Room @ Le Quartier Français.)

The French Connection Bistro 48 Huguenot Street, Franschhoek ▪ French bistro ▪ Open daily, lunch 12–3.30 & dinner 6–9.30 ▪ Booking advised ▪ Children welcome ▪ Major credit cards accepted ▪ Corkage R40 (1 bottle per 4 guests) ▪ Owner Matthew Gordon ▪ GM Jason Ratner ▪ info@frenchconnection.co.za ▪ www. frenchconnection.co.za ▪ **T +27 (0)21-876-4056** ▪ F +27 (0)86-591-4988

Recently renovated, Matthew Gordon's welcoming bistro at the heart of Franschhoek village offers a relaxed culinary experience. Appetising specialities range from French classics like traditional *moules* with *frites*; slow-roasted crispy duck with raspberry vinegar jus; and mouth-melting fillet mignon with three-mushroom sauce, to deliciously sea-fresh fish. Friendly and informative staff ensure that French Connection remains a popular stop in the 'Gourmet Capital of the Cape'. American Express Platinum Fine Dining Award 2007–2011.

The Tasting Room @ Le Quartier Français 16 Huguenot Street, Franschhoek ▪ Fine dining ▪ Dinner daily from 7pm ▪ Booking advised ▪ Children welcome ▪ Major credit cards accepted ▪ No BYO ▪ Owner Susan Huxter ▪ Chef Margot Janse ▪ restaurant@lqf.co.za ▪ www.lqf.co.za ▪ S 33° 912' 580" E 19° 121' 100" ▪ **T +27 (0)21-876-8442** ▪ F +27 (0)21-876-3105

Judged one of the Top 50 Restaurants in the world for the past eight years, this award-winning venue tantalises palates with creative, cutting-edge 'surprise' tasting menus. Expect an African-inspired epicurean journey, richly innovative in flavour pairing, matched to local wine. Each course is introduced by smiling staff, adding a personal touch to this gourmet celebration of South Africa and its indigenous produce, people and stories. S Pellegrino Top 50 Restaurants in the World 2002, 2005–'11; Diners Club International Diamond Award for winelist 2008–'10; *Wine Spectator* Award of Excellence 2008;

Best Culinary Experience – Virtuoso Best of the Best 2008. (See also Bread & Wine and The Common Room @ Le Quartier Français.)

Hermanus

La Vierge Restaurant & Champagne Verandah La Vierge Private Cellar, Hemel-en-Aarde Valley Road (R320), Hemel-en-Aarde Valley, Hermanus ▪ International cuisine with South African flavours ▪ Lunch Tue–Sun, dinner Fri–Sat ▪ Closed Mon ▪ Booking advised ▪ Ideal for weddings and corporate events ▪ Children welcome ▪ Major credit cards accepted ▪ No BYO, La Vierge wines served exclusively ▪ Owner La Vierge Wines ▪ restaurant@lavierge.co.za ▪ www. lavierge.co.za ▪ S 34° 22'22.3" E 019° 14'29.4" ▪ **T +27 (0)28-313-2007** ▪ F +27 (0)28-312-1388

Drink in vistas of Hemel-en-Aarde Valley and Atlantic ocean from this view-rich venue, while celebrity chef/author Shane Sauvage presents his eclectic brand of fusion dishes and classics with a local twist. Salmon sauvage, Aztec mushrooms and Afro-Parisian pastry share space on the menu with angel snails, strawberry and springbok carpaccio, and chocolate terrine. Or simply loiter legally on the champagne verandah, sipping MCC or Champagne. International Gourmand Award 2009. (See also A–Z section.)

Seafood at The Marine The Marine Hotel, cnr Marine Drive & Main Road, Hermanus ▪ Contemporary South African seafood ▪ Open daily, lunch 12–2. 30 & dinner 7–9.30 ▪ Booking advised ▪ Children 8+ welcome ▪ Major credit cards accepted ▪ Corkage R55 ▪ Owner Liz McGrath ▪ reservations@ collectionmcgrath.com ▪ www.collectionmcgrath. com ▪ S 34° 25'03.43" E 19° 14'41.11" ▪ **T +27 (0)28-313-1000** ▪ F +27 (0)28-313-0160).

Stylish, relaxed restaurant where the menu emphasis is on sea-fresh fish from Walker Bay. The open kitchen with talented young chefs provides a close-up of the organised energy that goes into meals. Evergreen favourites rule: Marine seafood soup with *rouille*, gruyere and croutons; and bunny chow (Cape Malay Seafood curry in homemade pot-bread). Accredited American Express Platinum Fine Dining Restaurant 2008 — 2011.

Hout Bay

Pure Hout Bay Manor, Baviaanskloof Road, off Main Road, Hout Bay ▪ Global cuisine, using local, fresh and organic produce ▪ Dinner Tue–Sat 6.30–10.30, lunch Sun 12–3 ▪ Closed Mon ▪ Booking advised ▪ Children welcome ▪ Major credit cards accepted ▪ No BYO, extensive wine list ▪ pure@houtbaymanor.co.za ▪ www.pure-restaurant.co.za ▪ S 34° 04'32.01" E 18° 36'06.38" ▪ T +27 (0)21-791-9393 ▪ F +27 (0)21-790-0118

Pure delight. Chef Ian Bergh pleasures palates against a soothing backdrop of creamy shades,

rustic driftwood dividers and shells appropriate to the hotel's seaside setting. Dishes burst with seasonal freshness, organic ingredients and intense, layered flavours – like gurnard, braised fennel and saffron velouté; or lamb rack, Jerusalem artichoke risotto, exotic mushrooms and garlic/thyme jus. Fascinating winelist, grouped by terroir, offers a Hout Bay wine. Diners Club Winelist Awards; Gold in 2009, Diamond in 2010. (See also Accommodation section.)

Kuils River

Zevenwacht Restaurant see under Stellenbosch

McGregor

Kingsriver Restaurant Kingsriver Estate, Koningriver Road, McGregor on Route 62 ▪ Sophisticated, wholesome country cuisine ▪ Open daily for breakfast, lunch & dinner ▪ Special wine and food events throughout the year ▪ Booking advised ▪ Children welcome ▪ Major credit cards accepted ▪ No BYO ▪ Owner Ruud de Clercq ▪ kingsriver-guesthouse@ breede.co.za ▪ www.kingsriver-estate.com ▪ S 33° 55' 18.7" E 019° 49' 46.2" ▪ **T +27 (0)23-625-1040** ▪ F +27 (0)23-625-1045

If gourmet picnics in a canyon, decadent breakfasts, lazy lunches and delectable dinners tickle your tastebuds, head for Kingsriver, where 380 ha of Karoo fynbos ensures your peace, and views from the à la carte restaurant extend across vineyards to distant mountains. Only the freshest farm produce is used in menus that combine comfort foods like bitterballen or lamb knuckle curry with appetising lighter options. (See also Accommodation & A–Z sections.)

Montagu

Mimosa Lodge Restaurant 19 Church Street, Montagu ▪ French continental ▪ Open daily for breakfast 8–10 & dinner from 7–9 ▪ Booking essential ▪ Children by prior arrangement ▪ Major credit cards accepted ▪ Corkage R45 ▪ Owners Bernhard & Fida Hess ▪ info@mimosa.co.za ▪ www.mimosa.co.za ▪ S 33° 47' 16.04" E 20° 7'9.03" ▪ **T +27 (0)23-614- 2351** ▪ F +27 (0)86-535-0722

Award-winning restaurant that put Montagu on the fine-dining culinary map. Setting is an elegant Edwardian double-storey guest house, where chef/ patron Bernhard specialises in French contemporary cuisine. Four-course, daily-changing menus feature fresh local ingredients and subtle sauces: gourmet highlights could include a crayfish tail enhanced by truffled sour-cream sauce, partnered with a seared scallop and langoustine skewer; or herb-marinated springbok loin, drizzled with honey/vinegar jus. American Express Platinum Fine Dining Award 2008–'11; AA Travel Fabulous Food Award 2008.

Overberg

Gordon Manuel @ The Venue see under Elgin

Paarl

Babel Restaurant at Babylonstoren Klapmuts-Simondium Road, Paarl ▪ Honest, organic produce from the 8 acre garden (tours offered) ▪ Open Wed–Sun 10–4 ▪ Closed Mon–Tue ▪ Booking advised ▪ Children welcome ▪ Major credit cards accepted ▪ Corkage R30 ▪ F&B Manager Anelle van Tonder ▪ reservations@babylonstoren.com ▪ www.babylonstoren.com ▪ S 33° 49′ 26.73″ E 18° 55′ 39.08″ ▪ **T +27 (0)21-863-3852** ▪ F +27 (0)21-863-1727

Your table decoration in the airy, glass walled restaurant could be a cabbage leaf; the menu showcases garden-fresh salads as signature dishes. No simple salads these, but nature's bounty; bursting with herbs, fruit, and vegetables, with chicken, trout or moist biltong as optional extras. Flavour-infused starters, soups to savour and pork belly to linger over. Don't miss the savoury dessert option. Your tastebuds will thank you. Hotel on the *Conde Nast Traveller's* 2011 Hot List in the UK and USA. (See also Accommodation and A–Z sections.)

Backsberg Restaurant Backsberg Estate Cellars, Simondium Road, Suider-Paarl ▪ Robust country cooking ▪ Open daily from 9.30–3.30 ▪ Booking advised ▪ Children welcome ▪ Major credit cards accepted (excl. American Express) ▪ No BYO ▪ Owner Michael Back ▪ restaurant@backsberg.co.za ▪ www.backsberg.co.za ▪ S 33° 49′ 684″ E 18° 54′ 917″ ▪ **T +27 (0)21-875-5952** ▪ F +27 (0)86-508-7622

Relaxed, rustic setting offering great value and wholesome country fare. Lunch under shady trees in the inviting garden in summer, in winter move indoors beside a crackling fire. Seasonal menus are livened by specials focused on fresh local produce. À la carte during the week and on Saturday; on Sunday enjoy live music at a hearty buffet featuring lamb on the spit with roast potatoes. (See also A–Z section.)

Bistro Allegro Plantasie Street, Paarl ▪ Casual dining ▪ Open daily from 12–close, with a lighter menu served from 2.30–6 ▪ Booking advised ▪ Children welcome ▪ Major credit cards accepted ▪ No BYO ▪ GM Anja Bosken ▪ F&B Co-ordinator Christine Visagie ▪ reserve@granderoche.co.za ▪ www.granderoche.com ▪ S 33° 45′ 02″ E 18° 57′ 35″ ▪ **T +27 (0)21-863-5100** ▪ F +27 (0)21-863-2220

Sit poolside under the frangipani trees in summer; in winter move into the cosy interior. Grande Roche's inviting bistro offers casual lunches and dinners at competitive prices, complemented by specially selected wines from the area. Order à la carte or from the special three-course menu – best sellers include slow-cooked lamb shank with crushed butter potatoes, gremolata beans and pancetta – and enjoy the informal dining experience. Diners Club winelist Platinum Award 2008 & '09; Diamond Award 2010. (See also Accommodation section for Grande Roche Hotel.)

Bosman's Restaurant Plantasie Street, Paarl ▪ Global cuisine ▪ Dinner daily 7–9 (mid Oct–mid Apr) & Thu–Sun (mid Apr–mid Oct) ▪ Booking advised ▪ Children 4+ welcome ▪ Major credit cards accepted ▪ No BYO ▪ GM Anja Bosken ▪ F&B Co-ordinator Christine Visagie ▪ reserve@granderoche.co.za ▪ www.granderoche.com ▪ S 33° 45′ 02″ E 18° 57′ 35″ ▪ **T +27 (0)21-863-5100** ▪ F +27 (0)21-863-2220

Enjoy state-of-the-art fine dining in a gracious gabled manor house, where an array of menus offers culinary delights complemented by splendid wines from a superbly stocked cellar. Butter-tender herb-poached veal fillet, and glazed sweetbread with truffle jus and cauliflower tempura, are among specialities from award-winning executive chef Roland Gorgosilich, who has represented Grande Roche and South Africa at numerous gastronomic events locally and abroad. Diners Club winelist Diamond Award for 2008 & '09; Best Wine List in South Africa 2010. *Wine Spectator's* Best of Award of Excellence 2008–'10 and in 2008, described as the restaurant with the 'best wine experience in South Africa', the only local restaurant to receive this Best of Award of Excellence. SA Tourism Award No. 1 Fine Dining Restaurant in SA, 2010; fourth place in *Eat Out* Top 10, 2010. (See also Accommodation section for Grande Roche Hotel.)

cosecha Restaurant see under Franschhoek

Freedom Hill Country Restaurant see under Franschhoek

Glen Carlou Restaurant Simondium Road, Klapmuts ▪ Contemporary cuisine ▪ Lunch daily 11–4 ▪ Booking advised ▪ Children welcome ▪ Major credit cards accepted ▪ No BYO ▪ Owner Hess Family Estates ▪ restaurant@glencarlou.co.za ▪ www.glencarlou.co.za ▪ S 33° 48′ 34.44″ E 18° 54′ 19.41″ ▪ **T +27 (0)21-875-5528** ▪ F +27 (0)21-875-5314

Family friendly glass-walled venue with panoramic views from an umbrella-shaded veranda in summer or in winter, from the fire-warmed interior flowing from the tasting room. The enlarged, updated kitchen allows for expanded menus: *foie gras* and mixed exotic mushrooms now share space with all-time favourites like rib-eye steak; kudu burgers with fries and salad; and for dessert, crème brûlée or a tempting selection of home-made ice-creams. (See also A–Z section.)

Joostenberg Bistro see under Stellenbosch

Marc's Mediterranean Cuisine and Garden 129 Main Street, Paarl ▪ Mediterranean cuisine/grill/pizza/mezze platters/specials ▪ Open daily for lunch, dinner Mon-Sat ▪ Closed Sun night, Easter Mon, 2 weeks during winter school holiday, Dec 26 & Jan 1 ▪ Booking advised ▪ Children welcome ▪ New delicatessen ▪ Major credit cards accepted ▪ Corkage R40 ▪ Owner Marc Friederich ▪ info@marcsrestaurant.co.za ▪ www.marcsrestaurant.co.za ▪ **T +27 (0)21-863-3982** ▪ F +27 (0)86-638-6458

A byword for best-selling paella, lavish Lebanese mezze, and scrumptious wood-fired pizzas, this friendly restaurant with inviting Mediterranean-style courtyard has enhanced its appeal. Try fragrant Thai green chicken and prawn curry from the wine-matching menu, or exotic *foie gras* crème brûlée with Maldon salt caramel and cinnamon toast. Do visit the newly-opened delicatessen extension, where irresistible temptation extends from hams cut sliver-thin to must-try cheeses. Diners Club Award of Excellence 2006-'07; Diamond Award 2008-2010.

Olivello Restaurant see under Stellenbosch

Seasons Restaurant see under Wellington

The Goatshed Restaurant Fairview Wine & Cheese Farm, Suid-Agter Paarl Road, Suider-Paarl ▪ Farm-style Mediterranean ▪ Open daily 9-5 (kitchen closes at 4.30) ▪ Closed Good Friday, Dec 25 & Jan 1 ▪ Booking advised ▪ Children welcome ▪ Major credit cards accepted ▪ Corkage R45 ▪ Owners Charles Back & Andy Küng ▪ goatshed@fairview.co.za ▪ www.goatshed.co.za ▪ S 33° 45.5'0.4" E 18° 55.10'0.56" ▪ **T +27 (0)21-863-3609** ▪ F +2 (0)21-863-2591

Named for Fairview's 750-strong herd of goats, this rustic, hospitable eateries in one of the farm's old wine cellars pulls the crowds with light and tasty lunches from locally-sourced seasonal produce, spilling on to a terrace in summer. Compile individual platters from just-baked breads and a choice of some 25 different cheeses from the farm's cheesery — best enjoyed with Fairview and Goats do Roam wines. *Eat Out* Top 10 Alfresco Restaurants 2010. (See also A–Z section.)

Robertson

Fraai Uitzicht 1798 Klaas Voogds East, on Route 62 between Robertson & Montagu ▪ Sophisticated Afro-Asian cuisine with Mediterranean influences ▪ Open Wed–Sun from 12 (Mon & Tue for resident guests only) ▪ Closed mid Jun–Aug, Dec 24/31 & Jan 1 ▪ Booking advised ▪ Children 12+ welcome ▪ Major credit cards accepted ▪ No BYO ▪ Owners Sandra & Karl Uwe Papesch ▪ info@fraaiuitzicht.com ▪ www.fraaiuitzicht.com ▪ S 33° 47'43.23" E 20° 00' 17.87" ▪ T +27 (0)23-626-6156 ▪ F +27 (0)86-662-5265

Relaxed owner-run restaurant on a historic wine and guest farm. Indulge in the 7-course degustation menu (with legendary dessert), enjoying Sandra's farm-fresh cooking and personal attention from her husband Karl Uwe. Or order Sandra's speciality: steak tartare as featured in BBC chef Justin Bonello's best-selling cookbook, *Out of the Frying Pan*. Extensive winelist showcasing the Roberson Wine Valley's best, including hand-crafted Fraai Uitzicht 1798 Merlot. American Express Platinum Fine Dining Programme 2003–'11; Rossouw's Restaurants 2 stars. (See also Accommodation & A–Z sections.)

Kingsriver Restaurant see under McGregor

Restaurant 1723 Jan Harmsgat Country House, On the R60 between Ashton and Swellendam ▪ Continental cuisine ▪ Open daily from 8am–10pm ▪ Booking advised ▪ Children welcome ▪ Visa & MasterCard accepted ▪ Corkage R25 ▪ Owners Willie & Camron Malherbe ▪ reservations@janharmsgat.com ▪ www.janharmsgat.com ▪ S 33° 56'48" E 20° 12'58" ▪ **T +27 (0)23-616-3407** ▪ F +27 (0)86-523-9284

Lunch or dine delectably. Set four-course menus change constantly as owner/chef Camron Malherbe and assistant Susan Daniels are inspired by fresh produce from the kitchen garden. Specialities include rack of lamb, seared tuna, signature kudu fillet and aged beef; all pastas are handmade and salad ingredients picked fresh daily. Don't miss the pecan pie with organically grown pecans from the farm, topped with homemade ice-cream. (See also Accommodation section.)

Reuben's at The Robertson Small Hotel 58 Van Reenen Street, Robertson ▪ Cosmopolitan cuisine ▪ Open daily for breakfast 8–10, lunch 12–3 & dinner 6–9 ▪ Booking advised ▪ Children by prior arrangement ▪ Major credit cards accepted ▪ Deli ▪ Corkage R40 ▪ Owners Reuben Riffel, Tim Rands, Marc Kent & Gys Naudé ▪ info@therobertsonsmallhotel.com ▪ www.therobertsonsmallhotel.com ▪ S 33° 48'1" E 19° 52'47" ▪ **T +27 (0)23-626-7200** ▪ F +27 (0)23-626-1680

Look forward to frequently changing menus in the popular chef's signature style, offering eclectic options to suit all palates. Focus is on the best local and seasonal produce, organic where possible; emphasis is on texture and flavour. Chilli salt squid remains entrenched as a starter; best-seller among mains is crispy duck breast with citrus-spiced jus. If available, chocoholics will rejoice in the decadent chocolate pavé. (See also Accommodation section.)

Rosendal Restaurant Rosendal Winery & Wellness Retreat, Robertson Wine Valley, between Robertson & Ashton on the R60, known as Route 62 ▪ Fusion of classical cuisine with a touch of Global & African ▪ Open daily for breakfast 8–10, lunch 12–2 & dinner from 6 ▪ Booking advised ▪ Children welcome ▪ Visa & MasterCard accepted ▪ No BYO ▪ Owners Geir & Sissel Tellefsen ▪ info@rosendalwinery.com ▪ www.rosendalwinery.com ▪ S 33° 48'7.8" E 019° 59'19.0" ▪ **T +27 (0)23-626-1570** ▪ F +27 (0)23-626-1571

Captivating cuisine adds an extra sparkle to your spa treatment at this relaxing getaway. The kitchen team is Belgian; inviting menus fuse exotic, contemporary flavours with African touches and classic favourites to tempt your tastebuds. Enjoy hearty breakfasts, appetising light lunches and delectable dinners, served with award-winning Rosendal wines in an ambience that's rustic by day, elegant by night. (See also Accommodation & A–Z sections.)

Somerset West

96 Winery Road Restaurant see under Stellenbosch

Sofia's @ Morgenster Morgenster Estate, Vergelegen Avenue, off Lournsford Road, Somerset West ▪ Contemporary global cuisine with local flair ▪ Lunch Wed–Mon (summer), Wed–Sun (winter); Dinner Wed & Sat; Special event dinners Fri (winter only) ▪ Closed Tue (summer); Mon–Tue (winter) & Jun–Aug ▪ Booking advised ▪ Regular salt & wine pairing evenings ▪ Wheelchair-friendly ▪ Children welcome ▪ Visa & MasterCard accepted ▪ Corkage R50 (wine), R85 (sparkling wine) ▪ Owner Craig Cormack ▪ sofiasatmorgenster@gmail.com ▪ twitter @01Sofias ▪ www.facebook.com/sofias.at.morgenster, www.morgenster.co.za ▪ S 34° 5' 2.9" E 018° 53' 7.8" ▪ **T/ F +27 (0)21-847-1993** ▪ F +27 (0)86-624-2615

Don't expect a plate of pasta. There could even be a tasty tagine on chef Craig Cormack's appetising weekly changing menus. While the name pays tribute to Sophia Loren, whose photographs grace the walls, this popular cottage restaurant offers tasty, contemporary global fare from prime local produce. The diverse, Morgenster-rich winelist is food-focused and "salt alchemist" Craig also specialises in pairing various salts with wines. (See also A–Z section.)

Taste Restaurant Corner Klein Helderberg Road (off R44), Somerset West ▪ French, bistro, global, eclectic, contemporary ▪ Open Thu–Mon for lunch 12–2 & dinner 6–8 (last table seated) ▪ Closed Tue & Wed ▪ Booking advised ▪ Children welcome (no kiddies menu) ▪ Major credit cards accepted (excl. Diners Club) ▪ Corkage R30 (1-2 bottles), R35 (3-4 bottles), R40 (5-6 bottles), R50 (7+ by arrangement only) ▪ Owners Ed Pearce & Anton Bekker ▪ tasteinfo@mweb.co.za ▪ www.tasterestaurant.co.za ▪ **T +27 (0)21-855-3686**

Décor has changed, but the house rule still stands: don't demand salt. Taste first. Flamboyant chef Anton prides himself on perfectly seasoned dishes; welcoming partner Ed handles front of house. Creative, constantly changing menus are classic in inspiration (regulars would riot should the half crispy duck disappear) but new taste-treats include home-cured pancetta and maturing cheeses. If available, order fresh tuna. It's served

superbly just-seared. *Eat Out* magazine Top 300 Restaurant 2010 & '11.

The Avontuur Estate Restaurant Avontuur Wine Estate, R44, Somerset West ▪ Contemporary country ▪ Open Mon–Sun 9–4; dinner Wed & Fri in summer ▪ Closed Good Fri, Dec 25 & Jan 1 ▪ Booking advised ▪ Children welcome ▪ Major credit cards accepted ▪ No BYO ▪ Chefs/patrons Zunia Boucher-Myers & Melanie Paltoglou ▪ openhand@polka.co.za ▪ www.avontuurestate.co.za ▪ S 34° 1' 33.2" E 018° 49' 23.8" ▪ **T +27 (0)21-855-4296** ▪ F +27 (0)21-855-4600

Celebrating its 10th anniversary in November, this popular estate restaurant with hands-on, people-friendly chef/patrons, specialises in value-for-money, appetising food, served at shady tables with a view. Seasonal menus, centred round organic produce, add new dishes to old favourites: tender fillet and crispy duck have been joined by lighter options like preserved figs, brie and mascarpone; and smoked salmon trout with grilled prawns. End indulgently with deep-fried ice-cream. 4-star rated by the Tourism Grading Council. (See also A–Z section.)

The Restaurant @ Lourensford Lourensford Wine Estate, Lourensford Road, Somerset West ▪ Modern European cuisine ▪ Deli with farm honey & cheese ▪ Coffee tasting ▪ Open daily 8–5 ▪ Closed Easter Fri, Dec 25 & Jan 1 ▪ Booking advised ▪ Children welcome ▪ Visa & MasterCard accepted ▪ No BYO ▪ Owner Christo Wiese ▪ chef@lourensford.co.za ▪ www.lourensford.co.za ▪ **T +27 (0)21-847-2328** ▪ F +27 (0)21-847-0910

Food rules. The successful recipequestion Match the palates of an exuberant chef and equally passionate winemaker. Tullishe le Roux, who worked with Marco Pierre White, and winemaker Hannes Nel start with a given (the wine), then brainstorm which spices and ingredients will enhance it. Whether fresh fish, risotto, iconic lamburgers or dreamy cheesecake, the result is flavour bliss. Fresh menus daily and friendly, informed service. (See also A–Z section.)

The Restaurant at Waterkloof Waterkloof Wines, Sir Lowry's Pass Village Road, Somerset West ▪ Contemporary with French influence ▪ Lunch daily, dinner Mon-Sat ▪ Closed Sun eve, Dec 25 & Jan 1 ▪ Booking advised ▪ Children welcome ▪ Major credit cards accepted ▪ No BYO ▪ Owner Paul Boutinot ▪ restaurant@waterkloofwines.co.za ▪ www.waterkloofwines.co.za ▪ **T +27 (0)21-858-1491** ▪ F +27 (0)21-858-1293

Here food is art, calling for unhurried appreciation; complemented by the estate's European-style wines and seamless service. Chef Grégory Czarnecki is from a 3-star Michelin background: close your eyes and you could be in Paris. But why close themquestion You're seated in a lofty glass promontory, flowing from the slick tasting lounge and state-of-the-art gravitational cellar, overlooking the amphitheatre of Waterkloof vineyards and False Bay. (See also A–Z section.)

The Vergelegen Restaurant Vergelegen Wines, Lourensford Road, Somerset West ▪ **The Vergelegen Restaurant** (B la carte/contemporary/ global) open daily for lunch 11.45–2.30, teas 10–11. 45 & 2.30–4; **Rose Terrace Bistro** (al fresco/light meals) 10–4 daily (Nov–Apr); **Camphor Forest Picnic** (luxury/elegant picnic) baskets available 12–1.30 (Nov–Apr) ▪ Closed Good Fri, May 1 & Dec 25 ▪ Reservations required for The Vergelegen Restaurant & Camphor Forest Picnic ▪ Children welcome ▪ Major credit cards accepted ▪ No BYO ▪ Owner Anglo American plc ▪ restaurant@vergelegen.co.za ▪ www.vergelegen.co.za ▪ S 34° 04'771" E 18° 53'244" ▪ **T +27 (0)21-847-1346** ▪ F +27 (0)21-847-1608

Three culinary experiences, very different in style but all with seasonal, country fresh menus developed to complement Vergelegen's award winning wines. In summer, lunch à la carte at Vergelegen Restaurant, on a patio sheltered by Liquid Amber trees beside manicured lawns; in winter reserve a table indoors in front of the fireplace. Lunch lightly *al fresco* at the Rose Terrace Bistro overlooking the acclaimed rose garden, or book a basket for an elegant picnic in the centuries-old camphor forest while the children amuse themselves with a treasure hunt. (See also A–Z section.)

Stellenbosch

96 Winery Road Restaurant Zandberg Farm, Winery Road, off the R44 between Somerset West & Stellenbosch ▪ Country cuisine, with influences from around the world ▪ Lunch daily 12-3.30, dinner Mon-Sat 6.30-8 ▪ Closed Dec 25 eve & Jan 1 ▪ Booking advised ▪ Children welcome ▪ Major credit cards accepted ▪ Corkage R40 ▪ Owners Ken & Allan Forrester, Martin Meinert & Natasha Wray ▪ wineryrd@mweb.co.za ▪ www.96wineryroad.co.za ▪ **T +27 (0)21-842-2020** ▪ F +27 (0)21-842-2050

Here local is *lekker*; ambience rustic, and best-sellers dry-aged organic beef, duck and cherry pie and crispy pork belly. But break out: choices range from regular, *degustation*, and 'fresh seasonal and inspired' menus to a lighter 'what's for lunch?' Hollandse pepper fillet is flamed at the table; in winter, *potjies* simmer over the fire, while summer brings fresh trout and pasture-fed chicken. Outstanding winelist. Diners Club winelist Diamond Award 2006-10 and *Wine Spectator* Grand Award 2006–'11.

La Provence Road, Stellenbosch (behind Polkadraai farm stall on the M12 Stellenbosch–Kuils River) ▪ Now a functions venue ▪ Authentic Indonesian food for groups of 8–10 or more ▪ Vegan-friendly ▪ Booking essential – owners have their spontaneous sabbatical breaks; seasonal closure ▪ Catered functions

also welcome ▪ Fully licensed ▪ sunhillf@iafrica.com ▪ www.jakarta.co.za ▪ S 33° 57'41.5" E 18° 44'35.8" ▪ **T +27 (0)21-881-3243/+27 (0)79-868-2425** ▪ F +27 (0)21-881-3299

Popular for authentic Indonesian *rijsttafel*, this refreshingly uncommercial restaurant has evolved into a functions venue with wine of your choice provided by Jakarta-born Dutch owner/patron Duncan Fransz. Book for *rijsttafel* for a group of friends; hire for private events or corporate functions with outside caterers. You'll eat al fresco or amid a mix of antiques and art: everything you see is for sale – except the staff.

Barouche Restaurant Blaauwklippen Estate, on the R44 between Stellenbosch & Somerset West, opposite Techno Park ▪ Continental/European breakfast & lunch; South African dinner ▪ Breakfast & lunch (Sep–Apr) Mon–Fri 9–4 Sunset hour 4–6 Sat–Sun 12–3 & lunch (May–Aug) Wed–Sun 12–4; Dinner (Oct–Apr) Wed–Fri 6–9 ▪ Closed Mon & Tue (May–Aug); Jan 1 ▪ Booking advised ▪ Children welcome ▪ Major credit cards accepted ▪ Corkage R45 ▪ Horse-drawn carriage rides through the vineyards ▪ Picnics ▪ Cellar tours & wine tasting at the Wine Centre ▪ Weddings, functions & conferences ▪ Owners Farmers Markt Landhandel GMbh ▪ mail@blaauwklippen.com ▪ www.blaauwklippen.com ▪ S 33° 58'23.3" E 018° 50'51.0" ▪ **T +27 (0)21-880-8222** ▪ F +27 (0)21-880-1246

Family friendly, indoor-outdoor restaurant with tasty options and wine-pairing suggestions to suit all palates. Kick-start your day with breakfast (special kids combo available); lunch à la carte on choices from pesto-crusted linefish to grills and platters, and round-off your meal with a horse-drawn carriage ride. At dinner, savour traditional favourites like *bredie*, *lams skilpadjie* and *pampoen poffertjies* (glossary provided) ending with a *springbokkie* parfait. (See also A–Z section.)

Cuvée Restaurant Simonsig Wine Estate, Kromme Rhee Road, Koelenhof, Stellenbosch ▪ Traditional/local cuisine with a French touch ▪ Lunch Tue–Sat 12–3 Sun 12–2; dinner Wed, Fri & Sat 7–10 ▪ Closed Mon, Good Fri, Dec 25 & Jan 1 ▪ Booking advised ▪ Children welcome ▪ Major credit cards accepted ▪ No BYO ▪ Owners Francois, Johan & Pieter Malan ▪ cuvee@simonsig.co.za ▪ www.cuveeatsimonsig.co.za ▪ S 33° 52'322" E 018° 49'473" ▪ **T +27 (0)21-888-4932** ▪ F +27 (0)21-888-4909

Simonsig's signature restaurant captivates with a quirky mix of nostalgia and Cape Dutch modernism, blended with wine-knowledgeable service and Winelands hospitality. Décor is eclectic; the locally inspired menus country-fresh. Relax over a flute of *Kaapse Vonkel*, study the palate-titillating combos, and treat your tastebuds to delicately spiced free-range beef tatare, or flame-grilled fillet of beef with slow- roasted vine tomatoes and Café de Paris butter. 2 stars in *Rossouw's Restaurants* 2010. (See also A–Z section.)

Delaire Graff Restaurant Delaire Graff Estate, R310, Helshoogte Pass, Banhoek Valley, Stellenbosch ▪ Bistro-chic ▪ Lunch daily 12–2.30, dinner Mon–Sat 6.30–9.30 ▪ Closed Sun eve ▪ Booking advised ▪ Children welcome ▪ Major credit cards accepted ▪ No BYO ▪ Owner Laurence Graff ▪ reservations@delaire.co.za ▪ www.delaire.co.za ▪ S 33° 55' 236" E 18° 55' 207" ▪ **T +27 (0)21-885-8160**

A trio of attractions: the spectacular view, the striking art-rich décor that juxtaposes happily with the mountain and vineyard panorama, and signature wine-friendly 'bistro chic' cuisine from exec chef Christiaan Campbell. This implies beautifully presented yet simple seasonal dishes from 'green' farmers and organic suppliers, combined with flair and flavour. Indulge in decadent dessert and end with tea. The selection's wide and the ceremony delightful. (See also Accommodation & A–Z sections.)

De Oewer Aan de Wagen Road (next to De Volkskombuis), Stellenbosch ▪ Global contemporary cuisine ▪ Lunch daily 12–3, dinner Mon–Sat 6.30–10 & Sun (Nov–Apr) ▪ Closed Good Friday, Jun–Sep ▪ Booking advised ▪ Children welcome ▪ Major credit cards accepted ▪ Corkage R30 ▪ Owners Dawid & Christelle Kriel ▪ oewer@volkskombuis.co.za ▪ www.deoewer.co.za ▪ **T +27 (0)21-886-5431** ▪ F +2 (0)86-582-5128

Alfresco-style lunch and dinners in the inviting setting of a food and wine garden on the banks of the Eerste River, shaded by venerable oaks. Seasonal menus focus on Mediterranean-style dishes — even a juicy Med burger! — while making the most of fresh produce. All-time favourites include warm lamb salad, fresh grilled linefish and matured beef. Buffet menus for groups of over 15, by prior arrangement. (See also Accommodation section for Oak Village B&B.)

De Volkskombuis Aan de Wagen Road, Stellenbosch ▪ SA cuisine ▪ Lunch 7 days a week 12–3, dinner Mon–Sat 6.30–10 & Sun (Nov–Apr) ▪ Closed Good Fri ▪ Booking advised ▪ Children welcome ▪ Major credit cards accepted ▪ Corkage R30 ▪ Owners Dawid & Christelle Kriel ▪ mail@volkskombuis.co.za ▪ www.volkskombuis.co.za ▪ **T +27 (0)21-887-2121** ▪ F +27 (0)86-582-5128

Well-established restaurant, quintessentially Cape in setting, menus and extensive winelist. Hospitable second-generation owners Dawid and Christelle Kriel ensure that the quality and authenticity this evergreen venue, started 34 years ago, is still maintained today. Take hearty appetites and enjoy dishes like Karoo lamb rib, *kerrie*, richly satisfying oxtail stew and the popular 'Cape country sampler'. Do leave room for the

killer Cape brandy pudding. (See also Accommodation section for Oak Village B&B.)

Eight Restaurant Spier, R310 Lynedoch Road, Stellenbosch ▪ Farm to table ▪ Open Tue–Sun for brunch 10–12.30, lunch 12.30–3 & tea 3–4 ▪ Closed Mon ▪ Booking advised ▪ Children welcome: jungle gym, toys & healthy treats ▪ Major credit cards accepted ▪ No BYO ▪ eight@spier.co.za ▪ www.spier.co.za ▪ S 33° 58' 379" E 18° 46' 944" ▪ **T +27 (0)21-809-1188** ▪ F +27 (0)21-809-1134

Eight symbolises infinity, harmony and plenty: all abundant at this light, airy restaurant on the Eerste River banks. Feast on fresh, tempting farm-to-table fare, with most ingredients sourced from Spier. Move from just-squeezed juices to Spier organic wine; taste the difference in biodynamic veg and pasture-fed chicken (best-seller is chicken pie) and end blissfully with flour-free chocolate cake (70% organic chocolate/30% free-range eggs). See also A–Z section.

Flavours at The Devon Valley Hotel Devon Valley Road, Devon Valley, Stellenbosch ▪ Contemporary Cape cuisine ▪ Open daily 6.30–10.30 for breakfast, lunch & dinner ▪ Booking advised ▪ Children welcome ▪ Major credit cards accepted ▪ BYO not encouraged, corkage R35 ▪ Owner Louis Group Hotels, Spa's & Vineyards ▪ info@devonvalleyhotel.com ▪ www.devonvalleyhotel.com ▪ S 33° 54' 12.64" E 18° 48' 53.03" ▪ **T +27 (0)21-865-2012** ▪ F +27 (0)21-865-2610

Friendly, relaxed restaurant, specialising in authentic contemporary Cape cuisine, that brings people together to celebrate the good things in life — in one of the Winelands' most beautiful valleys. Be guided by the wine-pairing suggestions and dine on dishes like fresh Saldanha Bay mussels in Pernot cream sauce, and basil-topped rack of Karoo lamb with pine-kernels; lunch lightly or enjoy drinks on the view-rich Vineyard terrace. Diners Club winelist Diamond Award 2009 & '10. (See also Accommodation section & A–Z for SylvanVale.)

Guardian Peak Restaurant Guardian Peak, Annandale Road, Stellenbosch ▪ South African food & wine experience — hearty, wholesome dishes paired with Guardian Peak wines ▪ Open Tue–Sat 9–5 ▪ Closed Sun/Mon, Good Fri & Dec 25 ▪ Booking advised ▪ Children welcome ▪ Major credit cards accepted ▪ No BYO ▪ Owner Jean Engelbrecht ▪ info@guardianpeak.com ▪ www.guardianpeak.com ▪ S 34° 0' 40.48" E 18° 50' 31.29" ▪ **T +27 (0)21-881-3899** ▪ F +27 (0)21-881-3388

Inviting combo of vineyard vistas, tables on a wide veranda, and menus focused on wine. Breakfasts range from light and healthy to a hearty 'Kalahari Lion'; lunches are wine-inspired, with dishes listed under the wine labels. Try herb-crusted smoked trout or grilled beef ribeye with Malbec

Tannat; goats cheese wontons or grilled pork fillet with Guardian Peak Frontier; and duck leg confit with Merlot. (See also A–Z section.)

Indochine Restaurant Delaire Graff Estate, R310, Helshoogte Pass, Banhoek Valley, Stellenbosch ▪ Asian-inspired cuisine ▪ Open daily for lunch 12–2.30 & dinner 6.30–9.30 ▪ Booking advised ▪ Children welcome ▪ Major credit cards accepted ▪ No BYO ▪ Owner Laurence Graff ▪ guest.relations@delaire.co.za ▪ www.delaire.co.za ▪ S 33° 55' 236" E 18° 55' 207" ▪ **T +27 (0)21-885-8160**

Asian-inspired cuisine is perfectly placed in this serene, art-studded ambience, under a flight of swallows suspended from the ceiling. Wrap-round views over Stellenbosch valley, a focused winelist and organic ingredients from the estate greenhouse, root you in the Cape. But picture-perfect, aromatic dishes like ponzu duck salad, tamarind sirloin, and Burmese linefish, with an array of tempting side-dishes, waft your tastebuds swiftly to the East. (See also Accommodation & A–Z sections.)

Joostenberg Bistro Klein Joostenberg Farm, R304, Muldersvlei ▪ Country bistro ▪ Open daily from 8–5 ▪ Booking advised ▪ Children welcome ▪ Major credit cards accepted ▪ Corkage R35 ▪ Owners Philip Myburgh, Susan Dehosse/Christophe Dehosse ▪ bistro@joostenberg.co.za ▪ **T +27 (0)21-884-4208** ▪ F +27 (0)21-884-4135

Unpretentious, family-friendly Boland bistro, specialising in farm-reared pork and fresh local produce. À la carte menus change with the seasons: summer brings three-course set Sunday lunches on the vine-shaded stoep, overlooking lawns with space for kids to play. In winter, indoor tables beckon, warmed by a huge fireplace. Taste Joostenberg wines in the tempting deli; enjoy by the glass or bottle at the table. (See also A–Z section.)

Jordan Restaurant Jordan Wine Estate, Stellenbosch Kloof Road, Vlottenburg, Stellenbosch ▪ Continental / Modern European cuisine ▪ Lunch Mon-Sun 12–3, dinner Thu & Fri from 6.30 ▪ Booking advised ▪ Children welcome ▪ Major credit cards accepted ▪ No BYO ▪ Owners George & Louise Jardine ▪ restaurant@jordanwines.com ▪ www.jordanrestaurant.co.za ▪ S 33° 36' 33.7" E 018° 44' 41.3" ▪ **T +27 (0)21-881-3612**

Chef/patron George Jardine breaks barriers (his treatment of sago with barrel-smoked yellowtail banishes boarding-school memories) but admire the view before feasting your eyes on your plate. While daily-changing menus capture seasonal freshness (try Saldanha Bay mussels *en papillote* with ginger, garlic and fragrant lemongrass), hallmarks remain faultless flavours and featherlight soufflés. New for summer is a 'Bus Stop' menu, to share at a communal table. *Eat Out* magazine's Top

Ten (ranked no 3) & American Express Platinum Card Fine Dining Award 2011. (See also A–Z section.)

Morgenhof Restaurant Morgenhof Wine Estate, Klapmuts Road (R44), Stellenbosch ▪ Country – fresh seasonal ▪ Open daily for breakfast 9–11, lunch 12–3 (Nov–Apr) & 12–2.30 (May–Oct); Coffee shop 9–4.30 daily ▪ Closed Mondays (May–end Aug), Good Friday, Dec 25 & Jan 1 ▪ Booking advised ▪ Children welcome (kiddies menu) ▪ Major credit cards accepted ▪ No BYO ▪ Owner Anne Cointreau ▪ info@morgenhof.com ▪ www.morgenhof.com ▪ S 33° 53' 38.5" E 018° 51' 39.2" ▪ **T +27 (0)21-889-5510** ▪ F +27 (0)21-889-5266

Popular year-round venue where flavour sets seasonal menus from exec chef Siraaj Allie. Enjoy signature chicken salad; pan-fried duck breast with chilli sweet-potato mash, pak choi and verjuice reduction; or a seafood platter laden with grilled linefish, black tiger prawns and pan-fried Patagonia squid, seated at garden tables in summer; under a vine canopy in winter sunshine; or banishing the chill beside log fires indoors. (See also Accommodation & A–Z sections.)

Olivello Restaurant Marianne Wine Estate, Valley Road, off R44, between Klapmuts & Stellenbosch ▪ Cape Mediterranean ▪ Seasonal opening times, generally closed Mon & Tue ▪ Booking advised ▪ Children welcome ▪ Wheelchair-friendly ▪ German, Italian & French spoken ▪ Visa & MasterCard accepted ▪ Corkage R40 ▪ Owners Laurille Krug & Lynne Aberdeen ▪ restaurant@olivello.co.za ▪ www.olivello.co.za ▪ S 33° 49' 46.88" E 18° 53' 19.93" ▪ **T +27 (0)21-875-5443**

Their hallmark is generosity. Partners Laurille and Lynne specialise in retro food of the most comforting kind — deliciously fresh and redolent of the Med — on the shores of a reed-sheltered, water lily-strewn pond. Menu must is melt-in-the-mouth fillet draped in creamy, black pepper and brandy-laced sauce; a Sunday buffet-style Mediterranean Table is a robust feast for the senses. Relax, laze on the lawns, or play *boule*. Selected as one of Wine Magazine's 2009 'Hidden Gems for Weddings and Functions'. (See also Accommodation & A–Z sections.)

Raphael's Restaurant Asara Wine Estate & Hotel, Polkadraai Road (M12), Stellenbosch ▪ Flavourful dishes from locally sourced produce ▪ Open daily 7 am–9.30 pm ▪ Booking advised ▪ Children welcome ▪ Major credit cards accepted ▪ Corkage R35 ▪ Owner Markus Rahmann ▪ info@asara.co.za ▪ www.asara.co.za ▪ S 33° 56' 35.00" E 18° 48' 31.00" ▪ **T +27 (0)21-888-8000**

Fresh, flavour-driven menus from new internationally experienced exec chef Archie Mclean (ex The Tasting Room), complement lighter décor framing spectacular views of vineyards and mountains, while summery terrace tables capitalise on the peaceful waterside setting. Relish mushrooms in marrow bones; attempt 700g of mouth-melting Nguni beef rib-eye, carved at your table (doggy bag available), and introduce your tastebuds to dessert speciality: gluten-free mielie-meal chocolate fondant. Diners Club Diamond Winelist Award 2008 & '10; Platinum Award 2009. (See also Accommodation & A–Z sections.)

Rust en Vrede Restaurant Rust en Vrede Wine Estate, Annandale Road (off R44), Stellenbosch ▪ Fine dining, contemporary take on the classics ▪ Dinner Tue-Sat from 7 to close ▪ Closed Sun/Mon, Good Fri & Dec 25 ▪ Booking advised ▪ Major credit cards accepted ▪ No BYO ▪ Owner Jean Engelbrecht ▪ dining@rustenvrede.com ▪ www.rustenvrede.com ▪ S 33° 59'54" E 18° 51'21" ▪ **T +27 (0)21-881-3757** ▪ F +27 (0)21-881-3000

Stylish fine dining in the original wine cellar, where décor and custom-designed tableware enhance contemporary cuisine. Four- and six-course menus (with well-chosen wine) combine freshness, flavour and prime ingredients, while new exec chef John Shuttleworth brings enticing delicacy and subtle touches to perfectly plated food-pairing. Savour smoked tuna with scallop tartare; roasted monkfish with braised oxtail; or butter-tender lamb rump and neck with fennel fondant. S Pellegrino Top 100 restaurants in the world 2009–'11; *Eat Out* Best Chef 2010, Best Restaurant 2010, Best Service 2009–'11; *Rossouw's Restaurants* 3 stars 2009–'11. (See also A–Z section.)

Spier Hotel Restaurant R310 Lynedoch Road, Stellenbosch ▪ Fine dining ▪ Open daily for breakfast 6.30–10.30, wine bar 12–6 & dinner 6–10 ▪ Booking advised ▪ Children welcome ▪ Major credit cards accepted ▪ No BYO ▪ info@spier.co.za ▪ www.spier.co.za ▪ S 33° 58'379" E 18° 46'944" ▪ **T +27 (0)21-809-1100** ▪ F +27 (0)21-809-1134

A softer look to the dining room, terrace tables for sunny days, and smiling, helpful service. Menus, matched to Spier wines, focus on fresh, seasonal produce from the Spier farm or neighbouring producers: organic fruit and vegetables, hand-picked herbs, pasture-fed chicken and eggs, and sustainable fish. Helpings are generous, with runaway best-sellers tasty short-rib pot pie in pastry-topped individual *potjies*, and pan-seared, Hollandaise-draped Franschhoek trout. (See also A–Z section.)

Terroir Restaurant Kleine Zalze Wines, R44, Technopark, Stellenbosch ▪ Provençal ▪ Lunch Mon-Sun 12–2.30, dinner Mon-Sat 7–9 ▪ Closed Sun eve ▪ Booking advised ▪ Children welcome ▪ Major credit cards accepted ▪ Corkage R50 ▪ Owner Kleine Zalze Wines ▪ Chef Michael Broughton ▪ terroir@kleinezalze.co.za ▪ www.kleinezalze.co.za ▪ S 33° 56'

16.51" E 18° 51'06.70" ▪ **T +27 (0)21-880-8167** ▪ F +27 (0)21-880-0862

The terroir is decidedly Cape in flavour and setting; so are the food-friendly, highly-rated Kleine Zalze wines. Though deceptively simple dishes are French-inspired, fresh seasonal ingredients are local, showcasing chef Michael Broughton's award-winning culinary skill and impeccably judged sauces. The come-as-you-are ambience encourages lingering over chalkboard offerings such as miso glazed salmon with smoked potato, tempura tomatoes and truffled asparagus, or pork belly with braised apples and cider sauce. *Eat Out* Awards' Top 10 2006–'07, '09–'11. (See also A–Z section.)

The Avontuur Estate Restaurant see under Somerset West

The Big Easy Restaurant and Wine Bar 95 Dorp Street, Stellenbosch ▪ Up-market and contemporary ▪ Breakfast Mon-Fri 7.30-10, Sat/Sun & public holidays 8.30–11; lunch 12–3, tapas 3–7 & dinner 6–10 daily ▪ Closed Dec 25 ▪ Retail store (Ernie Els memorabilia & proprietor's wine) open daily from 9–5 ▪ Closed Dec 25 ▪ Booking advised ▪ Children welcome ▪ Major credit cards accepted ▪ No BYO ▪ Owners Jean Engelbrecht, Ernie Els, Johann Rupert, Paul Harris & Giuseppe Cuicci ▪ info@thebigeasy.co.za ▪ **T +27 (0)21-887-3462** ▪ F +27 (0)21-887-3470

Relax and enjoy generous dishes in a laid-back ambience rich in history. Setting is a gracious gabled house with interleading rooms, service is friendly and constantly changing menus celebrate flavour, whether mixed mushrooms in an exotic truffle-creamed risotto, a speciality burger, or Belgian chocolate fondant with iced Amaretto cream. Best-sellers are prime char-grilled rump, sirloin or fillet steaks, with fries and a choice of sauces. (See also A–Z section for Ernie Els Wines.)

The Duck Pond Restaurant Welmoed Winery, R310, Baden-Powell Drive, Stellenbosch ▪ Traditional South African cuisine ▪ Open daily from 10–5 (Oct-Apr), Wed-Mon 10–4 (May-Sep) ▪ Closed Tue (May-Sep) ▪ Booking advised ▪ Children welcome ▪ Major credit cards accepted ▪ Corkage R20 ▪ Owners Ronel & Charlene van der Walt ▪ info@duckpond.co.za ▪ www.duckpond.co.za ▪ **T/F 021-881-3310**

Calling comfort-food fans. You'll find slow-roasted lamb shank, roast duck with port and berry sauce, chicken and mushroom pie, plus traditional *snoek* pâté, in hearty helpings at Welmoed Winery, where the restaurant in the Wine Tasting centre overlooks a large duck pond. The relaxed setting (and friendly ducks) make this an ideal family venue. Indoor and lawn seating, with new enclosed veranda for weddings or functions. (See also A–Z section.)

Umami Restaurant Black Horse Centre, corner Dorp & Market Street, Stellenbosch ▪ Contemporary cuisine ▪ Open Mon–Sat for lunch 12–2.30 & dinner 6–9 ▪ Closed Sun ▪ Secure parking available ▪ Booking advised ▪ Children welcome ▪ Major credit cards accepted ▪ Corkage R35 ▪ Owner Toerie van der Merwe ▪ info@umamirestaurant.co.za ▪ www. umamirestaurant.co.za ▪ **T** +27 (0)21-887-5204 ▪ F +27 (0)21-887-5208

Popular mid-town food haven, enticing both locals and visitors intent on experiencing 'umami' (the fifth taste). Here chefs tempt tastebuds by using local products in seasonal menus with one overriding objective — to unlock and accentuate each dish's 'deliciousness'. For maximum effect opt for wine pairing: carefully chosen wines are well-priced and exclusively from the Stellenbosch region. Eat indoors or at tables in the shady courtyard.

Wild Peacock Food Emporium 32 Piet Retief Street, Stellenbosch ▪ Brasserie – Del Foods and Mediterranean ▪ Open Mon–Tue 7.30–6, Wed–Fri 7.30–10pm & Sat 8–4 ▪ Closed Sun & religious holidays ▪ Booking advised evenings ▪ Children welcome ▪ Visa & MasterCard accepted ▪ No BYO ▪ Owner Baker Family Trust ▪ sarah@wildpeacock.co.za ▪ www. wildpeacock.co.za ▪ S 33° 56′ 24″ E 18° 51′ 34″ ▪ **T** +27 (0)21-887-7585 ▪ F +27 (0)86-577-3663

This enticing French-style brasserie-cum-deli oozes temptation, whether shopping for specialities like oysters, snails, fresh duck, quail, fish, free-range poultry, artisinal cheeses and fine wine, or sitting down to eat. Breakfasts are scrumptious; lunches deliciously light or a filling, flavoursome *plat de jour* (pots of Ma Baker's mussels are a must). Excellent, well-priced wine-by-the-glass selection, plus a specialised retail wine boutique focused on the Stellenbosch area.

Zevenwacht Restaurant Zevenwacht Wine Farm, Langverwacht Road, Kuils River ▪ Global contemporary cuisine ▪ Breakfast Mon–Fri 7–10, Sat/Sun 8–11; lunch 12–3 & dinner 6–10 daily ▪ Garden picnics ▪ Booking advised ▪ Children welcome ▪ Major credit cards accepted ▪ No BYO ▪ Owner Manie Wolmarans ▪ restaurant@zevenwacht.co.za ▪ www.zevenwacht. co.za ▪ **T** +27 (0)21-903-5123 ▪ F +27 (0)21-903-5257

The setting is idyllic: a gabled manor house on the lawns of a lake. Happily, under passionate new chef Justin Pillay (ex Buitenverwachting) contemporary cuisine now matches the ambience. Wine-pairing suggestions are made with élan; sauces and

foams show a deliciously delicate touch; herb-rich lamb and fillet are mouth-melting, and sinful desserts irresistible. Estate, vegetarian and braai picnic baskets available to enjoy in the garden. (See also Accommodation & A–Z sections.)

Swellendam
Restaurant 1723 see under Robertson

Wellington
Seasons Restaurant Diemersfontein Wine & Country Estate, R301 Jan van Riebeeck Road, Wellington ▪ Mediterranean cuisine with a traditional South African twist ▪ Open daily for breakfast, lunch & dinner ▪ Booking advised ▪ Children welcome ▪ Major credit cards accepted ▪ Corkage R20 ▪ Owners David & Sue Sonnenberg ▪ Chef Eddie Maqegu ▪ restaurant@ diemersfontein.co.za ▪ www.diemersfontein.co.za ▪ **T** +27 (0)21-864-5060 ▪ F +27 (0)21-864-2095

Relaxed restaurant overlooking the paddocks on tranquil Diemersfontein Wine and Country Estate, long a local favourite as a hospitable meeting place with good food at good value. Breakfast beautifully on Boland eggs Benedict; enjoy the estate's highly rated wines with Mediterranean-style tapas bites, fresh linefish and locally sourced beef steaks; and savour Diemersfontein pinotage by the glass — or in signature oxtail and chocolate mousse. (See also Accommodation & A–Z sections.)

The Stone Kitchen on Dunstone Dunstone Winery, Bovlei Road, Wellington ▪ Café style ▪ Open Wed–Sun 8am–4pm, Thu 8am–10pm ▪ Closed Mon & Tue ▪ Booking advised ▪ Children welcome ▪ Major credit cards accepted ▪ Corkage R20 ▪ Owner Johan van Schalkwyk ▪ stonekitchen@dunstone.co.za ▪ www. thestonekitchen.co.za ▪ S 33° 38′01″ E 19° 03′ 41″ ▪ **T/ F** +27 (0)21-864-2451

Hospitable café-style eateries in Dunstone wine cellar, doubling as tasting room, with stainless steel tanks as décor feature. Ideal view-rich 'pitstop' when exploring Wellington wine route (especially during harvest, when you can *stomp* grapes). Inviting ingredient mixes on blackboard menus change as valley-proud chef/patron Johan draws on fresh produce from surrounding farms. Fun play area to occupy offspring; legendary breakfasts and best-selling wild boar burger. (See also Accommodation section for Bovlei Valley Retreat & A–Z section.)

Accommodation in the Winelands and Cape Town

Featured below are some guest lodges, hotels, country inns, B&Bs and self-catering cottages in the winelands, many of them on wine farms (look for the 🏠 symbol beside the individual entries in the A–Z section of this guide). These are paid entries. The venues supplied information on their facilities and attractions, which was then edited for consistency of style. Unless stated to the contrary, all speak English and Afrikaans, have parking and gardens/terraces. Rates are for standard double rooms unless otherwise specified — for example per person (pp) or breakfast included (B&B). Tourism Grading Council of South Africa (TGCSA) ratings where provided. Should you wish to know about wheelchair access, please discuss with the relevant venue.

Index of accommodation
Listed alphabetically, with region.

Ashton
Pat Busch Private Nature Reserve see under Robertson

Bonnievale
Bushmanspad Estate see under Montagu

Calitzdorp
The Retreat at Groenfontein Groenfontein Farm, District Calitzdorp (20km from Calitzdorp, off Route 62) ▪ TGCSA 3 & 4-star guest house ▪ 8 rooms — luxury & standard ▪ Low season: double R480–R620 pps DB&B, single R630–R1,110 DB&B; High season: double R710–R910 pps DB&B, single R860–R1,640 DB&B ▪ Visa & MasterCard accepted ▪ Restaurant (problem diets catered for — advise when booking) ▪ Pool ▪ Children welcome ▪ Walking trails ▪ River with rock pools ▪ Observatory for star gazing ▪ French, German, Italian & Swedish spoken ▪ Owner Marie Holstensson ▪ info@ groenfontein.com ▪ www.groenfontein.com ▪ S 33° 26′ 15.6″ E 21° 47′ 20.9″ ▪ **T +27 (0)44-213-3880** ▪ F +27 (0)86-271-5373

   A consistent award-winner, this welcoming, personally run 3 and 4-star graded Victorian farmhouse offers both standard and luxury rooms. You'll enjoy personal pampering, hearty breakfasts and tasty dinners. The inviting lounge and dining room overlook sweeping lawns and the majestic Swartberg. Take leisurely walks, challenging trails, explore the rockpools in the bird-rich river, or simply laze at the pool, soaking up the peace and silence. AA Hall of Fame award 2010.

Camps Bay

The Twelve Apostles Hotel and Spa Victoria Road, Camps Bay, Cape Town ▪ TGCSA 5-star boutique hotel; Leading Hotels of the World & part of the family-run Red Carnation Hotel Collection ▪ 70 rooms & suites ▪ Rates on request ▪ Major credit cards accepted ▪ Azure Restaurant; The Café Grill; The Leopard Bar (live music) ▪ Banqueting & conferences (8 function rooms) ▪ Weddings ▪ Luxury spa ▪ 2 pools (1 heated) ▪ Cinema ▪ Garden hammocks ▪ Hiking trails ▪ Picnics on mountainside ▪ Helicopter flips ▪ Shuttle service ▪ Childcare ▪ Air-conditioning ▪ WIFI ▪ TV ▪ German spoken ▪ Owner The Tollman Family ▪ bookta@12apostles.co.za ▪ www.12apostleshotel.com ▪ S 33° 58' 59.37" E 18° 21' 31.43" ▪ **T +27 (0)21-437-9000** ▪ F +27 (0)21-437-9055

Spoil yourself. Set on the mountainside between Table Mountain National Park and Atlantic breakers, this 5-star boutique hotel has one of the world's most dramatic locations. Views are spectacular; light, airy rooms offer luxurious comfort, up-to-the-minute technology and 24-hour service, while world-class facilities include a cinema and newly renovated seven treatment-room spa. The V&A Waterfront and Cape Town's bikini beaches are a few minutes away. Voted one of The 'Best Places to Stay in the World' *Condé Nast Traveler's* Gold List 2011. (See also Restaurants section.)

Cape Town

African Pride Crystal Towers Hotel & Spa Corner Century Boulevard & Rialto Road, Century City, Cape Town ▪ 180 rooms ▪ Seasonal rates: double R1,700–R4,350 per room B&B, single R1,350–R4,000 B&B ▪ Major credit cards accepted ▪ The Towers Restaurant, The Deli & The Ruby Bar ▪ Convention Centre ▪ Suspended swimming pool ▪ DVD library ▪ Wii Game, Playstation & Board Games for in room use ▪ Safe ▪ Air-conditioning ▪ Life Day Spa ▪ French spoken ▪ Owner Protea Hospitality Group (Pty) Ltd ▪ reservations@crystaltowershotel.com ▪ www.africanpridehotels.com/crystaltowers ▪ S 33° 89' 23.62" E 18° 51' 23.06" ▪ **T +27 (0)21-525-3888** ▪ F +27 (0)21-525-3889

Expect streamlined simplicity emphasised by bright colour; lofty volumes and innovative lighting. In rooms, soft shades form a restful backdrop to fittings and accessories essential for a luxurious/business stay, including a freestanding shower with soothing 'raindrop' showerhead. Enjoy the variety of eating options, revitalise at the state-of-the-art

spa, work out in the gym, and laze poolside with cocktails at sunset. World-class convention facilities. (See also Restaurants section.)

Brooklands House Guest House 3 Surbiton Road, Rondebosch, Cape Town ▪ TGCSA 4-star guest house ▪ 4 en-suite rooms ▪ Seasonal rates: double R550-R595 pps B&B; single R615-R735 B&B ▪ Major credit cards accepted ▪ Conferences ▪ Pool ▪ Boule court ▪ TV ▪ Ceiling fans ▪ Owners Philip & Sandra Engelen ▪ brooklands@mweb.co.za ▪ www.brooklands-guesthouse.co.za ▪ **T/F +27 (0)21-689-3594 ▪ Mobile +27 (0)82-659-6659**

Charming Victorian villa, within walking distance of some 7 restaurants, near Newlands rugby and cricket grounds, and less than 15 mins drive from CT international airport. Breakfast in the sunroom overlooking the garden; dine by prior arrangement; in winter relax beside the drawing room fire. If you're planning Winelands excursions, consult your hosts, wine enthusiasts who planted a petit shiraz vineyard beside the boule court.

Cape Grace West Quay Road, V&A Waterfront, Cape Town ▪ TGCSA 5-star boutique hotel ▪ 120 rooms ▪ Seasonal rates: R5,290-R5,450 per room B&B, single R4,350-R4,510 B&B ▪ Major credit cards accepted ▪ Signal Restaurant; Bascule Whisky, Wine and Cocktail Bar ▪ Conferences ▪ Communication Centre with 24-hour complimentary Internet access ▪ Outdoor heated pool ▪ Satellite TV ▪ Air-conditioning ▪ Spa ▪ Luxury yacht 'Spirit of the Cape' for chartering ▪ French, German, Italian, Korean, Maltese, Portuguese, Shona, Spanish, Swedish, Xhosa & Zulu spoken ▪ Owner Meikles Ltd ▪ reservations@capegrace.com ▪ www.capegrace.com ▪ S 33° 54' 29" E 18° 25' 12" ▪ **T +27 (0)21-410-7100** ▪ F +27 (0)21-419-7622

Setting is a private quay of an international yacht marina, against the backdrop of Table Mountain, between Cape Town's working harbour and bustling Victoria & Alfred Waterfront. Ambience is gracious, capturing the essence of the Cape in furnishings and fabrics that combine local creativity with seductive luxury, reinforcing the warm atmosphere and personalised service that have for years defined the hotel. Contemporary restaurant and whisky bar. Annual awards since opening: latest are Best Hotel in Africa *US Celebrated Living* 2011; Best Hotel in Africa *UK Daily Telegraph Ultra Travel Awards* May 2011; Third Best Hotel in Africa and the Middle East *Travel & Leisure Service Awards* 2011; 500 World Best Hotels *Travel & Leisure* 2011; Gold List *Condé Nast Traveler* 2011; Best For Food in Africa, Middle East & Indian Ocean *Conde Nast Traveller* 2011; Favourite Worldwide City Hotels *The UK Sunday Times Travel Magazine* 2011.

Hout Bay Manor see under Hout Bay

One&Only Cape Town Dock Road, V&A Waterfront, Cape Town ▪ TGCSA 5-star luxury hotel/resort ▪ 131 guest rooms & suites ▪ Seasonal rates from R5,390 per room per night B&B ▪ Major credit cards accepted ▪ Restaurants: Nobu & Reuben's ▪ Conferences ▪ Pool ▪ Spa & Fitness Centre ▪ Air-conditioning ▪ Amenities include: multi-media entertainment system, 42-inch flat screen TV, DVD/CD player, iPod docking station, complimentary Wi-Fi access, in-room business services (multi-adaptor, fax/computer hook-ups, 3-phone/2-line communication system), Nespresso machine, hairdryer, safe ▪ Owner Kerzner International ▪ reservations@oneandonlycapetown. com ▪ www.oneandonlycapetown.com ▪ S 33° 54' 30" E 18° 24'59" ▪ **T +27 (0)21-431-5888** ▪ F +27 (0)21-431-5230

Succumb to pampering. Luxury, stylish African design, and personalised services are standard at the One&Only's majestic Marina Rise, where rooms and suites are the largest in Cape Town and windows overlook Table Mountain or the lively Waterfront. Spacious Island rooms and suites on an exclusive island, each with balcony or terrace overlooking the waterway, offer a peaceful haven a few steps from the world-class spa. (See also Restaurants section.)

The Twelve Apostles Hotel and Spa see under Camps Bay

Vineyard Hotel & Spa Colinton Road, Newlands, Cape Town ▪ TGCSA 4-star deluxe ▪ 207 rooms ▪ Double R973–R2,223 pps B&B; single R1,595–R3,995 B&B ▪ Major credit cards accepted ▪ 3 restaurants: The Square, Myoga & Splash Café ▪ Conferences ▪ Angsana Spa ▪ Health & fitness centre ▪ 2 pools: outdoor & heated indoor ▪ TV ▪ Air-conditioning ▪ Dutch, French, German & Xhosa spoken ▪ Owners Alexander & George Petousis ▪ hotel@vineyard.co.za ▪ www.vineyard.co.za ▪ **T +27 (0)21-657-4500** ▪ F +27 (0)21-657-4501

In 1800 Lady Anne Barnard and her husband Andrew named their new Cape residence The Vineyard after the property's 22 000 vines. In 2011 the charming Vineyard Hotel & Spa, set in landscaped gardens overlooking Table Mountain, celebrated its 117th anniversary as a hotel with a deluxe new wing and multi-car underground parking. A thriving mini-vineyard commemorates the venue's links to the past and to wine. (See also Restaurants section for The Square.)

Constantia
Constantia Uitsig Country Hotel and Spa Constantia Uitsig Wine Estate, Spaanschemat River Road, Constantia, Cape Town ▪ TGCSA 4-star country hotel ▪ 16 rooms ▪ Seasonal rates: from R1,750–R3,600 per room B&B, single from R1,300–R2,400

B&B ▪ Major credit cards accepted ▪ Three restaurants: Constantia Uitsig Restaurant, La Colombe & River Café ▪ The Wine Shop ▪ Pool ▪ Spa ▪ TV ▪ Air-conditioning ▪ Owner Constantia Uitsig Holdings (Pty) Ltd ▪ reservations@uitsig.co.za ▪ www.constantia-uitsig.com ▪ S 34° 02'45.28" E 18° 25'12.55" ▪ **T +27 (0)21-794-6500** ▪ F +27 (0)21-794-7605

Enjoy peace and gracious hospitality at this serene 16-bedroom hotel on a working wine estate in scenic Constantia valley, just minutes from the city centre and major tourist attractions. Seamless vistas encompass tranquil gardens, vineyards and a cricket oval; an award-winning spa invites relaxation, and highly acclaimed restaurants — La Colombe, Constantia Uitsig Restaurant and the River Café — entice. Ideal for exclusive events. (See also Restaurants & A–Z sections.)

Hampshire House 10 Willow Road, Constantia ▪ TGCSA 4-star guest house ▪ 5 rooms ▪ Seasonal rates: double R495–R595 pps B&B; single R650–R850 B&B ▪ Visa & MasterCard accepted ▪ Pool ▪ TV ▪ Air-conditioning ▪ Ceiling fans ▪ Owners Ricky & Carole Chapman ▪ stay@hampshirehouse.co.za ▪ www.hampshirehouse.co.za ▪ **T +27 (0)21-794-6288** ▪ F +27 (0)21-794-2934

Welcoming 4-star guesthouse, ideally placed for exploring the Cape Peninsula. Set in the peaceful Constantia wine valley, with six wineries just five minutes away, the lodge offers easy motorway access to Table Mountain, the Waterfront, Winelands, beaches and local restaurants. Five attractive, individually decorated en-suite bedrooms, both English and continental buffet breakfasts (Carole's fresh home-baked muffins are legendary), secluded swimming pool and secure off-street parking.

Darling
Darling Lodge 22 Pastorie Street, Darling ▪ TGCSA 4-star B&B; Greenwood Guide ▪ 6 rooms ▪ Double R440 pps B&B, single R550 B&B ▪ Major credit cards accepted (excl Diners Club) ▪ Conferences/functions ▪ Pool ▪ TV ▪ Ceiling fans ▪ Dutch, French and German spoken ▪ Owner Alfred Legner ▪ info@darlinglodge.co.za ▪ www.darlinglodge.co.za ▪ S 33° 22'44.78" E 18° 22'41.29" ▪ **T +27 (0)22-492-3062** ▪ F +27 (0)22-492-3665

Charmingly restored Victorian house in the gentle Darling valley offers a welcoming blend of old and new in an environment of vineyards, pastures, wheat fields and spectacular wild flower displays. Enjoy the area's award-winning wines and olives in a gorgeous garden with inviting pool. An hour from Cape Town and minutes from the Atlantic Ocean. Winelands, beaches, golf, whale watching, art galleries; 'Evita se Perron' nearby.

Elgin

South Hill Guest House South Hill Vineyards, 113 The Valley Road, Elgin ▪ TGCSA 4-star self-catering ▪ 6 rooms ▪ Double from R440–R780 pps B&B; single from R800–R1,400 B&B ▪ Major credit cards accepted ▪ Restaurant ▪ Conferences ▪ Pool ▪ TV ▪ Boule court ▪ Hiking & mountain bike trails ▪ Owner Kevin King ▪ info@southhill.co.za ▪ www.southhill.co.za ▪ S 34° 13'59.48" E 19°06'44.28" ▪ **T +27 (0)21-844-0033** ▪ F +27 (0)21-844-0959

Set amid vineyards and apple orchards, this 4-star, fully serviced guest house has four en-suite double rooms plus loft (with bathroom) that converts from lounge to sleepover area for five kids. Honeymoon suite with outdoor spa bath; inviting restaurant and catering on request. Bird watching, *boule* court and pool; mountain and quad biking or hiking for the energetic. All just an hour from Cape Town. (See also Restaurants section for Gordon Manuel @ The Venue and A–Z section.)

Franschhoek

Akkerdal Guest House Akkerdal Estate, R45 Franschhoek Road, Franschhoek ▪ 2 double rooms ▪ Rates on request ▪ Self-catering/continental breakfast ▪ Shuttle service to Franschhoek on request ▪ Visa & MasterCard accepted ▪ Conferences ▪ TV ▪ Air-conditioning ▪ Owner Pieter Hanekom ▪ wine@akkerdal.co. za ▪ www.akkerdal.co.za ▪ S 33° 52'43.40" E 19° 2' 58.50" ▪ **T +27 (0)21-876-3481** ▪ F +27 (0)21-876-3189

Escape city pressures to this peaceful guest house in the picturesque Franschhoek valley, sheltered by oaks beside the Berg river, with golf estates and luxury spas just minutes away. Taste the carefully crafted Akkerdal wines and watch the sun set over the mountains, glass in hand. Self-catering, though a continental breakfast will be supplied if requested, and Franschhoek, known for its restaurants, is only 6km from the farm. (See also A–Z section.)

Allée Bleue Kendall Cottage and Manor House T-junction R45 & R310, Groot Drakenstein ▪ TGCSA 5-star MESE ▪ 4 rooms ▪ **Kendall Cottage** accommodates max 4 guests; 15 guests for cocktail style function: R3,700 B&B for use of whole cottage per night (2 rooms) & R2,200 per night (one room only) ▪ **Manor House** accommodates max 4 guests; 40 guests for functions: R2,800 per room B&B (sleeps 2) ▪ Major credit cards accepted (excl. Diners Club) ▪ Bistro Allée Bleue ▪ Picnics ▪ Conferences ▪ Weddings/ functions ▪ TV ▪ Air-conditioning ▪ Wine cellar & tasting ▪ German spoken ▪ Owners Wilfred & Elke Dauphin ▪ info@alleebleue.com, esther.dewit@ alleebleue.com ▪ www.alleebleue.com ▪ S 33° 51'51. 02" E 18° 58'42.90" ▪ **T +27 (0)21-874-1021** ▪ F +27 (0)21-874-1850

Allée Bleue's signature shade is cleverly reflected in décor, furnishings and art in the estate's stylish accommodation. The gracious manor house, blending history with modern comforts, is ideal for functions. More intimate, revitalised Herbert Baker-designed Kendall cottage, linking two bedrooms through a spacious lounge, can be booked for a night, and will accommodate 15 for finger-food functions. Breakfast included in stayovers; additional meals by arrangement. (See also Restaurants & A–Z sections.)

Babylonstoren see under Paarl

Basse Provence Country House R45 Main Road, Franschhoek ▪ TGCSA 4-star B&B/guesthouse ▪ 9 rooms ▪ From R700–R1,350 per room B&B ▪ Visa & MasterCard accepted ▪ Rickety Bridge Restaurant ▪ Conferences ▪ Pool ▪ DSTV ▪ Air-conditioning ▪ Owner Rickety Bridge Properties ▪ booking@basseprovence. co.za ▪ www.basseprovence.co.za ▪ **T +27 (0)21-876-2994** ▪ F +27 (0)21-876-3673

Bed and breakfast à la carte in 4-star Winelands luxury, with the option of exclusive private dinners for guests. This tranquil retreat combines Cape Dutch hospitality with personalised service in a historic homestead shaded by 300 year-old oaks, surrounded by vines and framed by the Franschhoek mountains. Spacious, air-conditioned and elegantly decorated en-suite rooms with mini-bars, tea/coffee making facilities and DSTV; pool and sunny patio. (See also Restaurants section.)

Cabrière Cottage Franschhoek 47 Cabrière Street, Franschhoek ▪ 1 cottage, with 2 en-suite bedrooms ▪ Self-catering ▪ Seasonal rates: from R1,000–R1,300 per cottage ▪ No credit card facilities ▪ Plunge pool ▪ DSTV ▪ DVD player & iPod docking station ▪ Ceiling fans ▪ Fireplace ▪ Owners Matthew & Nicky Gordon ▪ info@cabrierecottage.com ▪ www.cabrierecottage. com ▪ **T +27 (0)82-455-6411**

Tranquil self-catering cottage in Franschhoek village, within walking distance of the addictive restaurants and antique shops that line the main road, offers visitors an ideal base for exploring all that Franschhoek has to offer. Two comfortable en-suite bedrooms, spacious open-plan lounge and fully fitted kitchen. Catch a tan in the private garden with plunge pool; enjoy a leisurely breakfast or sundowner on the large veranda.

Clouds Estate Guesthouse & Self-catering Chalets see under Stellenbosch

La Bourgogne Farm Riverside Cottages La Bourgogne Farm, Excelsior Road, Franschhoek ▪ TGCSA 3-star self-catering; AA Quality Assured — highly recommended ▪ 6 cottages/8 bedrooms ▪ Seasonal rates: from R600–R800 per 1-bedroomed cottage; R1,050–R1,200 per 2-bedroomed cottage ▪ Major credit cards accepted ▪ Pool ▪ Ceiling fans ▪ Owner

George Mayer ▪ info@labourgogne.co.za ▪ www.labourgogne.co.za ▪ S 33° 55' 28.0" E 019° 7' 15.0" ▪ **T +27 (0)21-876-3245** ▪ F +27 (0)86-542-3615

Relax on a deck overhanging a river between pear orchard, oaks and willows, watching the sunset tint the Middagkrans Mountains; or tan on loungers beside the pool. Charming self-catering cottages on a family wine farm just 1.5 km from Franschhoek Main Road, combine tranquility with a convenient base for exploring the Cape's French heritage, top restaurants and wine farms. Winetasting complimentary for stay-over guests. (See also A–Z section.)

La Petite Ferme Guest Suites La Petite Ferme, Franschhoek Pass Road, Franschhoek ▪ TGCSA 4 & 3-star B&B, self-catering and non-graded suites ▪ 15 rooms ▪ Low season: double R960–R2,560 pps B&B, single R672–R1,792 B&B; High Season: double R1,056–R2,816 pps B&B, single R739–R1,971 B&B ▪ Major credit cards accepted ▪ Restaurant ▪ Private plunge pools at vineyard suites & 2 ungraded cottages ▪ TV ▪ Minibar ▪ Air-conditioning ▪ Ceiling fans ▪ Fire places and/or under floor heating ▪ Complimentary cellar tours daily at 11am ▪ Owner Mark Dendy Young ▪ info@lapetiteferme.co.za ▪ www.lapetiteferme.co.za ▪ S 33° 55' 13" E 019° 08' 15" ▪ **T +27 (0)21-876-3016/18** ▪ F +27 (0)86-720-6284

Unwind in peaceful mountainside suites with panoramic views of Franschhoek valley, on a working wine farm with award-winning restaurant and boutique winery. La Petite Ferme offers relaxed family options; 4-star comfort; or tranquil lakeside lodges, high on the Franschhoek mountains. For those craving ocean views, their luxury seafront villa, La Petite Baleine, provides privacy and uninterrupted vistas of sea and sunsets over Walker Bay. (See also Restaurants & A–Z sections.)

Mont Rochelle Hotel & Mountain Vineyards Dassenberg Road, Franschhoek ▪ TGCSA 5-star hotel ▪ 16 rooms & 6 suites ▪ Seasonal rates from R2,300–R3,500 per room B&B ▪ Major credit cards accepted ▪ Two restaurants: Mange Tout & The Country Kitchen ▪ Boardroom ▪ Pool ▪ Gym ▪ Spa ▪ Satellite TV ▪ DVD players ▪ Wi-Fi ▪ Mini bar ▪ Safe ▪ Air-conditioning ▪ Under-floor heating ▪ Horse riding ▪ Hiking ▪ Cycling/mountain biking ▪ Wine tasting, also on horseback ▪ Herb garden ▪ Owners Erwin Schnitzler & Rwayitare family ▪ info@montrochelle.co.za ▪ www.montrochelle.co.za ▪ S 33° 92' 05.20" E 19° 10' 50.53" ▪ **T +27 (0)21-876-2770** ▪ F +27 (0)21-876-3788

Elegant 5-star boutique hotel with wrap-round vistas of vineyards and mountains. Attention to detail is paramount: sink into comfort in individually decorated rooms and luxury suites, each with every convenience. Expect fresh flowers, handmade chocolates and a welcome drink on arrival; a daily local

newspaper and scrumptious breakfast every morning; fine dining and rustic restaurants. Fishing, hiking and horse riding are part of everyday pleasure. AA Travel Guide & American Express Accommodation awards: Gold Achiever 2009; Great Wine Capitals Best of Wine Tourism 2008 & 2009 for Accommodation & Best Restaurant 2009. (See also Restaurants & A–Z sections.)

Rickety Bridge Manor House Rickety Bridge Wine Estate, R45 Main Road, Franschhoek ▪ TGCSA 4-star B&B/guesthouse ▪ 3 rooms ▪ From R1,600–R1,750 per room B&B ▪ Visa & MasterCard accepted ▪ Restaurant ▪ Conferences ▪ Pool ▪ Satellite TV ▪ Wi-Fi ▪ Air-conditioning ▪ Underfloor heating ▪ Owners DS Sarnia (Pty) Ltd ▪ shani@ricketybridge.com ▪ www.ricketybridge.com ▪ **T +27 (0)21-876-2994** ▪ F +27 (0)21-876-3673

Enjoy gracious living in a gabled manor house. Stylishly renovated 19th century rooms with four-star comforts encourage it; the ambience ensures it. You'll find yellow-wood beamed ceilings and pine floors polished with layers of history; Cape Dutch furniture and country kitchen. Breakfast in the quaint breakfast-room or beside the pool; picnic deliciously among vines; taste wine in the fire-warmed lounge and enjoy a private dinner. (See also Restaurants & A–Z sections.)

The Owner's Cottage at Grande Provence Grande Provence Heritage Wine Estate, Main Road, Franschhoek ▪ TGCSA 5-star guest house ▪ 4 rooms & 1 deluxe suite — exclusive use from 1 to 10 persons ▪ Seasonal rates: one room/one couple from R13,000–R16,000 to five rooms/five couples from R29,000–R42,000; full breakfast & 3-course dinner included ▪ Major credit cards accepted ▪ Butler service ▪ Restaurant ▪ Conferences ▪ Swimming & spa pool ▪ TV ▪ Air-conditioning ▪ Wireless Internet access ▪ Wine tasting, cellar tours & guided tour of The Gallery ▪ Dutch, French & German spoken ▪ Owner Grande Provence (Pty) Ltd ▪ ownerscottage@grandeprovence.co.za ▪ www.grandeprovence.co.za ▪ S 33° 53' 57.6" E 19° 06' 10.5" ▪ **T +27 (0)21-876-8600** ▪ F +27 (0)21-876-8601

Period elegance melds with contemporary luxury in this exclusive, superbly appointed 5-star retreat with four rooms, deluxe suite, conservatory, stylish lounge, swimming and spa pool area. Soothing charcoal grey and white décor suggests sophistication; furnishings promise an indulgent experience, with technology discreetly concealed. On lush lawns deck chairs and lounging areas beckon beside an inviting pool, with elevated spa area offering mountain and vineyard views. (See also Restaurants & A–Z sections.)

Whale Cottage Franschhoek 11 Akademie Street, Franschhoek ▪ 7 rooms + 1 luxury honeymoon suite ▪ Winter: rooms R350–R450 pp B&B, suite R550–R750; Summer: rooms R490–R600 pp B&B, suite R650–R800 pp B&B ▪ Visa & MasterCard accepted ▪ Whale Cottage Loyalty Card offers one night free for every 10 nights ▪

Pool ▪ Flat screen TV ▪ Air-conditioning ▪ Fireplace ▪ Free wireless Internet ▪ Secure parking ▪ Owner Chris von Ulmenstein, Whale Cottage Portfolio cc ▪ winelands@whalecottage.com ▪ www.whalecottage.com ▪ S 33° 54′41″ E 19° 07′22″ ▪ **T +27 (0)21-433-2100** ▪ F +27 (0)21-433-2101

Welcome to a whale of a stay at Whale Cottage Franschhoek, a country house with a delightful garden and babbling brook, in the heart of South Africa's gourmet village. Top restaurants Reuben's and Le Quartier Français are 200m away. Beautiful mountain views.

Hermanus

The Marine Hotel Cnr Marine Drive & Main Road, Hermanus ▪ TGCSA 5-star Relais & Chateaux Boutique Hotel ▪ 42 rooms ▪ Seasonal rates: double R2,600–R4,400 per room B&B; single R1,850–R2,650 B&B ▪ Major credit cards accepted ▪ Seafood at The Marine & The Pavilion restaurants ▪ Conferences ▪ Heated salt water pool & tidal pool ▪ Carchele Beauty Spa ▪ The Collection Boutique ▪ TV ▪ Air-conditioning ▪ Sun lounge and bar ▪ Internet lounge ▪ Wireless access ▪ German spoken ▪ Owner Liz McGrath ▪ reservations@collectionmcgrath.com ▪ www.collectionmcgrath.com ▪ S 34° 25′03.43″ E 19° 14′41.11″ ▪ **T +27 (0)28-313-1000** ▪ F +27 (0)28-313-0160

Set atop cliffs, this understated, luxury boutique hotel offers one of the most spectacular seascapes in the southern hemisphere — including the best possible land-based whale watching. Unwind: enjoy the view from inviting bedrooms or suites, or from the chic sun-lounge and bar; choose elegant or informal eating options; and shed stress at the spa, or in the heated salt water and tidal pools. (See also Restaurants section for Seafood at The Marine.)

Whale Cottage Hermanus 38 Westcliff Drive, Hermanus ▪ 6 rooms ▪ Winter R350–R450 pp B&B; summer R490–R600 pp B&B ▪ Visa & MasterCard accepted ▪ Whale Cottage Loyalty Card offers one night free for every 10 nights ▪ Pool ▪ Flat screen TV ▪ Air-conditioning ▪ Fireplace ▪ Free wireless Internet ▪ Secure parking ▪ Owner Chris von Ulmenstein, Whale Cottage Portfolio cc ▪ hermanus@whalecottage.com ▪ www.whalecottage.com ▪ S 34° 23′34″ E 19° 13′50″ ▪ **T +27 (0)21-433-2100** ▪ F +27 (0)21-433-2101

You'll have a whale of a stay at Whale Cottage Hermanus, a marine-themed beach house with magnificent views over Walker Bay, and of whales B & B (breaching and blowing). Hermanus is the whale capital of South Africa, and offers the best land-based whale watching in the world. Just a 1km walk to village centre and craft market. Welcome to a coastal home from home.

Hout Bay

Hout Bay Manor Baviaanskloof Road, off Main Road, Hout Bay ▪ TGCSA 5-star boutique hotel ▪ 19 rooms ▪ Family friendly ▪ Excellent rates on request ▪ Major credit cards accepted ▪ Pure restaurant ▪ Functions/executive meetings/private dinners (12 pax) ▪ Pool ▪ Inzolo Wellness Suite ▪ TV ▪ Air-conditioning ▪ WIFI ▪ GM Lucia Davadoss ▪ reservations@houtbaymanor.co.za ▪ www.houtbaymanor.com ▪ S 34° 04′32.01″ E 18° 36′06.38″ ▪ **T +27 (0)21-790-0116** ▪ F +27 (0)21-790-0118

Set between mountains and beach, the gracious 19th century gabled manor suggests tranquility. This appealing 5-star boutique hotel offers much more: expect personal pampering backed by a vibrant mix of fabrics, art, colonial and ethnic touches in individually decorated rooms and suites. Eat elegantly at Pure restaurant; indulge in soothing therapies at the wellness suite; laze at the pool or walk along pristine beaches. (See also Restaurants section.)

Kuils River

Zevenwacht Country Inn see under Stellenbosch

McGregor

Kingsriver Guest House Kingsriver Estate, Koningriver Road, McGregor on Route 62 ▪ TGCSA 4-star guesthouse ▪ 3 suites ▪ Seasonal rates from R999–R1,650 per room B&B ▪ Major credit cards accepted ▪ Restaurant ▪ Special wine and food events throughout the year ▪ Conferences ▪ Venue for small weddings ▪ TV ▪ Wi-Fi ▪ Air-conditioning ▪ Hiking ▪ Wine tasting ▪ Dutch, French & German spoken ▪ Owner Ruud de Clercq ▪ Manager Rodger Saunders ▪ kingsriver-guesthouse@breede.co.za ▪ www.kingsriver-estate.com ▪ S 33° 55′18.7″ E 019° 49′46.2″ ▪ **T +27 (0)23-625-1040** ▪ F +27 (0)23-625-1045

Relax body, mind and spirit in the nurturing peace of a 4-star guesthouse surrounded by 380 ha of unspoiled fynbos. Wake to country stillness in one of three comfortable suites; experience a therapeutic massage or beauty treatment; stroll through vineyards, hike mountain trails, discover Stone Age and San artifacts, and linger over farm-fresh meals with Kingsriver wines. Then adopt a vine and grow your own. (See also Restaurants & A–Z sections.)

Montagu

Bushmanspad Estate Route 60, Ashton — Swellendam ▪ TGCSA 4-star self-catering & B&B ▪ 5 cottages ▪ R750 per cottage ▪ Major credit cards accepted ▪ DSTV ▪ Internet ▪ Bird watching ▪ Hiking ▪ Mountain biking ▪ Dutch, French & German spoken ▪ Owner Menno Schaafsma ▪ info@bushmanspad.co.za ▪ www.bushmanspad.co.za ▪ S 33° 53′55.0″ E 020° 11′46.7″ ▪ **T +27 (0)23-616-2961** ▪ F +27 (0)23-616-3714

Escape to a wine estate high in the Langeberg Mountains, where en-suite cottages, easily accessible by car, are fully-equipped for self-catering. Breakfast in the 17th century farmhouse, taste wine in the 200 year-old cellar and braai on a wood fire in the barbeque area. Fish, swim, bird-watch and hike: or simply chill, enjoying 100 km vistas, breathtaking sunsets and peaceful nights under an African sky. (See also A–Z section.)

Les Hauts de Montagu 3km past Montagu, on Route 62 to Barrydale • TGCSA 4-star lodge • 10 rooms • Low season: R550–R600 pps B&B, single R700 B&B; High season: R800–R875 pps B&B, single R1,100 B&B • Visa & MasterCard accepted • Pool • TV in some rooms • Ceiling fans • Internet • Small chapel • 8 hiking trails • Bird watching • French spoken • Owners Eric & Myriam Brillant • info@leshautsdemontagu.co.za • www.leshautsdemontagu.co.za • S 33° 80' 58.96" E 20° 15'77.23" • **T +27 (0)23-614-2514** • F +27 (0)23-614-3517

Take time out in a tranquil 4-star lodge on a 600 ha olive farm on the slopes of the Langeberg, offering spectacular views of surrounding mountains and olive groves, and bird-rich hiking trails through fynbos. Romantic thatched cottages with spacious en-suite rooms have quaint Victorian bathtubs, plus outdoor showers that make the most of the view. Two hours from Cape Town on the scenic Route 62.

Montagu Country Hotel Cnr Bath & Kohler Street, Montagu • TGCSA 3-star hotel • 33 rooms • Seasonal rates: double R440–R530 pps B&B; single R495–R640 B&B • Major credit cards accepted • Restaurant • Conferences • Wellness centre • 2 pools • TV • Air-conditioning • Dutch spoken • Owner Gert Lubbe • GM P-J Basson • res@montagucountryhotel.co.za • www.montagucountryhotel.co.za • S 33° 44' 29" E 20° 27' 13" • **T +27 (0)23-614-3125** • F +27 (0)23-614-1905

Experience old-world charm in a country hotel where décor echoes Paris-inspired 1920s Art Deco style. Traditional cuisine is complemented by local wines, while Golden Oldies played on a Baby Grand again take you back in time. Relax at the pools in the shady garden; visit the wellness centre with its steam room and mineral bath; or enjoy exploring the wine route in chauffeur-driven classic cars.

Overberg
South Hill Guest House see under Elgin

Paarl
Babylonstoren Klapmuts-Simondium Road (R45), Paarl • 16 rooms: 6 x suites, 2 x 1-bedroom cottages & 4 x 2-bedroom cottages • Seasonal rates: double R2,970–R4,270 pps B&B, single R2,240–R3,205 B&B • Major credit cards accepted • Babel Restaurant • Conferences (12 executives) • Pool • Gym • Spa with

plunge pool, steam room, sauna, treatment rooms & Hammam • Guided garden tours • Wine tasting • Natural dam swimming pool • Hiking trails • Bicycles • Canoes • TV • Air-conditioning • Ceiling fans • Under floor heating • Owners Koos Bekker & Karen Roos • Hotel Manager Elmine Nel • reservations@babylonstoren.com • www.babylonstoren.com • S 33° 49' 26.73" E 18° 55' 39.08" • **T +27 (0)21-863-3852** • F +27 (0)21-863-1727

Relax, at one with nature, but with all modern extras (including spa and gym) on a 1692 farm where appealing en-suite guest accommodation echoes early whitewashed Cape Dutch farm buildings and a formal 8-acre fruit orchard was inspired by Cape Town's 17th century Company Gardens. Tour the garden, pick your own produce, and celebrate the seasons at Babel restaurant. Just 60 kms from Cape Town. (See also Restaurants & A–Z sections.)

Diemersfontein Country House see under Wellington

Hawksmoor at Matjieskuil see under Stellenbosch

Druk My Niet Wine Estate Bodal Road, Daljosafat, Paarl • 3 cottages • Self-catering • Protea R1,000 (sleeps 2), Guava R1,500 (sleeps 4) & Fynbos R2,500 (sleeps 6) • Major credit cards accepted • Pool • Wireless Lan, DSTV, DVD & Stereo • Ceiling fans • German spoken • Owners Georg & Dorothee Kirchner • georg.kirchner@dmnwines.co.za • www.dmnwines.co.za • S 33° 41' 25" E 19° 01' 42" • **T +27 (0)21-868-2393** • F +27 (0)21-868-2392

Move back in time – with all mod cons like washing machines, DSTV and DVD. Experience farm life in charming Cape Dutch thatched cottages on a historic wine farm, where original buildings date back to 1692. The area is a biosphere rich in fynbos; the three fully equipped self-catering cottages (from one-bedroomed to a refurbished larger cottage, sleeping six) enjoy beautiful views over Paarl valley. (See also A–Z section.)

Grande Roche Hotel Plantasie Street, Paarl • TGCSA 5-star hotel; Satour 5-star silver • 28 rooms • Seasonal rates: terrace suites R3,350–±R4,645 per suite B&B; duplex suites R2,915–R4,215 per suite B&B • Major credit cards accepted • Bosman's Restaurant & Bistro Allegro • Conferences • Fitness centre • Masseur on request • Sauna & steam room • 2 heated pools • TV • Air-conditioning • Horse riding, hot air ballooning (in season) and golf nearby • French, German, Italian & Swedish spoken • GM Anja Bosken • reserve@granderoche.co.za • www.granderoche.co.za • S 33° 45' 02" E 18° 57' 35" • **T +27 (0)21-863-5100** • F +27 (0)21-863-2220

A member of the Mantis Collection, this gracious 5-star estate hotel is a legend for luxury, attention to detail, beautiful gardens and award-winning culinary delights. Set in vineyards against the back-drop of Paarl Rock, it's an ideal base for exploring the Cape. Relax at the pools, go cycling, visit the fitness centre, enjoy excellent golf nearby or tour the numerous wine farms in close proximity. Named 5th best resort in Africa and 29th best property in the world by *Condé Nast Traveler* 2009. (See also Restaurants section.)

Marianne Wine Estate see under Stellenbosch

Robertson

Ballinderry, The Robertson Guest House 8 Le Roux Street, Robertson ▪ TGCSA 4-star guest house; Portfolio luxury ▪ 7 rooms ▪ Low season: double R375–R590 pps B&B, single R500–R750 B&B; High season: R420–R680 pps B&B; single R650–R900 B&B ▪ Major credit cards accepted ▪ Restaurant for stay-over guests ▪ Pool ▪ DSTV ▪ Air-conditioning & ceiling fans ▪ Free WIFI ▪ Off-street parking ▪ Flemish/Dutch, French & German spoken ▪ Owners Luc & Hilde Uyttenhove ▪ info@ballinderryguesthouse.com ▪ www.ballinderryguesthouse.com ▪ S 33° 48′ 02.40″ E 19° 53′ 13.58″ ▪ **T +27 (0)23-626-5365** ▪ F +27 (0)86-742-8692

Relish fine wines and delectable food at this contemporary guest house in the heart of Robertson, where hands-on Belgian owners, Luc and Hilde, pamper guests with personal service. The thatched villa in a large and tranquil tropical garden offers five double rooms and two pool suites. Near the region's best-known wineries and an 18-hole golf course. Champagne breakfast included in room rates; dinner reservations essential.

Fraai Uitzicht 1798 Klaas Voogds East, on Route 62 between Robertson & Montagu ▪ TGCSA 4-star guest house & AA Quality Assured Superior Accom-modation (2003–'10) ▪ 9 units consisting of luxury cottages & garden suites ▪ Double from R530 pps B&B; single from R800 B&B ▪ Major credit cards accepted ▪ Restaurant ▪ Pool ▪ DSTV in cottages ▪ Air-conditioning, fireplace & underfloor heating ▪ Two night 'Klaas Voogds Experience' package includes 7-course fine dine & wine dégustation menu, game drive as well as maze walk in botanical garden ▪ German, Xhosa & Zulu spoken ▪ Owner Sandra & Karl Uwe Papesch ▪ info@fraaiuitzicht.com ▪ www.fraaiuitzicht.com ▪ S 33° 47′ 43.23″ E 20° 00′ 17.87″ ▪ **T +27 (0)23-626-6156** ▪ F +27 (0)86-662-5265

Unwind and rejuvenate on this historic wine farm in the Langeberg hills. Cottages and suites amidst vineyards and orchards offer spectacular views of Robertson valley, and extensive recent renovation and refurbishment ensures a luxurious stay. Enjoy the view from an outside shower, eat at the award-winning restaurant, walk in the vineyards and explore the valley's oldest cellar, with original wine-making equipment. Game drives available nearby. (See also Restaurants & A–Z sections.)

Jan Harmsgat Country House On the R60 between Ashton and Swellendam ▪ TGCSA 5-star guest house ▪ Fair Trade accredited; Fedhasa ▪ 10 rooms ▪ Seasonal rates: double R900–R1,230 pps B&B, single R780–R1,090 B&B ▪ Visa & MasterCard accepted ▪ Restaurant 1723 ▪ Conferences ▪ Pool ▪ TV ▪ Air-conditioning/ceiling fans in some rooms ▪ Orchard walks ▪ Indigenous wildlife ▪ Acclaimed preserves ▪ Owners Willie & Camron Malherbe ▪ reservations@janharmsgat.com ▪ www.janharmsgat.com ▪ S 33° 56′ 48″ E 20° 12′ 58″ ▪ **T +27 (0)23-616-3407** ▪ F +27 (0)86-523-9284

Relive the past in charm and comfort. Dating back to 1723, this 5-star guest house, set among nut, fruit and olive trees, has been revitalised to retain its rich heritage while satisfying contemporary needs. Authentic Overberg style blends with space and elegance; original metre-thick walls and yellowwood combine with modern conveniences; and deliciously indulgent meals from owner/head chef Camron Malherbe will tempt you back. Awarded the Fair Trade in Tourism S.A. Trademark. (See also Restaurants section.)

Kingsriver Guest House see under McGregor

Pat Busch Private Nature Reserve Bergendal Farm, Klaas Voogds West, Breede River Valley, Robertson ▪ Sleeping 46 people in variety of cottages ▪ Self-catering ▪ Rates from R175–R350 pp ▪ Major credit cards accepted ▪ Conferences/functions ▪ Air-conditioning / ceiling fans in some cottages ▪ Wine tasting & cellar tours ▪ 4x4 route ▪ Hiking ▪ Swimming & fishing in mountain dams ▪ Birding ▪ Game drives ▪ Massages. ▪ German spoken ▪ Owners Stephan & Lindi Busch ▪ cottages@patbusch.co.za ▪ www.patbusch.co.za ▪ S 33° 46′ 34″ E 19° 59′ 47″ ▪ **T +27 (0)23-626-2033** ▪ F +27 (0)86-573-2156

A world in one valley, part of a 2 000 ha pristine mountain reserve on the fynbos-covered kloofs and slopes of the Langeberg, just beyond Robertson and 1.5 hours from Cape Town. Great rates for self-catering accommodation in comfortable cottages, larger farmhouse and luxury air-conditioned units with spa baths. Hiking trails, dams for swimming and fishing, birding, game drives, wine tastings and cellar tours.

Rosendal Winery & Wellness Retreat Robertson Wine Valley, between Robertson & Ashton on the R60, known as Route 62 ▪ TGCSA 4-star guesthouse ▪ 8 rooms ▪ Low season: R499–R599 pps B&B; High season: R730–R795 pps B&B ▪ Visa & MasterCard accepted ▪ Spa & Wellness Centre ▪ Boutique shop ▪ Conferences ▪ Restaurant ▪ Wine tasting ▪ Pool ▪ Ceiling fans ▪ Norwegian spoken ▪ Owners Geir & Sissel Tellefsen ▪ info@rosendalwinery.com ▪ www.

rosendalwinery.com ▪ S 33° 48′7.8″ E 019° 59′ 19.0″
▪ **T +27 (0)23-626-1570** ▪ F +27 (0)23-626-1571

Shed stress at this serene haven providing personal service, a wine bar and restaurant fusing global cuisine with African inspiration — plus grape-based treatments at the in-house spa and wellness centre. Eight en-suite rooms in the original farm house and new manor house, elegantly furnished with colonial pieces, overlook vineyards, pool or beautiful garden. A relaxing getaway and ideal base for Breede River excursions and wine tastings. (See also Restaurants & A–Z sections.)

The Robertson Small Hotel 58 Van Reenen Street, Robertson ▪ TGCSA 5-star hotel ▪ 10 rooms ▪ Seasonal rates: from R850–R1,450 pps B&B ▪ Major credit cards accepted ▪ Reuben's at The Robertson ▪ 2 pools ▪ Flat screen TV ▪ DVD player ▪ iPod docking station ▪ Wireless Internet ▪ Complimentary mini-bar contents ▪ Electronic safes in rooms ▪ Air-conditioning ▪ Wheelchair-friendly with suite specifically for the disabled ▪ Owners Tim Rands, Gys Naude & Marc Kent ▪ GM Riaan Kruger ▪ reservations@ therobertsonsmallhotel.com ▪ www. therobertsonsmallhotel.com ▪ S 33° 48′ 00.8″ E 19° 52 47.6″ ▪ **T +27 (0)23-626-7200** ▪ F +27 (0)23-626-1680

Chic sophistication meets Old World charm at this genuinely hospitable 5-star country retreat, a 'family of three' comprising a Victorian manor house (a national monument built in 1909); relaxing stable suites and cool, crisp poolside suites. Ten air-conditioned luxury rooms, linked by natural shades and textures, fuse eclectic yet comfortable furnishings with a sense of space, and are fitted with the latest business-friendly technology. (See also Restaurants section.)

Route 62
Les Hauts de Montagu see under Montagu

Montagu Country Hotel see under Montagu

Somerset West
Eikendal Lodge see under Stellenbosch

Lyngrove Country House see under Stellenbosch

Somerton Manor Guesthouse 13 Somerset Street, Bridgewater, Somerset West ▪ TGCSA 4-star guesthouse ▪ 12 rooms ▪ Seasonal rates: double R440–R600 pps B&B; single R595–R725 B&B ▪ Major credit cards accepted ▪ Conferences ▪ Heated pool ▪ Jacuzzi ▪ Sauna ▪ Spa ▪ Gymnasium ▪ TV ▪ Free Wi-Fi Internet ▪ Air-conditioning & ceiling fans ▪ Dutch & German spoken ▪ Owner Antonie van den Hurk ▪ info@somerton.co.za ▪ www.somerton.co.za ▪ S 34° 09′92.7″ E 018° 51′ 21.57″ ▪ **T +27 (0)21-851-4682** ▪ F +27 (0)21-851-4672

Styled with Cape Dutch elegance, blending old-world charm with modern facilities. Luxurious en-suite bedrooms; Jacuzzi, sauna, and heated-swimming pool; gym to keep toned. Wine from the cellar to enjoy in the tranquil garden, lapa, or on the veranda. A golfer's paradise: 20 courses nearby and reduced green fees at Erinvale golf club. 30 minutes from Cape Town international airport, with easy access to major tourist attractions.

Stellenbosch
Asara Wine Estate & Hotel Polkadraai Road (M12), Stellenbosch ▪ Relais & Chateaux; TGCSA 5-star hotel ▪ 29 deluxe rooms, 4 courtyard rooms & 3 suites ▪ Seasonal rates from R2,000–R3,750 per room/suite B&B ▪ Major credit cards accepted ▪ All bedrooms have mini bar, hairdryer, satellite TV/DVD, telephone, tea & coffee making facilities and electronic safe ▪ Air-conditioning ▪ Pool, steam bath & massage ▪ Raphael's Restaurant ▪ Sansibar & Grand Ballroom for events & conferences ▪ Weddings ▪ Deli & Confectionary ▪ Shopping emporium with premium table & kitchenware, Asara clothing, gifts ▪ Wine tasting ▪ German spoken ▪ Owner Markus Rahmann ▪ reservations@asara.co.za ▪ www.asara.co.za ▪ S 33° 56′ 35.00″ E 018° 48′ 31.00″ ▪ **T +27 (0)21-888-8000**

More than a hotel: a 5-star, Relais & Chateaux experience. This superbly fitted, chandelier-adorned lakeside hotel on a working wine estate provides luxury, tranquility and warm hospitality against a spectacular backdrop of rolling vineyards and mountains. Ballroom for events/conferences, gourmet and casual restaurants, 'Belle Époque' cigar/whisky lounge and 'arcade' with winetasting centre, inviting deli-cum-confectionary and deluxe kitchen showroom. 4km from Stellenbosch and 20 from CPT International. (See also Restaurants & A–Z sections.)

Caledon Villa 7 Neethling Street, Stellenbosch ▪ TGCSA 4-star guest house ▪ Portfolio 'great comfort' ▪ National monument ▪ 15 rooms ▪ Double R490–R650 pps B&B; single R650–R850 B&B ▪ Visa & MasterCard accepted ▪ Conferences ▪ Pool ▪ TV ▪ Air-conditioning / ceiling fans ▪ Wireless & Internet ▪ Dutch & German spoken ▪ Owners Johan & Ode Krige ▪ info@caledonvilla.co.za ▪ www.caledonvilla.co.za ▪ S 33° 56′ 15″ E 18° 51′55″ ▪ **T/ F +27 (0)21-883-8912**

Go walkabout from this splendid Edwardian villa and explore the historic heart of Stellenbosch, with its restaurants, shops and art galleries. Delight in the ambience of the century-old house, which reflects the owners' in-depth research in history, culture, genealogy, wine and art. Relax on the roof terrace, enjoying the colourplay of sunset on the mountains, and if planning outings and tours, expect expert assistance.

Clouds Estate Guesthouse & Self-catering Chalets Clouds Estate, Helshoogte Road (R310), Stellenbosch ▪ TGCSA 5-star guesthouse & 4-star chalets ▪ 5 luxury suites + 4 self-catering chalets ▪ Suites 1 May–30 Sep: R900–R1,500 for 2 persons sharing B&B, single supplement R200; 1 Oct–30 Apr: R1,200–R2,900 for 2 persons sharing B&B, single supplement R300 ▪ Chalets: seasonal rates from R850–R1,100 for 2 adults + 2 kids ▪ Major credit cards accepted ▪ Wedding venue: 70–100 guests, chapel (seats up to 150) ▪ Conferences ▪ High tea ▪ TV ▪ Air-conditioning ▪ 2 pools ▪ Surrounded by excellent restaurants & wine estates ▪ Walks, mountain biking, easy access to 15 golf courses ▪ Owners Bernard & Petro Immelman ▪ info@cloudsestate.co.za ▪ www.cloudsestate.co.za ▪ S 33° 55' 23.9" E 018° 55' 29.7" ▪ **T +27 (0)21-885-1819** ▪ F +27 (0)21-885-2829

Set at the highest point of the Helshoogte Pass, Clouds Estate is a place of 'just being', with panoramic views over the mountain-fringed Banhoek valley. Uncluttered décor encourages relaxation, creating a tranquil Mediterranean-inspired sense of space that permeates both guesthouse and four delightful guest chalets, fully fitted for self-catering. At five-star Clouds Villa, balconies from stylish en-suite bedrooms make the most of the breathtaking views. (See also A–Z section.)

Delaire Graff Lodges & Spa Delaire Graff Estate, R310, Helshoogte Pass, Banhoek Valley, Stellenbosch ▪ TGCSA 5-star lodge ▪ 10 lodges ▪ Seasonal rates: Deluxe lodges (x4) R7,150–R9,350; Luxury lodges (x4) R7,950–R10,400; Presidential lodge R16,200–R21,200 & Owners R20,250–R26,500 ▪ Major credit cards accepted ▪ Delaire Graff & Indochine Restaurants ▪ Art collection ▪ Conferences ▪ Private cinema ▪ Spa ▪ Gym ▪ Each lodge has private heated pool, butler's kitchen, en-suite bedrooms & separate sitting area ▪ Amenities include LED flat screen TV, wireless internet, iPod docking station & use of iPad ▪ Air-conditioning ▪ Owner Laurence Graff ▪ lodge.reservations@delaire.co.za ▪ www.delaire.co.za ▪ S 33° 55' 236" E 18° 55' 207" ▪ **T +27 (0)21-885-8160** ▪ F +27 (0)86-626-4403

Luxury meets serenity in a world-class destination. Centred around a main lodge with state-of-the-art spa, gym, private cinema, meeting facilities and Asian-inspired restaurant, ten superbly understated lodges offer an enticing, all-encompassing experience on a working wine estate. Windows overlook Stellenbosch valley to far-distant Table Mountain; sink-into-comfort interiors boast every current convenience (including a butler's kitchen) and an art collection personally selected by owner Laurence Graff. (See also Restaurants & A–Z sections.)

Eendracht Hotel & Self-catering 161 Dorp Street, Stellenbosch ▪ TGCSA 3-star hotel ▪ Superior –

small inn/hotel ▪ SATSA GreenStay 4-star ▪ 13 rooms; also three fully serviced, semi self-catering units in 1928 listed house ▪ Seasonal rates: double R469–R569 pps B&B; single R639–R799 B&B ▪ Major credit cards accepted ▪ Restaurant ▪ Pool ▪ TV ▪ Air-conditioning ▪ Free Wi-Fi ▪ Owner Daniel Lutz ▪ info@eendracht-hotel.com ▪ www.eendracht-hotel.com ▪ S 33° 56' 19.13" E 18° 51' 46.15" ▪ **T +27 (0)21-883-8843** ▪ F +27 (0)21-883-8842

Experience the historic ambience of Dorp Street in the comfort of a delightfully located owner-run boutique hotel next to the Village Museum. Award-winning service; friendly coffee bar offering breakfast, light lunch and traditional SA treats. Within easy walking distance of more than 60 restaurants, antique shops, museums, and art galleries. Centrally placed for the Stellenbosch Wine Route, with easy access to over 10 golf courses. AA Accommodation Award: winner in small hotel/inn category 2009 & '10.

Eikendal Lodge Eikendal Vineyards, R44, between Stellenbosch & Somerset West ▪ TGCSA 4-star lodge; AA Quality Assured 'Superior' Small Country Retreats ▪ 9 rooms ▪ Seasonal rates: from R630–R1,180 pps B&B; single from R565–R1,050 B&B ▪ Major credit cards accepted ▪ Restaurant ▪ Conferences ▪ Pool ▪ Hiking/jogging trails ▪ Fly fishing ▪ Complimentary cellar tours & wine tasting ▪ Boutique shop ▪ Willie Haas cheetah outreach facility ▪ German TV ▪ Free Wireless Internet ▪ Air-conditioning ▪ Safe ▪ Owner Ruedi Saager ▪ info@eikendallodge.co.za ▪ www.eikendallodge.co.za ▪ S 34° 00' 51.16" E 18° 49' 42.42" ▪ **T +27 (0)21-855-3617** ▪ F +27 (0)21-855-3862

Recharge in country-style luxury, experiencing a welcoming Winelands blend of fine wines and hospitality. Nine spacious en-suite rooms, each with private terrace, are surrounded by 'royalty', with noble cultivars at their door. Breakfast al fresco against the backdrop of the Helderberg; enjoy complimentary snacks and wine every evening. Meet cheetah cubs (seasonal); learn to fly-fish; hike through unspoiled *fynbos*; or take an enlightening cellar tour. (See also A–Z section.)

Hawksmoor House Matjieskuil Farm, R304, Klipheuwel Road, Stellenbosch ▪ 16 rooms ▪ Seasonal rates: double R1,500–R1,950 per room B&B; single R1,000–R1,450 B&B ▪ Visa, MasterCard & American Express accepted ▪ Pool ▪ Antiques ▪ French & German spoken ▪ Owners Mark Borrie & Simon Olding ▪ reservations@hawksmoor.co.za ▪ www.hawksmoor.co.za ▪ **T +27 (0)21-884-4815** ▪ F +27 (0)21-884-4816

If you enjoy spectacular sunsets, wine by candlelight, an owl outside your window, friendly dogs — and don't mind sharing the pool with the occasional disoriented frog — you'll love this tranquil Cape Dutch retreat. Set on a 220-hectare wine farm overlooking Table Mountain, Hawksmoor has been meticulously restored and beautifully decorated with antiques. Relax with an in-room massage and you'll not want to tear yourself away. (See also A–Z section.)

Laibach Vineyards Lodge Laibach Vineyards, R44 Klapmuts Road, Stellenbosch ▪ TGCSA 4-star self-catering ▪ 5 apartments ▪ Double R900 per room; single R700 ▪ Major credit cards accepted ▪ Pool ▪ LCD satellite TV ▪ Ceiling fans ▪ Owners Laibach family ▪ info@laibachwines.com ▪ www.laibachwines.com ▪ S 33°50'41.67" E 18°51'43.88" ▪ **T +27 (0)21-884-4511** ▪ F +27 (0)21-884-4848

Chill out among organic vines on a 50 ha wine farm. Spacious, comfortable self-catering apartments, each with en-suite bathroom with shower, open on to a deck with sweeping views. Taste wines, walk in the vineyards, mountain bike, or laze at the pool. Only 15 minutes from Stellenbosch and Paarl, 20 from Franschhoek and 40 from Cape Town. Golf courses, restaurants and wine estates within easy reach. (See also A–Z section.)

Lyngrove Country House Lyngrove Wines and Guesthouse, Raithby-Annandale Road, Raithby, Stellenbosch ▪ TGCSA 5-star guest house ▪ 9 rooms ▪ Seasonal rates: double R1,200–R1,900 per room B&B; single R700–R1,150 per room B&B ▪ Major credit cards accepted (excl. Diners Club) ▪ Conferences & meetings ▪ Functions & weddings ▪ Wine tasting & sales by appointment only ▪ Billiards room with bar ▪ Pool ▪ Tennis court with floodlights ▪ Satellite TV ▪ Air-conditioning ▪ Wireless Internet access ▪ lyngrove@iafrica.com ▪ www.lyngrove.co.za ▪ S 34°00'43.2" E 018°47'33.8" ▪ **T +27 (0)21-842-2116** ▪ F +27 (0)21-842-2118

Find peace on the patio of a charming country house, surrounded by vineyards and breathtaking mountains. Just 30 minutes from Cape Town airport and deep in the Winelands, this 5-star getaway with English colonial-style overtones, individually decorated en-suite bedrooms, comfortable lounge, billiards room and braai area is a perfect place to relax, glass of Lyngrove wine in hand. Full breakfast; lunch and dinner by arrangement. (See also A–Z section.)

Majeka House 26-32 Houtkapper Street, Paradyskloof, Stellenbosch ▪ TGCSA 5-star country house ▪ 22 rooms ▪ Low season: double from R820–R1,230 pps B&B, single from R1,225–R1,795 B&B; High season: double from R1,045–R1,550 pps B&B, single from R1,575–R2,300 B&B ▪ Major credit cards accepted ▪ Makaron Restaurant ▪ Business centre & boardroom ▪ Library ▪ 2 pools + 1 heated indoor pool ▪ Sanctuary Spa with full range of treatments, sauna, steamroom & fitness centre ▪ In room facilities include: DSTV, DVD player, free Wi-Fi, safe, laundry service & air-conditioning ▪ Secure onsite parking ▪ French spoken ▪ Owner Karine Dequeker ▪

reservations@majekahouse.co.za ▪ www.majekahouse.co.za ▪ S 33°58'04.07" E 18°51'39.64" ▪ **T +27 (0)21-880-1549** ▪ F +27 (0)21-880-1550

Spoil yourself in Stellenbosch in a graceful garden setting, 5 minutes from the town centre. Whether in a spacious en-suite room or the private, fully-equipped Villa, Majeka House marries past elegance with modern luxury — and a French touch. Linger over gourmet meals at the restaurant; shed kilos in the gym; swim (the roof in the heated indoor pool retracts); or indulge in soothing spa treatments.

Marianne Wine Estate Marianne Wine Estate, Valley Road, off the R44, between Stellenbosch & Klapmuts ▪ TGCSA 4-star B&B ▪ 4 en-suite superior loft apartments; luxury 3-double-bedroom manor house & honeymoon suite, as a whole, fully catered or separate ▪ Seasonal rates: double R750–R1,990 per room B&B; single occupancy R590–R1,190 B&B ▪ Major credit cards accepted ▪ Olivello Restaurant ▪ Conferences ▪ Pool & Braai ▪ Satellite TV ▪ Wireless Internet ▪ Air-conditioning ▪ Wine tasting & tours ▪ French & German spoken ▪ Owner Dauriac family ▪ info@mariannewinefarm.co.za ▪ www.mariannewinefarm.co.za ▪ **T +27 (0)21-875-5040** ▪ F +27 (0)21-875-5036

Unwind in the foothills of the Simonsberg, at this spacious 4-star guesthouse, surrounded by vineyards and citrus orchards. Savour estate-grown wines; sunbathe at the pool or amble through the vineyard; enjoy Mediterranean-style lunches at popular Olivello Restaurant in a restful setting among the vines. Just 35 minutes from Cape Town airport; perfectly situated for exploring the Winelands; numerous golf courses nearby. (See also Restaurants & A–Z sections.)

Morgenhof Manor House Morgenhof Wine Estate, Klapmuts Road (R44), Stellenbosch ▪ 5 en-suite rooms ▪ Double R495 pps B&B, R990 per room B&B; single R695 B&B ▪ No charge for tour guides with parties ▪ Major credit cards accepted ▪ Restaurant (lunch only) ▪ Coffee, tea & handmade biscotti offered in rooms ▪ Free wine tasting at Morgenhof ▪ Conferences ▪ Weddings/functions ▪ Pool ▪ 24 hour security on estate ▪ French & German spoken ▪ Owner Anne Cointreau ▪ info@morgenhof.com ▪ www.morgenhof.com ▪ S 33°53'38.5" E 18°51'39.2" ▪ **T +27 (0)21-889-2034** ▪ F +27 (0)21-889-5266

Absorb the relaxed food and wine lifestyle on a wine estate dating back to 1692, now offering accommodation in the refurbished, gabled manor house. Five en-suite double rooms (those upstairs are smaller and more informal) and well-equipped, self-catering kitchen. Cosy coffee shop breakfasts included and lunch available at the estate restaurant. An inviting tourist base, centrally located on the R44 just 4 km from Stellenbosch. (See also Restaurants & A–Z sections.)

Natte Valleij Farm Natte Valleij, Klapmuts Road (R44), between Stellenbosch and Paarl ▪ TGCSA 3-star

B&B & self-catering ▪ 2 cottages — both private with patio and BBQ — Vineyard cottage (sleeps 6) & Cellar cottage (sleeps 2 adults + 2 children) ▪ B&B R340–R360 pp; self-catering R220–R250 pp ▪ Owners Charles & Charlene Milner ▪ milner@intekom.co.za ▪ www.nattevalleij.co.za ▪ S 33° 50' 3.6" E 018° 52' 43.2" ▪ **T +27 (0)21-875-5171**

Step into the past. Ideal for families or a group of friends, this historic wine farm in the prime wine-making 'Muldersvlei bowl' area, with a magnificent Cape Dutch homestead, was the original land grant of the area. Relaxing rural ambience; secluded pool set in the large garden. Wonderful walking through vine-yards or the neighbouring game reserve where wilde-beest, zebra, springbok, bontebok, gemsbok and eland graze. (See also A–Z section.)

Oak Village B&B 7 Hamman Street, Stellenbosch ▪ TGCSA 3-star B&B ▪ 8 rooms ▪ Seasonal rates: double R900–R1,500 per room B&B; single R650–R1,200 B&B ▪ Also self-catering house (sleeps 4) R1,200–R1,800 ▪ Visa & MasterCard accepted ▪ TV ▪ Air-conditioning ▪ Tea/coffee making facilities ▪ Owners Dawid & Christelle Kriel ▪ oakvillage@volkskombuis.co.za ▪ www.oakvillage.co.za ▪ **T +27 (0)21-887-7889** ▪ F +27 (0)86-615-2095.

Hospitable Stellenbosch B&B (breakfasts are memorable) in quiet cul-de-sac near the town's historic core. Hosts Dawid & Christelle Kriel will make you feel at home, sharing their passion for food, wine and people. Or choose to self-cater in the next-door house, sharing the private garden and pool with B&B guests. (See also Restaurants section for De Volkskombuis & De Oewer.)

Ons Genot Country Lodge Bottelary Road (M23), Stellenbosch ▪ TGCSA 4-star guest house ▪ 9 rooms ▪ Low season: double from R390 pps B&B, single from R520 B&B; High season: double from R490 pps B&B, single from R750 B&B ▪ Visa & MasterCard accepted ▪ Restaurant ▪ Conferences ▪ Tennis court ▪ Pool ▪ TV ▪ Air-conditioning ▪ Ceiling fans ▪ Dutch, French & German spoken ▪ Owners Eric & Marleen Bovijn ▪ info@onsgenot.com ▪ www.onsgenot.com ▪ S 33° 52' 45.80" E 18° 47' 34.00" ▪ **T +27 (0)21-865-2233** ▪ F +27 (0)21-865-2250

'Where guests become friends' captures the warm, welcoming touch of this 4-star country retreat on the outskirts of Stellenbosch. Updated country fare at The Only One Restaurant adds a tasty touch and tours can be suggested to match individual interests. Luxury air-conditioned en-suite rooms with private terraces, attractive garden, TV, mini-bar, bathroom with bath and shower, Jacuzzi in the honeymoon suite. Conference room accommodates 20.

Sugarbird Manor Devon Valley Road, Stellenbosch ▪ TGCSA 4-star guesthouse ▪ 9 rooms ▪ Seasonal rates:

double R1,000–R1,450 per room B&B; single R700–R1,160 B&B ▪ Major credit cards accepted ▪ Conferences ▪ Weddings ▪ Hiking ▪ Pool ▪ DSTV ▪ Air-conditioning & ceiling fan ▪ Owner Ginny Povall ▪ reservations@sugarbirdmanor.co.za ▪ www.sugarbirdmanor.co.za ▪ S 33° 54' 18.5" E 18° 49' 25" ▪ **T +27 (0)21-865-2313** ▪ F +27 (0)21-865-2326

Comfortable meets chic; welcoming detail meets delightful destination. Eclectic in design, this 4-star guesthouse on a protea and wine farm adds a respectful twist of city sophistication to the Cape Wineland's country roots. Whether for a long holiday or short break, the 21 ha of gorgeous flowers and vineyards provides a perfect base for exploring the Winelands — or just chilling out in quiet luxury. (See also A–Z section for Botanica Wines.)

The Devon Valley Hotel Devon Valley Road, Devon Valley, Stellenbosch ▪ TGCSA 4-star hotel ▪ 50 rooms ▪ Low season: double from R635 pps B&B, single from R890 B&B; High season: double from R860 pps B&B, single from R1,250 B&B ▪ Major credit cards accepted ▪ Flavours Restaurant ▪ Conferences ▪ Communications centre with free Internet access ▪ Wireless Internet in main building ▪ Jacuzzi & 2 pools ▪ Children of all ages welcome ▪ Satellite TV ▪ Air-conditioning ▪ Boule/Petanque court ▪ Hiking trail ▪ Devon Valley Detour Transfers and day tours arranged on request ▪ German, Xhosa & Zulu spoken ▪ Owner Louis Group Hotels, Spa's & Vineyards ▪ info@devonvalleyhotel.com ▪ www.devonvalleyhotel.com ▪ S 33° 54' 12.64" E 18° 48' 53.03" ▪ **T +27 (0)21-865-2012** ▪ F +27 (0)21-865-2610

Enjoy handmade hospitality at this friendly hotel tucked away in a lush valley at the heart of the Stellenbosch Winelands, surrounded by SylvanVale working vineyard. Views from windows and terrace are spectacular; en-suite rooms blend style with comfort, and contemporary Cape cuisine is backed by an award–winning winelist. Savour a definitive collection of single malt whiskies: both wine and single malt tastings are available. Global Wine Capital's Best of Wine Tourisim Award in accommodation category 2010. Summit Hotels & Resorts 'Resort of the Year' 2010 by Preferred Hotel Group. Best Boutique Hotel finalist 2011 - South Africa, AA Travel Guide and American Express. (See also Restaurants section & A–Z for SylvanVale.)

The Wild Mushroom Boutique Hotel 39 Digteby Estate, Vlottenburg Road, Stellenbosch ▪ TGCSA 5-star hotel ▪ 6 rooms ▪ Seasonal rates: double R750–R1,300 pps B&B; single R1,300–R1,900 B&B ▪ Visa & MasterCard accepted ▪ Restaurant (full breakfast, and light lunch/dinner menu) ▪ Conferences ▪ Pool ▪ Plasma-screen TVs with DSTV ▪ Free Wi-Fi ▪ iPod-friendly music centres ▪ Air-conditioning & ceiling fans ▪ Owner Wynand Nel ▪ Manager Adriaan Smit (082-

749-8553) ▪ info@wildmushroom.co.za ▪ www.
wildmushroom.co.za ▪ S 33° 57' 31.52" E 18° 47' 47.
26" ▪ **T +27 (0)21-881-3586** ▪ F +27 (0)21-881-
3593

Unlock the world of gourmet mushrooms at this
unique Winelands boutique hotel. The first in the
world to offer mycotourism (a first-hand introduction
to cultivating and identifying edible exotic mushrooms), it blends information with luxury. Stylish
décor reflects specific species in colour and texture;
en-suite bedrooms have extra-length king-size beds
— and you can feast on gourmet mushrooms at a full
breakfast, light lunch and dinner. Nominated by Blue
Sky Publications in the UK as one of the Best Top Ten
Boutique Hotels in South Africa.

Zevenwacht Country Inn Zevenwacht Wine
Farm, Langverwacht Road, Kuils River ▪ TGCSA 4-star
country house ▪ 12 suites + 1 honeymoon suite
(deluxe), 7 three-bedroom cottages & 1 four-bed-
room self-catering chalet — 38 rooms in total ▪ Low
season: double from R315 pps B&B, single from R455
B&B; High season: double from R445 pps B&B, single
from R650 B&B ▪ Major credit cards accepted ▪ Restaurant ▪ Conferences ▪ Weddings ▪ Mangwanani Spa
▪ Gift shop ▪ Pool ▪ TV ▪ Air-conditioning ▪ Sauna ▪
Floodlit tennis court ▪ Picnics ▪ Cellar tours & wine
tasting ▪ MTB trials ▪ Xhosa spoken ▪ Owner Harold
Johnson ▪ info@zevenwacht.co.za ▪ www.
zevenwacht.co.za ▪ **T +27 (0)21-903-5123** ▪
F +27 (0)21-906-1570

A choice of accommodation on a multi-faceted
wine farm, from luxury suites in the Country Inn to
vineyard cottages and self-catering chalet with spectacular views of Table Bay and False Bay. Restaurant
in the historic manor house open daily for breakfast,
lunch & dinner; garden picnics also available. Facilities
for weddings, launches and conferences; cheesery,
wine tasting centre, gift shop, chef school, and African
Day Spa. Highly Recommended: Fine Country Estates.
(See also Restaurants & A–Z sections.)

Swellendam
Jan Harmsgat Country House see under
Robertson

Wellington
5 Mountains Lodge & Spa Bains Kloof Road,
Wellington ▪ intimate TGCSA 4-star country house &
AA highly recommended country style retreat ▪ 5
rooms, master suite and four en-suite cottages
accommodating 15 ▪ Seasonal rates: double R450–
R850 pps B&B, single R580–R650 B&B ▪ Visa &
MasterCard accepted ▪ Restaurant ▪ Conferences ▪
Pool ▪ Spa ▪ TV ▪ Air-conditioning ▪ Mini bar, tea /
coffee making facilities ▪ Owners Stuart & Louisa
McLachlan ▪ Manager Carole Rothery ▪ reservations@

5mountains.co.za ▪ www.5mountainslodge.com ▪
T +27 (0)21-864-3409 ▪ F +27 (0)21-873-7193

Luxury, tranquillity, and delicious food are corner-
stones of this 4-star Provençal-style sanctuary, set in
vineyards and manicured gardens and framed by
mountain scenery. A new multi-treatment spa now
adds to the attractions, encouraging guests to relax
under the skilful hands of professional staff. Combine
pampering with sightseeing, wine tours, mountain
biking, horse riding and walking, or simply chill out on
a sun-lounger beside the pool. (See also A–Z section.)

Bovlei Valley Retreat Bovlei Valley Retreat Estate,
Bovlei Road, Wellington ▪ TGCSA 4-star guesthouse ▪
7 rooms ▪ Seasonal rates: double R562–R750 pppn
B&B, single R850–R960 B&B ▪ Major credit cards
accepted ▪ Restaurant ▪ Pool ▪ TV ▪ DVD players ▪ Air-
conditioning/heating ▪ Owners Abbi & Lee Wallis ▪
info@bvr.co.za ▪ www.bvr.co.za ▪ S 33° 38'5.3" E
019° 3'36.88" ▪ **T/F +27 (0)21-864-1504**

You'll find a tea tray with home-made lavender
cookies in your room at this relaxing retreat at the
foot of the Limietberg, recently refurbished with no
loss of country hospitality. Added to the attraction of
mountains, vineyards and the scent of lavender, are
comforts like aircon/heating, fine linen, goose-down
duvets, luxury toiletries and colour TV – plus
appetising three-course set menus that change
every evening. (See also Restaurants section for The
Stone Kitchen & A–Z section for Dunstone Winery.)

Diemersfontein Country House Diemersfontein
Wine & Country Estate, R301 Jan van Riebeeck Drive,
Wellington ▪ TGCSA 4-star guest house ▪ 30 rooms ▪
Seasonal rates: double R650–R850 per room B&B; sin-
gle R450–R650 B&B ▪ Major credit cards accepted ▪
Seasons Restaurant ▪ Conferences ▪ Weddings ▪ Pool ▪
TV ▪ Air-conditioning/ceiling fan ▪ Wine tasting ▪
Horse riding ▪ Mountain biking ▪ Birding ▪ Owners
David & Susan Sonnenberg ▪ reception@
diemersfontein.co.za ▪ www.diemersfontein.co.za ▪
T +27 (0)21-864-5050 ▪ F +27 (0)21-864-2095

A gracious, tranquil haven, surrounded by
majestic mountain ranges, only 45 minutes from
Cape Town airport. Now a 4-star guest house, this
much-loved third generation family home is set
among tall palms and oaks, colourful flowerbeds
and manicured lawns. Taste country life in single
garden suites, cottages, or the historic manor house,
whether on holiday, conference or mini-break. A
perfect setting for romantic weddings. (See also
Restaurants & A–Z sections.)

Druk My Niet Wine Estate see under Paarl

Jacaranda Wine- and Guestfarm Old Hermon
Road, Voor Groenberg, Wellington ▪ 2 rooms in Manor
House & 2 cottage units ▪ Seasonal rates: double
R600-R650 per room B&B, single R500-R550 B&B ▪
No credit card facilities ▪ Lunch/dinner/picnics on

request ▪ Pool ▪ TV ▪ Wi-Fi hotspot ▪ Air-conditioning in cottages ▪ Ceiling fans ▪ French, German, Swiss-German & Mandarin spoken ▪ Owners René Reiser & Birgit Schmiederer-Reiser ▪ birgit@safinewines.co.za ▪ www.jacarandawines.co.za ▪ S 33° 36' 49.2" E 019° 0' 16.1" ▪ **T +27 (0)21-864-1235 or +27 (0)72-432-6716**

Welcoming wine farm offering lunch, dinner, picnics and wine tastings on request. Manor house guest rooms blend old world charm with a touch of Asia; charming cottage units have romantic bedrooms directly under the thatch, a private stoep, fully equipped kitchen and braai facilities. Reading room, tasting area and 15m pool at your disposal; biking, golf courses and the Winelands right at your doorstep. (See also A–Z section.)

Val du Charron Wine & Olive Estate Guesthouse Farm 256, Bovlei Road, Wellington ▪ TGCSA 4-star; AA Superior guesthouse ▪ 7 en-suite bedrooms & 2 family suites ▪ Rates – refer to website ▪ Major credit cards accepted ▪ Restaurant ▪ Conferences ▪ Weddings/functions ▪ Pool ▪ Air-conditioning ▪ Ceiling fans ▪ TV ▪ Library ▪ Games collection ▪ Wine tasting ▪ Cellar tours ▪ Walks ▪ Bass fishing ▪ Owner Val du Charron Wines (Pty) Ltd ▪ stay@vdcwines.com ▪ www.vdcwines.com ▪ S 33° 37' 28.14" E 019° 2' 55.32" ▪ **T +27 (0)21-873-1256** ▪ F +27 (0)86-535-4922 Relax in luxury on a working wine farm at the foot of Bainskloof, under an hour from Cape Town. This four-star guesthouse with spectacular views of Hawekwa Mountains, offers seven en-suite bedrooms and two family suites. Feast on a farmer's breakfast; tour the cellar, walk, swim, fish, explore the Winelands and Route 62 — or succumb to the appeal of the large library and games collection. (See also A–Z section.)

Disabled Access in SA Wineries

Now in its second decade, the guide's accessibility audit initiative is intended to verify that venues which are open to the public at set times, and aim to be disabled friendly, in fact are accessible — not only for wheelchairs but for all types of disability.

The initial audit project was carried out in stages in conjunction with disability consultant Guy Davies, and the results incorporated into successive editions as they became available. Practical difficulties intervened but, after a brief hiatus, the initiative was restarted.

This edition Guy and his Disability Solutions team again carried out the work, covering both new and recently upgraded venues. The results of their evaluations are incorporated into the relevant producer entries in the A–Z section of this book, as well as in the look-up tables which accompany the maps, in the form of the universally recognisable 'wheelchair' icon.

As before, wineries open only by appointment are excluded, as it is felt that in these cases visitors can ascertain their individual requirements when making an appointment.

While the team bases its assessments on local building regulations, it tries to be sensitive to the practical implications for each winery. In an agricultural/rural setting it can sometimes be quite a challenge to ensure that access is not compromised. Many tasting facilities occupy beautiful historic buildings, which were originally designed and built with no thought to accessibility, and it is acknowledged that providing good access can be a challenge for many wineries.

We would like to extend our appreciation and thanks to Guy, and invite readers who have comments or suggestions to contact him either through the guide's offices or directly on telephone +27 (0)21-872-1101, mobile +27 (0)83-289-1199 or email guy@disabilitysolutions.co.za.

In closing, it is important to emphasise that while the audits cover parking, the tasting area, toilet facilities and cellar tours, if offered, the focus is on the tasting area and, if this is accessible, the wheelchair icon is shown. Please phone ahead if in doubt.

Also bear in mind that wineries which are not flagged as accessible in the A–Z or the map tables do not necessarily have deficient or non-existent disabled facilities; it might simply be that we are not yet in a position to comment on them. Our intention remains to not only continue but if possible expand the present coverage of disabled facilities, and, as always, we welcome any suggestions on how to achieve this goal.

WINELANDS MAPS

The maps in this section show locales where wine is available for tasting/sale either at set times or by appointment. The larger-scale map below shows the areas covered by the maps, and the table starting on the next page lists some details for prospective visitors.

Areas covered by the maps

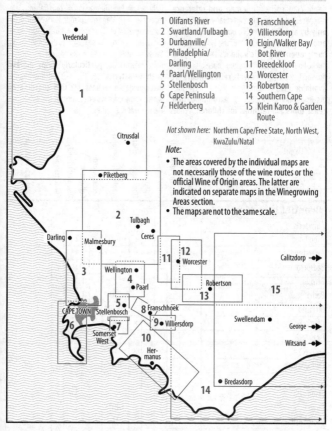

1 Olifants River
2 Swartland/Tulbagh
3 Durbanville/Philadelphia/Darling
4 Paarl/Wellington
5 Stellenbosch
6 Cape Peninsula
7 Helderberg
8 Franschhoek
9 Villiersdorp
10 Elgin/Walker Bay/Bot River
11 Breedekloof
12 Worcester
13 Robertson
14 Southern Cape
15 Klein Karoo & Garden Route

Not shown here: Northern Cape/Free State, North West, KwaZulu/Natal

Note:
• The areas covered by the individual maps are not necessarily those of the wine routes or the official Wine of Origin areas. The latter are indicated on separate maps in the Winegrowing Areas section.
• The maps are not to the same scale.

Some distances from Cape Town (kilometres)

Calitzdorp	370	Paarl	60	Tulbagh	120
Franschhoek	75	Robertson	160	Vredendal	300
Hermanus	120	Stellenbosch	45	Worcester	110

Key for maps

═══ Main access roads	R62 R60 Road numbers
─── Roads	Towns
······· Gravel roads	

Details of Locales Shown on Maps

The tables below are intended to facilitate winery visits by providing summary information about all the winetasting venues which are open to the public, either at set times or by appointment, and appear on our winelands maps. Venues are listed by region, and details provided include a **map grid-reference**, if applicable; whether the particular venue is **open only by appointment** (T); **open on Saturdays and/or Sundays** (✓ = at set times; T = by appointment); **open on public holidays** (✗ = closed all public holidays; otherwise assume open all or some holidays); and whether **meals/refreshments are available** (BYO = bring your own picnic). Other details include availability of **accommodation**, **cellar tours** and **facilities for children**. Venues

which are **friendly to individuals with reduced mobility**, as audited by our disability consultants, are highlighted. **Other languages spoken** (besides English and Afrikaans) are also noted (Danish = da, Dutch/Flemish = nl, French = fr, German = de, Hebrew = he, Hungarian = hu, Italian = it, Japanese = ja, Mandarin = mdr, Norwegian = nn, Portuguese = pt, Romanian = ro, Russian = ru, Setswana = tn, Spanish = sp, Swedish = sv, Swiss = gsw, isiXhosa = xh, isiZulu = zu). For more information, **particularly items marked with an asterisk**, see the A–Z and Restaurants/ Accommodation sections. For **GPS coordinates**, where known, for wineries open to the public, see the relevant A–Z entries.

	Grid reference	Open by appt. only	Open Saturdays	Open Sundays	Open public holidays	Meals/refreshments	Accomodation	Cellar tours	Disabled friendly	Child friendly	Languages spoken
Breedekloof Map											
Aufwaerts		T									
Avondrood			T			T/BYO*	✓	✓		✓	
Awendland		T						T			
Badsberg			✓		✗	T/BYO*		✓*	✓	✓	
Bergsig			✓			✓		T		✓	
Botha			✓			BYO		T			
Breëland		T*				T/BYO*	✓	T			
Dagbreek		T			✗	BYO		T			
De Breede		T									
Du Preez			✓		✗	BYO		T*	✓		
Du Toitskloof			✓			BYO		T	✓		de
Goudini			✓			✓		T			
Jason's Hill			✓*			✓		T	✓	✓	
Kirabo			T		✗	T/BYO		✓		✓	
Ladera Artisan		T*				T*		T			sp
Lateganskop								T	✓		
Lorraine					✗	T/BYO*		✓			
Merwida			✓				✓		✓		
Mountain Oaks		T						T			
Mountain Ridge					✗	BYO			✓		
Olifantsberg		T									
Opstal			✓	T		✓*		✓	✓	✓	
Rico Suter		T				T/BYO*	✓	T			de/fr/it
Seven Oaks		T									

	Grid reference	Open by appt. only	Open Saturdays	Open Sundays	Open public holidays	Meals/refreshments	Accomodation	Cellar tours	Disabled friendly	Child friendly	Languages spoken
Slanghoek			✓			T*		T	✓		de
TCB					x	BYO	✓	✓			
uniWines			✓			T/BYO*		T	✓*	✓	✓	
Waboomsrivier					x			T			
Cape Peninsula Map											
Ambeloui		T									
Beau Constantia		T*			x						
Buitenverwachting			✓		x	✓		T	✓		
Cape Point Vyds			✓	✓		✓			✓	✓	
Cape to Cairo		T									
Cheviot		T*			x						nl
Constantia Glen			✓	✓		✓					
Constantia Mist			✓	✓		BYO	✓		✓		
Constantia Uitsig			✓	✓		✓	✓		✓		
Eagles' Nest			✓	✓					✓		
Emineo		T									
Final Cut		T									
Groot Constantia			✓	✓		✓		✓	✓	✓	de/fr/nl
High Constantia			✓			T/BYO		✓			
Hout Bay Vyds		T						T		✓	de
Klein Constantia			✓		x				✓		fr/sv
Kling		T									
Mzoli's						✓					xh
Signal Hill			✓		x	✓		✓			fr
Steenberg			✓	✓		✓*	✓	✓	✓		
Vaughan Johnson											
Durbanville, Philadelphia & Darling Map											
Altydgedacht			✓			✓		T		✓	
Bloemendal			✓	✓		✓			✓		
Capaia			T	T	x			✓			de
Cloof			✓			✓		T	✓		
D'Aria			✓	✓		✓	✓				nl
Darling Cellars			✓					T	✓	✓	xh
De Grendel			✓	✓				T	✓		
De Vallei			✓	✓		✓		✓	✓		
Diemersdal			✓					T			
Durbanville Hills			✓	✓		✓		✓*	✓	✓	
Four Fields		T						T			
Franki's		T			x	T/BYO	✓	T			
Groote Post			✓	✓		T/BYO*		✓	✓	✓	

	Grid reference	Open by appt. only	Open Saturdays	Open Sundays	Open public holidays	Meals/refreshments	Accomodation	Cellar tours	Disabled friendly	Child friendly	Languages spoken
Hillcrest			✓	✓		✓		T			
Klein Roosboom			✓	✓		✓/BYO*		✓	✓		
Kronendal Boutique		T	✓			T*		T	✓		
Meerendal			✓	✓		✓		T	✓	✓	xh/zu
Nitida			✓	✓		✓			✓	✓	
Ormonde			✓			T/BYO		T*	✓	✓	
Phizante Kraal			✓								
Russo Family Vintners			T		✗			✓			
Signal Gun			✓			✓*					
Wines of Cape Town		T									
Withington			✓	✓							
Elgin, Walker Bay & Bot River Map											
Almenkerk			✓	T		T/BYO		✓			nl/fr
Arumdale Cool Climate		T*									
Ashbourne		T						T			
Ataraxia			✓	✓*							
Barry Gould		T				T	✓	T		✓	
Barton			✓			BYO*	✓	✓	✓		
Beaumont			✓			T*	✓	✓	✓		
Belfield		T						T			
Benguela Cove			✓*	✓*		BYO					
Birkenhead			✓	✓		✓/BYO		✓	✓	✓	
Blomendahl		T									de
Boschrivier De Villiers			✓	✓		✓/BYO	✓		✓		
Bouchard Finlayson			✓		✗	BYO		✓	✓		de/fr
Boutros Wine			✓								
Catherine Marshall		T				T		T			
COAV		T									
Creation			✓	✓		✓		✓	✓	✓	de/fr
Dispore Kamma		T						T			
Eerste Hoop		T*						T*			
Elgin Ridge		T*				✓/BYO*		T*			fr
Elgin Valley			T	T	✗						
Elgin Vintners		T				T*					
Feiteiras		T									pt
Gabriëlskloof			✓	✓		✓/BYO		T		✓	
Genevieve		T									
Glen Erskine		T				BYO		T			de
Goedvertrouw		T				T	✓			✓	
Hamilton Russell			✓					T			tn/xh

	Grid reference	Open by appt. only	Open Saturdays	Open Sundays	Open public holidays	Meals/refreshments	Accomodation	Cellar tours	Disabled friendly	Child friendly	Languages spoken
Hemelzicht		T									
Hermanuspietersfontein			✓	✓*		✓*	✓	T	✓		
Highlands Road			✓	✓		✓	✓	✓	✓	✓	
Hornbill			✓			✓		✓			
Iona			T		x			✓			
Keisseskraal			✓	✓		T/BYO*	✓	✓	✓	✓	de
La Vierge			✓	✓		✓		T	✓		fr
Luddite			T	T	T			✓*	✓		nl
Misty Mountains			✓			✓	✓	T			
Mount Babylon		T						T			
Newton Johnson			✓		x	✓			✓		
Oak Valley			✓	T			✓				it/fr
Paul Cluver			✓			✓/BYO*		✓			
Raka			✓			BYO		T			
Restless River		T*			x	T		T*			
Rivendell			✓	✓		✓				✓	
Robert Stanford			✓	✓		✓*				✓	
Ross Gower		T				T	✓	T			fr/de
Shannon		T									
South Hill			✓	✓		✓	✓		✓		
Southern Right			✓					✓	✓		
Spioenkop			T	T	x	BYO	✓	✓*		✓	fr/nl
Spookfontein		T			x		✓	T			
Springfontein			T*			BYO	✓	✓*			
Stanford Hills			✓		x	BYO	✓	✓	✓		
Sumaridge			✓	✓		✓				✓	
Thandi			✓	✓		✓/BYO			✓	✓	
Vaalvlei		T*					✓				
Valley Green			T	T		T/BYO*		T			
Whalehaven			✓	✓				T			
Wildekrans			✓	✓		BYO	✓	✓	✓		
William Everson		T						✓	T		
Wine Village			✓	✓					✓		
Franschhoek Map											
Akkerdal			✓		x		✓				
Allée Bleue			✓	✓		✓	✓	T	✓	✓	de
Anthonij Rupert			✓	✓		✓		✓			
Blueberry Hill		T					✓				
Boekenhoutskloof					x				✓		xh
Boschendal			✓	✓		✓		✓	✓	✓	

	Grid reference	Open by appt. only	Open Saturdays	Open Sundays	Open public holidays	Meals/refreshments	Accomodation	Cellar tours	Disabled friendly	Child friendly	Languages spoken
Cape Chamonix			✓	✓		✓	✓	T	✓		
Colmant		T*						T	✓		fr
Dieu Donné			✓	✓		✓		T*			
Eikehof		T						T			
Four Paws		T									
Franschhoek Cellar			✓	✓		✓/BYO			✓		
GlenWood			✓*	✓*		✓/BYO*		✓	✓		
Graham Beck			✓	✓					✓		
Grande Provence Heritage			✓	✓		✓	✓	✓*	✓		
Haut Espoir		T			✗			T	✓		
Haute Cabrière			✓	✓		✓		✓*	✓		Fr/De
Holden Manz			✓	✓		✓		✓	✓		de
La Bourgogne			✓				✓			✓	
La Bri			✓			✓/BYO*		✓			
La Chataigne			T	T	✗		✓				sv
La Chaumiere		T						T			
La Motte			✓			✓			✓	✓	xh
La Petite Ferme		T*			✗	✓	✓	✓			
La Petite Provence		T*									
La Petite Vigne			✓		✗		✓				
La Vigne		T						T			
Landau du Val		T									
Le Manoir de Brendel			✓	✓		T*	✓			✓	
Leopard's Leap			✓*								
Lynx			T	T	T	BYO		✓*			de/sp
Maison			✓	✓		✓					
Mont Rochelle			✓	✓		✓*	✓	✓			
Môreson			✓	✓		✓		✓	✓		
My Wyn			T	T	✗	T*		✓			
Plaisir de Merle			✓	T*		✓	T	✓	✓	✓	de
Rickety Bridge			✓	✓		✓	✓	✓	✓	✓	
Solms-Delta			✓	✓		✓		T			
Stony Brook			✓		✗		✓		✓		
The House of GM&Ahrens		T			✗	T		T			
Topiary			✓*			T/BYO		✓	✓		
Helderberg Map											
Aeternitas		T			✗			T			
Anatu		T			✗			T			fr/he
AntHill		T									
Anwilka		T			✗			T			

	Grid reference	Open by appt. only	Open Saturdays	Open Sundays	Open public holidays	Meals/refreshments	Accomodation	Cellar tours	Disabled friendly	Child friendly	Languages spoken
Avontuur			✓	✓		✓		T	✓		de/pt
Bayede!			✓	T	×	✓				✓	
BLANKbottle		T*									
Cape Classics		T									
Conspirare		T									
Croydon			T			T*		T	✓	✓	
Dellrust		T				✓					
Eikendal			✓	✓		✓*	✓	✓	✓	✓	de
Elberti		T									
Equitania		T			×		✓				
Grangehurst			✓	✓			✓				
Hathersage		T*			×	BYO*					
Heron Ridge		T			×	T*		T			
Idiom		T*									it
Journey's End		T*				T/BYO*	✓	T			
JP Bredell			T								
Ken Forrester			✓	✓*		✓*	✓		✓		
Longridge			✓			✓					
Lourensford			✓	✓		✓		✓			
Lyngrove		T					✓				
Micu Narunsky		T									
Miravel		T				T	✓				nl/fr
Moordenaarskop		T						T			
Morgenster			✓	✓		✓					
Onderkloof			T		×	T	✓	✓*			
Pfeifer's Boutique		T									gsw/de
Post House			✓		×	BYO	✓	✓	✓		
Revelation		T*						T*			
Ridgemor			✓	✓	×	BYO	✓				
Romond		T*					✓	T*			
Somerbosch			✓	✓		✓		T	✓	✓	
Stonewall		T*				T					
The Wnry of Gd Hope		T			×						fr/sv
Vergelegen			✓	✓		✓		✓*	✓	✓	
Waterkloof			✓	✓		✓		T	✓		
Waterstone		T			×		✓	T			
Wedderwill		T*			×	BYO	✓	T			de
Yonder Hill			✓*		×				✓		
Zandberg			✓	✓		✓	✓				

	Grid reference	Open by appt. only	Open Saturdays	Open Sundays	Open public holidays	Meals/refreshments	Accomodation	Cellar tours	Disabled friendly	Child friendly	Languages spoken
Klein Karoo & Garden Route Map											
Axe Hill		T						T			
Barrydale - SCV			✓			BYO		T			
Bergwater			✓			T/BYO	✓	T	✓		
Boplaas			✓					T			
Calitzdorp			✓			T/BYO		T			
De Krans			✓			✓/BYO*			✓	✓	
Domein Doornkraal			✓			✓*	✓				
Du'SwaRoo		T*			×						
Excelsior Vlakteplaas											
Garden Route			✓						✓		
Grundheim			✓						✓		
Herold			✓			✓/BYO*	✓	✓	✓	✓	
Hillock			✓	✓		✓/BYO	✓	✓			
Jakkalsvlei			✓			✓/BYO					
Joubert-Tradauw			✓			✓		✓	✓	✓	
Karusa			✓			✓			✓		
Ladismith - SCV			✓			✓		T			
LuKa											
Mimosa			✓	✓		✓	✓		✓	✓	de/gsw
Mons Ruber			✓				✓				
Montagu Wine & Spirits			✓						✓		
Montagu Wine Cellar			✓		×	BYO		T*	✓		
Oudtshoorn Cellar - SCV			✓			BYO		T	✓		
Packwood					×	T*	✓				
Peter Bayly		T						T			
Quinta do Sul		T									
SoetKaroo			✓						✓		de
Star Hill			✓	✓		✓	✓	T		✓	
The Goose		T				T	✓				
TTT			✓	T		BYO		✓			
Withoek		T					✓	T			
KwaZulu-Natal Map											
Abingdon		T*	✓	✓		✓*		✓	T		
Highgate			✓	✓		✓				✓	de
Northern Cape, Free State & North West Map											
Bezalel-Dyasonsklip			✓			✓*		✓		✓	nl
Die Mas van Kakamas			T	T		T/BYO*	✓	✓*		✓	
Douglas					×			T			
Hartswater								T			

	Grid reference	Open by appt. only	Open Saturdays	Open Sundays	Open public holidays	Meals/refreshments	Accomodation	Cellar tours	Disabled friendly	Child friendly	Languages spoken
Landzicht GWK					×	T		T*			
Orange River Wine Cellars			✓		×			✓*	✓		
Olifants River Map											
Bellpost		T						T			
Cape Rock		T				BYO		T			
Cecilia		T									
Cederberg			✓			BYO	✓				
Driehoek Family		T				BYO	✓			✓	
Fryer's Cove			✓			T/BYO		✓			
Klawer Wine Cellars			✓		×	BYO			✓	✓	
Lutzville Vyds			✓			✓		✓	✓		de
Matzikama		T									
Namaqua			✓			✓*		✓*	✓	✓	
Seal Breeze			✓			T/BYO		✓	✓	✓	
Sir Lambert			✓			BYO	✓			✓	
Stellar						BYO		T			
Stoumann's			T		×	T		✓			
Teubes Family			✓	✓		BYO	✓	T			
Tierhoek			T		×	BYO	✓	✓			
Vleiland		T*				BYO					
Wilgenhof		T									
Paarl & Wellington Map											
5 Mountains Lodge	G2		✓	✓		✓	✓	T			
African Terroir	C1	T*			×	BYO		T*			fr
Alkmaar	G2		✓					T			
Andreas	G1	T*			×		✓	T			sv
Anura	C7		✓	✓		✓		✓	✓		de
Appollis Fairtrade	G1	T						T			
Arra	C8		✓			BYO				✓	
Avondale	F6	T*						T	✓		
Avondvrede	C8	T				T		T			
Ayama	B2	T				T/BYO					it
BABISA	D7		✓	✓		✓*		✓			lt
Babylonstoren	D8		✓	✓		✓*	✓				
Backsberg	D8		✓	✓		✓/BYO		T	✓		
Bergheim	E6	T									
Bernheim	D1, E3	T			×			T	✓		
Black Pearl	D5	T*						T*	✓		
Blouvlei Wyne	G2		T		×			✓*			de
Boland	E4		✓					T	✓		

	Grid reference	Open by appt. only	Open Saturdays	Open Sundays	Open public holidays	Meals/refreshments	Accomodation	Cellar tours	Disabled friendly	Child friendly	Languages spoken
Bosman Family	G1	T						T			
Bovlei	G2		√					T	√		
Calais	F4	T					√				
Crows Nest	D3		T	T	T	T/BYO		√		√	
Damarakloof	A7	T*									
De Villiers	E6	T									
De Zoete Inval	E6	T									
Diemersfontein	F2		√	√		√	√	T			
Diners Club Bartho Eksteen	C3	T				T/BYO		T		√	
Domaine Brahms	C3	T			T			T			
Doolhof	H1		√	√		√*	√	T	√		
Doran	D1	T									
Druk My Niet	F4	T			×	T/BYO	√	T			de
Dunstone	H1		√	√		√	√	√		√	
Fairview	D6		√	√		√			√		
Freedom Hill	F7		√	√					√		
Glen Carlou	D7		√	√		√		T	√	√	de
Groot Parys	E5	T									nl
Hawksmoor	A7	T*					√				fr/de/ja
Helpmekaar	F2	T*			×			T*			
Hildenbrand	G2		√	√*		√	√		√		de
Imbuko	F4		T		×	T*					
Jacaranda	F1		√			T*	√				fr/de/mdr
Jacques Smit	F2	T						T	√		
Joostenberg	A8		√	√		√		T	√	√	
Juno	E5		√			√					
Klein Optenhorst	H1	T									
Klein Parys	E5		√			√/BYO*	√*	√		√	
Kleine Draken	D6				×	T*		T	√		
KWV	E6		√	√		√		√	√		de
La Ferme Derik	D3	T					√	T			
Laborie	E6		√	√		√	√	√*	√		de
Landskroon	D6		√			T/BYO*	√	T*		√	
Lazanou	F1	T*				T*					
Le Fût	F5	T									
Le Joubert	A4	T									
Lindhorst	D7	T*				T*	√	T	√		
Linton Park	G1	T*			×	BYO		T*			
Longbarn	F2							T			
Marianne	C8		√	√		√	√	√			de/fr
Maske	G2	T*				BYO					de

	Grid reference	Open by appt. only	Open Saturdays	Open Sundays	Open public holidays	Meals/refreshments	Accomodation	Cellar tours	Disabled friendly	Child friendly	Languages spoken
Mellasat	G5		✓			T*		T	✓		
Mischa	F1	T			×	T	✓	T*			
Mon Rêve	D7	T				BYO		T		✓	fr/de
Mont Destin	C8	T			×			T			de/fr
Mont du Toit	G2		T		×		✓	✓*			de
Mooi Bly	F4	T				BYO	✓	T			nl
Mount Vernon	C7	T						T			
Nabygelegen	H1		✓		×	T*	✓	✓			
Napier	G2		✓			✓*		✓	✓		
Nederburg	F5		✓	✓*		T*		✓	✓		de
Nelson	D3		T	T	×		✓	T	✓	✓	
Niel Joubert	C8	T*			×						
Noble Hil	D8		✓	✓		✓		T	✓	✓	fr
Nwanedi	E3		✓	T		✓	✓	T			
Olsen	G5	T				T*					
Oude Denneboom	C2	T					✓				
Oude Wellington	H2		✓	✓		✓	✓	T	✓	✓	de
Painted Wolf	E6	T*				T*					fr
Perdeberg	B3		✓			T/BYO*		T*			xh
Retief	E4		T	T	×						
Rhebokskloof	D3		✓	✓		✓	✓	T	✓	✓	
Ridgeback	D3		✓	✓		✓	✓	T			
Ruitersvlei	D6	T							✓		
Rupert & Rothschild	D8		✓*					✓*	✓		
Scali	C1	T			×		✓	T			
Schalk Burger & Sons	F1		✓			BYO		✓	✓		de
Seidelberg	D6		✓	✓							de/fr
Simonsvlei	D7		✓	✓		✓/BYO*			✓	✓	
Southern Sky	E5	T									
Spice Route	D6					✓					
Stone Ridge	D1	T									
Tempel	E3	T					✓	T			da/de/fr/nn/sv
The Mason's	E6	T				✓*					
Thembi & Co	E4		✓					T			
Thokozani	F2		✓	✓		✓	✓	T			
Upland Organic	G3	T			T		✓	T			
Val de Vie	F7		✓	✓		T*		T			
Val du Charron	H1		✓	✓		✓	✓	✓	✓		
Veenwouden	E3	T						T			
Vendôme	E6	T			×				✓		
Versailles	E1	T						T			

	Grid reference	Open by appt. only	Open Saturdays	Open Sundays	Open public holidays	Meals/refreshments	Accomodation	Cellar tours	Disabled friendly	Child friendly	Languages spoken
Vondeling	C1	T						T			
Vrede en Lust	D8		✓	✓		✓	✓	T*	✓	✓	
Welgegund	G2	T					✓				
Welgeleë	D7		✓	✓		T					
Welgemeend	C7		✓		×			✓	✓		
Wellington	E2		✓		×			T	✓		
Welvanpas	H1		✓	✓		✓/BYO				✓	nl
Windmeul	D3		✓		×	✓*		T	✓		
Zanddrift	E6					✓					
Robertson Map											
AlexKia		T*									it/fr
Arendsig		T					✓	T			
Ashton Wynkelder			✓				✓	T	✓	✓	
Bon Cap				✓		✓	✓	T	✓	✓	
Bon Courage			✓			✓			✓	✓	
Bonnievale Cellar			✓			✓*			✓	✓	
Buffalo Creek			✓	T				✓*			
BurCon			✓	T		✓	✓			✓	
Bushmanspad						BYO	✓				nl
Cape Dreams		T						T			
Clairvaux					×	BYO		T	✓		
Cloverfield								✓			
De Wetshof			✓					T*	✓		
DuVon		T					✓				
Excelsior			✓			T/BYO	✓			✓	
Fraai Uitzicht			✓	✓		✓*	✓				de
Goedverwacht			✓			T/BYO*		✓			
Golden Kaan			✓			T				✓	
Janeza		T*									
Jonkheer		T*			×		✓	T			
Kingsriver			✓	✓		✓/BYO	✓	✓	✓		nl
Kleinhoekkloof		T*									
Koningsrivier		T						T			
Kranskop			✓			BYO	✓	✓			de
Langverwacht					×			✓	✓		
Le Grand Chasseur		T			×				✓		
Lord's			✓*	✓*		✓*		✓			
McGregor			✓			BYO					
Mont Byrne		T					✓	T		✓	
Mooiuitsig							✓	T			

	Grid reference	Open by appt. only	Open Saturdays	Open Sundays	Open public holidays	Meals/refreshments	Accomodation	Cellar tours	Disabled friendly	Child friendly	Languages spoken
Quando		T			x						de
Rietvallei			√			√*		T	√		
Robertson			√	√				T			
Roodezandt					x			T	√	√	
Rooiberg			√			√/BYO			√	√	
Rosendal			√	√		√	√	√	√		nn
Rusticus			√*		x	BYO	√	√		√	de
Springfield			√			BYO		T			
Sumsaré		T*				BYO		T*	√		
Tanagra		T			T	T*	√	T			de
Van Loveren			√			√*	√	T	√		
Van Zylshof			√					T			
Viljoensdrift			√	√*		√	√			√	fr
Vruchtbaar		T			x			T			
Wandsbeck			T	T	x			T	√		de
Wederom		T			T	T	√	T			de
Weltevrede			√			√	√	T	√		
Windfall		T			x	BYO		T			
Wolfkloof		T				T/BYO		T		√	
Wolvendrift			√			T		T	√	√	
Wonderfontein			√								
Zandvliet			√			BYO			√		

Southern Cape Map

	Grid reference	Open by appt. only	Open Saturdays	Open Sundays	Open public holidays	Meals/refreshments	Accomodation	Cellar tours	Disabled friendly	Child friendly	Languages spoken
Andy Mitchell		T						T			
Black Oystercatcher			√	√		√*		√	√	√	
Brunia		T*				√*					
Jean Daneel			√			√		T			de
Lismore		T								√	
Oewerzicht			T	T			√				
Strandveld			√			BYO	√	√			
The Berrio		T*				T/BYO					
Zandfontein		T					√				
Zoetendal			√*				√	√			

Stellenbosch Map

	Grid reference	Open by appt. only	Open Saturdays	Open Sundays	Open public holidays	Meals/refreshments	Accomodation	Cellar tours	Disabled friendly	Child friendly	Languages spoken
Aaldering	D4	T*			x						
Accolade	F6							T			
Akkerdraai	E8		√								de
Alluvia	H5		√	√		T/BYO*	√	T		√	
Alto	E8		√	√		T*					
Amani	B6		√			BYO		√	√	√	

	Grid reference	Open by appt. only	Open Saturdays	Open Sundays	Open public holidays	Meals/refreshments	Accomodation	Cellar tours	Disabled friendly	Child friendly	Languages spoken
Amares	G4	T*			X	T*		T			nl
Annandale	E8		✓			BYO		✓	✓		
Asara	D6		✓	✓		✓	✓	T	✓	✓	de
Audacia	E7				X				✓		
Bartinney	H5				X			T	✓		
Beau Joubert	B6		T		X	BYO	✓	T			
Bein	B6	T						T			de/fr
Bellevue	C3		✓								
Beyerskloof	E3		✓			✓		T	✓		
Bilton	E8		✓	✓		✓*		T*	✓	✓	
Blaauwklippen	E6		✓	✓		✓		T	✓	✓	de
Blue Creek	E7	T						T			
Boer & Brit	F2		✓				✓	✓		✓	de/fr/nl/sp/xh
Bonfoi	C5		✓		X	BYO			✓		
Boschheim	E5	T									de
Boschkloof	C6		✓			BYO		✓			
Botanica	D4	T*				✓*	✓				
Bottelary Hills	D3		✓	✓							
Brampton	F5		✓			✓*					
Camberley	H5		✓	✓		T/BYO	✓	T			
Cape Gable	C5	T			X			T			
Cape Hutton	E7	T						T			
Carisbrooke	C6				X						
Casa Mori	D3	T				T		T			it/fr
Cirrus	E8		✓								
Clos Malverne	D4		✓	✓		✓		✓*			
Clouds	G5		✓			T*	✓				
Clovelly	D4	T						T			
Dalla Cia	E5		✓			✓					it
De Meye	E1		✓	✓		✓*		T*	✓		
De Toren	B6	T						T			
De Trafford	G8	T*	✓		X			✓*			
Delaire Graff	G5		✓	✓		✓*	✓	T*	✓		
Delheim	F2		✓	✓		✓	✓	✓	✓	✓	de
DeMorgenzon	C5		✓	✓				T			
Devon Rocks	D3	T					✓	T			de/sv
Devonair	D3	T			X		✓				
Devonvale	D3	T*				✓	✓		✓		de/fr
DeWaal	C5		✓*								
Die Bergkelder	E5		✓					✓	✓		
Dombeya	E8		✓	✓		✓*	✓	T	✓	✓	

	Grid reference	Open by appt. only	Open Saturdays	Open Sundays	Open public holidays	Meals/refreshments	Accomodation	Cellar tours	Disabled friendly	Child friendly	Languages spoken
Dormershire	A5		T					√*			
Dornier	F7		√	√		√*	√	T	√	√	
Eaglevlei	E1		√	√		√*			√	√	
Edgebaston	F3	T									
Elgin Heights	C6	T									
Ernie Els	F8		√			√		√	√		
Ernst Gouws	D1		√						√	√	de
Escapades	B4	T									
Fish Hoek	F6							T			
Flagstone	F6							T	√		
Fort Simon	C4		√		×	√*		T	√		
Francois la Garde	E5	T									
Gilga	D5	T									
Glenelly	F4		√					T	√		de/fr
Goede Hoop	C3		√			T/BYO*		√			
Graceland	E7	T*			×		√				
Groenland	B3		√			BYO		T	√		
Guardian Peak	E8		√			√					
Hartenberg	C4		√	√*		√		T	√	√	de
Haskell	E8		√	√		√*	√	T		√	
Hazendal	B3		√	√		√		√	√	√	de/ru
Hidden Valley–Land's End	F8		√	√		√		√	√		
Hoopenburg	E1				×	BYO	√	√			
Jacobsdal	B6										
Jordan	C5		√	√		√		T	√		
Kaapzicht	B4		√			BYO	√	T			de
Kanonkop	F2		√			T/BYO*			√		
Kanu	E3				×						
Katbakkies	D5	T*			×						
Keermont	F8	T						T			
Klein DasBosch	F7	T									
Klein Moerbei	C7	T					√				
Kleine Zalze	E6		√	√		√	√		√		
Knorhoek	F3		√	√		√*	√	√	√	√	
Koelenhof	D1		√					T	√	√	de
Koopmanskloof	C3				×	BYO	√	√			
Kumala	F6							T			
Kyburg	D4	T					√				fr/de
Laibach	F1		√*				√	T			
Lanzerac	G5		√	√		√	√	√	√		
L'Avenir	E3		√			BYO	√	T	√		fr

	Grid reference	Open by appt. only	Open Saturdays	Open Sundays	Open public holidays	Meals/refreshments	Accomodation	Cellar tours	Disabled friendly	Child friendly	Languages spoken
Le Bonheur	F1		✓	✓							
Le Pommier	H4		✓	✓		✓	✓			✓	
Le Riche	G6	T*			×			T			de
Lievland	F1		✓	✓		✓*	✓	✓	✓		
L'Olivier Wine & Olive	D5	T				✓	✓			✓	
Louiesenhof	E4		✓	✓*		✓*	✓		✓	✓	
Louisvale	D4				×	BYO		✓	✓		
Lovane	D6		✓	✓	×		✓	✓			
Malanot	E8	T*						T*	✓		
Marklew	F1	T						T			
Meerlust	B8		✓		×			T			
Meinert	D4	T*			×						de
M'hudi	B1		✓				✓				tn/xh/zu
Middelvlei	E4		✓	✓		✓*	✓	T	✓	✓	
Mitre's Edge	F1	T*					✓	T			
MolenVliet	H4	T					✓				
Monterosso	E4		T	T	T			T			it/zu
Mooiplaas	B4		✓			T/BYO*					
Morgenhof	F3		✓	✓		✓	✓	T	✓	✓	de/fr
Mostertsdrift	E4	T				T*		T	✓		
Mulderbosch	C6		✓								fr
Muratie	F2		✓	✓		✓	✓	T			
Mvemve Raats	B6	T			×						
Natte Valleij	F1		T			BYO	✓	✓*		✓	
Neethlingshof	D5		✓	✓		✓*		T	✓	✓	de
Neil Ellis	G5		✓			✓*			✓		
Nico vd Merwe	B6	T									fr/de
Nietvoorbij	F4		T		×			T*			
Oldenburg	H5		T		T	✓*			✓		
Origin Wine	D3	T									fr/de
Overgaauw	D5	✓*				BYO		✓			
Peter Falke	E8		✓	✓		✓*		T			
Quoin Rock	F3		✓	✓		✓*					
Raats Family	B6	T									
Rainbow's End	H5	T				BYO		T			
Remhoogte	E3		✓			✓*	✓	T			
Re'Mogo	E4		✓						✓		
Reyneke	B6		✓		T	BYO		✓			
Rozendal	G5	T				✓	✓	T			
Rust en Vrede	E8		✓			✓		T			
Rustenberg	G4		✓						✓		

	Grid reference	Open by appt. only	Open Saturdays	Open Sundays	Open public holidays	Meals/refreshments	Accomodation	Cellar tours	Disabled friendly	Child friendly	Languages spoken
Saxenburg	A5		√	√		√/BYO	√				
Seven Sisters	D7	T									
Simonsig	E2		√	√		√		√*	√	√	
Skilpadvlei	C6		√	√		√	√		√	√	
Slaley	E2		√			√		T			
Spier	C7		√	√		√	√		√	√	de/xh
Spring Grove	H4	T									
Stark-Condé	G6		√	√		√			√		ja
Stellekaya	E5				x	T*		√	√		zu
Stellenbosch Hills	D6		√						√		
Stbosch Univ. Welgevallen	F6		T		x						
Stellendrift — SHZ Cilliers/Kuün	C7	T						T			
StellenRust	E7		√			√/BYO*		T			xh
Stellenzicht	E7		√	√				T			
Sterhuis	C4	T						T	√	√	
Stonehill	D4	T									
StoneyCroft	D3	T									
Summerhill	E3				x	√*			√		
SylvanVale	D4		√	√		√	√		√	√	de/xh
Tamboerskloof Wine	F7				x			√			
The Co Wine People	C7		√	√		√			√	√	xh
The Foundry	B8	T			x						
The High Road	E5	T			x						
The House of JC le Roux	D4		√	√*		√		√*	√		
Thelema	G4		√		x	BYO			√		
Tokara	G4		√	√		√			√	√	
Topaz Wine	F2	T									de/fr
Uitkyk	F2		√	√		√/BYO*		√	√	√	
Usana	C5	T									
Uva Mira	F8		√	√		√			√		
Vergenoegd	B8		√	√		√		T	√	√	xh
Vilafonté	E5	T						T			
Villiera	D1		√			√/BYO*		√	√		fr
Vredenheim	D6		√*	√		√	√		√		
Vriesenhof	F7		T		x	T		T			
Vuurberg	H4	T			x			T			
Warwick	F1		√	√	x	√*		T	√	√	
Waterford	F7		√					√	√		
Webersburg	E8		√			√	√	√	√		
Welgevallen	F5				x			√			
Westbridge	E1	T				T*	√				

	Grid reference	Open by appt. only	Open Saturdays	Open Sundays	Open public holidays	Meals/refreshments	Accomodation	Cellar tours	Disabled friendly	Child friendly	Languages spoken
Zevenwacht	B5		✓	✓		✓	✓	✓	✓	✓	fr/xh
Zorgvliet	H4		✓	✓		✓	✓	T	✓	✓	
Swartland Map											
Abbottshill		T						T			
Allesverloren			✓			✓*		T	✓	✓	
Annex Kloof		T				BYO		T			
Babylon's Peak		T				T/BYO*	✓	T	✓		
Badenhorst		T			×		T	T			
Dragonridge		T				T/BYO	✓	T		✓	
Farm 1120			✓			✓*					
Het Vlock Casteel			✓			T*			✓		
Hofstraat		T						T			
Hughes Family		T									sp
Kloovenburg			✓	✓*		BYO	✓	✓	✓		
Lammershoek		T				T/BYO		T			de
Mac's Hill		T			×					✓	
Meerhof			✓	✓							
Mullineux Family		T*	✓	T				T*			
Nieuwedrift			✓			T/BYO		✓		✓	
Nuweland Wynkelder			✓	✓		✓*		T*		✓	
Orangerie		T						T			
Org de Rac			✓			T/BYO		✓			de
Pulpit Rock			✓			✓/BYO	✓	T	✓		
Riebeek			✓	✓		BYO		T			
Sadie Family		T									
Santa Cecilia			✓	✓		✓*	✓				
Sequillo		T*			×						
Swartland			✓						✓	✓	
Wedgewood											
Wildehurst			✓	✓		✓*	✓	T			
Winkelshoek			✓						✓		
Tulbagh Map											
Blue Crane			T					T			
Constantia de Tulbagh		T			×			T			
De Heuvel			✓					✓	✓		
Drostdy-Hof			✓						✓		
Fable		T*									
Koelfontein			✓		×	BYO	✓				
Lemberg			✓			T/BYO*	✓	✓			
Manley			✓			✓	✓	T			

	Grid reference	Open by appt. only	Open Saturdays	Open Sundays	Open public holidays	Meals/refreshments	Accomodation	Cellar tours	Disabled friendly	Child friendly	Languages spoken
Montpellier			✓		✗	✓*	✓	✓		✓	
Oude Compagnies Post		T						T			
Rijk's		T						T			
Rijk's			✓				✓	T	✓		
Saronsberg			✓			BYO		T			
Schalkenbosch		T			✗		✓	T			de
Theuniskraal			✓						✓		
Tulbagh			✓*	✓*		BYO		T	✓		
Twee Jonge Gezellen			✓					✓			de
Waverley			✓	✓		✓/BYO*		✓	✓	✓	
Badgerberg		T*				✓*				✓	
Villiersdorp Map											
Cranefields		T									
Faraway House		T									
Slowine			✓			✓			✓		
Villiersdorp			✓			✓			✓		
Worcester Map											
Aan de Doorns Cellar			✓		✗			✓*	✓		
Alvi's Drift		T						T			
Brandvlei			✓		✗				✓		
Conradie			✓	✓		✓/BYO	✓	✓		✓	
De Doorns Wynkelder			✓						✓		
De Wet			✓		✗	BYO		T	✓		
Eagle's Cliff					✗	✓			✓	✓	
Hex River Crossing			✓		✗	✓		T		✓	
Nuy			✓			BYO			✓		
Overhex			✓			✓*		T	✓	✓	
Stettyn			✓*		✗	T/BYO*		T*	✓	✓	

Cape Peninsula

ATLANTIC OCEAN

TABLE BAY

See Durbanville map

N7

N1

N7

See Stellenbosch map

● Cheviot
○ Vaughan Johnson
Signal Hill ●

M6

CAPE TOWN

N1

N2

CLIFTON

● Emineo-Cape to Cairo

M62

CAMPS BAY

N2

KLIPFONTEIN ROAD

○ Mzoli's

M63

M3 M4 M5

SANDY BAY

Ambeloui ○
Kling ○
Beau Constantia
Constantia Glen
Final Cut ○
Eagles' Nest ○ ○ Constantia Mist
Hout Bay Vyds ○ High Constantia ○
Groot Constantia ○

M6

Hout Bay

Constantia

Klein Constantia ○
Constantia Uitsig ○ ○ Buitenverwachting

HOUT BAY

M6

M4

● Steenberg

Cape Point

OU KAAPSE WEG

Noordhoek

Muizenberg

M4

M65

M6

Fish Hoek

M4

Simon's Town

M65

FALSE BAY

M4

M65

ATLANTIC OCEAN

ATLANTIC OCEAN

CAPE POINT

CAPE OF GOOD HOPE

Durbanville, Philadelphia & Darling

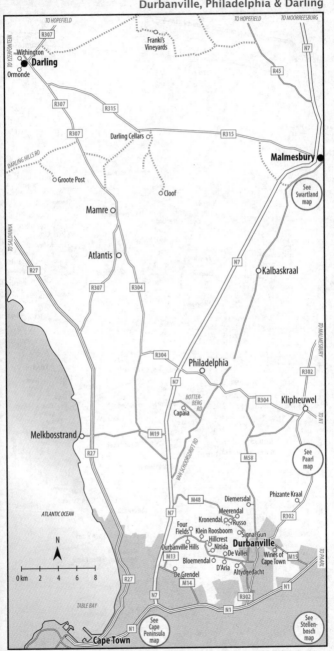

TO HOPEFIELD
TO HOPEFIELD
TO MOORREESBURG
R307
N7
TO YZERFONTEIN
Franki's Vineyards
Withington
Darling
Ormonde
R45
R307
R315
R307
Darling Cellars
R315
DARLING HILLS RD
Malmesbury
Groote Post
See Swartland map
Cloof
Mamre
Atlantis
N7
Kalbaskraal
TO SALDANHA
R27
R307
R304
TO MALMESBURY
R304
Philadelphia
N7
R302
BOTTER-BERG RD
Klipheuwel
Capaia
TO N1
R304
M19
Melkbosstrand
See Paarl map
R27
VAN SCHOORSDRIFT RD
M58
ATLANTIC OCEAN
Phizante Kraal
M48
Diemersdal
R302
N7
Meerendal
Kronendal
Russo
Four Fields
Klein Roosboom
Signal Gun
Hillcrest
Durbanville
Durbanville Hills
Nitida
Wines of Cape Town
M15
M13
De Vallei
TO PAARL
Bloemendal
D'Aria
Altydgedacht
N1
De Grendel
M14
N7
R302
N1
N1
TABLE BAY
See Cape Peninsula map
See Stellenbosch map
Cape Town

N

0 km 2 4 6 8

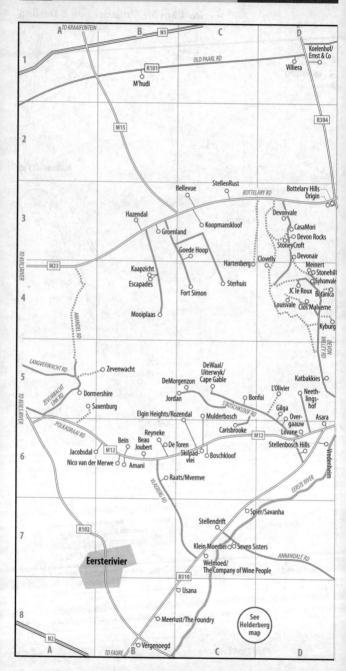

Stellenbosch

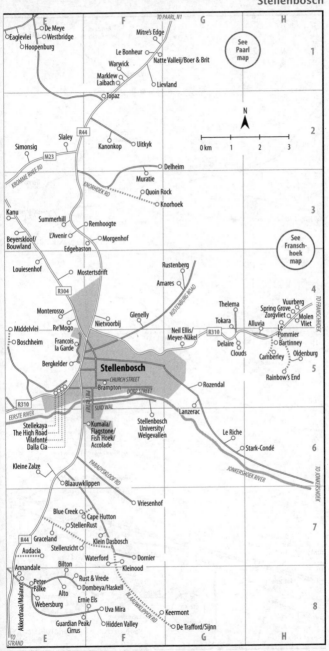

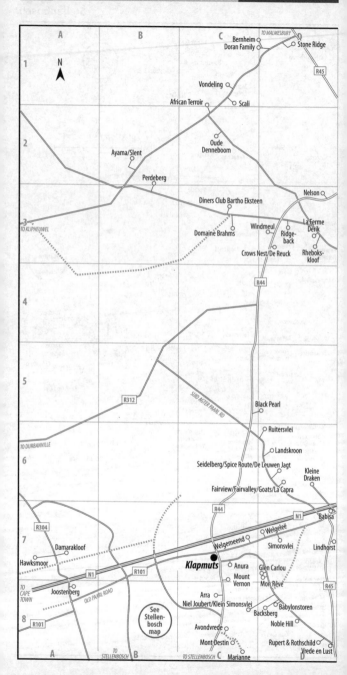

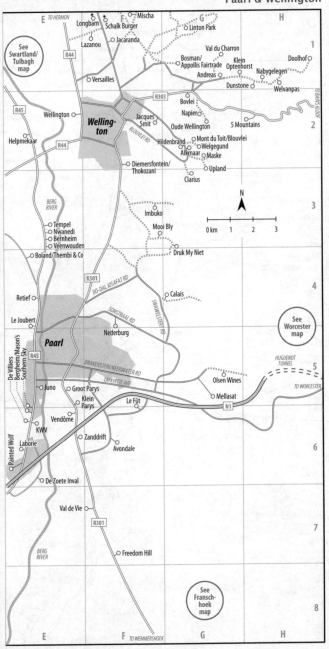

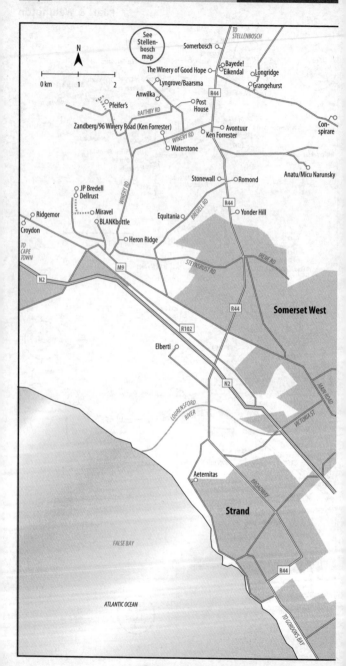

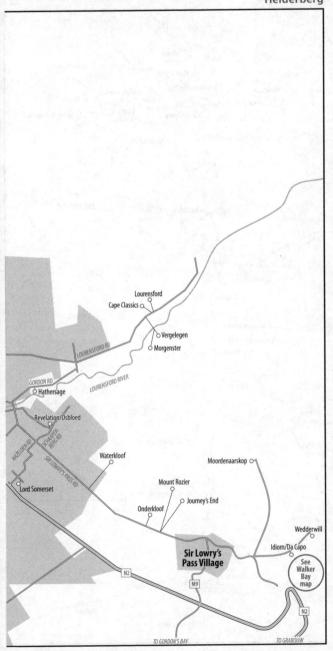

Lourensford
Cape Classics
Vergelegen
Morgenster
LOURENSFORD RD
GORDON RD
LOURENSFORD RIVER
Hathersage
Revelation/Osbloed
HAZEL DN RD
SCHAPEN BERG
SIR LOWRY'S PASS RD
Waterkloof
Moordenaarskop
Mount Rozier
Lord Somerset
Journey's End
Onderkloof
Wedderwill
Sir Lowry's Pass Village
Idiom/Da Capo
See Walker Bay map
N2
M9
N2
TO GORDON'S BAY
TO GRABOUW

Franschhoek

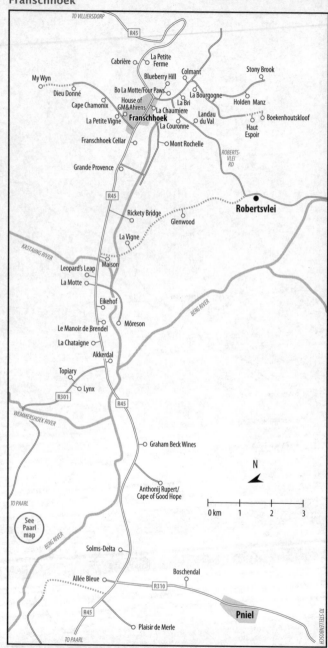

Elgin, Walker Bay & Bot River

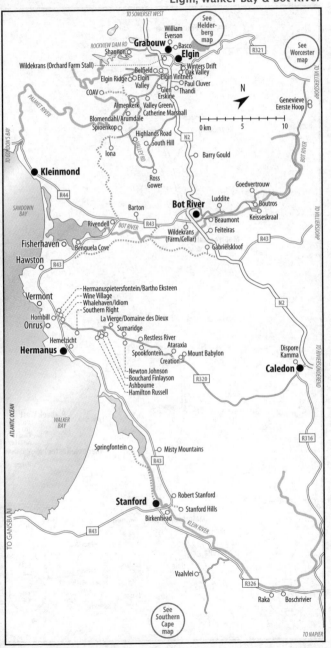

Swartland

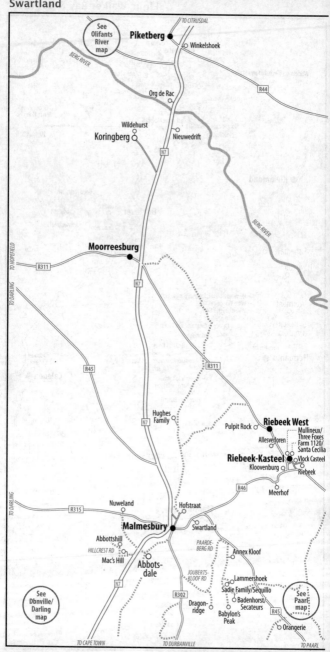

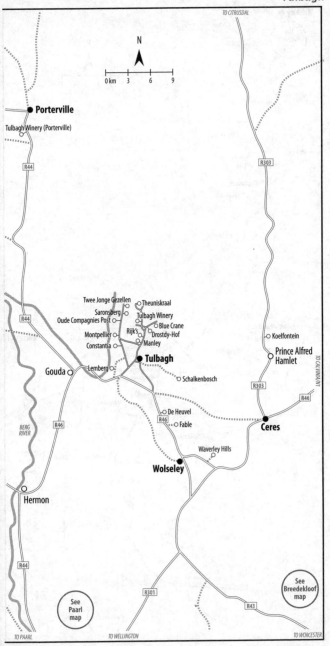

Breedekloof

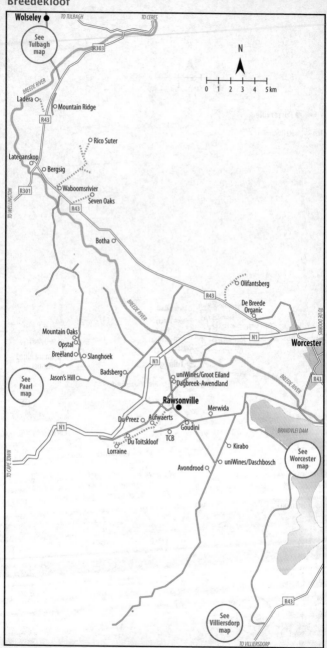

Worcester

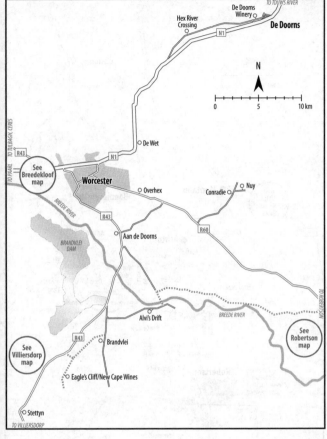

Villiersdorp

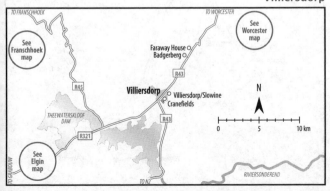

Robertson

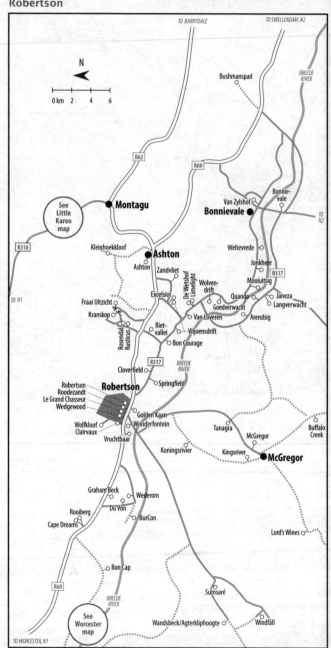

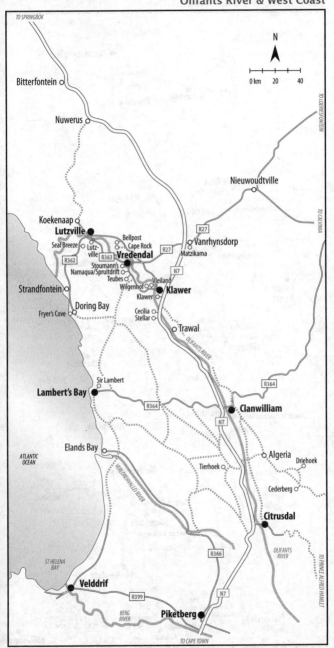

Klein Karoo & Garden Route

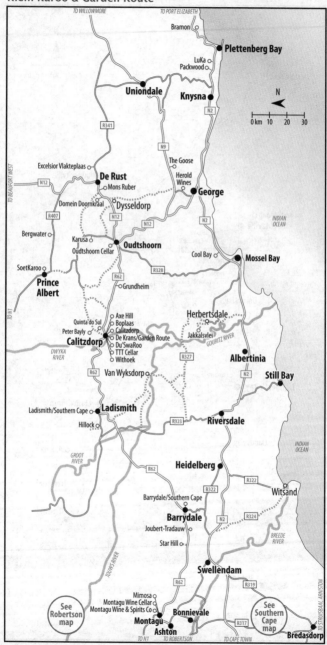

TO WILLOWMORE   TO PORT ELIZABETH

Bramon

Plettenberg Bay

LuKa
Packwood

Uniondale

Knysna

N

0 km 10   20   30

R341

N9

Excelsior Vlakteplaas

The Goose
Herold
Wines

De Rust
Mons Ruber

George

N12

TO BEAUFORT WEST

Domein Doornkraal

Dysseldorp

N12   N12

R407

Bergwater

Karusa
Oudtshoorn Cellar

Oudtshoorn

Cool Bay

Mossel Bay

INDIAN
OCEAN

SoetKaroo

R62

R328

**Prince
Albert**

Grundheim

TO N1

Herbertsdale

Axe Hill
Boplaas
Calitzdorp
De Krans/Garden Route
Du'SwaRoo
TTT Cellar
Withoek

Quinta do Sul
Peter Bayly

Jakkalsvlei

GOURITZ RIVER

Calitzdorp

DWYKA
RIVER

Albertinia

R327

Van Wyksdorp

Still Bay

R62

N2

Ladismith/Southern Cape

Ladismith

Hillock

R323

Riversdale

GROOT
RIVER

INDIAN
OCEAN

R62

Heidelberg

R322

Barrydale/Southern Cape

R322

Witsand

Barrydale

N2

R324

Joubert-Tradauw

BREEDE
RIVER

Star Hill

TOURNS RIVER

Swellendam

R319

TO STRUISBAAI, ARNISTON

See
Robertson
map

R62

See
Southern
Cape
map

Mimosa
Montagu Wine Cellar
Montagu Wine & Spirits Co

Bonnievale

R317

Montagu

Ashton

TO N1   TO ROBERTSON   TO CAPE TOWN

Bredasdorp

KwaZulu-Natal

Southern Cape

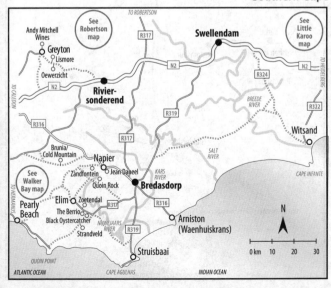

Northern Cape, Free State & North West

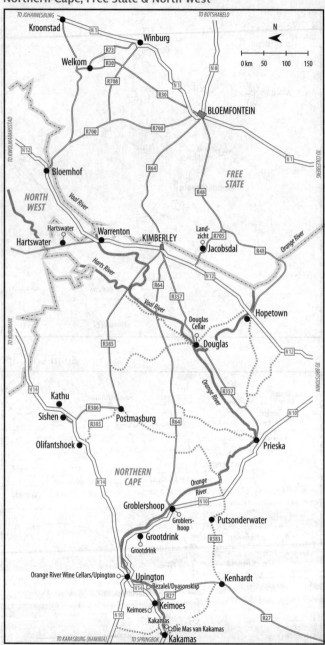

Our Track-Record-Based Rating System

All wines rated 4 stars or more are set in red type

General rating ★★★★ **Caldera**

For 4-star or better wines, we give the 'track-record rating' over two or more vintages in the margin.

Vintage-specific rating 06 (★★★☆)

Any differences from the general rating noted in brackets beside the particular vintage

★★★★★	Superlative. A South African classic
★★★★★	Outstanding
★★★★	Excellent
★★★★	Very good/promising
★★★	Characterful, appealing
★★★	Good everyday drinking
★★	Pleasant drinking
★★	Casual quaffing
★	Plain and simple
★	Very ordinary
No star	Somewhat less than ordinary

Abbreviations

% alc	Percentage alcohol by volume
1stB	First bottled vintage
BEE	Black Economic Empowerment
BWI	Biodiversity & Wine Initiative
BYO	Bring your own (wine, picnic)
Cs	Cases
CWG	Cape Winemakers Guild
CWM	Cape Wine Master
Est	Date established
g/l	Grams per litre
IPW	Integrated Production of Wine
IWC	International Wine Challenge
IWSC	International Wine & Spirit Competition
LBV	Late Bottled Vintage
Malo	Malolactic fermentation
MCC	Méthode cap classique
MW	Master of Wine
NLH	Noble Late Harvest
NV	Non-vintage. Year of harvest not stated on label
RS	Residual sugar
SAA	South African Airways (selected for First or Premium Class)
SLH	Special Late Harvest
Veritas	SA National Bottled Wine Show
WIETA	Wine & Agricultural Ethical Trade Association
Wine	Wine magazine (South African)
WO	Wine of Origin

cabernet/cab	cabernet sauvignon
pinot	pinot noir
chenin	chenin blanc
sauvignon/sauv	sauvignon blanc
riesling	Rhine/weisser riesling
touriga	touriga nacional
tinta	tinta barocca

Symbols

Winery symbols

🍶	Bottles own wine on property
⚲	Open for tasting (no fee unless noted)
☕	Restaurant/refreshments
⌂	Accommodation
📷	Other tourist attractions/amenities on the property
🌲	Bring your own (BYO) picnic
🧒	Child friendly
♿	Wheelchair friendly (see page 100)

Wine symbols

🗔	Screwcapped
✓	Good value
☺	Exceptionally drinkable and well priced
NEW	New wine
🌿	Organic
▨	Certified as sustainable (see www.swsa.co.za)

The text used here is illustrative and not complete. See A–Z for full details.

Location: nearest major centre to winery, vyd, head office. Map: See Maps section for winery's position.

WO: Wine of Origin geographical unit, region, district or ward; wines described/rated bear the first-mentioned WO certification unless noted.

Total hectares/hectares under vine (not necessarily in production); main varieties planted

GPS coordinates, based on Datum WGS 84

Our track-record-based rating system
See previous page for an explanation

Unless noted, red wines wooded; whites unoaked

Wine name, vintage, colour & style

Listings of wines available during the currency of the book

Symbols
See previous page for a complete list

See previous page for a list of abbreviations

Date established

T = Telephone number
F= Fax number

Producer's name

Fairview

Location/WO: Paarl ▪ Map: Paarl & Wellington ▪ E
30min before closing ▪ Fee R25 or R60 ▪ Closed Eas
Groups by appt only ▪ Tasting & sales of Fairview ch
Anthony de Jager (Dec 1996), with Adele Dunbar (2
Mouton ▪ 500ha/300ha (cab, barbera, merlot, m
sauv, viog) ▪ 1 850t 80% red 15% white 5% rosé ▪
accredited ▪ Export brand: Six Hats ▪ PO Box 583 Su
S 33° 46' 19.5" E 018° 55' 28.0" ▪ **T 021-863-24.!**

Fresh life is being fed into the entir
Paarl's distinctive granite dome and
form of uprooting blue gum trees an
dry as long as Charles Back can reca
plantings of Grenache blanc and rous
first tempranillo went to barrel.

Fairview range

★★★★ **Cabernet Sauvignon** ✓ Renamed S
some & approachable. Silky tannin frame from 5

★★★★ **Cyril Back** Flagship homage to Back
but gentle texture. Complex, dense & concentra
fruit. 18 mths in 30% new Fr oak. Needs time.

★★★★ **Sauvignon Blanc** ✓ 🗐 👒 Fig & gr
tact adds body to mid-palate. All Darling fruit.

Darling Chenin Blanc 😊 🗐 👒 ★★★ *
minerality with honeysuckle hint. Broad palate

Barbera ★★★★ **08** has ripe mulberry succulenc
mths old Fr oak. **Stellenbosch Merlot** 🗐 ★★★
tar intensity. Fr oak, 20% new, yr. **Mourv** NEW "d
08. Concentrated & slightly chunky but elegant. V
08's bold structure & density tempered by plum
Straw Wine ✓ ★★★★ Exotic lavender floral nos
Vanilla wafer too. Sweet (136g RS) but long, dry fi

False Bay Vineyards

Location: Somerset West ▪ WO: Coastal/Western
Boutinot ▪ Winemaker(s) Werner Engelbrecht (2C
70% white ▪ PO Box 2093 Somerset West 7129 ▪
T 021-858-1292 ▪ F 021-858-1293

A consistent range for the UK-owne
lar of sibling Waterkloof – with the
and often with the natural ferm
Engelbrecht. The grapes are, howeve

Tastings, sales & cellar tour times (closed Saturdays & Sundays but open public holidays unless noted)

Symbols
See previous page for a complete list

Other attractions or activities available on the property

▪ 1stB 1974 ▪ Tasting & sales daily 9–5, last tastings c 25, Jan 1 ▪ The Goatshed (see Restaurants section) ▪ wner(s) Charles Back ▪ Winemaker(s) Charles Back & tephanie Betts (2010) ▪ Vineyard manager(s) Donald t sirah, ptage, shiraz, chard, chenin, grenache b&n, 2001 & HACCP certified; IPW & BWI member; WIETA l 7624 ▪ info@fairview.co.za ▪ www.fairview.co.za ▪ 1-863-2591

Names of owner, winemaker, viticulturist & consultant/s; year/month of appointment in brackets

Postal & email address, website (see www.wineonaplatter.com for social media details)

view ecosystem on the rear slopes of tain. On the natural front it took the vegetation that has seen riverbeds — n with water again. In the cellar, new were vinified for the first time, and the

All wines dry unless noted

b. **08** is bold, leafy cassis & fruitcake galore. Sleek, lis-, brl-ferm fruit. 16 mths in 25% new Fr oak.

07's waxy plum segues to blueberry & pepper. Firm x yet full-bodied. Basket-pressed Paarl & Swartland

crispness on **10**. Lemon & flint minerality. Lees con-

anadilla & grapefruit zip on unoaked **10**. Fresh contact.

Exceptionally drinkable & well priced

mon spice over cocoa oak notes. Fine tannin from 12 lling 08. Cocoa earthiness set against ripe mulberry, ★★ Savoury soy & earth over black pepper & plum on . **Petite Sirah ★★★★** Floral lavender & blueberry. . Long mocha tail. Yr Fr oak, 40% new. **Hanepoot** eysugar, jasmine, ginger & peach abundance on **08**. epoot grapes ex-swartland. — FM

Taster/s initials

t/1stB 2000 ▪ Tasting at Waterkloof ▪ Owner(s) Paul culturist(s) Werner Engelbrecht ▪ 60,000cs 30% red aterkloofwines.co.za ▪ www.waterkloofwines.co.za ▪

Production, in tons and/or 12-bottle cases (cs) and red:white ratio

outinot portfolio and made in the cel-ttention to detail as the estate's wines n favoured by winemaker Werner e widely sourced.

Brief introduction/news update

■ **AA Badenhorst** *see* Badenhorst Family Wines

Aaldering Vineyards & Wines

Location/map/WO: Stellenbosch ▪ Est 2004 ▪ 1stB 2007 ▪ Tasting & sales by appt Mon–Fri 9-4 ▪ Closed all pub hols ▪ Owner(s) Marianne & Fons Aaldering ▪ Cellarmaster(s)/winemaker(s)/viticulturist(s) Dustin Osborne (Jul 2011) ▪ 24ha/21ha (cab, merlot, ptage, syrah, chard, sauv) ▪ ±120t/±9,150cs own label 70% red 30% white ▪ IPW ▪ PO Box 1068 Stellenbosch 7599 ▪ estate@aaldering.co.za ▪ www.aaldering.co.za ▪ S 33 55' 9.81" E 018 49' 8.14" ▪ **T +27 (0)79-526-8026**

Dutch owners Fons and Marianne Aaldering have appointed Dustin Osborne winemaker and general manager. Dustin brings extensive knowledge of winemaking in the Devon Valley area, and says he feels very at home with the classic, elegant house style. 'Quality grapes are key, and the vineyards here are known to produce top quality. My main aim therefore is to protect and nurture what we get during the vintage.' He's keen to see a cellar on site, to further enhance quality control.

Aaldering Vineyards & Wines range NEW

★★★★ **Shiraz** Juicy, ripe black berries on big & fruit-forward 07. Full bodied, boldly structured with a savoury Asian spice conclusion.

Pinotage ★★★ Dark plums & dusty aromas, 07 very ripe dark fruit with grainy tannins & warm dry finish. **Cabernet Sauvignon-Merlot** ★★★★ Big & bold 07 offers seductive blackcurrant, smoke & flashes of leafiness. Vanilla oak flavours balance black berry fruit. **Chardonnay** Fresh apple, vanilla oak & lime on medium-bodied preview 11, too young & unformed to rate conclusively. — Panel

Aan de Doorns Cellar

Location/map/WO: Worcester ▪ Est 1954 ▪ Tasting & sales Mon–Fri 8-5 Sat 10-1 ▪ Closed pub hols ▪ Tours during harvest by appt ▪ Owner(s) 58 members ▪ Cellarmaster(s) Johan Morkel (Nov 1993) ▪ Winemaker(s) Gert van Deventer (Sept 1997) & Ryno Booysen (Jan 2007) ▪ Viticulturist(s) Pierre Snyman ▪ 1,494ha (cab, ptage, chard, chenin, cbard) ▪ ±25,000t/10,300cs own label ▪ PO Box 235 Worcester 6849 ▪ info@aandedoorns.co.za ▪ www.aandedoorns.co.za ▪ S 33° 41'47.0" E 019° 29' 26.2" ▪ **T +27 (0)23-347-2301** ▪ F +27 (0)23-347-4629

The most important focus for this Worcester company of winegrowers, says veteran cellarmaster Johan Morkel, is supplying the best-quality wine to FirstCape, a highly successful joint marketing venture giving its five shareholders access to UK markets. A much smaller project now on the cards is the building of a farmstall and rustic bistro at the entrance to the winery, aimed at boosting trade.

Chenin Blanc ☺ 🍷 ★★★ 11 best dry wine in easy-drinking, well-priced line-up. Melon & clove, satisfying, bone-dry yet flavoursome. **Sauvignon Blanc** ☺ 🍷 ★★★ 11 continues upward path with attractive, pungent asparagus & khaki bush, fair weight.

Pinotage ★★★ Berry-nuanced 10 is soft & supple for uncomplicated sipping. **Doornroodt** ★★★ 09 mixes ruby cab & merlot, has jam & vanilla tones, stalky edge. **Blanc de Noir** 🍷 ★★★ Grapey, spicy muscat fruitiness & sweetness, 11 quick-quaff is the perfect curry companion. **Colombar Semi-Sweet** 🍷 ★★ 11 leaner than previous vintages, sweetness seems overdone. **Sparkling** ★★★ Overtly sweet & frothy NV party bubbly from colombard & ruby cab. **Muscat d'Alexandrie** ✓ 🍷 ★★★★ Aromatic 10 fortified dessert, glacé pineapple & citrus rind, unctuous & rich yet wonderfully fresh, zippy. More layers than 09 (★★★). **Red Muscadel** 🍷 ★★★ Consistent fortified dessert is sunshine in a bottle. 10 well-rounded, with peppery notes. **Cape Ruby** 🍷 ★★★ Uncomplex port-style tinta, touriga. Dark & plummy 10 has liquorice accents. — Panel

Abbottshill

Location: Malmesbury ▪ Map/WO: Swartland ▪ Est/1stB 2004 ▪ Tasting, sales & tours by appt ▪ BYO picnic ▪ Owner(s) CA Bain & SP Graham ▪ Winemaker(s) CA Bain ▪ Viticulturist(s) Klaas Coetzee (Swartland Winery) ▪ 112ha/10ha (cab, mourv, shiraz) ▪ 625cs own label 100% red ▪ PO Box 433 Malmesbury 7299 ▪ cameron@empa.co.za ▪ S 33° 29' 26.4" E 018° 39' 25.3" ▪ **T +27 (0)22-485-7080** ▪ F +27 (0)22-485-7080

Winemaker (and chief bottle-washer) Cameron Bain initially only drank the stuff. Then he started making some in a bathtub, then graduated to a converted dairy -

even better than an actual garage and not quite disqualifying 'garagiste' claims for what he does with grapes off his ten hectares of maturing Malmesbury vines.

Cabernet Sauvignon ★★★ Last year unwooded sample **09** looked promising, yet needing time to show its best. **Shiraz** ★★★ Rich, powerful **09** shows very ripe blackberry & tar, high alcohol adding to sweet impression & warming (slightly bitter) finish. **Shiraz-Cabernet Sauvignon** Await next. **Bosstok Boogie** ★★ **10** red blend, off-dry, alcoholic, oaky & awkward. **Rosé** NEW ★★★ Juicy, easy-going, appealing **11** from shiraz is dry, with lemon twist on fresh finish. — JPf

Abingdon Wine Estate

Location: Lions River ▪ Map: KwaZulu-Natal ▪ Est 2004 ▪ 1stB 2007 ▪ Tasting, sales & cellar tours Mon-Fri by appt (T. 083-463-8503) ▪ Tasting room & restaurant open Sat/Sun & pub hols 10-5 for personalised tastings & fresh country meals ▪ Picnics by pre-arrangement ▪ Self-catering accommodation ▪ Owner(s) Ian & Jane Smorthwaite ▪ Winemaker(s) Ian Smorthwaite ▪ Marketing Jane Smorthwaite ▪ Viticulturist(s) Ian Smorthwaite ▪ 7ha/2.5ha (cab, syrah, chard, sauv, viog) ▪ Lions River KZN Midlands ▪ jane@abingdonestate.co.za, ian@abingdonestate.co.za ▪ www.abingdonestate.co.za ▪ S 29° 26' 36.71" E 030° 09' 14.18" ▪ **T** +27 (0)33-234-4335/+27 (0)83-463-8503 ▪ F +27 (0)33-234-4797

Continuing media interest in Abingdon's wines, the only certified single-vineyard estate bottlings coming out of KwaZulu-Natal, keeps the visitors calling and the shelves forever emptying. 'A great place to be, but a tight spot to be in!' is co-owner, winemaker and viticulturist Ian Smorthwaite's wry comment.

Cabernet Sauvignon Newer vintages of this, **Syrah**, **Sauvignon Blanc** & **Viognier**, not ready at press time. In the wings are a maiden **Rosé Chardonnay** & debut **Chardonnay-Viognier**.

■ **Above the Mist** *see Retief Wines*

Accolade Wines South Africa

Stellenbosch ▪ Tasting & sales Mon-Fri 10-4 at Doornbosch Centre, Strand Rd, Stellenbosch ▪ Fee R20, waived on purchase ▪ Closed Dec 25 to Jan 2 ▪ Cellar tours by appt ▪ Owner(s) Champ Private Equity based in Australia ▪ Winemaker(s) Bruce Jack, Gerhard Swart, Ben Jordaan & Karen Bruwer ▪ Viticulturist(s) Chris Keet ▪ 3.2m cs own label ▪ PO Box 769 Stellenbosch 7599 ▪ hannelize.mouton@accolade-wines.com ▪ www.accolade-wines.com ▪ S 33° 56' 44.93" E 018° 51' 17.29" ▪ **T** +27 (0)21-882-8177 ▪ F +27 (0)21-882-8176

Accolade Wines South Africa is a new entity created by the 80% acquisition in January 2011 of Constellation Wines South Africa by Australian private equity fund CHAMP. Constellation Brands entered the South African wine market in 2006 by buying Kumala brand's Canadian parent Vincor International, and added Bruce Jack's Flagstone Winery in 2008, putting him at the winemaking helm of both brands. Former Constellation brands (including Fish Hoek) thus join Accolade's comprehensive portfolio and will benefit from the company's access to important growth markets. See separate listings.

Adoro Wines

Location: Stellenbosch ▪ WO: Western Cape ▪ Est 2005 ▪ 1stB 2004 ▪ Closed to public ▪ Owner(s) Intra International ▪ Winemaker(s) Ian Naudé (May 2005) ▪ Viticulturist(s) Lucas de Kock (Aug 2005) ▪ 40% red 60% white ▪ PO Box 982 Stellenbosch 7599 ▪ adorowines@iafrica.com ▪ www.adorowines.co.za ▪ **T** +27 (0)83-630-3794 ▪ F +27 (0)21-880-1585

Adoro Wines, sibling of Benriach Distillery in Speyside, Scotland, owns no vines but instead harnesses long-term relationships with vinegrowers in a variety of regions. For their new creation, winemaker Ian Naudé and viticulturist Lucas de Kock identified a block of Swartland mourvèdre, and vinified it Natural Sweet style to meet a challenge from the sommelier of a restaurant in London's Belgravia: make an unfortified wine that works with not just one, but a range of cheese.

★★★★ **Red Blend** When tasted last edition, soft & accessible **06** (★★★★) had more overt oak masking the delicate red-berry fragrance we admired in **05**.

★★★★ **Sauvignon Blanc** 🔖 With 'Three Regions' prefix last time. **10** (★★★★) steely, but fleshy fruit & year in bottle soften brisk acid, so not as penetrating as **09**.

★★★★☆ **Naudé White** 🏳 The 'magician of layering flavour' at work: **10** has chalky, mineral, floral, waxy & fruity elements held together by fresh acidity, & background wood. Balanced & lingering. Very lightly wooded chenin, semillon, sauvignon, roughly equal portions.

Natural Sweet Mourvèdre NEW ★★★★ The brief: a made-for-cheese wine, 'neither fortified nor overly dry or sweet'. The **09** reply: jostling ripe fruit, sweetness & oak, singular, & (atypically for this house) unsubtle. —DS

Aeternitas Wines

Location: Strand ▪ Map: Helderberg ▪ WO: Swartland ▪ Est 2005 ▪ 1stB 2007 ▪ Tasting & cellar tours by appt ▪ Closed all pub hols ▪ Owner(s) Johan & Michelle Grimbeek ▪ Cellarmaster(s) Johan Grimbeek (Jan 2005) ▪ Winemaker(s) Johan Grimbeek, with Michelle Grimbeek (both Jan 2005) ▪ Viticulturist(s) Various ▪ 4t/320cs own label 50% red 45% white ▪ 21 Livingstone Street Strand 7140 ▪ aeternitaswines@telkomsa.net ▪ S 34° 6' 3.3" E 018° 49' 35.6" ▪ **T +27 (0)21-853-7312**

After six crushes in their suburban garage, Kanu winemaker Johan Grimbeek and wife Michelle hoped to graduate to a cellar in the Swartland, source of their grapes. But Kanu's relocation last year demanded so much attention, he gave his own wine 'a break'. No matter, plans to escape the suburbs remain on the table.

Syrah ★★★★ Naturally fermented **07** showed ripe red fruit & oriental spicing previously. **Blanc** 🏳 📷 ★★★★ Lavish **10** billows summer fruit, shows amazing balance considering ripeness, oak & 14% alc. Ex chenin. —DS

▪ **A Few Good Men** *see* Riebeek Cellars
▪ **Africa** *see* Waterstone Wines
▪ **Africa Five** *see* Waterstone Wines
▪ **African Dawn** *see* Rooiberg Winery
▪ **African Gold** *see* Old Bridge Wines
▪ **African Lizard** *see* Waterstone Wines

African Pride Wines

Location: Constantia ▪ WO: Western Cape/Coastal ▪ Est/1stB 2002 ▪ Closed to public ▪ Owner(s) Afrifresh Group ▪ Winemaker(s) Mike Graham (May 2002) ▪ 240,000cs ▪ PO Box 518 Constantia 7848 ▪ info@africanpridewines. za ▪ www.africanpridewines.co.za ▪ **T +27 (0)21-887-2204** ▪ F +27 (0)21-887-2204

Export driven from inception, African Pride's wines can be found in well over 30 countries - and more's to come: a new office in Bonn, Germany, serves to grow market share as well as develop new opportunities in Europe. The upgraded Cape Grace Sugarbird range replaces export-only Cape Grace.

Lady Anne Barnard range
★★★★ **Cabernet Sauvignon** ✓ **08** worthy successor to **07** with classic rich cab fruit from Helderberg, toasty oak in support. Supple tannin structure for early enjoyment.
★★★★ **Sauvignon Blanc** ✓ 📷 Serious cooler-climate expression, **10** vibrant capsicum & tropical fruit in luscious (lees-influenced) & textured frame. Firm & generous. From Darling vines.
Syrah ✓ ★★★★ Ripe, fruit-forward, juicy & spicy **08** offers lush, concentrated berry flavours, full & round in the mouth with a lipsmacking spicy lift. Stellenbosch fruit.

Footprint Impression range
Shiraz-Mourvèdre-Viognier ★★★ Attractively lean **08** had savouriness from shiraz, floral note ex viognier; like next, not revisited. **Viognier** ★★★★ Judiciously oaked **08** had distinct varietal stonefruit & jasmine, characterful flavours with fresh acid lift. Discontinued: **Petit Verdot-Shiraz**.

Footprint range

Merlot ☺ 📷 ★★★ **10** trumps previous: sweet upfront fruit, juicy, soft & balanced. **Chardonnay** ☺ 📷 ★★★ **11** opulent yellow peaches & plums, silky mouthfeel with a touch of oak. Moreish!

Cabernet Sauvignon ★★★ Berry fruit appeal, unoaked **10** grippy tannins plumped by juicy fruit. **09** (★★) lightly wooded, leaner version with drying finish. Neither revisited, as for next. **Shiraz** ★★ Lightly oaked **09** ripe, smoky, brambly & grippy. **10** similarly perfumed but softer; unoaked. Perfect for the braai. **Merlot-Pinotage** 🏳 📷 ★★ **11** ripe, fun & fruity. Unoaked. A summer sipper. **Pinotage Rosé** 🏳 ★★ **10** fruit-shy & dry last edition, savoury flavours dominated. **Sauvignon Blanc** ★★★ Passionfruit, grassy notes on piercing, super-lean **10** previous edition. **Chenin Blanc-Semillon** 🏳 📷 ★★ Fruity & zippy **11**, perfect for picnic.

Cape Grace Sugarbird range NEW
Pinotage 🍷 🏵 ★★ Unoaked perky **10** with understated plum flavours. **Shiraz** 🍷 🏵 ★★ Brusque dark fruit on **10** with smoky end. **Chenin Blanc** 🍷 🏵 ★★ Summery & fruity **10**, easy sipper.

Cape Grace range
Now discontinued. — WB

■ **African Roots** *see* Seven Sisters
■ **African Star** *see* Stellar Winery

African Terroir

Location: Paarl ▪ Map: Paarl & Wellington ▪ WO: Western Cape/Paarl/Stellenbosch/Elgin/Simonsberg-Paarl ▪ Est/1stB 1991 ▪ Tasting, sales & cellar tours Mon-Fri 8.30-4 strictly by appt ▪ Closed all pub hols ▪ BYO picnic ▪ Conferences ▪ Conservation area ▪ Owner(s) Jacques Germanier ▪ Winemaker(s) Stéphane de Saint Salvy (Oct 2010), with Marco Swartz (Feb 2009) ▪ Viticulturist(s) Johan Barnard (Nov 2009) ▪ 118ha/75ha (cab, merlot, ptage, shiraz, chard, cbard, sauv, viog) ▪ 540t ▪ Brands for clients: Hunting Owl (Woolworths), Mwitu (USA) ▪ ISO 22000 in process, BWI, BRC, Fairtrade, FFF, FOA, HACCP, IPN, Organic ▪ PO Box 2029 Windmeul Paarl 7630 ▪ office@african-terroir.co.za ▪ www.african-terroir.co.za ▪ S 33° 37' 1.8" E 018° 50' 38.4" ▪ **T +27 (0)21-869-8103** ▪ F +27 (0)21-869-8104

Established in 1991 on the 130ha wine farm Sonop near Paarl, African Terroir celebrates 21 years of organic grape growing this year. Milestones include exporting most of its 540t harvest to more than 20 countries worldwide, and an impressive array of environmentally and socially responsible accreditations. The Swiss-owned winery's mission remains the same: to help wine lovers discover the richness of the Cape's diverse terroirs.

Azania range
Shiraz ★★ Ripe malt, raisin notes last year on supple **09** from Stellenbosch.

Big Five range
Cabernet Sauvignon ★★★ Previously, **10**'s lush red berries coated by firm tannin. All in range still selling, none retasted. **Pinotage** ★★ Strawberry-toned **10** slips down easily. **Shiraz** ★★ Dusty red fruit, **10** shy & tad bitter. **Chardonnay** ★★★ Baked apple appeal on brisk **10**. **Sauvignon Blanc** ★★ Pear-drop delicacy on **10**, with lunchtime friendly 12% alc. WO W Cape for all these.

Out of Africa range

Cabernet Sauvignon ☺ ★★★ Uncomplex & unoaked **11**, ex-tank, strawberry flavoured with affable grip. WO Elgin.

Shiraz 🍷 ★★ **10** slightly warm, with strong tannic grip on review. **Chardonnay** ★★★ Last edition, confident **10** preview had lemon blossom whiffs. **Sauvignon Blanc** ★ **11** light, tropical & gentle dry white off Paarl-area vines. Not revisited, as all this range.

Sonop Organic range

Cabernet Sauvignon ☺ ❀ 🏵 ★★★ Juicy, red berry-nuanced **11** unoaked, like all reds in range, for immediate enjoyment. This, **Merlot**, **Viognier** previewed; all others not reassessed & still available. **Viognier** ☺ ❀ 🏵 ★★★ **11** best in line-up. Enticing orange & apricot, good weight & length.

Merlot ❀ 🏵 ★★ Demure **11** has zesty acidity, tad stalky finish. **Pinotage** ❀ 🏵 ★★ Pervasive lemony acidity on strawberry-infused **10**. **Shiraz** ❀ 🏵 ★★★ Unpretentious **10** last year scored with tealeaf & cranberry aromas, firm tannins. **Viognier-Merlot Rosé** NEW 🍷 ❀ 🏵 ★ **10** more 'light red' than 'rosé', perfumed, lacks verve. **Chardonnay** ❀ 🏵 ★★★ Last edition, **10** was fresh & demanded attention. **Sauvignon Blanc** ❀ 🏵 ★★ Wallet-pleasing **10** is zingy, with khaki bush aromas. WO Paarl, as for all.

Tribal range
Merlot 🍷 ★★ Preview **11** soft & plummy quick-quaff, unfettered by oak. WO Paarl, rest of range W Cape. **Pinotage** 🍷 ★★ **10** simple party red with strawberry highlights. Not retasted, like all following. **Dry Red** Unwooded **NV** from cinsaut, pinotage & shiraz. **Rosé** Await next, as for **Dry White**, **Sparkling White Dry**, **Sparkling Semi-Sweet** & **Sparkling Rosé Dry**. **Sauvignon Blanc-Colombard Fairtrade** ★★ Ex tank, **10** previously brisk, light & grassy. **Chenin Blanc-Colombar** ★ **10** preview was reticent, floral toned.

Winds of Change Fairtrade Organic range
Cabernet Sauvignon ☺ ★★★ Improved **10** has spice highlights to red fruit. Still selling & not revisited, as for all except Chardonnay, Chardonnay-Viognier. WO W Cape for all unless noted. **Merlot** ☺ ★★ **10**'s soft plums offset by firm tannins. **Pinotage** ☺ ★★ Lemon acidity adds zest to strawberry flavours in **10**. **Shiraz** ☺ ★★★ Interesting scrub & sour cherry notes, firm tannins on **10**. **Pinotage-Shiraz** ☺ ⊠ ★★★ **10** preview lightly flavoured, touch astringent. **Chardonnay** ☺ ⊠ ★★ Intense lemon, spice highlights on slick **11** unwooded crowd pleaser, tasted ex tank. WO Paarl. **Sauvignon Blanc** ☺ ★★ Grassy **10** tangy & dry. **Chardonnay-Viognier** ☺ ⊠ ★ Fragrant **11** preview has bold, plump palate. WO Paarl. **Sparkling Cabernet Sauvignon Rosé** ☺ ★★ **NV** sparkler an appealing celebration package. — CvZ

African Wines & Spirits

Cape Town ▪ Est 1999 ▪ Closed to public ▪ Owner(s) Edward Snell & Co ▪ Directors D Asherson, DV Hooper, IV Hooper, JM Pousson & CC Weeden ▪ 40% red 60% white ▪ PO Box 318 Paarden Eiland ▪ chrisw@esnell.co.za ▪ T +27 (0)21-506-2600 ▪ F +27 (0)21-510-4560 / +27 (0)86-682-4922

This wholesaling and marketing company is owned by Edward Snell & Co, and is responsible for the good-value range, Craighall, among other popular brands.

■ **Agterkliphoogte** *see Wandsbeck Wyne Koöp Bpk*

Agterplaas Wines

Location/WO: Stellenbosch ▪ 1stB 2003 ▪ Tasting by appt ▪ Owner(s)/winemaker(s) James Basson ▪ 2t/150cs own label 60% red 40% white ▪ PO Box 863 Stellenbosch 7599 ▪ agterplaas@adept.co.za ▪ T +27 (0)21-886-5446 ▪ F +27 (0)21-886-5446

Architectural designer James Basson vinifies only 2 tons of grapes - the chenin picked personally - in rented space at Hidden Valley. Aiming for elegance and longevity, he says: 'I don't believe in here today, gone tomorrow fruit-bomb wines, but rather wines that drink at their best after five years or more in bottle.'

Cabernet Sauvignon ★★★ Returns to the guide with **09**, blackberry & spice, dry tannin still a bit grippy. Medium body & length. **Agterplaas** 🔲 ★★★ Mainly cab & merlot, dashes cab franc, malbec & petit verdot. **06** savoury plum spice, silky tannin & integrated oak last time. **Chenin Blanc** NEW ★★★ Oatmeal & apricot on toasty backing of wooded **10**. Good length & structure, tangy acidity adds freshness. — FM

■ **Agulhas Wines** *see Strandveld Wines*

Akkerdal Wine Estate

Location/map/WO: Franschhoek ▪ Est 2000 ▪ 1stB 2001 ▪ Tasting & sales Mon-Fri 9–5 Sat 9–1 ▪ Fee R20pp ▪ Closed all pub hols ▪ Akkerdal Guest House, self-catering (see Accommodation section) ▪ Owner(s)/cellarmaster(s)/winemaker(s) Pieter Hanekom ▪ Viticulturist(s) Pieter Hanekom, advised by Eben Archer, Bennie Liebenberg & Dawid Saayman ▪ 18ha (barbera, cab f, carignan, durif, grenache noir, malbec, merlot, mourv, p verdot, roobernet, shiraz, tannat, tempranillo, chard, nouvelle, sauv, sem, viog) ▪ 3,000cs own label 95% red 4% white 1% rosé ▪ IPW 📖 ▪ PO Box 36 La Motte 7691 ▪ wine@akkerdal.co.za ▪ www.akkerdal.co.za ▪ S 33° 52'50.9" E 019° 3'3.8" ▪ T +27 (0)21-876-3481 ▪ F +27 (0)21-876-3189

Pieter Hanekom tends this small Franschhoek property, bottling only the best portions under own label, the rest bound for big brands. He's inclined to go on gut-feel rather than follow a recipe and the results are generally a little quirky but if you're tired of same old, same old then Hanekom's your man.

★★★★ **Merlot** Last-tasted **05** opulent yet elegant, polished tannins, good prospects.
★★★★ **Syrah** Sweet, round, accessible **05**, previously had fynbos & fennel edge, malty toast finish.
★★★★ **Wild Boar 09** conforms to no conventional template, with 5 different varieties inc roobernet & tempranillo. Fruit driven but not facile, with fresh acidity, dry finish. 2 years oak, 40% new. No **07**, **08**.
★★★★ **Sophia's Blush** NEW ✓ ⊠ **10** a blend of 91% pinotage & 9% grenache, this dry rosé shows real imagination. Layers of flavour inc red fruit, spice. Focused & fresh. Long, saline finish.
Petit Noir ⊠ ★★★ Malbec-led **10** shows dark fruit, herbal note on nose & palate. Rustic but not without charm.
Passion Red ★★★★ Intriguing 5-way, shiraz-led **08** shows red fruit & spice on palate. Medium bodied with well-judged oak. No **06**, **07**. **Kallie's Dream Red** ★★★ **06** blend shiraz, mourvèdre, merlot, malbec. Sweet

fruited, with serious oak when last tasted. **Sauvignon Blanc ★★ 10** understated herbal quality, gentle acidity last edition. **Kallie's Dream White ★★★ NV** blend of viognier, sauvignon, chardonnay & semillon. Not retasted, as for next. **Passion White ★★★ 05** different proportions, same varieties as above. — CE

Akkerdraai

Location/map/WO: Stellenbosch ▪ Est 1956 ▪ 1stB 2007 ▪ Tasting Mon-Fri 9-5 Sat 9-12:30 ▪ Closed Easter Fri-Mon, Dec 25 & Jan 1 ▪ Fee R20, refundable on purchase ▪ Walking/hiking trails ▪ Owner(s)/cellarmaster(s) Salie de Swardt ▪ Winemaker(s) Marius Malan (consultant), with Salie de Swardt (both Jan 2004) ▪ Viticulturist(s) Marius Malan (Jan 2004, consultant) ▪ 1.75ha (cab) ▪ 12t 100% red ▪ PO Box 22 Lynedoch 7603 ▪ saliedes@ mweb.co.za ▪ S 33° 59′ 53.52″ E 018° 49′ 50.94″ ▪ **T +27 (0)21-881-3861/+27 (0)83-264-1463** ▪ F +27 (0)21-881-3861

Retirement is supposed to be 'redelik rustig' (relatively peaceful) and that's the way former media man Salie de Swardt likes it. His smallholding off Annandale Road in the Helderberg foothills is planted solely with cab, so making wine with Marius Malan of Malanot is very much a boutique-style hobby.

★★★★ **Cabernet Sauvignon** Fynbos whiff to intense, richly fruited **08** tasted last year. Blackcurrant, white pepper, cigarbox; firm grip of well-judged oak (30% new), restrained 13% alc. Sleek, lithe frame. — FM

■ **Alexandersfontein** see Ormonde Private Cellar

AlexKia Estate

Location/map/WO: Robertson ▪ Est 2004 ▪ 1stB 2006 ▪ Tasting by appt at La Verne, Robertson ▪ Owner(s) Carla Maestroni ▪ Winemaker(s) André van Dyk (Rooiberg) ▪ ±90ha/7ha (cab, chard) ▪ ±70t/5,000cs own label 50% red 50% white + 4,000cs for clients ▪ PO Box 101 Robertson 6705 ▪ franco@alexkia.co.za ▪ www.alexkia.co.za ▪ S 33° 46′ 52.4″ E 19° 41′ 00.36″ ▪ **T +27 (0)82-575-9578, +27 (0)82-783-9825**

On the 'retirement' farm near Robertson they named after their granddaughters, Carla and Franco Maestroni are still working harder than ever. In addition to establishing a network of wine distributors in Europe, they have now planted nine hectares of rosemary for its extract, a powerful antioxidant. But wine remains the focus: 'It is the essential part of our business and pleasure.'

Alexandra Cabernet Sauvignon ⌾ ★★★ Candyfloss fragrance on easy-sipping **10**, but enough flavour & grip to take to a braai. **Merlot Reserve** ⌾ ★★★ Plush-fruited **10** billows dried herbs & spices; new oak character is attractive & restrained, commendably doesn't add vanilla sweetness to finish. **Chiara Chardonnay** ⌾ ★★★ Much-improved unoaked **11**, acacia & thatch bouquet, keenly focused acidity for seafood. — Panel

Alkmaar Boutique Vineyard

Location/WO: Wellington ▪ Map: Paarl & Wellington ▪ Est 2001 ▪ 1stB 2005 ▪ Tasting & sales Mon-Fri 10-4 Sat 10-2 ▪ Closed all religious pub hols ▪ Cellar tours by appt ▪ Walks (part of Wellington Wine Walk) ▪ Owner(s) Bouwer & Janet Nell ▪ Winemaker(s) Pieter-Niel Rossouw (Jan 2010, consultant), with Dawid Futhwa (Jan 2010) ▪ Viticulturist(s) Dawid Futhwa (Jan 2003) ▪ 7.6ha (cab, merlot, mourv, p verdot, ptage, shiraz, chard, viog) ▪ 35t/380cs own label 83% red 17% white + 12,000L bulk ▪ PO Box 1273 Blouvlei Road Wellington 7654 ▪ janet@ alkmaarwines.co.za ▪ www.alkmaarwines.co.za ▪ S 33° 39′ 37.98″ E 019° 1′ 55.14″ ▪ **T +27 (0)21-873-0191**

The didactic references in the Alkmaar wine branding recall Hollander Marinus Stucki, who founded a school on the Wellington property in the 1860s. Look out for a new shiraz-viognier-mourvèdre, The Old School Mistress, and an as yet unnamed sparkling, originally made for co-owner Bouwer Nell's 50th birthday.

The Old School Master ★★★★ Bordeaux-style red blend, **09** ripe berry fruit, dusty oak on the nose; good fruit concentration, smooth texture, soft acidity. No **08**. **The Old School Reunion** 🗐 ★★★ Shy, unevolved **10** unoaked chardonnay with citrus flavour, bright acidity, appealing if not hugely complex. — CE

Allée Bleue Wines

Location/map: Franschhoek ▪ WO: Franschhoek/Western Cape/Walker Bay/Stellenbosch ▪ Est 1690 ▪ 1stB 2001 ▪ Tasting & sales Mon-Fri 9-5 Sat 10-5 Sun 10-4 ▪ Fee R20/4 wines ▪ Closed Easter Fri ▪ Cellar tours by appt ▪ Bistro Allée Bleue open daily (see Restaurants section) ▪ Wine tasting courtyard, light lunches in summer ▪ Picnic's, booking required ▪ Jungle gym ▪ Farm produce ▪ Conferences ▪ Weddings ▪ Kendal Cottage & Manor House (see Accommodation section) ▪ Owner(s) DAUPHIN Entwicklungs-und Beteiligungs GMH (Germany) ▪ Winemaker(s) Van Zyl du Toit (Jul 2009) ▪ Viticulturist(s) Douw Willemse (Sep 2008) ▪ 135ha/30ha (cab, merlot, ptage, pinot, shiraz, chard, chenin, sauv, viog) ▪ 380t/18,000cs own label 34.5% red 55% white 5% rosé 5% MCC 0.5% fortified ▪ IPW ▪ PO Box 100 Groot Drakenstein 7680 ▪ info@alleebleue.com ▪ www.alleebleue.com ▪ S 33° 51′29.0″ E 018° 59′12.9″ ▪ **T +27 (0)21-874-1021** ▪ F +27 (0)21-874-1850

Owned by the Dauphin family from Germany, operations at this winery in Franschhoek have gone from strength to strength. To this end two senior sales and marketing managers have been appointed in the local and European offices to oversee the ever-expanding markets in Germany, Switzerland, Sweden, Canada and Denmark. Firmly established as a wedding, conference and function venue, two new méthode cap classique sparklers will be added to its range.

Allée Bleue range

★★★★ **Chenin Blanc** ✓ ▤ Rich & bold **10** bursts with tropical fruit salad, round & creamy texture with vanilla touch & perky acid. Will age well. From Walker Bay & Franschhoek.

★★★★ **Sauvignon Blanc** ✓ ▤ Tropical, herbal & mineral notes on **10** from Walker Bay, lipsmacking acidity & silky mouthfeel plumped by some sweetness, finishes with vibrant grapefruit lift.

★★★★ **Isabeau** ✓ Powerful aromas of pear, stonefruit & lanolin on **10** semillon, chardonnay & viognier flagship white. Rich, silky mouthfeel layered with creamy flavours, a citrus tang in the dry finish. WO W Cape.

Cabernet Sauvignon Await next. **Pinotage** ★★★★ Juicy plums, ripe berries & lively spice, **08** luscious & ripe last edition, but more balanced than **07** (★★★★). **Shiraz** ✓ ▤ ★★★★ Fruit-driven **10** offers ripe dark berries & spice in medium-bodied, rich & balanced offering. **Cabernet Sauvignon–Merlot** ✓ ★★★★ Cassis, dark choc & brambleberries vie for attention in **09** from Stellenbosch, harmoniously oaked & balanced. No-nonsense versatility. Delicious! **L'Amour Toujours** ✓ ★★★★ Red flagship. Cab/merlot-led blend **08** more complex than **07** (★★★★), intense ripe berry flavours, super oak balance & structure. WO W Cape. **Brut Rosé Méthode Cap Classique** [NEW] ★★★ 2 vintages reviewed: faintest onionskin **09** from chenin, pinotage, oozes green apple & plum, creamy mousse & a zesty finish. WO Coastal. Gear up **10** (★★★★) adds 15% pinot noir; soft pink, more complex & full; fine creamy bubbles & zingy finish. Franschhoek & Walker Bay vines. Both for earlier drinking. **Cape Ruby** Untasted. Discontinued: **Rosé, Pinotage Natural Sweet**.

Starlette range

Starlette Pinotage ☺ ★★★ Easy-drinking style. Ripe cherry & strawberry, **10** is juicy, popping with fruit, balanced by soft tannins. **Starlette Rosé** [NEW] ☺ ▤ ★★★ Turkish Delight flavours on bright pink **11**, from shiraz & sauvignon. Just off-dry, vivacious, fresh & spicy. A delight! **Starlette Blanc** ☺ ▤ ★★★ Pungent grapefruit & quince; though off-dry, **10** sauvignon & chenin mix is bright & focused. Perfect for summer pool party.

Starlette Rouge ★★★ Cab/merlot blend for early consumption. Earthy red berries, **08** balanced soft tannins & mouthwatering acidity when last tasted. — WB

Allesverloren Estate

Location: Riebeek West ▪ Map/WO: Swartland ▪ Est 1704 ▪ Tasting & sales Mon-Fri 8.30–5 Sat 8.30–2 ▪ Fee R15pp for groups of 10 and more ▪ Closed Easter Fri/Mon, Dec 25 & Jan 1 ▪ Cellar tours by appt ▪ Pleasant Pheasant Restaurant Tue 10.30–3 Wed-Sat 9-3 & 6-10 Sun 9-4 ▪ Facilities for children ▪ Conference/function venue ▪ Owner(s) Malan Boerdery Trust ▪ Cellarmaster(s) Danie Malan (Nov 1987) ▪ Winemaker(s) Danie Malan (Nov 1987) & Louis van Riet ▪ 227ha/187ha (cab, shiraz & various port varieties) ▪ 50,000cs own label 100% red ▪ PO Box 23 Riebeek West 7306 ▪ info@allesverloren.co.za ▪ www.allesverloren.co.za ▪ S 33° 21′32.5″ E 018° 52′24.1″ ▪ **T +27 (0)22-461-2320** ▪ F +27 (0)22-461-2444

This estate, the oldest in the Swartland, acquired its name in the 18th century when one of its owners returned from a church visit to Stellenbosch to find the property devastated in a raid by San hunters, causing him to observe 'Allesverloren' (All is lost). It's been in the Malan family since 1872, current cellarmaster Danie the sixth generation to farm here. Unshowy, honest wines, and function facilities which now include an outdoor chapel.

★★★★ **Shiraz** Understated **10**, berries, vanilla & fynbos; medium bodied & well balanced with juicy fruit, fresh acidity & fine tannins.

★★★★☆ **Port 07** more smoothly approachable, delicious in youth than many Vintage ports, yet complex when last tasted.

Cabernet Sauvignon ★★★ 09 appears old-fashioned, ungiving but should open up in a few years. Medium bodied, some blackcurrant flavour, very firm tannins. **Tinta Barocca ★★★** One of the original unfortified varietal bottlings of Portuguese red-wine grape in Cape. **08** still selling; lightly juicy, modest oak, acidity a little sharp. **Touriga Nacional ★★★ 09** rustic & youthfully introverted, dark fruit with spice & pronounced acidity. — CE

Alluvia Winery & Private Residence Club

Location/map: Stellenbosch ▪ WO: Stellenbosch/Western Cape/Banghoek ▪ Est 2002 ▪ 1stB 2005 ▪ Tasting & sales daily 9-5 ▪ Fee R30 ▪ Closed Easter Fri & Dec 25 ▪ Cellar tours by appt ▪ Two 5-star self-catering houses & five 4-star suites ▪ Breakfast & picnic baskets for stay-over guests ▪ Day & estate spa ▪ Facilities for children ▪ Tour groups ▪ Gift shop ▪ BYO picnic ▪ Conferences ▪ Hiking & mountain biking trails ▪ Helipad ▪ Fly fishing ▪ PGA golf tee & green ▪ Owner(s) Brugman family ▪ Cellarmaster(s) Delarey Brugman ▪ Winemaker(s) Delarey Brugman & Neil Moorhouse ▪ Viticulturist(s) Bennie Booysen (Jan 2009, consultant) ▪ 11ha/7ha (cabs s/f, sauv) ▪ 30t/1,800cs own label 85% red 10% white 5% straw wine ▪ PO Box 6365 Uniedal 7612 ▪ wine@alluvia.co.za ▪ www.alluvia.co.za ▪ S 33° 55' 4.7" E 018° 55' 37.1" ▪ **T +27 (0)21-885-1661** ▪ F +27 (0)21-885-2064

The luxury guest house and residence club are central to this tiny property, explaining the many facilities on offer. On the wine side, only three varieties are planted, cab, cab franc, both single-vineyards, and sauvignon, and co-owner/cellarmaster Delarey Brugman believes in keeping them in the family. Ilka is named after twin daughters Ilsa and Karla, Lisa is the youngest daughter and Sandie is his wife. The Give Me a Chance range funds a social upliftment programme.

Princess range

★★★★ **Ilka Cabernet Sauvignon** Intense blackcurrant with cedar spicing, vintage-influenced **08** is more tightly held, lacks the silkiness, finesse of **07** (★★★★★), but still offers a flavourful mouthful. WO W Cape.

★★★★ **Lisa Vineyard Cabernet Franc** Lovely purity on **09**, template for the variety; herbal notes & brambleberry, tobacco savouriness, yet the ripeness is there in the curvaceous body, soft finish. WO Banghoek.

★★★★ **Ilka Sauvignon Blanc** Individual, another take on sauvignon, **11** preview shows yellow apple & melon, with freshening acidity giving it focus & length.

Queen range

★★★★ **Sandie Viognier Straw Wine** Tasted from barrel, where it will spend year, **10** (★★★★★) is richer than **09**, reflects apricot, peach & quince preserves - & barley sugar. Syrupy in its richness, it has an intriguing olive oil note at the end. Superb. 375ml.

Give Me A Chance range

Red Blend 🪣 ★★★ Last tasted was easy-drinking **07** mix Bordeaux varieties; packed with red & black berries, dusty note from year oak-staving. **Sauvignon Blanc** 🪣 **11** not tasted this edition. — CR

■ **Almara** *see Southern Sky Wines*

Almenkerk Wine Estate

Location/WO: Elgin ▪ Map: Elgin, Walker Bay & Bot River ▪ Est 2004 ▪ 1stB 2009 ▪ Tasting, sales & cellar tours Tue-Sat 10-4 Sun/Mon by appt only; open pub hols but call ahead during winter ▪ Meals/picnics by prior booking or BYO picnic ▪ Walking/hiking trails ▪ Conservation area ▪ Heliport ▪ Boules court ▪ Owner(s) Van Almenkerk family ▪ Cellarmaster(s) Joris van Almenkerk ▪ Winemaker(s) Joris van Almenkerk, with Danver van Wyk (Feb 2009) ▪ Viticulturist(s) Neil de Beer (May 2010) & Kevin Watt (consultant) ▪ 104.2ha/15ha (cabs s/f, malbec, merlot, mourv, p verdot, shiraz, chard, sauv, viog) ▪ 90t/705cs own label 50% red 40% white 10% rosé ▪ Brand for client: De Mikke Patron ▪ BWI ▪ PO Box 1129 Grabouw 7160 ▪ info@almenkerk.co.za ▪ www.almenkerk.co.za ▪ S 34° 12'55" E 019° 01'57" ▪ **T +27 (0)21-848-9844** ▪ F +27 (0)86-523-0877

A local attending the opening a while back of the Almenkerk cellar and visitor centre remarked that the spacious architect-designed complex represented a coming of age for the Elgin wine ward. Symbolism aside, the hillside facility is performing as intended, cellarmaster Joris van Almenkerk vinifing the own-brands ('Lace' an allusion to the Belgian family origins) as well as other vintners' labels. No way in the available space can we summarise the Almenkerks' news and plans. Suffice to say no Elgin trip would be complete without a visit and catch-up.

Almenkerk Wine Estate range

★★★★ **Sauvignon Blanc** ✓ 🔲 🎖 Understated, dry **10** follows previous: nettle & green fig, 'wet stone' minerality & seabreeze complexity, a pleasing gravelly texture & persistence. Worth seeking out.

Chardonnay NEW 🎖 ★★★★ One to watch. **10** has lemon-lime & coconut flavours, brisk acidity refreshes off-dry dollop sugar, a little new oak gives both weight & spice. Discontinued: **Merlot Rosé**.

Lace range NEW

Lace Red Blend 🔲 ★★★ Bordeaux-style blend, **09** meaty aromas & blackcurrant flavours, smooth & easy.

Yvonne range

Discontinued: **Sauvignon Blanc**. — CvZ

Alto Wine Estate

Location/map/WO: Stellenbosch ▪ Est 1693 ▪ 1stB 1921 ▪ Tasting & sales Mon-Fri 9–5 Sat/Sun10–4 ▪ Fee R10 wine tasting/ R10 port tasting ▪ Closed Easter Fri, Dec 25 ▪ Pâté & wine pairing R50pp, advance booking required ▪ Hiking trail ▪ Owner(s) Lusan Premium Wines ▪ Cellarmaster(s)/winemaker(s) Schalk van der Westhuizen (Jun 2000) ▪ Viticulturist(s) Eben Archer (consultant) ▪ 191ha/93ha (cabs s/f, merlot, shiraz) ▪ 800t/50,000cs own label 100% red ▪ PO Box 104 Stellenbosch 7599 ▪ info@alto.co.za ▪ www.alto.co.za ▪ S 34° 0' 10.4" E 018° 50' 49. 4" ▪ **T +27 (0)21-881-3884** ▪ F +27 (0)21-881-3894

A special wine (untasted this edition) has been released by this historic Helderberg farm, its name, MPHS, being the initials of past and incumbent winemakers. It's a Bordeaux-style red, nodding to Margaux in style (and price!), and honouring the legacy of fine-wine making at the estate over the past century. The other, equally elegant - and more pocket-friendly - reds, plus optional pâté pairings, are another good reason to visit.

★★★★ **Cabernet Sauvignon** ✓ From Stellenbosch's reputed 'Golden Triangle', **09** is classically structured & taut. Elegant, despite youth, with characteristic blackcurrant & subtle oak nuance. Cellarworthy table mate.

★★★★ **Alto Rouge** Previously tasted **08** (★★★★) was less graceful than **07**, but still an amenable, fruity shiraz/Bordeaux blend.

Shiraz ★★★★ No newer vintage tasted since firm, but ripe & tasty **08**. Not revisited, nor next. **Port** ★★★★ **06** from shiraz, previously was light with gentle grip. — MW

Altydgedacht Estate

Location/WO: Durbanville ▪ Map: Durbanville, Philadelphia & Darling ▪ Est 1698 ▪ 1stB 1981 ▪ Tasting & sales Mon-Fri 9–5 Sat 9–3 ▪ Closed Easter Fri/Sun, Dec 25 & Jan 1 ▪ Cellar tours by appt ▪ Breakfast & light lunches Mon-Sat 9.30-4 T +27 (0)975-7815 eat@altydgedacht.co.za ▪ Facilities for children ▪ Conferences ▪ Weddings/functions ▪ Conservation area ▪ Owner(s) Parker family ▪ Cellarmaster(s) Oliver Parker (1981) ▪ Winemaker(s) Etienne Louw (Jan 2006) ▪ Viticulturist(s) John Parker (1981) ▪ 412ha/180ha (16 varieties, r/w) ▪ 1,500t total 125t/ 9,000cs own label 30% red 65% white 5% rosé ▪ Other export brand: Ralph Parker ▪ PO Box 213 Durbanville 7551 ▪ altydgedacht@mweb.co.za ▪ www.altydgedacht.co.za ▪ S 33° 50' 46.6" E 018° 37' 26.4" ▪ **T +27 (0)21-976-1295** ▪ F +27 (0)21-976-4318

In response to surging demand, Altydgedacht's owners, the Parker family, have upgraded the packaging, and almost doubled production, of their niche varieties. Winemaker Etienne Louw is enjoying being kept on his toes with a trio of new styles: an MCC, a Cape blend (with trademark barbera) and a dessert wine, and is even considering a rendition of the heartbreak grape - pinot noir. He's proudest though of his Pinotage, which has begun earning him a number of accolades.

Parker Family Reserve range

★★★★ **Tintoretto** NEW Revival of flagship red label not seen for 20 years. **09** pinotage-led with barbera, spicy shiraz & cab; judicious oaking frames supple, succulent flavours.

★★★★ **The Ollo Estate White** ✓ Aromatic viognier adds charm to dry **11** flagship white semillon-led blend, with chardonnay & chenin. Fermentation in barrel broadens flavours, provides weight & firm texture.

★★★★ **MCC Blanc de Blanc** NEW All-chardonnay maiden **08** bubbly commendably complex with attractive yeastiness & refreshing thread of acidity throughout.

Semillon NLH NEW ★★★ Lightly spicy, soft **11** dessert wine has easy, pleasingly sweet & simple charm balanced by sufficient acidity to prevent cloying finish.

Altydgedacht Cultivar range

★★★★ **Cabernet Sauvignon Limited Release** NEW Appetisingly fresh 09 hits the spot with ample succulent fruit supported by fine tannins & savoury acidity to create stylishly elegant impression.

★★★★ **Barbera** Smoky, mocha-laced 10 (★★★★) exhibits variety's appetisingly fresh acidity. Lighter, simpler than last tasted 08. Pioneers of barbera in SA.

★★★★ **Sauvignon Blanc** 🍸 Tricky 11 (★★★★) vintage prompts dip in complexity. 10 reflected generally improved ratings for this well-made sauvignon, with dash semillon & lees contact for breadth.

Merlot Limited Release NEW ★★★ 09 in light herbaceous style, savoury & elegant but perhaps too light & insufficiently ripe to entice. **Pinotage** ★★★★ Elegantly-styled 10 shows wonderful balance, freshness & purity of fruit. More expressive than 09 (★★★★), shows what variety offers in cooler climate with judicious oaking. **Shiraz** ★★★ Lean, supple, vanilla-spiced 08 not re-tasted. Spicy freshness & savoury acidity lent elegance. **Gewürztraminer** 🍸 ★★★ Lightly aromatic 11 pleasantly dry & fresh, though less flavour concentration & weight than usual.

Tygerberg range

> **Gamay Noir** ☺🍸 ★★★ Pale, unoaked 11 from 24 yr-old estate vines offers light, sour-cherry quaffer can be served chilled any time of day. **Blanc de Blanc** ☺🍸 ★★★ Aromatic 11 blend press portions of all white varieties grown here, delightfully dry sipper. **Chatelaine** ☺🍸 ★★★ Spicy off-dry 11 meets demand for aromatic whites. Riesling-led blend, plus gewurtz & muscat delivers fresh charmer.

Cabernet Franc Rosé 🍸 ★★★ Delightfully aromatic, dry, juicy & fresh 10 tasted last year. — IM

Alvi's Drift Private Cellar

Location/map: Worcester ▪ WO: Worcester/Western Cape ▪ Est 1928 ▪ 1stB 2004 ▪ Tasting, sales & tours by appt ▪ Closed all pub hols ▪ Farm produce ▪ Owner(s) Bertie, Alvi & Johan van der Merwe ▪ Cellarmaster(s) Henk Swart ▪ Winemaker(s) Henk Swart, Alvi van der Merwe & Linley Schultz, with Freddie Scanlen ▪ Viticulturist(s) Pierre Snyman (consultant) & Jan du Toit ▪ 6,000ha/400ha (ptage, shiraz, chard, chenin, muscat de F) ▪ ±5,000t/25,000cs own label ▪ IPW ▪ PO Box 126 Worcester 6850 ▪ info@alvisdrift.co.za ▪ www.alvisdrift.co.za ▪ S 33° 46' 25.8" E 019° 31'53.7" ▪ **T +27 (0)23-340-4117** ▪ F +27 (0)86-654-9425

A fresh team, which includes accomplished former Distell group winemaker Linley Schultz, is transforming this family winery into one of the most dynamic in the Breede River Valley. Grapes are grown in an environmentally friendly, sustainable way, and in the cellar they're experimenting with wild-yeast fermentations. Highlights last year were their first exports to Europe and Asia, and the launch of Naughty Girl sparkling rosé – a huge hit at the inaugural Gugulethu Wine Festival.

AD range

★★★★ **Drift Fusion** 50/50 mix of cab & pinotge. Bold & very ripe 08 still selling, showed chunky spice & choc, earthy intensity, tannic grip mid-2010.

★★★★ **CVC** 🍸 ⌘ Elegant chenin/viognier blend with dash chardonnay. 10 rich & fruit-filled, with lingering spicy flavours. Something special, to sip attentively.

Chardonnay 🍸 ⌘ ★★★★ Moves from Premium range. Up on last 07 (★★★), 10 delivers an exceptional taste experience, with restrained oak embellishment to buttery orange flavours. **SVC** 🍸 Await next.

Premium Selection

★★★★☆ **Muscat de Frontignan White** Alluring fortified dessert with sherry-like oxidative notes, 07 exceptionally sweet & viscous yet delightfully clean & fresh, as was seductive, mouthcoating 06.
Discontinued: Cape Fusion, Chardonnay-Viognier, Muscat de Frontignan Red.

Signature range

Cabernet Sauvignon 🍸 ⌘ ★★★ Fruit-bomb 10 dusted with oak spice, quaffable despite tad unknit tannins. **Pinotage** 🍸 ⌘ ★★ Vanilla-toned 10 for early drinking. **Shiraz** 🍸 ⌘ ★★★ Faint 'wild' hint on cherry-fruited 10. **Chenin Blanc Unwooded** ✓🍸 ⌘ ★★★★ 10 punches above its price bracket. Oxidative styling, almond/marzipan & pineapple character, pleasing savoury conclusion. **Sauvignon Blanc** 🍸 ⌘ ★★★ 10 very sippable, with asparagus & grass, ripely rounded mouthfeel. Shows signs of evolution, so drink soon. WO W Cape. **Viognier** ✓🍸 ⌘ ★★★★ Oak & ginger spice, attractive stonefruit on zesty 10. Improves on last-tasted 07 (★★★); deft handling of a variety that can be blowsy. Lightly oak-chipped, like the reds in this range.

Alvi's Drift Private Cellar range

Naughty Girl ★★★ Delightful off-dry **NV** rosé sparkler, just 7.5% alc & 'berryful'. — Panel

■ **Amalienstein** *see* Ladismith Cellar - SCV
■ **Amandalia** *see* Rooiberg Winery

Amani Vineyards

Location/map: Stellenbosch ▪ WO: Stellenbosch/Coastal ▪ Est/1stB 1997 ▪ Tasting, sales & cellar tours Mon-Fri 9–4.30 Sat 10-4 ▪ Closed Easter Fri-Mon, Dec 25/26 & Jan 1 ▪ Facilities for children ▪ BYO picnic ▪ Walks/hikes ▪ Owner(s) Lynde & Rusty Myers ▪ Cellarmaster(s) Carmen Stevens (Jul 2005) ▪ Winemaker(s) Carmen Stevens (Jul 2005), with Chris van Reenen (Jan 2011) ▪ Viticulturist(s) JD Stassen (Apr 2006) ▪ 38ha/32ha (cabs s/f, merlot, mourv, shiraz, chard, sauv, viog) ▪ 217t/10,000cs own label 70% red 29% white 1% rosé ▪ EnviroWines ▪ PO Box 12422 Die Boord 7613 ▪ wine@amani.co.za ▪ www.amani.co.za ▪ S 33° 57' 54.3" E 018° 43' 59.5" ▪ **T +27 (0)21-881-3930** ▪ F +27 (0)21-881-3931

This boutique cellar has flourished with their low-volume, high-quality approach, but yet the wines have still to reach their full potential. Holistic and biological methods in managing that vital element - soil, as well as harvesting decisions based on infrared images (each vigour level is picked separately), manifests clearly in the resulting wines. Amani's reputation was built on chardonnay and merlot, since when they have added two accomplished, similarly styled shirazes and various blends to their portfolio.

Atkinson Ridge range

Chardonnay ★★★★ Savoury, nutty **06** showed generous oak easily handled by fruit when last tasted. **04** (★★★★) savoury & steely. **Sauvignon Blanc** Await next.

Amani range

★★★★☆ **Merlot** Plummy, savoury **09** includes cab, petit verdot, mourvèdre. Core red fruit supported by seamless oak tannins & fine acidity. Vineyard care shows in this tricky variety's supple, expressive & vivid fruit.

★★★★ **Cabernet Franc-Merlot** Leafy aromas in classic **09**, with cab& drop of petit verdot. Spicy oak gives structure to plush plum appeal, reminiscent of Bordeaux; acid thread ensures appetising whole.

★★★★ **Jordan Myers** Previously, like last-tasted **06**, with 'Shiraz-Cab' in name. But **09** (★★★★★) version of best-years-only label is merlot-led Bordeaux blend. Core plush red fruit has classic appeal & appetising herbal edge. Serious structure & depth of fruit bode augur well.

★★★★ **I Am 1** **09** blends 5 Bordeaux varieties + spicy shiraz. Ingratiating richness structured by oaking (a third of the barrels new). Delivers layered flavours, as harmonious as name suggests.

★★★★ **Chardonnay** ✓ 🈂 Excellent track record since maiden **98**. Deliciously rich **10** epitome of harmony. Full texture from natural yeasts, lees & oak. Bright lime acidity lifts richness.

★★★★ **Kamili Chardonnay-Viognier** ✓ Gold coloured, oaked **11**; 55% wild ferment, leesy chardonnay, with partly vine-dried viognier. Intriguingly complex, richly textured, with lively acidity to harmonise.

> **Poppy Blush** **NEW** ☺ ★★★ Weighty, flavourful preview **11** shiraz, dollop viognier. Sweet impression from sugar & 15% alc.

Forest Myers ★★★★ Renamed from FM 'Shiraz' to reflect other varieties' bigger input, notably mourvèdre & viognier. More favourable **09** vintage has splash of cab too, with more depth & structure than riper, softer, more effusive **08** with less mourvèdre, more shiraz (★★★★). **Pendana Shiraz** ★★★★ Spicy, relaxed, soft-fruited **09** less focused than **08** (★★★★) but enjoyable. As with other wines here, judiciously oaked to preserve fruit expression. **Chardonnay Reserve** Occasional release. **Sauvignon Blanc** ★★★★ Preview **11** in fresh, quiet, unshowy style. Lighter than previous **09** (★★★★) though barrel fermented portion gives breadth. — IM

Amares Wines

Location/map: Stellenbosch ▪ WO: Simonsberg–Stellenbosch/Stellenbosch ▪ Est 2005 ▪ 1stB 2006 ▪ Tasting, sales & cellar tours Mon-Sat by appt ▪ Closed all pub hols ▪ Cheese & olive platters by appt ▪ Owner(s) Amares Wines (Pty) Ltd ▪ Winemaker(s) Neville Koudstaal (Mar 2006) ▪ Viticulturist(s) TC Botha (Mar 2005, consultant) ▪ 5ha/ 2ha (cab) ▪ 4t/375cs own label 100% red ▪ PO Box 7253 Stellenbosch 7599 ▪ info@amares.co.za ▪ www.amares. co.za ▪ S 33° 54' 30.30" E 018° 53' 27.21" ▪ **T +27 (0)21-887-9414** ▪ F +27 (0)21-413-0854

This partnership of 'family and friends who cherish all things decadent' moved in 2005 to a 5-hectare farm surrounded by famous Rustenberg estate, aiming to 'experience the things we value most in life'. It's all small-scale and hands-on – and environmentally careful: although the cabernet vineyard is not certified, organic principles guide the farming practices. Shiraz grapes are brought in.

Cabernet Sauvignon ★★★★ Solidly built, tasty **08** neither stern nor frivolous. Firmly built & sweet-fruited, slightly drying finish. Both these pleasingly savoury. **Syrah** ★★★★ Ripe, bold, rich & full-flavoured **08** has more power than finesse. As with the Cab, the oak is well calculated. — TJ

■ **Ama Ulibo** *see Goedverwacht Wine Estate*

Ambeloui Wine Cellar

Location: Hout Bay ▪ Map: Cape Peninsula ▪ WO: Western Cape ▪ Est 1994 ▪ 1stB 1998 ▪ Tasting by appt ▪ Sales once a year on new wine release date (1st Sat in Nov) ▪ Owner(s) Nick & Ann Christodoulou ▪ Cellarmaster(s)/viticulturist(s) Nick Christodoulou (1994) ▪ Winemaker(s) Nick Christodoulou (2005), with Alexis & Christo Christodoulou ▪ 1ha/0.5ha (pinot, chard) ▪ 15t/1,500cs own label 5% white 95% MCC ▪ PO Box 26800 Hout Bay 7872 ▪ wine@ambeloui.co.za ▪ www.ambeloui.co.za ▪ S 34° 0' 49.5" E 018° 22' 55.4" ▪ **T +27 (0)21-790-7386/+27 (0)82-880-1715/+27 (0)82-460-8399** ▪ F +27 (0)88-021-790-7386

Nick Christodolou's top quality range of bubblies shows what focusing on a single style (and upgrading to a modern MCC-tuned bag press) can achieve, though his twin sons Alexis and Christo are intent on adding a still chardonnay-pinot blend to the portfolio - to be called, aptly, Didima (twins in Greek).

★★★★☆ **MCC** ✓ Richly aromatic, complex **09** 'Nicholas' close to French benchmark. Harmonious, classy & stylish: bubbles finely beaded, half pinot adds fine backbone to deliciously creamy chardonnay, while integrated oak adds breadth, complexity to refined finish.

★★★★☆ **Rosanne Rosé** ✓ Dazzling, fine-beaded, salmon-pink **NV** disgorged **11** shows usual impressive harmony & poise. Vibrant, (equal portion) chardonnay & pinot flavours effortlessly supported by oak fermentation, adding breadth & creaminess to long, racy conclusion. — IM

■ **Amira** *see Avondale Bio-LOGIC & Organic Wines*

Anatu Wines

Location: Stellenbosch ▪ Map: Helderberg ▪ WO: Coastal ▪ Est/1stB 2002 ▪ Tasting, sales & cellar tours by appt ▪ Closed all pub hols ▪ Owner(s) André & Freda Hamersma ▪ Winemaker(s) Micu Narunsky (Jan 2009) ▪ 40t/2,800cs own label 40% red 40% white 20% rosé ▪ Other export brand: Sereia ▪ Postnet Suite 246 Private Bag X5061 Stellenbosch 7599 ▪ sales@anatu.co.za ▪ www.anatu.co.za ▪ S 34° 1' 52.20" E 018° 50' 46.73" ▪ **T +27 (0)83-307-9333** ▪ F +27 (0)86-577-5019

Former Johannesburg bankers André and Freda Hamersma have moved their winemaking operations to the old Cordoba cellar in the Helderberg, revamped the Anatu branding and website, increased production, launched the first white wine, and at press time were set to plant their first 'own vines' on 4.5 hectares in the Paarl area. With winemaker Micu Narunsky (who now also vinifies his eponymous own-range here), they're creating a new entry-level brand, Sereia, with labels inspired by Khoisan rock paintings of mermaids found deep in the arid Karoo.

Family Blend range

★★★★☆ **Red** *Previously listed as 'Family Blend'.* Full-bodied, modern but elegant mix of grenache, shiraz, dash mourvèdre from Paarl & Swartland vines. Last-tasted **08** returned to form after **07** (★★★★), concentrated black fruit & excellent oaking.

Anatu Wines range

★★★★ **Shiraz** Heady scents of black berries, violets & pepper on **08**, with dollops grenache & mourvèdre ex Paarl. Balanced, elegant & moreish. For the long haul. Not retasted.

★★★★☆ **Fugue** NEW ✓ Debut stunner! **10** blend of roussanne, chenin & grenache blanc is rich & mouthfilling, waxy ripe-fruit flavours supported by precise oaking. Will reward ageing.

Rosé ★★★★ Still-available **09** from mourvèdre & shiraz (ex Swartland), spicy strawberry & cherry with a delicate, lingering perfume. — WB

■ **Ancient Africa** *see Baarsma Wine Group*

Andreas Wines

Location/WO: Wellington ▪ Map: Paarl & Wellington ▪ Est 2003 ▪ 1stB 2004 ▪ Tasting & sales by appt Mon–Fri 9–5 ▪ Fee R10 ▪ Closed all pub hols ▪ Cellar tours by appt ▪ Accommodation ▪ Weddings/functions ▪ Owner(s) Jan & Anita Bokdal ▪ Cellarmaster(s) Howard Heughs, Eugenie Ellis & Bertus Fourie (consultant) ▪ Winemaker(s) Howard Heughs & Ettienne Malan (consultant) ▪ Viticulturist(s) Howard Heughs ▪ 6ha/4.5ha (mourv, shiraz) ▪ 48t/1,584cs own label 100% red ▪ andreas@ezinet.co.za ▪ www.andreas.co.za ▪ S 33° 37'52.0" E 019° 2'50.1" ▪ **T +27 (0)21-873-2286** ▪ F +27 (0)86-664-5087

Vineyards planted in 2002 are now in full production at Jan and Anita Bokdal's biodynamic-influenced estate in the Bovlei area of Wellington, prompting the Swedish couple to contemplate a cellar upgrade. As the vines mature, American oak and new barrels are being scaled back 'to keep the balance between fruit and wood, and the wine slightly feminine for a shiraz'.

★★★★ **Andreas Shiraz** Higher general rating for highly individual shiraz. Intense choc-dipped strawberry & liquorice, **09** super-silky, with well-judged oak & wine's signature blackberry liqueur aftertaste. — WB

Andy Mitchell Wines

Location: Greyton ▪ Map: Southern Cape ▪ WO: Bamboes Bay/Stellenbosch ▪ Est/1stB 2003 ▪ Tasting, sales & tours by appt ▪ Closed Easter Fri/Sun & Dec 25 ▪ Owner(s) Andy & Vikki Mitchell ▪ Cellarmaster(s) Andy Mitchell (Jan 2003) ▪ Winemaker(s) Andy Mitchell (Jan 2003), with Olivia Mitchell (Jan 2008) ▪ 7t/350cs own label 41% red 25% white 18% rosé 16% MCC + 75cs for clients ▪ PO Box 543 Paarden Eiland 7420 ▪ andy@andymitchellwines.com ▪ www.andymitchellwines.com ▪ S 34° 2'26.3" E 019° 37'2.6" ▪ **T +27 (0)28-254-9045** ▪ F +27 (0)86-611-3106

Greyton winemaker since 2003, Andy Mitchell's business model builds on the freedom of owning no vines himself, to source 'small parcels of spectacular fruit which will make standout wines'. He rings the changes often to keep the interest up, but his winemaking lodestars remain minimal intervention and finely judged oaking.

★★★★ **Crooked Path Shiraz** Ripeness on still-selling **06** reined in by savoury acidity & tannin backbone, lifted by dash viognier. Like all except Nerina, not revisited. All WO Stellenbosch unless noted.

★★★★ **Chenin Blanc** 🔲 Partially barrel-fermented **09**'s (★★★★) steely presence layered with vanilla. Lacked dimension of **08** mid-2010 but may have developed complexity with cellaring.

Pinot Noir ★★★ Forest floor & cherry nuanced **09**, from Bamboes Bay fruit, in scarce supply as remaining stock is Andy's 'house wine'. **Breakfast Rock Syrah** ★★★★ Last-tasted **07** dark fruited & lithe but bold courtesy 15. 2% alc, so not as balanced as **05** (★★★★). **Nerina Shiraz Rosé** 🔲 ★★★ **10**, now bottled, appealing dry berry flavours for al fresco sipping. — Panel

Angels Tears Wines

WO: Western Cape/Franschhoek ▪ Closed to public ▪ Owner(s) Dutch & Belgium consortium ▪ Cellarmaster(s) Jaco Marais (Nov 2003) ▪ Winemaker(s) Jaco Marais ▪ Viticulturist(s) Jaco Marais (Jun 2005) ▪ 32ha/22ha (cab, merlot, chard, sauv) ▪ 600t/30,000cs own label 30% red 60% white 10% rosé ▪ PO Box 102 Franschhoek 7690 ▪ enquiries@grandeprovence.co.za ▪ www.angelstears.co.za ▪ **T +27 (0)21-876-8600** ▪ F +27 (0)21-876-8601

Under the mantle of Grande Provence in Franschhoek, this budget-conscious range focuses on unashamedly New World styles, concentrating on retail and restaurant trade locally while probing export markets on five continents. Grande Provence winemaker Jaco Marais is now running both operations.

White Chenin Blanc-Muscat d'Alexandrie ☺ 🔲 ★★★ 'White' last year. Spicy muscat fruit dominates **10** off-dry crowd-pleaser.

Red Merlot-Cabernet Sauvignon 🔲 ★★ Just 'Red' previously. **10** merlot-based blend improved, but still light & nutty. WO Franschhoek. **Pink Chenin Blanc-Pinotage** 🔲 ★★ 'Pink' last time. Undemanding, tutti-frutti **11** off-dry quaffer. **Sauvignon Blanc** 🔲 ★★★ Previously tasted **10** from sauvignon, crisp acid, dusty granadilla flavour. — GdB

■ **Ankerman** *see uniWines Marketing*

Annandale Wines

Location/map: Stellenbosch ▪ Est/1stB 1996 ▪ Tasting, sales & cellar tours Mon-Sat 9–5 ▪ Fee R20 ▪ Closed Easter Fri-Mon, Ascension Day & Dec 25 ▪ Farm produce ▪ BYO picnic ▪ Owner(s) Hempies du Toit ▪ Winemaker(s)/viticulturist(s) Hempies du Toit (1996) ▪ 72ha/45ha (cabs s/f, merlot, shiraz) ▪ 250t/5,000cs own label 100% red ▪ PO Box 12681 Stellenbosch 7613 ▪ info@annandale.co.za ▪ www.annandale.co.za ▪ S 33° 59'49.2" E 018° 49'50.9" ▪ **T +27 (0)21-881-3560** ▪ F +27 (0)21-881-3562

Grapes from the charming, ever-welcoming Helderberg farm of former rugby Springbok Hempies du Toit find their way into the bottles of some very grand producers. And, of course, into his own small range of wines, which have the great advantage of becoming available when nicely mature. One of them (the merlot below, but under a special name) was served at the 2011 royal wedding in Monaco.

★★★★ **Shiraz** Spicy, oaky complexity added to fruit on last-tasted satisfying, unshowy & firmly built **03**.

Cabernet Sauvignon ★★★★ Usual serious-minded, dry classicism on big, spicy **04**. Like Merlot & Sauvignon, tasted pre-bottling - after long wait in barrel, which exposes tannins from drying out effect on fruit - but still some sweet succulence here. **03** (★★★★) was bottled earlier. **Merlot** NEW ★★★★ Big, burly **05**'s herbal-edged fruit has survived 6 years in oak, but mouth-drying finish. Ready now, but like all these should keep well. **Cavalier** ★★★★ Last-tasted **01** was balanced Bordeaux blend + shiraz. **Nostalgia** NEW ★★★★ A tribute to old-style Cape reds, from cab, shiraz & cinsaut - latter adding lovely wild, raspberry notes. **NV**, from various years; mature but not dried out; power but also charm. Only in magnum. Old-timers would have liked it too. Sample tasted, so provisional rating. **Sauvignon Blanc** NEW ★★★☆ Unusual, successful take on variety in **11**. Oxidative styling lessens fruitiness, not flavour. Lightly rich, dry, savoury; herbal acidity shows at end. Coastal WO. **CVP** ★★★★ 'Cape Vintage Port' from shiraz; richly spicy **03** was last tasted. — TJ

Annex Kloof Wines

Location: Malmesbury ▪ Map/WO: Swartland ▪ Est/1stB 2006 ▪ Tasting, sales & cellar tours by appt ▪ Closed Easter Fri-Mon, Ascension day, Pentecost, Dec 16/25/26 & Jan 1 ▪ BYO picnic ▪ Walking/hiking & 4x4 trails ▪ Conservation area ▪ Owner(s) Toeloe Basson with sons Thys, Hugo & Tobie Basson ▪ Winemaker(s) Hugo Basson (Jan 2006) ▪ 450ha (cab, malbec, merlot, ptage, shiraz, chard, chenin, sauv) ▪ 4,300t/625cs own label 100% red ▪ PO Box 772 Malmesbury 7299 ▪ hugo@annexkloofwines.co.za ▪ S 33° 30' 39.1" E 018° 48' 22.5" ▪ **T +27 (0)22-487-3870** ▪ F +27 (0)22-487-3870

Inspired by the quality coming out of the revolutionised Perdeberg part of the Swartland, these farmers supplying big merchants set aside some vineyards where only quality counted. Their choice of malbec as a flagship surprised some, but recently-tasted earlier vintages of Hugo Basson's delightful, naturally fermented and well-structured wine revealed its ageability too.

★★★★ **Malbec** ✓ **09** shows usual flavour profile: mulberry, loganberry, black plum, lingering dry finish. But more depth & intensity, & firmer, confident structure; the best yet. Delicious now, will keep.

★★★★ **Red Blend** Still-selling **07** (★★★★), as tasty as **06**, has ultra-ripe component, so a touch hollower. But not unfresh; plenty of good flavour, with typical fine, firm Perdeberg tannins. Shiraz, with cab, merlot.

White Blend ★★★★ Last tasted was unshowy, vibrant **08** blend of sauvignon, chenin & chardonnay. — TJ

AntHill Wines

Location: Somerset West ▪ Map: Helderberg ▪ WO: Stellenbosch ▪ Est 1999 ▪ 1stB 2000 ▪ Tasting by appt ▪ Owner(s) Mark Howell & Hylton Schwenk ▪ Winemaker(s) Mark Howell (Feb 2000) ▪ 300cs own label 100% red ▪ 19 Immelman Rd Somerset West 7130 ▪ anthill@absamail.co.za ▪ S 34° 4'30.8" E 018° 52'37.6" ▪ **T +27 (0)82-895-9008** ▪ F +27 (0)21-851-5914

Garagiste vintners Mark Howell and Hylton Schwenk have a loyal following built up over more than a decade. 'We'd like to see wine as well televised as food and cooking shows have become,' says Mark. 'Moves by the industry to pair food and wine add to the education of the consumer, and allow for more experimentation.'

★★★★ **Cabernet Sauvignon Entre Nous** Last edition, **07**'s was a bold Helderberg cab with lush, minty black berry fruit. Had seductive charm, fine tannin grip. Should drink well now.

Shiraz Entre Nous ★★★☆ Super-extracted **07**, rich port-like aromas, fruit flavours ripe but well framed by firm tannins. Not retasted. **The Persian Shiraz** 🔲 ★★★ Deep, dense smoky black fruit, **08** rich & sweet with supporting round, spicy tannins. For early enjoyment. **Whitestone Sauvignon Blanc** Occasional release. — WB

Anthonij Rupert Wines

Location/map: Franschhoek ▪ WO: Coastal/Western Cape ▪ Est 1714 ▪ 1stB 1982 ▪ Tastings Mon-Fri 9–4.30 Sat/Sun 10–3 ▪ Fee R30 ▪ Closed Easter Fri & Dec 25 ▪ Light meals (gourmet sandwiches; cheese & meat platters) & refreshments ▪ Cheese, olive oil & honey ▪ Franschhoek Motor Museum Mon-Fri 10-4 Sat/Sun 10-3; admittance R60 adults R50 senior R30 kids (3-12) ▪ Owner(s) Johann Rupert ▪ Cellarmaster(s) Neil Patterson (Jan 2003) ▪ Winemaker(s) Dawie Botha (Jan 2005) & Christo Hamerse (Jan 1997), with Melanie Sauerman (Sep 2009) & Zanie Viljoen (Jan 2007) ▪ Viticulturist(s) Rosa Kruger (May 2004) ▪ 4 farms: total ±1,100ha/±210ha (cabs s/f, carignan, cinsaut, grenache, merlot, mourv, pinot, sangio, shiraz, chard, chenin, pinot grigio, rouss) ▪ ISO 14001:2009 ▪ PO Box 435 Franschhoek 7690 ▪ tasting@rupertwines.com ▪ www.rupertwines.com ▪ S 33° 53' 13.51" E 019° 0' 20.31" ▪ **T +27 (0)21-874-9000** ▪ F +27 (0)21-874-9111

With four exceptional farms supplying grapes – L'Ormarins (Franschhoek), Riebeecksrivier (Riebeek-Kasteel), Elandskloof (Villiersdorp) and Rooderust (Darling) – the team at this showpiece winery is spoilt for choice - but they need to be to satisfy the different demands of its three tiers. At the top, aged minimum four years before release, are the Anthonij Rupert wines, named for the late founder and brother of current owner Johann. Terra del Capo, inspired by the traditional Italian proclivity for combining wine and food, tends towards restraint. Lighter, and for earlier enjoyment, is good-value Protea, after the remarkably varied indigenous flower whose name in turn recalls the shape-shifting deity Proteus.

Anthonij Rupert range

★★★★ **Cabernet Franc** Accomplished & polished modern take on the variety, **07** black fruit & echoes of scrub & forest floor, tad confected finish. Powerful, tight, would benefit from hour/2 decanting, as all these.

★★★★ **Merlot 07** silky & hedonistic, noticeable fruit & oak sweetness balanced by savoury tomato-like hint & mineral texture. WO W Cape. 2 years new wood, followed by 2 years bottle-age prior to release for all these.

★★★★ **Optima** One of S Africa's favourite sons. **07** mainly cab plus merlot, cab franc, petit verdot; similar to taut **06** but offering less sweet fruit, more tannic firmness than stablemates. Deserves time.

Cabernet Sauvignon ★★★★ Recent releases emphasise power, structure & opulent oak seasoning, so **07**'s blackcurrant fruit broods in a savoury, almost malty cocoon, waiting to emerge. **Syrah** ★★★★ Shy **07** opens in glass to lovely lily/blackcurrant aroma, broad & generous flavours, let down a bit by overt oak char in conclusion.

Terra Del Capo range

Sangiovese ★★★★ Whiffs sour cherry & (attractive) metallic edge last time to delicate but persistent **08**. **Arné** ★★★★ Tribute to late Norwegian Everest summiteer Arné Naess. Fruitful marriage of merlot's plum & 'rock pool' character with sangiovese's zip & grip in **07** raised the bar on **06** (★★★★). **Pinot Grigio** 🔲 ★★★ Previewed **11** is fresh, with Granny Smith apple, light nut/geranium character. Very sippable courtesy lowish 12.5% alc. WO W Cape, as all these.

Protea range

Shiraz ☺ 🔲 ★★★ **09** ultra-ripe prune flavours with twist of black pepper & scrub, supple drinkability aided by few grams sugar. Lightly oaked, as all these reds.

Cabernet Sauvignon ✓ 🔲 ★★★★ Improved **09** greets with blackcurrant & liquorice, follows with restrained fruitiness, gentle but firm grip. Able flag waver for this well-priced range targeting wine-by-the-glass market. All previewed unless stated, mainly WO W Cape. **Merlot** 🔲 **09** to young & unformed to rate. **Reserve** NEW ★★★★ Ready-to-drink combo shiraz, mourvèdre & drop viognier. **09** food-friendly savouriness & restraint, hint strawberry fruit. **Chardonnay** ★★★ **10** carbon copy of debut **09**: timid lemon blossom aroma followed by burst of flavour, freshness, even some tannin. **Chenin Blanc** ✓ 🔲 ★★★★ Satisfying **10** has gained complexity & presence since previewed last time: quince flavour complements crisp acidity, firm structure. **Sauvignon Blanc** ✓ 🔲 ★★★★ Lemon & greengage-toned **11** is delicious: crunchy cool fruit, vibrant acidity, bone-dry finish. Over-delivers, like most in this range. — CvZ

Anthony de Jager Wines

Location: Paarl ▪ Est/1stB 2001 ▪ Closed to public ▪ Owner(s)/winemaker(s) Anthony de Jager ▪ 180cs own label 100% red ▪ PO Box 583 Suider-Paarl 7624 ▪ homtini@absamail.co.za ▪ **T +27 (0)21-863-2450** ▪ F +27 (0)21-863-2591

There's not much news about Fairview winemaker Anthony de Jager's own brand, Homtini. In fact, since he's no longer selling direct to the public, he asked us to withdraw our description and rating. But that doesn't mean you shouldn't add it to your shopping basket when you come across it: it's a very fine shiraz indeed.

Anthony Smook Wines

Location/WO: Paarl ▪ Est/1stB 2000 ▪ Tasting by appt ▪ Owner(s) Winefolk Brands (Pty) Ltd ▪ Cellarmaster(s) Anthony Smook ▪ Viticulturist(s) Johan Wiese (2001, consultant) ▪ 30t from various vyds ▪ PO Box 7038 Northern Paarl 7623 ▪ anthony@smookwines.co.za ▪ www.smookwines.co.za ▪ **T +27 (0)21-872-3232** ▪ F +27 (0)21-872-3235

Paarl-based negociant Anthony Smook has been concentrating on his more commercial brands, and handcrafts wines for his eponymous range only in small quantities: 'It's taken a bit of a back seat. Because my name is on the label, I bottle only when it's something very, very special.'

Shiraz Reserve Await next, as for **Shiraz. Chardonnay** ★★★ Last time, **06** was approachable, had ripe pear nuances & integrated oaking. — DB

Anura Vineyards

Location: Paarl ▪ Map: Paarl & Wellington ▪ WO: Simonsberg-Paarl/Western Cape/Coastal/Paarl/Darling/Swartland ▪ Est 1990 ▪ 1stB 2001 ▪ Tasting, sales & cellar tours daily 9.30–5 ▪ Closed Easter Fri, Dec 25 & Jan 1 ▪ Fee R30 (cheese & wine) ▪ Lilly Pad Restaurant ▪ Tour groups ▪ Farm produce ▪ Conference facilities ▪ Owner(s) Tymen Bouma ▪ Cellarmaster(s) Tymen Bouma (1990) ▪ Winemaker(s) Johnnie Calitz & Lance Bouma (Jan 2007), with Inga Rix (Jan 2011) ▪ Viticulturist(s) Hannes Kloppers (Oct 1997) ▪ 240ha/120ha (cab, carignan, grenache, malbec, merlot, mourv, p verdot, ptage, pinot, sangio, shiraz, tempranillo, chard, chenin, sauv) ▪ 750t/50,000cs own label 80% red 17% white 2% rosé 1% fortified + 10,000cs for clients ▪ Other export brands: LB, Zee ▪ Brands for clients: Heart & Soul, Joy, Kiss My Springbok ▪ IPW ▪ PO Box 244 Klapmuts 7625 ▪ info@anura.co.za, wine@anura.co.za ▪ www.anura.co.za ▪ S 33° 48' 41.4" E 018° 53' 19.8" ▪ **T +27 (0)21-875-5360** ▪ F +27 (0)21-875-5657

This family winery in the Simonsberg foothills is nothing if not diverse, with no fewer than 15 grape varieties planted (and more planned), extensive wine ranges and customer labels, the Forest Hill Cheesery, Lilly Pad Restaurant, Froggit Food Deli and, soon, the Twelve Pigs Smoked Meat Emporium. Wine quality continues to rise, as evidenced by their impressive top 5 achievement at Veritas. Looking ahead, the emphasis will be on raising the status and profile of the reserve ranges.

Reserves & Limited Releases

★★★★ **Merlot Reserve** ✓ Minty, fruity, full-bodied **08**, first tasted since **05**, shows opulent ripeness & firm tannic grip. Easily outperforms standard range, but still great value.

★★★★ **Syrah Limited Release 07**, not revisited, was big yet rich & multi-dimensional; tannins, oak integrated, allowing peep of sombre, unevolved dark choc, spice.

Cabernet Sauvignon ✓ ★★★★ Pleasant if rather meaty-savoury **07** follows previous form, with dark chocolate notes & chalky tannins. **Malbec Limited Release** ✓ ★★★★ **08** improves on tangy **07** (★★★★), shows lots of concentration, honest black fruit & elegant structure. Deep & dark, with brooding liquorice notes & firm tannic grip. **Petit Verdot Limited Release** ✓ ★★★★ Elegantly handled varietal rarity, **08** has rich exotic fruit & thick tannin cloak. **Pinotage Reserve** ★★★★ **09** last year boasted fresher raspberry focus than **08** (★★★★). Concentrated & creamy, with supportive structure. Coastal WO. **Syrah-Mourvèdre** ★★★★ Elegance & fruit combined in last-tasted **05**. **Chardonnay Limited Release** ✓ 🏅 ★★★★ More subdued **10** reflects lighter vintage but retains nutty-oaky mantle. Pleasing leesy weight & texture. Western Cape WO. **Chenin Blanc Limited Release** 🏅 ★★★★ Big-boned, sweetly fruity barrel-fermented **10** is perhaps a little overstated, ripe & forceful for top-tier range. WO Coastal. **Sauvignon Blanc Unfiltered Reserve** 🏅 ★★★★ Stylish flag-bearer from Darling vineyards, previewed **11** shows greater depth & complexity than siblings. Notch up on **10** (★★★★), with focused fruit & lingering finish.

Signature Series

Grenache ★★★☆ 07 previously showed elegance with palate power. Grapes from Swartland, as for Maestro. **Pinot Noir ★★★** Last tasted was firm **06**; 14.5% alc out of sorts. **Sangiovese ★★★ 06** tasted mid-2008, with pale reticence belying saucy texture. **Maestro ★★★★** Big dry tannins, sweet fruit noted previously on **05** shiraz, mourvèdre & grenache blend. **La Traviata ★★★☆ 07** from nebbiolo, grenache, mourvèdre & viognier not retasted. **La Traviata White ★★★★** Oaked **09** based on roussanne, grenache blanc, with chenin & telling 8% viog. Not retasted. WO Coastal.

Anura range

Merlot ☺ **★★★** Quaffable price-conscious **09** rushed onto market to replace sold-out stocks. Chalky textured, minty & berry-rich. **Pinotage-Syrah** ☺ 🍴 🥂 **★★★** Appealing 2-part Cape Blend, **10** is harmonious & juicy. Shows potential as a braai companion or fireside sipper. WO Western Cape, as for Chardonnay. **Rosé** ☺ 🍴 🥂 **★★★** Impressive previewed **11**. Now dry, grenache with splash hanepoot, from Darling vineyards. Fullish, fruity & satisfying. **Chardonnay** ☺ 🥂 **★★★** Bright & fruity **10** has zesty citrus fruit, modest weight, lots of appeal. Anytime, anywhere quaffer. **Sauvignon Blanc** ☺ 🍴 🥂 **★★★** Unassuming, fresh & crisp, **11** is a cut above price-peers.

Pinotage 🍴 **★★★★** Last **08** was ripe & bold but with carefully judged extraction, oaking. **Legato** ✓ 🍴 **★★★★** Aromatic, spicy scents lend appeal to ripe, fruity core of modestly positioned **08** cab-merlot blend. Paarl WO. **Viognier Barrel Selection** 🥂 **★★★** Rather heavy oaking on **10**, from Swartland vines, mars otherwise promising fruity & aromatic profile. **Méthode Cap Classique Brut ★★★★** Like **06** (★★★★), previously tasted bottle-fermented sparkling **08** was classic chard, pinot mix. Generous brioche, bruised apple aromas, oak-enriched. WO Western Cape. **Cape Ruby Port ★★★ 08** last edition was suitably if not classically from ruby cab. Fruity, smoothed by noticeable brandy spirit.

Frog Hill range

Pinotage ☺ 🍴 🥂 **★★★** Nicely formed, overtly fruity **10** over-delivers for base-level range. Mostly for export to Netherlands.

Cabernet Sauvignon-Merlot 🍴 **★★★** Easy-drinking **08** had ripe dark berry fruits last time. **Sauvignon Blanc** 🍴 🥂 **★★★** Light-bodied & brief but balanced entry-level **11** preview. — GdB

Anwilka

Location: Somerset West ▪ Map: Helderberg ▪ WO: Stellenbosch ▪ Est 1997 ▪ 1stB 2005 ▪ Tasting & sales by appt at Klein Constantia ▪ Closed all pub hols ▪ Cellar tours by appt ▪ Owner(s) Bruno Prats, Hubert de Boüard & Lowell Jooste ▪ Cellarmaster(s) Bruno Prats & Hubert de Boüard (both Oct 2004) ▪ Winemaker(s) Jean du Plessis (Aug 2008, consultant) ▪ Viticulturist(s) Piet Neethling, with Johan Wiese (consultant, both 1997) ▪ 48ha/±39ha (cab, merlot, p verdot, shiraz) ▪ 200t/±12,000cs own label 100% red ▪ Other export brand: AmododA ▪ PO Box 5298 Helderberg 7135 ▪ anwilka@mweb.co.za ▪ www.anwilka.com ▪ S 34° 1'8.77" E 018° 48'9.54" ▪ **T +27 (0)21-842-3225** ▪ F +27 (0)21-842-3983

Continuity and change: the owners remain two eminent Bordelais (Hubert de Boüard and Bruno Prats) and one local (Lowell Jooste), all with impeccable wine connections; a winemaker (Jean du Plessis) whose first vintage is the current release. This vintage promises even better things from Anwilka, whose wine had sometimes seemed undeniably good, but a little too easy for greatness. Also new are plantings of shiraz and petit verdot ('with huge potential in terms of quality'), and fancy grape-sorting technology. But, as Jean du Plessis says, everything is always new in producing wine: after four years, 'I am now really starting to get to know the vineyards, a never-ending and humbling learning curve'. The Ugaba, noted by us for the first time below, was first produced in 2006.

★★★★☆ Anwilka 09 a break-through vintage - adding more depth, seriousness & structure to usual ripe, dense fruit. From 56% shiraz + cab (**08** included merlot). Plenty of new oak used, but integrated. Supple & flowing, on implacable but graceful infrastructure. A modern classic; will mature many years.

★★★★ Ugaba NEW **09** from same grapes as senior, with 69% shiraz & just 25% new oak. Less intense & deep, but lovely & seamless; smooth, sweet-fruited, dry-finishing (a touch too drying). — TJ

■ **Appaloosa** see Mon Rêve Estate

Appollis Fairtrade

Location/WO: Wellington ▪ Map: Paarl & Wellington ▪ Est 1699 ▪ 1stB 2009 ▪ Tasting by appt ▪ Fee R50pp, waived on purchase ▪ Closed Easter Fri-Mon, Dec 22 to Jan 4 ▪ Sales Mon-Thu 8-5 Fri 8-4.30 ▪ Cellar tours by appt ▪ Conservation area ▪ Festivals: 'The Long Lunch' (Mar) & 'Release Weekend' (Sep) ▪ Owner(s) Bosman Family & Adama Workers Trust ▪ Cellarmaster(s) Petrus Bosman (Nov 2003) ▪ Winemaker(s) Corlea Fourie (Nov 2006), with Charlene Ferreira (Nov 2006) ▪ Viticulturist(s) Heinie Nel & Pierre Carstens (Jan 2000) ▪ 1,000ha/280ha (46 varieties r/w) ▪ 3,000t/10,000cs own label 70% red 25% white 5% rosé + 1,000cs for clients ▪ Brands for clients: Co-op & Sainsbury ▪ BRC, BWI, Fairtrade ▪ PO Box 9 Wellington 7654 ▪ info@bosmanwines.com ▪ www.bosmanwines.com ▪ S33° 37' 34.7" E019° 01' 28.9" ▪ **T +27 (0)21-873-3170** ▪ F +27 (0)21-873-2517

There are 111 families resident on Lelienfontein farm, the Wellington home of Bosman Family Vineyards, and most trace their ancestry to Adam Appollis. With the Bosman family as partners, the kinsfolk have created the Appollis Fairtrade brand for consumers in Europe (and now South Africa). Though still young, the initiative's financial benefits are already evident: computers and books in the library, sports kit, music (62 different instruments are played!), daycare and more.

Cabernet Sauvignon Blend 🍷 ⊠ ★★★ Spicy blackcurrant & cocoa richness on **10** 5-way Bordeaux blend, supple & rounded with touch of char grip from French oak, 20% new. **Shiraz Blend** 🍷 ⊠ ★★★ Juicy, gentle plum spice on **10**'s shiraz-led oaked blend. **Chardonnay Blend** 🍷 ⊠ ★★★ Chardonnay, chenin & viognier deliver light tropicality, subtle oak sheen in **10**. — FM

◼ **Aprilskloof** *see Lammershoek Winery*
◼ **Arbelos Wines** *see Botha Wine Cellar*

Arendsig Handcrafted Wines

Location/map: Robertson ▪ Est/1stB 2004 ▪ Tasting & cellar tours by appt ▪ Tour groups ▪ Gift shop ▪ BYO picnic ▪ Wedding/function venue ▪ Farmhouse (sleeps up to 10 people) ▪ Owner(s) Lourens & Frikkie van der Westhuizen ▪ Cellarmaster(s)/viticulturist(s) Lourens van der Westhuizen (2004) ▪ 95ha/12ha (cab, shiraz, chard, sauv) ▪ 80t/2,500cs own label 50% red 50% white + 120t/500cs for clients ▪ Brands for clients: Eyona, Mimosa, Star Hill ▪ PO Box 170 Robertson 6705 ▪ info@arendsig.co.za ▪ www.arendsig.co.za ▪ S 33° 55' 37.9" E 020° 0' 47.6" ▪ **T +27 (0)84-200-2163/+27 (0)23-616-2835** ▪ F +27 (0)86-535-0693/+27 (0)23-616-2090

Boutique winemaker Lourens van der Westhuizen is winning friends and influencing people with his focus on single-vineyard wines. Mimosa, Star Hill and newcomer Eyona all benefit from his expertise, and Woolworths stores (unusually) carry his wines under their original Arendsig label. Last year he found the perfect site to plant pinot noir on the Robertson family farm, and vinified a maiden shiraz blanc de noir from – yes, a single vineyard.

◼ **Arendskloof** *see Eagle's Cliff Wines-New Cape Wines*

Arniston Bay

A flagship brand of The Company of Wine People, Arniston Bay was recently voted 41st among the 50 Most Admired Brands by a Drinks International poll of experts. The brand is now sold in 35 countries and has a Facebook page with close to 6,000 fans. A lot to 'like', apparently, such as a commitment to eco-friendly practices and a social conscience that includes participation in development initiatives.

Bush Vine range

Pinotage 🍷 ★★★ 09 appealing juicy/spicy red fruit, balanced & structured, promise of easy drinkability. **Chenin Blanc** 🍷 ⊠ ★★★★ Back on track last year, **10** showed serious intent; ripe & juicy, with tangy acidity. Oak (50% new) well integrated. WO Western Cape for all ranges.

Original range

> **Cabernet Sauvignon-Merlot** ☺ 🍷 ⊠ ★★★ Vibrant berries on **10**, unwooded, with lively juicy drinkability.

Cabernet Sauvignon 🍷 ⊠ ★★★ 10 preview reveals leafy walnut aromas, freshness & balance for early enjoyment. **Merlot** 🍷 ⊠ ★★ 10 savoury & dry, with core of dark fruit, needs bit more time or food. **Shiraz** 🍷

★★★ Previewed **10**, lively & frisky with savoury smoky edge. **Shiraz-Pinotage** ☐ ★★★ Balanced **10** spicy & savoury; fruity approachable braai companion. **Shiraz-Merlot** ☐ ★★ **10** shy but friendly everyday dry red. **Cabernet Sauvignon-Shiraz** ☐ ★★★ **10** quite characterful, juicy & vibrant for easy drinking. **Rosé** ☐ ★★★ 'Pinotage Rosé' last time. Still mostly from pinotage, fragrant **11** is an off-dry yet crisp summer quaffer. **Chardonnay** ✓ ☐ ★★★★ Standout in line-up. Limy vibrant fruit on preview unoaked **11**. Zesty & vivacious. **Sauvignon Blanc** ☐ ★★★ Crunchy crisp freshness on **11**, sampled from tank. **Sauvignon Blanc-Semillon** ☐ ★★★ **11** crisp & waxy, balanced, with soft-toned green fruit. **Chenin Blanc-Chardonnay** ☐ ★★★ Pre-bottling, **11** succulent apple & pear flavours, good mouthfeel & aromatic lift.

The Shore range
Red ☐ ★★ Gentle structure, mellow, easy drinking. **NV**. **Rosé** ☐ ★★ Light, sweetish strawberry-fruited sipper. **NV**. **White** ☐ ★★★ Crisp & fruity poolside quaffer. **NV**.

Sparkling range
Méthode Charmat Brut ★★ Bubbly from chardonnay with refreshing fruit flavour. **NV**. Not retasted, as next. **Méthode Charmat Rosé** ★★ Pretty packaging reflects in gently frothy, fruitily sweet **NV**.

Limited Releases
Occasional bottlings.

Reserve range
Now discontinued. — MW

Arra Vineyards

Location: Paarl ▪ Map: Paarl & Wellington ▪ WO: Paarl/Coastal ▪ Est 1998 ▪ 1stB 2001 ▪ Tasting & sales Tue-Thu & Sat 9-4.30 Fri 9-6 ▪ Facilities for children ▪ Tour groups ▪ Gifts ▪ Farm produce ▪ BYO picnic ▪ Conferences ▪ Walks/ hikes & mountain biking ▪ 4x4 trail ▪ Conservation area ▪ Owner(s) Arra Vineyards (Pty) Ltd ▪ Cellarmaster(s) Dee Wentzel (2006) ▪ Viticulturist(s) Johan Southey (2000) ▪ 72ha/30ha (cab, merlot, mourv, ptage, ruby cab, shiraz, viog) ▪ 10,000cs ▪ PO Box 298 Klapmuts 7625 ▪ info@arrawines.com ▪ www.arrawines.com ▪ S 33° 49' 25.9" E 018° 51' 47.7" ▪ **T +27 (0)21-875-5363** ▪ F +27 (0)21-875-5866

With the opening of the new tasting room, Cellarmaster Dee Wentzel aims to offer a quality wine for every palate; certainly this extensive range should meet her goal though one can't helping thinking that making fewer wines would allow the promising quality to rise even higher. Much remains in the experimental stage, so it's possible the range will be more compact in future. Maybe not with viognier, a Wentzel favourite: with four different and interesting styles being offered, she obviously would have difficulty in deciding on only one representative.

Reserve range
★★★★☆ **Cabernet Sauvignon** 06 (★★★★) slightly less impressive than classic **05**. Like Barrel Select shows some evolution, well-integrated tannins; also bit more new oak. Unlikely to benefit from further ageing.

★★★★ **Shiraz** ✓ Savoury & well-spiced **06** smoothly rounded but still fresh. Welcoming medium-bodied feel. Enjoy over next yr/2.

★★★★ **Viognier** Expressive apricot pip, ginger tones noted last yr on **09**. Silky; 15% alc tempered by fresh acidity. Off-dry; barrel fermented.

Nobility NEW ★★★★ Apricot crème brulée features on silkily sweet **10** viognier. Flavours lifted, lengthened by bright, balanced acidity. 12.5% alc unusually modest for this variety.

Barrel Select range NEW
★★★★ **Cabernet Sauvignon** For those who enjoy reds with some age, traditionally-styled **06** shows some meaty, savoury evolution, complexity. Harmonious but no hurry to drink up.

★★★★ **Pinotage Barrel Select** ✓ One to please even non-pinotage lovers. **08** understated, more savoury spice than sweet red fruits; quite dense but fresh with beautifully polished tannins. Subtly oaked (20% new).

Arra Vineyards range
Cabernet Sauvignon ✓ ★★★★ **09** fresh, ripe blackberry scents, firm but not intimidating. Dash merlot, malbec add interest. **08** (★★★) smooth, approachable. **Merlot** ★★★ **09** uncomplicated drinking. Ripe dark berry aromas; very fresh, simple flavours. **Pinotage** ★★★ **08**'s earthy nose refrained on **09**. Plainer, sweetish red fruit, soft, ready. **Shiraz** ★★★ Blended with grenache noir, mourvèdre & noticeably peachy viognier in tail, **09** ripely juicy & ready. **Cabernet Sauvignon-Merlot** NEW ★★★ **09** unoaked 85/15 blend; satisfying ripe fruit, structure for

current enjoyment. **Red Blend** 🍷 ★★★ Hearty, country-style **09** headed by well-disguised pinotage with shiraz, cab, merlot. Richly flavoured, chewy tannins. **Shiraz-Cabernet Sauvignon** ✓ ★★★★ Usual happy pairing of bright cassis fruit overlay to textured savouriness in **09**. Beneficial French oak, 10% new. **Shiraz-Mourvèdre-Carignan** ✓ ★★★★ Comfortably padded **09** with rich yet fresh gamey, spicy flavours & tasty savoury tail. Like Shiraz, WO Coastal. **Blanc de Noir** 🍷 ★★ Plain, dryish **11** from shiraz. **Viognier** ★★★ Ginger spice hint on partially oaked, sweetish **10**. **Natural Sweet Viognier** NEW 🍷 ★★★★ Honeyed apricot sweetness cut by refreshing acidity provide enjoyable drinking in **10**; lightly spiced dishes recommended. **Natural Sweet Red Blend** ★★★ **09** spicy shiraz-led septet; ideal candidate for mulled wine. — AL

■ **Arthouse** *see Juno Wine Company*

Arumdale Cool Climate Wines

Location/WO: Elgin • Map: Elgin, Walker Bay & Bot River • Est 1962 • 1stB 2003 • Tasting & sales by appt Mon-Sat 8-5 Sun 10-5 • Fee R15/5 wines, waived on purchase (2 or more bottles) • Closed Easter Fri-Mon, Dec 25/26 & Jan 1 • Owner(s) Mark Simpson • Cellarmaster(s) Franz Josef Blomendahl (2005, consultant) • Viticulturist(s) Paul Wallace (Nov 2008, consultant) • 90ha/10ha (cab, merlot, shiraz, sauv) • 70t/4,000cs own label 80% red 10% white 10% rosé • PO Box 2 Elgin 7180 • royalwine@arumdale.co.za • www.arumdale.co.za • S 34° 13'11.3" E 019° 2'31.3" • **T +27 (0)21-848-9880** • F +27 (0)21-848-9683

Owner Mark Simpson has introduced an 'informal' label, the Robin Hood Legendary Wine Series, promoted on Facebook. It comprises wines named for Sherwood Forest's fabulous folk, either single varieties or blends, depending on what doesn't fit into the Arumdale range and what's bought in. Winemaker Franz Blomendahl vinifies in a refurbished apple-packing shed on the Simpsons' Elgin farm, its underground concrete structure providing more than satisfactory cellar space.

St. Andrews Blend ★★★ No newer release since **06** oaked cab, merlot & shiraz blend. — MW

Asara Wine Estate & Hotel 🍴🍷🛏️🏊📷🍽️♿

Location/map: Stellenbosch • WO: Western Cape • Est/1stB 2001 • Tasting Mon-Sat 10-6 Sun 10-4 • Fee R20 (3 wines), R30 (5 wines) • Sales 10-5 • Closed Good Fri & Dec 25 • Cellar tours by appt • Tour groups • Five star hotel (see Accommodation section) • Raphael's (see Restaurants section) • Sansibar Cigar & Whisky Lounge • Deli • Gift shop • Wine Bar • Function & banqueting facilities • Conferences • Weddings • Owner(s) Markus & Christiane Rahmann • Cellarmaster(s) Francois Joubert (Sep 2009) • Winemaker(s) Francois Joubert (Sep 2009), with Tanja-Mari Goedhart (Oct 2010) • Viticulturist(s) Henk Agenbach (Oct 2009) • 180ha/102ha (cab, merlot, p verdot, chard, sauv) • 800t/22,500cs own label 73% red 25% white 2% rosé • IPW • PO Box 882 Stellenbosch 7599 • info@asara. co.za • www.asarawine.co.za • S 33° 56'35.00" E 018° 48'31.00" • **T +27 (0)21-888-8000** • F +27 (0)21-888-8001

The gates to this Stellenbosch historic estate – granted in 1691 – were shut to the public under some previous owners, but current proprietors Markus and Christiane Rahmann over the past decade have thrown them wide open. (Sited at the confluence of two major access roads into Stellenbosch, they're easy to find, too.) Once inside, a cornucopia of upmarket hospitality awaits, including a new lakeside wine bar. The wine team has earmarked special blocks for a new single-vineyard range in the pipeline. They're also working on a roll-out in the local market, and 'big global expansion plans with a particular focus on Asia'.

Bell Tower Collection

★★★★ **Estate Wine** Malbec-led blend of 5 Bordeaux red varieties; **07** wet-leaf characters when last tasted, but with enough bramble fruit in balance with pliable tannins.

★★★★ **Avalon** Extraordinary vine-dried pinotage & shiraz in Amarone style, 3 years oak, half new. **07** bold, sweet & warmly alcoholic (15%). The team's equally unusual food suggestion: springbok pizza.

Petit Verdot Await new vintage.

Asara Wine Estate & Hotel range

★★★★ **Cabernet Sauvignon** ✓ **09** tightly wound - even a bit angular - mid-2011 but promises elegance in 3-5 years. Improves on softer, less enduring **08** (★★★☆).

Ivory ☺ 🍷 📖 ★★★ **11** refreshing, fruity chenin fleshes out steely sauvignon for poolside pleasure.

Merlot ✓ ★★★★ Scrumptious **09**, succulence & meaty flesh are like a bear hug with big tannins too. For food. **Shiraz** ★★★★ **09** back to form after barnyardy **07**, (no **08**), polished spice & savoury fruit limited only by 'wild' edginess. **Ebony** 🔲 ★★★ Full-frontal **09**, plummy mocha in supple mouthful previously. **Cape Fusion** ★★★ Cape Blend of pinotage, merlot, shiraz & cab, **09** plummy & touch rustic last edition, just-dry. **Cabernet Sauvignon Blanc** ✓ 🖉 ★★★★ Unusual white wine from black grape. Greenpepper-fresh **10**, nutty interest in firm texture. **Rosé** 🖉 ★★★ Ruby-hued, just-dry **10** had fresh nutmeg fillip when last tasted. **Chardonnay Reserve** 🖉 ★★★★ Now bottled (preview last edition), **10** broad buttered brioche flavour, cleaned up by vibrant citrus fruit & fresh acid. **Chardonnay Unwooded** 🔲 🖉 ★★★ Agreeable if workmanlike, **11** typical lemon/lime profile. **Sauvignon Blanc** 🔲 🖉 ★★★ Straightforward **11**, tropical tones & grassy hints, clean & dry. **Noble Late Harvest** Await next. **Spirit of Chenin** ★★★★ Port-style fortified white from chenin, 2 years older cask. Nutty **08** previously was really interesting & more attractive than last-tasted **04** (★★★★). — DS

Ashbourne

Location: Hermanus ▪ Map: Elgin, Walker Bay & Bot River ▪ WO: Hemel-en-Aarde Valley/Walker Bay ▪ Est 1996 ▪ 1stB 2001 ▪ Tasting, sales & tours by appt ▪ Owner(s) Anthony Hamilton Russell ▪ Winemaker(s) Hannes Storm (2004) ▪ Viticulturist(s) Johan Montgomery (2005) ▪ 113ha/24.35ha (cabs s/f, malbec, p verdot, ptage, shiraz, sauv, sem) ▪ 20t/1,000cs own label 50% red 50% white ▪ PO Box 158 Hermanus 7200 ▪ hrv@hermanus.co.za ▪ **T +27 (0)28-312-3595** ▪ F +27 (0)28-312-1797

After realising they'd taken the pinotage from this property as far as it could go unblended, owner Anthony Hamilton Russell and winemaker Hannes Storm added small portions of shiraz and cab in 07, and envisage that future Ashbournes, vintage permitting, will be at least 75% pinotage with souçpons of the two cabernets, malbec, petit verdot and shiraz. Unchanged is Hannes's mission to retain a European styling and avoid Anthony's pet hate: easy-going blandness (however 'correct') which, he says, originally put Australia on the map and 'has to be resisted'. He's adamant: 'Ashbourne will always fly a South African flag. And making strongly European-styled wine in South Africa is a South African thing to do; just consider those great wines of the early and mid 1970s.'

★★★★☆ **Ashbourne** Sumptuous **05** & previous straight pinotage, **07** (★★★★) enriched with equal dabs (9%) shiraz & cabernet. Cool black cherry & clean leather coupled with Old World savouriness, subtle oaking & leafy tannins. Poised; deserves 5+ years cellaring. Moderate ±13% alcohol for this & stablemate.

★★★★☆ **Sandstone** Seamless **08** masterly blend of sauvignon (77%) & drops chardonnay & semillon fermented in clay amphoras. Enticing now, with vibrant acid structure & flavour depth (asparagus, fennel) to reward good few years ageing. — CvZ

Ashton Wynkelder

Location: Ashton ▪ Map/WO: Robertson ▪ Est 1962 ▪ 1stB 1970 ▪ Tasting & sales Mon-Fri 8-5 Sat 9-2 (summer) & 10-2 (winter) ▪ Closed Easter Fri/Sat & Dec 25/26 ▪ Cellar tours by appt ▪ Facilities for children ▪ Tour groups ▪ Farm produce ▪ Conferences ▪ Walks/hikes ▪ 4x4 trail ▪ Mountain biking ▪ Conservation area ▪ Accommodation ▪ Owner(s) 52 shareholders ▪ Cellarmaster(s) Sterik de Wet (Oct 2009) ▪ Winemaker(s) Simon Basson (Nov 2007) & Roy Thorne (Oct 2011) ▪ Viticulturist(s) Hennie Visser (Vinpro) ▪ 1,200ha (cab, ruby cab, shiraz, chard, chenin) ▪ 20,183t/10,000cs own label 37% red 55% white 6% rosé 2% other; 3,300cs & 12m L bulk for clients ▪ Other export brands: Berryfields, Mountain Stream ▪ ISO 22000, BWI, HACCP ▪ PO Box 40 Ashton 6715 ▪ info@ ashtonkelder.co.za ▪ www.ashtonkelder.co.za ▪ S 33° 50' 12.1" E 020° 1' 48.3" ▪ **T +27 (0)23-615-1135** ▪ F +27 (0)23-615-1284

Francois Bezuidenhout, who vinified the reds from this grower-owned cellar, has departed (Roy Thorne has taken his place), leaving a wine that colleague Simon Basson, overseeing white-wine making, describes as the best yet from this winery. It's the Limited Release Pinotage, made from a little left in barrel after the bottling of the standard - 'a move on and up' from other's fashionable mocha styling.

Reserve range

★★★★ **Pinotage Limited Release** [NEW] Inky **10** boasts luscious wild berry fruit, exotic spices. Like Shiraz below, muscular & powerful with dense tannins needing year/2 to mellow.

Shiraz Reserve ★★★ Last edition, full-bodied & aromatic **07** reeled under weighty oak spices & solid tannins; we suggested may emerge given time. **Roodewal** ✓ ★★★★ Switches to Cape Blend in **10**, cab (60%), pinotage

(30%) & dash merlot. Rich, well-composed & smooth for comfortable, rewarding sipping. Discontinued: **Cabernet Sauvignon Reserve**.

Ashton Kelder range

Cabernet Sauvignon ★★★ Ripe blackcurrant fruit on **09**, faint oak influence; for early drinking. Not retasted, as for Chardonnay. **Pinotage** 🌱 **★★** Banana-toned **11** oozes blackberry jam, billows savoury spice. **Shiraz** 🌱 **★★★ 10** in footsteps of solid, black cherry fruited **09**, with shapely body & firm tannins. **Cabernet Sauvignon-Merlot ★★★ 09** quaffer has sweet fruit, slightly astringent mouthfeel. **Satynrooi** 🍷 **★★** Party/everyday red blend, **11** unoaked & uncomplicatedly enjoyable. **Satynrosé NEW** 🍷 **★★ 11** light-bodied rosé for the sweet-toothed, from pinotage. **Chardonnay Unwooded** 🍷 🌱 **★★★ 10** slightly muted but had sense of elegance last year. **Chenin Blanc** 🍷 🌱 **★★** White nuts, apple blossom & light alc on **11**, for drinking soon. **Sauvignon Blanc** 🍷 🌱 **★★★** Loses 'Winemaker's Choice' suffix in **11**. Bone-dry, lowish-alc al fresco white. **Satynwit** 🍷 🌱 **★★** Straightforward dry white, **11** mostly from colombard. **Satynperlé NEW** 🍷 **★★ 11** spritzy, gently sweet chenin. **Bonica Vin Doux** Frivolous **10** sweet fizz. **Red Muscadel Jerepigo ★★** Floral whiffs, grapey flavour, syrupy texture on **09** fortified dessert. **White Muskadel Jerepiko ★★★** Fortified dessert steps up in **06**: ripe & sunny, with lively acidity refreshing the unctuous grape/orange flavours. Discontinued: **Pétillant Blanc, Pascali, Special Late Harvest, Port**. — Panel

Assegai Selection

Location: Somerset West ▪ Est 1999 ▪ Sales by appt ▪ Owner(s) Woodlands Import Export ▪ Cellarmaster(s) Zakkie Bester ▪ Winemaker(s) Eric Saayman ▪ 20,000cs 80% red 20% white ▪ 67 Oakbridge Village Bizweni Ave Somerset West 7130 ▪ rbuchner@worldonline.co.za ▪ S 34° 3'9.2" E 018° 49'58.3" ▪ **T +27 (0)21-851-0552** ▪ F +27 (0)86-616-1743

His new sparkling wines met with the sort of reception that a strong rand and a patchy Euro-economy offer, exporter Raimund Buchner is biding his time and thanking Bacchus that he has no stock gathering cobwebs. Inbetween whiles, he's turned his trilingualism to good account, selling ad space for German print media.

Ataraxia Wines

Location: Hermanus ▪ Map: Elgin, Walker Bay & Bot River ▪ WO: Western Cape ▪ Est 2004 ▪ 1stB 2005 ▪ Tasting & sales Mon-Fri 9-4 Sat 10-3.30 Sun (Sep-Apr) 10-3.30 ▪ Fee R15pp for groups of 10 or more, refunded with individual purchase ▪ Closed Easter Fri/Mon, Dec 25 & Jan 1 ▪ Art exhibition ▪ Owner(s) Kevin Grant Wines (Pty) Ltd ▪ Cellarmaster(s)/winemaker(s)/viticulturist(s) Kevin Grant (Sep 2004) ▪ 47ha/12ha (pinot, chard) ▪ 83t/6,000cs 40% red 60% white ▪ PO Box 603 Hermanus 7200 ▪ info@ataraxiawines.co.za ▪ www.ataraxiawines.co.za ▪ S 34° 20'27.0" E 019° 18'30.8" ▪ **T +27 (0)28-212-2007** ▪ F +27 (0)28-212-1921

Kevin Grant established his own farm and winery in the Hemel-en-Aarde area in 2004, not far from where he'd been winemaker at Hamilton Russell. With him he brought his particular passion for chardonnay and pinot noir. Nowadays, visitors are warned, Kevin can only be glimpsed 'in a blur of movement'. Busy as he is with the elegant wines which are winning a fine reputation for Ataraxia, his heart is with a wine yet to be made - from the farm's young pinot vines. Small precursor batches have in fact been vinified since 2010, in anticipation of the wine that will meet his expectations and demands. If you want to taste these experiments and be 'part of his learning curve' you must join the Ataraxia Pinot Noir Club.

Ataraxia range

★★★★ Serenity Like **07**, impressive **08 (★★★★★)** unspecified red blend, WO Western Cape. Tasted last year, refined & polished, but powerful in structure, intense in flavour. Well balanced, should age well.

★★★★☆ Chardonnay In lesser vintage, **10** has perhaps less substance & long-term potential than **09** (though still needs year/2 to start showing its best). But it is still very fine & elegant with subtly expressive fruit & a lemony, mineral freshness, gently supported by oak. Local, Elgin grapes.

★★★★☆ Sauvignon Blanc 🍷 These invariably tasted ex-tank, so ratings provisional. Incisive **11** from Elgin. Fairly weighty & intense, with nothing too obvious or showy; penetrating but fine & unabrasive acidity, succulent conclusion. — TJ

- **Atkinson Ridge** *see* Amani Vineyards
- **Attie's Long Shadow** *see* Opstal Estate
- **Auberge du Paysan** *see* L'Auberge du Paysan

Audacia Wines

Location/map/WO: Stellenbosch ▪ Est 1930 ▪ Tasting & sales Mon-Fri 9–4 ▪ Fee R20, waived on purchase ▪ Closed all pub hols ▪ Owner(s) Strydom & Harris families ▪ Cellarmaster(s)/winemaker(s)/viticulturist(s) Michael van Niekerk (Aug 2009) ▪ 32ha/20ha (cabs s/f, malbec, merlot, p verdot, roobernet, shiraz) ▪ 120t/9,000c own label 100% red ▪ IPW ▪ PO Box 12679 Die Boord 7613 ▪ info@audacia.co.za ▪ www.audacia.co.za ▪ S 33° 59' 45.7" E 018° 50' 2.9" ▪ **T +27 (0)21-881-3052** ▪ F +27 (0)21-881-3137

Improved visibility and branding of this boutique red-wine specialist coincides with plans to relocate the tasting venue closer to the well-travelled R44 between Stellenbosch and Somerset West. Further consolidation sees the range trimmed to just five wines. 'Retro New World' is co-owner Trevor Strydom's description of their approach. 'Delicious, smooth easy-drinking style.'

Malbec ★★★★ Meaty **05** noted previously as quintessential malbec: dark plums & hedgerow berries, lively & drinkable. **Merlot ★★★** Shy mulberry smoke on **09**. Lighter, softer body than previous. **Shiraz ★★★** Ripe but restrained **09**, savoury but straightforward, lighter than previous. **Rouge Noble ★★★** Easy 6-way shiraz-led **NV** blend, with sweet berry fruit appeal. **Jeté ★★★★** Juicy, off-dry red blend from unspecified varieties. Last **NV** offered appealing plum & spice flavours. Discontinued: **Cabernet Sauvignon**. — FM

Aufwaerts Co-operative

Location: Rawsonville ▪ Map: Breedekloof ▪ Tasting by appt ▪ Winemaker(s) Hennie de Villiers ▪ PO Box 15 Rawsonville 6845 ▪ aufwaerts@breede.co.za ▪ S 33° 41' 42.4" E 019° 17' 33.7" ▪ **T +27 (0)23-349-1202** ▪ F +27 (0)23-349-1202

The De Villiers family welcomes visitors for by-appointment tastings of their Dry Red and Dry White, and newer Semi-Sweet White and Full-Sweet Hanepoot.

■ **Austin** see Noble Hill Wine Estate

Autumn Harvest Crackling

Long-established perlé wines by Distell, from widely scattered vineyards.

Autumn Harvest Crackling 🗒 **★★** Light & spritzy chenin, colombard & crouchen. Latest **NV** is off-dry yet crisp & fresh. 750ml, 1L & 1.5L. **Autumn Harvest Rosé** 🗒 **★★** Semi-sweet perlé, a blend red & white wine, newest **NV** is like a gush of fresh strawberry juice. Also 1.5L. — Panel

Avondale Bio-LOGIC & Organic Wines

Location/WO: Paarl ▪ Map: Paarl & Wellington ▪ Est 1996 ▪ 1stB 1999 ▪ Tasting & sales Mon-Sat by appt ▪ Tasting R50pp, Eco Tour R200pp ▪ Closed Easter Fri-Mon, Dec 25 & Jan 1 ▪ Cellar & Eco Tours by appt only ▪ Art exhibit ▪ Owner(s) Grieve Family / The Avondale Trust ▪ Winemaker(s) Corné Marais (Oct 2008), with Clarise Sciocatti (Dec 2008) ▪ Viticulturist(s) Johnathan Grieve (Jul 1999) ▪ 300ha/100ha (cabs s/f, grenache, merlot, mourv, shiraz, chard, chenin, rouss, sem, viog) ▪ 500t/25,000c own label 50% red 38% white 2% rosé 10% MCC ▪ EU Organic and USDA NOP organic, LEAF ▪ PO Box 602 Suider-Paarl 7624 ▪ wine@avondalewine.co.za ▪ www.avondalewine.co.za ▪ S 33° 45' 52.9" E 019° 0' 4.7" ▪ **T +27 (0)21-863-1976** ▪ F +27 (0)21-863-1534

As the name of their Paarl winery suggests, the Grieve family are Cape pioneers of science-supported organic and biodynamic winegrowing. Now, a long-gestated makeover and streamlining aims 'to develop Avondale into a leading winery in South Africa'. GM/viticulturist Johnathan Grieve elaborates: 'We have reinvented our range to something that we believe is truly what we do well and, more specifically, what is perfectly suited for Avondale. All seven wines have a unique offering and an individual story to tell.' The make-over includes packaging, so each wine's identity (the armillary sphere, Gaelic tree of life, rebirth, soul etc) is reflected on the label. Innovatively, all branding features smartphone-scannable Quick Response (QR) codes linking to pages on Avondale's website.

Avondale range NEW

★★★★ Samsara 100% shiraz, restraint obvious on **06**, ripe plum & berry fruit with white pepper & fynbos below. Supple yet strong - just 20% new oak for 14-16 months. Elegant now but will cellar well.

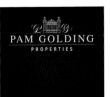

Chenin blanc champion **Ken Forrester** is intent on converting the world, 'just one bottle at a time'. He's among a group of visionaries who have advanced this noble variety's cause by giving it the royal treatment to produce iconic wines, and seeking out and saving old chenin vineyards. Over the years, the accomplished vintner and restaurateur, who co-owns 96 Winery Road Restaurant near Somerset West, has become synonymous with food, and his favourite variety certainly holds its own in that context. No doubt the chenin sparkling, in the pipeline for his eponymous range, will do the same.

vineyard hotel & spa
the perfect setting

Tastes of 2012
eat, sip, savour

diarise your fridays for 2012

27 april	vineyard hotel's five partners *
11 may	villiera wines
25 may	ernst gouws & co. family wines
08 june	creation wines
22 june	elgin valley, paul cluver & iona vineyards
13 july	muratie wine estate
27 july	hartenberg estate
10 aug	oldenburg vineyards
24 aug	mooiplaas estate
07 sept	anthonij rupert wines
21 sept	boutique wine makers
05 oct	haut espoir wines
26 oct	constantia valley wines

*Klein Constantia, Meerlust, Simonsig, Warwick, Waterford

Join us at the square to taste the latest
and greatest from top estates and fêted winemakers. Then enjoy a 4 or 5-course gourmet excursion
with our acclaimed Chef
and complimentary wines to accompany each
course. Booking is essential for these popular
events, so call us on 021 657 4500 or
e-mail us at eat@vineyard.co.za.

Weekly wine tastings in the garden lounge Improve your
wine know-how with complimentary tastings every Monday
at 18h00 throughout the year.

Pop in.

the SQUARE

An early and innovative adopter of digital technology, Creation Wines in bucolic Hemel-en-Aarde Ridge is reaching out to wine lovers around the world through an ever-expanding array of channels, including video, QR codes on bottle labels, social media and iPads strategically placed around the stylish tasting room. Which means (among others) you can view video clips about the farm on your smartphone, go online to rate your food-and-wine pairing experience, or join fellow tweeters at the 'Twittertable' as an invited guest during functions. 'The idea is to bring the human aspect back into technology and make Creation more accessible in the process,' says co-owner **Carolyn Martin** (foreground), pictured with marketing assistant **Salome Geldenhuys**.

Metro Liquor

We stock a wide range of Wines to suit all Occasions!

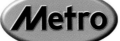

Best Quality at the Best Prices!

YOUR

Grandfather's
Name

MERLOT

WEALTH LEGACY MANAGEMENT

MANAGE. PROTECT. GROW.

YOUR FATHER'S FATHER CREATED IT,
YOUR FATHER NURTURED IT,
YOU GLOBALISED IT
AND YOUR CHILDREN WILL INHERIT IT.

Possessions passed from generation to generation have a

value that is so much more precious than mere financial worth,

they are part of the fabric that holds families together.

Managing, protecting and growing them is no small responsibility.

At RMB Private Bank, we understand wealth legacies and what they mean

to each one of our clients individually… it's how we've built our business.

And even though we don't pretend to be able to see into your future, we

do make it our business to fully understand your current legacy aspirations

so that we can help you build wealth creating plans that shape them.

www.rmbprivatebank.com

RMB
PRIVATE BANK
A division of FirstRand Bank Limited

Traditional values. Innovative ideas.

Thinking that can change your world

Having gone green on various levels, from making eco-friendly wines to installing the largest roof-mounted photovoltaic solar panel in South Africa, the Grier family, owners of Villiera Wines, are now helping persuade wine lovers to buy into a better future too, via the 220ha Villiera Wildlife Sanctuary. Visitors are guaranteed fantastic sightings of buck, hartebeest and zebra, as well as birdlife attracted to 12 dams and marsh areas, as staff members **Pascal El Azzi** and **Heidi Cilliers** discovered during a tour with viticulturist **Simon Grier** (right) in the venture's first electric-propelled vehicle.

It's all about continuing the 'Circle of Life' (also the name of their red and white blends) at Waterkloof in the Helderberg, where a natural, traditional approach is followed. Farm manager **Christiaan Loots**, a proponent of biodynamic farming, encourages Louis the Percheron as he pulls the country's first horse-drawn spray pump, with **Paul Arendse**, one of the team dedicated to working with the horses, aboard. A growing stable of these draft horses is reducing usage of heavy machinery at the pioneering estate.

Riedel recognises that the bouquet, taste, balance and finish of a wine is affected by the shape of the glass from which it is drunk. Over forty years ago Claus Riedel began his pioneering work to create stemware that would match and complement different wines and spirits.

"The Finest glasses for both technical and hedonistic purposes are those made by RIEDEL. The effect of these glasses on fine wine is profound.

I cannot emphasize enough what a difference they make."
Robert M.Parker Jr –
The Wine Advocate.

THE VINEYARD
CONNECTION

021 884 4360
info@vineyardconnection.co.za

EXPORTERS OF WINES FROM THE CAPE

TO CAPE TOWN

R44 TO PAARL

exit 47

N1

R101

KLAPMUT

KLAPMUTSKOP

LIEVLAND

MULDERSVLEI ROAD

THE VINEYARD CONNECTION AT DELVERA

BOTTELARY ROAD

R44

KANONKOP

SIMONSIG

TO STELLENBOSCH

KROMME RHEE ROAD

★★★★ **La Luna** 🍃 Cab, cab franc, merlot, petit verdot blend. Celery, blackcurrant & herbs with violet edge. **06** is soft yet firm, ripe & juicy, with dark cocoa concentration, rich but not bulky.

★★★★ **Navitas** Previewed **08** is spicy mix of shiraz, mourvèdre, grenache, with cranberry tang, cedar & buchu. Lithe, but with firm core of fruit & oak tannin (14 months, 30% new).

★★★★ **Cyclus** 🍃 Viognier-led (60%) mix, chenin, chardonnay & semillon bit players in **09**. Lime zest, pepper & nettle; mineral, textured, with body & length. 40% unwooded portion adds freshness.

Camissa 🍃🍃 ★★★ Nuanced rosé from unusual combo muscat de Frontignan & mourvèdre. Sumptuous Turkish Delight & flowers on **10** but dry (just 4g sugar) & fresh. **Anima** 🍃 ★★★★ From chenin, naturally fermented, as with all these. **09** tarte tatin & apricot richness, 10 months lees-ageing & 20% new oak add body, elegance. **Armilla Méthode Cap Classique** ★★★★ Rich yet tangy **NV** sparkling from chardonnay, 2 years on lees. Vibrant citrus freshness & integration, great length. 10% oaked.

Les Pleurs range
Discontinued: **Syrah, Chenin Blanc, White.**

Avondale Reserve range
Discontinued: **The Owl House Cabernet Sauvignon, Camissa Syrah, Graham, The Weir Chardonnay, MCC Brut.**

The Green Duck range
Discontinued: **Green Ducks The Duke, Green Ducks The Duchess.**

Organic range
Discontinued: **Jonty's Ducks.**

Avondale Premium range
Discontinued: **Julia, Rosé, Chenin Blanc, Sauvignon Blanc.**

Fortified Sweet range
Discontinued: **Muscat Rouge, Muscat Blanc.** — FM

Avondrood Vineyards

Location: Rawsonville ▪ Map: Breedekloof ▪ Est/1stB 2005 ▪ Tasting, sales & tours Mon-Fri 8-12 & 1.30-5 Sat by appt (phone +27 (0)82-578-6841) ▪ Closed most pub hols ▪ Refreshments/food-and-wine tastings by appt or BYO picnic ▪ Hewn-stone Mountain Cottage ▪ Conferences ▪ Walks/hikes ▪ Facilities for children ▪ Owner(s) Albertus van Rensburg ▪ Winemaker(s) Albertus van Rensburg, with Johannes Damane ▪ Viticulturist(s) Pierre Snyman ▪ 80ha (cab, ptage, shiraz, chard, sauv, viog) ▪ 30t/2,100cs 40% red 60% white ▪ PO Box 277 Worcester 6849 ▪ vineyards@avondrood.co.za ▪ www.avondrood.co.za ▪ S 33° 43'32.9" E 019° 20'18.7" ▪ **T +27 (0)23-349-1858** ▪ F +27 (0)86-210-5806

From their boutique winery in the Goudini Valley, Albertus van Rensburg and his wife Minett travel the country to present their wines paired with food, which has proved particularly popular in Pretoria. Robust sales in Gauteng confirm the success of these personalised tastings. This harvest, malbec, mourvèdre and tannat coming on stream will add variety to his winemaker's palette.

Avondvrede

Location: Paarl ▪ Map: Paarl & Wellington ▪ Est 1995 ▪ 1stB 1999 ▪ Tasting, sales, cellar tours & light lunches by appt ▪ Tour groups ▪ Function room ▪ Owner(s) John & Christine Enthoven ▪ Winemaker(s) John Enthoven ▪ Vineyard manager(s) Gerardus van Zyl ▪ 3ha (cabs s/f, merlot) ▪ ±250cs own label 100% red ▪ PO Box 152 Klapmuts 7625 ▪ S 33° 49'47.2" E 018° 53'8.3" ▪ **T +27 (0)83-658-0595** ▪ F +27 (0)21-875-5609

The Enthoven family vinify tiny quantities of cab and merlot (2010 is current vintage) mainly for export to Europe and some for own consumption.

Avontuur Estate

Location: Somerset West ▪ Map: Helderberg ▪ WO: Stellenbosch ▪ Est 1850 ▪ 1stB 1990 ▪ Tasting & sales Mon-Fri 8. 30-5 Sat/Sun 9-4 ▪ Fee R20/5 wines, R40/premier range, brandy & bubbly ▪ Closed Easter Fri, Dec 25 & Jan 1 ▪ Cellar tours by appt ▪ The Avontuur Restaurant (see Restaurants section) ▪ Small conference venue ▪ Thoroughbred stud ▪ Owner(s) Taberer family ▪ Winemaker(s) Jan van Rooyen (Jan 2011) ▪ Viticulturist(s) Pippa

Mickleburgh (Sep 1999) • 104ha/74ha (cabs s/f, merlot, ptage, pinot, shiraz, chard, sauv) • 300t/30,000cs own label 60% red 40% white • PO Box 1128 Somerset West 7129 • info@avontuurestate.co.za • www. avontuurestate.co.za • S 34° 1' 33.2" E 018° 49' 23.8" • **T** +27 (0)21-855-3450 • F +27 (0)21-855-4600

It was a break with a traditional tendency to female dominance over the wine part of this Helderberg farm when Jan van Rooyen was appointed winemaker in time for the 2011 harvest - but Pippa Mickleburgh continues to rule the vineyards. The other part of the farm – the horse stud – is duly recognised in the winery, with the (established) wines in the newly constituted Premiere Range named for 'five of the finest horses to have passed through the farm': Baccarat, Luna de Miel, Sarabande, Dominion Royale and Minelli.

Avontuur Premiere range

★★★★ **Dominion Royale (Shiraz Reserve)** Tasted last year, **08** full bodied & powerful (15.5% alc), with attractive wealth of fruit, raspberry liqueur; vanilla & coconut scents from oak. Fine, firm tannin structure.

Minelli (Pinot Noir Reserve) ★★★★ Fresh & food-friendly **09** offers delicate cherry & raspberry. Modest alcohol, unobtrusive oaking & soft tannin make it very accessible. **Baccarat** ★★★★ **08** Bordeaux blend led by cab franc. Just-dry, with ripe fruit & spicy notes, the finish a bit warm from 14.5% alc. **Luna de Miel (Chardonnay Reserve)** ★★★★ **09** tasted last year was less oaky than previously. Pleasant & dry, if slightly dilute, with ripe pear & faint floral notes. **Sarabande (Sauvignon Blanc Reserve)** ★★★★ **10**, with mineral-toned blackcurrant flavours, was fresh & dry, last year looked likely to gain complexity with time.

Avontuur Estate range

★★★★ **Brut Cap Classique NV** from chardonnay, tasted last time, with aromas of ripe apple, pear & spicy gingerbread. Creamy mouthfeel, showing yeasty notes, & a good dry finish.

Cabernet Sauvignon ★★★ Last tasted was hefty, ultra-ripe & oaky **07**. **Cabernet Franc** ★★★★ Last year **08**'s redcurrant & plum aromas had spicy fynbos undertones. Hot finish ex 15.5% alc. **Pinotage** ★★★ **08** was last sampled, its raspberry fruit dominated by oak & dry tannin. **Shiraz** ★★★ **08** last year loaded with jammy fruit & spicy oak. Dry, but big alc left sweet impression. **Cabernet Sauvignon-Merlot** ★★★ Just-off-dry **08**. Firmly built with support from older oak & some awkward acid balanced by sweetness on the frail finish. **Vintner's Red** ▤ ★★★ Off-dry **07** cab-shiraz (different wine from last year's version), easy drinking but fades fast. **Vintner's Blend** ▤ Await next. **Sauvignon Blanc** ▤ ★★★ Gently mannered, bone-dry **11** with boiled sweet & grassy aromas & limy finish. **Above Royalty (Noble Late Harvest)** ★★★ Occasional release. **01** (★★★★☆) from riesling, **09** tasted last year from chenin. Strange raisiny aromas but fresh acidity. — JPf

---

Awendland

Location: Rawsonville • Map/WO: Breedekloof • Est/1stB 2006 • Tasting, sales & tours by appt • Owner(s) André van der Walt • Cellarmaster(s)/winemaker(s) André van der Walt (Jan 2009) • Viticulturist(s) Peet Smith (Jan 2009) • 10ha total • 10t/2,000cs own label 50% red 50% white • PO Box 237 Rawsonville 6845 • utilitas@iafrica.com, dagbreek@compnet.co.za • S 33° 39' 57.7" E 019° 18' 8.43" • **T** +27 (0)21-887-2713 • F +27 (0)21-887-2710

'The queen is resting and not to be disturbed!' quips André van der Walt of the rare-in-the-Cape nebbiolo grown and vinified on his Breedekloof farm. 'Nebbiolo needs at least two years in the barrel. Once bottled, the 2009 will be fantastic.'

Nebbia Reserve Await next. **Shiraz** In abeyance, as for **Cab-Merlot Unfiltered**, **Cab-Merlot** & **Sauvignon Blanc**. **Chenin Blanc Reserve** ★★★★ Seriously styled **10** rich glacé pineapple & lime flavour balanced by tangy acid. Previewed & provisionally rated last year. — MW

Axe Hill

Location/WO: Calitzdorp • Map: Klein Karoo & Garden Route • Est 1993 • 1stB 1997 • Tasting, sales & cellar tours by appt Mon-Sat • Owner(s) Axe Hill Winery (Pty) Ltd • Cellarmaster(s)/winemaker(s) Mike Neebe (Oct 2007) • Viticulturist(s) Johannes Mellet (Aug 2009, consultant) • ±60ha/1.3ha (souzão, tinta barocca, touriga nacional) • ±5t/±2,000cs own label 70% red 30% white • Wesoewer Road Calitzdorp 6660 • info@axehill.co.za • www. axehill.co.za • S 33° 30' 54.6" E 021° 41' 23.0" • **T** +27 (0)11-447-4366, +27 (0)44-213-3585 • F +27 (0)11-447-3219

Mike Neebe, owner/winemaker at this boutique cellar in the Klein Karoo, remains fired-up with enthusiasm from his trip to the Douro two years ago and now, having seen the successes in Portugal, has added the first still wines to Axe Hill's port-based portfolio. The final goal is a 'Calitzdorp Blend' – a still wine made using only Portuguese varieties, but in the meantime he continues to experiment with new wines including a 'Cape Pink' port, made in a drier style. He describes his winemaking philosophy as 'less is more' and tries to intervene as little as possible throughout the whole process.

★★★★ **Shiraz** NEW ✓ Cellar's first unfortified red worth the wait. This **10** especially impressive: dark fruit & bouillon, 50% new oak deftly judged, adds structure & light seasoning; great concentration & prospects.

★★★★☆ **Cape Vintage Port** Classic Cape port style, with souzão (39%) leading touriga & tinta for 1st time in **09** (★★★★), also one of their driest (mere 88g/l RS). Plump fruit, dried herb & spice overlay, good complexity but shade off **08**.

★★★★ **Cape Ruby Port** NEW ✓ Touriga flies solo in ripe & rich **NV**, permeated by Karoo scrub, buoyed by exceptionally pure fruit, elegant & accessible - & delicious!

Machado NEW ★★★ Their 2nd unfortified offering, estate's trio port grapes & shiraz (33%). Lightly oaked **10** reticent, faintly spicy, burly alc evident. May simply need time to settle. **Cape White** ★★★ Fortified chenin aged in a solera. Latest **NV** bottling dips slightly, lacks complexity, depth & power of previous. — Panel

Ayama Wines

Location/WO: Paarl ▪ Map: Paarl & Wellington ▪ Est 2005 ▪ 1stB 2006 ▪ Tasting by appt ▪ Closed all pub hols ▪ Meals/refreshments by appt; or BYO picnic ▪ Walking/hiking trails ▪ Conservation area ▪ Owner(s) Slent Farms (Pty) Ltd (6 partners) ▪ Cellarmaster(s)/winemaker(s) Michela Sfiligoi (2005) ▪ Viticulturist(s) Attilio Dalpiaz (2005) ▪ 172ha/37ha (cab, merlot, shiraz, chenin) ▪ 300t/20,000cs own label 30% red 68% white 2% rosé ▪ Suite 106 Private Bag X3041 Paarl 7620 ▪ info@slentfarms.com ▪ www.slentfarms.com ▪ S 33° 37'22.5" E 018° 49'19" ▪ T +27 (0)21-869-8313 ▪ F +27 (0)21-869-8313

Italian passion gushes forth here at Slent Farm on the Perdeberg slopes, where the spanking new winery is eagerly awaited. The Dalpiaz family have bought into the South African lifestyle in every way, and intend bringing a bit of Italy into the mix: the first plantings of the trendy vermentino grape.

Leopard range NEW

★★★★ **Shiraz-Pinotage-Mourvèdre** ✓ 🗐 🖾 Appealing blend with ripe dark berry fruit & soft texture, **10** shows classic Old-World touch. Elegant & balanced, eminently drinkable.

Chardonnay-Chenin Blanc-Viognier ✓ 🗐 🖾 ★★★★ First tasting, alluringly scented **10** shows richly ripe fruit, thick texture & elegantly balanced acidity.

Ayama Wines range

> **Merlot** ☺ 🗐 ★★★ Reticent, lean **10** shows restrained handling, cooler vintage. Still appealing, but understated, begging meaty, saucy dishes. **Sauvignon Blanc** ☺ 🗐 ★★★ Waxy, mineral **10** has distinctive flavour profile nodding at Swartland new-wave. Fullish, gently acidic & appealing.

Cabernet Sauvignon ★★★ Unwooded **09** was soft, pliable, had slightly bland fruit profile. This & next 2 from previous edition. **Pinotage** ★★★ Unoaked **09** expressed ripe berry fruit with edgy spiciness & commendable body. **Shiraz** ★★★★ Fruit-driven unwooded **09** had depth & substance, appealing peppery centre & black cherries. **Baboon's Back** ✓ ★★★★ Previously 'Shiraz Barrel Selection'. Still from shiraz, satisfyingly smoky **09** holds back on fruit but expresses varietal herbaceousness. Should develop. **Pinotage-Shiraz** Await new vintage. **Rosé** 🗐 ★★ Spicy, fruity **10** from pinotage showed variety's brisk acidity. Not retasted, as next 4. **Chardonnay** 🗐 ★★★ Unoaked **10**, had fullish body with intense apricot notes. WO Swartland. **Chenin Blanc** 🗐 ★★★ Nice floral scents, greengage & lime cordial noted on bracingly fresh **10**. **Viognier** Await next. **Chenin Blanc-Sauvignon Blanc** 🗐 Await next. — GdB

■ **Azania** see African Terroir

Baarsma Wine Group

Closed to public ▪ Owner(s) Baarsma Wine Group B.V. ▪ MD Chris Rabie ▪ Cellarmaster(s) Hannes Louw (since Jan 2005) ▪ PO Box 7275 Stellenbosch 7599 ▪ info@baarsma.co.za ▪ www.baarsma.co.za ▪ T +27 (0)21-880-1221 ▪ F +27 (0)21-880-0851

Stellenbosch-based Baarsma SA is a major export marketer of SA wines, shipping more than 1m cases a year to the major international wine markets, notably Europe. Ranges owned or exported include Ancient Africa, Blydskap, Cape Reality, Goede Moed, Goedgenoegen, Lazy Bay, Lyngrove (see entry), Meerland, Rotsvast, Stonechurch, Veelplesier and Voorspoed. Baarsma also represents a number of top SA brands in Europe.

BABISA - Born & Bred in South Africa

Location/WO: Paarl ▪ Map: Paarl & Wellington ▪ Est 2008 ▪ 1stB 2007 ▪ Tasting, sales & cellar tours daily 9-5 ▪ Fee R15pp ▪ Closed Easter Sun, Dec 25 & Jan 1 ▪ Light meals/refreshments ▪ Tour groups ▪ Owner(s) BABISA Brand Innovation Holdings Ltd ▪ Cellarmaster(s)/winemaker(s)/viticulturist(s) Various ▪ 5,000cs 60% red 30% white 10% rosé ▪ Export brand: BABISA - Lifestyle (UK & Europe) ▪ PO Box 52185 Waterfront 8002 ▪ wines@babisa.com ▪ www.babisa.com ▪ S 33° 46' 57.00" E 018° 57' 6.12" ▪ **T +27 (0)71-232-8840** ▪ F +27 (0)86-616-2794

Paul Burger, proprietor of the BABISA lifestyle brand, has big plans for a worldwide network of outlets, showcasing a range of SA commodities, including an 'icon' wine. Details are not public yet, but he promises 'little corners of Africa' everywhere. In the meantime, he's scouring the winelands for suitable products.

★★★★ **Valerie Reserve** Now with 'Reserve' suffix. Serious, appealing shiraz-led 6-way blend from Paarl, **09** repeats previous formula. Heavily oaky, but should evolve. Big, ripe & lingering.
Discontinued: **Cabernet Sauvignon**, **Shiraz**, **Gloria Rouge Wooded**. — GdB

Babylon's Peak Private Cellar

Location: Malmesbury ▪ Map: Swartland ▪ WO: Swartland/Western Cape ▪ Est/1stB 2003 ▪ Tasting, sales & cellar tours by appt ▪ Closed Easter Fri-Mon, Dec 25 & Jan 1 ▪ Pre-booked light refreshments for groups ▪ Olives ▪ BYO picnic ▪ Walking/hiking trails ▪ Conservation area ▪ Self-catering Cottage ▪ Dams for fishing ▪ Owner(s) Stephan Basson ▪ Cellarmaster(s)/winemaker(s)/viticulturist(s) Stephan Basson (Jan 2003) ▪ 580ha/230ha (carignan, grenache, mourv, ptage, shiraz, chenin, rouss, viog) ▪ 10,000cs own label 65% red 35% white + 500,000L bulk ▪ PO Box 161 Malmesbury 7299 ▪ info@babylonspeak.co.za ▪ S 33° 33' 40.8" E 018° 48' 38.6" ▪ **T +27 (0)21-300-1052** ▪ F +27 (0)86-518-3773

A 'boutique' winery amid big vineyards - with roussanne recently planted to augment the mix of southern French varieties flourishing here. The focus remains on viticulture as the belief is that good wine is made in the vineyard. It means there's quality and also great value to be found in these Basson family offerings.

★★★★ **Shiraz-Mourvèdre-Grenache** NEW ✓ Very good exposition of modern Swartland Rhône style. **09** 87% shiraz. Savoury spice, fynbos & contained ripe berries meld into rich, dry palate. WO W Cape.
★★★★ **Chenin Blanc** ✓ 🍏 Old-vineyard intensity shines on **11**, peachy fruit introduces crisp, refreshing palate with dry pebbly length, typical of Swartland chenin. Zesty acid keeps fruit weight in check.

Shiraz-Carignan 😊 🍏 ★★★ Lovely nose of ripe dark fruits, some plums & good earthy support. **09** balancing acid foil to sweetish end. Mostly shiraz.

Syrah ★★★☆ Showy **07** with succulent dark fruit tasted last year. **Babylon** ★★★☆ Last **06** pinotage-led with cab, shiraz. **Viognier** ★★★★ Vibrant **09** last year had all varietal hallmarks; up on **08** (★★★★). — JP

Babylonstoren NEW

Location: Paarl ▪ Map: Paarl & Wellington ▪ Est 2011 ▪ Tasting & sales Wed-Sun 10-4 from Dec 2011 ▪ Tour groups ▪ Gift shop ▪ Hiking/walking trails ▪ Guesthouse & Spa (see Accommodation section) ▪ Babel Restaurant (see Restaurants section) ▪ Guided garden tours ▪ Winemaker(s) Charl Coetzee (Nov 2010), with Wian Mouton (Jan 2011) ▪ Viticulturist(s) Hannes Aucamp (Jan 2010) ▪ 200ha/±62ha (mourv, shiraz, chard) ▪ PO Box 167 Simondium 7670 ▪ cellar@babylonstoren.com ▪ www.babylonstoren.com ▪ S 33° 49' 26.73" E 018° 55' 39.08" ▪ **T +27 (0)21-863-1804** ▪ F +27 (0)21-863-1727

Cape Town media man Koos Bekker and former journalist wife Karen Roos have injected money, style and return-to-their-farming-roots gusto into this 17th-century Cape Dutch property in the Simonsberg foothills, and won acclaim for the rustic-chic guest lodgings, restaurant (Babel) and organic farm garden from the likes of

Travel & Leisure and Harper's Bazaar. Seasoned (Kaapzicht, Clos Malverne) cellar chief Charl Coetzee's maiden 2011 shiraz and chardonnay, made in a facility 'equipped with everything a winemaker could possibly want', are destined for a premium label.

■ **Babylons Toren** *see* Backsberg Estate Cellars
■ **Babylon's Vineyards** *see* Mount Babylon Vineyards

Backsberg Estate Cellars

Location: Paarl ▪ Map: Paarl & Wellington ▪ WO: Western Cape/Coastal/Paarl ▪ Est 1916 ▪ 1stB 1970 ▪ Tasting & sales Mon-Fri 8-5 Sat 9.30-4.30 Sun 10.30-4.30 ▪ Fee R15 ▪ Open 365 days a year ▪ Cellar tours by appt ▪ Backsberg Restaurant (see Restaurants section) ▪ Tour groups ▪ Gift shop ▪ Figs & preserves for sale ▪ BYO picnic ▪ Conferences ▪ Weddings & functions ▪ Conservation area ▪ Sunday picnic concerts (Dec-Jan) ▪ Owner(s) Michael Back ▪ Winemaker(s) Guillaume Nell (Jan 2008) ▪ Viticulturist(s) Clive Trent (Jul 1992) ▪ 130ha (cab, merlot, shiraz, chard) ▪ 900t/80,000cs own label 65% red 30% white 5% rosé ▪ PO Box 537 Suider-Paarl 7624 ▪ info@backsberg.co.za ▪ www.backsberg.co.za ▪ S 33° 49' 42.9" E 018° 54' 56.9" ▪ **T +27 (0)21-875-5141** ▪ F +27 (0)21-875-5144

This established family winery has continued getting recognition for environmental innovation, winning the 2011 Climate Change Leadership Award in the Agriculture sector. 'Our composting initiative is well underway, and we're developing our cooling systems for red-wine fermenters using dam water rather than air-conditioned water,' says Simon Back, marketing manager. 'Currently the cellar is in the middle of the first phase of a redesign that will see it become, to a large extent, gravity-fed.' Winemaker Guillaume Nell notes that although they're pressing almost 1,000t, it is 'in the manner of a boutique cellar'. The Summer Picnic Concerts remain a success, with Sunday afternoon audiences relaxing to some of South Africa's favourite musicians and sipping Backsberg wine.

Flagship - Backsberg Family Reserve range

★★★★ **Red Blend** Impressive quartet Bordeaux varieties, dollop shiraz. **05** opulently fruited, full bodied & complex, lingering savoury finish. Coastal WO, as for John Martin. Like next, tasted last year.

★★★★ **White Blend** ▣ Adds 'Blend' to name, as did Red. Chardonnay/roussanne-driven **09**'s waxy overlay complements boldly flavoured yet balanced profile, refreshing acid zing. Drop viognier for floral lift.

Black Label range

★★★★ **Klein Babylonstoren** Graceful cab/merlot blend. **05** expressive cassis, lead pencil & herbal notes; balanced flavours, long savoury conclusion. None in this range retasted except Sauvignon, MCC, Elbar.

★★★★ **Elbar** ✓ Malbec & mourvèdre 70% of **07**'s 7-way blend, tasted as preview last year. Hedgerow fruit, sprinkle of dried herbs, supple oak add savoury flavours, long silky flourish.

★★★★ **John Martin Reserve Sauvignon Blanc** ✓ Now bottled, **10** displays intense capsicum, gooseberry, lime aromas, with vanilla note from oak. Mouthfilling, stylishly complex, snappy mineral finish.

★★★★ **Hillside Viognier** ▣ Vanilla notes to **09**'s peach/apricot medley. Delicately textured, smooth balanced acidity from 14% roussanne, lingering nutty finish.

Pumphouse Shiraz ★★★ Last-tasted **07** offered blackberries, spice & herbs, friendly tannins. **Bella Rosa** ▣ ★★★ Light & fruity **09** rosé ex viognier & Italian reds. **Aldorina** ▣ In abeyance. **Brut MCC** ★★★★ **08** blends chardonnay & pinot: yeasty biscuit aromas, vibrant melon/apple flavours, persistent lemon-drop conclusion.

Premium range

Dry Red ☺ ▣ ★★★ **NV** quaffer has sweet berries & a hint of vanilla. **Rosé** ☺ ▣ ★★★ Semi-sweet **NV** from white aromatic varieties with shiraz, gentle & charming. **Sauvignon Blanc** ☺ ▣ ★★★ **11** citrus, melon & gooseberry notes leading to a long fresh, zesty conclusion.

Cabernet Sauvignon ★★★ Mint & cassis, dry & savoury firm structure on **07** tasted last edition. **Merlot** ✓ ★★★★ **09** earth/plum/vanilla sipper. Elegant, with firm dusty farewell. **Pinotage** ▣ ★★★ **09** in usual sweetly ripe, smooth easy-going mode. WO Coastal. **Chardonnay** ★★★ Now bottled, oaked **09** has developed nicely, with same buttered toast, baked apple & cinnamon character. **Chenin Blanc** ▣ ★★★ Tasted last year, fruit-pure & full-flavoured **10** exuded pineapple & melon. **Special Late Harvest** Await new.

Kosher range

Merlot ★★ Lightly oaked & easy **10**. WO Paarl for this, still wines following. **Pinotage** ★★★ **10** is fresh & fruity, with good dry finish. **Chardonnay** 🔖 ★★ Easy-drinking, unwooded **10** tasted last year, as was... **Brut MCC** ★★★ 1st kosher bubbly in SA. 100% chardonnay **08** frothy, light & fruitily crisp.

Fortified range

Pinneau ★★★ Fortified semillon grape juice; Last tasted was **04** with fruit, toffee, medicinal notes. **Port** ★★★★ From cab franc, **06** last year was like drinking brandy-doused fruitcake: full-bodied, rich. — WB

Badenhorst Family Wines

Location: Malmesbury ▪ Map: Swartland ▪ WO: Coastal ▪ Est 2007 ▪ 1stB 2006 ▪ Tasting, sales & tours by appt ▪ Closed all pub hols ▪ Conferences ▪ Conservation area ▪ Guest cottages ▪ Owner(s) Adi & Hein Badenhorst ▪ Winemaker(s) Adi Badenhorst (2006), with Jasper Wickens (2008) ▪ Viticulturist(s) Pierre Rossouw (Jan 1975) ▪ 60ha/23ha (cinsaut, grenache, shiraz, chard, chenin, rouss) ▪ 1,800cs own label 60% red 40% white ▪ PO Box 1177 Malmesbury 7299 ▪ adi@iafrica.com ▪ www.aabadenhorst.com ▪ S 33° 32'38.01" E 018° 49'7.42" ▪ **T +27 (0)82-373-5038** ▪ F +27 (0)21-794-5196

In 2007/8, Adi Badenhorst swapped life as winemaker at Rustenberg for a 60ha piece of the Perdeberg with an abandoned winery and a 'dodgy 1960s house'. Because he's a rebel? That too. It was the 20-plus hectares of old Swartland dryland bushvines that attracted him: chenin in the 60s, cinsaut from 1957 and grenache planted in 1951. And, one senses, the chance to embrace traditional winemaking without (too much) regard for commercial imperatives. Grapes are picked early for fresher wines – 'psychological versus physiological ripeness,' he quips. And 'sorry for those who like new oak', cellar vessels are all large old vats or concrete tanks. Badenhorst, who breeds parrots in his spare time, is usually joking and hard to take seriously. The antithesis of his wines.

AA Badenhorst range

★★★★ **Red** Shiraz shepherds cinsaut, grenache & mourvèdre in disarmingly fruity, delightfully savoury **08**. Accessible to drink mid-2011, with palate-purchase for food. Only big older oak used.

★★★★☆ **White** Elegant power: subtle weight & texture, nothing gauche. Chenin-led **09** (with nine partners including roussanne & rarity in the Cape grenache gris) is big but smooth & complex, held together by minerality. 20 months in old cask/concrete tank allows chalky, tarragon-scented features centre stage.

★★★★ **Funky White Wine** NEW NV from 11 varieties vinified in 5-vintage 'solera' (500L drawn off & 500L fresh wine added to system each year). Oxidised styling; nutty, salty, near-tarry tones. — DS

Badgerberg Estate NEW

Location/map: Villiersdorp ▪ WO: Overberg ▪ Est 2000 ▪ 1stB 2009 ▪ Tasting & sales Mon-Sat by appt ▪ Light German refreshments, sausages, cheese breads, cold cuts - Sat during summer or by appt from 10-4 ▪ Facilities for children ▪ Gift shop ▪ Walking/hiking trails ▪ German October fest annually & bimonthly charity high tea ▪ Owner(s) Heinz & Lynnette Mederer ▪ Winemaker(s) Ryan Puttick (Villiersdorp Cellar) ▪ Viticulturist(s) Andre Bruyns (Villiersdorp Cellar) ▪ 35ha/9ha (cab, merlot, shiraz, sauv) ▪ 100t/634cs own label 53% red 47% white ▪ PO Box 2605 Somerset West 7129 ▪ info@badgerberg.co.za, lynnettem@badgerberg.co.za ▪ www.badgerberg.co.za ▪ S 33° 57'07.5" E 19° 19'29.5" ▪ **T +27 (0)21-852-1150, +27 (0)83-263-2783** ▪ F +27 (0)86-586-2237

Exploring the potential of their newly bought estate, owners Heinz and Lynnette Mederer first had a red blend made at nearby Villiersdorp Cellar in 2009, joined in 2010 by a sauvignon and a sauvignon-based méthode cap classique due for release as the guide went to press. See contacts section above for more about their German heritage offerings and bimonthly charity high teas.

Prima ★★★ **09** merlot, cab blend oozes red fruit. Bright & uncomplicated with supple fruit flavours balanced by fresh acidity & firm vanilla oak. **Sauvignon Blanc** 🔖 ★★★ Lightly fruited, easy lunchtime **10** white. — Panel

Badsberg Wine Cellar

Location: Rawsonville ▪ Map/WO: Breedekloof ▪ Est 1951 ▪ 1stB 1958 ▪ Tasting & sales Mon-Fri 8-5 Sat 10-1 ▪ Fee R20pp for groups of 8+ ▪ Closed all pub hols ▪ Cellar tours Mon-Fri between 2-3 (Feb-Mar only) ▪ Picnics by appt during harvest; or BYO picnic ▪ Facilities for children ▪ Farm produce ▪ Conference facilities (40 pax) ▪ Conservation area ▪ Cloudy Nouveau (Mar), Soetes & Soup (Jul) & Outdoor festivals (Oct) ▪ Owner(s) 26 members ▪ Cellarmaster(s) Willie Burger (1998) ▪ Winemaker(s) Henri Swiegers (2002) & De Wet Hugo (Dec 2006), with Jaco Booysen (Jan 2007) ▪ Viticulturist(s) De Wet Hugo (Dec 2006) ▪ ±1,500ha/±1,300ha (ptage, shiraz, chenin, cbard) ▪ ±23,000t own label 15% red 60% white 10% rosé 15% fortified ▪ ISO 22000:2009 ▪ PO Box 72 Rawsonville 6845 ▪ enquiries@badsberg.co.za ▪ www.badsberg.co.za ▪ S 33° 39′ 40.1″   E 019° 16′ 9.2″ ▪ **T +27 (0)23-344-3021** ▪ F +27 (0)23-344-3023

Traditionally a large-scale producer and exporter (Netherlands, UK, Germany, China) supplied by Breedekloof grape growers, Badsberg intends expanding its bottled wine range and distribution locally. The aim is 'to have a bottle of Badsberg at hand, whenever the occasion requires it'. Going green is another theme of this member of the Badsberg Bewarea Nature Reserve, through indigenous species conservation, eco-friendly cellar practices and lower sulphites in their wines.

★★★★★ **Badslese** NEW ✓ Our White Wine of the Year is this outstanding, elegantly presented Natural Sweet dessert from chenin. **09** great concentration & spread of flavour, from floral to spicy, huge sweetness concludes on a tangy savoury/leafy note, which is uncloying & decidedly moreish. With 10% hanepoot, unwooded.

★★★★ **Noble Late Harvest** ✓ Deliciously soft & sweet after-dinner treat from (unwooded) chenin, **07** lots of good things - honey, apricot, marmalade - to smell & taste; clean & uplifting. 375ml disappears so quickly...

★★★★ **Noble Late Harvest Limited Edition** ✓ Wooded version, also chenin, 3 years barrelled (!) hence **05**'s caramel tone, but there's also loads of fruit (fresh, dried & candied!), & palate-cleansing freshness. 750ml.

★★★★ **Red Muscadel** ✓ 📖 They do this fortified dessert style so well: everything in place & contributing to delicious, sweet, smooth, fragrant mouthful. Liquid Turkish Delight. **10** irresistible now & for many winters.

★★★★ **Red Jerepigo** ✓ 📖 Attractive sipper from pinotage, **10** candyfloss & plums, tad sweeter than the other fortifieds but still delightful, lively, thanks to spirity grip.

> **Merlot** ☺ 🖫 ★★★ **09** smoky, light, with food-inviting freshness; 'perfect for barbecues' say winemakers. **Vin Doux** ☺ 🖫 ★★★ Semi-sweet sparkling from hanepoot, **10** zesty, light fun in the sun.

Pinotage-Mocha Fusion NEW 📖 ★★★★ Juicy **10** leaves no doubt about 'coffee' styling: oak char, espresso &, yes, mocha too. But good fruit to back it up. **Belladonna** ★★★ Three Bordeaux reds & shiraz, **09** dusty, dry, shows cab's chunky tannins. **Rosé** NEW 🖫 📖 ★★★ Off-dry **10** from merlot, light body, strawberry flavour, appealing tang on finish. **Chardonnay Sur Lie** 📖 ★★★★ Barrel-fermented **11** rich, buttery & oaky, enough crisp acid to balance, nice lime cordial aftertaste. **Chenin Blanc** 🖫 📖 ★★☆ Light, uncomplicated **11**, everyday dry white. **Sauvignon Blanc** 🖫 ★★★ **10** light bodied & very fresh, needs a summer salad. **Special Late Harvest** 📖 ★★★ Pleasant barley sugar flavours from equal mix chenin & hanepoot, **10** light, fresh, not oversweet. **Hanepoot Jerepigo** ✓ 📖 ★★★★ Fortified dessert **10**, lovely sweet grapey character, refreshing savoury finish in which judicious 15% alc is well integrated. **Vintage Port** ★★★★ Touch sweeter & lighter than conventional 'vintage' style but **05** perfectly pleasant, nice herby/spicy touch. — Panel

■ **Bain's Way** see Wellington Wines
■ **Bakenskop** see Jonkheer
■ **Balance** see Overhex Wines International
■ **Balthazar** see Roodezandt Wines
■ **Bandana** see Klein Roosboom
■ **Barefoot Wine Company** see Catherine Marshall Wines

Barista

Location: Paarl ▪ WO: Western Cape ▪ Est/1stB 2009 ▪ Tasting at Val de Vie & Robertson Winery ▪ Owner(s) Vinimark ▪ Winemaker(s) Bertus Fourie ▪ Viticulturist(s) Briaan Stipp ▪ 600t/30,000cs own label ▪ PO Box 6223 Paarl 7620 ▪ info@vinimark.co.za ▪ www.baristawine.co.za ▪ **T +27 (0)21-883-8043** ▪ F +27 (0)21-886-4708

You could be forgiven for thinking Bertus Fourie (nicknamed 'Starbucks' for pioneering the much-emulated 'coffee' pinotage style) runs on java: he manages to successfully juggle lecturing at Elsenburg oenology faculty, winemaking for the Barista brand and consulting to several wineries (and being snapped for our Photo Gallery this edition). The fruity coffee pinotage below is flying - and three different areas supply grapes: Darling, Robertson and Wellington, where it all began.

Pinotage 🍷📷 ★★★ Mocha-chocolate, raspberries & caramel on **10**, juicy & agile quaffer. Attractively light but not frivolous. —FM

■ **Barn Find** *see* Franki's Vineyards
■ **Baroness** *see* Oudtshoorn Cellar - SCV
■ **Barony** *see* Rosendal Winery

Barrydale Cellar - SCV

Location: Barrydale ▪ Map: Klein Karoo & Garden Route ▪ WO: Tradouw/Western Cape/Klein Karoo ▪ Est 1941 ▪ 1stB 1976 ▪ Tasting & sales Mon–Fri 9–5 Sat 9–3 ▪ Fee R20 for groups of 5 or more ▪ Closed Easter Fri–Mon, Dec 25/ 26 & Jan 1 ▪ Book ahead for cellar tours ▪ BYO picnic ▪ Conservation area ▪ Owner(s) 75 members ▪ Cellarmaster(s) Riaan Marais (Jan 1999) ▪ Winemaker(s) Ferdi Smit (May 1985) ▪ Viticulturist(s) Hermias Vollgraaff (2009) ▪ ±102ha (cab, merlot, shiraz, chard, cbard, sauv) ▪ ±997t/5,000cs own label 56% red 43% white 1% rosé + 500cs for clients ▪ Other export brand: Joseph Barry ▪ PO Box 59 Barrydale 6750 ▪ sales@scv.co.za ▪ www. barrydalewines.co.za ▪ S 33°54'35.83" E 020°42'45.20" ▪ **T +27 (0)28-572-1012** ▪ F +27 (0)28-572-1541

What was a two-cellar operation has become a trio: Barrydale, Ladismith and Oudtshoorn wineries now comprise the Southern Cape Vineyards (SCV) grower-owned company. CEO Riaan Marais is optimistic about this year's performance and the chances for success of Barrydale's newly launched grappa-style Joseph Barry Husk Spirit, which joins two other brandies in the Joseph Barry range.

Merchant's Mark range

Cabernet Sauvignon NEW ★★ **08** dry & medium bodied for solo sunset sipping. **Merlot** ★★ **10** fresh & fruity fun, but ends quite quickly. **Pinot Noir** ★★★ **10** first since **05**; attractive dark cherry/earth fragrance, easy to like, good varietal flavours linger pleasantly. WO W Cape. **Ruby Cabernet** NEW 🍷 ★★ Upbeat fruit, rounded mouthfeel on friendly **09**. Klein Karoo WO, like next. **Shiraz** ★★ Revisited **08** has improved in bottle; now has black pepper dusting, softer mouthfeel. **Sauvignon Blanc** ★★ Light acid bite to breezy **11**. **Chardonnay-Viognier** ★★ Peach-toned **10** is a juicy, bright quick-sip.

Decent range NEW

Decent Red 🍷 ★★ **NV** combo red varieties soft & easy for uncomplicated enjoyment. **Decent White** 🍷 ★★ Pot-pourri bouquet on gently sweet **NV** trio white varieties. —Panel

Barry Gould Family Wines

Location: Elgin ▪ Map: Elgin, Walker Bay & Bot River ▪ Est 2003 ▪ 1stB 2004 ▪ Tasting, sales & cellar tours by appt ▪ Closed Easter Fri, Dec 25 & Jan 1 ▪ Meals/functions by arrangement (up to 20 pax) ▪ Wildekrans Country House (B&B) + self-catering cottage ▪ Child-friendly ▪ Gifts ▪ Farm produce ▪ Conference venue (20 pax) ▪ 4-day fully guided slack-packing trail ▪ Owner(s) Barry Gould & Alison Green ▪ Cellarmaster(s) Barry Gould (2003) ▪ Winemaker(s) Barry Gould (2003), with family (2004) ▪ Viticulturist(s) Barry Gould (2003) ▪ ±2t/160cs own label 70% red 30% white ▪ PO Box 7 Elgin 7180 ▪ gould.arc@wildekrans.co.za ▪ S 34°12'12.7" E 019°8'53.6" ▪ **T +27 (0)21-848-9788 / +27 (0)82-901-4896** ▪ F +27 (0)21-848-9788

'As a small-scale winemaker, one has to innovate every step of the way,' says architect-by-day Barry Gould, ably assisted by his family. 'Hands in, hands on, and hand made' is how he describes their low-tech approach. But who needs fancy equipment? 'My first-ever wine tasting was at Muratie. I was a teenager on holiday from Natal. None of the tasting glasses matched. It was a highlight of my life.'

A Simple Red Unready, as for **Chenin Blanc** & maiden **Sauvignon Blanc**. Discontinued: **Chardonnay**. —

Bartinney Private Cellar

Location/map/WO: Stellenbosch ▪ Est 2006 ▪ 1stB 2008 ▪ Tasting & sales Mon–Fri 10–4 ▪ Closed all pub hols ▪ Cellar tours by appt ▪ Owner(s) Rose & Michael Jordaan ▪ Cellarmaster(s) Therese de Beer (Jan 2009) ▪ Viticulturist(s) Ryno Maree (Oct 2010) ▪ 38ha/±17ha (cab, chard, sauv) ▪ 118t/2,000cs own label 50% red 50% white + 20,000L bulk ▪ BWI champion ▪ Postnet Suite 231 Private Bag X5061 Stellenbosch 7599 ▪ info@bartinney.co.za ▪ www.bartinney.co.za ▪ S 33°55'6.7" E 018°55'52.2" ▪ **T +27 (0)21-885-1013** ▪ F +27 (0)21-885-2852

Long-desired Biodiversity & Wine Initiative Championship status was achieved at the Jordaan family's winery below the brow of Stellenbosch's Helshoogte Pass, along with continued certified carbon neutrality. That, and solar panels added to the cellar's roof to reduce electricity usage by a third, and an awarded indigenous vegetation planting programme initiated by co-owner and architect Rose Jordaan, indicate how seriously green issues are taken here.

★★★★ **Cabernet Sauvignon** NEW 09 blackberry & cigar spice on gentle, textured mouthful, oak (40% new) enrobes ripe fruit. Lovely concentration & depth. Powerful but refined & restrained, lovely long aftertaste. **Elevage** 09 cab-based blend not reviewed. **Chardonnay** ★★★★ 09 last edition offered fresh lime & tangerine offset by cashew creaminess, marmalade & lemongrass tang on oak frame. Richer than 08 (★★★★). **Sauvignon Blanc** Ⓐ ★★★★ 10, step up on 09 (★★★★), previously had gorgeous fig & gooseberry richness balanced by acidity, textured mineral notes. — FM

Barton Vineyards

Location: Bot River ▪ Map: Elgin, Walker Bay & Bot River ▪ WO: Walker Bay/Western Cape ▪ Est 2001 ▪ 1stB 2003 ▪ Tasting, sales & cellar tours Mon-Fri 9–5 Sat 9–1 ▪ Fee R20 for 5 wines ▪ Closed Easter Sun, Dec 25 & Jan 1 ▪ Lavender products (hand/body cream, liquid soap, shampoo & essential oils), Olive oil, proteas ▪ BYO picnic ▪ Four 4-star self-catering villas (www.bartonvillas.co.za) ▪ Owner(s) Peter J Neill ▪ Cellarmaster(s)/winemaker(s)/viticulturist(s) PJ Geyer (Oct 2010) ▪ 200ha/28ha (cab, malbec, merlot, mourv, shiraz, chenin, sauv, sem) ▪ 100t/5,500cs own label 40% red 50% white 10% rosé ▪ IPW ▪ PO Box 100 Bot River 7185 ▪ info@bartonvineyards.co.za ▪ www.bartonvineyards.co.za ▪ S 34° 15' 43.8" E 019° 10' 29.2" ▪ **T +27 (0)28-284-9283** ▪ F +27 (0)28-284-9776

A new team, including French-trained winemaker, PJ Geyer, and plenty of new ideas at this well-positioned winery on the main road to Hermanus. The new white blend and the merlot might particularly benefit from Geyer's eight years as a flying winemaker with Bordeaux's Moueix family. As well as wine, olive products and honey are offered, while walking routes and mountain biking trails are being developed, with spots for bird watching and picnic areas. The idea is to offer a total working farm experience. A winery to watch.

★★★★ **Shiraz-Cabernet Sauvignon** ✓ Cool-climate white spice mixed with supple, rich flavours forges harmonious, tasty 09. Good drinking now but no hurry to open.

Merlot NEW ★★★★ Rich, simple dark berry fruit on 09, its full ripeness salvaged by enlivening acid. Needs no longer than year/2 softening. **Shiraz Rosé** 🍷 Ⓐ ★★★ 11 echoes 10's vivid ruby hue, spicy strawberry concentration. Tangily dry. **Chenin Blanc** 🍷 Ⓐ ★★★★ 11 (ex-tank, as is following wine) adds whiff oak spice to ripe but gentle floral tones. Quite rich, concentrated, with bright acid aiding honeyed conclusion. **Sauvignon Blanc** 🍷 Ⓐ ★★★ 11 riper-fruit style with few grams sugar to balance vigorous acid. Rating provisional. **Sauvignon Blanc-Semillon** NEW Not tasted. — AL

◼ **Basco** see Blomendahl Vineyards

Bayede!

Location: Somerset West ▪ Map: Helderberg ▪ WO: Paarl/Western Cape/Franschhoek ▪ Est 2008 ▪ Tasting & sales at Eikendal Vineyards Mon-Fri 10-4 Sat 10-1 Sun by appt only ▪ Fee R25 ▪ Closed all pub hols ▪ Bayede! Restaurant Tue-Sun 12-4; boutique & conference centre ▪ Facilities for children ▪ Tour groups ▪ Walks/hikes ▪ 70% red 20% white 10% rosé ▪ 510 Main Road Paarl 7646 ▪ anto@bayede.co.za ▪ www.bayede.co.za ▪ **T +27 (0)21-870-1686** ▪ F +27 (0)21-871-1105

Named for the traditional greeting 'Hail the King' and based at Eikendal Vineyards, with its own visitor amenities, Bayede! is a job creation initiative endorsed by Zulu monarch Goodwill Zwelethini KaBhekuzulu. To celebrate his 40-year reign, a new range, Royal Wine, was launched and overseas distribution plans formulated. The established wines were listed by retail chain Pick 'n Pay, exported to China and poured at international wine shows.

HM King Goodwill range

Merlot ★★★ Ripe 09 needs time to settle, earthy & savoury styling with hints of dark chocolate. WO Western Cape, like next. **Pinotage Reserve** NEW Ⓐ ★★★★ Hinting at blackcurrant & lavender, 10 shows promise, deserves more time for oak to fully integrate. **Shiraz** Not tasted, like **Chardonnay**.

Bayede! range

King Shaka Jubilee ★★★ Mainly cab & merlot, **06** prune & leather notes with dry cedary tannin. Enjoy soon with a meal. WO Franschhoek. Not retasted this edition, as for all in this range. **The Prince Red** 🍷 ★★★ **09** fruity, off-dry cab/shiraz, very lightly oaked. **Queen Thomo Sauvignon Blanc** 🍷 🛇 ★★ **10** ripe, gently crisp & light. **The Prince White** 🍷 ★★★ Refreshing melon fruit on **09** off-dry sipper from chenin & sauvignon. **Queen Mantfombi Brut Rosé** Dry sparkling not tasted. —DB

◼ **BC Wines** see Brandvlei Cellar
◼ **Beacon Hill** see Jonkheer

Beau Constantia

Location/WO: Constantia ▪ Map: Cape Peninsula ▪ Est 2003 ▪ 1stB 2010 ▪ Tasting & sales by appt Mon–Fri ▪ Closed all pub hols ▪ Spa by appt, T +27 (0)21-794-3376 (Anda) ▪ Owner(s) Dormell Properties 139 (Pty) Ltd ▪ Winemaker(s) Justin van Wyk (Sep 2010) ▪ Viticulturist(s) Japie Bronn (Sep 2002) ▪ 22ha/±11ha (cabs s/f, malbec, merlot, p verdot, shiraz, sauv, viog) ▪ 20t/900cs own label 80% red 20% white ▪ 1043 Constantia Main Road Constantia 7806 ▪ justin@beauconstantia.com ▪ www.beauconstantia.com ▪ S 34° 0' 48.57" E 018° 24' 21.67" ▪ **T +27 (0)21-794-7061** ▪ F +27 (0)21-794-0534

As the youngest estate in South Africa's oldest wine area, Beau Constantia aims to 'create a contemporary wine brand that fits in with the very modern architecture and design achieved on the farm', which sits in the 'saddle' atop Constantia Mountain. This strategy, says winemaker Justin van Wyk, 'is a bold move in a very classical region' but hopefully also 'a breath of fresh air'. The first release was from 7-year-old viognier vines, and the current focus is on their sauvignon blocks, rising up to 350m above sea level. A spa is open (by appointment), and the next step is a tasting and sales venue with 'magnificent views'.

Beau Constantia range `NEW`

★★★★ **Cecily** 🍷 Lovely **10** from viognier ably showcases variety's peach & stonefruit, well-judged oak & perky acidity balance ripe fruit flavours to lengthy pithy mineral finish. —Panel

Beau Joubert Vineyards & Winery

Location/map: Stellenbosch ▪ WO: Polkadraai Hills ▪ Est 1695 ▪ 1stB 2000 ▪ Tasting & sales Mon–Fri 8-5 Sat by appt ▪ Fee R15 ▪ Closed all pub hols ▪ Cellar tours by appt ▪ BYO picnic ▪ Walking/hiking trails ▪ Self-catering guest cottage ▪ Conference facility (max 100 guests) ▪ Functions & weddings (max 150 guests) ▪ Owner(s) Joubert family & US investors led by Andrew Hilliard ▪ Cellarmaster(s)/winemaker(s) Christian Kuun (Dec 2006) ▪ Viticulturist(s) Ian Engelbrecht (Nov 2010) ▪ 105ha/50ha (cabs s/f, merlot, pinot, shiraz, chard, chenin, sauv) ▪ 280t/20,000cs own label 60% red 35% white 5% rosé + 10,000 litres for clients ▪ Other export brand: Joubert Brothers ▪ Ranges for customers: Infusino's, Polkadraai Road ▪ PO Box 1114 Stellenbosch 7599 ▪ info@beaujoubert.com ▪ www.beaujoubert.com ▪ S 33° 57'11.6" E 018° 44'25.5" ▪ **T +27 (0)21-881-3103** ▪ F +27 (0)21-881-3377

'A bustling year it has been - exports soaring, heaps of ventures into new markets and local sales increasing dramatically' is the upbeat report from the American-South African joint venture in Stellenbosch's Polkadraai wine ward. Cellarmaster Chris Kuun says: 'The production team is optimising and upscaling the vineyard and winemaking programs, while the marketing division continues to perform at 110%.' In the pipeline is a conservation area around the natural spring.

Beau Joubert range

★★★★ **Reserve** `NEW` Elegant merlot blend (81%), plus cab & shiraz, **09** debuts with bright ripe berries, soft spice. Balanced & understated, vanilla-dipped berry aftertaste lingers tastily. Ageworthy.

Cabernet Sauvignon ★★★★ **09** seduces with upfront blackcurrant & fresh herbal notes, balanced by spicy oaky grip. Needs year/2 for optimum enjoyment. **Christmas Cabernet** ★★ Herbal & cassis edge, charry edge to **NV** quaffer last edition. **Merlot** ★★★ Smoky mulberry, plum & cocoa richness on soft & succulent **08** last year. **Shiraz** ★★★ **09** a step up; sweet earthy black fruit, vanilla oak flavours & a sprinkle of dry herbs. **Chardonnay** 🍷 ★★★ Gently oaked **09** stepped up last guide, showed citrus & creamy lees on structured palate. **Sauvignon Blanc** 🍷 ★★ Fresh green grass, fig on **11** preview, crisp yet juicy quaffer. **Fat Pig** `NEW` ★★★ Light-bodied port from pinotage. Sweet fruitcake & cinnamon on previewed **07**, for fireside enjoyment.

Oak Lane range

> **Shiraz-Cabernet Sauvignon** ☺ ★★★ **10** appealing earthiness & spice, blackcurrant pastilles & cigarbox notes, silky texture.

Pinot Noir NEW ★★★ Uncomplicated but pleasant **10**, earthy strawberries & firm oaky goodbye. **Merlot-Cabernet Sauvignon** ✓ ★★★☆ Herbs & smoky plums, **10** is smooth, ends with light grip, lovely balance for early drinking. **Rosé** 🍽🏠 ★★ Red fruit simplicity to **10**'s 100% cab offering last year. **Chenin Blanc-Sauvignon Blanc** 🍽 ★★☆ Soft melon & apple flavours on light **11** summer sipper. Tasted from tank. — WB

Beaumont Wines

Location: Bot River ▪ Map: Elgin, Walker Bay & Bot River ▪ WO: Bot River/Walker Bay ▪ Est 1750 ▪ 1stB 1994 ▪ Tasting, sales & cellar tours Mon-Fri 9.30–4.30 Sat 10–3 ▪ Fee R20pp for groups 10 ▪ Closed Easter Sun, Dec 25 & Jan 1 ▪ Meals by prior arrangement ▪ Farm produce ▪ Walking/hiking trails ▪ Conservation area ▪ 200-year old watermill ▪ Art/jewelly exhibits ▪ 2 historic self-catering guest cottages ▪ Owner(s) Beaumont family ▪ Cellarmaster(s) Sebastian Beaumont (Jun 2003) ▪ Winemaker(s) Marelise Jansen van Rensburg (Jan 2007) ▪ Viticulturist(s) Sebastian Beaumont (Jun 1999) ▪ 500ha/34ha (mourv, ptage, chenin) ▪ 200t/12,000cs own label 45% red 45% white 10% rosé ▪ BWI, IPW ▪ PO Box 3 Bot River 7185 ▪ info@beaumont.co.za ▪ www.beaumont.co.za ▪ S 34° 13′ 27.2″ E 019° 12′ 24.9″ ▪ **T +27 (0)28-284-9194** ▪ F +27 (0)28-284-9733

For Sebastian Beaumont, in the cellar as much of an artist as his mother, painter Jayne, and sister, jewellery designer Ariane, seeing Hope Marguerite recognised as one of the purest expressions of South African chenin – this is the 15th vintage and the second five star – is a career highlight to date. Taking Vitruvian, a distinctive and different Cape Blend, to similar status would be his next. 'The pendulum swung from the lean, green wines of the 1990s to the fruit-bombs of the 2000s; even Beaumont got caught up in the quest for phenolic ripeness. Now, we're trying to find the true expression of our terroir in greater fruit purity and less new wood, somewhere in the middle. That can only augur well for all our wines, and especially for Vitruvian.'

Beaumont range

★★★★☆ **Mourvèdre** Leads the (small) pack of varietal bottlings in SA. **09** maintains standard set by explosive **08**. Lipsmacking black fruit, satiny texture & endless satisfyingly dry finish.

★★★★ **Pinotage 09** back on track: as generously fruited but softer than **08** (★★★★). Good expression of variety's acetone/mulberry tones, could gain complexity with year/2 ageing.

★★★★ **Ariane 08** a 5-way Bordeaux blend, previous **06** being mainly merlot & duo cabs. Last year was fresh, approachable; lithe tannins wrapped compact black plum/berry fruit.

★★★★☆ **Vitruvian 08** authoritative & distinctive mix mourvèdre & pinotage, dashes shiraz, cab franc, petit verdot (latter not present in fine **06**; **07** not reviewed). Well composed, with firm tannin grip, subtle sour cherry & amaretto tones. Worth seeking out (& cellaring).

★★★★ **Shiraz-Mourvèdre** Preview **09** too unformed to rate. Lithe **08** was initially shy but opened in glass, left soulful, brooding impression; might since have perked up & become more expressive.

★★★★★ **Hope Marguerite Chenin Blanc** 🍷 Benchmark barrel fermented/aged chenin deserving to be cellared. **10** precise but rich; masterly balance of tannin, acid & fruit, seamless finish. Shares custard, cinnamon & clove profile with enticing **09** (★★★★★) & equally stellar **08**.

★★★★ **Chenin Blanc** ✓ 🍷 Step-up **11** (★★★★★) star bright & though slightly reticent on nose, gloriously steely & focused on palate. Quince-like puckering acidity, compact fruit from older vines promise to reward cellaring. **10** was similarly taut, **09** more honeyed.

★★★★ **Goutte d'Or** Consistently delicious botrytised dessert. Semillon & sauvignon as always in **08** &, like previous, neither overtly sweet nor heavy, just satiny fruit over fine acidity.

Cape Vintage ★★★ Port-style **07** preview warming mix tinta & pinotage, cherry highlights, lengthy farewell.

Raoul's range

Constable House Shiraz-Cabernet Sauvignon ★★★★ **09** dominated by shiraz; bursts with licorice, finishes with leafy tannins. Tasted ex barrel. Previously mainly WO W Cape, these now Walker Bay. **Red** 🍽🏠 ★★ **10** French-Portuguese blend offers melange berry flavours, firm smoky conclusion. **Shiraz Rosé** 🍽🏠 ★★★ Raspberry sherbet & bubblegum, coral hue, light dry flavour in **11**. **White** 🍽🏠 ★★★ Plenty of zesty appeal in **11**'s tangerine & lemon blossom glassful. — CvZ

Bein Wine Cellar

Location/map/WO: Stellenbosch • Est 2002 • 1stB 2004 • Tasting, sales & cellar tours Mon-Sat by appt • R20pp, waived on purchase of R100 • Closed Easter Fri, Dec 25 & Jan 1 • Owner(s)/cellarmaster(s)/winemaker(s) Luca & Ingrid Bein • Viticulturist(s) Luca Bein • 3ha/2.2ha (merlot) • 16t/1,200cs 750ml, 80cs 375ml & 290 magnums own label 80% red 20% rosé • IPW • PO Box 3408 Matieland 7602 • lib@beinwine.com • www.beinwine.com • S 33°57'40.0" E 018°44'12.0" • **T +27 (0)21-881-3025** • F +27 (0)88-021-881-3025

So perfect are their two hectares of merlot, one can imagine the Beins tending their vineyards with nail scissors! In pursuing premium quality reds in the style of Pomerol, a Swiss work ethic and computer modelling of their vineyard has enabled this ex-veterinerian couple to improve quality with nearly each vintage since the maiden 2002. Infrared imaging allows them to stagger pickings based on vigour, and decide which vines will be destined for each of their four bottlings.

Bein Wine range

★★★★ **Little Merlot** ✓ Stylishly elegant, classic 'little brother' from more vigorous vines, treated as for flag-ship until oaking. Accessible **10** maintains quality of fruit, harmoniously balanced by finely textured tannins.

★★★★☆ **Merlot** ✓ Classically-styled flagship **09** delivered depth, harmony & complexity last year. Polished tannins from splash cab & judicious oaking framed spicy succulent fruit. **07** (★★★★) touch less impressive.

★★★★☆ **Merlot Reserve** Handsome, new-oaked **08** tasted mid-09. Best-quality fruit imparts lovely bit-ter-choc richness, intensity checked by freshness & fine, polished tannins. Needed year/2 for oak to integrate.

Pink Merlot ☺ ★★★ Fragrant, crisp **11** harvested early for lightness. Satisfyingly dry & flavoursome con-clusion. — IM

Belbon Hills Private Cellar

Location: Cape Town • WO: Western Cape • Est/1stB 1999 • Closed to public • Owner(s) Pedro Estrada Belli • Winemaker(s) Outsourced, with Pedro Estrada Belli • 10,000cs own label 70% red 25% white 5% dessert • Other export brand: Gugu • PO Box 457 Bloubergstrand 7436 • info@belbonhills.com • www.belbonhills.com • **T +27 (0)21-557-7143** • F +27 (0)21-557-1351

'The export market is tough,' says owner and assistant winemaker Pedro Estrada Belli, and the Cape Town-based Italian importer/exporter should know. But his des-sert wines have good support in niche EU markets: 'Quality always prevails, and innovation sometimes isn't about trying to create the next storm but finding the way forward from your heritage.'

Belbon Hills range

Cabernet Sauvignon ★★☆ Easy-drinking **08** had red cherry & mulberry appeal previously. Still selling, as fol-lowing. **Shiraz** ★★★ Spicy nuances, juicy finish to last-tasted **08**. **Red** Await new release, as for **White**, **Che-nin Blanc** & **Sauvignon Blanc**.

South African Soul range

Gewürztraminer New bottling of this & **Passito** not available at press time. — DB

Belfield Wines

Location/WO: Elgin • Map: Elgin, Walker Bay & Bot River • Est 2000 • 1stB 2005 • Tasting, sales & tours by appt • Closed Dec 25 • Owner(s) Mike & Mel Kreft • Cellarmaster(s)/winemaker(s) Mike Kreft • Viticulturist(s) Paul Wallace (2002, consultant) • 5.5ha/2.5ha (cab, merlot, shiraz) • 20t/1,000cs own label 100% red • PO Box 191 Elgin 7180 • mike@belfield.co.za • www.belfield.co.za • S 34° 10' 20.9" E 019° 1' 45.8" • **T +27 (0)21-848-9840** • F +27 (0)86-613-3108

These Elgin red wine specialists are delighted they're no longer 'squatters' – they now have their own cellar. With just 2.5ha under vine, 20 tons of grapes and 1,000 cases in bottle, it's a true blue boutique. Co-owner Mike Kreft believes wine rests at the confluence of science and the natural world, with 'a bit of artistry thrown in!'

Belfield range

★★★★☆ **Magnifica** All-cab, bears Queen Protea moniker. **08** (★★★★) was redolent of tangy blackberry when last reviewed; fresh, very measured. Like **07**, a tad less intense than previous.

★★★★ **Aristata** 'Blend' last edition. Coolly composed Bordeaux-style red now named for an indigenous aloe. Well-defined merlot drove the **07**, with cab, when last tasted.

Merlot ★★★★ **08** quiet previously, with promise of voluptuous, velvety fruit given enough time. — DS

■ **Bellemore** *see* Bellevue Estate Stellenbosch

Bellevue Estate Stellenbosch

Location/map/WO: Stellenbosch ▪ Est 1701 ▪ 1stB 1999 ▪ Tasting & sales Mon-Fri 10–4 Sat 10–3 ▪ Fee R10, waived on purchase ▪ Closed Good Fri, Dec 25 & Jan 1 ▪ Owner(s) Dirkie Morkel ▪ Winemaker(s) Wilhelm Kritzinger (Feb 2002), Anneke Potgieter (Feb 2003) ▪ Viticulturist(s) Dirkie Morkel (Jan 1979) ▪ 291ha/151ha (cabs s/f, cinsaut, malbec, merlot, p verdot, ptage, pinot, shiraz, chenin, sauv) ▪ ±750t/±10,000cs own label 97% red 3% white; ±20,000cs for clients; balance in bulk wine & grapes ▪ Export brands: Bellemore, Bellemore Family Selection, Houdamond, Morkel, Tumara ▪ Labels for clients: Cap du Vin, Marks & Spencer, Provoyeur, Pure African, Sizanani, Woolworths ▪ WIETA, IPW, BWI ▪ PO Box 33 Koelenhof 7605 ▪ info@bellevue.co.za ▪ www.bellevue.co.za ▪ S 33° 52' 48.48" E 018° 45' 50.40" ▪ **T +27 (0)21-865-2055** ▪ F +27 (0)21-865-2899

In the Morkel family since 1860, last year the enlightened step was taken to transfer ownership of the easy-drinking Sizanani brand (see separate entry) to a trust with shareholders comprised entirely of current and former farmworkers. Bellevue produces around half a million litres of wine a year but only some 10,000 cases appear under the own label. When it comes to the top range, winemakers Wilhelm Kritzinger and Anneke Potgieter strive to make site-specific wines. Exciting to learn then that a Pinotage from a block planted in 1953, apparently the world's oldest, is in the pipeline.

PK Morkel range

★★★★ **Petit Verdot** NEW Very sexy **09** preview, aromas of dark fruit, attractive herbal note. Big & bold, good fruit expression, oak-derived chocolate (2 years in barrel, 100% new), fresh acidity & smooth tannins.

★★★★ **Pinotage** Red cherry & some vanilla, **08** pre-bottling balanced, good concentration, bright acidity & fine mouthcoating tannins. 34 months oak, 100% new, creates sound platform for ageing.

Tumara NEW ★★★ **05** Bordeaux blend cab & petit verdot-led, with dark fruit, chocolate & mint, & touch tart acidity. Oak as for Pinotage.

Morkel range

★★★★ **Pinotage** Previewed **09** (★★★) is earthy, oak dominated, lacks vinosity of **08**.

Malbec ★★★ Tasted pre-bottling, discordant green note, tart acidity on medium-bodied **09**. **Shiraz** NEW 🔲 📖 ★★ Red fruit, vague herbal note, vanilla on medium-bodied, easy **10**, sampled from tank. **Atticus Cape Blend** ★★★ Likeable pinotage-driven **09** is plump & fruit-driven, with soft tannins. **Sauvignon Blanc** ✓ 🔲 📖 ★★★★ Subtle herbal note on **11** before a palate of purity & focus. Lime flavour, great line of acidity, pithy finish. More winning than austere **09**. No **10**. — CE

Bellingham

Location: Wellington ▪ WO: Coastal/Western Cape/Paarl ▪ Est 1693 ▪ 1stB 1947 ▪ Closed to public ▪ Owner(s) DGB ▪ Winemaker(s) Niël Groenewald, with Mario Damon (Jul 2004, Jan 2002) ▪ Viticulturist(s) Stephan Joubert (2006) ▪ 4,000t/280,000cs own label 50% red 49% white 1% rosé ▪ ISO 9001:2000, HACCP, IPW, WIETA ▪ Private Bag X03 Groot Drakenstein 7680 ▪ bellingham@dgb.co.za ▪ www.bellinghamwines.com ▪ **T +27 (0)21-870-4200** ▪ F +27 (0)21-874-1531

The DGB-owned Bellingham brand is renowned for its accessible wines locally, and one of the larger South African brands in the international market. Focusing on vineyard selection and understanding the characteristics and flavour profiles of the various varieties, especially during ripening, has resulted in wines with better balance at an earlier stage. A new mocha-toned merlot, the product of creative fermentation techniques, is also sure to be popular. Bellingham should soon achieve another of its goals: official carbon-neutral status. Large tracts of bamboo, planted in Natal and planned for the Eastern Cape, help offset the brand's carbon footprint and also provide the local communities with both a source of income and building material. See separate listing for The Bernard Series.

The Legends Collection

★★★★ **Fair Maiden** Delicious & unusual **08** oaked blend roussanne, chenin, verdelho, grenache blanc & viognier still selling, not retasted, as all these.

St Georges ★★★☆ No newer vintage since fruity pinotage-led **06** blend, with shiraz, cab & merlot. **Dragon's Lair** ★★★☆ Smooth & satisfying **06** shiraz-based blend still available.

Fusion range

Cabernet Sauvignon with a splash of Cabernet Franc ✓ ★★★☆ Good vintage shows in deliciously juicy **09**, with supple, serious structure. Enjoy now & next few years. All in range WO Coastal, except Shiraz. **Pinotage with a dash of Petit Verdot** ★★ Ripe & rustic **09** needs time or a meal for harmony. **Shiraz with a splash of Viognier** ✓ ★★★☆ Now bottled, **08** adds mocha tone to aromatic & spicy flavours. Structure & drinkability intact, plus few years. WO Paarl. **Merlot with a dash of Malbec** ★★★ **09** preview quietly confident structure, dark fruit & touch minerality. Succulent & balanced, solo or with food. **Chardonnay with a splash of Viognier** ★★★★ **09** still selling. Rich waxy tone was spiced with aromatic tangy flavours when last previewed. **Sauvignon Blanc with a dash of Semillon** ✓ 🍽 ★★★☆ Bottled **10** confirms preview's vivacious styling. Crisp & grassy, green fig & semillon's waxy tone.

The Blends range

Rosé Sec 😊 🍽 ★★★ **11** a tangy, light cranberry quaffer, refreshingly dry. **Chardonnay-Semillon** NEW 😊 🍽 🍷 ★★★ Juicy & quaffable **10**, plump pear & melon flavours freshened by zesty acidity.

Cabernet Sauvignon-Merlot ★★★ Now bottled, **09** cool leafy elegance & structure to bright fruit. Balanced tablemate. WO W Cape, as all unless noted. **Shiraz-Cabernet Sauvignon** 🍽 ★★★ **09** less taut after bottling. A more amenable & savoury braai mate. **Shiraz-Pinotage** NEW 🍽 🍷 ★★ **10** light & savoury with mocha tone. Wispy dry texture – vinous espresso! WO Coastal. **Pinotage Rosé** 🍽 🍷 ★★ Delicate, light & bright red fruit, same dry style in **11** as last. **Rosé** 🍽 🍷 ★★ **10** tangy & light semi-sweet, still available. **Sauvignon Blanc-Chardonnay** 🍽 🍷 ★★★ **10** gently crisp & tropical blend, still selling. **Chenin Blanc-Viognier** 🍽 🍷 ★★★ Plumper & peachy **10** a tad less vibrant since bottled. Still good spicy/fusion food partner. **Premier Grand Cru** NEW ★★★ Lightish NV has tangy melange of fruit with fresh & pithy grip for food.

Insignia Series NEW

Mocha Java Merlot 🍽 🍷 ★★★ Aptly named **10** has distinct roasted coffee bean tone. Merlot, dash malbec, one of more appealing additions to popular, accessible & smooth 'café culture' category. WO Coastal. — MW

Bellpost

Location: Vredendal ▪ Map/WO: Olifants River ▪ Est/1stB 2005 ▪ Tasting, sales & cellar tours by appt ▪ Owner(s) Lollies Thiart ▪ Winemaker(s) Koos Thiart (Jan 2005) ▪ Viticulturist(s) Nico Thiart (Jan 2005) ▪ 5ha/2ha (merlot, ruby cab, shiraz, chard, nouvelle, viog) ▪ 12t/900cs own label 80% red 20% white ▪ PO Box 39 Vredendal 8160 ▪ bellpost@starmail.co.za ▪ www.bellpost.co.za ▪ S 31° 36' 24.1" E 018° 25' 0.6" ▪ **T +27 (0)27-213-2562** ▪ F +27 (0)27-213-2562

The brothers Thiart share duties on their small West Coast farm, Koos making the wine and Nico looking after the vines. 'It's a dream doing what I do,' says Koos, adding that vinifying is the easy part: it's finding a market that's hard work. However, a new agent in the Western Cape and their Gauteng representative extending feelers into KwaZulu-Natal are making a difference.

Merlot ★★★ Touch more savoury in **08**, salty sour-fig character a food style compared with previous' solo-quaffable ripe fruit. **Ruby Cabernet** ★★★ Step-up **08** is expressive & packed with mulberry flavour, engaging despite slight bitter edge. **Shiraz** ★★★★ **08** back on track with typical leather, bacon & smoke; black plum & liquorice complexity, house's signature big alc (15%) well contained. Seek out. **Chardonnay** ★★ Ripe & leesy **10** has earthy lemon sherbet notes, lacks precision, freshness of previous. **C'est la Vie** ★★ Apricotty viognier smallest (22%) but dominant partner in aromatic **10** white blend. Waxy, broad, yet tad disjointed. — Panel

■ **Bell Tower** see Asara Wine Estate & Hotel

Benguela Cove

Location: Bot River ▪ Map: Elgin, Walker Bay & Bot River ▪ WO: Walker Bay ▪ Est 2004 ▪ 1stB 2007 ▪ Tasting Mid Sep-Apr: Mon-Fri 9-5 Sat/Sun 11-3; May-mid Sep: Mon-Sun by appt T +27 (0)83-645-6198 with 24 hours notice ▪ Fee R20pp, waived on purchase ▪ Sales Mon-Fri 9-5 Sat/Sun (mid Sep-Apr) 11-3 ▪ Closed Easter Fri/Sun,

Dec 25/26 & Jan 1 ▪ BYO picnic ▪ Owner(s) Benguela Cove Investments (Pty) Limited (Flora Drummond) ▪ Winemaker(s) Johan Joubert (2006, Kleine Zalze), Cathy Marshall (2009, Cathy Marshall Wines), Niels Verburg (2009, Luddite) & Thys Louw (2009, Diemersdal), with Zara Conradie (Kleine Zalze) & Mari van der Merwe (Diemersdal) ▪ Viticulturist(s) Paul Wallace & Schalk du Toit (both 2011, consultants) ▪ 206ha/66ha (cabs s/f, malbec, merlot, p verdot, pinot, shiraz, chard, sauv, sem, viog) ▪ 592t/2,200cs own label 60% red 30% white 10% rosé ▪ PO Box 112 Onrusriver 7201 ▪ info@benguelacove.co.za ▪ www.benguelacove.co.za ▪ S 34° 20'45.0" E 019° 8'15.7" ▪ **T** +27 (0)83-645-6198 ▪ F +27 (0)21-671-5229

Beyond Bot River as you drive to Hermanus you pass a picturesque lagoon just inland from the sea, around which is an upmarket residential estate. This is the setting for Benguela Cove's vineyards, which explains the wine styles produced here. Sea proximity and open slopes give the grapes cool growing conditions, which reflect as long, slow ripening and good fruit development. In order to use the skills of experts in their fields, wines are made by a number of specialist winemakers, either completely or in part and then blended for added complexity.

★★★★ **Sauvignon Blanc** ✓ 🍷 From tank, **11** promises well, passionfruit with an intriguing lemongrass nuance, racy acidity that fits the profile. Will age well.

Cabernet Sauvignon Await next, as for **Rosé** & **Chardonnay-Semillon**. **Cabernet Franc** NEW Unrated preview **10** variety-true leafy note in the berries, but grape tannins still chunky, planned oaking could soften. **Shiraz** ✓ ★★★★ Rich & ripe, mocha choc & vanilla-toned **10** ex barrel is warm hearted, generous; supple tannins allow early enjoyment. — CR

▪ **Ben Hur** *see* Blomendahl Vineyards
▪ **Berg en Dal** *see* Wine-of-the-Month Club

Bergheim

Location: Paarl ▪ Map: Paarl & Wellington ▪ WO: Western Cape/Paarl ▪ Est/1stB 2000 ▪ Tasting by appt ▪ Owner(s) Edwin Jordaan ▪ Cellarmaster(s)/winemaker(s) Edwin Jordaan (Jan 2000) ▪ 4-6t/500cs own label 66% red 34% white ▪ PO Box 6020 Paarl 7622 ▪ drjordaan@gmail.com ▪ S 33° 45'20.2" E 018° 57'42.5" ▪ **T** +27 (0)82-923-3115, +27 (0)21-863-1529 ▪ F +27 (0)21-862-7852

Sharing cellar facilities in Paarl's Main Road with three other winemakers, each doing his own thing, winemaking for Edwin Jordaan is a solitary pursuit. He believes wines reflect their creator's personality and his is 'reserved' but two additions this year reveal a more thoughtful, social side. Ben and Celia are sold as a pair for when couples have different tastes.

Bergheim range

★★★★ **Mignon** NEW ✓ 'Darling' in French, how winemaker regards semillon, 80% of **10** (rest sauvignon, all barrel fermented). Sparks with vitality; complex, interwoven oatmeal, minerality, lemongrass.

Pinotage ★★★ Only 2 barrels made, **08** full-ripe plums, older-oak-spiced. Paarl vines, as for Shiraz. **Shiraz** ✓ ★★★★ **08** perfect now, tannins fully integrated, exuberant fruit & spice. Lovely. Discontinued: **Semillon**.

Couple's Wine range NEW

Dry Red Ben ✓ ★★★★ Same wine as **08** Shiraz. Tall 500ml bottle to partner Celia when couples want different wines. **Dry White Celia** ★★★ Appley, leafy & bone-dry **10**, friendly 12% alc. 500ml. — CR

▪ **Berghuis** *see* Groupe LFE South Africa
▪ **Bergkelder** *see* Die Bergkelder Wine Centre

Bergsig Estate

Location: Worcester ▪ Map/WO: Breedekloof ▪ Est 1843 ▪ 1stB 1977 ▪ Tasting & sales Mon-Fri 8–5 Sat & pub hols 9–5 ▪ Fee R20 for groups of 10+ ▪ Closed Easter Fri, Dec 25 & Jan 1 ▪ Cellar tours by appt ▪ Bergsig Bistro ▪ Facilities for children ▪ Farm produce ▪ Conferences ▪ Self-guided birdwatching route ▪ Conservation area, visits by appt ▪ Lategan history & historical artifacts on display ▪ Festivals: Cloudy Nouveau (Apr); Soetes & Soup (Jul); Outdoor (Oct) ▪ Owner(s) Lategan family ▪ Cellarmaster(s) De Wet Lategan (Jan 1989) ▪ Winemaker(s) Chris du Toit (Jul 2003) ▪ Viticulturist(s) Louis & Plum Lategan (1991) ▪ ±400ha/253ha (cab, ptage, shiraz, touriga nacional, chard, chenin, sauv) ▪ 3,200t/50,000cs own label 35% red 60% white 4% rosé 1% other + 70,000cs for clients ▪ Other export brand: White River ▪ Brands for clients: Woolworths ▪ BWI, BRC, Fairtrade, IPW ▪ PO Box 15 Breërivier 6858

■ wine@bergsig.co.za ■ www.bergsig.co.za ■ S 33° 31'9.4" E 019° 11'38.7" ■ **T +27 (0)23-355-1603** ■ F +27 (0)23-355-1658

At this 6th generation family estate, wine matters because, 'while water slakes your thirst and cleans your body, wine enhances your feeling of well-being'. But personal well-being is certainly not the only driver here; the Lategans strive to ensure the welfare of their employees (through the Fynbos Vrugte & Wyn Boerdery empowerment company) and the planet. Here, Bergsig's most recent accomplishment is becoming the first winery to receive Woolworths' Farming for the Future sustainability accreditation.

Bergsig Estate range

★★★★ **Cabernet Sauvignon Reserve NEW** ✓ Commendable combo intense creamy fruit & judicious oak (30 months, all new). **08** restrained & satisfyingly dry, exceptionally persistent: a nod to the classics.

★★★★ **Icarus** Seductive **08** from cab & touriga (85:15) nudges next level with sweet cassis & exotic spice profile. Unashamedly modern & lush, lifted by vibrant acidity, smart oaking.

★★★★ **Chardonnay** 🔲 **10** (★★★★) in footsteps of bold **09**: similar ebullient lemon/butter notes & lime acidity to cut rich fruit-laden palate, but oak more noticeable.

★★★★ **Cape Vintage** Succulent, smooth & spicy **04** from tinta similar to last-tasted **00**. Generously flavoured but not sweet, sufficient fire to warm a winter night.

★★★★ **Cape LBV** ✓ **01** from tinta entices with molasses & nut bouquet, charms with well-knit tannins & alc, seduces with bitter choc-orange farewell. At 88g/l sugar, drier than most. Drinking well.

Gewürztraminer ☺ 🔲 ★★★ **11**'s litchi & rosepetal fragrance, soft sweetness & light grip tick all the right drinkability boxes. **Sauvignon Blanc** ☺ 🔲 ★★★ Interesting peppery nasturtium nuance, hint mint & persistent firm acidity raise the bar in **11**.

Cabernet Sauvignon ✓ ★★★★ Appealing **09** dark fruited & youthful, 14.5% alc well disguised but charry tannins need year/2 to assimilate. **Pinotage** ★★★ Quintessential strawberry & banana character, slight bitter touch on **09**, uncomplex, for early enjoyment. **Bulldozer Pinotage** ★★★ Exuberant **10** unfettered by oak, enlivened by zesty acidity. Previewed last edition & not revisited, as Ruby Cab-Merlot, Chenin, White River Chenin, Bouquet Light & Brut. **Ruby Cabernet-Merlot** ★★★ Easy-sipping **08**, red cherries & plums, firm yet amenable tannins. **Shiraz Rosé** 🔲 ★★ Understated **11**, whisper of red berries, gentle just-dry leafy farewell. **Chenin Blanc** 🔲 ★★★ Crunchy apple fruit, crisp acidity, **10** uncomplicated sipping. **White River Chenin Blanc** ★★★ **10** engaging marriage crackling acidity & pithy goodbye. **Bouquet Light** 🔲 ★★ Sweet, tingly perlé **NV** from muscat. **Sauvignon Blanc Brut** ★★ Last was **06**. **Special Late Harvest** ★★★ Previously reviewed was **07** from botrytised chenin. **Cape Ruby** ★★★★ Unoaked **NV** from tinta packed with berries, Xmas cake fruits & nuts. Delicious, approachable as this style should be.

Lategan Family Reserve range

Barrel Aged Chardonnay Await next. Discontinued: MCC Chardonnay Brut. — CvZ

Bergwater Vineyards

Location: Prince Albert ■ Map: Klein Karoo & Garden Route ■ WO: Prince Albert Valley/Western Cape ■ Est 1999 ■ 1stB 2003 ■ Tasting & sales Mon-Thu 9-4.30 Fri 9-4 Sat 10-3 ■ Fee R15 for groups, free for individuals ■ Cellar tours by appt ■ Meals by prior arrangement ■ BYO picnic ■ Gifts ■ Olives & olive oil ■ Wedding/conference/function venue (up to 250 pax) ■ 2 x self-catering guesthouses ■ Gravel airstrip for light aircraft (phone ahead) ■ Hiking/mountain biking & 4x4 trail by arrangement ■ Owner(s) Heimie & Stephan Schoeman ■ Cellarmaster(s)/winemaker(s) Mariska Vorster (Jan 2003) ■ Viticulturist(s) Adan Liepner (Jan 2005) ■ 1,500ha/72ha (cab, merlot, shiraz, chard, sauv) ■ 126t/±1,000cs own label 80% red 15% white 5% rosé + 70,000L bulk ■ PO Box 40 Prince Albert 6930 ■ wine@bergwater.com ■ www.bergwater.com ■ S 33° 16'46.3" E 022° 13'55.7" ■ **T +27 (0)23-541-1703** ■ F +27 (0)23-541-1081 / +27 (0)86-541-7335

New from this mainly red-wine cellar in Prince Albert Valley is a fortified muscat d'Alexandrie, described by winemaker Mariska Vorster as 'particularly satisfying'. Last harvest brought a double whammy of drought *and* hail, but the cellardoor remains wide open for visitors and if you prefer to fly in, just phone ahead for the co-ordinates of the gravel airstrip.

Reserve range

Cabernet Sauvignon 🍷 ★★ Last edition, blackcurrant-infused **09** needed time for oak tannins to mellow. **Merlot** 🍷 Previewed **09** fresh & fruit-filled, but too unformed to rate mid-2011. **Shiraz** 🍷 ★★★ Pre-bottling, **09** is supple, red-fruited & crisp but needs bit more time to open up & show best. **Royal Reserve** Untasted. **Sauvignon Blanc** ✓ 🍷 ★★★★ Appealing **11** preview is the star of the line-up. Karoo scrub, lime & grapefruit flavours, zesty acidity & long aftertaste.

Bergwater Vineyards range

Merlot 🍷 Blackcurrant & vanilla **08**, chunky, brisk & dry. Still selling & not revisited. **Shiraz** 🍷 In abeyance, like **Organic Shiraz**, **Chardonnay** & **Rendezvous White**. **Rendezvous Red** 🍷 ★★ Plummy **08** merlot & shiraz mix, harmonious & earthy last edition. **Muscat D'Alexandrie** NEW ★★★ Spicy highlight to grapey **10** fortified dessert, lovely length & light textured. Wo W Cape. Discontinued: **Sauvignon Blanc**.

Pienk Pikkewyn range NEW

Pienk Pikkewyn 🍷 ★ Previously named 'Rosé', the 'Pink Penguin' is gently sweet **10** party in a box. **Sparkling Brut Rosé** ★★ Ebullient **10** bubbly with faint red-berry notes & lowish alc (12%) for anytime fun. — Panel

Bernheim Wines

Location: Paarl ▪ Map: Paarl & Wellington ▪ WO: Voor Paardeberg/Paarl ▪ Est/1stB 2004 ▪ Tasting, sales & tours by appt ▪ Closed all pub hols ▪ Conservation area ▪ Owner(s) Pacas Winery (Pty) Ltd (Pieter Taljaard, Hermann Helmbold, Jacques Kruger) ▪ Cellarmaster(s)/winemaker(s) Jacques Kruger ▪ Viticulturist(s) Morné van Greunen (Feb 2009) ▪ 133ha/50ha (cabs s/f, merlot, ptage, p verdot, shiraz) ▪ 6,000cs own label 95% red 5% rosé à% port ▪ BWI, IPW ▪ PO Box 7274 Noorder-Paarl 7623 ▪ bernheim@iafrica.com ▪ www.bernheimwines. com ▪ S 33° 35' 22.5" E 018° 52' 45.0" (VP), S 33° 40' 54.73" E 018° 58' 20.92" (P) ▪ T +27 (0)21-869-8384 ▪ F +27 (0)21-869-8365

Joining the growing worldwide green awareness campaign, Bernheim signed up for the Biodiversity & Wine Initiative, having set aside 10 of their total 130 hectares for conservation. Changes in the past 12 months include two new wines and the Casual Collection, which features specially designed fun and funky labels.

JH Pacas & Co range

Cabernet Sauvignon ★★★★ Charry oak on **04** matched by ripe blackcurrant, refreshing cab acidity. Not retasted, like next. **Shiraz** ★★★★ **05** long & firm flavours, lavender & red berry hints, 14.5% alc hardly noticeable.

Vintners Selection

Cabernet Sauvignon ★★★ Violet & lavender previously noted on **03**. Ripe blackcurrant, olive & dry oak tannin.

Bernheim range

Merlot-Cabernet Sauvignon ★★★ **06** noted last edition as light & uncomplicated, with herbal edge to mulberry fruit. **Classique** NEW 🍷 ★★★★ Fruitcake & nutmeg appeal, **08** firm frame from cab, merlot & cab franc but with gentle texture on ripe finish. **Dry Red** Await next. **Shiraz-Cabernet Sauvignon** 🍷 ★★★ Cheery cranberry & salami combo on still-selling **08**. Shiraz edges cab in the blend, adding pepper spice. **Pinotage Rosé** 🍷 ★★★ Off-dry **10** offers raspberry & candyfloss with light succulence. **Cape Vintage** ★★★ Listed as 'Port' previously. 5 barrels of cab & shiraz, **08** fiery cherry plum & spice.

Casual Collection

> **Red Select** NEW ☺ 🍷 ★★★ NV merlot, pinotage & cab blend mirrors its fun label. Light red fruit, cinnamon & a touch of dry tannin on medium end.

Pinotage ★★★ Moves here from Bernheim range. **10** a step up, offers smoky plum & spice appeal. — FM

BerRaz   NEW

Named for its berry-like shiraz character, this KWV brand is aimed at young, trendy consumers just starting to enjoy wine - and those who prefer it sweet.

BerRaz 🍷 ★★ NV Berry-sweet red from shiraz, grape juice. Ex-tank juicily gluggable; best chilled. — AL

■ **Berrio** see The Berrio Wines

■ **Berryfields** *see Ashton Wynkelder*

Beyerskloof

Location/map: Stellenbosch ▪ WO: Stellenbosch/Western Cape/Coastal ▪ Est 1988 ▪ 1stB 1989 ▪ Tasting & sales Mon-Fri 8.30–4.30 Sat 10–4.30 ▪ Closed Easter Fri-Mon, Dec 25/26 & Jan 1 ▪ Cellar tours by appt ▪ Red Leaf Restaurant (T +27 (0)21-865-2685) Tue–Fri 9–3.30 Sat 10–3 ▪ Farm produce ▪ Conference facilities (30 pax) ▪ Owner(s) Beyers Truter & Simon Halliday ▪ Cellarmaster(s) Beyers Truter (Jan 1988) ▪ Winemaker(s) Anri Truter (Jan 2004) & Travis Langley (Jan 2009), with Buddy Hendricks (Jan 2010) ▪ Viticulturist(s) Johan Pienaar (2000, consultant) ▪ 130ha/94ha (cab, merlot, ptage) ▪ 750t/120,000cs own label 96% red 2% white 2% rosé + 5,000cs for clients ▪ Brands for clients: Pick's Pick, Tesco ▪ WIETA ▪ PO Box 107 Koelenhof 7605 ▪ wine@beyerskloof.co.za ▪ www.beyerskloof.co.za ▪ S 33°53'28.0" E 018° 49'23.6" ▪ **T +27 (0)21-865-2135** ▪ F +27 (0)21-865-2683

This high-flying Stellenbosch producer is not planning any major changes in the near future, but with their enviable range, reputation and market penetration, that's not surprising. Perennial champions of the pinotage cause, Beyers Truters and his winery set the standard, bear the flag and sing the praises of the indigenous variety. They produce it in an array of styles: Cape Blend, rosé, port, white blend, sparkling and even single varietal. To further the campaign, they've been instrumental in launching the Cape Blend Trophy Challenge, where understandably they're hot contenders. Their ultra-premium labels, Faith and Diesel, are approaching icon status in their fields, and were the first sold-out items at the cellar last year.

★★★★☆ **Pinotage Reserve** ✓ Maestro's serious offering; **08** shows intent, with dark, noble fruit & precise, elegant structure. Just coming into drinking form, promises years of improvement.

★★★★★ **Diesel Pinotage** Flag-bearing masterpiece from Cape's foremost proponent of the variety. After stately **08**, great **09** (★★★★★) vintage shows impossible concentration of dark, layered fruit & chocolate, cloaked in dense tannic structure. Year's 15 best barrels (French, 22 months matured).

★★★★☆ **Field Blend** Stunning cab-led Bordeaux red, from 5ha interplanted cab & merlot vineyard. **07** continues noble lineage: huge, New-World classic delivers rich, layered fruit on endless finish. Expertly crafted to deliver balance & silky texture with weight.

★★★★★ **Synergy Cape Blend** ✓ Double vintage review: **08** shows savoury overtones; **09** (more pinotage-driven) is ripe & rich. Both finely constructed, deftly blended, reflecting potential of pinotage blends in Cape.

★★★★☆ **Faith** Massive, brooding thumper, **08** flagship Cape Blend still shows great elegance & balance. Huge wine in equally huge packaging, crafted to impress in every way. The new definitive expression of the genre. Near equal cab & pinotage, 15% merlot. 10 barrels made.

> **Pinotage Rosé** ☺ 🍴 🎨 ★★★ Light-bodied, flavoursome **11** is dry, crisp & refreshing. Fun alternative to producer's many interpretations of variety.

Pinotage ✓ 🍴 ★★★★ Legendary brand with perennial appeal. Huge volumes of dependable quality & distinctive house style. **10** follows form. **Bowland Cabernet Sauvignon-Merlot** ★★★ **09** previously showed primary grape-berry edginess, hard tannins. **Chenin Blanc-Pinotage** 🍴 🎨 ★★★ More chenin, more balance in quirky **11** blend. Fresh & friendly, undemanding, with honest fruity core. **Pinotage Rosé Brut** ★★★ Bright & cheerful **09** charmat-method bubbly gushed strawberry jam flavour on lively mousse last edition. **Lagare Cape Vintage** ★★★☆ **09** not retasted. Overtly sweet, edgy port-style fortified from touriga & ptage. Discontinued: **Synergy Cape Blend Reserve**. — GdB

Bezalel-Dyasonsklip Wine Cellar

Location: Upington ▪ Map: Northern Cape, Free State & North West ▪ Est 1949 (farm)/1997 (cellar) ▪ 1stB 1998 ▪ Tasting, sales & cellar tours Mon-Fri 9–5 Sat 9–1 ▪ Fee R15pp ▪ Professional tasting by appt ▪ Closed Easter Fri-Sun, May 1, Dec 16/25 & Jan 1 ▪ Green Fig Café - breakfast & light meals ▪ Venue for conferences & weddings up to 250 people ▪ Owner(s) Bezuidenhout family ▪ Cellarmaster(s)/winemaker(s)/viticulturist(s) Inus Bezuidenhout (1989), with Jan-Adriaan Bezuidenhout (2005) ▪ 60ha/44ha (cab, cornifesto, merlot, pinot, ptage, sangio, shiraz, touriga, chard, cbard, gewürz, merbein, sultana) ▪ ±500cs own label 100% red ▪ Eurogap certified ▪ PO Dyasonsklip 8805 ▪ info@bezalel.co.za ▪ www.bezalel.co.za ▪ S 28° 36'28.69" E 021° 6'19.01" ▪ **T +27 (0)54-491-1325, +27 (0)83-310-4763** ▪ F +27 (0)54-491-1141

Awarded a PMR Golden Arrow Award last year for stimulating the economic growth and development of the Northern Cape, this hospitable Orange River family farm – where father-and-son team Inus and Jan-Adriaan Bezuidenhout produce an array of boutique wines, as well as 'rather adventurous' brandies and liqueurs – also cares for the environment by practising sustainable viticulture.

■ **Big Five** *see African Terroir*
■ **BIG Flower** *see Botanica Wines*
■ **Big Six** *see Old Bridge Wines*

Bilton Wines

Location/map/WO: Stellenbosch ▪ Est 1964 ▪ 1stB 1998 ▪ Tasting & sales Mon-Fri 9–5 Sat/Sun 10–4 ▪ Fee R35/6 wines, R50 dark Belgian chocolate & wine pairing (4 wines) ▪ Closed Easter Fri, Dec 25/26 & Jan 1 ▪ Cellar tours Mon-Fri by appt ▪ Vintage D'Vine restaurant Tue-Fri 9–4 Sat/Sun 9–3; also picnics by appt ▪ Jungle gym & play area for children ▪ Vineyard walk ▪ Mountain bike route - booking required ▪ Owner(s) Mark Bilton ▪ Winemaker(s) Rudolf de Wet (Nov 2005) & Elizma van der Mescht (Jan 2010), with Giorgio Dalla Cia (consultant) ▪ Viticulturist(s) Ruan du Plessis (Dec 2004) ▪ 377ha/69ha (cabs s/f, merlot, mourv, p verdot, ptage, pinot, shiraz, chenin, sauv, sem, viog) ▪ 390t/7,500cs own label 80% red 20% white ▪ BWI, IPW ▪ PO Box 60 Lynedoch 7603 ▪ info@biltonwines.com, sales@biltonwines.com ▪ www.biltonwines.com ▪ S 33° 59' 52.9" E 018° 50' 58.3" ▪ **T +27 (0)21-881-3714** ▪ F +27 (0)21-881-3801

The launch of their controversial, extreme-priced The Bilton flagship red has garnered most of the publicity, but other things are happening at Mark Bilton's Helderberg estate too. Aggressive export marketing has seen recognition and awards across much of Europe and the US, while on the local scene, the focus is on terroir, classic styling and exclusive quality. Recently Biodiversity & Wine Initiative-certified, the estate is concentrating on reinstating indigenous vegetation in its conservation areas after the wildfire horrors of last year.

Private Collection

★★★★ **The Bilton** 100% cab, **06** matured 3 years in '500% new oak' produced porty, inky, tannic leviathan, hopefully to emerge with grace.

★★★★☆ **Sir Percy 07** Bordeaux-style red blend last year presented a beautiful expression of classic form. Big bodied & intense. Not retasted, like next 5 wines.

★★★★ **Viognier** Pricey **08** white flagship was impossibly spicy & intense last edition, with ripe peach fruit.

Cellar Selection

★★★★ **Cabernet Sauvignon 07** (★★★★☆) stepped up to the big league after ripe & satisfying **06**, with inky iodine notes tempering thumping black fruit. Big & tough yet beguiling.

★★★★ **Merlot** Rustic farmyard whiff on **07** (★★★★), with robust tannins & ripe fruit centre noted last time. **06** was fuller & more succulent.

★★★★ **Shiraz 07** had farmyard hint, but delivered intense cherry fruit with wild herbaceous scents.

Pinotage ★★★★ Youthful & fruity **08** on review was appealingly fragrant & spicy. **Matt Black** 🗐 ★★★★ 6-way merlot-led blend, **08** is long on ripe fruity appeal. 2nd tier, but seriously handled, showing balance & finesse. **Sauvignon Blanc** ✓ 🗐 🏵 ★★★★ Change in style & pitch, **11** is fresh, crisp & accessible. Pleasant, light-hearted, for early drinking. — GdB

■ **Birdfield** *see Klawer Wine Cellars*

Birkenhead Estate & Brewery

Location: Stanford ▪ Map: Elgin, Walker Bay & Bot River ▪ WO: Walker Bay ▪ Est 1997 ▪ 1stB 2007 ▪ Tasting, sales & tours Mon-Sat 10–5 Sun 11–4 ▪ Fee R20 wine/beer ▪ Closed Easter Fri & Dec 25/26 ▪ Micro brewery ▪ Restaurant ▪ BYO picnic ▪ Facilities for children ▪ Tour groups ▪ Owner(s) Birkenhead Holdings Ltd (Isle of Man) ▪ Cellarmaster(s) Josef Dreyer (Apr 2007, consultant) ▪ Winemaker(s)/viticulturist(s) Niell Ferreira (Jul 2009) ▪ 300ha/22ha (cab, merlot, p verdot, pinot, shiraz, chard, sauv, sem) ▪ 72t/6,000cs own label 40% red 60% white ▪ PO Box 530 Stanford 7210 ▪ info@birkenhead.co.za ▪ www.birkenhead.co.za ▪ S 34°26'30.5" E 019°27'40.5" ▪ **T +27 (0)28-341-0183** ▪ F +27 (0)28-341-0196

Niell Ferreira's appointment as viticulturist-winemaker at Birkenhead is clearly paying dividends, with quality racheting up thanks to his care in the vineyards. With their own cellar due to come online in 2012 and more plantings afoot, this Stanford wine and micro-brewing outfit is upbeat about the future.

Walker Bay Vineyards range

Sauvignon Blanc ☺ 🍷 ★★★ Satisfyingly full **10** delightfully harmonious, freshly herbaceous with light tropicality ensuring friendliness.

Cabernet Sauvignon NEW ★★★★ Brightly spicy red-fruited **10** deliciously accessible. Integrated tannins gently restrain appetisingly ripe flavours. **Amesteca** Await next. **Rosé** ★★ **10** sample fruity & dry last year. **Chardonnay** 🍷 ★★★ Oak-scented **10** pleasantly fruity with brisk finish. **Chardonnay** NEW 🍷 ★★★ Unwooded version. Sample **11**'s tropical flavours cheerful & unpretentious. — IM

■ **Bistro** *see* Zandvliet Wine Estate & Thoroughbred Stud

Bizoe Wines

Location: Somerset West ▪ WO: Western Cape ▪ Est/1stB 2008 ▪ Tasting & sales by appt or during tailor-made tours - booking essential ▪ Fee R1,500 pp incl transport & lunch ▪ Owner(s)/cellarmaster(s)/winemaker(s) Rikus Neethling ▪ Viticulturist(s) Org Viljoen ▪ 1,000cs ▪ Unit 189 Croydon Vineyard Estate Somerset West 7130 ▪ info@bizoe.co.za ▪ www.bizoe.co.za ▪ T +27 (0)21-843-3307 ▪ F +27 (0)86-653-8186

Benoni-born boutique winemaker and tour guide Rikus Neethling likes to show off the natural beauty of his adopted home to Americans and Europeans visiting the Cape. And if they ship a few bottles of his internationally acclaimed wines back to their homes, he reckons they're his best salespeople.

★★★★ **Estalet Shiraz 09** without cab & malbec dabs of previous. US oak dropped too - now only French. But still Breedekloof grapes. Blackcurrant & lily, an attractive 'wild' note, loads of gentle fruit give juicy appeal.

★★★★☆ **Henriëtta** Accomplished, deftly oaked semillon/sauvignon blend (70/30). **10** bone-dry, yet plush & rich, its weight & breadth belying the lowish (for SA) ±13% alc. Franschhoek, Elgin grapes. — CvZ

Blaauwklippen Agricultural Estate

Location/map: Stellenbosch ▪ WO: Stellenbosch/Western Cape ▪ Est 1682 ▪ 1stB 1974 ▪ Tasting & sales Mon-Fri 9-5 Sat 10-5 Sun & pub hols 10-4 (all subject to change on market days) ▪ Fee R25/informal, R35/formal, R50/tour & formal tasting ▪ Closed Dec 25 & Jan 1 ▪ Cellar tours by appt (48-hr advance notice) ▪ Barouche Restaurant open daily for breakfast & lunch (see Restaurants section); Cape Kitchen open Wed-Fri evenings 6-9 (mid Oct–mid Apr); mini cheese boards in wine centre ▪ Facilities for children ▪ Pony & carriage rides ▪ Gift shop ▪ Conferences ▪ Weddings/functions ▪ Walks/hikes & mountain biking by appt ▪ Permanent carriage museum ▪ Regular market days ▪ Owner(s) Blue Lion GmbH ▪ Cellarmaster(s) Rolf Zeitvogel (Sep 2003, consultant) ▪ Winemaker(s) Rolf Zeitvogel (Sep 2003, consultant), with Albert Basson (Jul 2007, consultant) ▪ Viticulturist(s) Christo Hamman (Jan 2009) ▪ 180ha/103ha ▪ cabs s/f, malbec, merlot, p verdot, shiraz, zin, viog ▪ 550t/35,000cs own label 89% red 3% white 6% rosé 2% other & 11,000cs for clients ▪ Brands for clients: Blue Rock (Germany), Eagle Canyon (China) ▪ IPW ▪ PO Box 54 Stellenbosch 7599 ▪ marketing@blaauwklippen.com ▪ www.blaauwklippen.com ▪ S 33° 58' 23.3" E 018° 50' 51.0" ▪ T +27 (0)21-880-0133 ▪ F +27 (0)21-880-0136

A big property by any standards, over 100ha of vineyards, which makes the specialisation all the more admirable. At a time when other Cape producers uprooted theirs, Blaauwklippen made zinfandel a key part of the range, from a white (well, pale pink, to be accurate), to two versions of red, to Noble Late Harvest. The trick here is location. The fruity exuberance of the variety is tempered by the terroir, giving balance and a serious aspect to the wines. With 2012 marking the 330th anniversary of this farm, a number of new products have been launched, 'Before & After' below, and Eight and Ten Year-Old Brandies.

Icon range NEW

★★★★ **Shiraz** Differs from its sibling in the fruit concentration, oak treatment, savoury fynbos finish. Attractive **09** is elegantly smooth, with layered dark fruit & dried herbs.

★★★★ **Zinfandel** Although still youthful, with 6+ years potential, **09** shows fruit purity & concentration, proving how good this variety can be with grape selection & careful handling.

Blaauwklippen Vineyard Selection (BVS)

★★★★ **Cabernet Sauvignon** Last year, 07 (★★★★) had layered cassis & cedar but also firm tannins which may since have softened. Followed Old World 05's silky tannins.

★★★★ **Cabriolet** Changing blend, malbec with cab, petit verdot in 07. Last year showed deepened, darkened succulent fruit. Built to age 8+ years, mainly new barrels 17 months but deftly done, approachable.

Shiraz ★★★★ Last 07 had blackberries & fennel, elegant oak & Rhône-style peppery complexity. Improved on jammy 06 (★★★★). **Zinfandel** ★★★☆ Dusty cranberries, intense & insistent, anchored by 08's youthfully firm tannins, ideal for rich stews or further cellaring. **White Zinfandel** 🌟 ★★★ Hint of pink, red berries in distinctive 10's aromas; the touch of sweetness good match for spicy Asian food.

Blaauwklippen Blending Competition

BBC 27 ★★★★ Winner of 27th annual wine club blending competition. PE's Engineers Wine Society's zinfandel/shiraz mix, dab others, 09 shows fruitcake ripeness, retains balance, succulence, making drinking this 1.5L easy.

Blaauwklippen Cultivar Selection

Cabernet Sauvignon ★★★ Last was 07, showed black plums & liquorice, trademark dry tannins. **Malbec** ★★★★ Always intense, & ex-barrel 08 last edition didn't disappoint: dark fruit juiciness, cedar-savoury input from new oak. **Merlot** ★★★ Last 07 showed svelte lines, berries & spice, youthful tannins. **Shiraz** ★★★ Designed to please, 09 has a generous nose & palate, the ripe plummy fruit gently spiced from year in big oak. **Rosé** NEW ★★ 10 fruity off-dry shiraz/zinfandel, nice sweet/sour finish. **Chenin Blanc** NEW ★★☆ 11 perky lemon-fresh, full mouthfeel despite low alc. **Sauvignon Blanc** 🌟 ★★★ In prime of youth, dry 11 preview from Slanghoek is light with palate minerality. **Viognier** NEW ✓ ★★★★ Peach pip & lavender, previewed 11 is more Old World than New, has a delicacy, refinement setting it apart.

Landau range

Red 🌟 ★★★ Shiraz/cab-led 4-part blend, dark fruited 07 ex-tank drinks well. WO W Cape for these. **White** 🌟 ★★ 11 ex-tank, fruity chenin, sauvignon, viognier dry quaffer. **Semi-Sweet** 🌟 ★★ Chenin, sauvignon & viognier, 10's profile is gently sweet summer fruit. Discontinued: **Rosé**.

Noble Late Harvests

★★★★ **Malbec** Rare bottling from minuscule yields, as both these reds. Prunes & black pepper on 10, luscious body, mouthfilling richness, all vindicate the huge effort to make this wine.

★★★★ **Zinfandel** Macerated berries infused with a whopping 240g/l sugar, yet 10's zesty freshness makes it deliciously drinkable. Shows the essence of zinfandel fruit. 375ml, as both these reds.

Discontinued: **Viognier**.

Aperitif range NEW

★★★★☆ **Before & After** Handsome packaging for this aptly named berry & spice saturated beauty; cloves, cinnamon, the palate silky sweet & very moreish. Fortified to 16% alc, brandy-like notes on finish. **NV**. — CR

■ **Black Box** *see Wineways Marketing*

Black Forest   NEW

Location: Stellenbosch ▪ Est 2010 ▪ 1stB 2011 ▪ Closed to public ▪ Owner(s) Louis Nel ▪ Cellarmaster(s)/winemaker(s) Louis Nel (Jan 2011) ▪ 8t/500cs own label 100% red ▪ 3 Chestnut Lane Stellenbosch 7600 ▪ info@blackforestwines.com ▪ www.blackforestwines.com ▪ T +27 (0)21-889-5555

When your wine tastes like cherries and chocolate, Black Forest is a pretty apt name for the brand! Winemaker Louis Nel's strategy for dealing with the economic downturn is to create this new, lower-priced wine, offering 'great value for money'. Now both he and savvy consumers can have their cake... Unready for tasting, we'll get our slice next time. Meanwhile see separate listing for 'Louis'.

Black Knight Wine

Location: Cape Town ▪ 22 Kildare Road Newlands 7700 ▪ jane@garyplayer.co.za ▪ www.playerwine.com, www.garyplayer.com ▪ T +27 (0)21-671-5159 ▪ F +27 (0)21-671-2250

This series of wines (18 are contemplated) is well underway with their commemoration of golfing great Gary Player's Major Championship victories. Made at Quoin Rock in Stellenbosch, the wines are also pretty deft, with their balance between classic refinement and more showy modernism.

★★★★ **Gary Player Major Championship Series** 05 named for Aronimink 1962, half shiraz, with cab, merlot, pinotage. Tasted last year, seriously built but approachable; ripe & big but balanced; good oaking. — TJ

■ **Black Label** *see Backsberg Estate Cellars*

Black Oystercatcher Wines

Location/WO: Elim ▪ Map: Southern Cape ▪ Est 1996 ▪ 1stB 2003 ▪ Tasting, sales & cellar tours Mon-Fri 9-5 Sat/Sun 10-3.30 ▪ Closed Easter Fri & Dec 25 ▪ Restaurant, function & wedding venue: kitchen open daily 11-2.30 - booking essential ▪ Facilities for children ▪ Tour groups ▪ Conferences ▪ Conservation area ▪ Annual Sauvignon Blanc & Oyster Festival (Dec); peak season programme ▪ Owner(s)/cellarmaster(s)/winemaker(s)/viticulturist(s) Dirk Human ▪ 1,550ha/18.5ha (cab, merlot, shiraz, sauv, white pearl) ▪ ±90t/±3,300cs own label 17% red 73% white 10% rosé ▪ BWI, IPW, WIETA ▪ PO Box 199 Bredasdorp 7280 ▪ venue@blackoystercatcher.co.za, wine@blackoystercatcher.co.za ▪ www.blackoystercatcher.co.za ▪ S 34° 37'58.0" E 019° 49'39.9" ▪ **T +27 (0)28-482-1618 ▪** F +27 (0)86-666-7954

Black Oystercatcher prime mover Dirk Human's tiny cellar and thriving restaurant and function venue are the social hub for locals and visitors to Elim wine ward's vast, unspoilt coastal plains. Only here you'll find his latest single-barrel specialities - a Reserve Blanc Fumé and Reserve Semillon ('barrel-fermented, unfiltered, hand-bottled, -corked, -labelled'). One of his major passions is the government-approved, privately initiated Nuwejaars Wetland Special Management Area, and he's delighted that about 24 other landowners have committed nearly 45,000ha, worth some R1-billion, to this landmark conservation effort. Newly stocked with buffalo, hippo and large buck, it's earmarked for public recreational use.

Black Oystercatcher range

★★★★ **Triton** ✓ 🗎 Liquorice-toned 08 mixes shiraz (41%), cab & merlot to deliver impressive, restrained & cellarworthy red. Still tightly wound, needs few years to soften as did cab-dominated 07 (★★★★).

★★★★☆ **Sauvignon Blanc** ✓ 🗎 🕲 Shy & reserved 10 (★★★★) fine effort in difficult vintage, with satisfying vinosity, flinty 'oystershell' persistence, but not as much intensity or precision as standout 09.

★★★★☆ **White Pearl** ✓ 🗎 Highly pedigreed blend semillon & sauvignon heads the excellent, focused line-up from this Elim stalwart. Partly oaked 09 is 70/30 blend, with khaki bush & white peach notes, extra weight from older oak, endless finish. Still unevolved compared to 08 at this stage, will reward patience.

Cabernet Sauvignon-Merlot 🗎 ★★★ Fruit-filled & satisfying 08, mineral & cedar notes from French oak, cab's drying tannin & merlot's plum fruit. **Rosé** 🗎 🕲 ★★★ Bone-dry 10 equal portions early-picked cab & merlot, savoury & zesty for summer sipping. — Panel

Black Pearl Vineyards

Location/WO: Paarl ▪ Map: Paarl & Wellington ▪ Est 1998 ▪ 1stB 2001 ▪ Tasting, sales & tours just about anytime but phone ahead (no credit cards) ▪ Closed Dec 25 ▪ Walks ▪ Conservation area ▪ Owner(s) Lance & Mary-Lou Nash ▪ Winemaker(s)/viticulturist(s) Mary-Lou Nash ▪ 240ha/7.2ha (cab, shiraz) ▪ ±1,800cs own label 100% red ▪ BWI member ▪ PO Box 609 Suider-Paarl 7624 ▪ info@blackpearlwines.com ▪ www.blackpearlwines.com ▪ S 33° 44'10.5" E 018° 53'40.8" ▪ **T +27 (0)83-297-9796, +27 (0)83-395-6999 ▪** F +27 (0)86-617-8507

Recently invested Cape Wine Master Mary-Lou Nash's involvements range from making wine and distilling brandy to brewing beer and growing proteas. Equally varied are the attractions at the family farm near Paarl: a new Nguni herd joins the alpacas, and the first hiking trail traverses the nature reserve. A natural approach is followed, and the aim is to produce terroir-driven wines.

Black Pearl range

★★★★ **Shiraz** ✓ 🗎 09 impresses with sweet mulberries, brambleberries & spice. Elegant & silky mouthfeel with precise oaking & lingering berry flavours.

★★★★ **Oro** 🗎 Very ripe dark berries, sweet & slightly jammy 09 (★★★★), tad off 07. Soft, smooth mouthfeel. Drink now.

Cabernet Sauvignon 🗎 Await next.

Conservation range

Nash Family Vineyards Rhinoceros Shiraz 🗎 ★★★ Enticing 09 has juicy black fruit, hint of oak. Medium-bodied & cheerful. — WB

■ **Black Rock** *see* The Winery of Good Hope
■ **Black Tie** *see* Wineways Marketing

BLANKbottle

Location: Somerset West ▪ Map: Helderberg ▪ WO: Western Cape/Wellington/Swartland/Piekenierskloof/Stellenbosch ▪ Est 2005 ▪ 1stB 2003 ▪ Tasting & sales Mon-Sat by appt ▪ Sales also via website ▪ Owner(s)/cellarmaster(s)/winemaker(s) Pieter H Walser ▪ Viticulturist(s) Various ▪ 2,000cs own label 70% red 30% white ▪ Lanrust Wine Estate Winery Road Somerset West 7129 ▪ pieter@blankbottle.co.za ▪ www.blankbottle.co.za ▪ S 34° 2' 41.1" E 018° 47' 16.0" ▪ **T +27 (0)21-842-2747/+27 (0)82-872-8658** ▪ F +27 (0)86-503-0974

There's always something innovative from Pieter Walser, proprietor and marketing pioneer of internet communication in the local wine industry: website, blog, YouTube, email-shots, education and now even wine movies. The range is constantly changing and the operation has grown, from little batches of bought-in oddities to serious ranges of impressive quality, value and diversity. Now he's supplying Woolworths, exporting his first consignments and endlessly informing anybody out there who will listen.

BLANKbottle range

★★★★ **Batavia NV** Cape blend previously was spicy & aromatic, mocha & toasty oak notes, big, brawny structure. This & next 3 not retasted.

★★★★ **Black 08** shiraz with bits of mourvèdre, carignan, grenache, all from Swartland last time was substantial, well-judged, with rich primary berry fruit.

★★★★ **The Spaniard** Mourvèdre-fronted red Mediterranean quartet in spicy, characterful 07, berry & scrub notes with coconut waft.

★★★★ **The White Black** Rich, buttery blend of chardonnay, chenin, viognier, clairette blanche, 09 showed class last year. Primary tropical fruit mingled easily with lees fatness.

★★★★ **The Big Spaniard** NEW ✓ Rhône-style 4-way red blend continues blending experiment - see Educational range. This, the more serious, fuller 09 sibling, shows dividends from ripe vintage & longer oaking.

> **Mnr Professor** NEW ☺ ★★★ 08 cab-led Bordeaux-style blend ex Stellenbosch has surprising weight & substance. Meaty & dry with chalky tannins.

Midnight Call ★★★ Cab-led Bordeaux blend 07 from very ripe Wellington fruit was judiciously oaked last edition. **Moment of Silence** 🌐 ★★★★ 10 Wellington-sourced, chenin-led wooded blend shows individuality & charm. Improves on 09 (★★★★). Well-judged oak lifts & spices up big but elegant & rounded body. **The Misfit** NEW ★★★★ Inky, intense newcomer, 09 is Swartland carignan. Thickly tannic, with sombre black fruit & aromatic oak. **Nothing To Declare** NEW ✓ ★★★★ Stylish (old) barrel-fermented chenin from Swartland vines, 10 is full-bodied, ripe & spicy, with creamy lees texture.

Educational range

Mourvèdre ★★★★ This & 3 below thematic set of Mediterranean blend components tasted last ed. 07 showed spicy plum pudding. Wellington grapes. **Carignan** ★★★★ Part 2 was 07 Swartland fruit. Steely, ink & sundried tomatoes. Medium bodied, fruit driven, ripe & sunny. **Grenache** ★★★★ 07 from Piekernierskloof, showed redcurrants & strawberry jam with racy acid, lighter body. **Cinsaut** ★★★ 07 hailed from Wellington. Juicy-fruity, with peppery notes. Light, fresh, accessible. — GdB

Bloemendal Estate

Location/WO: Durbanville ▪ Map: Durbanville, Philadelphia & Darling ▪ Est 1902 ▪ 1stB 1987 ▪ Tasting & sales Mon-Fri 9-5 Sat 9-4 Sun 11-3 ▪ Fee R10pp tasting, R20 cellar tour & tasting ▪ Closed Dec 25 ▪ Deli/oyster bar, weddings, evening functions & conference facilities ▪ Owner(s) Spirito Trade 82 (Pty) Ltd ▪ Winemaker(s) Christie Langeveld & Juli Slabbert ▪ Vineyard manager(s) Juli Slabbert ▪ 154ha (cab, merlot, shiraz, sauv) ▪ 5,000cs own label 75% red 25% white ▪ PO Box 466 Durbanville 7551 ▪ juli@bloemendalwines.co.za ▪ www.bloemendalwines.co.za ▪ S 33° 50' 22.1" E 018° 36' 1.4" ▪ **T +27 (0)21-976-2682** ▪ F +27 (0)86-615-7020

Keen on driving sales through the cellardoor (a smart strategy, given its proximity to the large and thriving Durbanville and Bellville communities), the new owners and management team of this historic estate have revamped the restaurant and tasting room. To further tickle visitors' wallets, cellar stalwart Christie 'Boetman' Langeveld has a Méthode Cap Classique sparkling on the lees and a Sauvignon Blanc

Natural Sweet awaiting release. They'll join the farm's first Chardonnay and Pinotage reviewed below.

★★★★ **Sauvignon Blanc Suider Terras** Previewed last edition, **10** (★★★★) was a punchy guava & fig fruit-bomb with broad, creamy texture, short finish compared with **09**.

Cabernet Sauvignon ★★★★ Classically scented & styled **05** firm & dry last year. **Merlot** ★★★ Slightly meaty/oxidative notes on **05** suggested previously it should be drunk soon. **Pinotage** NEW ★★★ Estery **10** easy-sipper has complex bouquet musk sweets, curry leaf & banana; fruit-filled palate enlivened by bright acidity, slight bitter nudge on finish. Only this & Chardonnay tasted this year. **Chardonnay** NEW ★★★ **11** pleasant lunchtime white with brisk lemon flavour, very dry finish; interesting bouquet of pear, blackcurrant & coconut. **Semillon** ★★★★ Unwooded & undemanding **10** preview last year was for youthful enjoyment. **Bloemenblanc** ★★★ Previewed **10** from sauvignon with dash semillon; fruity (& big, at 15% alc) with savoury notes from lees-ageing. — CvZ

Blomendahl Vineyards

Location: Elgin ▪ Map: Elgin, Walker Bay & Bot River ▪ WO: Elgin/Simonsberg-Paarl/Swartland/Western Cape ▪ Est 2003 ▪ 1stB 2006 ▪ Tasting by appt ▪ Owner(s) Blomendahl Trust ▪ Cellarmaster(s)/winemaker(s)/viticulturist(s) Franz Josef Blomendahl ▪ 126ha (cab, merlot, ptage, shiraz, chard, chenin) ▪ 480t/35,000cs 90% red 10% white ▪ PO Box 52019 Waterfront Cape Town 8002 ▪ info@basco.co.za ▪ www.blomendahl.de ▪ S 34° 13′ 12.2″ E 019° 2′ 28.8″ ▪ T +27 (0)21-859-1411/+27 (0)72-692-6229/+49 (0)44-45-14-11 ▪ F +27 (0)21-848-9679

Having established his specialist range of estate labels (including Basco from his farm in Grabouw, Môrewag from Paarl, Blue Bay from the West Coast and Bonny Bay from a farm overlooking False Bay), Franz Blomendahl now invites friends, clients and the general public to visit his 'very, very small' boutique winery on Basco farm. 'We are busy preparing the guest rooms and building a very nice tasting venue, and everything should be ready by mid-2012.'

Ben Hur range
Quadrega ★★★ Black-fruited **06** trio cab, merlot & shiraz showed sleek oak tannins when last tasted.

Estate Collection
Basco Merlot ★★★ As for all wines below, previously tasted. **07** for early enjoyment, sweetness held in firm tannic grip. Elgin WO for this label. **Môrewag Pinotage** ★★ Sturdy, strapping, spicy **05** had ripe fruitcake character. **06** (★★★) shy by comparison, less extracted, with firm tannins. Simonsberg-Paarl WO for Môrewag wines. **Basco Pinotage** 🍷 ★★ Acid dominated youthful, magenta-hued, spicy **10**. **Blue Bay Shiraz** ★★★ Ripe, dark fruit in juicy, accessible **06**. Ex West Coast vines. **Môrewag Rosé** 🍷 **09** had sweet impression from fruitiness but dry & nicely structured. **Basco Rosé** 🍷 ★★★ Light pink **10** delighted with off-dry fruity flavours. **Basco Chardonnay** 🍷 ★★★ Green-apple toned **10** was pleasant summertime sipper. **Bonny Bay Bushvine Chenin Blanc** 🍷 ★★★ Tad unexpressive for bushvines, but **09** was pleasantly dry food wine. WO Stbosch for this brand. **Basco Sauvignon Blanc** 🍷 ★★★★ **09** attractive stony acidity & minerality when tasted mid-10. Good table companion. **Môrewag Shiraz** ★★★ Natural Sweet **08** had savoury hints; sweet, but good grip added balancing savouriness. **Môrewag Cabernet Sauvignon** ★★★ Natural Sweet **08** brimmed with fruit, sweetness checked by leafy dry savouriness.

Prime Bin range
Cabernet Sauvignon-Merlot ★★★ Mix cab & merlot in black-fruited **06**, was dense & closely knit, must since have softened. **Lady in Red Rosé** 🍷 ★★★ Attractively different: more 'light red' than 'rosé', **09** had plenty cab fruit for flavour & structure.

Bonolo range
Cabernet Sauvignon ★★☆ Ex Helderberg **06** was variety-true, with ample structure. — IM

▪ **Blouberg** see Graça

Blouvlei Wyne

Location: Wellington ▪ Map: Paarl & Wellington ▪ WO: Paarl ▪ Est/1stB 2003 ▪ Tasting, sales & cellar tours Mon-Fri 9-4.30 Sat by appt ▪ Fee R15 ▪ Closed all pub hols ▪ Picnic area by arrangement ▪ Owner(s) BEE Company ▪ Winemaker(s) Abraham Cloete (Marinus Bredell) ▪ Viticulturist(s) Ettienne Barnard (Oct 2010) ▪ ±40ha/28ha (alicante bouschet, cabs s/f, merlot, mourv, p verdot, shiraz, tinta barocca) ▪ ±150t/5,000cs own label 50% red 50% white ▪ IPW ▪ PO Box 817 Wellington 7654 ▪ blouvlei@cknet.co.za ▪ www.montdutoit.co.za ▪ S 33° 39′31.3" E 019° 2′2.6" ▪ **T +27 (0)21-873-7745** ▪ F +27 (0)21-864-2737

The workers of Mont du Toit winery in Wellington are shareholders in this enter-prise making wines for easy, everyday drinking. Red grapes come partly from the parent farm (which shares its production and sales facilities with Blouvlei) but, as Mont du Toit is all-red, the sauvignon blanc grapes must be bought in.

Sauvignon Blanc ☺ 🍽 🌿 ★★★ **11** tends to the greener side of the sauvignon spectrum, but has a bit of weight & is crisply & tastily succulent. WO Paarl.

Blouvlei Red 🍽 ★★ Warm-hearted **09** from cab & merlot plus shiraz, for youthful enjoyment. Like all, except sauvignon, not retasted. **Klassique** 🍽 ★★★ Characterful **05** dark-fruited, chunky & rustic. **Rosé** 🍽 ★★★☆ Uncomplicated **10** dry, zesty & fruity. — TJ

■ **Blue Bay** *see* Blomendahl Vineyards

Blueberry Hill Estate

Location/map/WO: Franschhoek ▪ Est 1998 ▪ 1stB 2005 ▪ Tasting & sales by appt ▪ 3 self-catering cottages (T 078-148-2749 Claire van Zyl) ▪ Owner(s) Proximitas Investments 106 (Pty) Ltd ▪ Winemaker(s)/viticulturist(s) Oswald Sauermann (Nov 2008, La Vigne) ▪ 0.6ha (merlot) ▪ 4t/250cs own label 100% red ▪ PO Box 383 Franschhoek 7690 ▪ blueberryhill@telkomsa.net ▪ www.blueberryhillcottages.co.za ▪ S 33° 55′19.14" E 019° 8′4.92" ▪ **T +27 (0)21-876-3362** ▪ F +27 (0)21-876-3341

'Dynamite comes in small packages,' says Claire van Zyl, manager of this boutique estate in Franschhoek. 'Even though we are not organically certified, we like to let nature take its course.' Winemaking interventions are minimised to reflect the terroir of this 'little piece of heaven' – which visitors can now experience overnight in any of three luxuriously appointed cottages. 'It'll give you a new perspective on the growing of what we think is a world-class merlot.'

Merlot ★★★★ **06** shows more structure than fruit at this stage, firm tannins need more time (or aeration, if broaching now) to soften. — Panel

Blue Crane Vineyards

Location/map/WO: Tulbagh ▪ Est 2001 ▪ 1stB 2004 ▪ Visitors welcome but phone ahead ▪ Owner(s) Fred & Manuela Crabbia ▪ Cellarmaster(s)/winemaker(s) Zia Pienaar ▪ Viticulturist(s) Chris Fox, advised by Andrew Teubes & suppliers ▪ 138ha/6ha (cab, merlot, shiraz, sauv) ▪ 2,000cs own label 75% red 25% white ▪ BWI ▪ PO Box 306 Tulbagh 6820 ▪ info@bluecrane.co.za ▪ www.bluecrane.co.za ▪ S 33° 14′34.7" E 019° 9′49.4" ▪ **T +27 (0)23-230-0823** ▪ F +27 (0)23-230-0825

Owned by the Crabbia family, boutique winery Blue Crane Vineyards near Tulbagh is undergoing change under the guidance of cellarmaster Zia Pienaar and farm man-ager Chris Fox. Underway are the planting of more vines and indigenous trees, development of the farm's biodiversity, and improvement of the natural environ-ment. A new cellar, tasting room and coffee shop are on the cards.

Blue Crane range
Cabernet Sauvignon ✓ ★★★★ Blueberries & herbs excite on **10** gluggable offering. Mouthfilling fruit tem-pered by firm tannins, lingering exit. Previewed, as for rest of range. **Merlot** ★★★ Rounded & accessible **10**, attractive cherry fruit & lightly spiced vanilla notes, dry tannins. **Shiraz** ✓ ★★★★ **10** exudes ripe blueberry, smoke & vanilla. Smooth & balanced, with fruit purity & vibrant savoury lift. **Full Flight** 🍽 ★★★ Food-friendly cab, shiraz/merlot **08** last year was chunky & fleshy, with ripe blackcurrant & savoury spice.

Strelizia range
Shiraz-Merlot [NEW] 🍽 ★★★ Juicy, fruity **NV**, easy sipper with earthy & spicy aftertaste. **Shiraz-Cabernet Sauvignon-Merlot** 🍽 ★★★ **07** blend offered dry & spicy fruit with evident tannins last edition. **Sauvignon Blanc** 🍽 🌿 ★★★ **10** greengage, citrus & mineral flavours, silky acidity & zingy tail. — WB

Blue Creek Wines

Location/map/WO: Stellenbosch ▪ Est 1995 ▪ 1stB 1996 ▪ Tasting, sales & tours by appt ▪ Owner(s) Piet & Liezl Smal ▪ Winemaker(s) Piet Smal ▪ Viticulturist(s) Johan Smith (1996, consultant) ▪ 7.5ha (cab, merlot, ptage) ▪ 1,000cs own label 100% red ▪ 26 Piet Retief Str Stellenbosch 7600 ▪ liezl@eject.co.za ▪ S 33° 58' 14.1" E 018° 51' 13.4" ▪ **T +27 (0)21-880-0522, +27 (0)82-857-6683** ▪ F +27 (0)21-886-5462

Piet Smal is an after-hours winemaker, but seeing he not only vinifies at this boutique family holding in the Blaauwklippen Valley but also lends a hand at Cape Hutton (where he's responsible for another Cabernet), it's likely that his dental practice is the part-time activity during harvest at least.

★★★★ **Cabernet Sauvignon** Previous edition **06** was restrained, with shy redcurrant, liquorice & earthy notes. Elegant & refreshing; tannins should be approachable now. — WB

▪ **Blue Grove Hill** see Capaia Wine Estate
▪ **Blydskap** see Baarsma Wine Group
▪ **Bob's Your Uncle** see Boer & Brit

Boekenhoutskloof Winery

Location/map: Franschhoek ▪ WO: Western Cape/Coastal/Franschhoek/Swartland ▪ Est 1994 ▪ 1stB 1996 ▪ Tasting & sales Mon-Fri 9-5 ▪ Closed all pub hols ▪ Owner(s) Boekenhoutskloof Winery (Pty) Ltd ▪ Cellarmaster(s) Marc Kent (1994) ▪ Winemaker(s) Jean Smit, Johan Nesenberend & Elsabé Engelbrecht ▪ Viticulturist(s) Heini Tait ▪ 71ha/20ha (cabs s/f) ▪ 3,000t/250,000cs own label 60% red 39% white 1% rosé ▪ BDOCA, BRC, HACCP ▪ PO Box 433 Franschhoek 7690 ▪ info@boekenhoutskloof.co.za ▪ www.boekenhoutskloof.co.za ▪ S 33° 56'33.0" E 019° 6' 28.0" ▪ **T +27 (0)21-876-3320** ▪ F +27 (0)21-876-3793

The innovative move is back to artisanal first principles for Marc Kent and his widely acclaimed team: experimental fermentation and maturation techniques are moving from stainless steel and oak barrels to concrete 'kuipe' and large wooden 'foudres' in an effort to express the grapes' character more authentically. Continuing this back-to-basics theme, the Franschhoek vineyards have now achieved organic certification and every stage of production strives to optimise sustainable practice. Progressive marketing sees their wines on shelves in 35 countries worldwide. Adding significantly to production scope and capacity is the recent acquisition of Helderberg Wijnmakerij near Firgrove (see entry). Boekenhoutskloof is one of the all-time star champions of this guide, having previously achieved maximum points no fewer than 11 times. This edition they add a further trio of five star ratings, plus the Superquaffer of the Year garland as well as the ultimate accolade, Winery of the Year 2012.

Boekenhoutskloof range

★★★★★ **Cabernet Sauvignon** Tightly focused **09** blockbuster maintains great lineage. Riper, more opulent than **08**, yet elegantly herbaceous & supple. Just beginning to emerge after 2+ years in new oak, promises even finer things to come. Franschhoek grapes.

★★★★☆ **Syrah** Iconic label revels in ripeness of **09** (★★★★★) vintage. Reticent & understated, unfurls slowly in glass to reveal grace, complexity & subtlety. Seamless, silky texture masks deceptively full body. Like **08**, textbook Rhône styling, from Wellington fruit.

★★★★ **The Chocolate Block** Shiraz-led 5-way blend has attracted a loyal following. Seriously conceived & crafted **10** is elegantly balanced, richly ripe, deeply satisfying. WO W Cape, mostly Swartland.

★★★★ **Semillon** Substantial but understated **09** shows serious intent through dominant spicy oak. Restrained fruit, silky texture & intriguingly aromatic finish. Needs time. WO Franschhoek.

★★★★☆ **Noble Late Harvest** From Franschhoek semillon; like **07**, sumptuous **08** (★★★★★) in less-syrupy Sauternes style, with honeyed almonds, citrus zest. Perennially stately, beautifully expressed varietal form, with depth & complexity after 30 months in new oak.

The Wolftrap range

The Wolftrap ☺ 🍽 ★★★ Great-value lower tier still shows class. Shiraz, mourvèdre & viognier, **10** from Malmesbury vineyards a bit chewy, but characterful & fruity. **The Wolftrap White** NEW ☺ 🍽 ★★★ Budget-level Swartland-style newcomer is our Superquaffer of the Year. Mainly viognier, splashes chenin, grenache blanc, **10** offers great value. Creamy, leesy body with ripe stonefruit. Delicious. WO W Cape.

Porcupine Ridge range

Sauvignon Blanc ☺ 🍷 ★★★ Dependable, undemanding **11** WO W Cape follows house form. Light in body & alc, but refreshingly fruity & crisp.

Cabernet Sauvignon ✓ 🍷 ★★★★ **10** shows finesse & balance, lacks intensity of **09**. Aromatic tobacco & blackcurrants, with oak spices. WO Coastal. **Merlot** 🍷 ★★★ Good varietal form on **10** mix of own & Malmesbury fruit. Plush berry flavours with hints of mocha & aromatic herbs. **Syrah** ✓ 🍷 ★★★★ Supple, fruity **10** off Malmesbury vines has charming white pepper spiciness with wild herbs. Juicy & approachable. **Syrah-Viognier** ✓ 🍷 ★★★★ Charred nutty notes on **10** spice up sweetly fruity flavours, with appealing fragrant lift. Ex Swartland vineyards. **Viognier-Grenache Blanc** NEW ✓ 🍷 ★★★★ Charred oak entry on **10** Swartland/Citrusdal-sourced blend gives way to rich, lengthy lemon-tinged body with hints of terpene. — GdB

Boer & Brit

Location: Paarl ▪ Map: Stellenbosch ▪ WO: Western Cape ▪ Est 2010 ▪ 1stB 2008 ▪ Tasting, sales & cellar tours Mon-Fri 9-4 Sat 10-3 ▪ Closed Ash Wed, Mar 21, Easter Fri-Mon, Ascension day, Apr 27, May 1, Dec 16/25/26 & Jan 1 ▪ Child-friendly ▪ BYO picnic ▪ Conference/indaba venue ▪ Boer War artifacts & various paintings ▪ Natte Valleij B&B (see Accommodation section) ▪ Vintage furniture shop ▪ Art gallery & art classes ▪ Owner(s) Stefan Gerber & Alexander Milner ▪ Winemaker(s) Stefan Gerber, Alex Milner (both Jul 2010) & Marco Benjamin (2011) ▪ Viticulturist(s) Leon Coetzee (Jul 2010) ▪ 30t own label 70% red 30% white ▪ Other export label: Bob's Your Uncle ▪ PO Box 4 Klapmuts 7625 ▪ contact@boerandbrit.com ▪ www.boerandbrit.com ▪ S 33° 50' 3.6" E 018° 52' 43.2" ▪ **T +27 (0)21-875-5824** ▪ F +27 (0)86-531-7137

Boer & Brit represents a 'truly South African story of optimism, reconciliation and the indomitable spirit of young South Africans', according to Stefan Gerber and Alexander Milner, their great-great-grandfathers having been President Paul Kruger and Field Marshal John French, who opposed each other in the Anglo-Boer War. From 'two barrels of wine and a little bit of social media activity' in July 2010 to processing 30t from eight different areas around the winelands in 2011, business seems to be booming.

Boer & Brit range

★★★★ **The General** 🍷 New version of **09** Bordeaux-style red improves on previous. Violets, attractive herbal note, medium body, accessible but not simple. Elgin, Stellenbosch fruit. Mainly cab franc, older oak. **The Field Marshall** 🍷 ★★★ Likeable if straightforward red from 3 Rhône varieties & 12% tinta amarela. **09** sweet red fruit, spice, soft tannins. **Gezina** 🍷 ★★★ **10** sauvignon is intriguing but awkward with both green and riper notes.

Suikerbossie Ek Wil Jou Hê range NEW

Cap Classique Brut ★★★ Ebullient **NV** sparkling is mainly chardonnay, dash pinotage, off Northern Cape vines. Juicy ripe tropical fruit, tangy acidity, slightly coarse bubble.

Transkaroo-Bring My Huis Toe/Take Me Home range

Pinotage ★★★ Earthy banana whiffs on **08**, gentle tannins, hints of elegant pinot parentage last edition. — CE

■ **Boland Cellar** see Boland Kelder

Boland Kelder

Location/WO: Paarl ▪ Map: Paarl & Wellington ▪ Est/1stB 1947 ▪ Tasting & sales Mon-Fri 8–5 Sat & pub hols 9–1 ▪ Closed Easter Fri-Sun, Ascension day, Sep 24, Dec 25/26 & Jan 1 ▪ Cellar tours by appt ▪ Wynvlieg cellar theatre (www.ticketbreak.co.za) ▪ Owner(s) 96 producing shareholders ▪ Cellarmaster(s) Jurie Germishuys (Jul 2008) ▪ Winemaker(s) JD Rossouw (Sep 2007) & Bernard Smuts (Dec 2001), with Heidi Dietstein, Burger Badenhorst & Handré Barkhuizen (all Dec 2009) ▪ Viticulturist(s) Jurie Germishuys (Jul 1998) ▪ 2,210ha (cab, merlot, ptage, shiraz, chard, chenin, nouvelle, sauv, viog) ▪ 21,976t/120,000cs own label 50% red 40% white 10% rosé + 200,000cs for clients ▪ Other export brands: Lindenhof, Montestell ▪ WIETA ▪ PO Box 7007 Noorder-Paarl 7623 ▪ info@bolandkelder.co.za ▪ www.bolandkelder.co.za, www.bolandcellar.co.za, www.bolandwines.co.za ▪ S 33° 41' 19.6" E 018° 57' 20.1" ▪ **T +27 (0)21-862-6190** ▪ F +27 (0)21-862-5379

At this large winery which routinely uses staves as part of its oaking regime, there were boards of a different sort introduced half-way through last year: an unused storage area was converted into the Wynvlieg Cellar Theatre, and numerous well-known performers have since trodden the boards there in a variety of productions. Patrons are treated to an hour-long tasting and dinner before the show. Boland's winemaking cast of five vinifies a whopping 22,000 tonnes annually, all of which now perform in 22 different international theatres worldwide, including a large chunk of former Eastern Bloc countries. The dark continent has proved a thirsty market for this go-ahead former Paarl cooperative's accessible and fruity product, with exports going to five African countries.

Cellar Reserve range

★★★★ **Cabernet Sauvignon 08** (★★★★) floral touch to blackcurrant & tobacco, shows effect of ±2 new-oak ageing rather more than **06** did, needs more time to mellow. No **07**.

★★★★ **Shiraz** ✓ Ample plum & blackberry spice on **09**. Juicy & plush, with a peppery twist & firm concentrated middle. Oak supports fruit well. Long chocolatey aftertaste.

Merlot ★★★★ **09** ripe mulberry & some beetroot earthiness. Intense, concentrated & long but textured. Improves on previous. **Pinotage** ★★★★ **09** raspberry with earthy overlay, tangy succulence & softness. Same gentleness & plush fruit as delicious & persistent **08** (★★★★) (both vintages tasted). **Chardonnay** ★★★★ Appetising & rich combo marmalade & banana toast, yet **10** is light, zesty & fresh too. Oaking shows restraint.

Five Climates Single Varietal range

Chenin Blanc ☺ 🍴 🌿 ★★★ Zesty melon & pear, **11** leesy breadth yet refreshing lime acidity.

Cabernet Sauvignon ✓ 🍴 ★★★★ **09** keeps up the standard, with velvety blackberry spice abundance. Dry, earthy concentration & long tail. **Merlot** 🍴 ★★★ **09** maintains tone of previous: savoury tang & delicate fynbos, char hint. Gently firm structure & persistence. **Pinotage** 🍴 ★★★ **09** offers cocoa grip to piquant raspberry fruit. Approachable, like previous, but shade less concentrated. **Shiraz** ✓ 🍴 ★★★★ **09** retains standard with its accessible black cherry fruit. Good body, density & depth. Light oak sheen. **Chardonnay** 🍴 🌿 ★★★ Tangerine cream tang on crisp, light **11**, accessible & easy. **Sauvignon Blanc** 🍴 🌿 ★★★ Grassy gooseberry typicity, **11** zippy energetic acidity. **Red Muscadel** 🌿 ★★★ Lovely lavender & jasmine perfume on **11** fortified dessert. Barley sugar sweetness, full flavoured but ends clean, dry. **Cape Ruby Port** ★★★ Return to form for renamed 'Port', from shiraz. Plum & tealeaf mouthful of sweetness in **09**, spice & fire with chalky texture.

Cappupinoccinotage range

Cappupinoccinotage 🍴 🌿 ★★★ 100% pinotage, 'decaffeinated' (compared to last year's overt cappuccino character) **11** preview dials up berry fruit & earthy appeal, succulent to end.

Sixty 40 Blend range

Cabernet Sauvignon-Shiraz 🍴 🌿 ★★★ **10** sweet juicy plum & berry, simple immediate accessibility. **Rosé** 🍴 🌿 ★★ Fizz-pop sherbet tang simplicity to **11**. Modest 11% alc. **Chenin Blanc-Sauvignon Blanc** 🍴 🌿 ★★ **11** uncomplex tropical fruit & sweetish edge but still tastes fresh, clean.

Flutterby range NEW

Merlot 🍴 🌿 ★★★ Approachable black fruit, chocolate & char on **10**, long & likeable. **Sauvignon Blanc** 🍴 🌿 ★★ Previewed **11**'s fig & gooseberry tang offers accessible refreshment.

Bon Vino range

Dry Red ☺ 🍴 ★★★ NV succulent spicy, smoke & berry. Solid commercial appeal. 500ml.

Rosé 🍴 ★★ Lollipop & strawberry attractiveness to light, sweet **NV** pink quaffer. 500ml. **Dry White** 🍴 ★★ Uncomplicated **NV** crowd pleaser. Tropical fruit with light acid zip. 500ml. **Natural Sweet** 🍴 ★★ NV Natural Sweet offers crisp, tangy pineapple taste, clean finish. 500ml. — FM

Bon Cap Organic Winery   🍴🍷🛋️📷🎾♿

Location/map: Robertson • WO: Eilandia • Est 2001 • 1stB 2002 • Tasting & sales Mon-Fri 8–5 Sun 8–4 • Closed Sat due to weddings & functions • Cellar tours by appt • Bon Rouge Bistro • Facilities for children • Gifts • Cheese platters • Guesthouse • Owner(s) Roelf & Michelle du Preez/SHZ Winery (Pty) Ltd • Winemaker(s) Marinus Potgieter (Jan 2008) • Viticulturist(s) Roelf du Preez • 460ha/40ha (cab, p verdot, ptage, shiraz, chard, cbard, sauv, viog) • 295t/21,000cs own label 60% red 35% white 5% rosé • Other export brand: The Greenhouse • Brands for clients;

Matto H Barfuss, The Societies ▪ SGS ▪ PO Box 356 Robertson 6705 ▪ info@boncap.co.za ▪ www.boncaporganic. co.za ▪ S 33° 47' 1.0" E 019° 40' 53.2" ▪ **T +27 (0)23-626-2073** ▪ F +27 (0)23-626-5789

'Sustainability is important,' says winemaker Marinus Potgieter, an understatement given that this is one of South Africa's largest privately owned organic wineries. Co-proprietor Michelle du Preez explains that farming in low-rainfall Eilandia gives them a 'natural' advantage: 'It means low impact with regards to diseases like powdery mildew. Also, high rainfall tends to compact the soil and wash the nutrients out.' Showcasing the healthy soil is key to the philosophy of 'terroir-driven rather than over-wooded' wine.

Bon Cap range

★★★★ **Cape Blend** ✓ ☼ Pinotage heads 07 (★★★☆) with petit verdot, cab; unusual combo but works. Polished & fresh, vanilla oak gloss adding to the modern persona. 1st tasted since 05 (06 sold out untasted). **The Perfect Blend** ★★★★ Mid-2010, well-composed 09, cab (51%), pinotage & shiraz dusted with cinnamon, plump, with blueberry & choc-raisin. **Viognier** ☼ ◪ ★★☆ Misreported as discontinued last time. 10 full-bore varietal apricot but not much else, oak tad unknit, allow time to come together. **Méthode Cap Classique** NEW ☼ ★★★★ Butterscotch & lemon zest on 06 traditional-method sparkling from chardonnay (82%) & pinot. Rich & satisfying, attractively dry celebrator.

The Ruins range

Rosé ☺ 🍴 ☼ ◪ ★★★ Savoury & dry 11 from shiraz, compact & fruity anytime sipper. **Sauvignon Blanc** ☺ 🍴 ☼ ◪ ★★★ Step up for personality-laden 11. Zesty & slightly savoury seafood partner or aperitif, bone-dry & light.

Pinotage 🍴 ☼ ◪ ★★★ 10's mulberry jam, smoky overlay, crisp acidity hit right drinkability notes. **Syrah-Cabernet Sauvignon** ✓ 🍴 ☼ ◪ ★★★★ Accomplished 10 vivacious & elegant, unforced versus warm & raisined 09 (★★★★). Scrubby/meaty complexity from shiraz (60%), medium body, well-judged new oak. **Chardonnay-Viognier** ✓ 🍴 ☼ ◪ ★★★★ Poise, restraint from lightly oaked 11 combo. Vibrant, juicy yet well-contained (12.5% alc), endless dry tail; a notch up. **Sparkling Brut** ☼ ◪ ★★ Yeasty aromas on lively lemon-toned 10 sparkler ex colombard. Some of these available under The Greenhouse label in Checkers retail stores. Discontinued: **CVV.** — Panel

Bon Courage Estate

Location/map/WO: Robertson ▪ Est 1927 ▪ 1stB 1983 ▪ Tasting & sales Mon-Fri 8–5 Sat 9–3 ▪ Fee R10pp for groups of 10+ ▪ Closed Easter Fri, Dec 25 & Jan 1 ▪ Café Maude T +27 (0)23-626-6806 ▪ Facilities for children ▪ Owner(s) André & Jacques Bruwer ▪ Winemaker(s) Jacques Bruwer ▪ Viticulturist(s) André Bruwer ▪ 150ha (cab, pinot, shiraz, chard) ▪ 40% red 50% white 10% rosé ▪ Export brand: Three Rivers ▪ PO Box 589 Robertson 6705 ▪ wine@ boncourage.co.za ▪ www.boncourage.co.za ▪ S 33° 50' 43.8" E 019° 57' 38.0" ▪ **T +27 (0)23-626-4178** ▪ F +27 (0)23-626-3581

'What you see is what you get' is what the Bruwer father-and-son team of owner/viticulturist André and winemaker Jacques say about themselves and their value-for-money wines. They achieve consistent success at competitions, especially with their bubbly (repeat winner of Wine magazine's annual Cap Classique Challenge, among others). 'My approach is to work with what nature offers me,' explains Jacques. 'Keep it simple and you get a complex wine that's lekker to drink.'

Inkará range

★★★★ **Cabernet Sauvignon** 09 similar to concentrated & taut 08. Eucalyptus, forest floor whiffs to dusty cassis fruit; as always, signature sweetness tempered by minerality; endless savoury finish.

★★★★☆ **Shiraz** Harmonious 09 retains elegance, sense of accomplishment despite being full & bold (±15% alc). Intense mulberry & violets lead to velvet palate. Like 08, lingering lift in tail. Will reward cellaring 5+ years.

Bon Courage Estate range

★★★★ **Cap Classique Jacques Bruère Brut Reserve Blanc de Blancs** Champagne-method sparkling from chardonnay still available; last year 07 noted as sophisticated & balanced.

★★★★☆ **Cap Classique Jacques Bruére Brut Reserve** Traditional-method sparkling from pinot noir/chardonnay (60/40); base wine barrel fermented/aged, 3/4 years on lees in bottle. 07 beautifully fresh & lively last edition, persistent fine mousse, creamy conclusion. As fine, complex, as 06. Not revisited.

★★★★ **Noble Late Harvest** Refined & poised unoaked botrytised riesling. Mouthfilling marmalade, apricot preserve & fynbos honey on **10** (★★★★★) seamed with piercing lime acidity to deliver uncloying flavour. Smooth, succulent, as was **09**.

★★★★ **White Muscadel** Voluptuous & seductive **11** perfect marriage of fruity sweetness, zingy acidity & integrated spirit. Sun-warmed honey & apricot delight. Offers as much complexity, length than enduring **10**.

Pinotage ☺ ★★★ **09** plush & generous: violets & fynbos aromas, chocolate-dipped cherries. **André's Fame Colombard** ☺ 🔖 ★★★ Guava & green-apple perkiness, clean finish to light-bodied & off-dry **11** sipper. **Blush Vin Doux** ☺ ★★★ Grapey, light, sweet **NV** carbonated sparkling, Turkish Delight infused, a real crowd pleaser.

Cabernet Sauvignon ✓ ★★★★ Affable **09** continues on improved path with dark fruit, earthy tones, approachable tannins. **Bruère Gold Reserve Pinot Noir** Await new. **Shiraz** ✓ ★★★★ Another cellar stalwart; everyday **10** food friendly & balanced, engaging coriander & dark berry notes. Nudges next level. **Hillside Red** ✓ ★★★★ Estate's hallmark earth/smoke scents on bouncy **10** cab (65%), shiraz combo. Red fruited & juicy, seamless finish take it up a rung. **Chardonnay Prestige Cuvée** ★★★★ Baked apple, cinnamon, oak-derived toffee on **10**, ebullient fruit dominated by wood mid-2011; should settle within year/2. **Chardonnay** ✓ 🔖 ★★★★ Unwooded version; **11** exudes lemon blossom, lime perfume; white peach & spice end. For more than just casual sipping. **Sauvignon Blanc** 🔖 ★★★★ Tropical fruit salad, feisty acidity & pithy texture tick all drinkability boxes on **11**. **Hillside White** 🔖 ★★★ Light casual quaffer **11** from colombard & chardonnay (85/15), spicy pineapple, mango & papaya flavours spiked with clove. **Gewürztraminer Special Late Harvest** ★★★★ Charming, light **11** laced with rosepetal & litchi, ends dry thanks to crackling acidity; perfect sunset enjoyment. **Red Muscadel** ★★★★ Intense muscat, red berry & spicy enticement on still-selling fortified **10**; sweet yet delicate, spirity afterglow. **Cape Vintage Port** ★★★ Foursquare yet amicable **09** from touriga & tinta packed with Christmas cake nuts, marzipan & cherries; needs year/2 for tannins to mesh with fiery tail. Discontinued: **Riesling**, **Bruére Gold Reserve Chenin Blanc**.

Like Father Like Son range

Cabernet Sauvignon-Merlot ☺ 🔖 ★★★ **11** a happy picnic companion: all juiciness & joie de vivre. **Chenin Blanc-Colombard** ☺ 🔖 ★★★ **11** cheerful, semi-dry lunchtime-friendly (12% alc) tipple.

Rosé 🔖 ★★ **11** light-bodied quick-quaff with dusty, sweet edge; from pinotage. — Panel

Bonfoi Estate

Location/map: Stellenbosch ▪ Est 1699 ▪ 1stB 1974 ▪ Tasting & sales Mon-Fri 9–5 Sat 10–2.30 ▪ Closed pub hols ▪ BYO picnic ▪ Walks ▪ Conservation area ▪ Owner(s)/winemaker(s)/viticulturist(s) Johannes van der Westhuizen ▪ 200ha/101ha (cabs s/f, merlot, pinot, pinot meunier, ptage, shiraz, chard, chenin, sauv, sem) ▪ 700t/3,000cs own label 60% red 40% white ▪ BWI ▪ PO Box 9 Vlottenburg 7604 ▪ bonfoi@mweb.co.za ▪ www.bonfoiwines.co.za ▪ S 33° 56' 29.1" E 018° 46' 29.8" ▪ **T +27 (0)21-881-3774** ▪ F +27 (0)21-881-3807

This family boutique winery boasts a rich history dating back to 1699 and with a name that means 'Good Faith' one is bound to have an authentic experience. Worth a visit for the beautiful views alone, but also for the chance to get your hands on some lovely mature wines.

★★★★ **Cabernet Sauvignon** 04 previously tasted, still available at time of press.

★★★★ **Shiraz** In abeyance. Previous was fine & dry **04**.

★★★★ **Ouverture** Previously reviewed was stylish **04**, still selling.

Merlot Sold out await new. **Chardonnay** New vintage not ready at presstime. **Sauvignon Blanc** Sold out, await new. — JP

Bonnievale Cellar

Location: Bonnievale ▪ Map/WO: Robertson ▪ Est 1951 ▪ 1stB 1977 ▪ Tasting & sales Mon-Fri 8–5 Sat 10–1 ▪ Closed Easter Fri-Mon, Dec 25/26 & Jan 1 ▪ Cheese platters, biltong/droëwors & mini cheese platters ▪ Facilities for children ▪ Tour groups ▪ Conferences (12 pax) ▪ CCC Christmas Market ▪ Owner(s) 110 members ▪ Winemaker(s) Esmarie Smuts, Jolene Calitz Le Roux & Eduard Malherbe (Jan 2002/Aug 2007/Dec 2007), with Marthinus Rademeyer (Dec 2009) ▪ Viticulturist(s) Sakkie Bosman (Nov 2006) ▪ 1,754ha (cab, ruby cab, shiraz, chard, chenin, cbard, sauv) ▪ 25,000t/25,000cs own label 32% red 52% white 10% brut 1% port 5% juice + 300cs for clients ▪ Brands for clients: Simola Hotel ▪ WIETA ▪ PO Box 206 Bonnievale 6730 ▪ sales@bonnievalecellar.co.za ▪ www.

bonnievalecellar.co.za ▪ S 33° 57' 26.2" E 020° 6' 7.6" ▪ **T** +27 (0)23-616-2795/2800/2359 ▪ F +27 (0)23-616-2332

'Value for money, exceptional quality and a touch of hospitality' are what the grower-owned winery on the ridge above Bonnievale aspires to, so new brand custodian Lidelle Rheeders is understandably pleased about all the good things visitors are saying about the refurbishments that (among others) have transformed the old tasting area into something vastly more airy, stylish and inviting. Positive vibes are also being experienced on Facebook and Twitter, where followers and fans are being added 'by the day'.

Vertex Reserve range

Cabernet Sauvignon ★★★ Well-made **08** shows ripeness of vintage in plush fruit & suppleness. Dense, concentrated, would benefit from a more savoury conclusion. Revisited, like next. **Shiraz** ★★★ Lifted, leafy aroma, 'graphite' minerality on modern **08**, juicy, with lovely clean lines & freshness.

Bonnievale range

> **Cabernet Sauvignon-Shiraz** ☺ 🍽 ★★★ A candidate for our Superquaffer of the Year, any-occasion **09** artfully arranges chocolate & ripe black fruit in a succulent, well-priced package.

Shiraz ✓ 🍽 ★★★★ Modern, well-made **09** inspired by the Rhône: lilies & slightly dusty red fruit, crisp & medium-bodied enjoyment. **Cabernet Sauvignon-Merlot** 🍽 ★★ Lavender infused **11**, juicy fruit centre wrapped in perhaps too much of cab's bold tannins, needs time or a meal. **Chardonnay** 🍽 ★★ Faint lemon & beeswax on reticent **11**, fair length & nutty oak complexity but still unknit mid-2011, deserves more time. **Sauvignon Blanc** 🍽 ◎ ★★★★ Dusty & engaging **11**, zesty green-fruit flavours, savoury & refreshing easy-drinker. **Sauvignon Blanc Brut** ★★ Lively dry sparkling, **NV** crisp & balanced, though variety's capsicum pungency might be too much for some. **Cape Ruby** Untasted. Discontinued: **Kelkierooi, Kelkiewit.**

CCC range

Red 🍽 ★★ Trio red varieties make for uncomplicated berry tones & early drinking in **10**. **White** 🍽 ★★★ Fruit salad **11** ripe & smooth, engaging acid zip in tail. **Semi-Sweet** 🍽 ★★ Quietly & softly sweet **NV**, with lemony lift, designed for Thai green curry. — Panel

- **Bonny Bay** see Blomendahl Vineyards
- **Bonolo** see Blomendahl Vineyards
- **Bonsella** see Overhex Wines International

Bon Terroir

Location/WO: Stellenbosch ▪ Est 2002 ▪ 1stB 2007 ▪ Closed to public ▪ Owner(s) Agri Marketing Exchange (Pty) Ltd, with shareholder Will-Mag Holdings Ltd ▪ Winemaker(s) Bruwer Raats (2007, consultant) ▪ Viticulturist(s) Dricus van der Westhuizen (2007, consultant) ▪ 15.5ha/4ha (cabs s/f) ▪ 5t/300cs own label 100% red ▪ PO Box 2996 Knysna 6570 ▪ willie@willmag.co.za ▪ www.bonterroir.co.za ▪ **T** +27 (0)44-382-1686 ▪ F +27 (0)86-622-8254

This tiny farm, revelling in name and deed in the soils of Stellenbosch, has a new owner. Willie Dique, MD of the proprietory company, is pleased that continuity will be given in the vineyard by Drikus Hattingh and in the cellar by renowned consultant Bruwer Raats – understandably so, given the high standards they set.

★★★★☆ **Cabernet Sauvignon** Modern, big, sweet-fruited **09** (★★★★), showing tobacco & spice from effective oaking, seems riper, bolder & heavier than **08** - & a touch clumsier. — TJ

- **Bon Vino** see Boland Kelder

Boplaas Family Vineyards

Location: Calitzdorp ▪ Map: Klein Karoo & Garden Route ▪ WO: Calitzdorp/Coastal/Western Cape ▪ Est 1880 ▪ 1stB 1982 ▪ Tasting & sales Mon-Fri 8-5 Sat 9-3 ▪ Fee R20pp ▪ Closed Easter Fri & Dec 25 ▪ Cellar tours by appt ▪ Gifts ▪ Farm produce ▪ Walks/hikes ▪ Conservation area ▪ Ring of Rocks ▪ Owner(s) Carel Nel ▪ Cellarmaster(s) Carel Nel (1982) ▪ Winemaker(s) Margaux Nel (Dec 2006) ▪ Viticulturist(s) Johannes Mellet (Vinpro) ▪ 2,300ha/70ha (cab, ptage, shiraz, tinta barocca, touriga nacional, chard, cbard, sauv) ▪ 55% red 45% white ▪ BWI, IPW ▪ PO Box 156

Calitzdorp 6660 ▪ info@boplaas.co.za ▪ www.boplaas.co.za, www.coolbay.co.za ▪ S 33° 32'8.0" E 021° 41'1.9" ▪
T +27 (0)44-213-3326 ▪ F +27 (0)44-213-3750

Amid ongoing innovation (such as a 'chocolate' tinta barocca) by the Nel family, 5th
and 6th generations, Boplaas remains one of South Africa's pre-eminent port producers, reaffirmed by the annual string of competition accolades both for their
young wines and their market-ready releases. Regular trips by Carel Nel and
winemaker daughter Margaux to the Douro (climatically similar to their semi-arid
Klein Karoo) inspire and instruct: a recent highlight was sharing an 1863 vintage
Niepoort 'still in brilliant condition'. Marketer daughter Rozanne keeps an eye on
the big picture, including the Cool Bay range sourced from maritime vineyards. Says
proud father: 'We are a wine family.'

Family Reserve range

★★★★ **Shiraz** Previously we noted that svelte & balanced **07** was structured for few years cellaring, showed
lovely depth of fruit, leather & pepper seasoning; should be drinking well now.

★★★★ **Ring of Rocks** From cab, merlot, touriga, **07** (★★★★) dark & brooding, restrained, promised
slower evolution than **06**. This, all in range except Pinot Noir MCC, still selling, not revisited.

★★★★ **Cabernet Sauvignon-Shiraz 07** 60/40 duo from Bo-Langkloof/home vineyards elegant without
sacrificing ripeness.

Cabernet Sauvignon ★★★★ Well-toned **06** (★★★★) followed by slightly medicinal **08**, noted last time as
needing year/2 for muscular grip to relax. **Pinotage** ★★★★ From Stellenbosch grapes, **08** previously bright &
well composed, vanilla edge to mulberry fruit. **Pinot Noir Méthode Cap Classique** NEW ★★★★ Forthcoming, pale pink **09** champagne-method sparkling with bready/honeyed bottle-age notes, fair yeasty complexity;
lovely pinot noir weight but tad sweeter than usual for this style. Discontinued: **Sauvignon Blanc**.

Boplaas range

★★★★ **Hanepoot Reserve** ✓ **11** (★★★★★) fortified dessert more complex & persistent than last **09**.
Litchi, orange & raisin flavours coupled with measured sweetness ensure each mouthful is fresh & uncloying.

★★★★★ **Red Muscadel Vintners Reserve** Senior citizen **75** suave, engaging, with fully integrated dried
fruit flavour, tannin & alc. Tasted previously, not revisted, as for Cabernet Sauvignon, Merlot, Pinotage, Shiraz,
Tinta Barocca, Touriga Nacional, Cape Tawny Port Vintners Reserve, Cape Tawny Port, Cape Tawny Show Reserve,
Pink Port & Cape White Port.

★★★★☆ **Muscadel Reserve** ✓ Latest releases of fortified dessert thoroughly worthy of 'reserve' status.
10's shy gingery/grapey bouquet belies a beautiful acid structure, complex spicy & balanced palate (even at
213g/l sugar). Poise in a glass.

★★★★★ **Cape Vintage Reserve Port** ✓ Cape benchmark for this style. **09** another brilliant & ageworthy
vintage expression: black-as-night touriga, tinta & droplet souzão again show Old World restraint; taut, firm &
powerful, promises long & rewarding life. WO W Cape.

★★★★☆ **Cape Tawny Port** ✓ Sexy **NV** from tinta, touriga, souzão, latest bottling festooned with awards
including SAA's Port of the Year. Nutty & spicy from long ageing in barrel, wonderfully balanced, shows mere
hint of sweetness on the aftertaste. WO W Cape.

★★★★☆ **Cape Vintage Port** ✓ Xmas cake fruits & spice, tealeaf complexity make **09** a delight. Same
grapes as Reserve bottling but bigger fractions tinta & souzão, structured to reward 10+ years cellaring. WO W
Cape.

★★★★ **Cape Ruby Port** ✓ Shy **NV** raises the bar on previous bottling but needs time to realise its full
potential; soft, sweet & juicy, with just a nip of tannin on finish.

★★★★ **Cape Tawny Port Vintners Reserve** Tinta & touriga duo in **NV** 375ml bottle. Unctuous yet
sprightly, mocha flavours spiked with tangy citrus rind & deliciously warming swirl of peppery spirit.

★★★★★ **Cape Tawny Port** A tinta, touriga, souzão mix (90/8/2), **97** is the classiest of the tawny quartet.
Previously rich & sleek, infused with caramel, choc/orange & cinnamon, all elegantly focused by deft spirit integration (19.2%) from 12 yrs in old barrels. W Cape WO.

★★★★ **Cape Tawny Show Reserve** Same blend as **NV** Tawny but more sugar (105g/l) mid-2009
imparted greater richness, creamier tones to nut & citrus melange.

★★★★☆ **Chocolate Cape Vintage Port** ✓ Dark & tarry **09** (★★★★) is plump, with milk chocolate &
maraschino cherry lushness; firm tannins (auguring well for cellaring) & char on palate. For the hedonist, as was
08 with choc hint to pure black-plum fruit.

Sauvignon Blanc ☺ 🍴 ★★★ Grassy & brisk **11** for everyday enjoyment. **Viognier** ☺ ★★★ Apricot & rosepetal on aromatic **10**, attractive, not blowsy; dry & zesty early drinking.

Cabernet Sauvignon ★★ Savoury **08** had blueberry nuance & tight dusty tannin previously. **Merlot** ★★★ Briefly oaked, lithe **09** was prune & malt infused last time. **Pinotage** ★★★★ Light-textured **09** supple, well-composed plum & redcurrant sipper. **Shiraz** ★★★★ Polished tannins, dense plum centre, earth & floral notes on peppery **08**. **Tinta Barocca** ★★★ Lightly-wooded **09**, savoury, refreshing & friendly. **Tinta Chocolat** ★★★ 'New-style' tinta, flamboyant **10** oozes plum fruit, has lashings of chocolate flavour. One of the better-made & more convincing examples. **Touriga Nacional** ★★★★ Fragrant **09** more interesting than previous, with orange peel hint, vibrant red-berry acidity & fair grip. **Chardonnay Unwooded** 🈺 ★★ Quiet **11**, some nut, lemon & citrus tones, faint musky sweetness on finish. **Pinot Noir Sparkling** ★★ **11** pink & frothy cherry-flavoured bubbly with sweetish finish. **Hanepoot** ★★★★ Uncomplicated but delicious fortified dessert, toffee & ripe sultanas, zingy lime acidity makes **11** bright & refreshing. **Muscadel** ★★★★ Quiet raisin charm on **11** fortified winter warmer from white muscadel, uncloying but rather reticent for the style, unlike luscious & persistent **10** (★★★★). **Pink Port** ★★★ Tinta, touriga, souzão combo is tangy, with interesting watermelon suggestion. **NV**. **Cape White Port** ★★★ **NV** from chard, with ginger & melon appeal. Discontinued: **Blanc de Noir**, **Red Dessert**.

Cool Bay range
★★★★ **Sauvignon Blanc Reserve** ✓ Mineral & precise, **11** continues along path of step-up **10** with 'oystershell' & wet stone vivacity, lovely concentration & enduring flavour.

Reserve Shiraz NEW ★★★ Forthcoming tar on nose, oak char on palate of cool-climate **08**, lean & taut, with gentle red fruit. These all WO Coastal. **Sauvignon Blanc** NEW ★★★ Cool, green **11**, similar pebbly notes to sibling but fruitier, with hint of blackcurrant in aftertaste. — Panel

■ **Borg Family Wines** *see Painted Wolf Wines*
■ **Born & Bred in South Africa** *see BABISA - Born & Bred in South Africa*

Boschendal Wines   🏠 🍷 ☕ 📷 🍴 ♿

Location/map: Franschhoek ▪ WO: Coastal/Western Cape/Stellenbosch ▪ Est 1685 ▪ 1stB 1975 ▪ Tasting & sales daily May-Oct 9-4.30 Nov-Apr 10-6.30 ▪ Fee R20pp ▪ Closed Mar 21, Easter Fri, May 1 & Dec 25 ▪ Cellar tours daily 10.30, 11.30 & 3 ▪ Cheese platters on request ▪ Restaurant ▪ Facilities for children ▪ Tour groups ▪ Gifts ▪ Farm produce ▪ Conservation area ▪ Museum ▪ Owner(s) DGB (Pty) Ltd ▪ Cellarmaster(s) JC Bekker (1986) ▪ Winemaker(s) Lizelle Gerber (whites, 2006) & Thinus Kruger (reds, 2008), with Lionel Leibrandt (1999) ▪ Viticulturist(s) Stephan Joubert (2006) ▪ 2,240ha/200ha (shiraz, sauv) ▪ 3,100t/250,000cs own label 32% red 43% white 14% rosé 11% sparkling ▪ WIETA ▪ Private Bag X03 Groot Drakenstein 7680 ▪ cellardoor@dgb.co.za ▪ www.boschendalwines. com ▪ S 33° 52' 27.5"   E 018° 58' 34.4" ▪ **T** +27 (0)21-870-4200 ▪ F +27 (0)21-874-5130

With a winemaking history dating back to 1685, Boschendal has long been a showpiece for the traditional heritage of the South African wine industry. The focus here is on shiraz and sauvignon blanc, with a few tiers celebrating these varieties in different dress. Currently the standout wines are from shiraz and the excellent Grande Cuvée Brut (the 2007 was given joint top score in the 2011 Amorim MCC Challenge). The Reserve Collection range has been expanded with the addition of a Chardonnay and the revived Vin d'Or, while the 1685 range now includes a varietal Merlot. These wine ranges are well thought out, with each performing to expectations, conveying a sense of confidence at this grande dame presiding at the point where Franschhoek, Paarl and Stellenbosch meet.

Cecil John Reserve range
★★★★☆ **Shiraz** **09** follows fine **08** (★★★★★) with lovely white pepper spice & perfumed aromas. Palate exudes poised focus, fine tannins, excellent oak use & fresh acidity for harmonious whole. Subtle & long finish is hallmark of accomplished effort. WO Stbosch.

★★★★☆ **Sauvignon Blanc** Last tasted was restrained, vibrant, tangy **08**.

Reserve Collection
★★★★ **Cabernet Sauvignon** Last tasted was brooding, dark **03**.

★★★★☆ **Shiraz** Smart **09** in riper mould than flagship above, but still well composed. Tobacco, forest floor notes enhanced by fine vibrant red berry. Fresh red cherry follows, serving as foil to alcoholic weight & supportive oak; stays fresh & dry to the end. This & next WO Stbosch.

★★★★ **Grande Reserve** Ripe fruit profile on **09** combo cab & shiraz in fleshier mould than previous. Composed, plush & concentrated palate evolves to fine tannin finish. Polished oaking adds to weight.

★★★★ **Chardonnay** NEW Sophisticated **09** shows bright, restrained fruit, gentle toasty overlay leading to textured, fine & focused palate. Juicy flavours & good oak support rounds out end.

★★★★☆ **MCC Grande Cuvée Brut** Classically from chardonnay & pinot noir, **07** exudes charming baked apple & brioche with fresh appeal from delicate persistent mousse to long-lingering finish. Fine effort.

★★★★ **Vin d'Or** NEW ✓ **09** Natural Sweet dessert wine; intense grapey aromas, heather perfume, honey & hints of lavender. Pure fruit, with delicious sun-ripe viscosity. Welcome rebirth of old label.

Sauvignon Blanc 🍷 ★★★★ Subtle, clean & zesty entry to **10** has vibrant acidity balanced by good texture, ending with good focus & precision. WO W Cape. **MCC Le Grande Pavillion Brut Rosé** ★★★★ With pleasant salmon hue, latest **NV** has red berry lift leading to well balanced lively mousse & rounded softness.

1685 range

Merlot NEW ★★★ Lovely plums with coffee notes in support, leads to pleasantly juicy flavours & clean fresh acid lift on **09**. **Shiraz** ★★★ **09** hits the spot with smoky spice & wild berry fruit mix. Harnessed tannins end dry & rather firm. **Shiraz-Cabernet Sauvignon** ★★★★ Toasty rich-fruited **09** shows good harmony of cab's dark fruit & structure, complemented by shiraz spice & savoury thread. **Chardonnay** ★★★★ Oaky style will satisfy followers of rounded richer vanilla & toasty offerings. **10** leaves sweetish impression, but dry. WO W Cape. **Sauvignon Blanc Grand Vin Blanc** ★★★★ **10** riper in style than siblings above with fruit-forward tropical aromas, cut by zingy citrus acidity & soft send-off. **Chardonnay-Pinot Noir** ★★★★ Good example of this popular style. **10** mostly from chardonnay presents as a white with fresh crispness & hint of red berry.

Boschendal Favourites

Lanoy ★★★☆ Indeed an old favourite; **09** last year taut & elegant. **Blanc de Noir** 🍷 ★★★ Shy spicy nose with delicate florals. **10** in usual more winey than fruity mould. Good crisp dry food partner. **Chenin Blanc** ✓ 🍷 ★★★★ **10** good exposition of the variety, with floral perfume, ripe fruits followed by focused, pithy & fuller palate. **Boschen Blanc** 🍷 ★★★ Previously known as Blanc de Blanc. **10** proffers subtle fruity nose, rounded palate with a touch of pleasant sweetness. This, next, WO W Cape. **Le Bouquet** 🍷 ★★★ Delicately fragrant muscat whiffs, combine with soft off-dry entry rounded out by potpourri spice on pleasing **10**.

The Pavillion range

Shiraz-Cabernet Sauvignon ☺ ★★★ Shiraz dominated **09** shows good mix fruit & structure with fresh bounce keeping all well-knit. Oak in subtle support. This, Blanc, WO W Cape. **Rosé** ☺ 🍷 ★★★ Delicate floral intro with spicy whiffs on appealingly soft but dry-ending **10**; balanced & vinous. **Pavillion Blanc** ☺ 🍷 ★★★ Chenin-based **10** has soft fruit, with dash viognier adding spice. Good acid line combines with saline edge. — JP

■ **Boschetto** see Stellekaya Winery

Boschheim 🍷

Location/map/WO: Stellenbosch ▪ 1stB 2003 ▪ Tasting & sales by appt ▪ Owner(s)/winemaker(s) Andy Roediger ▪ 900cs 85% red ▪ PO Box 3202 Matieland 7602 ▪ andy@roedigeragencies.co.za ▪ S 33°51'54.9" E 018°50'10.5" ▪ **T +27 (0)21-808-3175** ▪ F +27 (0)21-886-4731

Andy Roediger, polymer scientist, phenolic ripeness expert and Cape Wine Master started this garagiste operation which has since expanded into a fully-fledged boutique winery. Grapes are bought in from his many contacts in the winelands. The range is ever-evolving: newcomer Muse was vinified with local businessman Mark Philp, who wanted to make his own wine. Next is a chardonnay.

Cabernet Sauvignon ★★★★ Less new oak than sibling, **09** is savoury & grassy rather than fruity; still withdrawn, would benefit from year/2 in bottle. **Muse** NEW ★★★★ 100% cab. Lots on offer in **09**, including juicy appeal, cassis & nutmeg/cinnamon spicing. Tannins are supple & integrated. **Merlot** ★★★ Red fruited **08** was last; youthfully shy, firm structure invited further cellaring. **Elemental Shiraz** ★★★ Plums & white pepper, sprinkle dried herbs, **09** has the palate freshness for food, but dry tannins require rich dishes. **Ella Marie** ★★★ Shiraz/cab blend (45/40, plus dollop merlot); last tasted **07** was soft & easy, with attractive cassis & cedar aromas. **Verdelho** ★★★ Individually styled **07** previously showed dried peach tones & obvious but balanced sweetness. **Viognier** 🍷 ★★★ Last was **08**, oak masked apricot flavour; good body, but acid low . — CR

Boschkloof Wines

Location/map: Stellenbosch ▪ WO: Western Cape/Stellenbosch ▪ Est/1stB 1996 ▪ Tasting, sales & cellar tours Mon-Fri 9-5 Sat 9-1 ▪ Fee R20 ▪ Closed Easter Fri-Sun, Dec 25 & Jan 1 ▪ BYO picnic ▪ Owner(s)/cellarmaster(s)/viticulturist(s) Jacques Borman ▪ Winemaker(s) Jacques Borman, with Reenen Borman (Jun 2010) ▪ 30ha/19ha (cabs s/f, merlot, shiraz, chard) ▪ ±80-120t/3-4,000cs own label 90% red 10% white ▪ PO Box 1340 Stellenbosch 7599 ▪ boschkloof@adept.co.za, info@boschkloofwines.com ▪ www.boschkloofwines.com ▪ S 33° 57' 37.0" E 018° 46' 11.8" ▪ **T +27 (0)21-881-3293 (office)/+27 (0)21-881-3268 (cellar)** ▪ F +27 (0)21-881-3032

Having his youngest son Reenen join him in the cellar last year was a career highlight for Stellenbosch cellarmaster and co-owner Jacques Borman. They're aiming for more elegance in their wines, with better expression of the Boschkloof terroir. 'We've all been through a period of ultra-ripe harvesting and high extraction; now we're moving back to lower alcohols and wines that are not so fully ripe.'

★★★★ **Syrah** Subdued red fruits, lilies & cream on bold but balanced **08**. Like all these reds, matured in oak, with a small percentage of the barrels new.

★★★★ **Conclusion** Last edition, powerful **06** Bordeaux-style blend needed time to harmonise.

★★★★ **Chardonnay ✓ 10** continues on the path blazed by rich **09**. A burst of citrus fruit, vanilla & nutty oak seasoning (though only older oak barrels used) lead on to a limy finish.

Cabernet Sauvignon ★★★★ 08 similar to brooding **06** (**07** skipped): extremely ripe yet not jammy, some leafiness & a tad unyielding. Allow time to soften. **Merlot ★★★ 07** not for the faint-hearted: big tannins & 14. 8% alc dominate gentle prune, malt & clean leather flavours. **Cabernet Sauvignon-Merlot ★★★★** Tasted last year, serious **08**'s restrained oaking left the fruit very alive. Discontinued: **Five Acres Shiraz-Viognier.** — CvZ

Boschrivier De Villiers Family Vineyards

Location: Stanford ▪ Map: Elgin, Walker Bay & Bot River ▪ WO: Overberg ▪ Est 1998 ▪ 1stB 2002 ▪ Tasting & sales Mon-Fri 8-5 Sat 9-5 Sun 10—1 ▪ Fee R5 ▪ Closed Dec 25 ▪ Light meals during tasting hours; or BYO picnic ▪ Gift shop ▪ Farm produce ▪ Conference facilities (20 pax) ▪ Walking/hiking & 4x4 trails ▪ 4-bedroom self-catering Farm House (sleeps 9) ▪ Owner(s)/viticulturist(s) Theodore de Villiers ▪ Winemaker(s) Clinton le Sueur (Jan 2010, Longridge) ▪ 14ha (cab, shiraz) ▪ 7t/ha 464cs own label 100% red ▪ Remhoogte Caledon p/a 70 Fairbairn Street Worcester 6850 ▪ drnjtdevilliers@mweb.co.za ▪ www.boschrivier.co.za ▪ S 34°23'19.4" E 019°37'51.0" ▪ **T +27 (0)23-347-3313/2 ext 3; +27 (0)76-736-0351** ▪ F +27 (0)23-342-2215

When Doctor Theo de Villiers inherited two farms between Stanford and Caledon in the late 1990s, it allowed him to fulfil a dream of making wine and he planted vineyards accordingly. To date, there has only been a shiraz but plans are afoot for a cabernet sauvignon.

★★★★ **Shiraz ✓** Youthful & moreish **08** shows red fruit & spice, medium body, well-expressed fruit, fresh acidity, fine tannins. 20 months in oak, 64% new. — CE

Bosman Family Vineyards

Location: Wellington ▪ Map: Paarl & Wellington ▪ WO: Wellington/Upper Hemel-en-Aarde Valley/Western Cape ▪ Est 1699 ▪ 1stB 2004 ▪ Tasting by appt ▪ Fee R50pp, waived on purchase ▪ Closed Easter Fri-Mon, Dec 22 to Jan 4 ▪ Sales Mon-Thu 8-5 Fri 8-4.30 ▪ Cellar tours by appt ▪ Conservation area ▪ Festivals: 'The Long Lunch' (Mar) & 'Release Weekend' (Sep) ▪ Owner(s) Bosman Family & Adama Workers Trust ▪ Cellarmaster(s) Petrus Bosman (Nov 2003) ▪ Winemaker(s) Corlea Fourie (Nov 2006), with Charlene Ferreira (Nov 2006) ▪ Viticulturist(s) Heinie Nel & Pierre Carstens (Jan 2000) ▪ 1,000ha/280ha (46 varieties r/w) ▪ 3,000t/10,000cs own label 70% red 25% white 5% rosé ▪ Other export brand: Appollis ▪ Brands for clients: Sainsbury Supermarkets ▪ Fairtrade, BWI ▪ PO Box 9 Wellington 7654 ▪ info@bosmanwines.com ▪ www.bosmanwines.com ▪ S33° 37'34.7" E019° 01'28.9" ▪ **T +27 (0)21-873-3170** ▪ F +27 (0)21-873-2517

Two-year-old Jan Bosman is the 9th generation on Lelienfontein farm, which dates back to 1699. Not mired in the past, the Bosmans look to the future with (among others) innovative blends, social media and marketing programmes, and strong Fairtrade support (see under Appollis Fairtrade). The wine team have access to an extraordinary palette of almost 50 varieties in the Wellington nursery and 'vineyard garden' in Upper Hemel-en-Aarde Valley. The Rosé, featuring 30 different grapes, was such a hit at 2011 J&B Met race day that it sold out.

Unique Innovation range

★★★★ **Adama Red** ✓ Just 'Adama' previously. Shiraz (81%) leads 5-way blend in **09**. Velvety mouthful of spicy plum compote, French/American oak, half new, adds backbone, exotic edge from mourvèdre & primitivo.

★★★★ **Adama White** NEW ✓ 🌣 Full bodied but lithe, dry & structured blend chenin & 4 others. **10** nectarine & lemongrass with light oak sheen, 30% new. Zesty nettle liveliness, long peppery finish. WO W Cape.

Single Vineyard range

★★★★ **Pinotage** 09 (★★★★) soft blueberry fruit & vanilla, wood (100% new, French/American) a bit strong mid-2011 & needs time to assimilate fully. **08** was more nuanced.

Cabernet Sauvignon ★★★★ **07** notch up on previous. Cassis & fynbos overlay, last year showed posture & elegance from French oak, 33% new. **Optenhorst Chenin Blanc** ★★★★ From chenin vineyard planted 1952, 4th oldest in SA. Last edition we noted creamy apricot & oatmeal on naturally fermented **09**, step up on previous.

Dolce Primitivo ★★★ Unusual sweet red from botrytised primitivo. Last time **07**'s spicy blackcurrant & cherry got dry tannin backbone from 2 years all-new extra-charred oak.

Bosman Family Vineyards range

30 Rosé NEW 🍽 🌣 ★★★ Ruby grapefruit & cranberry **10**, mix of 30 different varieties! Dry & zesty. Upper Hemel-en-Aarde Valley WO. — FM

■ **Bosman's Hill** *see* Saxenburg

Botanica Wines

Location/map: Stellenbosch ▪ WO: Banghoek/Citrusdal Mountain/Elgin ▪ Est/1stB 2008 ▪ Tasting by appt ▪ Wine sales Mon-Fri 8-5 ▪ Farm produce ▪ Conferences ▪ Walks/hikes ▪ Mountain biking trail ▪ Refreshments offered at Sugarbird Manor guesthouse (see Accommodation section) ▪ Owner(s) Virginia C Povall ▪ Winemaker(s) Virginia Povall (Jan 2008) ▪ Viticulturist(s) Johan Viljoen (Jul 2008, consultant) ▪ 21.6ha/5ha (cabs s/f, merlot, p verdot, pinot) ▪ PO Box 12523 Die Boord 7613 ▪ ginny@botanicawines.com ▪ www.botanicawines.com ▪ S 33° 54' 18.5" E 018° 49' 25.4" ▪ **T +27 (0)21-865-2313** ▪ F +27 (0)21-865-2326

The five star rating last year for her debut chenin had owner/winemaker Ginny Povall beaming. This edition another of her passions makes an entrance: an Elgin pinot noir. Quality grapes are sourced while young vines mature at Protea Heights flower farm and luxury guest house in Stellenbosch's Devon Valley, where New York-based Ginny spends the other (better?) part of her year. She incorporates organic and biodynamic principles in both viti and floriculture, goats recently being enlisted for weed control.

Botanica Wines range

★★★★☆ **Pinot Noir** NEW ✓ Stunning **10** from Elgin debuts with soft, spicy strawberries - a very delicate wine, well structured, carefully oaked (9 months, French) with perfumed sour cherry grip to lingering savoury conclusion. Regal, elegant, complemented by beautiful, thoughtful packaging.

★★★★★ **Chenin Blanc** ✓ Subtly sublime **09** followed by only marginally less brilliant **10** (★★★★★), also from ±50 year old dry-farmed bushvines near Clanwilliam. Delicate sweet floral & honeyed tones, minerals building in the mouth, part barrel ferment adding to harmony & promise of greater pleasure with time.

BIG Flower range NEW

★★★★ **Cabernet Sauvignon** ✓ Bright character of ripe dark berry fruit & sweet spice. **08** rich, medium bodied yet complex with a dusty, savoury finish which begs for simply grilled meat. Stellenbosch vines. — WB

Botha Wine Cellar

Location: Worcester ▪ Map: Breedekloof ▪ WO: Breedekloof/Breede River Valley ▪ Est 1949 ▪ 1stB 1974 ▪ Tasting & sales Mon-Fri 8–5 Sat 10–1 ▪ Closed Easter Fri-Sun & Dec 25 ▪ Cellar tours by appt ▪ BYO picnic ▪ Conservation area ▪ Soetes & Soup; Breedekloof Outdoor & Wine Festival ▪ Owner(s) Botha Wynkelder (Edms) Bpk ▪ Cellarmaster(s) Gerrit van Zyl (Nov 2007) ▪ Winemaker(s) Johan Linde & Michiel Visser (Nov 1996/Nov 1999), with Annamarie van Niekerk & Pierre Hugo (Dec 2009/Jan 2001) ▪ Viticulturist(s) Jan-Carel Coetzee (Nov 2010) ▪ 1,969ha (cab, cinsaut, chard, chenin, cbard) ▪ 29,778t/10,000cs own label 80% red 15% white 1% rosé 4% fortified; 900cs for clients ▪ ISO 22000:2009 ▪ BWI, IPW, WIETA ▪ PO Box 30 PK Botha 6857 ▪ admin@bothakelder.co.za ▪ www.bothakelder.co.za ▪ S 33° 34' 1.5" E 019° 15' 27.5" ▪ **T +27 (0)23-355-1740** ▪ F +27 (0)23-355-1615

Production may be large, but the emphasis for this Breedekloof giant's own range is on small batches of quality labels, now aiming at export markets. The corporate remodelling is complete; now the facilities are getting an upgrade. In the vineyards (all 1,800+ ha) conditions were tough last season, with weather extremes taking their toll.

Reserve range

Cabernet Sauvignon ★★★★ Big & gutsy **07**, blackberry fruit well matched by oak. Noted previously as worth cellaring few years.

Dassie's Reserve range

Dassie's Rood 🖿 ★★★ Juicy cranberries on **09** last year, with dash sweetness adding drinkability. **Dassie's Rosé** NEW 🖿 ◪ ★★ Semi-sweet **10** has floral scents with light berry fruit. **Dassie's Blanc** 🖿 ◪ Await next.

Botha range

> **Merlot** ☺ ◪ ★★★ Sweet-spicy **10** still oak-dominated but shows underlying ripe berry fruit. Light, unserious quaffer. **Sauvignon Blanc** ☺ 🖿 ◪ ★★★ **11** is fresh & vibrant, with aromatic fruitiness. Appealing rounded ripeness & solid body.

Cabernet Sauvignon ★★★★ **07** invitingly berry fruited, showed potential when reviewed. This & next 4 previously tasted. **Pinotage** ★★★ Ripe plum-fruited **09** last year was pleasingly juicy & drinkabile. **Shiraz** ★★★ **09** was smoky with spicy tones & succulent sipability. **Chenin Blanc** 🖿 ◪ Await new release. **White Light** NEW 🖿 ◪ ★★ Light, low-alc **10** shows green fruit on sweetish edge. **Chardonnay Brut** ★★★ Fresh lime notes to dry **NV** celebratory sparkler. **Red Jerepigo** ★★★ Oddly structured pinotage fortified dessert, **08** somewhat 'wild', with green-grass notes. **Hanepoot Jerepigo** ✓ ★★★★ Rich, honeyed nectar with beguiling grapey 'moskonfyt' fragrance, **08** reflects the pride of the region. Undiscovered treasure. Even more charming than sunshine-in-a-bottle **06**. **Late Bottled Vintage Port** Await next release. Discontinued: **Chardonnay**. — GdB

■ **Bottega Family Wines** see Idiom Wines

Bottelary Hills Wines

Location/map: Stellenbosch ▪ WO: Stellenbosch/Bottelary ▪ Tasting & sales Mon-Sat 9-6 Sun & pub hols 10-3 ▪ Closed Easter Fri, Dec 25 & Jan 1 ▪ Owner(s) Bottelary farmers ▪ Cellarmaster(s) Danie Steytler ▪ PO Box 35 Koelenhof 7605 ▪ bhwc@telkomsa.net ▪ www.bhwc.co.za ▪ S 33° 52' 34.6" E 018° 48' 47.2" ▪ **T +27 (0)21-865-2955** ▪ F +27 (0)21-865-2885

No new releases from this informal grouping of winemaker friends, guided by Kaapzicht's Danie Steytler. Wines are mostly in the everyday drinking category and serve to celebrate the terroir of Stellenbosch's Bottelary wine ward, best known for reds, sauvignon and chenin.

Pinotage Await new. **Shiraz** ★★★ We last tasted **03** whose seductive dark fruit should since have asserted itself. **Merlot-Cabernet Sauvignon** ★★ Last time we noted mature **02** ready to enjoy, with plummy appeal. **Cabernet Sauvignon-Pinotage** Untasted. **Hillside Red** 🖿 ★★★ Previously **07** 5-way merlot-led blend had savoury capsicum, plum & mocha tones. **Sauvignon Blanc** 🖿 ★★★★ Fruit-forward **09** for summer enjoyment when last tasted. **Chenin Blanc-Sauvignon Blanc** 🖿 Unready. **Limerick** 🖿 ★★★ Zippy **09** 50/50 mix sauvignon & chenin, was tart with pineapple ripeness. **Natural Sweet Chenin Blanc** Not ready. — JP

Bottelary Winery

Location: Paarl ▪ WO: Paarl/Western Cape ▪ Tasting & sales at Perdeberg Winery ▪ Owner(s) Perdeberg Winery ▪ Cellarmaster(s) Albertus Louw (Oct 2008) ▪ Winemaker(s) Riaan Möller (Dec 2006) & Carla Herbst (Jun 2008) ▪ Viticulturist(s) Jaco Engelbrecht (Nov 2011) ▪ PO Box 214 Paarl 7620 ▪ info@perdeberg.co.za ▪ www.bottelary. com ▪ **T +27 (0)21-869-8244** ▪ F +27 (0)21-869-8245

Previously a co-operative and one of the oldest cellars in Stellenbosch's Bottelary wine ward, then shut down for a period, Bottelary found a new lease on life when it joined Perdeberg Winery, where the wines are now made. A value-for-money brand, it can be found in selected Panarottis and Spur family restaurants.

Bottelary Winery range

Rosé☺🍽 ★★★ Vibrantly fruity, sweet, low-alcohol quaffer from pinotage. **NV**. W Cape WO, as for Semi-Sweet. **Soft Smooth Red**☺🍽🥛 ★★★ Tasty partygoer, plump off-dry **10**, smoky dark-fruit flavours.

Merlot 🍽🥛 ★★★ **10** ripe & juicy, touch of oak adds backbone, savoury note. These listed as 'Value for Money' range last time. **Classic Red** 🍽 ★★★ Cab/merlot **09** has meaty, dark-plum tones, smooth appeal. **Chenin Blanc** 🍽🥛 ★★★ Apple & pear freshness in **10** makes for perky summer fare. **Semi-Sweet** 🍽🥛 ★★★ Chenin-based **10** attractively fresh & thus not as sweet as name suggests. Discontinued: **Shiraz**. — CR

Bouchard Finlayson

Location: Hermanus ▪ Map: Elgin, Walker Bay & Bot River ▪ WO: Walker Bay/Overberg/Hemel-en-Aarde Valley/Western Cape ▪ Est 1989 ▪ 1stB 1991 ▪ Tasting, sales & cellar tours Mon–Fri 9–5 Sat 9.30–12.30 ▪ Fee R40pp for groups of 6+ ▪ Closed all pub hols ▪ Cheese platters ▪ Gift shop ▪ BYO picnic ▪ Conservation area ▪ Owner(s) Bouchard Finlayson (Pty) Ltd ▪ Cellarmaster(s)/viticulturist(s) Peter Finlayson (1989) ▪ Winemaker(s) Peter Finlayson (1989), with Chris Albrecht (Nov 2010) ▪ 125ha/20ha (barbera, nebbiolo, pinot, sangio, chard, sauv) ▪ 210t/16,500cs own label 25% red 75% white ▪ BWI, IPW ▪ PO Box 303 Hermanus 7200 ▪ info@bouchardfinlayson.co.za ▪ www.bouchardfinlayson.co.za ▪ S 34° 22'54.0" E 019° 14'30.9" ▪ **T +27 (0)28-312-3515** ▪ F +27 (0)28-312-2317

Knowing the origin of this Hemel-en-Aarde Valley property is key to understanding the wines. Burgundian Paul Bouchard and Peter Finlayson started it together in 1989 and Peter's passion for chardonnay and pinot noir deepened as a result and has never wavered. A range of four chardonnays and three pinot noirs bears testimony to that. He says: 'I approach my winemaking most of all with a desire to achieve structure and then balance, while taste will naturally follow.' Exports now reach 30 countries, and the accolades keep pouring in, most recently for both Kaaimansgat versions and for Galpin Peak, which got its highest ever Wine Spectator rating, 92 points. Interestingly, this guide's 5 star ranking is not for any of them but the unique and aromatic Hannibal, a blend of sangiovese and five other varieties.

★★★★☆ **Galpin Peak Pinot Noir** 🥛 Tasted from barrel, **10** already shows the class you expect from this label; succulent red berries & supple tannins, a polished, poised beauty. Retasted **09** (★★★★) shows better integration year later, spicy cherry fruit meshed with the oak. Not yet at full potential.

★★★★☆ **Tête de Cuvée Galpin Peak Pinot Noir** 🥛 Barrel selection & double new oak (75%) of siblings, **10** preview rich, dark styling: black cherries, mocha whiffs, but same sure hand captures the variety's finesse, balance, innate controlled power. Approachable but needs time to show its best.

★★★★☆ **Hannibal** 🥛 The blender's art in exceptional **10** (★★★★★), luscious dark fruit, nuances of liquorice, espresso, smoky notes. Wonderful palate appeal, juicy, sleekly curvaceous, lots of drinking pleasure. Half sangiovese, with pinot noir, nebbiolo, mourvèdre, barbera, shiraz, as was last **08**.

★★★★☆ **Kaaimansgat/Crocodile's Lair Chardonnay** Beginning with lime & passionfruit, an oak-influenced gentle hazelnut overlay, sleekly muscular **10** develops some minerality in the glass. More expressive than its stablemate, as delicious & admirable. Both from reputed Elandskloof vines (Overberg WO), like Sans Barrique.

★★★★☆ **Kaaimansgat Chardonnay Limited Edition** Citrus rind & buttered toast, **10** has forthcoming perfume but flavours are subtler: crushed almonds, a slatey note. Textured mouthfeel from 60% new oak portion. Masterly construction, layers of interest, speaks in a quiet but authoritative voice.

★★★★ **Missionvale Chardonnay** 🥛 A different style to other chardonnays from this cellar, upfront, more New World, **10**'s toastiness from barrel ferment/maturation a strong component, tropical fruit in support.

★★★★ **Sauvignon Blanc Reserve** Previewed last edition, now bottled, **10** continues to impress with its gooseberry flavours, gunflint smokiness. Bone-dry but palate weight & finish are extended by 14% semillon.

★★★★ **Sauvignon Blanc** ✓ 🥛 Fresh apples & pears, with a leafy, dill top note, pre-bottled **11** is in the prime of health. Tangy fresh, youthfully vibrant, deliciously food friendly. WO Hemel-en-Aarde Valley.

Galpin Peak Pinot Noir Unfiltered Limited Edition Not tasted. **Sans Barrique Chardonnay** ★★★★ Unoaked but 6 months lees-ageing gives **10** a creamy lime/fig leaf character. Good freshness, length, a match for seafood. **Blanc de Mer** ✓ ★★★★ Highly perfumed, courtesy of 71% riesling/viognier, previewed **11**'s flavours a melange of fruits, yet it's unexpectedly dry, elegant. WO W Cape. — CR

Boutros Wine

Location: Bot River ▪ Map: Elgin, Walker Bay & Bot River ▪ 1stB 2006 ▪ Tasting & sales Mon-Fri 9-4 Sat 9-1 ▪ Closed Easter Fri/Sun, Dec 25 & Jan 1 ▪ Owner(s) Pieter & Bonnie Meiring ▪ Winemaker(s) Niels Verburg (consultant) ▪ 2.6ha (cab, shiraz) ▪ 14t 100% red ▪ PO Box 622 Bot River 7185 ▪ boutroswine@mweb.co.za ▪ S 34° 10' 31.63" E 019° 13' 33.95" ▪ **T +27 (0)28-284-9871** ▪ F +27 (0)28-284-9871

Pieter and Bonnie Meiring wanted a product that can be produced on a small scale, yet provide sufficient income to cover costs; hence their decision to plant vines. While the blend will remain the flagship, they are encouraged by some experimental cabernet - 'a really special wine'. Look out for this, and a shiraz.

Shiraz-Cabernet Sauvignon ★★★☆ Last year, **06** showed refreshing acid, fine tannins & impressive length to rich, sweet fruit. — AL

Bovlei Cellar

Location/WO: Wellington ▪ Map: Paarl & Wellington ▪ Est 1907 ▪ Tasting & sales Mon-Fri 8–5 Sat 8.30–12.30 pub hols 9–4 ▪ Closed Easter Fri/Sun, Dec 25/26 & Jan 1 ▪ Cellar tours by appt ▪ Owner(s) 32 members ▪ Cellarmaster(s) Frank Meaker ▪ Winemaker(s) Frank Meaker, with Jacques Theron ▪ Viticulturist(s) Dawie le Roux (consultant) ▪ 920ha ▪ 8,000t/7m L 52% red 48% white ▪ PO Box 82 Wellington 7654 ▪ info@bovlei.co.za, wines@bovlei.co.za ▪ www.bovlei.co.za ▪ S 33° 38' 18.4" E 019° 1' 54.2" ▪ **T +27 (0)21-873-1567/+27 (0)21-864-1283** ▪ F +27 (0)21-864-1483

The grand old lady of the Hawekwa Valley in Wellington is in her 106th year and still going strong. The 'Centenary' labelling of the premium range, commemorating the 100th vintage, has given way to the new 'Vineyard Selected' line-up, with the extensive second tier now branded 'Lifestyle'.

Bovlei Vineyard Selected range

★★★★ Shiraz-Mourvèdre Last-tasted 60/40 combo **06** was star of line-up. Pepper, lily & dark plum notes mingled with gentle oak nuances.

Merlot ☺ ★★★ 07 more conventional than previous, generous juicy berry fruit. Light, gentle tannins.

Cabernet Sauvignon ★★★ Friendly **07**, succulent dark blackberries, oak-spice highlights, firm tannins.
Pinotage ★★★ Plum & mulberry-toned **08** had vanilla sweetness from sojourn in oak, good lingering grip.
Shiraz ★★★ Juicy **07** packed with ripe blackberries & savoury spices, refreshing acidity. These 3 tasted last time.

Bovlei Lifestyle range

Cabernet Sauvignon ☺ ★★★ 09 appealing cherry-juicy fruitiness with cheerfully light body. **Merlot ☺ ★★★** Ripe & full-bodied, **09** is robustly fruity & generous, with big tannins. Exuberantly enjoyable braai companion. **Pinotage ☺ ▨ ★★★ 10** shows lively well berry fruit with steely edge. **Gewürztraminer ☺ ▤ ▨ ★★★** Distinctive spicy floral scents on off-dry **10**. Try with spicy food. **Sauvignon Blanc ☺ ▤ ▨ ★★★ 11** is fresh, uncomplicated good value. Pleasantly dry & crisp. **Special Late Harvest ☺ ▤ ▨ ★★★** Straightforward, honest sweet chenin, **11** is fresh & crisp. **Hanepoot Jerepiko NEW ☺ ★★★** Opulent, spicy muscat fruit on **10** borne on honeyed sweetness. Satisfying fortified winter warmer.

Vin Rouge ▤ ★★ Ebullient **NV** poolside quaffer ex pinotage in 500ml bottle. Not retasted. **Shiraz ✓ ★★★★ 09**'s 16% alc somehow seems less massive in the glass than on paper, shows delightful Rhône-like pepper & wild herb character. **Pinotage Rosé ▤** Await next. **Rosé ▤** Untasted. **Chardonnay ▤ ★★** Mineral appeal on unwooded **10**, with hint of marzipan. **Chenin Blanc ▤** Await next. **Vin Blanc ▤ ★★ NV** easy picnic-style dry white in 500ml format. This & next 3 not tasted this edition. **Beaukett ▤ ★★★** Appealing tropical, floral notes & honey melon delights on **NV** from chenin (80%) & muscat d'Alexandrie. **Pinotage Rosé Sparkling ★★ 09** upbeat sweet carbonated bubbly from pinotage. **Port ★★** Plump, soft after-dinner treat. **NV**. — GdB

Bowwood Mountain Vineyards

Location: Paarl ▪ Est 2002 ▪ 1stB 2004 ▪ Closed to public ▪ Owner(s) Julian Johnsen & Bruce Jack ▪ Cellarmaster(s) Bruce Jack ▪ Winemaker(s) Bruce Jack & Adi Badenhorst ▪ Viticulturist(s) Julian Johnsen ▪ 5ha (cab, merlot, mourv, shiraz, chard, viog) ▪ 40t/1,100cs own label 100% red ▪ Voor Paardeberg Agter Paarl 7630 ▪ jjohnsen@telkomsa.net ▪ www.bowwoodwines.co.za ▪ **T +27 (0)21-869-8179** ▪ F +27 (0)21-869-8219

The joint venture between Agter Paarl-based Julian and Bridget Johnsen and Bruce Jack is quiet but not moribund. 'We made wine last year but it was snapped up in bulk - for a nice price,' says Julian Johnsen, also viticulturist at nearby Vondeling. Bruce Jack's day job of keeping the Accolade South Africa wines ticking over, several thousand cases at a time, precludes extra-curricular experimentation. The Cab-Merlot previously listed here can now be found under The Drift, the Jack family home-farm in the Napier area.

■ **Bradgate** *see* Jordan Wine Estate
■ **Brahms** *see* Domaine Brahms Wineries

Bramon Wines

Location/WO: Plettenberg Bay ▪ Est 2000 ▪ 1stB 2004 ▪ Tasting & sales daily 9-5.30 ▪ Fee R5 per tasting glass ▪ Closed Dec 25 ▪ Cellar tours by appt ▪ Restaurant: 11-5 daily ▪ Facilities for children ▪ Southern Crags Conservation ▪ Owner(s) Private company ▪ Cellarmaster(s)/winemaker(s) Anton Smal (Feb 2010) ▪ Viticulturist(s) Peter Thorpe (2000) ▪ 26ha/13ha (chard, sauv) ▪ 21t/2,200cs own label 100% white ▪ PO Box 1606 Plettenberg Bay 6602 ▪ accounts@bramonwines.co.za ▪ www.bramonwines.co.za ▪ S 33° 57' 20.30" E 023° 28' 45.02" ▪ **T +27 (0)44-534-8007** ▪ F +27 (0)86-589-6816

Last year marked a milestone for this white-wine boutique as their new cellar swung into operation – the first wines ever made in Plettenberg Bay. GM Danny van Deventer expects quality to rise even higher now they can set their own pace, and looks forward to new wines made from chardonnay and pinot noir.

The Crags Sauvignon Blanc ★★★ Light-bodied **11** has enough tangy herbaceous freshness for the richest seafood lunches. **Méthode Cap Classique** ★★★ Dry, fresh **08** bottle-fermented bubbly from sauvignon (unusually - most MCCs ex chardonnay &/or pinot noir). Crisp, clean & noted last time as great with sushi. —IM

Brampton

Location/map: Stellenbosch ▪ WO: Stellenbosch/Coastal/Western Cape ▪ Est/1stB 1996 ▪ Tasting & sales Mon-Fri 10-7 Sat 10-2 ▪ Fee R15/3 wines R25/5 wines R45 food & wine pairing ▪ Dec 25 ▪ Light lunches 10-4.15; snacks (cheese platters, pistachio nuts, biltong, olives, etc) & refreshments all day ▪ Owner(s) DGB (Pty) Ltd ▪ Winemaker(s) Thinus Krüger (Sep 2007) ▪ Viticulturist(s) Stephan Joubert (Nov 2006) ▪ 500t/40,000cs own label 40% red 55% white 5% rosé ▪ WIETA ▪ Private Bag X3 Groot Drakenstein 7680 ▪ brampton@dgb.co.za ▪ www.brampton.co.za ▪ S 33°56'17.42" E 018°51'38.08" ▪ **T +27 (0)21-883-9097**

Owner DGB has gone to town on Brampton, the brand it acquired from Rustenberg Wines in 2010 – literally: a Brampton Wine Studio, recently opened in the heart of Stellenbosch, offers tastings, sales, wine-and-food pairings, lunches, snacks, board games to accompany a glass or bottle of wine, and a venue for private functions. 'Green is the new black' here, with chalk and boards as promotional materials, rather than printed paper, and recycling and electricity saving a priority.

★★★★ **Cabernet Sauvignon** ✓ 🗏 Food-friendly **09** captures the variety's charm. Rich & layered, its focused fruit provides texture & structure for ageing.

★★★★ **Shiraz** 🗏 Savoury, earthy & leathery **08** (★★★★) is supple but lacks the ebullience of **07**.

★★★★ **OVR** ✓ 🗏 Well-made, juicy & accessible merlot-led Bordeaux blend, **09** rich fruit with underlying serious structure & oaking.

Unoaked Chardonnay ☺ 🗏 ★★★ Sampled from tank, **11** shows good varietal character. Fresh & juicy, if touch less rich than previous.

Rosé 🗏 ★★★ **10**, previewed last year, mainly from shiraz with merlot & cab. Cranberry flavour & lovely fresh acidity. This & Viognier WO Coastal. **Sauvignon Blanc** 🗏 ★★★★ Elgin & Stellenbosch grapes last edition combined in crisp & grassy **10** preview; lively, balanced, with hint of minerality. **Viognier** 🗏 ★★★ **09** last edition noted as less harmonious & engaging than previous, gentle & understated, faint apricot kernel hint. —MW

Brandvlei Cellar

Location/map/WO: Worcester ▪ Est 1955 ▪ Tasting & sales Mon-Thu 8-5 Fri 8-4.30 Sat 9-1 ▪ Closed all pub hols ▪ Conference facilities ▪ Owner(s) 19 members ▪ Cellarmaster(s) Jean le Roux (Aug 1995) ▪ Winemaker(s) Willie

Biggs (Sep 2009) & Daneel Jacobs ▪ Viticulturist(s) Danie Conradie (Sep 2004) ▪ 1,600ha (cab, ptage, chard, chenin, cbard, sauv) ▪ 23,500t 15% red 80% white 5% rosé ▪ PO Box 595 Worcester 6849 ▪ sales@bcwines.co.za ▪ www.bcwines.co.za ▪ S 33° 48' 19.5" E 019° 28' 8.1" ▪ **T +27 (0)23-340-4215** ▪ F +27 (0)23-340-4332

The spruced up labels on this Worcester cellar's good-value wines depict the surrounding mountains and their pinnacle, Jonaskop, frequently dusted with snow in winter. Viticulturist Danie Conradie last year oversaw limited grubbing up and replanting, and a small vineyard addition. 'In line with demand more white than red went into the ground, mostly chenin and colombard.'

BC Wines range

Shiraz Rosé ☺ 🇿 🄴 ★★★ Step-up **11** has juicy berry fruitiness, refreshing acid zing. **Chenin Blanc** ☺ 🇿 🄴 ★★★ Honey melon & apricot, bright acidity in **11** promise uncomplicated enjoyment. **Bacchanté** ☺ 🇿 🄴 ★★★ **NV (11)** from chenin raises the bar with fresh apple & grass, gentle sweetness. Perfect budget summer sipping, like most BC wines.

Cabernet Sauvignon 🄴 ★★★ Tutti-frutti **10** offers effortless drinkability but also pleasing weight & grip for food pairing. **Ruby Cabernet-Merlot** 🇿 🄴 ★★ Rum & raisin nuanced **10** has intense oak char aroma, slight spritz & hard tannin/acid end. **Chardonnay** 🇿 🄴 ★★★ Unoaked (& just bottled) **11** bursts with lemongrass & musk, zesty freshness for anytime enjoyment. **Sauvignon Blanc** 🇿 🄴 ★★ Understated **11** has quiet blackcurrant aromas/flavours, lots of freshness. **Hanepoot Jerepigo** 🄴 ★★★ **11** fortified dessert is intensely raisined but uncloying, dusted with nutmeg. — Panel

■ **Bredell's** *see* JP Bredell Wines
■ **Brederode** *see* Groupe LFE South Africa
■ **Breede Valley Wines** *see* Wedgewood Wines

Breëland Winery   🍴 🥢 🎋 ⛲ 📷

Location: Rawsonville ▪ Map: Breedekloof ▪ WO: Slanghoek ▪ Est 1825 ▪ 1stB 2010 ▪ Tasting, sales & cellar tours Mon-Sat by appt ▪ Fee R10 pp tour & tasting ▪ Closed Ash Wed, Easter Fri-Mon, Ascension Day, Dec 25 & Jan 1 ▪ Pre-booked lunches (5 days prior notice) ▪ BYO picnic ▪ Walking/hiking ▪ Mountain biking & 4x4 trails ▪ Conservation area ▪ Guest accommodation (mountain hut/B&B villa/farm house/camping) ▪ Owner(s) Kosie & Lizelle Marias ▪ Cellarmaster(s) Wickus Erasmus (Dec 2008) ▪ Winemaker(s) Wickus Erasmus (Dec 2008), with Jefry Fry (Jan 2009) ▪ Viticulturist(s) Wickus Erasmus / Kosie Marais ▪ 1,000ha/100ha (cab, cinsaut, ptage, shiraz, chenin, cbard, hanepoot, sauv, sem) ▪ 1,750t/250cs own label 20% red 80% white ▪ 250cs for clients ▪ Brands for clients: Kaap Agri ▪ PO Box 26 Rawsonville 6845 ▪ wine@boegoekloof.co.za ▪ www.buchukloof.co.za ▪ **T +27 (0)23-344-3129** ▪ F +27 (0)23-344-3671

The shared delight of co-owner Kosie Marais and winemaker Wickus Erasmus in developments on this newly renovated Slanghoek Valley wine farm and conservation area is palpable. Following selective and intensive vineyard plantings and cellar modernisations, came their 2010 Young Wine Show champion white blend (from 3-year-old sauvignon and chenin); the 2011 release of maiden bottlings; a regulation soccer pitch for staff; and triathlons and mountain bike marathons for 'active' nature lovers.

Breëland range NEW

Cabernet Sauvignon 🄴 ★★★ Delicate swan motif on label doesn't prepare for beefy wine within, **09** attractive mulberry flavour, racy freshness good foil for meaty stews. **Pinotage** 🄴 ★★★ Effortless **09**, juicy plum, mocha & hint vanilla, perfect pepperoni pizza partner. **Sauvignon Blanc-Chenin Blanc** 🄴 ★★ Guava & other ripe tropical fruit flavours, **10** easy to drink, refreshing sherbety aftertaste. — Panel

Brenthurst Winery   ▯

Location: Paarl ▪ Est 1993 ▪ 1stB 1994 ▪ Open to public only by special appt ▪ Owner(s) José Jordaan ▪ Winemaker(s) José Jordaan with advisers ▪ Viticulturist(s) Johan Wiese (1991, consultant) ▪ 5ha (cabs s/f, merlot, p verdot) ▪ 50-70t ▪ PO Box 6091 Paarl 7622 ▪ **T +27 (0)21-863-1154/1375** ▪ F +27 (0)21-424-5666

With returns on South Africa's bottled wine exports what he calls 'marginal' and no desire to sit on stock, Cape Town attorney-cum-vintner José Jordaan is happy to bide his time and leave his current three Brenthurst vintages (2009 on) in barrel until the general situation improves or he's made an offer he can't refuse.

■ **Brink Family** *see Pulpit Rock Winery*
■ **Bristle** *see Stonehill*
■ **Broad Reach** *see Devonvale Golf & Wine Estate*
■ **Broken Rock** *see Riebeek Cellars*
■ **Broken Stone** *see Slaley*

Brunia Wines

Location: Stanford ▪ Map: Southern Cape ▪ WO: Walker Bay ▪ Est 2005 ▪ 1stB 2009 ▪ Tasting & sales by appt Tue-Sun 10-4 & daily during holidays ▪ Closed Dec 25/26 ▪ Light lunches, picnics & tractor rides ▪ Self-guided hiking trails ▪ Mountain biking ▪ Conservation area ▪ Owner(s) W P du Preez ▪ Winemaker(s) Kobie Viljoen (Gabriëlskloof) ▪ Viticulturist(s) Andrew Teubes (consultant) ▪ 417ha/17ha (pinot, shiraz, chard, sauv, sem) ▪ 75t/2,800cs own label 16% red 84% white ▪ PO Box 368 Stanford 7210 ▪ info@bruniawines.co.za ▪ www.bruniawines.co.za ▪ S 34° 28'9.25" E 019° 39'42.60" ▪ **T +27 (0)28-341-0432** ▪ F +27 (0)86-669-6064

Baby steps patter on at Willie du Preez's Cold Mountain farm near Stanford, home of Brunia Wines. Pinot noir and chardonnay have been established 'for MCC purposes as well as single varieties' says the former Eastern Cape cattle farmer, tasting facilities have been upgraded, and (seasonally) light lunches, picnics and vineyard tractor rides are now offered. Willie's philosophy: 'To produce premium quality wines in harmony with nature at sustainable margins. That's a mouthful!'

★★★★ **Shiraz** ✓ Previewed last year, **09** now well-knit & elegantly proportioned. Smoky bacon, white pepper & clean leather make for suave & appealing solo sip or dinner companion.

Sauvignon Blanc ✓ 🍽 ★★★★ **10** flying high with British Airways & UK's prestigious Wine Society; white asparagus character & softer acidity distinguish it from other sauvignons from the area. — Panel

Buffalo Creek Wines

Location: McGregor ▪ Map: Robertson ▪ WO: McGregor/Malgas ▪ Est/1stB 2005 ▪ Tasting, sales & cellar tours Mon-Fri 9-6 Sat 9-12.30 Sun by appt only ▪ Closed Easter Sun, Dec 25 & Jan 1 ▪ Owner(s) Leroy & Mark Tolmay ▪ Cellarmaster(s)/winemaker(s) Mark Tolmay (Jun 2005) ▪ 1,328ha/30ha (p verdot, ptage, pinot, merlot, chard, chenin, cbard, sauv) ▪ ±350-380t/250-300cs own label 65% red 25% white 10% rosé ▪ PO Box 124 McGregor 6708 ▪ info@buffalocreek.co.za ▪ S 34° 0'2.97" E 019°53'11.94" ▪ **T +27 (0)23-625-1727** ▪ F +27 (0)23-625-1727

This boutique winery in McGregor is sending the youngest Tolmay family member, Mark jnr, out on the road to visit several safari lodges to try and capitalise on the Big Five connection. His ex-restaurateur father concentrates on winemaking whilst grandfather Leroy returns to his farming roots in the vineyards.

Merlot ★★ Meaty & brisk **07** tasted previously, not revisited, as all. **Pinotage** ★★ Last year **07** was strawberry toned with herbaceous flavours. **Dry Red** NEW Uncertified **NV** blend of pinot noir, petit verdot. Also NEW & not reviewed **Sweet Rosé** & **Crispy Dry White**. **Chardonnay** ★★★ **10** was fresh & very sippable last edition, with vivacious lime freshness. **Sauvignon Blanc** ★★★ Easy-drinking **10** previously was faintly grassy. — DB

■ **Buitenstekloof** *see Le Roux & Fourie Vignerons*

Buitenverwachting

Location: Constantia ▪ Map: Cape Peninsula ▪ WO: Constantia/Coastal ▪ Est 1796 ▪ 1stB 1985 ▪ Tasting & sales Mon-Fri 9-5 Sat 10-3 ▪ Closed all pub hols ▪ Cellar tours by appt ▪ Buitenverwachting Restaurant (see Restaurants section) ▪ Conference facilities ▪ Owner(s) Richard & Sieglinde (Christine) Mueller, Lars Maack ▪ Cellarmaster(s) Hermann Kirschbaum (Jan 1993) ▪ Winemaker(s) Brad Paton (Jan 2005) ▪ Viticulturist(s) Peter Reynolds (Jan 2001) ▪ 147ha/105ha (cab, chard, sauv) ▪ 500t/100,000cs own label 8% red 90% white 2% rosé ▪ PO Box 281 Constantia 7848 ▪ www.buitenverwachting.com ▪ S 34° 2'30.4" E 018° 25'1.5" ▪ **T +27 (0)21-794-5190/1** ▪ F +27 (0)21-794-1351

While Christine, this farm's flagship red wine, is regarded as among the Cape's best, some 90% of the farm's production is white, with Constantia's signature sauvignon blanc dominating. In a major replanting drive, other varieties are making way for sauvignon to play an even stronger role. Unlike many, the team here prefers younger vines for their sauvignon, saying 'they tend to produce the best quality'. Vines themselves are making way for indigenous vegetation and dams to attract insects and wildlife that will act as natural predators on unwanted bugs on the vines. Eco-friendly methods extend to generating power; external solar lights have been installed and solar panels for the cellar are being investigated. Renewable energy generally will be a focus of attention over the coming year.

★★★★ **Cabernet Sauvignon** Last yr austere **07** with fine, dark-berried fruit promised tannic grip would integrate, benefit from 3 - 4 yrs in bottle.

★★★★ **Cabernet Franc** Attractive, if not very complex, **08**'s light texture, soft core, fine tannins focus leafy, spicy fragrance, sweet fruit. Good now, further 2-3 yrs.

★★★★ **Merlot** Quiet dark fruits, cedary oak introduction to **08** (★★★★). Brighter ripe fruit flavours edged out by brisk acid in tail. No **07**; **06** fresh vibrant.

★★★★☆ **Christine** Refined cool-climate benchmark. Benefits of blending evident in **08** where cab, cab franc, merlot & a drop of petit verdot make a whole greater than the sum of the parts. Subtly complex; sweet flesh contrasted by well-balanced freshness, fine tannin. All-new oak seamlessly absorbed.

★★★★ **Chardonnay** Delicious buttered crumpet with lime marmalade nose tempts on seriously oaked **10**. Fruitier, zesty flavours fleshed out by creamy undertones.

★★★★ **G** NEW 🌿 G for gewürztraminer; no mistaking the distinctive yet unblowsy litchi, Turkish Delight aromas on **10**; smoothed by older oak, persistent & bone dry. WO Coastal.

★★★★☆ **Husseys Vlei Sauvignon Blanc 10** captured typical greengage, lime aromatics, crystalline mineral palate, emphasised on fantail finish. Noted previously as benefiting from few years.

★★★★☆ **Sauvignon Blanc** 🌿 Vintage rather than quality differences reflected here. Thus **11** shows the fruity succulence of the year; a bone-dry, bracing finish lengthens those juicy lime, grassy tones.

★★★★☆ **1769** Natural Sweet dessert from oaked muscat de Frontignan. Clean, long **08** tasted last year. New vintage unavailable for tasting. **07** (★★★★★) amazingly elegant.

Meifort ★★★★ Dusty overlay to spicy, fresh red fruit attractions on **08**. Bone dry with savoury richness aiding accessibility. Cab franc, petit verdot with merlot, cab. **Rough Diamond** Await next vintage. **Blanc de Noir** Await next. **Buiten Blanc** Await next of this reliable blend. **Batavia** ★★★★ 'White Blend' as tasted last year. Experimental riesling, oaked viognier, chenin blend. Freshness & silken viscosity on off-dry **09**. **White Blend** NEW 🌿 ★★★★ Temporary name for oaked chenin with unoaked semillon - latter batting above its 8% input. **10** ripe & rich, firm acid clips off-dry finish. WO Coastal. **Maximus** NEW ★★★★ Ripe tangerine flavours, sumptuous texture feature on persistent **09** sauvignon (86%), semillon mix. Just-dry. Older oak ferment. **Brut MCC** ★★★★ Touch more brioche character, richness on latest **NV** from chardonnay & pinot. Exuberant bubble, bright acidity provide refreshment. Discontinued: **Husseys Vlei Chardonnay**, **Rhine Riesling**. — AL

BurCon Wines

Location/map/WO: Robertson ▪ 1stB 2004 ▪ Tasting Tue-Fri 9-4 Sat 10-2 Sun by appt only ▪ Restaurant ▪ Conference facilities ▪ Farm produce ▪ Facilities for children & tour groups ▪ Walking/hiking & mountain biking trails ▪ Guided horseback trails ▪ Owner(s) Frans & Amanda Conradie, Renée Burger ▪ Winemaker(s) Christie Steytler (Feb 2004, Roodezandt) ▪ 234ha/25ha (ptage, shiraz, muscadel) ▪ 16t/1,250cs own label ▪ PO Box 86 Robertson 6705 ▪ info@nerinaguestfarm.com ▪ www.nerinaguestfarm.com ▪ S 33° 50'5.2" E 019° 45'55.3" ▪ **T +27 (0)23-626-2012** ▪ F +27 (0)23-626-2012

If it's a relaxing, wholesome holiday in the country you're after, you'll find it at this riverside Robertson guest farm with floating restaurant, horseback riding, hiking and mountain biking trails, fresh farm produce, and playfully named wine, made to spec by Christie Steytler at Roodezandt Wines.

Oompie se Oeps 🍴 ★★ **NV** (**09**) pinotage (85%) & shiraz (co-planted in error!) very sippable unwooded plummy fruit & spice mix. Like following, not revisited. **Miskien Christien** ★★★ Rich fortified red muscadel, **09** unctuous raisined & honeyed, in 2L pack. —Panel

Burgershof

Location/WO: Robertson ▪ Est 1864 ▪ 1stB 2000 ▪ Closed to public ▪ Sales: see intro ▪ Owner(s) HJ Reynecke ▪ Cellarmaster(s)/winemaker(s)/viticulturist(s) Hennie Reynecke (Jan 1979) ▪ 68ha (cab, merlot, muscadel r/w, ptage, ruby cab, shiraz, chard, chenin, cbard, sauv) ▪ IPW ▪ PO Box 72 Klaasvoogds River 6707 ▪ burgershof@barvallei.co.za ▪ **T +27 (0)23-626-5433** ▪ F +27 (0)23-626-5433

Having 'grown up in the vine and wine culture', it's the 'creativity of winemaking' that continues to inspire Hennie Reynecke. Father Ben's traditional Cape muscadels were once SA champion wines, but Hennie struck out with classic varieties and found a niche in Holland's Jumbo supermarkets, where he's currently selling most of the wines listed below. Sole SA stockists remain La Verne and Wine Boutique in nearby Robertson and Ashton respectively.

Burgershof range NEW

Pinotage ☺ ▤ ▨ ★★★ Youthful & brightly fruited, **10** juicy & generous with variety's firm braai-friendly tannins. **Sauvignon Blanc** ☺ ☺ ▨ ★★★ **11** fragrant, floral & fresh with vivacious green edge.

Merlot ★★ Mature **08** has forest floor, bouillon overlay to plum jam fruit, best enjoyed soon. **Reserve Shiraz** ★ Mature **07** starting to tire, Marmite & tealeaf, drink soonest. **Cabernet Sauvignon- Shiraz** ★★ Plum & prune-toned **09** for campfires & winter casseroles. **Chardonnay** ▤ ▨ ★★ Intended for those who enjoy 'a slightly heavier wine', **11** makes its 5% new oak go a long way but peachy fruit peeps through. — Panel

■ **Bush Camp** *see Landskroon Wines*
■ **Bushman's Creek** *see Wines of Cape Town*

Bushmanspad Estate

Location: Bonnievale ▪ Map/WO: Robertson ▪ Est 2000 ▪ 1stB 2006 ▪ Tasting & sales Mon-Fri 8.30–5 ▪ Fee R15/6 wines ▪ BYO picnic ▪ Walks/hikes ▪ 4-star B&B/self-catering cottages (see Accommodation section) ▪ Owner(s) Menno Schaafsma ▪ Cellarmaster(s)/winemaker(s)/viticulturist(s) Arthur Basson (Feb 2011) ▪ 52ha (cabs s/f, malbec, merlot, mourv, shiraz, sauv) ▪ 400t own label 80% red 15% white 5% rosé ▪ PO Box 227 Bonnievale 6705 ▪ info@bushmanspad.co.za ▪ www.bushmanspad.co.za ▪ S 33° 53'55.0" E 020° 11'46.7" ▪ **T +27 (0)23-616-2961** ▪ F +27 (0)23-616-3714

Recently appointed winemaker/viticulturist Arthur Basson describes every day at this Langeberg foothills property as a blessing. 'I keep everything as natural as possible to capture the unique character of our grapes,' he says. 'All winemaking processes are important. There are no shortcuts.' His wine style: New World fruit and Old World structure.

Bushmanspad Estate range

★★★★ **The Menno** Flagship **09** red fruit & spice, medium bodied & elegant, chewy tannins to accompany red meat dishes. Not retasted, as for all reds below.
Cabernet Sauvignon ★★★★ Well-put-together **09** judiciously oaked, satisfying & refreshing everyday red.
Cabernet Franc ★★★ **09** herbal edge to red fruit, unyielding tannins mid-2010 may since have softened. **Rosé** NEW ▤ ★★ Dusky pink **11** from shiraz, in reticent youth hints at creamy berry, gently sweet delights to follow.
Sauvignon Blanc ▤ ★★★★ Peppery notes to dust & khaki bush, **11** fruity & lingering with pebbly finish, lowish 12% alc ideal for summer refreshment.

Red Gold range

Cabernet Sauvignon ★★★ Appealing **07**, red fruit, fresh acidity, soft tannins last edition. Mainly exported to China, like next. **Shiraz** ★★★ Black berry & pepper bouquet, fine tannins on smart **07** sipper. — Panel

■ **Buthelezi** *see Signal Hill Wines*
■ **BWC Wines** *see Catherine Marshall Wines*
■ **Cabrière** *see Haute Cabrière*
■ **Café Collection** *see FirstCape Vineyards*

Café Culture

It's not only South Africans who enjoy this KWV coffee/mocha-redolent drink; Canadians and, in bag-in-a-box format, Swedes have taken to it too. In October 2011 it was joined by Café Culture Choc Mousse, a sparkling version, untried by us.

Café Culture range

Pinotage ▤ ▨ ★★ **10** espresso flavours ex-oak with peep of ripe red fruit. — AL

Calais Wine Estate

Location/WO: Paarl • Map: Paarl & Wellington • Est/1stB 2000 • Tasting by appt • Sales daily 8-1 • Guest accommodation • Owner(s) Calais Wine Estate shareholders • Winemaker(s)/viticulturist(s) Philip Costandius (consultant) • 28ha (cab, malbec, merlot, p verdot, ptage, shiraz, chard) • 50t/1,500cs 90% red 10% white • PO Box 9006 Klein Drakenstein 7628 • info@calais.co.za • www.calais.co.za • S 33° 42' 32.1" E 019° 1' 24.6" • **T +27 (0)21-868-3888, +27 (0)82-835-3511** • F +27 (0)21-868-1400

On this farm at the foot of the Drakenstein Mountains in Paarl they were growing grapes three centuries ago. The current owners are expanding the capacity of the cellar (more space, more tanks for Philip Costandius) as well as producing new wines from young vineyards of petit verdot, chenin blanc and sauvignon.

Cabernet Sauvignon ★★★ Unwooded '& unplugged' 06 showed succulent, lively fruit when tasted mid-09. Only Merlot and 'new' wines tasted for this edition. **Merlot ✓ ★★★★** Rustic, nicely mature 05 with plum, coffee & green olives, the flavour experience supported by firm but fine tannins. **Petit Verdot NEW ★★★** 08 shows molasses, black fruits & hint of green nettle. Rich & ripe but, again, some awkward acidity. **Pinotage ★★★** Fresh, drinkable, lightly oaked 06. **Shiraz ★★★** Unadorned fruit in 06, juicy smooth drinking. **Applause ★★★★** Serious oaking was apparent in 05's bold spicing, firm structure, matched by rich cab/shiraz fruit. **Bel Canto ★★★** 06 combo cab, shiraz, merlot had lovely drinkability; cassis with good oak support. **Cape Riesling ★★** Delicate 08, crisp & dry. WO Wellington. **Chardonnay** Await next. **Chenin Blanc NEW ★★** Easy 10 attractive & restrained, but a warming finish. **Sauvignon Blanc NEW ★★★** Light & easy, yellow-fruited, softish 11 from Stellenbosch. Also light, but greener 10 (★★) ex Paarl, with awkward acidity. — JPf

Calitzdorp Cellar

Location/WO: Calitzdorp • Map: Klein Karoo & Garden Route • Est 1928 • 1stB 1976 • Tasting & sales Mon-Fri 8-5 Sat 8-1 • Closed Easter Fri & Dec 25 • Cellar tours by appt • Tour groups • Farm produce • Picnics/meals by appt; or BYO picnic • Conference facilities • Succulent garden • Owner(s) 39 members • Cellarmaster(s)/winemaker(s) Alwyn Burger (1990) • Viticulturist(s) Johannes Mellet (2005, consultant) • 286ha (13 varieties, r/w) • ±4,000t/3,500cs own label 34% red 17% white 11% rosé 38% other • IPW • PO Box 193 Calitzdorp 6660 • manager@calitzdorpwine.co.za • www.calitzdorpwine.co.za • S 33° 32' 18.9" E 021° 41' 10.6" • **T +27 (0)44-213-3301** • F +27 (0)44-213-3328

'It was a good year,' says winemaker Alwyn Burger of the 2011 season, the dams of his owner-growers full and production up by 15%. There were extended plantings, too, mainly of chenin, with a little sauvignon blanc and pinotage going into new vineyards. Cherry on the top was last year's even more successful port festival.

★★★★ Hanepoot Fortified dessert; previewed & provisionally rated 11 (★★★), floral & overflowing with honey flavours but shorter, less complex than standout NV version we tasted last time.

★★★★ Hanepoot-Muskadel Reserve NEW ✓ ⏀ Fortified delight from equal portions muscats de Frontignan & d'Alexandrie, 10 pure fruit, great intensity & poise courtesy zesty acidity. Rivals the region's finest.

★★★★ Red Muscadel NEW ✓ ⏀ Smoke & geranium billow from red-fruited 10 fortified muscat; unctuous, mouthcoating but not cloying. Go on, spoil yourself.

★★★★ White Muscadel ⏀ Fragrant & spicy fortified dessert, 10 (★★★) attractive but shows a touch too much freshness, gear down from liquid sunshine 09.

Cabernet Sauvignon ★★★★ Not revisited 08, for early drinking; had ripe cab fruit, supple tannin, sweetish impression from 15% alc & oak vanilla last edition. **Merlot ⏀ ★★** Super-ripe dark berry fruit on 10 sipper, slightly astringent finish would suit rich meat dishes. **Pinotage ⏀ ★★★** Step up for vanilla-plum 10, smooth & very accessible. **Shiraz ★★** Ultra-ripe (15% alc) 09 is sweet & juicy but uncomplex. **Touriga Nacional ⏀ ★★** Plummy 10 juicy; brief farewell. **Rosé** Not tasted. **Chardonnay ▤ ⏀ ★★★** Very subdued 11 not quite up to speed of previous. **Sauvignon Blanc ▤ ⏀ ★★** Weight watcher's friend 11 is light (11% alc) if somewhat neutral. **White Muscadel NEW ⏀ ★★★** Lauded by SA Muscadel Ass & Young Wine Show, 10 sweetie in 500ml bottle unctuous & lingering, bursts with sultana & white peach. **Golden Jerepigo ★★★** Junior version of above Hanepoot-Muskadel Reserve. Latest NV bottling gorgeous sultana & mandarin appeal, rich & full mouthfeel. **Vintage Port ★★★** Equal touriga & tinta in 09, lavishly fruited & concentrated, extended dry finish. **Ruby Port ★★★** Latest NV same make-up as Vintage, seductive jam-chocolate notes layered with Xmas cake spice & marzipan, but not as smoothly sophisticated as previous. Discontinued: **Dry Red, Dry White**. — Panel

Callender Peak

Location: Ceres ▪ Est/1stB 2007 ▪ Closed to public ▪ Owner(s) MacDonald & Jeffrey families ▪ Cellarmaster(s)/winemaker(s) Johan Kruger (whites, Sterhuis 2007) & Clive Torr (reds, Topaz 2007) ▪ Viticulturist(s) Willem Mouton (1990) ▪ 2ha (cab, merlot, pinot, chard) ▪ 2t/200cs 50% red 50% white ▪ clive@topazwines.co.za ▪ **T +27 (0)21-855-5086** ▪ F +27 (0)21-855-5086

Just last edition, Johan Kruger was commenting on the amazing consistency of fruit from these Winterhoek Mountain vineyards. This year, co-winemaker Clive Torr observes wryly: 'Some years the birds decimate the grapes and there is no crop - nothing to report'. Such are the vagaries of living in harmony with nature!

★★★★ **Merlot** Deep & dark **07**, old-style leather, oak spice & juicy, plummy fruit. These reds all tasted pvsly.

★★★★ **Pinot Noir** Light-bodied, elegant **07** showed leafy red-berry fruit; supple & savoury with good tannic grip & spicy tail.

★★★★ **Chardonnay** Previewed **09** last yr was heavily oaky, rather dumb, but showed serious fruit lurking with intent.

Cabernet Sauvignon ★★★★ Leafy, savoury **07** dominated mid-2008 by all-new oak & astringent tannins - but fruit to balance, given time. — GdB

Camanga Wine & Olives

Location: Tulbagh ▪ Est 2003 ▪ 1stB 2005 ▪ Closed to public ▪ Owner(s) Colin & Charlotte Richardson ▪ Winemaker(s) Dewaldt Heyns (Feb 2010, Saronsberg) ▪ Viticulturist(s) Grant Clack (Jun 2003, consultant) ▪ 34ha/1ha (shiraz) ▪ 3t/200cs own label ▪ info@camanga.co.za ▪ www.camanga.co.za

Colin and Charlotte Richardson have endured a calamitous time on their tiny Tulbagh property recently: no 2009 (due to an error in the cellar) or 2010 (runaway cows destroyed the crop) but the accomplished Dewaldt Heyns of nearby Saronsberg oversaw production for 2011 which no doubt relieved some stress.

Camanga range
Shiraz Await next. — CE

Camberley Wines

Location/map/WO: Stellenbosch ▪ Est 1990 ▪ 1stB 1996 ▪ Tasting & sales Mon-Sat & pub hols 9-5 Sun 9-3 ▪ Fee R40 max (depending on wine choice), waived on purchase ▪ Closed Dec 25 & Jan 1 ▪ Cellar tours by appt ▪ Lunch/refreshments by appt; or BYO picnic ▪ Boule court for hire ▪ B&B guest cottage ▪ Owner(s) John & Gaël Nel ▪ Winemaker(s) John Nel, with Louis Koch ▪ Viticulturist(s) Jaco van der Westhuizen ▪ 7ha (cabs s/f, merlot, p verdot, ptage, shiraz, touriga) ▪ ±35t/3,200cs own label 100% red ▪ PO Box 6120 Uniedal 7612 ▪ john@camberley.co.za ▪ www.camberley.co.za ▪ S 33° 55' 8.9" E 018° 55' 58.3" ▪ **T +27 (0)21-885-1176** ▪ F +27 (0)21-885-1822

'We have decided to sell wines, called Prohibition, at the same cost per millilitre as beer at the local student pub,' says Stellenbosch boutique vintner John Nel. 'And it has worked brilliantly. But we are battling to keep up with the demand, as not only students are looking for a bargain.' A forthcoming attraction is a wine called The Fifth Element, a selection of the best barrels. Meanwhile the upgraded tasting room now has a snack bar, extra boules court, beer pub and video wall.

Camberley Wines range
★★★★ **Pinotage 09** (★★★★) oozes sweet, pungent plums. Rich, powerful & fruity. Firm tannic grip with a warming finish (16% alc). Trumped by **08**.

★★★★☆ **Shiraz** Bold, robust & inky **09** (★★★★) lacks complexity of **08**. Ripe, fully extracted dark fruit & spice fills the mouth. Well structured with firm tannins. Alc (just on 16%) well hidden.

★★★★☆ **Philosophers' Stone** Merlot-led Bordeaux blend **08** was classic Camberley last year: bold (alc 15%), opulent & velvet textured, hints of plum, lead pencil & vanilla oak.

★★★★ **Cabernet Sauvignon-Merlot** 2 vintages reviewed: **08** upfront bright New World fruit, bold & sweet, balanced oak & smoky conclusion. **09** same vein, firm tannin grip. Needs time to develop & show charms. Good food wines.

★★★★ **Charisma** ✓ Gorgeous mint, herbs & red berry flavours on classy **08** blend cabs sauvignon & franc (first since **04**). Juicy & balanced, smooth vanilla finish. Should age well.

Cabernet Sauvignon Reserve Await next **Elm Tree Merlot** Await next. **Sparkling Shiraz** ★★★ Rare shiraz bubbly. **04** (2 years longer than last-tasted of this vintage): bright cherry flavours, light & elegant, savoury & dusty finish. **Elixir Fortified Red** ★★★ Spirited port-style dessert from shiraz with a sweet finish on **05** tasted last year.

Prohibition range NEW

> Red ☺ 🍷 ★★★ NV easy-drinking quaffer from shiraz & pinotage, juicy & soft with earthy finish. **White** ☺ 🍷 ★★★ Bright & crisp NV from sauvignon; depth & full-flavoured grassy, lemony freshness; slips down easily. — WB

Cameradi Wines

Location: Wellington ▪ Est 1999 ▪ 1stB 2000 ▪ Closed to public ▪ Owner(s) Stelvest cc (Nic Swingler, Hendrik du Preez & Casper Lategan) ▪ Winemaker(s) Casper Lategan (Jan 1999) ▪ 2t/130cs 100% red ▪ 48 Bain Str Wellington 7655 ▪ cas@lategans.co.za ▪ **T +27 (0)21-873-1225** ▪ F +27 (0)21-873-4910

There's not been much acitivity in recent years in the cellar behind Casper Lategan's Wellington house, but a 2008 Shiraz has been bottled – not in time for us to taste, unfortunately.

Shiraz ★★★★ Last was previewed (and now sold out) **05**. Discontinued: **Cabernet Sauvignon-Shiraz**. — JPf

Capaia Wine Estate

Location/WO: Philadelphia ▪ Map: Durbanville, Philadelphia & Darling ▪ Est 1997 ▪ 1stB 2003 ▪ Tasting, sales & cellar tours Mon-Fri 8-5 Sat/Sun on request ▪ Closed all pub hols ▪ Tour groups ▪ Owner(s) Ingrid & Alexander Baron von Essen ▪ Cellarmaster(s) Bernabé Strydom (Oct 2006), assisted by Stephan von Neipperg (consultant) ▪ Winemaker(s) Adriaan Burger (Oct 2010) ▪ Viticulturist(s) Schalk du Toit (2009, consultant) ▪ 140ha/60ha (cabs s/f, merlot, p verdot, shiraz, sauv) ▪ 260t/13,000cs own label 85% red 15% white ▪ IPW ▪ PO Box 25 Philadelphia 7304 ▪ info@capaia.co.za ▪ www.capaia.co.za, www.capaia.com ▪ S 33° 42'45.9" E 018° 34'6.9" ▪ **T +27 (0)21-972-1081** ▪ F +27 (0)21-972-1894

While Bordeaux's Count Stephan von Neipperg consults on the reds, young Armin Tement from Austrian sauvignon producer Weingut Tement has been (successfully) working on raising the quality of the sauvignon. With the youngest vines now over a decade old, second label Blue Grove Hill has been phased out, expressing a determination to grow and vinify outstanding grapes.

Capaia Wine Estate range

★★★★☆ **ONE** Formerly 'Capaia'. Brooding **09** (★★★★) from merlot, can, cab franc, petit verdot plus 5% shiraz. Unyielding tannins mask ultra-ripe fruit, lacks freshness. **08** more impressive.

Merlot-Cabernet Sauvignon ★★★★ Softly ripe **09** blend redeemed by sufficient tannin structure to underpin sweet fruit flavours; firm, savoury conclusion. Same varieties as above. **08** (★★★★) more assertive. **Sauvignon Blanc** 🔎 ★★★★ Herbaceous previewed **11** big step-up from **10** (★★★). Has steely resolve. Firm acid controls fruit, light oaking adds dimension to austere food-style intended by winemaker. — IM

▪ **Cap du Vin** see Bellevue Estate Stellenbosch
▪ **Cape Elephant** see Lutzville Cape Diamond Vineyards
▪ **Cape Auction** see Jonkheer
▪ **Cape Avocet** see Rooiberg Winery
▪ **Cape Bay** see FirstCape Vineyards

Cape Chamonix Wine Farm

Location/map/WO: Franschhoek ▪ Est 1991 ▪ 1stB 1992 ▪ Tasting & sales Mon-Sat 9.30-4.30 Sun 9.30-4 ▪ Fee R15 ▪ Closed Dec 25 & Jan 1 ▪ Cellar tours by appt ▪ Mon Plaisir Restaurant T +27 (0)21-876-2393 ▪ Conservation area ▪ Fully equipped self-catering cottages ▪ Owner(s) Chris Hellinger ▪ Cellarmaster(s)/viticulturist(s) Gottfried Mocke (Sep 2001) ▪ Winemaker(s) Gottfried Mocke (Sep 2001), with Emul Ross (Jun 2011) ▪ 300ha/50ha (cabs s/f, malbec, merlot, p verdot, ptage, pinot, chard, chenin, sauv, sem) ▪ 220-250t/20,000cs own label 60% red 40% white ▪ IPW ▪ PO Box 28 Franschhoek 7690 ▪ marketing@chamonix.co.za ▪ www.chamonix.co.za ▪ S 33° 53' 60.0" E 019° 7'34.0" ▪ **T +27 (0)21-876-8400** ▪ F +27 (0)21-876-3237

This year celebrating two decades since its first vintage, Chamonix is a well-established feature of a rejuvenated industry. With a decade of continuous improvement since Gottfried Mocke took over both vineyards and cellar for the 2002 vintage, it now ranks high among that industry's elite, with a classic approach. Without discounting the achievements in the cellar (the innovative, unique approach to pinotage, for example), it seems that the major advances have been in the vineyards. Amongst the changes here have been higher-altitude plantings and working with compost and soil preparations to create more active organisms. Why? 'We have realised', says Gottfried, 'that if you really want to crack individual, site-specific wines, one needs to have the fruit quality to do this.'

★★★★ **Cabernet Sauvignon** ✓ Blackcurrant, lead pencil & leafy notes dominate this austere, fragrant, spicy & classic **09**, with an extra green lift from 10% cab franc. 50% new oak evident, but integrating.

★★★★★ **Pinot Noir Reserve 10** (★★★★★), our Red Wine of the Year, shows savoury cedar whiffs, with bright cherry & strawberry aromas powering through tealeaf cigarbox spice. Plush tannins, sweet berry notes. Integrated 80% new French oak; natural ferment. Even more vibrant & detailed than finely managed **09**.

★★★★☆ **Greywacke Pinotage** ✓ Sweet red fruit notes on still-oaky tank sample **09** (so rating remains provisional). Might prove less beguiling, intense than brilliant **08**. Earthy but slightly puckering. Intricate technique involves mix of early-picked & desiccated grapes. Includes 10% pinot.

★★★★☆ **Troika** Intense, unyielding **09**; spice-driven with 54% bright yet brooding cab franc, the sweeter cab & merlot bringing more fruit, texture. All-new oak still harmonising.

★★★★ **Chardonnay** Beautifully interwoven **10**, though still youthfully shy tasted from barrel; creamy breadth, with lemon brulée notes. Always a slow-evolving wine, but this plusher, less charry than **09**.

★★★★☆ **Chardonnay Reserve** Grapefruit & tropical notes the hallmark of this subtle, finely balanced classic. **10**'s aromas now morphing into grilled hazelnut, peardrop & spice. 80% new oak (standard version 50% new). Natural ferment brings sweet-citrus freshness, length. More luminous than **09**.

★★★★☆ **Sauvignon Blanc Reserve** ✓ One of the leading Cape examples of oaked sauvignon. **10**'s white peach & vanilla aromas herald profound, harmonious (though still integrating) flavours. Ageworthy, with 13% semillon contributing edginess, length. Showing less exuberance, more restraint than **09**.

★★★★ **Sauvignon Blanc** ✓ 🔲 **11** tasted from tank, but looks a touch off fine, last-tasted **09** (★★★★★). Crushed nettle, green fig aromas; extraordinary viscosity masks slight oaking, but a balancing zestiness.

★★★★ **MCC Blanc de Blancs** Finely styled **06** from chardonnay, tasted last year. Restrained classical freshness, with zesty, citrus notes, stony fragrance.

Rouge ✓ ★★★★ **09** as usual a savoury, merlot-led Bordeaux blend, showing tobacco, tealeaf & plum, with a fine-tannined structure. **Blanc** ✓ 🔲 ★★★☆ **11** sample shows light melon, apricot notes, good intensity, freshness & length. From chardonnay, chenin, sauvignon. — MF

Cape Classics   🍷🍷

Location: Somerset West ▪ Map: Helderberg ▪ WO: Western Cape ▪ Est 1991 ▪ 1stB 1996 ▪ Tasting by appt only ▪ Owner(s) André Shearer ▪ Winemaker(s) Bruwer Raats (May 2010) ▪ 120,000cs own label 50% red 50% white ▪ Other export brand: Beyond ▪ PO Box 1695 Somerset West 7129 ▪ info@capeclassics.com ▪ www.capeclassics.com, www.indabawines.com ▪ S 34° 4' 5.9" E 018° 53' 38.2" ▪ **T +27 (0)21-847-2400** ▪ F +27 (0)21-847-2414

Individual brands should lead the way into the American market believes US-focused Cape Classics, and their sweet red, Jam Jar Shiraz, is blazing a 100,000 case trail as the No. 1 South African brand. Plans for a similarly sweet white Jam Jar are in the advanced stage. A packaging revamp enforced by a US jam company had an unexpected spin-off (and additional exposure) when the new look was featured on the most visited packaging design website in the world, Dieline. Indaba not only continues to rake in best buy accolades, but also provides post-graduate funding for three Stellenbosch University winemaking students. Another Classic spin-off is a US-based outbound travel venture, with the winelands the main destination.

Indaba range

Merlot ☺ 🔲 ★★★ Easy drinker with plush plum fruit, **10** light cocoa concentration on platform of oak.
Chenin Blanc ☺ 🔲☺ ★★★ **11** fig & apricot zip, ideal zesty summer pool sipper. WO W Cape for all.

Shiraz 🍷 ★★★ Focused on enjoyment & texture, **10** tender blackberry & earth, middling body & grip from 5 months oak. **Jam Jar Sweet Shiraz** 🍷🖼 ★★ Easy glugger **10** continues the crowd pleasing fizzpop sweetness. **Chardonnay** 🍷🖼 ★★★ **10** keeps up the standard. Marmalade delicacy & light oak sheen. Creamy & lingering while also fresh & full. **Sauvignon Blanc** 🍷 ★★★ Light, crisp grapefruit & flint **10** not revisited. —FM

- **Cape Crossings** *see Arniston Bay*
- **Cape Diamond** *see Lutzville Cape Diamond Vineyards*
- **Cape Discovery** *see Waterstone Wines*
- **Cape Diversity** *see Withington*

Cape Dreams

Location/map/WO: Robertson ▪ Est/1stB 2009 ▪ Tasting & cellar tours by appt ▪ Owner(s) Bunty Khan ▪ Cellarmaster(s) André van Dyk ▪ 600ha (cab, merlot, ptage, shiraz, chard, chenin, sauv) ▪ 60% red 40% white ▪ ISO 9001, HACCP, BEE, BWI ▪ croftsales@telkomsa.net ▪ www.croftsales.co.za ▪ T +27 (0)21-531-2016 ▪ F +27 (0)88-021-531-2016

For Bunty Khan, owning and developing her wine brand is a dream come true – hence the name of this mainly export label. The wines are made in partnership with Rooiberg Winery, the aim being to offer quality at competitive prices, and a percentage of profits go to fund community upliftment projects.

Shiraz 😊 ★★★ One of several savoury reds in this line-up: tar & bacon combo in **09**, sprinkle of coriander, ripe flavour refreshed by acidity. **Chardonnay** 😊 🖼 ★★★ Citrus plus tropical tones on well-wooded, medium-bodied **10**, with creamy lemon butter aftertaste.

Cabernet Sauvignon 🖼 ★★ Vanilla sheen, herbal notes to fruit on firm **10**; ready, enjoy soon. **Merlot** NEW ★★ Spice & dried meat savouriness on food-styled **09**. **Pinotage** ★★★ Quaffable **09** has forward berry fruit, whiffs bouillon & banana, noticeable alc (14%). Pleasant but fading; drink up. **Pinotage Rosé** 🍷 ★★ Previously reviewed **09** was bone-dry, lightish. Small quantities, bottled on demand, as for Chenin Blanc. **Chenin Blanc** 🍷🖼 ★★ Last edition, **10** crisp & crunchy, apple fresh. **Sauvignon Blanc** 🖼 ★★ Effusive **11** intriguing white pepper nuance, plump fruit cushions brisk acidity for comfortable sipping. —Panel

- **Cape Elements** *see Nico van der Merwe Wines*
- **Cape Frizzante** *see Groupe LFE South Africa*

Cape Gable Wines

Location/map/WO: Stellenbosch ▪ Est/1stB 2009 ▪ Tasting, sales & tours by appt ▪ Fee R15 ▪ Closed all pub hols ▪ Owner(s) Chris & Daniël de Waal ▪ Cellarmaster(s)/winemaker(s)/viticulturist(s) Chris & Daniël de Waal (both Jan 2009) ▪ 55ha/50ha (cab, malbec, merlot, ptage, shiraz, chenin, sauv, viog) ▪ 385t/300cs own label 66% red 33% white ▪ PO Box 31 Vlottenburg 7604 ▪ info@capegable.co.za ▪ www.capegable.co.za ▪ S 33° 56' 29.3" E 018° 45' 59.9" ▪ T +27 (0)21-881-3700 ▪ F +27 (0)21-881-3700

Chris de Waal's fledgling venture, since the restructuring of the family estate, still maintains close ties with his siblings, while fashioning a new identity. The wines are made in the Uiterwyk Estate cellar in Stellenbosch Kloof, with brother Daniël consulting.

Cabernet Sauvignon ★★★ Forthcoming blackcurrant & spice on **08**, supple tannins complemented by fine fruit. This & next tasted last edition. **Pinotage** ★★ **07** had underlying plum/earth tones, drying tannins. **Sauvignon Blanc** 🍷 ★★★ Fresh, crisp & flavoursome **11** has appealing grassy notes. —GdB

- **Cape Grace** *see African Pride Wines*

Cape Hutton

Location/map: Stellenbosch ▪ Est 2003 ▪ 1stB 2004 ▪ Tasting, sales & tours by appt ▪ Deli & wine tasting 8-5 by appt (incl cheese, meats, jams & olives) ▪ Owner(s)/viticulturist(s) Gerrit & Lesley Wyma ▪ Winemaker(s) Piet Smal (cab), Wynand Hamman (sauv) & Hilko Hegewisch (merlot) ▪ 4ha (cab, merlot) ▪ PO Box 2200 Somerset West 7129 ▪ lesley@capehutton.com ▪ www.capehutton.com ▪ S 33° 58' 27.6" E 018° 51' 10.3" ▪ T +27 (0)21-880-0527 ▪ F +27 (0)21-880-0666

Dental specialist Gerrit Wyma and wife Lesley's property, nestled idyllically in the Blaauwklippen valley, derives its name from the soil type prevalent in the vineyards. The wines are made to order by a variety of well-known winemakers, including Fryer's Cove's Wynand Hamman and peripatetic dentist Piet Smal.

Cabernet Sauvignon ★★★★ Harmonious **08** showed classic cab aromas after **05** (★★★★). Blackcurrant, lead pencil & tobacco; firm tannic backbone; balanced, well-judged oak. **Merlot Rosé** 🍷 Await next. **Sauvignon Blanc** 🍷 ★★★ Cool green figs, grass, with riper tropical fruit on **09**, soft acidity, smooth citrus end. WO W Cape. **Veri Beri** ★★ **10** Natural Sweet from merlot. WO W Cape. None of these retasted. —GdB

■ **Capell's Court** see Linton Park Wines
■ **Cape Maidens** see Juno Wine Company

Capenheimer

South Africa's original perlé wine, launched in 1962. Made by Distell.

Capenheimer 🍷 ★★ Semi-sweet white, mainly chenin & colombard, **NV**. Lightly spritzy, with fresh green-apple flavour. Also 1.5L. —Panel

Cape of Good Hope

Location: Franschhoek ▪ WO: Citrusdal Mountain/Stellenbosch/Swartland/Overberg ▪ Tasting at Anthonij Rupert Wines (see entry) ▪ Owner(s) Johann Rupert ▪ Cellarmaster(s) Neil Patterson (Jan 2003) ▪ Winemaker(s) Dawie Botha (Jan 2005) & Christo Hamerse (Jan 1997), with Melanie Sauerman (Sep 2009) & Zanie Viljoen (Jan 2007) ▪ Viticulturist(s) Rosa Kruger (May 2004) ▪ (merlot, ptage, chard, chenin, sem) ▪ PO Box 435 Franschhoek Valley 7690 ▪ tasting@rupertwines.com ▪ www.rupertwines.com ▪ **T** +27 (0)21-874-9000 ▪ F +27 (0)21-874-9111

In its stylish but understated livery, and paying homage to those few people who have accepted responsibility as stewards of parcels of vines old enough to be considered 'venerable and old', this range fires the imagination. If you want to make your own pilgrimage, however, to meet these custodians and stand in the vineyards, best you realise a hired sedan won't do the job as it would in Bordeaux, Burgundy or the Loire; here you'll need a 4x4 – and a fast one at that – to keep pace with the no-nonsense viticulturist, Rosa Kruger, tasked with keeping a watchful eye on these gems. Also keep an eye out in the stores for Rhône-inspired white and red blends joining the line-up.

Parel Vallei Farmstead Merlot ★★★★ Step up for **07**; more restraint, less obvious power than spirity **06** (★★★★). Intriguing bouquet 'rock pool', iodine & curry leaf, slippery texture, chewy finish. New names for all in range; most reflect grower/source of fruit. This from Helderberg. **Basson Pinotage** ★★★★ **08** ex Swartland, similar to **07**: strawberry/acetone whiffs, juicy centre, measured (13.5% alc). Serious attempt though tad gruff, developed, probably not for keeping. **Serruria Chardonnay** ★★★★ Faint lemon & oatmeal on **10** from 10 year old vines in Elandskloof wine ward. Flavoursome, satisfying without being contrived; 11 months older oak add weight, subtle seasoning. Nudges next level. **Van Lill & Visser Chenin Blanc** ★★★★ **10** hinting at what this vineyard can achieve. Like exceptional Loire examples & **09** (★★★★), focus is on structure, not aroma. Taut, tempered, savoury, older oak in supportive role. **Laing Semillon** ★★★★ Judiciously oaked **10** raises bar on soft **09** (★★★★) with greater intensity, structure. Yellow peach/fennel hints, fine acid thread, presence & poise at moderate 13% alc. This & Chenin from Citrusdal Mountain. —CvZ

■ **Cape Orchards & Vineyards** see COAV
■ **Cape Original** see Origin Wine

Cape Point Vineyards

Location: Noordhoek ▪ Map: Cape Peninsula ▪ WO: Cape Point/Western Cape ▪ Est 1996 ▪ 1stB 2000 ▪ Tasting & sales Mon-Fri 9-5 Sat 10-5 Sun 10-4 ▪ Fee R10-R55 ▪ Closed Easter Fri, Dec 25 & Jan 1 ▪ Cheese/Antipasti platters available during tasting hours ▪ Facilities for children ▪ Farm produce ▪ Conservation area ▪ Owner(s) Sybrand van der Spuy ▪ Cellarmaster(s) Duncan Savage (Dec 2002) ▪ Winemaker(s) Duncan Savage (Dec 2002), with Jeremiah Mkhwanazi (Oct 2005) ▪ Viticulturist(s) Duncan Savage (Dec 2002), advised by Kevin Watt ▪ 60ha/32ha (cab, shiraz, chard, sauv, sem) ▪ ±232t/20,000cs own label 18% red 82% white + 2,450cs for clients ▪ Brands for clients: Bufo (Wine of the Month club), Foodbarn Restaurant, Woolworths ▪ BWI, IPW ▪ PO Box 100 Noordhoek 7985 ▪

info@cape-point.com ▪ www.capepointvineyards.co.za, www.splatteredtoad.co.za ▪ S 34° 5' 41.82" E 018° 22' 17.28" ▪ **T +27 (0)21-789-0900** ▪ F +27 (0)21-789-0614

Innovative techniques are always needed - just to keep the leaves and grapes on the vines, quips winemaker and surfer Duncan Savage, who masters wines and waves but not always the wind. Situated on the peninsula jutting out into the south Atlantic ocean, vineyards are buffeted by and (mostly) benefit from these cooling winds. The focus is on white wines and, a decade on, Duncan is now able to start selecting components for his acclaimed sauvignons and blends, in the vineyards rather than the cellar. He was one of the first South African winemakers to start experimentation with fermentation in clay amphoras, now fine-tuned to retain the wine's freshness. Perfect for enjoyment at the new picnic site on their Noordhoek farm.

Cape Point Vineyards range

★★★★ **Chardonnay** 🌱 Barrel-fermented **10** is more sumptuous than focused **09**. Still has succulent creamy texture with balancing lime & gooseberry flourish to complement spicy/fusion cuisine.

★★★★☆ **CWG Auction Reserve Sauvignon Blanc Barrel Fermented** NEW 🌱 Special **10** bottling, from low-yielding vineyards & full barrel treatment, is powerful & tightly woven. Core of intense lime fruit still masked by toasty butterscotch tone. Good structure & pedigree will handsomely reward cellaring.

★★★★☆ **Sauvignon Blanc Reserve** 🌱 Compelling **10** is riper & fuller than herbaceous **09**. Rich, creamy texture from full oak treatment doesn't detract from focused passionfruit & citrus fruit. Splash semillon adds extra zest. Mouthfilling, with good length.

★★★★ **Sauvignon Blanc** ✓ 🍷🌱 Elegant **10** has lovely fruit purity, with dash of semillon, as in **08**. (No 2009.) Greenpepper & fig flavours crisply balanced, with lightest brush of oak.

★★★★★ **Isliedh** 🌱 One of Cape's consistently highly rated white blends. **10** (★★★★★) is a sauvignon (75%), semillon mix. A clean flintiness adds tension to subtly oaked nectarine & lime flavours. Delicious, with good complexity & length, as in brilliant **09**.

Discontinued: **Semillon Noble Late Harvest**.

Splattered Toad range

Sauvignon Blanc ☺ 🍷🌱 ★★★ **11** fresh & crisp, this tangy quaffer's sales helps save the toads.

Shiraz-Cabernet Sauvignon 🍷🌱 ★★★ Ripe & hearty **10**, savoury & characterful. Enjoy solo or with a meal. WO W Cape for both; exported as 'Stonehaven'. — MW

Cape Promise

WO: Breedekloof ▪ Est 2002 ▪ Closed to public ▪ Owner(s) UK-based WaverleyTBS ▪ WaverleyTBS, Punchbowl Park, Cherry Tree Lane, Hemel Hempstead, Hertfordshire HP2 7EU ▪ elaine.taylor@waverleytbs.co.uk, julian. twaites@waverleytbs.co.uk ▪ www.waverleytbs.co.uk ▪ **T +27 (0)23-349-1110; 09-44-1442-206800** ▪ F +27 (0)23-349-1980; 09-44-1442-206888

This is the export-only brand for UK wholesaler WaverleyTBS, made to order at uniWines' Breedekloof winery (see entry), and aimed principally at the price-conscious restaurant and high street retail trade. Marketing centres on value and accessibility, with Fairtrade certification adding social credibility.

Cabernet Sauvignon-Merlot 🍷🌱 ★★★ Plummy, ripe, fruity **10** with hint of wood-spice. Undemanding, pleasant sipping. **Sauvignon Blanc** 🍷🌱 ★★★ Wild, aromatic **11** is palate- & budget-friendly. Commendable fruit intensity, lengthy finish. — GdB

▪ **Cape Reality** see Baarsma Wine Group

Cape Rock Wines

Location: Vredendal ▪ Map/WO: Olifants River ▪ Est 2001 ▪ 1stB 2002 ▪ Tasting, sales & cellar tours by appt ▪ Closed Easter Fri, Dec 25 & Jan 1 ▪ BYO picnic ▪ Owner(s) Willie Brand ▪ Cellarmaster(s) Willie Brand (Jan 2001) ▪ Winemaker(s) Willie Brand (Jan 2001) & Gavin Brand ▪ Viticulturist(s) Jeff Joubert (Jan 2001, consultant) ▪ 62ha/32ha (cab, grenache, merlot, mourv, ptage, roobernet, ruby cab, shiraz, chard, chenin, cbard, rouss, sauv, viog) ▪ 480t/250cs own label 75% red 25% white + 32,000 litres bulk ▪ PO Box 261 Vredendal 8160 ▪ caperockwines@gmail.com ▪ www.caperockwines.co.za ▪ S 31° 37' 24.0" E 018° 24' 52.9" ▪ **T +27 (0)27-213-2567** ▪ F +27 (0)27-213-5567

There are moves towards upping the percentage of white wine produced at this small West Coast family-owned winery, with a Rhône-style blend of viognier, grenache blanc and roussanne bottled last year by landscape architect Gavin Brand and his father Willie. Plans have been approved for a small cellar on another of the family's farms, where the winemakers will continue using 'simple, natural methods, which are ever harder to find'.

★★★★ **SMV** This, following, step up for this boutique producer. **09** shiraz, mourvèdre & viognier, co-fermented, dense & firm with scrubby savoury finish. Already elegant & composed, shows fine potential.

★★★★ **Capa Roca** NEW Once-off Portuguese blend touriga, souzão, dash tinta. **09** brooding cocoa & liquorice perfume, slippery & rich yet not porty. Delicious now, structure to improve 3+ years.

Cabernet Sauvignon ★★ Still-selling **09** not revisited, mid-2010 needed year/2 to knit, so should be more approachable now. **SGMV** ★★★★ Characterful **08** red blend shiraz, grenache, mourvèdre & viognier gave fine fruit expression last edition. **Red Shoe Cabernet Sauvignon** 🏷 Not reviewed. — Panel

■ **Cape Roots** see Quest Wines
■ **Cape Style** see Paarl Wine Company

Cape to Cairo Wines

Location: Cape Town ▪ Map: Cape Peninsula ▪ WO: Breede River Valley ▪ Est 2007 ▪ 1stB 2008 ▪ Tasting by appt ▪ Owner(s) Trans-Scripto (Pty) Ltd ▪ Winemaker(s) Nico van der Merwe (consultant) & Jolene Calitz-le Roux ▪ 3,500cs 100% red ▪ PO Box 1358 Cape Town 8000 ▪ sales@capetocairowines.com ▪ www.capetocairowines.com ▪ **T** +27 (0)82-579-4849 ▪ **F** +27 (0)86-660-4323

Inspired by the mystique of unexplored Africa in its labelling and image, Cape to Cairo shares resources with its sister brand, Emineo, also under the stewardship of intellectual property guru Otto Gerntholtz. Headline news for both is that the new tasting venue in the Cape Town city bowl has opened.

Syrah ★★★ Previously, **07** soft & accessible, very ripe fruit wrapped in sweet oak, lingering savouriness. — Panel

Cape Wine Works-Bardo Wines NEW

Closed to public ▪ Owner(s) Cape Wine Works (Pty) Ltd ▪ PO Box 36825 Chempet 7442 ▪ rein@ghib.com ▪ www.capewineworks.com ▪ **T** +27 (0)21-529-3990 ▪ **F** +27 (0)21-555-3033

Bardo means 'a space crammed with events and great significance'. The limited-release merlot and pinotage have a very special pedigree – the grapes are grown in the vineyards at L'Auberge du Paysan, owned by shareholder in this wine business Michael Kovensky, who also bottles wine under his Helderberg farm's name. And each variety that goes into the range of one-litre carton wine blends has been specially selected from the area most renowned for that particular variety.

■ **Cape Zebra** see Overhex Wines International
■ **Cappupinoccinotage** see Boland Kelder
■ **Cap Vino** see Winkelshoek Wine Cellar

Carisbrooke Wines

Location/map/WO: Stellenbosch ▪ Est 1989 ▪ 1stB 1996 ▪ Tasting & sales Mon-Fri 10-2 ▪ Closed all pub hols ▪ Owner(s) Willem Pretorius ▪ Cellarmaster(s)/winemaker(s) Kowie du Toit (1997), Willem Pretorius ▪ Viticulturist(s) Kowie du Toit (1997) ▪ 19ha/6ha (cab, sem) ▪ 50t/400cs own label 100% red ▪ PO Box 25 Vlottenburg 7604 ▪ willem@carisbrooke.co.za ▪ **T** +27 (0)21-881-3798 ▪ **F** +27 (0)21-881-3796 / +27 (0)86-518-8767

With his latest bottling, lawyer-winegrower Willem Pretorius continues to pay tribute to the ideals of the celebrated South African writer Alan Paton. Appropriate 'quality and equity', he says, are to be sought in the modest 250 cases of the wine he made from grapes off his small Stellenboschkloof farm.

Alan Paton Cabernet Sauvignon NEW ★★★ Varietally typical, pleasant-fruited **09**, with a little smokiness here & a vegetal touch there; decently balanced, but a drying effect on the finish recalls the 75% new oak. Discontinued: **Cabernet Sauvignon**, **Alan Paton Red Blend**. — TJ

■ **Carnival** see Orange River Wine Cellars

■ **Carpe Diem** *see* Diemersfontein Wines

Casa Mori

Location/map: Stellenbosch ▪ Est 1995 ▪ 1stB 2009 ▪ Tasting, sales & tours by appt ▪ Meals/refreshments by appt ▪ Farm produce ▪ Conferences/functions ▪ Artichoke Festival ▪ Owner(s) Eugene Mori ▪ Cellarmaster(s)/viticulturist(s) Bruno Julian Mori (1997) ▪ Winemaker(s) Bruno Julian Mori (1997), with Mori family ▪ 4.4ha/2.3ha (cab, malbec, sangio, syrah, viog) ▪ 5-8t/200cs own label 97% red 1% white 2% rosé ▪ Other export label: Mori ▪ PO Box 71 Koelenhof 7605 ▪ mori.wines@gmail.com, casamori@mweb.co.za ▪ www.casamori.co.za ▪ S 33° 53' 15.28" E 018° 48' 27.64" ▪ **T +27 (0)71-086-5003** ▪ F +27 (0)86-625-0080

Where there's an Italian, can olive oil, pasta and vino be far behind? Certainly not at Casa Mori Cucina, which offers all that as well as dolci. To top it off, there's Bruno the sangiovese/cab blend, which made it all the way to the 'Tomorrow's Stars' showcase tasting at last year's London International Wine Fair, to the delight of cellarmaster Bruno Julian Mori.

Bruno ★★★★ Unfiltered **NV** combo sangiovese/cab (78/22) elegant & dry when reviewed previously, attractive polished leather nuance, firm food-pairing tannins. — CvZ

■ **Casual Collection** *see* Bernheim Wines

Catch Of The Day

Location: Cape Town ▪ WO: Coastal/Stellenbosch ▪ Closed to public ▪ Owner(s) Cunicsar Vintners cc t/a Rainbow Nation Wines ▪ PO Box 44852 Claremont 7735 ▪ contact@rainbownationwines.com ▪ www.rainbownationwines.com ▪ **T +27 (0)21-671-6024/+27 (0)82-577-1608** ▪ F +27 (0)21-671-6036

This is the fastest-growing brand in a collection of wines sourced by a Cape Town-based negociant exclusively for restaurants and other on-consumption licensees. Other labels include The Shosholoza Collection, 100% Cape Town, Chef's Cellar and Gone Fishin'. Or the wines can be relabelled at no additional charge as restaurant house brands.

Shiraz ▤ ★★★ **08** one year on, more harmonious with accents of dark berries & liquorice. **Chenin Blanc** ★★★★ Bright apple notes last edition on balanced **10**, a characterful easy-drinker. **Sauvignon Blanc** ▤ ★★★ Fresh & lively **11**, attractive perfumes & crisp apple aftertaste. — DB

Cathedral Cellar

This range, which sits below The Mentors in the KWV hierarchy, has also benefited from the general improvement with more freshness, purer fruit and less overt oak. At its quality level, the range is the leading South African brand in Canada, Japan & Sweden. In South Africa it's available exclusively through TOPS at Spar.

★★★★ **Cabernet Sauvignon** Lovely vintage reflected in ripe yet firmly structured **09**. Modern, bright blackberry fruits; medium body, freshness, dry finish more traditional. 3-5 yrs potential.

★★★★ **Merlot 09** much improved on **07** (★★★). Ripely enticing red plum, mint choc tones; pure, silky & fresh with fine tannin, tapered fruity tail. All-new French oak well absorbed. No **08**.

★★★★ **Shiraz 09** (★★★★) clean, youthful & with light red fruits. Like **08** short on concentration, but less obvious oaking.

★★★★☆ **Triptych** Four rather than usual three varieties in **09** (★★★★); mainly cab, shiraz, splashes merlot, tannat. Friendly fragrant fruit steadied by minerally core, firm grip. **08** rich, savoury.

★★★★ **Sauvignon Blanc** ▨ Worthy example from difficult **10** vintage. Fragrant gooseberry, lemongrass medley; juicy succulence lifted & lengthened by mineral vitality. Clean, bone-dry finish.

★★★★ **MCC Brut** NEW Charming **09** from refreshing, lemony chardonnay with enriching 11% pinot noir. Fine, creamy mousse; properly brut. Potential to grow.

Pinotage ★★★★ Gentle pinot-like cherry fragrance on **09**. Smooth, fresh fruity flow to vibrant, light-tannin close. Harmonious & balanced. **Chardonnay** ★★★★ Big, bold style. **10** lashings of pickled lime, oak vanillins lacking subtlety, length. Sumptuous with very firm acid core. — AL

Catherine Marshall Wines

Location: Elgin • Map: Elgin, Walker Bay & Bot River • WO: Elgin/Swartland • Est/1stB 1997 • Tasting, sales & cellar tours by appt • Closed Easter Fri-Sun, Dec 25 & Jan 1 • Meals/refreshments by appt • Owner(s) Cathy Marshall, Greg Mitchell, Jonathan Oxenham & Jeff Jolly • Cellarmaster(s) Catherine Marshall (Oct 1996) • Winemaker(s) Shaun Fortuin (Jan 2010) • Viticulturist(s) Various • 40-50t/3,000cs own label 60% red 35% white 5% fortified • IPW • PO Box 30913 Tokai 7966 • cathy@cmwines.co.za • www.cmwines.co.za • S 34° 10'9.7" E 019° 0'29.8" • T +27 (0)83-258-1307 • F +27 (0)86-523-7479

Another move in Elgin sees Cathy Marshall on a farm with established vineyards and fully equipped cellar, which will allow for increased production and quality. 'It all came about two weeks before harvest and was pretty hair-raising to get sorted before grapes came in but well worth it!' First off the line is Marshall's distinctively Elgin sauvignon blanc from home vineyards. But clearly her first love is pinot noir. Why does wine matter? we asked. 'Wine, particularly pinot noir is like oxygen; without it, how do you survive?'

★★★★ **Pinot Noir** 🗒 **10** lighter vintage shows pleasant dark cherry aromatics, juicily fresh flavours & a nip of tannin. Benefits from being served properly cool.

★★★★ **Pinot Noir 6 Barrels Reserve 10** more introvert, viscous than regular version. Earthy notes, oak spice temper palate's brighter cherry flavours but ends distinctly savoury. Worth 2-3 yrs ageing.

★★★★ **SMG** Shiraz-led, homogenous trio (with mourvèdre, grenache). **09** shows freshness, purity associated with range. Ripe but unheavy; tasty savoury thread grows to expansive finish. WO Swartland.

★★★★ **Sauvignon Blanc** 🗒 Tasted just post-bottling, **11** captures Elgin's poise, minerality. Has weight to balance vivacity without spoiling fruit purity, length. **10** (★★★★) from Durbanville less balanced.

Merlot 🗒 ★★★★ Bright red fruits, juicy flavours noted last yr on **09**. Balanced tannin, oak, allowed for 2-3 yrs ageing. W Cape WO, as for Myriad. **Myriad** ★★★★ **07** showed toffee, nut tones last edition. Unheavy, clean fortified merlot/pinot; 3 yrs older oak. 69 g/l sugar. Discontinued: **Syrah**. — AL

■ **CCC Wines** *see* Bonnievale Cellar

Cecilia Wines

Location: Klawer • Map: Olifants River • WO: Western Cape • Est 2010 • 1stB 2007 • Tasting by appt • Owner(s) Cerina van Niekerk • Cellarmaster(s)/winemaker(s) Cerina van Niekerk (2007) • 2t/125cs own label 100% red • PO Box 23 Trawal 8147 • cecilia@mylan.co.za • www.ceciliawines.co.za • S 31° 51'32.16" E 018° 36'13.37" • T +27 (0)82-334-9422 • F +27 (0)86-617-0101

Klawer winemaker and concert pianist Cerina van Niekerk vinifies the Cecilia boutique wine for her own account (appropriately, it's named for the patron saint of music) in the Klawer cellar. While the 2010 harvest was 'satisfying', it wasn't good enough and she elected not to release it. Several changes to production were made in 2011, and she plans to tweak labelling to better differentiate her brand in a market where 'people choose wines in the supermarket as quickly as picking up a burger at a McDonald's Drive-Thru'.

Shiraz-Mourvèdre ★★★★ Loses malbec component in **11**, preview is very ripe but balanced, not at all warming - like last **06** (★★★★). Scrub highlight to the dark fruit, oak in supporting role. — Panel

■ **Cecil John** *see* Boschendal Wines

Cederberg Private Cellar

Location: Citrusdal • Map: Olifants River • WO: Cederberg/Elim • Est 1973 • 1stB 1977 • Tasting Mon-Sat 8-12; 2-4.30 pub hols 9-11.30; 4-5.30 • Fee R20 • Closed Easter Fri/Sun, Dec 25 & Jan 1 • Sales Mon-Sat 8-12.30; 2-5 Sun & pub hols 9-12; 4-6 • BYO picnic • Sanddrif Holiday Resort self-catering cottages; camping • Walks/hikes • Mountain biking • Conservation area • Rock climbing • Sport climbing • Observatory • Owner(s) Nieuwoudt family • Cellarmaster(s) David Nieuwoudt (Jan 1997) • Winemaker(s) David Nieuwoudt (Jan 1997), with Jan Taylor (Jan 2005) • Viticulturist(s) Ernst Nieuwoudt (Jan 1960) • 5,500ha/53ha (cab, shiraz, bukettraube, chenin, sauv) • 480t/26,000cs own label 50% red 50% white • PO Box 84 Clanwilliam 8135 • info@cederbergwine.com • www.cederbergwine.com • S 32° 30'12.8" E 019° 15'27.7" • T +27 (0)27-482-2827 • F +27 (0)86-531-0491

Representing the fifth generation of Niewoudts at this spectacular farm in the Cederberg Wilderness Area is David, who knows the highs and lows of winemaking. His home vineyards are no longer the absolute highest in the Cape (Sutherland now has higher ones) but very high – 'Vites Altae' proclaim the bottle capsules. He also makes wine from windswept vines in coastal Elim, about 1000 metres lower in altitude. Coolness is a crucial factor in both locations. Up high, new chenin and bukettraube vineyards have come into production and 'the bukettraube drought is nearly past'. One measure of the winery's success is the plan to massively extend and rebuild the cellar, as well as a new tasting centre. 'Visitors must be a little patient!' is the plea. But they can always look at the view.

Five Generations range

★★★★ **Cabernet Sauvignon** 09 in usual modern style: ripe, sweetly fruity (though dry) & oaky (all-new barrels). Undoubtedly impressive, with fruit power & structure to allow a good few years' maturation.

★★★★ **Chenin Blanc** 🔲 10 (★★★★★) even finer than 09. Richer, rounder than standard version, with floral complexity to the tropical notes, well supported by sensitive oaking (which adds a little nuttiness). Clean, dry & elegantly balanced, with a lovely ripple of fresh acidity.

David Nieuwoudt Ghost Corner range

★★★★ **Sauvignon Blanc** 🔳 This pair from Elim. 11 less fruity, more green, dusty & complex than home-grown version. Some might find it too bracingly austere; others will revel in the steely excitement.

★★★★ **Semillon** 🔳 In unkind vintage, 10 (★★★★) a little less substantial, greener-charactered than 09 (with dusty capsicum, lime). But bears new oak very well - might blossom with a year or 2 in bottle.

Cederberg Private Cellar range

★★★★ **Cabernet Sauvignon** 09 back to form after weaker 08 (★★★★). Sweet ripe fruit & oak showing, firmly built; on only slightly less powerful scale than top version, a little more approachable in youth.

★★★★ **CWG Auction Reserve Teen die Hoog Shiraz** 09 (★★★★★) the best yet, ripe-fruited but less showily so than 08, & carrying the all-new oak better. Concentrated flavours, impressive structure well balanced (on a big scale), with firm dry finish. Not exactly fresh, but lively enough.

★★★★ **Shiraz** Big, richly ripe, warm-fruited, oaky-spicy & extracted 09 not one for lovers of dry restraint, but will delight many others - especially after a few years in bottle.

★★★★ **Sauvignon Blanc** 🔲 11 seems almost fruity alongside Elim version, though fairly restrained in fact, with green fig & limy citrus in balanced whole - a touch green-sour on the bone-dry finish.

★★★★ **Blanc de Blancs** [NEW] Méthode cap classique from chardonnay. Mature biscuity notes from 4 years on lees mingle with citrus & pawpaw aromas on fresh, dry 06. Creamy texture, moderate depth & length.

Merlot-Shiraz ★★★★ Name change from 'Cederberg', 09 loses pinotage component, now 80% merlot. Ripe, sweetish flavours, decent structure - but unexciting. **Sustainable Rosé** 🔲 ★★★ Subtle, simple flavours on dryish 11 from shiraz, with a charming light charm. **Bukettraube** 🔲 ★★★ Perhaps less exuberant than previous, semi-sweet, 11 offers plenty of easy, fruity delight & doesn't quite cloy. **Chenin Blanc** 🔲 ★★★★ Tropical, showy aromas & flavours on fresh, tasty, dry-finishing 11. Deliciously, succulently piquant as ever. — TJ

Cellar Cask

Distell high-volume budget range, South Africa's first bag-in-box (1979), from widely sourced grapes. Available in 2L and 5L casks; also 750ml glass bottles.

Select Johannisberger Rosé ★★ Sweet, light & friendly NV, dollops ruby cab & pinotage for colour. **Select Johannisberger White** ★ Honey-tinged, sweet & fruity NV from chenin & colombard, dash riesling. **Select Johannisberger Red** ★ Surprising sweet/rough combo in spicy NV mix pinotage, ruby cab & cinsaut. —Panel

■ **Centennial** see Groupe LFE South Africa
■ **Chameleon** see Jordan Wine Estate
■ **Chamonix** see Cape Chamonix Wine Farm

Chanteclair Estate

Location/WO: Franschhoek • 1stB 2005 • 4-star L'Auberge Chanteclair Guest House • Owner(s) Chanteclair Estate (Pty) Ltd • Winemaker(s) DP Burger (Jul 2009) • 11ha/4ha (cab) • 200cs own label 100% red • PO Box 416 Franschhoek 7690 • chanteclair@mweb.co.za • www.chanteclair.co.za • T +27 (0)21-876-3685 • F +27 (0)21-876-2709

Replanting chenin and cabernet in these vineyards stretching up the mountainside behind the Franschhoek Monument continues. Chenin and shiraz will be the next additions to the wine range, giving guests at the Auberge Chanteclair a choice to sip as they stroll through the vineyards and admire the views down the valley towards the Simonsberg.

Cabernet Sauvignon ▤ ★★★ **09** less classic than previous, with uncomplicated dark berry fruit, medium body, & abundant dense, dry tannins. — AL

▪ **Chapel** *see* Robertson Winery
▪ **Chapel Cellar** *see* Zanddrift Vineyards

Chateau Libertas

Made uninterrupted since 1932, this Distell-owned paragon of value and drinkability turns 80 this year and gets a new label, but remains a cab-based blend.

Chateau Libertas ☺ ★★★ **09** & **10** tasted, both unpretentious but rewarding reds, lightly wooded. Creator Bill Winshaw would have been pleased with the consistency over 8 decades. Also in 5L. — Panel

Chateau Naudé Wine Creation

Location: Stellenbosch ▪ WO: Wellington/Coastal/Stellenbosch ▪ Est 2006 ▪ 1stB 2007 ▪ Closed to public ▪ Owner(s) Francois Naudé snr, Magda Naudé, Francois Naudé jnr, Melissa Naudé ▪ Cellarmaster(s) Francois Naudé (Jul 2007) ▪ 520cs own label 65% red 35% white ▪ Local/export brands: Le Vin de François, The Wingnut & nuts about ▪ 11 Weidenhof Street Stellenbosch 7600 ▪ naude@levindefrancois.co.za ▪ www.levindefrancois.com ▪ **T** +27 (0)21-883-8469 ▪ F +27 (0)86-651-3192

So much for retiring - ex-chemist and winemaker of two decades standing, Francois Naudé (along with his family) is busier than ever. This small family concern is as ambitious as many larger companies. 'My video talk' has been introduced on their website and the same facility will be used at the winery's annual auction, so buyers worldwide can participate live. Naudé's winemaking philosophy is far more down to earth: 'Wine is primarily made not to be sniffed and spat, but to be best enjoyed with food and friends.'

The Wingnut range NEW

★★★★ **Cabernet Sauvignon 08** satisfying example from lighter vintage. Bright, ripe cab fruit gripped by succulent grape tannin. Careful oaking enhancement. Good now & for 2-3 years. WO Stbosch.
Chardonnay ★★★★ Plush oatmeal & hazelnut features on **10**. Smooth yet fresh with fruitily dry tail. Barrel ferment, 25% new. **White Port** ★★★ Fruity, sweetish lightly oaked **10** from chenin. Natural ferment.

Chateau Naudé Wine Creation range

★★★★☆ **Le Vin de François 09** Rolls Royce of pinotages. Sleek & so well structured - tannins polished to a T — there's no feeling of heaviness despite core concentration of spicy, cherry fruit. Harmonious & classic. Wine ex 6 Stellenbosch farms, 1 Paarl. WO Coastal.

Nuts About range NEW

Shiraz Some promising dark spice, salami aromas on **10** from cask. Palate too unformed to rate. **Chenin Blanc** ▤ ★★★★ Quietly vinous **10** grows in flavour, textural richness, to clean, long finish. Modest 12.5% alc. — AL

▪ **Chatta Box** *see* Distell
▪ **Chef's Cellar** *see* Catch Of The Day
▪ **Cherry Hill** *see* Liquor World

Cheviot Winery

Location: Cape Town ▪ Map: Cape Peninsula ▪ WO: Stellenbosch ▪ Est/1stB 2004 ▪ Tasting & sales by appt Mon-Fri 9-12 ▪ Fee R20 p/p, refundable on purchase ▪ Closed pub hols & Christian religious days ▪ Owner(s)/winemaker(s) Elmari Swart & Jaap Scholten ▪ 150cs own label 100% red ▪ PO Box 5 Green Point 8051 ▪ winesales@cheviot-wines.com ▪ www.cheviot-wines.com ▪ S 33° 54' 59.06" E 018° 23' 43.61" ▪ **T** 082-553-4771, 082-698-4315 ▪ F 021-426 5889

There's been a change of thinking here, both in marketing and in winemaking. Co-owners and winemakers Jaap Scholten and Elmari Swart are holding their wines back, with the conviction that longer time in barrel improves their integration and longer in the bottle adds value, hence no wine release in this guide. And while conscious of the need to remain connected through social media, their marketing approach is increasingly more educational, through targeting private and corporate functions and tour groups.

★★★★ **Syrah** Last tasted was expressive & delicate **07** (★★★★★); had great purity, focus & resounding length. Improved on **06**. — CR

■ **Chris Keet** *see* Keets Wines

Christian Kuun Wines

Location/WO: Stellenbosch ▪ Est 2009 ▪ 1stB 2010 ▪ Tasting by appt ▪ Fee R20 ▪ Sales via 'Personal Wines' T +27 (0)21-552-6280, sales@baypointtrading.co.za ▪ Owner(s)/cellarmaster(s)/winemaker(s) Christian Kuun ▪ 140cs own label 100% red ▪ gumbootkuun@hotmail.com ▪ **T +27 (0)82-615-8105** ▪ F +27 (0)86-671-3363

'The wine will never have a single recipe,' says Christian Kuun, winemaker at Beau Joubert, of his own-label blend, though Stellenbosch cab will probably always feature, as he's 'a huge fan'. He'd had a lot of requests from family and friends to make his own wine. Finally, the birth of his son in 2009 inspired him to do so. 'Sales were slow initially and the financial strain from the capital invested had me bleeding. Luckily, when sales picked up they did so dramatically.'

Integra ★★★★ Tiny 140 cases of **09**, laudably not a blockbuster, just fine cab character, weight & depth; oak (though 75% new) complements the leafy, tobacco-fragrant blackcurrant fruit & lightish, open texture. — Panel

■ **Christina Van Loveren** *see* Van Loveren Private Cellar
■ **Christine-Marié** *see* Niel Joubert Estate

Christo Wiese Portfolio/CWP Wine Brands

Umbrella for businessman Christo Wiese's wine interests, including farms Lanzerac and Lourensford, and associated River Garden brand.

■ **Cilliers Cellars** *see* Stellendrift - SHZ Cilliers/Kuün Wyne
■ **Circumstance** *see* Waterkloof

Cirrus Wine Company

Map/WO: Stellenbosch ▪ Est/1stB 2003 ▪ Tasting & sales Mon-Sat 9-5 at Guardian Peak ▪ Fee R30 ▪ Closed Easter Fri/Sun, Dec 25 & Jan 1 ▪ Owner(s) Jean Engelbrecht & Ray Duncan ▪ Cellarmaster(s) Coenie Snyman (Jun 2010) ▪ Winemaker(s) Coenie Snyman (Jun 2010), with Schalk Opperman (Jun 2010) ▪ Viticulturist(s) Dirkie Mouton (Jun 2010) ▪ 5t/280cs own label 100% red ▪ IPW ▪ PO Box 473 Stellenbosch 7599 ▪ info@guardianpeak.com ▪ www.cirruswines.com ▪ S 34° 0' 44.31" E 018° 50' 33.22" ▪ **T +27 (0)21-881-3899** ▪ F +27 (0)21-881-3000

A joint venture between Ray Duncan of Silver Oaks Cellars in California and Jean Engelbrecht of Guardian Peak and Rust en Vrede - whose winemaker, Coenie Snyman, crafts the wine. Unsurprisingly the orientation tends to the plush, grand-scale American model, with its undeniable quality evidenced in the 2007 winning the Decanter regional trophy for Rhône variety.

★★★★ **Cirrus 09** from shiraz with a little viognier to augment perfume; opulent & polished, with super-ripe fruit. Flavour intensity holds the oak (60% new) & high alc (15.5%) with savoury aplomb. — MF

■ **Citrusdal Wines** *see* Six Hats

Claime d'Or

Location: Robertson ▪ WO: Robertson/Western Cape ▪ Est/1stB 2008 ▪ Tasting & sales at Rietvallei Wine Estate (see entry) ▪ Owner(s) Magriet de Wet & Bernardo Rapoport ▪ Cellarmaster(s)/winemaker(s) Kobus Burger (2002, Rietvallei) ▪ Viticulturist(s) Wilhelm Treurnicht (2007, Rietvallei) ▪ 10ha (cabs s/f, sauv) ▪ 30% red 60% white 10% rosé ▪ PO Box 2040 Parklands 2121 ▪ info@claimedorwines.co.za ▪ www.claimedorwines.co.za ▪

T +27 (0)23-626-3596/+27 (0)82-444-5473/+27 (0)82-567-5197 ▪ F +27 (0)23-626-4514/+27 (0)11-788-7346

The Sauvignon lived up to this Robertson boutique winery's name by claiming gold at Veritas last year, much to the satisfaction of the Burger family of Rietvallei, who manage the vineyards and make the wines, and Johannesburg-based owners Bernardo Rapoport and Magriet de Wet. A chardonnay and shiraz were launched as we went to press; a pinot noir is next.

★★★★ **Cabernet Franc** Previewed last edition, **08** now is a minty choc-berry delight with vibrant acid balance & fruit-filled conclusion.

★★★★ **Cabernet Sauvignon-Cabernet Franc** Listed in error as 'Cab Franc-Cab' last time. **08** now bottled & much improved. Beautifully integrated, fresh & herbal. Graceful companion at any dinner table.

Cabernet Sauvignon Rosé NEW 🍷 ★★★ Floral berry fragrance, cranberry flavours on **11** dry & savoury sipper. **Sauvignon Blanc** 🍷 ★★★★ Tasty **11** effusive & crisp, hallmark gooseberry this time mingles with cutgrass, zesty acidity & persistent end. Provisionally rated preview from Olifants River grapes. — Panel

Clairvaux Private Cellar

Location/map/WO: Robertson ▪ Est/1stB 2000 ▪ Tasting & sales Mon-Fri 8-5 ▪ Closed all pub hols ▪ Cellar tours by appt ▪ BYO picnic ▪ Owner(s) Wouter J de Wet snr, Wouter J de Wet jnr ▪ Cellarmaster(s) Pieter van Aarde (Dec 2004) ▪ Winemaker(s) Pieter van Aarde (Jan 2004) ▪ 200ha (cab, merlot, ptage, shiraz, chard, chenin, cbard, muscadel, sauv) ▪ 4,000t/500cs own label 40% red 40% white 5% red 15% white red + 2.5m L bulk ▪ PO Box 179 Robertson 6705 ▪ clairvaux@lando.co.za, appelsdrift@lando.co.za ▪ www.clairvauxcellar.co.za ▪ S 33° 48' 13.8" E 019° 52' 21.1" ▪ **T** +27 (0)23-626-3842 ▪ F +27 (0)23-626-1925

The De Wet family winery, a bulk wine producer bottling a smidgen under its own brand, is exploring alternative packaging 'to give people more for less', says Pieter van Aarde, a winemaker who believes 'wine makes friends' and whose life's highlight remains being at the birth of all three his little boys (the latest end 2010).

Sauvignon Blanc ☺ 🍷 ★★★ Spice & grass highlights to **11**'s sweet-sour flavours, exuberant mouthful. **Port** ☺ ★★★ Step up for **07** from ruby cab. Savoury nuance to dark chocolate & brandy pudding flavours; full body & firm tannins grab your attention.

Cabernet Sauvignon ★ Fruit-shy **09** firm, oak dominated. **Shiraz** ★★ Easy-drinking **08** lightly fruited, tad woody & developed. **Sand berg Purple** ★★ Cabernet, shiraz, merlot equal partners in aromatic **10**. **Chardonnay** ★★ Toasty **10** lemon curd & baked apple, charry tail. **Appelsdrift Dry White** 🍷 ★★★ Previously tasted, cheerful **NV** zesty quaffer from colombard. **Soleil** In abeyance. **Rosé** 🍷 ★★ **10** gently sweet & juicy; muscadel & colombard, shiraz for colour. **Good Night Irene** ★★★ Fortified fireside charmer from hanepoot tasted last edition. **10** honey & full-ripe raisins cleansed by zesty citrus. **Madonna's Kisses Golden Muscadel** ★★★ Fortified white muscadel, **10** bursts with uncomplicated sunny sweetness, could do with more zest. — Panel

Cloof Wine Estate

Location/WO: Darling ▪ Map: Durbanville, Philadelphia & Darling ▪ Est/1stB 1998 ▪ Tasting & sales Mon-Sat 10-4 ▪ Closed Easter Fri-Sun, Dec 25 & Jan 1 ▪ Cellar tours by appt ▪ Meals/refreshments Tue-Sat 10-3 ▪ Farm produce ▪ Conservation area ▪ Game & eco drives by appt ▪ Owner(s) Cloof Wine Estate (Pty) Ltd ▪ Winemaker(s) Christopher van Dieren (Jan 2002), with Frederick Kalumpie (Apr 1999) ▪ Viticulturist(s) Peter Duckitt (May 2004) ▪ 1,300ha/166ha (cabs s/f, cinsaut, merlot, ptage, shiraz, chard, chenin, viog) ▪ 600t/50,000cs own label 88% red 12% white ▪ BWI champion ▪ PO Box 269 Darling 7345 ▪ info@cloof.co.za ▪ www.cloof.co.za ▪ S 33° 28' 58.1" E 018° 31' 23.4" ▪ **T** +27 (0)22-492-2839 ▪ F +27 (0)22-492-3261

'Exports are doing well,' says Willem Wentzel, marketing manager, 'and our wines are flying off the shelves from Bryanston to Lithuania.' New labels have been launched and once again the creative energy behind the Cloof team is evident in the eye-catching packaging. The successful South African online shop has been duplicated in the UK, aimed at creating a close relationship with consumers internationally. The success of the annual Rocking the Daisies music festival on the property continues. As well as a wedding venue, visitors are able to enjoy leisurely lunches at the Cloof Kitchen.

Cloof range

★★★★☆ **Crucible Shiraz 06** (★★★★) last impressed with peppery dark fruit, prosciutto layers but was less harmonious than concentrated **04**; no **05**. This, Lynchpin & Duckitt not reassessed this edition.

★★★★ **Lynchpin** Named for vital cab franc role in merlot-led blend: 29% in last-tasted **06**. Interesting sipper, should be showing well now.

★★★★ **Duckitt Merlot-Cabernet Sauvignon** ✓ **07** was crafted with care, cedar-infused from serious oaking. Harmonious & lithe tannins should support 6+ years ageing.

> **Cab Cult Cabernet Sauvignon** NEW ☺ ★★★ Bright cassis, juicy blackberry, smoky oak on smooth & easy-drinking **09**. **Happy Dragon Pinotage-Shiraz** ☺ 🍴 ★★★ **10** unadorned juicy black plum fruit, enough bite to be food friendly. Unoaked. **Rosy Darling** ☺ 🍴 ★★★ **11** crammed with berries, comfortably dry for fun summer sipping. **Happy Dragon Chenin** NEW ☺ ★★★ Gentle apple & marzipan on friendly **10** picnic sipper. **Daisy Darling Chenin Blanc-Sauvignon Blanc** ☺ 🍴 ★★★ Cheerful **11** picnic wine from chenin, sauvignon, summer's day delight: tropical fruit, zippy acidity, dry tail.

Pinotage ✓ ★★★★ 2 vintages reviewed: **08** with juicy dense plums, touch of chocolate, mouthfilling & rounded savouriness. To drink soon. **09** younger sibling oozes fresh juicy plums & spice, shows lovely balance. **The Very Posh Pinotage** NEW ✓ ★★★★ **09** offers juicy plums, spice & chocolate notes, mouthfilling & silky with perky smoky end. Good everyday drinking. **The Very Sexy Shiraz** ✓ 🍴 ★★★★ Sweet & succulent **09** packed with sweet spicy black fruit, dusted with fynbos, pepper & vanilla. Finishes with chunky dry bite. **Cellar Blend** 🍴 ★★★ All-sorts red blend from press juice in preview **09**; dark, brooding berries, chunky solid finish; extracted fruit needs hearty food. **Inkspot Vin Noir** ✓ 🍴 ★★★★ Ever-popular pinotage, shiraz, cinsaut mix, **09** delights with succulent plums, fresh berries & vanilla oak conclusion. Yum! **Kalumpie & Co** ✓ ★★★★ **05** married cab, shiraz, merlot in medium-bodied anytime red last edition. Crunchy berry fruit, taut tannins, refreshing acid lift. **The Dark Side Cabernet Sauvignon-Shiraz** ✓ 🍴 ★★★★ Smoke-infused **08** nicely structured: fleshy, rich black berry fruit, smooth entry, firm finish. Appealing savoury tone. Stock up! **Summertime Sauvignon Blanc** NEW ★★★ From tank, **11** bursts with tropical fruit, zippy & fresh summer sipper. Funky packaging! **The Very Vivacious Viognier** ★★★ Just 'Viognier' previously. Fragrant peach & apricot intermingle with creamy vanilla on part-oaked off-dry **11**. **40 Days Natural Sweet** 🍴 ★★★★ Listed as 'Chenin Blanc Natural Sweet' previously & noted as exuding barley sugar, peach & lime; barrel-aged **09**'s richness lifted by tangy acidity. — WB

Clos Malverne   🍴🍷☕🏠📷

Location/map: Stellenbosch ▪ WO: Stellenbosch/Western Cape ▪ Est/1stB 1986 ▪ Tasting & sales Mon-Sat 10-5 Sun 10-4.30 ▪ Fee R25/4 wines ▪ Closed Easter Fri, Dec 25 & Jan 1 ▪ Cellar tours Mon-Fri ▪ Restaurant: lunch Tue-Sun ▪ Tour groups ▪ Gifts ▪ Farm produce ▪ Conferences ▪ Walks/hikes ▪ Wellness Day Spa ▪ Owner(s) Seymour & Sophia Pritchard ▪ Cellarmaster(s)/viticulturist(s) Suzanne Coetzee (Oct 2010) ▪ Winemaker(s) Suzanne Coetzee (Oct 2010), with Mynardt Hitchcock (1999) ▪ 27ha/18ha (cab, ptage, sauv) ▪ ±200t/40,000cs own label 50% red 50% white ▪ PO Box 187 Stellenbosch 7599 ▪ info@closmalverne.co.za ▪ www.closmalverne.co.za; www.capeblend.co.za ▪ S 33° 54' 38.0" E 018° 48' 49.2" ▪ **T +27 (0)21-865-2022** ▪ F +27 (0)21-865-2518

2011 heralded a quarter century of vintages for this picturesque, visitor-friendly estate in Devon Valley. The strong suit here has always been pinotage, in its various guises, and this year sees the release of (surprise) a coffee-flavoured version. Newly appointed winemaker Suzanne Coetzee presided, also embarking on the estate's first MCC sparkling project, from shiraz grapes, which they hope to release in three years time. The swish new restaurant is now open for lunch on Sundays.

Clos Malverne range

★★★★ **Pinotage Reserve** Inky, intense & spicy **09** proclaims its provenance: ripeness of vintage shows, with satin tannin cloak on sumptuous black berries. Youthful but focused, needs time.

★★★★ **Sophia Limited Release** Silky, elegantly shaped **08** cab/merlot is cut above other labels. Appealingly dry & focused, medium bodied, showing ripe, healthy fruit. Only 2nd Ltd Release in producer's history.

★★★★ **Auret** Pioneer Cape Blend is perennially classy. Cab-driven (65%, 25% pinotage, rest merlot) **09** follows form, with ripe, healthy fruit reflecting vintage. Fresh, spicy & nicely balanced.

★★★★ **Auret Limited Release** NEW Small-production reserve release, **08** (similar ratios to sibling) shows little more weight, lots more oaky spiciness. Hard to justify extra cost, but honest effort to raise bar.

Merlot NEW ★★★★ **09** shows promising ripe plummy fruit with rounded body. Bit of edgy acidity, but good varietal form. **Le Café Pinotage** NEW ★★★ Exaggeratedly mocha-flavoured **10** newcomer, appealing to some palates. Ripe & well-formed, but hard to take seriously. **Cabernet Sauvignon-Merlot** ★★★

Unexpectedly lean, ungenerous **09** still retains good balance & texture. Food-friendly profile, begs red meat partnership. **Cabernet Sauvignon-Shiraz** ★★★ Rather chewy, oak-spiced **08** lacks wow factor. **Chardonnay** ★★★★ **10** follows previous elegant, mineral style. Commendably restrained oak, but lighter body reflecting vintage. Robertson vines. **Sauvignon Blanc** 🍴 🔲 ★★★★ Spicy, asparagus-rich **10** has impressive weight & intensity. Shows unusual ripeness for vintage, with food-friendly acidity. Discontinued: **Shiraz**.

Devonet range

Merlot-Pinotage None since **07**. Discontinued: **Chardonnay**.

Heron's Nest range

Cabernet Sauvignon-Pinotage Not tasted, as for **Chardonnay**. — GdB

Clouds Vineyards

Location/map/WO: Stellenbosch ▪ Est/1stB 1993 ▪ Tasting & sales Mon-Sat 10-5 ▪ Fee R10 ▪ Closed Easter Fri-Mon, Dec 25 & Jan 1 ▪ Breakfast, lunch & dinner by appt for non residents/visitors ▪ Clouds Estate Guesthouse & Self-catering Chalets (see Accommodation section) ▪ Conferences ▪ Weddings & functions ▪ Chapel ▪ Owner(s) Bernard & Petro Immelman ▪ Cellarmaster(s) Neil Moorhouse (Jan 2010, Zorgvliet) ▪ Winemaker(s) Neil Moorhouse (Jan 2010, Zorgvliet), with Bernard Immelman (Jan 2010) ▪ Viticulturist(s) Wynand Pienaar (Aug 2009, consultant) ▪ 4.5ha/2.5 ha (sauv) ▪ 24t/1,000cs own label 100% white ▪ PO Box 540 Stellenbosch 7599 ▪ bernard@cloudsestate.co.za ▪ www.cloudsestate.co.za ▪ S 33° 55' 23.9" E 018° 55' 29.7" ▪ **T +27 (0)21-885-1819** ▪ F +27 (0)21-885-2829

High up in the Helshoogte Pass, rubbing shoulders with the chic super-wineries of the area, Bernard and Petro Immelman run their beautiful guest-house and functions venue, while their wines are made at neighbouring Zorgvliet. This year they're looking for ways to cut production costs to keep their wines affordable.

★★★★ **Sauvignon Blanc** ✓ 🔲 Single-vyd free-run **11** shows precise focus without frills. Fully ripe, fruity & aromatic, yet restrained & elegant, with perky acid lingering on finish.

Pink Sauvignon Blanc 🔲 ★★★★ Addition of 4% shiraz transforms otherwise identical sibling. **11** seems rounder, juicier & softer than pure sauv. Prettier too. — GdB

Clovelly Wines

Location/map/WO: Stellenbosch ▪ Est/1stB 2000 ▪ Tasting, sales & tours strictly by appt ▪ Owner(s) York Partnership t/a Clovelly Wines ▪ Winemaker(s)/viticulturist(s) Jacques Fourie ▪ 4ha/3ha (cab) ▪ 90% red 10% white ▪ Postnet Suite 215 Private Bag X5061 Stellenbosch 7599 ▪ info@clovellywines.com ▪ www.clovellywines.com ▪ S 33° 53' 54.1" E 018° 47' 52.3" ▪ **T +27 (0)82-853-7190** ▪ F +27 (0)21-865-2511

With just 3 hectares of cabernet on this family farm in Devon Valley (triangle-shaped – hence the name of the blend), Jacques Fourie sources red grapes from elsewhere in Stellenbosch and chardonnay from Robertson. 'We work in a wonderful industry', he muses. 'But have we made wine too much of a snob thing?'

★★★★ **Cabernet Sauvignon** Full-bodied **08** boasts blackcurrant, toasty oak & scorched earth. Impressive & concentrated, plush & rounded with ripe tannins, but the acidity is rather marked.

Patina Shiraz ★★★★ **05** dense & brooding. Like others below, not tasted this year. **The Three Sides Vineyard Blend** ★★★★ Pvsly 'Family Red' - last was lean NV (★★★). Firm, tasty **05** cab, merlot, shiraz blend has concentrated fruit & characterful rusticity, with a warming finish. **Chardonnay** ★★★ **09** with appealing aromas, but lacking balance & length. Not up to **07** (★★★★). — JPf

Cloverfield Private Cellar

Location/map/WO: Robertson ▪ Est 1945 ▪ 1stB 2002 ▪ Tasting & sales Mon-Fri 9-5 ▪ Closed Easter Fri-Mon, Dec 25 & Jan 1 ▪ Owner(s)/viticulturist(s) Pieter Marais ▪ Cellarmaster(s) Cobus Marais (2002) ▪ Winemaker(s) Cobus Marais (2002), with Gerald Smith (Jun 2009) ▪ ±200ha total (shiraz, chard, chenin, sauv) ▪ 40% red 60% white ▪ PO Box 429 Robertson 6705 ▪ info@cloverfield.co.za ▪ www.cloverfield.co.za ▪ S 33° 49' 57.3" E 019° 55' 34.1" ▪ **T +27 (0)23-626-4118** ▪ F +27 (0)23-626-3203

Brothers Cobus and Pieter Marais make a small, affordable range of wine under the Cloverfield branding, an allusion to the four-leaf clover and the good luck that Liz, Irish wife of patriarch Pietie Marais, is said to have brought to the operation. This

Huguenot family has farmed in view of the Langeberg mountains near Robertson for three centuries, and the portfolio includes an aptly named Shamrock Red.

Winemaker Selection

Shiraz ★★★ Smoke & red fruit, pleasantly firm tannin grip on **09** satisfying sipper. **Chardonnay Wooded** 🗄 ★★★★ Oak-driven **08** early-drinker had vanilla overtones & pleasant citrus fruit last edition.

Vineyard Selection

Chenin Blanc NEW ☺ 🗄 ★★★ Shy **11** soft thatchy floral bouquet, gentle sweet conclusion. **Sauvignon Blanc** ☺ 🗄 ★★★ Muted **11** has pleasant light vinosity, zesty tail to wake up your taste buds. This & Chardonnay are bone-dry slimmer's friends.

Shamrock Red 🗄 ★★ Now bottled, **09** has fruit sweet finish, slightly high-toned aromas. **Chardonnay Unwooded** ✓ 🗄 ★★★★ Unexpected sauvignon-like blackcurrant note on lemon-lime **11**, focused & refreshing, dry & persistent, over-delivers at the price. — Panel

COAV

Location/WO: Elgin ▪ Map: Elgin, Walker Bay & Bot River ▪ Est 2005 ▪ 1stB 2009 ▪ Open by appt ▪ Owner(s) James & Mark Simpson, James Craven ▪ Cellarmaster(s)/winemaker(s) Joris van Almenkerk (consultant) ▪ Viticulturist(s) Hannes Louw (Jun 2005) ▪ 165ha/11ha (cab, shiraz, sauv) ▪ 36t/1,000cs own label 100% white + 1,000cs for clients ▪ Viljoenshoop Road 50 Elgin Valley 7180 ▪ james@thecravens.co.za ▪ www.coav.co.za ▪ S 34° 14' 14. 08" E 019° 00'00" ▪ **T +27 (0)82-801-8811** ▪ F +27 (0)21-683-0776

There are three things you need to know about me and wine, says James Craven, co-owner of COAV (Cape Orchards & Vineyards) along with brothers James and Mark Simpson: 'I love drinking it. I like making it. I *hate* selling it!' Fortunately the strikingly packaged sauvignon, vinified by Joris van Almenkerk at nearby Almenkerk Wine Estate, could just about sell itself. Primarily an apple and pear farm with 11ha of vines, the Elgin property on the Palmiet River borders the Kogelberg Biosphere Reserve.

Sauvignon Blanc 🗄 ★★★★ Racy, lean, light textured, more mineral than overtly fruity - **10** is the essence of cool Elgin sauvignon. One senses there's more in store, though, so give time to settle & fill out. — Panel

▪ **Cocoa Hill** *see* Dornier Wines
▪ **Cogmanskloof** *see* Zandvliet Wine Estate & Thoroughbred Stud

Cold Duck (5th Avenue)

Enduring sweet, low-alcohol carbonated sparkling brand owned by Distell.

5th Avenue Cold Duck ★★ Frothy, unashamedly frivolous **NV**, pinotage gives the rosy hue. — Panel

▪ **Cold Mountain** *see* Brunia Wines

Colmant Cap Classique & Champagne

Location/map: Franschhoek ▪ Est 2005 ▪ 1stB 2006 ▪ Tasting & cellar tours daily by appt ▪ Fee R10 (½ glass bubbly) ▪ Sales Mon-Fri 9-4.30 Sat 10-1 ▪ Owner(s) Jean-Philippe & Isabelle Colmant ▪ Cellarmaster(s) Jean-Philippe Colmant ▪ Viticulturist(s) Paul Wallace (consultant) ▪ 5ha/3ha (pinot, chard) ▪ 3,400cs own label 100% MCC ▪ PO Box 602 Franschhoek 7690 ▪ info@colmant.co.za ▪ www.colmant.co.za ▪ S 33° 55'22.4" E 019° 7'37.3" ▪ **T +27 (0)21-876-4348/+27 (0)72-368-4942** ▪ F +27 (0)21-876-3732

A decade ago, Jean-Philippe and Isabelle Colmant, plus five children, made the leap from a stone-working factory in Belgium to the lovely Franschhoek valley. There they set about planting vines and building that rare thing in the Cape, a cellar solely dedicated to serious sparkling wines from classic varieties. The value of their focus, and of their genuine dedication to quality (witness the increasingly long time their wines are left on the lees before disgorging), is there to taste.

★★★★☆ **Brut Reserve** ✓ Classically styled, creamy & with a fine persistent mousse. Current **NV** near-equal blend pinot & chardonnay, includes 25% reserve from earlier vintages, spent 32 months in oak on lees. Elegant yet edgy with delicate, almost limey finish.

★★★★★ **Brut Chardonnay** Made for ageing (45 months on the fermentation lees in wood). Limy notes dominating on current **NV** despite 15% new oak. Super-fine mousse reveals dab hand of winemaker. Crisp, taut & bone-dry - a delicious, impressive & serious bubbly, finer & better integrated than previous.

★★★★ **Brut Rosé** Salmon pink with coppery flecks on **NV** from pinot noir, chardonnay; raspberry/baked bread aromas. 2 years on lees. Perhaps bolder, less nuanced than previous, but will develop. — MF

■ **Compagnies Wijn** *see* Oude Compagnies Post Private Cellar
■ **Condé** *see* Stark-Condé Wines

Conradie Family Vineyards

Location/map: Worcester ▪ WO: Nuy/Western Cape ▪ Est/1stB 2004 ▪ Tasting, sales & cellar tours Mon-Fri 9-5 Sat 9-3 Sun 11-2; after-hours by appt ▪ Closed Good Fri, Ascension day, Dec 25 & Jan 1 ▪ Nuy Vallei Restaurant & Guest House: meals daily 8-5, or by appt ▪ Facilities for children ▪ Tour groups ▪ Gift shop ▪ Farm produce ▪ BYO picnic ▪ Conference facilities ▪ Walks/hikes ▪ Mountain biking & 4x4 trails ▪ Conservation area ▪ Annual Nuy Valley Feast (May) ▪ Owner(s) Conradie family ▪ Cellarmaster(s) CP Conradie (Jan 2004) ▪ Winemaker(s) Elsabé Conradie (Jan 2007), with Colin Cilliers (Jan 2004, consultant) ▪ Viticulturist(s) CP Conradie (Jan 2000) ▪ 4,500ha/80ha (cab, ptage, chenin, cbard, crouchen, muscadel w, pinot gris, sauv) ▪ 1,400t total 70t/2,700cs own label 50% red 25% white 25% rosé ▪ BWI ▪ PO Box 5298 Worcester 6851 ▪ wine@conradievineyards.co.za ▪ www.conradie-vineyards.co.za ▪ S 33° 39'28.0" E 019° 37'59.6" ▪ **T +27 (0)23-342-7025** ▪ F +27 (0)86-509-4911

Six generations of Conradies have grown grapes here in the Nuy Valley near Worcester since 1871. 'Wine is in our blood, but no more than the legal limit!' laughs cellarmaster CP Conradie. Also strictly limited are the volumes produced to ensure quality and exclusivity, with no expansion planned other than an underground vinoteque for maturing the award-winning wines.

Single Vineyard Barrel Selection Reserve Cabernet Sauvignon ★★★ 'Cabernet Sauvignon' last time. **09** is powerful (±15% alc) & concentrated, with amarone-like richness which slips down easily but finishes a tad sweet. **Single Vineyard Barrel Selection Reserve Pinotage** ★★★☆ 'Pinotage' previous edition. **09** intense, with banana & acetone lift, structurally very impressive & appealing but let down by overripe fruit. **Pinotage-Cabernet Sauvignon** ★★★ Not revisited **08** had lush dark fruit, fleshy appeal mid-2009. **Single Vineyard Chardonnay** 🍷 📷 ★★★ Just 'Chardonnay' previously. Tangerine & lime appeal, **10** well-judged coconut oak, slightly warming tail & sweet impression. **Sauvignon Blanc** ✓ 🍷 📷 ★★★★ Attractive tropical aroma, **11** full body (despite lowish alc), vibrant fruit, lipsmacking dry finish. **Sweet Rosaline Perlé Rosé** 🍷 ★★ Thatch & cranberry scents on light, gently sweet, softly spritzy **11** from sauvignon, muscadel & pinotage. Discontinued: **Chenin Blanc, Werdoux Semi-Sweet.** — Panel

Conspirare

Location: Somerset West ▪ Map: Helderberg ▪ Est/1stB 2002 ▪ Tasting by appt ▪ Owner(s) HB Dowling/LRD Trust ▪ Winemaker(s) Henry Dowling ▪ Viticulturist(s) Francois de Villiers ▪ 24ha (cab s/f, merlot, shiraz, chenin) ▪ 250t/425cs own label 100% red ▪ PO Box 1210 Stellenbosch 7599 ▪ dowls@mweb.co.za ▪ S 34° 1'18.4" E 018° 50'54.6" ▪ **T +27 (0)21-855-0706** ▪ F +27 (0)21-855-0706

Boutique winemaker Henry Dowling hasn't vinified his blended red Conspirare ('Breathing Together') in several years, but the 02 is still available from the farm in the Helderberg heights.

Constantia de Tulbagh

Location/map/WO: Tulbagh ▪ Est 1965 ▪ 1stB 2000 ▪ Tasting, sales & tours by appt ▪ Closed all pub hols ▪ Owner(s) Lucas J van Tonder ▪ Cellarmaster(s) Theo Brink (Jan 2008) ▪ Winemaker(s) Theo Brink (Jan 2008), with Mynhardt van der Merwe (Dec 2009) ▪ Viticulturist(s) Mynhardt van der Merwe (Dec 2009) ▪ 330ha/35ha (cab, merlot, pinot, chenin, riesling, sauv) ▪ 3–5,000cs own label 20% red 80% white ▪ PO Box 79 Tulbagh 6820 ▪ montpellier@montpellier.co.za ▪ www.montpellier.co.za ▪ S 33° 17'21.3" E 019° 6'30.7" ▪ **T +27 (0)23-230-0656** ▪ F +27 (0)23-230-1574

Since purchasing this sibling estate to Montpellier (see entry) in 2004, owner Lucas van Tonder has concentrated on raising quality standards and restoring the historic buildings. Both entities are overseen by veteran cellarmaster Theo Brink (of Uitkyk renown), who has groomed his former assistant, Mynhardt van der Merwe, to take the reins.

Cabernet Sauvignon ★★★★ Previously, debut **04** married toasty aromas & fleshy dark berries, firm but yielding tannins. — GdB

Constantia Glen

Location/WO: Constantia ▪ Map: Cape Peninsula ▪ Est 2000 ▪ 1stB 2005 ▪ Tasting & sales Mon-Fri 10-5 Sat/Sun 10-4 ▪ Fee R30, waived on purchase ▪ Closed Easter Fri & Dec 25 ▪ Coffee & hot chocolate R10/cup (free to designated drivers); cheese platters ▪ Owner(s) Tumado Investments (Pty) Ltd ▪ Winemaker(s) Karl Lambour (Nov 2006) ▪ Viticulturist(s) Andrew Teubes (consultant) ▪ 60ha/28.5ha (cabs s/f, malbec, merlot, p verdot, sauv, sem) ▪ 160t/10,000cs own label 70% red 30% white ▪ PO Box 780 Constantia 7848 ▪ wine@constantiaglen.com ▪ www.constantiaglen.com ▪ S 34°0'39.6" E 018°24'30.6" ▪ **T +27 (0)21-795-6100** ▪ F +27 (0)21-795-6101

Anyone who mentions to bordelais consultant Dominique Hebrard that these reds could be French will be gentle rebuked: 'They are Constantia Glen, not Bordeaux.' Hebrard has a sincere interest in helping this property reach its own very promising potential. The established reputation enjoyed by the Sauvignon Blanc should soon apply to the reds too; every vintage brings a greater understanding of the vineyards and their performance for winemaker Karl Lambour and Hebrard. A new tasting room allows visitors not only to appreciate the different aspects and slopes which help create the differences, as well as the splendid views, but taste the wines as they do so. Bearing in mind the dangers of drinking and driving, coffee or hot chocolate is provided free for non-tasting, designated drivers.

★★★★☆ **Constantia Glen Five** Used to just bear estate name. New one, with **08**, refers to Bordeaux quintet make-up. Deep, spice-laden fragrance sets classy tone for this sleek, cab franc-led blend. Ample sweet flesh, complexities need further 4-6 yrs to emerge from vibrant, taut structure.

★★★★☆ **Constantia Glen Three** Previously 'Saddle'. Merlot's plush, ripe tones & flesh bring ready appeal to **08**. Cab, cab franc & smart French oak lend gravitas, spice, structure & good 3-5 yr potential.

★★★★☆ **Sauvignon Blanc** Gently fresh **10** (★★★★) with riper tropical citrus profile than assured **09**. Small but noticeable portion oaked semillon adds weight, dimension to food-friendly style. — AL

Constantia Mist

Location: Constantia ▪ Map: Cape Peninsula ▪ Est 2004 ▪ 1stB 2009 ▪ Tasting & sales daily 10-5 ▪ Fee R30 ▪ Closed Easter Fri & Dec ▪ BYO picnic ▪ 4-star Guest House (self-catering) ▪ Owner(s) Eagles Nest Property Investments (Pty) Ltd ▪ Cellarmaster(s) John Schooling (2009), with Justin van Wyk (2009) ▪ Winemaker(s) Karl Lambour (2009) ▪ Viticulturist(s) Alan Cockroft (2009) ▪ 6.6ha/2.8ha (sauv) ▪ 6t/ha 560cs own label 100% white ▪ Postnet Suite 96 Private Bag X16 Constantia 7848 ▪ johns@stagprop.com ▪ www.constantiamist.co.za ▪ **T +27 (0)21-794-0904** ▪ F +27 (0)21-794-4123

From managing a property developer and construction company to owning a wine label - it's been an eye-opener for John Schooling. 'I'm surprised how difficult it is to sell large quantities of wine,' he comments. Any tips for newcomers? 'It's all about developing new markets and sales', is his no-nonsense advice.

★★★★☆ **Sauvignon Blanc** Riper tropical profile on **11** (★★★★). Bone-dry & bracing, with some toasty lees extras, but it lacks the intensity & length of **10**.

Discontinued: **Red Blend**. — AL

Constantia Uitsig

Location/WO: Constantia ▪ Map: Cape Peninsula ▪ Est 1980 ▪ 1stB 1988 ▪ Tasting Mon-Fri 9-5 Sat/Sun & pub hols 10-5 ▪ Fee R25 ▪ Closed Easter Fri, Dec 25/26 & Jan 1 ▪ Wine Shop: cheese platters, deli items, gifts ▪ Hanepoot grapes sold annually ▪ Tour groups ▪ Conferences ▪ Horse livery facilities ▪ Cricket oval ▪ La Colombe, Constantia Uitsig Restaurant & River Café (see Restaurants section) ▪ Constantia Uitsig Hotel & Spa (see Accommodation section) ▪ Owner(s) Constantia Uitsig Wine Estate (Pty) Limited ▪ Cellarmaster(s) John Loubser (2003) ▪ Winemaker(s) André Rousseau (2003) ▪ Viticulturist(s) André Rousseau (1997) ▪ 60ha/32ha (cabs s/f, merlot, chard, Muscat d'A, sauv, sem) ▪ 140t/1,000cs own label 16% red 84% white ▪ WIETA ▪ PO Box 32 Constantia 7848

▪ marketingmanager@uitsig.co.za, andre@uitsig.co.za ▪ www.constantia-uitsig.com ▪ S 34° 2′51.9″ E 018° 25′ 27.5″ ▪ **T** +27 (0)21-794-6500 ▪ F +27 (0)21-794-7605

They don't come more committed than André Rousseau. Viticulturist and joint-winemaker here since 2003, he describes the highlight of his career to date as 'most certainly being part of the Constantia Uitsig brand'. And what a brand to be associated with. The property's luxury offerings include a hotel, spa and three restaurants, not to mention wine. Rousseau tends 32ha of vine (including a small block of hanepoot planted some 40 years ago) and the wines are made at nearby Steenberg. 'It's important not to be complacent,' he says, a recent innovation in the cellar being the introduction of large-format barrels which has led to greater 'complexity and depth' in both red and whites.

★★★★ **Constantia Red** Sophisticated Bordeaux blend, mostly merlot (57%) & cab, dash cab franc. Exceptional **07** (★★★★★) shows pure red & black fruit, great freshness, fine tannins; medium body with a long, dry finish. Fully assimilated 15 months French oak, 70% new, add to the overall elegance. Less austere than **06**.

★★★★ **Chardonnay Unwooded** 🍴 🍷 Unsullied by wood, **11** citrus blossom aromas before concentrated lemon flavour, tangy acidity on the palate. Return to form after leaner **10** (★★★★).

★★★★ **Sauvignon Blanc** 🍴 🍷 Well-rounded **11** shows dusty nose before rich & concentrated but well-balanced palate; lime & herbaceous flavours, good weight, moderate acidity.

★★★★☆ **Semillon** 🍴 🍷 A South African benchmark, though **10** (★★★★) off the pace of **09** & previous. Lacking concentration, nuance. Tangerine, herbal flavours, broad in structure with gentle acidity, a little short.

★★★★ **Constantia White** 🍴 🍷 **10** from 60% semillon & sauvignon very expressive but mid-2011 bit unknit: lime, melon, asparagus & herbal notes; rich, full, with moderate acidity, oak needs time to fully integrate.

★★★★ **Méthode Cap Classique** Champagne-method sparkling from chardonnay. Carefully conceived **08**; citrus & hint baked bread; good fruit delineation, fresh & soft; barrelled portion adds attractive weight.

★★★★☆ **Red Muscat d'Alexandrie** Irresistibly fortified dessert from 40 year old block of rare-in-Cape red hanepoot. Current incarnation (**NV** blend of 2008, 2010 & 2011) relatively light body but intense red fruit & spice flavour. Even more wow-factor than previous bottling. — CE

▪ **Constellation Wines South Africa** *see* Accolade Wines South Africa
▪ **Constitution Road** *see* Robertson Winery

Conviction

WO: Elgin ▪ Est/1stB 2009 ▪ Closed to public ▪ Winemaker(s) Clive Torr, with Anne Howell ▪ 10ha ▪ 50cs ▪ 26 Topaz Street Heldervue 7130 ▪ clivetorr@bigfoot.com ▪ **T** +27 (0)82-557-0826

Clive Torr believes wine brings people together, as it did when he and American friends David Brown and Anne Howell convened in his Somerset West cellar to make just two barrels of Conviction (last year noted in the Topaz range). 'We set out to make Screaming Eagle,' he enthuses about the deliciously ripe cabernet that resulted; 'from Elgin grapes, nogal!' That he wouldn't make a wine he wouldn't drink himself is endorsement enough.

★★★★☆ **Cabernet Sauvignon** Classic **10** (★★★★) deceptively accessible given youth, new oaking & cool climate origin. Very harmonious with lovely minty edge, perhaps a tad less concentration than **09**. — IM

▪ **Cool Bay** *see* Boplaas Family Vineyards
▪ **Coral Reef** *see* Wineways Marketing
▪ **Country Cellars** *see* Orange River Wine Cellars
▪ **Couple's Wine** *see* Bergheim

Craighall

First listed in 1994, the perennially good-value white blend was a response to the high-priced chardonnay of the day, to allow a wider market to experience the must-have of the wine trade. Their winning formula has remained remarkably consistent through the years. Produced by African Wine & Spirits (E Snell).

Cabernet Sauvignon-Merlot ☺ ★★★ Sweet berry fruit with nutty hints on **10** undemanding quaffer.
Sauvignon Blanc ☺ ★★★ Light-bodied, nervously fresh **11** shows gentle floral notes. **Chardonnay-**

Sauvignon Blanc 😊 🍴 ★★★ Formula-driven chardonnay-led blend. **11** offers usual zesty, fruit-laden appeal. WO W Cape as all. — GdB

Cranefields Wine

Location/map: Villiersdorp • Est/1st B 1995 • Tasting by appt only • Owner(s) SJ Greve & CJ Roux • Winemaker(s) Riaan Wassüng (consultant, Jan 2005) • Viticulturist(s) Charl Roux (Feb 1998) • 35ha (cab, merlot, shiraz) • 272t/ 3 000cs own label 100% red • PO Box 417 Villiersdorp 6846 • info@cranefields.com • www.cranefields.com • S 34° 2' 45.99" E 019°13'59.64" • **T +27 (0)28-840-2565** • F +27 (0)28-840-0440

Much of the harvest off this all-red estate bordering the huge Theewaterskloof Dam goes elsewhere, with just a little made into Cranefields wine at Stellenbosch University's Welgevallen facility. On those bottles is (in gold) a beautifully stylised depiction of the blue crane, the elegant bird which gives the farm its name.

Cabernet Sauvignon ★★★ Plum & berry-nuanced **06** had firm tannins mid-2008; should since have softened. This, Red Bishop, still selling. **Merlot** Like **Shiraz**, new vintage not ready at press time. **Red Bishop** ★★★ Cassis-rich **06** cabernet-led with splashes merlot & shiraz; was refreshing & balanced last time. — Panel

Creation Wines

Location: Hermanus • Map: Elgin, Walker Bay & Bot River • WO: Walker Bay • Est 2002 • 1stB 2006 • Tasting, sales & cellar tours daily 10-5 • Closed Dec 25 & Jan 1 • Lunch; Wine & Canapés/'Éclat de Chocolat' pairing • Kiddies menu & designated play area • Tour groups • Wine accessories, books & souvenirs on sale • Walking/hiking trails • Conservation area • Art exhibition (paintings & sculptures) • Events: blend your own bottle; barrel/true terroir tasting; regular musical performances & themed cultural events • Owner(s) Jean-Claude & Carolyn Martin, Heidi Kellerhals Kaser & Christoph Kaser • Cellarmaster(s) Jean-Claude Martin & Christoph Kaser (both Jan 2005) • Winemaker(s) Jean-Claude Martin & Christoph Kaser, with Kevin Baatjies (all Jan 2006) • Viticulturist(s) Jean-Claude Martin, Christoph Kaser & Peter Davison (consultant), advised by Johan Pienaar (all 2002) • 35ha/30ha (cab, grenache, merlot, p verdot, pinot, syrah, chard, sauv, sem, viog) • 170t/14,000cs own label 65% red 35% white • BWI, IPW • PO Box 1772 Hermanus 7200 • info@creationwines.com • www.creationwines.com • S 34° 19' 51.5" E 019° 19'33.8" • **T +27 (0)28-212-1107** • F +27 (0)28-212-1127

Carolyn Martin would not trade Creation's idyllic Hemel-en-Aarde location for the world, nor would winemaking husband Jean-Claude or their wine-partners Heidi and Christoph Kaser. Visitors - 200 to 300 a day in peak season - happily tackle the dirt road to sample not just the ever-improving wines (perfectly paired with bite-sized food morsels and, now, chocolate) but also the fine-art displays, occasionally including sculptures in the fynbos garden and stunning surrounds.

★★★★ **Merlot** 🧿 **10** (★★★★☆) ratchets the bar higher still, improving on **09**. Rich, rounded & restrained, it's pure black-fruit elegance. Succulent & integrated, with structure to last for 5+ years.

★★★★ **Pinot Noir** 🧿 Variety's forest floor & red cherry aplenty on polished, modern **10**. Balance of firm fruit core with gossamer suppleness. Inky blackness & concentration. Just 25% new oak used. Pure lengthy tail.

★★★★☆ **Pinot Noir Reserve** NEW 🧿 Minx of a wine! **10** shows a velvety European influence: smoky morello cherry, plum fruit with spice & tobacco leaf. Intense, rigid yet sinuous. Dense, dark & brooding yet with a soft generous charm. Toned oak (30% new), so will age well.

★★★★ **Syrah** 🧿 Soft black berry fruit with fynbos overlay on **10**. Gymnastic sleekness & pure fruit concentration. Length, body & integrated oak (25% new). Supple & rewarding. Like **09**, will age well.

★★★★ **Syrah-Grenache** ✓ 🧿 Inexorable rise in quality sees **10** (★★★★★) improve on perfumed **09**. Rich spice lifts red & black berry succulence. Plump fullness but with firm oak backbone, just 25% new. Herbal pepper zing tussles fleshy fruit without either gaining dominance. Delicious.

★★★★ **Chardonnay** 🧿 Old World template for **10**: rich but reined-in citrus rind & smoke, creamy texture & oak platform (30% new) all create a delicious tension between fruit & wood, as seen in **09**.

★★★★ **Sauvignon Blanc** 🧿 **11** shows typical pungent flint, lemon & herb but good length. Body & acidity to comfortably take it beyond cricket season. **10** impressed with elderflower scent & zesty acidity.

★★★★ **Viognier** ✓ 🧿 **11** whispers its typicity: nuanced nectarine, peach richness, poised flinty minerality & zesty lightness, lingering elegant spicy aftertaste.

Merlot-Cabernet Sauvignon-Petit Verdot ★★★★ Name change signals merlot leadership of **09**, where cab helmed **08** (★★★★★). Fynbos nuance to full mulberry fruit, complex, svelte with grip & length. **Semillon** 🧿

Untasted. **Sauvignon Blanc-Semillon** NEW ⊗ ★★★★ Gravel minerality to **11**, tangy nettle & herb zestiness. No rush: it'll gain complexity with age. — FM

Crios Bríde

Location: Stellenbosch • WO: Swartland • Est/1stB 2007 • Closed to public • Owner(s) Yorke-Smith Family & Martin Bates • Winemaker(s) Carla Pauw (Jan 2007, consultant) • 1,250cs own label 15% red 25% white 60% MCC • PO Box 2290 Dennesig Stellenbosch 7601 • info@criosbride.com • **T +27 (0)21-883-9568** • F +27 (0)88-021-883-9568

Not all SA MCC's enjoy lengthy lees ageing, but this is the style the brand owners and winemaker Carla Pauw, prefers, especially after her regular visits to the Champagne region. The next wine release to receive the blessing of the symbolic Crios Bride will be another MCC, including some magnum bottlings, enriched by 4 yrs lees contact.

★★★★ **Syrah-Carignan** Powerful **07** still available. Showed concentrated molten dark fruit, good structure & ageability when previously tasted.

Chenin Blanc ★★★★ Sumptuous & robust **07** ex Swartland vines still selling, not retasted. **Sauvignon Blanc** ★★★★ No newer vintage since previously tasted single-vineyard **08** from Darling, with gentle asparagus tone. **Méthode Cap Classique** ★★★★ Traditional-method sparkling **07** from chardonnay & pinot noir, made extra-dry & perfect with oysters, still available. — MW

■ Cross Collection *see* Dieu Donné Vineyards

Crows Nest

Location: Paarl • Map: Paarl & Wellington • WO: Coastal • Est/1stB 2002 • Tasting, sales & cellar tours Mon-Fri 10-5 Sat/Sun & pub hols by appt • Fee R25, waived on purchase • Meals by appt; or BYO picnic • Facilities for children • Farm produce • Walking/hiking trails • Conservation area • Owner(s) Marcel & Deidre de Reuck • Winemaker(s) Marcel de Reuck • 33.6ha/11.5ha (cab, shiraz) • 60t/5,000cs own label 90% red 5% white 5% port • PO Box 2571 Paarl 7620 • dereuck@mweb.co.za • www.dereuckwines.co.za • S 33° 40'33.0" E 018° 54'25.4" • **T +27 (0)21-869-8712** • F +27 (0)21-869-8714

Coming soon from this Paarl winefarm: free-range pork from 'happy hogs', as Marcel de Reuck says. And perhaps more white wine, 'using our chardonnay and viognier instead of selling or blending it away. Main focus has been on reds – blockbuster-style ones, for this may be a small farm, but the wines are very big!

Marcel de Reuck range

★★★★ **Cabernet Sauvignon** Charming red & black cherry fruit, oak spice on grippy **07** (★★★), though warming 15.7% alcohol detracts. Less elegant than last-tasted **04**. These all WO Coastal.

Syrah ★★★ Ultra-ripe, blockbusterish **07** offers 16% alcohol & sweet, raisiny & tired black fruit. **Cabernet Sauvignon-Merlot** ★★★ Youthful, bold **07** last year had tannins to balance rich fruit but big alcohol evident. **Chardonnay** Await new. Discontinued: **Sauvignon Blanc**.

Torres Claude range NEW

Crow's Nest ★★★ Rhône-inspired **07** blend with forward fruit; rich, densely packed, with simple flavours & sweetish hot finish from 15.4% alcohol. — JPf

Croydon Vineyard Residential Estate

Location: Somerset West • Map: Helderberg • WO: Stellenbosch • Est/1stB 2004 • Tasting & sales Mon-Fri 8-5 Sat by appt • Closed all religious holidays • Cellar tours by appt • Meals/refreshments on request • Weekly family dinners Wed & winemakers luncheons Fri • Facilities for children • Tour groups • Conference facilities • Owner(s) Croydon Vineyard Estate Homeowners Association • Cellarmaster(s) Beyers Truter (2004) • Winemaker(s) Corius Visser (2004) • 43ha/7.5ha (cabs s/f, malbec, merlot, ptage, shiraz) • 65t/2,000cs own label 100% red • Unit 1 Croydon Vineyard Estate Croydon Somerset West 7130 • info@croydon-estate.co.za • www.croydon-estate.co.za • S 34° 2'23.3" E 018° 45'5.5" • **T +27 (0)21-843-3610** • F +27 (0)21-843-3609

Since the property owners of this residential estate are also shareholders in the vineyards and winery, there are regular social activities planned here, like weekly family dinners and winemaker lunches, as well as monthy get-togethers with music. Winemaker Corius Visser intends to widen the reach to the local Helderberg area, no hardship with the continually improving wine quality. Pinotage features strongly in order to remain 'true to the Cape', all under the watchful eye of consultant and Pinotage guru Beyers Truter.

Title Deed range

★★★★ **Cape Blend** Pinotage partners cab & merlot in **10**, glossy blueberries & refreshing acidity more than a match for muscular tannins, promises well for the future. This & Covenant sampled from barrel.

Rhône Blend Await next.

Croydon Vineyard Residential Estate range

★★★★ **Covenant** Such intense fruit demands respect: crushed berries & 20 months new barrels, **09** (last-tasted was **05**) is a serious pinotage. Beautifully made, has a 10 year future. Nudges next level. — CR

Crystallum

Location: Hermanus ▪ WO: Western Cape/Hemel-en-Aarde Valley/Walker Bay/Walker Bay ▪ Est 2006 ▪ 1stB 2007 ▪ Closed to public ▪ Owner(s) Crystallum Coastal Vineyards (Pty) Ltd ▪ Winemaker(s) Peter-Allan Finlayson (2006) ▪ 20t/1,300cs own label 60% red 40% white ▪ PO Box 857 Hermanus 7200 ▪ info@crystallumwines.com ▪ www.crystallumwines.com

Furthering the commitment to sustainability here, they plan to install turbines to power the straw-bale cellar via the river flowing through Crystal Kloof. In the cellar Peter-Allan Finlayson continually experiments - 'never at the expense of the laws of making fine wine, but small improvements at each stage of the process must always be a focus'. Another element in the refined Crystallum wines reflects philosophy as much as technique: 'The challenge in our conditions is to not be seduced by the abundant sunshine into making ripe, confected wines, but rather to make ones that are restrained and complex.'

★★★★☆ **Cuvée Cinéma Pinot Noir 10**'s plush strawberry & cherry fruit carries generous oaking (65% new) with ease. Massively perfumed & textured, refined despite being a big wine (14.7% alc); pinot delicacy perfectly captured; no jagged edges, seamlessly managed. From Hemel-en-Aarde Ridge fruit.

★★★★ **Peter Max Pinot Noir** Cedarwood, tobacco spice rather than the red fruit of Cinema on light (racy & slightly insubstantial) yet savoury **10**, hauntingly aromatic. Brings in some Elgin grapes.

★★★★☆ **Clay Shales Chardonnay** Refreshingly sweet-fruited **09**, sumptuously oaked (14 months, 50% new), but fine limy notes lifting dense, creamy textures. Worthy successor to **08**, combining bold aromas with an elegant persistent palate. Hemel-en-Aarde Ridge grapes.

★★★★ **The Agnes Chardonnay** Harmonious & masterly crafted **10**, showing dollops of tropical lime fruit, finely layered oak (25% new) adding grip to plushness. Not simple, but amply fruited. Widely sourced grapes.

Sauvignon Blanc Last tasted was **09**. — MF

Culemborg

Produced by DGB for export only. Established range of easy-drinking wines with main markets including the Netherlands and Germany.

Blanc de Noir ☺ 🍷 🥂 ★★★ Charming off-dry summer quaffer. **11** appealing combo of savouriness & fresh red berries. WO Western Cape, as for all below.

Cabernet Sauvignon 🥂 ★★ **10** brush of blackcurrant, appealing & ready to drink. **Pinotage** 🥂 ★★ Succulent easy-drinking **10**, with spicy plum flavours. **Cape Red** 🍷 🥂 ★★ Savoury & bright al fresco sipper, **10** well padded with plum & spice. **Chenin Blanc** 🍷 🥂 ★★ **11** light, clean & fresh anytime white. **Muscat du Cap** NEW 🥂 ★★★ **10**, from hanepoot, like liquidised tropical fruit salad with a twist of tangy passionfruit to balance the sweetness. **Sauvignon Blanc** 🍷 🥂 ★★ Previewed **11** ripe & gentle, soft fruity flavour. **Cape White** 🥂 ★★ Perfumed **11** crisp yet gentle summer picnic wine. **Sweet Red** NEW 🥂 ★★ **10** spicy winter warmer for the sweeter tooth. Discontinued: **Cinsault, Merlot, Shiraz, Chardonnay**. — MW

Dâbar   NEW

Location/WO: Napier ▪ 1stB 2010 ▪ Closed to public ▪ Owner(s) Kevin Snyman & Jannie Gutter ▪ Winemaker(s) Jean Daneel (Jean Daneel Wines) ▪ Viticulturist(s) Dawie le Roux (consultant) ▪ 50/50 white/red ▪ kevinsnyman@telkomsa.net ▪ T +27 (0)82-926-8459

Dâbar ('Promise' in Hebrew) is a new wine venture on the farm Vierfontein in the mountains above Napier, where owner Kevin Snyman also grows pomegranates, figs and flowers. The maiden sauvignon was made by good friend Jean Daneel in his boutique cellar in the town, though ultimately Kevin wants to vinify on site. He plans to make 'top wines', in a location that is 'even cooler than Constantia'. He's so confident of the potential, he's supported the creation of a new wine ward 'for future wine producers in the Napier area'.

Sauvignon Blanc ★★★ 10 will be appreciated by Old World fans for its lightish (12.5% alc) body & tone, racy freshness; hay, wax & cream in satisfying, moreish package. Vinified by Napier neighbour Jean Daneel. — Panel

■ **Da Capo Vineyards** *see* Idiom Wines

Dagbreek

Location: Rawsonville ▪ Map/WO: Breedekloof ▪ Est/1stB 2009 ▪ Tasting, sales & cellar tours Mon-Sat by appt ▪ Closed all pub hols ▪ BYO picnic ▪ Walking/hiking trails ▪ Owner(s) Peet Smith ▪ Cellarmaster(s)/winemaker(s) Peet Smith (2009) ▪ Viticulturist(s) Leon Dippenaar (2009, consultant) ▪ 108ha/48ha ▪ 7t/500cs own label 70% red 30% white ▪ WIETA ▪ PO Box 237 Rawsonville 6845 ▪ dagbreek@compnet.co.za ▪ www.dagbreek.co.za ▪ S 33° 39'56.20" E 019°18'26.99" ▪ **T +27 (0)82-820-2256** ▪ F +27 (0)86-529-2865

'Wine gets made on the vine,' says Breedekloof boutique winemaker Peet Smith, therefore delighted that his vines include a block of 40 year old bushvine chenin. But Peet is even prouder of his gold medal from the 2010 Michelangelo Awards for his Nebbiolo: 'It was a highlight, seeing it was the first wine I produced.'

Nebbiolo ★★★ 10 inky blueberry with variety's typical bright acidity, still unsettled in youth, needs time or food. **Touriga Nacional ★★★★ 10** black scrubby fruit plumped by tad sugar, juicy & flavoursome, shows potential. **Chenin Blanc Barrel Selection NEW ✓ ★★★★** Lovely balance & integration of flavours on previewed **10**, fine fruit purity from old vines, not overwhelmed by oak; quite a rich style. — MW

Dalla Cia Wine & Spirit Company

Location/map/WO: Stellenbosch ▪ Est 2004 ▪ Tasting, sales & traditional Italian meals at Pane E Vino Food & Wine Bar, Mon-Fri 10-6 Sat 10-5 ▪ Owner(s)/winemaker(s) Giorgio Dalla Cia ▪ 9,000cs ▪ 7A Lower Dorp Street Bosman's Crossing Stellenbosch ▪ info@dallacia.com ▪ www.dallacia.com ▪ S33° 56'25.8" E018° 50'50.1" ▪ **T +27 (0)21-888-4120** ▪ F +27 (0)21-887-2621

This Italianate winery and distillery is situated in the trendy Bosman's Crossing area of Stellenbosch which has commercial, retail and residential components combined together. Run by Giorgio Dalla Cia, previously the winemaker at illustrious Meerlust for many years, and family, they produce their own range of wine and grappa as well as providing a consultancy service and operating a small café called Pane E Vino. Here you can enjoy the recently introduced Grappa Tasting Menu: chocolates, biscuits and ice-cream all featuring the fiery spirit as well as a glass of grappa and a single espresso in order to perform caffè corretto (grappa added to the coffee).

★★★★ **Cabernet Sauvignon 06** sensual combo blue/blackberries, cigarbox & spice, all precisely drawn, & framed by ultra-fine tannins. 70% new wood, 18 months. This, next two tasted for last edition.

★★★★☆ **Giorgio** Bordeaux-blend maestro Giorgio Dalla Cia's hand shows in **06**, ripe plum, rich choc-coffee & meaty notes all easily assimilate 80% new oak, Italian-style dry tannins for pleasure at table. Preview **07** juicy, bolder (15% alc).

Chardonnay 🍷 ★★★★ Previewed **10** offers round quince notes, just 5% wooded portion more subtle, agreeable than **09**. **Sauvignon Blanc 🍷 ★★★** Relatively weighty & rich **10** shows granadilla, some asparagus, moderate acidity before savoury finish. — CE

Damarakloof

Location/WO: Paarl ▪ Map: Paarl & Wellington ▪ Est/1stB 2006 ▪ Function venue by appt ▪ Owner(s) Agnes de Vos ▪ Winemaker(s) Carla Pauw (Jan 2006) ▪ 19ha (cabs s/f, merlot, chenin) ▪ 10t/650cs own label 50% red 50% white ▪ PO Box 38 Elsenburg 7607 ▪ agnesdevos@mweb.co.za, carlapauw@gmail.com ▪ S 33° 48'41.79" E 018° 47'21.19" ▪ **T +27 (0)21-884-4304** ▪ F +27 (0)21-884-4304

This diverse Paarl agricultural spread has been home to Agnes de Vos's family for over a century. Her grandfather turned the local racetrack – originally deemed unfit for vines due to its gravel soils – into a chenin vineyard of note, but it's quiet for now. The dignified Bordeaux-style red blend 'Regale' continues to fly the flag.

Racetrack range

Regale ★★★★ **08** back in elegant style after hiatus; no **07**, last **06** (★★★★) was lesser. Very fragrant, refreshingly demure & altogether delightful to drink, even in youth. Discontinued: **Chenin Blanc**. — DS

■ **Dam Good** *see* Villiersdorp Cellar
■ **Danie de Wet** *see* De Wetshof Estate
■ **Danie se Withond** *see* Grundheim Wines

D'Aria Winery

Location/WO: Durbanville ▪ Map: Durbanville, Philadelphia & Darling ▪ Est/1stB 2007 ▪ Tasting & sales Mon-Fri 10-6 (Sep-Apr) & 9-5 (May-Aug) Sat 10-5 Sun 10-4 ▪ Fee R10 ▪ Closed Dec 25 & Jan 1 ▪ Cheese platters & oysters served in tasting room ▪ Poplars Restaurant ▪ Conference/function venue ▪ Walking/hiking & mountain biking trails ▪ 4-star Guest Cottages ▪ Music concerts (summer months) ▪ Owner(s) Barinor Holdings ▪ Winemaker(s) Rudi von Waltsleben (Nov 2007), with Nicola Viljoen (Apr 2010) ▪ Viticulturist(s) Johan von Waltsleben (1998) ▪ 63ha (cab, merlot, shiraz, sauv) ▪ 400t/10,000cs own label 67% red 30% white 3% rosé + 200cs for clients ▪ Brands for clients: Doilie Klub (Elzabé Zietsman) ▪ M13 Racecourse Road Durbanville 7550 ▪ tasting@daria.co.za ▪ www.dariawinery.co.za ▪ S 33° 50' 28.6" E 018° 36' 36.2" ▪ **T +27 (0)21-801-6772** ▪ F +27 (0)86-539-4519

Composer and guitar-playing winemaker, Rudi von Waltsleben sees his two pursuits as a 'coming together of the senses,' something he hopes the wines' musical names and the muse logo conveys. With their cool-climate origin, the generous expression shown by the range should indeed touch the senses.

★★★★☆ **The Soprano Shiraz** Bold, generously-oaked (only 40% new) **09** (★★★★) a dense pliable mouthful. Good fruit but lacks freshness, with a rather cloying finish. Less successful than powerful **08**.

★★★★ **Songbird Sauvignon Blanc** 🔲 After initial sweaty notes, **10** reveals expressive passionfruit. Fine, steely support for lemongrass, asparagus attractions broadened by 5% oaked component.

> **Music Red** ☺🔲 ★★★ **10** ticks all boxes for delicious drinkability. Bright, spice-led scents, rich fruit flavours, chewy & supple.

Merlot ★★★☆ Cool climate vibrancy, minty notes on **09**. Juicy with lively, supportive tannins; fruitily dry. Better balance than **08** (★★★). **Cabernet Sauvignon-Merlot** ★★★★ Fruit-driven **08** last year showed dark fruits, hint green pepper, & toasty coffee notes. **Shiraz-Viognier** ★★★★ Some complexity, polish on previously tasted **08**. Fine tannin, integrated oak lead to bitter-sweet finish. **Blush** 🔲 ★★ **11** mildly fruity, sweetish quaffer from merlot, sauvignon. **Sauvignon Blanc** 🔲 ★★★★ Lively, uncomplicated **10**; ripe figgy notes, leesy bounce & a little sugar trim steely acid's aggression. **The Following White Blend** 🔲 ★★★★ Aromatic viognier with semillon, sauvignon. Near-dry, oaked **09** noted last year as opulent, rich. Discontinued: **Music White**. — AL

Darling Cellars

Location: Darling ▪ Map: Durbanville, Philadelphia & Darling ▪ WO: Darling/Groenekloof/Coastal ▪ Est 1948 ▪ 1stB 1996 ▪ Tasting & sales Mon-Fri 8-5 Sat 10-2 ▪ Closed Easter Fri, Dec 25 & Jan 1 ▪ Cellar tours by appt ▪ Wine & food pairing/sampling, no meals ▪ Facilities for children ▪ Owner(s) 20 shareholders ▪ Cellarmaster(s) Abé Beukes (Dec 1997) ▪ Winemaker(s) Welma Visser & Carel Hugo (Nov 2007/Jun 2009) ▪ Viticulturist(s) Jaco Engelbrecht (Jan 2008) ▪ 1,300ha (cab, cinsaut, grenache, merlot, ptage, shiraz, chard, chenin, sauv) ▪ 7,500-8,500t/350,000cs own label 70% red 28% white 2% rosé ▪ Export brands: Alta Casa, Cellar Road, Fountain Crossing, Mamre Vale, Victoria Bay ▪ BRC, BWI, WIETA ▪ PO Box 114 Darling 7345 ▪ info@darlingcellars.co.za ▪ www.darlingcellars.co.za ▪ S 33° 26' 25.7" E 018° 31' 25.1" ▪ **T +27 (0)22-492-2276** ▪ F +27 (0)22-492-2647

Abé Beukes raised some eyebrows when he set forth from Stellenbosch to the forsaken frontiers of Mamreweg back in 1997; now the floodgates have opened to the Swartland, and the Darling Cellars operation remains in the forefront. Its metamorphosis has been extraordinary over the years, from a minor co-op to a major industry player, offering some of the best value in the Cape. Out in the field, their composting project, recycling all grape waste for use in the vineyards, is up and running. The Onyx range has been renamed simply Premium and the DC line-up of site-specific varietal wines is now the Reserve label.

Limited Releases

★★★★☆ **Sir Charles Henry Darling** 08 now cab-led, Bordeaux-style blend is finely balanced, mellow & elegant. Substantial but focused, showing ripe spectrum of berry fruit, silky tannins, lingering finish. Great example of Groenekloof finesse. DC's top-tier wines continue to impress.

★★★★☆ **Lime Kilns** ✓ Very special range-topping member of the elite new club of great SA white blends. **10**, chenin-based with chardonnay & viognier, is rich & supple, plush yet restrained & mineral. Distinctly West Coast in character.

★★★★ **Blanc de Blancs Brut** NEW ✓ Rich & leesy, maiden 08 méthode cap classique sparkling is a laudable effort. All-chardonnay, crisply dry, with a creamy mousse & elegant mineral finish.

Cellarmaster's Signature Selection No. 1 ★★★★ 08, from petit verdot, bit uncomfortable as standalone when tasted last year. Groenekloof WO.

Darling Cellars Premium range

★★★★☆ **Cabernet Sauvignon** ✓ These previously under respected good-value Onyx branding. Classy preview 09 (★★★★) ex Groenekloof brims with ripeness. Classic leafy herbaceousness laced with blackcurrant fruit. Follows finer **08**.

★★★★ **Shiraz** Satisfyingly fruit-driven **08** not revisited. Faint hints of pepper & fynbos on dark berries, gently textured tannins.

★★★★ **Sauvignon Blanc** Tank sample **10** last year had hints of peas & asparagus harmonising with leesy minerality. Finely knit fruit layering & noble stature.

★★★★ **Noble Late Harvest** ✓ Impressive Sauternes-styled **10** from Groenekloof chenin & riesling. Honeyed, concentrated dried-fruit flavours linger on unctuous sweetness. Bigger, richer than previous.

Pinotage ★★★★ Steely 09 shows hefty wild berry fruit, with faint malt whiff. Big, exuberant & spicy, expressing Swartland sunshine. **Kroon** ★★★★ Mediterranean varietal compote in last-tasted **07**. Reverted to chunkier profile of **05** after elegant 06 (★★★★).

Darling Cellars Reserve range

Six Tonner Merlot ☺ 🗏 ★★★ Middle range showcases Swartland sites & vines. **10** is gently fruity, with spicy notes & pleasing tarry core. Serve at the braai. This & entire range are remarkable value. **Black Granite Shiraz** ☺ 🗏 ★★★ **10** is softer & lighter than previous, but retains enticing peppery aromas. Eminently quaffable. **Quercus Gold Chardonnay** ☺ 🗏 ★★★ Restrained, unassuming **11** still generous in ripeness & body. Atypical yet pleasing white fruit profile. **Arum Fields Chenin Blanc** ☺ 🗏 ★★★ **11** is full of ripe tropical fruit, nicely balanced & quaffable.

Terra Hutton Cabernet Sauvignon ✓ 🗏 ★★★★ Well-defined varietal currants & spicy-savoury aromas on latest **10**. **Old Block Pinotage** ★★★★ Last year **09** showed deft touches. Harnessed, well-directed fruit with tobacco & sweet spices. **Bush Vine Sauvignon Blanc** ✓ 🗏 ★★★★ Charming, typical Swartland dusty-grassy aromas on **11** follow to bracing fresh crispness & satisfyingly ripe fruit.

Flamingo Bay range

Cabernet Sauvignon-Merlot ☺ 🗏 ★★★ Entry level range of reliable quaffers at rock-bottom prices. **10** is solid & pleasant everyday drinking. **Cinsaut-Cabernet Sauvignon** ☺ 🗏 ★★★ A gush of dark berries & oaky spices on **10** emphasise cinsaut drinkability. Appealing anytime quaffer. WO Coastal. **Merlot Rosé** ☺ 🗏 ★★★ Refreshingly dry juicy-berry summer cooler, **11** pocket-pleaser over-delivers. Swartland sunshine in a bottle.

Chenin Blanc-Sauvignon Blanc 🗏 ★★ **11** unpretentious everyday quaffer. Coastal WO.

Zantsi Africa Natural Sweet range

Rosé 🗏 ★★ **11** sweet strawberry gusher. **White** 🗏 ★★ **11** low-alc refresher from bukettraube. **Pettillant White** NEW 🗏 ★★ Spritzy **11** as above, new to range. — GdB

■ **Darlington** *see* Withington
■ **Daschbosch** *see* uniWines Marketing
■ **Dassie's Reserve** *see* Botha Wine Cellar

D'Athis Wines SA Negociants

Location: Stellenbosch ▪ Est 2008 ▪ Tasting & sales by appt only ▪ Owner(s) Marcel du Preez & Jacques du Preez ▪ Winemaker(s)/viticulturist(s) Jan du Preez (consulting) ▪ PO Box 7210 Stellenbosch 7599 ▪ dathiswines@vodamail.co.za ▪ www.dathiswines.co.za ▪ **T** +27 (0)82-856-3560/+27 (0)79-053-3193 ▪ **F** +27 (0)86-588-3482

While Jacques du Preez continues as winemaker in the family wine business in Stellenbosch, advised by his father Jan, younger brother Marcel who managed marketing and logistics is now the rugby relations manager for Puma SA, a dream job for this rugger fanatic, who also plays for Pirates. Wine ranges produced are Headbutt, Leidersburg and Migration.

David   `NEW`

Location: Tulbagh ▪ WO: Swartland ▪ Est/1stB 2010 ▪ Closed to public ▪ Wines availbable at Lemberg Wine Estate ▪ Owner(s)/winemaker(s)/viticulturist(s) David & Nadia Sadie ▪ (chenin) ▪ 6t/320cs own label 45% red 55% white ▪ wine@davidsadie.co.za ▪ www.davidsadie.co.za ▪ **T** +27 (0)72-375-4336 ▪ **F** +27 (0)86-512-4903

Inspired by a crush in the Rhône Valley, David and Nadia Sadie are making their own wines from grapes sourced (initially) in the Swartland, where David grew up. First steps have been learning to understand the vineyards they're buying grapes from, and their philosophy is about 'balance in the soil, vineyard, grapes and people' to create balanced wines, while striving for freshness and terroir expression. Their wines, for now, are available (and made) at Lemberg in Tulbagh. Much further afield, their maiden 2010 Aristargos blend was one of Tomorrow's Stars at the London International Wine Fair, sticking a wedge in the door of the UK market.

★★★★☆ **Aristargos** ✓ If you're wondering why all the fuss about new-wave Swartland, try this perfumed & exotic beauty from **10** chenin (51%), viognier, verhelho: boldly ripe, concentrated, but so firmly anchored by acidity & textured minerality, the rich dried-fruit flavours trip lightly - & moreishly - on the palate. — Panel

David Frost Signature Series

Location: Paarl ▪ WO: Paarl/Western Cape ▪ Est/1stB 2007 ▪ Tasting & sales at Perdeberg Winery ▪ Owner(s) PDF Trading ▪ Cellarmaster(s) Albertus Louw (Oct 2008) ▪ Winemaker(s) Riaan Möller (Dec 2006) & Carla Herbst (Jun 2008) ▪ Viticulturist(s) Jaco Engelbrecht (Nov 2011) ▪ PO Box 214 Paarl 7620 ▪ info@perdeberg.co.za ▪ www.davidfrostwine.com ▪ **T** +27 (0)21-869-8244 ▪ **F** +27 (0)21-869-8245

This is one of Perdeberg Winery's joint ventures, here with pro golfer David Frost, a neighbour. He gets access to their vineyards, winemaking and marketing skills, while Perdeberg, where the wines are made, gets a name known across the globe. Further synergy is found in retail chain Pick 'n Pay, where R1 from each bottle's sale is donated to the Raymond Ackerman Golf Academy.

David Frost Signature range

Soft Smooth Red ☺ 🍴 📖 ★★★ Generously fruity off-dry red, **10** is perfect winter fare.

Shiraz 🍴 📖 ★★★ Designed to please, **10**'s smoke-infused berries have soft, easy drinkability. **Classic Red** 🍴 ★★ Cab, merlot in last-tasted **09**, herbal touch to red fruit. **Chenin Blanc** 🍴 📖 ★★★ Apple & pear flavours, **10** has nice fruity freshness. This range previously listed as 'Value for Money'. — CR

■ **David Nieuwoudt** *see* Cederberg Private Cellar
■ **Dawning** *see* Elberti Wines
■ **DC Wines** *see* Darling Cellars

DeanDavid Wines

Location: Riebeek-Kasteel ▪ WO: Swartland ▪ Est/1stB 2003 ▪ Closed to public ▪ Wines available at the Wine Kollective, Riebeek-Kasteel ▪ Owner(s) Dean & David Thompson ▪ Cellarmaster(s)/winemaker(s) Dean Thompson ▪ 8t/400cs own label 100% red ▪ PO Box 355 Riebeek-Kasteel 7307 ▪ dean@unwined.co.za ▪ www.unwined.co.za ▪ **T** +27 (0)71-233-8261

Dean Thompson is the winemaking (and marketing-reluctant) son, David his father who has long had a share in a grape farm just outside Riebeek-Kasteel. Some delightful wines have emerged, in tiny quantities. The Syrah is off five blocks, 'close to organic and in great balance' says Dean – a balance reflected in the wine.

★★★★ **2 Mile Square Swartland Syrah** Honest, delightfully pure **09** last year showed fresh, sweet-fruited but thoughtful charm. Warm, ripe tannins from the grapes, not the modest oaking. — TJ

■ **De B** see De Breede Organic Vineyards

De Breede Organic Vineyards

Location: Worcester ▪ Map/WO: Breedekloof ▪ Est 2006 ▪ 1stB 2009 ▪ Tasting by appt ▪ Owner(s) Tim & Debbie Alcock ▪ Cellarmaster(s)/viticulturist(s) Tim Alcock (2006) ▪ Winemaker(s) Tim Alcock (2006), with Isaac Mabeta (2009) ▪ 26ha/2,5ha (cab, malbec, merlot, p verdot) ▪ 6t/250cs 99% red 1% rosé ▪ Certified organic by BCS ▪ PO Box 511 Worcester 6849 ▪ debreede@burchells.co.za ▪ www.debreedevineyards.co.za ▪ S 33° 37' 10.69" E 019° 22' 44.79" ▪ **T +27 (0)23-342-5388** ▪ F +27 (0)86-684-7778

Working organically means problems for Tim and Debbie Alcock on their young, boutique-scale Worcester vineyards – 'particularly with weedfighting!' Although, Tim adds, 'the grapes are small and full of flavour as a result of the struggle'. And thriving: bigger cabernet yields in 2011, and now a little malbec. Keeping things in the family, artist son James designs the labels.

De B range

1st XI Merlot NEW 粻 ★★★★ Softer than the blend, **09**'s velvet wraps a very firm core. Pleasant herbal hint. From first eleven rows of vineyard - hence name. **Little Red Rooster** 粻 ★★★ Merlot-based Bordeaux blend **10** juicy, flavoursome. More extracted power than intensity - rather macho (but friendly!). — TJ

■ **Decent** see Ladismith Cellar - SCV

De Doorns Wynkelder (Koöp) Bpk

Location/map/WO: Worcester ▪ Est 1968 ▪ Tasting & sales Mon-Fri 8–5 Sat 8–12 ▪ Cellarmaster(s) Danie Koen ▪ Winemaker(s) Danie Koen, with Peter James Thomson ▪ PO Box 129 De Doorns 6875 ▪ ddwk@hexvallei.co.za ▪ www.dedoornscellar.co.za ▪ S 33° 29' 10.3" E 019° 39' 43.2" ▪ **T +27 (0)23-356-2835** ▪ F +27 (0)86-579-1310

'2011 was the second-largest harvest in our history,' says Danie Koen, with satisfaction. Cellarmaster of this grower-owned winery north of Worcester, Danie oversaw the production of close to 35,000t of bulk-wine last year, some of it for new contract holders. Also new is a dam on the cellar premises, an element of a waste water treatment project.

Cabernet Sauvignon ☺ ★★★ Very sippable **09**, gentle spicy eucalyptus notes, fresh berry centre & slight grip.

Roodehof 🍷 ★★ Unoaked & quaffable **10**, mainly cab & pinotage, with smoky bacon savouriness. — Panel

De Grendel Wines

Location: Durbanville ▪ Map: Durbanville, Philadelphia & Darling ▪ WO: Durbanville/Coastal/Western Cape ▪ Est 1720 ▪ 1stB 2005 ▪ Tasting & sales Mon-Fri 9–5 Sat/Sun 10–4 ▪ Fee R20/3 wines & R50/complete range, waived on purchase ▪ Closed Dec 25 ▪ Cellar tours by appt ▪ Conference facilities ▪ Owner(s) David Graaff ▪ Cellarmaster(s) Charles Hopkins (Oct 2005) ▪ Winemaker(s) Elzette du Preez (Jan 2006) ▪ Viticulturist(s) Douglas Muzengeza (2008) & Kudzai Mwerenga (2009) ▪ 800ha/110ha (cabs s/f, malbec, merlot, mourv, p verdot, ptage, pinot noir/gris, shiraz, chard, sauv, sem, viog) ▪ 550t/25,000cs own label 35% red 45% white 20% rosé ▪ 112 Plattekloof Road Panorama 7505 ▪ info@degrendel.co.za ▪ www.degrendel.co.za ▪ S 33° 51' 2.5" E 018° 34' 18.4" ▪ **T +27 (0)21-558-6280** ▪ F +27 (0)21-558-7083

De Grendel is a sprawling 800ha of Durbanville land owned by Sir David Graaff, son of the late Sir De Villiers Graaff, leader of the opposition party during the mid-20th century. Mixed farming is practised here, 110ha under vine and larger-than-life Charles Hopkins in charge of winemaking. He relates that because of De Grendel's cool-climate location, meticulous vineyard work is required to avoid a 'green' quality in the red wines, and pays particular tribute to Douglas Muzengeza and Kudzai Mwerenga, both of whom used to farm tobacco and roses in Zimbabwe. 'Two of the best vineyard managers I've ever worked with. Their attention to detail is extraordinary.'

★★★★ **Op Die Berg Pinot Noir** 🍷 **09** red cherry flavour, good fruit definition, fresh acidity, oak carefully observed. More precise than **08** (★★★★).

★★★★ **Shiraz 08** displays black fruit, pepper & fynbos on the nose. Intensely flavoured, with fresh acidity, pleasing tannic grip before long, saline finish. WO Coastal, like Sauvignon.

★★★★ **Rubáiyát 08** tight & demanding, this classically styled Bordeaux-style red needs time. Dark fruit, attractive oak, intensely flavoured but not weighty, finishes long & dry. 86% Stellenbosch cab, rest own fruit.

★★★★ **Sauvignon Blanc** ✓ 🍷 **11** appears ripe & full with pronounced grenadilla. Juicy fruit, acidity more than adequate but not hard, aggressive. Delicious!

★★★★☆ **Koetshuis Sauvignon Blanc** 🍷 **11** shows dusty note on nose. Elegant, with great complexity thanks to a range of subtle flavours inc lime, paprika & some grenadilla. Pure & refined & not as overtly green, piercing as previous. Includes portion Darling fruit.

★★★★☆ **Viognier** NEW 🍷 **11** surprisingly understated nose for the variety. Peach & peach kernel flavour, thick but not unctuous texture; tangy, well integrated acidity while a touch of oak lends interest. Substantial but not overdone.

★★★★ **Winifred** 🍷 **10** (★★★★) idiosyncratic blend of 43% chardonnay, 39% semillon, 18% viognier, much like **09**. Range of flavour from herbal through citrus to peach a little awkward. WO W Cape.

Merlot ★★★ Red berries, herbal note on nose of **09**. Juicy fruit, soft tannins on palate but green character persists. Oak well judged. **Rosé** 🍷 ★★★ Abundant strawberry on clean, fresh, dry **11**. **Pinot Gris** 🍷 ★★★ **11** juicy & fresh, an easy summer quaffer. **Méthode Cap Classique Brut** ★★★★ Fresh, youthful **09** traditional-method sparkling (68% chardonnay, 32% pinot noir), lime, green apple, fine mousse, bracing acidity. — CE

■ **De Haas** *see* Hazendal

De Heuvel Wine & Olive Estate

Location/map: Tulbagh ▪ WO: Tulbagh/Walker Bay/Swartland/Darling/Western Cape ▪ Est/1stB 1997 ▪ Tasting & sales Mon-Fri 8.30–5 Sat 9–2 ▪ Fee R30 p/p for groups ▪ Closed Easter Fri/Sun, Dec 25 & Jan 1 ▪ Tours Mon-Fri 9–4.30 ▪ Olive oil/olive products ▪ Owner(s) Gaëtan Bovit ▪ Cellarmaster(s)/winemaker(s)/viticulturist(s) Johan Meyer (2008) ▪ 16ha (cab, nebbiolo, ptage, shiraz) ▪ 70t/6,000cs 70% red 30% white ▪ BWI member ▪ PO Box 103 Tulbagh 6820 ▪ info@deheuvelestate.co.za ▪ www.deheuvelestate.co.za ▪ S 33° 20′ 57.1″   E 019° 10′ 20.3″ ▪ **T +27 (0)23-231-0350** ▪ F +27 (0)23-231-0938

Quality at this family-owned Tulbagh winery is on the rise. 'Manage your vineyards well and 80% of the wine makes itself,' is winemaker/viticulturist Johan Meyer's explanation. They're working on an 'exiting new reserve range' and Rhône-style white blend. Also watch this space, urges Johan, for 'a unique wedding venue - first in the Western Cape'.

★★★★ **Chenin Blanc Barrel Fermented** ✓ Delicious **10**, from Swartland grapes (as debut **09**) maintains high standard with candied lemon & rich vanilla overlay. Serious structure, limy/toasty finish. Good future. Yum!

Cabernet Sauvignon ★★★ Restrained, leaner style, last edition **07** was leafy & herbaceous, showed hint dark fruit, good structure. **Pinotage** ★★★ **08** previously was densely packed with smoky mulberries, firm chalky grip which may have softened by now. **Shiraz** ★★★ Savoury **08**, with polished leather & smoky bacon character, underpinned by robust tannin when last tasted. **Cape Blend** 🍷 ★★★ Shiraz (50%), pinotage & cab. Improved & promising preview **09** appealing dusty dark berries, chunky savoury fruit. **Rosé** 🍷 ★★ Previewed **11**, from pinotage, light & dry lower-alc sipper. **Chardonnay** ★★★★ Now bottled, **10** from Walker Bay grapes is smooth & creamy, mouthfilling, a vanilla hint combines with lemon in the aftertaste. **Chenin Blanc** 🍷 ★★★ **10** juicy lime/quince with hints of almond, lively acidity, athletic poise last time. WO Swartland. **Sauvignon Blanc** ✓ 🍷 ★★★★ Groenekloof fruit character shows in now-bottled **10**'s dusty ripe passionfruit & greenpepper; nicely balanced, engaging zippy conclusion. Lovely development in the bottle. Notch above debut **09** (★★★★). **White Blend** NEW ★★★★ Chenin & 3 others; full body, sweet ripe fruit, vanilla oak; **10** balanced, mouthfilling, lifted lime marmalade conclusion. WO W Cape. Discontinued: **Semi-Sweet Muscat, Dry Muscat.** — WB

■ **Dekker's Valley** *see* Mellasat Vineyards

De Krans

Location/WO: Calitzdorp ▪ Map: Klein Karoo & Garden Route ▪ Est 1964 ▪ 1stB 1977 ▪ Tasting & sales Mon-Fri 8–5 Sat 9–3 ▪ Fee R20pp for groups, free for individuals ▪ Closed Easter Fri/Sun & Dec 25 ▪ Pick your own apricots (last week Nov, 1st week Dec) & hanepoot grapes (±8 Feb-3 Mar) ▪ 'Braaivleis' available during picking; Vygieshof Home for the Aged also offer meals Wed & Sat during this period ▪ Facilities for children school hols ▪ BYO picnic ▪ Walking/hiking trails ▪ Owner(s) De Krans Wines (MD Boets Nel & Directors Stroebel Nel & René Oosthuizen) ▪ Cellarmaster(s) Boets Nel (Jan 1982) ▪ Winemaker(s) Boets & Stroebel Nel (Jan 1982/Jan 1988) ▪ Viticulturist(s) Stroebel Nel (Jan 1988) & Johannes Mellet (2007, Vinpro) ▪ 78ha/45ha (cab, ptage, tempranillo & port varieties, chard, chenin & muscats) ▪ 500t/20–25,000cs 50% red 10% white 3% rosé 37% fortifieds ▪ IPW, BWI ▪ PO Box 28 Calitzdorp 6660 ▪ dekrans@mweb.co.za ▪ www.dekrans.co.za ▪ S 33° 32′ 6.3″ E 021° 41′ 9.0″ ▪ **T +27 (0)44-213-3314** ▪ F +27 (0)44-213-3562

If owning shares in, and a home among the vineyards of one of South Africa's finest port producers appeals, the conversion of De Krans into a company with potential for minority stakeholders now makes it possible. Winemaker Boets Nel is managing director (and sole owner of separately listed Garden Route); viticulturist brother Stroebel and René Oosthuizen are directors. In the past year exports picked up, domestic sales were boosted by an improved distribution arrangement, and a slew of competition honours confirmed De Krans' reputation for outstanding dessert wines. Two new bottlings, Espresso and Tinta Mocha, joined the established Pink Port in the drive to acquaint the younger market with De Krans and the pleasures of drinking fortified wines. Wary of creating homogenised wines by inter-regional blending, Boets says he believes in Calitzdorp terroir and wants to showcase it in his wines.

★★★★ **Touriga Nacional** ✓ 'Our flagship' says Boets Nel. Much lauded **10** appealing plum & red-berry fruit, savoury edge to juicy centre; balanced & refreshing, malleable tannins. Should improve few years in bottle.

★★★★ **Red Stone Reserve** Satisfying mouthful, **06** touriga & 30% cab blend still selling. Dense dark fruit underpinned by tannin, should be drinking well now. Not revisited.

★★★★ **Reserve Muscat** ❧ Very appealing fortified pudding wine. Preview **11**, from 30 year old vines, tad shy but shows more presence & character than **10** (★★★); sweet ginger-spiced flavours, great poise.

★★★★ **White Muscadel Jerepigo** ✓ Picked before too raisined to preserve intense muscat flavour. Creamy orange-lime fruit on back-on-track **11** highlighted by nutty passionfruit nuance. Slippery-sweet & fiery - & more focused than **10** (★★★).

★★★★★ **Cape Vintage Reserve Port** ✓ A Cape benchmark from touriga, tinta, souzão (62:36:2), invariably impressive, delicious & ageworthy port-style fortified. Restrained, almost aloof as ever, **09** opens in glass to reveal a potent centre of scrubby/plummy fruit encased in a tannin structure designed to age decade & more.

★★★★☆ **Cape Vintage Port** ✓ Recent vintages snap at heels of regal Vintage Reserve - astonishing depth of quality (& value) from this cellar. Opaque, brooding & black-fruited **10** continues on path set by beautifully integrated **09**. Tannins, velvet fruit & spirit in perfect balance. Allow plenty of time to grow, improve.

★★★★☆ **Cape Tawny Port** ✓ Latest NV shade less oxidative than other awarded examples from area but retains fire, relative sweetness (98g/l RS). Mainly tinta, plus touriga, tinta roriz; aged average 8 years.

★★★★ **Cape Ruby Port** Previewed NV from tinta, touriga, souzão (50/45/5), year oak. Fruit-packed & fiery, shows house's fine balance between sweetness, alc punch & approachability. Delicious!

Pinotage ☺ 🍽 ★★★ Acetone & banana, full body, **10** slips down easily solo, & accompanies venison & casseroles. **Tempranillo** ☺ 🍽 ★★★ Vanilla tone from dab American oak, **10** fruity & refreshing, straightforwardly tasty & appealing.

Cabernet Sauvignon 🍽 ★★☆ Deep & brooding **10** has tealeaf nuance, drying tannins, anticlimactic end. **Tinta Mocha** ✓ 🍽 ★★★★ Fashionably 'coffee'styled (& renamed from 'Tinta Barocca') **10**, laudably restrained, zesty & bright fruit is the focus, soft tannin grip. **Relishing Red** 🍽 ★★★ Unpretentious off-dry everyday red, raspberry & cherry flavours, slight bitter nuance on finish. NV. **Cabernet Sauvignon Rosé** 🍽 ❧ ★★★ Delicately blushing **11** billows rosepetals & boiled sweets, finishes semi-dry & rather quickly. **Chardonnay** 🍽 ❧ ★★★ Shy white blossoms, otherwise neutral **11** animated by lemony acidity. **Chenin Blanc** 🍽 ❧ ★★★ Faint floral & smoky notes, **11** brief but juicy quick-quaff. **Golden Harvest** 🍽 ★★ Equal muscat d'Alexandrie & chenin in latest spicy, gently sweet NV, for sipping lightly chilled. **Pink Port** NV preview too young & unformed to rate, as for **Cape White Port** Discontinued: **Merlot**. — Panel

Delaire Graff Estate

Location/map: Stellenbosch ▪ WO: Stellenbosch/Western Cape/Coastal/Swartland ▪ Est 1983 ▪ 1stB 1984 ▪ Tasting & sales Mon-Sat 10-5 Sun 10-4 ▪ Fee R30/3 wines R40/4 wines R50/5 wines ▪ Cellar tours by appt (no tours during harvest) ▪ Salads/cheese platters on request ▪ Gifts ▪ Farm produce ▪ Conferences ▪ Walks/hikes ▪ Art collection ▪ Delaire Graff & Indochine Restaurants (see Restaurants section) ▪ 5-star Lodges & Spa (see Accommodation section) ▪ Owner(s) Laurence Graff ▪ Winemaker(s) Morné Vrey (Jul 2009) ▪ Viticulturist(s) Kallie Fernhout (Jun 2010) ▪ 38ha/20ha (cabs s/f, malbec, merlot, p verdot, chard, sauv) ▪ 280t/17,000cs own label 40% red 55% white 5% rosé ▪ WIETA ▪ PO Box 3058 Stellenbosch 7602 ▪ info@delaire.co.za ▪ www.delaire.co.za ▪ S 33° 55'20.4" E 018° 55' 26.0" ▪ **T +27 (0)21-885-8160** ▪ F +27 (0)21-885-1270

While we're not taking any bets on whether the building storm is over here, this grand mountainside establishment, owned by jeweller Laurence Graff, has certainly started picking up awards for work done so far. The Lodges and Spa have been listed by two publications as among the best new hotels in the world: Conde Nast Traveler's 2011 Hot List and Travel & Leisure's 'IT' list. Morné Vrey's wines have maintained this pace - see below, but also note Coastal Cuvée Sauvignon Blanc 2010 taking the trophy for best Sauvignon Blanc on the Trophy Wine Show.

★★★★★ **Cabernet Sauvignon Reserve** 09 (★★★★★) after initial reticence, gains gravitas, more nuanced dark berry scents, flavours; all harmonise with the succulent, chalky tannins, fresh acid & oak enrichment (80% new). Promises greater rewards, maybe more than **08**, after 5-8 years.

★★★★ **Shiraz** 🍷 Last year 09 noted as youthfully accessible yet ageworthy. Comfortable, fresh and balanced with persistent spice, salami appeal. All-new oak well assimilated.

★★★★☆ **Botmaskop** 09 cab-led Bordeaux quintet with shiraz in seamless, flavoursome composition. More plush, softer tannined than **08**. Drinks well now; has concentration, firm acid for 5-6 years development.

★★★★ **Chardonnay** 🍷 After pleasing citrusy aromas, 10 (★★★★) on richer, more buttery side; touch of limy lift freshens, trims sweeter finishing notes. 09 more elegant, poised.

★★★★ **Chenin Blanc** NEW 🍷 Sophisticated, ageworthy style; **10** from Swartland savoury, rich & vinous with firming mineral core. Oak (40% new) yet to harmonise - but has the substance to do so.

★★★★ **Sauvignon Blanc** 🍷 Widely sourced 11 with splash oaked semillon. Just post-bottling (like next) still edgy but promising unshowy, pure greengage, citrus fruit; more sauvage notes tempered by firm flesh. WO W Cape.

★★★★ **Coastal Cuvée Sauvignon Blanc** 🍷 11 unoaked with 5% semillon lending extra weight. More minerals, fumé tones, less obvious fruit than partner. Balanced, juicy & food-friendly. WO Coastal.

★★★★ **Semillon-Sauvignon Blanc** 🍷 Touch less semillon in **10** than 09 (55% vs 60%) though has initial fatter feel. With more sauvignon brings more focus, freshness and dimension; maybe less ageworthy than **09**. WO W Cape.

★★★★☆ **Cape Vintage Port** 09 touriga, tinta barocca blend. Initially more forward, fragrant fruit than 2088, less alc grip, but closes with fine chainmail of tannin. Drinkable, but 6-7 year wait would be rewarded.

Merlot NEW ★★★★ Dense, velvety 09; straightforward dark soft berries, chocolate opulence freshened by lemony acid. **Red Blend** Await next. **Cabernet Franc Rosé** 🍷 ★★★ Dry 11 echoes softer, fruitier style of **10**. Extended lees contact provides weight necessary for food; good solo too. **Chardonnay Reserve** Await next. **Noble Late Harvest Semillon** In abeyance. — AL

■ **De Leuwen Jagt** see Seidelberg Wine Estate

Delheim Wines

Location/map: Stellenbosch ▪ WO: Simonsberg–Stellenbosch/Stellenbosch ▪ Est 1971 ▪ 1stB 1961 ▪ Tasting & sales daily 9-5 ▪ Fee R25 tasting/R35 tasting & cellar tour ▪ Closed Easter Fri/Sun, Dec 25 & Jan 1 ▪ Cellar tours daily at 10.30 & 2.30 ▪ Delheim Restaurant open daily for breakfast 9.30-11.30 lunch 12-3.30 snacks & cheese platters 3.30-4.30, booking essential Sat/Sun & hols T +27 (0)21-888-4607, restaurant@delheim.com ▪ Facilities for children ▪ Tour groups ▪ Gifts ▪ Farm produce ▪ Conferences ▪ Conservation area ▪ Oakleaf Lodge B&B at Delvera ▪ Events: see website for schedule ▪ Owner(s) Sperling family ▪ Cellarmaster(s) Brenda van Niekerk (Oct 2002) ▪ Winemaker(s) Brenda van Niekerk (Oct 2002), with Marius Prins (Jul 2007) ▪ Viticulturist(s) Victor Sperling (Aug 1993) ▪ 375ha/148ha (cab, ptage, shiraz, chard, chenin, riesling, sauv) ▪ 980t/60,000cs own label 50% red 30% white 20% rosé ▪ Brands for client: Woolworths ▪ BWI champion, WIETA ▪ PO Box 210 Stellenbosch 7599 ▪ delheim@delheim.com ▪ www.delheim.com ▪ S 33° 52'10.1" E 018° 53'9.8" ▪ **T +27 (0)21-888-4600** ▪ F +27 (0)21-888-4601

Wine matters for the Sperling family at Delheim, because 'its rich heritage brings people from across the world together'. This is exactly what patriarch Spatz Sperling did, being one of the founders of the first wine route (Stellenbosch) in 1972, when tourists cars were counted in by staff putting stones in a bucket! Thousands of visitors now flock here annually, for a whole range of wine-based entertainment. 82 year old Spatz was recently honoured as the Institute of Cape Wine Masters Wine Personality of the Year. His mentorship has benefited both top South African winemakers and his family, who have added their creative energy to this successful, multi-faceted venture.

Vera Cruz Estate range

★★★★☆ **Shiraz 08** low-yielding single-vineyard delivers consistent quality. Cured meat, polished leather & spice, enhanced by integrated new oak. Elegant & poised, with layers of complexity, for next 3-5 years.

Delheim range

★★★★ **Cabernet Sauvignon ✓ 09** suave & streamlined, good depth of fruit, subtle oaking & long finish. Confident, ageworthy style. Upholds estate's reputation for top-quality cab.

★★★★ **Shiraz 08** still current. Harmonious, accessible & stylish, savoury tone when last tasted.

★★★★☆ **Grand Reserve 08** flagship red, mostly cab & dab merlot, classically styled. Inky, dark fruit, leather & cedar oak, all elegantly restrained. So suave & well groomed, disguises inherent power. Cellarworthy.

★★★★ **Spatzendreck Late Harvest ✓ 🖉** Now all chenin, **11** pre-bottling a step up on **10** (★★★). Sweet but zesty & uncloying glacé pineapple & quince flavours. Great aperitif or fusion/Thai partner.

★★★★☆ **Edelspatz Noble Late Harvest 🖉** Preview of single-vineyard riesling, tad riper in **11** (★★★★). Similar rich & tangy glacé pineapple & tropical flavours to **10**, but less vibrancy. Still elegant & delicious.

Merlot ★★★ Heady red berry & minty preview jostles with **09**'s firmer structure. Tad unknit, with alc afterglow. Food & time may harmonise. **Pinotage ✓ 🖉** ★★★★ Riper but sprightly **10** has more fruit depth & harmony than previous. Medium bodied, long, spicy but warm farewell. WO Stellenbosch, as for Gewürztraminer. **Chardonnay 🗐 🖉 11** sample too unformed to rate. **Chardonnay Sur Lie 🖉** ★★★★ **10** rich toasty oak currently masks core of marmalade fruit, from low-yielding vines. Time will bring harmony (& higher rating?). **Gewürztraminer 🗐 🖉** Early **11** tank sample too unformed to rate, but shares fruit profile of elegant & piquantly balanced **10** (★★★★). **Sauvignon Blanc 🗐 🖉** Like previous, current **11** preview too young to rate.

Lifestyle range

Pinotage Rosé ☺ 🗐 🖉 ★★★ **11** ever popular just-off-dry quaffer with tangy red-berry appeal.

Cabernet Sauvignon-Shiraz ✓ 🗐 🖉 ★★★★ Preview even brighter & juicier in **10**. Flavoursome & supple 6-way blend for attractive easy drinking, solo or with a meal. WO Stellenbosch, as for Pinotage Rosé. **Chenin Blanc 🗐 🖉** ★★★ **11** warmer vintage less crisp, with apple cider & almond flavours. **Heerenwijn Sauvignon Blanc-Chenin Blanc 🗐 🖉** ★★★ Gets 'Heerenwijn' prefix this edition. Riper, succulent & amiable **11** has apple & marzipan nuance. — MW

Dellrust Wines

Location: Somerset West ▪ Map: Helderberg ▪ WO: Stellenbosch ▪ Est/1stB 1998 ▪ Tasting & sales by appt ▪ Owner(s)/winemaker(s)/viticulturist(s) Albert Bredell ▪ 50ha/±37ha (cab, merlot, ptage, shiraz, sauv) ▪ 200t/5,000cs own label 90% red 10% white ▪ PO Box 5666 Helderberg 7135 ▪ albert.b@dellrust.co.za ▪ www.dellrust.co.za ▪ S 34° 1' 58.7" E 018° 46' 46.9" ▪ **T +27 (0)82-771-3090** ▪ F +27 (0)86-695-9615

Albert Bredell has hit the 'pause' button on his boutique-scale operation in the Faure area of Stellenbosch. Right now he's too busy with viticultural and farming consulting to give it the necessary focus. It's only temporary, he avers, and fans of fiery fortifieds should now there's something in the pipeline.

Merlot ★★★ Ripe brambly **08** with fynbos & char, light & juicy. Not revisited. **Shiraz** ★★ Still-selling **06**, first since **98**. Gamey, ripe & tad porty. **Three Vines Limited Release** ★★★ Still-listed **05** shiraz-led (70%) blend with merlot & cab. Pvsly noted as meaty, with determined wood tannins which may since have settled. **Sauvignon Blanc** Not tasted, as for Jerepigo. **Jerepigo** Not tasted. **Cape Vintage** ★★★★ Last ed noted **06**'s tinta & touriga mix has spicy Xmas pud, raisin & choc notes. Touch light, lacks grip & fire. 36 mths older Fr brls. Discontinued: **Rosé**. —

De Meye Wines

Location/map/WO: Stellenbosch ▪ Est/1stB 1998 ▪ Tasting & sales Mon-Fri 9-4.45 Sat/Sun 11-4 ▪ Fee R15/5 wines ▪ Closed Easter Fri, Dec 25/26 & Jan 1 ▪ Cellar tours Mon-Fri by appt ▪ 'The Table at De Meye' open for lunch Sat-Sun, booking essential (www.thetablerestaurant.co.za) ▪ Farm produce ▪ Owner(s) Jan Myburgh Family Trust ▪ Winemaker(s) Marcus Milner (Sep 1999), with Aby Bodlani (Sep 2000) ▪ Viticulturist(s) Johan Pienaar (Jan 2006, consultant) ▪ 100ha/65ha (cabs s/f, merlot, shiraz, chard, chenin) ▪ 300t/18,000cs own label 65% red 25% white 10% rosé ▪ IPW ▪ PO Box 20 Elsenburg 7607 ▪ info@demeye.co.za ▪ www.demeye.co.za ▪ S 33° 49'0.7" E 018° 49'48.8" ▪ **T +27 (0)21-884-4131** ▪ F +27 (0)21-884-4154

The long-standing team at this quaint assemblage of recycled farm buildings has focused on a distinctive house style for their wines, and change is now more evolutionary. Environmental considerations have always been a priority, and every step of the production process takes note of the carbon footprint it leaves. Their recently opened little restaurant, The Table at De Meye, is attracting favourable attention for its simple but sophisticated take on fresh, natural ingredients.

De Meye range

★★★★ **Cabernet Sauvignon** ✓ Lighter-bodied than previous, **08** expresses leafy, herbaceous notes, has elegant balance with commendable dryness. Lots of dark fruit lingers to satisfying finish.

★★★★☆ **Trutina** ✓ Rich, plush & generous **09** oozes appeal. Flag-bearer blend of Bordeaux varieties with a dash of shiraz avoids fruit-bomb pitfalls, but offers complete, well-rounded body with spicy/aromatic core.

Shiraz Rosé ☺ 🗐 📖 ★★★ **11** is reliably fresh & fruity, with fragrant scents & gentle acidity. Ideal summertime dry sipping.

Merlot ✓ ★★★★ Full, ripe **09** already showing class of the vintage. Bigger in body & fruit than **08** (★★★★), but retaining focus & elegance. Oak needs time to integrate. **Shiraz** ✓ ★★★★ Richly fruity middleweight with spicy notes, **09** reflects ripeness of vintage. Elegant, well judged, shapely. **Chardonnay Unwooded** 🗐 📖 ★★★ Cheerful, uncomplicated **11** retains form & zesty citrus flavours of previous years. Lean, sprightly & appealing. **Chenin Blanc** 🗐 📖 ★★★ Latest **11** rather lean after richer, tropical **10**. From 35 year old bushvines.

Little River range

Cabernet Sauvignon ☺ 🗐 ★★★ Quality second-tier perennially over-delivers. **10** is first since **07**, fresh & juicy, with just a hint of seriousness. **Shiraz** ☺ 🗐 📖 ★★★ Despite modest aspirations, new **10** shows distinct varietal form, with generous weight & structure.

Discontinued: **Cabernet Sauvignon-Shiraz**. — GdB

DeMorgenzon

Location/map: Stellenbosch ▪ WO: Stellenbosch/Western Cape ▪ Est 2003 ▪ 1stB 2005 ▪ Tasting & sales daily 10-5 ▪ Fee R15-R25 ▪ Closed Easter Fri, Dec 25/26 & Jan 1 ▪ Cellar tours on request ▪ Conservation area ▪ Owner(s) Wendy & Hylton Appelbaum ▪ Cellarmaster(s) /GM Carl van der Merwe (Jul 2010) ▪ Winemaker(s) Carl van der Merwe (Jul 2010), with L'Ré Burger (Dec 2010) ▪ Viticulturist(s) David van Schalkwyk (Aug 2010) & Kevin Watt (consultant) ▪ 91ha/52ha (cab, grenache, merlot, mourv, syrah, chard, chenin, rouss, sauv, viog) ▪ 252t/15,000cs own label 56% red 33% white 8% rosé 3% other ▪ BWI, IPW ▪ PO Box 1388 Stellenbosch 7599 ▪ info@demorgenzon.co.za ▪ www.demorgenzon.co.za ▪ S 33°56'22.99" E 018°45'0.17"E ▪ **T +27 (0)21-881-3030** ▪ F +27 (0)21-881-3773

The enthusiasm generated by Hylton and Wendy Appelbaum for this Stelleboschkloof property is evident throughout: in the flowers, fynbos and trees proliferating beyond and alongside the vineyards, the vines themselves, the staff and new winemaker, Carl van der Merwe. Music is seen as a good motivator for vines, cellar staff and wines; speakers in the vineyards and the cellar play baroque works 24 hours a day. Syrah and Scarlatti anyone? Except not on the harpsichord, deemed an unpleasant sound by the workers.

★★★★ **DMZ Syrah** NEW 🗐 **09** marked by its delicate yet convincing red fruits & spice purity, savoury tail & subtle oak enhancement. Early drinking permitted by suppleness, caressing tannins; will age well too.

★★★★ **DMZ Concerto** Rhône-like **08** still available. Perfumed with grippy yet polished red fruit; refreshing.

★★★★ **Chenin Blanc Reserve 09** noted last edition as seductive, opulent, with mineral core & good dollop sugar (8g/l). 11 mths oak, some new.

★★★★ **DMZ Sauvignon Blanc** 🖩 Despite aromatic grassy green hint, **10** fills out with well-textured, persistent ripe fruit on palate. Bracing but unharsh. Admirable interpretation from sometimes difficult vintage.

Garden Vineyards Rosé 🖩 ★★★ Classic salmon-colour on previously tasted **09** ex shiraz. Fresh, appetising & bone dry. **DMZ Chardonnay** 🖩 ★★★★ Elegant **10**; some complexity in citrus, ripe melon & oatmeal array. Plump, fresh thread, lees adding to savoury length. **09** (★★★★) slightly soapy finish. WO W Cape. — AL

■ **Denneboom** *see* Oude Denneboom
■ **De Oude Opstal** *see* Stellendrift - SHZ Cilliers/Kuün Wyne

Desert Rose Wines

Location: Vredendal ▪ WO: Western Cape ▪ Tasting by appt ▪ Owner(s) Alan van Niekerk & Herman Nel ▪ Winemaker(s) Herman Nel ▪ desertrose@nashuaisp.co.za ▪ **T +27 (0)82-809-2040/+27 (0)82-800-2270** ▪ F +27 (0)27-213-2858

This Olifants River garagiste winery is the brainchild of 'two 40-somethings who like 80s music' says co-owner Alan van Niekerk who, with grape-grower Herman Nel, decided to turn a dinner-party conversation into reality. It's a very hands-on affair which includes numbering bottles ('stops us drinking them all!'), licking labels, sealing cases – and plenty of tasting along the way.

Cabernet Sauvignon ★★★ Food-inviting **09** has walnut piquancy, sour cherry flavours, shows cool vintage's grip. **Shiraz** ★★★ In contrast to Cab, **09** is dense & powerful, savoury, still tight. Appealing roast beef, black pepper, scrub aromas, structure to develop interestingly. **Jada's Rose** ★★★★ Smooth **09**, happy marriage cab & shiraz (60/40), latter's spice & raspberry fruit plump out cab's robust grip. Good now & for few years. — Panel

De Toren Private Cellar

Location/map/WO: Stellenbosch ▪ Est 1994 ▪ 1stB 1999 ▪ Tasting, sales & cellar tours by appt ▪ Fee R180, waived on purchase ▪ Donkey Walk ▪ Owner(s) Edenhall Trust ▪ Cellarmaster(s) Albie Koch (Oct 1998) ▪ Winemaker(s) Charles Williams (Dec 2008, consultant) ▪ Viticulturist(s) Ernest Manuel (Mar 2003, consultant) ▪ 25ha/±21ha (cabs s/f, malbec, merlot, p verdot) ▪ 150t/8,000cs own label 100% red + 3,000cs for clients ▪ Brands for clients: Shoprite Checkers Odd Bins ▪ PO Box 48 Vlottenburg 7604 ▪ info@de-toren.com ▪ www.de-toren.com ▪ S 33° 57′ 34.5″ E 018° 45′7.5″ ▪ **T +27 (0)21-881-3119** ▪ F +27 (0)21-881-3335

Meticulous attention is paid to every aspect of De Toren's operation and they've had 18 years to get it right, so anything new is noteworthy. In this case, a malolactic fermentation room which allows complete temperature control of the process. All this trouble for just two wines, you might ask, but they're not ordinary wines, these are amongst the highest rated South African wines by the international media. Both classic 5-variety Bordeaux-type blends, but with different proportions, Fusion V usually Cabernet dominant, Z (named after its vineyard block, and pronounced 'Zee') with more Merlot. Most recent Fusion V awards include 5 star ratings in both Wine Magazine and Decanter and the only SA wine to appear on Wine Enthusiast's Top 100 Wines of the World. Both wines are regularly rated 90+ points in Wine Spectator, Wine Enthusiast and by Stephen Tanzer.

★★★★☆ **Fusion V 09** (★★★★★) 5-variety Bordeaux red, usually cab-led, as was **08**. Pure drinking pleasure, cassis & dark chocolate, with complex nuances keeping you involved. Structure strikes perfect balance between polished accessibility & ageing ability. Enjoy till ±2020.

★★★★ **Z** Earlier drinking 'Bordeaux 5' counterpoint to sibling. Merlot leads in **09**, succulent plums & berries, rich chocolate tones, beautifully presented in a smooth-textured body. — CR

De Trafford Wines

Location/map/WO: Stellenbosch ▪ Est/1stB 1992 ▪ Tasting, sales & tours Fri & Sat 10–1, or otherwise by appt ▪ Fee R50, waived on purchase ▪ Closed al pub hols ▪ Owner(s) David & Rita Trafford ▪ Winemaker(s) David Trafford ▪ Viticulturist(s) Schalk du Toit (consultant) ▪ 200ha/5ha (cabs s/f, merlot, pinot, shiraz) ▪ 71t/3,500cs own label 70% red 30% white ▪ PO Box 495 Stellenbosch 7599 ▪ info@detrafford.co.za ▪ www.detrafford.co.za ▪ S 34° 0′45.1″ E 018° 53′ 57.8″ ▪ **T +27 (0)21-880-1611** ▪ F +27 (0)21-880-1611

Spending too much time on admin is one of David Trafford's frustrations and he looks forward to getting back to the vineyards. Commenting on how much fruit can vary from one site to another, he's become so impatient with many journalists' contempt for the terroir concept outside traditional European areas, he decided to demonstrate its existence here. Sourcing enough 2010 Shiraz grapes for a 225l barrel each from two Swartland vineyards, from Chris Mullineux and Eben Sadie; two from Walker Bay, namely Benguela Cove and Springfontein; his own De Trafford 393 vineyard and Malgas, he produced them all in exactly the same way, from ripeness at picking; length of time on skins; temperature; time in barrels, and no new oak – to highlight the different sites. The 5 bottles will be released as a pack the end of 2011. And a recent highlight was representing South Africa, with six other producers, at The Wine Spectator's New World Wine Experience in Las Vegas.

★★★★☆ **Cabernet Sauvignon** Cassis & dark plums in **09**, ripeness tamed by firm dry tannins, no harshness but a vital force in the wine. Scrub & white pepper are a few of the many interwoven complex notes, with more to be revealed over the next 6+ years.

★★★★ **Merlot** Just-picked berries, some charcuterie notes in **09**, trademark polished lines. Still youthful tannins will soften over time, no barrier to current enjoyment.

★★★★ **Blueprint Syrah** Younger Keermont vineyard grapes fruitier than stablemates, but **09** doesn't lack savoury allspice to accompany the succulent berries, older oak fully integrated. 'Blueprint Shiraz' previously.

★★★★☆ **Syrah 393 08** & previous listed as 'Shiraz'. Natural balance best describes this vineyard, which includes full ripeness, but **09** offers more: espresso & smoky whiffs, Provençal herbs, the dark fruit's freshness a counterpoint to the supple tannins. Slightly less concentration than seminal **08** (★★★★★).

★★★★☆ **Elevation 393** Barrel selection, named for home-vineyard altitude. Cab-led Bordeaux blend & shiraz, each playing their part in **09**. Plush dark berries, whiffs of salty liquorice, scrub, backed by muscular tannins designed for long, slow, bottle evolution.

★★★★ **Chenin Blanc** From low-yielding older vines (25-40 years), showy **10** reflects the vintage's ripeness in its full body, fruit preserve flavours. Barrel fermented/matured, unfiltered. Can age good few years.

★★★★☆ **Straw Wine** Pioneer of style, in 12th year & always impressive. Honey & apricots, preserved quince, **09**'s powerful sweetness infused with an almond savoury seam. Enjoy on its own after a meal. Chenin air-dried on racks, 23 months in 50% new French oak.

Discontinued: **Pinot Noir**. — CR

De Vallei   ⅋ 🍴 🍷 📷 ⛏ ♿

Location/WO: Durbanville ▪ Map: Durbanville, Philadelphia & Darling ▪ Est/1stB 2006 ▪ Tasting, sales & cellar tours Wed-Fri 10-4 Sat/Sun 11-3 ▪ Fee R15 ▪ Closed Easter Fri/Mon, Dec 25/26 & Jan 1 ▪ Mezze platters ▪ Mountain biking ▪ Owner(s) De Vallei Wynlandgoed (Pty) Ltd ▪ Cellarmaster(s)/winemaker(s) Nikie de Villiers (Jan 2006) ▪ Viticulturist(s) Nikie & Koos de Villiers ▪ 140ha/100ha (cab, merlot, pinot, shiraz, chard, sauv) ▪ 500cs own label 36% red 64% white ▪ PO Box 488 Durbanville 7551 ▪ info@devallei.co.za ▪ www.devallei.co.za ▪ S 33° 50'22.3" E 018° 36'22.6" ▪ **T +27 (0)72-279-1429** ▪ F +27 (0)86-664-0881

Durbanville's signature sauvignon makes up half of this farm's vineyards, but a 20 year old block of pinot noir is a current focus for Nikie de Villiers. He made a wine from it in 2011 which 'looks promising, but I'll wait until 2012 to see how it develops.' If it's good enough, he hopes it will help establish their young brand.

★★★★ **Sur Lie Sauvignon Blanc** NEW Light oaking, 11 months on lees, hint of bottle age enhance individual **10**. Plump but not flabby, with honey-licked fig flavours extended by keen but well contained acidity. **Donum** 🍽 ★★★ Approachable **09** last year showed had bright cassis with herbaceous edge. **Cabernet Sauvignon** NEW ★★★★ Presently austere **09** leavened by sweet vanilla notes from oak (50% new). Blackberry fruit should emerge for pleasant drinking after year or 2. **Syrah** Await next release. **Jacobus** ★★★★ If it ain't broke, don't fix it; idiom applies to this cab, shiraz, merlot blend. **09** displays usual juiciness, modest alcohol & freshness. **Annerose Pinot Noir-Chardonnay** 🍽 ★★★ Soft **10** with red fruit fragrance still selling. **Sauvignon Blanc** ★★★ Simple, sweetish tropical tones on **11** cut by steely-edged acidity. — AL

De Villiers Wines   ⅋

Location: Paarl ▪ Map: Paarl & Wellington ▪ Est/1stB 1996 ▪ Tasting & sales by appt ▪ Owner(s) De Villiers Family Trust ▪ Cellarmaster(s)/winemaker(s)/viticulturist(s) Villiers de Villiers (1996) ▪ 25,000cs own label 80% red 20%

white ▪ Other export brand: Heeren van Oranje Nassau ▪ PO Box 659 Suider-Paarl 7624 ▪ vadev@mweb.co.za ▪ S 33° 45' 43.3" E 018° 57' 40.8" ▪ **T +27 (0)21-863-2175** ▪ F +27 (0)86-653-8988

Having secured a presence in most major supermarket chains locally, CEO Villiers is pleased to announce that 'De Villiers Wines is once again supplying China with wine; the last time we supplied the Chinese was via the envoy of the Dutch East India Company in 1789; to Peking'.

Cabernet Sauvignon ★★★ Intense berry jam flavours on **09**, firm tannin, brief finish. None of these retasted this ed. **Merlot ★★★** Berry-toned **09** had pleasant roundness & body, soft structure. **Pinotage ★★★ 09** showed deft touches: enticing spicy wild black fruits & juicy plumpness. **Shiraz ★★★** Generous **09** mixed black fruit, smooth texture, hint dark choc. **Sauvignon Blanc** 🗐 **★★★** Light & refreshing **10** was still quite restrained soon after btlng. Discontinued: **Pinotage Rosé, Paarl Riesling, Chardonnay, Chenin Blanc, Blanc de Blanc**. — GdB

■ **De Vloot** *see* Groupe LFE South Africa

Devonair

Location/map: Stellenbosch ▪ Est 1994 ▪ 1stB 2000 ▪ Tasting & sales by appt ▪ Closed all pub hols ▪ Conference facilities ▪ 2 self-catering cottages ▪ Owner(s) Leon & Rina de Wit ▪ Winemaker(s) Ernst Gouws (Mar 2006) ▪ Viticulturist(s) Frans Snyman (2011) ▪ 2.2ha (cab) ▪ 10t/460cs own label 100% red ▪ PO Box 1274 Stellenbosch 7599 ▪ alana@devonair.co.za ▪ www.devonair.co.za ▪ S 33°53'44.45" E 018°48'27.46" ▪ **T +27 (0)21-886-6830** ▪ F +27 (0)21-886-6855

Co-owner Leon de Wit believes in specialisation, hence only Cabernet plantings on this tiny Devon Valley property near Stellenbosch. SAA clearly approved, because The Cab 2006 is sold out ex-farm, snapped up as the category winner and served only to Premium Class passengers. Collectors need not panic, however, the 2006 Family Reserve and some older vintages of The Cab are still available here and through Cybercellar.

The Cab ★★★★ Last **06** showed serious intent in 2 yrs oaking, half new, but balanced by plush ripe fruit. **The Cab Family Reserve ★★★★** Good fruit in last **06**, cassis & plums, with sturdy oak providing structure, rewarding future. Own, Grangehurst vines. **The Rosé** Await next. — CR

■ **Devonet** *see* Clos Malverne

Devon Hill

Location/WO: Stellenbosch ▪ Est 1994 ▪ 1stB 1996 ▪ Closed to public ▪ Owner(s) Geir Tellefsen ▪ Cellarmaster(s)/ winemaker(s)/viticulturist(s) Philip Costandius (Jan 2010, consultant) ▪ 10,000cs own label 80% red 15% white 5% rosé ▪ info@devonhill.co.za ▪ www.devonhill.co.za ▪ **T +27 (0)21-424-4498** ▪ F +27 (0)21-424-1571

Existing stock, with its attractive packaging, and the right to produce under the Devon Hill label were acquired late last year by Geir Tellefsen of Rosendal Winery in Robertson. The new owner intends sourcing grapes from select growers in the Devon Valley and marketing the wines through his extremely active wine club using proven internet, email and telephone marketing techniques. 'This way, we boost quality/price ratios by ±50%, something our customers really appreciate.'

★★★★ **Bluebird** Like all reds, **02** ready now; well-knit merlot-led (73%) combo with plummy flavour. Grapes for these from Devon Valley.

Cabernet Sauvignon ★★★★ Good expression of mature SA cab, **03** tasted out of vintage sequence previously & noted as best enjoyed soon. Not revisited, as Shiraz, Pinotage. **Merlot ★★★★** Complex aromas fynbos, wet earth & plum on fruit-filled **10**, fresh & medium bodied to enjoy young. **Pinotage ★★★★ 02** acetone lift to strawberry & banana fruit, slightly medicinal, drink soon. **Shiraz ★★★★** Intense **03**'s ripe mouthful reined in by deft oak & tannins, vein of acidity. **Sauvignon Blanc ★★★** Shy tangerine & grass, **10** doesn't trumpet the variety but makes an appealing food companion. Discontinued: **Four Stars**. — CvZ

Devon Rocks

Location/map/WO: Stellenbosch ▪ Est 1998 ▪ 1stB 2003 ▪ Tasting, sales & tours by appt ▪ B&B accommodation ▪ Owner(s) Jürgen & Brita Heinrich ▪ Winemaker(s) Simon Smith (Louisvale) ▪ Viticulturist(s) Gawie du Bois & Paul

Wallace (advisers) ▪ 4ha/3.5ha (ptage, shiraz) ▪ 2,200cs 57% red 18% white 25% rosé ▪ PO Box 12483 Die Boord 7613 ▪ info@devonrocks.co.za ▪ www.devonrocks.co.za ▪ S 33° 53′ 19.9″ E 018° 48′ 30.1″ ▪ **T +27 (0)21-865-2536** ▪ F +27 (0)21-865-2621

New markets in Sweden and Switzerland, joint ventures for streamlining production and marketing, and a mission statement of quality as a priority; these may not seem particularly innovative concepts, but Devon Valley boutique vintners Jürgen and Brita Heinrich believe the basics should be respected and quality should take preference over change.

Pinotage ★★★★ Good varietal profile, crisp structure & drying tannins on **08** everyday uncomplicated red. **Shiraz Rosé** 🍷 ★★★ Semi-sweet **09**, juicy tutti-frutti style, good poolside thirst quencher. **Sauvignon Blanc** 🍷 ★★★ Notes of green beans & minerals. **09** crisp but tad austere. All above previously tasted. — GdB

Devonvale Golf & Wine Estate

Location/map/WO: Stellenbosch ▪ Est 1997 ▪ 1stB 2004 ▪ Tasting by appt ▪ Fee R10pp ▪ Sales Mon-Sat 11–6 ▪ Restaurant open daily for breakfast, lunch & dinner (Sep-Apr) & 7-3 (May-Aug) ▪ Tour groups ▪ Golf ▪ Pro shop ▪ Conferences ▪ Devonvale Lodge ▪ Owner(s) Devonmust (Pty) Ltd ▪ Winemaker(s) Wilhelm Kritzinger (2004, Bellevue Estate) ▪ Viticulturist(s) Ruben Nienaber (2000) ▪ 117ha/26.5ha (shiraz) ▪ 14t/950cs own label 100% red ▪ PO Box 77 Koelenhof 7605 ▪ info@devonvale.co.za ▪ www.devonvale.co.za ▪ S 33° 52′ 59.6″ E 018° 48′ 15.0″ ▪ **T +27 (0)21-865-2080** ▪ F +27 (0)21-865-2601

Residents of Devonvale housing estate, golf course and working wine farm outside Stellenbosch at harvest time roll up their sleeves and help bring in the crop from vines fringing some of the fairways, for vinification and bottling at Bellevue. The nautical connotations in the branding are to Devonvale founder and round-the-world yachtsman JJ Provoyeur, and to a particularly favourable angle in sailing.

Owner's Special Reserve range NEW
Shiraz ★★★★ Elegant & rounded **08**, good concentration of plums, savoury edge offset by showy oak.

Broad Reach range
Provoyeur Cabernet Sauvignon ★★★ **07** earthy notes, plummy centre, toasty new-oak seasoning & support noted last year. **Provoyeur Shiraz** ★★★ **09** shows the mocha/chocolate notes of previous but more balance, with smoky, plummy edge. — DB

DeWaal Wines

Location/map/WO: Stellenbosch ▪ Est 1682 ▪ 1stB 1972 ▪ Tasting & sales Mon-Fri 10–12.30 & 2–4.30 Sat 10–4.30 (Aug-Apr only) ▪ Fee R20 ▪ Closed Easter Fri-Mon, Jun 16, Dec 25/26 & Jan 1 ▪ Owner(s) Pieter de Waal ▪ Winemaker(s)/viticulturist(s) Chris de Waal & Daniël de Waal (whites/reds, consultants) ▪ 154ha/120ha (ptage, shiraz, sauv) ▪ 800t 50% red 50% white ▪ IPW ▪ PO Box 15 Vlottenburg 7604 ▪ info@dewaal.co.za ▪ www.dewaal.co.za ▪ S 33° 56′ 29.3″ E 018° 45′ 59.9″ ▪ **T +27 (0)21-881-3711** ▪ F +27 (0)21-881-3776

The DeWaal family business has undergone a revamp, with new brands being partitioned off from the jointly-owned estate and three separate arms of control (see Cape Gable and Super Singles). The original label is now under the control of Pieter, who sources wines from his brothers, Danie & Chris. The lovely old family farm, Uiterwyk, in the Stellenboschkloof area, still provides the grapes for wines in all three stables. This arrangement, according to Pieter, allows each to pursue his particular directions of interest, without the constraints of committee decision-making. For the moment, the sensibly positioned three-tier product range remains as before.

DeWaal range
★★★★ **Cabernet Sauvignon** Leafy, nutty aromas on **07** followed to bracing blackcurrant & wild herb flavours last year.

★★★★ **Merlot** ✓ Full-bodied, resolutely dry **09** shows old-world styling with solid, ripe black fruit. Emerging house style is a welcome change from fruit-driven rivals.

★★★★ **CT de Waal Pinotage** Meaty, robust **07** had noble structure & form last time, with blackberry pudding flavour. This & all following not retasted.

★★★★☆ **Top of the Hill Pinotage** 07 demanded attention last edition. Tiny yield off old vines, precisely handled. Complex mix spicy baked fruits, fresh crushed berries.

★★★★ **Signal Rock** Cab-driven 08 Bordeaux-style blend last year was big & angular, tealeaf & forest floor layers over rich blackcurrant fruit.

Pinotage ★★★★ Lighter-bodied 09 modestly oaked, highlighting appealing mulberry & cherry fruit. **Sauvignon Blanc** ★★★★ On review, striking asparagus aromas on 09 signalled new-found boldness with crisply satisfying palate. **Viognier** ★★★★ Back-to-basics unoaked 09, when last tasted emphasised varietal richness & ripe peach fruit.

Young Vines range

Merlot 🍷 ★★★ 09 lightweight, bit angular with dusty mulberry fruit. **Shiraz** 🍷 ★★★ 09 butterscotch surprise, juicy-fruity quaffer. **Chenin Blanc** 🍷 ★★★ Admirable consistency. **10** echoed previous, over-delivered on flavour & body mid-2010. **Sauvignon Blanc** 🍷 ★★★ Pungent, fresh & racy 10 pleasantly undemanding. — GdB

Dewaldt Heyns Family Wines

WO: Coastal/Swartland ▪ Est/1stB 2006 ▪ Tasting by appt at Saronsberg ▪ Owner(s) Dewaldt Heyns Family Wines ▪ Cellarmaster(s)/winemaker(s)/viticulturist(s) Dewaldt Heyns ▪ (shiraz, chenin) ▪ 15t/550cs own label 50% red 50% white ▪ dewaldt@saronsberg.com ▪ **T** +27 (0)82-441-4117

'My father's weathered hands testify to a lifetime of faithful toil among the vineyards of his Swartland farm,' says Dewaldt Heyns, owner/winemaker (and celebrated cellarmaster at Saronsberg). 'This stark region leaves its mark on all who call it home, and in this range I hope to express its unique and enduring character. I dedicate these wines to the man whose love for the vine was the start of my own.'

Weathered Hands range

★★★★ **Chenin Blanc** Joins upper echelon of Swartland terroir wines with 09, beautifully expresses the variety in pure tropical & apple fruit, lingering creamy vanilla flavours; complex structure will reward ageing.

Shiraz ★★★★ Plush New World style 07 is rich & full, suffused with dark berry fruit, black pepper & sweet spice. Well-judged oak, warm conclusion (15% alc) doesn't linger. Swartland grapes (certified as Coastal). — Panel

De Wetshof Estate

Location/map/WO: Robertson ▪ Est 1949 ▪ 1stB 1972 ▪ Tasting & sales Mon–Fri 8.30–4.30 Sat 9.30–12.30 ▪ Closed Easter Fri/Sun/Mon, May 1, Dec 25/26 & Jan 1 ▪ Cellar tours by appt Mon–Fri 8.30–4.30 ▪ Conservation area ▪ Owner(s) Danie de Wet, Peter de Wet & Johann de Wet ▪ Cellarmaster(s) Danie de Wet (Jan 1973) ▪ Winemaker(s) Danie de Wet (Jan 1973), Mervyn Williams (2001) & Peter de Wet (2007) ▪ Viticulturist(s) George Thom (1996), advised by Phil Freese & Francois Viljoen (both 1997) ▪ 600ha/180ha (cab, merlot, pinot, chard, riesling, sauv) ▪ 1,800t 8% red 90% white 1% rosé 1% cap classique ▪ ISO 9001:2008, ISO 22000:2005, BBBEE Grade 4, BWI, Enviro Scientific, Integrity & Sustainability, IPW ▪ PO Box 31 Robertson 6705 ▪ info@dewetshof.com ▪ www.dewetshof.com ▪ S 33° 52'38.0" E 020° 0'35.1" ▪ **T** +27 (0)23-615-1853 ▪ F +27 (0)23-615-1915

Nature in Concert is the name of both their acclaimed pinot noir and a Club where farmschool pupils and personnel alike are encouraged to adopt water conservation and sustainability generally. In the cellar, too, the goal is 'to partner nature with science to make the finest wines possible'. Marketing chief Lesca de Wet (wife of cellarmaster Danie, mother to winemakers Peter and Johann) highlights two non-negotiables in the family's quest for vinous excellence: 'One is managing the vineyards in tandem with our unique climate and natural limestone-rich soils. The other is implementing state-of-the art technology. Progress is embraced.'

De Wetshof range

★★★★ **Bateleur Chardonnay** Enduring & noble expression of barrel fermented/lees-aged chardonnay. **09** last year was restrained, lemon toned & tightly wound, needed year/2 to show better.

★★★★★ **The Site Chardonnay** NEW ✓ Another gem, this in Burgundian mould, from a Cape chardonnay pioneer. Tantalisingly subtle on the nose, yet 09 is full, lithe & silky in the mouth, generously layered with ripe citrus & gooseberry fruit. Unevolved mid-2011 but will richly reward patience.

★★★★ **Rhine Riesling** 🍷 Previously tasted 09 showed a spicy candied fruit character, smidgen sugar softened a steely edge; commendably moderate 12.5% alc.

★★★★★ **Edeloes** Exceptional botrytised dessert, occasional release. Last-tasted 05 (★★★★) charming, complex; previous was 00. 500ml.

Chardonnay D'Honneur ★★★★ Clotted cream, bruised apple hallmarks of French oak fermented/aged version. Previewed mid-2010, 07's vanilla & brioche seamed with zingy lime took it to the next level over 06 (★★★★). Ageworthy, like Bateleur. **Finesse Chardonnay** ⓦ ★★★★ 10 fatter & more buttery than previous release, engaging citrus zest refreshes, spicy notes extend the finish. **Bon Vallon Chardonnay** ✓ ⓦ ★★★★ Unwooded version. 11 continues along path struck by step-up 09. Fresh & supple, green apple acidity & leesy richness. **Sauvignon Blanc** ★★★ 11 raises the bar: aromatic & spicy, hint of dusty stone well-formed, substantial mouthful. **Méthode Cap Classique Brut** NEW ★★★★ Champagne-method sparkling from chardonnay (70%) & pinot noir, NV. Rich brioche, yeasty lees appeal & commendable dryness; tad brisk though.

Danie de Wet range

★★★★ **Naissance Cabernet Sauvignon** Previewed last time, 09 now reaps rewards of bottle-age. Classic structure & firm tannins, lead pencil fragrance; matches complexity, elegance of tasted-out-of-sequence 06.

★★★★ **Cape Muscadel** Last was sweetly simple 07 (★★★), missing complexity of 06 & previous.

Nature In Concert Pinot Noir 🍷 ★★★★ Not revisited cherry & choc-mocha 09 was firm, flavoursome, hid 14.5% alc well. **Rosé** 🍷 ★★★ 10 appealing summer sipper from cab franc, still selling & not retasted. **Chardonnay Sur Lie** ✓ 🍷 ⓦ ★★★★ Unwooded 11 has creamy richness laced with tangy lemon twist. Poised & elegant expression of fruit. **Limestone Hill Chardonnay** ✓ 🍷 ⓦ ★★★★ Unoaked, lees-aged 11 now bottled: vibrant & fruity, touch of buttery fatness, & the mineral chalkiness suggested in wine's name. **Sauvignon Blanc** 🍷 ⓦ ★★★ Lightish (±12% alc) 11 zesty sipper infused with ripe gooseberry & passionfruit. — Panel

---

De Wet Winery

Location/map/WO: Worcester ▪ Est 1946 ▪ 1stB 1964 ▪ Tasting & sales Mon-Fri 8–5 Sat 9–12 ▪ Fee R1/wine ▪ Closed all pub hols ▪ Cellar tour by appt ▪ BYO picnic ▪ Owner(s) 60 members ▪ Cellarmaster(s) Piet le Roux (Jan 2000) ▪ Winemaker(s) Tertius Jonck (Sep 2007) & Phillip Vercuiel (Dec 2007) ▪ Viticulturist(s) Hennie Visser (Jul 2008, Vinpro) ▪ 1,000ha (cab, shiraz, chard, chenin, sauv) ▪ 15,500t/15,000c. own label 29% red 36% white 5% rosé 30% fortified + 10m L bulk ▪ ISO 22000, SGS ▪ PO Box 16 De Wet 6853 ▪ admin@dewetcellar.co.za ▪ www.dewetcellar.co.za ▪ S 33° 36' 24.2" E 019° 30' 36.5" ▪ **T +27 (0)23-341-2710** ▪ F +27 (0)23-341-2762

New technology having lifted quality in the cellar, the focus is shifting to reducing the carbon footprint and optimising water management at this grower-owned cellar, a founder member of the highly successful export joint venture, FirstCape. Winemaker Tertius Jonck's enthusiasm for méthode cap classique saw them release a maiden bubbly, one of the first in the Worcester area.

★★★★ **White Muscadel** ✓ 🍷 High-toned almond, apricot & tangerine, 10 fortified after-dinner treat is sweet but clean, uncloying, offers delightful flavours of glacé pineapple & dried apple.

> **Pinotage** 😊 🍷 ★★★ Appealing 09, tasty spread of mulberry, vanilla & savoury, restrained & medium bodied. **Chenin Blanc** 😊 🍷 ⓦ ★★★ 11 says 'notice me': substantial appley mouthful, long juicy pineapple aftertaste. **Rosé** 😊 🍷 ★★ Gently sweet NV bubbly from pinotage, with understated berry taste.

Cabernet Sauvignon 🍷 ⓦ ★★ Mulberry & thatch notes on tad stalky 10, spicy-sweet style for early enjoyment. **Shiraz** 🍷 ⓦ ★★ Tutti-frutti style 10, vanilla-infused everyday red. **Dry Red** 🍷 ⓦ ★★ Attractive berry-honey aroma, candyfloss taste, bit hard finish on 10. **Chardonnay** NEW 🍷 ⓦ ★★★ Plenty vanilla & spicy oak, 10 creamy centre, slightly warm tail. **Sauvignon Blanc** 🍷 ⓦ ★★★ Preview 11 pear-drop fragrance, 'dusty pebble' flavour & nice lemony bite. **Petillant Fronté** 🍷 ★★ Aromatic, sweetish, spritzy NV from white muscadel, light (8% alc) & floral. **Cravate** NEW ★★★★ Among first méthode cap classique sparklings from the region is a fine effort. 100% chardonnay, 09 myriad tiny bubbles, fresh & vibrant. Not as much brioche flavour or weight as some but welcome addition to the category. **Hanepoot** ⓦ ★★★★ Fortified dessert with heady muscat aroma, lovely nutty aftertaste. 10 drier than stablemates but more warming. **Red Muscadel** 🍷 ★★★★ Delicious fortified dessert offering balanced raisin sweetness & weight, cranberry & tealeaf flavour. 10 steps up, delivers more complexity than honey-sweet 09 (★★★). Both muscat desserts & Cape Vintage worth stocking up on for good-value winter sipping. **Ruby Port** ★★★ Just 'Port' last time. NV from tinta & pontac is a tad tired, with garnet edge, almond & tealeaf flavours. **Cape Vintage** ✓ ★★★★ 08 fortified from now-uprooted pontac vineyard. Last edition had curry spice & Xmas cake, firm structure & luscious lingering flavour. Nudged next level. Discontinued: **Gewürztraminer Natural Sweet**. — Panel

De Zoete Inval Estate

Location/WO: Paarl ▪ Map: Paarl & Wellington ▪ Est 1878 ▪ 1stB 1976 ▪ Tastings & sales by appt ▪ Owner(s) DZI Agricultural Investments cc (John Robert & Eulalia Frater) ▪ Cellarmaster(s) John Robert Frater ▪ Winemaker(s) John Robert Frater (1999) ▪ Viticulturist(s) John Robert Frater (1999) / Dirk Blom (2007) ▪ 80ha/25ha (cab, grenache, malbec, p verdot, port varieties, sangio, shiraz, zinf, chard, sauv) ▪ 200t/8,000cs own label 50% red 50% white ▪ PO Box 591 Suider-Paarl 7624 ▪ info@dezoeteinval.co.za ▪ www.dezoeteinval.co.za ▪ S 33° 46′ 35.9″ E 018° 57′ 50.9″ ▪ T +27 (0)21-863-1535 ▪ F +27 (0)21-863-2158

The Frater family are going organic in their vineyards in Suider Paarl: permanent cover-crops, zero pesticide and minimal intervention are the new viticultural order. Recent plantings of sangiovese, malbec and grenache will be making their way into the blends planned for this vintage.

★★★★ **Pinotage Reserve** Spicy oak dominated **08** last year, with well-layered plummy fruit, meaty savoury notes. Supple body & texture. Simonsberg vines.

Pinotage ★ **05** noted previously as overripe & touch porty. **Cabernet Sauvignon-Shiraz** ★★★ **09** was medicinal, with sweet berry fruit. Heavy, full bodied. **Chardonnay** ★★ Reintroduced **10** has faint wet-wool notes on lean, mineral body. **Vintage Brut** ★★★ Bone-dry méthode cap classique sparkling from chardonnay. **04** apple aromas & racy acidity when last tasted. **Cape Vintage** ★★★ Elegant blend 7 port varieties; vines up to 80 years old. Previously **03** showed spicy fruitcake flavours, lowish alc. **Sweet Surrender Shiraz** ★★★ Fortified campfire warmer, **06** (reviewed out of vintage sequence) fruit-drop blackcurrant & solid spirit thump. Discontinued: **Sauvignon Blanc-Semillon-Chenin Blanc**. — GdB

DGB

Wellington ▪ Est 1942 ▪ Closed to public ▪ Owner(s) DGB Management, Brait Capital Partners & Kangra ▪ Winemaker(s)/viticulturist(s) see Bellingham & Boschendal ▪ PO Box 246 Wellington 7654 ▪ exports@dgb.co.za ▪ www.dgb.co.za ▪ T +27 (0)21-864-5300 ▪ F +27 (0)21-864-1287

Well-established merchant house with strong portfolio of premium and own-brand table wines, ports and sherries. See separate entries for Bellingham, Boschendal, Brampton, Culemborg, Douglas Green, Franschhoek Cellar, Legacy, Millstream, Oude Kaap, Tall Horse, The Bernard Series and The Saints.

▪ **Diamond Collection** *see Lutzville Cape Diamond Vineyards*
▪ **Dido** *see The Township Winery*

Die Bergkelder Wine Centre

Location/map: Stellenbosch ▪ All day tasting & sales Mon-Fri 8–5 Sat 9–2 ▪ Tour fee R25 ▪ Open non-religious pub hols ▪ Tours Mon-Fri 10, 11, 2 & 3; Sat 10, 11 & 12; incl AV presentation; bookings: info@bergkelder.co.za ▪ Tel +27 (0)21-809-8025 ▪ Special group tours, private tastings by appt ▪ Owner(s) Distell ▪ Cellarmaster(s) Andrea Freeborough ▪ Winemaker(s) Pieter Badenhorst (whites) & Justin Corrans (reds), with John November & Bradley van Niekerk ▪ Viticulturist(s) Bennie Liebenberg ▪ 2,500t/214,000cs 45% red 55% white ▪ PO Box 184 Stellenbosch 7599 ▪ info@bergkelder.co.za ▪ www.bergkelder.co.za ▪ S 33° 56′ 8.8″ E 018° 50′ 54.7″ ▪ T +27 (0)21-809-8025 ▪ F +27 (0)21-883-9533

Literally 'Mountain Cellar', after the maturation facilities deep within Stellenbosch's Papegaaiberg, Die Bergkelder is the home of Fleur du Cap, listed separately. FdC wines can be tasted during a cellar tour, while other premium and super-premium wines in the Distell portfolio can be tasted and purchased at Die Bergkelder Wine Centre. The Vinoteque, now in its 28th year, markets fine wines with the option of having purchases stored in perfect cellar conditions. T +27 (0)21-809-8281 • info@vinoteque.co.za • www.vinoteque.co.za.

▪ **Die Kaapse Seleksie** *see Linton Park Wines*
▪ **Die Krans** *see De Krans*
▪ **Die Laan** *see Stellenbosch University Welgevallen Vineyards & Cellar*

Die Mas van Kakamas

Location/WO: Northern Cape ▪ Map: Northern Cape, Free State & North West ▪ Est/1stB 2005 ▪ Tasting & sales Mon-Fri 8-5 Sat/Sun by appt ▪ Closed Easter Fri-Mon & Dec 25 ▪ 3-hr full farm tour on tractor-pulled wagon during tasting hours ▪ Meals/refreshments by appt ▪ Facilities for children ▪ Tour groups ▪ Gift shop ▪ Farm produce ▪ BYO picnic ▪ Conference facilities ▪ Walking/hiking/mountain biking trails ▪ Conservation area ▪ Camping facilities, 3 self-catering chalets & large lapa/bush pub ▪ Owner(s) Die Mas Boerdery (Pty) Ltd ▪ Cellarmaster(s)/winemaker(s)/viticulturist(s) Danie van der Westhuizen (May 2010) ▪ 1,400ha/80ha (cab, merlot, muscadel r/w, p verdot, pinot, ptage, sangio, shiraz, souzão, tinta barocca, touriga nacional, chard, chenin, cbard, sauv, viog) ▪ 350t/7,000cs own label 50% red 20% white 30% brandy ▪ PO Box 193 Kakamas 8870 ▪ winemaker@diemasvankakamas.co.za ▪ www.diemasvankakamas.co.za ▪ S 28° 45' 48.59" E 020° 38' 26.45" ▪ **T +27 (0)54-431-0245 / +27 (0)82-931-5902** ▪ F +27 (0)86-531-9243

Small blocks of an array of classic dry wine, sweet dessert, port and brandy varieties are starting to bear fruit on this holiday farm developed by intrepid former teachers Vlok and Welna Hanekom. Winemaker Danie van der Westhuizen is determined to prove the Orange River spread capable of producing fine wine.

Rooi Kalahari range NEW

Merlot ★★ Ripe & plummy **09**, soft & easy-drinking. **Shiraz** ◎ ★★ Very ripe berry flavours on effortless **10**. **Port** ★★★ Fruitcake & spice on **09** appealing fireside warmer. Well developed, with smooth chocolate finish.

Groen Kalahari range NEW

Chardonnay ◎ ★★ Uncomplicated dry **11** sipper. **Sauvignon Blanc** ◎ ★★ Tropical **11**, crisp summer white.

Goue Kalahari range NEW

Hanepoot ✓ ★★★★ Northern Cape sunshine in a bottle. **09** oozes fragrant pineapple & boiled sweets. Unctuous & mouthfilling yet lively, a velvety texture. — Panel

Diemersdal Estate

Location: Durbanville ▪ Map: Durbanville, Philadelphia & Darling ▪ WO: Durbanville/Western Cape ▪ Est 1698 ▪ 1stB 1979 ▪ Tasting & sales Mon-Fri 9–5 Sat 9–3 ▪ Closed Easter Fri/Sun, Dec 25 & Jan 1 ▪ Tours by appt ▪ BYO picnic ▪ Walks ▪ Owner(s) Tienie Louw ▪ Winemaker(s) Thys Louw & Mari van der Merwe ▪ Viticulturist(s) Div van Niekerk (1980) ▪ 400ha/172ha (cab, grenache, malbec, merlot, mourv, p verdot, ptage, shiraz, chard, sauv) ▪ 1,750t 70% red 30% white ▪ BWI, BRC, HACCIP ▪ PO Box 27 Durbanville 7551 ▪ thys@diemersdal.co.za ▪ www.diemersdal.co.za ▪ S 33° 48' 6.3" E 018° 38' 25.1" ▪ **T +27 (0)21-976-3361** ▪ F +27 (0)21-976-1810

Increasing export sales for this 6th generation family estate was high on incumbent winemaker Thys Louw's to do list in 2011, and achieved - not readily but convincingly - thanks to travel, travel and more travel. When the going gets tough, relationships are your weapon of choice, he says, so there's always someone heading off to put in some 'face-time' with distributors. Also contributing to sales was the unusual sauvignon rosé and a maiden grenache, which found a ready market in Belgium. And the year ahead? Travel, travel and more travel...

MM Louw range

★★★★☆ **Red Blend** 🍷 Restraint, elegance, hallmarks of this Bordeaux blend. **09** subtle mint & cassis, lively acidity, fine tannins; structure to reward few years cellaring. **07** classic cedar/cigarbox complexity; **08** sold untasted.

★★★★☆ **Sauvignon Blanc** There's a sauvignon to suit every palate & wallet at Diemersdal; this usually the most ageworthy. Last time **09** a star in stellar vintage for the variety: fragrant & green fruited but with a savoury nuance, pinpoint balance & distinct minerality.

Reserve range

★★★★ **Private Collection** Cab-led Bordeaux blend, exceptional **09** (★★★★★) evokes Old World in herbaceous wafts to subtle black fruit/lead pencil bouquet, smartly managed tannins, oak seasoning a mere suggestion (20 months 60% new Fr). More complex than **08**. This, others unless stated, previously in Estate range.

★★★★ **Chardonnay Reserve** Tasted previously, **09** nudged standard set by standout **07** (★★★★★): pineapple & melon glacé complexity plus firm acidity; caramel ex 9 months new French oak.

★★★★☆ **Sauvignon Blanc** Expresses character of low-bearing, 25 year old single-vineyard. Quince/ greengage on **11** in footsteps of **10**: tinged with distinctive 'Durbanville dust', soy & green olive notes; slight blackcurrant exclamation on persistent, crystalline finish.

Grenache NEW ★★★★ Translucent **10** vibrant & engaging, raspberry fruit, soft & rounded flavours with little oak influence. A first for the property; augurs well for future vintages. **Pinotage Reserve** NEW 🖲 ★★★☆ **10** modern & youthful, densely packed with fruit & oak (14 months, 50% new), satisfying dry conclusion. Could score higher after year/2 cellaring; one to watch.

Diemersdal Estate range

★★★★ **Merlot** ✓ **10** (★★★★) ticks all the right boxes: leafy cool mint to ripe Ribena nose, pleasant grip; is let down by sweet farewell. **08**, **07** were soft but savoury. **09** sold out untasted.

★★★★ **Pinotage** ✓ 🖲 Traditional style very well done. **10** crafted to showcase ripe mulberry & banana, smoky overtones; satisfying dry finish.

★★★★ **Shiraz 09** (★★★★) worth seeking out for drinkablity & varietal expression: black pepper & lily; plump palate & endless goodbye. **08**, too, very accessible, more knit.

★★★★ **Sauvignon Rosé** ☺🍽 Food-friendly marriage sauvignon (73%), cab. Boiled sweets, passion-fruit overlain with coffee & cashew nut aromas in **11** (★★★). Follows serious dinner companion **10**.

★★★★ **Chardonnay Unwooded** ✓ 🍽 🖲 Cool lime whiff on reticent **11** followed by thatch, musk notes, persistent mineral tail. Brisk aperitif style with structure to improve year/2.

★★★★☆ **Sauvignon Blanc** ✓ 🍽 🖲 Consistently over-delivers. **10** complex, vivacious; **11** (★★★★) green aromas & flavours, tropical fruit & gentle pithy nudge from pot-pourri of yeasts, 3 months lees-ageing.

★★★★☆ **Sauvignon Blanc 8 Rows** Row selection from single-vineyard, 25 years old, 4 months lees-aged for additional weight, texture. **11** back on track after broad **10** (★★★★). 'Wet pebble' minerality, firm acidity. Rewards undivided attention.

★★★★ **Matys Sauvignon Blanc** ☺🍽 🖲 Entry-level version. Cut-grass & nettles, zingy if brief farewell, **11** (★★★) good summertime fun, where **10** over-delivered.

Matys Cabernet Sauvignon-Merlot ☺🍽 🖲 ★★★ Name change (from 'Matys Cape Blend') for lightly oaked, early drinking combo. **10** uncomplex berry melange, sherbet edge. WO Coastal. — CvZ

Diemersfontein Wines

Location/WO: Wellington ▪ Map: Paarl & Wellington ▪ Est 2000 ▪ 1stB 2001 ▪ Tasting & sales daily 10–5 ▪ Fee R15 ▪ Closed Dec 25 ▪ Cellar tours by appt ▪ Seasons Restaurant (see Restaurants section) ▪ Tour groups ▪ Conferences ▪ Weddings ▪ Walks ▪ Mountain biking ▪ 4-star Diemersfontein Country House (see Accommodation section) ▪ Owner(s) David & Susan Sonnenberg ▪ Cellarmaster(s) Francois Roode (Sep 2011) & Brett Rightford (consultant) ▪ Winemaker(s) Francois Roode (Sep 2003), with Lauren Hulsman (2011) ▪ Viticulturist(s) Waldo Kellerman (Aug 2007) ▪ 180ha/60ha (cabs s/f, grenache, malbec, mourv, p verdot, ptage, roobernet, shiraz, chenin, viog) ▪ 600t/ 40,000cs own label 90% red 10% white ▪ ISO 22000 ▪ PO Box 41 Wellington 7654 ▪ wine@diemersfontein.co.za ▪ www.diemersfontein.co.za ▪ S 33°39'41.1" E 019°0'31.1" ▪ **T +27 (0)21-864-5050** ▪ F +27 (0)21-864-2095

Owned by the Sonnenberg family since the early 1940s, Diemersfontein lies in the shadow of the majestic Hawekwa Mountains, and is blessed with a panoramic view. 'We make our wines to show the unique Wellington terroir at its best - especially for pinotage and chenin,' says winemaker Francois Roode. A highlight since the last edition was the 10th anniversary of the original and trend-setting 'coffee' pinotage, born here and the object of an increasing fan base. In addition to the four-star guesthouse, wedding and conference facilities, visitors can enjoy pinotage truffles, exclusively made for Diemersfontein, with their favourite wine.

Carpe Diem range

★★★★ **Malbec** ✓ Bold **09** offers blueberry, roasted coffee bean, liquorice. Ripe, sappy & mouthfilling with a firm spine & warm finish. Needs time to deliver full potential.

★★★★☆ **Pinotage** Deep, rich & powerful **09**, dark choc, ripe plum & mocha smoothness, layers of brooding concentrated black fruit in a delicious tannic grip. Super expression of the variety. Will age gracefully.

★★★★☆ **Chenin Blanc** ✓ 🖲 Big, bold & showy **10** (★★★★★), with dashes chardonnay & viognier, like **09** has knock-out nose of orange marmalade, tropical fruit, green apple & vanilla biscuit. Great balance, smooth but firm acidity, 25% barrel-fermented portion & lees-ageing add complexity. Unflagging finish.

★★★★ **Viognier** ✓ Creamy peach, apricot & floral flavours dominate the palate of fragrant **10**, just off-dry but balanced, finishing on a luscious vanilla note. Dollops chenin, chardonnay add some zip.

Discontinued: **Cabernet Sauvignon**, **Shiraz**.

Diemersfontein range

★★★★ **Pinotage** ✓ Previewed **11** will not disappoint fans: espresso, tobacco & ripe plum seduce the senses. Oak still dominates, so will reward some patience. Sweet-savoury moreish finish, brisk tail.

★★★★ **Summer's Lease** ✓ Bright, pristine fruit on **09** Rhône-style red, shiraz, mourvèdre & viognier. Hints of fynbos, juicy & mouthfilling with lovely balance. Oak influence needs time to fully integrate & soften.

Cabernet Sauvignon ★★★ Bright plum, fine spice & cedar prelude to **10**, plush flavour, robust & firm tannin structure begs for food. Needs time. **Shiraz** ✓ ★★★★ Bold & spicy **09** with juicy black fruit, fynbos & dark chocolate flavours; prominent vanilla with lipsmacking savoury end. Needs 3+ years. **For The Birds** NEW ★★★ Fruity **09** merlot-led easy-drinker, light bodied & balanced for early enjoyment. **Maiden's Prayer Red** NEW ★★★ Bordeaux-style blend **10**, juicy with sweet dark fruit, balanced for easy enjoyment. Yummy! Discontinued: **Heaven's Eye**. — WB

■ **Die Tweede Droom** see Groot Parys Estate

Dieu Donné Vineyards

Map: Franschhoek ▪ Est 1984 ▪ 1stB 1986 ▪ Tasting & sales Mon-Fri 9–4 Sat/Sun 10.30–4 ▪ Fee R15 ▪ Closed Dec 25 & Jan 1 ▪ Cellar tours Mon-Fri by appt ▪ Cheese platters ▪ Gifts ▪ Micro Beer Brewery ▪ Dieu Donné Restaurant (see Restaurants section) ▪ Owner(s) Robert Maingard ▪ Cellarmaster(s)/winemaker(s) Stephan du Toit (May 1996) ▪ Viticulturist(s) Hennie du Toit (Apr 1988) ▪ 40ha (cab, merlot, shiraz, chard, sauv, viog) ▪ ±280t/16,500cs own label 60% red 32% white 3% rosé 5% MCC ▪ PO Box 94 Franschhoek 7690 ▪ info@dieudonnevineyards.com ▪ www.dieudonnevineyards.com ▪ S 33° 53'46.9" E 019° 7'45.0" ▪ **T +27 (0)21-876-2493** ▪ F +27 (0)21-876-2102

Winemaker and Cape Wine Master Stephan du Toit did himself proud with this Franschhoek mountainside's flagship Merlot 2008 over the past show season, earning a clutch of golds locally and internationally. Similar success came for ultra-premium, limited-release The Cross Collection's Shiraz-Viognier 2008. A new-look label has freshened up this enduring producer, exporting steadily to the UK, Netherlands, Germany, Taiwan and Ireland.

■ **Die Vlakte** see Cloverfield Private Cellar

Diners Club Bartho Eksteen Academy NEW

Map: Paarl & Wellington ▪ WO: Overberg/Paarl ▪ Est/1stB 2011 ▪ Tasting, sales & cellar tours by appt ▪ Meals/refreshments by pre-booking ▪ Facilities for children ▪ Farm produce ▪ BYO picnic ▪ Conference facilities ▪ Walking/hiking & mountain biking trails ▪ Nature reserve ▪ Owner(s) Bartho & Suné Eksteen with Hoër Landbouskool Boland & Diners Club ▪ Cellarmaster(s) Bartho Eksteen (Feb 2011) ▪ Winemaker(s) Bartho Eksteen, with Suné Eksteen (both Feb 2011) ▪ Viticulturist(s) Willie van der Linde (Hoër Landbouskool Boland); Rosa Kruger, Schalk du Toit & James Downes (bought in grapes) ▪ 1,300ha/20ha (cab, merlot, shiraz, chard, chenin) ▪ 10t/900cs own label 23% red 62% white 15% other ▪ PO Box 2244 Hermanus 7200 ▪ info@barthoeksteensavvycelebration.co.za ▪ www.barthoeksteensavvycelebration.co.za ▪ S 33° 39' 11.45" E 018° 52' 59.77" ▪ **T +27 (0)28-312-4612** ▪ F +27 (0)86-554-0896

'Time to plough back,' says Hermanuspietersfontein and 2010 Diners Club Winemaker of the Year Bartho Eksteen, who, having secured Diners Club sponsorship and wife Suné's support, has gone back to his old school in the Boland (Hoër Landbouskool Boland) and instituted a three-year winemaking course for pupils there. Officially opening this year, a 'wet run' course last harvest produced the wines tasted here, to be sold under a Wijnskool label.

Wijnskool Chenin Blanc ★★★ Light-hearted **11**, sunny pineapple & dried peach, interesting 'wet pebble' note. Tasted mere days after bottling (rating provisional), showed good potential. **Wijnskool Sauvignon Blanc** **11** off Overberg vines, too unsettled to rate but clearly starting well, showing serious intent. — Panel

Dispore Kamma Boutique Winery

Location: Caledon ▪ Map: Elgin, Walker Bay & Bot River ▪ WO: Paarl ▪ Est/1stB 2002 ▪ Tasting, sales & tours by appt ▪ Owner(s) Philip Mostert & Hannes Coetzee ▪ Winemaker(s) Philip Mostert (Jan 2002), with Hannes Coetzee

(Jun 2002) ▪ 75cs own label 100% red ▪ PO Box 272 Caledon 7230 ▪ disporekamma@overnet.co.za ▪ S 34° 13'40.
2" E 019° 25' 10.5" ▪ **T** +27 (0)28-212-1096 ▪ F +27 (0)28-214-1077

Philip Mostert, general practitioner and garagiste vintner with orthopaedic surgeon
Hannes Coetzee, at press time were awaiting confirmation of their first US export
order, raising the prospect of increased production (preceded, no doubt, by much
celebration). 'Innovation' here means minimal intervention during vinification, no
fining or filtration, and 'keeping our product as natural as possible'.

Dispore Kamma Boutique Winery range

★★★★ **Syrah Reserve** Only 25 cases of rich, ageworthy **09**, dark brooding spicy berries, floral scents &
liquorice. Juicy, complex & warm (15% alc), lingering in the mouth. From Paarl grapes, as is next.

Syrah ✓ ★★★★ Bold, juicy dark berries on full-bodied **09**. Well-judged oaking with a warm (15% alc) conclusion. — WB

Distell

PO Box 184 Stellenbosch 7599 ▪ info@distell.co.za ▪ www.distell.co.za ▪ **T** +27 (0)21-809-7000

Operating from two corporate-owned cellars in Stellenbosch (Bergkelder and Adam
Tas), Distell vinifies some of South Africa's most successful and enduring wine
brands. They include: 5th Avenue Cold Duck, Autumn Harvest Crackling,
Capenheimer, Cellar Cask, Chateau Libertas, Chatta Box, Drostdy-Hof, Fleur du Cap,
Graça, Grand Mousseux, Grünberger, Ixia, Kellerprinz, Kupferberger Auslese,
Libertas, Monis, Obikwa, Oom Tas, Oracle, Overmeer, Place in the Sun, Pongrácz,
Sedgwick's, Ship Sherry, Table Mountain, Tassenberg, Taverna, Two Oceans, Vir-
ginia and Zonnebloem. Distell also owns the House of JC le Roux, a dedicated spar-
kling-wine cellar in Devon Valley. Then there are the stand-alone 'estate' labels:
Nederburg, Plaisir de Merle and Lomond. Distell is also the co-owner, together with
Lusan Holdings, of a handful of top Stellenbosch properties (Alto, Le Bonheur,
Neethlingshof, Stellenzicht/Hill & Dale, Uitkyk/Flat Roof Manor), and, with several
local growers, of Durbanville Hills. Distell also has agreements with a few independently owned cellars (Allesverloren, Jacobsdal, Theuniskraal) for which it provides a
range of services. Finally, there's the black empowerment venture on
Papkuilsfontein farm near Darling, source of Tukulu wines. See Die Bergkelder for
details about the Vinoteque Wine Bank, and separate entries for most of the above
brands and properties.

■ **Dixon's Peak** see Waverley Hills Organic Wines & Olives
■ **Dolphin Bay** see Wines of Cape Town
■ **Dolphin Sands** see Wines of Cape Town

Domaine Brahms Wineries

Location/WO: Paarl ▪ Map: Paarl & Wellington ▪ Est 1998 ▪ 1stB 1999 ▪ Tours (vyd/cellar/wine) & tasting by appt ▪
Fee R5/wine ▪ Chapel & wedding/function venue ▪ Owner(s) Johan & Gesie van Deventer ▪ Winemaker(s)/viticul-
turist(s) Gesie van Deventer (1998) ▪ 12ha (cab, merlot, ptage, shiraz) ▪ 30,000L 90% red 10% white ▪ PO Box
2136 Windmeul 7630 ▪ brahms@iafrica.com ▪ www.domainebrahms.co.za ▪ S 33° 40' 27.28" E 18° 53' 29.24" ▪
T +27 (0)21-869-8555 ▪ F +27 (0)86-614-9445

Advocate-turned-vintner Gesie van Deventer, now also executive mayor of
Drakenstein, somehow finds time to nurture the vines and make wine on her and
husband Johan's Paarl property. 'I don't know how she does it,' marvels local wine
personality Victor Titus, who runs a vino-edutainment business from the farm,
where upgraded wedding and function facilities are doing 'exceptionally well'.

★★★★ **Shiraz 08** (★★★★) differs from last big & bold **05**: there's more red-fruit tang & chalkiness in the
texture, plus a sprinkle of turned earth below. Alc is big, though, at 15%. No 2006/7.

Cabernet Sauvignon ★★★ **06**'s fruit very ripe, but rather quiet & lean when last reviewed. **Merlot** ★★★ Ripe
berry fruit on debut **07**, dry spicy oak may have integrated since last tasted. **Pinotage** ★★★ **08** lighter styled
than previous but has a refreshing red-berry lift. Light hints of liquorice & ink. Alc is high at 15.6%. **Quartet**
★★★★ No update on **06** (ex-cask) tasted last time. Ripely fruity pinotage (40%) with cab, merlot, shiraz. Juicy
but serious, well oaked. **Sonato** ★★★★ **06** cab-based blend with ripely sweet but modest fruit, charry dry finish.

10% new oak; 15% alc. Not revisited. **Chenin Blanc** Await next. **Unwooded Chenin Blanc ★★★** A glass of kiwi, fig & melon, **11** acid freshness with honey after. Discontinued: **White**. — FM

Domaine des Dieux

WO: Walker Bay/Hemel-en-Aarde Ridge ▪ Est 2002 ▪ 1stB 2006 ▪ Tasting by appt or at La Vierge Wines ▪ Owner(s) Domaine des Dieux (Pty) Ltd ▪ Winemaker(s) Marc van Halderen ▪ Viticulturist(s) Andrew Teubes ▪ 28ha/20ha (pinot, shiraz & other red varieties, chard, sauv) ▪ 10,500cs own label 20% red 26% white 54% MCC ▪ PO Box 2082 Hermanus 7200 ▪ info@domainedesdieux.co.za ▪ www.domainedesdieux.co.za ▪ **T +27 (0)28-313-2126/+27 (0)83-536-5916** ▪ F +27 (0)86-552-9667

Sharon Parnell planted early-ripening clones at her farm in the high-altitude, ocean-cooled Hemel-en-Aarde Ridge ward 'because late-ripening ones wouldn't ripen at all!' Harvest occurs two weeks later than further down the valley, and winemaker Marc van Halderen values the natural acidity and modest alcohols which result – hallmarks likewise of his home cellar, La Vierge, just down the road.

★★★★ Syrah Mourvèdre NEW Well-constructed **09**, intriguing garrigue aromas, cool-climate red fruit purity reminiscent of Rhône models. Youthful tannins provide ample grip to charmingly fruity, spicy finish.

★★★★ Sauvignon Blanc Pungent herbaceousness in astonishingly vibrant **10**. Concentration & complexity improve each vintage, flinty minerality & grapefruit pithiness underpin richness from extended lees contact.

★★★★ Claudia MCC Despite 3-4 yrs on lees, **07** chardonnay-led blend still needs to harmonise edginess. Frothy mousse, fine bubbles please & carry flavours along firm pinot backbone to bone-dry finish.

★★★★ Rose of Sharon MCC Brut Rosé Steely, mineral **08** pinot-led, with chardonnay to plump out austere styling. Portion fermented in new oak & 3 yrs on lees adds necessary breadth & faintly creamy length. Walker Bay, Elgin grapes for this & sibling above.

Josephine Pinot Noir ★★★★ Earthy **10** up a solid notch on **09** (★★★★) with more substance & pizazz. Vibrant pure red fruit flavours & harmoniously supple tannins reflect excellent handling of tricky variety. **Chardonnay ★★★★** Subtle wood spice aromas signal expensive oaking & serious intent in **10** though surprisingly light fruit to match. Elegant, flinty style with appetising lime finish. — IM

Dombeya Wines

Location/map/WO: Stellenbosch ▪ Est 2005 ▪ 1stB 2006 ▪ Tasting & sales Tue-Fri 10-4.30 Sat/Sun 10-3 ▪ Closed Mon, Easter Fri-Mon, Dec 25 & Jan 1 ▪ Cellar tours on special request only ▪ The Long Table Restaurant & Café: Tue-Sun 9-5; sundowner evenings Thu-Fri (Sep-Mar) - booking essential ▪ Facilities for children ▪ Self-catering accommodation in 'The Residence' ▪ Owner(s) Preston Haskell ▪ Winemaker(s)/viticulturist(s) Wikus Pretorius (Dec 2005) ▪ Cellarmaster(s) Rianie Strydom (Jan 2005) ▪ 25ha/13.5ha (cabs s/f, merlot, shiraz, chard) ▪ ±80t/7,500cs own label 80% red 20% white ▪ PO Box 12766 Die Boord 7613 ▪ info@dombeyawines.com ▪ www.dombeyawines.com ▪ S 34° 0' 13.9"   E 018° 51' 38.4" ▪ **T +27 (0)21-881-3895** ▪ F +27 (0)21-881-3986

This rising star on the flank of the Helderberg (and sibling winery to Haskell Vineyards) has seen an 'exceptional' increase in visitors the past year. Not surprising, given the increasingly reputed wines (some served at last year's royal wedding in Monaco), the lovely views and varied attractions, which include leisurely Winemakers Lunches with Dombeya's celebrated oeno-consultant Rianie Strydom. Adept at interacting via social media, the team aims to help winelovers 'understand the processes and production methods of a wine farm', hence the regular posts on the website, blog, Facebook and Twitter.

★★★★ Boulder Road Shiraz Velvety **08** delivered inviting mouthful of blackberries, plums & meaty savouriness last edition; dash mourvèdre added interest & savouriness.

★★★★☆ Chardonnay 🍇 **10** (★★★★), while not quite as complex as super **09**, is still bright & fruity, seduces with glazed apricot & pineapple centre, finishes with citrus zing & hint of vanilla.

Cabernet Sauvignon ★★★★ 08 greater fruit clarity than engaging **07** (★★★★); well-composed tannins, refreshing lift in tail add to cedary charm. Not retasted, like most of these. **Merlot ★★★★☆ 08** last year convincingly trumped **07** (★★★★): concentrated fruit, ripe tannins, balancing spicy freshness. Already complex, should improve 5+ years. **Altus ★★★★** Previously named 'Samara'. **07** elegantly taut Bordeaux red up a notch from **06** (★★★★). Cab's clean blackcurrant, polished tannins, silky texture & complexity. **Sauvignon Blanc ✓ ★★★★** Refreshing acidity, ebullient lemon/grapefruit aromas, **11** improved on **10** (★★★★). — WB

Domein Doornkraal

Location: De Rust ▪ Map: Klein Karoo & Garden Route ▪ Est 1880 ▪ 1stB 1973 ▪ Tasting & sales Mon–Fri 9–5 Sat 9–1 ▪ Closed Easter Fri/Sun & Dec 25 ▪ Light refreshments ▪ Farm produce ▪ Gifts ▪ Conference facility on farm ▪ Self-catering farm cottages & B&B ▪ Owner(s) Swepie & Piet le Roux ▪ Cellarmaster(s) Swepie le Roux (Apr 2011) ▪ Winemaker(s) Swepie & Piet le Roux, with Kobie Adams (2008) ▪ Viticulturist(s) Danie Theron (2008) & Hugo Steyn (2009, consultant) ▪ 2,000ha/17ha (cab, merlot, muscadel, ptage, chard, chenin, cbard) ▪ 90t/2,000cs own label 15% red 15% white 70% fortified ▪ PO Box 14 De Rust 6650 ▪ wyn@doornkraal.co.za ▪ www.doornkraal.co.za ▪ S 33° 32' 43.5" E 022° 26' 42.6" ▪ **T** +27 (0)44-251-6715 ▪ F +27 (0)86-528-5633

The Le Rouxs, headed by jovial patriarch Oom Swepie, are expanding their wine business to tap into wine tourism and give visitors a 'taste of the Klein Karoo'. Self-catering farmhouse accommodation, hikes and mountain bike routes, and a winetasting locale enlarged to include snacks and traditional farm produce complement a wine range known for 'Tickled Pink' bubbly and luscious dessert wines.

▪ **Donatus** *see Dornier Wines*

Doolhof Wine Estate

Location: Wellington ▪ Map: Paarl & Wellington ▪ WO: Wellington/Paarl ▪ Est 1995 ▪ 1stB 2003 ▪ Tasting & sales Mon–Sat 10–5 Sun 10–4 ▪ Fee R20/5 wines ▪ Closed Easter Fri, Dec 25/26 & Jan 1 ▪ Cellar tours by appt ▪ Light lunches Tue–Sun 11–3; picnics by appt ▪ Conference facilities ▪ Walking/hiking/mountain biking & 4x4 trails ▪ 5-star Grand Dédale Country House (www.granddedale.com) ▪ Owner(s) Dennis Kerrison ▪ Cellarmaster(s)/winemaker(s) Friedrich Kühne (Dec 2008) ▪ Viticulturist(s) Hendrik Laubscher (Aug 1996) ▪ 380ha/38ha (cabs s/f, malbec, merlot, p verdot, ptage, shiraz, chard, sauv) ▪ 180-220t/12,000cs own label 73% red 26% white 1% rosé ▪ BWI, IPW ▪ PO Box 157 Wellington 7654 ▪ office@doolhof.com ▪ www.doolhof.com ▪ S 33° 37' 35.6" E 019° 4' 58.7" ▪ **T** +27 (0)21-873-6911 ▪ F +27 (0)21-864-2321

Two major Decanter awards were among many garlands received the past year by owner Dennis Kerrison's team at the Doolhof ('Labyrinth') winery and luxe guest house in the Wellington heights. Doubtless the accolades abetted the impressive 36% sales growth achieved in a challenging market (the US particularly appreciative of Dark Lady pinotage). The plan is to 'continue to expand and establish our local and international footprint, and lure winelovers to our magical labyrinth'.

Signatures of Doolhof range

★★★★ **Chardonnay Wooded** Almond/lime nose on last edition's 08 (★★★★), with creamy mandarin flavour. Sleek & poised but shade less impressive than 06.

Cabernet Sauvignon ★★★★ Spice & fruitcake on 07, reviewed previously. Ripe, rich mouthful, smooth texture. **Malbec** ★★★★ Earthy cocoa, spice & blueberry, 09 is juicy, with depth & light tannic grip from year oak, 50% new; rich finish. Very good but misses savoury complexity of 08 (★★★★★). **Merlot** ★★★ Smoky mulberry & herb with cocoa tang on medium-bodied 07, reviewed last time. **Petit Verdot** NEW ★★★ Sweet ripe blackberry & light smoky note, 08 dry grip, doesn't linger. **Pinotage** ★★★★ 09's ripe charry red & black fruit much like 08. Light bodied but with grip from year French oak, 50% new. **Shiraz** ★★★★ Firm frame of black fruit with herbs & spice on 07, previously tasted. Grip & earthy char from 50% new French oak. Followed standout 06 (★★★★★). **Renaissance Cabernet Sauvignon-Merlot** ★★★★ After generous 06 (★★★★★), last-tasted 07 had blackcurrant & cigarbox, ripeness balanced by char from year in 40% new French oak. **Chardonnay Unwooded** 🔲 ★★★ Citrus & hot earth, 09 tangy green bean & pomelo last edition. **Sauvignon Blanc** 🔲🔲 ★★★ Lively grass pungency & zesty flint on 10 last edition. Smoked lemon hint too. Moderate 12.5% alc.

Legends of the Labyrinth range

★★★★ **The Minotaur** Meaty plum spice when reviewed; 08 (★★★★) soft, light-bodied Bordeaux red, less structure than juicy 07.

Dark Lady of the Labyrinth ★★★ 10 from pinotage, showing mocha/chocolate & mulberry plushness. Tannic caramel edge from 100% new oak. **Lady in Red** 🔲 ★★★★ Unusual jasmine note last time to juicy mulberry & mocha on seriously oaked 08, five-way Bordeaux blend. **Lady in White** NEW 🔲 ★★★ Chenin, semillon & sauvignon liaison. Lemon butter & nettle, 10 zingy yet also creamy from year 100% new oak.

Cape range

Robin ☺ 🍷 ★★★ Changes from pinotage/merlot to shiraz in **11**, dry spicy & plummy quaffer. **Loerie** ☺ 🍷 ★★★ Sauvignon's fig & pepper on **10**, crisp lemony easy-drinker with moderate 12.5% alc.

Boar √ 🍷 ★★★★ **09** step up on previous. Dried herb & red fruit on merlot, cab, petit verdot mix. Warm, soft texture from year in older oak. **Roan** 🍷 ★★★ Malbec-led **08** has pepper & blueberry with char from year older oak & spice from shiraz & mourvèdre. Rounded, smooth, nice length. **Eagle** NEW 🍷 ★★★ Tropical & tangy **10**, lightish unwooded chardonnay with splash of chenin. — FM

Doran Family Vineyards

Location: Paarl ▪ Map: Paarl & Wellington ▪ Est 2010 ▪ 1stB 2012 ▪ Tasting by appt ▪ Owner(s) Edwin Doran ▪ Winemaker(s) Charles Stassen ▪ Viticulturist(s) Marius Mouton (Jan 2000, consultant) ▪ 170ha/50ha (cabs s/f, merlot, ptage, shiraz) ▪ 620t/15,000cs own label ▪ Suite 310 Private Bag X16 Constantia 7848 ▪ andrebad@iafrica. com ▪ www.horsemountainwines.com ▪ S 33° 35′ 15.14″ E 018° 52′ 06.13″ ▪ **T +27 (0)21-869-8328** ▪ F +27 (0)21-869-8329

After selling his UK travel business, Irishman Edwin Doran bought the Voor Paardeberg farm Far Horizons and the Horse Mountain wine brand that went with it in 2010. He asked old friend André Badenhorst, who had a hand in setting up the top Constantia wineries Buitenverwachting and Constantia Uitsig, to come on board and the property is currently being entirely overhauled – a new cellar and guest house among some of the new developments.

Dormershire Estate

Location/map/WO: Stellenbosch ▪ Est 1996 ▪ 1stB 2001 ▪ Tasting, sales & tours Mon-Fri 8–5 Sat by appt 10–3 ▪ Fee R10pp ▪ Closed Easter Fri, Jun 16, Aug 9 & Dec 25 ▪ Owner(s) SPF Family Trust ▪ Winemaker(s) Michelle Loots (Apr 2007) ▪ Viticulturist(s) Johan Pienaar (consultant) ▪ 8ha/6ha (cab, shiraz, sauv) ▪ ±50t/4,000cs own label 85% red 10% white 5% rosé ▪ PO Box 491 Bellville 7535 ▪ wine@dormershire.co.za ▪ www.dormershire.com ▪ S 33° 56′ 27.0″ E 018° 42′ 54.7″ ▪ **T +27 (0)21-801-4677** ▪ F +27 (0)86-517-0716

Newly-wed winemaker Michelle Louw is very enthusiastic about the Barrel OwnersClub at this mainly red-wine farm, where winelovers from as far afield as Zimbabwe and Swaziland purchase a barrel of shiraz or cabernet 'en primeur.' The scheme offers tastings and discounts - and you get to keep your barrel afterwards too.

Cabernet Sauvignon 🍷 ★★★★ As expected, juicier & earlier accessible than the Reserve, a savoury note makes **07** a good food match. This, next 5 wines, not revisited. **Reserve Cabernet Sauvignon** ★★★★ Selection of best barrels, 18 months oak (as for all the reds). Despite big alc, **07** achieves elegance & poise. **Shiraz** 🍷 ★★★ **07** toasted bread & spicy cherry flavours, ending dry. Ideal winter casserole red. **Stoep Shiraz** ★★★ Wood here a toasty backdrop, **07** earthy & savoury blackberry fruit, pepper seasoning. **Reserve Shiraz** ★★★★ **05** deeply fruited with blackcurrant, scented with pencil shavings. **Cabernet Sauvignon-Shiraz** ★★★★ **07** has this estate's Old World character: peppery/dusty notes, cherry flavours & firm tannins. **Rosé** Await new vintage. **Sauvignon Blanc** ★★★ Previewed **11** textbook herbal tangy pineapple & green apple, succulent & fleshy. **Sweet Red** ★★★★ Listed last time as 'Sweet Shiraz'. Latest version of **NV** jerepiko-style fireside snuggler still from that variety, with intriguing savoury overlay. — DB

Dornier Wines

Location/map: Stellenbosch ▪ WO: Stellenbosch/Swartland/Western Cape ▪ Est 1995 ▪ 1stB 2002 ▪ Tasting & sales daily 10-5 ▪ Fee R30, waived on purchase ▪ Closed Jan 1 ▪ Cellar tours by appt ▪ Dornier Bodega Restaurant: lunch daily 12-5 dinner (Oct-Apr) Thu-Sat ▪ Facilities for children ▪ Gift shop ▪ Conference venue ▪ Conservation area ▪ 4x4 team building ▪ Homestead with 6 bedrooms & large entertainment areas offered ▪ Owner(s) Delfinarte Foundation ▪ Winemaker(s) JC Steyn (May 2005) ▪ Viticulturist(s) Theunis Bell (Sep 2009) ▪ 167ha/ 60ha (cabs s/f, malbec, merlot, p verdot, ptage, shiraz, tempranillo, chenin, sauv, sem) ▪ 440t 80% red 13% white 7% rosé ▪ PO Box 7518 Stellenbosch 7599 ▪ info@dornier.co.za ▪ www.dornier.co.za ▪ S 33° 59′ 31.00″ E 018° 52′ 19.00″ ▪ **T +27 (0)21-880-0557** ▪ F +27 (0)21-880-1499

Central to this property is the visually stunning cellar designed by the late owner, Swiss artist Christoph Dornier. You see it from the Bodega Restaurant, it houses the production facilities and now will be more prominently featured on the revamped labels. On the wine side, winemaker JC Steyn is delighted with the first crop of cab franc and tempranillo from high-density vineyard plantings, which are delivering their quality promise. The range will include small single-variety bottlings of the latter and malbec in the future. And making a reappearance due to public demand is cab/merlot, the last vintage was 2002.

Donatus range

★★★★ **Red** Showing youthful house-style restraint, previewed **09** still tightly structured. Has requisite fruit, amenable tannins but best is still to come. Drink in year or 2 till ±2020. Mainly cab, dashes malbec & cab franc.

★★★★ **White** ❷ As complex but more expressive than usual, oaked **10** showcases chenin (74%, rest semillon). Quince & almonds, lovely full palate, then an austere finish that welcomes food. WO Western Cape.

Dornier range

★★★★ **Cabernet Sauvignon** Following in **06**'s footsteps, complex **07**'s dark plum centre shows dried herb, allspice, even fynbos nuances. Tannins are supple with a good backbone for 6+ more years.

★★★★ **Pinotage** ❷ Individual **10** reveals the finesse pinotage can show in the right hands. Plums, smoke & spice all seamed into a lithe, sleekly muscled form. Previewed, as wines following.

★★★★ **Froschkoenig Natural Sweet** Occasional release, **09** (1 barrel rack-dried chenin) has melon preserve, baked apple tones in its richness, lovely barley sugar finish that stays. Aged 24 months.

Merlot ★★★★ Last edition **07** had berry-rich, herbal-tinged aromas & flavours; was savoury & firm, with modest fruit intensity. **Cabernet Sauvignon-Merlot** NEW ★★★★ Dusty overlay from barrel ageing, well handled by **09**'s fruit. Tannins dry, not edgy, give another year, drink till ±2016. **Chenin Blanc Bush Vine** ❷ ★★★★ Just 'Chenin Blanc' last time. Different styling to Cocoa Hill, **11** shows melon & thatch, more Old World than New, finishes with savoury notes. WO Swartland.

Cocoa Hill range

Chenin Blanc ☺ 🍽 ❷ ★★★ Apple & lime freshness to **11**, showing the attractive vibrancy of youth. These whites & Rosé tasted pre-bottling.

Red ★★★ Retasted **09**, bottled wine settled into warm-hearted style with curvy lines, nice dry finish. Mainly shiraz, merlot. WO Western Cape. **Rosé** 🍽 ❷ ★★★ From merlot, patio fare **11** shows red berries, nicely dry. **Sauvignon Blanc** 🍽 ❷ ★★★ Red apple & pear give **11** a gentle fruitiness, crisply dry. — CR

Douglas Green

Location: Wellington ▪ WO: Western Cape/Wellington/Coastal ▪ Est/1stB 1938 ▪ Closed to public ▪ Owner(s) DGB ▪ Cellarmaster(s) Gerhard Carstens, with Liezl Carstens (2000) ▪ Winemaker(s) Jaco Potgieter (oenologist, 2000) ▪ Viticulturist(s) Stephan Joubert (2006) ▪ 50% red 49% white 1% rosé ▪ ISO 9001:2000, Fairtrade, HACCP, WIETA ▪ PO Box 246 Wellington 7654 ▪ douglasgreen@dgb.co.za ▪ www.douglasgreenwines.com ▪ T +27 (0)21-864-5300 ▪ F +27 (0)21-864-1287

Having access to a wide range of grape sources around the Cape gives the wine team responsible for this venerable (1938) DGB-owned brand a full palette of options regarding styles, varieties and sites. The 30-plus wines listed below are linked by a common thread: affordable drinkability. The slew of best value awards locally and overseas bears testimony to this.

Reserve Selection

Merlot ★★★ Food-friendly **09** had tangy red fruit when previously tasted. **Shiraz** ❷ ★★★ Ripe & robust **10** has loads of smoky bacon flavours & chunky structure, for hearty fare. **Chardonnay** ★★★ **10** still available. Previously showed lime & buttered toast flavours.

Vineyard Creations

Cabernet Sauvignon ☺ 🍽 ❷ ★★★ Liquid fruit pastilles in a glass! **10** continues in super-quaffable, smooth & supple style. **Pinotage** ☺ 🍽 ❷ ★★★ Preview **10** has riper mulberry fruit than previous. Spicy & smooth for carefree quaffing.

Merlot ⍝ ★★★ **10** more fruit-filled & friendly than previous. Plummy pizza/pasta wine. **Shiraz** 🍷 ⍝ ★★★ Savoury, smoky **10** in ripe, undemanding, outdoors style. **Chardonnay** 🍷 ★★★ **10** still current. Was easy-drinking with lime & marmalade tones when last tasted. **Chenin Blanc** ⍝ ★★★ Crisp but plump, ripe melon on friendly **11** preview. **Sauvignon Blanc** 🍷 ⍝ ★★ **11** is a gentle tropical-toned quaffer with fresh finish.

Diversity range

Cabernet Sauvignon-Merlot ☺ 🍷 ⍝ ★★★ **10** rich & ripe dark berry fruit in supple, accessible style. Balanced, with food friendly dry finish. **Merlot-Malbec** ☺ 🍷 ⍝ ★★★ Ripe & characterful **10** has juicy, earthy flavours with dry, savoury farewell.

Cinsaut-Pinotage 🍷 ⍝ ★★ **11** smooth preview is light, with smoky red fruit. **Shiraz-Viognier** 🍷 ⍝ ★★★ Aromatic lift to savoury preview **10**. Juicy, rustic charm. **Pinotage Rosé** 🍷 ⍝ ★★★ Light & tangy **10** still available. Not retasted. **Chardonnay-Viognier** 🍷 ⍝ ★★★ **10** floral, spicy blend still selling. **Chenin Blanc-Sauvignon Blanc** 🍷 ⍝ ★★ Plumply ripe **11**, ex-tank is fruity, light & easy-drinking. **Chardonnay-Colombard** 🍷 ⍝ ★★ **11** preview is light & floral, for carefree sipping. **Sunkissed Natural Sweet Rosé** NEW 🍷 ★★ Sweet, low-alc pinotage/merlot NV sundowner. **Sunkissed Natural Sweet White** 🍷 ★★ NV aromatic charmer is smoothly sweet & tangy.

Douglas Green Signature Brands

The Beachhouse ☺ 🍷 ⍝ ★★★ Fresh & tangy, off-dry **11** white from sauvignon & semillon is tailor-made for summer.

The Delivery Cabernet Sauvignon-Merlot ★★ Less structured **10** preview is a ripe & rustic braai mate. **Ribshack Red** 🍷 ⍝ ★★★ Just 'Ribshack' last time. Savoury, smooth & smoky **10** aptly named, juicy pinotage/shiraz duo, spicy barbeque ribs in a glass! WO Wellington. **St Augustine** ★★★ **09** flavoursome cab, merlot, shiraz blend still available. **The Beachhouse Rosé** 🍷 ⍝ ★★ **11** a tutti-frutti sundowner. Light & semi-sweet, from pinotage. WO Wellington. **The Delivery Chenin Blanc** NEW 🍷 ★★★ Genial **10** preview is smooth with baked apple flavours. **The Delivery Chardonnay-Chenin Blanc** ★★ Previously tasted **10** preview was gently fruited & crisp. **Sprizzo Sweet Rosé** NEW 🍷 ★★ NV a sweet, aromatic bouquet that is light, fun & fizzy! **Cape Ruby Port** ★★★ NV blend tinta & souzão with fruitcake sweetness, not retasted.

Fairtrade range

The Principle Cabernet Sauvignon-Merlot 🍷 ★★★ Riper **10** has gentle berry tones in fresh & accessible style, for youthful enjoyment. WO Coastal. **The Principle Chenin Blanc-Sauvignon Blanc** ★★ **10** chenin/sauvignon blend still selling. Not retasted, nor the range below.

Enviro Pack

Cabernet Sauvignon ★★★ NV still available, was savoury & juicy last time. **Chardonnay** ★★★ Plump pear & citrus NV, still available in 3L enviro-friendly pouch, as for Cab. — MW

Douglas Wine Cellar

Location: Douglas ▪ Map: Northern Cape, Free State & North West ▪ Est 1968 ▪ 1stB 1977 ▪ Tasting & sales Mon-Fri 8–5 ▪ Fee R5 ▪ Closed pub hols ▪ Cellar tours by appt ▪ BYO picnic ▪ Gifts ▪ Owner(s) Shareholders ▪ Cellarmaster(s) Ian Sieg ▪ Winemaker(s) Ian Sieg & Winston Bailey ▪ Viticulturist(s) Johan Fourie ▪ Douglas + Landzicht GWK: 350ha (cab, ptage, ruby cab, shiraz, chard, chenin, cbard, gewürz, muscadels r/w) ▪ 20,000cs own label 20% red 40% white 5% rosé 35% fortified ▪ PO Box 47 Douglas 8730 ▪ wynkelder@gwk.co.za ▪ www.landzicht.co.za ▪ S 29° 3' 57.0" E 023° 46' 7.8" ▪ **T +27 (0)53-298-8314/5** ▪ F +27 (0)53-298-1845

Visitors are welcome at this 44 year-old winery, located near the confluence of South Africa's greatest rivers, the Orange and Vaal, in the Northern Cape agricultural town of Douglas. Owned by agribusiness GWK, ranges include Confluence and Barney Barnato, though cellarmaster Ian Sieg also handles vinification here of GWK's other wine interest, Landzicht, listed separately.

■ **Down to Earth** *see Villiera Wines*

Dragonridge

Location: Malmesbury ▪ Map: Swartland ▪ Est 2004 ▪ 1stB 2006 ▪ Tasting, sales & cellar tours by appt ▪ Fee R30, waived on purchase ▪ Closed Easter Fri, Dec 25/26 & Jan 1 ▪ Meals by arrangement ▪ Facilities for children ▪ Farm

produce ▪ BYO picnic ▪ Weddings/functions ▪ Conferences ▪ Walks/hikes ▪ Mountain biking trail ▪ Conservation area ▪ Guest House ▪ Owner(s) Fynbos Estate (3 partners) ▪ Cellarmaster(s)/winemaker(s) Johan Simons (Jan 2004) ▪ Viticulturist(s) Johan Simons (Jun 1997) ▪ 320ha/13ha (cab, mourv, ptage, sangio, shiraz, chard, chenin, viog) ▪ 35t/700cs own label 40% red 40% white 20% rosé ▪ P O Box 526 Malmesbury 7299 ▪ info@fynbosestate. co.za, info@dragonridge.co.za ▪ www.dragonridge.co.za ▪ S 33° 33'28.9" E 018° 47'5.6" ▪ **T +27 (0)22-487-1153** ▪ F +27 (0)86-611-5125

Some of the grapes grown on the tranquil Fynbos Estate on the Perdeberg are sent off to the local big winery. Others are made into wines by Johan Simons 'in the old traditional way'. And just as (referring to guests, conference delegates and the like) 'no-one leaves Fynbos hungry', presumably no one leaves thirsty either.

Dragonridge Winery range

Sangiovese ★★★ 09 with same dark cherry, pronounced acid & tarry notes as 08. Like all of these, tasted last year. **Jack's Red ★★** 10 blend offered juicy & spicy mouthful on preview. **Cosmos ★★★** 10 dry rosé with delicate red fruits. **Chenin Blanc ★★★** Oxidative almond & baked apple whiffs on 10, long spicy finish. **Galaxy ★★★★** Chardonnay, chenin & viognier blend; apple, honey, blossom & dried apricot on oaked 09, with broad texture & rich finish. — JPf

---

Driehoek Family Wines

Map: Olifants River ▪ WO: Cederberg ▪ Est/1stB 2009 ▪ Tasting by appt ▪ Closed Easter Fri & Dec 25 ▪ Facilities for children ▪ Gift shop ▪ BYO picnic ▪ Walking/hiking & mountain biking trails ▪ Horse riding ▪ Bird watching ▪ Fishing ▪ Bushman paintings ▪ Conservation area ▪ Self-catering cottages / camping ▪ Beauty treatments ▪ Owner(s) Du Toit Family ▪ Cellarmaster(s)/winemaker(s) David Nieuwoudt (Jan 2008, Cederberg) ▪ Viticulturist(s) Dawie Burger & Hennie Spamer (both Jun 2006), advised by David Nieuwoudt ▪ 375ha/4.5ha (pinot, shiraz, sauv) ▪ 1,250cs own label 50% red 50% white ▪ P O Box 89 Clanwilliam 8135 ▪ driehoekcederberg@gmail.com ▪ www. cederberg-accommodation.co.za ▪ S 32° 26'34.40" E 019° 11'24.32" ▪ **T +27 (0)27-482-2828** ▪ F +27 (0)86-720-2474

Like their neighbours (Cederberg Private Cellar's David Nieuwoudt makes their wines) the Du Toits have been here in the magnificent Cederberg mountains for five generations. The vineyards, however, date back only to 2006 - amongst the highest in the Cape. The grapes clearly revel in the heady atmosphere.

Driehoek range

★★★★☆ Shiraz Brooding 09 tasted last year. Still very young & reticent then, but savoury tannins, structure & dense core hinting at exciting future.

Sauvignon Blanc ⊛ ★★★★ Handsome 11 less sweatily tropical than 10 (★★★★), with citrus & lime abetting the passionfruit. A forceful acidity carries the persistent flavours to a fine conclusion. — TJ

■ **Drie Kleine Leeuwen** *see Leeuwenberg*
■ **Driftwood** *see Viljoensdrift Wines & Cruises*

Drostdy-Hof Wines

Location/map: Tulbagh ▪ WO: Western Cape ▪ Est 1804 ▪ Tasting & sales at De Oude Drostdy Mon-Fri 10-5 Sat 10-2 ▪ Fee R20pp, waived on purchase ▪ Closed Easter Fri, Dec 25 & Jan 1 ▪ Private functions by arrangement ▪ Owner(s) Distell ▪ Cellarmaster(s) Andrea Freeborough ▪ Winemaker(s) Deon Boshoff (whites) & Justin Corrans (reds) ▪ Viticulturist(s) Bennie Liebenberg ▪ P O Box 213 Tulbagh 6820 ▪ info@drostdywines.co.za ▪ www. drostdyhof.co.za ▪ S 33° 15'23.3" E 019° 8'57.5" ▪ **T +27 (0)23-230-0203** ▪ F +27 (0)23-230-0211

Distell's Tulbagh-linked Drostdy-Hof brand had its Slimpac-boxed sauvignon named Best White in the first local Bag-in-Box competition hosted by the Spit or Swallow website. That's a sign of the times: the aim is to move all three tiers of the range into a more contemporary space but keeping traditional cues like the image of the iconic De Oude Drostdy building. Another blend of trad and mod is the brand's ongoing sponsorship of the annual Aardklop arts festival in North West Province.

Winemaker's Collection range

Merlot ☺ **★★★** Softly smooth 10 shows balance, hint of sweetness on plummy fruit. **Pinotage** ☺ **★★★** Spicy wild berry fruit, near-dry 10 lifted by hint of oak. **Shiraz** ☺ **★★★** Lively cherry fruit with charry edge in improved **10**. **Chardonnay** ☺ 🍾 ★★★ Nicely shaped citrus-toned fruit with hints of oak spice, **10** is fresh & appealing. **Chardonnay-Viognier** ☺ ★★★ Impressively well-rounded **10** in 3L cask. Mineral, chardonnay-led blend with hints of oaky spice, lees richness.

Cabernet Sauvignon 🍾 Untasted. **Shiraz-Pinotage** ★★ **10** stalky, lean & light with sour-cherry fruit. **Cabernet Sauvignon Rosé** 🍾 ★★★ Wholesome, pleasant **10** from cab, lively & fresh last year. **Sauvignon Blanc** 🍾 ★★ **11**, as always, light, grassy & aromatic, with crisp acidity. **Sparkling Brut** Await next. **Adelpracht** ★★★ Late Harvest-style **10** from chenin, light body but quite intense dried fruit, crisp acidity.

Natural Sweet Light range

Extra Light Dry White ★ Lean & green-toned **NV** chenin. Low alcs (7-9%) for these. **Red** ★★ **NV** sweet mouthful of spicy muscat & sour cherry flavour. **Rosé** ★★ **NV** with flavour of sweet berry cordial. **White** ★★ Uncomplicated sweet sipper. **NV**. Like all these, also in 2L/5L.

Standard range

Cape Red ☺ 🍾 ★★★ Appealingly youthful, fresh **10** shows ripe spicy berries. **Chardonnay-Semillon** ☺ 🍾 ★★★ Restrained fruit with mineral centre, **10** offers good weight & freshness.

Claret Select ★★ Undemanding **NV**, soft & plummy. Like some in range, also in 2L/5L casks. **Rosé** 🍾 Untasted. **Steen/Chenin Blanc** 🍾 ★★ **11** is light, straightforward, near-dry & very refreshing. **Premier Grand Cru** 🍾 ★★ Formula-driven, undistinguished **NV** dry white blend. **Stein Select** ★★ Semi-sweet equivalent of PGC, **NV** shows hints of tropical fruit. **Late Harvest** 🍾 ★★ No-frills **NV** everyday sweetie. — Panel

Druk My Niet Wine Estate

Location: Wellington ▪ Map: Paarl & Wellington ▪ WO: Paarl ▪ Est 2003 ▪ 1stB 2009 ▪ Tasting, sales & cellar tours by appt ▪ Fee R20pp ▪ Closed all pub hols ▪ Meals/refreshments on request ▪ BYO picnic ▪ Tour groups ▪ Walking/hiking & mountain biking trails ▪ Conservation area ▪ 3 self-catering cottages (see Accommodation section) ▪ Owner/s Georg & Dorothee Kirchner, Jens-Peter & Kerstin Stein ▪ Cellarmaster(s)/winemaker(s)/viticulturist(s) Abraham de Klerk (Jun 2008) ▪ 24.5ha/9ha (cabs s/f, malbec, merlot, shiraz, tannat, tempranillo, tinto amerela, chenin, viog) ▪ 60t/1,750cs own label 80% red 20% white ▪ Other export brand: Mapoggo ▪ BWI, IPW ▪ PO Box 7383 Paarl 7620 ▪ georg.kirchner@dmnwines.co.za ▪ www.dmnwines.co.za ▪ S 33° 41'25" E 019° 1'42" ▪ **T** +27 **(0)21-868-2393** ▪ F +27 (0)21-868-2392

Georg and Dorothee Kirchner, co-owners of one of Paarl Valley's original estates, are as well as wine lovers, and their recent innovations include a three-wine Find Art Collection, whose labels will showcase different local artists every year. A new flagship, T3, is another first: a blend of tannat, tempranillo and tinta amarela ('the only one in the world'), varieties the Druk-My-Niet team have over the years found well suited to Paarl's climate.

Flagship range NEW

★★★★ **Invictus** Merlot-led **09** flagship blend (with cabs sauvignon & franc) in classic, plush Bordeaux style; serious & integrated (40% new oak well judged) with lengthy farewell.

★★★★ **T3** Intriguing red fruit & mint aromas on creative & unusual **09** equal tannat & tinta amarela blend with tempranillo (25%). Ripe berries are balanced by savoury acidity & firm tannins.

Find Art Collection NEW

★★★★ **Cabernet Sauvignon** Boldly fruited **09** exhibits lush dark-toned flavours. Balanced & integrated (though noticeable) vanilla oak.

★★★★ **Cabernet Franc** Excellent varietal expression on **09** - dust, leaf, mint, you name it. Elegant, harmonious & touch savoury. Definitely the 'find' among this trio.

Malbec ★★★★ While stablemates already integrated & complete, this **09** still a bit unformed, needs more time for cranberry fruit, acidity & (not unattractive) stalky element to mesh.

Mapoggo range NEW

Cabernet Sauvignon-Merlot-Cabernet Franc 🍾 ★★★☆ **09**, 81% cab with, fleshier, fruitier than red stablemate yet also with variety's firmness in slightly solid finish. Food wines both. **Cabernet Franc-Cabernet Sauvignon-Merlot** 🍾 ★★★ 67% cab franc, hence **08**'s herbaceous, leafy persona & dried herb twist. Well developed, with firm oak influence. **Sauvignon Blanc-Chenin Blanc-Viognier** 🍾 ★★★ Individually styled

09 intrigues with oxidative nutty character. **Chenin Blanc-Sauvignon Blanc-Viognier** 🍴 🏵 ★★★ With chenin behind wheel, **10** is fresher & more intense than counterpart, better balanced & focused. —Panel

■ **Dry Creek** *see* Du Preez Estate

Dunstone Winery 🍴🍷🛢🏠📷🎿

Location/WO: Wellington ▪ Map: Paarl & Wellington ▪ Est/1stB 2006 ▪ Tasting, sales & cellar tours Wed-Sun 8-4 ▪ Fee R10pp, waived on purchase ▪ Closed Easter Fri/Sun/Mon, Ascension day, Pentecost, Dec 25 & Jan 1 ▪ The Stone Kitchen (see Restaurants section) ▪ Facilities for children ▪ Conferences ▪ Bovlei Valley Retreat luxury B&B Guesthouse & self-catering Cottage (see Accommodation section) ▪ Owner(s) Abbi & Lee Wallis ▪ Winemaker(s) Lee Wallis, Robert Frith (Jun 2011) & Bertus Fourie (consultant), Neil Marais (Jun 2011) ▪ Viticulturist(s) Johan Viljoen (Jan 2008, Vinpro) ▪ 8.9ha/2.7ha (merlot, shiraz) ▪ 10t/1,160cs own label 90% red 10% rosé ▪ PO Box 901 Wellington 7654 ▪ wine@dunstone.co.za ▪ www.dunstone.co.za ▪ S 33° 38′5.3″ E 019° 3′36.8″ ▪ **T +27 (0)21-873-6770** ▪ F +27 (0)21-873-6770

For UK emigrés, Lee and Abbi Wallis, Dunstone recalls the name of the village where Lee bought his first house, and it was also the name of their first home. So logic dictated the name of their South African property. Logic and soil analysis led them to plant their favourite grape, shiraz - also the name of the weimaraner on the label. While hospitality-trained Abbi runs the guest house, Lee's professional life revolves around being a Professor of Emergency Medicine.

★★★★ **Shiraz** Brooding **09** just wins overripeness battle. Rich meaty, spice features in chewily smooth texture. Departs with hint of alcohol glow. Not in league of **08** (★★★★★); up on maiden **07** (★★★).
Merlot ★★★ Plummy, rich **09** noted last year as needing time to meld. Good structure bodes well. **Shiraz Rosé** 🍴 ★★★ Moderate body, spicy, cherry flavours on **11**; elegant, dry & persistent. —AL

■ **Du Plessis** *see* Havana Hills
■ **Du Plevaux** *see* Imbuko Wines

Du Preez Estate 🍴🍷🎋🛢

Location: Rawsonville ▪ Map/WO: Breedekloof ▪ Est 1926 - 1stB 1998 ▪ Tasting & sales Mon-Fri 8-5 Sat 10-1 ▪ Closed all pub hols ▪ Cellar tours by appt, 14-day prior notice required ▪ BYO picnic ▪ Tour groups (20 pax) ▪ Owner(s) Du Preez family ▪ Cellarmaster(s)/winemaker(s) Kobus van der Merwe (Dec 2008) ▪ Viticulturist(s) Jean du Preez ▪ 400ha (merlot, p verdot, ptage, shiraz, chard, chenin, cbard, nouvelle, sauv) ▪ 6,000t ▪ Other export brand: Maranda ▪ IPW ▪ PO Box 12 Route 101 Rawsonville 6845 ▪ info@dupreezestate.co.za ▪ www.dupreezestate.co.za ▪ S 33° 41′37.1″ E 019° 16′59.6″ ▪ **T +27 (0)23-349-1995** ▪ F +27 (0)86-654-7337/+27 (0)23-349-1923

This popular wine, function and wedding destination now produces two méthode cap classique sparklings, including the Rawsonville area's first rosé. 'Inspired by a young lady, worthy of admiration' – namely winemaker Hennie du Preez's five-year-old daughter Maranda – it's further evidence that family comes first at an estate where successive generations of Du Preez have grown wine since 1926.

Du Preez Estate range
★★★★ **Hendrik Lodewyk Méthode Cap Classique** Elegant & layered sparkler, lemon/lime & nutty aromas mingle with rich brioche flavour. 90% chard, with pinot noir, bottle-aged 48 months, **NV**.
★★★★ **Maranda Rosé Méthode Cap Classique** 🆕 Excellent addition to expanding pink sparkling category. Mainly pinot noir, 40% chardonnay, **NV**. Persistent mousse & delicate, lingering cherry flavours.
Hendrik Lodewyk Petit Verdot Await new vintage. **Chardonnay** Untasted. **Hanepoot** ★★★★ Generous **09** still selling, honey-sweet fortified pudding wine with hint of dried apricot. Discontinued: **Cabernet Sauvignon, Merlot, Shiraz**.

Du Preez Private Cellar range

Sauvignon Blanc ☺🍴🏵 ★★★ Light-bodied **11**, zesty & fresh with herbs & hint of tropical fruit salad.

Cabernet Sauvignon ★★★ **09** pleasing ripe berries with plum & mulberry tones, subtle oaking last edition. **Merlot** 🏵 ★★★★ Warm & alluring texture, dark chocolate & black cherry with mocha overlay. **10** big step up. **Shiraz** 🏵 ★★★★ Now from Breedekloof vines, improved **10** ripe mulberry fruit, soft mouthfeel & mocha nuances. **Polla's Red** ★★★ Appealing red blend, **09** last noted as softer than usual.

Rockfield range

Sauvignon Blanc ☺ 🍷 📖 ✱ ★★★ Epitomises early picked freshness, **11** guava & melon, juicy, sweet.

Cabernet Sauvignon 📖 ★★ 'Steak & braai wine' (said winemakers last year), **09** tasty sweet berries & fennel. **Merlot** 📖 🍷 ★★ Shy & gentle-fruited **10**, milk chocolate & hints coffee. Fresh & tasty table companion. **Shiraz** ★★★ Food-friendly **09**, earthy, with ripe & juicy mulberry fruit last time. **Dry Creek Red** ★★ Casual **09** is shiraz-led, has chocolate hint & juicy fruit. **Red Stone Blend** ★★ **09** plum-pudding aromas & soft berries when tasted. **Dry Creek Bouquet Blanc** Await next. — DB

Durbanville Hills

Location/WO: Durbanville ▪ Map: Durbanville, Philadelphia & Darling ▪ Est 1998 ▪ 1stB 1999 ▪ Tasting & sales Mon-Fri 9–4.30 Sat 10–3 Sun 11–3 ▪ Fee R40/15 wines incl glass ▪ Closed Easter Fri, Dec 25 & Jan 1 ▪ Cellar tours Mon-Fri 11 & 3; groups of 10+ to book ahead ▪ The Eatery Tue–Fri 11–3 Sat/Sun 8.30-3 ▪ Facilities for children ▪ Weddings & functions ▪ Owner(s) Distell, 9 Farmers & Workers Trust ▪ Cellarmaster(s) Martin Moore (Nov 1998) ▪ Winemaker(s) Wilhelm Coetzee (reds, Sep 2008) & Günther Kellerman (whites, Jul 2003) ▪ Viticulturist(s) Drikus Heyns (consultant) ▪ 770ha (merlot, sauv) ▪ 6,000t/150,000cs own label 40% red 58% white 2% rosé ▪ ISO 9000-1, ISO 14000-1, BWI, BRC, HACCP, IPW, WIETA ▪ PO Box 3276 Durbanville 7551 ▪ info@durbanvillehills.co. za ▪ www.durbanvillehills.co.za ▪ S 33° 49'29.9" E 018° 33'56.7" ▪ **T +27 (0)21-558-1300** ▪ F +27 (0)21-559-8169

Highlight of 2011 for this winery and its farmer members was winning the Ethical Award at the 2011 Drinks Business Awards. The winery established and supports the Durbanville Hills Share Purchase Trust which helps the disadvantaged community of the Durbanville area. One way funds are raised is via a percentage of the price of each bottle sold. With its wines often regarded as safe and steady rather than innovative and exciting, the team here is ready to produce some fireworks. 'There's much more we can do,' insists MD Albert Gerber; watch out for an individual blend with pinotage and a cabernet that will do more than prove the area is suitable for this variety. Both should help the Trust funds enormously.

Durbanville Hills Single Vineyard range

★★★★ **Luipaardsberg Merlot** Lead player in individual merlot trio. **09** biggest in richness, structure. Eucalyptus purity, mineral thread & dry finish add balance. 2 years new French oak seamlessly absorbed.

★★★★ **Caapmans Cabernet Sauvignon-Merlot** Classic cab-led **08** with 29% merlot. Ripe concentration, firm structure & ageworthy. 2 years new Fr oak. Not restasted.

★★★★ **Biesjes Craal Sauvignon Blanc** 📖 Billowing green bean perfume on **10** reflects cool climate source. Rich & flavoursome with keen mineral thread adding focus & length. Can age further. Previewed last year.

Rhinofields Reserve range

★★★★ **Merlot** Inviting dark mint chocolate introduction to **09**. Soft & velvety with fresh, minerally lift to dry finish. Subtle oak polish. Good now, 5-6 years.

★★★★ **Chardonnay** 📖 bigger than **09**; still captures usual lime/lees poise, depth of rich flavour.

★★★★ **Sauvignon Blanc** 📖 Styled between Hills & Biesjes Craal. **11** (★★★★) pretty if light tropical grassy mix; few grams sugar softens briskish acid. **10** deeper, really dry.

Pinotage 📖 ★★★ Extravagance of ripe raspberry features on silky **10**; extra sweetening from French oak (50% new). Dry, firm finish. **Shiraz** ★★★★ Elegance with red/black berry substance noted last year on **08**. **Inner Valley Sauvignon Blanc** Occasional release. **Outer Valley Sauvignon Blanc** Occasional release.

Durbanville Hills range

Chardonnay ☺ 🍷 📖 ★★★ Always satisfying, drinkable. Lightly oaked **10** creamy lees, juicy melon, citrus lift in comfortable harmony. Loves spiced dishes.

Cabernet Sauvignon ★★★ More concentrated, ripe dark-berried fruit on **09** than previous balances cab's assertive tannins. **Merlot** ★★★ Very fresh **09**; light mint, plum features; firm finish. **Pinotage** ★★★★ **09** raises bar with its pinot-like elegance. Pure cherry, raspberry fruit; fresh with fine, polished tannins. **Shiraz** ★★★ Supple, satisfying **09**. Good concentration, rich cured meat tones, savoury length. **Bastion** ★★★ Cabernet/shiraz blend. Neither American oak dominated **09** nor better balanced, savoury **10** (★★★) as satisfying as **08** (★★★★). **Merlot Rosé** NEW 📖 ★★★ Electric pink **11**. Hint of spritz to candy flavours; fruitily dry.

. Sauvignon Blanc 🍷 🎍 ★★★ As usual, **11** styled for ripe, tropical approachability, but less intense than previous. — AL

Dusty Heath Vineyard [NEW]

Est 2009 ▪ Closed to public ▪ Owner(s) Mark & Paula Haldane ▪ Cellarmaster(s) Paula Haldane (Aug 2009) ▪ Winemaker(s) Paula Haldane (Aug 2009), with Maqua Madlala (Aug 2009) ▪ Viticulturist(s) Mark Haldane (Aug 2009) ▪ 20ha/2ha (cabs s/f, merlot, p verdot) ▪ 100% red ▪ dhvineyard@sai.co.za ▪ **T +27 (0)33-383-0361/2** ▪ F +27 (0)86-542-8704

Mark and Paula Haldane are part of the small band of producers intent on making wine in the summer-rainfall and hence unconventional Midlands region of KwaZulu-Natal. They bought their property in 2008 and planted varieties for a Bordeaux-style blend, first harvest this year. 'It's a challenge to get big suppliers to take us seriously,' says winemaker Paula. On the plus side? The property is located close to the famous private schools of the area and affluent parents should make for a ready market.

▪ **Dusty Rhino** *see* United Nations of Wine
▪ **Dusty Road** *see* Cloof Wine Estate

Du'SwaRoo

Location/WO: Calitzdorp ▪ Map: Klein Karoo & Garden Route ▪ Est/1stB 2008 ▪ Tasting & sales by appt Mon-Fri 9-5 Sat 9-1 ▪ Closed all pub hols ▪ Wines also available at Withoek Cellar ▪ Farm produce - olives, olive oil, atchars, jellies ▪ Owner(s) Tony Bailey ▪ Cellarmaster(s)/winemaker(s)/viticulturist(s) Tony Bailey (2008) ▪ 7ha/2ha (hanepoot, shiraz, tinta, touriga) ▪ ±20t/150-180cs own label 50% red 10% rosé 40% port ▪ PO Box 279 Calitzdorp 6660 ▪ duswaroo@telkomsa.net ▪ www.kleinkaroowines.co.za/cellars/duswaroo.asp ▪ S 33° 30' 58.7" E 021° 41' 39.5" ▪ **T +27 (0)44-213-3137** ▪ F +27 (0)44-213-3137

A few years into his transition from water scientist to Calitzdorp vintner, Tony Bailey – who came to the Klein Karoo via Durban and Namibia (formerly SWA), hence the quirky name – has produced something new: a 'Cape blend' that reflects this distinctive area. Named after the Weimaraner-mad family's youngest, Sirocco is a port-variety blend with a noble red cultivar. We think he's onto something...

Sirocco [NEW] ☺ ★★★ Chocolate & Karoo scrub notes on three-way **NV (10)** combo shiraz (50%), touriga, tinta. With sweet-fruit end, soft tannins, slips down easily.

Cabernet Sauvignon Untasted. **Shiraz** ★★★ Lavender & fynbos nuanced **09** had savoury appeal, robust tannins mid-2010. Still selling, not revisited, as for Khamsin & Cape Vintage. **Shiloh Shiraz Reserve** [NEW] ★★★★ Rich chocolate notes on plush **09** preview; successful bold 'Australian' style with noticeable alc. Drink now & for year/2. **Khamsin** ★★★ From touriga, **NV (09)** firm & fiery (15.2% alc) to carry very ripe Xmas cake fruit. **Mistral** ★★ **NV (11)** rosé from shiraz; bright & friendly (12.5% alc), commendably savoury al fresco sipper. **Cape Vintage** ★★★★ Tealeaf-toned port-style fortified from 66/34 touriga & tinta. Last edition, we noted **09** would be even better in a few years. **Cape Ruby** [NEW] ★ 60/40 touriga/tinta mix **10** tired, unexciting. Discontinued: **Cabernet Sauvignon-Shiraz**. — Panel

▪ **Du Toit Family Wines** *see* Driehoek Family Wines

Du Toitskloof Winery

Location: Rawsonville ▪ Map: Breedekloof ▪ WO: Western Cape/Wellington/Western Cape/Breedekloof ▪ Est 1962 ▪ Tasting & sales Mon-Fri 8-5 Sat 9-3.30 ▪ Closed Easter Fri, Dec 25 & Jan 1 ▪ Cellar tours by appt ▪ Cheese platters ▪ BYO picnic ▪ Owner(s) 22 members ▪ Cellarmaster(s) Shawn Thomson (Oct 1999) ▪ Winemaker(s) Chris Geldenhuys (Mar 2005) & Willie Stofberg (Feb 2011), with Derrick Cupido (Jan 1993) ▪ Viticulturist(s) Leon Dippenaar (Jan 2005, consultant) ▪ 900ha (cab, merlot, ptage, shiraz, chard, chenin, cbard, sauv) ▪ 14,000t/ ±261,952cs own label 33% red 61% white 4.8% rosé 1.2% grape juice ▪ Fairtrade ▪ PO Box 55 Rawsonville 6845 ▪ info@dutoitskloof.co.za ▪ www.dutoitskloof.co.za ▪ S 33° 42' 9.2" E 019° 16' 8.9" ▪ **T +27 (0)23-349-1601** ▪ F +27 (0)23-349-1581

This famously value-giving winery at the entrance to the Du Toitskloof Mountain Pass was established exactly 50 years ago as a co-operative, with six members. Now

22 farmers contribute grapes. A neat, tripartite mantra is invoked at the winery: 'Vineyard to bottle with minimum interference. Quality always above price. Fruit above wood.' It seems to work fine for very many Du Toitskloof fans.

Reserve Collection

★★★★ **Nebbiolo 09** (★★★★) tasted last year, a toned down version of bold **08**: briefer oak sojourn, lower alcohol. Earthy tones with nuts & spice overlay, firm acidity, balanced 14% alc.

★★★★ **Dimension** Blend cab, merlot, shiraz plus a drop petit verdot. Easy-drinking **07** (★★★) last year showed a tad less structure, staying power than previous **04**.

Sauvignon Blanc 🔲 🈂 ★★★ Undemanding **10**'s guava & ripe honeydew leads to fresh, clean, short finish. Notably modest alcohol (12.2%). **Chardonnay-Viognier** ★★★★ Fruit-forward & well-rounded **08** combo, lightly oaked. Not retasted.

Du Toitskloof range

> **Cabernet Sauvignon** 😊 🔲 ★★★ Juicy, straightforward **09** with cranberry & wood spice notes. **Merlot** 😊 🔲 🈂 ★★★ Ready to drink **10** offers dark fruit, dark choc & a little wood spice. **Pinotage** 😊 🔲 🈂 ★★★ Fruity, spicy **10** fresh & well structured, though a bitter note intrudes. **Shiraz** 😊 🔲 ★★★ Balanced but uncomplicated **08** with pleasant hints of mulberry, black pepper & oak.

Pinotage-Merlot-Ruby Cabernet 🔲 🈂 ★★★ Inviting ripe plum/prune & crisp cranberry flavours on **10** tasted last year; a perfect braai companion. **Cabernet Sauvignon-Shiraz** 🔲 🈂 ★★ Modest **10** with just-off-dry finish. **Rosé** 🔲 🈂 ★★★ Tasted last year, fruity-floral **10** softly off-dry. **Chardonnay** 🔲 ★★ Nearly-dry, lightly oaked, easy **11**. **Chenin Blanc** 🔲 🈂 ★★ Juicy, off-dry **11** with naartjie tones. **Sauvignon Blanc** 🔲 ★★ Uncomplicated, tropical **11**; typically just off-dry. **Beaukett** 🔲 🈂 ★★ Flamboyant **11** blend with usual rosepetal & orange sweetness. **Sparkling Brut** ★★★ Crisply dry sauvignon-led **NV** fizz tasted last year.

Dessert Wine range

★★★★ **Hanepoot Jerepigo** 🈂 Rich, highly perfumed **10** (★★★) billowing Turkish Delight and oranges - but lacks complexity; sweetness perhaps more cloying than **09**. Best left to mature for many years.

★★★★ **Red Muscadel** ✓ 🈂 Sweet-scented **10** (★★★★) with floral & spiced red fruit aromas. More interesting than white version but also slightly cloying finish. Warm-hearted, as was **09**.

Noble Late Harvest ★★★★ Last tasted was sleek **07** from muscat & chenin. **Cape Ruby** ★★★ Fruity, slightly pruney **08** from tinta barocca, souzão, touriga. Not too sweet. WO Breedekloof.

Perlé Wines range NEW

Cape Secco Rosé ★★ Modest perlé from white & red grape mix. These both **NV**, both off-dry, both WO Breedekloof. **Cape Secco Blanc** ★★ Easy, light semi-sparkler with floral suggestions. — JPf

DuVon Wines

Map/WO: Robertson ▪ Est/1stB 2003 ▪ Tasting & sales by appt ▪ DuVon Guesthouse ▪ Owner(s) Du Toit & Von Klopmann families ▪ Cellarmaster(s)/winemaker(s)/viticulturist(s) Armand du Toit (2003) ▪ 42ha/29ha (cab, ruby cab, chenin, cbard, sauv) ▪ 450t/±625cs own label 70% red 30% white ▪ PO Box 348 Robertson 6705 ▪ info@duvon.co.za ▪ www.duvon.co.za ▪ S 33° 48'46.8" E 019° 47'4.1" ▪ **T +27 (0)82-341-1059** ▪ F +27 (0)86-626-1490

Armand du Toit and his uncle Alex von Klopmann put their middle names together to christen the wines they make from this revitalised Robertson farm. Francisca Nel has recently joined the team as admin, managing the new 200-guest wedding venue and freeing Armand to get the best out of the grapes.

Cabernet Sauvignon ★★★ **08** not a shy wine: peppery blackberries, robust tannins & 15.5% alc. Not retasted. **Shiraz** ★★★★ Dark, inviting **08** offered ripe blackberries & plums last time, well spiced by Fr/Am oak. **Chenin Blanc** ★★★ Last year **10** had subtle floral tones, fresh & dry finish. **Sauvignon Blanc** Await next. — DB

▪ **Dwyka Hills** *see Eagle's Cliff Wines-New Cape Wines*
▪ **Dyasonsklip** *see Bezalel-Dyasonsklip Wine Cellar*

Eagle's Cliff Wines-New Cape Wines

Map: Worcester ▪ WO: Breede River Valley/Western Cape ▪ Est 2000 ▪ Tasting & sales Mon-Fri 8-4.30 ▪ Closed all pub hols ▪ Light meals Mon-Fri 10-2.30 ▪ Facilities for children ▪ Tour groups ▪ Owner(s)/winemaker(s) Christiaan

Groenewald ▪ 600ha/80ha ▪ 40% red 60% white ▪ PO Box 898 Worcester 6849 ▪ christiaan@ncw.co.za ▪ www.eaglescliff.co.za ▪ S 33° 50' 25.4" E 019° 25' 7.4" ▪ T +27 (0)23-340-4112 ▪ F +27 (0)23-340-4132

Owner-winemaker Christiaan Groenewald takes his cue from the eagles that loop and swoop high in the mountain eyries above his farm Welgemoed between Villiersdorp and Worcester in the Breede River Valley. The three ranges - Eagle's Cliff, Dwyka Hills and new Arendskloof - all celebrate nature's majesty. On the property are a restaurant, tasting and wedding venues, and facilities for children.

Eagle's Cliff Reserve range

Cabernet Sauvignon ★★★ 05 perfect steak companion, with succulent flavours, well-managed tannins. Still selling, not revisited. **Shiraz** Await next.

Arendskloof range [NEW]

★★★★ Syrah-Tannat Unusual & ambitious blend, **09** has noble black plum & prune bouquet, firm tannins (as expected from tannat) yet hedonistic cherry fruit, well composed despite 15% alc. WO W Cape.

Eagle's Cliff range

Shiraz Rosé ☺ ★★★ Coral-hued **11**, dusty terpene edge, hint of tannin creates appealing & quaffable semi-dry effect.

Pinotage ★★★ 10 meaty & savoury, dense & long with satisfying weight. **Cabernet Sauvignon-Merlot** 🗎 **★★★** Still-available **09** attractive easy-sipper with black cherry & chocolate. **Shiraz-Pinotage ★★☆ 08** was supple coffee & red berry quaffer last year. **Chardonnay** Await next. **Chenin Blanc ★★ 11** generous sweet-sour candy apple flavour, uncomplex but enjoyable. **Sauvignon Blanc ★★★** Step-up **11** has faint hay & greenpepper bouquet, engaging & well-balanced peppery taste.

Dwyka Hills range

Shiraz ★★★ Old school leather-&-smoke style **10** lifts the bar, bright red-fruit flavour & bready/tarry complexity. WO W Cape. — Panel

Eagles' Nest

Location/WO: Constantia ▪ Map: Cape Peninsula ▪ Est 2001 ▪ 1stB 2005 ▪ Tasting & sales daily 10-4.30 ▪ Fee R30pp, waived on purchase of R300+ ▪ Closed Easter Fri, Dec 25 & Jan 1 ▪ Farm produce ▪ Owner(s) The Mylrea Family ▪ Cellarmaster(s) Martin Meinert (2005) ▪ Winemaker(s) Stuart Botha (2007) ▪ Viticulturist(s) Kobus Jordaan (2008) ▪ 38ha/12ha (merlot, shiraz, viog) ▪ 90t/7,500cs own label 85% red 15% white ▪ PO Box 535 Constantia 7848 ▪ info@eaglesnestwines.com ▪ www.eaglesnestwines.com ▪ S 34° 0' 54.2" E 018° 24' 54.3" ▪ T +27 (0)21-794-4095 ▪ F +27 (0)21-794-7113

Shiraz has clearly found a home on this relatively new wine-producing mountaintop Constantia property. Since its maiden 2005 vintage, there have been two Platter five stars, 2005 and 2008, half of the releases, a record most established cellars would envy. Winemaker Stuart Botha counts amongst his proudest moments picking up the 2010 Old Mutual trophy for Best Red Wine for the 2008 Shiraz, and then later in the year for the same wine getting Best Red as well as Winemaker of the Year at Winemakers Choice. With that kind of encouragement, we are sure the track record has only just begun.

★★★★★ Shiraz 🗎 After oakier **07** (★★★★★), last **08** (just 30% new wood) was back to purer style. Violets, black pepper intro to creamy elegant wine, hinted at complexity - fruit-filled but subtle, ultra-soft tannins.

★★★★ Verreaux 🗎 Developing blend as young vineyards mature, last **08** added dollops cab, cab franc. Modest oaking (35% new), good plum cake fruit with herbal dimension.

★★★★☆ Viognier 🗎 Template for the variety, oaked **10** shows how it should be done; peach pip austerity as the central theme, jasmine flower lifts the aroma while gentle dried peach flavours help soften the bone-dry finish. Individual & impressive.

The Little Eagle 🗎 **★★★☆** Merlot with cab, dab petit verdot. Last edition **08** was tastily ripe, fruity, fragrant, soft but well structured. **Sauvignon Blanc ★★★☆** Last-tasted **10** had fresh grass-tinged passionfruit, was cleanly dry, with penetrating delicacy. — CR

Eaglevlei Wines SA

Location/map: Stellenbosch ▪ Est/1stB 1997 ▪ Tasting & sales Wed–Sun 10–5 ▪ Fee R20 ▪ Closed Jan 1 ▪ Eaglevlei Restaurant Wed–Sun 10–5 ▪ Facilities for children ▪ Tour groups ▪ Conferences ▪ Weddings/functions ▪ Art Gallery ▪ Owner(s) Nigel Smith & Bill Oldfield ▪ Cellarmaster(s)/winemaker(s) Marcus Milner (Aug 2009, consultant) ▪ Viti-culturist(s) Johan Pienaar (1997, consultant) ▪ 50ha/±8ha (cab, merlot, ptage) ▪ 70t/49,000L own label 90% red 5% white 5% rosé ▪ PO Box 969 Stellenbosch 7599 ▪ enquiries@eaglevlei.com ▪ www.eaglevlei.com ▪ S 33° 49′ 33.5″ E 018° 48′ 52.2″ ▪ **T** +27 (0)21-884-4713 ▪ F +27 (0)21-884-4716

This northern Stellenbosch property, on the Old Paarl Road, is looking for a new owner, so any plans for innovation are on hold. In the meantime, winemaking control has been placed in the hands of estimable Marcus Milner from neighbouring De Meye, and it's business as usual on the estate.

Cabernet Sauvignon ★★★★ Focused, enticing blackcurrant fruitiness on **07** showed through hefty tannins & oak, needed time to meld when tasted. Not revisited, as for all below. **Pinotage** ★★★★ Full-bodied **07** domi-nated by heavily toasted oak, but sweet black plum fruit showing through. **Special No 7 Shiraz** Await next. **Shiraz** ★★★ **07** sweet berry fruit couched in heady oak aromas. Neatly formed, lightish body. **Red Affair** 🍷 ★★★★ **07** had ponderous oak over lively, ripe juicy fruit. Blend cab, merlot, shiraz & pinotage. **Pink** 🍷 Ex-tank **09**, from pinotage, still rather angular, too unformed to rate previously. **Viognier** 🍷 ★★★ Elegant, restrained **09** ex-tank rounded body, quite neutral fruit, well-judged oak. **Muscat D' Alexandrie** ★★★★ Limited-release fortified dessert. **08** had unctuous sweetness & intense hanepoot fruit, with gentle spirit tang. — GdB

▪ **Edenhof** see Schalkenbosch Wines
▪ **Eden's Vineyards** see Women in Wine

Edgebaston

Map: Stellenbosch ▪ WO: Stellenbosch/Coastal ▪ Est/1stB 2004 ▪ Tasting by appt only ▪ Owner(s) David Finlayson ▪ Cellarmaster(s) David Finlayson (Jan 2004) ▪ Winemaker(s) David Finlayson (Jan 2004), with Mark Goldsworthy (Nov 2008) ▪ Viticulturist(s) Mark Goldsworthy (Nov 2008) ▪ 30ha/24ha (cab, shiraz, chard, sauv) ▪ 180t/ 14,000cs own label 60% red 40% white ▪ PO Box 2033 Dennesig 7601 ▪ david@edgebaston.co.za ▪ www. edgebaston.co.za ▪ S 33° 53′ 33.82″ E 018° 51′ 17.61″ ▪ **T** +27 **(0)**21-889-9572 / +27 (0)83-263-4353 ▪ F +27 (0)21-889-9572

Production at the top-rank Finlayson family's hillside farm near Stellenbosch has reached its target, and owner/cellarmaster David Finlayson is now sourcing small parcels from selected growers to experiment with. A pinot noir will be bottled this year, followed by zinfandel and perhaps petite sirah. Innovation here is 'actually going back in time to what works best on our land and with our grapes', such as man-ual punch-downs as opposed to pump-overs, natural yeast fermentations, and large wooden vats for maturation. 'It makes wines with more character and personality.' Holistic in approach, David embraces aspects of biodynamics, organics and scientific winegrowing 'for my own peace of mind, not marketing purposes'.

★★★★☆ **'GS' Cabernet Sauvignon** Named after SA wine legend George Spies. Rich & silky, **08** deliciously accessible in youth last edition. Very fine & tailored; fruit, bright acid, 14.5% alc & oak in complete harmony.

★★★★ **Cabernet Sauvignon** ✓ Model Stellenbosch cabernet, arms more open than flagship above. **09** dusty edge to clean blackcurrant flavour, touch of herbs, hint of mint, substantial alc (15%) evident in lush finish.

★★★★ **Shiraz** Elegant **08** more floral in character than the usual berry-&-spice; classy layers of flavour noted last year. No **07**.

★★★★ **Chardonnay** ✓ 🍷 Deft bridge of the Old/New World divide. **10** has oodles of oatmeal richness cut by citrus tang, all tied up with mouthwatering acidity. Perfect food wine.

The Pepper Pot ✓ 🍷 ★★★★ Unusual mix of shiraz, mourvèdre & tannat, with the expected (white) pepper spicing in **10**. Easy to drink but there's more to the wine than the rustic front label suggests. WO Coastal. **The Berry Box** ✓ 🍷 ★★★★ Juicy partner to the spicy 'Pot'; **09**, from 6 red varieties, packs lugs of plump berries into a hip, knock-back glass. **Sauvignon Blanc** ✓ 🍷 ★★★★ Steely edge to **10**'s greengage fruit; usual 10% semil-lon addition fills out bone-dry finish. **Honey Pot** NEW ✓ 🍷 ★★★★ Label suggests something sweet but **10** far from it: dusty semillon & flinty sauvignon keep boisterous viognier in check. — DS

Eerste Hoop Wine Cellar

Location: Villiersdorp ▪ Map: Elgin, Walker Bay & Bot River ▪ WO: Theewater/Bot River/Western Cape ▪ 1stB 2006 ▪ Tasting, sales & tours Mon-Sat by appt ▪ Owner(s) Belgium owners ▪ Cellarmaster(s) Philip Costandius (Mar 2006, consultant) ▪ Winemaker(s)/viticulturist(s) Leon Engelke (Mar 2007) ▪ 24.5ha/11ha (cab, grenache, mourv, pinot, shiraz, chard, chenin, viog) ▪ 95t/7,000cs 55% red 42% white 3% rosé ▪ Brands for clients: Oggendau, Skoon Vallei, Stilfontein ▪ IPW ▪ PO Box 89 Elgin 7180 ▪ leon@eerstehoop.co.za ▪ www.eerstehoop.co.za ▪ S 34° 5'23.7" E 019° 11'50.7" ▪ **T +27 (0)28-841-4190/+27 (0)82-742-4793** ▪ F +27 (0)86-625-6028

Commenting on 2011 being the driest season in 30 years, winemaker Leon Engelke who doubles up as the cellar's viticulturist, also says the small berries were 'bursting with flavour'. Lots then to look forward to, including new varieties grenache, mourvedre and viognier harvested this year as blending partners for Shiraz, and a Pinot Noir already in barrel.

Eerste Hoop range

Cabernet Sauvignon ★★★★ Year later, **08**'s meatiness more pronounced, interleaved with herbs & black-currant. Supple tannins give immediate enjoyment. **Shiraz** ★★★★ Retasted **08**, liquorice & black berries, intriguing earthy note. Firm tannins offset by creamy fruit. Has 4+ year future. **Blushing Bride Rosé** 🍷 ★★★ Revisited **10** more expressive; red berries & food dryness. **Wooded Chardonnay** ★★★★ Now bottled, **10** shows better oak integration. Crisp & dry, with vanilla & citrus flavours; for fans of bold chardonnay. **Viognier** ★★ Perfumed **10** shows jasmine & peach, a softly rounded body. Tiny portion wooded.

Witklip range

Shiraz 🍷 ★★ Retasted **09** toasty oak & plums; tannins remain chunky. **Chardonnay** 🍷 ★★ Last was unwooded **10**, shy apple & lemon tones for easy sipping. — CR

▪ 1855 *see* Hermanuspietersfontein Wynkelder

Eikehof Wines

Location/map/WO: Franschhoek ▪ Est 1903 ▪ 1stB 1992 ▪ Tasting, sales & tours by appt ▪ Closed Easter Fri/Sat/Sun, Ascension Day, Pentecost & Dec 25 ▪ Owner(s)/cellarmaster(s)/winemaker(s) Francois Malherbe ▪ 29ha/24ha (cab, merlot, pinot, shiraz, chard, sem) ▪ 21t/1,500cs own label 80% red 20% white ▪ PO Box 222 Franschhoek 7690 ▪ eikehof@mweb.co.za ▪ www.eikehof.com ▪ S 33° 52'53.3" E 019° 3'52.0" ▪ **T +27 (0)21-876-2469** ▪ F +27 (0)21-876-2469

Francois Malherbe's love of hiking and mountain-biking keeps him close to nature, and this directness and simplicity feed through into his winemaking. The family vinify only about 20% of their 30ha grape crop; some routine Cabernet Sauvignon replanting happened this year. An eight-hectare peach orchard consumes the rest of Francois' time.

Cabernet Sauvignon ★★★ Sweet fruit in spicy **08**, charry staves & savoury acid grip. **Merlot** ★★★ Earthy **09** in savoury mould with plenty of fresh acidity. **Shiraz** ★★★ Smoky mocha dominates sweet spicy fruit in **08**. Slightly astringent finish. **Chardonnay** 🍷 ★★ Unoaked **10** pleasantly light, crisp everyday quaffing. — IM

Eikendal Vineyards

Location: Somerset West ▪ Map: Helderberg ▪ WO: Stellenbosch/Western Cape ▪ Est 1981 ▪ 1stB 1984 ▪ Tasting & sales Mon-Sat 9.30-4.30 (Sep-May) & 10-4 (Jun-Aug); Sun 10-4 ▪ Fee R20/5 wines ▪ Closed Easter Fri, Dec 25/26 & Jan 1 ▪ Cellar tours Mon-Fri 10 & 2.30 ▪ Restaurant T +27 (0)21-855-5033: lunch Tue-Sun & dinner Wed ▪ Facilities for children ▪ Tour groups ▪ Gift shop ▪ Conferences ▪ Walks/hikes ▪ Mountain biking trail ▪ Flywaters fly fishing ▪ Cheetah Outreach ▪ Eikendal Lodge (see Accommodation section) ▪ Owner(s) Substantia AG ▪ Winemaker(s)/viticulturist(s) Nico Grobler (2007), with Edward Jonsson (2009) ▪ 78ha/±56ha (cabs s/f, malbec, merlot, p verdot, chard) ▪ 250t/35-40,000cs own label 70% red 30% white ▪ IPW ▪ PO Box 2261 Stellenbosch 7601 ▪ info@eikendal.co.za ▪ www.eikendal.com ▪ S 34° 0'46.7" E 018° 49'24.5" ▪ **T +27 (0)21-855-1422** ▪ F +27 (0)21-855-1027

There's an air of change about this Helderberg property, with the emphasis firmly on raising the quality bar. Enthusiastic winemaker Nico Grobler, together with manager Stuart Buchan, has set himself high goals, and is working on achieving them through a radical overhaul of the vineyards, focusing the house style on tautness, purity and elegance. They eschew the big, intense style prevalent in this area in favour of finesse and balance, tweaking the vines to achieve ripeness at lower sugar levels. Outside the winery, there are diverse ecological programmes involving chee-tahs, waterfowl and Anatolian Shepherd dogs.

Limited Release range

★★★★ **Réserve du Patron** Dense, concentrated & extracted **05**, last year had very ripe, rich & brooding dark fruit, powdery tannins.

Flagship range

★★★★☆ **Classique** Elegant & focused cab blend shows perennial class. **08** cellar standard is intensely aro-matic & lithe, with generous ripe fruit despite lighter vintage. Uncompromisingly dry Bordeaux style, should develop & improve for several years.

★★★★ **Chardonnay** Promising change in direction here: taut, lean & minerally **10** shows focus, restraint & elegance but retains varietal character. Includes Franschhoek grapes.

★★★★ **Noble Late Harvest** Classic pineapple & candied peel character on previous **08**, from chenin. **Methodé Cap Classique** ✓ ★★★★ Appealing **08** sparkling from chardonnay shows class, leesy richness on creamy mousse. Improves on previous **05** (★★★☆). Delightful aperitif or sunset sipper.

Signature range

★★★★ **Merlot** 🔲 Previewed **09** reflects fine vintage's generous ripeness, but retains producer's wild berry & minty style. Approachable now, but should improve 3+ years.

Cabernet Sauvignon ✓ ★★★★ Solid, darkly rich **08** reflects prime cab neighbourhood. Ripe & earthy, satisfy-ingly big after mintier **07** (★★★★). Youthful fruit layers integrating nicely - should develop. **Cabernet Franc** ★★★★ **05**'s sappy austerity overpowered by spicy fennel features last edition. **Pinotage** ★★★★ Perfumed **08** had sweet dark-berried base. More characteristic varietal smoke & strawberry in **09**. Both tasted last year. **Shiraz** 🖼 ★★★★ Spicy, racy **10** has appealing fynbos spice over solid red-fruit centre. Shows generous ripeness. Own & Franschhoek grapes. **Cabernet Sauvignon-Merlot** NEW ★★★ Light-bodied **09** is pleasant without gravitas. Tends to crushed-berry juiciness rather than intensity. Drink now. **Janina Unwooded Chardonnay** ✓ 🔲 🖼 ★★★★ Much improved **11** tank sample shows leesy structure with bracing freshness. Welcome new direction. **Sauvignon Blanc** 🔲 🖼 ★★★ Ripe, pliant quaffer off Lutzville vines. Typical West Coast gravel & nettle. Latest **11** misses focus of **09**. Discontinued: **Semillon**.

Eikendal Wines

Rosé ☺ 🔲 🖼 ★★★ Pale salmon poolside sipper, **11** is fresher, fuller bodied. Persistently dry, with muted berry fruit. **Blanc** ☺ 🔲 🖼 ★★★ Pleasant everyday quaffing, **11** from sauvignon & chardonnay.

Rouge 🔲 🖼 ★★ Rather stewy base-level **10** merlot/shiraz fruitbomb. **Brut Sparkling** 🖼 ★★★ **10** includes brace of varieties, expresses roasted nuts & frothy charm. Undemanding & easy-drinking. WO W Cape. — GdB

🔲 **Eksteens' Family Vineyards** see Stone Ridge Wines
🔲 **Elandsberg** see Viljoensdrift Wines & Cruises

Elberti Wines

Location: Somerset West ▪ Map: Helderberg ▪ Est 2005 ▪ Tasting & sales by appt ▪ Owner(s)/cellarmaster(s)/ winemaker(s)/viticulturist(s) Pieter Steyn ▪ 1,000cs own label 90% red 10% white ▪ PO Box 70 Somerset Mall 7137 ▪ info@elbertiwines.com ▪ www.elbertiwines.com ▪ S 34° 4'39.0" E 018° 49'4.0" ▪ **T +27 (0)21-851-4760** ▪ F +27 (0)21-851-4761

Though based in Somerset West, Pieter and Eppie Steyn's efforts in gaining recogni-tion for their pioneering vineyards on the Theewaterskloof lakeside near Villiersdorp are reaping rewards, with the 2011 sauvignon sold out and incubating 2010 reds 'sure to turn a few heads'. Henceforth, all wines grown at the waterfront property will be 'estate' certified.

Dawning range

Merlot ★★★★ Previously, **06** raised the bar on last-tasted **03** with sugar plum bouquet & well-judged oak. **Sauvignon Blanc** ★★★★ **10**, previewed last year, showed promise: restrained & elegant, with body, balance & presence. Theewater fruit. Note: Sojourn range discontinued. — GdB

Elemental Bob

Location: Hermanus ▪ WO: Walker Bay/Durbanville ▪ Est/1stB 2004 ▪ Closed to public ▪ Owner(s)/winemaker(s) Craig Sheard ▪ 50-75cs own label 75% red 20% white 5% port ▪ elementalbob@gmail.com ▪ **T +27 (0)82-265-1071**

Craig Sheard can experiment at his own garagiste venture in ways he can't at his Spookfontein day job, and does so – sometimes radically (as some of the blends below show), often successfully. Always tending to the natural: no additions of acid or enzymes; fermentation with wild yeasts; no filtration.

Retro Series
The 1st Chardonnay ★★★★ Last year, fruit & spice on richly austere, even steely **09** from Elgin. Older oak.

Wood-cut Series 3
★★★★ **The Delight** Warm, engaging **08** from barbera with 10% shiraz. Beautifully fresh; also charming & well-balanced, sweet fruit supported by older oak. Like all these, not retasted this year.
The Ratio 20:80 ★★★★ Ratio of merlot to cab, that is. Big, macho, tannic **07**, has fruit to hopefully justify rating in year/2. **The Ratio 80:20** ★★★ Inverse of previous; characterful but over-chunky, extracted **07**. **The Turkish** ★★★★ Eccentric, delicious **08** blend barbera (for colour & quietly assertive tannins) & gewürztraminer (floral notes). Like Delight, WO Durbanville. — TJ

▪ **Elements** see Hartswater Wine Cellar
▪ **Elephantasy** see Groupe LFE South Africa

Elgin Grove

Location/WO: Elgin ▪ Est 2004 ▪ 1stB 2007 ▪ Closed to public ▪ Owner(s) Nigel McNaught, BDO & Tony Davis ▪ Winemaker(s) Nigel McNaught ▪ Viticulturist(s) Paul Wallace (2004, consultant) ▪ 20ha/6ha (sauv) ▪ 40t/500cs own label 100% white ▪ c/o Stony Brook PO Box 22 Franschhoek 7690 ▪ nigel@stonybrook.co.za ▪ **T +27 (0)21-876-2182** ▪ F +27 (0)21-876-2182

Elgin has developed a good reputation for sauvignon and this steep 6ha vineyard, lying behind the coastal mountains of the UNESCO registered Kogelberg Biosphere Reserve, is designed to prove a point. Co-owner Nigel McNaught of Stony Brook in Franschhoek (where this wine is made by him) believes sauvignon has a much better ageing potential than commonly believed.

Sauvignon Blanc 🍷 ★★★ Improving on the maiden release, latest **10**'s asparagus perfume transforms to gentle minerality on the palate. — CR

Elgin Heights

Location/map: Stellenbosch ▪ WO: Elgin ▪ 1stB 2007 ▪ Tasting & sales by appt ▪ Conference facilities ▪ Owner(s) Ryk Joubert ▪ Winemaker(s) Andries Burger, Kobie Viljoen & Corne Marais (sauv/shiraz/MCC, consultants) ▪ Viticulturist(s) DD Joubert ▪ 111ha/70ha (cab, merlot, shiraz, chard, sauv, viog) ▪ PO Box 52 Vlottenburg 7604 ▪ wine@elginheights.co.za ▪ www.elginheights.co.za ▪ S 33° 57' 2.60" E 018° 45' 28.91" ▪ **T +27 (0)84-517-9300** ▪ F +27 (0)86-648-1704

The Joubert family from Stellenbosch purchased this farm in 1966. Until 1999 it grew purely deciduous fruit; then, as on many Elgin farms, vines were introduced. As these mature, so the range grows. The new Cap Classique is named Emerald after the Afrikaans name of the farm, Smarag.

★★★★ **Sauvignon Blanc** 🍷 ▨ **11** (preview) consistent with previous: full bodied, with luscious gooseberry, fig flavours enlivened by keen mineral thread.
Shiraz NEW ▨ ★★★★ **10** full of ready, youthful appeal. Crackles with spicy aromas; a touch of sugar emphasises sweet red-fruit flavours; smoothly textured with nip of form-giving tannin. **Emerald Cap Classique Chardonnay** NEW ★★★★ Subtle, refreshing **09** MCC from 100% chardonnay. Whiff of cream, ginger biscuit; vivacious bubble leads to clean, tingling departure. — AL

Elgin Ridge

Location/WO: Elgin ▪ Map: Elgin, Walker Bay & Bot River ▪ Est 2007 ▪ 1stB 2009 ▪ Tasting, sales & tours Mon-Fri 10-4 by appt Sat/Sun & pub hols by appt only ▪ Food & wine pairings during Elgin Open Gardens weekends 10-4 ▪ Farm produce ▪ BYO picnic ▪ Owner(s) Brian & Marion Smith ▪ Winemaker(s) Niels Verburg (Aug 2009, consultant), with Brian Smith ▪ Viticulturist(s) Kevin Watt (Apr 2007, consultant), with Marion Smith ▪ 10.2ha/4.5ha (pinot, chard, sauv, sem) ▪ 14.5t/1,000cs own label 100% white ▪ PO Box 143 Elgin 7180 ▪ info@elginridge.com ▪ www.elginridge.com ▪ S 34 12′15″ E 19 00′18″ ▪ **T +27 (0)21-846-8060** ▪ F +27 (0)21-846-8060

The wine dream keeps evolving on this tiny Elgin property owned by Londoners Marion and Brian Smith. A small but fully equipped cellar has been built, despite miniscule production, and the 2010 vintage was made there by Brian and advisor Niels Verburg. Marion's vineyards, supervised by consultant Kevin Watt, are still young but show promise. In the pipeline is a pinot noir slated for release in 2015.

282 Chardonnay NEW ▤ ★★★ Unoaked **10** is delicately perfumed but not simple: white peach & a tangy acidity that extends the finish, refreshes. **282 Sauvignon Blanc** ▤ ★★★★ Organically grown **10** shows pear, passionfruit, limy freshness. Food friendly - sold mainly in restaurants & hotels. — CR

Elgin Valley Vineyards

Location/WO: Elgin ▪ Map: Elgin, Walker Bay & Bot River ▪ Est 2003 ▪ 1stB 2007 ▪ Tasting & sales Mon-Fri 9-2 Sat/Sun by appt ▪ Closed all pub hols ▪ Owner(s) Ian & Anette Corder ▪ Cellarmaster(s)/winemaker(s) Joris van Almenkerk (Mar 2010) ▪ Viticulturist(s) Kevin Watt (2004) ▪ 40ha/14ha (pinot, shiraz, chard, sauv) ▪ 90t ▪ own label 20% red 80% white ▪ PO Box 169 Elgin 7180 ▪ admin@elginvalleyvineyards.co.za ▪ www.elginvalleyvineyards.co.za ▪ **T +27 (0)21-846-8083** ▪ F +27 (0)21-846-8460

Ian Corder's career in marketing and advertising has included plenty of work on wine accounts while wife Anette originally had a travel company with a focus on wine tourism, so no surprise when they decided to buy this Elgin property in 2003 and set up vineyards. Highlight to date? 'Making our first wine.'

Elgin Valley Vineyards range

★★★★☆ **Corder Barrel Crafted Viognier** ▤ Simply 'Viognier' last time. Peach & hint of spice, **10** preview (★★★) is creamy but lacks intensity & freshness of last **08**.

Corder Special Reserve Shiraz ▤ Just 'Shiraz' last time. Await new vintage. **Sauvignon Blanc** ▤ ★★★ **10** wonderfully complex aroma with notes of citrus blossom, grapefruit & passionfruit but shade less substance & verve than last time. Name changes to 'Corder Cool Climate Sauvignon Blanc' from **11**.

Lorry range

Red Lorry Easy Red NEW ▤ ★★ From shiraz, **NV** is plain, straightforward. **Yellow Lorry Sauvignon Blanc** ▤ ★★ Very ripe **11** preview appears sweeter than previous, misses its easy-drinking charm. — CE

Elgin Vintners

Location/WO: Elgin ▪ Map: Elgin, Walker Bay & Bot River ▪ Est 2003 ▪ 1stB 2004 ▪ Tasting & sales by appt ▪ Closed Easter Fri/Sun/Mon, Dec 25 & Jan 1 ▪ Light meals by arrangement for tasting groups (12-20 pax) ▪ Owner(s) Derek Corder, Max Hahn, Alastair Moodie, James Rawbone-Viljoen, Rob Semple & Paul Wallace ▪ Cellarmaster(s)/winemaker(s) Various (Kevin Grant, Gavin Patterson, Jeff Grier, Nico Grobler, Martin Meinert, Niels Verburg, Joris van Almenkerk) ▪ Viticulturist(s) Paul Wallace ▪ 1,379ha/±102ha (cab, malbec, merlot, pinot, shiraz, chard, riesling, sauv, sem, viog) ▪ 800t/8,000cs own label ▪ BWI, IPW ▪ PO Box 121 Elgin 7180 ▪ elginvintner@mweb.co.za ▪ www.elginvintners.co.za ▪ S 34° 10′4.9″ E 019° 2′1.3″ ▪ **T +27 (0)21-859-2779** ▪ F +27 (0)86-646-3693

A busy and exciting 2011 saw the group win their first Swedish tender for the Chardonnay 2009, their most expensive wine, and ship their first orders to the US and Mauritius. Africa and Asia are their next target export markets. Upgrades include an online ordering facility, and codes on back labels which link directly to wine notes on the website. Much anticipated has been a flagship sauvignon blanc-semillon blend, launched too late in 2011 for us to try.

★★★★ **Agama** Previously tasted **07** (★★★★) from cab, merlot; unshowy aromas, simple & austere flavours. Less stylish than **06**.

★★★★ **Chardonnay** 🍸 ⍟ Expressive limy, buttery nose; good juicy fruity acids with subtle oaking add dimension, weight to **10**. Satisfying rather than complex.

★★★★ **Viognier** 🍸 Tasty if simple ripe fruit on dry **10** (★★★★) somewhat overwhelmed by buttery oak (50% new). Cloying farewell despite good acidity. **09** was elegant, aromatic.

Cabernet Sauvignon ★★★ Austere **07** last yr showed straightforward cassis; lacked guts for smoothing effects of age. **Merlot** ★★★★ Pleasing ripe yet fresh fruit notes introduce **08**; perhaps a little light for the assertive tannins that follow. May benefit from further year/2. **Pinot Noir** 🍸 ⍟ ★★★★ Fresh & fruity style; subtle oaking (30% new) on **10** adds balanced enrichment. **Shiraz** 🍸 ★★★★ Powerful spice, gamey features on **08**. Richly mouthfilling, supple & savoury with roundly dry finish. **07** (★★★★). **Rosé** 🍸 ★★★ Pretty pink **11** sample from merlot. Tangy wild strawberry flavours, lively & fruitily dry. **Sauvignon Blanc** 🍸 ⍟ ★★★ Tasted as sample last year, **10** now has simple fig, gooseberry aromas, fresh acidity but fruit tiring. — AL

Emineo Wines

Location: Cape Town ▪ Map: Cape Peninsula ▪ WO: Durbanville/Coastal ▪ Est 2004 ▪ 1stB 2006 ▪ Tasting by appt ▪ Owner(s) Trans-Scripto (Pty) Ltd ▪ Winemaker(s) Nico van der Merwe & Thys Louw ▪ 750cs own label 100% red ▪ PO Box 1358 Cape Town 8000 ▪ info@emineo.com ▪ www.emineo.com ▪ **T +27 (0)82-579-4849** ▪ F +27 (0)86-660-4323

The Liber red blends of this legally-themed brand, under the aegis of patent attorney Otto Gerntholtz, are made by the highly regarded Nico van der Merwe (Saxenburg, Mas Nicolas). Together with its sister brand, Cape to Cairo, its public profile is being raised through exposure, targeted marketing and a new centre-city tasting venue.

★★★★ **Liber II JLS** Poised **07** cab (65%) with merlot & pinotage. Minty chocolate aromas, lively cassis underpinned by acidity & tannin. Not retasted, like others in range.

★★★★ **Liber III RG 07** big, ebullient shiraz with splash mourvèdre, ex-Durbanville & Swartland. Seriously styled, with polished oak.

Liber I OCG ★★★★ Soft & approachable **06**, 5-way Bordeaux blend mostly cab. — GdB

▪ **Enon** *see* Zandvliet Wine Estate & Thoroughbred Stud
▪ **Enoteca Bottega** *see* Idiom Wines

Epicurean Wines

WO: Western Cape ▪ Est 2001 ▪ 1stB 2003 ▪ Closed to public ▪ Owner(s) Global Pact Trading 125 (Pty) Ltd ▪ Cellarmaster(s) Mutle Mogase, Mbhazima Shilowa, Moss Ngoasheng, Ron Gault (Nov 2002) ▪ Winemaker(s) Schalk Willem Joubert (consultant) ▪ 250cs own label 100% red ▪ WIETA ▪ PO Box 280 Parklands 2121 Johannesburg ▪ info@epicureanwine.co.za ▪ www.epicureanwine.co.za ▪ **T +27 (0)11-530-9100** ▪ F +27 (0)11-530-9101

'A great wine is conspicuous by its perfect balance which is aromatically harmonious, pure, powerful, and above all complex.' For six vintages, the four owners have aimed to meet the challenge of creating such a wine, helped by Schalk-Willem Joubert of Rupert & Rothschild. They plan to convert 'sophisticated consumers who might otherwise have ordered a Jack Daniels or Southern Comfort'.

★★★★ **Epicurean** More lightweight **08** reflects the vintage. Pretty mint-lifted red berry tones are held by a challenging structure. Best opened 2012-14. — AL

Equitana

Location: Somerset West ▪ Map: Helderberg ▪ WO: Stellenbosch ▪ Est 2000 ▪ 1stB 2008 ▪ Tasting & sales by appt ▪ Fee R10 ▪ Closed all pub hols ▪ B&B ▪ Function venue ▪ BYO picnic ▪ Walking/hiking trails ▪ Owner(s) Equitana (Pty) Ltd, Johann & Esme de Beer ▪ Viticulturist(s) Gavin Dun (May 2007) ▪ 4.65ha/1.38ha (cabs s/f) ▪ 10.54t/6,000cs own label 100% red ▪ PO Box 5308 Helderberg 7135 ▪ equitania@mweb.co.za ▪ www.equitania.co.za ▪ **T +27 (0)21-842-3756** ▪ F +27 (0)21-842-2766

The De Beer family farm is a stone's throw from suburbia but, with its views of the majestic Helderberg, the convenience of having a shopping mall just five minutes away is forgotten. Instead, the focus is on enjoying the gifts wine brings – the opportunity to meet interesting people, to share a meal, create memories and dream of future vintages... which may include merlot and pinot noir.

★★★★ **Flag** NEW New French oak component distinguishes this from sibling Bordeaux blend. Chocolate-toned 08 touch more serious, savoury, yet still smooth & engaging.

Fluke ★★★ Last edition franc led 09 (★★★★) blend - since renamed - of the two cabs. Tasted out of sequence, 08 ups cab sauvignon to 60%, shows appealing creamy berry-mousse character, ripe & rounded. — CvZ

Ernie Els Wines

Location/map: Stellenbosch • WO: Stellenbosch/Western Cape • Est 1999 • 1stB 2000 • Tasting, sales & cellar tours Mon-Sat 9-5 • Fee R30 • Closed Easter Fri/Sun, Dec 25 & Jan 1 • Light lunches & cheese platters Tue-Sat • Tour groups • Gift shop • Corporate events & functions • Small conference facilities • Mountain biking trail • Ernie Els's Trophy Room • The Big Easy Restaurant at 95 Dorp Str (see Restaurants section) • Owner(s) Ernie Els • Cellarmaster(s) Louis Strydom (Dec 1999) • Winemaker(s) Louis Strydom (Dec 1999), with Klaas Stoffberg (2009) • Viticulturist(s) Charl van Reenen (2008) • 72ha/45ha (cab, merlot, shiraz) • 250t/9,000cs own label 90% red 10% white + 750cs for clients • Brand for client: SA Rugby • PO Box 7595 Stellenbosch 7599 • info@ernieelswines.com • www.ernieelswines.com • S 34°0'52.8" E 018°50'53.5" • **T +27 (0)21-881-3588** • F +27 (0)21-881-3688

Ernie Els is one of the world's top professional golfers, career wins including three major championships and his nickname being 'The Big Easy' due to his fluid, seemingly effortless golf swing. An eponymous winery was established in Stellenbosch in 1999, Louis Strydom the winemaker since inception and now managing director as well. Originally, there was just one Bordeaux-style red blend made in a modern, full-bodied style and carrying an ultra-premium price tag but the range has grown over time and now includes a number of more modestly conceived, medium-priced wines. 'We're looking to reduce alcohol levels and that has to happen in the vineyard. It's about managing our sunshine more effectively.'

★★★★ **Cabernet Sauvignon** Big, ripe 09 packed with flavour & oaked accordingly, noted last year.

★★★★ **Merlot** 10 (★★★★) shows red fruit, slight herbal edge. Medium- to full-bodied with fresh acidity, fine tannins. Classically styled but lacks 09's gravitas.

★★★★☆ **Ernie Els Signature** Ambitious take on Bordeaux-style blend, 08 has forthcoming nose of ripe dark fruit & oak spice. Opulent & polished with huge flavour concentration, smooth texture & gentle acidity. Big 15% alc & a few grams of sugar have their influence.

★★★★ **Big Easy Red** 10 (★★★☆) is 6-way blend, led by shiraz. Sexy rather than profound, with sweet, juicy red fruit & fine tannins. Includes some Piekenierskloof fruit. Less weight than 08; 09 not tasted.

★★★★☆ **Proprietor's Blend** 09 is 62% cab, with shiraz, cab franc, merlot, malbec. Brooding nose of dark fruit, herbs, graphite. Palate shows good concentration, fresh acidity, firm but fine tannins. Long, dry finish.

★★★★☆ **CWG** NEW 09 is 60% cab, 30% shiraz, 10% merlot. Focus & precision are what impress; full but well balanced with fresh acidity & smooth but not slippery tannins. Layers of flavour including red & black fruit, attractive herbal note & oak spice.

Proprietor's Syrah Await next. **Big Easy White** NEW ✓ 🗒 ★★★★ From chenin, 11 shows yellow apple aromas & flavours. Pure and intense with good line of acidity - very rewarding. **Sauvignon Blanc** NEW 🗒 ★★★ Intense pineapple on appealing 11. Juicy fruit, soft acidity. These last two WO W Cape. — CE

Ernst Gouws & Co Wines

Location/map: Stellenbosch • WO: Malmesbury/Stellenbosch/Coastal/Koekenaap • Est/1stB 2003 • Tasting & sales at Koelenhof Winery Mon-Thu 9-5 Fri 9-4 Sat 10-2 • Fee R15pp • Closed Easter Fri/Sun, Ascension Day, Dec 25/26 & Jan 1 • Facilities for children • Owner(s) Ernst & Gwenda Gouws • Cellarmaster(s) Ernst Gouws • Winemaker(s) Ernst Gouws snr, with Ezanne Gouws-Du Toit & Ernst Gouws jnr • 72ha total • 30,000cs own label 40% red 60% white • Other export brands: New Gate, Timbili • IPW • PO Box 7450 Stellenbosch 7599 • ernst@ ernstgouws.co.za • www.ernstgouws.co.za • S 33° 50'3.4" E 018° 47'52.7" • **T +27 (0)21-865-2895** • F +27 (0)21-865-2894

This well-established family-owned and -run winery in Stellenbosch boasts three qualified winemakers: father Ernst Gouws, daughter Ezanne and most recently son Ernst jnr, 'the soul and drive' behind BulkIt, their new bulk wine brokering subsidiary. Also new are the New Gate brand, spreadheading the Gouws' entry to the Asian market, and a Reserve range poised for launch as the guide went to press.

Chenin Blanc ☺ 🗒 ★★★ Delicate tropical fruit salad & cream, zesty acidity on 11.

Merlot ★★★★ Ripe black cherry, hints cappuccino & chocolate, **08** smooth & lingering last edition. WO Coastal. **Pinot Noir** ★★★ Ripe & big **08** preview is earthy, spicy cherry with savoury mushroom & oaky finish. WO Western Cape. **Shiraz** ✓ ★★★★ Friendly & fragrant **09** is fruity, spicy & soft. Creamy lingering savoury finish. WO Malmesbury. **Chardonnay** ✓ ⌦ ★★★★ From Swartland bushvines, **10** is rich & buttery, mouthfilling, with a delicious citrus & vanilla conclusion. **Sauvignon Blanc** ✓ 🦘 ★★★★ Fresh & fruity **11**, succulent fruit/acid balance. A real crowd pleaser. WO Stellenbosch, like Chenin. — WB

Escapades Winery

Location/map: Stellenbosch ▪ WO: Stellenbosch/Coastal ▪ Est/1stB 2006 ▪ Tasting by appt ▪ Owner(s) Evangelos Gerovassiliou, Vassilis Tsaktsarlis & Takis Soldatos ▪ Cellarmaster(s) Vassilis Tsaktsarlis & Evangelos Gerovassiliou (both 2006) ▪ Winemaker(s) Chris Kelly (Oct 2010, consultant) ▪ (cab, grenache, malbec, melot, mourv, ptage, shiraz, sauv, sem) ▪ 87t/3,000cs own label 30% red 60% white 10% rosé ▪ PO Box 5 Sanlamhof 7532 ▪ info@escapadewinery.com ▪ www.escapadewinery.com ▪ S 33° 54'47.7" E 018° 44'7.7" ▪ **T +27 (0)82-569-3371** ▪ F +27 (0)86-585-6549

Evangelos Gerovassiliou and Vassilis Tsaktsarlis, the two Greek winemakers who decided to explore the vinous possibilities of 'an ancient continent', have now brought in a New Zealander – the locally well-experienced and well-reputed Chris Kelly – to help them. They're ranging far and wide from their Stellenbosch base for grapes, 'partnering with growers that use sustainable practices, to produce internationally acceptable styles', fast adding more wines to their range.

★★★★ **Semillon-Sauvignon Blanc** NEW ▤ **11**'s 75% semillon gives richness, sauvignon adds vibrancy; more delicacy than power. Balanced, lingering. Like Semillon, subtly oaked. Partly ex-Franschhoek. **Cabernet Sauvignon** ★★★ **06** was fruity, zesty, rather oaky. All these reds tasted last year. **Merlot** ★★★ Uncomplicated **07**, its opulence cut by highish acid. **Pinotage** ★★★ Juicy, balanced **07** with typical bright raspberry tones & a gentle nip of bitterness. **Shiraz** ★★★ Pleasing varietal clarity & well-judged oak on accessible, supple **07**. **Rosé** NEW ▤ ★★★ **11** ex-Franschhoek has pinotage's earth-tinged raspberry. Dry, but soft & easygoing. **Sauvignon Blanc** ▤ ★★★★ **10** untasted; **11** juicy & bright-fruited, cutting its rich tropicality with fresh greenness – though acidity well controlled. **Semillon** NEW ▤ ★★★★ Lemony **11** in youth shows touch less intensity, interest & harmony than the blend, but bolder, broader & softer. — TJ

◾ **Eskdale** *see De Zoete Inval Estate*

Esona   NEW

Location/WO: Robertson ▪ Est 2002 ▪ 1stB 2010 ▪ Closed to public ▪ Owner(s) Rowan & Caryl Beattie ▪ Winemaker(s) Lourens van der Westhuizen (Jan 2010, Arendsig) ▪ Viticulturist(s) Frikkie Bruwer (Sep 2009) ▪ 17ha/9.83ha (shiraz, chard, chenin, cbard, raisin blanc, sauv) ▪ ±250t/3,000cs own label 34% red 66% white ▪ PO Box 2619 Clareinch 7400 ▪ info@eyonawine.co.za ▪ www.eyonawine.co.za ▪ **T +27 (0)82-417-5362** ▪ F +27 (0)21-787-3792

Esona (Xhosa for 'The Very One'), situated overlooking the Breede River between Robertson and Bonnievale, is owned by Cape Town businessman Rowan Beattie and wife Caryl. In order to make their farming operation more viable, they enlisted the services of nearby Arendsig winemaker Lourens van der Westhuizen and set about making a range of wines from specially selected vineyard blocks on the farm. As for the overall philosophy behind the brand, Rowan is succinct: 'Superior quality, limited quantity, realistic price'.

Shiraz ★★★ Blackcurrant **10** fruit-filled & well balanced, sweet impression on finish. **Chardonnay** ★★★ Good fruity intro to **10** persists to palate, zippy acidity balances the few grams of sugar & active 14.5% alc. **Sauvignon Blanc** ★★★ Year bottle-age adds extra interest, honeysuckle & toasty dimension to crisp & refreshing **10** sipper. Enjoy soon. — Panel

◾ **Eternal** *see Kumala*

Eve Bubbly   NEW

Est 2006 ▪ Closed to public ▪ Owner(s) Eve Sparkling (Pty) Ltd (6 shareholders) ▪ Cellarmaster(s) Shawn Lucus (2009) ▪ PO Box 66442 Highveld 0169 ▪ info@evebubbly.co.za ▪ www.evebubbly.co.za ▪ **T +27 (0)12-661-5077** ▪ F +27 (0)86-569-3078

Inspired by the need for a 'mobile, trendy product that ladies could enjoy anywhere, anytime', the Eve brand is directed at new/emerging wine drinkers and making wine more accessible and fashionable. To that end the six wines - half still and half sparkling - are packaged in pretty 250ml slimline aluminium cans. These, brand manager Marisca Biagio says, are not only fun, easy-drinking entrées to wine but also space-saving, easy-to-chill housewines for restaurants, lodges, hotels and function venues, where 'the bubbly is a great welcome drink'.

Eve range

Dry Red ★★ Friendly, slightly savoury dry red, **NV**, food friendly & best lightly chilled in summer. Both ranges sourced from Orange River Wine Cellars. **Rosé** ★★ Subtle strawberry hints on gently sweet low-alc **NV** sipper. **Dry White** ★★ Light, easy **NV** dry white designed for sushi & Thai-style butterfish.

Eve Bubbly range

Brut ★★★ Frothy **NV** sipper, not too dry, refreshing, hint of lemon in the lively bubbles. **Vin Doux** ★★ Sweet but refreshing **NV** bubbly with low alc (8.5%) & lemon-drop flavour. **Rosé** ★★★ The prettiest & tastiest of these: streams of fresh prickly bubbles; sweet, grapey, strawberry bubblegum flavours. **NV**. Serve well chilled. —Panel

■ **Eventide Cellar** *see* Mischa Estate

Excelsior Estate

Location/map/WO: Robertson ▪ Est 1859 ▪ 1stB 1990 ▪ Tasting & sales Mon-Fri 10-4 Sat 10-3 ▪ Picnics available on request, also BYO picnic ▪ Facilities for children ▪ Conference venue ▪ 4-star Excelsior Manor Guesthouse (see Accommodation section) ▪ Owner(s) Freddie & Peter de Wet ▪ Cellarmaster(s) Johan Stemmet (Aug 2003) ▪ Winemaker(s) Johan Stemmet (Aug 2003), with Kelly Gova (2005) ▪ Viticulturist(s) Freddie de Wet (1970) ▪ 320ha/220ha (cab, merlot, p verdot, shiraz, chard, sauv) ▪ 2,200t/160,000cs own label 75% red 25% white ▪ Other export brand: Stablemate ▪ BRC ▪ PO Box 17 Ashton 6715 ▪ info@excelsior.co.za ▪ www.excelsior.co.za ▪ S 33°51'15.1" E 020°0'25.6" ▪ **T +27 (0)23-615-1980** ▪ F +27 (0)23-615-2019

Co-owner Peter de Wet reveals the latest secret ingredient at this engaging Robertson estate: 'worm wee'. Gathered from worm farms, it's used to fertilise the soil, increase its microbial life and improve the overall health of the vines. Sights set on cracking Asian markets, Peter, viticulturist Freddie de Wet and winemaker Johan Stemmet are keen to increase the complexity and elegance of their 'full, rich New World style wines', and are picking varieties like shiraz 'a week or two earlier'.

★★★★ **Evanthuis Cabernet Sauvignon** Last edition, we noted classy **07** following in **06**'s elegant footsteps: smooth, svelte texture; tannin & fruit in perfect balance.

★★★★ **San Louis Shiraz Reserve** Gets 'San Louis' prefix in **09** (★★★★), liquorice & tar, still a bit gruff, needs year/2 to integrate fully, show as well as dense & smoky **07**.

Merlot ☺ 🍷 ★★★ Black cherry **10** soft & gentle, with nutty twist; medium bodied & undemanding for anytime relaxation. **Paddock Shiraz** ☺ 🍷 ★★★ Bouncy & extrovert, **09** sweet plums & sour cherries spiced with black pepper & a (good) hint of tar. **Sauvignon Blanc** ☺ 🍷 ★★★ Steely **11** raises the bar; feisty but poised, with lemon blossom, mineral suggestion.

Cabernet Sauvignon 🍷 ★★★ Everyday companion **09**'s fruitiness accented by tealeaf & smoky whiffs. **Gondolier Merlot Reserve** 🍷 ★★★ 'Merlot Reserve' last time. **08** mocha-dusted baked plum, softer than previous, remains an appealing drink. **Purebred Red** ✓ 🍷 ★★★★ Always a wallet friendly easy-drinker. **10** shiraz with dash viognier, floral, peppery & packed with flavour. **Chardonnay** 🍷 ★★★ **11** fruit forward & uncomplex, body & grip from brush of oak. **Viognier** 🍷 ★★★ Fragrant **11**'s generous 14.5% alc warms & smooths the palate. —Panel

Excelsior Vlakteplaas

Location: Oudtshoorn ▪ Map: Klein Karoo & Garden Route ▪ Est 1934 ▪ 1stB 1998 ▪ Tasting & sales Mon-Fri 9-5 ▪ Closed Easter Fri-Mon, Ascension day, Dec 16/25/26 & Jan 1 ▪ Owner(s)/winemaker(s) Danie Schoeman ▪ 41ha (merlot, ptage, ruby cab, chenin, muscadel r/w) ▪ 490t/1,000cs own label 50% red 50% white ▪ PO Box 112 De Rust 6650 ▪ jjschoeman@telkomsa.net ▪ S 33°29'16.74" E 022°35'25.50" ▪ **T +27 (0)82-821-3556** ▪ F +27 (0)44-241-2569

Klein Karoo farmer Danie Schoeman resolutely adheres to his policy of bottling under his own label only in even years. So the muscadels from the 2010 vintage were dressed in His Master's Choice livery, while those from the 2011 harvest were sold in bulk. 'There's a big demand for muscadel,' he notes.

His Master's Choice range

Red Muscadel Only bottled in even years; **10** sold out, await next. **White Muscadel ★★★** Sweet but lively **06** still selling; barley sugar & orange zest treat, especially over crushed ice. —Panel

Fable

Location/map/WO: Tulbagh ▪ 1stB 2009 ▪ Tasting Sat/Sun & pub hols by appt ▪ Owner(s) Terroir Capital ▪ Winemaker(s) Rebecca Tanner (Jul 2009) ▪ Viticulturist(s) Paul Nicholls (Jul 2009) ▪ 185ha/10ha (mourv, syrah), planting another 20ha (grenache, syrah, viog) ▪ PO Box 19 Tulbagh 6820 ▪ rebecca@fablewines.com ▪ www. fablewines.com ▪ S 33° 21'7.9" E 019° 12' 46.1" ▪ **T** +27 (0)78-315-3861, +27 (0)73-768-1600 ▪ F +27 (0)86-660-9288

A recommendation by Jancis Robinson of it as 'an interesting place' and an email from the previous owner asking if he might be interested in the property, led Terroir Capital's Charles Banks to buy the Tulbagh Mountain Vineyards farm in 2010, and reinvent the wines under a new label. (The previous home-grown wines were discontinued; see under TMV Wines for the former negociant range.) Coming from a previous owner of Californian cult winery Screaming Eagle, this investment in the Cape winelands augurs well - as do the first, distinctive wines under the new label. Banks lost no time in starting an overhaul, including new vineyard plantings, refitting and extending the cellar. Environment-friendly practices continue; the intention is to sign on to the UN global compact, which promotes environmental, social and economic sustainability.

Fable range NEW

★★★★☆ **Bobbejaan 09** shiraz of great delicacy & freshness, despite 14.9% alc. Intricate mélange dark spice, roast game; caressing mouthfeel, tannins ease to savoury length. Lovely now; good potential.

★★★★☆ **Lion's Whisker** Expressive, elegant syrah/mourvèdre blend in fresh, easy-drinking yet satisfying Côtes du Rhône style. **09** broad, supple texture backdrop to fullsome, savoury flavours.

★★★★★ **Jackal Bird** Chenin, chardonnay might fill core role but **10**'s warm-climate distinction derives from roussanne, viognier, grenache blanc trim. Earth & minerals wrapped in soft, silky viscosity; rich (there's a little residual sugar) but not heavy, with pithy finish giving form. WO Coastal. — AL

■ **Fairhills** *see* Origin Wine

Fairseat Cellars

Location: Cape Town ▪ Closed to public ▪ Owner(s) Dick Davidson ▪ PO Box 53058 Kenilworth 7745 ▪ fairseat@ mweb.co.za ▪ **T** +27 (0)21-797-1951

Negociant and Cape Wine Master Dick Davidson sources wines locally for export to Europe, chiefly buyers' own brands (BOBs) for the German market. He is also the South African importer for the wines of Domaines Schlumberger from Alsace.

Fairvalley Wines

Location: Paarl ▪ WO: Western Cape ▪ Est 1997 ▪ 1stB 1998 ▪ Tasting by appt only ▪ Fee R25 ▪ Sales daily 9-4.30 at Fairview ▪ Closed Easter Fri, Dec 25 & Jan 1 ▪ Owner(s) Fairvalley Farmworkers Association ▪ Cellarmaster(s) Awie Adolf (Feb 1998) ▪ Winemaker(s) Jaco Brand (Nov 2009) ▪ 15,000c own label 50% red 50% white ▪ Fairtrade ▪ PO Box 6219 Paarl 7620 ▪ wine@fairvalley.co.za ▪ www.fairvalley.co.za ▪ **T** +27 (0)21-863-2450 ▪ F +27 (0)21-863-2591

Significant changes for this pioneering farmworker upliftment venture established under the aegis of Fairview in 1997: it's entered into a marketing partnership with Citrusdal Wines and moved production there as well. As one of a handful of black-owned companies with Fairtrade wines, Fairvalley is upbeat about the future and aims to be self-supporting within the next year.

Sauvignon Blanc ☺ 🍽 ★★★ Zesty fig & flint, **11** showing improved complexity & length, zippy acidity.

Cabernet Sauvignon ✓ 🍽 ★★★★ **10** preview a step up on previous. Tangy, savoury black fruit & cigarbox, concentrated density. 6 months oak adds firm body. **Pinotage** 🍽 🥂 ★★★ Ripe berries galore, **10** gentle vanilla caramel edge from French/American oak staves, medium length. **Shiraz** NEW 🍽 ★★★ Smoky plum & dense fruit, previewed **10** is warm & soft textured, light vanilla grip from oak. **Chardonnay** 🍽 ★★★ Tropical fruit & sherbet, **10** fresh naartjie tang. Previewed last year, still selling. **Chenin Blanc** 🍽 ★★★ Juicy melon & vibrant ruby grapefruit tang on **11**. Sampled from tank, like Sauvignon. — FM

Fairview

Location: Paarl ▪ Map: Paarl & Wellington ▪ WO: Paarl/Coastal/Darling/Swartland/Stellenbosch ▪ Est 1693 ▪ 1stB 1974 ▪ Tasting & sales daily 9–5, last tasting 30min before closing ▪ R25/standard tasting, R60/master tasting ▪ Closed Easter Fri, Dec 25 & Jan 1 ▪ The Goatshed Restaurant (see Restaurants section) ▪ Tour groups by appt only ▪ Farm produce ▪ Museum: history of farm with photos in tasting room ▪ Owner(s) Charles Back ▪ Winemaker(s) Anthony de Jager (Dec 1996), with Adele Dunbar (2006) & Stephanie Betts (2010) ▪ 500ha/300ha (cab, carignan, grenache, merlot, mourv, p sirah, ptage, shiraz, tannat, tempranillo, chenin, sauv, viog) ▪ 2,100t/130cs own label 80% red 15% white 5% rosé ▪ ISO 9001:2001, BWI, BRC, HACCP, IPW, WIETA ▪ PO Box 583 Suider-Paarl 7624 ▪ info@fairview.co.za ▪ www.fairview.co.za ▪ S 33°46′19.16″ E018° 55′25.26″ ▪ **T +27 (0)21-863-2450** ▪ F +27 (0)21-863-2591

At Fairview's core are values, family, community and hard work. The growth and evolution of this family brand - now exported to 27 countries - is detailed in pen sketches on a simple brown paper placemat in The Goatshed, the popular eatery adjacent to the wine (and cheese) tasting room below Paarl mountain's distinctive granite dome. Charles Back II's ancestor, Charles I from Lithuania, bought Fairview - then called Bloemkoolfontein - in 1937. He'd be hard pressed to recognise the place with its 6m tall goat tower, emphasis on shiraz and unusual grape varieties, as well as fully-fledged offshoots La Capra and Goats do Roam. Labels have been tweaked - and, as ever, there are a few new wines in bottle too.

Fairview range

★★★★ **Cabernet Sauvignon** ✓ 09 dark, earthy & luxuriantly complex. Cassis & char offer interest & concentration. Fir, with tannin as smooth as 08 yet less time in oak; 15 months 25% new. WO Stellenbosch.

★★★★ **Pegleg Carignan** 09 returns to form after 08 (★★★★). Remarkable old Swartland bushvines still produce the goods. Ripe red berry fruit & spice with choc richness. Broad yet lean, structured.

★★★★☆ **Primo Pinotage** ✓ Big but genteel & refined 09 maintains usual high standards. Savoury black fruit with fresh acidity supplemented by tobacco leaf & smoke character from oaking - 40% new barrels, both French & American. Coriander spice adds lift on a long ripe aftertaste. This, Shiraz, Caldera, Barbera, Merlot, Pinotage-Viognier & Oom Pagel Semillon all WO Coastal.

★★★★☆ **Eenzaamheid Shiraz** Serious styling on 09 (first since 06), which is all dark, concentrated black fruit but elegant. Light char/smoke from 45% new oak barrels but ample pure fruit ensures equilibrium. Textured & refreshing. Not over-extracted, it should age well for 5+ years.

★★★★☆ **The Beacon Shiraz** Like formidable 07, 08 (★★★★★) from a single Paarl vineyard is the proverbial iron fist in a velvet glove. Nuanced & complex with spicy, pepper & violets over liquorice & juicy black fruit. Oak (45% new) is toned & enhances the whole. Gentle & seamlessly lithe yet powerful, dark & dense.

★★★★ **Jakkalsfontein Shiraz** 07 made as always from Swartland bushvines. Plush fruit pastille succulence with cedar spice & peppery fynbos notes. Rich but showing finesse. Sleek yet concentrated. As with previous vintages, powerfully soft. No 06 made.

★★★★ **Shiraz** ✓ 09 (★★★★) has a floral violet lightness. Plum fruit vies with earthy intensity, on a platform from 14 months in oak. Not as polished or rich as 08.

★★★★ **Cyril Back** Flagship homage to Back patriarch, 07 (★★★★★) tasted last edition. From Paarl & Swartland shiraz. Firm but gentle texture; complex, dense, concentrated. Needing time, as did 06.

★★★★☆ **Caldera** ✓ Last year 08 preview needed time. It's now matured to display generous spicy flavour. Cranberry dryness with lively cinnamon zip on old vine grenache, shiraz, mourvèdre blend. Opulent yet fresh & sinuously lean.

★★★★☆ **La Beryl Blanc** 🥂 10 sees sugar down from glorious 09 (★★★★★) - that was 194g/l, this is 140g/l. Unctuous rich sundried pineapple & apricot but superbly balanced by fresh acidity. All chenin, from 33-year-old home bushvines. Finishes clean but flavour memory lingers long.

★★★★ 09 follows the trend set by **08**. Juicy black berries, cocoa richness & yielding texture; fresh & ~~...~~s. **Merlot** 🗎 **★★★★** Previously 'Stellenbosch' in name. Herbs & fynbos on **09**, lead to deep tarry density very like **08**'s. **Mourvèdre ★★★★ 09** is tangy, succulent & very spicy, with ample plum & pepper fruit. With a firm grip & density obvious. **Petite Sirah ★★★★ 09** a pre-bottling sample. Like **08** spicy but juicy. Firm core yet delicate blueberry, vanilla appeal & length. **Pinotage** 🗎 **★★★★** Red berry with subtle mocha on **10**. Light grip & texture with brambly concentration supported by modest oaking. **Sangiovese ★★★** Cherry & gluhwein spice on **09** from Darling grapes. Dry, herbal edge yet supple body & texture. Year in old oak strengthens structure. **Pinotage-Viognier** 🗎 🍷 **★★★★** Consistent as ever, **10** has usual juicy vibrancy. Buoyant red fruit, yet earthy concentration below. **Chardonnay** 🗎 🍷 **★★★★ 10** with creamy citrus character. Textured breadth & richness from 8 months lees contact. Darling fruit. **Darling Chenin Blanc** 🗎 🍷 **★★★** Preserved lemon & pear on **11**. Light acidity matches breadth & gentle creamy softness courtesy of 3 months lees contact. **Riesling** 🗎 🍷 **★★★★ 11** sample shows typical green apple/strudel tang. Spicy & off-dry with balanced acidity & zip. From Darling. **Darling Sauvignon Blanc** 🗎 🍷 **★★★ 11** is first with 'Darling' in name. Vibrant grass & fig aromas, & altogether zesty with good acidity, succulence & some weight. **Oom Pagel Semillon** 🗎 🍷 **★★★★ 10** has ample nettle & herb, a waxy hint at the end. Serious, dry & light, deftly blending tank & oaked portions. **Viognier** 🗎 🍷 **★★★★ 10** with customary restraint, though nectarine-redolent. Rich, broad & well structured, helped by partial oaking. **Viognier Special Late Harvest** 🗎 **★★★ 11** with tarte tatin charm of previous. Poised balance between sweet fruit & acid, then a lingering dry finish. **Sweet Red** 🗎 **★★★ 09** sees Swartland souzão fortified to 17% alc (last was shiraz), with almond, raisin & spice notes. **La Beryl Rouge ★★★ 10** shiraz straw wine returns after 2 year absence. Savoury olive & a touch chalky with a dry grass undertone to its sweet richness. Discontinued: Petit Verdot, Tannat, Rosé. — FM

■ **Faithful Hound** *see Mulderbosch Vineyards*

False Bay Vineyards

Location: Somerset West ▪ WO: Western Cape ▪ Est/1stB 2000 ▪ Tasting at Waterkloof ▪ Owner(s) Paul Boutinot ▪ Cellarmaster(s)/viticulturist(s) Werner Engelbrecht (Jun 2004) ▪ Winemaker(s) Werner Engelbrecht (Jun 2004), with Nadia Barnard (Dec 2008) ▪ 75,000cs own label 30% red 65% white 5% rosé ▪ PO Box 2093 Somerset West 7129 ▪ info@waterkloofwines.co.za ▪ www.falsebayvineyards.co.za ▪ **T +27 (0)21-858-1292** ▪ F +27 (0)21-858-1293

These unshowy and quietly satisfying wines are made for British wine importer Paul Boutinot at his splendid Somerset West winery, Waterkloof. There Werner Engelbrecht treats the grapes (mostly widely sourced) with the respect shown for the home-farm's labels – even using natural fermentation in many cases.

Shiraz ☺ 🗎 **★★★** Supple, lightly textured, balanced & essentially modest - as with previous vintage, **10** as elegant as you can get at this level.

Pinotage 🗎 **★★★** Aromas on **10** allude to coffee idea (although scarcely any oak influence) alongside the clean understated fruit. **Rosé** 🗎 **★★** Pre-bottling, **11** mostly shiraz; as usual, softly dry, fresh & vaguely pleasant. **Chardonnay** 🗎 **★★★ 11** preview an unassuming, unimposing & delightful dinner partner. Dry & unoaked. Confidently easy-going. **Chenin Blanc** 🗎 **★★★** Poised, balanced **10** tasted last year. Smooth & gentle, but piquant acid assures food compatibility. **Sauvignon Blanc** 🗎 **★★★** In established style, **11** delivers clean varietal character plus a little more, in a friendly way. Modest 12% alcohol. — TJ

■ **Fantail** *see Morgenhof Wine Estate*

Faraway House Wine Estate

Location/map: Villiersdorp ▪ WO: Overberg ▪ Est 2002 ▪ 1stB 2008 ▪ Tasting by appt ▪ Closed Easter Fri-Mon, Ascension day, Pentecost & Dec 25/26 ▪ Owner(s) Faraway House Estate Pty Ltd ▪ Winemaker(s) Nicolas Follet & David Ciry ▪ Viticulturist(s) Willem Pelser ▪ 90ha/14ha (cab, merlot, ptage, shiraz, sauv) ▪ 50t/2,000cs own label 80% red 15% white 5% rosé ▪ PO Box 403 Villiersdorp 6848 ▪ info@farawayhouse.co.za ▪ www.farawayhouse.co.za ▪ S 33°56'24.63" E 019°19'39.41" ▪ **T +27 (0)76-558-9112** ▪ F +27 (0)28-840-2740

Located high in the mountains between Villiersdorp and Worcester, this farm is aptly named. Only 30 of its 94 ha are cultivated, with figs, pomegranates, olives and Mediterranean vegetables joining the vines. Biodiversity and sustainability are watchwords: fynbos is planted between new vineyards, and solar-powered pumping of irrigation water has also cut electricity costs.

Shiraz ✓ ★★★★ Vivid, cool climate spice distinguishes youthful, fresh **09**. A drying, rather tannic finish slightly detracts. **Quadrille** ✓ ★★★★ Scented, merlot-led **09**, with shiraz, pinotage & cab. Less austere than **08**, but a tannin kick trims the sweeter tones. **Classic** ✓ ★★★★ Plenty of shiraz pizazz in combo with cab, merlot (45/25), enlivening **09**. Fresh, flavoursome & mouthfilling. Good now, better in year/2. **08** (★★★★). — AL

Farm 1120

Map: Swartland ▪ Est 2005 ▪ 1stB 2006 ▪ Tasting facility in The Wine Kollective: Mon-Sat 10-5 Sun 10-3 ▪ Closed Easter Fri, Dec 25 & Jan 1 ▪ Gifts ▪ Farm produce ▪ Bar Bar Black Sheep Restaurant adjacent to tasting facility ▪ Winemaker(s) Anton Espost (2005) ▪ Viticulturist(s) Thys Greeff (Feb 2008, Outback Viticulture) ▪ 70ha/22ha (ptage, shiraz, chenin) ▪ 180t total 10t/500cs own label 100% red ▪ PO Box 61 Riebeek-Kasteel 7307 ▪ espost@ telkomsa.net ▪ S 33° 23′ 1.48″ E 018° 53′ 46.54″ ▪ **T +27 (0)22-448-1008/+27 (0)82-776-9366**

From vineyards planted high on the western slope of the Kasteelberg, biodynamically grown grapes are sold to the 'Swartland rock stars'. But some are used for the Santa Cecilia wines (see separate entry) and now a tiny percentage is kept aside for this label, exclusively available in Riebeek-Kasteel: 'We leave no stone unturned to ensure that only quality grapes are used,' says co-owner/winemaker Anton Espost. Intervention is otherwise minimal: natural yeasts, no additives, no filtering or stabilisation.

Fat Bastard

The jocular comparison of a chardonnay which UK vintner Guy Anderson was blending in France one afternoon in 1995 with a somewhat similar Bâtard-Montrachet begat the 'Fat Bastard' brand, now marketed throughout the English-speaking world. In South Africa, it's made by Robertson Winery.

Shiraz ▨ ★★★ Perfumed **10**, ripe & juicy easy-sipper with touch coffee. **Chardonnay** ▨ ★★★★ Well-handled new oak, smidgen sugar add to the appeal of seductive **10**. Vanilla intro, lemon marmalade, pear & peach middle, generous end. Very satisfying. **Sauvignon Blanc** ▨ ★★★ **11** preview grassy greenpepper pungency, perky acidity. Stock up for summer fun. Robertson WO for all. — Panel

Feiteiras Vineyards

Location/WO: Bot River ▪ Map: Elgin, Walker Bay & Bot River ▪ Est 2003 ▪ 1stB 2004 ▪ Tasting & sales by appt ▪ Owner(s) De Andrade Family ▪ Cellarmaster(s)/winemaker(s) Jose de Andrade ▪ Viticulturist(s) Manuel de Andrade ▪ 16.2ha/4.2ha (cab, merlot, mourv, shiraz, verdelho) ▪ 600cs own label 65% red 15% white 20% rosé ▪ PO Box 234 Bot River 7185 ▪ feiteiraswine@icon.co.za ▪ www.feiteiraswine.co.za ▪ S 34° 14′3.6″ E 019° 12′33.3″ ▪ **T +27 (0)82-453-1597** ▪ F +27 (0)28-284-9525

São Vicente, patron saint of winemakers, gave his name to the Madeira home of the De Andrade family. Brothers Manuel and Jose have continued Portuguese winemaking traditions on their Bot River enclave, using a pole-operated basket press (thought to be the only working example in the Cape) to make, among others, characterful fortified wines and a rare in the Cape verdelho.

Côr de Rosa ☺ ▤ ★★★ Strawberry pink from merlot; previewed **11** has grip from seasoned casks that fills out the cherry fruit in a bone-dry 'food please' flourish.

Cabernet Sauvignon ★★★★ Vibrant bramble fruit was tucked into tailored, food-friendly **09** when tasted last edition. **Troca Tintas** ✓ ▨ ★★★★ Merlot, petit verdot & cab trio give grilled meat interest to **10**, perfect for espetada - even spicy trinchado. **Verdelho** ✓ ▤ ★★★★ A tonic for jaded palates: individual **11**'s spicy centre has a dash of sauvignon adding zip. **Vinho Forte Tinto** ★★★★ **06** fortified mourvèdre. Lush, earthy chocolate featured in warm 19% alc bite previously. These 375ml. **Vinho Forte Branco** ★★★★ Fortified **06** verdelho had a clean nutty toffee note to its spiritous aftertaste when last reviewed. — DS

Felicité

These easy-going, elegantly labelled wines are made by the Newton Johnson family of the fine eponymous winery in the Hemel-en-Aarde area. Some of the grapes come from the Robertson Valley, where Nadia NJ's family has grown vineyards for 6 generations. Others are brought in from other sources to the home cellar.

Pinot Noir 🔲 ★★★ 11's Robertson grapes supplemented by Hemel-en-Aarde. Rustic, moderately fruity aromas; somewhat unharmonious with light boiled-sweet flavours. **Rosé** 🔲 🌣 ★★★ Gently fruity, just-dry 11 from mixed shiraz, sauvignon Elgin grapes. **Chardonnay** 🔲 ★★★★ Striking 09 last tasted. Next vintage not ready for sampling. — TJ

■ **FIFA 2010** *see* Nederburg Wines
■ **5th Avenue Cold Duck** *see* Cold Duck (5th Avenue)

Final Cut Wines

Location: Hout Bay ▪ Map: Cape Peninsula ▪ WO: Stellenbosch ▪ Est 2006 ▪ 1stB 2007 ▪ Tasting by appt ▪ Owner(s) Iain & Julie Anderson ▪ Winemaker(s) Teddy Hall (Sep 2006, consultant) ▪ PO Box 12077 Hout Bay 7806 ▪ iain@finalcutwines.co.za ▪ S 34°01'07.26" E 018°22'52.58" ▪ **T +27 (0)21-790-8808**

'Films' – the bread and butter of Hout Bay garagistes Iain and Julie Anderson – 'are an effective marketing tool that can be used in all social media', and they plan to promote these wines with the medium. As their bistro, Wild Woods, has closed, Final Cut is now available for tasting and purchase only by appointment.

Shiraz Await next. **Chenin Blanc** ★★★★ 10 in groove of improved 09, an opulent mouthful, peachy fruit packed into bold finish, tensioned by brisk acidity. — DS

■ **Find Art Collection** *see* Druk My Niet Wine Estate
■ **Finest (Tesco)** *see* Ken Forrester Wines

FirstCape Vineyards

Location: Paarl ▪ Est 2002 ▪ Closed to public ▪ Owner(s) De Wet, Aan de Doorns, Stettyn, Goudini & Badsberg co-op wineries ▪ Winemaker(s) David Smit ▪ WIETA accredited ▪ PO Box 62 Simondium 7670 ▪ david@firstcape.com ▪ www.firstcape.com ▪ **T +27 (0)21-874-8340** ▪ F +27 (0)21-874-8344

This joint venture between five Breede Valley cellars and British marketer BrandPhoenix was begun in 2002 and is today the biggest-selling South African wine brand in the UK, with well over 40m bottles a year, and the 4th largest light wine brand overall in the British off-trade. It's a remarkable achievement, and intrinsic quality and value, plus canny marketing are calculated to maintain the upward trajectory. The wines, for export only, are available as FirstCape (Entry, Limited Release, First Selection, Winemaker's Selection and Sparkling), Millstone, Cape Bay and new additions Blue Range, President's Selection and low-alcohol (5.5%) Café Collection.

■ **First Dawn** *see* Nwanedi Estate
■ **First Sighting** *see* Strandveld Wines

Fish Hoek Wines

Location/map: Stellenbosch ▪ WO: Western Cape ▪ Tasting & sales Mon-Fri 10-4 at Doornbosch Centre, Strand Rd, Stellenbosch ▪ Fee R20, waived on purchase ▪ Closed Dec 25 to Jan 2 ▪ Cellar tours by appt ▪ Owner(s) Accolade Wines South Africa ▪ Winemaker(s) Gerhard Swart (Sep 2008) & Bruce Jack (1998) ▪ 50% red 50% white ▪ PO Box 769 Stellenbosch 7599 ▪ hannelize.mouton@accolade-wines.com ▪ S 33° 56' 44.93" E 018° 51' 17.29" ▪ **T +27 (0)21-882-8177** ▪ F +27 (0)21-882-8176

Now under Accolade Wines' aegis, this internationally exported mid-tier brand (says winemaker Bruce Jack) is about 'simple excellence', aiming for the 'yum' factor, and offering good value for money.

> **Pinotage** ☺ 🔲 ★★★ Blueberries & creamy spice, 09 offers a warm-hearted welcome. Soft vivacious tannins, this is an anytime wine. W Cape WO, as for all. **Shiraz** ☺ 🔲 🌣 ★★★ Appealing 10 offers plump juicy bramble fruit & spice. An easy-sipping joy!

Merlot 🔲 🌣 ★★★ Soft, sweet plummy fruit on 10, well balanced for easy drinking. **Pinotage Rosé** 🔲 ★★★ Vibrant berries, 09 surprised last edition with dry savoury finish; good food match. **Chenin Blanc** 🔲 ★★★

Crisply dry **10**, crunchy fruit salad flavour last time, clean & bright. **Sauvignon Blanc** 🍷 ★★★ Gooseberry & green apple in **10**, nice palate fullness despite lowish 12.6% alc, previously drank easily & well. — WB

■ **Five Climates** *see* Boland Kelder
■ **Five Generations** *see* Cederberg Private Cellar

5 Mountains Lodge

Location/WO: Wellington ▪ Map: Paarl & Wellington ▪ Est 2002 ▪ 1stB 2004 ▪ Tasting Tue-Sat 9-5.30 Sun 9-2 ▪ Fee R20 ▪ Closed Easter Fri/Sun/Mon & Dec 25/26 ▪ Cellar tours by appt ▪ Meals & refreshments 9-5 daily ▪ Conference facilities ▪ Guest House & Spa (see Accommodation section) ▪ Owner(s) Stuart & Louisa McLachlan ▪ Winemaker(s) Corlea Fourie (2004, Bosman Family Vineyards) ▪ 7.5ha/1ha (chenin) ▪ 2.5t/150cs own label 100% white ▪ PO Box 691 Wellington 7654 ▪ carole@5mountains.co.za ▪ www.exclusiveescapes.com ▪ S 33° 38′ 38.34″ E 019° 2′ 21.19″ ▪ **T +27 (0)21-864-3409** ▪ F +27 (0)21-873-7193

When British couple Stuart and Louisa McLachlan bought this Wellington property in 2002 to run as the 5 Mountains Lodge guest house and spa, they almost uprooted its patch of old bushvine chenin. A neighbour's foresight saw them save the now 25-year-old vines, the source since 2004 of a wooded Chenin (and one vintage of Natural Sweet) made by Corlea Fourie at nearby Bosman Family Vineyards.

> **Chenin Blanc** 😊 😋 🍷 ★★★ Attractive barrel-fermented **10** is more mineral than fruity, shows 'stony' aromas, pleasantly textured mouthfeel & a dry finish. — Panel

■ **Five's Reserve** *see* Van Loveren Private Cellar

Flagstone Winery

Location/map: Stellenbosch ▪ WO: Western Cape/Elgin/Stellenbosch/Tulbagh/Elim ▪ Est 1998 ▪ 1stB 1999 ▪ Tasting & sales Mon-Fri 10-4 at Doornbosch Centre, Strand Rd, Stellenbosch ▪ Fee R20, waived on purchase ▪ Closed Dec 25 to Jan 2 ▪ Cellar tours by appt ▪ Owner(s) Accolade Wines South Africa ▪ Winemaker(s) Gerhard Swart (Sep 2008) & Bruce Jack (1998), with Gerald Cakijana (Jan 2000) ▪ Viticulturist(s) Chris Keet (consultant) ▪ 70% red 30% white ▪ PO Box 769 Stellenbosch 7599 ▪ hannelize.mouton@accolade-wines.com ▪ www.flagstonewines. com ▪ S 33° 56′ 44.93″ E 018° 51′ 17.29″ ▪ **T +27 (0)21-882-8177** ▪ F +27 (0)021-882-8176

Flagstone last year completed its 13th vintage. 'A very lucky number for us,' says founder and cellarmaster Bruce Jack. 'The first forklift I bought was marked 13; if you add the 2 of 2011 to its makes 13; and we have 13 staff members.' Last year also saw the realisation of some of the huge opportunities in Russia: 'They are drinking their fair share of Flagstone wine,' says Bruce. Innovation is the order of the day here: 'We perfected the soft destemming of red grapes in our very own 'laundromat'; the first white and red wines from Elim were bottled here, as well as the first viognier. We are looking forward to launching a sparkling sherry this year. I am also pleased to see interns from 'Flagstone University' go on to become brilliant winemakers elsewhere in South Africa and abroad.'

Flagstone Winery range

★★★★ **Music Room Cabernet Sauvignon** 🍷 Blackcurrant, tealeaf & sweet tobacco, full-bodied **09**, deep blackberry flavours & rich vanilla oak roundness, lingering blackberry liqueur conclusion.

★★★★ **Fiona Pinot Noir** 🍷 Previously we noted delicate strawberries, deft oaking, enticing firm grip on layered **08**, mainly Elim fruit. Elegant, but missed **07**'s (★★★★☆) harmony.

★★★★☆ **Writer's Block Pinotage** 🍷 **09** offers sumptuous chocolate-dipped plums, hedgerow fruit, nutmeg & fynbos. Full on the palate, with deep plum & silky vanilla flavours (from American oak, hallmark of this winery's reds), delicious grip on lengthy finish. Will reward good few years cellaring.

★★★★ **Dark Horse Shiraz** 🍷 Inky black, with smoky mulberry & dark choc. Muscular yet balanced **08** typical bright berry fruit, soft lingering spicy conclusion. Ideal with a barbecue.

★★★★ **Dragon Tree** 🍷 Last edition intense dark berries & chocolate on **08** cab, shiraz, pinotage & merlot combo, taut tannins added tension to otherwise pillow-soft fruity mouthful.

★★★★ **Free Run Sauvignon Blanc** 🍷 Highly perfumed **11** preview from Elgin is crisp, minerally & overflows with lime, capsicum, greengage & quince; fruit intensity countered by balanced freshness.

★★★★ **Word of Mouth Viognier** 🍷 ☟ Seductive **10** off Stellenbosch vines is creamy & full bodied, spicy floral charm, balanced & elegant. Peach melba finish.

★★★★ **Treaty Tree Reserve White** 🍷 ☟ Listed as 'Treaty Tree Reserve' last time, **10** is sophisticated, serious blend sauvignon & semillon from Elim & Elgin fruit. Creamy & full, yet fresh & vibrant, with hint of oak.

★★★★★ **CWG Auction Reserve Happy Hour** 🍷 Seductive sauvignon, semillon & viognier blend is a real gem. **09** fresh & aromatic, lemon, lime, peach blossom & a toasty richness. Impressive depth, excellent balance & super-delicious length.

Treaty Tree Reserve Red NEW 🍷 ★★★☆ **05** cab, merlot blend from Elim, Tulbagh & Constantia vines, developed dark smoky berry flavours, firm grip. Exclusive to Wine-Of-The-Month Club, for drinking soon. **Longitude** ✓ 🍷 ☟ ★★★★ Consistent value from shiraz, cab, malbec blend, smoky berry melange & friendly tannins in **10. Noon Gun** 🍷 ★★★ Floral & peachy appeal on stalwart blend sauvignon & chenin, dash viognier, **10** is delightfully zingy. **Last Word** 🍷 ★★★★ Port-style fortified from Tulbagh shiraz, **06** hedonistic, slippery & sweetly delicious, not overly serious. Discontinued: **Field Day Pinot Blanc**.

Knockon Wood range

★★★★ **Red Blend** 🍷 Enticing plum, cinnamon, cigarbox tones on previously tasted **08** troika cab, pinotage, shiraz. Voluptuous fruit, athletic tannins, lipsmacking savoury tail. This range & next export only.

★★★★ **Sauvignon Blanc-Semillon** 🍷 Feisty lemon-lime aromas, citrus finish, **09** mouthfilling & rich, orchard fruit flavours wrapped in toasty cloak. Not retasted.

The Strata Series

★★★★ **The BDX Blend Reserve** NEW 🍷 Mainly cab, dashes merlot & cab franc. Ripe blackcurrant & savoury plum, **04** fine & complex, good fruit purity, balance & length. Drink soon. Range exclusive to Makro.

★★★★ **Cool Clime Sauvignon Blanc** NEW 🍷 ☟ Bright, crisp **10** with depth, elegance. Full flavoured, tropical fruit aromas & lemon freshness. A lipsmacking acidity rounds off this balanced offering from Elim.

Stumble Vineyards range

Malbec 🍷 ★★★ Mulberry compote, Indian spices ooze from **10**, pliable tannins for laid-back sipping. Not retasted, as for all. **Chardonnay** 🍷 ★★★ **10** subtle whiteflower scents, delicate palate, perky farewell. **Sauvignon Blanc** 🍷 ★★★ **10** greenpepper & lemon zest, balanced if uncomplex tipple. Like all the range, for enjoying soon. **Viognier** 🍷 ★★★ Peachy fragrance, **10** soft & juicy, dab oak for weight, flavour. — WB

■   **Flame** *see Linton Park Wines*
■   **Flamingo Bay** *see Darling Cellars*

Flat Roof Manor

These are honest and well placed easier drinking wines from the Uitkyk wine estate. Packaging suggests fun and, in keeping with this, the range has been expanded to include an ultra-light Sauvignon Blanc for the more health conscious. With Estelle Lourens at the helm these wines are going from strength to strength.

Merlot ☺ 🍷 ☟ ★★★ Chocolate earthy aromatics lead to soft palate with rounded texture. **10** offers balanced easy drinking. **Pinot Grigio** ☺ 🍷 ☟ ★★★ Dollops sauvignon & chenin in **11** adds some complexity. Well balanced with rounded, fleshy palate. Ends dry. WO W Cape.

Shiraz-Mourvèdre-Viognier 🍷 ★★★☆ Attractive **09** made in same ilk as previous. Successfully combines ripe fruits, spice & herbal freshness. WO W Cape. **Pinot Rosé** 🍷 ☟ ★★★ **10** still selling & was a red-white marriage of pinotage & pinot gris, dry & fruity. **Sauvignon Blanc Light** NEW 🍷 ☟ ★★★ As name suggests, **11** sample under 10% alc; dry summer quaffer. Discontinued: **Cabernet Sauvignon-Sangiovese**. — JP

Fleur du Cap

Location: Stellenbosch ▪ WO: Western Cape/Stellenbosch/Coastal ▪ Est 1968 ▪ 1stB 1969 ▪ Tasting, sales & tours at Die Bergkelder Wine Centre (see entry) ▪ Owner(s) Distell ▪ Cellarmaster(s) Andrea Freeborough (Aug 2005) ▪ Winemaker(s) Justin Corrans (Aug 2005, red wines), Pieter Badenhorst (Dec 2006, white wines), with John November (Jan 2008) & Christoff de Wet (Sep 2010) ▪ Viticulturist(s) Bennie Liebenberg (Apr 2001) ▪ ±17,000t/ ±145,000cs own label 47% red 53% white ▪ ISO 14001, BRC, IFS, HACCP, ISO 9001 ▪ info@fleurducap.co.za ▪ www.fleurducap.co.za ▪ **T +27 (0)21-809-8025** ▪ F +27 (0)21-887-9081

The renaissance continues for this well-established Distell-owned brand, headquartered at Die Bergkelder in Stellenboch. Instrumental in that revival has been cellarmaster Andrea Freeborough, but she's quick to credit her team. So much so, she shared the 2010 SA Woman Winemaker of the Year R25,000 prize money with her charges by way of international wine exposure. Joining the squad is Praisy Dlamini, first female graduate of the Cape Winemakers Guild Protégé Programme which supports emerging winemakers through an internship in members' cellars. The luminary in the galaxy of this cellar is the Noble Late Harvest, a serial five-star stunner from 2006-2010. The former, made from riesling, was recently selected for Cathay Pacific's front-end guests, while the 2009 – our White Wine of the Year last year – was instrumental in securing 2010 SA Producer of the Year status status for Freeborough and team at the International Wine & Spirit Competition.

Unfiltered Collection

★★★★☆ **Cabernet Sauvignon** ✓ Classic, stylish Stellenbosch cab. **09** very fine; manicured minty blueberry fruit in yielding tannic framework, compelling length of flavour. Promises much pleasure over 4-7 years.

★★★★ **Merlot** ✓ Tightly wound **09** back to form after gentler **08** (★★★★); plum fruit wrapped up in supple tannins with a graceful seam of freshness. WO Stellenbosch.

★★★★ **Chardonnay** ✓ 🍽 🖼 Closed **10** has fine gravelly texture, oak (8 months, 35% new) cosseting lime fruit. Very good, but lacks intensity of beautifully balanced **09** (★★★★★).

★★★★☆ **Sauvignon Blanc** ✓ 🍽 🖼 Steely-dry, with cool grassy features, just-bottled **11** enjoys textural support from lees-ageing & vitality from racy acidity. Like **10**, yard off brilliant **09** (★★★★★). Includes 5% nouvelle.

★★★★☆ **Sauvignon Blanc Limited Release** ✓ 🍽 🖼 Sleek, & as sophisticated as cellar siblings, **11** is richer, more weighty; mineral, fresh, structured for development. From Agulhas & Darling.

★★★★ **Semillon** ✓ 🍽 🖼 Gear up from **08**, **10** has buffed hay tones with a stony mineral heart. Classy, far from simply fruity, but not quite as brilliant as **09** (★★★★★), which is a magnificent albeit understated wine.

★★★★ **Viognier** ✓ 🍽 🖼 Boisterous **10** a kaleidoscopic array of apricot & pungent peach-pip flavours barely contained by tangy acid; not subtle, but outrageously enjoyable!

★★★★ **Sauvignon Blanc-Chardonnay-Semillon-Viognier** ✓ 🍽 🖼 Fabulous interplay of near-equal parts of four grapes makes for interesting **10** (★★★★★). Grassy tang tempered by waxy notes, with broader oatmeal overlay to a fruity finish, its balance takes it beyond riotous **09**.

Fleur du Cap Bergkelder Selection

★★★★☆ **Laszlo** Powerful cab-led Bordeaux quartet, with 18% shiraz. Generously oaked (100% new, 18 months) **06** had a cedary polish to its sumptuous fruit/grape tannins previously.

★★★★ **Chenin Blanc** ✓ 🍽 🖼 Less oak, more fruit in latest **11** (★★★★); tropical laced guava fruit balanced by firm acidity, but shade less convincing than **09** & **08**. (**10** sold out before tasting.)

★★★★★ **Noble Late Harvest** ✓ 🖼 Outstanding botrytised dessert from chenin, dashes semillon & muscat in **10**; bold orange & jasmine aromas, full-sweet & weighty, extraordinary intensity of flavour & arresting balance. Tad more grapey but just as mesmerising as its five-star predecessors **09**, **08**, **07** & **06**.

Chardonnay 😊 🍽 🖼 ★★★ Ripe **10** enlivened by tangy lemon/lime fruit expression & oak vanilla. **Sauvignon Blanc** 😊 🍽 🖼 ★★★ Hints of ripe fig in grassy **11**, gentle capsicum nip is nicely judged for wide appeal.

Cabernet Sauvignon ✓ ★★★☆ Plum fruited & open textured, **09** less compelling than flag-bearer above, but cheerily generous. **Merlot** ✓ ★★★★ Mulberry & dark chocolate allure on **09**, gentle tannic grip for early access. **Pinotage** ✓ ★★★★ Uncomplicated **09** satisfies, unfettered cranberry succulence to polished tannins. WO Coastal. **Shiraz** ✓ ★★★★ Savoury **09** has red berry fruit in open-grained oak frame. **Natural Light** 🖼 ★★ Dainty **11** fresh & fruity, semi-dry with low ±10% alc. — DS

- ◼ **Flutterby** *see* Boland Kelder
- ◼ **Foot of Africa** *see* Kleine Zalze Wines
- ◼ **Footprint** *see* African Pride Wines
- ◼ **Forresters** *see* Ken Forrester Wines
- ◼ **Fortress Hill** *see* Fort Simon Wine Estate

Fort Simon Wine Estate

Location/map: Stellenbosch ▪ WO: Stellenbosch/Western Cape ▪ Est 1997 ▪ 1stB 1998 ▪ Tasting & sales Mon-Fri 9. 30–5 Sat 10–2 ▪ Fee R10/5wines ▪ Closed all pub hols ▪ Cellar tours by appt ▪ Cheese platters ▪ Farm produce ▪ Venue for after-hours receptions & conferences (max 40 guests) by appt ▪ Owner(s) Renier, Petrus & Michéle Uys ▪ Winemaker(s) Stander Maass (Sep 2006) ▪ Viticulturist(s) Renier Uys ▪ 110ha/80ha (cabs s/f, malbec, merlot, p verdot, ptage, shiraz, chard, chenin, sauv, viog) ▪ 800t/40,000cs own label 60% red 30% white 10% rosé ▪ PO Box 43 Sanlamhof 7532 ▪ accounts@fortsimon.com ▪ www.fortsimon.co.za ▪ S 33° 55' 9.5" E 018° 45' 19.4" ▪ **T +27 (0)21-906-0304** ▪ F +27 (0)21-903-8034

Named after founder Simon Uys and the crenelated cellar, built from rocks on the farm, this family-owned winery is one of the top performers in Stellenbosch's Bottelary Hills. Production is increasing to supply existing export markets, most recently China, and the focus is on developing new opportunities in the BRICS and other emerging nations, as well as creating new blends for these markets.

Platinum Collection

★★★★ **Viognier** Last year, complex & harmonious **09** was layered, appealed with creamy peach & pineapple flavours, lengthy perfumed aftertaste.

Viognier Noble Late Harvest Await next.

Fort Simon Estate range

★★★★ **Shiraz** ✓ Pungent, spicy dark fruit on **07**. Suave & balanced, with spicy cinnamon finish. Not retasted.

★★★★ **Chardonnay** ✓ Pre-bottling **10** (★★★★) delivers fresh, crunchy apple & citrus with zingy lemon finish. **09** more elegant & stylish, concentrated.

★★★★ **Sauvignon Blanc** ✓ Upfront greengage & gooseberry flavoured **10** is harmonious & moreish, with smooth acidity. Priced to enjoy all summer long.

Cabernet Sauvignon ★★★ Tad off well-structured **07** (★★★★), **08** offers rich black-fruit & vanilla flavours. Full bodied, bold & sweet. **Merlot** ✓ ★★★★ Delightfully juicy **09**, sampled from barrel, ripe plum & spice cake aromas; soft & balanced for easy drinking. **Pinotage** ✓ ★★★★ Juicy plum & mocha on **08**. Polished, ripe & rich, lingering savoury farewell. **Rosé** ★★★ Previewed from tank, **11** oozes pinotage's ripe strawberries. Easy dry summer sipper. **Chenin Blanc** ✓ ★★★★ Up a notch from **09** (★★★★), barrel preview **10** is rich & concentrated, lemon & apple with vanilla from well-judged oaking. Rounded & yummy! Discontinued: **Barrel Select**.

Fortress Hill range

Shiraz ☺ ★★★ Barrel sample of **08** promises spicy dark berries & black pepper. Second glass is inevitable. **Sauvignon Blanc** ☺ ★★★ Tropical fruit & easy-sipping charm, **10** juicy & not too fresh, for early enjoyment.

Merlot ★★★ When last tasted, delightfully juicy & smooth **09** was soft & invited early enjoyment, as for all in this range. **Chardonnay** ★★★ Expressive **09**, lemon/lime, pineapple & vanilla wafts from light oaking. Not retasted. **Chenin Blanc** ★★★★ When tasted last year, **09** hit the spot with tropical fruit ripeness, lime & hint spicy oak. Nice! **Natural Sweet Rosé** ★★★ Soft, sweet red-fruit flavours on **08** when previously tasted. Discontinued: **Pinotage**. — WB

■ **Four Cousins** *see* Van Loveren Private Cellar

Four Fields Vineyards

Location/WO: Durbanville ▪ Map: Durbanville, Philadelphia & Darling ▪ Est/1st B 2004 ▪ Tasting & tours by appt only ▪ Sales mainly via Wine Concepts, Cape Town ▪ Owner(s) 8 shareholders ▪ Cellarmaster(s)/winemaker(s) Chris Kuhn (Sep 2004) ▪ 5t 100% red ▪ 59 Bethanie Road Sonstraal 7550 ▪ dockuhn@gmail.com ▪ S 33° 48' 56" E 018° 33' 15" ▪ **T +27 (0)83-929-9199** ▪ F +27 (0)21-557-2608

Retired insurance professional Chris Kuhn gave winemaking a rest last year, but intends getting back into his private cellar for the current vintage. His wines continue to win friends and are on several restaurant wine lists, and he hopes to add a chenin if plans to source the right grapes come to fruition.

Cabernet Sauvignon-Cabernet Franc ★★★ Herbal/perfume contrast on mulberry-fruited **08** previous edition. **Chardonnay** 🍸 ★ Barrel-aged **08** had overt oak patina when last tasted. — Panel

Four Paws Wines

Location/map: Franschhoek ▪ WO: Piekenierskloof/Western Cape/Franschhoek ▪ Est 2005 ▪ 1stB 2006 ▪ Tasting by appt at Bo La Motte Farm (contact Anne +27 (0)83-447-1376 or Gerda +27 (0)82-375-0524) ▪ Owner(s) Rob Meihuizen, Gerda Willers & Anne Jakubiec ▪ Winemaker(s) Gerda Willers (2005) ▪ Viticulturist(s) Gerda Willers ▪ 60t/6,000cs own label 70% red 30% white ▪ PO Box 69 Simondium 7670 ▪ anne@southerntrade.co.za ▪ www.fourpawswines.co.za ▪ S 33° 55' 15.6" E 019° 7' 39.9" ▪ **T +27 (0)21-874-1033** ▪ F +27 (0)21-874-2110

With two harvests under the belt (collar?) of a trio of wine and cat lovers on Bo La Motte farm, the new storage facility is complete, tasting amenities are in the works and winemaking partner Gerda Willers can get back into the vineyards. Newly named Calico is the epitome of the promised 'good quality, value for money wines'.

★★★★ **Pablo** Cab, plus shiraz & merlot. Meaty **08** (★★★★) lighter, easier than **07** (with dab grenache) when tasted last year. No **09**.

> **Sauvignon Blanc** ☺ 🍷 ★★★ Preview **11** has palate-clucking steely freshness to whet the appetite or rejuvenate. WO Western Cape. **Calico** ☺ 🍷 ★★★ 'White Blend' last edition; previewed **11** a veritable fruit-cup of flavours, nicely tied together by acid seam. Mainly chenin, WO Franschhoek.

Pinotage ★★★ **10** clove-studded plummy fruit ordered by firm wooding. **09** held back for later release. **Chardonnay** NEW ✓ ★★★★ Wake-me-up freshness balanced by leesy girth, **10** very promising just days after bottling. Year 40% new wood already absorbed. — DS

Fraai Uitzicht 1798

Location/map: Robertson ▪ WO: Klaasvoogds ▪ 1stB 2000 ▪ Tasting & sales daily 10-6 ▪ Closed Easter Fri/Sun, Dec 25/31 & Jan 1 ▪ Restaurant Wed-Sun (see Restaurants section) ▪ 4-star guesthouse: for amenities & activities, see Accommodation section ▪ Owner(s) Karl Uwe Papesch ▪ Winemaker(s) Karl Uwe Papesch (2005) ▪ Viticulturist(s) Michael Marson ▪ 175ha/10ha (grenache, merlot, shiraz, touriga nacional) ▪ 500cs own label 100% red ▪ PO Box 97 Robertson 6705 ▪ info@fraaiuitzicht.com ▪ www.fraaiuitzicht.com ▪ S 33° 47' 43.0" E 020° 0' 18.2" ▪ **T +27 (0)23-626-6156** ▪ F +27 (0)86-662-5265

Karl and Sandra Papesch have enjoyed increasing success with both their luxury guesthouse and their wines in recent years. A visit to their cellar under the restaurant is always exciting, and Karl is enthusiastic about stocking it with Rhône-blends in years to come. He's planted grenache, and more varieties are on the way.

Merlot ★★★★ Plenty of spice & plum interest last year on **08**, 12 months oak enhanced juicy accessibility. We said drink early before 15+% alc dominates. **Prima** NEW ★★★★ 100% merlot aged 2 years in French oak. Generous **08** satisfies with food or solo. Fresh & balanced, firm tannins offset by zesty acidity. — Panel

Francois La Garde

 NEW

Location/map: Stellenbosch ▪ WO: Franschhoek/Western Cape ▪ Est 2004 ▪ Tasting by appt ▪ Owner(s) PL Matthée ▪ Cellarmaster(s)/winemaker(s) Piet Matthée (Jan 2009) ▪ 15t/800cs own label 100% white ▪ PO Box 12366 Die Boord 7613 ▪ admin@technofill.co.za ▪ www.francois-lagarde.com ▪ **T +27 (0)21-887-3674** ▪ F +27 (0)21-887-5274

Originally an oenology lecturer at Elsenburg Agricultural College, Piet Matthée's day job currently involves running his own mobile bottling and labelling company in Stellenbosch. However he's passionate about méthode cap classique and has been making it on the side for many years. Now he's gone public with an own-brand, naming it after an ancestor who shared his love for bubbly.

String of Pearls range

★★★★ **Blanc de Blancs** ✓ Bottle-fermented sparkling from Franschhoek semillon, 48 months on lees. Lemongrass & lanolin, snaky strings of fine mousse, rich, long lime marmalade flavour. **05** structured for ageing.

★★★★ **Brut Méthode Cap Classique** ✓ Classic champagne-method bubbly, equal pinot noir & chardonnay, 36 months on lees. **07** strawberry flavours, fine yeasty mousse & balance show elegance, class. — Panel

Franki's Vineyards

Location: Malmesbury ▪ Map: Durbanville, Philadelphia & Darling ▪ WO: Swartland ▪ Est 2004 ▪ 1stB 2007 ▪ Tasting, sales & cellar tours by appt Mon-Fri 8-5 ▪ Closed all pub hols ▪ Meals by arrangement ▪ Tour groups ▪ BYO picnic ▪ Conference facilities ▪ Walking/hiking ▪ Conservation area ▪ Classic car museum ▪ 4-star Franki's Guest Lodge (10 bedrooms) & Solitude @ Franki's B&B (4 bedrooms) ▪ Owner(s) Franco Afrique Technologies (Pty) Ltd ▪ Winemaker(s) Erica Joubert (Jan 2004), with Nicolaas Hanekom (Jan 2004) ▪ 700ha/22ha (grenache, mourv, viog) ▪ 80t/175cs own label 100% red ▪ PO Box 972 Malmesbury 7299 ▪ erica.joubert@cropspec.co.za ▪ www.frankisvineyards.co.za ▪ S 33° 20' 59.5" E 018° 32' 12.4" ▪ **T +27 (0)22-482-2837** ▪ F +27 (0)86-660-3677

Franki's Vineyards near Darling stands out with its large collection of classic cars, 4-star accommodation, rooibos tea estate, and winemaker Erica Joubert's unusual mourvèdre-grenache blend. The estate will stand out even more from this year, when ground is broken for what's set to be South Africa's largest (5MW, 7ha) privately owned photovoltaic solar energy farm.

Barn Find range

Grenache NEW ★★★ Appealing & rich, hint of blackcurrant sweetness, spread of berries on debut **10**. **Mourvèdre-Grenache** ★★★ Still-available **09** 75/25 blend, gentle fruitcake aroma; textured & ripe, with kick of 16% alc. — DB

Franschhoek Cellar

Location/map: Franschhoek ▪ WO: Western Cape ▪ Est 1945 ▪ Tasting & sales Mon-Fri 9.30-5 (Apr-Sep) & 10-6 (Oct-Mar) Sat 10-3 Sun 11-4 ▪ Fee R20/6 wines, R35/6 wines with 6 cheeses ▪ Closed Easter Fri, May 1, Jun 16 & Dec 25 ▪ Cheese platters daily during tasting hours ▪ Farm produce ▪ BYO picnic ▪ Owner(s) DGB (Pty) Ltd ▪ Winemaker(s) Richard Duckitt (Dec 2005) ▪ Viticulturist(s) Stephan Joubert (Nov 2006) ▪ 300ha (cab, merlot, shiraz, chard, chenin, sauv, sem) ▪ 30,000t 49% red 50% white 1% rosé ▪ ISO 9001:2001, IPW ▪ PO Box 52 Franschhoek 7690 ▪ fhcellardoor@dgb.co.za ▪ www.franschhoekcellar.co.za ▪ S 33° 54' 16.4" E 019° 6' 40.7" ▪ **T +27 (0)21-876-2086** ▪ F +27 (0)21-876-4107

While the cellar is deservedly popular for its flavoursome and unpretentious wines, international awards for last year's shiraz and unwooded chardonnay show that the wines punch above their weight. A convivial restaurant is planned, where guests can enjoy their food cooked on an open fire, hosted by staff known for their enthusiasm and efficiency.

Franschhoek Vineyards range NEW

Shiraz Reserve 🍽 🖾 ★★★ **10** tank sample has good varietal pepper & savouriness, enhanced by oak. Supple, respectable structure doesn't sacrifice accessibility. **Semillon** 🍽 🖾 ★★★★ Low yields reward **10** with rich, waxy texture & tangy marmalade flavours. Balanced & subtly oaked, enjoy now or over next few years.

The Village Walk range

Cabernet Sauvignon ☺ 🍽 🖾 ★★★ Friendly & juicy **10** preview continues in cellar's popular accessible style. Balanced, with bright blackcurrant, enjoy solo or with food. **Shiraz** ☺ 🍽 🖾 ★★★ **10**, from tank, is amiable, with dusty red berry flavours. **Chardonnay** ☺ 🍽 🖾 ★★★ Creamy, ripe pear toned **11**, sampled pre-release, has silky drinkability. **Sauvignon Blanc** ☺ 🍽 🖾 ★★★ **11** preview is a fruit-filled, crisp & juicy quaffer.

Merlot 🍽 🖾 ★★★ Pre-bottling, **10** is supple with complementary red berry fruit. **Chenin Blanc** 🍽 🖾 ★★ Ultra-soft styling on **11** preview. Plump, with gentle apple tone. — MW

Freedom Hill Wines

Location: Paarl ▪ Map: Paarl & Wellington ▪ WO: Paarl/Stellenbosch ▪ Est 1997 ▪ 1stB 2000 ▪ Tasting Mon-Sat 10-5 Sun 11-3 ▪ Fee R20pp ▪ Sales Mon-Fri 8-5 Sat 10-5 Sun 11-3 ▪ Closed Easter Fri/Sun & Dec 25 ▪ Freedom Hill Country Restaurant (see Restaurants section) ▪ Farm produce ▪ Freedom Day Festival ▪ Owner(s) Francois Klomp ▪ Cellarmaster(s) Francois Naudé (Jan 2007, consultant) ▪ Winemaker(s) Kowie du Toit (Feb 2007) ▪ Viticulturist(s) Chris Immelman (June 2006) ▪ 82ha/19ha (cab, ptage, shiraz) ▪ ±70t/6,000cs own label 100% red ▪ PO Box 6126 Paarl 7620 ▪ info@freedomhill.co.za, suretha@freedomhill.co.za ▪ www.freedomhill.co.za ▪ S 33° 49' 49.9" E 019° 0' 37.7" ▪ **T +27 (0)21-867-0085** ▪ F +27 (0)21-882-8207

This family-owned Paarl boutique winery overlooks the Victor Verster (now Drakenstein) Prison from where Nelson Mandela took his historic first steps to freedom, an event that inspired the naming of the new wine range, Freedom Walk 1335/88 (Mandela's prison number). Cheese platters and picnics are now offered in season.

Freedom Hill Wines range

Pinotage ★★★★ 07 had intriguing earthy/mushroom introduction to sweet plum & cranberry centre last year. Big boned, mouthfilling (15% alc). More substance & interest than 08 (★★★★). **Shiraz ★★★** 09 smooth & easy-drinking, chocolate accented prunes & plums with smoky leather. **Shiraz Reserve Magnum ★★★☆** Ripe & well-rounded 05 still selling, concentrated plum flavours, overlay of vanilla & oak from portion American barrels. **Shiraz-Cabernet Sauvignon ★★★** 09 shiraz-led combo, fresh berries & pepper, dry tannins encountered last year may have softened. **Sauvignon Blanc** 🗎 🖾 **★★★** 10 lime & pineapple toned, friendly & pleasing. **Sauvignon Blanc Reserve** 🗎 Await next.

Freedom Walk 1335/88 range

Cape Blend ★★★ New blend of 06, shiraz now in the saddle, cab & pinotage adding to the established warm, rounded, spicy & dark-fruited persona. **Cabernet-Sauvignon-Pinotage ★★★** Variation on 09 blend previewed last time (& listed as 'Freedom Walk 1335/88'), cab more prominent (66%). Understated, with vanilla & ripe plum, subtle oaking. — DB

- **Freedom Walk** *see* Freedom Hill Wines
- **Frisky Zebras** *see* United Nations of Wine
- **Frog Hill** *see* Anura Vineyards
- **Frost Vineyards** *see* David Frost Signature Series

Fryer's Cove Vineyards

Location: Strandfontein ▪ Map: Olifants River ▪ WO: Bamboes Bay/Western Cape ▪ Est 1999 ▪ 1stB 2002 ▪ Tasting, sales & cellar tours Mon-Fri 8-5 Sat 10-5 ▪ Fee R15 ▪ Closed most pub hols ▪ Pre-booked cheese platters & picnics; or BYO picnic ▪ Farm produce ▪ West Coast walking trail ▪ Owner(s) Jan Ponk Trust, JH Laubscher Family Trust & Wynand Hamman ▪ Cellarmaster(s) Wynand Hamman (Apr 1999) ▪ Viticulturist(s) Jan van Zyl (Apr 1999) ▪ 10ha/6ha (pinot, sauv) ▪ 50t/3,000cs own label 20% red 80% white ▪ PO Box 93 Vredendal 8160 ▪ janponk1@kingsley.co.za, fryerscove@mylan.co.za ▪ www.fryerscove.co.za ▪ S 31°45'53.1" E 018° 13'55.8" ▪ **T +27 (0)27-213-2312 (office)/+27 (0)27-215-1092 (tasting)** ▪ F +27 (0)27-213-2212

The first crush last year at own premises in Doring Bay's old harbour, and the opening of tasting facilities in time for Easter were milestones for brothers-in-law and co-owners Wynand Hamman, winemaker, and Jan 'Ponk' van Zyl, viticulturist. The news reverberated locally and up and down the West Coast, with more good tidings to follow: in conjunction with the Department of Trade & Industry, plans are afoot to open a community-run restaurant on site.

★★★★ Sauvignon Blanc 🖾 Only Bamboes Bay grapes, provisionally rated preview 11 is intense & mouthfilling, shows greater presence & length of flavour than stablemate. As engaging as lipsmackingly dry 10. **Pinot Noir** 🖾 **★★★☆** 11 preview slightly funky from natural ferment. Appealing pinot cherry fruit with earth, mocha hints, crunchy acidity & sweet fruit. Shows promise, nudges next level. **Bay To Bay Sauvignon Blanc** 🗎 🖾 **★★★★** This version combo Bamboes/Lamberts Bay fruit. Bone-dry 11 preview restrained & herbaceous, subtle pineapple hint, lovely weight, food-friendly snap in the aftertaste. — Panel

Fundi

Location: Stellenbosch ▪ WO: Stellenbosch/Coastal ▪ Est 2008 ▪ Closed to public ▪ Wine distributed through Vinimark ▪ Owner(s) Section 21 Company ▪ Directors Paul Cluver snr, Tim Rands (Vinimark), Joachim Sa (Amorim Cork), Michael Lutzeyer (Grootbos), Valli Moosa & Su Birch (WOSA) ▪ 100% red ▪ PO Box 987 Stellenbosch 7599 ▪ info@fundiwine.co.za ▪ www.fundiwine.co.za ▪ **T +27 (0)21-883-3860** ▪ F +27 (0)21-883-3861

The Fundi ('Learner') project aims to plough money earned from sales of the premium reds listed below into meaningful change in the lives of unemployed South Africans. To date the project has provided on-the-job training for 2,095 individuals, setting them on track for careers in the hospitality business as wine waiters. This

exceeds the initial target set by generic wine marketing organisation Wines of South
Africa.

★★★★ **Cabernet Sauvignon-Shiraz-Merlot** By Anwilka; **07** offers dark, dense black fruit with firm, lingering meaty mocha & oak flavours. Well-made & oaked. Not revisited, as for all.

Cabernet Sauvignon-Merlot ★★★★ **06** plummy & ripe, with rich spicy fruit, but dry-finishing. By Company of Wine People. WO Coastal, as for next. **'Bordeaux Blend'** ★★★★ **07** led (unusually) by petit verdot. Sweet liquorice aromas; plenty of spicy ripe red fruit; savoury & bright. By Waterkloof/False Bay. **Merlot-Cabernet Sauvignon-Pinotage** ★★★ Spicy berries & red sour-plums on Stellekaya's accessible **07**; soft, rich mouthfeel. **Cabernet Sauvignon-Shiraz-Merlot** ★★★★ Previously tasted **06** is supple, richly fruited & gently savoury with leafy cassis, white choc tones. By Hartenberg. — Panel

■ **Fynbos** see Mitre's Edge

Gabriëlskloof

Location/WO: Bot River ▪ Map: Elgin, Walker Bay & Bot River ▪ Est 2002 ▪ 1stB 2007 ▪ Tasting & sales Mon-Fri 9-5 Sat/Sun 10-2 ▪ Fee R15, waived on purchase ▪ Closed Dec 25 & Jan 1 ▪ Cellar tours by appt ▪ Restaurant open daily 9-5 ▪ Deli ▪ BYO picnic ▪ Child-friendly & dogs welcome ▪ Conferences (12 pax) ▪ Weddings ▪ Annual market (Dec) ▪ Owner(s) Bernhard Heyns & shareholders Johan Heyns, Barry Anderson & Wally Clarke ▪ Winemaker(s) Kobie Viljoen (Jun 2008), with Christiaan van der Merwe (Jan 2011) ▪ Viticulturist(s) Barry Anderson (2001) ▪ 150ha/68ha (cabs s/f, malbec, merlot, mourv, p verdot, pinot, syrah, sauv, sem, viog) ▪ PO Box 499 Kleinmond 7195 ▪ info@gabrielskloof.co.za ▪ www.gabrielskloof.co.za ▪ S 34° 15'20.3" E 019° 15'31.9" ▪ **T +27 (0)28-284-9865** ▪ F +27 (0)28-284-9864

Much has been accomplished here in a few short years. The first wines were bottled only in 2008 and now there's a cellar, tasting venue overlooking the vineyards, restaurant, and the range is growing apace. Winemaker Kobie Viljoen is happy with the quality and potential of the young vineyards; low rainfall reduces the yield and the cool ocean-influenced climate gives the wines a particular style. At the top end of the range, the wines get a lot of attention, with long barrel-ageing and use of new oak. Early days certainly, but clearly heading in the right direction.

Ultra Premium range NEW

★★★★ **Syrah** Spice-laden **08**'s dark fruit masks big alc, shows powerful meaty tones from 2 years in barrel, half new. Smoothly polished, ready, but 5+ year future. Inc small portions mourvèdre & viognier.

★★★★☆ **Five Arches** Flagship 5-part Bordeaux blend, streets ahead of version below. Near equal portions cabs franc & sauvignon, malbec give **08** different styling: fynbos, dark chocolate, pepper. Already delicious, fine tannins give 8+ years further potential.

Premium range

Shiraz NEW ✓ ★★★★ Mulberries, hints of beef extract & earthiness in **09** courtesy of ripeness (14.8% alc) & dabs mourvèdre & viognier. **The Blend** 🍽 ★★★ Cab leads in **09**'s classic 5-way Bordeaux mix. Blackcurrants & creamy chocolate, firm flesh, youthful. Drink or keep few years. **Sauvignon Blanc** NEW 🍽 ★★★ Flinty style **10** given palate weight by partially oaked semillon addition. Ultra-dry finish. **Viognier** ★★★☆ Fusion-cuisine partner, **09** with sumptuous peach flavours overlain with oak-spice when last tasted. **Magdalena** ★★★★ Blend of sauvignon & semillon, former's crisp green tone in **09** dominated latter's waxy note when last tasted. — CR

■ **Galantskloof** see Keisseskraal Vineyards

Galleon Wines

Location/WO: Durbanville ▪ Est 2003 ▪ 1stB 2004 ▪ Tasting by appt at Diemersdal ▪ Owner(s) BK Investments/Andries Brink/Thys Louw ▪ Winemaker(s) Andries Brink, Thys Louw & Mari van der Merwe ▪ Viticulturist(s) Div van Niekerk ▪ 850cs own label 50% red 50% white ▪ PO Box 62 Durbanville 7551 ▪ info@galleonwines.co.za ▪ www.galleonwines.co.za ▪ **T +27 (0)21-976-8129** ▪ F +27 (0)21-976-8129

Durbanville garagiste winemaker Andries Brink has released the 09 vintage of his cab, the first since 05, and is putting the final touches to a maiden pinotage. 'Research statistics show,' the retired cardiologist says, 'that the life extension of people who drink wine daily in moderation with food increases by 30%.'

Cabernet Sauvignon ★★★ Subtle oaking supports ripe mulberry aromas & savoury overlay in **09**. **Cabernet Sauvignon Reserve** Await next. **Shiraz** ★★★ Less juicy than previous, **08** mocha & coffee, some earthiness, robust spicy aftertaste. **Chardonnay ★★★** Mid-2009, charry oak on **08** dominated limy fruit but should have harmonised by now. **Sauvignon Blanc 🗒 ★★★** Still-available **10** tad less vivacious than **09** (**★★★★**). Fynbos & herbs, medium body, racy acidity noted last year. — DB

■ **Ganzekraal** *see* The Goose Wines

Garden Route

Location: Calitzdorp ▪ Map: Klein Karoo & Garden Route ▪ WO: Durbanville/Outeniqua ▪ Est/1stB 2008 ▪ Tasting & sales Mon-Fri 8-5 Sat 9-3 at De Krans ▪ Fee for groups R20pp, free for individuals ▪ Closed Easter Fri/Sun & Dec 25 ▪ BYO picnic ▪ Walking/hiking trails ▪ Owner(s) Boets Nel ▪ Cellarmaster(s) Boets Nel (2008) ▪ Viticulturist(s) Jean Fourie (Jan 2011) ▪ 9ha (shiraz, chard, sauv) ▪ 80t/±1,500cs own label 40% red 60% white ▪ PO Box 28 Calitzdorp 6660 ▪ dekrans@mweb.co.za ▪ S 33° 32' 6.3" E 021° 41' 9.0" ▪ **T +27 (0)44-213-3314 ▪** F +27 (0)44-213-3562

Garden Route is made from bought-in grapes at De Krans cellar by leading port exponent Boets Nel, who says it's 'quite a change but very exciting' to vinify fruit from cool areas (Outeniqua wine ward for 2011 vintage) compared with the home-vineyards at Calitzdorp. Main markets are the Southern Cape and Germany; tasting and sales also at De Krans.

Shiraz 🗒 ★★★★ Savoury & moreish **07** from Durbanville grapes still selling, plum & black pepper balanced with rich vanilla oak & soft tannins. **Sauvignon Blanc 🗒 📷 ★★★★** Appealing white peach & blackcurrant, moderate 12.5% alc, preview **11** racy freshness, focus & charm in one package. — Panel

■ **Gary Player** *see* Black Knight Wine
■ **Gecko Ridge** *see* Long Mountain Wine Company

Genevieve Méthode Cap Classique

Location: Elgin ▪ Map: Elgin, Walker Bay & Bot River ▪ Est/1stB 2009 ▪ Tasting by appt ▪ Owner(s)/winemaker(s) Melissa Nelsen ▪ Cellarmaster(s) Melissa Nelson, Robert Gower (2008, Ross Gower Wines) ▪ Viticulturist(s) Leon Engelke (2008, consultant) ▪ 10t/600cs own label 100% MCC ▪ PO Box 122 Elgin 7180 ▪ melissa@genevievemcc.co.za ▪ www.genevievemcc.co.za ▪ S 34° 5' 23.7" E 019° 11' 50.7" ▪ **T +27 (0)83-302-6562 ▪** F +27 (0)28-841-4190

Melissa Nelsen's day job involves promoting the wines of various Bot River producers but a love for bubbly saw her launch her own label, Genevieve - also her middle name after the patron saint of Paris, the city much visited by her parents. Her Méthode Cap Classique is made at Ross Gower Wines in Elgin and production has jumped from 5,500 bottles of the maiden 2008 vintage to 10,000 of 2010.

■ **GEPA** *see* Koopmanskloof Wingerde
■ **Ghost Corner** *see* Cederberg Private Cellar
■ **Giant's Peak** *see* Wine-of-the-Month Club

Gilga Wines

Location/map/WO: Stellenbosch ▪ Est/1stB 2002 ▪ Tasting & sales by appt ▪ Owner(s) John Rowan ▪ Cellarmaster(s)/viticulturist(s) Stefan Gerber (Jun 2010, consultant) ▪ Winemaker(s) Stefan Gerber (Jun 2010, consultant), with Marco Benjamin (Dec 2010, consultant) ▪ 4ha/3.5ha (grenache, mourv, shiraz, tempranillo) ▪ 10t/550cs own label 100% red ▪ PO Box 871 Stellenbosch 7599 ▪ stefan@gilga.co.za, stefan@boerandbrit.com ▪ www.gilga.co.za ▪ S 33° 56' 46.1" E 018° 47' 20.6" ▪ **T +27 (0)21-875-5824 ▪** F +27 (0)86-531-7137

New broom treatment at Gilga: tempranillo, grenache and mourvèdre have been planted with a blend in mind; a homestead and barrel ageing cellar are planned and new packaging was launched in 2011. But as far as the wines go, Chris Joubert wants to cut artificial influences and 'bring back the Old World charm.'

★★★★ Gilga Syrah Bold, intensely-spiced **06** follows trend of **05**. Big 15% alcohol, new French oak (40%) & solid grippy tannins add to blockbuster impression.

Discontinued: **Amurabi.** — AL

■ **Gilysipao** *see* Orange River Wine Cellars
■ **Give Me A Chance** *see* Alluvia Winery & Private Residence Club

■ **Glass Collection** *see Glenelly Cellars*

Glen Carlou

Location: Paarl ▪ Map: Paarl & Wellington ▪ WO: Paarl/Coastal ▪ Est 1985 ▪ 1stB 1988 ▪ Tasting & sales Mon-Fri 8.30-5 Sat/Sun 10-4 ▪ Fee R25-R50 ▪ Closed Easter Fri, Dec 25/26 & Jan 1 ▪ Cellar tours by appt ▪ Restaurant Mon-Sun 11-3 (see Restaurants section) ▪ Facilities for children ▪ Tour groups ▪ Gifts ▪ Honey ▪ Conferences ▪ Conservation area ▪ Hess Art Collection Museum ▪ Owner(s) Hess Family Estates Ltd (Switzerland) ▪ Cellarmaster(s) Arco Laarman (Jan 2000) ▪ Winemaker(s) Arco Laarman (Jan 2000), with Bertus van Zyl (Jul 2009) ▪ Viticulturist(s) Marius Cloete (2000) ▪ 145ha/62ha (cabs s/f, malbec, mourv, p verdot, pinot, shiraz, chard) ▪ ±700t/50,000cs own label ▪ PO Box 23 Klapmuts 7625 ▪ welcome@glencarlou.co.za ▪ www.glencarlou.co.za ▪ S 33° 48' 44.2" E 018° 54' 14.0" ▪ **T** +27 (0)21-875-5528 ▪ F +27 (0)21-875-5314

There have been only three winemakers at this Paarl vineyard – founder Walter and son David Finlayson, and incumbent Arco Laarman who is planning its 25th vintage this year. Recent exports have 'soared', thanks no doubt to parent Hess Family Estates' winemaking presence on four continents, but Arco's tracking consumer trends toward less wooded wine styles. Two new Nomblot concrete fermenters offer opportunity in the cellar, and the property's first unwooded chardonnay will be released exclusively off the farm. Looking ahead, less successful varieties and 'problem' blocks face renewal, while Arco has eyes for cooler climes: 'I think more wineries will seek out land south, toward Cape Agulhas'.

Prestige range

★★★★☆ **Gravel Quarry Cabernet Sauvignon** Power of farm's top cab in handsome **08** was brooding last edition; classy cassis flavours in fine tannic frame had great grip for cellaring.

★★★★☆ **Quartz Stone Chardonnay** Modern & chicly attired, super **10** leans more toward 'fine white wine' than just 'chardonnay': subtle, no obvious citrus fruit or butterscotch, rather a rich fabric with layers of textured minerality.

The Welder ★★★★ Unwooded sweet chenin named for winemaker who shares first name with US welding supplies company! **09**'s tropical flavours zapped by fresh acidity previously. **08** (★★★☆) less intense.

Classic range

★★★★ **Cabernet Sauvignon** ✓ Back with flashy **09**. Delicious redcurrant & cranberry styling in a pliable frame, more open & generous than previous. No **08**.

★★★★ **Syrah** Broad bacon, pepper & red fruit flavours in open-hearted **07** (★★★☆) when last tasted. Less structured than **06** & previous.

★★★★ **Grand Classique** Svelte cab-driven blend of 5 Bordeaux red varieties, accessible **08** is stiffened by fresh & fragrant petit verdot (13%). Like **07**, shade lighter than classical **06** (★★★★☆).

★★★★ **Chardonnay** ✓ 目 ⊠ Rich & creamy, butterscotch nuances a trademark. **10** a broad New World mouthful, its zesty lime preserve balanced by snappy acidity. 10 months in 30% new oak.

Pinot Noir 目 ⊠ ★★★★ Demure **10**, sour cherry interest to open texture, lighter styling. **Sauvignon Blanc** 目 ⊠ ★★★ Ripe fruit-salad flavours take the edge of **11**'s grassy zing. WO Coastal. Discontinued: **Zinfandel**.

Contemporary range

Tortoise Hill White ☺ 目 ⊠ ★★★ Juicy guava & pear - & hint of pineapple - to racy, dry viognier-led **11** preview, with splashes semillon & verdelho. WO Coastal.

Tortoise Hill Red 目 ★★★ Merlot-led **08** was well fruited but savoury & contained last edition. — DS

Glenelly Cellars

Location/map: Stellenbosch ▪ WO: Stellenbosch/Western Cape ▪ Est/1stB 2003 ▪ Tasting & sales Mon-Fri 10-4.30 Sat 10-2.30 ▪ Closed Easter Fri/Sun, Dec 25/26 & Jan 1 ▪ Cellar tours by appt ▪ Gift shop ▪ Glass Museum ▪ Owner(s) May-Eliane de Lencquesaing ▪ Cellarmaster(s) Luke O'Cuinneagain (Jan 2008) ▪ Winemaker(s) Luke O'Cuinneagain (Jan 2008), with Jerome Likwa (Jan 2008) ▪ Viticulturist(s) Heinrich Louw (2003) ▪ 128ha/65ha (cabs s/f, merlot, p verdot, shiraz, chard) ▪ 400t/27,667cs own label 95% red 5% white ▪ PO Box 1079 Stellenbosch 7599 ▪ info@glenelly.co.za ▪ www.glenellyestate.com ▪ S 33° 55' 6.1" E 018° 52' 45.1" ▪ **T** +27 **(0)21-809-6440** ▪ F +27 (0)21-809-6448

'South African wine with a French touch.' When May-Eliane de Lencquesaing, former owner of Château Pichon-Longueville, started converting orchard to vineyard here just north of Stellenbosch, many expected another replication of the Bordeaux paradigm in the Cape. Eight years on, while the Gallic touch is manifest, the eclectic offering is in response to the land, not one imposed on it. The red Grand Vin, for example, is not classic in the Bordeaux genre, being shiraz driven. There's no sign of lookalike Bordeaux white either, rather a top-end rendition of Burgundy's chardonnay. And The Glass Collection, after May's antique stemware – some of which is displayed in the winery – is a New World take on the 'second wine' concept: a varietal range under screwcap with serious wine at sensible prices.

Glenelly range

★★★★☆ **Lady May** Grace & style defined. Like 08, mainly cab, dash petit verdot, individual **09** (★★★★★) is a carefully composed ensemble, all the components – pure berry fruit, clean oak, fine tannins, fresh acid, supportive 14.8% alc – contribute, none dominate, in textured sensory splendour.

★★★★☆ **Grand Vin de Glenelly** Elegant & accessible shiraz/Bordeaux blend. **08** (★★★★) a lighter touch than **07**, but supple now while waiting for 'Madame' above to mature. WO Western Cape.

★★★★ **Grand Vin de Glenelly Chardonnay** NEW Creamy texture (ferment/9 months lees-ageing in oak) gives girth to **10**'s tight citrus fruit profile; complexity unfurls with length of flavour.

The Glass Collection

Chardonnay ☺ 🍷 ★★★ Now bottled, **10** loaded with vibrant citrus flavour, eminently drinkable.

Cabernet Sauvignon ✓ 🍷 ★★★★ Ripe blackcurrant tightly packed into muscular structure – with finesse. **09** buttoned up mid-2011; like rest of this trio, for 3 years cellaring or with food now. **Merlot** ✓ 🍷 ★★★★ Full-bodied but demure, preview **10** offers floral violet charm to firm texture. **Shiraz** ✓ 🍷 ★★★★ **10** more peppery than rich **09**, roasted nut & spicy warmth, dense tannins need time. — DS

Glen Erskine Estate

Location/WO: Elgin ▪ Map: Elgin, Walker Bay & Bot River ▪ Est 2005 ▪ 1stB 2009 ▪ Tasting, sales & cellar tours by appt ▪ Closed Easter Fri/Sun, Dec 25 & Jan 1 ▪ BYO picnic ▪ Owner(s) Reine & Annalien Dalton ▪ Cellarmaster(s) Annalien Dalton ▪ Winemaker(s) Annalien Dalton, with Rikus Neethling (Sep 2009, Bizoe Wines) ▪ Viticulturist(s) Reine Dalton ▪ 14.6ha/4.93ha (sauv, sem, viog) ▪ 28t/475cs own label 100% white + 115cs for clients ▪ Ranges for customers: Kievits Kroon ▪ PO Box 111 Elgin 7180 ▪ annalien.dalton@gmail.com, reinedalton@gmail.com ▪ S 34°10'34.94" E 019° 2'12.75" ▪ **T +27 (0)21-848-9632** ▪ F +27 (0)86-547-4473

The first crops from Elgin grape and apple farmers Reine and Annalien Dalton's semillon and viognier vines last year joined sauvignon in their new Reserve, while they and rising star consultant Rikus Neethling teamed up with an upscale Gauteng lodge to supply its house wines.

Sauvignon Blanc ✓ 🍷 ★★★★ Quince fruit flavour softens the austerity of cool-climate **10**, flinty & food-friendly. **Glen Erskine Reserve** NEW ✓ 🍷 ★★★★ **10** sauvignon gains fuller, multi-faceted nuances from lightly oaked partners viognier & semillon. Promising debut. — DS

▪ **Glenhurst** *see Quoin Rock Winery*

Glenview Wines

Location: Cape Town ▪ WO: Coastal ▪ Est/1stB 1998 ▪ Closed to public ▪ Owner(s) Robin Marks ▪ Winemaker(s) Frank Meaker (Nov 2010, consultant) ▪ 7,000cs own label 50% red 50% white ▪ PO Box 32234 Camps Bay 8040 ▪ bayexport@kingsley.co.za ▪ **T +27 (0)21-438-1080** ▪ F +27 (0)21-511-2545

Robin Marks believes his online wine business to be the best way to offer consumers affordable wines without compromising on quality. After much debate, he has decided to add sauvignon to his portfolio, as he believes he has finally found the right quality at the right price – no easy feat.

Merlot 🍷 🖉 ★★ Ready-to-drink **10** repeats **09**'s chocolate tones, food-friendly savouriness. **Chenin Blanc** 🍷 🖉 ★★★ Soft peachy summer quaffer. Previewed **11** tad less expressive than previous. **Sauvignon Blanc** NEW 🍷 🖉 ★★ **11** undemanding, with light tropical taste. — DB

GlenWood

Location/map: Franschhoek ▪ WO: Franschhoek/Coastal ▪ Est/1stB 2002 ▪ Tasting & sales Mon-Fri 11–4 Sat/Sun (Sep-Apr only) 11-3 ▪ Closed Easter Fri/Sun, Dec 25 & Jan 1 ▪ Tasting R30/R50 incl cellar tour ▪ Tours daily at 11 ▪ Cheese platters ▪ BYO picnic ▪ Hikes ▪ Owner(s) Alastair G Wood ▪ Cellarmaster(s)/viticulturist(s) DP Burger (Apr 1991) ▪ Winemaker(s) DP Burger (Apr 1991), with Justin Jacobs (Jan 2011) ▪ 49ha/30ha (chard, sauv, sem) ▪ 200t/8,000cs own label 50% red 50% white ▪ BWI, IPW ▪ PO Box 204 Franschhoek 7690 ▪ info@glenwoodvineyards.co.za ▪ www.glenwoodvineyards.co.za ▪ S 33° 54′ 56.7″ E 019° 4′ 57.0″ ▪ **T +27 (0)21-876-2044** ▪ F +27 (0)21-876-3338

'Look out for a refreshed GlenWood brand in this, our 10th year, and a Premium Chardonnay and Syrah,' says DP Burger, winemaker/general manager of this scenically situated Franschhoek estate. Objectives for the year include Biodiversity & Wine Initiative Champion status, and increased visibility throughout South Africa and in social media (having successfully ventured into the Garden Route and KwaZulu Natal markets). With full marks for his SKOP1 senior cellar staff training programme, new assistant winemaker Justin Jacobs gives notice of future stardom.

★★★★ **Merlot** ✓ **08** is well defined, with ripe plums & dark chocolate. Mouthfilling & firm, long savoury conclusion. Enjoy now with robust meat dishes or give time to reveal all charms.

★★★★☆ **Syrah Vigneron's Selection 08** had impressive depth, sour plum notes & peppery complexity last time.

★★★★☆ **Chardonnay Vigneron's Selection** 🌱 **10** (★★★★) tad off showstopping **09**. Bold & powerful citrus burst, mouthfillingly rich & creamy vanilla, judicious wooding needs time to integrate.

★★★★ **Unwooded Chardonnay** ✓ Charming **11** lean & lithe, delicate green apple & citrus, lingering lemon cream conclusion. Cries out for sushi. Also enough structure & flavour to age a few years.

★★★★ **Semillon Vigneron's Selection** Classy **09** shows lingering peach & floral scents. Full-bodied, smooth & creamy with a toasty oak conclusion. Good food partner.

> **Sauvignon Blanc** ☺ ★★★ Ebullient **11**, ripe tropical fruit flavours; crisp & lean, zesty lemon finish, modest 12.5% alc.

Shiraz ★★★★☆ **08** last edition took a big step up, was much more complex & elegant than **07** (★★★). WO Coastal, as for Unwooded Chardonnay. **Shiraz-Merlot** NEW 🍷 ★★★ Easy-drinking, cheerful **10** is medium bodied, balanced, fruit-sweet & juicy, with soft vanilla wafts. — WB

Goats do Roam Wine Company

WO: Coastal/Western Cape ▪ Est/1stB 1998 ▪ Tasting & sales at Fairview ▪ Owner(s) Charles Back ▪ Winemaker(s) Anthony de Jager, with Adele Dunbar & Stephanie Betts ▪ PO Box 583 Suider-Paarl 7624 ▪ info@goatsdoroam.com ▪ www.goatsdoroam.com ▪ **T +27 (0)21-863-2450** ▪ F +27 (0)21-863-2591

Good-naturedly cocking a snook at Old World wine icons with punning labels inspired by the goat herd at his Fairview farm in Paarl, Charles Back's Goats do Roam range has been an international hit for almost 15 years. Now the Goatfather has decided that three members of the Roaming range have served their cheeky purpose and put them out to pasture. But in the Back universe, as one goat door closes, another opens - in the shape of fashionable variety roussanne, playing a maiden cameo role in the white blend.

★★★★ **Bored Doe** ✓ Petit verdot (49%) vaults cab to lead serious **09** Bordeaux blend. Bold yet soft fruitcake & herb flavour, dark & dense yet elegant. Older oak (15 months) well integrated.

★★★★ **Goat-Roti** 🍷 Shiraz & viognier co-fermented; peppery **09** (★★★★) shows earth, plum & 'graphite' minerality but less sleekness than **08**, more overt char from French/American oak, 10% new.

Goats do Roam Red 🍷🌱 ★★★★ The first goat: **10** retains serious Rhône styling - dry, spicy & dark fruited. Rounded yet firm, seasoning from 7 months older French/American oak. **The Goatfather** 🍷 ★★★★ Juicy blueberry, cocoa & tobacco density on **09**, unusual sangiovese, barbera, cab mix. Gentle long finish. **Goats do Roam Rosé** 🍷🌱 ★★★ Fresh, zesty berry & rhubarb dryness on shiraz-led **11**. **Goats do Roam White** 🍷 ★★★ Green peach & lime on previewed **11**, viognier-led 3-way Rhône blend. Zesty chalk dryness on medium body. Refreshing, lively & long. WO Coastal/W Cape for all Goats. Discontinued: **Goats in Villages Shiraz-Pinotage, Goat Door, Goats in Villages Viognier**. — FM

Goede Hoop Estate

Location/map: Stellenbosch ▪ WO: Bottelary/Stellenbosch ▪ Est 1928 ▪ 1stB 1974 ▪ Tasting, sales & cellar tours Mon-Fri 9-4 Sat 10-1 ▪ Closed Easter Fri-Sun, Dec 25/26 & Jan 1 ▪ Pieter's Private Cellar: monthly 4-course gourmet meal & wine (1st Thu of each month) R285pp, booking essential (12 seats only) ▪ BYO picnic ▪ Conference facilities ▪ Mountain biking trail ▪ Owner(s) Pieter Bestbier ▪ Winemaker(s) Albert Ahrens (Jun 2009) ▪ Viticulturist(s) Altus van Lill (May 2011) ▪ 122ha/80ha (cab, malbec, merlot, ptage, shiraz, chard, chenin, sauv) ▪ ±600t/ 10,000cs own label 91% red 9% white & ±200,000L bulk ▪ PO Box 25 Kuils River 7579 ▪ goede@adept.co.za ▪ www.goedehoop.co.za ▪ S 33° 54'32.0" E 018° 45'14.0" ▪ **T +27 (0)21-903-6286** ▪ F +27 (0)21-906-1553

The old cellar has had a general revamp, the maiden straw wine has been released and the labels are getting a makeover. In a novel fine-dining event, once a month proprietor Pieter Bestbier opens his private cellar to 12 guests, allows them to select wines to accompany their meal from his forty-year collection and guides them through the pairings.

Goede Hoop Estate range

★★★★ Merlot-Cabernet Sauvignon Leafy mineral notes last year on remarkably youthful **02**, caressed by silky tannin. Accessible & appealing.

★★★★ Estate Straw Wine NEW Estate's first release of fashionable style, **10** from air-dried chenin. Hugely sweet & concentrated, with healthy ripe fruit flavours. To be enjoyed in small helpings.

Cabernet Sauvignon ★★★ 02 showed signs of tricky vintage on review. Intact, evolved, well-measured but not for keeping. This & next 3 not revisited. **Pinotage ★★★** 05 was developed last we tried, with evolved black fruit on still-firm tannins. **Shiraz ★★★** 03 showed sprightly fruit last edition, lovely integration, velvety tannins & spicy/smoky notes. **Chardonnay ★★★** 09 had generous citrus fruit when sampled, but floundered in pervasive oak which may since have settled. **Sauvignon Blanc ★★★** Pungent asparagus & mineral/dusty notes on **10** follow onto fruity but crisply tart palate. Needs food. **Shiraz LBV Port** NEW **★★★★** Big & ripe maiden **07** emerges after lengthy stay in barrel, revealing modest sweetness & evolved fruit with firm spirit grip.

Domaine range

Red ☺ ▤ **★★★** Uncomplicated, pleasant & easy-sipping lower tier range, **10** delivers well on value. Soft & savoury, but big on fruit. **White** ☺ ▤ **★★★ 10** sauvignon-chenin blend echoes previous. Distinctive & characterful, with pungent wild aromas & fullish body. — GdB

▪ **Goede Moed** see Baarsma Wine Group
▪ **Goedgenoegen** see Baarsma Wine Group

Goedvertrouw Estate

Location: Bot River ▪ Map: Elgin, Walker Bay & Bot River ▪ Est 1990 ▪ 1stB 1991 ▪ Tasting & sales by appt ▪ Home-cooked meals & accommodation by appt ▪ Play area for children ▪ Walks ▪ Farm produce ▪ Small conferences ▪ Conservation area ▪ Small art gallery ▪ Owner(s)/winemaker(s)/viticulturist(s) Elreda Pillmann ▪ 8ha (cab, pinot, chard, sauv) ▪ 70% red 30% white ▪ PO Box 37 Bot River 7185 ▪ goedvertrouwwineestate@telkomsa.net ▪ S 34° 9' 56.7" E 019° 13'24.1" ▪ **T +27 (0)28-284-9769** ▪ F +27 (0)28-284-9769

Situated on the Van der Stel Pass between Bot River and Villiersdorp, Goedvertrouw Estate allows Elreda Pillmann to continue living the dream she and late husband, Arthur shared. What Elreda today uses as a wine cellar still has the original 'skietgate' (holes for shooting) used during World War II. Be sure to stay for a meal (by appointment) at this tranquil venue.

Cabernet Sauvignon ★★★ 06 yeasty aromas, pure fruit & ripe tannins. Should be harmonious now. Not retasted, as for all. **Pinot Noir ★★** Fragrantly mineral **04**, hints of game & damp earth. **Chardonnay ★★★** Orange peel & biscuit tones waft out of nicely round **06**. **Sauvignon Blanc ★★★** Previewed **08** finished satisfyingly dry. — WB

Goedverwacht Wine Estate

Location: Bonnievale ▪ Map/WO: Robertson ▪ Est 1960's ▪ 1stB 1994 ▪ Tasting, sales & tours Mon-Fri 8.30-4.30 Sat 10-1 ▪ Closed Easter Fri/Sun, Dec 25/26 & Jan 1 ▪ Mediterranean or quiche & salad platter; picnic basket for 2 (incl bottle sparkling wine) - booking essential 2 days prior ▪ BYO picnic ▪ Tour groups ▪ Conservation area ▪ Owner(s) Jan du Toit & Sons (Pty) Ltd ▪ Winemaker(s) Henry Conradie (Aug 2005), with Charles Petrus Adam (Jan 2003) ▪

Viticulturist(s) Jan du Toit, advised by Francois Viljoen ▪ 220ha/130ha (cab, merlot, shiraz, chard, cbard, sauv) ▪ 1,600t/1 million litres 43% red 50% white 7% rosé ▪ Other export brands: Ama Ulibo, Misty Kloof's, Mzansi's, Soek die Geluk ▪ Brands for clients: Vinimark Trading ▪ PO Box 128 Bonnievale 6730 ▪ goedverwachtestate@lando. co.za, info.goedverwacht@breede.co.za ▪ www.goedverwacht.co.za ▪ S 33° 55' 11.3" E 020° 0' 19.1" ▪ **T +27 (0)23-616-3430** ▪ F +27 (0)23-616-2073

One of a string of farms on the route between Robertson and Bonnievale, the Du Toit family business did well last year, with increased exports to Europe, particularly Germany, and extended plantings of chardonnay and merlot (the latter being a best seller). The focus is on drinkability in the lower- to middle-range wines, and classic structure and longevity in the flagships.

★★★★ **Maxim Cabernet Sauvignon 07** is a rung above firmer **06** (★★★★), similar to stylish **04**. Enticed with coffee & smoke, soft mouthfeel, layered flavours last time.

★★★★ **Maxim Chardonnay** 🕸 **10** (★★★★) shade off generous **07**. Toasty, with lemon curd & baked apple character, vanilla in tangy tail.

Great Expectations Chardonnay ☺ 🍷 🕸 ★★☆ Friendly **10**'s citrus highlighted by buttered toast.

Crane Red Merlot 🍷 🕸 ★★ **11** has savoury red berry fruit, quince-like acidity, uncomplicated quaffing red. **An Acre of Stone Shiraz** 🍷 🕸 ★★☆ Easy-drinking **10** fresh & light toned, spicy flick in tail. **Triangle** ★☆ Leafy **09** Bordeaux blend led by cab. **Shiraz Rosé** 🍷 🕸 ★★★ **11** poolside sipper, just off-dry & lightish. **Crane White Colombar** 🍷 🕸 ★★ **11** attractively lean & bursting with tart apple exuberance. **The Good Earth Sauvignon Blanc** 🍷 🕸 ★★ Early picked **11** very light, shy & faintly grassy. **Crane Brut Sparkling** 🕸 ★★ Last edition, **10** off-dry sparkler from colombard had frothy but rapidly dissipating mousse. **Crane Rosé Brut Sparkling** 🕸 ★★ From shiraz, **10** off-dry strawberry fruit-bomb fizz still selling. — Panel

◼ **Goeie Tye** see Rooiberg Winery

Golden Kaan

Location/map: Robertson ▪ WO: Western Cape ▪ Est/1stB 2002 ▪ Tasting & sales at 9 Voortrekker Rd Robertson Mon-Fri 8.30-5 Sat 9-2 ▪ Fee R15 for large groups ▪ Food & Wine pairing by appt ▪ Closed Sun, Easter Fri, Dec 25 & Jan 1 ▪ Facilities for children ▪ Gifts ▪ Art exhibitions ▪ Conference room (14 pax) ▪ Owner(s) KWV ▪ Winemaker(s) Richard Rowe ▪ Viticulturist(s) Cobus van Graan ▪ PO Box 892 Robertson 6905 ▪ info@goldenkaan.co.za ▪ www. goldenkaan.com ▪ S 33° 48' 29.9" E 019° 52' 40.0" ▪ **T +27 (0)23-626-1511** ▪ F +27 (0)23-626-1517

This KWV range is designed to offer winelovers readily drinkable and unchallenging wines - many of them definitely off-dry. Germany and Eastern Europe are popular hunting grounds for Golden Kaan, while newly introduced African Passion is proving popular at entry level, with further labels on the cards.

Golden Kaan range

Cabernet Sauvignon 🕸 ★★ Light fruit on **10** lifted by few grams sugar. **Merlot** 🕸 ★★★ Smooth, fleshy red plums, **10** can take light chilling. **Pinotage** 🕸 ★★ Portily ripe **10**, hard finish to sweet fruit. **Shiraz** 🕸 ★★★ Comfortable padding to **10**'s savoury & red fruit. **Pinotage Rosé** 🍷 🕸 ★★ Raspberries & cream flavours on previewed off-dry **11**. **Chardonnay** 🕸 ★★ Fruitily sweet **10** with hint oak spice. **Chenin Blanc** 🕸 ★★ Softly dry **11** with lush fruit salad flavours. **Sauvignon Blanc** 🍷 🕸 ★★ Smooth, nettly sweet **11**.

African Passion range NEW

Cabernet Sauvignon-Merlot 🍷 ★★☆ Sweetish **10**, with contrasting dry tannins. **Chenin Blanc** 🍷 ★★ Melon-toned, juicy, off-dry **11**. Both these tasted pre-bottling. — AL

◼ **Golden Triangle** see Stellenzicht Vineyards
◼ **Golden Vine** see Waterstone Wines
◼ **Gone Fishin'** see Catch Of The Day

Goudini Wines

Location: Rawsonville ▪ Map: Breedekloof ▪ WO: Goudini ▪ Est 1948 ▪ Tasting & sales Mon-Fri 8-5 Sat 9.30-12.30 ▪ Closed Easter Fri, Dec 25/26 & Jan 1 ▪ Cellar tours by appt ▪ Coffee shop: light meals during tasting hours ▪ Conference facility ▪ Owner(s) 40 members ▪ Cellarmaster(s) Hennie Hugo (Dec 1984) ▪ Winemaker(s) Ruaan Terblanche (Nov 2001), with Tinus le Roux & Gerhard Rossouw (Jan/Oct 2010) ▪ Viticulturist(s) Hendrik Myburgh (Nov 2001) ▪ 1,000ha (merlot, ruby cab, shiraz, chard, chenin, sauv) ▪ 20,000t/33,000cs own label 45% red 45%

offering the full platter

of legal services

The Samsung RW52DASS Wine Chiller with multi temperature control creates an optimal wine storage environment for both red and white wine by allowing the top and bottom compartment

Customer Care 0860 726 786

Grapes are the most noble and challenging of all fruits. They deserve a good home.

temperatures to be individually controlled. It's a long journey for the grape, and undeniably it deserves a happy ending.

www.samsung.com

Drinking wine with food is hardly novel but making it specifically with food pairing in mind is the more innovative idea served up by collaborators and friends **Peter Tempelhoff** (left), executive chef for The Collection by Liz McGrath, and **Adam Mason**, winemaker at Klein Constantia, via their Yardstick brand. In the Greenhouse's kitchen at the Cellars-Hohenort Hotel in Constantia, they partner the Yardstick Pinot Noir and Kaboom! Cabernet Sauvignon-Merlot with their respective signature dishes: honey-glazed duck breast and slow-cooked beef shortrib.

INTELLECTUAL PROPERTY ASPECT

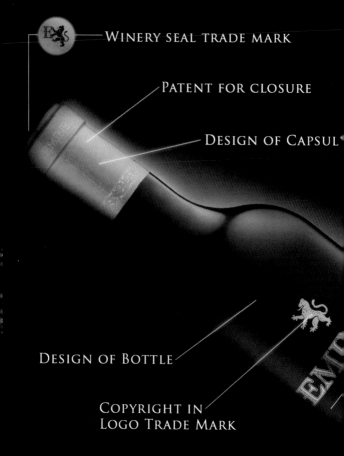

WINERY SEAL TRADE MARK

PATENT FOR CLOSURE

DESIGN OF CAPSUL

DESIGN OF BOTTLE

COPYRIGHT IN
LOGO TRADE MARK

BOTTLE AS CONTAINER
TRADE MARK

DR GERNTHOLTZ INC
INTELLECTUAL PROPERTY LAWYERS
PATENTS • DESIGNS • TRADE MARKS • COPYRIGHT

OF A WINE BOTTLE AND LABEL

PRIMARY TRADE MARK

DOMAIN NAME
(WWW.EMINEO.COM)

SECONDARY TRADE MARK

COPYRIGHT IN LABEL
DESIGN

(+27 (021) 551 2650
+27 (021) 551 2960
+27 (021) 551 2974
info@gerntholtz.com
www.gerntholtz.com
PO Box 8, Cape Town 8000, South Africa
30 Union Road, Milnerton 7441, South Africa

Using a coffee pot to decant wine is somewhat unconventional, but then so is **Bertus Fourie**. The wine-maker and -educator, nicknamed 'Starbucks', is the creator of an entirely new wine category, the 'coffee pinotage'. He discovered the recipe for this 'brew' by accident in 2001, after trying many combinations of yeasts, oak types and varieties. Though Bertus, who makes this style of wine under the Barista label, believes only pinotage presents a very specific coffee profile, all sorts of taste-alikes, across numerous varieties and blends, are pouring forth faster than you can say cuppa java. And consumers love them.

A sophisticated turn-on

Sophistication is about refinement, perfection, ingenuity, taste and a little touch of style. Most importantly, sophistication is about meeting these high standards with absolutely no fuss.

When it comes to your wine, no words could ring more true, which is why Nampak Closures' range of screw caps are designed to give your wine a perfect sense of style that appeals to even the most sophisticated connoisseur.

Our screw cap closures are impermeable, eliminate the high risk of cork taint, experience no loss of resilience and have no finicky storage requirements. They are effortless to open and re-close, and offer beautiful high-end printing and finishes. With our screw caps, there are sure to be no unpleasant surprises, just a refined little twist to top off that perfect wine experience.

For more information, contact us on +27 21 507 8411 or email:
Madene.Koen@za.nampak.com
William.Footman@za.nampak.com
Barry.Erasmus@za.nampak.com

At MAN Vintners, they're thinking out of the box, with an innovative carton that promises to reduce the packaging and transport footprint of their wines by more than 50%, according to some measures. Trials in key markets have proved promising and already represent about 5% of MAN Vintners' fast expanding business, according to marketing manager **Matthew Cooke** (right), pictured here with winemaker **Francois Bezuidenhout**.

Bringing a fresh approach to wine tourism is Opstal Estate in the scenic Slanghoek Valley with their latest visitor offering, the appropriately named Opstal Fresh. It' a quarterly farmer's market, intended as 'a meeting place for fresh produce, fresh ideas and, of course, fresh people'. Visitors can sample and purchase everything from biltong to coffee, mainly from artisanal suppliers in the area, as well as Opstal wines. We snapped Opstal winemaker and marketer **Attie Louw** and **PR Helga Croucher** (left) at Worcester resident **Charina Jonker**'s stall, piled with delicious – fresh – produce.

Experience the true taste of South Africa

KARIBU
South African Dining

Come dine with magnificent views of Table Mountain
while indulging in the best our country has to offer

- Traditional South African Cuisine
- Award-Winning Restaurant
- Daimond Award Wine List

- Ostrich and Venison
- Bobotie and Bredies (stews)
- Springbok Shank
- South African Braai (BBQ)
- A-Grade Karan Steaks
- Top quality Seafood
- Local Desserts

  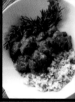 

Our menu might bring you in, but our excellent, friendly
service and great-tasting food will surely bring you back

V&A Waterfront, Cape Town, South Africa
Tel: +27 21 421 7005/6 • E-mail: kariburestaurant@mweb.co.za
www.kariburestaurant.co.za

white 10% rosé + 7,000cs for clients ▪ PO Box 132 Rawsonville 6845 ▪ winesales@goudiniwine.co.za ▪ www. goudiniwine.co.za ▪ S 33° 41'37.8" E 019° 19'9.5" ▪ **T +27 (0)23-349-1090** ▪ F +27 (0)23-349-1988

The practice of harvesting at night - a first for a large commercial winery in the Breedekloof Valley - continues, as cellarmaster Hennie Hugo believes it's resulting in a discernible improvement in the quality of the wine (40% of it going to FirstCape, in which Goudini is one of five shareholders, for export to the UK).

Goudini range

Pinotage ⊞ ★★ Fresh & spicy **10**, plum flavours for early drinking. **Shiraz** Await new vintage. **Ruby Cabernet-Merlot** ⊞ ★★ **10** red berries in light, tangy aperitif/al fresco style. **Rosé** NEW ⊟ ⊞ ★★ **11** from pinotage; light berry tones with sweet-sour twist. **Unwooded Chardonnay** Occasional release. **Chenin Blanc** ⊟ ⊞ ★★ Off-dry & tropical, **11** tangy easy-drinking style. **Sauvignon Blanc** ⊟ ⊞ ★★★ **11** soft herb & tropical tones, nice tangy tail. **Brut Sparkling** ★★ Less fresh appeal than previous, more broad-based waxy, nutty character. **NV**. **Natural Sweet** ⊟ ⊞ ★★ Ripe tropical tones on previewed **11**, fresh & nicely balanced. **Hanepoot** ★★★ Last year **06** was a balanced fortified dessert with gentle barley sugar & lemon tastes, best enjoyed soon. **Cape Ruby Port** ★★★ Sweet winter warmer. Thatch & ripe red-fruit flavours with a touch of mocha. **NV**. Discontinued: **Reserve Ruby Cabernet**, **Blanc de Noir**, **Ruby Cabernet-Merlot Semi-Sweet**, **Port**.

Umfiki range

Cabernet Sauvignon ★★★ Friendly barbecue wine with smoky blackcurrant flavour. **NV**, as for all these. **Merlot** ★★ Light & juicy red with appealing red-berry taste. **Dry White** ⊟ ★★ From chenin; softly tropical, gentle yet crisp. **Semi Sweet Chenin Blanc** ★★ When last tasted, a pleasant semi-sweet white for the poolside. **Sauvignon Blanc** ⊟ ★★ Light, tart & tangy dry white. — MW

▪ **Goudriaan** *see* Groupe LFE South Africa
▪ **Gouverneurs** *see* Groot Constantia Estate

Graça

Portuguese-inspired, lightly spritzy sippers, the original white version after nearly 30 years still South Africa's top-selling cork-closed wine. By Distell.

Rosé ☺ ★★★ Semi-sweet strawberry fruit-bomb with sherbety twist, & blush from ruby cab. **NV**. **Graça** ☺ ★★★ Consistent & appealing white, off-dry, crisp & lively, mainly sauvignon & two others. **NV**. —Panel

Graceland Vineyards

Location/map/WO: Stellenbosch ▪ Est/1stB 1998 ▪ Tasting & sales Mon-Fri by appt ▪ Fee R30 ▪ Closed all pub hols ▪ B&B, two self-catering cottages ▪ Owner(s) Paul & Susan McNaughton ▪ Cellarmaster(s)/winemaker(s)/viticulturist(s) Susan McNaughton (2001) ▪ 18ha/10ha (cab, merlot, shiraz) ▪ 55t/4,000cs own label 100% red ▪ Suite 144 Private Bag X4 Die Boord 7613 ▪ graceland@iafrica.com ▪ www.gracelandvineyards.com ▪ S 33° 59'37.5" E 018° 50'3.1" ▪ **T +27 (0)21-881-3121** ▪ F +27 (0)86-556-4600

This petite winery is a real gem, situated in the heart of the storied 'Golden Triangle' on Stellenbosch's hilly southern periphery. Graceland is the culmination of 14 years of dedication by Paul McNaughton and winemaking wife Susan, who declare 'we have had to box smart in this competitive market'. They certainly punch above their weight, having built a successful wine venture (growing from 600 to 4,000 cases), a loving family home and luxury accommodation.

★★★★ **Cabernet Sauvignon** Cool vintage adds polish to opulent, well-groomed **09**. Fine varietal character with cassis & pencil shavings. Harmonious even in youth, with structure for enjoyment over good few years.

★★★★ **Strawberry Fields** 09 shiraz (70%) & cab blend, raises the bar on **08** (★★★★), recalls focused **07**. Retro floral label belies gravitas of rich melange of savoury dark fruit. Supple & flavoursome.

★★★★ **Three Graces** 09 first tasted since **06**, captures spirit of Regnault's eponymous painting depicted on the label. Barrel selection of cab, merlot & shiraz has layers of flavour in supple & streamlined elegance.

Merlot ★★★★ Restrained **09** has a 'graphite' mineral tone. Somewhat unknit in youth, time will reward greater fruit (& rating). **Shiraz** ⊞ ★★★★ Ripe & unashamedly New World styled **10** has brambly fruit & robust structure, afterglow favours hearty fare. — MW

Graham Beck Wines

Location: Franschhoek/Robertson ▪ Maps: Franschhoek & Robertson ▪ WO: Western Cape/Robertson/Coastal/
Stellenbosch/Paarl ▪ Est 1983 ▪ 1stB 1991 ▪ Robertson & Franschhoek: Tasting & sales Mon-Fri 9–5 Sat/Sun 10–4 ▪
Tasting fees: Classic is complimentary; Deluxe R50, waived on purchase of R200 or more; MCC R75; Master Class
R75 ▪ Closed Easter Fri & Dec 25 ▪ Owner(s) Graham Beck Enterprises ▪ Cellarmaster(s) Pieter Ferreira (Aug 1990)
& Erika Obermeyer (Jan 2005) ▪ Winemaker(s) Robertson: Pierre de Klerk (Oct 2010) ▪ Viticulturist(s) Leon
Dippenaar (consultant) ▪ 3,904ha/264ha (cab, pinot, shiraz, chard, sauv) ▪ 2,734t/200,000cs own label 52% red
48% white 2% rosé ▪ ISO 14001, BWI champion (Robertson), IPW, SABS 1841, WIETA ▪ PO Box 724 Robertson
6705/PO Box 134 Franschhoek 7690 ▪ cellar@grahambeckwines.co.za, market@grahambeckwines.co.za ▪
www.grahambeckwines.com ▪ Fhoek: S 33°52'56.2" E 019°1'27.2" Rbtson: S 33°48'14.95" E 019°48'1.41" ▪ T
+27 (0)23-626-1214, +27 (0)21-874-1258 ▪ F +27 (0)23-626-5164, +27 (0)21-874-1712

Geographical changes are occurring on the wine side of Graham Beck Enterprises
(three-pronged, with racehorse studs and hospitality) after the death in 2010 of its
visionary founder. Now owned by a family trust, GB has consolidated its assets and
divested itself of its Franschhoek winery. Final handover to another SA tycoon,
Johann Rupert (of neighbouring Anthonij Rupert Wines) happens mid 2012. Facilities are being expanded at GB-owned Steenberg in Constantia to handle premium
Graham Beck wines, directed by cellarmaster Erika Obermeyer, from fruit on GB's
Stellenbosch farms. GB's cellar in Robertson, with its stylish tasting room, will
increasingly emphasise its bubbly production (2011 saw the million-bottle mark
reached under cellarmaster Pieter 'Bubbles' Ferreira). Robertson terroir wines will
still be made here with winemaker Pierre de Klerk's help.

Icon Wines

★★★★★ **Ad Honorem** 07 *Grand vin* spicy & aromatic, noble cab-shiraz blend (72:28). Fruitcake with
blackcurrant edge, iodine minerality & silky tannins. Still selling, not revisited, as for next.

★★★★☆ **Cuvée Clive** Flagship of accomplished méthode cap classique sparkling range. 05 finely crafted,
with dense, profound minerality & richness courtesy fruit purity, 5 yrs on lees. Robertson chardonnay (80%) &
Firgrove pinot noir.

Ultra Premium range

★★★★ **Coffeestone Cabernet Sauvignon** Appealing cedar, pencil shaving notes to 07's pristine blackberry Stellenbosch fruit; taut tannin structure augurs well for future. 06 (★★★★☆) showed greater focus.

★★★★☆ **The Joshua** 08 (★★★★) co-fermented shiraz, 5% viognier. Engaging mix lavender & red berries,
sweet fruit & savoury tail; svelte tannins. 07 had a dark heart of black cherry, roast beef & mocha. WO Coastal.

★★★★☆ **The Ridge Syrah** From Robertson, 08 as expressive, opulent as smoky meat, pepper & fynbos 06.
Rich & spicy, with finesse & length. Drinking well now but with 3+ yrs to go. 07 skipped.

★★★★☆ **The William** Still available & not reassessed 08 blend cabernet (70%) & pinotage. Aristocratic,
ageworthy attention-seeker from Stellenbosch vines; mulberries & blackcurrants cloaked in satin tannins.

★★★★ **Lonehill Chardonnay** 🍃 Partially oak fermented/aged version. 10 (★★★★) less complex than
finely layered 09. Quiet, earthy whiffs; creamy lemon/lime flavours & lingering finish. WO Robertson.

★★★★☆ **Bowed Head Chenin Blanc** 🍃 Paarl grapes in precisely-oaked example. 10 (★★★★) melange
fruit; noticeable barrel-derived aromas/flavours for complexity, texture. 09 an exercise in concentration.

★★★★★ **Pheasants' Run Sauvignon Blanc** 🍃🍃 Vivacious follow-up to 10: 11 wafts lime, gooseberry, quince; has impressive concentration & a bracing jolt of minerality, leading to a juicy conclusion. Currently
nervy & finely-strung, it's structured for 3+ yrs cellaring. Blends Darling, Durbanville, Stellenbosch grapes.

Discontinued: **The Old Road Pinotage**, **The Andrew**.

Super Premium range

★★★★☆ **The Game Reserve Cabernet Sauvignon** Leafy 09 (★★★★) cabernet with attitude; angular,
austere but rewarding. Robertson fruit, as for more powerful, expressive maiden 08; not revisited.

★★★★ **Cabernet Sauvignon** ✓ Herb & dust undertones to 08's voluptuous blackberry core; impressively
dry with firm tannin handshake. Follows in footsteps of muscular 08; also from Stellenbosch.

★★★★ **The Game Reserve Chenin Blanc** 🍃🍃 10 (★★★★) a contradiction: barely-there nose, concentrated & subtly oaked palate. Complete & balanced 09 delivered on both fronts. Paarl fruit.

Merlot ★★★★ Tasted last edition, fresh minty notes, solid but supple shape & texture in 08; 15% cab franc
added extra leafiness. **Pinotage** 🍃🍃 ★★★★ Savoury tinges on 10 recall pinot noir ancestry. Easy-drinking
style: ebullient plummy fruit reined in by friendly tannins. WO Coastal. **Shiraz** ★★★ Warm, spicy mulberry hints

in unassuming **08** from Stellenbosch roughed up by slightly grainy end. **Chardonnay** ✓ 🖹 ⬚ ★★★★ Step up for **10** ex Robertson. Vanilla, lemon curd nuances; mouth-filling lime flavours marry with sympathetic oak detail & lengthy lees-ageing, refreshing acidity. Finer than generous **09** (★★★). **Sauvignon Blanc** ✓ 🖹 ⬚ ★★★★ **11** raises the bar on nettly **10** (★★★) with intensity & length: green pepper/herb accents, crackling acidity & dusty pebble farewell courtesy Darling, Durbanville fruit. **Viognier** 🖹 ⬚ ★★★ Oak far more in play on peach kernel **10** than gently-brushed **09**; the former also borders on austere, not a character typical of this variety. Robertson grapes.

Chalkboard range NEW

★★★★★ **Series #3 Cabernet Sauvignon** Regal **07** a study in concentration, elegance & power. Stern but unobtrusive tannins enclose blackcurrant-toned Rubenesque curves, promise long life. Stellenbosch fruit.

★★★★ **Series # 4 Shiraz** Like #2 sibling **08** from Paarl, as fruit-packed & approachable but quieter & smoother with greater elegance & complexity.

★★★★☆ **Series #1 Sauvignon Blanc-Chenin Blanc-Viognier** ✓ Serious **09** with 85% sauvignon; varieties barrel-fermented separately, aged 9 months. Commanding presence, crackling acidity; oak well judged for weight & structure - not for flavour. WO Coastal.

Series # 2 Shiraz ★★★★ Accessible ambassador for the variety, Paarl vineyards. **07** smoky & succulent, shot through with feisty acidity that extends the finish, enlivens the palate.

Premium range

> **Pinno** ☺ ⬚ ★★★ Cheerful quick-sip **10** plum-cake flavoured pinotage with nudge of espresso. **Rosé** ☺ 🖹 ⬚ ★★★ Charming **11** ideal al fresco sipper or picnic companion: crisp, fruitful, dry. **Waterside Chardonnay** ☺ 🖹 ⬚ ★★★ Exuberant unoaked sipping from Robertson vineyards. **11** floral, apple & lemon melange; lightish 12% alc.

Shiraz-Cabernet Sauvignon 🖹 ⬚ This, **Shiraz-Viognier** & **Chardonnay-Viognier** for export only. Not reviewed. **Railroad Red** 🖹 ★★★ Stalwart juicy favourite; 6-way blend. Sample **09** bouncy & fresh, has cranberry highlights & sweet vanilla thanks to portion US oak.

Méthode Cap Classique range

★★★★ **Brut** ✓ The house's mainstay **NV**, latest slightly more pinot noir (sweet strawberries) than chardonnay (lemon acidity). Bitingly dry with persistent fine bead & brioche richness.

★★★★☆ **Brut Blanc de Blancs** Delicious clove & pear, hazelnut praline flavours in elegant **08** (★★★★) from Robertson; unusually soft mouthfeel for the style but, like **07**, richness & delicate mousse underscore class.

★★★★ **Brut Zero** NEW Chardonnay, 15% pinot in impressive **05** disgorged after 5 years on lees. Subtle, pure & bone-dry with fragile oystershell nuances, demonstrating cellarmaster's light touch. Only in best yrs.

★★★★ **Brut Rosé** Stylish **09** 82% pinot noir, chardonnay co-fermented ('a first for South Africa'). Palest onionskin hue, tiny bubbles & strawberry/cherry vivacity.

★★★★ **Brut Rosé** Cherry & Karoo dust on poised **NV** bubbly. Latest bottling 51:49 chardonnay-pinot noir; explosive mousse, intensely savoury & generous finish. For those who like to indulge themselves.

Bliss Demi Sec ★★★★ Latest **NV** same varietal make-up as Brut, 38g/l sugar; step up on previous (★★★). Charming barley-sugar scents, creamy strawberry-mousse, fresh & slightly frivolous for immediate consumption.

Dessert Wines

★★★★ **Rhona Muscadel** Hedonistic muscat fruit on grippy spirit in **08**, first since **04**. Poised & elegant, with rich marmalade finish. Still selling, not retasted, as for following.

Cape LBV ★★★★ From Stellenbosch tinta. **07** plum pudding fruit, sturdy tannins; at 90g/l sugar, one of drier versions. — Panel

Grande Provence Heritage Wine Estate 

Location/map: Franschhoek ▪ WO: Franschhoek/Western Cape ▪ Est 1694 ▪ 1stB 2004 ▪ Tasting & sales Mon-Sat 10-6 (Apr-Oct) & 10-7 (Nov-Mar); Sun 10-6 ▪ Fee R20/4 wines, R40/7 wines, R80/food & wine pairing ▪ Cellar tours Mon-Fri 11 & 3 Sat/Sun by appt ▪ Restaurant & Owners Cottage guest house/villa (see Restaurants & Accommodation sections) ▪ Tour groups ▪ Gift shop ▪ Farm produce ▪ Conferences ▪ Art gallery ▪ Harvest festival ▪ Owner(s) Dutch & Belgium Consortium ▪ Cellarmaster(s) Jaco Marais (Nov 2003) ▪ Winemaker(s) Jaco Marais ▪ Viticulturist(s) Jaco Marais (Jun 2005) ▪ 32ha/22ha (cab, merlot, chard, sauv) ▪ 120t/5,000cs own label 60% red

40% white ▪ PO Box 102 Franschhoek 7690 ▪ enquiries@grandeprovence.co.za ▪ www.grandeprovence.co.za ▪ S 33° 53' 57.6" E 19° 06' 10.5" ▪ T +27 (0)21-876-8600 ▪ F +27 (0)21-876-8601

Part of the tourist heartland of Franschhoek, with restaurant and visitor facilities of the highest order, this pretty estate beckons travellers entering and leaving the village. They've launched their über-premium Estate blend in its imposing livery, and next they'll unveil a méthode cap classique sparkling. Cellarmaster/viticulturist Jaco Marais has taken overall control of production for both this range and (separately listed) sister brand, Angels Tears.

Premier range

★★★★ **Pinot Noir** NEW 🍷 Fruit & fragrant aromatics are allowed to dominate in laudable maiden **09**, from own vines. Rare substance from this variety & area, with judicious, modest barrel-oaking.

★★★★ **Shiraz** 🍷 Finely structured **07** raised the bar on **06** (★★★★) last edition. Lithe & elegant Rhône style from Stellenbosch grapes.

★★★★☆ **The Grande Provence** NEW Ambitiously conceived (& priced) debut flagship, **06** sets a new standard for the producer. Merlot-cab blend with power & grace; layered fruit, rich tannins & long, lingering finish. Retains signature minty hints.

★★★★ **Chardonnay** 🍷 Closely modelled on big-bodied, oaky **09**, current **10** shows youth, but should soften & mellow with time. Satisfying, grippy citrus fruit lingers to long, elegant finish.

★★★★ **Chenin Blanc-Viognier** NEW ✓🍷 Elegant, reserved newcomer in minerally, less-oaked style à la Swartland. **10** impressive texture & weight, lingering finish.

Cabernet Sauvignon 🍷 ★★★★ Familiar leafy-minty fruit cordial aromas on **08**, typical of house style. Brash & youthful, may integrate with time. **Sauvignon Blanc** 🍷 ★★★☆ Consistent, understated house style is elegant, with balance & weight. Durbanville fruit. **11** shows class in restraint. — GdB

Grand Mousseux

Enduring anytime, anywhere carbonated budget bubbly by Distell.

Vin Doux ★★ Evergreen sweet **NV** offers frothy ripe-apple fruit flavour. — Panel

Grangehurst

Location: Somerset West ▪ Map: Helderberg ▪ WO: Stellenbosch ▪ Est/1stB 1992 ▪ Tasting & sales Mon-Fri 9–4 Sat/Sun 10-3 ▪ Fee charged for group tastings depends on wines being presented ▪ Closed Easter Fri-Mon, Dec 25/25 & Jan 1 ▪ Self-catering guest cottages ▪ Owner(s) Grangehurst Winery (Pty) Ltd ▪ Cellarmaster(s) Jeremy Walker (Jan 1992) ▪ Winemaker(s) Jeremy Walker (Jan 1992), with Gladys Brown (Jan 2002) ▪ Viticulturist(s) Gary Probert (2008, consultant) ▪ ±13ha/6ha own (cab) + 8ha bought in grapes (merlot, p verdot, ptage, shiraz) ▪ 80t/5,500cs own label 90% red 10% rosé + 900cs for clients ▪ Brands for clients: Auslese (Aubergine Restaurant), Woolworths ▪ PO Box 206 Stellenbosch 7599 ▪ winery@grangehurst.co.za ▪ www.grangehurst.co.za ▪ S 34° 01' 02.9" E 018° 49' 50.5" ▪ T +27 (0)21-855-3625 ▪ F +27 (0)21-855-2143

Only cabernet sauvignon grows on this Helderberg property; other grapes are sourced from elsewhere in Stellenbosch. Sadly, a substantial block of bushvines on the edge of Stellenbosch town had to be uprooted, nature and man providing two reasons for this. Strong spring winds made the creation of decent shaped vines impossible; economically, it was unviable to convert to trellised vines, as human neighbours find the poles, vines (for firewood) and fruit too tempting! Also tempting in their traditional, classic style, Grangehurst wines are always among the most mature on release. 'We aim for elegance, structure and good evolution, so the second glass tastes better than the first, and the third better than the second', explains Jeremy Walker.

Grangehurst range

★★★★ **Cabernet Sauvignon Reserve** After charming **05**, classic **06** (★★★★★) showed bold ripe tannins, delicate blackcurrant fruit with extended finish. Like next wine, tasted last year.

★★★★ **Pinotage** Pinot noir parentage clear in complexity of **03** (★★★★★). Like **02**, 12% cab.

★★★★ **Cabernet Sauvignon-Merlot** Increased merlot on **05** (now 32%) lends fleshier, more open texture to lighter-weight fruit. Poised & balanced for lovely current drinking. No **04**. **03** (★★★★★).

★★★★☆ **Grangehurst** Last tasted was cab-led **05** - complex, mineral & long. Still available.

★★★★ **Nikela** **05** (no **04**) announced by pinotage's sweet raspberry scent. Usual partners cab, shiraz & merlot imbue savouriness, some richness but lacks depth of **03** (★★★★). Best over next year/2.

★★★★☆ **Shiraz-Cabernet Sauvignon Reserve** Complex cassis & red pepper spice, leather & earthy tobacco notes on **05** (★★★★) 63/35 blend. First since finer **03**. Like next wine, not retasted.

★★★★ **Cape Rosé Blend** 🍴 Crisp & light-bodied **09**, from cab + 4 others, showing real personality.

Reserve Cape Blend In abeyance; await new release. — AL

■ **Greenacres Fine Wines** see Jacob's Quest Wines
■ **Greendale** see Withington
■ **Green Duck** see Avondale Bio-LOGIC & Organic Wines
■ **Greenfield Organic** see Origin Wine
■ **Griekwaland West Co-op** see Douglas Wine Cellar
■ **Groblershoop** see Orange River Wine Cellars

Groenland

Location/map/WO: Stellenbosch ▪ Est 1932 ▪ 1stB 1997 ▪ Tasting & sales Mon-Fri 10–4 Sat 10–1 ▪ Fee R10pp for groups of 6+ ▪ Closed Easter Fri/Sun & Dec 25 ▪ Cellar tours by appt ▪ BYO picnic by appt ▪ Conference/function venue (20-60 pax) ▪ Owner(s) Kosie Steenkamp ▪ Cellarmaster(s) Kosie Steenkamp (Feb 1975) ▪ Winemaker(s) Kosie Steenkamp (Feb 1975), with Piet Steenkamp (Jan 2001) ▪ Viticulturist(s) Piet Steenkamp (Jan 2001) ▪ 188ha/152ha (cab, merlot, ptage, shiraz, chenin, sauv) ▪ 1,500t/±6,500cs own label 75% red 25% white ▪ BEE level 3, BWI, IPW ▪ PO Box 4 Kuils River 7579 ▪ steenkamp@groenland.co.za ▪ www.groenland.co.za ▪ S 33° 53′ 48.9″ E 018° 44′5.3″ ▪ **T +27 (0)21-903-8203** ▪ F +27 (0)21-903-0250/+27 (0)86-571-4969

Bottelary Hills father and son winegrowers Kosie and Piet Steenkamp aim for fruity, delicate and soft wines. Accolades for the quality of their merlot persuaded them to age the 2009 vintage in 100% new barrels for bottling under the Premium label. Kosie is proud to have achieved Level 3 BEE status, and aims to reach L2 this year. Most of all, Kosie is delighted that Piet's 'dedication and hard work' are set to carry the venture into the future.

Premium range

★★★★ **Antoinette Marié** ✓ **08** equal blend shiraz, cab, merlot; more extract & depth, powerful & enhanced by all-new oak. Concentrated fruit shows more modern approach vs classic-style Groenland range.

Cabernet Sauvignon ★★★ **08** shows riper vintage, vanilla enhancement (from year new French oak), modern styling with fruit-forward texture. **Merlot** NEW ★★★ **09** exudes varietal minty fruit, chocolate/mocha farewell; balanced & juicy drinkability. **Shiraz** ✓ ★★★★ **08** now American oak (100% new), absorbs ripeness of vintage, rich juicy supple tannins, enjoy with hearty meals.

Classic range

Sauvignon Blanc 😊 🍴 ★★★ **11** ripe tropical style, gentle & crisp.

Cabernet Sauvignon ✓ ★★★★ **07** juicy & elegant, slightly dusty tones. Balanced & supple supportive structure. **Shiraz** ✓ ★★★★ Tighter **07**, shows restraint & cool tones with savoury, dusty overlay; food style. **Antoinette Marié** ✓ ★★★★ **08** half shiraz & equal cab/merlot; ripe, with juicy exuberance, pliable tannins, so easy to drink! **Chenin Blanc** ★★★ Ripe, plump **11**, apple & marzipan tones, friendly summer quaffer. — MW

Groot Constantia Estate

Location/WO: Constantia ▪ Map: Cape Peninsula ▪ Est 1685 ▪ 1stB 1688 ▪ Tasting & sales daily 9–6 (Oct-Apr) & 9–5 (May-Sep) ▪ Fee R25, R33 incl glass, R38 tasting & tour ▪ Closed Easter Fri, Dec 25 & Jan 1 ▪ Cellar tours 10–4 on the hour, every hour ▪ Simon's at Groot Constantia Restaurant; Jonkershuis Restaurant ▪ Facilities for children ▪ Tour groups ▪ Gifts ▪ Farm produce ▪ Conferences ▪ Walks/hikes ▪ Conservation area ▪ Manor House, historic buildings & orientation centre ▪ Owner(s) Groot Constantia Trust NPC RF ▪ Winemaker(s) Boela Gerber (Jan 2001), with Daniel Keulder (Sep 2009) ▪ Viticulturist(s) Andrew Teubes (2009) ▪ 170ha/±90ha (cab, ptage, shiraz, sauv) ▪ 493t/ 34,000cs ▪ Private Bag X1 Constantia 7848 ▪ enquiries@grootconstantia.co.za ▪ www.grootconstantia.co.za ▪ S 34° 1′36.5″ E 018° 25′27.3″ ▪ **T +27 (0)21-794-5128** ▪ F +27 (0)21-794-1999

The grand-daddy of them all, Governor Simon van der Stel's estate, circa 1685, is content to leave innovation to the others, concentrating instead on its enviable tradition and heritage. This beautiful historic icon deserves a visit in its own right, for the fine Cape Dutch homestead. Change has come to the vineyards, though, which are constantly being assessed and fine-tuned; 40ha have been replanted in the ten years of winemaker Boela Gerber's stewardship. The results can be judged by their wines' relentless march into red ink. After the heady tourist rush of World Cup 2010, the tasting room is in line for an upgrade this year to maintain focus on the important visitor trade.

Gouverneurs range

★★★★☆ **Reserve Red** Near-iconic flag-bearer. Bordeaux blend fronted by cabs sauvignon & franc. Ripe, voluptuous **09** lives up to vintage expectations. Beautifully wrought, with weight & complexity in perfect balance. Cellar-treasure for very special occasions.

★★★★☆ **Chardonnay** 🥂 Showy, confident New-World expression of variety, **10** follows lofty standards of previous. Rich, buttery & full, yet layered & complex, demands attention. Underlines area's reputation for great cool-climate whites.

★★★★ **Sauvignon Blanc** 🥂 Fragrant & flavoursome **10**, welcome change in style. Elegance above power, depth & finesse in place of raw aromatic force. Whole-bottle enjoyment from obviously cool-climate vines.

★★★★☆ **Reserve White** Classy, polished example of a Constantia speciality: semillon-dominated Bordeaux-style blend. **10** has robust varietal character, shaped & enriched by precise oak regimen. Understated & poised, with lingering finish.

Shiraz Await next.

Groot Constantia range

★★★★☆ **Sauvignon Blanc** 🥂 Youthful, vibrant **11** still unsettled, but showing spicy promise. Intensely aromatic, with shades of citrus & dusty pebbles. Impressive weight & substance with lingering finish; an exercise in force with control.

★★★★ **Grand Constance** Gorgeous dessert from muscat de Frontignan, partly sun-dried, always zesty, balanced. Exceptional **08** (★★★★★), complex, engaging, delicate yet with presence. More complexity than **07**. **Cabernet Sauvignon** ★★★★ Classically formed **09** reflects vintage's ripeness after lighter **08** (★★★☆). Deep & dark, with stately bearing, enticing liquorice & tealeaf notes. Should improve further with cellaring. **Merlot** ★★★★ Generously ripe, meaty **09** a step up from **08** (★★★☆). Now from own vines, shows finely focused structure & elegance. **Pinotage** New vintage missed our deadline. **Shiraz** ★★★★ Smoky, meaty, big-boned **09** is cloaked in chalky tannins. Should emerge with cellaring, already shows promising red berry fruit & spiciness. Riper, richer than **07** (★★★★). **Constantia Rood** ★★★ House standard 6-way blend, **09** shows little distinctive style. **Blanc de Noir** 🥂 ★★★ Previewed **11** merlot-cab blend is light, dry, & refreshing, with charming strawberry fruit. Pretty pale coral hue. **Semillon-Sauvignon Blanc** ★★★★ **10** blend previously had intense white pepper, grass whiffs, vivacious acidity & gentle fruit-sweet lift. **Méthode Cap Classique** ★★★★ First since **04** (★★★★), champagne-method sparkling **07** now 100% chardonnay, far more focussed & refined. Lively bead, appealing baked fruit with creamy texture. Tiny 200 case production. **Port** ★★★★ Enticing liquorice, chocolate & sweet cherry fruitiness on **09**, repositioned from 'Ruby'. Deeper, fuller than last. — GdB

■ **Grootdrink** see Orange River Wine Cellars
■ **Groot Eiland** see uniWines Marketing

Groote Post Vineyards

Location: Darling ▪ Map: Durbanville, Philadelphia & Darling ▪ WO: Darling/Coastal ▪ 1stB 1999 ▪ Tasting, sales & cellar tours Mon-Fri 9–5 Sat/Sun 10–4 ▪ Fee R20 for groups of 10+ ▪ Closed Easter Fri, Dec 25 & Jan 1 ▪ Hilda's Kitchen open for lunch Wed-Sun, booking essential ▪ Facilities for children ▪ BYO picnic ▪ Conference facilities ▪ Walks/hikes ▪ Conservation area & bird hide ▪ Owner(s) Peter & Nicholas Pentz ▪ Winemaker(s) Lukas Wentzel (Nov 2000) ▪ Viticulturist(s) Jannie de Clerk (1999), advised by Johan Pienaar ▪ 4,000ha/107ha (cabs s/f, merlot, pinot, shiraz, chard, riesling, sauv, sem) ▪ 580t/32,000cs own label ▪ Brands for clients: Woolworths ▪ PO Box 103 Darling 7345 ▪ wine@grootepost.co.za ▪ www.grootepost.com ▪ S 33° 29'0.5" E 018° 24'35.0" ▪ **T +27 (0)22-492-2825** ▪ F +27 (0)22-492-2693

It might be off the beaten track, but the Pentz family has made sure there's plenty to do once you're here. Having 4,000ha to play with allows space for game drives, bird viewing from the hide, walks through the conservation area (they're BWI members), followed by a lunch made from freshly sourced local ingredients, at Hilda's Kitchen. None of this crowds the vineyards or winemaking, where the quest to continually upgrade quality continues. The riesling style has changed to provide one off-dry wine in a dry range, and viticultural improvements are impacting on other varieties. The well-priced Old Man's range, named after patriarch Peter who is still involved in blending, has grown apace and received a Méthode Cap Classique bubbly this year, because that's another style he likes to drink!

The Reserve range

★★★★ **Pinot Noir** Previewed **09**, now bottled, lost none of its charm or elegance & refinement but quite restrained, has a delicacy that suggests earlier drinking rather than keeping.

★★★★ **Wooded Chardonnay** Last ed **09** (★★★★★) was more intense than **08**; minerality added interest to spicy richness & impressive depth. Sympathetic oak detail: 7 mths Fr, 50% new.

★★★★ **Sauvignon Blanc Reserve** ⏳ Selection of top vineyard blocks, last **10** was mineral with green-gage fruit, racy saline conclusion. Should improve year/2 in bottle.

The Groote Post range

★★★★ **Unwooded Chardonnay** ⏳ Last-tasted **10** preview was still oxidative in style, but presented touch more fruit than **09**. Lovely richness from 3 months lees-ageing.

★★★★ **Chenin Blanc** ✓ 📋 ⏳ A fresh rather than opulent style & **11** does it beautifully. Fruit essence, pineapple & melon, is shot through with racy acidity, adding a vital spark & length. WO Coastal.

★★★★ **Riesling** ✓ ⏳ Retasted **10** even more aromatic than last year's preview; preserved quince & citrus peel, gingerbeer, mouthwateringly tempting. 12g/l sugar meets its match in brisk acidity, tastes almost dry.

★★★★ **Sauvignon Blanc** ✓ 📋 ⏳ Staying true to its terroir, **11** shows passionfruit & mineral notes, streamlined & pure, lipsmackingly delicious on its own or with food.

Merlot ⏳ ★★★ Lush & full-ripe (15.6% alc), **10**'s plum & white pepper tones have gentle oak support for earlier enjoyment. **Shiraz** ✓ ★★★★★ Finished wine **09** confirms preview's rating; plush mulberries, an array of spices, sweet & savoury plus a prosciutto tone that prepares the tastebuds for food. Svelte, polished, totally delicious. **08** (★★★★) was less ripe, expressive. **Noble Late Harvest** Occasional release.

The Old Man's Blend range

★★★★ **The Old Man's Blend Red** ✓ 📋 ⏳ For early drinking but not simple. Cab-led Bordeaux blend **10** has more restrained oak than other reds here, lovely blackcurrant & peppery spice.

★★★★ **The Old Man's Blend White** ✓ 📋 ⏳ Designed to please, well put together & balanced **11**'s litchi & pear tones come from sauvignon, body from chenin, semillon. Zesty, delicious. This, Red, WO Coastal.

The Old Man's Sparkle Brut Rosé Méthode Cap Classique ★★★ Pink-hued & fruity from majority merlot, latest **NV** has all the zinging freshness you look for in an anytime sparkler. — CR

Groot Parys Estate

Location/WO: Paarl ▪ Map: Paarl & Wellington ▪ Est 1699 ▪ 1stB 1709 ▪ Tasting & sales by appt ▪ Owner(s) Eric Verhaak, Mariëtte Ras, Peter Ras ▪ Winemaker(s) JD Rossouw, with Heidi Dietstein ▪ Viticulturist(s) Gawie Kriel (consultant) ▪ 81ha/45ha (ptage, ruby cab, chard, chenin, cbard) ▪ 105t 90% white 10% rosé ▪ Debio internationally certified organic ▪ PO Box 82 Huguenot 7645 ▪ grootparys@wam.co.za ▪ www.grootparys.co.za ▪ S 33° 44'48.0" E 018° 58'41.6" ▪ **T +27 (0)21-873-5818**

Now that Dutch co-owner Mariëtte Ras' dream of going totally organic has been realised, demand is taking off in this Paarl property's European markets, and she feels it's all coming together rather nicely. The wines, made with minimal sulphur and minimal interference of any kind, are light and fresh in style - the exception being the unctuous Straw Wine made from gnarled 30-year-old chenin bushvines.

Die Tweede Droom range

★★★★ **Chenin Blanc Wooded Wild Yeast** ⏳ Previously tasted **09** fermented in barrel with natural yeast; zesty acid concealed fruit, showed textured, stony minerality.

★★★★ **Straw Wine** ⏳ Was 'Vin de Paille'. Bronze **10** from air-dried, oaked chenin sweet & delightful. Sufficient acidity to balance viscosity, though not quite as poised as **09**. Savoury, flavourful conclusion.

Rosé NEW 📋 ⏳ ★★ Bone-dry, light **11** a crisp pink quaffer from ruby cab. **Chardonnay Wooded Wild Yeast** ★★★★ Steely, oaked **09** previously showed delightful citrus flavours, structured by crunchy acidity & line of minerality. **Chardonnay Unwooded** NEW 📋 ⏳ ★★★ Pear-drop **11** offers plenty of flavour, but needs to settle. **Chenin Blanc Unwooded** 📋 ⏳ ★★★ Tropical **11** uncomplicated & racily fresh. **Chenin Blanc Unwooded Wild Yeast** 📋 ⏳ ★★★ Unpretentious, light **11** offers zesty chenin acidity & freshness. All wines from this vintage tasted as pre-bottling samples. — IM

Groupe LFE South Africa

Location: Somerset West ▪ WO: Western Cape/Swartland/Stellenbosch ▪ Est/1stB 2006 ▪ Closed to public ▪ Owner(s) Groupe LFE Netherlands ▪ Cellarmaster(s) Malcolm Human & Kobus Rossouw (consultant) ▪ 600,000cs own label 60% red 35% white 5% rosé ▪ Fairtrade ▪ PO Box 88 Somerset Mall 7137 ▪ malcolm@groupelfe.co.za ▪ www.groupelfe.co.za ▪ T +27 (0)21-850-0160 ▪ F +27 (0)21-851-3578

'People like that style, especially on pinotage,' says consultant winemaker Kobus Rossouw of the new 'coffee-style' Expresso Mokka Pinotage, which is redolent of espresso and chocolate, and particularly popular in Finland and Sweden. The wine is among a number of new listings in Europe for the 'proudly South African' arm of Netherlands-based Groupe LFE.

Berghuis range

Cabernet Sauvignon 🍽 📖 ★★ Undemanding ripe-fruited **10**, lightly oaked. Stellenbosch WOs for these. **Pinotage Rosé** 🍽 📖 ★★ **10** had delicate strawberry notes, satisfactory dry end last edition. **Chenin Blanc** 🍽 📖 ★★ Light-textured **11**, peachy lunchtime white.

Centennial 5 Barrel Reserve range

Shiraz ★★★ Vibrant **08** previously had red berries & savoury nuances; ripe creamy tannins for early enjoyment.

Elephantasy range

Big Ears Dry Red Await new, as for **Long Nose Gewürztraminer**. **Short Tail Rosé** 🍽 📖 ★★ **11** perky dry rosé, light strawberry summer sipper. **Long Nose Dry White** 🍽 📖 ★★ **11** light easy-drinker from chenin, with intriguing dusty herb hint.

Groupe LFE South Africa range

Grâce Blanche Natural Sweet 🍽 📖 ★★★ Juicy, sweet & easy-to-drink **10** from chenin, offers ripe apricot & lime. Discontinued: **Tonight Sweet Dreams**.

Kaaps Geskenk range

Cape Red NEW 🍽 📖 ★ **10** earthy red berries in uncomplicated braai red. **Cape Rosé** 🍽 📖 ★★ **11** dry, strawberry-toned lunchtime sipper. **Cape White** 🍽 📖 ★★ **11** light textured picnic partner from chenin.

Klein Kasteelberg Private Bin range NEW

Merlot 🍽 📖 ★★ Ripe & dark berried, hint of chocolate on **10**. WO Swartland, as all these. **Pinotage** 🍽 📖 ★★★ Fresh mulberry-toned, **10** juicy & accessible. **Expresso Mokka Pinotage** Not reviewed. **Shiraz Rosé** 🍽 📖 Not tasted. **Chardonnay** 🍽 📖 ★★ Brisk & fresh **10** with lemon/lime twist. **Secco** ★★★ Bouncy peach-toned **NV**, dry & lightly spritzy

Klein Kasteelberg range

Merlot 🍽 📖 ★★ **10** plum & milk chocolate on easy quaffer. Swartland WO, as all these. **Pinotage** 🍽 📖 ★★ Plum, prune & pepper combo in **10**, enough tannins for hearty fare. **Shiraz Rosé** 🍽 📖 ★★ Fresh & dry **10** with candyfloss flavour. **Chardonnay** 🍽 📖 ★★★ Unwooded **10**, pleasant melon & marmalade with nutty overlay. **Chenin Blanc** 🍽 📖 ★★★ **10** softly dry & fresh cling peach-toned thirst quencher.

Songloed range

Pinotage-Ruby Cabernet ★★ **10**, ripe & dark-berried, nice fruity mouthful. **Shiraz-Merlot** 🍽 📖 ★★★ Earthy & savoury intro, followed by mulberry & black cherry in **10**. **Shiraz-Merlot Rosé** 🍽 📖 ★★ Now bottled, coral pink **10** is fresh & crisp with hints of spicy strawberry. **Colombar-Chardonnay** ★★ Now bottled, accessible **10** crisp with fresh summer fruit. **Chenin Blanc-Viognier** Not ready at press time. — DB

Grünberger

Frankish 'bocksbeutel' flagons for most of these are a nod to the German oenologist who developed the Grünberger brand for what is now Distell in 1953.

Spritziger 🍽 ★★ **10** is a spritzy, off-dry yet tartly bracing white from chenin. WO W Cape for all. **Spritziger Rosé** ★★ Pinotage supplies the rouge for slightly spritzy **11**, sweeter & fuller than previous, with tangy berry edge. **Rosenlese** ★★ Sweetly blushing rosé, **11** is candyfloss light, low in alc, quaffable. **Freudenlese** ★★ Sweet white, with spicy gewürztraminer showing through on low-alc, no-frills **11**. — Panel

Grundheim Wines

Location: Oudtshoorn ▪ Map: Klein Karoo & Garden Route ▪ Est/1stB 1995 ▪ Tasting & sales Mon-Fri 9-5 Sat 9-1 ▪ Fee R15 for groups of 10+ ▪ Closed Easter Fri/Sun, Dec 25 & Jan 1 ▪ Owner(s) Danie Grundling ▪ Winemaker(s) Dys Grundling (1997) ▪ 25ha (cinsaut, muscadel r/w, ruby cab, tinta, touriga, cbard, hanepoot, palomino) ▪ 360t/ 10,000L own label 100% fortified ▪ PO Box 400 Oudtshoorn 6620 ▪ grundheim@absamail.co.za ▪ S 33° 37' 40.1" E 022° 3' 54.6" ▪ **T +27 (0)44-272-6927** ▪ F +27 (0)86-616-6311

'Old World' is their style and they're sticking to it, say the Grundling family, owners of Sandkoppies vineyards near Oudtshoorn and custodians of Grundheim, Danie se Withond and Happy Cow brands. 'Anyway,' comments manager Elana Grundling, 'our cellar won't allow us to change.' Said facility houses an antique copper potstill, used for their extensive range of brandies, liqueurs and fortifieds.

★★★★ **Red Jerepiko** Interesting NV from touriga & pinotage; mid-2010 had stewed fruit flavours, substantial sugar balanced by crisp acidity, punchy alc. Not revisited, nor were Ruby, Vintage & Late Bottled.

★★★★ **Late Bottled Vintage** 05 winter-warming port-style from touriga; complex, gripping, with attractive fiery heart (20.5% alc).

Red Muscadel ★★★ Latest NV bottling of fortified firesider shade off the mark, needs more acidity to cope with the nutty/spicy richness, lower invigorating alc. **White Muscadel** ★★★ Nutty development on understated NV fortified; faint floral notes, little of the complexity usually delivered by this style. **Cape Ruby Port** ★★★ Easy-drinking NV from touriga, spiced plum jam, balanced finish. **Cape Vintage Port** ★★★★ Bit soft for style, but **09** good dense fruit from touriga, layered with chocolate. Discontinued: **White Muscadel Reserve**. — Panel

■ **G Spot** *see* United Nations of Wine

Guardian Peak Wines

Location/map: Stellenbosch ▪ WO: Western Cape/Stellenbosch/Piekenierskloof/Wellington ▪ Est 1998 ▪ 1stB 2000 ▪ Tasting & sales Mon-Sat 9-5 ▪ Fee R30 ▪ Closed Easter Fri/Sun, Dec 25 & Jan 1 ▪ Guardian Peak Restaurant (see Restaurants section) ▪ Owner(s) Jean Engelbrecht ▪ Winemaker(s) Philip van Staden (Jan 2009), with Jacques Maree (Jan 2009) ▪ Viticulturist(s) Dirkie Mouton (Jun 2010) ▪ 25,000cs own label 100% red ▪ Brands for clients: Pick's Pick ▪ IPW ▪ PO Box 473 Stellenbosch 7599 ▪ info@guardianpeak.com ▪ www.guardianpeak.com ▪ S 34° 0' 44.31" E 018° 50' 33.22" ▪ **T +27 (0)21-881-3899** ▪ F +27 (0)21-881-3000

They're reducing their impact on the environment in vineyards supplying Guardian Peak – cutting the amount of herbicides and insecticides for example, and composting winery and garden waste. The bottles that the wine goes into, however, are still in a less environment-friendly massive style! Perhaps they need to be to contain the wine from this all-red producer (owned by Jean Engelbrecht of another all-red winery, Rust en Vrede) - it is mostly pretty big itself, tending to tasty blockbusterism: ripe, powerful and often with a definite sweetness. The aim is to 'introduce more people to the fascinating lifestyle and culture of wine'.

★★★★ **Lapa Cabernet Sauvignon** 09 brash but not brusque; sweet though slightly herbal notes add freshness to massive 15.4% alc & generous all-new oak. Hints of stewed fruit, crème caramel evolving. WO Stbosch.

★★★★ **SMG** Polished & harmonious, delicate aromatic 09 (★★★★). Like 08, includes some grenache. Raisiny notes from extreme ripeness (15+% alc). From Stellenbosch, Piekenierskloof.

★★★★ **Frontier** ✓ 🍴 📖 **10** cab/shiraz/merlot combo harmoniously assembled. Savoury, persistent, polished & plush, juicy yet restrained. Almost dry.

★★★★ **Tannat-Malbec** Reverses name in 09 for 60% tannat. Sappy yet firm, with juicy edge. Bold, but more classic & dry than some here, grippy & savoury. Wellington/Stellenbosch fruit, plenty of oak (60% new).

Merlot ✓ 🍴 📖 ★★★★ **10** made for instant gratification: attractive, clean fruit, lightly oaked, just-dry. Undemanding but not entirely simple. **Shiraz** ✓ 📖 📖 ★★★★ **10** seductive Xmas pudding aromas, vanilla, cloves; big 14.7% alc & evident sugar sweetness provide velvety finish. — MF

■ **Guinea Fowl** *see* Saxenburg
■ **Guru** *see* Hoopenburg Wines
■ **Gwendolyn** *see* Saxenburg
■ **Hagelsberg** *see* Middelvlei Estate
■ **Hakuna Matata** *see* Remhoogte Wine Estate

Halala Afrika/Lula Afrika

These wines, produced by Rudera, are in the easy-drinking mould, offering purity and freshness. The name means 'Celebrate Africa' and evokes the spirit of sunny warmth from the fertile African soils. The wines are for export only.

Shiraz 🗒 ★★★★ Dark berries hint at full ripeness on **10** tasted ex-barrel. Palate shows off savoury notes over medium body with fine tannins. **Chenin Blanc** 🗒 ★★★ Apple fresh notes, with zesty lime entry on **11**, ex-tank. Soft tropically fruited palate ends crisp & assertively dry. — JP

Hamilton Russell Vineyards

Location: Hermanus ▪ Map: Elgin, Walker Bay & Bot River ▪ WO: Hemel-en-Aarde Valley ▪ Est 1975 ▪ 1stB 1981 ▪ Tasting & sales Mon-Fri 9–5 Sat 9–1 ▪ Closed Easter Fri/Mon, Dec 26 & Jan 1 ▪ Tours by appt ▪ Fynbos reserve & 2 wetlands ▪ Owner(s) Anthony Hamilton Russell ▪ Winemaker(s) Hannes Storm (2004) ▪ Viticulturist(s) Johan Montgomery (2005) ▪ 170ha/52ha (pinot, chard) ▪ 9,352cs own label 50% red 50% white ▪ PO Box 158 Hermanus 7200 ▪ hrv@hermanus.co.za ▪ www.hamiltonrussellvineyards.com ▪ S 34° 23'23.0" E 019° 14'30.6" ▪ **T +27 (0)28-312-3595** ▪ F +27 (0)28-312-1797

'No reserves, no second labels, just two exceptional estate-grown wines.' This comment by owner proprietor Anthony Hamilton Russell could be an advertising slogan, especially given his father and founder of the property, Tim, was in that game. But it isn't, it's a promise. One wine lovers everywhere celebrate, and critics like those at the World Chardonnay Championships in Denmark and Wine Spectator's New York Wine Experience applaud. And, while some raise eyebrows at Anthony's pursuit of the Burgundian style in a New World terroir, all respect his commitment to his soil and to innovation – fermentation in stoneware amphoras lined with clay, trials with yeasts indigenous to his vineyards, and a programme to find a HRV clone using vineyard propagation to name but a few ongoing projects.

★★★★ **Pinot Noir** 📖 **10** juxtaposes power & restraint: compact raspberry/cherry core, feisty acidity, assertive & yet well-controlled tannins augur well for 5+ years development. **09** (★★★★★) more silken, supple.

★★★★☆ **Chardonnay** 📖 Outstanding barrel-fermented version, consistently among SA's best. **10** slowly unveils its charms: creamy lime/lemon notes give way to spicier cardamom, fenugreek & fennel. Pure fruit, taut acidity meld with tempered oak tannins, controlled savoury finish. Will please for many years. — CvZ

▪ **Hands on Wine** see The Parlotones
▪ **Hannay Wines** see Valley Green Winery
▪ **Happy Cow** see Grundheim Wines
▪ **Harmony Tree** see United Nations of Wine

Harrison Hope

Location: Queenstown ▪ Est 2000 ▪ 1stB 2009 ▪ Tasting & tours by appt ▪ Accommodation ▪ Owner(s) Ronnie & Janet Vehorn ▪ Cellarmaster(s)/winemaker(s)/viticulturist(s) Ronnie Vehorn ▪ 2ha (merlot, ptage, chard) ▪ 1,000cs own label ▪ PO Box 1394 Queenstown 5320 ▪ rvehorn@gmail.com ▪ www.harrisonhope.com ▪ S 32 10' 01.11" E 026 50'28.28" ▪ **T +27 (0)40-842-9444** ▪ F +27 (0)40-842-9200

Harrison Hope continues to test the terroir and terrors of introducing vines and wines to the Eastern Cape's mountainous interior, with the 2011 chardonnay, pinotage and merlot now in barrel and improving with age. Top of the wish-list is a liquor license, still un-issued by the local authorities after two years of conscientious effort.

Hartenberg Estate

Location/map/WO: Stellenbosch ▪ Est/1stB 1978 ▪ Tasting & sales Mon-Fri 9–5 (Nov to Easter 9–5.30) Sat 9–3 Sun 1 Dec till Easter 10–4 ▪ Closed all other Sundays, Easter Fri, Dec 25 & Jan 1 ▪ Tasting fee for groups, refunded with purchase ▪ Cellar tours by appt ▪ Vintner's lunches 12-2, menu changes for winter months ▪ Facilities for children ▪ Farm produce ▪ Conference facility by appt only ▪ Walking/hiking trail ▪ Bottelary Renosterveld Conservancy ▪ Monthly tapas & jazz evenings in summer; soirées in winter ▪ Owner(s) Hartenberg Holdings ▪ Cellarmaster(s) Carl Schultz (Nov 1993) ▪ Winemaker(s) Patrick Ngamane (Jan 2001), with Oscar Robyn (Nov 2010) ▪ Viticulturist(s) Wilhelm Joubert (May 2006) ▪ 187ha/85ha (cab, merlot, shiraz, chard, riesling, sauv) ▪ 550t/30,000-

40,000cs own label 80% red 20% white ▪ BWI, IPW ▪ PO Box 12756 Die Boord 7613 ▪ info@hartenbergestate.com ▪ www.hartenbergestate.com ▪ S 33° 53'52.5" E 018° 47'30.4" ▪ **T +27 (0)21-865-2541** ▪ F +27 (0)21-865-2153

As plaudits continue to roll in – most recently for shiraz, sauvignon and mature riesling – this acclaimed but modest Bottelary Hill team has embarked on the next step in moving on, moving up: packaging. The familiar premium-range oval label has been revamped, and a 'key' motif (derived from the underground cellar door, originally in the Castle of Good Hope) used to differentiate the cabernet, shiraz and sauvignon. The upper-echelon 'named' wines have their own identities. In the tasting room, bespoke olive, charcuterie and wine matches are on offer (book ahead), and innovation continues with a 'closed cycle' system that purifies cellar water via a natural reed bed filter, for reuse in the vineyard.

★★★★ **Cabernet Sauvignon** Blackcurrant-toned **08** noted last edition as more accessible & fresher than previous.

★★★★ **Merlot** Gentle violet perfume leads out lovely red-berry fruit in **09** but a tannic kick reminds this is serious wine. Elegant, certainly, but needs ample time - 4 years minimum.

★★★★☆ **Gravel Hill Shiraz** One of a trio of very different shirazes. From estate's best site - dry, gravelly, strewn with *koffieklip* ('coffee stones')- yielding appropriately mineral, savoury, elegant shiraz. **07** is winemaking at its zenith: ethereal, spicy, very polished, with powerful length of flavour.

★★★★ **Shiraz** Fruitiest of the shiraz trio; really tasty **08**, like **07**, in more athletic, carry-no-excess-baggage style. Still juicy though, with 15% alc to boot!

★★★★★ **The Mackenzie Cabernet Sauvignon-Merlot** The classic red Bordeaux associations - cigarbox, pencil lead, clean blackcurrant - all apply to immensely pleasurable **08** (★★★★★), but lighter on its feet than stellar **07**, which was fine-grained & showed dazzling fruit purity.

★★★★ **Chardonnay** Full yet elegant **09** showed creamy vanilla patina to brisk lemon/lime flavours last edition; length to savoury complexity.

★★★★☆ **The Eleanor Chardonnay** Stately restraint, wonderful depth of flavour in textured **08** when tasted previously; all-new wood gave gravitas to enduring, viscous finish. **09** missed our deadline.

★★★★☆ **Riesling** ✓ 📖 Respected track record under previous 'Weisser Riesling' branding. Quality continues in just-dry **10**, delicate stonefruit flavour, fresh acid grip satisfies & offers partnership at meal-time.

★★★★☆ **The Stork Shiraz** From heavier clay soil, & a marked contrast to Gravel Hill: this an Aussie-style extrovert, with upfront vanilla-oak, open almost gulpable texture - though pimento-toned **08** is shade more elegant, less opulent than previous, reflecting vintage.

★★★★ **Sauvignon Blanc** ✓ Bone-dry **10** (★★★★) softer, more tropical than super, steely **09**.

Snuffbox Merlot Await new vintage. **Cabernet Sauvignon-Shiraz** ✓ ★★★★ Enduring favourite; **09** smoky plum aromas & ripe berry flavours, with enough tannins to serve with food or age a few years. Discontinued: **Pinotage**. — DS

Hartswater Wine Cellar

Location: Hartswater ▪ Map: Northern Cape, Free State & North West ▪ WO: Northern Cape ▪ Tasting & sales Mon-Fri 8.30-1, 2-5 ▪ Sales also from outlet in Hartswater town; orders delivered to liquor stores in Northern Cape (350km radius), Free State & North West ▪ Tours by appt ▪ Owner(s) Senwes ▪ Winemaker(s) Deon Truter ▪ 3,500t ▪ PO Box 2335 Hartswater 8570 ▪ deon@wynkelder.co.za ▪ S 27° 55'2.2" E 024° 49'38.2" ▪ **T +27 (0)53-474-0700** ▪ F +27 (0)53-474-0975

This far-flung winery north of Kimberley in the Spitskop Dam irrigation region has recently come under the control of Orange River Wine Cellars. For the present, the range designations remain as before, but reconfiguration and bigger volumes, made for ORWC, are planned in the near future.

Elements range

Cabernet Sauvignon 🍷 Await next. **Earth** 🍷 ★★ Friendly NV braai pal from ruby cab. Not revisited, as all. **Fire** 🍷 ★★ Sweet NV rosé ex ruby cab & pinotage with mulberry notes. **Chenin Blanc** 🍷 Await next. **Wind** 🍷 ★★ Floral, lowish-alc dry NV picnic sipper from colombard. **Rain** 🍷 ★★ Undemanding NV lowish-alc semi-sweet colombard. **Chardonnay-Colombar** 🍷 ★★ Delicate, fruit-salady **08**. **Thunder** 🍷 ★★ Sweet, light-bodied NV from ruby cab.

Overvaal range

Red Jerepico ★★★ Raisin-sweet **NV** warmer from ruby cab, more complex than previous. **White Jerepico** 🗐 ★★ Fleshy raisiny sweetness, **NV** from fernão pires. — GdB

Haskell Vineyards

Location/map/WO: Stellenbosch ▪ Est 2002 ▪ 1stB 2008 ▪ Tasting & sales Tue-Fri 10–4.30 Sat/Sun 10-3 ▪ Fee R40 - only for tasting on weekends ▪ Closed Mon, Easter Fri-Mon, Dec 25 & Jan 1 ▪ Cellar tours on special request only ▪ The Long Table Restaurant & Café Tue-Sun 9-5; aundowner evenings Thu-Fri (Sep-Mar) - booking essential ▪ Facilities for children ▪ Self-catering accommodation in 'The Residence' ▪ Owner(s) Preston Haskell ▪ Cellar-master(s) Rianie Strydom (Jan 2005) ▪ Winemaker(s)/viticulturist(s) Wikus Pretorius (Dec 2005) ▪ 25ha/13.5ha (cabs s/f, merlot, shiraz, chard) ▪ ±80t/1,800cs own label 80% red 20% white ▪ PO Box 12766 Die Boord 7613 ▪ info@haskellvineyards.com ▪ www.haskellvineyards.com ▪ S 34° 0' 13.9" E 018° 51' 38.4" ▪ **T +27 (0)21-881-3895** ▪ F +27 (0)21-881-3986

Sibling to separately listed Dombeya, the Haskell label has been garnering major recognition worldwide under the aegis of consultant winemaker Rianie Strydom: from back-to-back five stars in this guide to the first ever South African overall winner at the Tri-Nations Challenge. At the Helderberg estate, a weekend highlight is the Tri-Nations Tasting where Haskell wines come up against New Zealand and Australian examples. The Rare & Distinguished Tasting explores historical wines from South Africa and France. Sustainability is a strong focus, hence the well-established composting system which processes all cellar and restaurant wastes. The cellar approach is 'as natural as possible', with natural fermentations for some blocks, and oaking regimes finely adjusted to match fruit quality. As with the new Anvil Chardonnay and Haskell II red blend, the stylistic aim is elegance.

★★★★★ **Pillars Syrah** Following showstopper debut **07**, equally brilliant **08** (listed as 'Pillars Shiraz') last year opened to explosive aromas of blackberry, liquorice & floral essences. Complex & restrained, excellent concentration of berry flavours on well-developed tannin frame.

★★★★☆ **Aeon Syrah** Heady array of berries, violets, dark choc, leather & gunflint on previously tasted **08**, with dollop mourvèdre. Enticing spice cake flavour complemented by supple tannins & refreshing acidity.

★★★★ **Haskell IV** Powerful **07** cab-led Bordeaux red last edition was elegant, almost austere, though flavours built on the palate. Deserved time to show true potential.

★★★★☆ **Haskell II** NEW Debut **09** from shiraz, cab & mourvèdre oozes class. Elegant, sweet, clean lines of ripe juicy black fruit, luscious vanilla tannins & a nutty, creamy finish with a hint of black pepper.

★★★★☆ **Anvil Chardonnay** NEW ⌁ Stunning newcomer from eponymous vineyard, whose shape resembles a hammering block. **10** palate explodes with powerful exotic fruit tamed by a fine silky oakiness & creamy, lingering finish. Great depth, richness & elegance, will develop beautifully. — WB

Hathersage

Location: Somerset West ▪ Map: Helderberg ▪ WO: Stellenbosch ▪ 1stB 2007 ▪ Tasting by appt only ▪ Sales Mon-Sat 9-5 ▪ Closed all pub hols ▪ Tour groups ▪ BYO picnic ▪ Conference & wedding/function venue with catering (10-200 pax) ▪ Conservation area ▪ Owner(s) Stephan Holdings cc & Stephan Brothers (Pty) Ltd ▪ Winemaker(s) Michael Liedtke (Jan 2010, consultant) ▪ 40ha/12ha (cabs s/f, merlot, p verdot, shiraz, chard, sauv, sem) ▪ 52t/1,518cs own label 43% red 57% white ▪ PO Box 2517 Somerset West 7129 ▪ info@hathersage.co.za ▪ www.hathersage.co.za ▪ S 34° 4'54.42" E 018°51'55.32" ▪ **T +27 (0)21-851-1644/+27 (0)21-851-5076** ▪ F +27 (0)21-851-8382

On the Lourensford River is Hathersage House, named after an English village whose church is depicted on the wine labels. The range produced in Michael Liedtke's cellar continues to expand, and this year the wines tasted (all as pre-bottling samples) seem to have benefited from the ageing of the barrels, with less new wood to mask a lighter, fresher expression of the vineyards.

★★★★ **Cabernet Sauvignon** ✓ **09** delicately herbal, with fine licorice spice. Too restrained to be instantly attractive, but quietly seductive. More perfumed, less smoky than previous **07**. Except for Red Blend, all these samples.

★★★★ **Merlot** ✓ Bright, though light, plum fruit on amply spiced **09**; delicate tannins, but oak dominates otherwise elegant barrel sample - fresher & finer than previous **07**.

Special Edition Red Blend 🍷 ★★★☆ Fine-textured old-oaked **08** merlot-cab. Spicy, delicious drinking tasted last year. **Chardonnay** NEW 🍷 ★★ **11** with leesy, light citrus fruit, faint smoky whiffs. **Sauvignon Blanc** ✓ 🍷 ★★★★ Tropical & ripe **11**, with gooseberry & melon notes, after greener **10**. Splash of semillon adds weight. **Semillon** ✓ 🍷 ★★★★ **11**, with splash of sauvignon, shows fresh-mown hay aromas; 20% oak-fermented portion adds vanilla, persistence, & bitter hint. **White Reserve** 🍷 ★★★ Was 'Special Edition White Blend'. Fresh green edged to **11** blend sauvignon(80%), semillon; zesty but insubstantial. — MF

Haute Cabrière

Location/map: Franschhoek • WO: Western Cape/Franschhoek • Est 1982 • 1stB 1984 • Tasting & sales Mon-Fri 9-5 Sat & pub hols 10-4 Sun 11-4 • Fee R20pp for 3 wines, R30pp for 5 wines • Formal tour/tasting Mon-Fri 11 & 3 R50pp • Private tasting/tour (pre-booked) R60pp • Achim/Takuan's tasting/tour Sat 11 R50pp • Closed Good Fri, Dec 25 & Jan 1 • Haute Cabrière Restaurant (see Restaurants section) • Tour groups • Conferencing for groups of max 120 • Owner(s) Clos Cabrière Ltd • Cellarmaster(s)/winemaker(s) Achim von Arnim (1984), with Takuan von Arnim (2005) • Viticulturist(s) Sakkie Lourens (May 2002) • 30ha (pinot, chard) • 40% red 60% white • PO Box 245 Franschhoek 7690 • marketing@cabriere.co.za • www.cabriere.co.za • S 33° 54'51.8" E 019° 8'8.2" • **T +27 (0)21-876-8500** • F +27 (0)21-876-8501

Now called Haute Cabrière (as it appears on the wine label) this family-owned farm's entire wine portfolio comprises only two varieties: chardonnay and pinot noir – alone and in various blends and styles: still, sparkling and fortified, dry to sweet. Smart, traditional packaging is common to both ranges, which enjoy a loyal local following. Demand for a light, less tannic red has been answered with an unwooded pinot. Extra maturation on the lees of the bubblies has necessitated extending the Pierre Jourdan cellar. Meanwhile, both Achim and son Takuan stress they are growers: the word 'winemaking', they insist, doesn't exist in the European vintner's vocabulary.

Arnim range
Discontinued: **Arnim Sauvignon Rouge**.

Haute Cabrière range
Pinot Noir ★★★★ Pale **08** from own vines. Fresh acidity threads soft cherry flavours to silky textured finish, oak adds sufficient grip. **Unwooded Pinot Noir** NEW 🍷 ★★★ Tank sample off-dry **11** could pass for deep rosé. Soft, light, cherry-fruited. Perfect chilled any time of the day. **Chardonnay-Pinot Noir** 🍷 ★★★ Faint blush in pretty, just off-dry **11** light lunchtime sipper, slips down easily.

Pierre Jourdan range
★★★★ **Blanc de Blancs** Persistent mousse in 100% chardonnay **NV** MCC. Softly fruited, rounded mouthfeel from oaking & time spent on lees.
★★★★ **Cuvée Reserve NV** chardonnay spends 85 months on lees, so would expect more lees complexity, though attractive floral freshness, fine mousse & light harmonious finish compensates.
★★★★ **Ratafia** Chardonnay fortified with own potstill chardonnay brandy. Sweet & inviting **NV** stylishly packaged in bubbly bottle.
Tranquille 🍷 ★★ Still, dry simple **NV** blend chardonnay & pinot noir, as for next two. **Brut** ★★★ Popular **NV** bottle-fermented blend has sweet entry, shy apple flavours & brisk finish. Lees character not evident. **Brut Sauvage** ★★★★ Fine bubbles in pale gold **NV**, zero dosage MCC. More aromatic complexity than last bottling, firm, edgy finish. **Cuvée Belle Rose** ★★★★ Pretty salmon-pink pinot noir MCC **NV**. Persistent mousse persists through subtle flavours to clean, dry finish. — IM

Haut Espoir

Location/map: Franschhoek • Est 1999 • 1stB 2004 • Tastings, sales & cellar tours by appt • Closed all pub hols • Fynbos walks • Conservation area • Owner(s) Armstrong family • Cellarmaster(s)/winemaker(s)/viticulturist(s) Nikey van Zyl (Jan 2003) • ±23ha/12ha (cab, merlot, p verdot, shiraz) • 70t/5,000cs own label 70% red 30% white • BWI • PO Box 681 Franschhoek 7690 • wine@hautespoir.co.za • www.hautespoir.co.za • S 33° 56'23.6" E 019° 6'20.9" • **T +27 (0)21-876-4000** • F +27 (0)21-876-4038

Gentle giant Rob Armstrong's love of nature is tangible. Not only are moves afoot to proclaim a conservancy with neighbouring Boekenhoutskloof but biodiversity initiatives proceed apace. Just one example is the wetland which processes waste water, cellar and farm effluent. There's also a semillon-driven white blend gestating quietly.

★★★★ **Chardonnay** Previously, **08**'s citrus gleamed through serious oaking (11 months Hungarian & French) to elegant spicy finish. Broad, balanced & complex. 40% wild yeast, barrel ferment. WO Coastal. **Cabernet Sauvignon** ★★★★ Last tasted was **05**, with oak providing backbone for pure, ripe & rich black fruits. **Malbec** Await next, as for **Petit Verdot**. **Syrah** ★★★ Last-tasted **06**'s leather & spice lifted by florals. **Shiraz** ★★★★ Last reviewed **06** big jump in quality from restrained **05** (★★★). Full bodied, concentrated & rich, with ripe berry & sweet spice flavours. Part carbonic maceration. **Gentle Giant** ★★★ Step-up **07** merlot-dominated blend of 5 red varieties tasted previously. Bright sweet ripe berries, spicy oak, good intensity. **Shiraz Rosé** ★★ **09** toffee apple, tealeaf & spice, tasted last ed bit rough & short. **Sauvignon Blanc** ★★★ Fleshy **08** holding up well on review. Savoury notes from 7 months lees-ageing. **Semillon Reserve** ★★★ Shy, crisp **07** last showed clear fruit with typical lanolin & fynbos notes. Lightly oaked; 12.5% alc. **Viognier** ★★★ oak-fermented **08** last showed forward oak & spice. Full bodied with oily texture. Warm finish ex 14.3% alc. — FM

Havana Hills

Location: Philadelphia ▪ WO: Philadelphia/Coastal ▪ Est 1999 ▪ 1stB 2000 ▪ Closed to public ▪ Owner(s) Kobus du Plessis ▪ Winemaker(s) Piet Kleinhans (Sep 2008) & Joseph Gertse (Jan 2000) ▪ Viticulturist(s) Rudi Benn (Jan 2001) ▪ 260ha/60ha (barbera, cabs s/f, merlot, mourv, sangio, shiraz, sauv) ▪ 35,000cs own label 50% red 20% white 30% rosé ▪ IPW, WIETA ▪ Postnet Suite #57 Private Bag X18 Milnerton 7435 ▪ sales@havanahills.co.za ▪ www.havanahills.co.za ▪ **T +27 (0)21-972-1110** ▪ F +27 (0)21-972-1105

Owner Kobus du Plessis might not make the wine but he's involved in its strategy and has a presence: flagship Kobus is named after him, as is new red blend Du Plessis. Other changes include the transfer of the Pinot Noir to Virgin Earth, the range from Kobus' wine and game farm in the Langeberg foothills, and a number of new Havana Hills labels shortly to be released: two further rosés, from cab and mourvèdre, to provide a choice of pinks for both the local and export markets; a chardonnay/pinot noir blend and an interesting sounding cab/barbera. The focus on reducing alcohol in the wines through viticultural and winemaking practices is bearing fruit, as aptly demonstrated by the sauvignons this year.

Kobus range

★★★★★ **Red** Flagship only in best vintages. Last-tasted majestic **05** was 4-way Bordeaux blend, seamless tannins cosseting sweet fruit.

★★★★ **Chardonnay** Last was **10**, crushed hazelnuts & lemon preserve, satisfying palate weight from dab sugar, extended acid-brightened farewell.

Havana Hills range

★★★★ **Du Plessis Reserve** NEW ✓ Lovely mix plush berries, pepper & prosciutto reflects **07** blend shiraz, cab, merlot, with fruit deepening on palate. Silky seduction, already drinking well & will do till ±2018.

Merlot ☺ ★★★ Creamy berries with vanilla & spice infusion, **08** instantly appeals, has softly smooth drinkability.

Cabernet Sauvignon ★★★ Last was plump & juicy **08**, had blackcurrant & slight sweetness; 18 months oaking added grip. Coastal WO, like Du Plessis Reserve. **Shiraz** ★★★ Light, mulberry-toned **09** is for drinking rather than keeping. Oak provides a dusty note, dry finish, ideal for food. **Sauvignon Blanc** ✓ 🍷 ★★★★ Asparagus & lime, off-dry to balance acidity, **11** has cool-climate styling. Crackles with vitality; friendly 12% alc.

Lime Road range

Shiraz ☺ ★★★ **09** is spot on, ripe dark plums, smoky spice, fleshy & smooth.

Cabernet Sauvignon-Merlot-Cabernet Franc ★★★ Last edition, **08**'s plummy fruit enfolded tannins, gave generous drinkability. WO Coastal. **Merlot Rosé** 🍷 ★★ Previously zesty **10** was off-dry, light patio fare. **Cabernet Sauvignon Rosé** NEW 🍷 ★★ Off-dry **11**'s cranberry styling ideal for summer quaffing. **Sauvignon Blanc** 🍷 ★★★ Grassy lime cordial, dab sugar offsets **10**'s acidity. Lowish 12.4% alc. — CR

Hawksmoor at Matjieskuil

Location: Paarl ▪ Map: Paarl & Wellington ▪ WO: Paarl/Coastal ▪ Est 1692 ▪ 1stB 2005 ▪ Tasting by appt 10–4 daily; sales by appt Mon-Sat ▪ Fee R20 refunded with purchase ▪ Closed Easter Fri-Sun, Dec 25/31 & Jan 1 ▪ Luxury guest house (see Accommodation section) ▪ Owner(s) Brameld Haigh ▪ Farm manager Jan Lategan ▪ Winemaker(s) Various ▪ Viticulturist(s) Paul Wallace (2004) ▪ ±23ha (cab f, mourv, ptage, shiraz, chenin) ▪ ±130t/500cs own label 65% red 25% white 10% rosé ▪ PO Box 9 Elsenburg 7607 ▪ wines@hawksmoor.co.za ▪ www.hawksmoor. co.za ▪ S 33° 48′ 47.4″ E 018° 46′ 14.1″ ▪ **T +27 (0)21-884-4587** ▪ F +27 (0)21-884-4465

Last year's wine releases saw a sharp rise in quality, which has been reflected in critical recognition. These tiny batches are custom-crafted by various winemakers from Matjieskuil's grapes as interpretations of their sites. The restoration of the 18th century Cape Dutch country house is complete, and it will soon be hosting traditional dinners to showcase the wines.

Limited Releases

★★★★ **Barrel 59** 📗 Just one (French) barrel of **08** shiraz. Fynbos & lavender, meaty-tarry core, black cherry juiciness. Intensely spicy, velvety tannins. Not revisited this edition, as all below.

★★★★☆ **Barrel 69** 📗 Farm manager's Jan Lategan's best American oak barrel of shiraz, **08** ethereal fragrance, floral notes, intense black fruit centre. Noble & elegant, yet powerful.

★★★★ **Saint Alfege's** 📗 Mediterranean scrub, morello cherries on poised **08**. Lightness with athletic substance. 85% shiraz, rest mourvèdre.

★★★★ **Algernon Stitch** 📗 **08** shiraz/mourvèdre (90/10) was dark, intense & savoury. Robust, yet refined, with subtle aromatic lift.

Mourvèdre 📗 ★★★★ Appealing soft damson fruit, spicy aromatics on **08**, structure showed ripeness & poise. **Pinotage** 📗 Await new. **Vanbrugh** 📗 ★★★ From pinotage, **07** was shy & restrained, with muted berry fruit encased by rigid tannins. **Shiraz** 📗 Await new. **Rosé** 📗 ★★★ Pleasantly plump **09** from mourvèdre & sauvignon, restrained strawberry notes. WO Coastal. **Edward Goudge** 📗 ★★ Chenin from quarter-century-old bushvines, **09** was oaky & oxidative, lacking charm.

Classic range

Pinotage 📗 ★★★ Accessible **06** plummy, rich & earthy, lively tannins & judicious oaking. **Mourvèdre Rosé** Await next. **Chenin Blanc** 📗 ★★★ **08** had warm hay wafts, apple ripeness, crisp acidity. — GdB

Hazendal

Location/map/WO: Stellenbosch ▪ Est 1699 ▪ 1stB 1950 ▪ Tasting & sales daily 9–4.30 ▪ Fee R10/5 wines ▪ Closed Easter Fri & Jan 1 ▪ Cellar tours Mon-Fri 11-3 ▪ Hermitage Restaurant Tue-Sun 9-4.30 ▪ Facilities for children ▪ Tour groups ▪ Gifts ▪ Cheese platters ▪ Conferences ▪ Mountain biking trail ▪ Russian Arts & Culture Museum ▪ Owner(s) Voloshin & Schumacher families ▪ Winemaker(s) Ronell Wiid (Jan 1998), with Werner du Plessis ▪ 140ha/52ha (cab, merlot, pinot, shiraz, chenin, sauv) ▪ 350t/25,000cs own label 40% red 60% white ▪ PO Box 336 Stellenbosch 7599 ▪ info@hazendal.co.za ▪ www.hazendal.co.za ▪ S 33° 54′ 2.7″ E 018° 43′ 9.1″ ▪ **T +27 (0)21-903-5112** ▪ F +27 (0)21-903-0057

2011 was the Chinese Year of the Rabbit, which was seen as an auspicious sign at the 'Dale of Rabbits' estate in Stellenbosch's Bottelary wine ward. To celebrate, they launched the new pocket-friendly De Haas range and ratcheted up their export initiatives to the Far East. Longtime winemaker Ronell Wiid cites the tough market conditions as her main preoccupation, and believes innovative thinking will be the key to increasing sales - 'pulling a rabbit out of the hat'. In other news, cellar hands Rollie and Hope are achieving renown as drag queens, depicted in the new gay art-movie, The Sisterhood.

Hazendal range

★★★★ **Shiraz** Supple, juicy **08** (★★★★) last edition had savoury centre of red fruit, spicy dry tannins & bright acidity.

★★★★ **Shiraz-Cabernet Sauvignon** ✓ **08** (★★★★) a tad meaty-savoury after riper **07**, with promising red berries showing through. Solid, weighty, with hefty tannins. Needs time.

★★★★☆ **The Last Straw** Unbotrytised dessert from air-dried grapes. Massively sweet, viscous nectar, **08** is pure delight, expressing chenin's typical dried apricot fruit in an embrace of honey. A leader in this emerging category.

Merlot ✓ ★★★★ Satisfyingly full & intense, **09** ratchets up on **07** (★★★★). Savoury hints & black fruit on substantial tannins. Noble, classically styled, for more serious moments. **Pinotage** Await new release. **Marvol Pinotage** ★★★★ Limited bottling, mainly for Russian & German markets. **07** was sumptuous, dark & sleek last time. **Reserve Red** ★★★ **08** on review was sappy merlot-led blend with cab & shiraz. Savoury & approachable. **Chenin Blanc Wooded** ✓ ★★★★ Richly ripe tropical fruit shows through oaky mantle on **09**. Character wrought from low-yielding old bushvines. **Bushvine Chenin Blanc** ✓ ★★★★ Dense, ripe **10** unwooded, from 30 year old vines. Over-delivers at price, gushes warm tropical fruit. **Sauvignon Blanc** ✓ ★★★ Previewed **11** shows lovely freshness, elegant structure. Commendably gentle acidity, with ripe tropical fruit. **White Nights Brut Cap Classique** ★★★★ Champagne-method sparkling **07** (80% chard, with pinot noir) in classy livery, last edition showed clean apple & brioche flavours. Discontinued: **Rosé**.

De Haas range NEW

Red ☺ 🍷 ★★☆ Base-level line of price-friendly quaffers. Meaty-spicy **NV** blend is pocket friendly, fresh & undemanding. **Rosé** ☺ ★★☆ Berry flavoured, salmon hued, semi-dry, with substance. **NV**. **White** ☺ 🍷 ★★☆ **NV** white from chenin-sauvignon is high on drinkability. — GdB

■   **Headbutt** *see* D'Athis Wines SA Negociants
■   **Heart & Soul** *see* Anura Vineyards

Helderberg Wijnmakerij

Location: Somerset West ▪ WO: Stellenbosch ▪ Est 2010 ▪ 1stB 2009 ▪ Closed to public ▪ Owner(s) Boekenhoutskloof Winery (Pty) Ltd ▪ Winemaker(s) Heinrich Hugo (Sep 2010) ▪ 75% red 25% white ▪ BRC, HACCP ▪ PO Box 1037 Stellenbosch 7130 ▪ info@helderbergwijnmakerij.com ▪ www.helderbergwijnmakerij.com ▪ **T +27 (0)21-842-2371** ▪ F +27 (0)21-842-2373

Now part of the Boekenhoutskloof stable, this venerable old lady of the Helderberg (circa 1906) is being reinvented as a specialised red-wine facility, particularly for cab. All due respect has been paid to its heritage, while tweaking and augmenting the equipment for its new, higher calling. The current releases, by resident winemaker Heinrich Hugo, feature distinctive new livery in an unmistakeably African theme.

Cabernet Sauvignon ▤ ★★★ **09** last edition charmed with jammy fruit, vanilla oak notes, good structure. Not retasted, as all reds. **Merlot** ▤ ★★ Chunky, perfumed **09** showed bright red-plum fruit & hint of dates. **Shiraz** ▤ ★★ Tutti-frutti fun, friendly tannin on **09**. These 3 not retasted. **Sauvignon Blanc** ▤ ★★★ Youthfully introverted grassy aroma, asparagus whiff, **11** is wholesome & ripe, refreshing crisp acidity. — GdB

Helpmekaar Wines

Location: Wellington ▪ Map: Paarl & Wellington ▪ Est 2007 ▪ 1stB 2008 ▪ Tasting, sales & tours by appt Mon–Fri 8-5 ▪ Closed all pub hols ▪ Function venue ▪ Owner(s) Hennie Lategan ▪ Winemaker(s) Hennie Lategan, Francois Louw & Daan Rossouw ▪ 25ha (cab, cinsaut, shiraz) ▪ 250t/150cs own label 100% red ▪ PO Box 2976 Paarl 7620 ▪ psycholat@telkomsa.net ▪ S 33°38'28.64" E 018°57'1.81" ▪ **T +27 (0)21-864-1041** ▪ F +27 (0)21-864-1041

Although the challenges of the 'bigger harvest' for commercial purposes occupied more of his time than the 'smaller process' of vinifying a portion of the grapes from his Wellington farm, psychologist Hennie Lategan and his wine-loving friends made wine again last year, he reports; the resultant cab resting in barrel, awaiting their assessment.

Shiraz ★★★☆ Previously we noted herbaceous notes on **07**, used-barrel oaking provided support, didn't intrude on berry flavours. — DB

Hemelzicht

Location: Hermanus ▪ Map: Elgin, Walker Bay & Bot River ▪ Est 1998 ▪ 1stB 2003 ▪ Tasting by appt ▪ Owner(s) Louis Saaiman ▪ PO Box 469 Onrusrivier 7201 ▪ S 34° 25' 8.2" E 019° 14' 27.9" ▪ **T +27 (0)28-313-2215** ▪ F +27 (0)28-313-2215

Louis Saaiman sold the portion of his Hermanus farm with vineyards on, which meant sitting out a harvest. Last year it was back to business as usual and the brand continues with wine made from bought-in grapes, until the land he retained is planted and the vineyards matured. The soil analyses completed, it was time to decide which variety would fare best where, and get cracking.

■ **Hendrik Lodewyk** *see Du Preez Estate*
■ **Hercules Paragon** *see Simonsvlei International*

Hermanuspietersfontein Wynkelder

Location: Hermanus ▪ Map: Elgin, Walker Bay & Bot River ▪ WO: Sunday's Glen/Western Cape/Walker Bay ▪ Est 2005 ▪ 1stB 2006 ▪ Tasting & sales Mon-Fri 9-5 Sat 9-4 Sun (15 Dec-15 Jan) 10.30-3 ▪ Closed Easter Fri/Sun/Mon & Dec 25/26 ▪ Cellar tours on request ▪ Food & Wine Market Sat 9-2 ▪ 3-star self-catering Cottages ▪ Owner/s Johan & Mariette Pretorius, Bartho Eksteen ▪ Winemaker(s) Bartho Eksteen, with Kim McFarlane (Feb 2006) ▪ Viticulturist(s) Ernst Bruwer (Oct 2009) ▪ 320ha/±61ha (cabs s/f, grenache, malbec, merlot, mourv, p verdot, shiraz, nouvelle, sauv, sem, viog) ▪ 200t/13,000c own label 55% red 40% white 5% rosé ▪ BWI champion ▪ Hemel en Aarde Village Suite 47 Private Bag X15 Hermanus 7200 ▪ kelder@hpf1855.co.za ▪ www.hpf1855.co.za ▪ S 34° 24'38.7" E 019° 11'51.7" ▪ **T +27 (0)28-316-1875** ▪ F +27 (0)28-316-1293

How appropriate that Bartho Eksteen was named Diners Club Winemaker of the Year in 2010 for his 2009 Sauvignon Blanc No 5 and the 2010 receives five stars in this guide. He is one of the variety's most ardent supporters: for many years he has held an annual Celebration of Sauvignon, pitting his own wines against other locals and some of the world's best. As with the entire range, these sauvignons, all from the home farm in the Sunday's Glen ward, receive fine honing, nothing left to chance. 'There's a lot of effort in choosing the right wood; size, age and toasting – it must be slow-toasted - they all matter,' says Eksteen of No 5. Such detail pushes the range to a position among the country's best.

Flagship Wines

★★★★ **Die Arnoldus** Cab-led Bordeaux quintet; 08 captures 'clairet' lightness of touch, freshness without lacking ripe fruit complexity. Polish of 100% new oak lends final stamp to flagship status. This, next & Kleonboet WO Western Cape.

★★★★ **Die Martha** Rich & supple, 08 boasts a generosity of dark spice, cured meat & clean leather in a savoury medley. Lots of sensual & fresh appeal in this shiraz, mourvèdre, viognier blend.

★★★★☆ **Die Bartho** 🍷 📖 Among best of SA's Bordeaux-style dry white blends, a splash of nouvelle adding local flavour. 10 in chrysalis stage: lovely aromatic purity; tighter, edgier feel. Textural richness waiting in wings for year or 2. Perhaps without depth of 09 (★★★★★).

Classic Wines

★★★★ **Swartskaap** Dark - yes; brooding - yes; perfectly behaved - yes. 09 cab franc individual but no black sheep; worthy solo player. Rich concentration lifted by lively spice, fine tannins.

★★★★ **Kleinboet** ✓ Approachable yet classy 08 from merlot-led Bordeaux quartet. Cedar, ripe plum, dark berry medley squeezed into classically dry, elegant frame. Smart 'little brother' to Arnoldus!

★★★★ **Sauvignon Blanc No 5** ✓ 🍷 📖 Oak-matured 10 (★★★★★) has Bordeaux class written all over it. Ripe, but not over the top; cleansing acid thread, bone dry finish pave way for fruity persistence. Includes 15% semillon. 09 billowing vanilla, with bristling grassy spikes.

★★★★ **Sauvignon Blanc No 3** 🍷 Tasted just post-bottling (as was No 7 below), 11 a charming apple blossom, fig medley; this, juicy succulence fulfills 'tropical' style indicated on back label. Lingering & dry.

★★★★ **Sauvignon Blanc No 7** 🍷 Sweet nettle & greengage rather than overt green grass, 11 no less vivacious, juicy for it. Closes pithy & dry.

Bloos 🍷 📖 ★★★★ Rosé from 'bled-off' juice of Bordeaux red varieties, fermented on oak chips. Spicy, tangy 11 with joie de vivre & quaffability.

Lifestyle Wines

1855 Posmeester ☺ 🍷 ★★★ 09 smoothly ripe-fruited cab, petit verdot, malbec with tannat adding twist in dry tail. WO Western Cape.

Sonner Nommer 🍷 📖 ★★★★ 'Without a number', appetising, lipsmackingly fresh 11 sauvignon with greengage, citrus notes. Under 12% alc, clean fruity finish. — AL

Hermit on the Hill Wines

Location: Durbanville ▪ WO: Coastal/Paarl/Stellenbosch/Durbanville ▪ Est/1stB 2000 ▪ Tasting & sales by appt ▪ Owner(s)/cellarmaster(s) Pieter de Waal ▪ Winemaker(s) Pieter de Waal & Lohra de Waal ▪ Cinsaut, grenache, mourv, pinot n, syrah, sauv, muscat b, viog ▪ 15t/800cs own label 60% red 40% white ▪ PO Box 995 Bellville 7535 ▪ pieter@dw.co.za ▪ www.hermitonthehill.co.za ▪ **T +27 (0)83-357-3864 ▪** F +27 (0)21-948-3441

The Hermit on the Hill team doubled last year when Pieter de Waal, the label's insti- gator, married Lohra, Pilates instructor and passionate garagiste winemaker herself. Pieter previously avoided the critical searchlight but recent rave reviews in the UK, in particular, saw the omertà broken and these amazing-value gems arrive on our tasting bench. Our recommendation: Buy! And don't pass up the opportunity to meet a truly engaging and thoughtful winelands personality.

Hermit on the Hill range NEW

★★★★☆ **Stellenbosch Syrah ✓** The 'Hill' in branding a reference to famous Hermitage in the Rhône, so no surprise pure & focused **07** is from shiraz; impresses with concentrated dark fruit, attractive herbal note, fresh acidity & fine tannins. Grapes from Post House in the Helderberg, year older oak.

★★★★ **The Second Crusade ✓** Shiraz, the Hermit's signature red grape, combo with third each grenache, mourvèdre. Pretty **08** red fruit, floral fragrance; fresh, with fine tannins; natural ferment, 15 months in older oak.

★★★★ **Aurora Blanc ✓** De Waal's favoured white grape is sauvignon. This the tank-fermented version, aged older barrels 9 months. Durbanville grapes, **10** complex & unusual, broad structure, spicy but balanced.

★★★★ **The Infidel ✓** More traditional take on sauvignon: Stellenbosch grapes spontaneously fermented, 'oxygen welcome' signs on the older barrels. Arresting **10** lime, green melon & peppery notes, bracing acidity.

★★★★☆ **The White Knight ✓** Sauvignon in its ultimate expression here: Bordeaux style, with 31% semil- lon, both fermented in older oak (with 5% muscat). **09** lime, tangerine & spice, hint of development; great fruit expression & many layers of flavour, riveting line of acidity.

Paarl Syrah ✓ ★★★★ 07 is shiraz & 9% mourvèdre; rich & broad in structure with dark fruit & spice, followed by long savoury finish. **The Red Knight ★★★** The family wild child: 85% shiraz, 15% cinsaut, **09** earthy, meaty character to go with dark cherry, tart acidity, firm tannins. **The Sauvignier ★★★** The workaday sauvignon: **09** with 48% viognier, plenty of peach & green melon flavour, soft acidity. — CE

Herold Wines

Location: George ▪ Map: Klein Karoo & Garden Route ▪ WO: Outeniqua/Klein Karoo ▪ Est 1999 ▪ 1stB 2003 ▪ Tast- ing, sales & cellar tours Mon–Sat 10-4 ▪ Fee R15, waived on purchase ▪ Closed Easter Sun, Dec 25 & Jan 1 ▪ Light refreshments/cheese platters during opening hours ▪ Picnic baskets/farm lunches with 2 days prior notice ▪ BYO picnic ▪ Facilities for children ▪ Tour groups ▪ Gifts ▪ Farm produce ▪ Walks/hikes ▪ Mountain biking ▪ Conservation area ▪ Self-catering Flufftail Cottage (sleeps 4) ▪ Owner(s) Nico & Maureen Fourie ▪ Winemaker(s) Nico Fourie (Jul 2011) & Vivien Harpur (consultant) ▪ Viticulturist(s) Nico Fourie (Jul 2011) ▪ 324ha/6ha (cab, merlot, pinot, shiraz, chard, sauv) ▪ 30t/1,700cs own label 55% red 25% white 20% rosé ▪ PO Box 10 Herold 6615 ▪ heroldwines@ xsinet.co.za, www.heroldwines.co.za ▪ S 33° 51'49.4" E 022° 28'9.9" ▪ **T +27 (0)72- 833-8223 ▪** F +27 (0)86-698-6607

After two years of 'tears, tantrums and panic attacks' since the former owners decided to sell this scenic farm in the Outeniqua Mountains, Nico and Maureen Fourie have 'signed the adoption papers'. Changes aren't high on the agenda (aside from restoring the bridge between cellar and vineyard which washed away after 192mm of rain) but the Fouries are excited about 'enhancing the great experience that Herold already is' wherever possible.

★★★★ **Sauvignon Blanc** Preview **10** last time delivered ripe tropical flavours, zesty acidity, excel- lent body & gravelly finish. Like all, described as 'vegetarian friendly'. Not revisited this edition, as all.

Pinot Noir 'Screwcap' ★★★★ 2nd-label pinot noir returned previous edition after hiatus under tentative name to differentiate from cork-closed flagship. **09** earth & smoke, bright fruit & acidity, may have softened & filled out since last time. **Pinot Noir ★★★★** The cellar's flagship, showing more minerality than New World fruit. Last edition **09** was light & ethereal yet with damp earth complexity & structure, lovely vinosity. Improved on **08** (★★★★). **Red Men ★★★★ 08** mix of shiraz, cab, merlot, lightly seasoned with oak, ±30% new. Lively, bal- anced, slipped down easily last time. WO Klein Karoo. **Skaam Skaap** ★★★★ Sauvignon, pinot noir, char- donnay, partly oaked. **09**, previewed mid-2009, showed slight blush after too-keen pressing of pinot, prompting name change from 'White Sheep' to 'Bashful Sheep'. Ex-tank **10** a deliberate reprise, equally tasty, charming.

Gertrude ★★★☆ Possibly unique sweet dessert from naturally dried pinot noir, 11 months older oak. **09** faint cherry nose, sweet berry palate, pleasant hint of tannin in finish. — Panel

Heron Ridge

Location: Somerset West ▪ Map: Helderberg ▪ WO: Stellenbosch ▪ Est 1997 ▪ 1stB 2001 ▪ Tasting, sales & cellar tours by appt ▪ Fee R20 ▪ Closed all pub hols ▪ Cheese lunches on Saturdays by appt ▪ Owner(s) Orpen family ▪ Cellarmaster(s)/winemaker(s) Pippa Orpen (May 2006) ▪ Viticulturist(s) Paul Wallace (Sep 1999, consultant) ▪ 4. 29ha/4ha (cab, shiraz) ▪ 20t/150cs own label 100% red ▪ PO Box 5181 Helderberg 7135 ▪ orps@xsinet.co.za ▪ www.heronridge.co.za ▪ S 34° 2′ 45.6″ E 018° 47′ 58.1″ ▪ **T +27 (0)21-842-2501** ▪ F +27 (0)86-613-6960

Winelovers Jane and the late Peter Orpen left Cape Town to live on a small Stellenbosch farm in 1997. Today their daughter Pippa is winemaker, vinifying some 20t a year. The farm was certified organic in 2010 and biodynamic principles are practised.

Shiraz ★★★★ 07 showed attractive rusticity and real liveliness, interest when last tasted. Very ripe fruit, spicy earthy undertones, 30% oak well integrated. **The Flight ★★★★** Spicy, well-built **06** shiraz/cab still selling. Peppery red fruit with slightly drying tannins but good savouriness. — CE

■ **Heron's Nest** *see* Clos Malverne

Het Vlock Casteel

Location: Riebeek-Kasteel ▪ Map: Swartland ▪ WO: Swartland/Coastal ▪ Est/1stB 2005 ▪ Tasting & sales Mon-Fri 9-5 Sat 9-2 ▪ Closed Easter Fri & Dec 25 ▪ Tour groups ▪ Gift shop ▪ Farm produce: olives, olive oil, jams, chutneys etc - sampling available in shop ▪ Conferences ▪ Café Merlot functions: by appt only ▪ Owner(s) Johan Louw Vlok ▪ Winemaker(s) Alicia Boshoff & Louwtjie Vlok ▪ Viticulturist(s) Johan Vlok (snr) & Johan Vlok (jnr) ▪ 100ha (cab, merlot, ptage, shiraz, chard) ▪ 1,300t/7,000cs own label 100% red ▪ PO Box 8 Riebeek-Kasteel 7307 ▪ info@ hetvlockcasteel.co.za ▪ www.hetvlockcasteel.co.za ▪ S 33° 23′ 22.74″ E 018° 53′ 40.75″ ▪ **T +27 (0)22-448-1433 / +27 (0)72-314-4184** ▪ F +27 (0)22-448-1610

Boasting wine, olives and fruit in their produce basket, and a function venue, shop, and accommodation in their service offerings, Johan and Ansie Vlok and family don't have an idle moment. Their own-brand is made by Alicia Boshoff at Riebeek Cellars, who also take up the rest of their grapes.

Cabernet Sauvignon ★★★★ 08 shows good varietal character, ripe blackberry flavours balanced by spicy aromas. **Merlot ★★★** Generous ripe mocha, chocolate & dark fruit, **08** satisfying everyday red. **Shiraz ★★★** Ebullient **08** bursting with smoky/savoury edged red fruit. **Sauvignon Blanc 📖 ★★★** Juicy tropical freshness on pleasant, easy-drinking **11**. — DB

Hex River Crossing Private Cellar

Location/map: Worcester ▪ WO: Western Cape ▪ Est 2003 ▪ 1stB 2004 ▪ Tasting & sales Mon-Fri 9-5 Sat 9-2 ▪ Closed all pub hols ▪ Cellar tours by appt ▪ Bistro 'Inspirati' ▪ Facilities for children ▪ Tour groups ▪ Gifts ▪ Farm produce ▪ Owner(s) De Villiers Graaff, AJ Reyneke & Leon Dippenaar ▪ Cellarmaster(s)/winemaker(s)/viticulturist(s) Leon Dippenaar (Aug 2004) ▪ ±41ha/2ha (mourv, shiraz, viog) ▪ 10t/2,000cs own label 75% red 25% white ▪ The Pines PO Box 5 Hex River 6855 ▪ auctioncrossing@hexvalley.co.za ▪ www.auctioncrossing.co.za ▪ S 33° 29′ 42.8″ E 019° 34′ 32.7″ ▪ **T +27 (0)23-357-9655** ▪ F +27 (0)23-357-9255

Hex River Crossing winemaker Leon Dippennar produces just two wines, modelled on French Côte Rôtie and Condrieu examples. He buys in grapes from different regions for greater complexity and interest, and makes the carefully oaked wines – both Fairtrade accredited – in traditional open kuipe.

The Auction Crossing range

Syrah-Viognier ★★★★ Co-fermented, aromatic **09** well made & accessible, pleasingly positive spicy finish as tannins tug sweetly ripe, dark fruit. **Viognier 📖 ◉ ★★★** Variety's exotic fruity, floral aromas belie bone-dry savouriness in lightly-oaked **10** with nice underlying pithiness. — IM

Hidden Valley Wines-Land's End Wines

Location/map: Stellenbosch ▪ WO: Stellenbosch/Western Cape/Elim ▪ Est/1stB 1995 ▪ Tasting, sales & cellar tours Mon-Fri 9-6 (summer) & 9-5 (winter) Sat/Sun 9-5 ▪ Fee R30pp ▪ Closed Dec 25/26 & Jan 1 ▪ Overture Restaurant ▪ Cheese/chocolate platters ▪ Picnics, to be pre-booked ▪ Table olives & olive oil ▪ Tour groups ▪ Conferences ▪ Weddings/functions ▪ Walks/hikes ▪ Conservation area ▪ Owner(s) David Hidden ▪ Winemaker(s) Emma Moffat (May 2010) & Louis Nel (consultant) ▪ Viticulturist(s) Johan 'Grobbie' Grobbelaar (Feb 1999) ▪ STB: 28ha/15ha (cab, merlot, p verdot, shiraz, tannat, sauv, viog); ELIM: 56ha/13ha (cab, p verdot, shiraz, sauv, sem) ▪ 120t/6,000cs own label 60% red 35% white 5% rosé ▪ BWI ▪ PO Box 12577 Die Boord 7613 ▪ info@hiddenvalleywines.com ▪ www.hiddenvalleywines.com ▪ S 34° 1'15.3" E 018° 51'13.9" ▪ **T +27 (0)21-880-2646** ▪ F +27 (0)21-880-2645

Dave Hidden's twin properties, in Elim and on the northern slopes of the Helderberg, offer an enviable range of vineyard sites. These are expressed in the terroir-specific eponymous and Land's End ranges, which grow in stature each vintage. The stylish contemporary cellar, with its sweeping views to the Bottelary Hills and perennial top ten restaurant, Overture, is well established as a tourist, wedding and function destination. The entire operation is committed to eco-responsibility, with the 'reuse, repair and recycle' philosophy deeply entrenched. For the intrepid, there is a nature trail, with secluded picnic sites.

Hidden Valley range

★★★★ **Barbera** Charming debut 08 Piedmontese offering had supple berry fruit with sundried tomato layers last year. Silky tannins, lingering finish.

★★★★ **Pinotage** ✓ Smoky, meaty, big-boned 09 shows complex layers of spices, ripe fruit & preserves. Substantial, solid & satisfyingly complete, reflecting fine vintage.

★★★★ **Hidden Gems** 📖 'Bordeaux Blend' last time. Big, thick & dark, overtly New-World 08 (★★★★☆) cab & petit verdot, satisfies on many levels. Great depth & intensity, complex liquorice/currant interplay & lingering finish on silky tannins. Less oak clout than 07 improves balance.

★★★★ **Hidden Secret** Listed as 'Mediterranean Blend' past editions. Dark, brooding 08 from shiraz & tannat bursts with black cherry fruit & Rhône-like spiciness. Rounded, smooth & satisfying.

★★★★ **Sauvignon Blanc** 📖 🌿 10 (★★★★) not revisited; ripe gooseberry & passionfruit, soft acidity. Follows pure yet unshowy 08.

Land's End range

★★★★ **Syrah** Riper, fuller 08 augers well for cool-region shiraz. Pleasant peppery herbaceous notes, robust tannins with sweet berry fruit, deserves year/2 to reveal its hidden charms.

★★★★ **Sauvignon Blanc** 📖 🌿 10 last year was rung above 08 (★★★★), had wild nettle & khaki bush notes over ripe, solid centre of bellpepper, lime & fig. From Elim grapes, as all these.

Rosé 📖 Await next. — GdB

High Constantia Wine Cellar

Location: Constantia ▪ Map: Cape Peninsula ▪ WO: Constantia/Coastal ▪ Est 1693 ▪ 1stB 2000 ▪ Tasting, sales & cellar tours Mon-Fri 8-5 Sat 10-1 ▪ Fee R40 ▪ Closed Easter Sun, Dec 25 & Jan 1 ▪ BYO picnic ▪ Meals pre-arranged with private chef, Marc Wassung ▪ Owner(s) David van Niekerk ▪ Cellarmaster/viticulturist(s) David van Niekerk (Jan 1999) ▪ Winemaker(s) David van Niekerk (Jan 1999) & Roger Arendse (Jan 2001) ▪ 14.5ha (cabs s/f, malbec, merlot, pinot, chard, sauv) ▪ 70t/5,500cs own label 52% red 15% white 3% rosé 30% MCC + 1,900cs for clients ▪ Brands for clients: Richeneau, Terra Madre ▪ Groot Constantia Rd Constantia 7800 ▪ david@highconstantia.co.za ▪ www.highconstantia.co.za ▪ S 34° 1'31.3" E 018° 25'36.1" ▪ **T +27 (0)21-794-7171/+27 (0)83-300-2064** ▪ F +27 (0)21-794-7999

The great days of Constantia's past are evoked here. Some of the vineyards leased by David van Niekerk were part of one of the famous old estates – its farmhouse has gone but its name lives on in this label, and that of its founder, Sebastiaan van Reenen, is honoured in the flagship red. No wines were tasted for this edition.

High Constantia range

★★★★ **Cabernet Franc** Lovely leafy aromatics & sweet fruit on 06 (★★★★) soon dissipate, losing out to ultra-savoury, wild undertones & dry tannic force. Leaner than pvs 04.

★★★★ **Malbec** Plush, aromatic, sweet-fruited 06 with big acid, dry tannins.

★★★★☆ **Sebastiaan** Well structured **06** (★★★★) blend 5 Bordeaux red varieties; but fugitive fruit leaves bones exposed, along with non-fruity elements. Less handsome than pvs **04**.

★★★★☆ **Sauvignon Blanc** 🍷 Creamy & fresh **10** sample with poise, balance & harmony.

★★★★ **Clos André MCC** Last tasted was dry but rich **07** (★★★★★). Like **06**, 70% chard & pinot.

Cabernet Sauvignon ★★★ Austere, simple **06** last tasted. **Merlot** 🍷 Await next, as for **Rosé** & **Viognier** in this range & **Viognier** in next.

Silverhurst range
Merlot 🍷 ★★★ Easy charm on **07**. **Rosé** 🍷 ★★★ Raspberry-fruited **07**. **Sauvignon Blanc** 🍷 ★★★ Delicious grassy-tropical **08**. — TJ

Highgate Wine Estate
 **NEW**

Location: Howick ▪ Map/WO: KwaZulu-Natal ▪ Est/1stB 2010 ▪ Tasting & sales daily 8-5 ▪ Closed Dec 25 & Jan 1 ▪ Facilities for children ▪ Coffee shop (see www.pigglywiggly.co.za) ▪ Wine, ceramics, gifts, linen, etc ▪ Garden centre ▪ Farm stall ▪ Owner(s) Rudi & Cindy Kassier ▪ Winemaker(s) Rudi Kassier, with Wal Bornheimer ▪ Viticulturist(s) Rudi Kassier ▪ 57ha/3ha (cab, merlot, ptage, shiraz, chard) ▪ 2.5t/420cs own label 50% red 50% white ▪ PO Box 1025 Howick 3290 ▪ rudi@pigglywiggly.co.za ▪ www.highgatewineestate.co.za ▪ S 29° 27' 29.92" E 030° 8' 8.66" ▪ **T +27 (0)82-895-1667** / **+27 (0)33-234-4323** ▪ F +27 (0)86-535-3187

In collaboration with the KwaZulu-Natal Department of Agriculture, Midlands Meander fresh-produce grower Rudi Kassier planted a single trial hectare of assorted wine grapes in 2005. They thrived, and Highgate Wine Estate now produces the areas's first certified chardonnay. Uncertified pinotage, merlot and shiraz sells as plain Dry Red, but will be better distinguished soon. All are shaped by Rudi's winemaking philosophy: 'Share information and don't be afraid to try something different.'

Lions River Chardonnay ★★ Characterful **10** is trim & firm with citrus fruit aromas. — Panel

---

Highlands Road Estate

Location/WO: Elgin ▪ Map: Elgin, Walker Bay & Bot River ▪ Est 2005 ▪ 1stB 2007 ▪ Tasting & cellar tours Wed-Sun 9-3 ▪ Sales daily 9-5 ▪ Closed Easter Sun/Mon, Jun 21, Jul 19, Dec 25 & Jan 1 ▪ Breakfast & light lunches ▪ Facilities for children ▪ Self-catering cottage (sleeps 4) ▪ Kayaking ▪ Fly fishing ▪ Boule ▪ Owner(s) Justin & Mary Hoy, Michael White ▪ Cellarmaster(s)/viticulturist(s) Justin Hoy (2007) ▪ Winemaker(s) Justin Hoy (2007), with Jacob September (2011) ▪ 28ha/9ha (pinot, chard, sauv) ▪ 60t/4,000cs own label 25% red 50% white 25% rosé ▪ PO Box 94 Elgin 7180 ▪ info@highlandsroadestate.co.za ▪ www.highlandsroadestate.co.za ▪ S 34° 14' 4.4" E 019° 4' 14.3" ▪ **T +27 (0)21-849-8699** ▪ F +27 (0)21-849-8699

The clan, as the word suggests, has a certain Gaelic ring, and some members are indeed Scottish; hence some of the wine names too. Ruadh means red and the new Cap Classique bubbly, Slainte, suitably means 'cheers!'. New marketing and sales lady, Joyan Balt, employed her creative talents in painting each bottle by hand.

Highlands Road range
Pinot Noir 🍷 **10** ex-tank, densely-hued with muted but ripe aromas, flavours. Too unformed to rate. **08** (★★★★); no **09**. **Ruadh** 🍷 ★★★ Straightforward **09** shiraz/merlot blend; juicy blackberry, smoky tones dimmed by roughish, dry tannins. **Rosé** 🍷 ★★★★ Fragrant, lightly spicy & dry **09** from merlot. Not re-tasted. **Sauvignon Blanc** 🍷 ★★★ Elgin's lively minerality on otherwise muted, short **10**. **Free Run Sauvignon Blanc** 🍷 Awaiting next release. **Sine Cera** 🍷 ★★★ **10** sauvignon-semillon blend less expressive than **09**. Quiet dried grass, earthy tones; lightish & briskly dry. **Slainte** **NEW** ★★★ NV MCC sparkler from Franschhoek chardonnay. Real pick-me-up style: lemony fresh, brisk pins-&-needles bubble, bone dry. — AL

Hildenbrand Wine & Olive Estate

Location/WO: Wellington ▪ Map: Paarl & Wellington ▪ Est 1991 ▪ 1stB 1999 ▪ Tasting & sales Mon-Sat 10-4 Sun 9-12 or by appt ▪ Fee R15pp wine tasting, R10pp olive & oil tasting ▪ Closed Easter Sat/Sun, Dec 24/25 & Jan 1 ▪ Restaurant open daily for breakfast, lunch & dinner ▪ Klein Rhebokskloof Country & Guest House ▪ Owner(s)/cellarmaster(s)/winemaker(s) Reni Hildenbrand ▪ ±4,167cs ▪ PO Box 270 Wellington 7654 ▪ info@wine-estate-hildenbrand.co.za ▪ www.wine-estate-hildenbrand.co.za ▪ S 33° 39'33.3" E 019° 1'46.3" ▪ **T +27 (0)82-656-6007**

2011 probably ranks as Wellington boutique winegrower Reni Hildenbrand's worst ever: her winemaker quit by SMS the day harvest started, a foreign student drafted in from Germany had to be bailed out of jail after smashing her pickup days later - and then fled without trace. Ever upbeat, Reni was bullish about 2011 quality and continued exports to Thailand.

★★★★ **Shiraz** Big wine though not bold, more understated in **07**. Cracked pepper, black cherry & warm spice meld in ripe palate. Not revisited.

Cabernet Sauvignon Barrique ★★★★ Plush blueberry texture to **07**'s muscular frame noted previously. Savoury, ripe, dry tannins from 17 months French oak, just 25% new. **Cabernet Sauvignon Unwooded** Await next. **Malbec** ◙ ★★★★ Bold blueberry & raisin vie with tangy acidity on **10**. Follows **07**, as preceding vintages sold out unreviewed. **Shiraz Rosé** 🔲 ◙ ★★★ **11** smoky raspberry flavours followed by dry grip. Tad less impressive than previous. **Chardonnay Barrique** ◙ ★★★★ **10** has nutty tangerine vibrancy, creamy rich vanilla from older oak & lees-ageing. **Chardonnay Unwooded** ★★★ Last reviewed **08** had zippy grapefruit freshness, substance & interest. **Chenin Blanc** ◙ ★★★ Toasty apricot with ripe mouthfeel, structure & breadth on **10**, long aftertaste. Only Hungarian oak used, mainly older. **Semillon** ★★★★ Last edition **08** continued tradition of lime zest & herbs on creamy, toasty palate from fermentation & 8 months ageing in oak, quarter new. **Lady Jemaima Cuvée** Untasted. **Bonnie & Claire** Await next vintage. **Sleepless Nights Semillon Noble Late Harvest** ★★★ **07** laudable effort, the name tells it all! Less sweet, hint of estate's distinctive grassiness a distraction on previous review. — FM

Hill & Dale

Easy-drinking wines vinified from grapes off selected Stellenbosch vineyards at Stellenzicht (see that entry for tasting/sales information).

Merlot ◙ ★★★ Uncomplicated **10** shows ripe red fruit, some herbal lift. **Pinotage** ★★★ **09** is medium bodied with plenty of red cherry flavour, fresh acidity & fine tannins. **Kosher Vin Rouge** New vintage not available. **Cabernet Sauvignon-Shiraz** 🔲 ◙ ★★★ **09** intense dark fruit, soft, little tannic structure. **Dry Rosé Merlot** 🔲 ◙ ★★★ Uncomplicated **11** has juicy red fruit, bright acidity. **Chardonnay** 🔲 ◙ ★★★ Plenty of citrus flavour on cleverly made, lightly wooded **11**, includes dash of semillon for freshness. **Sauvignon Blanc** 🔲 ◙ ★★ Neutral **11** lacks verve, doesn't linger. **Kosher Vin Blanc** Await new. — CE

Hillcrest Estate

Location/WO: Durbanville ▪ Map: Durbanville, Philadelphia & Darling ▪ Est/1stB 2002 ▪ Tasting & sales daily 9–5 ▪ Fee R100, waived on purchase ▪ Closed Easter Fri, Dec 25 & Jan 1 ▪ Cellar tours by appt ▪ Restaurant (T +27 (0)21-975-2346) open daily for breakfast & lunch ▪ Wedding/function venue ▪ Farm produce ▪ Walking/hiking & mountain biking trails ▪ Conservation area ▪ Owner(s) PD Inglis, R Haw & G du Toit ▪ Winemaker(s) Graeme Read (Jan 2003) ▪ Viticulturist(s) G du Toit ▪ 25ha (cabs s/f, malbec, merlot, p verdot, chard, sauv) ▪ 60t/±3,000cs own label 45% red 55% white ▪ Private Bag X3 Durbanville 7551 ▪ cellardoor@hillcrestfarm.co.za ▪ www.hillcrestfarm.co.za ▪ S 33° 49' 38.2" E 018° 35' 25.9" ▪ **T +27 (0)21-976-1110** ▪ F +27 (0)21-975-2195

The star of this small-scale Durbanville farm continues to rise. Recently rated one of the most successful wineries at the Trophy Show, taking top honours for its merlot (as in 2007) and gold for its Bordeaux blend. Red wines that 'warm the soul' are what really fire up self-trained winemaker and former marine biologist, Graeme Read. Since his first vinous epiphany in the 70s and making his own wine in 2002, he has continued to fine-tune these vineyards and wines. Bottlings of individual Bordeaux varieties from small experimental plots debut this edition. Equally creative is the conversion of an old quarry into a stylish visitor venue and showcase for the special metamorphosed rock that gives the wines that 'x' factor.

Metamorphic Collection

Quarry ★★★★★ Highly acclaimed **09** merlot raises the bar on **08** (★★★★). Lovely purity of fruit, with violets & minerality, complemented by new oak. Complex & polished, it is balanced in youth with pedigree to age. **Hornfels** ★★★★★ Serious & structured **09** a step up on **08** (★★★★). Powerful, ripe & complex 5-way Bordeaux blend with layers of dark berries & cedar from 100% new oak. Youthful & cellarworthy.

Hillcrest Estate range

Cabernet Franc NEW ✓ ★★★★ **10** cooler vintage, cab franc debuts with perfumed, pristine fruit. Refined, balanced & juicy. **Malbec** NEW ◙ ★★★ Meaty dark fruit & leather on brooding **10**. Tad gruff in youth, time will harmonise & allow fruit to shine. **Petit Verdot** NEW ✓ ★★★★ **10** good varietal inky/blueberry fruit & structure. Streamlined drinkability, for the table & few years cellaring. **Cabernet Sauvignon-Merlot** ★★★ **08** was a savoury, tight 5-way Bordeaux blend when tasted. **Cabernet Sauvignon Rosé** 🖿 ★★★ Al fresco style **11** is creamy, with savoury red berry tone. **Sauvignon Blanc** ✓ 🖿 ★★★★ **10** shows Durbanville's dusty, flinty character. Quite intense, with grapefruit tang & food-pairing pithy grip. Discontinued: **Chardonnay**. — MW

Hillock Wines

Map: Klein Karoo & Garden Route ▪ Est 2010 ▪ 1stB 2011 ▪ Tasting, sales & cellar tours daily 10-5 ▪ Closed Dec 25 ▪ Light lunches & refreshments 10-5 daily; or BYO picnic ▪ Tour groups ▪ Gifts ▪ Farm produce ▪ Guided hikes & vineyard tours ▪ Mountain biking ▪ 4-star Guest House (sleeps 14), Mymering Estate www.mymering.com ▪ Owner(s) Andy & Penny Hillock ▪ Cellarmaster(s) Mark Carmichael Green (Nov 2010, consultant) ▪ Winemaker(s) Duan Brits (Oct 2010, consultant) ▪ Viticulturist(s) Riaan Steyn (consultant) ▪ 400ha/50ha (shiraz, chard, chenin) ▪ 20t/ 1,800cs own label 25% red 75% white ▪ PO Box 278 Ladismith 6655 ▪ penny@mymering.com ▪ www. hillockwines.com ▪ S 33° 29′ 55.24″ E 021° 10′ 18.65″ ▪ **T +27 (0)21-551-1548** ▪ F +27 (0)28-551-1313

Situated on Mymering Guest Farm on the outskirts of Ladismith, this boutique operation has been growing grapes for twenty years, before finally taking the plunge and making wine themselves. For co-owner Dr Andy Hillock, a retired surgeon, this is the fulfilment of a lifelong dream and he and wife Penny believe the region has a big future. Visitors to the farm can expect a warm welcome, especially from manager Barend's pair of black king poodles!

▪ **Hilltop** *see* Rosendal Winery
▪ **Hippo Creek** *see* PicardiRebel
▪ **His Master's Choice** *see* Excelsior Vlakteplaas

Hofstraat Kelder

Location: Malmesbury ▪ Map/WO: Swartland ▪ Est 2002 ▪ 1stB 2003 ▪ Tasting, sales & tours by appt ▪ Owner(s)/ cellarmaster(s)/winemaker(s) Wim Smit, Jack de Clercq & Jerry Finley ▪ 2.5t/125cs own label 100% red ▪ PO Box 1172 Malmesbury 7299 ▪ renosterbos@cornergate.com ▪ S 33° 26′ 56.1″ E 018° 44′ 1.8″ ▪ **T +27 (0)83-270-2352** ▪ F +27 (0)22-487-3202

Last vintage saw the construction of a new cellar by these boutique vintners in Malmesbury. 'It's small, but big enough for our needs,' says co-owner and winemaker Wim Smit. Winemaking is as natural and traditional as possible, producing remarkable food-friendly combinations.

Renosterbos range
★★★★ **Barbera** Bold & powerful **10** misses the elegance of **09** (★★★★★). Ripe intense black cherries, firm assertive tannins & warm grip. Not for the faint-hearted (15.2% alc).
Cabernet Sauvignon ★★★ **10** not the same complexity as **09** (★★★★★). Ripe blackcurrant & fynbos, good balance, ripe tannin structure & oaky finish. Like all reds following, needs 2-3 years to develop fully. **Merlot** ★★★★ **09** last year was improvement on **08** (★★★★): complex aromas delicately supported by bright acidity & well-managed tannins. **Pinotage** NEW ★★★★ Dark & brooding **10** brims with plum, spicy fynbos & hint of coffee. Lovely acid balance to mop up ripe, sweet fruit. **Shiraz** ★★★ Bold **10** with house-style hefty alc (15.3%), still a wild child - needs a hearty meat dish. Discontinued: **Cape Vintage**. — WB

Holden Manz Wine Estate

Location/map/WO: Franschhoek ▪ Est 1999 ▪ 1stB 2005 ▪ Tasting, sales & cellar tours daily 10-5 ▪ Fee R10 ▪ Franschhoek Kitchen Restaurant lunch Tue-Sun 12-3 dinner Tue-Sat 6-10 ▪ Spa ▪ Picnic area ▪ Farmer's market ▪ Owner(s) Gerard Holden & Migo Manz ▪ Cellarmaster(s) Mark Carmichael-Green (Aug 2004, consultant) ▪ Winemaker(s) Mark Carmichael-Green (Aug 2004, consultant), with Melvin Davids (Jan 2009) ▪ Viticulturist(s) Tertius Oosthuizen (Sep 2010) ▪ 20ha/16ha (cabs s/f, merlot, shiraz) ▪ 110t/6,666cs own label 90% red 5% rosé 5% port ▪ IPW ▪ PO Box 620 Franschhoek 7690 ▪ info@holdenmanz.com ▪ www.holdenmanz.com ▪ S 33° 56′ 6. 3″ E 019° 7′ 8.3″ ▪ **T +27 (0)21-876-2738** ▪ F +27 (0)21-876-4624

In August 2010 Gerard Holden and Migo Manz bought Klein Genot (under which name this entry last appeared). They changed the name and a new brand was born. 2010 also saw the birth of the French Kitchen run by young Bjorn Dingemans, an establishment focusing on serving produce sourced directly from the organic garden. Looking to the future this new team looks to add fun, enhance their social media footprint and build on their Decanter Wine Award successes.

Holden Manz range NEW

★★★★ **Shiraz** 08 exudes savoury varietal notes. Palate follows with & supple tannins. Sweet impression from oak & poised ripeness rounds off a focused red.

Big G ★★★★ 09 equal parts cab & cab franc. Rich & confident in style with fresh herbal lift. **Rosé** ☐ ★★★ From cab, **10** has winey nose with firm dry tannins. **Good Sport Cape Vintage** ★★★ 09 serious port-style intention, but dense fruit, brandy spirit & obvious oak need to meld. Broach in 5 years. From shiraz.

Klein Genot range

Cabernet Sauvignon ★★★★ Blueberries & liquorice, creamy oak, rich fruitful finish on **08**. All in this range tasted last edition. **Merlot** ★★ 08 savoury & a touch developed; drink up. **Shiraz** ★★★ Bright & plush **08** melds showy oak (20% new) with ripe fruit. **Dry Cabernet Sauvignon Rosé** ☐ ★★★ Oaked 09's red & dark fruit v appealing, red-wine like. — JP

■ **Homtini** see Anthony de Jager Wines
■ **Honeypot** see Origin Wine

Hoopenburg Wines   🍷🎋⛏📷

Location/map: Stellenbosch ▪ WO: Stellenbosch/Coastal ▪ Est/1stB 1992 ▪ Tasting, sales & cellar tours Mon-Fri 8. 30-4 ▪ Fee R20/6-8 wines ▪ Closed all pub hols ▪ BYO picnic ▪ Conference facilities ▪ Guest house T +27 (0)21-884-4534 ▪ Owner(s) Gregor Schmitz ▪ Cellarmaster(s) Anton Beukes (Aug 2009) ▪ Viticulturist(s) Gert Snyders ▪ 70ha/30ha (cab, merlot, shiraz, chard) ▪ 180t/20,000cs own label 80% red 18% white 2% MCC ▪ Transit Organic - Control Union ▪ PO Box 1233 Stellenbosch 7599 ▪ info@hoopenburg.com ▪ www.hoopenburgwines.co.za ▪ S 33° 49'33.4" E 018° 49'9.3" ▪ **T +27 (0)21-884-4221** ▪ F +27 (0)21-884-4904

In these economic times not a lot of cellars can post 'Sold Out' on some of their top wines. In Hoopenburg's case it's attributable to the pricing and quality from all-bushvine vineyards, which clearly resonates with the buying public locally and overseas. The Integer range production is small and you know that because each label records exactly how many barrels were produced. An MCC was added here, and not neglecting other ranges, a new Rosé widens the Guru taste spectrum.

Integer range

★★★★☆ **Cabernet Sauvignon** Remarkable fruit intensity on **08**, with a stage on which to shine provided by finely judged oak. Seamed-in savouriness part of the appeal, as is sleekness (only 13% alcohol), an almost nervy tension, like a well-bred racehorse.

★★★★ **Syrah-Mourvèdre-Carignan** Name change from 'Red'. Not to be hurried, plenty in store, **09** (★★★★★) improves on **08** with layered dried herbs, spice, lush berries that already seduce & will continue to do so till ±2016, firmly ripe tannins almost guarantee it. WO Coastal.

★★★★ **Chardonnay** As always from this cellar, **08** is a triumph of layered complexity. Hazelnuts & preserved citrus peel, touch of lime, yet the finish manages to retain a savouriness, dry edge. Perfect for fine dining.

★★★★ **White** Chenin-led blend from Swartland, oaked 18 months. Last **08** was dry, but the restraint stopped there. Honey nougat & shortbread became more lemony on the palate, a savoury textured mouthfeel.

★★★★ **Méthode Cap Classique Brut** NEW Bone-dry NV made with care, chardonnay & pinot noir, part oak-ferment, 2 years on lees. Classic toasted brioche & lemon zest, good acid underpin gives freshness, length.

Syrah ★★★★ Stylistically different to previous, **07** has asphalt & smoky tones in its wild berries, more Old World than New, savoury & lithe.

Hoopenburg Bush Vine range

Cabernet Sauvignon ✓ ★★★★ Inviting plums, blackcurrants, **08** is tasty & smoothly accessible, amenable tannins a hidden backbone. **Merlot** ★★★ White pepper & plums, nice palate freshness, 09's youthful tannins best matched to rich casseroles. **Pinot Noir** ☐ ★★★★ From 18 year old vineyard, **09** has classic styling, red berries & forest floor, firm but ripe tannins finishing nicely dry. **Shiraz** ✓ ★★★★ Sleek & streamlined, **08** gives pure drinking pleasure, smoky dark fruit capturing the essence of shiraz. WO Coastal. **Chardonnay** ★★★★ Lemon preserve & shortbread, an attractive savoury/fruit juxtaposition in last tasted **08**. **Sauvignon Blanc** ★★★★ Previously trim **10** preview showed greengage fruit with a mineral underpin, good reflection of Elgin provenance.

Guru range

Merlot ★★★ Last was **08**, dark-fruit warmth, some oak & a friendly dab of sugar. **Cabernet Sauvignon-Merlot** Await next. **Rosé NEW** 🍷 ★★★ **11** cranberries in a dry package, fresh & fruity summer fare. WO Coastal. **Sauvignon Blanc** ★★★★ Previously elegant **10** had nettles & greenpepper perfume, flavours, was quintessential sauvignon, pure & bright. WO W Cape. — CR

Hornbill Garagiste Winery

Location: Hermanus ▪ Map: Elgin, Walker Bay & Bot River ▪ WO: Walker Bay ▪ Est 2004 ▪ 1stB 2005 ▪ Tasting, sales & tours Mon-Fri 9-5 Sat 9-2 ▪ Closed Easter Fri/Sun, Dec 25 & Jan 1 ▪ Gifts ▪ Art gallery & ceramic studio ▪ Restaurant ▪ Owner(s) John Dry ▪ Winemaker(s) John Dry (2004) ▪ 6t/400cs own label 100% red ▪ PO Box 4 Hermanus 7200 ▪ hornbill@intekom.co.za ▪ www.hornbillhouse.co.za ▪ S 34° 24′ 46.3″ E 019° 11′ 54.4″ ▪ **T +27 (0)28-316-2696** ▪ F +27 (0)28-316-3794

Family and friends help produce these truly artisanal wines, dovetailing perfectly with John Dry's established ceramic craftsmanship. Grapes are selected and sourced from different sites in the Hemel-en-Aarde Valley and produced in the absence of modern technology, thus ensuring that the wines have real personality.

Hornbill Garagiste Winery range

Reinet ★★★ Like next, previously tasted. **08** from merlot with dab cab showed plush fruit & a savoury end. **Milan** ★★★★ Ripe & fruity, individual **07** from merlot, cab, shiraz. Discontinued: **Merlot**.

The Naked Vines Collection range NEW

Merlot-Mystique ★★★ Dry-finishing **09** has sweet plummy fruit; ripe & extracted. — JP

▪ **Horse Mountain** *see Doran Family Vineyards*
▪ **Houdamond** *see Bellevue Estate Stellenbosch*
▪ **Houdconstant** *see Jacob's Quest Wines*

House of Mandela

WO: Stellenbosch/Coastal/Elgin ▪ Est/1stB 2009 ▪ Closed to public ▪ Owner(s) Makaziwe Mandela, Mandla Mandela & Tukwini Mandela ▪ Cellarmaster(s) Charles Back, Gyles Webb & Carl Schultz (Jun 2009, Fairview/Thelema/Hartenberg) ▪ Winemaker(s) Anthony de Jager, Rudi Schultz & Patrick Ngamane (Jun 2009, Fairview/Thelema/Hartenberg) ▪ Viticulturist(s) Various ▪ 62.5% red 37.5% white ▪ info@houseofmandela.com ▪ www.houseofmandela.com

For this young negociant business, owned by Nelson Mandela's children Tukwini, Mandla and Makaziwe, 2012 will be not only the Chinese Year of the Dragon but also their 'Year of the Launch': into the Chinese and US markets, and of an affordable wine range tentatively named Thembu. Hopefully the Dragon Year, associated with leadership and authority, will prove auspicious for the family of South Africa's former president and one of the most revered men on the planet.

Royal Reserve range

★★★★☆ **Cabernet Sauvignon** Seductive **08** classic cab nuances of cassis, lead pencil; silky precision, fine tannins, harmonious oak. Not revisited, like siblings. WO Stellenbosch.

★★★★ **Shiraz** From Paarl single-vineyard, **07**'s brooding black fruits wrapped in powerful, solid tannins. Rich, with savoury grip. WO Coastal.

★★★★ **Chardonnay 09** barrel-fermented, aged 10 months for vanilla glow to apple blossom & citrus; crisp lemony tail follows creamy core. From Elgin vines. — CvZ

Hout Bay Vineyards

Location: Hout Bay ▪ Map: Cape Peninsula ▪ WO: Hout Bay/Western Cape/Paarl/Stellenbosch ▪ Est/1stB 2004 ▪ Tasting, sales & cellar tours by appt ▪ Fee R30, refunded when case is purchased ▪ Closed Easter Fri-Mon, Dec 25/26 & Jan 1 ▪ Facilities for children ▪ Owner(s) Peter & Catharine Roeloffze ▪ Cellarmaster(s)/winemaker(s)/viticulturist(s) Peter & Catharine Roeloffze (Jan 2004) ▪ 1.5ha/1.1ha (pinot, pinot meunier, chard) ▪ 7.2t/1,400cs own label 47% red 22% white 7% rosé 24% MCC ▪ Other export brand: HB Vineyards ▪ PO Box 26659 Hout Bay 7872 ▪ cathy@4mb.co.za ▪ www.houtbayvineyards.co.za ▪ S 34° 1′ 31.0″ E 018° 22′ 31.0″ ▪ **T +27 (0)83-790-2372** ▪ F +27 (0)86-514-9861

This is very much a hands-on operation. Peter and Cathy Roeloffze have built everything - from their home, to vineyard terraces on the mountainside (each vine tied to a single stake), to bringing back machinery in their hand luggage! As their range grows, from their tiny, often improvised cellar, so does their confidence.

Cabernet Sauvignon ★★★ Ex-barrel, bold **09** shows very ripe dense fruit & tannins needing long time to soften. Reds except Shiraz from bought-in grapes. This, next, WO W Cape. **Merlot** ✓ ★★★★ Ripe & fruitily rich **09** sample nicely reined in by fresh, savoury acid, firm structure. 2 years oak adds classy dimension. **Shiraz** NEW ★★★★ Preview of **09** from maiden harvest reveals attractive, if simple spicy fragrance, clean, fresh flavours and comfortably cushioned tannins. **Petrus** ★★★★ Opulent 5-varietal Bordeaux blend **09** from Paarl fruit tasted pre-bottling. Good concentration, balance & structure augur well. **08** (★★★) opulent, from just 3 varieties. **Blush** ★★★ Raspberries & cream **11** slips down with easy charm. Dry but smooth & just 11% alc. Chardonnay, pinot noir/meunier blend. **Sauvignon Blanc** ★★★★ **11** quieter, more elegant, food friendly than **10**. Gentle tropical tones enlivened by taut mineral thread, subtly spiced by Acacia wooded portion. **Klasiek by Catherine** ★★★★ **08** zero dosage chardonnay, pinot blend with 3 yrs on lees. Crisply dry with creamy mousse, attractive fresh brioche nose, delicate baked apple fruit. **Black Swan Vintage Port** NEW ★★★★ Equal parts 5 port varieties infuses fortified **10** with aromatic interest. Properly dry, good fruit; perhaps lacks grip for long ageing. WO Stellenbosch. Discontinued: **Bordeaux Blend**. — AL

Howard Booysen Boutique Wines

Location: Stellenbosch ▪ WO: Swartberg/Stellenbosch ▪ Est 2009 ▪ 1stB 2010 ▪ Sales by appt ▪ Owner(s) Howard Booysen ▪ Cellarmaster(s)/winemaker(s)/viticulturist(s) Howard Booysen (Nov 2009) ▪ (cinsaut, riesling) ▪ 1,400cs own label 50% red 50% white ▪ howard@howardbooysenwines.com ▪ www.howardbooysenwines. com ▪ T +27 (0)72-414-5458

Boutique winemaker Howard Booysen has two preoccupations: cinsaut and riesling. The latter is destined for bottling in magnums as collector's items, a rather unique concept in South Africa; and he wants to (re)kindle the consumer's enthusiasm for the former. 'If you ask me in 20 years' time what has been my greatest achievement, I want to answer simply 'making cinsaut and riesling'.'

★★★★★ **Weisser Riesling** 🖼 Takes its lead from Germany's sweeter QmP styles rather than Australia's drier versions. Still-selling **10** persistent lime cordial flavours, finish; floral & Turkish Delight nuances mid-2010. **Cinsaut** NEW 🖼 ★★★★ Premium-priced **11** a blueprint for the variety: expressive & soft-centred; creamy red berry & hint black olive; light oaking, lowish alc, gentle sweetness - delightful & incredibly easy to drink. — CvZ

Hughes Family Wines

Location: Malmesbury ▪ Map/WO: Swartland ▪ Est 2000 ▪ 1stB 2004 ▪ Tasting by appt ▪ Owner(s) Billy & Penny Hughes ▪ Cellarmaster(s) Billy Hughes ▪ Winemaker(s) Billy Hughes & Jeremy Borg ▪ Viticulturist(s) Kevin Watt (Jul 2005, consultant) ▪ 52ha/27ha (grenache, merlot, mourv, ptage, tempranillo, shiraz, chenin, grenache b, rouss, viog) ▪ 180t total 25t/1,800cs own label 85% red 15% white ▪ 6 Riverstone Road Tierboskloof Hout Bay 7806 ▪ penny@nativo.co.za ▪ www.nativo.co.za ▪ S 33° 20'37.71" E 018° 43'45.09" ▪ T +27 (0)21-790-4824 ▪ F +27 (0)86-549-1080

Billy Hughes's farm should receive full organic accreditation this year. His grapes will receive endorsement from the leading Swartland producers he supplies, as well as going into his own ever-improving wines, which in style and spirit are well attuned to the excitement of this dynamic area. 'To make life more interesting' there are new plantings of unusual varieties, as well as developments in the cellar, where Billy seeks 'better ways to natural winemaking'.

Nativo range

★★★★ **White Blend** 🖼 As before, **10** has rich, powerful, dry presence. 75% oaked viognier well disciplined, plus chenin. Less oxidative than many neighbours, but not simply fruity. Best after year or two. **Red Blend** ★★★★ **09** shiraz-led blend (plus 4 others) has pure freshness of **08** (★★★★), promises more. Unshowy - just honest, lovely new-wave Swartland wine. These gain complexity with few years. — TJ

Huguenot Wine Farmers

Closed to public ▪ Owner(s) Kosie Botha ▪ Cellarmaster(s) Bill Matthee (1984) ▪ Trade enquiries Gert Brynard ▪ PO Box 275 Wellington 7654 ▪ jcb@mynet.co.za ▪ **T** +27 (0)21-864-1293 ▪ F +27 (0)21-873-2075

Privately owned wholesalers, blending, marketing and distributing a wide range of wines, liqueurs and spirits. Own wine brands include Huguenot and Zellerhof.

- **100% Cape Town** *see* Catch Of The Day
- **Hunting Family** *see* Slaley
- **Husseys Vlei** *see* Buitenverwachting
- **Idelia** *see* Swartland Winery

Idiom Wines

Location: Somerset West ▪ Map: Helderberg ▪ WO: Stellenbosch ▪ Est 1999/1stB 2003 ▪ Tasting & sales: see Whalehaven ▪ Vineyard tours by appt (Sir Lowry's Pass) ▪ Owner(s) Bottega Family Wines ▪ Winemaker(s) Reino Thiart ▪ Vineyard manager(s) Tim Clark ▪ 35ha (barbera, cabs s/f, merlot, mourv, nebbiolo, p verdot, ptage, sangio, shiraz, zin, sauv, sem, viog) ▪ 85% red 15% white ▪ PO Box 3802 Somerset West 7129 ▪ wine@idiom.co.za ▪ www.idiom.co.za, www.bottegafamilywine.co.za ▪ S 34° 6' 14.1" E 018° 56' 12.4" ▪ **T** +27 (0)21-858-1088 **(vyds)**, +27 (0)21-852-3590 **(sales)**, +27 (0)28-316-1633 **(tasting)** ▪ F +27 (0)21-858-1089 (vyds), +27 (0)21-851-5891 (sales), +27 (0)28-316-1640 (winery)

Much happening at Da Capo Vineyards, Helderberg home to Idiom Wines. Owners Bottega Family Wines now host the annual La Vendemmia harvest festival here in the first weekend of March to celebrate their Italian heritage. Then there's the introduction of two new entry-level Italian varietal blends. 'Rosso di Montalcino? No, Rosso di Stellenbosch!' says co-proprietor Roberto Bottega. The family now also distribute wines for 15 top Italian producers in a bid to create more awareness around Italian varieties.

Idiom range

★★★★ **900 Series Cabernet Sauvignon 05** still selling. Rich & full, with ultra-ripe fruit, high alc, 2 years new oak.

★★★★ **900 Series Nebbiolo 07** was serious proposition last edition with dark cherry fruit, fresh acidity & firm but fine tannins.

★★★★ **Merlot-Pinotage-Cabernet Sauvignon-Petit Verdot** After accomplished **07** (★★★★★), exuberant **08** shows wide array of aroma & flavour: plums, red cherry, fynbos & toasty oak. Rich & full, good intensity before savoury finish.

★★★★ **Viognier** Rich, broad **09** (★★★★) lacks elegance of **08**. Peach, touch of honey, soft acidity.

900 Series Cabernet Franc ★★★ Some attractive red fruit on last **06**, overwhelming oak may since have settled & integrated. **900 Series Barbera** ★★★★ Last edition **08** noted for concentrated red & black fruit, smooth tannins, soft acidity. **900 Series Mourvèdre** NEW ★★ Ultra-ripe, meaty **08** appears excessively weighty, tired. **Sangiovese** ★★ Meaty, savoury **08** lacks purity of fruit, richness of previous. **900 Series Shiraz** NEW ★★ Ponderous **07** displays jammy character, lacks refreshment. **Zinfandel** ★★★★ **07** last time was textured, with grip & fresh acidity. Followed mammoth **06** (★★★★). **Cabernet Sauvignon-Merlot-Cabernet Franc-Petit Verdot** ★★★ Fragrant, medium-bodied **08** is step back from ultra-ripeness of retasted **07** (★★★★) but seems a little developed, not for further keeping. **Shiraz-Mourvèdre-Viognier** ★★★★ Soft & accessible **08** shows juicy red & black fruit, some floral fragrance & spice. **900 Series SMV** ★★★ **05** broad red-fruit flavour, some savouriness & lots of oak when last tasted.

Enoteca Bottega range

Super Rosso 🍷 ★★★ Pizza-friendly **09** from 83% sangiovese, rest cab, merlot is fruit-driven yet not overly sweet. Follows last-tasted, powerful cab-led **05** (★★★★). **Rosso** 🍷 ★★★ **10** from 4 Italian varieties not as interesting as might be hoped for. — CE

- **Ikapa** *see* Handcrafted Wines

Imbuko Wines

Map: Paarl & Wellington ▪ WO: Western Cape ▪ Est/1stB 2004 ▪ Tasting Mon-Fri 9-4 Sat by appt ▪ Fee R15 for 5 wines ▪ Closed all pub hols & Dec 25 to Jan 1 ▪ Sales 8-5 ▪ Meals/refreshments by appt (48hr notice) ▪ Olives, olive oil, pinotage/merlot/shiraz jams, pinotage relish ▪ Owner(s) Imbuko Wines (Pty) Ltd ▪ Cellarmaster(s) Theunis van Zyl (2004) ▪ Viticulturist(s) Jan-Louw du Plessis ▪ 60ha (cab, cinsaut, merlot, ptage, shiraz, chenin, sauv, viog) ▪ 570t/40,000cs own label 60% red 40% white ▪ Other export brands: Makulu, Releaf Organic & Rebourne Fairtrade, Van Zijls Family Vintners ▪ Fairtrade, IPW, Organic ▪ PO Box 810 Wellington 7654 ▪ crm@imbuko.co.za ▪ www.imbuko.co.za ▪ S 33 40'30.84" E 019 01'18.87" ▪ **T +27 (0)21-873-7350** ▪ F +27 (0)21-873-7351

The Du Plessis family farm, home to son-in-law Theunis van Zyl's thriving wine export business, is now part of the Wellington Wine Walk vineyard trail. Visitors can add the (untasted by us) Van Zijls Family Vintners blends - honouring the winemaker's branch of the family - and the Pomüla pink pétillant muscat to the vinous choice, accompanied by pre-ordered, deli-sourced platters and picnics.

Du Plevaux range

Pinotage ⧈ ★★★ **10**, previewed from barrel, earthy mocha styling, ripe plum & berry-edged savoury twist. **Shiraz** ⧈ ★★★ Sampled pre-bottling, **10** offers strawberry jam & chocolate juiciness. **Sauvignon Blanc** ⧈ ★★★ **11** pungent herbal aromas, full body & nettly flavour.

Imbuko range

Cabernet Sauvignon ▤⧈ ★★ Easy-drinking & fruity **10**, with fresh blackberry aromas. **Pinotage Rosé** ▤ ★★ **10** was a fresh, off-dry strawberry quaffer last year. **Chardonnay** NEW ▤⧈ ★★★ Appealing fresh-baked bread & peach styling, **11** is charming & relaxed. **Sauvignon Blanc** ▤⧈ ★★ **11** crisp lunchtime sipper with summer fruit salad flavours. — DB

■ **Indaba** *see* Cape Classics
■ **Indalo** *see* Swartland Winery
■ **Infiniti** *see* Kumkani
■ **Infusino's** *see* Beau Joubert Vineyards & Winery
■ **Ingenuity** *see* Nederburg Wines
■ **Inkará** *see* Bon Courage Estate
■ **Integer** *see* Hoopenburg Wines

Intellego Wines

Location: Tulbagh ▪ Est/1stB 2009 ▪ Closed to public ▪ Owner(s) Jurgen Gouws ▪ 30cs own label 100% white ▪ jurgen@intellegowines.co.za ▪ **T +27 (0)82-392-3258**

Jurgen Gouws, owner of boutique brand Intellego ('Understand'), has added a year at Swartland rising-star winery Lammershoek to his CV. A Swartland devotee, with old-vine chenin as one of his calling cards, Jurgen is well placed to be part of the back-to-basics movement that's revitalising and transforming the area. We look forward to his next instalments.

■ **Interlude** *see* Nwanedi Estate
■ **Intulo** *see* Kumala

Iona Vineyards

Location/WO: Elgin ▪ Map: Elgin, Walker Bay & Bot River ▪ Est 1997 ▪ 1stB 2001 ▪ Tasting, sales & tours Mon-Fri 8-5 Sat by appt ▪ Closed all pub hols ▪ Walks/hikes ▪ Mountain biking ▪ Conservation area ▪ Owner(s) Andrew & Rozanne Gunn, Workers Trust ▪ Winemaker(s) Werner Muller (May 2011), with Thapelo Hlasa (Jun 1997) ▪ Viticulturist(s) Kevin Watt (Jan 2002, consultant) ▪ 100ha/40ha (cab, merlot, mourv, p verdot, pinot, shiraz, chard, sauv) ▪ 250t/12,000cs own label 25% red 75% white ▪ BWI ▪ PO Box 527 Grabouw 7160 ▪ orders@iona.co.za ▪ www.iona.co.za ▪ S 34° 16'42.2" E 019° 4'58.2" ▪ **T +27 (0)28-284-9678** ▪ F +27 (0)28-284-9078

Iona's wines could feature prominently in a SA vs France taste-off of classic regions: Bordeaux, Burgundy, Sancerre, Northern Rhône (both white and red). Andrew Gunn is vehement about his property's climate being at least as cool as Bordeaux's, allowing for long ripening periods and therefore able to produce fruit of comparable elegance, purity and concentration. Influenced by high altitude and a cool, proximate ocean, the natural fruit acidity of the vineyards is a winner, as is the judicious oaking in John Seccombe's cellar.

★★★★ **Syrah** Convincing **06**, then classic **07** (★★★★★) tasted last year. Fruit purity, boosted by splash mourvèdre. Supporting oak let compact fruit & mineral core lead to long clean finish.

★★★★ **The Gunnar** ✓ 'Elgin too cool for cab' sceptics proved wrong in savoury **07** Bordeaux style blend. Merlot, petit verdot add aromatic complexity & soften cab's youthfully austere edge.

★★★★☆ **Chardonnay** Exquisite **09** had tightly wound mineral, citrus core last edition. Piercing flavours structured by taut acidity & well-measured oak. Poised, expressive finish; needed time to show full complexity.

★★★★☆ **Sauvignon Blanc** ✓ 🍾 Flinty, vibrant **10** with dash semillon & lees contact to add dimension to lean, bone dry style. Steely minerality & acid core conceals apple fruit which needs year at least to show full promise - this wine often underestimated when sampled too early.

★★★★ **Viognier** NEW Exotically spicy & overtly floral, oaked **09** pithy & stylish with minerality more obvious than fruit. Ripe viognier's high alcohol integrated; low acid softens austerity.

Discontinued: **Noble Iona**. — IM

■ **Isis** see Schalkenbosch Wines
■ **Island View** see Orange River Wine Cellars
■ **Ivy Du Toit** see Jason's Hill Private Cellar
■ **Ixia** see Distell

Izak van der Vyver Wines

Location/WO: Elgin ▪ 1stB 2002 ▪ Closed to public ▪ Owner(s) Izak van der Vyver ▪ Cellarmaster(s) Andries Burger (Paul Cluver Wines) ▪ Winemaker(s) Izak van der Vyver (Jan 2002) ▪ 1.4t/75cs own label ▪ PO Box 42 Grabouw 7160 ▪ drs@telkomsa.net ▪ **T +27 (0)21-859-2508** ▪ F +27 (0)21-859-3607

Dr Izak van der Vyver laments he can only harvest 1.5 tons of grapes on account of his work – as a busy Grabouw general practitioner. He gathers faultless fruit from rows 13 and 14 on nearby Elgin farm Smarag in the early morning, and has the cool juice in the Paul Cluver cellar, where he crafts his 900 bottle haul by morning tea.

Sauvignon Blanc 🍷 ★★★★ River-stone & gunflint notes to grapefruit profile in tense **10** last edition. — DS

■ **Jabulani** see Winegro Marketing

Jacaranda Wine & Guest Farm

Location/WO: Wellington ▪ Map: Paarl & Wellington ▪ Est/1stB 2009 ▪ Tasting & sales Mon-Sat 10-5 ▪ Fee R15/3 wines, served with olives & bread ▪ Closed Easter Fri/Sun, Dec 25 & Jan 1 ▪ Vineyard tours ▪ Mediterranean/cheese platters & picnic baskets by appt ▪ B&B: 2 rooms in Manor House & 2 cottage units (see Accommodation section) ▪ Owner(s) René & Birgit Reiser ▪ Cellarmaster(s)/winemaker(s)/viticulturist(s) René Reiser (Jun 2009) ▪ 4.5ha/4ha (cab, merlot, shiraz, chenin, viog) ▪ 9t/750cs own label 50% red 40% white 10% rosé ▪ PO Box 121 Wellington 7654 ▪ jacarandawines@gmail.com ▪ www.jacarandawines.co.za ▪ S 33° 36' 49.2" E 019° 0' 16.1" ▪ **T +27 (0)21-864-1235**

Under new ownership since 2009, the Wellington farm's 20 to 30-year-old vines are being pampered back to their former glory and the cellar is slated for renovation. A B&B, forerunner of an agro-tourist venture, is now in operation, while dynamic owners René and Birgit Reiser have still found time to open a Wine Discoveries Vinothek in Shanghai to store-front their Asian wine export business.

Jacaranda range NEW

Cuvée Rouge 🍷 ★★★ Juicy, fruity uncomplicated Bordeaux blend **09** made for early drinking. **Pinotage Rosé** 🍷 🍾 ★★ Casual easy-sipping **10**, sweet red-fruit flavour & dry finish. **Chenin Blanc** 🍷 🍾 ★★ **10**, with splash viognier, in Old World un-fruity style, quite evolved but still pleasant & food amenable. — Panel

■ **Jackals River** see Beaumont Wines
■ **Jackleberry** see Saam Mountain Vineyards
■ **Jacksons** see Stanford Hills Winery

Jacobsdal Estate

Location/map/WO: Stellenbosch ▪ Est 1916 ▪ 1stB 1974 ▪ Tasting & sales at Bergkelder (see entry) ▪ Owner(s) Dumas Ondernemings (Pty) Ltd ▪ Cellarmaster(s) Cornelis Dumas ▪ Winemaker(s)/viticulturist(s) Cornelis Dumas, with Hannes Dumas ▪ 100ha (cab, ptage, chenin, sauv) ▪ 600t/13,000cs own label 100% red ▪ PO Box 11 Kuils River 7579 ▪ info@jacobsdal.co.za ▪ www.jacobsdal.co.za ▪ S 33° 58' 4.9" E 018° 43' 34.6" ▪ **T +27 (0)21-881-3336** ▪ F +27 (0)21-881-3337

Jacobsdal, in the Dumas family for three generations, is as typical a farm as you can imagine. There are sheep, cattle, a roomy homestead and, of course, vines. First bottling under own label was in 1974 and current winemaker is Cornelis, in charge since the 1960s. Bushvines grown in the meagre soil get no irrigation and have to fend for themselves. In the cellar only open cement fermenters are used, and all fermentation is natural. It doesn't get more old school.

Cabernet Sauvignon ★★★ Classically styled **07** exhibits blackcurrant, dusty oak; light bodied & well balanced. **Pinotage** ★★★ Pleasant, straightforward **08** has plum, red cherry & clove flavours; medium bodied & fruit driven, with fresh acidity. — CE

Jacob's Quest Wines

Location: Malmesbury ▪ WO: Swartland ▪ Est/1stB 2008 ▪ Tasting & tours by appt at Greenacres Garagiste @ Houdconstand (T +27 (0)22-931-2213) ▪ Winemaking during harvest time by appt ▪ Closed all pub hols ▪ Picnic baskets (pre-booked) ▪ Self-catering 'Owl Cottage' on Houdconstand farm ▪ Owner(s) 5 shareholders ▪ Winemaker(s) Dico du Toit ▪ 30ha (cab, chard, chenin) ▪ 300t/1,500cs own label 10% red 30% white 60% rosé + 150,000L bulk ▪ PO Box 727 Malmesbury 7299 ▪ sales@greencorp.co.za ▪ www.jacobsquest.com ▪ **T +27 (0)22-487-2233** ▪ F +27 (0)22-487-1916

In a quest to develop a wine brand specifically for the emerging black market, co-owner Jacob Peu joined forces with Des Green and grape growers in the Porterville area. In a short time, they succeeded beyond expectation, attracting a following among a wide spectrum of young South Africans. Encouraged, they're now thinking bigger and want JQW to become a household name.

Right of Passage Cabernet Sauvignon 🍷 ★★★ Briefly oaked **09** appealing combo sherbety strawberry favour, vanilla tail. Not revisited, as all. **Pétillant White Wine (Semi-Sweet)** 🍷 ★★★ Breezy & spritzy semisweet. **NV** to enjoy well chilled, like next. **Natural Sweet Pétillant Rosé** 🍷 ★★★ Strawberry hues & flavours, gently sweet, appealing prickle on the tongue. **NV**. — CvZ

■ **Jacoline Haasbroek Wines** *see* My Wyn

Jacques Smit Wines

Location/WO: Wellington ▪ Map: Paarl & Wellington ▪ Est/1stB 2003 ▪ Tasting, sales & tours by appt ▪ Closed Easter Fri/Sun/Mon, Ascension Day, Dec 25/26 & Jan 1 ▪ Facilities for children ▪ Owner(s) Jacques & Marina Smit ▪ Cellarmaster(s)/winemaker(s)/viticulturist(s) Jacques Smit ▪ 60ha/32ha (cab, roobernet, shiraz, chenin, Cape riesling) ▪ 300t total 100% red ▪ Welvanpas PO Box 137 Wellington 7654 ▪ info@vines2wine.com ▪ www.vines2wine.com ▪ S 33° 39′ 2.2″ E 019° 1′ 9.0″ ▪ **T +27 (0)21-873-1265** ▪ F +27 (0)21-873-2143

'Nurtured from only the best rootstock' is Jacques Smit's motto. As he is also a vine nurseryman, his wines start in the nursery, then the vineyard and in the cellar he brings what nature has to offer into the wine glass. 'Back to the basics, soil slope and sun, we use what we have to make natural wines.'

Limited Releases

Cabernet Sauvignon ★★★★ Juicy & appealing **07** easy-going mealtime companion. Like most others, still selling & not revisited. **Shiraz** ★★★★ Last-tasted **05** had lively palate, intense fruit hiding heavy 16% alc. **Vine Valley** ★★★★ Boldly fruited **06** blend cab (67%) & shiraz nicely integrated, pleasing firm handshake. **Chenin Blanc** Await new. **Cape Ruby Roobernet Port** ★★★★ Exuberantly fruity **07** given ageability by firm tannins. Also in 375ml.

Jacques Smit Wines range

Discontinued: **Cabernet Sauvignon**. — DB

■ **Jake White** *see* Wildekrans Wine Estate

Jakkalsvlei Private Cellar

Location: Herbertsdale ▪ Map: Klein Karoo & Garden Route ▪ Est 1987 ▪ 1stB 2008 ▪ Tasting & sales Mon-Fri 9.30-5 Sat 9.30-3 ▪ Closed Easter Fri & Dec 25 ▪ Cheese platters ▪ Deli ▪ BYO picnic ▪ Walks/hikes ▪ Mountain biking ▪ Owner(s)/cellarmaster(s)/viticulturist(s) JG Jonker ▪ 80ha/26ha (merlot, ptage, hanepoot) ▪ 280t/2,500cs own label 35% red 23% white 12% rosé 30% dessert + 125,000L bulk ▪ PO Box 79 Herbertsdale 6505 ▪ info@

jakkalsvlei.co.za ▪ www.jakkalsvlei.co.za ▪ S 33° 59' 15.31" E 021° 43' 9.33" ▪ **T +27 (0)28-735-2061** ▪ F +27 (0)86-593-0123

Jantjie Jonker's pleasure in sharing 'being part of everything to do with wine: soil preparation, planting, pruning, winemaking, marketing' is palpable in his standing invitation to all to join in all sorts of activities, including the annual Barefoot Grape Dance (helping make your own bottle of wine) and the Jakkalsvlei Mountain Bike Challenge. His small 'domain' range (available in shops between Riversdale and Plettenberg Bay) is the cherry on the top of the farm's bulk-wine business as supplier to Distell since 1983.

Jakob's Vineyards

Location: Hermanus ▪ WO: Walker Bay ▪ Est 2002 ▪ 1stB 2006 ▪ Closed to public ▪ Owner(s) André & Yvonne de Lange ▪ Winemaker(s) Peter-Allan Finlayson (consultant, 2010) ▪ Viticulturist(s) Johan Pienaar (consultant, Jun 2003) ▪ 5ha/2ha (cabs s/f, merlot) ▪ 12t/±500cs 100% red ▪ PO Box 15885 Vlaeberg 8018 ▪ wine@jakobsvineyards.co.za ▪ www.jakobsvineyards.co.za ▪ **T +27 (0)82-371-5686** ▪ F +27 (0)86-589-4619

Named after his father, this tiny Walker Bay vineyard was owner André de Lange's childhood dream. The young vines are delivering better fruit, and since the 2010 vintage, the wine has been made by Peter-Allan Finlayson of Crystallum (see separate listing), son of neighbour Peter. The focus is back on a single wine, the Bordeaux blend, its 2008 not ready for tasting this edition but due for release early 2012.

Cabernet Sauvignon ★★★★ Last was **06**, firm but amenable tannins, allowed full expression to spice & red berry fruit. **Bordeaux Blend ★★★★** Last **07** cab-led blend showed layered fennel, earthy & brambleberry styling, elegance. Oak supported 4+ years cellaring. — CR

Janeza Private Cellar

Location: Bonnievale ▪ Map/WO: Robertson ▪ Est 2000 ▪ 1stB 2001 ▪ Tasting & sales by appt Mon-Sat ▪ Fee R5 p/p for tour groups ▪ Owner(s) Jan & Eza Wentzel ▪ Winemaker(s) Jan Wentzel ▪ Viticulturist(s) Hennie Visser (consultant) ▪ 6ha (cab, merlot, shiraz) ▪ 3,200cs own label 100% red ▪ BWI member ▪ PO Box 306 Bonnievale 6730 ▪ jan.eza@lando.co.za ▪ www.janeza.co.za ▪ S 33° 57' 36.3" E 020° 1' 38.2" ▪ **T +27 (0)23-616-3547** ▪ F +27 (0)23-616-3547

The name of this small Robertson cellar is a combination of the first names of owners Jan and Eza Wentzel, who both grew up in this wine valley. They favour traditional winemaking methods, and personally welcome visitors (by appointment) to their tasting room in a restored stable.

Tresuva ★★★ Cab (48%), merlot & shiraz are 'Three Grapes' in Spanish name. Dark & spicy **07**'s firm tannins noted last time may have softened, showing wine's potential. **Dulcevida ★★★** Fortified dessert from red muscadel & muscat de Hambourg; previously **07** was ebullient with sunny fruit, cleansing acidity. — Panel

  ◼ **Jardin** *see* Jordan Wine Estate
  ◼ **Jason's Creek** *see* Jason's Hill Private Cellar

Jason's Hill Private Cellar

Location: Rawsonville ▪ Map: Breedekloof ▪ WO: Slanghoek/Breedekloof ▪ Est/1stB 2001 ▪ Tasting & sales Mon-Fri 8-5 Sat 10-3 (summer) & 10-1 (winter) ▪ Fee R10 ▪ Closed Easter Fri-Sun, Dec 25 & Jan 1 ▪ Cellar tours by appt ▪ Bistro Tue-Sun 10-3 ▪ Shop ▪ Facilities for children ▪ Weddings/functions ▪ 6.5km hiking trail ▪ Owner(s) Du Toit family ▪ Cellarmaster(s)/winemaker(s) Ivy du Toit (Jan 2001) ▪ Viticulturist(s) Alister Oates (Jan 2004) ▪ 100ha (shiraz, chenin) ▪ 800t 45% red 50% white 5% rosé ▪ Other export brands: Jason's Creek, Meme, Soet Izak, Stout Izak & Wolvenbosch ▪ PO Box 14 Rawsonville 6845 ▪ info@jasonshill.co.za ▪ www.jasonshill.com ▪ S 33° 39' 52.3" E 019° 13' 40.6" ▪ **T +27 (0)23-344-3256** ▪ F +27 (0)86-523-6655

'Wine is our life,' says Ivy du Toit, winemaker at the family farm in the scenic Slanghoek Valley, where a new wedding venue has been added to the varied visitor facilities. The Cape Leopard Trust set up cameras on the hiking route to survey faunal biodiversity, and among the animals caught on this 'candid camera' have been the rare honey badger and Cape fox, as well as a beautiful adult male leopard.

Jason's Hill range

Merlot ★★ Sweet berry notes on uncomplicated **09**. **Pinotage** ★★ Jammy, charred character on **09**. **Shiraz** ★★★ **09** offers meaty, smoky-savoury notes with sweet berry fruit for easy quaffing. **Classic Red** ★★★ Nutty **09** with red berry compote, minty hint, ripe winter warmer. Breedekloof WO. **Chenin Blanc** 🍽 🌿 ★★ Subtle floral notes on fresh & undemanding **11**. **Sauvignon Blanc** 🍽 🌿 ★★ Light, green & crisp **11**. — Panel

▪ **JC Kannemeyer** *see* Wolfkloof
▪ **JC le Roux** *see* The House of JC le Roux

Jean Daneel Wines

Location: Napier ▪ Map: Southern Cape ▪ WO: Western Cape/Coastal ▪ Est/1stB 1997 ▪ Tasting & sales Tue-Sat 8-4 ▪ Closed Dec 25 & Jan 1 ▪ Cellar tours by appt ▪ Restaurant & deli ▪ Owner(s) Jean & René Daneel ▪ Winemaker(s) Jean-Pierre Daneel ▪ 30t 50% red 50% white ▪ PO Box 200 Napier 7270 ▪ info@jdwines.co.za ▪ www.jdwines.co.za ▪ S 34° 27′55.7″ E 019° 53′45.4″ ▪ **T +27 (0)28-423-3724** ▪ F +27 (0)28-423-3197

Jean Daneel's son, Jean-Pierre, has had a sterling first year back in the cellar, 'sterling' being an appropriate word, given that Jean Daneel Wines is once again selling in the UK after a break. New markets have opened up in Asia and the US as well, and local sales are up: 'We're completely sold out'. Volumes are also up, with 15% more chenin in the bottle last year, thanks to a buy-in from a 65-year-old Malmesbury vineyard. The hunt is now on for even older Swartland vines.

Signature Series

★★★★ **Red** ✓ Perfumed & savoury blend cab, merlot & shiraz, lengthy (33 months) barrel maturation yields standout **08** (★★★★★), showing beautifully knit tannins & velvet texture. Superb. Follows more powerful & fruity **05**. WO W Cape.

★★★★ **Directors Signature Red** Statuesque **05** from cab, merlot & shiraz not revisited; on review, needed few years for athletic tannins to meld with plush fruit. WO Coastal.

★★★★☆ **Chenin Blanc 10** tour de force in challenging vintage, small oak fermented/aged portion (some new barrels) noticeable but doesn't overpower chenin's bruised apple & quince character. Wonderful dry & savoury conclusion. Attractively steely, like **09**, will reward ageing.

★★★★ **Brut** Méthode cap classique sparkling from chenin, base wine fermented & aged year in oak. Last edition, **05**'s weight & creaminess from 4 years lees-ageing gave pleasing balance.

Discontinued: **Shiraz, Chardonnay Brut**.

JD Initial Series

Red ★★★★ **10** merlot-led blend with healthy dollop cab, ripe but not jammy, bright acid profile ensuring refreshment. **White** ✓ ★★★★ Upbeat **10** unoaked pairing of chenin, colombard, sauvignon & chardonnay, for early drinking. Enough weight & fruit for solo sipping or spicy foods. **Port** ★★★ Last was fiery & sweet **02** from Franschhoek pinotage, tasted previously. — Panel

▪ **Jemma** *see* Painted Wolf Wines
▪ **JH Pacas & Co** *see* Bernheim Wines
▪ **Jil's Dune** *see* Springfontein Wine Estate
▪ **JJ Handmade Wines** *see* StellenRust
▪ **Johan de Wet Wines** *see* Lorraine Private Cellar
▪ **John Brutus** *see* Seven Sisters
▪ **John B** *see* Kaapzicht Wine Estate
▪ **Jonathan's Ridge** *see* Springfontein Wine Estate

Jonkheer

Location: Bonnievale ▪ Map: Robertson ▪ WO: Robertson/Western Cape ▪ Est 1912 ▪ 1stB 1956 ▪ Tasting & cellar tours by appt ▪ Wine sales Mon-Fri 8-5 at Jonkheer offices in Main Str ▪ Closed all pub hols ▪ 4 self-catering Guest Houses ▪ Lifestyle Centre ▪ Owner(s) Andries Jonker & Dirk Du Plessis Jonker ▪ Cellarmaster(s)/winemaker(s) Erhard Roothman (Feb 1971) ▪ Viticulturist(s) Andries Jonker (1984) ▪ 300ha/130ha (cab, merlot, muscadel r/w, ptage, chard, pinot grigio, sauv) ▪ 1,500t/17,000cs own label 25% red 65% white 10% rosé ▪ PO Box 13 Bonnievale 6730 ▪ info@jonkheer.co.za ▪ www.jonkheer.co.za ▪ S 33° 56′54.9″ E 020° 2′48.4″ ▪ **T +27 (0)23-616-2137/8/9** ▪ F +27 (0)23-616-3146

Jonkheer turns 100 this year and, to celebrate, owners Dirk and Andries Jonker invite you to come over to the family spread near Bonnievale and have a glass of wine. You'll find expanded guest accommodation, including a new honeymoon suite overlooking the Breede River, and, converted from an old, unused part of the cellar, a lifestyle centre stocked with imported furniture and interior items. And to drink there is the popular Es la Vida lifestyle perlé range, now rebranded.

Jonkheer range

★★★★ **Muscatheer** From 30+ year old muscat de Frontignan bushvines. **05** (★★★★) first since maiden **00**, shade less elegant. Not revisited, as for Chardonnay below.

Pinotage Await new, as for **Shiraz Family Reserve**. **Chardonnay Family Reserve** ★★★ Zesty **09** had buttered pear flavours mid-2010. **Buccanheer Touriga Nacional** ★★★★ Individual & attractive lighter styled fortified dessert, **04** shows a combination of port, sherry & jerepiko characters. At peak, enjoy soon. Robertson WO. Last-tasted **02** (★★★★) offered Xmas-cake flavours.

Bakenskop range

Cabernet Sauvignon ★★ Easy-drinking **10** clean blackcurrant with hint of oak. Like Merlot, Shiraz & Chardonnay, not revisited. **Merlot** ★ **10** berry-tinged & very light. **Pinotage** ✓ 🔲 🔊 ★★★☆ Unapologetically pinotage, decidedly good & a huge bargain. **11** fleshy banana & strawberry fruit, slippery as Teflon. W Cape WO, as most of these. **Shiraz** ★★ **10** amiable savoury braai mate. **Chardonnay** ★★ Gentle, pear-toned & light **10**. **Sauvignon Blanc** 🔲 🔊 ★★ Previewed **11** in lighter, more delicate style. **Es la Vida Blanca** 🔲 ★ 'Es la Vida Perlé' last time. Lightly spritzy low-alc sweet white from muscadel, current **NV** bottling more flavoursome than new red sibling. **Es la Vida Rosa** NEW ★ Tingly-on-tongue sweet red, **NV**, with muscadel's fragrant grapiness. **Red Muscadel** Await new. **White Muscadel** 🔲 Untasted.

Beacon Hill range

Sauvignon Blanc In abeyance.

Cape Auction range

Red 🔲 ★★ No newer versions tasted of this plummy **NV** crowd pleaser, nor rest of range. **Rosé** ★★ Rosé from pinotage & muscat for the sweet-toothed. **NV**. **White** 🔲 ★★ Last **NV** showed soft quaffability. **Late Harvest** ★★ Previously **NV** was an affable chenin/semillon duo. — Panel

Joostenberg Wines

Location: Paarl ▪ Map: Paarl & Wellington ▪ WO: Paarl/Western Cape ▪ Est/1stB 1999 ▪ Tasting & sales daily 9–5 at the Deli on Klein Joostenberg Farm ▪ Cellar tours by appt ▪ Closed Dec 25 & Jan 1 ▪ Joostenberg Bistro (see Restaurants section) ▪ Facilities for children ▪ Tour groups ▪ Gifts ▪ Farm produce ▪ Honey shop ▪ Conferences ▪ Ludwigs rose nursery & Van den Berg garden centre ▪ Owner(s) Philip & Tyrrel Myburgh ▪ Cellarmaster(s)/viticulturist(s) Tyrrel Myburgh (1999) ▪ 31ha (cab, merlot, mourv, shiraz, touriga nacional, chenin, rouss, viog) ▪ 120t/8,000cs own label 35% red 50% white 15% NLH ▪ PO Box 82 Elsenburg 7607 ▪ winery@joostenberg.co.za ▪ www. joostenberg.co.za ▪ S 33° 49' 34.8" E 018° 47' 45.5" ▪ **T +27 (0)21-884-4141** ▪ F +27 (0021-884-4135

Joostenberg has been in the Myburgh family since 1877 but customers rarely see the grand old buildings of the farm itself (you can visit them on the attractive website). The wines are sold in the nearby hugely popular Deli and Bistro, dedicated to selling 'the best possible agricultural products' and run with flair by the family with chef-extraordinarie and son-in-law Christophe Dehosse. Under the sensitive care of Tyrrel Myburgh, the wines also show flair without excess.

Joostenberg Wines range

★★★★ **Syrah** 🔲 Last tasted was fresh, vibrant **07**, co-fermented with viognier.

★★★★ **Bakermat** 🔲 **09** reflects cab's firm structure (52%) with syrah, splashes merlot, touriga, viognier for aromatic interest. Full-bodied but unheavy; great balance & great drink after yr/2. No **08**.

★★★★ **Fairhead** 🔲 Chenin-based **10** joined by viognier & a litle roussanne. More pronounced aromatics than **09**, still refined; gently creamy with purity, freshness. Natural ferment in barrel.

★★★★☆ **Chenin Blanc Noble Late Harvest** Golden nectar from single old chenin vyd. Touch less botrytis to fresh lime marmalade scents on **10**; still beguiling, with poise that belies its full body, rich sweetness. Natural ferment/9 months in oak.

Shiraz-Merlot 🗎 ★★★★ Attractive interplay of spice & dark soft berries on **09**. Rich & ripe with fresh core, lively tannins; digestibly dry. **Chenin Blanc-Viognier** 🗎 ★★★★ **10** includes usual precisely judged splash oaked viognier; lifts chenin's tropical/melon aromas, adds texture. Quietly delicious.

Little J range

> **Red** ☺ 🗎 ★★★ Lots of warm, spicy appeal in **09** shiraz-led blend. Rounded, accessible.

Rosé 🗎 ★★★ **10** from cinsaut. Juicy red fruits, just-dry spicy tail. This range all WO W Cape. **White** 🗎 ★★★ Mainly chenin, hint aromatic interest from viognier. **10** fruitily dry, easy. — AL

Jordan Wine Estate

Location/map/WO: Stellenbosch ▪ Est 1982 ▪ 1stB 1993 ▪ Tasting & sales daily 9.30–4.30 ▪ Fee R25pp, waived on purchase ▪ Closed Easter Fri-Mon, Dec 25 & Jan 1 ▪ Cellar tours by appt Mon-Fri 9.30–4.30 ▪ Jordan Restaurant (see Restaurants section) ▪ Farm produce ▪ Conferences (60 pax) ▪ Walks/hikes ▪ Mountain biking ▪ Conservation area ▪ Visits to old prospector's mine shafts ▪ Fly fishing (catch & release) R100/adult & R50/child under 12, booking essential ▪ Owner(s) Jordan family ▪ Cellarmaster(s) Gary & Kathy Jordan (1993) ▪ Winemaker(s) Sjaak Nelson (Jan 2002), with Brendan Butler (Feb 2009) ▪ Viticulturist(s) Gary Jordan (1983) ▪ 146ha/105ha (cab, merlot, syrah, chard, sauv) ▪ 850-950t/50,000c own label 45% red 54% white 1% rosé ▪ Other export brand: Jardin ▪ Brands for clients: Pick's Pick, Woolworths ▪ BWI, HACCP ▪ PO Box 12592 Die Boord Stellenbosch 7613 ▪ info@ jordanwines.com ▪ www.jordanwines.com ▪ S 33° 56'33.7" E 018° 44'41.3" ▪ **T +27 (0)21-881-3441** ▪ F +27 (0)21-881-3426

Wine names are always significant at this top-rank Stellenboschkloof estate. While Cobblers Hill is a reference to the family's footwear history and Sophia the mother of Faith, Hope and Charity (the three best barrels are chosen for this Cape Winemakers Guild wine), Gary Jordan's geological training and interest pops up in the naming of two wines, Outlier Sauvignon Blanc - the vineyard situated on a geological outlier with a 360° view of the Cape Peninsula - and Prospector Syrah which is in the centre of 2010's failed tin mining attempt. To show visitors some of the old prospector mine shafts on the estate, a 'Big 5' wine, fauna and flora trail is planned. On the food front, Jordan Restaurant made the SA top 3 in at the Eat Out Awards, and High Timber in London is now listed in the Michelin Guide.

Jordan Estate range

★★★★ **Cabernet Sauvignon** ✓ 🗎 Year later, **08** has many layers of interest, blackcurrants, beef biltong, dried herbs. Harmoniously oaked, it is smooth textured, perfect for current enjoyment.

★★★★ **Merlot** ✓ 🗎 Cassis & mocha chocolate, seductive **09** has had a lot of attention, 2 years French barriques, 80% new, but well integrated with the plush fruit. Drink now till ±2016.

★★★★☆ **Cobblers Hill** Barrel-selected Bordeaux blend carefully made, 2 years new French barriques, aims for harmony & cracks it. Lush dark berries in **08**, cedar-spice, tobacco leaf; admirable polish, supple tannins provide current enjoyment, an 8 year future.

★★★★☆ **Sophia** Blend of best Cobblers Hill barrels & a reserve cab. Dark chocolate & black cherries, complex & involving **08** hovers between savoury & fruity; grassy/herb whiffs add a further dimension. Sleekly muscular, one to keep, but already delicious. Small French oak 26 months.

★★★★ **Chardonnay Barrel Fermented** 🗎 🎨 Just 'Chardonnay' previously. Shortbread & citrus, **10** back on track after **09**'s (★★★★) lack of depth; sparks with vitality, freshness & flavour, delicious to drink.

★★★★☆ **CWG Auction Reserve Chardonnay** Best Nine Yards barrels. Less overt, more sophisticated than sibling, **10**'s (★★★★★) aroma is ever changing: citrus, pears, crushed almonds, hint of vanilla. Tighter focus on palate gives limy freshness, silky tension, oak never intrudes. Even better than compelling powerhouse **08**.

★★★★☆ **Nine Yards Chardonnay** 🗎 🎨 Ex single-vineyard, **10** fermented/matured 95% new Burgundian oak, portion natural ferment. Clementine & lemon preserve, toasted brioche, rich & powerful but plenty palate appeal, sleekly curvaceous, flavours laced with bright acidity.

★★★★ **The Outlier Sauvignon Blanc** 🗎 🎨 A different take on sauvignon, one that can age 3/4 years. Barrel fermented/matured, gives **10** a smoky character, but gooseberries are there as a broad base of fruit.

★★★★ **Sauvignon Blanc** 🗎 🎨 Green figs, some passionfruit in **11** preview; has attractive palate roundness to accompany the tangy citrus-toned acidity, an ultra long finish.

★★★★ **Mellifera Noble Late Harvest** 🔒 **11** (★★★★★), more intense than **10**, shows riesling aromas with consummate style: floral notes & cardamom spicing, a perfume delicacy counterpoint to rich, intense pineapple flavours. Brightening acidity leaves a delicious tanginess.

The Prospector Syrah 🍷 ★★★★ Name change from 'Syrah'. Lovely ripe fruit on **09**, creamy cappuccino & supple tannins; earlier drinking than red siblings. **Unoaked Chardonnay** 🍷 🔒 ★★★★ Bright-fruited **11** shows the fresh, unadorned face of chardonnay. Tropical toned with lemon acidity, & very tasty. **Chenin Blanc** 🍷 ★★★★ Fruit-driven, last-tasted **09** had quince & melon, a touch of spice. Combo older barrels & tank. **The Real McCoy Riesling** 🍷 🔒 ★★★★ Just 'Riesling' previously. Nice floral & tropical aromas, off-dry **10** continues appeal with pineapple flavours. Racy acidity keeps it fresh.

Bradgate range

> **Syrah** ☺ 🍷 ★★★ Good rendition **09** is smoky, dark-fruited & succulent; has enough grip for few years ageing. French barriques, 40% new. **Cabernet Sauvignon-Merlot** ☺ 🍷 ★★★ Showing blackcurrant intensity from major partner, **09**'s immediate appeal belies the oaking (50% new), could age 3-4 years.

Sauvignon Blanc-Chenin Blanc 🍷 🔒 ★★★ Tropical-toned **10** has appealing fruity freshness.

Chameleon range

> **Cabernet Sauvignon-Merlot** ☺ 🍷 ★★★ Dusty, earthy overlay to **09**'s red berries, the oak (50% new) showing in the sturdy structure. Youthful, drink till 2016. **Sauvignon Blanc-Chardonnay** ☺ 🍷 🔒 ★★★ Drinkability is key in **11** preview; fig & lime flavours add interest, there is good palate weight, freshness.

Rosé ✓ 🍷 🔒 ★★★★ Admirable restraint in **11** from merlot & shiraz, exactly right for food, enough berries for perfume/flavour, light enough for more than a glass. — CR

■ **Joubert Brothers** *see Beau Joubert Vineyards & Winery*

Joubert-Tradauw Private Cellar

Location: Barrydale ▪ Map: Klein Karoo & Garden Route ▪ WO: Tradouw ▪ Est/1stB 1999 ▪ Tasting, sales & cellar tours Mon-Fri 9-5 Sat 10-2 ▪ Closed Easter Fri/Sun & Dec 25 ▪ R62 Deli Mon-Fri 9-3 Sat 10-1 breakfasts, lunches & Klein Karoo tapas ▪ Walks/hikes ▪ Mountain biking ▪ Conservation area ▪ Lentelus B&B (www.lentelus.co.za) ▪ Owner(s) Lentelus Family Trust ▪ Cellarmaster(s)/winemaker(s)/viticulturist(s) Meyer Joubert (1999) ▪ 1,100ha/ 30ha (cab, merlot, shiraz, chard) ▪ 2,500cs own label 70% red 30% white ▪ PO Box 15 Barrydale 6750 ▪ info@ joubert-tradauw.co.za ▪ www.joubert-tradauw.co.za ▪ S 33° 55' 26.4" E 020° 35' 40.6" ▪ **T +27 (0)28-572-1619** ▪ F +27 (0)86-555-3558

Friendly and affordable wines are complemented at the Jouberts' scenic family estate by their R62 Deli, where you can tuck into 'Karoo tapas' and a slice of French chocolate cake. The former humble tin-roofed dwelling has been transformed into a Mediterranean farm kitchen, with fireplace and suitably rustic decor. Dine inside or out under the *afdak* with a Langeberg Mountain view. You can pick your own seasonal fruit here, milk a cow, and even view rock paintings.

Joubert-Tradauw Private Cellar range

★★★★ **Syrah** 🍷 One of the region's most accomplished unfortified reds. Dense black fruit & well-managed tannins in **08**, tasted out of vintage sequence. Smoky berries & cured meat, poise & focus.

★★★★ **Chardonnay 10** (★★★★) characterised by restraint & precision. Lemon fruit lightly seasoned with oak, long finish, modest 12.7% alc. Only missing complexity of **09**.

R62 ★★★★ Characterful '2nd red', usually Bordeaux blend but **08** is 100% cab, flagged last year as 'drink up'.

Unplugged 62 range

Red ★★ Previously, **07** shiraz had clean leather & forest floor notes, prominent alc (14%). **Sauvignon Blanc** 🍷 ★★★★ From venerable vines, **10** last year mixed cool fig & asparagus, had plenty of zingy appeal. — Panel

Journey's End Vineyards

Location: Somerset West ▪ Map: Helderberg ▪ WO: Stellenbosch ▪ Est 1995 ▪ 1stB 2001 ▪ Tasting, sales & cellar tours by appt Mon-Fri 9-5 Sat 9-1 ▪ Fee R50pp (incl cellar tour) ▪ Closed Easter Fri-Mon, Dec 25 & Jan 1 ▪ Cheese platters & snacks by appt; or BYO picnic ▪ Conferences (80 pax) ▪ Wedding venue (100 pax) ▪ Walks/hikes ▪ Mountain biking ▪ Conservation area ▪ Peacock Cottage with private pool (min 2 nights) ▪ Owner(s) Gabb family ▪ Cellarmaster(s)/winemaker(s) Leon Esterhuizen (Jun 2006) ▪ Viticulturist(s) Lodewyk Retief (Jun 2011) ▪ 50ha/ 32ha (cabs s/f, merlot, mourv, shiraz, chard, pinot gris, sauv, viog) ▪ 175t/15,000cs own label 80% red 20% white ▪ IPW ▪ PO BoX 3040 Somerset West 7129 ▪ info@journeysend.co.za ▪ www.journeysend.co.za ▪ S 34° 6'35.11" E 18°54'54.06" ▪ **T +27 (0)21-858-1929** ▪ F +27 (0)86-613-2164

This farm, high on the Schaapenberg, is fully exposed to the summer south-easterly wind blowing off False Bay. Dubbed the Cape Doctor, as it cools and helps prevent disease, it was an obvious name for the flagship wines. The Gabb family now have similar vistas with the purchase of neighbouring Mount Rozier; they also have what is probably the Cape's oldest pinot gris vineyard, planted in 1986.

Reserve range

★★★★☆ **Cape Doctor Cabernet Sauvignon** NEW **07** classically structured with its sweet, fresh fruit shielded by finely-grained tannins. Minty suggestion adds touch of modernity but savouriness is lasting memory. Well-judged oak (40% new) reinforces status.

★★★★ **The Cape Doctor Shiraz** Finely spiced, long **05** still selling. Last bottling under varietal label. From **10** will be blended with cab.

★★★★☆ **Destination Chardonnay** Infant **10** (★★★★) still tight. A little limey substance, but bold spice, vanilla sweetness from all-new oak more obvious - may harmonise with year/2. **06** was last tasted.

Journey's End range

★★★★ **Merlot** ✓ **06** was dominated by mint, herbal notes, but red fruits & meaty fragrance, bare trace of mint on **07**. Still tight, fresh; underlying gentle waves ripe fruit. Good presence, future prospects.

★★★★ **Chardonnay** ✓ 🍷 🎨 Unshowy limey, oatmeal purity on **10**. Supple, bouncy feel lifted by minerally core, very long. All-new French oak happily harmonised. Very good from a difficult vintge.

Cabernet Sauvignon ✓ ★★★★ Unshowy yet pure cab scents, flavours on **07**. Rounded tannins, some interesting savoury development make for tasty current drinking, 2-3 yrs potential. **06** (★★★★). **Shiraz** ★★★ Austere, mint-toned **06** still selling.

Cellar range

The Pastor's Blend 😊 📖 ★★★ Minty hint on **09** lifts merlot's rich meaty tones. Smoothly accessible with savoury, dry finish. Includes cab, shiraz. **Haystack Chardonnay** 😊 📖 ★★★ Plentiful peachy flavours on juicy **10**. Medium body, zesty; straightforward & accessible enjoyment. Aged in older oak. — AL

■ **Joy** see Anura Vineyards

JP Bredell Wines

Location: Somerset West ▪ Map: Helderberg ▪ 1stB 1991 ▪ Tasting & sales Mon-Fri 9-5 Sat by appt ▪ Owner(s) Helderzicht Trust ▪ Cellarmaster(s)/viticulturist(s) Anton Bredell ▪ Winemaker(s) Denzil Tromp ▪ 50ha/13ha (cab, merlot, ptage, pinot) ▪ 5,000cs own label 60% red 40% port ▪ PO Box 5266 Helderberg 7135 ▪ info@ bredellwines.co.za ▪ www.bredellwines.co.za ▪ S 34° 1'29.04" E 018° 46'18.72" ▪ **T +27 (0)21-842-2478** ▪ F +27 (0)21-842-3124

This property excels at producing port style wines and is one of the very few that consistently garner top awards besides the producers from the established Caltizdorp area. With no new releases available at time of going to press, one senses that here is a good opportunity to get a couple of mature ports and still wines that would be ready to drink. Wines are handcrafted with composed and balanced skill. Certainly worth searching out.

Bredell's range

★★★★ **De Rigueur** **08** cab-led blend still available at going to press. Tasted last edition.

★★★★ **Late Bottled Vintage** **04** still selling, in previous edition was as seductive as ever.

★★★★☆ **Cape Tawny Port** NV, 10 yrs in oak, still available at press time.

★★★★★ **Cape Vintage Reserve** Splendid **07** usual blend tinta, touriga, souzão. Intriguing, ripely dark dried-fruit aromas, orange-peel note highlighting complexity. Fiery in richly fruity-spicy & balanced style. Tasted last edition & still selling.

Cabernet Sauvignon Sold out, latest offering not ready. **Shiraz** ★★★★ Same vintage still selling, last tasted was **03**. **Cape Vintage** Await next. Discontinued: **Merlot**. — JP

■ **JP le Hanie Wines** *see* Vredevol Private Wine Cellar
■ **J Sainsbury's** *see* Saam Mountain Vineyards

Julien Schaal

WO: Elgin/Hemel-en-Aarde Valley ▪ Est 2004 ▪ 1stB 2005 ▪ Sales from Paul Cluver Estate (see entry) ▪ Tasting by appt only ▪ Owner(s)/winemaker(s) Julien Schaal ▪ 28t/2,000cs own label 85% red 15% white ▪ c/o PO Box 48 Grabouw 7160 ▪ julien@vins-schaal.com ▪ www.vins-schaal.com ▪ **T +33 (0)9-53-09-37-75** ▪ F +33 (0)3-90-29-81-27

Young Frenchman Julien Schaal travels south frequently from his wine estate in Alsace to make and nurture small volumes of wine in the Paul Cluver cellar. His working relationship there prompted an intercontinental joint venture – its first wine features below; the second will be a riesling made by Cluver winemaker Andries Burger in Alsace. Julien's quest for balance involves freshness, lowish alcohol and increasingly less new oak – but, he says, 'making an elegant wine is far more challenging and complicated!'

Julien Schaal range

★★★★ **Syrah** 🌣 What appeals most in sophisticated **10** (Hemel-en-Aarde fruit) is the light, supple freshness, with a firm basis of fruit & subtly strong structure. Will benefit from few years in bottle.

★★★★☆ **Chardonnay** 🌣 Impressive, rather grand **10** seems riper & richer than brilliant **09** (★★★★★), so a shade less focused, precise. But it's bright & forceful, the florality, citrus & understated oak support delivering a real treat - will improve 5+ years.

Schaal-Cluver range NEW

★★★★ **Shiraz** Schaal's **10** Elgin version promises more finesse, structure, intensity. Peppery, herbaceous notes & red fruit tell of cool origin. A little oaky now, but the fruit should win. — TJ

Juno Wine Company

Location: Paarl ▪ Map: Paarl & Wellington ▪ WO: Western Cape ▪ Est/1stB 2004 ▪ Tasting & sales at 191 Main Str Paarl Mon-Fri 8–5 Sat 9–1 ▪ Open most pub hols ▪ Café Juno ▪ Winemaker(s) Anthony de Jager ▪ Viticulturist(s) Thys Greeff ▪ ±50,000cs own label 40% red 54% white 6% rosé ▪ PO Box 68 Main Road Paarl 7622 ▪ info@junowines.com ▪ www.junowines.com ▪ S 33° 44' 36.9" E 018° 57' 46.1" ▪ **T +27 (0)21-872-0697** ▪ F +27 (0)21-872-1863

'In transition' is the word on Juno, the range of wines vibrantly illustrated by a bevy of buxom Cape beauties which even spawned a wine bar and cafe. The banners still wave from their negociant HQ in Paarl but there's a strategic realignment courtesy of Fairview's mastermind Charles Back who upped his stake and now owns the majority of this funky brand.

Juno range NEW

Cabernet Sauvignon ✓ 🍴 🌣 ★★★★ Complex blackcurrant, spice & plum pudding combo, **10** textured, dry but concentrated, has the structure to last a few years. **Shiraz** 🍴 🌣 ★★★★ Supple black fruit & cracked pepper on **10**, step up on previous. Dry, with firm tannic grip & density. **Sauvignon Blanc** 🍴 🌣 ★★ Lemon zest & grass on **11** from Darling fruit, lively & fresh.

Cape Maidens range

Rosé ☺ 🍴 🌣 ★★★ Cranberry cherry cheer on dry **10**, light & lively for summer. **Chardonnay** ☺ 🍴 🌣 ★★★ Zippy fresh grapefruit tang on **10**. Unoaked, with light body & structure. Ideal for ABC club members! **Chenin Blanc** ☺ 🍴 🌣 ★★★ Tangy appeal to **10**'s apricot & tangerine flavour. Unpretentious & fun. Succulent, with honeyed length.

Shiraz-Mourvèdre-Viognier 🍴 Occasional release. **Cabernet Sauvignon-Shiraz-Merlot** 🍴 🌣 ★★★★ Steady as she goes for cab-led (50%) **10**. Berry cocoa richness, with spicy density & grip, well knit components. — FM

■ **Kaap Agri** *see* Breëland Winery
■ **Kaapdal** *see* Robertson Wide River Export Company
■ **Kaaps Geskenk** *see* Groupe LFE South Africa

Kaapzicht Wine Estate

Location/map: Stellenbosch ▪ WO: Bottelary/Stellenbosch ▪ Est 1946 ▪ 1stB 1984 ▪ Tasting & sales Mon-Fri 9–4.30 Sat 9–12 ▪ Fee R20pp, waived on purchase ▪ Closed Easter Fri/Sun & Dec 25/26 ▪ Cellar tours by appt ▪ BYO picnic ▪ Conference/function/wedding & braai venues ▪ Walking/hiking & mountain biking trails ▪ Conservation area ▪ 2 self-catering cottages ▪ Scenic wine tours with 4x4 overlander ▪ 'Booze-Bus' (16 pax) with wine guide/winemaker on fun & informative tour, with option to braai & wine pair ▪ Owner(s) Steytdal Farm (Pty) Ltd/Steytler Family Trusts ▪ Cellarmaster(s) Danie Steytler snr (Jan 1979) ▪ Winemaker(s) Danie Steytler jnr (Feb 2009) ▪ Viticulturist(s) George Steytler (Jan 1984) & Schalk du Toit (Jun 2003) ▪ 190ha/162ha (cabs s/f, cincaut, malbec, merlot, p verdot, ptage, shiraz, chard, chenin, hanepoot, rouss, sauv, sem, verdelho) ▪ 1,100t/30,000cs own label 70% red 30% white + 10,000cs for clients ▪ Other export brands: Cape View, Friesland ▪ Brands for clients: Escapades, Handmade ▪ IPW ▪ PO Box 35 Koelenhof 7605 ▪ kaapzicht@mweb.co.za ▪ www.kaapzicht.co.za ▪ S 33° 54' 47.7" E 018° 44' 7.7" ▪ **T +27 (0)21-906-1620/1** ▪ F +27 (0)21-906-1622

The Steytlers don't rest on their considerable laurels. Interestingly, much of the development relates to white wines, although the estate's reputation rests mainly on its reds - some 70% of production, made in a rather massive, plush, darkly sweet-fruited (but impeccably dry) style. Now a 2011 sparkling wine is resting on its lees, and some interesting white varieties, roussanne and verdelho, have been planted. The idea is to develop a top-level multi-varietal white blend, based on their chenin off what is one of the oldest blocks of this variety in the Cape. A joint venture with a winery in Germany looks promising, and back home you can now take tours around the Bottelary area in the 'Booze Bus' (actually 'our old 4x4 Overlander'), with genial Danie Steytler dealing deftly with any questions.

Steytler range

★★★★☆ **Pinotage** Intense, sweet-fruited (but bone-dry) 08 with lime & raspberry notes. A lock-forward of a wine, unashamedly old-fashioned, with big oak (2 years all-new) now integrating, & big 14.6% alcohol. Brooding cab component (14%) adds middle & length.

★★★★☆ **Pentagon** 08 (★★★★) muscular & plush. Cab (70%) drives the cassis & cherry character, with merlot in support, as with 07. Huge oak influence (2 yrs all-new) delivers texture, masks the powerful acidity & alcohol - overall massive & lacking subtlety.

★★★★☆ **Vision** Harmoniously cab, pinotage, merlot 07 blend tasted last year. In trademark New World style, flaunting bright dark cherry notes; broad & bold, yet fresh to taste, oak & alcohol integrated.

Kaapzicht range

★★★★ **Merlot** ✓ 08 offers plum & mulberry notes, with tobacco & earthiness. The handsomely oaked ample sweet fruit is cut by a slightly clumsy dry, tannic finish.

★★★★ **Pinotage** Last-tasted 08 showing complex combo of strawberry & dark cherry, with a herbal touch. Almost lithe, so good the balance of ripeness, acid & oak nuance.

★★★★ **Shiraz** Ripe & plush-fruited 07 last year showed earthy black fruits cut by juicy acid. Harmoniously fruity, with balanced seductive sweet impression. Like 06 (★★★★), 2 yrs oak, half new.

★★★★ **Celebration** Last tasted was plush 06 cab, pinotage, merlot blend.

Kaleidoscope ☺ 🍽 ★★★ Name-change from 'Classic Red', still a cab-based blend of 4 well-married grapes. 10 sweet-fruited & chunky. **Chenin Blanc** ☺ 🍽 📷 ★★★ Lemon zest, apricot & peardrop on 11 in lean, taut style - even unyielding. **Sauvignon Blanc** ☺ 🍽 📷 ★★★ Intensely herbaceous 11 is austere and crisp. **Combination** ☺ 🍽 📷 ★★★ Of sauvignon & chenin. 11's fruit bright-edged, slightly grassy.

Cabernet Sauvignon ✓ ★★★★ On 08 vanilla oak (2 years, half new) dominates fruit & vinosity. Not the vibrancy, juiciness of 07. **Bin-3** ✓ ★★★★ Like previous, 08 from merlot plus cab & dollop pinotage. Developed, mouth-filling, with robust rich textures softened by juicy berry layerings. **Estate Red** ✓ ★★★★ Harmoniously composed 09 from 68% shiraz, cab & drop merlot. Ample fruit, restrained wooding (only older barrels), spicy, with powdery, slightly puckering finish. Step up on 08 (★★★★). **Shiraz Rosé** ★★★ Last tasted was light, dry 08. **Chardonnay** ✓ ★★★★ Lightly oaked 09 caramel toffee whiffs, buttered toast, rich lime tropical notes evident & evolving. **Natural Sweet** ★★★ Last tasted was succulent 07. **Hanepoot Jerepigo** ★★★ Over-done 08, gooey but spice still evident. **Tawny Port** ★★★★ Fresh 06 previewed some years ago. — MF

▪ **Kakamas** see Orange River Wine Cellars
▪ **Kamina** see Overhex Wines International
▪ **Kango** see Oudtshoorn Cellar - SCV

Kanonkop Estate

Location/map: Stellenbosch ▪ WO: Simonsberg–Stellenbosch ▪ Est 1910 ▪ 1stB 1973 ▪ Tasting & sales Mon-Fri 9–5 Sat 9–2 pub hols 10-4 ▪ Fee R10 ▪ Closed Easter Fri, Dec 25 & Jan 1 ▪ Cheese platters in summer; traditional snoek barbecues by appt (min 15 people); or BYO picnic ▪ Conservation area ▪ Art gallery ▪ Owner(s) Johann & Paul Krige ▪ Cellarmaster(s) Abrie Beeslaar (Jan 2002) ▪ Winemaker(s) Abrie Beeslaar (Jan 2002), with Jeremy Arries (2007) & Frikkie Elias (1992) ▪ Viticulturist(s) Koos du Toit (Jan 2004) ▪ 120ha/100ha (cabs s/f, merlot, ptage) ▪ 1,200t/ 85,000cs own label 98% red 2% rosé ▪ WIETA ▪ PO Box 19 Elsenburg 7607 ▪ wine@kanonkop.co.za ▪ www. kanonkop.co.za ▪ S 33° 51' 18.4" E 018° 51' 36.1" ▪ **T +27 (0)21-884-4656** ▪ F +27 (0)21-884-4719

One of the legendary red-wine estates of South Africa, Kanonkop is currently owned by Johann and Paul Krige, their grandfather being the late Paul Sauer, a former cabinet minister, who lends his name to the flagship Bordeaux-style blend. First bottling under own label was in 1973 and the property has since had only three winemakers: former rugby Springbok Jan 'Boland' Coetzee (now of Vriesenhof), Beyers Truter (now of Beyerskloof) and Abrie Beeslaar, incumbent since 2002. Abrie might seem mild-mannered but don't be deceived. A rugby nut, he says his future plan for Kanonkop is 'to build a team that scrum the hell out the best the world can offer'. Asked why wine matters, he answers rhetorically 'Why does oxygen matter?'

★★★★★ **Cabernet Sauvignon** 08 (★★★★★) appears to have near-perfect elaboration, with intense cassis, fresh acidity & fine tannins (23 months in French oak, 50% new). All of a piece, great elegance, just not quite as arresting as **07**.

★★★★★ **Pinotage** Showstopper 09 (★★★★★) has spectacular fruit purity, impeccably judged oak & great freshness. Medium bodied & well balanced, it's almost impossible to resist now but optimal drinking doubtless many years off. 16 months in French oak, 70% new. Convincingly trumps savoury **08**.

★★★★☆ **Paul Sauer** Intricate 08 (69% cab, 22% cab franc, 9% merlot) is medium bodied yet intensely flavoured. Violets, ripe red & black berries, vanilla & pencil shavings on the nose; excellent fruit expression, fresh acidity, ever so fine tannins before saline finish. 2 years in French oak, 100% new.

Kadette Dry Red ★★★★ Pinotage-led 09 showed succulent fruit lurking behind austere spicy tannins when last tasted. **Kadette Pinotage Dry Rosé** ★★★☆ 11 is substantial without being weighty, has great fruit purity, freshness. — CE

Kanu Private Cellar & Vineyards

Location/map/WO: Stellenbosch ▪ Est/1stB 1998 ▪ Tasting & sales Mon-Fri 9.30–4.30 ▪ Fee R30/5 wines ▪ Closed all pub hols ▪ Owner(s) Ben Truter ▪ Cellarmaster(s)/winemaker(s)/viticulturist(s) Johan Grimbeek (Jan 2002) ▪ 48ha/26ha (cab, merlot, chard, sauv) ▪ 200t/30,000cs own label 50% red 45% white 5% rosé + 4,000cs for clients ▪ BWI ▪ PO Box 548 Stellenbosch 7599 ▪ info@kanu.co.za ▪ www.kanu.co.za ▪ S 33° 53' 23.35" E 018°49'8. 44" ▪ **T +27 (0)21-865-2488** ▪ F +27 (0)21-865-2351

It's out with the old and in with the new, as the mythical Kanu bird (now fledged from the Mulderbosch family) sets about remodeling the ex parental nest on the R304 outside Stellenbosch. A multi-faceted, tourist-friendly village featuring a restaurant, conference and wedding venue, chapel and hiking trails is under construction, including an innovative viognier/malbec méthode cap classique, Giselle.

Premium range

★★★★ **Keystone** Leaner 06 (★★★★) a 5-way, mostly Bordeaux red blend, with piquant blackcurrant flavours, was a shade off **05**. Neither retasted.

★★★★ **KCB Chenin Blanc** Off-dry 08 still available. When last tasted, needed time for oak to harmonise with tangy quince flavours & warm afterglow.

★★★★ **Kia-Ora Noble Late Harvest** 08 still selling. Previously showed vivaciously balanced oak & piquant kumquat, glacé pineapple flavours.

Merlot NEW ☺ ★★★ Bright as a button, **10** has balanced juicy red fruit. For light meal or solo.

Cabernet Sauvignon NEW ✓ ★★★★ 08 is accessible, honest & appealing, with bright blackcurrant fruit & supple structure, for early enjoyment. **Shiraz** ★★★ 06 is ripe & savoury, with an earthy, leathery nuance. Ready to drink, warm farewell favours a hearty meal. **Sauvignon Blanc** NEW ★★★ Demure **11**, with a dab semillon, is gently fruity & crisp. **Viognier** NEW ★★★ **10** bursts with tangy apricot. Mouthfilling & ripe if tad boisterous. Good potential once settled. **Giselle Méthode Cap Classique** NEW ★★★★ Brut-style but friendly & characterful traditional-method bubbly. **08**'s unusual duo of early picked viognier & malbec (51/49) delivers more savoury than fruit flavours. Has just a tinge of spice & appealing biscuity nuance.

Prime range

> **Rockwood** ☺ 🍴 ★★★ **08** shiraz spices up Bordeaux mix. Round, ripe & accessible quaffer.

Chenin Blanc ✓ 🍴 ★★★★ Voluptuous & aromatic **10** is just off-dry & flavoursome. A dash of viognier adds tangy, spicy panache for fusion food.

Pouring range NEW

Merlot Rosé 🍴 ★★★ **NV** is crisply off-dry & plump, with savoury cranberry tone. — MW

■ **Karoo Classique** *see* Karusa Vineyards

Karusa Vineyards

Location: Oudtshoorn • Map: Klein Karoo & Garden Route • WO: Klein Karoo/Western Cape • Est/1stB 2004 • Tasting & sales Mon-Fri 9.30-4 Sat 10-2.30 • Closed Easter Fri & Dec 25 • Karoo Tapas Restaurant & Deli • Microbrewery • Conferences (30-40 pax) • Owner(s) Karusa Partnership • Cellarmaster(s) Jacques Conradie (2004) • 8ha (grenache, mourv, muscadel r, ptage, shiraz, touriga nacional, chard, sauv, viog) • 50-70t/2,500cs own label 30% red 50% white 5% rosé 15% other • PO Box 1061 Oudtshoorn 6620 • info@karusa.co.za • www.karusa.co.za • S 33° 28'36.0" E 022° 14'33.2" • **T +27 (0)44-272-8717** • F +27 (0)86-600-3167

This tiny but dynamic family winery echoes Jacques and Saretha Conradie's strong emphasis on wine tourism. Ideally placed en route to the famous Cango Caves in a lush valley amid the surrounding semi-arid and viticulturally 'harsh and extreme' Klein Karoo, the broadly accredited, marketing and environmentally savvy Karusa has added to its diverse mix of delights a satellite exhibition of nearby Oudtshoorn Art Karoo Gallery and the region's first full-grain microbrewery.

Reserve Collection

★★★★ **The 5th Element Syrah-Viognier** Co-fermented shiraz & 5% viognier, **08** (★★★) spicy & floral but doesn't attain complexity or intensity of **07**. Not revisited, nor was Blanc de Noir in range below.

Earth's Art Chardonnay-Viognier 🍴 ★★★ Buttery **10** has pleasant ripe orange & apricot complexity but insufficient fruit to back the oak, mask the alc.

Varietal Collection

★★★★ **Terre Noire Syrah** Dark & brooding **10** (★★★) black-fruit centre & rounded mouthfeel but lightish, not for keeping. **08** had lovely fruit clarity, savouriness; **09** not reviewed.

One Tree Hill Pinotage 🍴 ★★ Named for olive tree spared when vineyard established. Opaque **10** opens to baked bread nose, almost jammy fruit. W Cape WO. **Aloe Ridge Unwooded Chardonnay** NEW 🍴 ★★★ **11** faint lemon/lime notes, slight creaminess; promising; higher rating will come with more concentration, complexity. **Southern Slope Sauvignon Blanc** ✓ 🍴 🈂 ★★★★ Step up for just-bottled **11**, unfolds in glass to (attractive) cat's pee aroma, lipsmacking freshness, stony finish. **Stonerock Viognier** 🍴 ★★★★ **11** restrained peach & apricot tones, well-handled oak gives structure & gentle seasoning, zesty end.

Lifestyle Collection

> **Muscat Rosé** NEW ☺ 🍴 ★★★ Pleasant grapey tones on **11** sipper from unusual red muscat d'Alexandrie. Quaffability ensured by vibrant acidity that slices through touch sugar. **Muscat Blanc** NEW ☺ 🍴 ★★★ **11** light & engaging floral notes, gentle sweetness. **Sauvignon Blanc-Chenin Blanc** ☺ 🍴 ★★★ Fruit-filled **11** perfect for summer sipping, quite zesty acidity, interesting gentle pithy aftertaste.

Shiraz-Cabernet Sauvignon 🍴 ★★ Oak on **10** Rhône/Bordeaux marriage well handled, adds spice seasoning & structure but doesn't mask funky notes. W Cape WO. Discontinued: **Pinotage Rosé Off-Dry**.

Karoo Classique Collection

House Brut ★★★★ Name change from 'Chardonnay-Pinot Noir Brut' for traditional-method sparkling. Latest **NV** (**10**) 100% chardonnay: restrained, elegant with mouthfilling mousse & lemony conclusion. **Prestige Cuvée Blanc de Blancs** ★★★★ More serious version, gets extended lees-ageing. Last time **06** was poised & complex, lemon biscuit & earthy notes, mouthfilling & persistent flavour. **Pinot Noir Rosé Brut** ★★★★ Dusky-hued **10** bottle-fermented sparkling has berry aroma, red-fruit palate. Not as delicately structured as some but certainly well flavoured. —Panel

Katbakkies Wine

Location/map/WO: Stellenbosch ▪ Est/1stB 1999 ▪ Tasting & sales Mon-Sat by appt ▪ Closed all pub hols ▪ Owner(s) Andries van der Walt ▪ Cellarmaster(s) Andries van der Walt (1999) ▪ Winemaker(s) Teddy Hall (2002, consultant) & Andries van der Walt (1999) ▪ 29ha/10ha (cab, merlot, syrah) ▪ 500cs own label 40% red 60% white ▪ PO Box 305 Stellenbosch 7599 ▪ info@katbakkies.co.za, avdwalt@inds-ct.co.za ▪ www.katbakkies.co.za ▪ S 33° 55′37.4″ E 018° 49′14.6″ ▪ **T +27 (0)21-886-5452** ▪ F +27 (0)21-557-0597

The Devon Valley HQ is finally taking shape, and 'we are slowly settling in on the farm', says Andries van der Walt. 'The micro cellar has been dug into the slope of an earthbank, the tasting facility and house are framed against the skyline.' Here he, with illustrious consultant Teddy Hall, seeks 'to craft memories in complexity'.

★★★★ **Cabernet Sauvignon** Classic, understated character on mature **05** rather than overt fruitiness. Certainly pleasing, but on the austere side, with some drying tannins, though which the sweet fruit peeks.

★★★★ **Syrah Reserve** Dense, complex **04**, firm structure, bold but balanced; older oak. Not retasted.

★★★★ **Chenin Blanc** 09 (★★★★) more obviously off-dry than **08**; good depth of flavour, but the soft sweetness slightly awkwardly jostling some hard acidity. Pleasant enough, however.

★★★★ **Viognier 08** was elegant & fresh (despite 15.8% alc!) when tasted previously, with subtle, precise flavours. Off-dry sugar level giving richness; oak well absorbed. **07** was clumsy, oversweet (★★).

Syrah ★★★★ Last was deliciously suave, spicy & unshowily fruity **08**. **Perpendiculum Viognier** NEW ★★★ Quiet varietal character on **NV** blend of vintages 05 to 09, & quietly attractive in a dull way; just off-dry. —TJ

▪ **Kaya** see Overhex Wines International
▪ **KC** see Klein Constantia Estate

Keermont Vineyards

Location/map/WO: Stellenbosch ▪ Est 2005 ▪ 1stB 2007 ▪ Tasting, sales & cellar tours by appt ▪ Owner(s) Wraith family ▪ Winemaker(s)/viticulturist(s) Alex Starey (Jan 2005) ▪ 156ha/27ha (cab, merlot, syrah, chenin) ▪ 50t/ 1,000cs own label 65% red 33% white 2% sticky white ▪ BWI, IPW ▪ PO Box 713 Stellenbosch 7599 ▪ alex@keermont.co.za ▪ www.keermont.co.za ▪ S 34° 0′27.0″ E 018° 53′39.0″ ▪ **T +27 (0)21-880-0397** ▪ F +27 (0)21-880-0566

'Keermont is an actual place. It's not another generic 'Ridge' or 'Blue Sky',' says winegrower Alex Starey, gazing out of the tasting room window at vineyards in the heights above Stellenbosch's Blaauwklippen Valley. It's this steeply sloping mountain terroir that he and co-owner Mark Wraith consider unique, and 'our whole operation revolves around expressing it'. Hence the new chenin blend, whose name translates as 'Terraces', and vine-dried dessert wine, from another vertiginous site, both coaxed from tiny yields.

★★★★ **Syrah** 09 (★★★★★) even more exhilarating than **08** debut. An elegant spiciness pervades the pimento fruit, 22 months seasoned oak & 14.5% alc are fully absorbed.

★★★★ **Keermont** Premium Bordeaux/shiraz blend made in the naturally vinified, unfined/filtered house style. **08** had well-defined blackcurrant fruit, elegant spice, racy freshness when tasted last edition.

★★★★ **Terrasse** NEW 🐝 Barrel-fermented, chenin-driven white from four terraced blocks will win many adherents. **10** polished oatmeal coating to bold, ripe but balanced fruit. Minuscule yields - 1,575 bottles made.

★★★★ **Fleurfontein** NEW ✓ 🐝 Admirable **10**, chenin & sauvignon desiccated on the vine, the 'syrup' then oak-fermented for mere 580 half-bottles of decadent, not-too-sweet delight. —DS

Keets Wines

Location: Somerset West ▪ WO: Stellenbosch ▪ Est 2008 ▪ 1stB 2010 ▪ Closed to public ▪ Owner(s) Christopher Keet ▪ Cellarmaster(s)/winemaker(s)/viticulturist(s) Christopher Keet (Oct 2008) ▪ 10t/500cs own label 100% red ▪ PO Box 5508 Helderberg 7135 ▪ chris@keetswines.co.za ▪ **T +27 (0)21-851-9844** ▪ F +27 (0)86-544-3347

A three-year sabbatical has given ex-Cordoba winemaker/viticulturist Chris Keet plenty of time to plan the first release under his own name. The result - a five-way Bordeaux blend - has been sourced from many different vineyards, something which Chris says has opened his eyes to a new understanding of the influence of terroir - and human intervention - on wine style and flavour profile. His ultimate aim? 'To combine modern technology and traditional methods in order to make wines with soul.'

Keets Wines range NEW

★★★★☆ **First Verse 09** cab franc-led, 5-way Bordeaux red is like an expensive Swiss watch: classy, elegant & perfect, all the little details present & polished, harmonious: the blackcurrant, the cedary spice (from French oak, none new!), the herbal freshness, the yielding grip. Asks question: If this is *first* verse, what's next? —Panel

■ **Keimoes** see Orange River Wine Cellars

Keisseskraal Vineyards

Location: Bot River ■ Map: Elgin, Walker Bay & Bot River ■ WO: Western Cape ■ Est 2004 ■ 1stB 2005 ■ Tasting, sales & cellar tours daily 10-5 ■ Meals/refreshments by 24 hrs prior booking ■ Facilities for children ■ Farm produce ■ BYO picnic ■ Walking/hiking/4x4 & mountain biking trails ■ Owner(s) Johann & Ulrike Mendelsöhn ■ Cellarmaster(s) Johann Mendelsöhn (2004) ■ Winemaker(s)/viticulturist(s) Johann Mendelsöhn (1998) ■ 245ha/1. 6ha (shiraz) ■ 4t/250cs own label 100% red + 100cs for clients ■ PO Box 85 Botrivier 7185 ■ petitverdot@breede. co.za ■ S 34° 10' 37.6" E 019° 13' 50.0" ■ **T +27 (0)28-284-9219**

An architect by profession, Johann Mendelsöhn was inspired by the pinot noir made by the late Arthur Pillmann on neighbouring Bot River property Goedvertrouw to try his own hand. He has just under 2ha of vineyard planted but he says he's compelled to buy in grapes as the birds take most of what he grows.

Galantskloof Cabernet Sauvignon Await new vintage. **Galantskloof Shiraz** ★★★ 'Galantskloof Syrah' previous editions. Earthy, rustic **09** shows dark fruit & spice, but oak dominates. **Deep Red Shiraz** NEW ★★★ Ripe dark fruit on **09** but coffee, chocolate is over-riding impression. **Black & Red** NEW ★★ Mainly shiraz & cab, nutty **08** lacks freshness, appears coarse. Discontinued: **Pinot Noir**. — CE

■ **Keizer's Creek** see Roodezandt Wines

Kellerprinz

High-volume semi-sweet white from widely sourced grapes, by Distell.

Late Harvest ★★ Simple, light melon flavour on fruity **NV** quaffer from chenin & colombard. 2L box. —Panel

---

Ken Forrester Wines

Location: Stellenbosch ■ Map: Helderberg ■ WO: Western Cape/Stellenbosch/Coastal ■ Est/1stB 1994 ■ Tasting & sales on home farm, cnr R44 & Winery Rd: Mon-Fri 9-5 Sat 9.30-3.30; Sun & after hours at 96 Winery Rd Restaurant, T +27 (0)21-842-2020 (see Restaurants section) ■ Fee R30 KF & Petit range/R30 Icon tasting/R50 entire range ■ Closed Easter Fri, Dec 25 & Jan 1 ■ Cheese platters ■ Self-catering 3-bedroom cottage ■ Owner(s) Ken & Teresa Forrester ■ Cellarmaster(s) Ken Forrester (1994) ■ Winemaker(s) Ken Forrester (1994) & Martin Meinert ■ Viticulturist(s) Pieter Rossouw (Oct 2009) ■ 33ha/24ha (cab f, grenache, merlot, mourv, shiraz, chenin, sauv) ■ 200t/70,000cs own label 35% red 65% white + 30,000cs for clients ■ Other export brands: Finest (Tesco), Work horse (Marks & Spencer) ■ Brands for clients: Woolworths ■ ISO 9001:2000, WIETA, HACCP, SEDEX, BWI ■ PO Box 1253 Stellenbosch 7599 ■ info@kenforresterwines.com ■ www.kenforresterwines.com ■ S 34° 1' 31.06" E 018° 49' 05.92" ■ **T +27 (0)21-855-2374** ■ F +27 (0)21-855-2373

When gallivanting then-restaurateur Ken Forrester arrived at Winery Road in the early 1990s, it was Johannesburg diners' loss, and chenin blanc's gain! Together with vintner Martin Meinert (the 'M' of FMC), he helped put 'sexy' into the lexicon of this Cape workhorse grape. 2011 saw the 10th vintage of The FMC icon, and with it refreshed – more classic – logo and packaging. Ken's also adopted another variety, grenache, and the range now boasts a (unique?) trio of grenache, shiraz and mourvèdre blends: the bold Gypsy, sultry new Three Halves (with mourvèdre in the lead) and robust (rebranded) shiraz-grenache Renegade.

Icon range

★★★★☆ **The Gypsy** 🗒 Flamboyant, named for 'Bohemian character' of grenache, now 52% with shiraz & mourvèdre. Pre-bottling **08** retains rating of previous in the interim; spicy leather tones brooding for now. Big-boned **07** was generous, dark & haunting last edition. Year all-new wood, then second year older cask.

★★★★ **Three Halves** [NEW] 🗒 Mourvèdre (55%), grenache & shiraz interleaved in sultry **07**, complex but soft & ready for intimate dinners.

★★★★ **The FMC** 🗒 Emphatic, unequivocal, individual; not for the faint-hearted! Sensational **09** old gold in colour & character: a rich melange of leesy textures, round citrus fruit & glossy oak all brushed with botrytis, drawn together in a not-quite-dry tail. WO Stellenbosch.

★★★★☆ **'T' Noble Late Harvest** Named for Mrs Forrester - 'sweet, subtle, delicate & charming' the goal. **09** adds poise & balance to full botrytis blast. Chenin, as always, fermented with natural yeasts in 100% new French oak. Stellenbosch vines (but WO Coastal).

Ken Forrester range

★★★★ **Reserve Chenin Blanc** ✓ 🗒 🏵 Gains deserved 'Reserve' status from **10**. Most stately of the cellar's trio, an ensemble of polished apricot tints, super new (20%) oak & refreshing balance. Stellenbosch grapes. **Merlot** ✓ 🗒 ★★★★ High-toned violets feature in elegant **09**; supple, ready, just needs roast lamb. WO Stellenbosch. **Renegade** ✓ 🗒 ★★★★ 'Shiraz-Grenache' previously. Equal partners with mourvèdre in **07**. The outlier in the grenache trio, touch rustic, 'unshaven', but approachable, easy to like. **Sauvignon Blanc** 🗒 ★★★★ Still tight & flinty when previewed, **11** - with dash viognier - should unfurl when bottled to reveal broader herb/fig flavours. Stellenbosch vines.

Petit range

Pinotage ☺ 🗒 🏵 ★★☆ Clove spice & tropical banana features, **10** unencumbered by wood or tannin. **Cabernet Sauvignon-Merlot** ☺ 🗒 🏵 ★★★ **10** a juicy quaffer with dry, dusty, food-friendly structure. **Rosé** [NEW] ☺ 🗒 🏵 ★★★ Sample **11** a crisp red-berry mouthful, enough grip for a gingham picnic. **Chenin Blanc** ☺ 🗒 🏵 ★★★ Boisterous **11** preview brims with agile tropical fruit. — DS

■ **Kevin Arnold** *see* Waterford Estate
■ **Kievits Kroon** *see* Glen Erskine Estate

Kingsriver Estate

Location/WO: McGregor ▪ Map: Robertson ▪ Est 2003 ▪ 1stB 2005 ▪ Tasting & sales Mon-Sat 8-9 Sun 8-5 ▪ Cellar tours daily 8-5 ▪ Tour groups ▪ Farm produce ▪ BYO picnic ▪ Hiking trails ▪ Conferences ▪ 4-star Kingsriver Guest House & Restaurant (see Accommodation & Restaurants sections) ▪ Owner(s) De Clercq family ▪ Cellarmaster(s) Ruud de Clercq & Patrick Julius ▪ Winemaker(s) Ruud de Clercq (2005) ▪ Viticulturist(s) Patrick Julius (2005) ▪ 348ha/38ha (cab, ptage, ruby cab, shiraz, tannat, chard, chenin, cbard) ▪ 190t/5,000cs own label 80% red 20% white ▪ Other export label: Mzansi ▪ PO Box 203 McGregor 6708 ▪ kingsriver-office@breede.co.za ▪ www.kingsriver-estate.com ▪ S 33° 55' 19.5" E 019° 49' 45.5" ▪ **T +27 (0)23-625-1040** ▪ F +27 (0)23-625-1045

Keeping everything natural on this organic, historic (circa 1831) estate extends to the cellar, where Ruud de Clerq's 'classical approach' to winemaking includes natural fermentation. If five new guest cottages built in the quaint McGregor style don't tempt you to visit, how about a taste of their new apricot dessert wine?

Kingsriver Estate range [NEW]

Ruby Cabernet ★★ **06** has balsamic whiffs, sweetish conclusion, needs drinking soon. **Shiraz** ★★★ **07** Aussie-style bluegum & charry oak, smoke & nutty nuances for added appeal. Like sibling red, slightly warming alc. **Chardonnay** ★★ Ripe tangerine fruit, vanilla highlights on crisp **10** crowd pleaser. **Sauvignon Blanc** ★★☆ Blackcurrant twist on **11**, soft-centred & gentle everyday sipper. — Panel

Kirabo Private Cellar

Location: Rawsonville ▪ Map: Breedekloof ▪ Est 2002 ▪ 1stB 2003 ▪ Tasting, sales & cellar/vineyard tours Mon-Fri 8.30-5 Sat by appt ▪ Closed all pub hols ▪ Meals by appt only ▪ Facilities for children ▪ Tour groups ▪ Gift shop ▪ Farm produce ▪ BYO picnic ▪ Walking/hiking/4x4 trails ▪ Conservation area ▪ Owner(s) Pieter & Karen le Roux ▪ Cellarmaster(s) Pieter le Roux (2002) ▪ Winemaker(s) Pieter & Karen le Roux (2002) ▪ Viticulturist(s) Pieter le Roux ▪ 1,000t/6,000L total ▪ 10t own label 100% red ▪ IPW ▪ PO Box 96 Rawsonville 6845 ▪ info@kirabocellar.co.za ▪ www.kirabocellar.co.za ▪ S 33° 42' 36.68" E 019° 21' 27.55" ▪ **T +27 (0)23-349-6764** ▪ F +27 (0)23-349-6764

Pieter and Karen le Roux have created a function area beside their boutique cellar near Rawsonville with facilities for about 80 guests, complementing an array of seasonal attractions like a summer picnic area with pool, and winter log fires and home-made soups. They also host interesting tastings, and plan to introduce 'information evenings' about the Breedekloof and its wines.

■ **Kiss My Springbok** *see Anura Vineyards*

Klawer Wine Cellars

Location: Klawer ▪ Map/WO: Olifants River ▪ Est 1956 ▪ Tasting & sales Mon-Fri 8–5 Sat 9–1 ▪ Fee R5 pp for groups of 5+ ▪ Closed all pub hols ▪ Facilities for children ▪ BYO picnic ▪ Conferences (office hours only) ▪ Owner(s) 96 members ▪ Cellarmaster(s) Hermias Hugo (Dec 2002) ▪ Winemaker(s) Roelof van Schalkwyk & Cerina van Niekerk, with Christo Beukes & Richard Sewell ▪ Viticulturist(s) MG van der Westhuizen ▪ 2,095ha (cab, merlot, ptage, ruby cab, shiraz, chard, chenin, cbard, hanepoot, sauv) ▪ 43,000t/30,000cs own label 40% red 40% white 5% rosé 15% other ▪ Other export brand: Travino ▪ ISO 22000:2009, Organic, DLG, IPW ▪ PO Box 8 Klawer 8145 ▪ klawerwyn@kingsley.co.za ▪ www.klawerwine.co.za ▪ S 31° 47′ 34.9″ E 018° 37′ 36.1″ ▪ **T +27 (0)27-216-1530** ▪ F +27 (0)27-216-1561

It's cellarmaster Hermias Hugo's 10th anniversary at this Olifants River cellar (now changed from co-op to company), and he reflects: 'A decade ago perceptions of this area were negative - it was seen as nothing more than a place for bulk wine. Now there's quality in the mix, and more stability, and growth - sales of our Birdfield range have increased by 15% to 20% annually.' Staff have increased too, and with the addition of harvest-hand-promoted-to-winemaker Richard Sewell, 'we have a woman and an Englishman making wine here!'

Birdfield range

> **Sauvignon Blanc** ☺ 🍷 ★★★ 11 punches above its weight with attractive spread of grass & tropical fruit, great balance of freshness & flavour. Light, early-drinking satisfaction. **Viognier** ☺ 🍷 ★★★ Floral 11 is poised & fruit-filled yet not blowsy as variety can be in SA. Lovely apricot flavour, ends dry.

Cabernet Sauvignon ★★★ Drops 'Reserve' from name. Freshly brewed coffee & salty liquorice on ripe 08; leafy eucalyptus finish. **Merlot** ★★★ 08 medium bodied, slightly savoury & food friendly. Like following reds, still selling & not retasted. **Pinotage** ★★★ Mid-2010, unwooded 08 was riper & tastier than previous, had friendly tannin. **Shiraz** ★★★ 08 dry & smoky-spicy, with black cherry flavour. **Shiraz-Merlot** 🍷 Untasted. **Blanc de Noir** 🍷 ★★☆ Pale coral 11 from grenache, with off-dry pomegranate flavour, rung up on previous. **Chardonnay** 🍷 🍇 ★★★ Previewed last edition, 10 affirms provisional rating with vivacious biscuit/lemon combo, nicely balanced oak. **Chenin Blanc** 🍷 ★★ 11 early picked for fresh, lightish (12% alc) al fresco sipping. **Michelle Sparkling** 🍇 ★★★ Still-available 10, low-alc fizz from red muscadel. Vivacious, sweet & delicate. **Hanepoot** ✓ ★★★★ Light & uncloying fortified, 08's honeysuckle sweetness refreshed by zingy citrus acidity. Lightly chill & enjoy. Typifies value in this range; affirms all-round improvement, particularly whites. **Red Muscadel** ✓ ★★★☆ Sweet fortified dessert 09 is complex, with tealeaf & dried apricot aromas, berry & molasses flavours. **White Muscadel** ★★★★ Fortified dessert a real treat, 08 rich, ripe & lingering last year - perfect with crème brûlée. — Panel

Kleinbosch

Marketed by Winegro, the easy-drinking Kleinbosch reds, whites and rosé are named after the dryland bushvines common in the Wellington area, where the brand was born. No new vintages available for review this edition.

■ **Klein Centennial** *see Groupe LFE South Africa*

Klein Constantia Estate

Location: Constantia ▪ Map: Cape Peninsula ▪ WO: Constantia/Coastal/Stellenbosch ▪ Est 1823 ▪ 1stB 1986 ▪ Tasting & sales Mon-Fri 9–5 Sat 9–1 ▪ Fee R20 for groups ▪ Closed all pub hols ▪ Collection of original Constantia bottles on display ▪ Owner(s) Zdenek Bakala & Charles Harman ▪ Winemaker(s) Adam Mason (Jul 2003), Matthew Day (2009) ▪ Viticulturist(s) Stiaan Cloete (Jul 2008) ▪ 146ha/82ha (cabs s/f, malbec, merlot, p verdot, shiraz, chard, muscat de F, riesling, sauv, sem) ▪ 500t/40,000cs own label 30% red 70% white ▪ BWI champion ▪ PO Box 375

Constantia 7848 ▪ info@kleinconstantia.com ▪ www.kleinconstantia.com ▪ S 34° 2' 19.0" E 018° 24' 46.5" ▪ **T +27 (0)21-794-5188** ▪ F +27 (0)21-794-2464

The South African flag has been lowered at this legendary estate, world renowned for its iconic elixir, Vin de Constance. The Jooste family, having dedicated the past 32 years to restoring the estate, have now sold the farm to Czech-born Zdenek Bakala and Charles Harman from the UK. This is, however, anything but a hostile takeover by these two investment bankers, who both love the Cape and have bought second homes here. They are committed to preserving the property in its entirety and to the continued development of the winery. 'We are privileged to be custodians of one of the most historic properties in the Cape and regard the preservation of this heritage as a serious responsibility.' Lowell Jooste remains the CEO, working with long-time winemaker Adam Mason and his creative team.

Marlbrook range

★★★★ **Marlbrook** Flagship red named after victorious military duke. Preview **09** is a merlot-led mostly Bordeaux blend, now without cab. Streamlined & confident, with a core of dark fruit & cocoa, but a shade off powerfully structured cabernet-led **08** (★★★★☆).

★★★★ **Mme Marlbrook** Elegant **09** is the most balanced of all the whites. Mostly semillon with sauvignon & dab chardonnay, shows grapefruit tension leavened by subtle oak & rich lanolin & pear flavours.

Klein Constantia range

★★★★ **Cabernet Sauvignon** **09** very restrained in youth & more unyielding than generous, modern & sleek (★★★★★) **08**. Cassis core tightly cosseted in supportive tannin structure. More classical styling, but needs cellaring to harmonise & show full potential.

★★★★ **Riesling** 🌿 Appealing floral tone & viscosity on **11** (★★★☆) preview. Appears riper, less piquant & zesty than **09**. (**10** sold out untasted.)

★★★★☆ **Perdeblokke Sauvignon Blanc** Selection from high-altitude vines rewards with concentration, elegance & ageability. **09** (★★★★★), successor to fine **07**, last edition quivered with cool freshness & tension. Flinty, mineral overlay to herb & passionfruit flavours, with brush of older oak. **10** not yet released.

★★★★ **Sauvignon Blanc** 📗 🌿 Riper-styled **11** (★★★★) has breadth & presence courtesy of the vintage & dab semillon, but lacks vibrancy & fruit concentration of **10** (★★★★★) and **09**.

★★★★ **Brut Méthode Cap Classique** None since **07** (★★★☆), a gently creamy chardonnay/pinot bubbly, with crisp lemon/green apple tone. Not retasted, was previously a shade off all-chardonnay **06**.

★★★★☆ **Vin de Constance** Iconic dessert wine from unbotrytised muscat de Fontignan. Previewed **07** shade less fruit weight & vibrant acidity than exceptional **06** (★★★★★). Riper & still decadently delicious, glacé pineapple, caramel & barley sugar beautifully complemented by increased oaking (50% new, 48 months).

Discontinued: **Chardonnay**, **Chardonnay Reserve**.

KC range

Cabernet Sauvignon-Merlot ✓ 📗 ★★★★ Widely sourced grapes for WO Coastal **09** give succulent ripe berry & chocolate flavours. Firm but supple & ready for a meal. **Rosé** ★★★ Light al fresco styled **11** has zesty cranberry/savoury tone. Dual Stellenbosch/Constantia WO. **Sauvignon Blanc** ✓ 📗 🌿 ★★★★ Preview of WO Coastal **11** shows appealing dusty, flinty nuance with mouthfilling cool, green-fruited focus. — MW

■ **Kleindal** *see Robertson Wide River Export Company*

Klein DasBosch

Location/map: Stellenbosch ▪ Tasting by appt ▪ Owner(s) James Wellwood Basson ▪ Marketing director Nikki Basson-Herbst ▪ Viti/vini consultant Jan Coetzee (1997) ▪ Winemaker(s) Jan Coetzee (1994) ▪ 5.5ha ▪ 35t/ 3,200cs own label 90% red 10% white ▪ PO Box 12320 Stellenbosch 7613 ▪ dasbosch@telkomsa.net ▪ www. kleindasbosch.co.za ▪ S 33° 58' 56.0" E 018° 51' 44.5" ▪ **T +27 (0)21-880-0128, +27 (0)83-406-8836** ▪ F +27 (0)21-880-0999

Label vinified at Vriesenhof by Jan Coetzee for neighbour James 'Whitey' Basson, CEO of retailing empire Shoprite/Checkers. Current releases include 08/09 Merlot and 10 Chardonnay. Most are exported, though some do appear on selected local restaurant lists and wine shops. The wines can be tasted by appointment.

Klein Dauphine

Location/WO: Franschhoek ▪ Est 2001 ▪ 1stB 2003 ▪ Closed to public ▪ Fully equipped self-catering cottage (sleeps 2) ▪ Owner(s) John & Liz Atkins ▪ Winemaker(s) Justin Hoy (consultant) ▪ 2ha/0.5ha (cab, merlot) ▪ 3t 50% red 50% rosé ▪ PO Box 151 Franschhoek 7690 ▪ john@kleindauphine.co.za ▪ www.kleindauphine.co.za ▪ **T +27 (0)21-876-2244** ▪ F +27 (0)21-876-2398

Franschhoek couple John and Liz Atkins' boutique winery (just 0.5ha under vine) has no tasting venue but you can get your hands on their unusual wines (vinified by Justin Hoy of Highlands Road) by staying at their self-catering Plumtree Cottage, with its own plunge pool and tranquil setting among orchards and vineyards.

Cabernet Sauvignon NEW ☺ 🍷 ★★★ Gutsy **08** ideal for those who enjoy a few years bottle-age *and* tannic grip in their glass.

2's Company Cabernet Sauvignon-Merlot ★★★ **07** should be peaking now. This, following, not revisited. **Merlot Rosé** ★★★ The Atkins believe their rosés deserve keeping year/2, & vinify accordingly. This is the oaked version, **09** distinctive, very dry & nutty. **Cabernet Sauvignon Rosé** 🍷 ★★★★ The unwooded version; **09** also bold & savoury. Both rosés from single-vineyards, full-bodied, good with food. — CvZ

Kleine Draken

Location/WO: Paarl ▪ Map: Paarl & Wellington ▪ Est 1983 ▪ 1stB 1988 ▪ Tasting & sales Mon-Fri 8–4 ▪ Closed all pub hols & Jewish holy days ▪ Cellar tours by appt ▪ Pre-booked kosher picnics available ▪ Owner(s) Cape Gate (Pty) Ltd ▪ Winemaker(s) Jean van Rooyen (Dec 2007) ▪ Viticulturist(s) Frank Pietersen (1984) ▪ 12.5ha/5ha under vine ▪ 55t/10,000cs own label 50% red 47% white 3% rosé ▪ IPW ▪ PO Box 2674 Paarl 7620 ▪ zandwijk@capegate.co.za ▪ www.kosherwines.co.za ▪ S 33° 46'33.3" E 018° 56'50.4" ▪ **T +27 (0)21-863-2368** ▪ F +27 (0)21-863-1884

Kleine Draken have added the promised Merlot to their portfolio,

all of which is made by Jean van Rooyen at Zandwijk farm in Paarl under the supervision of the Cape Beth Din and complies with Kosher le Pesach dietary laws. Kosher juices and pre-booked picnics are also available at the farm. **Cabernet Sauvignon** ★★★ Cedary **06** with fynbos hint, firm dry tannins. All reds except next tasted previously. **Merlot** NEW 🍷 🖻 ★★ Pale, simple **11** sweetly oaky & fruity. **Pinotage** ★★ Big-tannin, touch bitter **04**. **Shiraz** ★ Red-berried **05** still selling. **Dry Red** ★★ Mature, merlot-led **06**, savoury, with bitter hint. **Rosé** 🍷 🖻 ★★ Light semi-sweet **10**, blend of red & white varieties. **Chardonnay** 🍷 🖻 ★★ Lightly oaked tropical **11**. **Sauvignon Blanc** 🍷 🖻 ★★ Uncomplicated, dry **11** quaffer. **Vin Doux** ★★ Carbonated **NV** version of Natural Sweet White. **Natural Sweet Red** 🍷 ★★ Sweet, light **NV** from pinotage, cab. **Natural Sweet White** 🍷 🖻 ★ Sweet & spicy, light **10** blend. **Kiddush** 🍷 ★★ Sacramental **NV** wine from cab & pinotage, mahogany hued & dulcet. Above sweet wines not retasted. — IM

■ **Kleine Parys** *see* Klein Parys Vineyards
■ **Kleine Rust** *see* StellenRust

Kleine Zalze Wines

Location/map: Stellenbosch ▪ WO: Coastal/Western Cape/Stellenbosch ▪ Est 1695 ▪ 1stB 1997 ▪ Tasting & sales Mon-Sat 9-6 Sun 11-6 ▪ R15/5 wines ▪ Closed Easter Fri & Dec 25 ▪ Terroir Restaurant (see Restaurants section) ▪ Kleine Zalze Lodge ▪ De Zalze Golf Course ▪ Conference/function venue ▪ Owner(s) Kobus Basson & Rolf Schulz ▪ Cellarmaster(s) Johan Joubert (Nov 2002) ▪ Winemaker(s) Bertho van der Westhuizen (Dec 2004), with Zara Conradie (Feb 2008) ▪ Viticulturist(s) Henning Retief (May 2006) ▪ 90ha/84ha (cab, merlot, shiraz, chenin, sauv) ▪ 2,300t/90,000cs own label 40% red 50% white 10% rosé ▪ PO Box 12837 Die Boord 7613 ▪ quality@kleinezalze.co.za ▪ www.kleinezalze.co.za ▪ S 33° 58'14.1" E 018° 50'8.9" ▪ **T +27 (0)21-880-0717** ▪ F +27 (0)21-880-0716

While the estate just 3km south of Stellenbosch is over three centuries old, its modern revival is recent, being only in its second decade. But the scope of what has been achieved – Top 10 restaurant Terroir, golf estate, luxury lodge and function venue – and the entrenchment of the wine business in the vanguard of Cape wine, is truly remarkable. One wonders where cellarmaster Johan Joubert found space for the most recent hat-trick of Veritas double-gold awards in the cluttered trophy cabinet.

But he's surely delighted – eyeing his tenth harvest here this year – at being invited into membership of the prestigious Cape Winemakers Guild.

Family Reserve range

★★★★ **Cabernet Sauvignon** Sweet-fruited **08** reflects vintage: less intense than multi-awarded **07** (★★★★★) with waves of flavour & interest in deep-piled structure. WO Stellenbosch.

★★★★ **Pinotage** NEW There's no doubting the variety: banana & plum fruit, hint of clove – but bold, out-the-blocks **09** has alluring sweet perfumes & a finely meshed structure to contain – just – its 15+% alc.

★★★★☆ **Shiraz** **08** (★★★★) retains trademark swirling spice focus, as elegant but easier, fruitier than thrilling **07**, which mastered black berry fruits in firm tannic support. WO Stellenbosch.

★★★★★ **Sauvignon Blanc** ✓ 🍷 Full flavoured, fatter style with ringing minerality. **10** has flinty 'river stone' backbone for brimming asparagus & bluegum flavour, all cleaned up by tingling acidity in long finish. WO W Cape.

Vineyard Selection

★★★★ **Cabernet Sauvignon Barrel Matured** ✓ Polished Stellenbosch cab; **09** blackcurrant woven into elegant fabric. A classy & svelte glassful despite 15% alc.

★★★★ **Chardonnay Barrel Fermented** ✓ 🍷 Obvious oak (7 months 30% new) fits tightly – just – into sleek flavour profile of **10**, finely textured finish. WO W Cape.

★★★★ **Chenin Blanc Barrel Fermented** ✓ Chenin with attitude. **10** gorgeous tropical tones buffed by subtle toasty oak (10 months, 20% new). Big but contained. WO Stellenbosch.

Pinot Noir ★★★★ Russet **09** in wet-earth bucolic genre, now all barrelled in seasoned casks. **Shiraz Barrel Matured** ★★★★ **09** back in spicy mould after broadly fruity **08**, balance – & higher rating – unhinged by heavy 15.5% alc. WO Stellenbosch. **Shiraz-Mourvèdre-Viognier** 🔲 ★★★★ Competition-garlanded maiden **09**, spice & plum pudding features, feisty dry tannins last edition. WO W Cape.

Cellar Selection

Gamay Noir ☺ 🔲 ★★★ Rustic **11** preview has enough clean plum fruit for easy enjoyment. **Merlot** ☺ 🔲 ★★★ **10** floral, with smoked-bacon interest, good at table. **Gamay Noir Rosé** ☺ 🔲 ★★★ Vibrant coral **11** brims with crisp, dry picnic-friendly fruit. **Chardonnay** ☺ 🔲 🍷 ★★★ Unwooded, but 4 months on lees adds oatmeal texture to light, tight, lemon/lime-tinged **11**. WO W Cape. **Chenin Blanc Bush Vines** ☺ 🔲 🍷 ★★★ An enduring favourite; **11**'s lush fruit amped by some botrytis, tempered with zippy acidity. WO Stellenbosch. **Sauvignon Blanc** ☺ 🔲 ★★★ Grassy **11** plumped by passionfruit, zinging finish. WO W Cape.

Cabernet Sauvignon 🔲 ★★★ **09** tad awkward when last tasted, sweet fruit, austere tannins & beefy 15% alc not yet in accord. **Pinotage** ✓ 🔲 ★★★★ Emphatic **10**, cinnamon & sweet-sour character in muscular frame. **Cabernet Sauvignon-Merlot** ✓ 🔲 ★★★★ Stylish medium-full **09**, clean blackberry fruit & savoury tannins, pliable & satisfying.

Foot of Africa range

Shiraz-Viognier ★★★ Purple berries bulge from ripe **10**, alc just under 15%, just-dry. **Chenin Blanc** 🔲 🍷 ★★ **11** peach & pear notes in lean body. These for export only. WO W Cape.

Zalze range

Pinotage 🔲 ★★★ **10** sweet-fruited & ripe, usual light oak seasoning. **Shiraz-Mourvèdre-Viognier** 🔲 ★★★ Fresh mulberries & touch of spice in medium bodied **10**. WO W Cape. **Cabernet Sauvignon-Shiraz Rosé** 🔲 🍷 ★★★ Pretty pink with cherry charm, **11** semi-dry. **Bush Vine Chenin Blanc** 🔲 🍷 ★★★ Ripe botrytis glaze to **11**, with clean acid swish. These exclusively for export. — DS

Kleinfontein

Location/WO: Wellington ▪ Est 1995 ▪ 1stB 2003 ▪ Closed to public ▪ Guesthouse ▪ Owner(s) Tim & Caroline Holdcroft ▪ Winemaker(s) Charles Stassen (May 2004, Nabygelegen) ▪ Viticulturist(s) Tim Holdcroft (Aug 1998) ▪ 12ha/1ha (cab, merlot) ▪ 5–8t/420cs own label 65% red 35% rosé ▪ IPW ▪ PO Box 578 Wellington 7654 ▪ kleinfon@iafrica.com ▪ www.kleinfontein.com ▪ T +27 (0)21-864-1202 ▪ F +27 (0)86-587-2675

Tim Holdcroft, an engineer by profession, left England in 1965 to have the 'African adventure'. His wife Caroline was born in Kenya, where she was involved in the tourism industry. They lived all over Africa before ending up at Kleinfontein, where they cultivate vines, olives and guavas as well as providing accommodation.

★★★★ Eminence Merlot & cab combo, 07 last year had integrated oak supporting rich, mouthfilling red & black fruit.

Cabernet Sauvignon ★★ Somewhat lean 09 shows red fruit, overt mint. **Merlot ★★★** Modest but likeable 07 exhibits dark fruit, firm tannins before long, dry finish. **Rosé 🖹 ★★★ 10** from merlot, refreshing & dry, still selling mid-2011. — CE

■ **Klein Genot** *see* Holden Manz Wine Estate

Klein Gustrouw Estate

Location: Stellenbosch ▪ WO: Stellenbosch/Jonkershoek Valley ▪ Est 1817 ▪ 1stB 1993 ▪ Closed to public ▪ Owner(s) Klein Gustrouw (Pty) Ltd ▪ Winemaker(s) Reg Holder (2008, consultant) ▪ Viticulturist(s) Pieter Smit (consultant) ▪ ±23ha/±14ha under vine ▪ 70% red 30% white ▪ PO Box 6168 Uniedal 7612 ▪ suzanne.slabbert@gmail.com ▪ **T +27 (0)21-882-8152 ▪** F +27 (0)21-882-8433 / +27 (0)86-609-7229

When business executives and longstanding friends Jannie Mouton and Markus Jooste bought this Jonkershoek property in 2007, major replanting took place. After a long wait, during which wines were made from grapes sourced in the valley, the team are looking forward to their first own-harvest this year.

Reserve NEW ★★★★ Savoury Bordeaux-shiraz blend 08 ripe & spicy, good dark-fruit concentration & medium body for current enjoyment. **Sauvignon Blanc ✓ 🖹 🖾 ★★★★ 10** step up from 08 (★★★), excellent spread capsicum, tropical & stonefruit flavours. Balanced acidity & lees-age complexity contribute to mouthfilling offering. 09 sold out untasted. WO Stellenbosch. Discontinued: **Cabernet Sauvignon-Merlot**. — Panel

Kleinhoekkloof

Location: Ashton ▪ Map: Robertson ▪ Est 2004 ▪ 1stB 2006 ▪ Phone ahead for opening hours ▪ Owner(s) Raudan Trust ▪ Cellarmaster(s) Theunis de Jongh (2010) ▪ Winemaker(s) Theunis de Jongh (2011) ▪ Viticulturist(s) Loure van Zyl (Mar 2004, consultant) ▪ 114ha/11.8ha (merlot, p verdot, pinot, shiraz, sauv, viog) ▪ 110t/1,200cs own label 45% red 40% white 15% rosé ▪ Other export brand: Mountain Eye ▪ PO Box 95134 Waterkloof 0145 ▪ theunis@khk.co.za ▪ www.kleinhoekkloof.co.za ▪ S 33° 46′ 51.87″ E 020° 03′ 17.30″ ▪ **T +27 (0)23-615-2121 ▪** F +27 (0)86-677-5399

Last year, Theunis de Jongh made the wines – a sauvignon, merlot, shiraz and shiraz-led blend – on this mountainside farm in Ashton for the first time (previous vintages were made at Graham Beck Wines and Viljoensdrift Wines). The family were eagerly awaiting the day they could bottle and present them.

■ **Klein Kasteelberg** *see* Groupe LFE South Africa

Klein Moerbei Estate

Location/map/WO: Stellenbosch ▪ Est 1998 ▪ 1stB 2007 ▪ Tasting & sales by appt ▪ Guesthouse ▪ Owner(s) Rahmatallah/O'Riordan families (beneficial ownership) ▪ Cellarmaster(s)/winemaker(s) Willie Stofberg (Jun 2008, consultant) ▪ 40ha/22ha (cab, merlot, ptage, sangiovese, shiraz, chard, chenin, sauv, sem) ▪ 160t/1,500cs own label 60% red 40% white ▪ PO Box 871 Stellenbosch 7599 ▪ moerbei@kleinmoerbei.com ▪ www.kleinmoerbei.com ▪ S 33° 59′ 38.30″ E 018° 46′ 20.23″ ▪ **T +27 (0)21-881-3381**

Positive reports from this Stellenbosch boutique winery (and grape supplier to big-name cellars): sales and 2011-vintage own-brand production both up, and now listed with a leading UK online retailer. New sauvignon blanc and cabernet single-varieties and a red blend will widen the range to five wines.

Moerbei Sable ★★★ From shiraz. Pale red, spicy 09, dominated by brisk acidity. **Moerbei White Gold ★★★** Quirky, water-white 10 oaked chardonnay, semillon blend, with intense litchi & wintergreen aromas, pithy lemon aftertaste. — IM

■ **Kleinood** *see* Tamboerskloof Wine

Klein Optenhorst

Location: Wellington ▪ Map: Paarl & Wellington ▪ Est/1stB 2001 ▪ Tasting & sales by appt ▪ Owner(s) Naas Ferreira ▪ Cellarmaster(s)/winemaker(s) Pieter Ferreira (2009, consultant) ▪ Viticulturist(s) Naas Ferreira (2001) ▪ 1ha/0.

25ha (pinot) ▪ ±2t/80cs own label 100% rosé ▪ PO Box 681 Wellington 7654 ▪ kleinoptenhorstwines@gmail.com ▪ www.kleinoptenhorst.com ▪ S 33° 37' 48.60" E 019° 3' 19.54" ▪ **T +27 (0)21-864-1210**

The note from Wellington's Klein Optenhorst estate, home to a tiny parcel of mature pinot noir, vinified since 2009 into champagne-method sparkling, read: 'The Ferreira family has decided to keep the 2010 vintage on its lees for a longer period to deliver greater complexity in the final wine.' So, sadly, nothing new to taste but, of course, our expectations have now been raised...

Pinot Noir Méthode Cap Classique ★★★★ Berry-toned **09** bottle-fermented sparkling last edition had pleasing weight & length, needed year or 2 to gain complexity. — CvZ

Klein Parys Vineyards

Location: Paarl ▪ Map: Paarl & Wellington ▪ WO: Paarl/Coastal ▪ Est 1692 ▪ 1stB 2002 ▪ Tasting, sales & cellar tours Mon-Fri 10-5 Sat 10-3 ▪ Fee R20/4 wines ▪ Closed Easter Fri, Dec 25 & Jan 1 ▪ Cheese platters; or BYO picnic ▪ Facilities for children ▪ Conferences ▪ Weddings/functions ▪ Live music evenings (every 2nd Fri) ▪ Accommodation from Jan 2012 ▪ Owner(s) Kosie Möller ▪ Cellarmaster(s) Kosie Möller (2002) ▪ Winemaker(s) Kosie Möller (2002), with Nicolas Husselman (Dec 2010) ▪ Viticulturist(s) Wilhelm van Reenen (Mar 2009) ▪ 56ha/45ha (cab, shiraz, chard, chenin) ▪ 1,800t/250,000cs own label 48% red 48% white 4% sparkling + 500,000cs for clients ▪ Brands for clients: Tokolosh, Tooverberg ▪ PO Box 1362 Suider-Paarl 7624 ▪ froux@kparys.co.za ▪ www.kleinparysvineyards.co.za ▪ S 33° 45'0.2" E 018° 58'48.6" ▪ **T +27 (0)21-872-9848** ▪ F +27 (0)21-872-8527

To further boost its share of the wine tourist's wallet, this scenic Paarl property intends adding a restaurant and accommodation to the live entertainment, function, conference and family-friendly facilities it already offers. To ensure they also increase their 'share of throat', they've added a voguish coffee-style pinotage and méthode cap classique.

Family Selection

★★★★ **Jacob Selection** Attractive **09** combo mainly pinotage, shiraz, cabernet franc & petit verdot last edition, still selling.

Beatrix Selection ★★★ Last tasted was very ripe shiraz-dominated **07**. Newer vintages of this, **Niclas Selection** & most below available but not tasted unless noted.

Kleine Parys Selection

> **Pinotage Coffee Style** NEW ☺ ⌾ ★★★ Rich cherry mocha **11** good example of this popular style. Sweet-fruited mouthful offset by firm tannins.

Cabernet Sauvignon ★★★ Previously **08** was tad developed & atypical. **Merlot** ★★ Last reviewed was fruit shy **09**. **Pinotage** ★★ Sweet-fruited **08** had edgy tannins, needed time to knit previously. **Shiraz** ★★ Juicy **09** an easy-sipper. **Chardonnay** 🍷 ★★★ Peach blossom, ripe pears & vanilla oak (5 months new French/American) on last-tasted **10**. **Chenin Blanc** 🍷 ★★★★ Just-dry **10** was pretty & full, with spicy note from 10% barrel-fermented portion. **Sauvignon Blanc** 🍷 ★★ Softly sweet **10** WO W Cape. **Méthode Cap Classique** NEW ★★★ Shortbread-infused **08** bottle-fermented sparkling shot through with chardonnay's lemon freshness, satisfyingly dry & complex. **Cuvée Brut** ★★★ Crisp **NV** sparkling still available at press time. **Red Muscadel** ★★★ Fortified **NV** dessert. Same bottling still available, was toffee rich last time.

Tooverberg range

Contour Merlot ★★★ Last reviewed was **09**, showing plum pudding richness. **Contour Chenin Blanc** 🍷 ★★★★ Lighter-style **10** had good balance & vibrancy previously. — JP

Klein Roosboom

Location/WO: Durbanville ▪ Map: Durbanville, Philadelphia & Darling ▪ Est 1984 ▪ 1stB 2007 ▪ Tasting, sales & cellar tours Tue-Fri 9-5 Sat/Sun 10.30-3 ▪ Fee R10, waived on purchase ▪ Closed Easter Fri, Dec 25/26 & Jan 1 ▪ Cheese platters Sat/Sun; soup & bread in winter ▪ Facilities for children ▪ Tour groups ▪ Rubies & Roses: gifts, interior, deli & more ▪ BYO picnic ▪ Owner(s) Jean de Villiers Trust ▪ Cellarmaster(s)/winemaker(s) Karin de Villiers (2007) ▪ Viticulturist(s) Jean de Villiers (1984) ▪ 260ha/130ha (cab, merlot, shiraz, chard, sauv) ▪ 1,500cs own label 40% red 60% white ▪ Postnet Suite #3 Private Bag X19 Durbanville 7551 ▪ cellar@kleinroosboom.co.za ▪ www.kleinroosboom.co.za ▪ S 33°49'6.24" E 018° 34'25.86" ▪ **T +27 (0)82-784-5102** ▪ F +27 (0)21-975-7417

This small-scale, family-run winery hosted a double celebration when they popped the corks of their maiden méthode cap classique sparkling, named after their daughter, Marné, on her 21st birthday. She in turn added another creative string to the family bow by opening a new deli/craft shop, Rubies & Roses, while winemaking mother Karin has a new oaked shiraz ready for release.

Klein Roosboom range

★★★★ **Cabernet Sauvignon** Elegant & well-composed **09**, dark berries & dusty minerality, still selling, not retasted, as for Merlot.

★★★★ **Merlot** No newer vintage since spicy & sweet-fruited **09**, supple & light, with savoury farewell.

★★★★ **Sauvignon Blanc** ✓ **10** (★★★★) riper & less mineral than **09**. Still shows area's hallmark zesty acidity & extract, just in lower key.

Marné Brut Méthode Cap Classique NEW ★★★★ Champagne-method sparkling **07** in 'extra-brut' style, but ample brioche breadth to balance the dryness. Fresh & savoury food partner from chardonnay & pinot noir.

Bandana range

Blanc 😊 🍷 ★★★ From sauvignon; riper **10** is still fresh, crunchy & flavoursome. As depicted on quaint & quirky label, for carefree Cape-style sipping. — MW

■ **Klein Simonsvlei** see Niel Joubert Estate
■ **Klein Tulbagh** see Tulbagh Winery

Kling

Location: Hout Bay ▪ Map: Cape Peninsula ▪ Est 1984 ▪ Tasting & sales by appt but always welcome ▪ Owner(s) Gordon Kling ▪ Winemaker(s) Elena Corzana ▪ Viticulturist(s) Gawie Kriel (consultant, Jan 2005) ▪ 4ha/3.5ha (cab, merlot, shiraz, sauv, viog) ▪ 3t/70cs own label 70% red 30% white ▪ Constantia Nek Farm (Houtkappersport entrance) Hout Bay Main Road Constantia Nek ▪ wine@kling.co.za ▪ S 34° 0'41.0" E 018° 24'3.7" ▪ **T +27 (0)21-794-3108** ▪ F +27 (0)21-794-0140

After Constantia's heights, where the roads turns down to Hout Bay, are the vines that Gordon Kling started planting in 2005. They've already delivered fruit that speaks of cool conditions; as they mature they'll do so more eloquently. There's no winery – after some false starts, from 2010 winemaking is at Buitenverwachting.

Merlot ★★★★ **09** has good fruit, but is restrained & light-footed, even a little lean, with a pleasant herbal note. Ready now. Like next two, retasted - last year tasted as pre-bottling samples. **Shiraz** ★★★★ Most attractive pure-fruited aromas & flavours on tactfully oaked, rather elegant **09**. A hint of green acidity on the unlingering finish. **Sauvignon Blanc** ★★★★ **10** now less showy, more subtle, with an earthy-tropical succulence to its fleshy weight, finishing off with quite a green bite. **Viognier** 🍷 ★★★ Rich **09** last year showed excessive oakiness, but otherwise balanced. — TJ

■ **Kloof Street** see Mullineux Family Wines

Kloovenburg Wine & Olives

Location: Riebeek-Kasteel ▪ Map/WO: Swartland ▪ Est 1704 ▪ 1stB 1998 ▪ Tasting & sales Mon-Fri 9-4.30 Sat 9–2 Sun at Kloovenburg Pastorie Guesthouse 10.30-2 ▪ Fee R10 wine/olive tasting ▪ Closed Easter Fri-Mon, Dec 25/26 & Jan 1 ▪ Cellar tours during tasting hours ▪ Tour groups ▪ Gift shop ▪ Farm produce/olive products ▪ BYO picnic ▪ Walks/hikes ▪ Conservation area ▪ Christmas Market (Dec) ▪ Owner(s) Pieter du Toit ▪ Cellarmaster(s)/ winemaker(s) Pieter du Toit (Jan 1998) ▪ Viticulturist(s) Kobus van Graan (Jan 1998, consultant) ▪ 300ha/130ha (cab, merlot, shiraz, chard, sauv) ▪ 229t/12,000cs own label 55% red 40% white 4% rosé 1% sparkling ▪ PO Box 2 Riebeek-Kasteel 7307 ▪ info@kloovenburg.com ▪ www.kloovenburg.com ▪ S 33° 23'36.3" E 018° 53'27.5" ▪ **T +27 (0)22-448-1635** ▪ F +27 (0)22-448-1035

With plans for hiking trails and wine tastings among the vineyards on this 'place in the ravine', as Pieter du Toit translates Kloovenburg, visitors will be able to appreciate the aspects, elevations and soils of this mountainside property. Why north-easterly slopes favour cabernet, and why shiraz thrives on south-westerly and easterly ones, should be clearer after tasting the wine in situ.

Kloovenburg Vineyards range

★★★★ **Cabernet Sauvignon** Quiet, fairly simple fruit on 09 (★★★★) backed by chunky yet approachable tannins. Best enjoyed next year/2. 08 juicy, rich.

★★★★ **Shiraz** 09 echoes approachable style of 08. Even more reined-in body, oak (10% new) focuses on fruit purity, supple texture. Rounded & fruitily dry.

★★★★ **Barrel Fermented Chardonnay** 🍷 🈁 11 (★★★★) ex-barrel (rating provisional) shows bold, ripe pear, spice & lime fruit. Full body accentuated by finishing sweetness. Fruit-driven 09 last tested.

Merlot ★★★ Musty note to earthy 09; very light fruit, dry tannins. **Eight Feet** ★★★ 09 switches to 80/20 shiraz/cab blend; 08 (★★★★) cab/merlot. Smooth & chocolatey with rounded chalky tannins. Year oak. **Shiraz Rosé** 🍷 ★★ Dry, savoury 11. Hint of pink & freshness. **Unwooded Chardonnay** 🍷 🈁 ★★★ Pleasant pear, pickled lime on 11; simple, juicy & dry. **Sauvignon Blanc** 🍷 🈁 ★★★ Bone-dry 11; moderate alcohol with quiet fruit to match. **White From Red Brut** ★★★ Fruity NV from shiraz. Frothy mousse adds to cheerful, just-dry quaffer. — AL

■ **Knockon Wood** *see Flagstone Winery*

Knorhoek Wines

Location/map: Stellenbosch ▪ WO: Simonsberg–Stellenbosch ▪ Est 1827 ▪ 1stB 1997 ▪ Tasting, sales & cellar tours daily 10–5 ▪ Fee R15/5 wines ▪ Closed Easter Fri/Sun & Dec 25 ▪ Towerbosch Restaurant Wed-Sun 11.30-3.30, booking essential Sat/Sun (T +27 (0)21-865-2958) ▪ Facilities for children ▪ Tour groups ▪ Gift shop ▪ Weddings/conferences ▪ Hiking trail ▪ Conservation area ▪ 3-star Guesthouse & self-catering Cottages ▪ Owner(s) Hansie & James van Niekerk ▪ Cellarmaster(s)/winemaker(s) Arno Albertyn (April 2005) ▪ Viticulturist(s) James van Niekerk (1977) ▪ ±80ha (cabs s/f, merlot, ptage, shiraz, chenin, sauv) ▪ 640t/12,000cs own label 51% red 42% white 4.65% rosé 2.35% sparkling & 184,500L bulk ▪ BWI ▪ PO Box 2 Koelenhof 7605 ▪ office@knorhoek.co.za, cellar@knorhoek.co.za, towerbosch@knorhoek.co.za ▪ www.knorhoek.co.za ▪ S 33° 52' 44.8" E 018° 52' 19.1" ▪ **T** +27 (0)21-865-2114 ▪ F +27 (0)21-865-2627

'Wine has the ability to bring people together, to make food taste better and make time stand still'. So quotes winemaker Arno Albertyn, who observes this firsthand, because besides the normal quota of visitors, Knorhoek has become a very popular wedding destination. Not surprisingly, given the restaurant setting next to a lake and many other facilities on offer, including a specialised wedding venue.

Knorhoek Wines range

★★★★ **Cabernet Sauvignon** Elegant styling on 07 last edition, with blackcurrant & leafy nuances. Structure enhanced by 20 months French oak, 30% new. Dashes merlot & cab franc add balance.

★★★★ **Cabernet Franc** Last tasted 06, classic styling saw fruit in the lead, oak (18 months, 20% new) in supporting role; 10% merlot added flesh & meaty nuance.

Pinotage ★★★ Dark tones in 09, mulberries & smoked meat but palate is juicy, vibrant, all light & laughter. Good oak foundation. **Shiraz** ✓ ★★★★ Ripe & fleshy, toned by 18 months in barrel, 09 is that irresistible force: classic shiraz appeal with a serious touch. **Pantére** ★★★★ Cab-led Bordeaux blend, long skin contact & 22 months in French barrels, half new - warns you to take 07 seriously. Polished, dark-fruit, delicious; long life ahead. Big jump from 06 (★★★). **Reserve** ★★★★ Last tasted 04, Bordeaux blend, dash shiraz. Layered with blueberry & wet earth, gamey nuance, firm savoury tannins. **Chenin Blanc** 🍷 🈁 ★★★★ Elegant, thatch-toned 10 spent 10 months on lees, has a nice mineral austerity, an edginess to the flavours & finish. **Sauvignon Blanc** 🍷 🈁 ★★★ Nothing overt, green figs & fynbos, crisp 11 leaves the mouth refreshed, ready for food.

Two Cubs range

Red Blend 🍷 ★★★ Unusual blend at this price level, cab franc, merlot gives grassy edge to 09's berries; meaty tones from 15 months oak. **Rosé** 🍷 🈁 ★★ 11 berry-rich, thanks to shiraz & merlot; off-dry & easy. **White Blend** 🍷 🈁 ★★★ Light-textured & leafy, ideal for a quaffer. Blend sauvignon, chenin, 11 preview has a touch of plumping sugar, finishes dry. — CR

■ **Koelenbosch** *see Koelenhof Winery*

Koelenhof Winery

Location/map/WO: Stellenbosch ▪ Est 1941 ▪ 1stB 1970's ▪ Tasting & sales Mon-Thu 9–5 Fri 9–4 Sat 10–2 ▪ Fee R15pp ▪ Closed Easter Fri/Sun, Ascension Day, Dec 25/26 & Jan 1 ▪ Cellar tours by appt ▪ Facilities for children ▪ Gift shop ▪ Farm produce ▪ BYO picnic ▪ Conference/function venue ▪ Owner(s) 67 shareholders ▪ Cellarmaster(s) Martin Stevens (Nov 2003) & Wilhelm de Vries (2002) ▪ Winemaker(s) Martin Stevens (Nov 2003) & Wilhelm de Vries (2002), with Erika van Zyl (Jun 2011) ▪ Viticulturist(s) Wilhelm de Vries (2010) ▪ 14,000t/11,000cs own label 45% red 45% white 8% rosé 2% fortified + 1,000cs for clients & 100,000 litres bulk ▪ Other export brand: Simonsbosch ▪ IPW ▪ PO Box 1 Koelenhof 7605 ▪ koelwyn@mweb.co.za ▪ www.koelenhof.co.za ▪ S 33° 50′5.2″ E 018° 47′52.7″ ▪ **T +27 (0)21-865-2020/1** ▪ F +27 (0)21-865-2796

Growing demand for their good-value own-label wines, notably from China, and for their outsource services and facilities have persuaded the grower-owners of this Stellenbosch winery to increase bottling and storage capacity, with a new warehouse that can house 1,600 barrels, 2,500 bins and 200,000 cases of their own and clients' wine. Winemaking wise, they stick to the basics and have 'the luxury of sourcing grapes from wherever we get the best for a specific product'.

Koelenbosch range

Merlot ★★★ Chocolate-dipped **08** still selling; fine dry tannins, nervy acidity, commendably modest 13% alc. **Pinotage** ★★★ Creamy vanilla oak dominates previewed **09**, masks core of rich mulberry fruit. **Sangiovese** 🍇 ★★★ Bright cherry flavours on **10**, perfect antipasto partner. **Shiraz** ★★★ **08** last year was rich & balanced, showed smoky bacon complexity to bright red fruit. **Nineteenfortyone** ★★★★ Red blend honouring cellar's founding date. Shiraz dominates **08** (with cab, petit verdot), robust & packed with fruit, needs food & time. Potential for higher rating. **Pinotage Rosé** NEW 🍱 🍇 ★ Light-textured & dry **11**. **Chenin Blanc Wooded** 🍇 ★★ **10** undemanding, with gentle nutty texture. **Sauvignon Blanc** 🍱 🍇 ★★ Gentle grassy tones, **11** crisp summer quaffer.

Koelenhof range

Sauvignon Blanc Vin-sec ☺ 🍱 🍇 ★★★ Sweet but lively fizz, light & tropical-toned **11** a spring celebration. **Pinotage Rosé Vin-sec** ☺ 🍇 ★★★ **11** effervescent berry bonanza, fresh, light & inviting.

Koelenberg ★★★ Shiraz-led juicy BBQ quaffer, briefly oaked. **09** still selling. **Pinotage Rosé** 🍇 ★★ Semisweet **11** with brush of red berries. **Koelenhoffer** 🍱 🍇 ★★ From sauvignon, **11** delicate & herbaceous poolside dry white. **Koelnektar** 🍇 ★★★ Sweetly crisp white, ideal for fusion food. **11** with gewürztraminer's rosepetal, riesling's spice, chenin's tropical fruit. **Pino Porto** ✓ ★★★ **08** true ruby-style port: balanced, warming, savoury edge & cinnamon spice take edge off the sweetness. Discontinued: **Hanepoot**. — MW

Koelfontein

Location/WO: Ceres ▪ Map: Tulbagh ▪ Est 1832 ▪ 1stB 2002 ▪ Tasting & sales Mon-Fri 9-1 Sat 10-1 ▪ Closed all pub hols ▪ Farm produce ▪ BYO picnic ▪ Walks/hikes ▪ Conservation area ▪ Die Kloof self-catering historic house (sleeps 6) ▪ Owner(s) Handri Conradie ▪ Winemaker(s) Dewaldt Heyns (2004) ▪ Viticulturist(s) Hennie van Noordwyk ▪ 950ha/±9ha (cab, merlot, shiraz, chard) ▪ ±24t/1,200cs own label 50% red 50% white ▪ PO Box 4 Prince Alfred's Hamlet 6840 ▪ wine@koelfontein.co.za ▪ www.koelfontein.co.za ▪ S 33° 15′54.70″ E 019° 19′29.28″ ▪ **T +27 (0)23-313-3304/+27 (0)23-313-3538** ▪ F +27 (0)23-313-3137

This high-lying farm has been in the Conradie family for seven generations. It's 10 years since they started to produce their own wine, encouraged by the awards for their chardonnay when vinified at the co-op. Helping encourage visitors to come to the farm and experience their wines, a historic house on the property has been renovated and turned into self-catering accommodation.

★★★★ **Shiraz** Very ripe, soft **07** (★★★). Jammy red fruits just about hold out against drying tannins & the alcohol glow. Follows **06**'s smouldering depth, fine tannins.

★★★★ **Chardonnay** ✓ Cool climate precision & minerality in happy marriage with barrel-ferment leesy richness on **09** (★★★★★). Limy, hazelnut tones with spicy oak promise more complexity over 3-4 yrs. Sophisticated, like **08**.

Merlot ★★★★ **06**, elegant despite 15% alc, sold out. Next vintage unavailable for tasting. — AL

▪ **Kogmans Kloof** see Zandvliet Wine Estate & Thoroughbred Stud
▪ **Koningshof** see Avondvrede

Koningsrivier Wines

Location: McGregor ▪ Map: Robertson ▪ Est/1stB 2002 ▪ Tasting, sales & tours by appt ▪ Owner(s) SW Colyn ▪ Cellarmaster(s)/winemaker(s) Niël Colyn ▪ Viticulturist(s) Briaan Stipp (consultant) ▪ 9ha (cab) ▪ 435cs own label

100% red ▪ PO Box 144 Robertson 6705 ▪ koningsrivier@barvallei.co.za ▪ S 33° 54'3.0" E 019° 51'45.9" ▪ **T +27 (0)23-625-1748** ▪ F +27 (0)23-625-1748

Niël Colyn is feeling positive about the 2011 crush on the family farm between Robertson and McGregor. A higher yield with smaller berries produced reds with concentrated flavours. 'The wines are looking very good, especially the shiraz.' Latest vintages of Cabernet, Shiraz and Merlot-Cabernet unready for tasting this edition.

Koopmanskloof Wingerde

Location/map/WO: Stellenbosch ▪ Est 1801 ▪ 1stB 1970 ▪ Tasting & cellar tours Mon-Fri 9-4 ▪ Fee R20 ▪ Sales 8-5 ▪ Closed all pub hols ▪ Farm produce ▪ BYO picnic ▪ Walking/hiking trails ▪ Mountain biking ▪ Private Nature Reserve with self-catering Berghuis lapa, accommodate 35 people with overnight facilities for 16 ▪ Owner(s) WS Smit Family Trust ▪ Cellarmaster(s) Louwtjie Vlok (1992) ▪ Winemaker(s) Louwtjie Vlok (1992), with Anriënka Vlok (Oct 2006) ▪ Viticulturist(s) Vinpro consultants (Nov 2010) ▪ ±690ha/520ha (cab, merlot, ptage, shiraz, chard, chenin, sauv) ▪ ±4,000t/±1 million litre 30% red 60% white 15% rosé ▪ Brands for clients: GEPA, One World Fairtrade, WIETA, IPW ▪ PO Box 19 Koelenhof 7605 ▪ info@koopmanskloof.co.za ▪ www.koopmanskloof.co.za ▪ S 33° 53'54.7" E 018° 45'36.7" ▪ **T +27 (0)21-865-2355** ▪ F +27 (0)21-876-2421

Wine has been made at the Smit family's two-century-old farm in the Bottelary Hills since 1970, and these days there is much attention to conservation, with hiking trails and mountain biking enabling visitors to enjoy nature's spoils. Growing interest in their (Fairtrade-accredited) wines in Europe has persuaded them to develop 'a light, fruity yet full and elegant style' for those markets.

Dry Red ☺ 🍷 ★★★ Fragrant, juicy **10** blend of pinotage, merlot, cab & savoury shiraz.

Cabernet Sauvignon 🍷 🍷 ★★★ Abundant sweet fruit in friendly, refreshing **10**. **Pinotage** 🍷 🍷 ★★ Youthful **10** offers oaky, sweet-fruited freshness. **Shiraz** 🍷 🍷 ★★ Spicy sweetness in oaky **10** quaffer. **Pinotage Rosé** 🍷 🍷 ★★ Uncomplicated, dry, raspberry flavoured **11**. **Chardonnay** NEW 🍷 🍷 ★★ Unassuming, freshly tropical unoaked **11**. **Chenin Blanc** 🍷 🍷 ★★ Straightforward **11**, fresh & light sipper. **Sauvignon Blanc** 🍷 🍷 ★★ Tropical **11**, fresh & simple. Sampled pre-bottling, as for all above. — IM

Kranskop Wines

Location/map: Robertson ▪ WO: Klaasvoogds ▪ Est 2001 ▪ 1stB 2003 ▪ Tasting, sales & tours Mon-Fri 10-4.30 Sat & pub hols 10-2 ▪ Closed Easter Sun & Dec 25 ▪ BYO picnic ▪ Walking/hiking trails ▪ Self-catering Klaasvoogds Cottage, www.klaasvoogdscottage.co.za ▪ Owner(s) Newald Marais ▪ Cellarmaster(s)/winemaker(s) Newald Marais (2008) ▪ Viticulturist(s) Francois Muller (2008) ▪ 43ha/30ha (cab, merlot, pinot, shiraz, tannat, chard, sauv, viog) ▪ 240t/1,500cs own label 75% red 25% white ▪ IPW, BWI ▪ PO Box 49 Klaasvoogds 6707 ▪ newald@kranskopwines.co.za ▪ www.kranskopwines.co.za ▪ S 33° 47'53.1" E 019° 59'56.6" ▪ **T +27 (0)23-626-3200** ▪ F +27 (0)23-626-3200

Robertson owner/winemaker Newald Marais' first Viognier Noble Late Harvest set a sweet seal on last year's season, which also saw the maiden crush of pinot noir, launched after our deadline, and tannat (too little for commercial release). A visitor favourite is the Marais' Great Dane, Jono, who's inspired a special bottling of red muscadel intended to benefit the SPCA.

Cabernet Sauvignon ☺ ★★★ Restrained **09** has dark berry & plum aromas, voluptuous centre reined in by firm but friendly tannins. **Sauvignon Blanc** ☺ ★★★ Interesting mix jasmine, lime & wet clay on crisp **10**, five months lees-ageing add satisfying breadth.

Merlot ✓ ★★★★ Opaque **09** chocolaty, smooth & sweet-fruited. Plush offering with creamy conclusion. **Shiraz** ✓ ★★★★ Perfumed **09** quite soft & narrow shouldered for this variety, very sippable. Raises the bar, like the other reds & Sauvignon. **Chardonnay** ★★★ Well-handled barrel fermentation lets **10** fruit shine through, oak a touch sweet on finish though. **Viognier** NEW Preview barrel-fermented **11** distinctive apricot & 'pine nut' character but mid-2011 too unformed to rate. — Panel

■ **Krone** *see* Twee Jonge Gezellen Estate-The House of Krone

Kronendal Boutique Winery

Location/WO: Durbanville • Map: Durbanville, Philadelphia & Darling • Est 2003 • 1stB 2006 • Tasting & sales Mon-Fri by appt Sat 10-3 • Fee R30/6 wines • Closed Easter Fri/Sun, Ascension Day, Dec 25/26 & Jan 1 • Cellar tours by appt • Cheese platters by prior arrangement • Conference facilities • Art • Seasonal 'langtafel' lunches • Owner(s) Pieter & Magdaleen Kroon • Winemaker(s) Magdaleen Kroon • 2ha/0.6ha (mourv, shiraz, tempranillo, viog) • 4t/260cs own label 100% red • PO Box 4433 Durbanville 7551 • info@kronendalwine.co.za • http://kronendal.belmet.co.za • S 33° 48' 30.78" E 018° 36' 50.82" • **T +27 (0)82-499-0198** • F +27 (0)086-603-1170

It appears contradictory: adopting low-tech, minimalist principles in the vineyard and cellar only to explore high-tech avenues powered by the internet, such as Facebook, to interact and market. But it isn't, as Pieter and Magdaleen Kroon have proven with each successive vintage from their tiny Tygerberg Hills vineyard. The wine gains elegance and finesse, and many more people get to experience it.

Westerdale range

★★★★ **Mirari** ✓ As Latin name suggests, increasingly a wine 'to wonder at'. Mainly shiraz co-fermented with 12% mourvèdre, 1% viognier. **08** (★★★★☆) perhaps the most Rhône-like yet; distinctive fynbos scent, restrained fruit, melded oak (French, 50% new). Fine & savoury, like appealing **07** & debut **06** (★★★★).

Impromptu ★★★ Debut **07** from cab (77%) & petit verdot off neighbouring farm. Less depth, complexity & new oak than stablemate; still charms. Not revisited. — CvZ

Kumala

Location/map: Stellenbosch • WO: Western Cape/Worcester/Robertson/Lutzville • Tasting & sales Mon-Fri 10-4 at Doornbosch Centre, Strand Rd, Stellenbosch • Fee R20, waived on purchase • Closed Dec 25 to Jan 2 • Cellar tours by appt • Owner(s) Accolade Wines South Africa • Winemaker(s) Ben Jordaan (Jul 2002), Bruce Jack (Feb 2008) & Karen Bruwer (Oct 2008) • 50% red 50% white • PO Box 769 Stellenbosch 7599 • hannelize.mouton@accolade-wines.com • www.kumala.co.za • S 33° 56' 44.93" E 018° 51' 17.29" • **T +27 (0)21-882-8177** • F +27 (0)21-882-8176

A global sell-off saw this internationally popular, multi-million case South African brand change hands last year. Now under the banner of Accolade, the less corporate and more entrepreneurial ethic suits the team's 'can do' flexibility ideally, says winemaker Bruce Jack. Good growth continues in Japan, Russia & China, spurred on by an appreciation of traceability and authenticity (one of the reasons much of Kumala's production is still bottled at home, rather than overseas). Jack concedes it affects profits but gels with their ethics, integrated production and sustainability values. Kumala's challenge is to deliver consistent quality and 'be a wine South Africans can be proud of' while also being a fast-moving consumer good 'with soul'.

Zenith range

Chenin Blanc-Chardonnay ☺ 🍷 📖 ★★★ **11**, pre-bottling, takes quality up a notch; lively melon length with some body & breadth.

Merlot-Cabernet Sauvignon-Shiraz 📖 ★★★ **11** preview has mulberry richness; soft & rounded, with some depth & density; splash viognier adds interest. **Rosé** 📖 ★★★ Cherry fizzpop pleasure on **11**, sampled from tank, light bodied, dry & fresh.

Regional Selection

Pier 42 Chardonnay 📖 ★★★ Pre-bottling, **11** is rich & ripe, marmalade tang & good width on palate. Lively, long aftertaste. Export only, as for next. **Pier 42 Sauvignon Blanc** 📖 ★★★ Grassy green bean on **11** preview, tangy typicity & crispness.

Core range

Merlot-Pinotage 📖 ★★★ **10** 50/50 mix ratchets up on previous. Soft red berry, cocoa richness & earthy density, rounded body. Export only. **Pinotage-Shiraz** 📖 ★★★ Waxy berry blaze on ex-tank **11**, light bodied & ripe. Exported. **Shiraz-Mourvèdre** 📖 ★★★ **10** peppery plum with cocoa richness. 2 months oak-ageing adds structure & body. Rich but supple. **Cabernet Sauvignon-Shiraz** ✓ 📖 ★★★★ **11** preview over-delivers. Typical cab with shiraz mocha spice lift; gentle body, firm core & concentration. Long finish. **Merlot-Ruby Cabernet** 📖 ★★★ **11**, from tank, improves on previous. Ripe mulberry & herb edge, textured density to medium aftertaste. **Rosé** 🍷 ⚖ ★★★ Dry berry/cherry mouthful on **11** preview, lively full body. **Chardonnay-Semillon** 🍷⚖ ★★★ **10** tad less impressive than last year; fruity citrus & nettle zip. Exported, like rest. **Chenin Blanc-Chardonnay** 🍷⚖ ★★★ Chenin leads **10** with crisp kiwi flavour, zesty & dry simplicity. **Colombard-Chardonnay** 🍷⚖ ★★★ **10** improves on previous, full-ripe melon & acid lift. **Sauvignon Blanc-Colombard** 🍷⚖ ★★ Quaffable **10**, nimble peppery zip & lime zest. **Sauvignon Blanc-Semillon** 🍷⚖ ★★★ Dusty nettle & herb on juicy **10**. A touch mute & shy. **Chenin Blanc-Viognier** 🍷⚖ ★★★ Welcome return for zippy apple & stonefruit charmer in **10**, a step up, lively & full. Discontinued: **Pinotage-Cinsaut**.

Eternal range

Eternal Merlot-Cabernet Sauvignon-Shiraz NEW ⚖ ★★★ Rich blackberry & cinnamon, **11** fleshy yet supple & gentle. Nuanced blend of merlot, cab, shiraz & dab viognier sampled from tank. **Eternal Chenin Blanc-Chardonnay-Semillon** 🍷 ★★★ Tangy fruit salad on previewed **11**, improvement on previous. Discontinued: **Eternal Shiraz-Cabernet Sauvignon**.

Intulo range

Intulo Red 🍷⚖ ★★★ **11** preview improves on last year's version. Rich berry & gentle grip. **Intulo White** 🍷 ⚖ ★★★ Muscat perfume on ex-tank **11**, lively & fresh. — FM

Kumkani

Derived from the Xhosa word meaning 'king', Kumkani is the flagship brand of The Company of Wine People, celebrating South Africa's rich heritage. Winemaker Bernard Claasen now joins the royal court, as do the thousands of Facebook and blogsite fans who recognise the quality derived from specially selected vineyards, and value the brand offers.

Kumkani Single Vineyard range

★★★★ **Cradle Hill Cabernet Sauvignon** Previewed **09** youthful, complex if less rich, tighter than **07** (★★★★★). Core of ripe blackcurrant sheathed in vintage's firm tannic structure. Deserves time. No **08**.

★★★★ **Triple J Shiraz** Powerful **09** preview's spicy, smoky bacon flavours reined in by firm structure & cedary oak. Pedigree of single-vineyard & good vintage will show with cellaring. Stellenbosch WO, as for Cab.

★★★★☆ **Lanner Hill Sauvignon Blanc** **10** (★★★★) pre-bottling sample riper, less vivacious than **09**. Still shows Groenekloof's minerality but with a rounder, silky texture.

Kumkani Reflections range

★★★★ **VVS** None since **09**'s vivacious viognier, verdelho, sauvignon mix, with piquant apricot, lime tones.

Kumkani Infiniti Méthode Cap Classique range

Brut ✓ ★★★★ **07** sparkling step up on last-tasted **04** (★★★★). Rich, creamy texture with ripe stonefruit, brioche & toasted nuts. Mostly chardonnay with pinots noir & meunier. WO Western Cape.

Kumkani Single Varietal range

★★★★ **Sauvignon Blanc** ✓ 🍷 **10** tank sample continues the company's success with this variety. Lively gooseberry fruit with flinty tinge. Balanced & crisp for early enjoyment. WO Coastal.

Pinotage 🍷 ★★★ **09** tank sample a step up. Fresh berry, plum tones in streamlined & restrained style. Clean fruited, fresh & balanced. **Shiraz** 🍷 ★★★ Dusty, savoury & taut **09** needs time & a meal to relax. WO Stellenbosch, as for all single-variety reds. **Chenin Blanc** 🍷⚖ ★★★★ **10** previously rated preview was plump, with crisp apple flavours. **Viognier** 🍷 ★★★ None tasted since tangy **09**, with apricot, Earl Grey tones.

Kumkani Dual Varietal range

★★★★ **Chardonnay-Viognier** **10** (★★★) sample lacks verve of vibrant **09**. Viognier dominates with plump & peachy, toasty nuance.

Merlot-Pinotage 🍷 ★★★ Last available was **08** preview with plush, juicy berry appeal. **Shiraz-Cabernet Sauvignon** ✓ 🍷 ★★★★ Muscular cab tones shiraz's spicy, savoury flavours on pre-bottling **09**. Youthful, balanced but still tight. Needs time. **Shiraz-Viognier** 🍷 ★★★★ No newer vintage tasted since tangy, floral **07**. Coastal WOs for these. — MW

Kupferberger Auslese

Crowd-pleasing chenin-sauvignon blend by Distell, from many Coastal vineyards.

Kupferberger Auslese ★★ Pleasant semi-sweet **NV** with sweet melon & light grassy flavours. — Panel

■ **Kuun Wines** *see* Christian Kuun Wines

KWV

Map: Paarl & Wellington ▪ KWV Wine Emporium: Kohler Street, T +27 (0)21-807-3007/8 F +27 (0)21-807-3119 ▪ Tasting & sales Mon-Sat 9–4.30 Sun 11-4 ▪ Fee R15 for 5 products; R35 chocolate & brandy ▪ Cellar tour R30 ▪ Tours: Eng Mon-Sat 10, 10.30 & 2.15; Ger 10.15; Sun Eng 11 ▪ Tour groups by appt ▪ Closed Easter Fri, Dec 25 & Jan 1 ▪ Owner(s) KWV (Pty) Ltd ▪ Cellarmaster(s) Richard Rowe ▪ Winemaker(s) Thys Loubser, Johann Fourie, Nomonde Kubeka, Anneke du Plessis, Izelle van Blerk, Nadia Bouwer, Christiaan Coetzee ▪ Viticulturist(s) Unathi Mantshongo ▪ PO Box 528 Suider-Paarl 7624 ▪ customer@kwv.co.za ▪ www.kwv-wines.com, www.cafeculturewines.com, www.cathedralcellarwines.com, www.roodeberg.com, www.kwv.co.za ▪ S 33° 45' 46.87" E 018° 57' 59.92" ▪ **T +27 (0)21-807-3911 (Office)** ▪ F +27 0)21-807-3000

It's been 20 years since SA's quota system, administered by then 'super co-op' KWV for most of the last century, was scrapped. Since transformed into a private company, boasting the biggest cellar complex in the world (which you can tour when you visit the KWV Wine Emporium in Paarl), this wine and spirits giant now has a new majority share holder, investment company HCI. But it's business as usual for chief winemaker Richard Rowe and team, focusing on 'global wine styles', and also for recently appointed brand directors Jeff Gradwell, De Bruyn Steenkamp, Gareth Haarhoff and Werner Swanepoel, who are 'making great progress in rejuvenating KWV's major brands', namely Roodeberg, Cathedral Cellar, Café Culture, Golden Kaan, Pearly Bay, flagship Laborie and of course the KWV wines. See separate entries for these, and for newcomer BerRaz.

KWV Wines

If improvement in quality can be measured by awards, then Richard Rowe and his team are rocketing up the scale. Apart from their first five star wine in this guide, The Mentors range has picked up top awards in virtually every local and international competition the wines have been entered in. But across the board the aim is freshness, crisp acid, elegant flavours in whites; the same for reds, plus sweet fruit and balanced tannins, with easy drinkability a focus in the more commercial ranges. The following notes should confirm these goals are increasingly being achieved. Future challenges? 'To develop Mentors into a global brand, volumes need to increase but on the back of quality fruit,' says Rowe. 'We also need to continue to finesse our winemaking and develop a culture of excellence.'

Heritage range

★★★★☆ **Abraham Perold Shiraz** Opulent, thrusting **06** ex Paarl last tasted. Should still have year/2 to go.

Reserve Collection

Cabernet Sauvignon √ ★★★★ Abundance fresh cassis, blackberry features on **09**. Straightforward but persistent & with firm, lively tannins. **Merlot** ★★★ Fresh & fruity **09**. Simple sweet 'n sour plums, herbal twist in tail. **Shiraz** √ ★★★★ Bright choc, berry aromas & flavours on **09**. Lightish body; rounded & savoury. **Shiraz-Tannat-Cabernet Franc** Await next. **Chardonnay** √ 🖾 ★★★★ Extravagant lime marmalade & spice aromas introduce **10**. Matured in older oak barrels. Zestily fresh, concentrated & long. **Sauvignon Blanc** 🖥 🖾 ★★★ **10** for easy drinking, with straightforward ripe & persistent figgy flavours. **White Blend** Await next. **MCC Brut** NEW ★★★★ **09** refreshingly dry champagne-method sparkling. Chardonnay's limy/creamy features lifted by bright, brisk bubble. With 11% pinot. Could beneficially mellow with short ageing.

Mentors range

★★★★ **Petit Verdot** 🖥 **09** lithe & lively. Delicate floral, wild dark berry scents yield to similar, refreshing flavours; the vitality theme ends with succulent yet vibrant tannins. Like next, WO Stellenbosch.

★★★★ **Pinotage** 🖥 **09** reflects its pinot noir parentage with a wealth of pure, bright raspberry/cherry fruit, silkily laid over buzz of well-managed tannins reminding one of actual varietal origin! No **08**.

★★★★ **Shiraz 09** builds on **08**; echoes lily, red fruit attractions with more substance, depth & youthful feel. Big 14.7% alcohol but balanced; best cellared for year/2 before opening. WO Coastal.

★★★★ **Chardonnay** NEW 🖥 🖾 Unshowy, mellow oatmeal, pickled lime aromas on **10** from Elgin. Poised & refreshing with elegant, silky mouthfeel, subtly enriched by oak. Lovely broad & sustained finish.

★★★★ **Chenin Blanc** 🖥 Pungent complexity on **08** tasted last year; rather fat & full.

★★★★★ **Grenache Blanc** NEW ✓ 🍾 🏵 Wonderfully expressive individual, **10** with wet earth & fresh hay aromas. These are subtly expanded on the silkily weighted palate which also shimmers with clean, mineral vitality. Should fascinate for several years. From Paarl grapes.

★★★★ **Sauvignon Blanc** 🍾 Refined green pea fragrance, taut mineral core & well-weighted fruit noted last year on **09**. WO Stellenbosch.

★★★★ **Semillon** 🍾 🏵 Distinguished by well-defined varietal honeycomb/lemongrass on **10** enlivened, lengthened by balanced freshness. Just short of complexity of **09** (★★★★★). WO Lutzville.

★★★★ **Sauvignon Blanc-Semillon** 🍾 **09** last year showed sauvignon's freshness well-matched with richer semillon; crescendo of intense tangerine, honey flavours.

Orchestra 🍾 ★★★★ Bordeaux-style quintet; **09** modern in its bright tangy plum/cassis purity, more classic in its medium body, freshness & austerity. Smart French oak, all new, well absorbed. **08** (★★★★) less complex. WO Coastal. **Canvas** Await next. **Viognier** 🍾 🏵 ★★★★ Fresher, less heavy style. Lightly oaked **10** notable for delicacy of dried peach features lifted by well-masked few grams sugar (officially off-dry).

Classic Collection

Cabernet Sauvignon ☺ 🏵 ★★★ Sound mouthfilling crunchy, juicy blackcurrants & lively tannin backing on previewed **10**. **Pinotage** ☺ 🏵 ★★★ **10** mouthful ripe juicy raspberries; fresh & lively with sustained finish. **Chardonnay** ☺ 🏵 ★★★ Fruit-driven **10**. Oaked portion (40%) lends breadth to easy-going melon, oatmeal tones. **Chenin Blanc** ☺ 🏵 ★★★ Generous ripe melon, honey fruit on **11**. Light, fresh, crisp; just off-dry.

Merlot 🏵 ★★ Smooth, sweet **10** with some alcohol glow. **Shiraz** 🏵 ★★★ Previewed **10** smooth-textured with bright spice, red fruits. **Pinotage Rosé** 🍾 ★★★ Raspberry flavours on off-dry but crisp, quaffable **11** tasted from tank. **Chêne** 🍾 ★★★ Gentle spice, floral & honeyed features on **10** tasted last year. **Sauvignon Blanc** 🏵 ★★ Light flavours on sprightly, sweetish **11**. **Cuvee Brut** ★★ Fruity NV from chenin at the sweeter end of Brut. **Sparkling Demi-Sec** ★★ Creamy fizz on sweetish **NV** from chenin. **Vin Doux** ★★ Sweet but clean, frothy **NV** still selling. **Sparkling Rosé** ★★ Tangy off-dry **NV** bubbly tasted last year. **Late Harvest** 🍾 🏵 ★★ Fresh & grapey **10** previously previewed.

Vintage Reserves
Discontinued: **Vintage White Muscadel**.

Dessert range
★★★★ **White Muscadel** 🍾 **NV** rich but not over-unctuous with complex flavours tasted last year. Warmingly long.

Cape Ruby ☺ ★★★ Solid ruby hue on **NV** dessert. Simple red plums, earthy tones; smooth & sweet. **Cape Tawny** ☺ ★★★ Some nice aged nutty, floor polish notes on unheavy **NV** mostly from tinta barocca. Smooth & very sweet. 8 yrs older oak.

Red Muscadel 🍾 ★★★ Latest **NV** with fresher muscat fruit than previous. Not too heavy or sweet. Now 2 rather than 5 years older oak.

Contemporary Collection NEW
Cabernet Sauvignon-Merlot 🍾 🏵 ★★★ Ripe, soft & accessible, very lightly oaked **10**; rounded & dry. **Shiraz-Cabernet Sauvignon** 🏵 ★★ Choc & red berries on robust off-dry **10** ex-tank. **Chenin Blanc-Chardonnay** 🍾 🏵 ★★★ Off-dry **10** (sample last year) now shows fresh, tropical juiciness, light creamy feel. **Chenin Blanc-Muscat** 🍾 🏵 ★★ Previewed **11** grapey & sweet. — AL

Kyburg Wine Estate

Location/map: Stellenbosch ▪ WO: Devon Valley/Stellenbosch ▪ Est 1998 ▪ 1stB 2006 ▪ Tasting & sales by appt ▪ Closed Easter Sun, Dec 25/26 & Jan 1 ▪ Fully furnished self-catering guesthouse (exclusive, rental min 2 weeks) ▪ Owner(s) Fred & Rosmarie Ruest ▪ Cellarmaster(s)/winemaker(s) Jacques Fourie (Jan 2006, consultant) ▪ Viticulturist(s) Frans Snyman (Jul 2006, consultant) ▪ 28ha/18ha (cab, merlot, shiraz) ▪ 150-160t/3,750cs own label 100% red ▪ PO Box 12799 Die Boord 7613 ▪ info@kyburgwine.com ▪ www.kyburgwine.com ▪ S 33° 54' 59.3" E 018° 49' 28.4" ▪ **T** +27 (0)21-865-2876

Only 30 percent of this farm's production goes under its own label, the balance being sold to well-reputed Stellenbosch wineries. Winemaker Jacques Fourie is determined to further improve quality in the vineyard, especially looking to 'more focus on balance between vines and fruit and how to retain that from the vine to the table'. The already promising wines should respond accordingly.

Kyburg range
Cabernet Sauvignon ★★★★ Bright, fresh cassis flavours, good fruit richness in balance with generous tannic base on **09**. Promising development potential. **Merlot** ★★★★ **09** displays rich, ripe fruit with sweet length & firm tannin support. **Shiraz** ★★★★ Spicy whiff livens up slightly jammy notes on **09**. Tasty, if simple; far fist of tannin requires time to soften. **08** (★★★★) was more complex. **33 Latitude** ★★★★ Fruity, savoury mix of cab with shiraz, merlot on **09**. Soft core with grippy tannin contrast. — AL

■ **La Bonne Vigne** *see Wonderfontein*

Laborie Wine Farm

Location: Paarl ▪ Map: Paarl & Wellington ▪ WO: Western Cape ▪ Est 1691 ▪ Tasting & sales Mon-Sat 9-5 Sun 11-3 ▪ Fee R15/5 wines R25/8 wines R25/tour + tasting ▪ Closed all Christian pub hols ▪ Tours for large groups by appt ▪ Laborie Restaurant T +27 (0)21-807-3095: lunch Tue-Sun 11.30-3 dinner Wed-Sun 6-10 ▪ Lazy Day Markets (Sat) ▪ Carols by Candlelight ▪ Conferences ▪ Weddings/functions ▪ Accommodation ▪ Owner(s) KWV (Pty) Ltd ▪ Winemaker(s) Johan Fourie & Anneke du Plessis ▪ Viticulturist(s) Marco Ventrella, with Unathi Mantshongo ▪ 59ha/30ha (ptage, pinot noir, pinot meunier, shiraz, chard, sauv) ▪ 40,000cs ▪ BWI, IPW, WIETA ▪ PO Box 528 Suider Paarl 7624 ▪ info@laboriewines.co.za ▪ www.laboriewines.co.za ▪ S 33°45'55.2" E 018°57'27.6" ▪ **T +27 (0)21-807-3390** ▪ F +27 (0)21-863-1955

Stretching up the north-facing slopes of Paarl Mountain, this farm was first granted to Isaac Taillefert in 1691; it has produced wine since 1698 and was acquired by the KWV in 1971. Perhaps better known for its restaurant than its wines until recently when, under the new winemaking team, there are notable improvements with shiraz and Cap Classique bubblies showing particular promise. The restaurant is also undergoing refurbishment and a weekly Lazy Day's fresh food market is proving another drawcard.

Laborie Cellar range
★★★★ **Jean Taillefert** Modern shiraz, **09** shows plenty of bright sweet fruit, spice augmented by French & American oak maturation (60% new). Bigger, denser than last **06**, but supple bounce & rounded finish.
★★★★ **Blanc de Blanc Brut** Some evolution shows in bright golden hue, oxidative/leesy flavours of **07** (★★★★). Brisk bubble; unaggressively dry. **06** was beautifully balanced.
★★★★ **Pineau de Laborie** 🍷 Dessert with both fortifying spirit & base wine from pinotage. **11** already smoothly, silkily integrated; warming & long macerated mulberry flavours. Not too sweet. First since **04**.
Cabernet Sauvignon ✓ 🗒 ★★★★ Medium-bodied **09** displays similar fresh brambleberry/cassis features as previous. Lively tannins need yr/2 to settle. **Merlot** 🗒 ★★★ **09** light tomato leaf, sour plum tones; simple & short. **Shiraz** ✓ 🗒 ★★★★ Full-bodied **09** with supple, spicy red fruit flavours to fore. Firm yet accessible build. Rounded by older oak. **Limited Collection Shiraz** ★★★★ **09** still youthful, gawky. Once settled its pretty oak-laced spice, red fruits, gentle texture should offer few years pleasure. **Merlot-Cabernet Sauvignon** 🗒 ★★★★ Fleshy, bright-fruited merlot framed by cab's lively, ripe tannins. Subtly oaked **09** flavoursome & long. **Chardon-nay** 🗒 🍷 ★★★ Juicy pear, citrus flavours on easy-drinking **10**. Portion briefly oaked. **Limited Collection Chardonnay** 🍷 ★★★ Generous sweet vanilla oak (40% new) overpowers lightish, brisk fruit on **10**. May bene-fit from short ageing. **Sauvignon Blanc** 🗒 ★★★ Riper tropical style, though sample **11** medium bodied. Few grams sugar lengthens juicy fruit. **MCC Brut** ✓ ★★★★ Elegant **08** creamy yet invigorating. Gentle brioche scents, soupcon red fruit flavours. Very dry, persistent. Like **07** (★★★★) from pinot & chardonnay. **MCC Brut Rosé** ★★★★ Last tasted **08** from pinot, chardonnay & 3% pinotage had biscuity, red fruit appeal. Discontinued: **Chardonnay-Chenin Blanc**. — AL

La Bourgogne Farm

Location/map/WO: Franschhoek ▪ Est 1694 ▪ 1stB 1902 ▪ Tasting & sales Mon-Sat 10-3 ▪ Fee R30 ▪ Closed Easter Fri-Sun, Ascension day, Dec 25/26 & Jan 1 ▪ Facilities for children ▪ Farm produce ▪ Olive & olive oil tasting ▪ Walk-ing/hiking trail ▪ Conservation area ▪ 6 self-catering riverside cottages (see Accommodation section) ▪ Owner(s) La Bourgogne Farm (Pty) Ltd ▪ Winemaker(s) DP Burger (2008, consultant) ▪ Viticulturist(s) Gappie le Roux (2003, consultant) ▪ 22ha/4ha (malbec, shiraz, chard, sem, viog) ▪ PO Box 96 Franschhoek 7690 ▪ info@labourgogne.co.za ▪ www.labourgogne.co.za ▪ S 33° 55' 28.0" E 019° 7' 15.0" ▪ **T +27 (0)21-876-3245** ▪ F +27 (0)86-542-3615

A diversity of agriculture ensures the economic viability of this historic farm, dating back to 1694. Fruit is the main focus, followed by olives and just 4ha of vines. Six self-catering cottages allow guests to enjoy both olive oil and wine tastings in this beautiful Franschhoek setting.

Progeny Semillon ★★★ Over-cropping (20T) dilutes fruit in **09**, but old vines retain varietal dignity with viscosity & lanolin nuance. **Progeny White Honey** Occasional release. — MW

La Bri Estate

Location/map/WO: Franschhoek ▪ Est 1694 ▪ Tasting, sales & cellar tours Mon-Fri 10-5 Sat 10.30-3.30 ▪ Fee R20pp, waived on purchase ▪ Closed Easter Fri/Sun, Dec 25 & Jan 1 ▪ Cheese platters ▪ BYO picnic (sites along the river) ▪ Bicycle friendly ▪ Old wine cellar & tasting room open by appt ▪ Owner(s) Robin Hamilton ▪ Cellarmaster(s) Irene Waller (Oct 2010) ▪ Winemaker(s) Glen Isaacs (Jun 2009) ▪ Viticulturist(s) Gerard Olivier (Oct 2010) ▪ ±24ha/±15ha (cabs s/f, merlot, p verdot, shiraz, chard, viog) ▪ 91t/2,500cs own label 80% red 20% white ▪ PO Box 180 Franschhoek 7690 ▪ info@labri.co.za ▪ www.labri.co.za ▪ S 33° 55' 18.3" E 019° 7' 1.5" ▪ **T +27 (0)21-876-2593** ▪ F +27 (0)86-275-9753

News of old and new from this riverside Franschoek property. Restoration of the old cellar will lead to a self-guided tour through to the state-of-the-art new one; new too are picnic sites along the river. A longer wait – until around 2013 - will be required for the first Cap Classique from experienced bubbly maker Irene Waller.

★★★★ **Chardonnay 10** (★★★☆) in accord with usual unshowy, pure-fruited, subtly oaked style. Less depth than **09**, but fresh, creamily rounded & ready.

Cabernet Sauvignon ★★★ Simple, strawberry-toned **08** not in same league as complex **07** (★★★★). Light fruit, dry tannins; for early drinking. **Merlot** ★★★ **09** sample shows attractive spicy perfume, rich dark berry flavours. Fuller than previous but with balanced freshness, oak. **Syrah** ★★★ Previously 'Shiraz-Viognier' (now still has 3% viognier). Oak rather than fruit lends light spicy edge to simple, sweetish **08**. **07** was more generous. **Affinity** ★★★★ Creamy dark fruit, fine, savoury tannins on merlot-led blend **06** tasted last year. Previous was **04** (★★★★). **Viognier** ★★★ Last tasted was quiet **08**. **09** sold out. — AL

La Capra

 NEW

La Capra began life as the youngest member of Charles Back's phenomenally successful vinous goat herd. Careful consideration was the watchword for this new kid: Capra is the word for wild goats and the label's precariously-poised stack (including a missing-fingered man) is highly symbolic. The inaugural La Capra festival celebrated its mantra of magic, laughter in the air and dancing till sunrise with a glass in hand. No surprise that entries for the annual Goat Run tripled.

★★★★ **Hanepoot Straw Wine** ✓ **09** (★★★★) apricot, butterscotch & ginger zestiness. Touch less complex than **08**. Creamy texture to clean, dry finish.

Malbec ☺ 🗎 🖉 ★★★ Blueberry galore on juicy, lightly oaked **10**, & light choc notes. Very approachable. **Merlot** ☺ 🗎 🖉 ★★★ **10** is tasty plum & mulberry spice exemplified. Light tannins helped by a little oak. Nice depth & length. **Pinotage** ☺ 🗎 🖉 ★★★ **10** a notch up on last tasted **08**. Succulent raspberry & blueberry pastille. Light-bodied, delicious quaffer. **Pinotage Rosé** ☺ 🗎 🖉 ★★★ **11** light powdery strawberry & sherbet tang. Simply tasty. **Chenin Blanc** ☺ 🗎 🖉 ★★★ **11** offers green apricot tang & medium body. Fresh & lively with crisp finish.

Cabernet Sauvignon ✓ 🗎 🖉 ★★★★ **10** fruitcake richness, with good density & depth. **09** sold out unreviewed (as for malbec, merlot & pinotage). **Chardonnay** ✓ 🗎 🖉 ★★★★ Rich citrus fruit & zesty life on **10**. Creamy breadth from 4 months on the lees & gentle part-oaking. **Pinot Gris** 🗎 🖉 ★★ Lively, tangy simplicity on **11**. **Viognier** 🗎 🖉 ★★★ **11** has tangy peach vibrancy. Pre-bottling sample still on lees, so might well improve. Touch chalky & short. **Shiraz** ✓ 🗎 ★★★★ Lovely pepper bite on liquorice & black-fruited **09**. Step up on **08**, with good dry concentration & texture. — FM

▪ **La Cave** see Wellington Wines
▪ **Lace** see Almenkerk Wine Estate

La Chataigne

Location/map/WO: Franschhoek ▪ Est 1972 ▪ 1stB 2003 ▪ Tasting & sales Mon-Fri 10-4 Sat/Sun by appt ▪ Closed all pub hols ▪ 3 guest cottages ▪ Owner(s) Parkfelt family ▪ Winemaker(s) Gerda Willers (2003, consultant) ▪ 27ha/17ha (cab, merlot, ptage, shiraz, chenin, sauv, sem) ▪ 150t/2,000cs own label 25% red 65% white 10% rosé ▪ PO Box 7 La Motte 7691 ▪ office@lachat.co.za ▪ www.lachat.co.za ▪ S 33° 52'43.8" E 019° 3'34.1" ▪ **T +27 (0)21-876-3220** ▪ F +27 (0)21-876-3220

'The biggest client for my wine is myself and the next biggest is my mother,' laughs Richard Parkfelt as he gives the credit for the vinous success of this family boutique to wine consultant Gerda Willers' creativity and talent. An unusual amarone-style wine is on the cards, whilst exports to home-country Sweden continue apace.

Marron ★★★★ Elegant **08** merlot, pinotage, cab combo with sweet-sour cherry flavours, tasted previously. **Kastanje** ✓ 🍷 ★★★★ Chenin from old dryland bushvines. **10** just off-dry, freshness & textured baked apple flavour make a distinctly individual wine. **Sauvignon Blanc** 🍷 ★★★★ Wild herbaceousness in **10** boosts fresh appeal, as does vibrant acidity & stony minerality. Mouthwatering. Discontinued: **Rosé**. — IM

La Chaumiere Estate

Location/map: Franschhoek ▪ Est 2001 ▪ 1stB 2003 ▪ Tasting & tours by appt ▪ Sales from local outlets ▪ Owner(s) Michael Pawlowski ▪ Winemaker(s)/viticulturist(s) Wynand Pienaar (consultant) ▪ 2ha (pinot, chard) ▪ 18t/900cs own label ▪ PO Box 601 Franschhoek 7690 ▪ wynlpers@iafrica.com ▪ S 33° 54'34.0" E 019° 6'54.9" ▪ **T +27 (0)21-876-4830/31** ▪ F +27 (0)21-876-2135

Last crush, farm manager and consultant winemaker Wynand Pienaar vinified chardonnay, pinot noir and a chardonnay-pinot noir méthode cap classique sparkling, all from grapes grown on this boutique Franschhoek estate. This year, he can add cabernet, shiraz and viognier to the line-up, from vineyards at La Grange, another property in the Franschhoek Valley owned by Michael Pawlowski.

Ladera Artisan Wines

 NEW

Location: Wolseley ▪ Map: Breedekloof ▪ WO: Coastal ▪ Est/1stB 2009 ▪ Tasting, sales & cellar tours Mon-Sat by appt ▪ Picnics & longtable lunches by prior booking ▪ Owner(s) Charles Ochse ▪ Cellarmaster(s)/winemaker(s) Charles Ochse (2003) ▪ 115ha total ▪ 6-8t/400cs own label 51% red 33% white 16% rosé ▪ PO Box 193 Wolseley 6830 ▪ info@ladera.co.za ▪ www.ladera.co.za ▪ S 33° 28'20.66" E 019° 11'27.45" ▪ **T +27 (0)72-536-0055**

In 2009, Charles Ochse was asked by his father to leave his post in charge of white wines at Franschhoek Cellar to take over the running of the family fruit farm in Wolseley. Charles found it impossible to forsake winemaking entirely and decided to start his own label. He says his biggest challenge is devoting enough time to the new project but nevertheless finds it fulfilling having to switch from farmer to winemaker to marketer.

★★★★ **Zahir Syrah** ✓ Boldly styled **09** is fruit-ripe, with meaty flavours. High alc (±15%) well assimilated, vanilla oak (none new) provides attractive veneer to rich fruit. — Panel

Ladismith Cellar - SCV

Location: Ladismith ▪ Map: Klein Karoo & Garden Route ▪ WO: Klein Karoo/Western Cape ▪ Est 1941 ▪ 1stB 1988 ▪ Tasting & sales Mon-Fri 9–5 Sat 9–3 ▪ Fee R20 for groups of 5 or more ▪ Closed Easter Fri-Mon, Dec 25/26 & Jan 1 ▪ Book ahead for cellar tours ▪ Restaurant ▪ Owner(s) 75 members ▪ Cellarmaster(s) Hermias Vollgraaff (2011) ▪ Winemaker(s) Hermias Vollgraaff (2010), with William Harvey (2011) ▪ Viticulturist(s) Hermias Vollgraaff (2009) ▪ 600ha/520ha (cab, merlot, ptage, ruby cab, shiraz, chard, chenin, cbard, viog) ▪ 4,800t/10,000cs own label 20. 25% red 79.75% white ▪ Other export brand: Decent ▪ PO Box 56 Ladismith 6655 ▪ info@scv.co.za ▪ www. ladismithwines.co.za ▪ S 33° 29'49.38" E 021° 15'59.40" ▪ **T +27 (0)28-551-1042** ▪ F +27 (0)28-551-1930

One of three wineries in the Southern Cape Vineyards stable, Ladismith Cellar has restored the old parsonage on the main street of its Klein Karoo home town, and now has a new tasting and sales area, restaurant and 'an exciting vehicle' for presenting its wines with the renowned local cheeses. Also new is the Ladismith 8-Year Old Brandy, already a gold winner at a couple of international shows.

Towerkop range

Pinotage NEW ☺ 🍴 ★★★ **11** healthy colour & laudably restrained aroma, this & following unoaked to let pristine fruit shine through.

Cabernet Sauvignon NEW ★★★ **11** provisionally rated preview is characterful, with juicy & clean fruit flavour. **Merlot** NEW ★★★ Light-hued **10** pleasant to sip, its plum fruit unfettered by oak. **Ruby Cabernet** 🍴 ★★ Preview **11** packed with berries, supple & juicy for anytime enjoyment. **Shiraz** ★★★ Still-selling **09** commendably dry, firm tannins rein in plush fruit. **Touriga Nacional** NEW ★★ (Unfortified) **09** slight malty overtone to jammy fruit. **Rosé** 🍴 ★★★ **10** semi-dry pretty pink sipper from shiraz had slight pétillance, finished crisp last edition. **Chardonnay** 🍴 ★★ Unwooded **11** preview quiet lemon/nut aromas, insubstantial flavours. **Chenin Blanc** 🍴 ★★ Karoo scrub & nuts, preview **11** bracing acidity from early picked grapes. **Sauvignon Blanc** ★★ Pre-bottling, **11** cool green varietal fruit, bright acidity, lowish 12% alc for anytime enjoyment. Ratings for previewed wines provisional. **Viognier** Await next. **Chardonnay-Sauvignon Blanc** 🍴 ★★★ Previously tasted **10** good early drinking style; chardonnay's citrus aroma & palate weight balanced by sauvignon's green fruit & zestiness. **Aristaat** 🍴 ★★ Sweetish white named for rare protea, uncomplicated, drink-soon **10** features dash muscadel. **Towersoet** ✓ 🍴 ★★★★ Fortified dessert from muscat d'Alexandrie. Improved **09** is bottled sunshine: ripe & juicy grape flavours, creamy texture, lovely clean fresh finish, whereas **07** (★★★) was cloying. WO W Cape. **Amalienstein Muscadel** ✓ 🍴 ★★★★ Delightful **10** fortified after-dinner treat again raises the bar. Bursts with enough lemon, lime, nutty complexity to brighten any dull winter's day. More depth & verve than last-tasted **06** (★★★). — Panel

▪ **Lady Anne Barnard** *see African Pride Wines*
▪ **Lady May** *see Glenelly Cellars*

La Ferme Derik

Location: Paarl ▪ Map: Paarl & Wellington ▪ WO: Paarl/Western Cape ▪ Est 1695 ▪ 1stB 1895 ▪ Tasting, sales & cellar tours by appt ▪ Function venue for 160 guests ▪ Guest house ▪ Owner(s) Hardus Otto ▪ Winemaker(s)/viticulturist(s) Eurica Scholtz ▪ 7ha (shiraz, grenache b/n, roussanne, viog) + 45ha export table grapes & macadamia nuts ▪ 35t 10% red 90% white ▪ PO Box 2008 Windmeul 7630 ▪ lafermederik@absamail.co.za ▪ www.lafermederik. com ▪ S 33° 40′ 33.348″ E 18° 55′ 56.964″ ▪ **T +27 (0)21-869-8380 / +27 (0)82-953-0185** ▪ F +27 (0)21-869-8433

Wine is a small part of family-owned La Ferme Derik, which also has table grapes and macadamia nuts under cultivation in addition to providing conference, function and accommodation facilities. Eurica Scholtz, family of owner Hardus Otto, is winemaker along with having a hand in just about everything else. As for what to expect from the wines, they're not mainstream and all the better for that.

Adagio ★★★★ Generous, open-structured **08** includes shiraz (85%), mourvèdre, viognier. Ripe red & black fruit, soft tannins, slightly hot finish. All wines listed here tasted for last edition. **Vlinnay** ★★★ Ex viognier, **08** rich, oxidative style; flavours of peach, spice; good palate weight, smooth texture, soft acidity. **Chénine** ★★★★ **09** a blend of old-vine chenin & viognier (80/20). Intense peach & apricot, rich & full with soft acidity. **Concerto 'les Quatre Saisons'** ★★★★ 5-way blend in **09** with sauvignon in lead (48%). Step up on **08** (★★★) with good fruit integrity, full body & balanced zesty acidity. Adventurous winemaking. **Vivace** ★★★★ Blend of chenin (52%) & 4 other whites. **09** better concentration, more layers of flavour than maiden **08** (★★★), tangy acidity lends balance. — CE

Laibach Vineyards

Location/map: Stellenbosch ▪ WO: Simonsberg-Stellenbosch/Western Cape/Stellenbosch ▪ Est 1994 ▪ 1stB 1997 ▪ Tasting & sales Mon-Fri 10-5 Sat 10-1 (Nov-Apr) pub hols 10-1 ▪ Fee R10/4 wines ▪ Closed Easter Fri/Sun, Dec 25/26 & Jan 1 ▪ Cellar tours by appt ▪ Laibach Vineyards Lodge (see Accommodation section) ▪ Owner(s) Petra Laibach-Kühner & Rudolf Kühner; consultant Stefan Dorst ▪ Cellarmaster(s)/winemaker(s) Francois van Zyl (Jan 2000) ▪ Viticulturist(s)/MD Michael Malherbe (Jun 1994) ▪ 50ha/37ha (cabs s/f, malbec, merlot, p verdot, ptage, chard, chenin, viog) ▪ 300t/24,000cs own label 70% red 30% white + 2,700cs for Woolworths ▪ BWI, Organic ▪ PO Box 7109 Stellenbosch 7599 ▪ info@laibachwines.com ▪ www.laibachwines.com ▪ S 33° 50′ 43.3″ E 018° 51′ 44.2″ ▪ **T +27 (0)21-884-4511** ▪ F +27 (0)21-884-4848

German family owned Laibach was one of the first in the Cape to embrace organic viticulture. Now, after several years in conversion, all blocks are fully certified (so expect to see more organic icons beside the wines in future editions). Understandably, GM/viticulturist Michael Malherbe's is delighted, and says he's keen to see how well liquid fertiliser diligently gathered from a wormery will work in the vineyards. It's just one of a series of innovations at the Stellenbosch estate, a first being the introduction of The Ladybird Red, with its early emphasis on natural winegrowing, back in 2002/3. Significantly, it and Ladybird White now account for 60% of total production.

★★★★ **Merlot** ✓ Combo own & Ceres grapes maintain track record in 09 with sexy mulberry/cocoa fruit purity. Concentrated depth yet satin-sleek in texture, oak finesse adds body & lengthy charm to spice appeal.

★★★★ **Claypot Merlot** 09 invites with cinnamon, plum & earth attractions. Serious savoury style with brush of tar. Oak again toned down from 08 - now 50%. Harmonious, balanced & wonderfully long.

★★★★ **Pinotage** ✓ 10 improves on last-tasted 08 (★★★★). Red berry & forest floor density & richness countered by nimble oaking (40% new). Nuanced, serious wine made with restraint. No 09.

★★★★ **Friedrich Laibach** 08 (★★★★★) first with merlot steering 5-way Bordeaux blend, & step up on cab-dominant 07. Velvety blueberry & cassis, bold & rich but toned, elegant, restrained. Fine tannin underscores ripe fruit. Oak (75% new) dialled down from previous.

★★★★ **Red Ladybird** ☙ Merlot, cab franc & cab almost equal partners (with malbec, petit verdot) in Bordeaux-style 10, ripe berries, tobacco leaf & earthy notes. Firm body & slight chunky texture, but nice freshness.

Cabernet Sauvignon ✓ ★★★★ 08 vaults last tasted 05 (★★★★). Rich blackcurrant, spice & velvety warm texture. Refined & elegant with good concentration. Just 10% new oak. Sadly, last bottling ever. **Widow's Block Cabernet Sauvignon** Await new vintage. **Chenin Blanc** ✓ 🗏 ★★★★ 11 ups the ante on 10 (★★★). Rich apricot purity from old bushvines in Bottelary Hills. Lovely acid tang (all natural), full of sunshine boldness yet rounded & stylish. Long & rewarding. **White Ladybird** 🗏 ★★★★ Chardonnay leads chenin & (Wellington) viognier in 10 mix. Agile peach/apricot & honey with biscuit nuance. Tangy vibrancy & oak veneer. — FM

La Kavayan

Location/WO: Stellenbosch ▪ Est 1999 ▪ 1stB 2001 ▪ Closed to public ▪ Owner(s) Gabriël Kriel & Theo Beukes ▪ Winemaker(s) PG Slabbert (2001, consultant) ▪ Viticulturist(s) Gabriël Kriel ▪ 4ha (cab, shiraz) ▪ ±10,000L own label 100% red ▪ PO Box 321 Stellenbosch 7599 ▪ wine@lakavayan.co.za ▪ **T +27 (0)21-881-3289/+27 (0)21-881-3246** ▪ F +27 (0)21-881-3095/+27 (0)21-881-3211

Friends and fellow vintners Theo Beukes and Gabriël Kriel secured an exclusive listing for their 2008 vintage with nationwide retailer Tops at Spar. Doubtless the boutique red-wine specialists celebrated by drawing the corks on some of their bottles – no screwcaps for these traditionalists, whose motto is 'timeless quality'.

Cabernet Sauvignon ✓ ★★★★ Classic violet & blackcurrant scents, supple tannins on medium-bodied 09, in mould of previous. **Cabernet Sauvignon-Shiraz** ✓ ★★★★ 09 back on track with red/black fruit complexity, more presence than 08. Both this & Cab commendably savoury & dry, not a fruit-bomb in sight. — CvZ

Lammershoek Winery

Location: Malmesbury ▪ Map: Swartland ▪ WO: Swartland/Swartberg ▪ Est 1999 ▪ 1stB 2000 ▪ Tasting, sales & cellar tours by appt ▪ Light lunch platters by appt (R100pp incl wine tasting); or BYO picnic ▪ Owner(s) Paul & Anna Kretzel, Stephan family ▪ Cellarmaster(s)/viticulturist(s) Craig Hawkins (Oct 2009) ▪ Winemaker(s) Craig Hawkins (Oct 2009), with Jurgen Gouws (Jan 2010) ▪ 210ha/96ha (cab, carignan, grenache, merlot, mourv, ptage, syrah, tinta barocca, zin, chard, chenin, hárslevelü, sauv, viog) ▪ 150t/10,000cs own label 65% red 30% white 5% rosé ▪ PO Box 597 Malmesbury 7299 ▪ info@lammershoek.co.za ▪ www.lammershoek.co.za ▪ S 33° 31'30.2" E 018° 48' 21.1" ▪ **T +27 (0)22-482-2835** ▪ F +27 (0)22-487-2702

The LAM show has started. Four exciting wines have been added. These are not seen as a second-level range but rather as a vehicle to express and use younger vineyards. The wines offer exceptional value and most strikingly share a fresh vinosity and low alcohol levels that offer great drinkability for serious consumers. As with winemaking in the past, Craig Hawkins continues and takes forward the wonderful experimental craft that has become synonymous with Lammershoek. The top echelon has markedly improved over the last few vintages and offers an exellent example of why the Swartland wine region has become so important.

Lammershoek range

★★★★ **Syrah** Still selling, last was **08** indicating shift to restraint, though big 14.5% alc; had shy raspberry & mulberry notes, supported by bright red cherry, savoury minerality.

★★★★☆ **Roulette** ✓ Complex shiraz-based Rhône style with carignan, grenache, mourvedre & viognier in support. **08** offers cold coffee overlay with fine underlying fruit & spice. Complex palate follows with fine tailored tannins, refreshing acidity. Clever oak.

★★★★☆ **Chenin Blanc** ✓ Very youthful, complex **10**, has tinned apple, sunny fruit perfectly poised to unfold to full flavoured & layered mouthfeel. Swartland minerality completes dry, serious effort. Overall impression of lingering freshness & focus. 13.5% alc modest for this area. With 13% chardonnay.

★★★★☆ **Roulette Blanc 10** Rhône-styled white continues on form of previous **09** (★★★★★) with fine oxidative stylistics. Mostly chenin & chardonnay with dash each viognier & clairette. Winemaking in natural idiom produces layers of flavours with super focused dry end; moderate 13% alc.

★★★★☆ **Straw Wine 10** (★★★★) sample tasted from chenin less convincing than **09**. Exudes rich sun ripened peaches, ultra-light with only 7.5% alc & lovely acid-balanced viscosity. Rating provisional.

Discontinued: **Pinotage**, **Tinta Barocca**, **Zinfandel-Syrah**, **Pinodoux**.

LAM range NEW

Pinotage ✓ 🔲 ★★★★ Wonderful exponent of the delicate side of the variety (13% alc). **10** sample has floral & red berry perfume, with attractive savoury entry leading to fine dry & mineral finish. Fresh throughout. **Syrah** ✓ 🔲 ★★★★ Vibrant entry to this young **10** shiraz ex-tank. Made in fresh & approachable style from younger vineyards. Exudes a wonderful winey character, with great fruit/spicy intensity. **Rosé** ✓ 🔲 ★★★★ Pale onionskin hue on savoury & dry **10** from shiraz. Light 11.5% alc with delicate red fruit & spice harmony. **White** ✓ 🔲 ★★★★ **10** from chenin, viognier in broad food-friendly style; oxidative yet fresh, more vinous than fruity. Just 12.5% alcohol. — JP

La Motte

Location/map: Franschhoek ▪ WO: Western Cape/Franschhoek/Walker Bay ▪ Est 1969 ▪ 1stB 1984 ▪ Tasting & sales Mon-Sat 9–5 ▪ Fee R30 ▪ Closed Easter Fri/Sun & Dec 25 ▪ Pierneef à La Motte restaurant (see Restaurants section) ▪ Facilities for children ▪ Tour groups (max 16) booking essential ▪ Farm shop: lavender, vegetables, bread ▪ Walking trail Mon-Sat 9-2 R50pp (duration 2-3hrs, not recommended for children under 10) ▪ 35ha conservation area ▪ Museum Tue-Sun 9-5: Rupert family, history of La Motte, Cape Dutch architecture, life/art of JH Pierneef & other SA artists ▪ Monthly classical music concerts ▪ Owner(s) Hanneli Rupert-Koegelenberg ▪ CEO Hein Koegelenberg ▪ Cellarmaster(s) Edmund Terblanche (Dec 2000) ▪ Winemaker(s) Michael Langenhoven (Dec 2006) ▪ Viticulturist(s) Pietie le Roux (May 1986) ▪ 170ha/35ha (merlot, pinot, shiraz, chard, sauv) ▪ 1,200t/60,000cs own label 30% red 69.6% white 0.4% sparkling + 15,000cs for clients ▪ Other export brand: Schoone Gevel ▪ Brands for clients: Woolworths ▪ ISO 14001:2003, BWI champion, EU & NOP Organic Certification, Farming for the Future: Woolworths, Global GAP, HACCP, IPW, WIETA ▪ PO Box 685 Franschhoek 7690 ▪ cellar@la-motte.co.za ▪ www.la-motte.com ▪ S 33°52'49.9" E 019°4'28.3" ▪ **T +27 (0)21-876-8000** ▪ F +27 (0)21-876-3446

The renaissance at this Franschhoek showpiece has been two-pronged. First, to 'get out there', taking control of marketing, sales and distribution, which increased production twenty fold over the ten years to 2009. The second – 'La Motte Redefined' – to 'get them in here'. Visitors can enjoy the Pierneef à La Motte Restaurant complementing a 'tasting room with a view' (and Shiraz Studio – Pierneef enhanced, again); a museum tracking the Rupert family and the life and art of JH Pierneef, a local artist for whom the admiration is 'a signature of our joint love of the South African land'; and the Farm Shop. There's also a hiking trail celebrating Biodiversity & Wine Initiative Champion status, and monthly classical music concerts. Each new addition to the re-delineation emerges from classic, understated style. Precisely what you'll find in the bottle.

Pierneef Collection

★★★★☆ **Shiraz-Viognier** Elegant, polished, a fresh & spicy flagship. **09** (★★★★★) offers piercing pimento features, but fruit tightly buttoned down mid-2011, needs many years from harvest to show its best. **08** more yielding in mocha-mulberry mode. Potentially peachy viognier (10% in **09**) doesn't detract.

★★★★ **Shiraz-Grenache** Earthy **08** had piquant spice & gamey tannin grip with a sweet liquorice tail when last tasted. A 53/29 blend, dashes mourvèdre & carignan.

★★★★ **Sauvignon Blanc (Organically Grown)** ✓ 🍷📖🌿🍇 Fuller than cellarmate - and many peers - **11** nicely weighted gooseberry character lifted by lingering minerality. Walker Bay vineyards.

Classic Collection

★★★★ **Cabernet Sauvignon** ✓ Suave 09 (★★★★★) rachets up on **08** with fine but still pliable tannins, fleshed out by clean blackcurrant fruit, tight-grained oak (50% new) in support. Impressive.

★★★★☆ **Shiraz** ✓ Follows urbane house style. Blueberry succulence marks **09**, yet the tannins are tighter than in 08 (★★★★), so the overall effect is one of svelte refinement.

★★★★ **Millennium** ✓ 5-variety Bordeaux red, led by 44% cab franc & 26% merlot. Open **08** followed by tighter **09**, plush red-berry fruit currently guarded by tannins, will need some years to open & reveal full charm.

★★★★ **Chardonnay** ✓ 🍷📖🌿 Initially full **10** proffers oak vanilla aromas, butterscotch breadth reined in by citrus freshness, ends with cellar's signature balance. Year 30% new wood. Franschhoek vines.

Sauvignon Blanc ✓ 📖🌿 ★★★★ Grassy winter-melon coolness to **11**, tastes sweeter than its 2.6 g/l sugar would suggest. **Méthode Cap Classique** ★★★★ Longer lees-ageing (30 months) gives **08** champagne-method sparkling more gravitas than maiden 07 (★★★★). 60% pinot noir, chardonnay. WO Franschhoek. —DS

■ **Landau** see Blaauwklippen Agricultural Estate

Landau du Val

Location/map/WO: Franschhoek ▪ Tasting by appt ▪ Sales at La Cotte Wine Sales, Franschhoek ▪ Owner(s) Basil & Jane Landau ▪ Winemaker(s) Anina Guelpa ▪ Viticulturist(s) Martin du Plessis ▪ 15ha under vine ▪ La Brie Robertsvlei Road Franschhoek 7690 ▪ basillandau@mweb.co.za ▪ S 33° 55′34.3″ E 019° 6′34.1″ ▪ **T +27 (0)82-410-1130** ▪ F +27 (0)21-876-3369

The venerable bushvines (105 years old must count as pretty ancient) on Basil Landau's Franschhoek farm took a breath in 2010, and rested. The minuscule crop of semillon was left to hang on the vines, for a little late-harvest sweet wine. Untasted by us, but as a variation on a fine theme it should be wonderful.

★★★★☆ **Semillon Private Selection** Always serene & lovely. Last year, **09** was no exception in its classic profile. Satisfying, easy drinking, with the force of ancient vines shown only in long-lingering subtlety. — TJ

■ **Land of Hope** see The Winery of Good Hope
■ **Land's End** see Hidden Valley Wines-Land's End Wines

Landskroon Wines

Location: Paarl ▪ Map: Paarl & Wellington ▪ WO: Paarl/Coastal/Western Cape ▪ Est 1874 ▪ 1stB 1974 ▪ Tasting & sales Mon-Fri 8.30-5 Sat 9-1 ▪ Fee R5pp for groups ▪ Closed Easter Fri, Dec 25 & Jan 1 ▪ Cellar tours Mon-Fri 8.30-5 by appt ▪ Picnics in summer by appt; or BYO picnic ▪ Play area for children ▪ Permanent display of Stone Age artefacts ▪ Self-catering Cottage ▪ Owner(s) Paul & Hugo de Villiers Family Trusts ▪ Cellarmaster(s) Paul de Villiers (Jan 1980) ▪ Winemaker(s) Abraham van Heerden (Sep 2007) ▪ Viticulturist(s) Hugo de Villiers jnr (1995) ▪ 330ha/200ha (cab, cinsaut, merlot, ptage, shiraz, chenin) ▪ 1,100t 74% red 19% white 7% port ▪ IPW ▪ PO Box 519 Suider-Paarl 7624 ▪ huguette@landskroonwines.com ▪ www.landskroonwines.com ▪ S 33° 45′38.2″ E 018° 55′0.8″ ▪ **T +27 (0)21-863-1039** ▪ F +27 (0)21-863-2810

Satisfactory market growth is being experienced in both Gauteng and Asia - two key markets considering current global economic trends. 'We aim to deliver attractive wines at attractive prices', says winemaker, Abraham van Heerden, now in his fifth year at Landskroon. Good value is achieved across all the ranges and the house style is true to their warmer Paarl climate, offering rich fruit forward wines with delicious richness. Don't miss out on their award-winning port.

Paul de Villiers range

★★★★ **Cabernet Sauvignon** 09 has gentle oaky intro to ripe style, expressing warm climate fruit-for-wardness, composed juicy fruit & balanced ripe tannins. Will evolve over next 5 years. 08 (★★★★) leaner.

★★★★ **Reserve** Confident combo shiraz, merlot & cab. **09** shows full ripeness of the region with dark brooding fruit leading to full-bodied & plush profile that will mature well into the future.

Shiraz ★★★★ Concentrated, flavoursome **09**, ripe black cherry with smoky & savoury notes, but a tad sweet.

Landskroon Wines range

★★★★ **Port** ✓ Blueberry fruit intensity, bold & focused with vibrant freshness. **07** still brooding but ready to broach. Established blend tintas barocca & amarela plus souzao & touriga nacional.

Pinotage ☺ 🍷 ★★★ Typical varietal notes on **10**, seduces with red berry freshness leading to firm, dry finish & lifted by brisk acid. **Cabernet Franc-Merlot** ☺ 🍷 ★★★ Cedar, perfume & floral aromas on attractive cab franc-based **10**, with merlot & splash shiraz. Medium body, balanced. **Chardonnay** ☺ 🍽 🍷 ★★★ Ticks all the boxes with ripe stonefruits, delicious ripe apple. **11** has fresh zippy palate & juicy, yet dry end. **Chenin Blanc Off-Dry** ☺ 🍽 🍷 ★★★ Fresh, juicy & clean **11** follows with fruity soft entry, well judged sweetness to complete summery off-dry sipper. **Bush Camp The Sundowner** 🍽 🍷 ★★★ Pleasing sweet-fruited chenin has good texture with cleansing acidity on well balanced **11**. **Paul Hugo White** ☺ 🍽 🍷 ★★★ **11** is youthful, vibrant, crisp & easy summer tipple. Like Sauvignon Blanc below, WO W Cape.

Cabernet Sauvignon ★★★★ Lovely hay, tobacco & dark cherry on ripe & fruity **09**. Has trademark rich fruit, but with serious & balanced tannins. **Cinsaut** ★★ Dusty choc-berry simple **09** quaffer. **Merlot** 🍷 ★★★ Bright & fruity **10** is fresh for easy, early enjoyment. **Shiraz** ★★★ **09** has some spice mingled with pleasant sweetish red fruits. **Cinsaut-Shiraz** ★★★ Shy spice intro on juicy & sweet-fruited **09**. **Paul Hugo Red** 🍽 ★★ **10** easy fruity, with soft end. **Bush Camp Our Daily Red** ★★★ Red berry & spicy **09** expresses easy soft & fruity palate. **Blanc de Noir Pinotage Off-Dry** 🍽 🍷 ★★ **11** fresh, floral & pleasant. **Bush Camp Blanc de Noir** 🍽 ★★ Off-dry fresh **11**, with berry twist. **Chenin Blanc Dry** 🍽 🍷 ★★★ Fresh & perfumed **11**, playful & crisp, patio pleaser. **Sauvignon Blanc** 🍽 🍷 ★★★ Shy blossom, ripe promise on **11** leads to dry zesty finish. — JP

Landzicht GWK Wines

Location: Jacobsdal ▪ Map: Northern Cape, Free State & North West ▪ Est 1976 ▪ 1stB ca 1980 ▪ Tasting & sales Mon-Fri 8-5 ▪ Fee R5 ▪ Closed pub hols ▪ Tours - bottling plant ▪ Meals/refreshments by appt ▪ Owner(s) GWK Ltd ▪ Winemaker(s) Ian Sieg ▪ Viticulturist(s) Johan Fourie ▪ Production: see under Douglas Wine Cellar ▪ PO Box 94 Jacobsdal 8710 ▪ landzicht@gwk.co.za ▪ www.landzicht.co.za ▪ S 29° 8′ 35.5″ E 024° 46′ 42.8″ ▪ **T +27 (0)53-591-0164** ▪ F +27 (0)53-591-0145

One of the first to have opened outside the Western Cape, this Free State winery is on many a tourist's 'must-do' list. While some past offerings were discontinued recently, there's still plenty to stock up on, notably the low-alcohol table wines and their speciality, fortified muscat desserts, none reviewed this year.

■ **Langeberg Wineries** see Wonderfontein

Langverwacht Koöp Wynmakery

Location: Bonnievale ▪ Map/WO: Robertson ▪ Est 1954 ▪ Tasting, sales & tours Mon-Fri 8-5 ▪ Closed all pub hols ▪ Owner(s) 25 members ▪ Cellarmaster(s) Johan Gerber (Dec 1986) ▪ Winemaker(s) Theunis Botha (Dec 2005) ▪ Viticulturist(s) Hennie Visser (Jul 2008) ▪ 640ha (cab, ruby cab, shiraz, chenin, chard, cbard, sauv) ▪ 10,500t/ 4,000cs own label 64% red 36% white ▪ IPW ▪ PO Box 87 Bonnievale 6730 ▪ info@langverwachtwines.co.za ▪ S 33° 57′ 32.8″ E 020° 1′ 35.3″ ▪ **T +27 (0)23-616-2815** ▪ F +27 (0)23-616-3059

More than a quarter century at this Robertson grower-owned winery, cellarmaster Johan Gerber says his career highlight has been 'surviving in the wine industry each year'. Only a fraction is marketed under the Langverwacht label, and the team (spurred on by a slew of recent awards) is determined to bottle only the best, and to continue with their consumer-dictated fruity, easy-drinking style.

Sauvignon Blanc ☺ 🍽 🍷 ★★★ **11** grapefruity charm, soft & dry, appealing weight & lingering flavour.

Cabernet Sauvignon 🍽 🍷 ★★ **11** high-toned & sweet-fruited quick-quaff, brief farewell. **Ruby Cabernet** ★★★ Shy casual sipper, **06** last year offered ripe berry fruit. Still selling, as for Shiraz & Chardonnay. **Shiraz** 🍽 ★★ Drying finish to **09**'s rich red fruit. **Chardonnay** 🍽 🍷 ★★★ **10**'s plump pear notes, mouthfilling 14.7% alc enlivened by crisp lemony acidity. **Chenin Blanc** 🍽 🍷 ★★ Green-apple coolness makes **11** ideal for sipping on a summer day. **Colombar** 🍽 🍷 ★★ Forthcoming guava, loads of flavour, fresh & fruity fun from **11**. —Panel

Lanner Hill

Location/WO: Darling ▪ Est 1999 ▪ 1stB 2002 ▪ Sales Mon-Fri 9-3 via email/phone; from farm by appt only ▪ Owner(s) David & Nicola Tullie ▪ Winemaker(s) Nicky Versfeld (2002) ▪ Viticulturist(s) David Tullie ▪ 91ha/51ha (cab, merlot, p verdot, shiraz, sauv, sem, viog) ▪ 450-500t/500cs own label ▪ PO Box 220 Darling 7345 ▪ tulliefamilyvineyards@gmail.com ▪ **T +27 (0)22-492-3662** ▪ F +27 (0)22-492-3664

Lanner Hill is the Tullie family farm in Darling's Groenekloof ward, where the Atlantic Ocean's cooling influence enhances the quality of both red and white varieties. Sauvignon is most prized (bemedalled locally and abroad under the Kumkani Lanner Hill label) and is now used exclusively by the Tullies in partnership with winemaker Nicky Versveld.

Lanner Hill range

★★★★ **The Yair** Elegant, succulent & structured **09** Bordeaux styled white (52% sauvignon, with semillon) exuded tropical & greenpepper flavours when last tasted.

Sauvignon Blanc NEW 🏵 ★★★★ **11** preview shining example of Groenekloof's compatibility with this variety, no matter what the vintage. Vivacious & racy, with mouthfilling passionfruit & lime flavours & good length. — MW

Lanzerac

Location/map/WO: Stellenbosch ▪ Est 1692 ▪ 1stB 1957 ▪ Tasting & sales daily 9.30-5 ▪ Fee R20 ▪ Cellar tours at 11 & 3 ▪ Closed Easter Fri, Dec 25 & Jan 1 ▪ Cheese platters; wine & chocolate tasting ▪ 5-star Lanzerac Hotel, Spa & Restaurant ▪ Conferences ▪ Weddings/functions ▪ Owner(s) Christo Wiese ▪ Winemaker(s) Wynand Lategan (Jan 2005, consultant) ▪ Viticulturist(s) Ronel Bester ▪ Vineyard manager Danie Malherbe ▪ 150ha/46ha (cab, merlot, ptage, chard) ▪ 300t/12-13,000cs own label 55% red 30% white 15% rosé ▪ BWI ▪ PO Box 6233 Uniedal 7612 ▪ winesales@lanzerac.co.za ▪ www.lanzeracwines.co.za ▪ S 33° 56' 14.7" E 018° 53' 35.5" ▪ **T +27 (0)21-886-5641** ▪ F +27 (0)21-887-6998

This gracious Cape Dutch-style estate at the entrance to Stellenbosch's Jonkershoek Valley is steeped in history, dating back to 1692. In addition to the conference, wedding and function venues, guests are able to experience the luxury of the five-star hotel and spa. The tasting room has had a makeover and now boasts a 'wall of chocolate', part of a choc-and-wine pairing offered. A style change is in progress as winemaker Wynand Lategan aims for 'balanced wine with more fruit concentration and polished tannin'.

★★★★ **Cabernet Sauvignon** ✓ Classic & restrained, **09** medley of bright black fruit, dark chocolate. Depth & complexity, fruit & fine oak balance boding well for the future.

★★★★ **Merlot** ✓ Black plums & savoury olives on vibrant **09**. Well integrated & complex, earthy notes mingle with aromatic oak. Fine balance.

★★★★ **Pinotage** ✓ Bright red berries, savoury meat notes. Elegant, stylish **09** understated, well-balanced with a fragrant plum pudding conclusion.

★★★★ **Pionier Pinotage 08** tad off showstopping **07** (★★★★★). Leaner, restrained style, sweet-sour black berry flavours, assertive oaking & a perky acid on the finish. Needs time & food.

★★★★☆ **Le Generale** Name change from 'Estate Red Blend' for **08**, which debuted spectacularly last time. 50% cab, partnering pinotage, shiraz & malbec, made a taut & complex assembly, fragrant & lingering, with grainy tannins.

★★★★ **Rosé** ✓ 🍷 South Africa's original dry rosé. **10** (★★★☆) from merlot & shiraz, shade off standout **09** (★★★★). Bright strawberry fruit, spicy grip, the perfect lunchtime wine.

★★★★ **Chardonnay** ✓ 🏵 Lime & buttered toast from barrel fermentation, **10** delicate hints of oak, honeyed complexity; good poise & balance. Delicious!

★★★★ **Sauvignon Blanc** 🏵 **11** (★★★★) preview not the intensity of **10**. More restrained gooseberry, grass & white peach fruitiness, perky lime twist. — WB

La Petite Ferme Winery

Location/map: Franschhoek ▪ WO: Franschhoek/Western Cape ▪ Est 1972 ▪ 1stB 1996 ▪ Tasting daily from 11 by appt ▪ Fee R50pp (complimentary if you book lunch) ▪ Sales daily 8.30-5 ▪ Cellar tours from 11-12.30 ▪ Closed all pub hols ▪ Restaurant & Guest Suites (see Restaurants & Accommodation sections) ▪ Gift shop ▪ Walking/hiking trails ▪ Owner(s) Dendy Young family ▪ Cellarmaster(s)/winemaker(s) Mark Dendy Young (1996) ▪ Viticulturist(s) John Dendy Young ▪ 16ha/14ha (cabs s/f, merlot, shiraz, chard, sauv, viog) ▪ 60-70t/6,000cs own label 40% red 50% white 10% rosé ▪ PO Box 55 Franschhoek 7690 ▪ jomark@mweb.co.za ▪ www.lapetiteferme.co.za ▪ S 33° 55'6.0" E 019° 8'9.5" ▪ **T** +27 (0)21-876-3016 ▪ F +27 (0)21-876-3624

'We were very proud when farm manager Frans Malies was awarded the Franschhoek Farm Worker of the Year award,' says Mark Dendy Young, proprietor and winemaker of this ever-popular Franschhoek food, wine and accommodation destination. 'The introduction of our Friday Night Live music evenings on our lawns in front of the restaurant/winery are a fantastic success. The Franschhoek summer calendar wouldn't be the same without them.'

La Petite Ferme range

★★★★ **Cabernet Franc** NEW   Gorgeous pristine red berry fruit, mint & leafy herbs, **10** elegant & understated with beautiful balance & a lingering herbal waft. Excellent varietal expression. Will reward ageing.

★★★★ **Barrel Fermented Chardonnay**   Exotic & creamy **09** last year burst with peaches & lemon cream, toasted nuts highlights from well-judged oak (50% new French). Back to form after **08** (★★★★).

★★★★ **Viognier** 🍷 **11** exudes white peach, soft vanilla & floral aromas. Fresh, rich & vibrant, with a crisp acidity & lingering lime & delicate stony notes. Great advertisement for the variety.

Cabernet Sauvignon NEW   ★★★★ Stylish aromas of blackcurrant & pencil shavings, **09** ripe dark-berry flavours balanced by well-judged oak & spice. **Merlot** ✓ ★★★★ **09** step up from **08** (★★★): plush, elegant, with rich fruitcake, spice & hint of sweet vanilla. Well-balanced &-structured, lingering savoury farewell. Will reward ageing. **Shiraz** ★★★★ **09** offers savoury olive, ripe mulberry & plum; vibrant & juicy with smooth, understated vanilla oak influence. **The Verdict** ★★★ Last edition, cab-based **07** with cab franc & merlot had elegant cherry notes; charry oak should have knit by now. **Baboon Rock Unwooded Chardonnay Wild Yeast Fermented** 🍷 Not ready. **Sauvignon Blanc** ✓ 🍷 ★★★★ Up a notch, **11** is fresh & floral showing citrus & ripe green-fruit flavours. Lovely balance, zippy ending. Discontinued: **Cabernet Sauvignon-Merlot**, **Blanc Fumé**.

Maison range

Blanc 😊 🍷 ★★★ Chenin-led **10** blend is light-hearted & fruity with tropical flavours & balanced, smooth acidity. Enjoy!

Rouge 🍷 ★★★ Unoaked, easy-drinking **10** cab, shiraz blend is ripe & fruity, with a smooth mouthfeel & soft, dry finish. WO W Cape, as Blanc. **Rosé** 🍷 ★★★★ Last edition **10** took big step up from summery **09** (★★★); crisp & dry sipper, cherry & Turkish Delight infused, lunchtime friendly lowish 11.5% alc. — WB

La Petite Provence Wine Company

Location/map/WO: Franschhoek ▪ Est 2001 ▪ 1stB 2005 ▪ Tasting & sales Mon-Sat by appt ▪ Owner(s) La Petite Provence Wine Trust ▪ Winemaker(s) Johan van Rensburg (2003, La Provence) ▪ 3.5ha (cab, merlot) ▪ 30t/450cs own label 90% red 10% rosé ▪ 2 Cabernet Drive La Petite Provence Franschhoek 7690 ▪ info@lapetiteprovence. co.za ▪ www.lapetiteprovence.co.za ▪ S 33° 53'59.1" E 019° 06'29.4" ▪ **T** +27 (0)21-876-4178 / +27 (0)21-876-3860

Membership of this exclusive wine-buying 'club' has reached 100 or so, mostly owners of homes on La Petite Provence Residential Estate in Franschhoek. Those who return to England for the summer have their wine imported; for the rest, it's a local market that tailors the product and snaps it up, hence last year's merlot rosé which sold out untasted by us.

Cabernet Sauvignon ★★★ Tannins still youthfully tight in **09**, masking savoury red fruit. Allow more time to soften. **Merlot** ★★★ Elegant, leafy **09**, fragrant & savoury, firm tannins add grip to fresh fruitiness. **Mélange** ★★★ Firm cab tannins lend seriousness & balance to well-integrated **09** blend with fruity merlot. — IM

La Petite Vigne

Location/map/WO: Franschhoek ▪ 1stB 2004 ▪ Tasting & sales Sat 10–5 ▪ Fee R10 ▪ Closed all pub hols ▪ Guesthouse ▪ Owner(s) Cyril & Kendal Shand ▪ Cellarmaster(s)/winemaker(s) Cyril Shand ▪ 3.3ha/2.5ha (cab) ▪ 10t/800cs own label 90% red 10% white ▪ PO Box 686 Franschhoek 7690 ▪ info@la-petite-vigne.co.za ▪ www.la-petite-vigne.co.za ▪ S 33° 54'9.0" E 019° 7'14.0" ▪ **T** +27 (0)21-876-2365 ▪ F +27 (0)86-538-7623

There's just a small unirrigated cabernet vineyard, and it was a 'small fascination' that developed into a 'grand passion' for Cyril and Kendal Shand, but the well-equipped cellar where the serious-minded wine is made pushes this winery beyond a garagiste dream. The Franschhoek setting is grand, too, of course.

La Petite Vigne range

> **Cabernet Sauvignon** ☺ ★★★ Ripe blackcurrant & graphite notes on properly dry **07**, but at this stage the oaking (one-third new barrels) dominates the finish.

Kendal range
Discontinued: **Semillon.** — MF

■ **Lategan Family** *see Bergsig Estate*

Lateganskop Winery

Location: Worcester ▪ Map/WO: Breedekloof ▪ Est 1969 ▪ 1stB 2004 ▪ Tasting & sales Mon-Fri 8–12 & 1–5 ▪ Closed Easter Fri-Mon, Dec 25/26 & Jan 1 ▪ Cellar tours by appt ▪ Owner(s) 5 members ▪ Cellarmaster(s) Heinrich Lategan (Oct 2008) ▪ Winemaker(s) Heinrich Lategan, with Kean Oosthuizen (May 2011) ▪ 238ha (cab, ptage, chard, chenin, sauv, sem) ▪ 2,900t/300cs own label 70% red 30% white + approx 2m L bulk ▪ PO Box 44 Breërivier 6858 ▪ lateganskop@breede.co.za ▪ S 33° 30' 57.27" E 019° 11'13.65" ▪ **T +27 (0)23-355-1719** ▪ F +27 (0)86-637-6603

Proud that the extended Lategan family has been making wine in the Breedekloof for over 100 years, cellarmaster Heinrich Lategan says: 'I would like to focus a lot more on our heritage and try to bring some of that into our wines.' To this end, he's experimenting with pinotage from bushvines planted in 1970, and, believing the area's chenin 'has a lot to offer', looking to consistently reflect this potential.

Lateganskop Winery range
The Zahir 🖉 ★★★ Fresh & appealing Cape Blend, equal cab & pinotage, **10** chocolate & ripe berry fruit.

Twin's Peak range
Chenin Blanc Await new vintage. **Sauvignon Blanc** 🖉 ★★ Previewed **11** is easy-drinking, crisp pineapple finish. **Chardonnay-Viognier** ★★★ **09** soft floral scents last edition, layers of honey, nutmeg & biscuits. **Hanepoot Jerepigo** ★★ Still-available full-sweet fortified **NV** dessert not revisited. — DB

La Terre La Mer

WO: Stellenbosch/Swartland ▪ Est/1stB 2008 ▪ Closed to public ▪ Owner(s) Deon le Roux, Charlie Benn, Mark Wiehahn, Stef Kriel & Adrian Toma ▪ Cellarmaster(s) Partners & Peter Turck (2008, consultant) ▪ Winemaker(s) Peter Turck (2008, consultant), with Deon le Roux, Charlie Benn, Mark Wiehahn, Stef & Fiona Kriel, Adrian Toma (all Jan 2008) ▪ Viticulturist(s) Grapes sourced from DeMorgenzon (2008/2009) & Mountain View (2010/2011) ▪ 2.5t/150cs own label 100% red ▪ 6 Princess Drive Bonza Bay East London 5241 ▪ dleroux@iafrica.com ▪ **T +27 (0)83-701-3148** ▪ F +27 (0)43-735-2494

The cellar closest to the sea (la Mer) and furthest from the vineyards (la Terre) overlooks East London's Quinera Lagoon and sources 2.5t of grapes from Stellenbosch (2008/9) and Swartland (2010/11) over 1,000km away. Guided by winemaker Pieter Turck and armed with Stellenbosch University's garagiste winemaking course, neurosurgeon Deon le Roux and wine-loving partners all get stuck into making their shiraz. Despite the challenge of logistics and grape transportation costs, it's about 'having fun while aiming to make a serious wine'.

Shiraz ★★ 3 vintages reviewed: **09** from Stellenbosch full bodied & meaty, savoury. Step up **10** (★★★) ripe red-fruit compote, leather & smoke, rounded, fuller, good length & texture. Swartland grapes, as for unrated preview **11**, light & juicy, still unformed. — Panel

Lathithá Wines

Location: Cape Town ▪ Tasting by appt only ▪ Owner(s) Sheila Hlanjwa ▪ Winemaker(s) Rolf Zeitvogel & Albert Basson (both Blaauwklippen) ▪ Viticulturist(s) Christo Hamman (Blaauwklippen) ▪ 100ha (cabs s/f, malbec, merlot, shiraz, zin, viog) ▪ Washington Shopping Centre Langa 7455 ▪ info@lathithawines.co.za ▪ **T +27 (0)21-556-6029** ▪ F +27 (0)21-695-1953

An empowerment project spearheaded by MD Sheila Hlanjwa who was introduced to wine through a wine marketing course at Stellenbosch University. Langa-based, but also with a presence at Blaauwklippen, which is a partner in wine supply and skills transfer in all aspects of the operation, including exports. The name is derived from a Xhosa expression meaning sunrise, and the project is intended to introduce local communities to wine.

Red 🍷 ★ Dense tannin overrode shy chocolate notes on **09** last edition. **Rosé** 🍷 ★★ Last was **09**, fruitily sweet wild strawberry flavours. — CR

L'Auberge du Paysan

Location: Somerset West ▪ WO: Stellenbosch ▪ Est 1995 ▪ 1stB 1998 ▪ Closed to public ▪ Owner(s) Michael Kovensky ▪ Cellarmaster(s) Tjuks Roos (consultant) ▪ Viticulturist(s) Tjuks Roos (1995, consultant) ▪ 7.3ha/5ha (merlot, ptage) ▪ 24t 100% red ▪ PO Box 204 Brackenfell 7561 ▪ kovensky@aroma.co.za ▪ **T +27 (0)21-529-3980** ▪ F +27 (0)21-555-3461

The small vineyard attached to the now defunct restaurant in Raithby still provides fruit for the wines sold under the house label, made by neighbour Tjuks Roos for owner Michael Kovensky. These are offered at son Paul Kovensky's chain of Cape Town restaurants and Aroma retail outlets.

Pinotage ★★★ The current release, **06**, was sampled last edition out of vintage sequence: dark fruit & mocha, rustically satisfying. Followed wild-berried **07** (★★★☆) & bolder, tighter **08** (★★★★). — GdB

L'Avenir Vineyards

Location/map: Stellenbosch ▪ WO: Stellenbosch/Western Cape ▪ Est/1stB 1992 ▪ Tasting & sales Mon-Fri 9–5 Sat 10–4 ▪ Fee R15 ▪ Closed Easter Fri/Sun, Dec 25 & Jan 1 ▪ Cellar tours by appt ▪ BYO picnic ▪ Luxury 4-star Country Lodge ▪ Owner(s) Advini ▪ Cellarmaster(s) Tinus Els (Sep 2005) ▪ Winemaker(s) Tinus Els (Sep 2005), with Dirk Coetzee & Mattheus Thabo (Aug 2009/Jan 2007) ▪ Viticulturist(s) Johan Pienaar (consultant) ▪ 64ha/34ha (cabs s/f, merlot, ptage, chenin, sauv) ▪ 320t/24,000cs own label 50% red 45% white 5% rosé ▪ IPW ▪ PO Box 7267 Stellenbosch 7599 ▪ info@lavenir.co.za ▪ www.lavenir-lodge.com ▪ S 33° 53′ 18.7″ E 018° 50′ 59.1″ ▪ **T +27 (0)21-889-5001/09** ▪ F +27 (0)21-889-5258

Perfectly situated on the prime lower slopes of the Simonsberg, L'Avenir ('The Future') supplied fruit to Nederburg until purchased by Mauritian Marc Wiehe in the early 1990s. Its reputation, especially with chenin and pinotage from old vines, was soon made under winemaker Francois Naudé. A reputation that has been maintained since 2005 under the new owner, Frenchman Michel Laroche (his company has since merged with French wine group, Jeanjean to form AdVini, the current owner) with cellarmaster Tinus Els. The wines are modern in their fruit purity but never showy – good food, as any Frenchman would require – being a necessary partner. A neighbouring farm was subsequently purchased; this has now been re-sold, taking L'Avenir back to its original size.

Icon range

★★★★☆ **Grand Vin Pinotage** Grand, as name implies, **08**; infused with plush, silky ripe fruit, spicy new oak. Small-grain tannins refresh, & will also benefit from few years ageing, as with **07** (★★★★).

★★★★☆ **Grand Vin Chenin Blanc** 🍷 From venerable vineyard. **08** last year showed floral yellow fruit aromas, creamy richness; drier than **07**. Finely balanced, long; potential for several years.

Platinum range

★★★★ **Cabernet Sauvignon** ✓ Unequivocal cassis, blackberry aromas elaborated with cedary complexity add distinction to classic **09**. Ripe, stentorian tannins need at least 3 years softening.

★★★★ **Pinotage** ✓ **09** engaging modern style. Plentiful yet refined oak-spiced cherry & raspberry features; firm, freshening tannins, balanced by sweet-fruited tail.

★★★★☆ **Stellenbosch Classic** 🍷 **08** (★★★★) cab softened by 20% cab franc, merlot; more obviously charming than varietal wine. Tasted last year. Previous was serious-minded **06**.

★★★★ **Chardonnay** 🗒 Nothing excessive in supple, silky **10** (★★★★) despite new oak component doubling to a mere 30%. Lacks depth of previous but agreeable early drinking. **09** elegant, understated.

★★★★ **Chenin Blanc** ✓ 🗒 **11** has usual unshowy refinement. Supple, lees-enriched base anchors gently persistent honey, floral features. Vibrant & dry; balanced to allow for delicious development. **10** untasted.

Merlot 🗒 ★★★ Dense & packed with luscious fruit, also squeeze of forming tannin, **10** offers uncomplicated satisfaction. **Sauvignon Blanc** 🗒 ★★★★ Riper, tropical flavours enhance juicily rounded **11**. Freshness nicely paced to lift but not disturb drinkability. **Brut Rosé MCC** ✓ ★★★★ Pretty blush pink belies more serious yeasty rich flavours, sprightly sparkle & clean, truly brut finish on **09**. Ptage 66%, with chenin. Step up from **08** (★★★★). Discontinued: **Cabernet Franc**.

Classic range

Chenin Blanc ☺ 🗒 ★★★ Readily recognisable melon, fresh honey tones on **11**. Juicy & long. Just-dry, with low (12%) alcohol.

Pinotage 🗒 ★★★ **11**, with some Swartland grapes, replete with ripe, succulent fruit. Rounded & dry. **Rosé de Pinotage** 🗒 ★★★ Vivid berry perfume, flavours on **11**. Rounded, dry, touch bitter. Swartland grapes. — AL

🔳 **Lavida** *see Overhex Wines International*

La Vierge Private Cellar

Location: Hermanus ▪ Map: Elgin, Walker Bay & Bot River ▪ WO: Hemel-en-Aarde Ridge/Hemel-en-Aarde Valley ▪ Est 1997 ▪ 1stB 2006 ▪ Tasting & sales daily 9–5 ▪ Closed Easter Fri & Dec 25 ▪ La Vierge Restaurant & Champagne Veranda (see Restaurants section) ▪ Tour groups by appt ▪ Cellar tours by appt ▪ Owner(s) La Vierge Wines (Pty) Ltd & Viking Pony Properties 355 (Pty) Ltd ▪ Winemaker(s) Marc van Halderen (Jun 2005), with Jan Fortuin (Jun 2009) ▪ Viticulturist(s) Johan Pienaar (Jul 2010) ▪ 90ha/40ha (pinot, sangio, shiraz, chard, riesling, sauv, sem) ▪ 75t 50% red 50% white ▪ PO Box 1580 Hermanus 7200 ▪ info@lavierge.co.za ▪ www.lavierge.co.za ▪ S 34° 22'22.3" E 019° 14' 29.4" ▪ **T +27 (0)28-313-0130** ▪ F +27 (0)28-312-1388

On the one hand, 2011 was challenging for this Hemel-en-Aarde Ridge producer, including as it did countless raids by birds. On the other, it yielded several characterful new wines and affirmation – in the form of Michelangelo gold for its 2009 maiden bottling – that pinot noir should be its focus. With 13 hectares under four clones and another 6 hectares being planted, Marc van Halderen and the team say they're set to produce a unique pinot style, influenced by the deep clay soils and varying aspects which characterise their location on the edge of the appellation.

La Vierge range

★★★★ **Redemption Sauvignon Blanc** Previously reviewed **08** from shy-bearing single-vineyard available only from cellardoor & restaurant. Restrained yet complex & mouthfilling.

Noir Pinot Noir ★★★★ **10** carbon copy of **09** (★★★★), but with greater depth; engaging cherry fruit, whiffs wet earth & gentle spice from brief sojourn oak. More delicate & approachable styling, drinks well now. **Nymphomane Cabernet Sauvignon-Malbec** NEW ★★★ Soft raspberry bouquet on **09**, interesting hint of leather, 70% cab portion means palate is unexpectedly firm, needs bit of time to soften. **Anthelia Shiraz-Mourvèdre** NEW ✓ ★★★★ Alluring **09** combo, 77% shiraz & well-judged year French oak deliver generous dark berry fruit with a savoury element, supple tannins complete competent package. **Satyricon Barbera-Sangiovese-Nebbiolo** NEW ★★★★ **09** powerful but clever mix of Italian varieties. Opaque, meaty, sour cherry twist, grape/oak tannins need year/2 to meld. **Jezebelle Chardonnay** NEW ✓ ★★★★ **10** ebullient lemon/lime sipper flamboyantly seasoned with vanilla oak. Well balanced; impressive length. **The Last Temptation Riesling** ★★★★ Unusual & attractive food-styled version, **10** savoury 'wet pebble' minerality, crackling lime acidity & pithy texture from long lees-ageing. **Original Sin Sauvignon Blanc** ✓ ★★★★ Increasingly serious expression. Sancerre-like scrub & earth on **09** (★★★★) also present in improved **10**; poised, intense, broadened by dash barrel-fermented semillon. — CvZ

La Vigne Estate

Location/map: Franschhoek ▪ WO: Western Cape/Franschhoek ▪ Est 2004 ▪ 1stB 2005 ▪ Tasting, sales & cellar tours by appt ▪ Fee R15pp ▪ Owner(s) Robert Joergensen ▪ Winemaker(s)/viticulturist(s) Oswald Sauermann (Mar 2006, consultant) ▪ 6.7ha/4.7ha (cab, shiraz, sem) ▪ 30t/1,500cs own label 85% red 15% white + 100cs for clients ▪ Brands for clients: Dutch East House ▪ PO Box 69 Simondium 7670 ▪ wine@lavigne.co.za ▪ www.lavigne.co.za ▪ S 33° 53' 28.0" E 019° 5' 0.5" ▪ **T +27 (0)21-876-3357** ▪ F +27 (0)86-548-9393

At La Vigne, they play music to their wines as they mature in barrel. Norwegian owner Robert Joergensen's background as a sound engineer has him convinced that the music will change the maturing wines 'in a harmonic way'. Slightly less alternative is an organically inclined approach in the vineyard.

★★★★ **Single Vineyard Shiraz** Young vineyard provides amazing depth in **07**, mulberry viscosity in tailored - yet refreshing - frame. This & below not retasted.

Owner's Selection Red ★★★☆ **06** Bordeaux blend let berry fruit outshine oak in medium-bodied balance mid-2009. WO W Cape, as for next. **Edvard Grieg Edition** ★★★ Cherry-fruited **06** as harmonious, elegant as its musical midwifery. **Owner's Selection White** ★★★ Broad **06** mainly semillon with 27% chardonnay, lightly oaked & waxy. **Musical Edition** ★★★★ **07** ex Citrusdal, impressive melding semillon (85%) & chard with brush new French oak. — DS

Lazanou Organic Vineyards

Location/WO: Wellington ▪ Map: Paarl & Wellington ▪ Est 2002 ▪ 1stB 2006 ▪ Tasting & sales by appt ▪ Open Days with wine & food pairing - booking required ▪ Tour groups ▪ Farm produce ▪ Owner(s) Josef Lazarus & Candice Stephanou ▪ Winemaker(s) Rolanie Lotz (Jan 2011, consultant) ▪ Viticulturist(s) Johan Wiese (Jan 2006, consultant) ▪ 8.48ha/5.54ha (mourv, shiraz, chard, chenin, viog) ▪ 50t/3,000cs own label 50% red 50% white ▪ Organic certification by SGS ▪ PO Box 834 Wellington 7654 ▪ wine@lazanou.co.za ▪ www.lazanou.co.za ▪ S 33°35'59.58" E 018°59'36.12" ▪ **T +27 (0)83-265-6341** ▪ F +27 (0)86-670-9213

Open days have become very popular at this Wellington winery. 'Visitors get a taste of organic viticulture and winemaking, and sustainable living,' says co-owner Josef Lazarus, 'together with award-winning wines paired with excellent food prepared from home-grown organic produce.' A viognier is in the pipeline - organic, of course - in line with Lazanou's mission 'to make excellent wines naturally'.

Syrah ✓ ☗ ★★★★ Fruit-driven style continues in single-vineyard **09**, with some spiciness, medium body, firm grip to finish. Attractive, but misses the complexity & minerality we admired in **08** (★★★★★). **Syrah-Mourvèdre** ☗ ★★★ **10** shade off the pace of wow-factor **09** (★★★★★). Soft, sweet-ripe berries, medium body & an espresso lift. **Chardonnay** ☗ ★★★★ Last edition, **08** blended white peach fruit with savoury tones from competent oaking. **Wooded Chenin Blanc** ☗ ★★★★★ Previously, fragrant peach & vanilla notes charmed on barrel-matured **09**, nuttiness from subtle oak, lively acidity integrated seamlessly with vibrant fruit. From a single-vineyard, like last **07** (★★★★). **Chenin Blanc** ☗ Await next. **Chenin Blanc-Chardonnay-Viognier** ☗ ★★★★ Name change indicates chenin leadership in aromatic **10** blend; stonefruit, citrus & baked apple, perky & oaky vanilla finish. — WB

▪ **Lazy Bay** *see* Baarsma Wine Group
▪ **LB** *see* Anura Vineyards
▪ **Leatherwood** *see* Prospect1870
▪ **Le Bistro** *see* Zandvliet Wine Estate & Thoroughbred Stud

Le Bonheur Wine Estate

Location/map: Stellenbosch ▪ Est 1790's ▪ 1stB 1972 ▪ Tasting & sales Mon-Fri 9–5 Sat/Sun 10–4 ▪ Fee R15/5 wines ▪ Closed Easter Fri ▪ Conference facilities ▪ Foreign Film Festival, every last Fri of the month - booking essential ▪ Owner(s) Lusan Premium Wines ▪ Cellarmaster(s)/winemaker(s)/viticulturist(s) Sakkie Kotze (Oct 1993) ▪ 163ha/72ha (cab, merlot, chard, sauv) ▪ 460t/20,000cs own label 30% red 65% white 5% rosé ▪ WIETA ▪ PO Box 104 Stellenbosch 7599 ▪ info@lebonheur.co.za ▪ www.lebonheur.co.za ▪ S 33° 50' 1.0" E 018° 52' 21.4" ▪ **T +27 (0)21-875-5478** ▪ F +27 (0)21-875-5624

The groundwork for this Stellenbosch property's wines was – literally – laid by Sakkie Kotze's soil-scientist predecessor. Extensive soil preparation, including addition of lime, in the 1970s, paved the way for today's well-regarded range. It started with the 1983 sauvignon, which was deemed one of the best in the country and opened winemakers' eyes to how well the grape could perform in the Cape. Quality reds soon followed and the present, consistent range has been in place since the 1989 vintage.

Le Bonheur Estate range

★★★★ **Cabernet Sauvignon** Inviting spice & cassis fruit on serious but approachable **08**. Effective structure in support; properly dry. This, all below not re-visited.

★★★★ **Prima** Unshowy, elegantly fresh **08**. Merlot-led but shows cab's strong, informing tannins. Drinkable but should improve for good few yrs.

Chardonnay ⚲ ★★★☆ Pleasant peach, citrus notes on **10**. Lightly rich, firm, fresh & dry, in unshowy house style. **Sauvignon Blanc** ⚲ ★★★☆ Typical aromas, flavours subtly expressed on **10**. Less aggressive than many, well balanced with with nice grapefruity finish. — AL

■ **Leeumasker** *see* Maske Wines

Leeuwenberg 🌶 NEW

WO: Western Cape ▪ Est/1stB 2010 ▪ Tasting only in Wiesbaden, Germany Mon-Fri 11-7 Sat 10-6 (T +49-(0)611-308-6778) ▪ Closed all pub hols ▪ Owner(s) Tanja Hilka ▪ Winemaker(s) Frank Kastien and Marcus Milner (Oct 2010, consultants) ▪ 1,000cs own label 70% red 30% white ▪ PO Box 50723 West Beach 7449 ▪ sales@leeuwenbergwines.com ▪ www.leeuwenbergwines.com ▪ **T +27 (0)73-645-3284**

Tanja Hilka's experience as a wine trader persuaded her that, from the German consumers' point of view, gaps still existed in South Africa's vinous offerings, and, mobilising her contacts in the SA wine industry, she started making and exporting an annual 1,000 cases of her own brand, Drie Kleine Leeuwen (after sons Yannick, Ben and Raphael), in 2010.

Drie Kleine Leeuwen range

Cape Blend ▤ ★★★ Ripe, dark stewed fruit aromas from **09** cab, pinotage, shiraz blend; fresh & uncomplicated, zingy finish. **Chardonnay Unwooded** ▤ ⚲ ★★★ Pear-drop aromas on fresh & crisp, pleasant **10** easy-drinker. — Panel

Leeuwenkuil Family Vineyards

Location: Paarl ▪ Est 2008 ▪ 1stB 2011 ▪ Closed to public ▪ Owner(s) Willie & Emma Dreyer ▪ MD Kobus de Kock ▪ Cellarmaster(s) Pieter Carstens (Aug 2008) ▪ Winemaker(s) Inge Terblanche (Nov 2010), with Jehan de Jongh (Aug 2008) ▪ Viticulturist(s) Koos van der Merwe (Dec 2008) ▪ 1,600ha/880ha (cab, merlot, ptage, shiraz, chenin) ▪ 14,500t 10.5m L 70% red 30% white ▪ WIETA ▪ PO Box 249 Koelenhof 7605 ▪ kobus@leeuwenkuilfv.co.za ▪ **T +27 (0)21-865-2455** ▪ F +27 (0)21-865-2780

Perdeberg's huge bulk wine producer is stepping into the retail sector this year, partnering with Vinimark in the launch of four wines – a chenin and a shiraz, as well as a red and a white blend under the Family Reserve label. They'll be bottled locally 'so that we have market-ready samples,' explains GM Kobus de Kock, but sold overseas. He dismisses the likelihood of cellar door sales any time soon.

Le Fût

Location/WO: Paarl ▪ Map: Paarl & Wellington ▪ Est 2004 ▪ 1stB 2005 ▪ Tasting by appt ▪ Conference/function/wedding venue ▪ Owner(s) Trevor & Joan Ernstzen ▪ Winemaker(s) Trevor Ernstzen (Nov 2004) ▪ Viticulturist(s) Joan Ernstzen (Nov 2004) ▪ ±17ha/10ha (shiraz, chenin, cbard, riesling) ▪ 120t/300cs own label 100% red ▪ PO Box 156 Paarl 7622 ▪ wine@lefut.co.za ▪ www.lefut.co.za ▪ S 33° 44'34.38" E 019° 0'39.90" ▪ **T +27 (0)83-561-1555** ▪ F +27 (0)86-675-5114

This boutique winery focuses on nurturing its older vineyards, yet allowing nature to play its hand. Owner-winemaker Trevor Ernstzen mentions plans to draw more visitors with a new 'unique' function venue, while his vinous highlight comes 'every moment he opens a bottle of his own wine'.

Shiraz Reserve ★★★ Development shows on interesting **07**. Medium-bodied (though big 15% alcohol), shy on fruit, with more savoury, smoky & earthy notes to follow. — JP

Legacy

South Africa's original 'Johannisberger' semi-sweet white, introduced in 1957 (under Bellingham). Now made and marketed by DGB.

Johannisberger ★★ Gently sweet **NV** not retasted for several editions. — MW

 Legends of the Labyrinth *see* Doolhof Wine Estate

Le Grand Chasseur Wine Estate

Location/map: Robertson ▪ Est 1881 ▪ 1stB 1999 ▪ Tasting by appt ▪ Closed all pub hols ▪ Owner(s) Albertus de Wet ▪ Cellarmaster(s)/winemaker(s) Carel Botha (Jan 2011) ▪ Viticulturist(s) Francois Viljoen (Jan 1998, consultant) ▪ ±1,300ha/300ha (cab, merlot, ptage, ruby cab, shiraz, chard, chenin, cbard, muscadel w, nouvelle, sauv) ▪ ±4,000t ▪ IPW ▪ PO Box 439 Robertson 6705 ▪ cellar@lgc.co.za, sales@lgc.co.za ▪ www.lgc.co.za ▪ S 33° 48′ 26.8″ E 019° 52′ 40.1″ ▪ **T +27 (0)23-626-1048** ▪ F +27 (0)23-626-1048

Carel Botha is the new broom sweeping clean in this Robertson cellar – and the vineyards too. Underperforming and unprofitable blocks were cleared to make way for new vines. He believes in getting the basics right from the start and not taking short cuts. 'It may look like more work but the end result definitely makes it worthwhile.' New vintages of Cabernet Sauvignon , Pinotage, Shiraz, Cap Classique and Sparkling not ready at press time.

 Leidersburg *see* D'Athis Wines SA Negociants

Le Joubert

Location/WO: Paarl ▪ Map: Paarl & Wellington ▪ Est 1693 ▪ 1stB 2007 ▪ Tasting & sales by appt ▪ Owner(s) Dawie & Alison Joubert ▪ Cellarmaster(s)/winemaker(s) Dawie Joubert ▪ 25ha/4ha (cab, p verdot) ▪ 20t/1,000cs own label 90% red 10% white ▪ PO Box 2963 Paarl 7620 ▪ alison@lejoubert.com ▪ www.lejoubert.com, www.lejoubert.co.za ▪ S 33° 43′ 24.97″ E 018° 57′ 27.98″ ▪ **T +27 (0)21-870-1070** ▪ F +27 (0)87-803-7886

A far cry from the Gauteng motor trade, this tranquil Paarl ex-table grape farm now occupies entrepreneur and car-racing buff Dawie Joubert's attention. The concrete tanks left from previous owners' forays into wine proved too tempting for this self-taught winemaker and the conversion back to wine production began. Vineyards are planted just to red varieties and production is small, available cellar door only.

1070 ★★★★ This & Shiraz named for number of days between harvest & release. Last-tasted **08** was bold cab-led Bordeaux blend. Stern oak tannins needed year or two to harmonise. **1070s** ★★★★ 'S' denotes the shiraz component in rich & assertive blend with 4 Bordeaux varieties. **08**, tasted previously, showed complexity & strong tannins from new oak. **Brillianté** NEW ✓ 🍷 ★★★★ Same varieties as 1070s, in different proportions, shiraz-led. **08** tasty, layered, & well structured from 22 months in new French oak. **Viognier** ★★★ Last edition **09** had gentle earthy aromas, dense fruit. Smart oaking & pithy tail deftly countered substantial 15% alc. — CR

Le Manoir de Brendel

Location/map: Franschhoek ▪ Est/1stB 2003 ▪ Tasting daily 12-4 ▪ Fee R40pp, waived on purchase ▪ Sales daily 7.30-4.30 ▪ Closed Easter Fri, Dec 25/26 & Jan 1; also closed when booked for weddings/conferences ▪ Group lunches on request, book ahead ▪ Facilities for children ▪ Gift shop ▪ Conference facilities: day package (60 pax)/overnight package incl 9 rooms ▪ Walking trail ▪ Wedding facilities (up to 60 pax) with chapel & wooden terrace on the river ▪ 5-star Guesthouse (10 suites) ▪ Spa, booking essential ▪ Owner(s) Christian & Maren Brendel ▪ Winemaker(s) Cerina de Jongh & André Bruyns ▪ Viticulturist(s) Paul Wallace (consultant) ▪ 30ha/±23ha (cab, merlot, ptage, shiraz, chard, chenin, sauv, sem) ▪ ±150t ▪ PO Box 117 La Motte Franschhoek 7691 ▪ lmb@brendel.co.za ▪ www.le-manoir-de-brendel.co.za ▪ S 33° 52′ 52.8″ E 019° 3′ 42.2″ ▪ **T +27 (0)21-876-4525** ▪ F +27 (0)21-876-4524

This Franschhoek luxury guesthouse and spa is now open daily for afternoon winetastings with the newly released Consul's Blend generally going down particularly well with visitors. Conferences and weddings keep owners Christian and Maren Brendel busy throughout the year, but they still find time to export wine to Grenada amongst other countries!

Lemberg Wine Estate

Location/map: Tulbagh ▪ WO: Tulbagh/Breedekloof ▪ Est 1978 ▪ Tasting, sales & tours Mon-Fri 9-5 Sat 10-3 ▪ Fee R15 waived on purchase ▪ Closed Easter Fri/Sat/Mon, Dec 25 & Jan 1 ▪ Meals, cheese platters & picnics by appt -

book prior to visit ▪ BYO picnic ▪ Table olives & olive oil ▪ Function venue (40 seats) ▪ 3 self-catering guest cottages (sleeps 2, 4 & 6 respectively) ▪ Fly fishing (equipment for hire) ▪ Sunset rowboat trips by prior arrangement ▪ Owner(s) Henk du Bruyn ▪ Winemaker(s) David Sadie (Feb 2011) ▪ Viticulturist(s) David Sadie (Feb 2011) & Consultants ▪ 21ha/9ha (ptage, pinot, shiraz, sauv, viog) ▪ 55t/3,300cs own label 60% red 25% white 10% rosé 5% sweet sauv ▪ IPW ▪ PO Box 69 Gordon's Bay 7151 ▪ lemberg@webafrica.org.za ▪ www.lemberg.co.za ▪ S 33° 18'8. 27" E 019° 6'23.06" ▪ T +27 (0)21-300-1130 ▪ F +27 (0)21-300-1131

The famously rustic winery has had a radical makeover, from lean-to shed to picture-pretty Cape country boutique cellar. Now Biodiversity & Wine Initiative-certified and tourism-orientated, the revitalised estate is working on the basics: healthy vineyards, sound viniculture (under the promising David Sadie) and focused marketing. Next is a patch of hárslevelü vines as a tribute to erstwhile owner Janey Muller.

Pinotage NEW ★★★★ Unmistakable but restrained & integrated, **10** has loads of body, lovely ripe berry fruit. Youthful, shows potential. **Private Bin 13** Await new vintage. **Syrah Blanc de Noir** NEW ★★★ Another debut in reinvented range, **11** offers bright, spicy berry fruit, satisfying weight. Anytime poolside companion. **Sauvignon Blanc** ★★★ Previewed **11** from 32 year old vines is much improved. Shows substance & character, with lean, almost salty minerality. **Viognier** NEW ✓ ★★★★ Delicately spicy, fragrant **11** barrel sample is auspicious debut. Restrained yet expressive, from Breedekloof vineyard. — GdB

Leopard Frog Vineyards

Location/WO: Stellenbosch ▪ Closed to public ▪ Owner(s) Dogwood Trust ▪ Cellarmaster(s)/winemaker(s) David John Bate (Jun 2005) ▪ 5,000cs own label 80% red 20% white ▪ 8 Royal Ascot Lane Sandown Sandton 2196 ▪ info@leopard-frog.com ▪ www.leopard-frog.com ▪ T +27 (0)11-884-3304 ▪ F +27 (0)11-883-0426

Canadian-born banker David Bate's wine production may be on the micro scale, but his creativity in crafting truly unique & interesting blends (and labels), is boundless. Innovative in either their varietal or multi-vintage make up, or lengthy oaking; not by artistic whim, but chosen design, drawing on his Bordeaux Wine Institute training.

★★★★ **Spellbinding Chenin Blanc** Once-off **NV** still available. Baked apple, oxidative tone & food-friendly acidity when last tasted.
Aphrodite Africa NEW ★★★★ Cab franc **04** emerges after 60 months beauty sleep in oak paler but perfumed, with enough vitality for mealtime entertainment. **Midnight Maasai Shiraz** ★★★★ Once-off **02** still selling. Previous tasting showed tertiary charcuterie flavours after house's lengthy oaking. **Tantra** ✓ ★★★★ **05** is a cab franc-led Bordeaux red with cab & petit verdot. Earthy dark fruit & serious cedary tannin undertone, still retains freshness & colour. Worthy dinner partner, step up on taut **04** (★★★). **Tribe** NEW ★★★★ **05** is an unusual, smooth & savoury blend of pinotage & its parents, pinot noir & cinsaut. Elegantly aged but fading. Enjoy now. **Kiss & Tell Reserve** ★★★ Approachable **05** is mostly shiraz & merlot, dashes malbec & mourvèdre. Savoury & polished, a comfortable confidant. **Singularity** NEW ★★★★ Another unusual offering: viognier from vintages 2005-2009 (thus **NV**), retains freshness & drinkability. Refined & light, with lemon & starfruit. — MW

Leopard's Leap Wines

Location/map: Franschhoek ▪ WO: Western Cape ▪ Est 2000 ▪ Tasting & sales Mon-Sat, phone ahead for hours ▪ World-class Culinary School, run by renowned chef Liam Tomlin ▪ Owner(s) Hanneli Rupert-Koegelenberg & Hein Koegelenberg ▪ Winemaker(s) Eugene van Zyl (Nov 2002) ▪ 250,000cs own label 60% red 39% white 1% rosé ▪ PO Box 1 La Motte 7691 ▪ info@leopardsleap.co.za ▪ www.leopards-leap.com ▪ S 33° 52'58.8" E 19° 04' 50" ▪ T +27 (0)21-876-8002 ▪ F +27 (0)21-876-4156

Drinkability – clean fruit, lower alcohols, finer tannins – is the hallmark of this relatively young Franschhoek venture, co-owned by Hein Koegelenberg and Hanneli Rupert-Koegelenberg of La Motte. Helping conserve the Cape leopard remains key, as is their interest in literary endeavours including an innovative '60 word back-label story' competition run in conjunction with LitNet. The new tasting facility was set to open as the guide went to press, with a cooking school directed by globe-trotting chef Liam Tomlin.

Classic range

Merlot ☺ 🍷 ★★★ **09** loaded with floral violet charm to plummy mushroom depth of flavour. Delicious.
Chenic Blanc NEW ☺ 🍷 ★★★ Unfettered tropical fruit characters converge in tasty dry tail of **11**.

Cabernet Sauvignon ✓ 🍷 ★★★★ Appealing, open styling of choc-mocha **09** means it's delicious in youth.
Shiraz 🍷 ★★★ Clean leather tones **09**, its peppery promise a little light for 40% new oak. **Cabernet Sauvignon-Merlot** ✓ 🍷 ★★★★ Upward trajectory of 60/40 blend on track in **09**; velvet feel to glossy red fruit in svelte tannins. Like all reds, commendably moderate (for SA) 13.5% alc. **Chardonnay** 🍷 ★★ Unwooded **11** low on fruit flavours. **Sauvignon Blanc** 🍷 ★★★ Tropical **11** beckons with peach & pear up front but doesn't linger. Discontinued: **Pinotage-Shiraz, Chardonnay-Viognier**.

Family Collection

Shiraz-Mourvèdre-Viognier ✓ 🍷 ★★★★ Red berry exuberance of **08** tethered by leather spice, earthy tones. Now all oaked, 20% new. Discontinued: **Sauvignon Blanc**.

Lookout range

Cabernet Sauvignon-Shiraz-Cinsaut 🍷 ★★★ Straightforward **10** fruity & light (12.5% alc). **Pinotage Rosé** 🍷 ★★ **11** strawberry charm, firm finish. **Chenin Blanc Semi Sweet** 🍷 ★★ Preview **11** bottled sunshine for the sweet-toothed. **Chenin Blanc-Chardonnay** 🍷 ★★ Bright **11** has clean melon thrust. — DS

■ **Le Pavillon** *see Boschendal Wines*

Le Pommier Wines

Location/map: Stellenbosch ▪ WO: Stellenbosch/Banghoek ▪ Est/1stB 2003 ▪ Tasting & sales Mon-Fri 10-6 Sat/Sun 11-3 ▪ Fee R10 ▪ Facilities for children ▪ Gift shop ▪ Spa ▪ Le Pommier Restaurant ▪ Guesthouse ▪ Picnics ▪ Wine lounge ▪ Owner(s) Melanie van der Merwe ▪ Winemaker(s) Neil Moorhouse ▪ Viticulturist(s) Kevin Watt (consultant) ▪ 16ha/4.8ha (cab f, malbec, sauv) ▪ 2,000cs own label 45% red 55% white ▪ PO Box 988 Stellenbosch 7599 ▪ info@lepommier.co.za ▪ www.lepommier.co.za ▪ S 33° 55' 8.58" E 018° 55' 43.14" ▪ **T +27 (0)21-885-1269/ +27 (0)21-885-1561** ▪ F +27 (0)21-885-1274

Previously an apple farm (hence its name) Le Pommier is these days more serious about providing a luxury lifestyle experience in a superb setting (the Zorgvliet Spa, for example). By contrast, the wines are easy-drinking and unpretentiously priced – try them paired with tapas and deli food at the new Wine Lounge.

Rosé NEW ☺ 🍷 ★★★ Dry, savoury **10** from cab franc is delightfully fresh & vibrant as well as prettily pink.

Cabernet Sauvignon Reserve 🍷 ★★★ Aromatic **08** shows serious intent but resolute tannin & firm acidity overwhelm fruit. **Jonathan's Malbec** ★★★★ Dark **09** delivered punchy plum, dark cherry fruit & pepper spice, austere tannins needing time. Like next, previewed last year. **Shiraz** ★★★ Bold, extracted **09** was overwhelmed by tannins, but plenty of mulberry fruit & spice. **Chenin Blanc** 🍷 ★★★★ Flavoursome **10** tasted last edition had frisky acidity enlivened by ripe tropical flavours. **Sauvignon Blanc** 🍷 ★★★ Easy, fresh, uncomplicated sample **11** needs to settle; less focus & vitality than previous vintages. Discontinued: **Chardonnay**. — IM

Le Riche Wines

Location/map/WO: Stellenbosch ▪ Est 1996 ▪ 1stB 1997 ▪ Tasting & cellar tours by appt only ▪ Sales Mon-Fri 8.30-4.30 ▪ Closed all pub hols ▪ Owner(s) Etienne le Riche ▪ Cellarmaster(s) Etienne le Riche (Jan 1997) ▪ Winemaker(s) Christo le Riche (Jan 2010), with Mark Daniels (Sep 2000) ▪ (cab) ▪ 70t/4,500cs own label 90% red 10% white ▪ PO Box 6295 Stellenbosch 7600 ▪ wine@leriche.co.za ▪ www.leriche.co.za ▪ S 33° 56' 26.5" E 018° 54' 14.3" ▪ **T +27 (0)21-887-0789** ▪ F +27 (0)21-887-0789

A slight tweak to stylistic approach under the influence of scions Yvonne and Christo should come into play from the 2009 vintages. The goal is to create modern wines offering more fruit character but staying true to the well-established elegance of the past. The latest wines offer slightly more fruit richness and power than usual due mostly to the impact of the 2008 ripening conditions. Having had the privilege in the past to scrutinize these wines in a vertical line-up it is clear that vintages are important as these top wines annually come from the same combination of Stellenbosch vineyards, serving as true reflections of harvest conditions. A highlight of 2011 for Etienne le Riche was to be invited to a 'Flagship Tasting' of South African wines in Copenhagen, Amsterdam, London and Brussels - a well deserved tribute.

★★★★☆ **Cabernet Sauvignon Reserve** 08 (★★★★) estate flagship in much riper, more alcoholic mould, in difficult vintage. Intense & sumptuous dark berries, powerful oak in support, but lacks elegance & freshness of **07**.

★★★★☆ **CWG Auction Reserve Cabernet Sauvignon** From single Helderberg vineyard. 08 exudes power & has concentrated fruit well integrated with all-new oak. Again, not as elegant as refined 07 (★★★★★), but shows fine tannins in support of brooding dark fruit, with attractive earthy undertone.

★★★★☆ **Cabernet Sauvignon** 08 (★★★★) like its big brothers exudes riper fruit profile than **07**. Plush, sweet cherry combines with dry cocoa, but lacks elegance of usual house style. Ends dry with firm tannins.

★★★★ **Cabernet Sauvignon-Merlot** Dry, savoury palate & vibrant acidity serves as foil to dark-fruited, modern ripe style of well balanced & approachable **09**. With dabs of cab franc & petit verdot.

★★★★ **Chardonnay** ✓ 10 leads with great citrus & stone fruit purity, while judicious wooding (half in 50%-new oak, rest in tank) adds to wonderful composure & subtly textured, fine dry finish. — JP

Le Roux & Fourie Vignerons

Location/WO: Robertson ▪ Est circa 1823 ▪ 1stB 2006 ▪ Closed for tasting/sales/tours ▪ Buitenstekloof Mountain Cottages (www.buitenstekloof.co.za) ▪ Walks/hikes ▪ Conservation area ▪ 100+ bird species, small game, mountain tortoises & many more ▪ Owner(s) Johan P & Le Roux Fourie ▪ Cellarmaster(s)/viticulturist(s) Johan Fourie (Mar 2003) ▪ Winemaker(s) Kobus van der Merwe (consultant) & Johan Fourie (both Mar 2003) ▪ 1,300ha/10ha (cab, carignan, grenache, mourv, ptage, shiraz, tinta amerela, chard, sauv, viog) ▪ 25t/1,100cs own label 80% red 20% white + 1,100cs for clients ▪ PO Box 765 Robertson 6705 ▪ info@buitenstekloof.co.za ▪ www.lerouxfourievignerons.com ▪ T +27 (0)23-626-5376 ▪ F +27 (0)86-619-0993

Not least amongst the attractions of this new boutique cellar in Robertson is the massive 9m-high straw bale winery – the tallest straw structure in South Africa. Owner/winemaker Johan Fourie's background is banking, so the thick walls which save up to 70% on his electricity bill are a bonus to his eco-friendly ideals. He and brother Le Roux have great faith in the limestone soils of the region and are excited about the potential of their handcrafted wines.

Carignina ★★ From carignan, **10** with savoury notes, needs hearty fare (like winemaker's suggested kudu steak). **Limestone Q** ★★★ Shiraz & 4 other reds plus soupçon viognier, **10** undemanding, with tarry hint. **Chardonnay** 🖩 **11** preview too young to rate, as for **Sauvignon Blanc 11**. — Panel

■ **Les Coteaux** see Mont du Toit Kelder

■ **Les Pleurs** see Avondale Bio-LOGIC & Organic Wines

■ **Le Vin de François** see Chateau Naudé Wine Creation

Libby's Pride Wines

Location: Wellington ▪ WO: Western Cape ▪ Tasting, sales & tours by appt ▪ Owner(s) Elizabeth Petersen ▪ Winemaker(s) Hennie Huskisson (Linton Park Wines) ▪ 750t/20,000cs own label 75% red 25% white ▪ info@libbyspridewines.com ▪ www.libbyspridewines.com ▪ T +27 (0)82-745-5550 ▪ F +27 (0)86-215-1811

Elizabeth 'Libby' Petersen's star sign is Leo, a symbol she associates with strength and pride - hence the name of the company she's intent on developing into South Africa's most successful black-woman-owned wine business. In this endeavour she's ably partnered by Linton Park winery near Wellington, where the wines are made to customer specifications.

Merlot ☺ ★★★ **10** is fun, fruit-forward & light-hearted, bursts with cherries & chocolate.

Cabernet Sauvignon ★★ Light, easy & noticeably dry, **10** is perfect with country fare. **Shiraz** ★★★ Easy-drinking **09** was balanced last year, had violet perfume, spicy lift. Not revisited, as for rest. **Signature Red** ★★ Fruity combo **09** from equal shiraz & merlot, savoury notes & tannic grip. **Chardonnay** ★★★ Lively unwooded **10**, fresh lime, apple & nectarine, zesty & seafood friendly. **Sauvignon Blanc** ★★ Shy, lightish **10**, faint grass & greenpepper, perky finish. — WB

■ **Libertas** see Distell

Lievland Estate

Location/map/WO: Stellenbosch ▪ Est/1stB 1982 ▪ Tasting, sales & tours Mon-Fri 9-5 Sat/Sun 10-4 ▪ Fee R10 ▪ Closed Dec 25 ▪ Summer picnic baskets ▪ B&B accommodation ▪ Owner(s) Susan Colley ▪ Winemaker(s) Kowie du Toit (2004) ▪ Viticulturist(s) Conrad Schutte (2010, Vinpro) ▪ 50ha (cab, merlot, shiraz) ▪ 250t/15,000cs own label 95% red 5% white ▪ PO Box 66 Klapmuts 7625 ▪ lievland@icon.co.za ▪ www.lievland.co.za ▪ S 33° 50′ 29.5″ E 018° 52′ 34.8″ ▪ **T +27 (0)21-875-5226** ▪ F +27 (0)21-875-5213

This mainly red-wine estate has been through several changes recently and winemaker Kowie du Toit is excited about now putting it firmly back on the map. The vineyards have been rejuvenated, and longer tasting hours, summer picnic baskets and a warming winter fire in the tasting room are proving attractive.

Shiraz ★★★☆ Latest of three bottlings of **05** is soft, silky & savoury, with appealing dark-fruit flavours. For drinking now. **Lievlander** ✓ 🍾 ★★★★ Equal parts shiraz & cab with dash merlot, **08** is savoury, juicy & supple with loads of berry fruit, drinking beautifully now. **Sauvignon Blanc** 🍾 ★★ **11** stonefruit flavours, soft & gentle for easy quaffing. Discontinued: **Owl's Own**, **Field Blend**. — MW

■ **Lifestyle** see Simonsvlei International
■ **Like Father Like Son** see Bon Courage Estate

L'illa

Location: Hermanus ▪ Est/1stB 2006 ▪ Tasting & sales at Newton Johnson Vineyards ▪ Owner(s)/winemaker(s) Gordon & Nadia Newton Johnson ▪ Viticulturist(s) AA Cilliers (Jan 1973) ▪ (chenin) ▪ 110cs (12 x 375ml) own label 100% white ▪ PO Box 225 Hermanus 7200 ▪ gordon@newtonjohnson.com, nadia@newtonjohnson.com ▪ www. newtonjohnson.com ▪ **T +27 (0)28-312-3862** ▪ F +27 (0)86-638-9673

The Cilliers have been farming in Robertson for six generations. Nadia Cilliers married into the Newton Johnson family of the eponymous winery near Hermanus and makes there this wine from her family farm's 40-year-old vineyard. It is, they say, 'the proverbial wine that makes itself'.

★★★★ **Noble Late Harvest** Botrytis subtly decorated chenin's peach aromas & succulence on **09** (★★★★★) tasted last year. Silky, lingering, with arresting acidity. Previously tasted **07** rich & unctuous. — TJ

Limelight

 NEW

Named for the limestone soils which characterise much of the Robertson Valley, this new standalone brand from chardonnay maestro and De Wetshof cellarmaster Danie de Wet celebrates the terroir in an easily accessible wine aimed at entry-level wine drinkers. See De Wetshof for contact and tasting details.

Chardonnay-Pinot Noir 🍾 ★★★ Unpretentious 80/20 mix, **11** light, with just a suggestion of sweetness, ideal for poolside sipping. — Panel

■ **Lime Road** see Havana Hills
■ **Lindenhof** see Boland Kelder

Lindhorst Wines

Location: Paarl ▪ Map: Paarl & Wellington ▪ WO: Paarl/Durbanville ▪ Est 1996 ▪ 1stB 2002 ▪ Tasting, sales & cellar tours by appt 11-5 daily ▪ Closed Dec 25 ▪ Meals by special request only ▪ Self-catering Cottage ▪ Owner(s) Mark & Belinda Lindhorst ▪ Winemaker(s) Mark Lindhorst, advised by Philip Costandius (Aug 2009, consultant) ▪ Viticulturist(s) Mark Lindhorst, advised by Kevin Watt (Jan 2001, consultant) ▪ 65ha/18ha (cab, merlot, mourv, ptage, pinot, shiraz, viog) ▪ 140t/4,000cs own label 100% red ▪ PO Box 1398 Southern Paarl 7624 ▪ mark@ lindhorstwines.com ▪ www.lindhorstwines.com ▪ S 33° 47′ 46.0″ E 018° 56′ 59.0″ ▪ **T +27 (0)21-863-0990** ▪ F +27 (0)21-863-3694

Co-owner Mark Lindhorst, a former auditor and management consultant, applies some unconventional thinking when it comes to marketing, eschewing wine shows for those of more general interest, his favourite being Sexpo! 'It's far better when there are not hundreds of competitors and thousands of possibly wine-soaked revellers.'

Cabernet Sauvignon ★★★ Uncomplicated **07** shows dark fruit, fresh acidity, firm tannins; needs time to lose slightly hard edges. **Merlot** ★★★ Rich & full **07** exhibits dark fruit & chocolate flavours; broad structured & smooth textured but lacks a little freshness. **Pinotage** ★★★★ Succulent yet complex, **07** had liquorice, graphite nuances alongside brambleberry fruit; previously tasted, as for next 2. **Shiraz** ★★★★ Earthy, with dried herbs & plums, **06** couldn't be more variety-true. **Max's Tribute** ★★★★ Blend, mainly shiraz in **06**. Admirable fruit purity, house-style fine tannins providing polished support. **Partner's Choice** NEW ★★★★ **07** from 49% cab, 49% shiraz, 2% pinotage. Red & black fruit, dusty oak on the nose; medium bodied & well balanced, with fresh acidity, fine tannins. **Statement** ★★★★ Shiraz blend with cab, merlot. **06** showed fleshy fruit, scrub & dark chocolate nuances, strong but not harsh oak. **05** (★★★★) had spice-layered red fruit. Neither retasted, as for all following. **Rosé** 🗒 ★★★ Shiraz-based **09** previously showed strawberry fruitiness; off-dry, with balancing freshness. **Sauvignon Blanc** ★★★★ On preview, **11** appears light and fresh with Muscat-like fragrance before green plum, herbal flavours, medium length. **Viognier** Await new vintage. — CE

Lingen

Location: Stellenbosch ▪ WO: Jonkershoek Valley ▪ Est 2003 ▪ 1stB 2008 ▪ Tasting & sales Mon-Sun 10-4 at Stark-Condé Wines ▪ Fee R30 ▪ Closed Easter Fri, Dec 25 & Jan 1 ▪ Owner(s) JD Krige Family Trust ▪ Cellarmaster(s)/winemaker(s) José Condé (Jan 2003) ▪ Viticulturist(s) Pieter Smit (Jan 2003, consultant) ▪ 7ha/2ha (cab, p verdot, shiraz) ▪ 14t/200cs own label 100% red ▪ PO Box 389 Stellenbosch 7599 ▪ info@stark-conde.co.za ▪ www.stark-conde.co.za ▪ **T** +27 (0)21-861-7700 / +27 (0)21-887-3665 ▪ **F** +27 (0)21-887-4340

Niel and Coreen Krige's Jonkershoek Valley vineyard is a stone's throw from Stark-Condé, where the grapes are vinified, but the soils are very different. Lingen's gravelly clay 'vilafonte' yields softer structure, with wild fynbos notes, explains winemaker José Condé. After maiden 2008's success, in 2011 all three varieties – cabernet, shiraz and petit verdot – were co-fermented for yet better integration.

★★★★ **Lingen** ✓ Poised **09** (★★★★★) Bordeaux/shiraz blend shows highly attractive bramble fruit & an alluring purple hue from petit verdot. Svelte & high toned, whereas ageworthy **08** more cocoa & spice. — DS

Linton Park Wines

Location: Wellington ▪ Map: Paarl & Wellington ▪ WO: Paarl/Western Cape/Wellington ▪ Est 1995 ▪ 1stB 1998 ▪ Tasting, sales & tours between 9-4 by appt ▪ Fee R50 pp ▪ Closed all pub hols ▪ BYO picnic ▪ Walking/hiking/4x4 & mountain biking trails ▪ Annual Harvest Festival Mar/Apr ▪ Owner(s) Camellia PLC UK ▪ Cellarmaster(s) Hennie Huskisson (2007) ▪ Winemaker(s) JG Auret (2007) ▪ Viticulturist(s) Vlok Hanekom (2006) ▪ 210ha/84ha (cab, merlot, pinot, shiraz, chard, sauv, viog) ▪ 650t/40,000cs own label 50% red 40% white 10% rosé ▪ Other export brands: Louis Fourie, The Rhino ▪ Brands for clients: Die Kaapse Seleksie, Flame, Mack Daddy, PieQue Select Wines, Vin d'Ester, Westerkaap ▪ PO Box 1234 Wellington 7654 ▪ sales@lintonparkwines.co.za, info@lintonparkwines.co.za ▪ www.lintonparkwines.co.za ▪ **S** 33° 36'40.1" **E** 019° 2'15.0" ▪ **T** +27 (0)21-873-1625 ▪ **F** +27 (0)21-873-0851

This UK-owned winery in Wellington's Slangrivier Valley is exploring new markets, obtaining Fairtrade certification, and reformatting its portfolio. The Capell's Court range is making way for new brand, Louis Fourie, and the established The Rhino line-up is being repackaged and relaunched, and a portion of sales being donated to Save the Rhino. 'Best value for money at affordable prices' is the goal.

Reserve range

★★★★ **Cabernet Sauvignon** Rich & full-bodied **08** dominated by blackcurrant, dark cherry & chocolate. Expressive fruit, firm centre of supple tannin, savoury tail. Not retasted, as for rest of range.

★★★★ **Merlot** When reviewed, **05** offered mint, liquorice & dark chocolate to vibrant wild-berry tone; firm tannins should be accessible now.

★★★★ **Shiraz** Oodles of violet, smoky, spicy plums in **07** last edition. Juicy, full-bodied, firm tannins & a savoury conclusion. Should be delicious now.

Linton Park range

Cabernet Sauvignon ✓ ★★★★ Well-made, gluggable **08** is ripe & dark-fruited, hints of blackcurrant & firm tannins. Lovely oaky finish. **Merlot** ✓ ★★★★ Dark & ripe spicy fruitcake & plums, **09** juicy fruit mingles with supple tannins, dry savoury conclusion. Super-drinkable! **Shiraz** ★★★★ Juicy plum, mulberry & spice last edition, **08** full-bodied, sweet fruit balanced by a refreshing acidity & smooth tannins. Paarl vines. **Chardonnay** ✓ ★★★★ **09** a step up from **08** (★★★★), appeals with ripe pineapple & vanilla biscuit. Round, fresh & creamy, lingering dry citrus aftertaste. **Private Bin 177 (Limited Release)** ★★★ From sauvignon, off highest vines on farm (±500m). Still-available **10** dry, food-friendly, with firm acidity.

Capell's Court range
Now discontinued. — WB

- **Lion Creek** *see* Napier Winery
- **Liquor City** *see* Orange River Wine Cellars

Lismore Estate Vineyards

Location: Greyton ▪ Map: Southern Cape ▪ Est 2003 ▪ 1stB 2006 ▪ Tasting & sales by appt ▪ Facilities for children ▪ Tour groups ▪ Walking/hiking & mountain biking trails ▪ Owner(s)/winemaker(s) Samantha O'Keefe ▪ Viticulturist(s) Andrew Teubes (consultant) ▪ 296ha/12ha (shiraz, chard, sauv, viog) ▪ 40t/2,000cs own label 15% red 85% white ▪ PO Box 76 Greyton 7233 ▪ wine@lismore.co.za ▪ www.lismore.co.za ▪ S 34° 4′ 25.23″ E 19° 41′ 16.83″ ▪ T +27 (0)28-254-9848 ▪ F +27 (0)28-254-9848

Lismore's Samantha O'Keefe doubled her production in 2011 to keep her existing clientele and growing export markets happy, and spent time wondering how to make more Viognier – sommelier Emily O'Hare of London's River Café is among its high-profile fans. With only .8ha at present, expanded plantings are naturally on the cards. The flagship Chardonnay and barrel-fermented Sauvignon Blanc continue to anchor the range.

- **Little River** *see* De Meye Wines
- **Live-A-Little** *see* Stellar Winery
- **Living Rock** *see* Withington

L'Olivier Wine & Olive Estate

Location/map/WO: Stellenbosch ▪ 1stB 2008 ▪ Tasting & sales by appt only ▪ Fee R50 ▪ Facilities for children ▪ Conference & wedding venue ▪ Walking/hiking & mountain biking trails ▪ Horse riding ▪ Accommodation in manor house/villa & two cottages ▪ Owner(s) Theuns Kuhn ▪ Winemaker(s) Mike Dobrovic ▪ Viticulturist(s) Jannie Lotter ▪ 30ha (cab, chard, sauv) ▪ ±128t/1,457cs own label 30% red 70% white ▪ Stellenbosch Kloof Road Stellenbosch 7600 ▪ carina@nonpareil.co.za, info@lolivierestate.com ▪ www.lolivierestate.com ▪ S 33° 55′ 37″ E 018° 46′ 54″ ▪ T +27 (0)21-794-1031 ▪ F +27 (0)21-794-1051

'Get that country feeling!' is the message from this Stellenboschkloof estate. By which is meant much more than the wine that has been made under their own label from their rolling vineyards, and more than the olive-oil from their groves. Think everything from smart accommodation to hiking. But don't forget the wine.

Non Pareil Boutique Wines
Cabernet Sauvignon ★★★ Cab astringency & freshness & plush fruit on last-tasted **07**. **Sauvignon Blanc** ★★★★ Drink soon, we said previously about green-toned, sugar-softened **09**. — Panel

Lomond

Location: Gansbaai ▪ WO: Cape Agulhas ▪ Est 1999 ▪ 1stB 2005 ▪ Tasting & sales at Farm 215 Mon-Sun 9-4 by appt ▪ Closed all pub hols ▪ Guest accommodation, restaurant, conferences, hiking trail, conservation area (www.farm215.co.za) ▪ Owner(s) Joint venture between Distell, Lomond Properties & Lomond Development Company ▪ Cellarmaster(s)/winemaker(s) Kobus Gerber (2004) ▪ Viticulturist(s) Wayne Gabb (1999) ▪ 800ha/120ha (merlot, syrah, nouvelle, sauv) ▪ 750t 40% red 60% white ▪ ISO 9002, BWI ▪ PO Box 184 Stellenbosch 7599 ▪ lomond@capelegends.co.za ▪ www.lomond.co.za ▪ S 34° 34′ 12″ E 019° 26′ 24.00″ ▪ T +27 (0)21-809-8330 ▪ F +27 (0)21-882-9575

This award-winning Distell farm in the Cape Agulhas district - member of the Biodiversity & Wine Initiative and part of the Walker Bay Fynbos Conservancy - keeps its viticulture 'clean and green'. 'We give life to the soil,' explains viticulturist Wayne Gabb, 'inoculating it with micro-organisms to increase organic matter, then create an environment that promotes self-induced resistance of the plants to the risk of disease. This approach is enhanced by a predator-release programme that allows insects to feed off otherwise destructive pests.'

★★★★ **Syrah 08** (★★★★☆) still selling. Previously had true shiraz structure, was delicately gripping & pure, & a shade finer than **07**.

★★★★☆ **Conebush Syrah** Previewed & provisionally rated **09** (★★★★) in cooler vintage is oak dominated, sweet-sour & taut, seems shade off juicy & complex **08**.

★★★★ **Pincushion Sauvignon Blanc** 🍷 🥂 **11** (★★★★) pre-bottling shows blackcurrant, fynbos & nectarine complexity, zesty acidity; ends tad warm (14.5% alc), less elegant than **10**.

★★★★☆ **Sugarbush Sauvignon Blanc** 🍷 **11** (★★★★) preview somewhat leaner & more mineral than siblings, but also very well balanced; light & crisp despite 14.3% alc, fullish fruity finish. However, not as enticing as **10**.

Merlot ★★★ Savoury & meaty **08**, rustic, tad insubstantial & green edged. **Cat's Tail Syrah** Untasted. **Sauvignon Blanc** 🍷 🥂 **★★★** Strong blackcurrant on this entry-level version. Previewed **11**, with dash nouvelle, less racy, waxier than single-vineyard stablemates, not as crisp & convincing as previous. **Snowbush** 🍷 **★★★★** Engaging **10** marries sauvignon with barrel-fermented semillon, nouvelle, smidgen viognier. Floral, bursting with fruit, less classically styled than others from the district but still very good. — Panel

Longbarn Winery

Location/WO: Wellington ▪ Map: Paarl & Wellington ▪ Est/1stB 2006 ▪ Cellar tours by appt ▪ Owner(s) David & Sue Power ▪ Winemaker(s) David Power (Feb 2006) ▪ Viticulturist(s) David Power (Sep 2003) ▪ 69ha/4ha (pinot, sauv) ▪ 7t/140cs own label 100% white ▪ PO Box 1295 Wellington 7654 ▪ david@longbarn.co.za ▪ www.longbarn.co.za ▪ S 33° 34' 13.6" E 019° 3' 53.6" ▪ **T +27 (0)21-873-6396** ▪ F +27 (0)86-611-1534

Set idyllically in the folds of the Agtergroenberg, north of Wellington, David Power's boutique winery turns out small volumes of sauvignon from a single hectare of vines (since the 07 vintage, his red-wine grapes are sold off). No changes or developments reported this year.

Pinot Noir 🍷 **★★★ 07**'s clean chocolate-cherry profile & crisp acid enlivened soft oak vanilla last time. **Sauvignon Blanc ✓** 🍷 **★★★★** Refreshing **11** preview shows added intensity of fruit, well tempered acidity. — GdB

Long Beach

Attractively packaged brand by Robertson Winery for Vinimark.

Sauvignon Blanc 🍷 🥂 **★★★ 11** overflows with greenpepper, grass & herbs, gooseberry & pineapple flavours. Perfect - chilled - anywhere, anytime, especially of course the beach. Robertson WO. — Panel

■ **Longmarket** see Woolworths

Long Mountain Wine Company

Location: Stellenbosch ▪ WO: Western Cape ▪ Est/1stB 1994 ▪ Closed to public ▪ Owner(s) Pernod Ricard South Africa ▪ Cellarmaster(s)/winemaker(s)/viticulturist(s) Emile Gentis (Oct 2006) ▪ 100,000cs own label 50% red 48% white 1% rosé 10% MCC ▪ 2nd Floor The Square Cape Quaters 27 Somerset Road De Waterkant Cape Town 8005 ▪ emile.gentis@pernod-ricard.com ▪ www.longmountain.co.za ▪ **T +27 (0)21-405-8800** ▪ F +27 (0)86-504-2052

Pernod Ricard's wine companies worldwide have joined forces under the Premium Wines Brands umbrella to enlarge their global footprint and share a common vision. That means change is in the air. 'The strategy is to 'premiumise' packaging, product and service,' says cellarmaster Emile Gentis, who'll no doubt approach the task with gusto given his reply to our stock question, Why does wine matter? 'Why does the sun come up? Every day, it's a miracle, as is wine each year we make it.'

Long Mountain Premium Reserve range

★★★★ **Chardonnay-Pinot Noir Cap Classique** Mid-2008, citrus & gooseberry nuanced **NV** traditional-method sparkling was noted as slightly sweeter than most 'brut' versions but still with good MCC character.

Pinotage 🥂 **★★★** National Young Wine Show champion **10** good expression of variety, example of smart oaking; has fruit intensity to match boldly flavoured dishes. **Shiraz** 🥂 **★★★** Preview **10** vibrant & pleasantly dry, balanced mouthful fruitcake & cinnamon. **Sauvignon Blanc** 🍷 🥂 **★★★★** Last edition, **10** preview's white asparagus richness was freshened by crisp acidity. Friendly sipper, similar to - but better than - **08** (★★★★).

Long Mountain range

Cabernet Sauvignon 😊 🍷 🖼 ★★★ Very satisfying **11** flash pasteurised to retain freshness, accentuate fruit. Unoaked, as all reds unless noted.

Pinotage 🍷 🖼 ★★★ Well-rounded, balanced **10** packed with raspberry & vanilla (ex French oak staves/chips) mid-2010. **Ruby Cabernet** 🍷 ★★★ Still-available **08** was easy & pasta friendly mid-2009. Best enjoyed soon. **Shiraz-Cabernet Sauvignon** 🍷 🖼 ★★★ **11** red plum flavour from 60% shiraz, sweetish tail, tad stalky tannin. **Merlot-Shiraz** 🍷 🖼 ★★★ Preview **11** lightly oak-staved, meaty & eminently drinkable (but note high 14.8% alc). **Chardonnay** 🍷 🖼 ★★★ **11** picked full-ripe for maximum flavour. Zippy acidity & brush of oak neutralise the dollop sugar. Previewed, as all the whites. **Chenin Blanc** 🍷 🖼 ★★ Granny Smith apple toned **11** is shy & retiring, light bodied at only ±12% alc. **Sauvignon Blanc** 🍷 🖼 ★★★ Dusty & green-fruited **11** has crisp acidity to complement rich seafood. **Semillon-Chardonnay** 🍷 🖼 ★★ Ultra-ripe chardonnay in **11** provides fatness, dashes zingy nouvelle & chenin ensure freshness. Deftly done. WO W Cape, as for all ranges.

Gecko Ridge Reserve range

Cabernet Sauvignon 🍷 ★★★ Well-priced range for export only. Faint metallic edge to jammy **10**. **Pinotage** 🍷 🖼 ★★★ Grippy **10** has banana, strawberry & smoke (& many fans in Sweden!). **Chardonnay** 🍷 🖼 ★★★ Lemony **11** pleasant, zingy unwooded al fresco lunch companion or solo sipper. **Chenin Blanc** 🍷 🖼 ★★★ Off-dry version **10** has creamy apricot aroma but not very intense flavours. Discontinued: **Shiraz-Pinotage**. — CvZ

Longridge Winery

Location: Somerset West ▪ Map: Helderberg ▪ WO: Western Cape/Stellenbosch ▪ Est 1994 ▪ Mon-Fri 9-5 Sat & pub hols 9-2 ▪ Closed Easter Fri/Sun, Dec 25 & Jan 1 ▪ Johan's Restaurant & Wine Bar ▪ Conference venue ▪ Owner(s) Aldo van der Laan ▪ Cellarmaster(s) Clinton le Seuer (Dec 2006) ▪ Winemaker(s) Clinton le Seuer (Dec 2006), with Hendrien de Munck (Jan 2009) ▪ Viticulturist(s) Johann Schloms (Dec 2006) ▪ 48ha/23ha (cab f, shiraz, chard, chenin, sauv, verdelho, viog) ▪ 201t/13,000cs own label 65% red 25% white 6% rosé 4% MCC ▪ Other export brands: Baaije Lekker, Bayridge, HPG, Santon, Verruklik ▪ PO Box 2023 Dennesig 7601 ▪ info@longridgewines.co.za ▪ www.longridge.co.za ▪ S 34°0'55.2" E 018°49'60.0" ▪ **T +27 (0)21-855-2005** ▪ F +27 (0)21-855-4083

It is now 20 years since the first Longridge wines appeared (they were made then from bought-in grapes). In the interim, the label has been through some complicated ownership set-ups, but since late 2006, when Aldo van der Laan bought the property, with Clinton le Seuer as winemaker, and Johann Schloms as viticulturist, things have settled. Throughout, the wines – chardonnay and pinotage in particular – have been remarkably and consistently good. A block of 30 year old chenin is among their own vineyards supplying the cellar.

★★★★ **Cabernet Sauvignon** 08 (★★★★) well-balanced with decent lightish cab fruit & well-judged tannins & oaking. Drink while waiting for elegant, complex **07** (★★★★).

★★★★ **Cabernet Franc** Fragrant cranberries, minty nuance on debut **07** in magnum. Firm tannins, lovely acidity deserve long cellaring. Still selling.

★★★★ **Pinotage** Returns to form with **08** after less complex **07** (★★★). Individual spicy, fresh mushroom features. Sweet, juicy core to pinotage's usual chainmail tannins. Even better with year/2.

★★★★ **Chardonnay** Silky **08** (★★★★★) followed vibrant **07**. Last yr, oak added toasty hazelnut, 5% viognier a perfumed nuance. All wines below, except Merlot, WO W Cape. Others WO Stellenbosch.

★★★★ **Chenin Blanc** 10 still oaky on nose, but more interesting earthy notes & textured feel beneath - a dollop of sugar showing rich more than sweet. Needs time; may not reach heights of (previewed) **09**.

★★★★ **Sauvignon Blanc** Cool, clean lines focus attractive dried fig bouquet on **10**. Fresh acid is assimilated well with the rich flavours; most pleasurable drinking. **09** (★★★★) was less balanced.

HPG Red NEW 😊 ★★★ Unoaked merlot-shiraz blend. **10** just-cooked plum jam nose (but not jammy). Full bodied, rich & spicy with decent grip.

Merlot ★★★ Light, simple fruit on **08**, with a sweetish finish, for early drinking. **Shiraz** ★★★★ Caressing crushed velvet feel highlights concentrated dark spice, salami & red fruits on well-structured, long **08**. Smart oak polish (52% new) rather than dryness of **07** (★★★★). **HPG Rosé** NEW ★★ Fiery pink, just-dry **10** blend. Maturing plum aromas; a bit flat. **HPG White** NEW ✓ ★★★★ Punches above its price. **10** from sauvignon, viognier, verdelho plus oaked chenin & chardonnay. Gutsy & moreish, with peachy, warm pebble & smoky intrigue. **Brut ★★★★** Salty sea & warm dough on chardonnay-based **08** MCC bubbly. Creaminess ex barrel ferment balanced by vivacious sparkle. Roundly dry. Discontinued: **Rosé**. — AL

■ **Lookout** *see* Leopard's Leap Wines

Loopspruit Winery

Location: Bronkhorstpruit ▪ Tastings, sales & tours by appt ▪ Restaurant lapa self-catering ▪ BYO picnic ▪ Conferences ▪ Owner(s) MEGA (Mpumalanga Economic Growth Agency) ▪ Winemaker(s) Ian Sieg, with Matthew Sibanyoni ▪ Viticulturist(s) Ian Sieg (adviser) ▪ 22ha (cabs s/f, ruby cab, shiraz, chard, chenin, cbard, hanepoot, raisin blanc) ▪ ±150t/±10,000cs ▪ PO Box 855 Bronkhorstpruit 1020 ▪ manie@madc.co.za ▪ www.madc.co.za ▪ **T +27 (0)13-930-7025** ▪ F +27 (0)86-610-8242

There's an air of renewal at one of the only wine estates north of the Vaal River, thanks to a substantial financial boost in the pipeline. 'We're looking at putting up chalets and opening the restaurant 24/7 again,' reports manager Manie Grobler. 'We've also added a Blanc de Blancs and a Rosé to the range.'

Lord Somerset ▪ NEW

Location: Somerset West ▪ WO: Western Cape ▪ Est 2010 ▪ 1stB 2011 ▪ Tasting & sales Mon-Fri 8.30-5 Sat 9-1 ▪ Closed all pub hols ▪ Tour groups ▪ Wine shop ▪ Owner(s) Boetie Rietoff ▪ Cellarmaster(s) Kobus Rossouw (Jan 2009, consultant) ▪ 100,000cs 80% red 20% white ▪ PO Box 2240 Somerset West 7129 ▪ info@somersetbeverages.co.za ▪ www.thewinegroup.co.za ▪ **T +27 (0)21-851-8188** ▪ F +27 (0)21-852-9563

There's heart in this Somerset West label which is all about marketing quality wines at affordable prices and giving something back to the community. Wines are selected from established wineries in the Helderberg basin and blended for local and export markets, and a percentage of sales goes to various local charities.

Shiraz Reserve ☺ **★★★** Ripe plums threaded through with savoury spice, **08** has enough succulent accessibility for everyday enjoyment.

Cabernet Sauvignon 🍷 🌿 **★★★** Dark fruit, well supported by oak, **10** could age a few years. **Merlot-Cabernet Sauvignon** 🍷 **★★★** Cherries & cloves, touch of mint in **10**, finishes firmly dry. **Soft Smooth Red** 🍷 **★★★** 11 light & juicy berries, plums, touch of sweetness aids appeal. **Chenin Blanc Bushvine** 🍷 🌿 **★★★** Pear-drops, clean & fresh **11** is light textured, easy drinking. **Sauvignon Blanc** 🍷 🌿 **★★★** Tropical notes within **11**'s freshness, food-friendly quaffer. — CR

Lord's Wines

Location: McGregor ▪ Map: Robertson ▪ WO: McGregor/Western Cape ▪ Est 2005 ▪ 1stB 2006 ▪ Cellar: Tasting, sales & cellar tours Mon-Fri 9-5 Sat/Sun by appt ▪ Lord's Wine Shop, Robertson: tasting & sales Mon-Fri 9-5 Sat/Sun 10-4, toffee & wine pairing R20, cheese platters ▪ Closed Easter Fri, Dec 25 & Jan 1 ▪ Tour groups ▪ Farm produce ▪ Owner(s) 12 shareholders ▪ Cellarmaster(s)/winemaker(s) Ilse van Dijk (Nov 2010) ▪ Viticulturist(s) Jacie Oosthuizen (Jan 2003) ▪ 33ha/13ha (pinot, shiraz, chard, chenin, sauv) ▪ 90t/6,600cs own label 50% red 45% white 5% rosé ▪ PO Box 165 McGregor 6708 ▪ ilse@lordswinery.com, sales@lordswinery.com ▪ www.lordswinery.com ▪ S 33° 59' 20.98" E 019° 44' 28.39" ▪ **T +27 (0)23-625-1265 (Cellar)/+27 (0)23-626-3202 (Wine Shop)** ▪ F +27 (0)86-514-2512

Besides characterful wine and superb vistas from the heights above McGregor, this young cellar offers a fresh enticement to visit: toffee-and-wine pairings. Winemaker/manager Ilse van Dijk's belief that 'wine should be enjoyed every day, not only on special occasions' no doubt extends to their trio of new bottlings: pinot noir rosé, chenin and (too late for our deadline) méthode cap classique sparkling.

The Wicked Maiden Rosé NEW ☺ **★★★** Elegant, bone-dry **11** from pinot noir, cranberry scented, ideal summer picnic pink. **Chardonnay Unwooded** ☺ 🍷 **★★★** Quiet citrus scents, burst of grapefruit in off-dry **10**, marmalade tang, herby flick in tail. **Sauvignon Blanc** ☺ 🍷 **★★★** Summer sipper **10**, pungent & cool green fruit, lemongrass seam ends with zingy dry flourish.

Pinot Noir ★★★ Fresh herb & earth highlights to sour cherry, strawberry fruit, **09** assertive grape tannins & overt oak flavours (despite no new oak) dominate mid-2011, allow more time to settle. **Shiraz ✓ ★★★★** Step up for **09**, with 50% Paarl grapes: engaging cigarbox, mulberry tones; understated oak spicing (no new wood), amenable tannin structure. Better focus than **08** (★★★★). WO W Cape. **Chardonnay Barrel Fermented** ★★★★ Vanilla-laden **10** plush & generous, but less so than boldly oaked **09**. Sufficient fruit & green apple/citrus acidity to benefit from cellaring few years. **Nectar Natural Sweet** ★★★ Don't be deceived by **11**'s pale hue, shy nose; there's a whack of peachy flavour, crackling acidity in this sweetie from nouvelle. — Panel

◼ **L'Ormarins** *see* Anthonij Rupert Wines
◼ **Lorna Hughes** *see* Stonehill

Lorraine Private Cellar

Location: Rawsonville • Map: Breedekloof • WO: Goudini • Est 1996 • 1stB 2002 • Tasting, sales & cellar tours Mon-Fri 8-1 • Closed all pub hols • Outdoor wine tasting & picnic by appt R200pp; or BYO picnic • Tour groups • Walking/hiking trails • Conservation area • Owner(s) Lorraine Trust (Johan & Lori Ann de Wet) • Cellarmaster(s)/winemaker(s) Johan de Wet (Jan 2002) • Viticulturist(s) Leon Dippenaar (2003, consultant) • ±417ha/155ha (cab f, merlot, p verdot, ptage, ruby cab, shiraz, chard, chenin, nouvelle, sauv, viog) • 2,000t total 50t/±4,200cs own label 45% red 50% white 5% rosé • Fairtrade • PO Box 2 Rawsonville 6845 • info@lorraine.co.za • www.lorraine.co.za • S 33° 42'43.14" E 019° 15'40.83" • **T +27 (0)23-349-1224** • F +27 (0)86-664-2279

As 5th generation owner of this large estate beneath the Du Toitskloof Mountains, Johan de Wet may well speak of 'a winemaking tradition'. De Wets have been 'loving wine since 1875', and for some ten years now Johan has been making wine from some of his own grapes in the refurbished cellar (it was built in 1875). Loving the land too, as the commitment to conservation shows.

★★★★ **Chardonnay 09** (★★★★) in classically New World style, with lime, spicy vanilla oak & honeysuckle amongst its charms. Creamy mouthfeel, but perhaps not as much freshness as last-tasted **07**.

★★★★ **Viognier** Intensely scented **10** (★★★★) less Old Worldish than last-tried **08**. Typical varietal character of apricot & orange blossom. Long-lingering flavours marked by high alcohol & ultra-ripeness.

Shiraz ★★★★ Tasted last year, **04** was opulent, velvety & seductive. **Cape Harmony** ★★★ **07** smooth & juicy blend pinotage, merlot & cab tasted last year. WO W Cape. **Love Of My Life Pinotage Rosé** ★★★ Previously **NV**, now dated. Fresh, off-dry & nicely balanced **10** offers easy summer fun. **Sauvignon Blanc** ★★★ Sample **11** mixes green & tropical notes. Moderate alc; some residual sugar but tastes dry enough. — JPf

◼ **Lorry** *see* Elgin Valley Vineyards

Louiesenhof Wines

Location/map/WO: Stellenbosch • Est/1stB 1992 • Tasting & sales daily 9–5 (summer) Mon-Sat 10–3 (winter) • Fee R10 • Closed Christian holidays • Louiesenhof B&B • Light meals in summer • Play area for children • Function facilities • Farm produce • Owner(s) WS Smit Watergang Trust • Cellarmaster(s) WS Smit • Winemaker(s) Jos le Roux • Viticulturist(s) Gawie Kriel (2000, consultant) • 130ha (cab, merlot, ptage, pinot gris, chard, chenin, sauv) • 1,000t/2,000cs own label 70% red 28% white 2% rosé • BWI • PO Box 2013 Stellenbosch 7601 • info@louiesenhof.co.za • www.louiesenhof.co.za • S 33° 53'34.7" E 018° 49'35.3" • **T +27 (0)21-865-2632/+27 (0)21-889-5550 (JIR)** • F +27 (0)21-865-2613

This Stellenbosch winery was two decades ahead of the pack in some ways. Stefan Smit was making a 'bio-organic wine' as far back as 1991. In keeping with established Cape tradition, though, there's also brandy in the range, and solid sweet reds to complement the standard output.

Pinotage ▤ ★★ **09** fresh, uncomplicated quaffing. All of these wines tasted few years back, apart from Bordeaux Blend, Roobernet & Sauvignon. **Cabernet Sauvignon-Cabernet Franc** ★★★ Prune fruit too modest to cover **06**'s oak frame & firm acidity. **Bordeaux Blend Premier Collection** NEW ★★★★ Mature **05** still fresh, with aromatic lift from cab franc & spicy, ripe fruit flavours to plump up dry, savoury conclusion. **Cape Blend** ▤ ★★ **09** pinotage, cab; juicy but brief flavours. **Perroquet Merlot Pétillant Rosé** ▤ ★★ **08** off-dry quaffer. **Chardonnay Sur-Lie** ▤ ★★★ Uncomplicated, tropical **08**. **Sauvignon Blanc** ▤ ★★★ **11** with unlingering tropical flavours for pleasant summertime sipping. **Sweet Red** ★★ Individual **NV** fortified dessert. **Perroquet Cape Tawny** ★★★★ **NV** rustic glow-inducer from tinta, with savoury touches. **Roobernet Cape Ruby** NEW ★★★ Youthful **10** fortified has spicy, medicinal notes. Pleasantly dry, dusty impression despite typical sweetness of style. — IM

Louis

Location/WO: Stellenbosch ▪ Est/1stB 2007 ▪ Closed to public ▪ Owner(s) Louis Nel ▪ Cellarmaster(s)/winemaker(s) Louis Nel (Jan 2007) ▪ 15t/1,500cs own label 50% red 50% white + 600cs for clients ▪ Brands for clients: Collaboration (Overture restaurant) ▪ 3 Chestnut Lane Stellenbosch 7600 ▪ louis@louiswines.com ▪ www.louiswines.com ▪ **T** +27 (0)21-889-5555

Louis Nel's resourceful mom used red wine to colour the icing on his first birthday cake (charmingly depicted on one of the wine labels). This creative spirit continues to shine in all his wines, from the two special Cape Winemakers Guild wines, Rebel Rebel and Turtles All the Way Down, to his Louis and Black Forest brands. Notwithstanding his success, Louis remains refreshingly humble, attributing success to sticking to the basics and respecting the grapes.

★★★★ **Cabernet Sauvignon 08** (★★★★★) raises the bar on **07**. Sweet reward from reprieved vineyard, the abundant blackcurrant fruit is suavely tailored, with supple tannin & oak structure. Silky texture tempts earlier enjoyment but complexity & fruit depth deserve good few years cellaring.

Cabernet Sauvignon-Merlot ✓ ★★★★ Ripe & succulent **08** is a step on **07** (★★★). Well groomed & streamlined but brimming with mint-tinged, juicy fruit. Bottled yumminess that will grace both table & cellar. **Sauvignon Blanc** Latest **11** missed our deadline. — MW

■ **Louis Fourie** see Linton Park Wines

Louisvale Wines

Location/map: Stellenbosch ▪ WO: Stellenbosch/Coastal ▪ Est/1stB 1989 ▪ Tasting, sales & cellar tours Mon-Fri 10-5 ▪ Fee R20 ▪ Closed all pub hols ▪ BYO picnic ▪ Owner(s) Louisvale Wines (Pty) Ltd ▪ Directors Altmann Allers, Hendrik Kluever, Johann Kirsten & Zane Meyer ▪ Winemaker(s)/viticulturist(s) Simon Smith (Jul 1997) ▪ 34ha/23ha (cab, merlot, chard) ▪ 220t/8,000cs own label 40% red 60% white ▪ PO Box 542 Stellenbosch 7599 ▪ winery@louisvale.com ▪ www.louisvale.com ▪ S 33° 54' 32.3" E 018° 48' 24.3" ▪ **T** +27 (0)21-865-2422 ▪ F +27 (0)21-865-2633

Louisvale's focus on chardonnay goes back to the earliest days in the late 1980s, when the property was owned by 'businessmen refugees from Johannesburg'. Ownership changed in 2002, and again in 2010, when it was bought by a company led by a four-strong team of 'friends and associates in diverse business environments'. Red grapes have long been sourced from a neighouring property and, from 2011 they will also take in grapes 'from a sister farm in Wellington'.

Chardonnay Unwooded ☺ ★★★ Easy-going **11** tasted ex-tank; vibrant with fresh green apple character leading to zesty finish. WO Coastal. **Stone Road Sauvignon Blanc** ☺ 🗐 ★★★ **11** sample shows flavour spectrum from greenpepper to gooseberry. Not complex, but lively, fresh, clean & enjoyable.

Stone Road Cabernet Sauvignon ★★★ Accessible, balanced **08** tasted last year. **Stone Road Merlot** ★★☆ Enjoyably rustic, firm & dry **10** sample. **Dominique** ★★★ Varietal make-up changes here. **09** a powerful, fleshy cab/shiraz blend, with rich fruit & firm tannin; moderate oaking. **Chardonnay** ★★★★ **10** the richest of the 3 chardonnays; 6 months half-new oak well integrated adding nutty complexity to citrus & spice. **Chavant** ✓ ★★★★ Crowd-pleasing **11** lightly oaked & light-bodied; lemon, apricot & floral notes, elegant soft finish. — JPf

Lourensford Wine Estate

Location: Somerset West ▪ Map: Helderberg ▪ WO: Stellenbosch/Western Cape ▪ Est 1999 ▪ 1stB 2003 ▪ Tasting, sales & cellar tours daily 9.30-4.30 ▪ Fee R25 ▪ Closed Easter Fri & Dec 25 ▪ The Restaurant @ Lourensford open daily 8-5 (see Restaurants section) ▪ Tour groups ▪ Art exhibition ▪ Coffee Roastery ▪ Cheesery ▪ Jewellery ▪ Conference facilities ▪ Conservation area ▪ Owner(s) Christo Wiese ▪ Cellarmaster(s) Chris Joubert (Oct 2007) ▪ Winemaker(s) Hannes Nel (Nov 2002), with Timothy Witbooi (May 2005) ▪ Viticulturist(s) Ronel Bester (Apr 2006) ▪ 4,000ha/217ha (cab, merlot, shiraz, chard, sauv, viog) ▪ 1,600t/120,000cs own label 40% red 58% white 2% rosé ▪ Brands for clients: Eden Crest (Checkers), Matumi (UK), Pracht Gaarden (Belgium), River Crossing (UK & Ireland) ▪ BRC, BWI champion, HACCP ▪ PO Box 16 Somerset West 7129 ▪ info@lourensford.co.za ▪ www.lourensford.com ▪ S 34° 4' 3.7" E 018° 53' 44.2" ▪ **T** +27 (0)21-847-2300 ▪ F + 27 (0)21-847-0910

This sprawling 4,000ha Somerset West property, owned by businessman Christo Wiese, has become a 'must visit' destination with entertainment for all - in and outdoors: aside from the permanent amenities listed above, there are mountain bike events, morning fresh produce markets, music and drama productions, even big expos. 'The past year has been good for us,' says general manager Koos Jordaan, 'and sales volumes year on year are up. Our River Garden range is doing very well, world-wide, because I think we deliver exceptional value for money. We have had very positive feedback from all our markets and media about the progress the brands have made in terms of quality and style. We continue focus on product development and a better understanding of terroir as a young brand.'

Loursford 1700 range

★★★★☆ **White Blend** 🅱 Blend of best barrel-fermented (older oak) sauvignon, chardonnay & viognier, **10** (★★★★) delivers intense tropical fruit & florals supported by subtle vanilla oak. Ageworthy, but not the complexity of **09**.

Red Blend In abeyance.

Loursford range

★★★★ **Cabernet Sauvignon** 🅱 Vibrant plum hue, ripe & smoky blackcurrant/floral note on **09** last year. Juicy, with soft oak influence, peppery aftertaste, fine profile.

★★★★ **Merlot** 🅱 🅱 Deep ruby **10** (★★★★), trumped by **09**, offers plum pudding, pepper & smoke. Grainy finish needs food or time.

★★★★ **Wine Makers Selection Syrah** Fruit-packed preview **09** (★★★★★) followed oaky **07** last year. Mulberry & brambleberry with savoury/earthy nuances & dry tannic grip. Soupçons merlot, cab & viognier added complexity & panache.

★★★★★ **Shiraz** 🅱 When last tasted, medium-bodied **08** offered intense & fragrant fruit, smoky & herbal notes & a long complex finish.

★★★★☆ **Shiraz-Mourvèdre-Viognier** ✓ 🅱 'Shiraz-Viognier' last time. **09** (★★★★) not same complexity as **08**, smoky, spicy notes & rich plummy fruit, good balance & earthy finish. Needs year/2. WO W Cape.

★★★★☆ **Chardonnay** ✓ 🅱 🅱 **10** (★★★★) shade off **09**, combines bright Granny Smith apple & lime fruit. Fresh, smooth & juicy, carefully oaked. Lovely balance. Lime marmalade note waves goodbye.

★★★★ **Wine Makers Selection Sauvignon Blanc** ✓ 🅱 **11**'s cool, fragrant white peach, gooseberry, lime fruit provides good structure for elegant offering. Dry, full & complex. Deserves time to reach potential.

★★★★ **Sauvignon Blanc** ✓ 🅱 🅱 **11** crammed with exuberant fruit: lime, gooseberry & nettle. Dry, with balance & depth - excellent food match. 10% semillon.

★★★★ **Wine Makers Selection Viognier** ✓ 🅱 Fine varietal character on single-vineyard **10**, spicy peach flavours enriched by creamy, subtle vanilla oak. Versatile with rich fish & poultry.

★★★★ **Méthode Cap Classique** Last a preview, chard/pinotage **07** striking green sheen & fine mousse. Crisp appley brioche from 36 months lees-ageing. Fresh & smooth, biscuity finish.

★★★★☆ **Semillon Noble Late Harvest** Unctuous botrytis dessert, **09** last year delighted with typical dried peach aroma & complex nuances of green tea & cedarwood. Long, juicy orange marmalade finish well balanced by fine acidity.

Wine Makers Selection Chardonnay Untasted.

River Garden range

★★★★ **Cabernet Sauvignon-Merlot** 🅱 Unexpectedly UN-tutti-frutti, **10** actually a fine glass of red with serious fruit concentration & a leafy pepper note previous edition.

★★★★ **Rosé** ✓ 🅱 🅱 Off-dry **11** (★★★★) from mourvèdre & shiraz offers zesty strawberries. Lively, light & friendly anytime rosé. Off the pace of **10**.

> **Chardonnay** ☺ 🅱 🅱 ★★★ Unwooded **11** crisp & limy, light & undemanding.

Shiraz-Cabernet Sauvignon 🅱 🅱 ★★★★ Last tasted **10** a Cinderella transformation after vin ordinaire **08** (★★★). Fragrant ripe plums, juicy berries heralding bold extrovert personality. **09** untasted. WO W Cape, as for Cab-Merlot. **Sauvignon Blanc** 🅱 🅱 ★★★ **11** step down from **10** (★★★★), straightforward green fruit flavours with a dry ending. — WB

Lovane Boutique Wine Estate

Location/map/WO: Stellenbosch ▪ Est 2003 ▪ 1stB 2006 ▪ Tasting, sales & cellar tours Mon-Sun 10-5 ▪ Tasting fee R20, waived on purchase ▪ Closed all pub hols ▪ Conferences ▪ Guesthouse & cottage ▪ Owner(s)/viticulturist(s) Philip & Gail Gous ▪ Winemaker(s) Philip Gous (2006), with Gail Gous (2006) ▪ 3.6ha/2.5ha (cabs s/f, p verdot) ▪

20t/1,400cs own label 90% red 5% white 5% rosé ▪ PO Box 91 Vlottenburg 7604 ▪ info@lovane.co.za ▪ www.lovane.co.za ▪ S 33° 57'09.74" E 018° 48'02.38" ▪ **T +27 (0)21-881-3827** ▪ F +27 (0)21-881-3546

This 3.6ha smallholding between established heavyweights Overgaauw and Neethlingshof was virgin earth when the Gouws family planted 2.5ha of it, mainly with cabernet, in 2003. Winemaking followed in 2006 and it now boasts a 4-star guest house and self-catering cottage, and chic conferencing amenities.

★★★★ **Cabernet Sauvignon Umbhidi Wholeberry** Fine **07** had a smoky oak depth to its juicy dark berries - with a buzz of supportive tannin - when tasted last year.

★★★★☆ **Isikhati** Cab-led **07** - with tiny but telling input from petit verdot & cab franc - was youthfully tight with a wealth of rich fruit promise previously.

Cabernet Sauvignon Isivuno ★★★★ Last tasted was mineral **06**. **Cabernet Franc Iliwa** ★★★★ **06**, with spicy interest, not retasted. **Petit Verdot Umama** ★★★★ Moderate alc & quiet vinosity, **06** satisfied previously. **Shiraz Lovane** ★★★★ **07** skipped, but **08** bounces back with perfume scents & chocolate warmth to big structure (34 months oak!). **Summer Mist** Next awaited. **Unfiltered Blanc de Noir** 🆕 ★★ Onionskin-hued, dry **10**, cherry fruit of cabernet lifts appeal. **Méthode Cap Classique** ★★★★ Dry NV sparkler returns in pink form (now from cab), last was a chardonnay. Latest bone-dry & refreshing, albeit loose-grained. Discontinued: **Blanc de Noir**. — DS

■ **Luca & Ingrid Bein** *see* Bein Wine Cellar

Luddite Wines

Location: Bot River ▪ Map: Elgin, Walker Bay & Bot River ▪ WO: Western Cape ▪ Est 1999 ▪ 1stB 2000 ▪ Tasting, sales & cellar tours Mon-Fri 9-1 or by appt Sat/Sun & pub hols by appt ▪ Charcuterie meats ▪ Walks/hikes & mountain biking ▪ Owner(s) Niels Verburg & Hillie Meyer ▪ Cellarmaster(s)/winemaker(s) Niels Verburg (1999) ▪ Viticulturist(s) Penny Verburg (1999) ▪ 17ha/5.5ha (cab, mourv, shiraz) ▪ 40t/2,500cs own label 100% red + 2,000cs for clients ▪ Brands for clients: Benguela Cove, Elgin Vintners, Ridgelands ▪ PO Box 656 Bot River 7185 ▪ luddite@telkomsa.net ▪ www.luddite.co.za ▪ S 34° 12'50.5" E 019° 12'24.1" ▪ **T +27 (0)28-284-9308/+27 (0)83-444-3537** ▪ F +27 (0)28-284-9045

Being Luddites, innovation is not high on Niels and Penny Verburg's agenda. But they do admit to supplementing their reds-only plantings by adding Chenin Blanc, believing their location on the slopes of the Houw Hoek Mountains near Bot River is suited to it. Two successive dry vintages might have affected grape yields but the interest in the charcuterie from their free-ranging pigs continues. Verburg quips that he delivers more meat than wine these days!

★★★★☆ **Shiraz** Powerful **07** (but just 14% alc) tasted last ed elegant & fresh. Dark fruit mingles with crushed black pepper, oriental spices. Broad palate, finely textured tannin; subtle oak (just 25% new). Lengthy finish. Stbosch, Bot R grapes. — FM

LuKa Wine Estate

Location/WO: Plettenberg Bay ▪ Map: Klein Karoo & Garden Route ▪ Est 2008 ▪ 1stB 2011 ▪ Tasting in Dec, Mar/Apr or by appt ▪ Owner(s) Hennie & Anita Kritzinger ▪ Cellarmaster(s)/winemaker(s) Anton Smal (Bramon Wines) ▪ Viticulturist(s) Hennie Kritzinger ▪ ±7ha/1.5ha (sauv) ▪ ±3t/211cs own label 100% white ▪ PO Box 2519 Plettenberg Bay 6600 ▪ henita@telkomsa.net ▪ www.lukawines.co.za ▪ S 34° 2'28.14" E 023° 15'57.56" ▪ **T +27 (0)82-457-8110/+27 (0)82-332-3299** ▪ F +27 (0)44-533-6782

Another fledgling winemaking venture along the southern Cape coast around holiday hotspot Plettenberg Bay: Hennie and Anita Kritzinger's small 'semi-retirement' property overlooking the Knysna Elephant Park. A love of 'space, gardening and a good wine' resulted in the planting of 3,000 sauvignon vines a few years ago. Vinified by Anton Smal (ex Villiera, now based at local Bramon Wines), the brand is an amalgam of the names of the Kritzingers' grandchildren, Luca and Kate.

Sauvignon Blanc 📖 ★★★ Fresh, fruity **11**, delicate & balanced, grassy & zesty conclusion. — Panel

■ **Lula Afrika** *see* Halala Afrika/Lula Afrika

Lusan Premium Wines

Closed to public ▪ clkirsten@distell.co.za ▪ **T +27 (0)21-883-8988** ▪ F +27 (0)21-883-8941

Umbrella organisation for Alto, Le Bonheur, Neethlingshof, Stellenzicht (and its value brand Hill & Dale) and Uitkyk (including Flat Roof Manor). See individual entries.

■ **Luscious Hippos** *see* United Nations of Wine

Lutzville Cape Diamond Vineyards

Location/WO: Lutzville ▪ Map: Olifants River ▪ Est 1961 ▪ 1stB 1980 ▪ Tasting, sales & tours Mon-Fri 9-5 Sat 10-2 ▪ Closed Sun, Easter Sat, Dec 25 & Jan 1 ▪ Coffee shop Mon-Fri 9-4 Sat 10-1 ▪ Function/conference venue ▪ Owner(s) Lutzville Cape Diamond Vineyards ▪ Cellarmaster(s) Gideon Theron (Nov 2005) ▪ Winemaker(s) Roy Thorne (Jan 2008), Jaco van Niekerk (Sep 2009) & Kenneth Wiley (Jun 2010) ▪ Viticulturist(s) Gideon Engelbrecht (Sep 2009) ▪ 2,100ha (cab, merlot, ptage, pinot, ruby cab, shiraz, chard, chenin, cbard, nouvelle, sauv, sem, viog) ▪ ±42,000t/ 112,000cs own label 11% red 89% white ▪ BRC ▪ PO Box 50 Lutzville 8165 ▪ info@lutzvillevineyards.com ▪ www. lutzvillevineyards.com ▪ S 31° 33'35.9" E 018° 21'0.2" ▪ **T +27 (0)27-217-1516** ▪ F +27 (0)27-217-1435

Cellarmaster Gideon Theron is challenging long-held perceptions about the well-priced wines emanating from the Olifants River Valley, and inviting consumers to take a fresh look in light of the changes they're ringing in vineyard and cellar. Close co-operation with growers and careful vineyard selection are improving quality; now gentler handling of grapes during vinification is set to further enhance this cultivar-driven range of wines.

The Diamond Collection

Cabernet Sauvignon Preview **09** too unformed to rate although shows glimpses blackcurrant & cab's austere backbone. Fruit selection, fraction new oak distinguish reds in range from that below. **Shiraz** 🗏 ★★★★ Sweet vanilla mingles with smoked meat, dark plum & prune on taut & youthful **09**. Dense fruit centre, structured for improvement 3+ years in bottle. **Ebenaezer NEW** 🖉 ★★★★ Six-way pinotage-led blend. Pre-bottling, **10** ripe & smoky, juicy & supple; fresh acid structure & concentration to improve few years in the cellar. **Chardonnay Wooded** ★★★ Oak influence obvious but not over-the-top on promising peachy **10** preview. **Sauvignon Blanc** 🖉 ★★★★ Step-up **11** powerfully aromatic & vibrant: cool green fruit & khaki bush, zingy freshness, packed with grassy capsicum flavour. Same early picked, light-bodied style as **10** (★★★). **Semillon NEW** 🗏 ★★★★ **10** preview enticing honey, nougat, nectarine aromas; early harvested & well-crafted for elegance & restraint (12.5% alc); may rate higher once bottled.

Cape Diamond range

Shiraz Rosé ☺ 🗏 🖉 ★★★ **11** preview lightish (12.5%) red berry-sipper with candyfloss/cinnamon dusting, strawberry-sweet end.

Cabernet Sauvignon 🗏 🖉 Baked blackcurrant & thatch on unfinished **10**, too young to rate but appealing. Like other reds, oak-staved for complexity. **Merlot** 🗏 🖉 ★ **10** astringent & green, lacks juiciness, bright acidity of previous. **Pinotage** 🗏 🖉 ★★★ Ripe & juicy **10** best of red line-up with typical mulberry, plummy notes; lively acidity. Slips down easily. **Shiraz** 🗏 🖉 ★★ Estery red fruit & toast on **10**; 14% alc warms the finish. **Chardonnay** ★★ **11** sample has some rough edges that should even out before bottling; is showing lovely pear/ lemon flavours. As with other samples, rating provisional. **Chenin Blanc** 🗏 🖉 **11** preview too young to score. **Sauvignon Blanc** 🗏 🖉 ★★★ Step-up **11** sample light & crisp with typical grassy notes, wonderful weight & pithy lees influence. **Muscadel** ✓ ★★★★ **10** from muscadel billows honey, barley sugar, litchees year on, has benefited from year in bottle. Rich & full but light-footed; uncloying delight. Discontinued: **Ruby Cabernet**, **Johannisberger**.

Cape Elephant Natural Sweet range

Red 🗏 Untasted. **Rosé** 🗏 ★★ Dash muscat d'A in low alc (8%), strawberry-infused **11** sipper; unashamedly sweet. This & next previewed. **White** 🗏 ★★★ **11** tropical fruit melange colombard & muscat d'A; invigorating lemon twist in tail. — Panel

Lyngrove

Location: Somerset West ▪ Map: Helderberg ▪ WO: Stellenbosch ▪ Est/1stB 2000 ▪ Tasting & sales by appt ▪ 5-star Lyngrove Country House (see Accommodation section) ▪ Conferences (12 pax) ▪ Walking/hiking trail (5km) ▪ Owner(s) Baarsma's Holdings B.V. ▪ Winemaker(s) Hannes Louw & Danielle le Roux (Jun 2006) ▪ Viticulturist(s) John Fullard ▪ 76ha (cab, merlot, p verdot, ptage, shiraz, chard, chenin, sauv) ▪ 50,000cs own label 70% red 20% white 10% rosé ▪ WIETA ▪ PO Box 7275 Stellenbosch 7599 ▪ wine@lyngrove.co.za ▪ www.lyngrove.co.za ▪ S 34° 1'8.7" E 018° 48' 10.2" ▪ **T +27 (0)21-880-1221** ▪ F +27 (0)21-880-0851

'A meal without wine is like a day without sunshine,' agree Danielle le Roux and Hannes Louw, co-winemakers at this brand in the Baarsma stable. Attempting to 'delight every wine lover' through three tiers of wine, their aim is for the most serious Platinum tier to 'reflect the character and soul of Lyngrove' with its upmarket guest lodge.

Platinum range

★★★★ **Latitude** Mainly cab fleshed out with touch merlot. Classic cedar & blackcurrant in **08** tasted previous edition, abundant sweet fruit checked by fresh acidity.

Pinotage ★★★★ Elegant, judiciously oaked **09**, dry & savoury, with plenty of freshness & bright red-fruit flavour. **Shiraz** ★★★★ Savoury, spicy **08** tasted last ed included dollop pinotage. Juicy red fruit cut by assertive acidity; missed complexity of **05** (★★★★). Discontinued: **Chardonnay**.

Reserve range

Shiraz-Pinotage 🗎 ★★★ **08** blend tasted previously showed smoky spiciness & ripe fruit, gathered by firm acidity. Also bottled under cork. **Chardonnay** ✓ 🗎 ★★★★ Seductively oaked **10** is agreeably fruity, time on lees adding breadth & complexity to charming, easy style.

Lyngrove Collection

Cabernet Sauvignon ☺ 🗎 🖾 ★★★ Ripe red fruit & herb appeal in **10**, firm texture invites robust/ meaty dishes. **Merlot** ☺ 🗎 🖾 ★★★ Herbal-edged **10**, abundant sweet fruit flavours, acidity providing fresh & savoury conclusion. **Pinotage** ☺ 🗎 🖾 ★★★ Dark, juicy, mocha-laced **10**'s ripeness pleasingly balanced by savoury freshness. **Chenin Blanc** ☺ 🗎 🖾 ★★★ Light & tasty **11** shows easy fruitiness. Ideal lunchtime wine. **Sauvignon Blanc** ☺ 🗎 🖾 ★★★ Reliably fresh, fragrant & well made. **11** vibrant, with ageing on lees adding a touch of balancing richness.

Shiraz 🗎 ★★★ Previously tasted **09** in popular ripe mocha style, held by soft tannins & firm acidity. — IM

Lynx Wines

Location/map/WO: Franschhoek ▪ Est/1stB 2002 ▪ Tasting, sales & cellar tours Mon-Fri 10–5 Sat/Sun & pub hols by appt ▪ Fee R30 (tasting & tour) ▪ BYO picnic ▪ Owner(s) Vista Hermosa (Pty) Ltd ▪ Cellarmaster(s) Dieter Sellmeyer (Jan 2002) ▪ Winemaker(s) Dieter Sellmeyer (Jan 2002), with Helgard van Schalkwyk (Nov 2010) ▪ Viticulturist(s) Theunis Brandt (Apr 2000) ▪ 26ha/11ha (cabs s/f, grenache, merlot, shiraz, viog) ▪ 90t/3,200cs own label 80% red 5% white 15% rosé ▪ IPW ▪ PO Box 566 Franschhoek 7690 ▪ winemaker@lynxwines.co.za ▪ www.lynxwines.co.za ▪ S 33° 51' 46.1" E 019° 2' 14.6" ▪ **T +27 (0)21-867-0406** ▪ F +27 (0)21-867-0397

Highlight of Franschhoek boutique vintner Dieter Sellmeyer's first ever European roadshow was a standing ovation and the sale of a pallet of wine in one evening in a packed yacht club in Denmark. 'Very satisfying!' comments the former engineer, who's encouraged not to mess with a winning formula of early accessible wine 'that expresses the fruit it is made from rather than the barrel that it sat in'.

Premium range

★★★★ **Cabernet Sauvignon** 🖾 **10** concentrated blackcurrant, tobacco & ripe plums. Fine tannins support & balance mouthfilling dark berry fruit. Lingering, grippy finish. Ageworthy.

★★★★ **Cabernet Franc** ✓ 🖾 Richly layered dark berries, herb tea & mint, **10** notable ripe tannins add to complexity on well-structured wine. Rich savoury finish.

★★★★ **Shiraz** 🖾 **10**'s dense, powerful & fruit-sweet. Firm, welcoming tannins offset by balanced acidity & lipsmacking blackberry & herbal finish.

★★★★ **Xanache** ✓ 🖾 Bordeaux blend **10** offers dark blackcurrant, cedar & sour cherry flavours. Mouthfilling, with integrated silky tannins. Yummy!

★★★★☆ **The Lynx** Flagship 09 Bordeaux blend (66% cab) oozes class & finesse. Concentrated, rich fragrant fruit; firmly structured, polished tannins, harmonious & balanced - superb!

★★★★ **Viognier** 🍷 ⌘ Spicy peach & apricot prelude to **10**, elegantly balances fruit with hints of creamy vanilla, finishes on lingering fragrant note.

Grenache 🍷 ⌘ ★★★★ Vibrant ruby, with upfront soft red berries & spice, **10** light-bodied yet serious, with a fresh oaky grip. **Merlot** ✓ 🍷 ★★★★ **10** back to form, packs rich, dark cherries, choc & minty flavours; medium-bodied & gentle, juicy farewell. **SMV** 🍷 ⌘ ★★★★ Mainly shiraz, dollops mourvèdre & viognier. Vibrant fresh red berries & peach blossom, **10** rounded silky tannins with a fresh, lipsmacking berry finish. **Sweet Lynx** ★★★ Last year's preview now bottled, **10** quirky sweet red from cab franc & shiraz, with berry flavours nicely melded.

Classic range

Vino Tinto ☺ 🍷 ⌘ ★★★ Easy-drinking **10** cab blend, improves on previous with upfront friendly berry fruit, savoury tannins, lovely balance. **Viognier Tardio** NEW ☺ 🍷 ⌘ ★★★ Fragrant Natural Sweet-style **11**, peaches & cream flavours, refreshingly dry finish to go with nutty frangipane tart.

Blanc de Noir 🍷 ⌘ ★★★ Palest pink **11** from merlot, delicate semi-dry summer fruit palate, mouthwatering zesty finish. Ideal for summer pool party. **Rosado** 🍷 ⌘ ★★★ Pink **10** cab & shiraz bursting with ripe strawberry flavours & tangy dry finish last edition. — WB

■ **Maankloof** see Mountain River Wines

Maastricht Estate

Location/WO: Durbanville ▪ Est 1702 ▪ 1stB 2009 ▪ Closed to public ▪ Owner(s) Wheaty Louw ▪ Cellarmaster(s) Thys Louw (Jan 2009) & Mari van der Merwe (Jan 2009) ▪ Viticulturist(s) Wheaty Louw (1986) ▪ 105ha (cab, ptage, shiraz, sauv) ▪ ±1,100t/1,500cs own label 40% red 60% white ▪ wine@maastricht.co.za ▪ **T +27 (0)21-975-1995** ▪ F +27 (0)21-976-7013

When developing new markets, it helps if your farm is named for a city in a country that produces very little wine itself. More so if both have a rich history. That's what the Louw family discovered when wines from their storied estate (circa 1702) landed in Maastricht, the Netherlands. Interest was high, and even the mayor attended the launch.

★★★★☆ **Pinotage** ✓ ⌘ Appealing curry leaf spicing, banana & strawberry on otherwise sterner **10** (★★★★), a serious but tight & oak-dominated wine mid-2011. Could match rating of silky & exuberant **09** if grip softens, wood integrates. Exceptional value, as all below.

★★★★☆ **Shiraz** ✓ 🍷 ⌘ Wet earth & raspberry nuances on baked plum fruit in **10** (★★★★). Medium bodied & supple, savoury but leafy, too. Shade of **09**'s exceptional fruit purity, depth & complexity.

★★★★ **Sauvignon Blanc** ✓ 🍷 ⌘ Good effort in difficult vintage, **11** (★★★☆) is green fruited, with all of **10**'s (★★★★☆) stony minerality but somewhat less of its ripe flavour & complexity, which in turn was an improvement on elegant debut **09**.

Cabernet Sauvignon NEW ✓ ⌘ ★★★★ Seductive mint & eucalyptus on blackcurrant-infused **10**. Well rounded & voluptuous, velvet finish. Nudges next level. — CvZ

■ **Mack Daddy** see Linton Park Wines

Mac's Hill Winery

Location: Malmesbury ▪ Map: Swartland ▪ Est 2004 ▪ 1stB 2005 ▪ Tasting by appt ▪ Closed all pub hols ▪ BYO picnic ▪ Facilities for children ▪ Olive & lavender oils ▪ Owner(s) Rick & Colleen McCrindle ▪ Winemaker(s)/viticulturist(s) Rick McCrindle ▪ 29ha (cab, cinsaut, shiraz, zinf, chenin, viog) ▪ 165t/250cs 100% red ▪ PO Box 630 Malmesbury 7299 ▪ hillsidevineyards@megaserve.net ▪ S 33° 29' 38.6"   E 018° 39' 29.4" ▪ **T +27 (0)22-485-7035** ▪ F +27 (0)22-485-7035

Most of the grapes off Rick and Colleen McCrindle's farm outside Malmesbury go to Swartland Winery, but Rick has made a few interesting blends over the years. All that we have previously listed are now sold out, and there's nothing new. 'We have a Cabernet and a Shiraz, both 2009,' says Rick, 'but not ready for tasting.'

■ **Madre's Kitchen** see Robert Stanford Estate

Maiden Wine Cellars

Location: Gordon's Bay ▪ Est 1995 ▪ 1stB 1999 ▪ Tasting/tours by appt; also tailor-made wine tours (max 6 people) ▪ Owner(s) Danie Hattingh ▪ 1,500cs 100% red ▪ PO Box 185 Gordon's Bay 7151 ▪ mwines@mweb.co.za ▪ www. maidenwines.co.za ▪ **T +27 (0)82-554-9395** ▪ F +27 (0)86-688-1177

Sales in America and Malaysia secure, exporter Danie Hattingh has been making headway in Angola; China, where they've appointed a South African as agent; and Poland. A new second label with the catchy name Iwayini, which means wine in Xhosa and Zulu, was developed specifically for these new markets.

Main Street Winery

Location: Paarl ▪ Est/1stB 1999 ▪ Tasting & tours by appt ▪ Owner(s)/winemaker(s) Marais de Villiers ▪ 700cs 50% red 50% white ▪ PO Box 2709 Paarl 7620 ▪ mainstreet@mweb.co.za ▪ **T +27 (0)21-872-3006** ▪ F +27 (0)21-872-3006

Marais de Villiers, purveyor of cellar equipment and production process advice to establishing wine producers, makes an occasional batch under his own name. In between, he's focusing on several properties in the Swartland, where he has a southern Rhône-style blend in barrel.

Main Street ★★ Bdx blend **05** bright cherry-red hue, herbal fruit & earthy note pvsly. — GdB

Maison

Location/map/WO: Franschhoek ▪ Est 2005 ▪ 1stB 2008 ▪ Tasting & sales Wed-Sun 10-5 ▪ Closed Dec 25 ▪ The Kitchen @ Maison (fusion bistro): lunch 12-5 ▪ Owner(s) Chris Weylandt & Kim Smith ▪ Winemaker(s)/viticulturist(s) Antwan Bondesio ▪ 11ha/4.5ha (shiraz, chard, chenin, viog) ▪ 50% red 50% white ▪ PO Box 587 Franschhoek 7690 ▪ sales@maisonestate.co.za ▪ www.maisonestate.co.za ▪ S 33°53'09.7" E 019° 4'39.80" ▪ **T +27 (0)21-876-2116** ▪ F +27 (0)21-876-2116

'Good living' is the philosophy of Maison co-owners Chris Weylandt (also founder and CEO of one of South Africa's leading furniture and homeware retailers) and partner Kim Smith. Hence the opening last year of fusion bistro The Kitchen at the store in Durbanville, and now at the wine estate in Franschhoek. Aside from the bottlings below, reflecting Weylandt's 'natural and contemporary' style, the new venue will also offer olive oil and lemon juice produced à la maison.

Vin Maison range
★★★★ **Shiraz** Modern **10** (★★★★) a tad jammy, with overt 15% alc, not as reined in as delicious, spicy **09**, Young Wine Show class winner.

Chenin Blanc ✓ ★★★★ Opulent **10** in tropical style, but with measured weight & enough freshness to retain elegance. Satisfies above its price point. — DS

Maison de Teijger   NEW

Location: Durbanville ▪ WO: Durbanville/Bottelary/Stellenbosch ▪ Est/1stB 2004 ▪ Closed to public ▪ Owner(s)/cellarmaster(s) Charl van Teijlingen ▪ Winemaker(s) Charl van Teijlingen, with Danél, Matthew & Elda-Marie van Teijlingen (all 2004) ▪ 6-9t/325-400cs own label 100% red ▪ PO Box 2703 Durbanville 7550 ▪ charlvt@kingsley. co.za ▪ **T +27 (0)83-456-9410** ▪ F +27 (0)21-975-0806

For Cape Wine Master Charl van Teijlingen it was a 'natural progression' to go from studying wine to specialising in anaesthetics to making his own healthy, natural soporific. Working since 2004 in his De Tyger Street home double-garage with a few tons of classic red varieties winkled from prime vineyards, the 'daredevil garagiste and his slaves' (wife Danél, children Matthew and Elda-Marie) are marketing their maiden selections off-site through group tastings such as wine clubs.

Stellenbosch range
Cabernet Sauvignon ★★★ Part of a tasting pack of components for Bordeaux-style red blend below sourced from selected Stellenbosch estates. **09** cab is from Cloetesdal; sweet blackcurrant, espresso & spice, tannic & charry. **Cabernet Franc** ✓ ★★★★ Darker fruit on well-structured **09**, full flavoured, solid vanilla oak & warm dustiness. From Bellevue, as for next. **Malbec ★★★ 09** full bodied & powerfully constructed, impressive berry

aromas, mouthfilling bramble fruit & oak. **Merlot** ✓ ★★★★ Bursting with ripe berries, **09** is serious yet supple, balanced, lingering vanilla finish. From Bottelary Hills farm Mesco, as next. **Petit Verdot** ★★★ Attractive spicy dark berries, **09** noticeable chunky oak & firm tail. **Voorout Bordeaux Blend** ✓ ★★★★ Malbec & merlot headline the blend from above Stellenbosch farms. Appropriately, **09** most complex of pack; dark berry fruit, firm structure & balance; promising but needs time to reveal charms.

Durbanville range

★★★★ **Malbec Diemersal** ✓ Pick of the pack is from Diemersdal. Fresh & complex **09**, good concentration of dark berries, rich spicy tobacco. Structured & balanced, excellent varietal expression bodes well.

Cabernet Sauvignon (Fermicru XL) ★★★ Part of 9-bottle tasting pack from top Durbanville estates, culminating in Bordeaux-style blend below. This from De Vallei/Morgenster, as next. Red fruit & blackcurrant, **09** fermented with Fermicru XL yeast. **Cabernet Sauvignon (NT 112)** ★★★ **09** fermented with NT 112 yeast is darker, brooding, integrated vanilla oak & savoury finish. **Cabernet Franc** ✓ ★★★★ Bramble, tobacco & violet notes on big **09**. Rich & smooth, warm slightly astringent finish. From Groot Roosboom farm. **Malbec Bloemendal** ✓ ★★★★ **09** oozes ripe plummy spice cake, creamy dark berry & chocolate. Full & rounded, firm finish. From Bloemendal. **Merlot Klein Roosboom** ★★★ Very ripe minty plums on sweet & spirity **09** from Klein Roosboom farm. **Merlot Meerendal** ★★ Porty & overripe **09**, not for the faint-hearted (16% alc). Meerendal grapes. **Petit Verdot** ★★★ Green spicy notes, **09** solid dark-berry fruit & obvious oak influence. Uncomplicated red from De Grendel. **Voorout Bordeaux Blend** ★★★ The Van Teijlingens settled on blend fronted by merlot, petit verdot & malbec for their 7-farm Durbanville **09** flagship. It's big & warm, touch rustic, needs time or food. — Panel

▪ **Makulu** ▪ see Imbuko Wines
▪ **Malagas Wine Company** see Sijnn
▪ **Malan de Versailles** ▪ see Versailles

Malan Family Vintners

Unpretentious easy-drinkers from the Simonsig estate, for export only.

Cape Rouge 🍷 ★★ A big softy: pleasant allsorts blend, not quite dry but totally easy. **Cape Blanc** 🍷 ★★ Rich, tasty, off-dry colombard-based blend. Both **NV** & from Stellenbosch. — TJ

Malanot Wines

Location/map: Stellenbosch ▪ WO: Western Cape/Stellenbosch ▪ Est/1stB 2006 ▪ Tasting & sales Mon-Sat by appt ▪ Fee R25 ▪ Cellar tours by appt & during harvest only ▪ Owner(s) Malanot cc ▪ Cellarmaster(s)/winemaker(s)/viticulturist(s) Marius Malan (Jan 2006) ▪ 3ha/1.5ha (cab) ▪ 60t/5,000cs own label 50% red 50% white + 1,000cs for clients ▪ Brands for clients: Selma ▪ PO Box 22 Lynedoch 7603 ▪ info@malanotwines.co.za ▪ www.malanotwines.co.za ▪ S 33° 59' 57.8" E 018° 49' 55.2" ▪ **T +27 (0)72-124-7462**

Marius Malan is spreading his activities around the Cape as a consultant (to previous full-time employer Slaley, among others) and own-brand vintner. His mainly-for-export range has grown, with some promising blends and varietal bottlings also available locally. He's enrolled in the Cape Wine Masters programme, and plans a wine warehouse selling Malanot and selected other brands.

Vior range

★★★★ **Cherry Blossom** NEW ✓ 🍷 Debut Rhône-style, shiraz-led blend, **09** shows big promise. Ripe, enticing cherry fruit with silky tannin texture. Paarl & Swartland vines.

Beanotage NEW 🍷 ★★★ New-style chocolate-coffee flavoured **10** for aficionados only. **Cabernet Sauvignon-Merlot** NEW 🍷 ★★★ Pretty, aromatic scents on **10**, with spicy oak condiment to ripe red fruit. Bit lightweight, with brief finish. **Bush Pig** NEW 🍷 ★★★ Seriously conceived **10** oaked chenin is big & full. Restrained fruit, from Wellington, emphasis on leesy weight. **Flower Pot** NEW 🍷 ★★★★ Barrel-fermented chenin/sauvignon-led blend, **10** ex Swartland & Paarl vines is oaky, full bodied & richly leesy. Discontinued: **Cabernet Sauvignon, Pinotage, Shiraz, Chenin Blanc, Sauvignon Blanc**.

Selma range NEW

Shiraz ★★★★ Wholesome, meaty **09** shows serious intent, with black cherry essence on velvet tannins. For Swedish & Norwegian markets. — GdB

▪ **Malgas** see Sijnn

Manley Private Cellar

Location/map: Tulbagh ▪ WO: Tulbagh/Coastal ▪ Est/1stB 2002 ▪ Tasting & sales Mon-Fri 9–5 Sat 10–3 ▪ Fee R25, waived on purchase ▪ Cellar tours by appt ▪ Closed Good Fri & Dec 25 ▪ Luxury B&B ▪ Restaurant ▪ Wedding & conference facilities ▪ Chapel ▪ Walks ▪ Owner(s) Bayaphambili Properties ▪ Winemaker(s)/viticulturist(s) Stefan Hartmann ▪ 38ha/7ha (cab, merlot, ptage, shiraz) ▪ PO Box 318 Tulbagh 6820 ▪ bookings@manleywinelodge.co. za ▪ www.manleywinelodge.co.za ▪ S 33° 16' 15.8" E 019° 8' 43.8" ▪ T +27 (0)23-230-0582 ▪ F +27 (0)23-230-0057

In the UK, the pinotage is pleasing crowds, while local sales are up too. Whether this is because Trevor the resident owl's invitation to visit (see the Thatch House label) is heeded by honeymooners and conference delegates, is moot - but this Tulbagh B&B and winery (75% foreign owned) is upping production accordingly.

★★★★ **Shiraz** 08 (★★★★) is a big spicy mouthful of ripe plum & black fruit. Succulent, but wood (90% French, 20 months) is still a tad dominant, unlike ready-on-release 07 (★★★★).

★★★★ **Merlot-Cabernet Sauvignon** Last edition, 07's dark plum, cherry & chocolate flowed through to accomplished fruit, textured but dry palate.

Cabernet Sauvignon ★★★★ Blackcurrant & bramble spice, 08 intense, ripe yet juicy & enduring, with good density. No 07 of this, other reds. **Merlot** ★★★ Cherry & curry leaf exoticism, 08 lithe structure & spicy finish, integrated oak. **Pinotage** ★★★ Light-bodied 09 differs from last-tasted voluptuous 06 (★★★★): red cherry & smoke appeal, soft tannic grip to end. **Thatch House Red** 🍷 ★★★ Shiraz leads 09 blend with cab, merlot. Bold red fruit, smoke & star anise, soft body & light appeal. **Sauvignon Blanc-Semillon** NEW ★★★ Crisp nettle & herbs, 10 lightly lees-aged & wooded. Coastal WO. **Thatch House White** 🍷 Await new vintage. — FM

▪ **Manor House** *see* Nederburg Wines

MAN Vintners

Location: Stellenbosch/Paarl ▪ WO: Coastal/Paarl/Western Cape ▪ Est 2001 ▪ Tasting & sales by appt ▪ Owner(s) MAN Vintners (Pty) Ltd ▪ Cellarmaster(s) Tyrrel Myburgh (2001) ▪ Winemaker(s) Francois Bezuidenhout (Jul 2011) ▪ 175,000cs own label 60% red 39% white 1% rosé ▪ Other export brand: Essay ▪ PO Box 389 Stellenbosch 7599 ▪ me@manvintners.co.za ▪ www.manvintners.co.za ▪ T +27 (0)21-861-7759 ▪ F +27 (0)21-887-4340

Sweeping into this Stellenbosch/Paarl-based wine partnership's good-value portfolio is a reserve range, taking its name from the Portuguese explorers who spoke of Cabo Tormentoso (Cape of Storms) when rounding the southern tip of Africa. Over the years the partners noticed a great source of old vine grapes being lost in bigger blends. Hey presto, Tormentoso's Old Vine Chenin was born - and went on to glory in the inaugural Top 100 selection.

Tormentoso range NEW

★★★★ **Cabernet Sauvignon** ✓ 🍷 Velvety feel to 09's spicy blackcurrant & light coconut, tobacco touch. Lovely oak platform (50% new) from 10 months ageing. Nuanced, gentle but also firm & supple. A keeper.

★★★★ **Syrah-Mourvèdre** 🍷 Plump black pastille & light violet, 09 bold spicy earthiness & liquorice adds depth to soft mouthfeel. Juicy & rich, with dry, nutty tannin. Persistent aftertaste.

★★★★ **Old Vine Chenin Blanc** 🍷 Rich stonefruit & nectarine, delicious complexity to the big creamy 10 mouthful from 40% new-oak fermentation. Zesty acidity brings balance to the structure.

Mourvèdre ✓ 🍷 ★★★★ Blue & black berry fruit, spicy 09 layered & nuanced with dab shiraz (12%). Elegant, shows fine dry tannin. **Bush Vine Pinotage** 🍷 ★★★★ 09 savoury black cherry fullness balanced by char, liquorice depth. Good intensity & spicy suppleness. WO Paarl for all these.

MAN Vintners range

Old Vine Rosé ☺ 🍷 ★★★ Just 'Rosé' last time. 10 cherry/berry abundance from cinsaut. Full, round, dry & long.

Cabernet Sauvignon ✓ 🍷 🖼 ★★★★ 10 blackcurrant, cocoa & cigarbox with light herbal edge - much like previous. Tactile, juicy, deep & long. WO Coastal for all, unless noted. **Merlot** 🍷 ★★★ Fruitcake, coffee & mulberry spice, 09 last year ticked all boxes: body, texture, drinkability. Tasted like more. **Pinotage** 🍷 🖼 ★★★ 10 cranberry & rhubarb tang. Dab shiraz & American oak add spice, as it did in 09. Medium bodied & very accessible. **Shiraz** ✓ 🍷 🖼 ★★★★ Bold blueberry & cocoa plum on spicy 10, gentle texture & savoury sweet/sour tang. Lengthy. **Chardonnay** 🍷 🖼 ★★★ Light tangerine & melon, 10 creamy texture balanced by light acid. Curvy body, good long finish. **Chenin Blanc** 🍷 📖 ★★★ Tropical guava & bruised apple, **11** fresh & crisp with light acidity. Old bushvines & lees contact make it rich, lengthy. **Cuvée V Chenin Blanc** NEW ✓ 🍷 📖 ★★★★ Elderflower & bruised apple, **11** rich, tangy pineapple. Rounded & full bodied but clean, crisp. **Sauvignon Blanc** 🍷 📖 ★★★ **11** granadilla & sundried pineapple followed by zesty grapefruit tang. Fresh & crisp, dash semillon (10%) like previous. WO W Cape. Discontinued: **Cabernet Sauvignon Reserve**, **Shiraz Reserve**. —FM

■ **Mapoggo** *see* Druk My Niet Wine Estate
■ **Marcel de Reuck** *see* Crows Nest

Marianne Wine Estate

Location: Stellenbosch ▪ Map: Paarl & Wellington ▪ WO: Simonsberg-Paarl/Paarl/Western Cape ▪ Est/1stB 2004 ▪ Tasting, sales & cellar tours Mon-Sat 9–6 Sun 9–5.30 ▪ Fee R20/5 wines, R45/9 wines ▪ Closed Easter Fri, Dec 25 & Jan 1 ▪ Olivello Restaurant (see Restaurants section) ▪ Tour groups ▪ Gift shop ▪ Conference facilities ▪ Art exhibition ▪ 1.5hr 'grape to wine' tour ▪ 4-star B&B guest apartments (see Accommodation section) ▪ Owner(s) Dauriac family ▪ Winemaker(s) Bertus Basson (2010) ▪ Viticulturist(s) André van den Berg (2004) ▪ 36ha/±18ha (cab, merlot, ptage, shiraz, sauv) ▪ 120t/10,000cs own label 90% red 5% white 5% rosé ▪ PO Box 7300 Stellenbosch 7599 ▪ info@mariannewinefarm.co.za ▪ www.mariannewinefarm.co.za ▪ S 33° 49' 57.6" E 018° 53' 37.4" ▪ **T +27 (0)21-875-5040** ▪ F +27 (0)21-875-5036

What's unlikely to change at French-owned Marianne, according to winemaker Bertus Basson, is the wine style: full, rich and big in structure. What has changed is the property's approach to wine tourism: extended opening hours for the tasting room and a 1½ hour 'Grape to Wine' tour of the Simonsberg foothills estate.

Cabernet Sauvignon ★★★★ Dramatic **09** shows blackcurrant & pencil shavings; plenty of fruit weight & power but still in balance thanks to fresh acidity, firm tannins. Better assembled than **08** (★★). **Merlot** ★★★★ Opulent but well-executed **09** displays ultra-ripe red & black fruit, full structure, smooth texture; fresh acidity ensures whole package doesn't overwhelm. More complete than **08** (★★★★). **Pinotage** ★★★ Rustic **09** shows jammy fruit, broad structure, slight bitterness. **Shiraz** ★★★ Unrestrained **09**, huge dark fruit concentration but appears weighty, lacks poise before somewhat astringent finish. **Cape Blend** ★★★ **09** approachable red including 30% pinotage is medium bodied, with juicy red & black fruit, moderate acidity, soft tannins. **Floreal** ★★★★ **09** from 40% cab, 40% merlot, 20% shiraz. Red & black fruit, vanilla flavours, full but balanced, soft tannins; relatively understated in context of big house style, not as oaky as **08** (★★★★). **Rosé** 📖 ★★ **10** light, dry, with soft acidity still selling mid-2011, as for next. **Sauvignon Blanc** 📖 ★★★ Herbal **10**, good palate weight, soft but sufficient freshness. Partly barrel fermented, matured. — CE

■ **Marimba** *see* Southern Sky Wines

Marklew Family Wines

Location/map: Stellenbosch ▪ WO: Simonsberg–Stellenbosch ▪ Est 1970 ▪ 1stB 2003 ▪ Tasting, sales & tours by appt ▪ Tour groups (max 20) ▪ Private/business functions for small groups ▪ Walks ▪ Mountain biking ▪ Conservation area ▪ Owner(s) Marklew family (Edward Dudley, Edward William, Lyn & Haidee) ▪ Winemaker(s) Henri Warren (Jan 2011) ▪ Viticulturist(s) Billy Marklew (Jun 2001), with Henri Warren (Jan 2011) ▪ 58ha/45ha (cabs s/f, merlot, ptage, shiraz, chard, sauv) ▪ ±300t/2,500cs own label 80% red 20% white ▪ IPW ▪ PO Box 17 Elsenburg 7607 ▪ wine@marklew.co.za ▪ www.marklew.co.za ▪ S 33° 50' 35.7" E 018° 51' 50.3" ▪ **T +27 (0)21-884-4412** ▪ F +27 (0)21-884-4412

The past year marked the 10th anniversary of Billy and Haidee Marklew taking the reins from their grape-growing parents at the established spread in Stellenbosch's hallowed Simonsberg wine ward, and the first season in the saddle for winemaking farm manager Henri Warren. Unchanged since maiden vintage 2003, Haidee says, is their terroir-dictated style 'between classical/elegant and modern'.

★★★★ **Cabernet Sauvignon** ✓ **07** in house style: elegant, polished & stylish. Clean blackcurrant flavour, a svelte body. For ageing as well as early enjoyment.

★★★★ **Merlot** ✓ Nuanced **08** is exemplary merlot, with floral silky juiciness, accessible & rewarding but not straightforward. Crafted, & beautiful to drink, as was step-up **07**.

★★★★ **Capensis Reserve 05** blend cab, merlot, shiraz & pinotage was back on form last edition, plush fruit stacked around a strong core, lavish oak fully absorbed. Improved on **04** (★★★★), with assertive tannins.

★★★★ **Chardonnay** ✓ ⊠ New World, certainly - expressive fruit, generous oaking - but with Old-World balance. **10** broad & welcoming, a fine dining partner.

Cape Flora Pinotage ✓ ★★★★ Evocative of (boot) leather & polish, **10** plummy fruit still toe-capped with strong tannin, needs plenty of time to soften. — DS

Mary Le Bow Trust

Location: Cape Town ▪ 1stB 2005 ▪ Wine sales Mon-Fri 8.30-4 ▪ Owner(s) The Frater Family ▪ Winemaker(s) Bruce Jack ▪ 258cs own label 100% red ▪ PO Box 3636 Somerset West 7129 ▪ catherine@terraceroad.com ▪ **T +27 (0)79-522-0597** ▪ F +27 (0)86-763-0960

The Mary Le Bow brand is owned by a trust, the beneficiaries of which are the Frater and Jack children: grapes come from Wildepaardekloof farm near Ashton owned by the Frater family; the winemaker Bruce Jack of Flagstone fame, the late James Frater and Jack having been good friends, and Jack godfather of Frater's daughter. Chris Keet (viticultural consultant for Flagstone's owners Accolade Wines) lends his experience in the vineyards.

★★★★★ **Mary le Bow** Elegant **07** blend still selling. Mint, chocolate-dipped raspberry & cassis; fine tannins, taut backbone from cab; dollops merlot & shiraz, dash cab franc promise complexity. — CE

Maske Wines

Location: Wellington ▪ Map: Paarl & Wellington ▪ WO: Wellington/Western Cape ▪ Est/1stB 2000 ▪ Tasting & sales Mon-Sun by appt ▪ Closed Ash Wed, Easter Fri/Sun & Dec 25 ▪ BYO picnic ▪ Owner(s) Erich Maske ▪ Winemaker(s)/viticulturist(s) Outsourced ▪ 7ha/5ha (cab, merlot, chenin) ▪ 80% red 20% white, blends outsourced ▪ Klein Waterval PO Box 206 Wellington 7654 ▪ laureat@iafrica.com ▪ www.maskewines.co.za ▪ S 33° 40' 4.2" E 019° 2' 37.3" ▪ **T +27 (0)21-873-3407** ▪ F +27 (0)21-873-3408

2012 sees a new winemaker bringing his expertise to this small Wellington winery, as De Meye's Marcus Milner joins with retailer Tanja Hilka (Leeuwenberg) to make a new range for German consumers. Similar schemes for other overseas markets are afoot and the plan is to take the winery beyond hobbyist proportions soon.

Leeumasker range NEW

Cape Blend ▦ ★★★ Medium bodied **09**, juicy mulberry of pinotage toned by structure of cab. Shows potential, deserves more time to develop.

Maske range

Cabernet Sauvignon ▦ ★★ **09** ripe-fruited, with chunky dry tannins, needed hearty fare when previewed last time. **Merlot** ▦ ★★★ Lively pizza partner, still-selling **09** vibrant & appealing cherry/red berry flavours. **Chenin Blanc** ▦ ★★ Tangy freshness & gentle apple notes on **09**, sampled from tank last time. — MW

▪ **Mason's Hill** *see* The Mason's Winery
▪ **Maties** *see* Stellenbosch University Welgevallen Vineyards & Cellar

Matuba

Owned by Winegro, Matuba ('Opportunity') wines are sourced from partner cellars in the Coastal region. New vintages not available for review this edition.

Matzikama Organic Cellar

Location: Vredendal ▪ Map: Olifants River ▪ Est/1stB 2001 ▪ Tasting by appt ▪ Owner(s)/winemaker(s)/viticulturist(s) Klaas Coetzee ▪ 12ha/2.5ha (cab, shiraz) ▪ 24t 100% red ▪ PO Box 387 Vredendal 8160 ▪ klaas@ matzikamawyn.co.za ▪ www.matzikamawyn.co.za ▪ S 31° 36' 34.37" E 018° 44' 11.32" ▪ **T +27 (0)82-801-3737**

After a fairly lengthy hiatus from making wine under his own organic boutique label, Klaas Coetzee plans an interesting project this season. 'It's still top secret but promises to get a few wine writers talking,' says Klaas, whose day job is as production manager at Stellar Winery in Olifants River Valley.

McGregor Wines

Location: McGregor ▪ Map: Robertson ▪ WO: McGregor/Western Cape ▪ Est 1948 ▪ 1stB 1978 ▪ Tasting & sales Mon–Fri 8–5 Sat 10–3 ▪ Closed Easter Fri, Dec 25/26 & Jan 1 ▪ BYO picnic ▪ Owner(s) 27 members ▪ Winemaker(s) Elmo du Plessis & Hugo Conradie ▪ Viticulturist(s) Jaco Lategan ▪ 12,000t 22% red 78% white ▪ IPW ▪ PO Box 519 McGregor 6708 ▪ info@mcgregorwinery.co.za ▪ www.mcgregorwinery.co.za ▪ S 33° 56′5.4″ E 019° 50′56.3″ ▪ **T +27 (0)23-625-1741/1109** ▪ F +27 (0)23-625-1829

The slogan of this grower-owned winery on the fringe of McGregor - 'In every bottle there's a story of a very special place' - refers not only to the picturesque village but also to the special sites from which the own-brand wines are selected and made, reveals winemaker Elmo du Plessis, whose focus is on quality and quantity: 'Better products, *and* more of those better products.'

Winemaker's Reserve range

Cabernet Sauvignon ★★★★ Last edition, 08's dark fruit interwoven with leather & vanilla from year older oak worked well, but alc gave a sightly hot finish. Still selling, as for Pinotage, Cab-Merlot, White Muscadel & Cape Ruby below.

McGregor range

Shiraz ☺ ★★★ Creamy blackberries & subtle tannin on 09 strike just the right drinkability notes.
Pinotage Rosé ☺ 🍷 🕮 ★★★ Light & not-too-dry 11 sunset sipper. Flowers, strawberries & candyfloss: very appealing.

Pinotage ★★★ Good dark-berried fruit on 09, tad disjointed acidity may since have assimilated. **Ruby Cabernet** 🕮 ★★ Almost overwhelming mulberry flavour untrammelled by oak, juicy delivery, 10 is the template for a (tasty!) fruit-bomb. **Cabernet Sauvignon-Merlot** ★★★ 09 well structured, lightly oaked & balanced Bordeaux red. **Chardonnay** ✓ 🍷 🕮 🌡 ★★★★ With its upfront (unoaked) fruit & bold 14% alc extrovert 11 leads the pack. Generous lime marmalade flavour, pithy tail adds interest. **Chenin Blanc** 🍷 🕮 ★★★ Thatch & florals, fruit-sweet conclusion for 11, lightish lunchtime companion. **Colombard** 🍷 🕮 ★★★ 11 tad shy mid-2011 but on track record should perk up & become appealing summer-fruit quaffer. **Sauvignon Blanc** 🍷 🕮 ★★ Youthfully muted 11 lighter styled yet zesty. **Red Muscadel** ★★★ 09 fortified winter warmer rather subdued for the style: pale hue, tealeaf & cranberry notes; opens to malva, raisins & toffee; sugar neutralised by piercing dried-apricot acidity. WO W Cape. **White Muscadel** ★★★ Previously previewed, 08 now packed with flavour richness; like drinking liquidised sultanas. **Cape Ruby Port** ★★★ Dark fruit, nice balance of intensity, weight & freshness on wallet-friendly 08, from ruby cab. Discontinued: **Colombar-Chardonnay**. — Panel

MC Square

Location: Somerset West ▪ WO: Stellenbosch ▪ Est/1stB 1996 ▪ Closed to public ▪ Owner(s)/winemaker(s)/viticulturist(s) Jean-Luc Sweerts ▪ 300cs 100% white ▪ PO Box 436 Somerset West 7129 ▪ mcsquare@iafrica.com ▪ **T +27 (0)83-303-5467**

'Why run off to Europe when we have such beautiful, evocative names for our wines right here in Africa?' asks DRC-born boutique winemaker Jean-Luc Sweerts. Hence Sophiatown, evoking the vibrant Johannesburg suburb demolished under apartheid, and Isandlwana, commemorating the famous 1879 Anglo-Zulu battle.

★★★★ **Sophiatown** NEW Classically styled 05 cab; dry, elegant & serious, but drink soon.

★★★★ **Red Square** Deep, opulent cab-dominated Bordeaux blend, with merlot & cab franc. 04 showed dark tones, espresso, wild scrub, hedgerow fruit. Not revisited, as all below.

★★★★ **Cuvée Chardonnay** Traditionally vinified sparkling. 04 full & rich citrus flavours, attractive toasty hint.

★★★★☆ **Cuvée Brut MCC** Classic & expressive 06 sparkling from pinot noir, chardonnay, pinot meunier. Persistent pinpoint bubbles & complex perfume; 3 years lees-ageing add richness & depth.

Isandlwana ★★★★ Delicious 07, sleek & supple, showcases pure shiraz fruit. — IM

Mea Culpa

WO: Stellenbosch ▪ Est 2003 ▪ 1stB 2005 ▪ Closed to public ▪ Owner(s) Eduard du Plessis ▪ Winemaker(s) Johan le Hanie ▪ 500cs 100% red ▪ PO Box 6458 Halfway House Midrand 1685 ▪ sales@meaculpa.co.za

For telecommunications businessman and brand owner, Eduard du Plessis, wine matters because it is one of the integral threads woven into the fabric of life. And Mea Culpa matters because it is the result of a search for something different, and it was created with the sole purpose of sharing with other winelovers.

Mea Culpa ★★★☆ 03 cab-led blend previously had mineral & liquorice tones, smooth savoury finish. — CvZ

■ **Meander** *see* uniWines Marketing
■ **Meditation** *see* Nwanedi Estate

Meerendal Wine Estate

Location/WO: Durbanville ▪ Map: Durbanville, Philadelphia & Darling ▪ Est 1702 ▪ 1stB 1969 ▪ Tasting & sales Tue-Sat 9-6 Sun 9-5 ▪ Fee R10, waived on 6 btl purchase ▪ Closed Easter Fri, Dec 25 & Jan 1 ▪ Cellar tours by appt ▪ Meerendal Manor House Restaurant & Deli Tue-Sun ▪ Barn & Lawn: Cape Table buffet Sun 12-3 ▪ Facilities for children ▪ Tour groups ▪ Farm produce ▪ Conferences ▪ Weddings/functions ▪ Walks/hikes ▪ Mountain biking ▪ Conservation area ▪ Owner(s) Coertze family ▪ Cellarmaster(s) Liza Goodwin (Sep 2006) ▪ Viticulturist(s) Kevin Watt (Jul 2005, consultant) ▪ 270ha/70ha (merlot, ptage, pinot, shiraz, chard, sauv) ▪ 650t/25,000cs own label 75% red 20% white 5% rosé ▪ IPW ▪ Private Bag X1702 Durbanville 7551 ▪ info@meerendal.co.za ▪ www.meerendal.co.za ▪ S 33° 47′ 55.8″ E 018° 37′ 26.2″ ▪ **T +27 (0)21-975-1655** ▪ F +27 (0)21-975-1657

The newest members of Meerendal's fan club are a group of gentlemen who've had some fans of their own over the past, well, four decades. Collectively, they're the pop band Smokie, and to a man ditched Australian shiraz as their tipple of choice for South African wine, preferably the product of this revitalised Durbanville property. The sponsorship is just one of the ways Meerendal maintains heightened consumer awareness. Others include Festival of the Grape, Sip, Soup & Bread, and Season of Sauvignon. No doubt festivities are planned, too, for the launch mid-year of the maiden pinot noir.

Prestige range

★★★★ **Heritage Block Pinotage** Statement 07 from 61 yr old vines: abundant spice & stewed plum flavours muted by grippy tannins. Like following, still selling, not revisited.

★★★★ **Blanc de Blancs Méthode Cap Classique** Well-structured 07, typical yeast, brioche & green apple notes; 6 months lees-ageing for breadth.

★★★★☆ **Natural Sweet** From naturally fermented chenin, older oak. 09 (★★★★) overly ripe marzipan flavours though enough acid to balance sugar & low alc. Last rated was medalled 06, also from chenin.

Merlot Reserve ★★★★ Bold & porty (ex 14.7% alc) 07's spiced plum ripeness was checked by big acid & tannin. **Bin159 Shiraz** ★★★★ Blockbuster styling of 07 also in ultra ripe 06 (★★★★); baked mulberry & fruitcake flavours, mouthfilling tannins. **Bin 242 Sauvignon Blanc** ★★★★ Last tasted was subtle, rich 07, more complex than 06 (★★★★).

Meerendal range

Pinotage Rosé ☺ 🍽 📖 ★★★ Off-dry quick-quaff 11 affable, flavoursome but brief.

Cabernet Sauvignon ★★★ Succulent blackberry fruit on 06 last time fleshed out firm tannins brisk acidity. Not reassessed, like Reserve Merlot, Cab-Merlot, Chenin, MCC & Natural Sweet. **Merlot** ★★★★ Step-up 09 more restrained & better knit than porty 07 (★★★★), nudges next level. Violet nuance to black plum fruit, avoids any leafy astringency. **Pinot Noir** NEW 📖 Unrated barrel sample 11 first crop off young vineyard shows promising black cherry fruit, fine tannins. **Pinotage** ✓ ★★★★ 09 back on track after blip in 06 (★★★). Appealing strawberry & sugared plum, composed tannins drink well now & bode well for few years cellaring. 08 & 07 sold on untasted. **Shiraz** ✓ ★★★★ Chocolate, leather, sour cherry & white pepper accents make 09 the most complex in the line-up. Convincingly raises bar on jammy/tarry 06 (★★★). **Cabernet Sauvignon-Merlot** ★★★★ 07 with 65% cabernet offers fresh blackcurrant, cedary spiciness. **Chardonnay Wooded** 📖 ★★★ Half-oaked 08 has breadth courtesy lees-ageing, though citrus-apple acidity tad pronounced. **Chardonnay Unwooded** 📖 11 charms with nuts & green hedge bouquet, finishes with racy grapefruit acidity. **Chenin Blanc** ★★★ White peach, apple on food-friendly, lightly oaked 09. **Sauvignon Blanc** 🍽 📖 ★★★★ Shy 11 doesn't show generosity, exuberance of 10 (★★★★), has similar tangy acidity, dry flinty conclusion. — CvZ

Meerhof Private Cellar

Location: Riebeek-Kasteel ▪ Map: Swartland ▪ WO: Western Cape ▪ Est/1stB 2000 ▪ Tasting & sales Fri-Sun & pub hols 10-4; open daily Dec 15-Jan 15 ▪ Fee R35 ▪ Closed Easter Fri & Dec 25 ▪ Walks/hikes ▪ Owner(s) Cobus Kotze, Herman Redelinghuys & Krige Visser ▪ Winemaker(s)/viticulturist(s) Rudi Wium ▪ 500ha/40ha (cab, cincaut, merlot, ptage, shiraz, chenin) ▪ 120t/500cs own label 80% red 20% white ▪ PO Box 1229 Malmesbury 7299 ▪ meerhof@wcaccess.co.za, meerhof@cinsaut.co.za ▪ www.cinsaut.co.za ▪ S 33° 24' 19.8" E 018° 52' 15.0" ▪ T +27 (0)22-487-2524 ▪ F +27 (0)86-683-8132

Renewed energy, with a focus on a natural winemaking approach and 'the forgotten cinsaut to be king again', is taking place at this Swartland winery. A major overhaul in the vineyards and in the cellar will pave the way for wines with lower alcohols, elegance and restraint.

★★★★ **Drège** Reserve in **11**. Shiraz-headed **08** offers appealing spicy, truffly notes, savoury persistence. Light touch from deftly handled tannins, tangy mineral thread prolong drinking pleasure. Merlot, cab other partners.

Syrah ★★★★ Admirably delicate **08** presents full, pure dark spice, truffle flavours. Fresh core, comfortably padded tannins add to current enjoyment. Includes splashes mourvèdre, viognier. Previous **06** (★★★☆). **Salomon** ★★★★ De la Caille in **11** edition. Fragrant **08** has firm structure associated with cab-led Bordeaux-style blends, still expressed with restraint, refinement. Focused, refreshing with sweet fruited persistence. — AL

▪ **Meerkat** see Schalk Burger & Sons Wine Cellar
▪ **Meerland** see Baarsma Wine Group

Meerlust Estate

Location/map/WO: Stellenbosch ▪ Est 1693 ▪ 1stB 1975 ▪ Tasting & sales Mon-Fri 9-5 Sat 10-2 ▪ Fee R30 ▪ Closed all pub hols ▪ Cellar tours by appt ▪ Owner(s) Hannes Myburgh ▪ Cellarmaster(s) Chris Williams (Jan 2004) ▪ Winemaker(s) Altus Treurnicht (assistant, 2008) ▪ Viticulturist(s) Roelie Joubert (2001) ▪ 400ha/106ha (cabs s/f, merlot, ptage, pinot, chard) ▪ 500t/25,000cs own label 90% red 10% white ▪ PO Box 7121 Stellenbosch 7599 ▪ info@meerlust.co.za ▪ www.meerlust.co.za ▪ S 34° 1'1.7" E 018° 45'24.7" ▪ T +27 (0)21-843-3587 ▪ F +27 (0)21-843-3274

Asked what makes his wines so remarkable, Chris Williams' response is predictably laconic: 'Gravel soils, mature vines, Roelie Joubert's green fingers (ask his wife who he loves more, the kids or the vines), low 35hl/ha yields, very good quality, properly seasoned oak, not stuffed up at bottling.' His own input unmentioned, he truly believes wine is made in the vineyard. As for the competent bottling, this is now the domain of Companjiesdrift Bottling & Logistics, a joint venture between the Meerlust Workers Trust and Myburgh Family Trust. Social and environmental sustainability are large on the agenda of this 8th generation family farm, as the wines must continue sustaining the 30 families living here.

★★★★☆ **Cabernet Sauvignon 09** first bottling since **05**, made only in excellent cab yrs, shows astonishing depth & concentration. Plenty of new (80%) & seasoned oak to seamlessly structure dense layers of succulent fruit flavours, resulting in impressive harmony & wholeness.

★★★★☆ **Merlot** Restrained, fine **08** with a little cab & cab franc, back on track after **07** (★★★★). Usual distinctive, classic styling gathers rich, dark fruit & fine tannins into complete, harmonious whole.

★★★★☆ **Pinot Noir** 🖋 Incredibly vibrant, youthful **10** (from 25 year old vines) delivers all the vivid fruit purity desired in pinot. Concentration focused by fine acidity. More herbal, austere **09** (★★★★) also tasted.

★★★★☆ **Rubicon** Approaching its 30th birthday, cab-based blend with merlot, cab franc still a Cape benchmark. Splendid **07** (★★★★★) reflects work in the vineyard, with remarkably intense fruit core, currently masked by firm, integrated tannin which should preserve charms to 2025. Like **06**, restrained not showy.

★★★★ **Chardonnay** Misleadingly unassuming **09** tasted last year; citrus with hazelnut biscuity notes. Crisp, yet creamy finish. Follows **08**'s (★★★★☆) style change to restrained elegance. — IM

Meinert Wines

Location/map: Stellenbosch ▪ WO: Devon Valley/Coastal ▪ Est 1987 ▪ 1stB 1997 ▪ Tasting Mon-Sat strictly by appt only ▪ Closed all pub hols ▪ Owner(s) Martin Meinert ▪ Cellarmaster(s)/winemaker(s) Martin Meinert (Nov 1997) ▪ Viticulturist(s) Henk Marconi (Jan 1991) ▪ 16ha/12ha (cabs s/f, merlot, p verdot, ptage, sem) ▪ 90t/7,000cs own label 65% red 35% white ▪ PO Box 7221 Stellenbosch 7599 ▪ info@meinertwines.com ▪ www.meinertwines. com ▪ S 33° 54'1.8" E 018° 48'50.2" ▪ **T +27 (0)21-865-2363** ▪ F +27 (0)21-865-2414

Asked about his winemaking approach, Martin Meinert is laconic: 'Much the same as it's been for at least the last 15 years'. If we can happily expect continuity in his rather traditional, classic-leaning style, it doesn't exclude experimentation and innovation (and escapism too, Meinert adds) at this small premium winery in Stellenbosch's Devon Valley. The FCM (Family Collection Meinert) range is the expanding place for such wines. Amongst them, in the near future, a sweet vine-dried semillon from a young home-vineyard, a chardonnay from Elgin, and perhaps even an Elgin pinot noir - 'if it passes my entirely personal quality test'.

★★★★ **Devon Crest** 06 tasted last edition. Blend cab with merlot, dash cab franc. Smartly built, fresh, elegant.

★★★★ **Synchronicity** Some grandeur here, with a note of aristocratic aloofness. **07** a handsome, well-structured cab-merlot blend, pinotage, cab franc in support. Dry, lingering finish. Should keep 10 years.

Cabernet Sauvignon 🗒 ★★★★ **07** last year showed improvement over **06** (★★★★), with classic flavours & judicious oaking. **Merlot** 🗒 ★★★★ **08** in usual lightish, elegant, red-fruited style, but herbaceous character notable this year, & ends rather mouth-drying. **Printer's Ink Pinotage** 🗒 ★★★★ The most easily charming in the range, with lovely berry aromas/flavours, but previewed **08** pleasingly fresh, with the Meinert fingertip of austerity. **Family Collection Meinert The Italian Job White Merlot** 🗒 ★★★ Light gold-coloured **09** from merlot - rare style. Unfruity and serious, with firm, biting mouth-grip. More like some chardonnays, chenins than merlot. **La Barry Sauvignon Blanc** 🗒 ★★★★ Light & juicy **10** from Elgin not retasted - last time promised to gain complexity over year or two. — TJ

Mellasat Vineyards

Location/WO: Paarl ▪ Map: Paarl & Wellington ▪ Est 1996 ▪ 1stB 1999 ▪ Tasting & sales Mon-Fri 9.30-5.30 Sat 9. 30-1 ▪ Closed Easter Fri/Sun, Dec 25 & Jan 1 ▪ Cellar tours by appt ▪ Light lunches for groups/tours or private dinner functions by appt; also food based events ▪ Tour groups ▪ Conference venue ▪ Paarl Ommiberg Festival ▪ Owner(s) Stephen Richardson ▪ Cellarmaster(s)/winemaker(s) Stephen Richardson (Jan 1999) ▪ Viticulturist(s) Poena Malherbe (Sep 1996) ▪ 13ha/8ha (cab, ptage, shiraz, tempranillo, chard, chenin, viog) ▪ 50t/3,500cs own label 50% red 40% white 10% rosé ▪ IPW ▪ PO Box 7169 Paarl 7623 ▪ mellasat@mweb.co.za ▪ www.mellasat. com ▪ S 33° 44'30.0" E 019° 2'31.0" ▪ **T +27 (0)21-862-4525** ▪ F +27 (0)21-862-4525

A new tasting centre, with function room and underground cellar, will play host to food-and-wine matching events with a twist, say owner Stephen Richardson and chef-wife Janet. The innovative white pinotage, now in its fifth vintage, will feature prominently with the new chardonnay and a gestating tempranillo.

Mellasat Premium range

'M' ★★★★ Shiraz-led **06** with cab & pinotage tasted last edition. Fresh acid enlivened spicy red fruit, 30 months French oak signalled serious intent. **'Sigma' White Pinotage** 🗒 ★★★★ Pinotage vinified in oak barrels as a white wine, **10** with unexpected structure & depth of flavour. Brisk acidity is evident in this interesting example. **Chardonnay** NEW ★★★★ Barrel-fermented &-matured **10** shows caramel & toffee, rich citrus flavour & firm acidity. **Tuin Wyn** 🗒 ★★★ Oak-matured **10** straw wine from air-dried chenin previewed last edition. Now bottled, nutty nougat flavours & light feel despite substantial 17% alc.

Dekker's Valley range

Revelation ☺ 🗒 ★★★ Harmonious cab, shiraz, pinotage **09** blend. Delightful fresh, vivid fruitiness in seamless partnership with oak.

Shiraz 🗒 ★★★ Mulberry & mocha in edgy **10** precede leather & fruit. **Shiraz Rosé** 🗒 ★★ Pale strawberry pink **11** a crisply dry & light lunchtime sipper. **Chenin Blanc** 🗒 ★★★ Simple apple & quince flavoured **11** enlivened by brisk acidity. — IM

▪ **MEME** see Jason's Hill Private Cellar
▪ **Merchant's Mark** see Barrydale Cellar - SCV
▪ **Merwespont Winery** see Bonnievale Cellar

Merwida Winery

Location: Rawsonville ▪ Map/WO: Breedekloof ▪ Est 1963 ▪ 1stB 1975 ▪ Tasting & sales Mon-Fri 8–12.30; 1.30-5 Sat 9-1 ▪ Fee R10 refunded on purchase ▪ Closed Easter Fri-Mon, Dec 25 & Jan 1 ▪ Merwida Country Lodge T 023-349-1435 ▪ Owner(s) Schalk van der Merwe & Pierre van der Merwe ▪ Cellarmaster(s)/viticulturist(s) Magnus Kriel ▪ Winemaker(s) Magnus Kriel (Dec 2000), with Sarel van Staden (Aug 1982) & Jacques Geldenhuys ▪ 630ha (cab, merlot, shiraz, chard, chenin, sauv, sem, viog) ▪ 10,000t/20,000cs own label 40% red 60% white ▪ BWI member ▪ PO Box 4 Rawsonville 6845 ▪ wines@merwida.com ▪ www.merwida.com ▪ S 33° 41'24.9" E 019° 20' 31.1" ▪ **T +27 (0)23-349-1144** ▪ F +27 (0)23-349-1953 / 086-538-1953

This family winery achieved last edition's plan to increase its markets from Rawsonville and the nearby Worcester area to selected restaurants, specialist wine shops and supermarkets in Cape Town. Jacques Geldenhuys joins as assistant winemaker, there's a push to find new markets, and a new baby in the form of a limited-edition pinotage.

★★★★ **Chardonnay** 🔲 Partially wooded **11** vibrant lemon zest with sweet oak spiciness; full, creamy texture with potent lemon-butter flavours. **10** sold out untasted.

Cuvée Brut ☺ ★★★ A crisp & lively party pleaser, elegantly dry, brims with happy bubbles. **NV.**

Cabernet Sauvignon ★★★ Appealing **09** still available; spice & smoky intro, blackberry fruit, firm but balanced tannins. **Barbera** ★★★★ **09** with sweet oaky notes which last year masked some of the ripe fleshy fruit which made **08** (★★★★) so attractive. Might since have integrated. **Pinotage Limited Edition** NEW ★★★ Debut **09** fleshy & succulent, toasty vanilla & dark ripe fruit with cedar edge. **Merlot Rosé** NEW 🔲 ★★☆ Strawberry & white chocolate on off-dry **11** party sipper. **Sauvignon Blanc** 🔲 ★★★ Crisp fruit salad & gooseberry freshness on **11**. **White Muscadel** ✓ 🔲 ★★★★ Utterly delicious fortified dessert, **11** lusciously sweet but balanced, lovely lemon & jasmine scents, lingering honeyed flavours. Even better than **09** (★★★★). — DB

▪ **Metamorphic** see Hillcrest Estate

Metzer Wines

Location: Somerset West ▪ WO: Stellenbosch ▪ Est/1stB 2004 ▪ Tasting by appt ▪ Owner(s)/winemaker(s) Wade Metzer ▪ 16t/1,200cs 100% red ▪ 3 Village Close 17 Drama Str Somerset West 7130 ▪ metzerwines@gmail.com ▪ www.metzerwines.com ▪ **T +27 (0)84-340-8278** ▪ F +27 (0)21-851-8245

Flying owner/winemaker Wade Metzer is now based in Switzerland to establish new markets for his brand in Europe. 'I will be returning to South Africa regularly for harvest, bottling, 'quality control' and surfing... in that particular order, though the last two are usually done simultaneously.' In the pipeline is Vit B Blanc, a chenin-based wine with viognier.

★★★★ **Vitamin B Syrah** Clean black fruit with herbal & savoury notes, velvety **09** delivered mouthful of mulberry, white pepper & spice that last year lingered impressively against refined tannins.

★★★★ **Syrah** ✓ Now bottled, **09** (★★★★★) flagship offers captivating perfumes of dark berries, flowers & spice. Strikingly pure, vibrant & juicy fruit around a core of well-handled tannins. Helderberg grapes (as for Vit B); last-tasted **07** was from Swartland. — WB

M'hudi Wines

Location/map: Stellenbosch ▪ WO: Stellenbosch/Western Cape ▪ Tasting & sales Mon-Sat 8.30-5 ▪ Guest accommodation ▪ Owner(s) Rangaka family ▪ Cellarmaster(s) Jeff Grier ▪ Winemaker(s) Jeff Grier ▪ Viticulturist(s) Yolande Marais (consultant) ▪ 43ha total ▪ 7,000cs own label 70% red 30% white ▪ WIETA ▪ PO Box 30 Koelenhof 7605 ▪ malmsey@mhudi.com ▪ www.mhudi.com ▪ S 33° 50'32.3" E 018° 45'13.9" ▪ **T +27 (0)21-988-6960** ▪ F +27 (0)86-582-8974

Matriarch and CEO Malmsey Rangaka's vision for M'hudi is to provide quality wines and family hospitality: 'We are a small business with a big vision and a big heart.' The family's diverse talents are employed: husband Diale tends the vineyards and manages exports, sons Tseliso and Senyane look after branding and marketing, while daughter Lebogang tends the ever-challenging local market.

Chenin Blanc ☺ ★★★ Rich & sweet-fruited, tropical **11** in rewardingly rounded, full fruity style.

Merlot ★★★★ Sleek merlot blueberry fruits given torque by portion cab. **06** firm yet accessible. This, Pinotage not retasted. **Pinotage** ★★★★ **07** previously tasted was extrovert, fresh & moreish. **Sauvignon Blanc** 🔖 ★★★★ Flavoursome **11** a well-balanced mix of tropical & herbaceous flavours with appetising, mouthwatering freshness to finish. — IM

Micu Narunsky Wines

Location: Somerset West ▪ Map: Helderberg ▪ WO: Coastal ▪ Est 2005 ▪ 1stB 2006 ▪ Tasting by appt ▪ Owner(s)/cellarmaster(s)/viticulturist(s) Micu Narunsky ▪ Winemaker(s) Micu Narunsky, advised by Francois Naudé ▪ 4.8t/225cs own label 85% red 15% white ▪ PO Box 427 Somerset Mall 7137 ▪ nmicu@hotmail.com ▪ www.micunarunsky.com ▪ S 34° 1'52.20" E 018° 50'46.73" ▪ **T +27 (0)73-600-3031 / +27 (0)21-855-2520**

Israeli-born jazz musician/composer and Portuguese-style reds specialist Micu Narunsky has realised his dream by coming to South Africa and creating his own wine label. Operations recently moved to the old Cordoba cellar in the Helderberg. In the pipeline is a joint venture with Anatu Wines, where he consults, to produce a new (Portuguese-named and mermaid-themed) label, Sereia.

★★★★ **lemanjá** Ever-improving touriga-led red (with 30% tinta), among handful such (unfortified) blends in SA. **09** brooding, sweet/spicy berries, robust, skilfully oaked - a food wine with ageing potential.
Olodum ✓ ★★★★ Mirror image of above blend: tinta leading, 17% touriga in **09**. Softer, juicy & spicy, medium bodied with well-judged oak. Delicious. — WB

Middelvlei Estate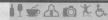

Location/map: Stellenbosch ▪ WO: Devon Valley/Stellenbosch/Stellenbosch ▪ Est 1941 ▪ 1stB 1973 ▪ Tasting & sales daily 10–4.30 ▪ Fee R15pp ▪ Closed Easter Fri, Dec 25 & Jan 1 ▪ Cellar tours by appt ▪ Traditional lunchtime braai on Sat & Sun; by prior arrangement for groups of 15+ on any other day ▪ Facilities for children ▪ Conferences ▪ Walking/hiking & mountain biking trails ▪ Cottage (2 pax) ▪ Owner(s) Momberg family ▪ Cellarmaster(s)/winemaker(s)/viticulturist(s) Tinnie Momberg (Feb 1992) ▪ 160ha/110ha (cab, merlot, ptage, shiraz, chard, sauv) ▪ 650t/30,000cs own label 95% red 5% white ▪ Other export brand: Hagelsberg ▪ IPW, WIETA ▪ PO Box 66 Stellenbosch 7599 ▪ info@middelvlei.co.za ▪ www.middelvlei.co.za ▪ S 33° 55'41.2" E 018° 49'55.9" ▪ **T +27 (0)21-883-2565** ▪ F +27 (0)21-883-9546

Bordering Stellenbosch's suburbia might tempt others to sell up and retire to a life of luxury, but that would go against the grain of the extended Momberg family who own and are involved in running this traditional estate. Besides weekend food events, visitors are offered hiking trails and mountain biking, there are animals galore to see and of course children are welcome. It is a family farm after all.

★★★★ **Shiraz** ✓ Unwavering quality, good shiraz track record at this cellar. **09** beef extract, cloves & black pepper, succulent fruit. So harmonious, already delicious, drink now till ±2016.
★★★★☆ **Momberg** Last was **07**, individual & impressive Cape blend, cab, pinotage & shiraz in total harmony. Smoky & peppery nuances vied with the hedgerow fruit, deep muscle tone from all-new oak.

Chardonnay ☺ 🔖 ★★★ Unwooded **11** the answer for those disliking oaked whites. Nothing but tasty tropical fruit, fresh & tangy.

Cabernet Sauvignon ★★★★ Opulence written all over it, still-selling **08**'s blackcurrant-laden richness easily handles the year oaking. **Pinotage** ★★★★ 'Free Run' on **09** label, so expect fruit focus; vivid blueberries, supple tannins. Part of sale goes to Endangered Wildlife Trust. **Pinotage-Merlot** ★★★★ Dark-fruited juicy styling from near-equal **09** blend; food-friendly tannins, finishes nicely dry. — CR

Migliarina Wines

WO: Stellenbosch ▪ Est 2001 ▪ 1stB 2002 ▪ Closed to public ▪ Owner(s)/winemaker(s) Carsten Migliarina ▪ 1,200cs own label 65% red 35% white + 105cs for clients ▪ Brands for clients: Kap Hase ▪ PO Box 673 Stellenbosch 7599 ▪ carsten@migliarina.co.za ▪ www.migliarina.co.za ▪ **T +27 (0)72-233-4138**

The sales trips locally and abroad have paid off for ex-sommelier Carsten Migliarina, doubtless aided by 94 point ratings on wineanorak.com from UK wine critic Jamie

Goode. Despite small production, his wine now sells in Switzerland, Germany and the UK, which includes Michelin-starred restaurant listings. All the more encouragement for range expansion beyond his favourite variety, shiraz. But he is first spending time consolidating, looking at operating costs and packaging, like any good businessman.

★★★★ **Shiraz** ✓ Packed with dark fruit, 08 wears its 21 months oaking with style; mocha & sweet spice, with just enough firmness for definition & 5+ years cellaring potential.

★★★★ **Migliarina** NEW Two-thirds shiraz with cab, 08 has deep opulent black fruit, espresso savouriness. Showy, impressive, made with lots of care; drink now till ±2016. — CR

■ **Migration** *see D'Athis Wines SA Negociants*

■ **Miko** *see Mont Rochelle Hotel & Mountain Vineyards* .

Miles Mossop Wines

Location: Stellenbosch ▪ WO: Stellenbosch/Coastal ▪ Est/1stB 2004 ▪ Closed to public ▪ Owner(s)/winemaker(s)/viticulturist(s) Miles Mossop ▪ 1t/1,000cs own label 47% red 48% white 5% NLH ▪ PO Box 7339 Stellenbosch 7599 ▪ miles@milesmossopwines.com ▪ www.milesmossopwines.com ▪ **T +27 (0)82-413-4335** ▪ F +27 (0)21-808-5900

Miles Mossop (also winemaker at Tokara) is creating a legacy. Three children, three distinctive wines. In his own words, 'the focus is on refinement rather than innovation'. The wines are getting better due to careful fruit selection and a confident, deft hand in the cellar. This is a trademark of these wines, each a very different expression of skill-set, certainly the upside of continued experience at the top end of wine crafting.

★★★★☆ **Max** Plush & modern 08 (★★★★★), in same mould as 07, with polished dark fruits. Tobacco & graphite whiffs from 50% cab with support from merlot & petit verdot. Perfectly poised ripeness runs to supple tannins showing very deft handling of excellent fruit.

★★★★☆ **Saskia** 🖉 Opulent & luxurious 10 has soft vanilla & toast intro. Floral, poised ripe fruit follow to creamy texture, celebrating luscious weight with harmonious sweetish send-off. Most from chenin with splash each of viognier & clairette blanche. WO Coastal.

★★★★☆ **Kika** 🖉 A botrytised chenin dessert wine with great purity of purpose, 10 with typical sweet/sour combo & a subtle oak overlay still to integrate. Powerful & viscous on the palate, but with fine cleaning acid on finish as part of accomplished effort. — JP

■ **Millstone** *see Stettyn Cellar*

Millstream

Established range produced by DGB for export chiefly to the UK, Ireland and the Netherlands.

Cinsaut-Ruby Cabernet 🍷🖉 ★★★ Approachable 10, appealing berry fruit for early drinking. **Rosé** 🍷🖉 ★★ From pinotage, sweetness of 11 balanced by fresh, tangy berry fruit. **Chenin Blanc** 🍷🖉 ★★★ 11 crunchy apple freshness in easy-drinking mode. Western Cape WOs for all these. — MW

Mimosa Boutique Wines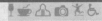

Location: Montagu ▪ Map: Klein Karoo & Garden Route ▪ WO: Robertson ▪ Est 2004 ▪ 1stB 2003 ▪ Tasting & sales daily 9-5 ▪ Facilities for children ▪ Tour groups ▪ Conservation area ▪ 4-star Mimosa Lodge: 23 rooms, conference centre, pool, boules pitch, wine cellar, tasting room & restaurant (see Restaurants section) ▪ Mimosa House: 4 rooms ▪ Mimosa Manor: includes tasting room, cellar, working wine farm, private butler & gourmet catering ▪ Owner(s) Bernhard Hess ▪ Cellarmaster(s)/viticulturist(s) Lourens van der Westhuizen (Jan 2006, consultant) ▪ Winemaker(s) Lourens van der Westhuizen (Jan 2006, consultant) & Bernhard Hess ▪ 5ha/3ha (cab, shiraz, chard, sauv) ▪ 20t/1,240cs own label 70% red 30% white ▪ PO Box 323 Montagu 6720 ▪ bernhard@mimosa.co.za ▪ www.mimosawines.co.za ▪ S 33°47'27.59" E 020°6'44.55" ▪ **T +27 (0)23-614-2351** ▪ F +27 (0)86-535-0720

'Seduction for the tongue and sunshine for the soul' is the aim of Montagu hotelier Bernhard Hess when it comes to his bespoke wine, vinified by Arendsig's Lourens van der Westhuizen. Much is consumed by guests of Bernhard's luxury Mimosa Lodge, but his greatest pleasure is enjoying a glass himself at the end of the day.

★★★★ **Shiraz** Deliciously savoury **09**, salami & ripe plum gently supported by vanilla oak & pliable tannins, zesty acidity & spicy tail add to appealing package.

★★★★ **Chardonnay** Judiciously oaked **09**, from limestone single-vineyard, not revisited. Buttered scone nuance, subtle spicing, poised & persistent with sweet suggestion on exit.

Cabernet Sauvignon ★★★★ Step-up **09**, classic pencil shavings & tobacco to brooding blackcurrant, sweet vanilla oak finish. Tannins friendly enough for standalone enjoyment. More complex than **08** (★★★★). **Hess Reserve** NEW Bordeaux blend missed our deadline. **Sauvignon Blanc** NEW ★★★ Muted aroma followed by burst of tropical & green fruit flavours, **11** good crisp & dry conclusion. — Panel

Miravel

Location: Somerset West ▪ Map: Helderberg ▪ WO: Stellenbosch ▪ Est 2002 ▪ 1stB 2005 ▪ Tasting & sales Mon-Sat & pub hols by appt ▪ Closed Ash Wed, Easter Fri-Mon, Ascension day, Pentecost, Dec 25/26 & Jan 1 ▪ Meals by prior arrangement ▪ Self-catering Fynbos Cottage ▪ Owner(s) Maarten van Beuningen ▪ Winemaker(s) Gerda Willers, Wynand Lategan & André Liebenberg (consultants) ▪ Viticulturist(s) Paul Wallace (Jun 2004, consultant) ▪ 39ha/27ha (cab, merlot, p verdot, ptage, chenin, sauv) ▪ 104t/270cs (sauv) & 450L (cab) own label 50% red 50% white ▪ PO Box 5144 Helderberg 7135 ▪ maarten@miravel.co.za ▪ www.miravel.co.za ▪ S 34° 1'58.7" E 018° 46'46.9" ▪ **T** +27 (0)21-842-3154 ▪ F +27 (0)21-842-3154

Being innovative for owner Maarten van Beuningen involves adding value to the grapes which he sells off - the majority of his yield. Careful site selection, especially for sauvignon blanc and cabernet, and 'maintaining edge and quality' ensures good prices from top wineries. 'Selling at premium prices needs patience and building a good relationship with the buyer; one has to go the extra mile.'

Cabernet Sauvignon ★★★★ **08** last year showed generous fresh fruit & firm tannins. Should age 3-4 years. **Ella Family Reserve** NEW ★★★★ Streamlined **08** from cab has pure fresh blackcurrant appeal. Gentle grip & modest oaking (no new barrels) allow for uncomplicated yet satisfying drinking. **Merlot** ★★★★ Last tasted was **06** with iron & spice aromas, bouncy grip. **Sauvignon Blanc** ▤ ★★★ Lightish grassy **10**, its briskness soothed by a little juicy sweetness. — AL

Mischa Estate

Location/WO: Wellington ▪ Map: Paarl & Wellington ▪ Est/1stB 1999 ▪ Tasting, sales & tours (vine nursery in winter & cellar in summer) by appt ▪ Fee R250, waived if purchase equals/exceed it ▪ Closed pub hols ▪ Snacks & meals by appt ▪ Walks ▪ Mountain biking ▪ Dunedin Manor House & Oak Tree Cottage; Talana Hill Cottage & Garden Room ▪ Owner(s) JA & GH Barns ▪ Cellarmaster(s)/winemaker(s) Andrew Barns (Jan 1999) ▪ Viticulturist(s) Ruiter Smit (Jun 1960) ▪ 40ha (cab, merlot, shiraz, sauv, viog) ▪ 97t/4,000cs own label 75% red 25% white ▪ PO Box 163 Wellington 7654 ▪ info@mischaestate.com ▪ www.mischaestate.com, www.mischawines.blogspot.com ▪ S 33° 36'13.1" E 019° 0'46.8" ▪ **T** +27 (0)21-864-1016/19/20 ▪ F +27 (0)21-864-2312 or +27 (0)86-514-9818

Mischa, named after a Russian ballet dancer, has been in the Barns family since 1947, and is first and foremost the site of a successful vine nursery. Own-label wine however is a relatively new endeavour with the first commercial bottling completed in 1999. Highlights to date? 'Every harvest is a highlight. It's a new beginning and another chance,' says winemaker Andrew.

Mischa Estate range

★★★★ **Cabernet Sauvignon** Exuberant **08** (★★★★) is full & intense, sweet dark fruit & smooth tannins; includes dashes cab franc, merlot. More powerful than balanced **07**.

★★★★ **Roussanne** NEW ▒ Expressive **10** displays melon, mango, honey & appealing yeasty character; rich & intense with soft but sufficient acidity before long, savoury finish. Has real interest.

Merlot ★★★ **09** red fruit but lacked freshness, appeared simple, short when last tasted. **Shiraz** ★★★ **08** sweet dark fruit & toasty oak make for appealing if rather obvious result.

Eventide Cellar range

★★★★ **Shiraz** NEW ▤ **08** fragrant aromas of red berries & fynbos; medium to full body with pure fruit, spice, fresh acidity & unobtrusive oak.

Sauvignon Blanc 🍷 ★★★ **09** was light bodied, refreshing with tropical fruit flavour. This & next tasted last edition. **Viognier** 🍷 ★★★ Elegant **09** peach flavour, smooth texture, gentle acidity. Includes 15% roussanne, 3 months barrel matured. — CE

◼ **Miss Molly** *see* Môreson
◼ **Misty Cliff** *see* Groupe LFE South Africa

Misty Mountains Estate

Location: Stanford ▪ Map: Elgin, Walker Bay & Bot River ▪ WO: Walker Bay ▪ Est 2004 ▪ 1stB 2008 ▪ Tasting & sales Mon-Fri 10-5 Sat 10-2 ▪ Closed Easter Fri & Dec 25 ▪ Barrel tasting on request ▪ Cellar tours by appt ▪ Accommodation ▪ Restaurant ▪ Conference venue ▪ Owner(s) Misty Mountains Estates ▪ Directors LL le Roux & A van Vuuren ▪ Winemaker(s) Philip Costandius ▪ Vineyard manager(s) Robert Davis ▪ 46ha/16ha (mourv, shiraz, sauv, sem) ▪ PO Box 1874 Hermanus 7200 ▪ info@mistymountains.co.za ▪ www.mistymountains.co.za ▪ S 34° 25'04" E 019° 25' 35" ▪ **T +27 (0)28-341-0486** ▪ F +27 (0)28-341-0561

Strangely perhaps, it was the discovery of a natural spring that led to once neglected land between Hermanus and Stanford now bearing vineyards, winery and tasting room - not to mention grand views (which were always there), a restaurant and other facilities and, of course, 'world class water'.

Single Vineyard range
Shiraz ★★★ **09** now bottled. Sweet-fruited, savoury, with rich meaty notes. 60% new oak hides 15% alc. **Sauvignon Blanc** ★★☆ Herbal, capsicum notes, pungent green fig on **10** tasted last year.

Misty Mountains range
Wooded Sauvignon Blanc ★★★★ **10** sample tasted last year. Seductive fruitiness integrating with butterscotch whiffs. **Sauvignon Blanc Reserve** ★★★★ Herbaceous, quince notes on grippy-textured grassy **10** last year. Ripe, but moderate intensity & concentration.

Misty Mountains Vineyards range
Pinotage 🍷 ★★★★ Huge step-up on previous bottling of **09**: ripe red fruit, fragrant & spicy. Off-dry plushness masks grippy finish, but oak evident. This, Shiraz above, WO Walker Bay. — MF

◼ **Misty Point** *see* Barrydale Cellar - SCV

Mitre's Edge

Location/map: Stellenbosch ▪ WO: Simonsberg-Paarl ▪ Est 1999 ▪ 1stB 2004 ▪ Tasting & sales by appt Mon-Fri 9-5 Sat 9-1 ▪ Cellar tours by appt ▪ Guesthouse B&B ▪ Olive oil ▪ Owner(s) Bernard & Lola Nicholls ▪ Winemaker(s) Lola Nicholls (2004), with Bernard Nicholls ▪ Viticulturist(s) Francois Roux (Consultant) ▪ 28ha/18ha (cabs s/f, malbec, merlot, p verdot, shiraz) ▪ 150t/1,000cs own label 95% red 5% rosé ▪ PO Box 12290 Die Boord 7613 ▪ info@ mitres-edge.co.za ▪ www.mitres-edge.co.za ▪ S 33° 49' 47.3" E 018° 52' 34.4" ▪ **T +27 (0)21-875-5960** ▪ F +27 (0)21-875-5965

'Blood Sweat & Secateurs' is the title of a Facebook album featuring images of premium-grape growers and boutique vintners Bernard and Lola Nicholls' current marketing focus: inviting corporates to make a barrel of wine as a team-building exercise. 'We want to provide a fun way for consumers to learn more about wine.'

Flagship range
Cabernet Sauvignon ★★★★ As noted last year, the Flagships characterised by vigorous tannin, needing time to soften. This despite cushion of sweetness (sugar & fruit) in appealing, well-composed **08**. **Merlot** Await next.

Mitre's Edge range
Shiraz ★★★ **08** plush fruit flavours but tad spiritous (15% alc), misses balance of previous. **Rosé** Untasted.

Fynbos range
Now discontinued. — CvZ

◼ **Moerbei** *see* Klein Moerbei Estate
◼ **Moja** *see* Waterstone Wines

MolenVliet Wine & Guest Estate

Location/map/WO: Stellenbosch ▪ Est/1stB 2005 ▪ Tasting & sales by appt ▪ Fee R50 ▪ Wedding/conference venue ▪ Self-catering accommodation / B&B ▪ Owner(s) Ockie & Susan Oosthuizen ▪ Winemaker(s) Ettienne Malan (2006, consultant) ▪ Viticulturist(s) Calvin Booysen (2005) ▪ 14ha/8ha (cab, merlot, shiraz) ▪ 13t/±1,250cs own label 100% red ▪ PO Box 6288 Uniedal 7612 ▪ info@molenvliet.co.za ▪ www.molenvliet.co.za ▪ S 33° 54'52.9" E 018° 56'30.6" ▪ **T** +27 (0)21-885-1597 ▪ F +27 (0)21-885-1684

The wine produced by this Banhoek Valley luxury estate is consumed mostly by guests at the many weddings and functions the Oosthuizen family owners host annually, and by visitors enjoying the four-star accommodation on the Dwars River banks. Private tastings up-country have had positive effects on brand awareness and sales, according to Ockie Oosthuizen jnr.

★★★★ **Cabernet Sauvignon** Despite 16% alc, **07** achieved elegance & fine balance last time. Full bodied & rounded, lingering flavours of spicy blackberry liqueur.

★★★★ **Shiraz 07** was rich, bold (16% alc) & complex on review, silky texture & lingering vanilla chocolate flavours, savoury conclusion.

★★★★ **Proprietors Blend 05** classy Bordeaux blend with enticing blackcurrant/plum & mineral bouquet, refreshing flavours & supple, balanced tannins previous editions.

★★★★ **Diagonal Reserve** Full-bodied, elegant shiraz/cab-led **07** offers upfront perfumed black fruit, spicy coffee & sweet vanilla oak. Ready to enjoy.

★★★★ **Meraz** Merlot & shiraz in equal proportion, finely structured **07** debuted previously with intense ripe plum flavour. Mouthfilling, enduring & moreish.

Proprietors Selection ★★★ **05** previously offered fresh herbal hints, plum & mulberry flavours & full mouthfeel from well-managed oak. — WB

■ **Moments Collection** see Teddy Hall Wines
■ **Monfort** see Ultra Liquors

Monis Wines

Location: Paarl ▪ WO: Breede River Valley/Calitzdorp ▪ Est 1906 ▪ Closed to public ▪ Owner(s) Distell ▪ Cellarmaster(s)/winemaker(s) Dirkie Christowitz (Aug 1979) ▪ 26,000cs 100% fortified ▪ PO Box 266 Paarl 7620 ▪ dchristowitz@distell.co.za ▪ www.moniswines.co.za ▪ **T** +27 (0)21-860-1601 ▪ F +27 (0)21-872-2790

The forerunner of this now Distell owned company, making only fortified wines, was started by Italian immigrant Roberto Moni in 1906. He sold the business to then Stellenbosch Farmers' Winery in 1966. Current winemaker, genial Dirkie Christowitz has lent this consistent range his considerable experience since 1979.

★★★★☆ **Wood Matured Muscadel** ✓ Flame-licked **04** 500ml of irresistible dried orange zest, spice, muscat complexity. Retasted, it's silkily smooth, the edge taken off its rich sweetness by 5 years in older oak, tangy acid. Delicious now, for many years to come. Fruit ex Breede River.

★★★★ **Tawny Port** Gorgeous **96** ex Paarlberg tinta & cinsaut still selling.

Vintage Port ★★★★ From Calitzdorp fruit. Dried fruit, leather with touriga's fragrance enhance retasted **06** with its warming spirity tail. Slightly more concentration would lead to higher rating. — AL

Mon Rêve Estate

Location: Paarl ▪ Map: Paarl & Wellington ▪ WO: Simonsberg-Paarl ▪ Est 2009 ▪ 1stB 2011 ▪ Tasting, sales & cellar tours by appt ▪ Fee R15pp, waived on purchase ▪ Closed Easter Fri/Sun, May 1, Dec 25 & Jan 1 ▪ Facilities for children ▪ BYO picnic ▪ Owner(s) Guillaume & Heidi Masson ▪ Cellarmaster(s)/winemaker(s)/viticulturist(s) Jomien Slabbert (Nov 2009) ▪ 12ha/±6ha (cab, merlot, shiraz, Muscat d'A) ▪ 8,000L own label 94% red 6% white + 12,000L for clients ▪ PO Box 438 Paarden Eiland 7420 ▪ jomienb@naturalstonewarehouse.com ▪ S 33° 49'4.98" E 018° 54'47.21" ▪ **T** +27 (0)84-513-2015 ▪ F +27 (0)21-511-0880

The dream alluded to in the name of tiling company owners Guillaume and Heidi Masson's young winery in the Simonsberg foothills became reality in mid-2011 with the bottling of their maiden vintage. Now the focus is on marketing and getting the brand known. But first, after the long, hard work, the thoughts of the Massons and winemaker Jomien Slabbert (who likes Mother Nature to have more reign than machinery and chemicals in the vineyard and cellar) turned to that well-deserved 'wyntjie'.

Mon Rêve Estate range NEW

Cabernet Sauvignon ★★★ Youthful **10** is ripe & bold, sweet red-fruit flavours still masked by firm oaking. Needs time. **Single Vineyard Merlot** ★★★ Very ripe **10** oozes dark fruit flavours with hint of cured meat smokiness & warm finish. **Appaloosa** ★★★ **10** from merlot, cab & splash of shiraz is bold with rich meaty red-berry fruit & firm finish. **Muscat D'Alexandrie** ★★★★ Grapey **10** fortified dessert is pretty & unctuous, slightly cloying, needs bit more zing in tail. — Panel

Mons Ruber Estate

Location: Oudtshoorn ▪ Map: Klein Karoo & Garden Route ▪ Est ca 1850 ▪ Tasting & sales Mon-Fri 9–5 Sat 9–1 ▪ Closed Easter Sun & Dec 25 ▪ Self-catering accommodation ▪ Farm produce ▪ Hiking trail in proclaimed conservation area ▪ Owner(s) Radé & Erhard Meyer ▪ Winemaker(s) Radé Meyer ▪ Viticulturist(s) Johannes Mellet (consultant) ▪ 38ha (cab, muscadel r/w, chard, chenin, hanepoot, palomino) ▪ ±500t/10,000cs own label 50% red 50% white ▪ BWI ▪ PO Box 1585 Oudtshoorn 6620 ▪ monsruber@gmail.com ▪ S 33° 32' 1.0" E 022° 28' 38.9" ▪ **T +27 (0)44-251-6550** ▪ F +27 (0)86-566-6550

A visit to this family farm's tranquil, quaint tasting room is a return to the pioneering past of the Klein Karoo. Variously a 19th-century toll house, watering hole of legendary scribes and politicos, and stop-over on Queen Elizabeth II's 1947 state visit, it offers wines, traditional fortifieds and potstill brandies.

Montagu Wine & Spirits Co

Location: Montagu ▪ Map: Klein Karoo & Garden Route ▪ WO: Klein Karoo/Montagu/Upper Langkloof ▪ Est 1941 ▪ Tasting & sales Mon-Fri 8-5 Sat 9-1 ▪ Owner(s) 79 members ▪ Cellarmaster(s) Christiaan van Tonder (Rietrivier) & Chris Crafford (Uitvlucht) ▪ 382ha ▪ 5,100t/15,000cs 28% red 22% white 50% muscadel ▪ PO Box 332 Montagu 6720 ▪ admin@mwsc.co.za ▪ www.montaguwinecompany.co.za ▪ S 33° 46' 59.8" E 020° 7' 53.6" ▪ **T +27 (0)23-614-1340** ▪ F +27 (0)86-556-1340

General manager Elsa Carstens has been hands-on (even in the cellar) since taking up the reins in early 2010, while maintaining a presence in the wider wine industry through judging at shows and serving on committees. While still mainly a bulk producer, MWSC produces a limited amount of own-brand wine from selected grapes, picked separately and vinified in small batches, the first of which was exported last year, to China.

Montagu Wine & Spirits Co range

Chenin Blanc ☺ 🍷 ★★★ Expressive bruised apple on step-up **11**, satisfying flavour & bright acidity.

Merlot Untasted, as for **Chardonnay**, **Viognier**, **Rietrivier Muscadel Red**, **Muscat de Frontignan** & **Port**. **Pinotage** ★★ Previously, **08** was wild & fresh - a more untamed version than the well-behaved **07**. Still selling, not revisited like Rietvivier Muscadel White & Vintage Port Revolution. **Red Muscadel** ★★★ **11** fortified winter warmer bursts with ripe red sultanas, Christmas cake & fiery spirit. **White Muscadel** 🍷 ★★ Reticent fortified dessert **11** has golden hue, Golden Syrup sweetness & warm farewell. **Rietrivier Muscadel White** ★★★★ Gorgeous peach & nectarine, candied tangerine peel on fortified **07**, very sweet yet not cloying, well-judged alc lends buoyancy to finish. **Jerepico Red** ★★ Fortified dessert from muscadel. Dusty tealeaf appeal, brandy-soaked sultana richness, fire on **11**. This, following, 500 ml. **Jerepico White** 🍷 ★★ Fortified from unspecified variety/s. **11** apricot & nut twist in tail, oxidative styling. **Vintage Port Revolution** ★★★ Multi-awarded version from touriga, **07** leafy hint, good structure & length. Should be peaking now. **Cape Ruby Port** NEW 🍷 ★★★ Chocolate-laden **NV** from touriga, tad old fashioned but pleasant, heart-warming conclusion.

Uitvlucht Wines range

Cabernet Sauvignon ★★★ **08** was light bodied, offered honest fruit mid-2009, firm tannins may since have softened. Upper Langkloof WO. **Shiraz** ★★★★ **08** deep, dark & voluptuous on review, with well-managed tannins, more serious than **07** (★★★). **Sauvignon Blanc** 🍷 Await next. — Panel

Montagu Wine Cellar

Location/WO: Montagu ▪ Map: Klein Karoo & Garden Route ▪ Est 1941 ▪ 1stB 1975 ▪ Tasting & sales Mon–Fri 8–5 Sat 9–12 ▪ Closed all pub hols ▪ Cellar tours by appt during harvest 10–4 ▪ Farm produce ▪ BYO picnic ▪ Owner(s) 68 members ▪ Cellarmaster(s) Eben Rademeyer (2006) ▪ Winemaker(s) Collin Wright (1990) & Cobus la Grange (2009) ▪ Viticulturist(s) Johannes Mellet (2005, consultant) ▪ 660ha (11 varieties r/w) ▪ 13,000t/5,500cs own label 12% red 82% white 6% muscadel ▪ IPW ▪ PO Box 29 Montagu 6720 ▪ sales@montaguwines.co.za ▪ www. montaguwines.co.za ▪ S 33° 46′ 37.3″ E 020° 7′ 58.4″ ▪ **T** +27 (0)23-614-1125 ▪ F +27 (0)23-614-1793

Modernisation of this venerable cellar in the eponymous Klein Karoo town continues. With an eye to environmental impact the effluent water treatment facility has been upgraded, and, believing that 'a healthy vine produces a quality wine', viticultural consultant Johannes Mellet has been piloting an intensified programme of vineyard care.

Chenin Blanc ☺ 📖 ▨ ★★★ Floral, beeswax & oranges, appealing **11** fresh acidity, zesty & clean. **White Muscadel** ☺ 📖 ▨ ★★★ Previewed **11** fortified dessert, lovely grapey flavour, light lime lift, long fresh finish.

Cabernet Sauvignon 📖 ★★★ Straightforward **08** was tad oaky mid-2009, still selling. **Merlot-Ruby Cabernet** 📖 ▨ Previewed **11** too unformed to rate. **Colombard** 📖 ★★ Lightly flavoured **11** with pineapple nuance, slimmer than previous. **Montagu Lover's Walk** Semi-sweet bubbly untasted. **Late Harvest** ★ Honey & wax on **09** sweet white, best enjoyed soon. **Hanepoot** Await new. **Red Muscadel** 📖 ▨ ★★ **10** fortified previewed last year was sweet & warming. Discontinued: **Cabernet Sauvignon-Shiraz**. — Panel

■ **Montagu Wine Company** *see* Montagu Wine & Spirits Co

Mont Byrne Estate

Location: Montagu ▪ Map: Robertson ▪ Est 2007 ▪ 1stB 2008 ▪ Tasting, sales & cellar tours by appt ▪ Guesthouses ▪ Children's play area ▪ Owner(s) Stuart & Sanet Byrne ▪ Winemaker(s) Stuart Byrne ▪ 20ha (ruby cab, chard, cbard) ▪ PO Box 387 Montagu 2952 ▪ sanet@kanonberg.co.za ▪ www.montbyrneestate.co.za ▪ **T** +27 **(0)83-287-1033** ▪ F +27 (0)23-614-3302

His maiden vintage port, the 2008, sold in its entirety to PPC for corporate gifting, owner/winemaker Stuart Byrne isn't sure where the 2009, now bottled, will find a home. Ditto the 2009 ruby cab. In fact, he's not sure when he'll have the time to launch either. The Montagu businessman is enjoying hugely his winefarming venture 'but it has a 3-year learning curve and a 5-year mistake list.'

Mont Destin

Location/WO: Paarl ▪ Map: Paarl & Wellington ▪ Est/1stB 1998 ▪ Tasting, sales & cellar tours by appt ▪ Closed all pub hols ▪ Open air wine bath ▪ Owner(s) Ernest & Samantha Bürgin ▪ Winemaker(s) Samantha Bürgin (May 1996) ▪ Viticulturist(s) Bertus de Clerk (2006, consultant) ▪ 10ha/7ha (cab, cinsaut, grenache, mourv, shiraz, viog) ▪ 15t/1,000cs own label 80% red 20% white ▪ IPW ▪ PO Box 1237 Stellenbosch 7599 ▪ info@montdestin.co.za ▪ www.montdestin.co.za ▪ S 33° 49′ 58.9″ E 018° 53′ 27.8″ ▪ **T** +27 (0)21-875-5870 ▪ F +27 (0)21-875-5870

Samantha and Ernest Bürgin's Stellenbosch boutique cellar has become the exclusive wine supplier to Skoda/Volkswagen automobile shows and launches worldwide, and has begun exporting to the US (having established itself in Belgium, Germany and Canada). The focus has turned to producing a 'unique, fabulously elegant South African Rhône-style blend'. The couple's out-the-box thinking has already produced a singular form of pampering: al fresco bathing in wine; now they're contemplating a further indulgence - bathing in chocolate.

★★★★☆ **Destiny Shiraz** Stepping up from **06**, elegant & serious **07** (★★★★★) shows exhilarating pristine fruit expression, excellent weight, velvety texture & balance. Lengthy blackberry & black pepper finish bodes well for the future.

★★★★☆ **Passioné** Generous & clever blend led by shiraz, cinsaut & mourvèdre. **09**'s rich & earthy, blackberry fruit concentration balanced by firm ripe tannins, moreish conclusion. **08** sold out untasted.

★★★★ **Chenin Blanc** ✓ ▨ Crisp apple & lemon on unoaked **10**. Impressive concentration, creaminess from lees-ageing, smooth acidity abets lingering citrus finish.

11 Barrels ✓ 🅑 ★★★☆ Shiraz & cinsaut-led unoaked blend a step up in **10**, accessible, light, spicy & fresh-fruited. — WB

■ **Mont d'Or** *see Makro*

Mont du Toit Kelder

Location: Wellington ▪ Map: Paarl & Wellington ▪ WO: Paarl ▪ Est 1996 ▪ 1stB 1998 ▪ Tasting, sales & cellar tours Mon-Fri 9-4.30 Sat by appt ▪ Fee R15/R35 ▪ Closed all pub hols ▪ Walking/hiking trails ▪ Picnic area by appt ▪ Guest cottages ▪ Owner(s) Stephan du Toit ▪ Cellarmaster(s) Bernd Philippi & Loftie Ellis (1997, consultants) ▪ Winemaker(s) Marinus Bredell (2011), with Abraham Cloete (Jan 2005) ▪ Viticulturist(s) Ettienne Barnard (Oct 2010) ▪ ±40ha/±28ha (alicante bouschet, cabs s/f, merlot, mourv, p verdot, shiraz, tinta barocca) ▪ ±150t/ ±8,000cs own label 100% red ▪ IPW ▪ PO Box 704 Wellington 7654 ▪ kelder@montdutoit.co.za ▪ www. montdutoit.co.za ▪ S 33° 39'31.2" E 019° 2'2.5" ▪ **T +27 (0)21-873-7745** ▪ F +27 (0)21-864-2737

The winery name is usually pronounced in the French way; that of the owner, Gauteng advocate Stephan du Toit, in the Afrikaans way. New winemaker Marinus Bredell (there's been some turnover recently) will no doubt manage both well. He will be expanding the production of single-cultivar reds introduced in 2010 to some acclaim (few ranges offer the quality:price ratio found in the Les Coteaux), after a decade of only blends from this corner of Wellington.

Mont du Toit Kelder range

★★★★ **Mont du Toit 06** (★★★★★) last year was a medley of brooding dark fruit, raspberries & tealeaves. Dense, complex & subtly oaked. Marries cab, merlot, alicante, shiraz, petit verdot, like powerhouse **05**.

★★★★☆ **Le Sommet** Ambitious blend. Last-tasted **03**'s (★★★★) composition was a secret, like **02**.

Hawequas ★★★ Cab-based combo destined for export markets. **07** had dark fruit, dry oaky end.

Les Coteaux range

★★★★☆ **Cabernet Sauvignon** ✓ **10** (★★★★) built to last in classic style, as was **09**. Handsome & serious - with even some elegant austerity which should start mellowing in a few years, given the good fruit.

★★★★ **Merlot** Very ripe fruit on attractive, open-textured **10** (★★★★). With acidity to freshen the ripeness, & a drying quality belying a touch of sugar, it has a lean element too. **09** perhaps lusher.

★★★★☆ **Shiraz** Ripe sweet fruit on **10** (★★★☆), less impressive than **09** but appealing & tasty. Dollop of sugar disguised by bony acidity, but great ripeness diminishes fruit intensity.

★★★★☆ **Sélection** ✓ **07** cab-based (69%) with merlot (18%) + 4 minor contributions. Drier, more elegant than others in range, but no less charming, & with bottle age augmenting classic, delicate fragrance of fruit & cedar. Lots of structure, subtly intense flavours. — TJ

■ **Montebello** *see Wine-of-the-Month Club*

Monterosso Estate

Location/map/WO: Stellenbosch ▪ Est/1stB 2000 ▪ Tasting, sales & cellar tours Mon-Fri 9-4 Sat/Sun & pub hols by appt only ▪ Fee R10pp ▪ Owner(s) Francesco, Socrate & Orneglio De Franchi ▪ Cellarmaster(s)/winemaker(s) Orneglio De Franchi (Jan 2000) ▪ Viticulturist(s) Francesco De Franchi & Orneglio De Franchi (both Jan 2000) ▪ 83ha/60ha (cab, merlot, ptage, sangio, shiraz, chard, chenin, riesling, sauv, sem) ▪ 540t/380cs own label 60% red 40% white ▪ PO Box 5 Stellenbosch 7599 ▪ defranchivin@mweb.co.za, monterosso@mweb.co.za ▪ www. monterosso.co.za ▪ S 33° 54'6.8" E 018° 50'10.4" ▪ **T +27 (0)21-889-7081 / +27 (0)21-889-5021** ▪ F +27 (0)21-889-7081 / +27 (0)21-889-5021

Socrate de Franchi bought this property in 1977, naming it after his Ligurian birth-place. An Italianesque cellar eventually grew on the Koelenhof Ridge, and the Italian flair is strengthened by the contribution of three sons. Now they're 'busy with plans and investors to establish a restaurant and function facilities'.

Sangiovese Socrate ☺ ★★★ **09**'s cherry & oak notes complemented by attractive but very firm tannins.
Chenin Blanc Old Bush Vine ☺ 🗏 🅑 ★★★ Easy-going **11** has fruit & freshness, less intensity & length.

Cabernet Sauvignon-Merlot ★★★★ Last year, honest **06** showed cassis & cherries on classic, balanced & firm structure, with integrated oak. **Sauvignon Blanc** 🗏 🅑 ★★ Grass & peardrop notes on soft **11**. — JPf

■ **Montestell** *see* Boland Kelder
■ **Mont Michele** *see* Leopard's Leap Wines

Montpellier

Location/map/WO: Tulbagh ▪ Est 1714 ▪ Tasting, sales & tours Mon-Fri 9–12; 2–5 Sat 9–12 ▪ Fee R10 ▪ Closed all pub hols ▪ Pre-booked cheese platters & light meals available during tasting hours ▪ Tour groups - gazebo with pizza oven ▪ Olives ▪ Walking/hiking trails ▪ Conservation area: Renosterbos ▪ Guesthouse/B&B/self-catering ▪ Weddings ▪ Owner(s) Lucas J van Tonder ▪ Cellarmaster(s) Theo Brink (Jan 2008) ▪ Winemaker(s) Theo Brink (Jan 2008), with Mynhardt van der Merwe (Dec 2009) ▪ Viticulturist(s) Mynhardt van der Merwe (Dec 2009) ▪ 482ha/60ha (cab, merlot, p verdot, pinot, shiraz, chard, chenin, gewürtz, viog) ▪ 300t/2,200cs own label 48% red 27% white 25% MCC + 150,000 litres in bulk ▪ PO Box 79 Tulbagh 6820 ▪ montpellier@montpellier.co.za ▪ www.montpellier.co.za ▪ S 33° 16' 30.4" E 019° 6' 40.0" ▪ **T +27 (0)23-230-0656 ▪** F +27 (0)23-230-1574

Cellarmaster Theo Brink has ramped up the méthode cap classique sparkling production, now comprising 25% of total output of this historic Tulbagh estate. A new barrel cellar has been built, using the eco-aware hay-bale construction system, and, to celebrate, a barrel-fermented chardonnay has been added to the listings.

Cabernet Sauvignon ★★★ Loud minty-nutty **09** masks ripe, enthusiastic blackcurrant fruit with layers of thick tannins. May emerge with time. **Shiraz ★★ 09** 1st since **05**, riper, fuller fruit, strong oaky tannins. **Chardonnay** NEW **★★★** Oaked **11** preview shows promise: rich, ripe & buttery, supple juicy body & ginger-spicy finish. **Chenin Blanc** 🔲 **★★★** Previewed **11** shows hint of tropical fruit. Lean, tart acidity. **Sauvignon Blanc** 🔲 Quirky **11** unrated tank sample has primary yeasty notes. **Theo's Synchrony** 🔲 **★★★** Chenin & gewürztraminer, off-dry **11** preview shows latter's appealing rosewater scents & former's tangy freshness. **Méthode Cap Classique ★★★** Traditional-method sparkling **NV** from pinot noir, apple & strawberry with lively mousse previously. **Port ★★ NV** fireside fortifier from shiraz last had dusty plum-pudding flavour. — GdB

Mont Rochelle Hotel & Mountain Vineyards

Location/map: Franschhoek ▪ WO: Franschhoek/Western Cape/Walker Bay ▪ Est 1994 ▪ 1stB 1996 ▪ Tasting & sales 10–7 daily ▪ Fee R20 ▪ Closed Dec 25 ▪ Cellar tours Mon-Fri 11, 12.30 & 3 Sat/Sun/pub hols 11 & 3 ▪ Mange Tout and Country Kitchen restaurants (see Restaurants section) ▪ Five-star hotel (see Accommodation section) ▪ Conference/function facilities ▪ Picnics ▪ Walking/hiking trails ▪ 'Tasting 101' monthly educational wine tastings ▪ Full moon hikes in summer ▪ Annual harvest festival ▪ Owner(s) Erwin Schnitzler & Rwayitare family ▪ Cellarmaster(s)/winemaker(s)/viticulturist(s) Darran Stone (Jun 2011) ▪ 33ha/16ha (cab, merlot, shiraz, chard, sauv, sem) ▪ 70t/6,000cs own label 60% red 35% white 5% rosé ▪ PO Box 334 Franschhoek 7690 ▪ wine@montrochelle.co.za ▪ www.montrochelle.co.za ▪ S 33° 54' 52.1" E 019° 6' 21.9" ▪ **T +27 (0)21-876-2770 ▪** F +27 (0)21-876-2362

At this small but upmarket establishment, guests enjoy magnificent views over the Franschhoek Valley, as well as internationally acclaimed 5-star accommodation and restaurants. The winery's success is based on sound viticultural practices, though 'some innovative adjustments are critical' according to new winemaker, Darren Stone, to maintain their desired style in challenging vintages, which already show the effects of global climate change. The themed 'Tasting 101' wine presentations are a new and educational way of experiencing their wines.

Miko Premier range

★★★★☆ **Chardonnay Sur Lie** Flagship white honours late co-owner. Cooler **09** (★★★★) has a tight centre of tangy citrus & pear enveloped by oak. Intense, youthful, needs time. Shade off previous elegant **06**.
Cabernet Sauvignon Await next.

Mont Rochelle Hotel & Mountain Vineyards range

★★★★ **Barrel Fermented Chardonnay 08** still current vintage. When last tasted, was medium bodied & elegant, with pear & vanilla flavours.
★★★★ **Sauvignon Blanc Reserve ✓** Bottled **10** (★★★★) retains preview's ripe & succulent texture, with tangy stonefruit flavours, but lacks the verve of **09**.
Cabernet Sauvignon ★★★ 06 is a ripe, sumptuous, dark berry compote. Best balance of the reds below, but all show more power than finesse. **Merlot ★★★ 05** ultra ripe, with brooding dark fruit & firm, brusque tone. **Syrah ★★★ 06** bold, ripe & flavoursome. Supple structure but big-boned with alc to match, demands hearty fare. WO W Cape, as for Artemis. **Artemis ★★★ 07** mostly Bordeaux blend, still available. When last tasted, had

appealing bramble, earthy notes. **Rosé ★★★ 10** bright, savoury & tangy shiraz-based dry quaffer. **Unwooded Chardonnay** 🎴 **★★★** Now bottled, **10** quieter than last year's preview, with creamy pear, touch of minerality & warm exit. WO Walker Bay. — MW

■ **Mooi** *see Flavors of Wine*

Mooi Bly Winery

Location/WO: Paarl ▪ Map: Paarl & Wellington ▪ Est/1stB 2005 ▪ Tasting, sales & cellar tours by appt ▪ Fee R50pp ▪ Closed Dec 25 & Jan 1 ▪ BYO picnic ▪ Walks ▪ 6 self-catering Cottages ▪ Owner(s) Wouters family ▪ Cellarmaster(s) Erik Schouteden (Jan 2005) ▪ Winemaker(s) Erik Schouteden ▪ Viticulturist(s) Erik Schouteden (Feb 2001) ▪ 32ha/18ha (cab, malbec, shiraz, tannat, chard, chenin) ▪ 70t/3,000cs own label 50% red 50% white ▪ PO Box 801 Huguenot 7645 ▪ wine@mooibly.com ▪ www.mooibly.com ▪ S 33° 41'7.0" E 019° 1'21.9" ▪ **T +27 (0)21-868-2808** ▪ F +27 (0)21-868-2808

The motto might be 'Honest wines for honest prices' but this family boutique cellar offers much more originality than that. It's one of the few producers of single bottled tannat and malbec, where demand outstrips supply, not suprisingly given the small volumes and quality produced from the 8 year old vineyards, 125 and 85 12- bottle cases respectively.

★★★★ Malbec ✓ Hedgerow fruit; intriguing wax polish note, **08** keeps in dark-toned character. Tasty accessibility via elegant oak-seamed succulence. Drink now till ±2015.
Cabernet Sauvignon Await next, as for **Shiraz**. **Tannat ★★★★** One of only few on market, **08** has earthy, green olive notes, smoky dark fruit. Dry finish from firm but ripe tannins. **Chardonnay ★★★** Easy-drinking **10** has touch of oak in tropical flavours. **Chenin Blanc ★★★★** From 35 year old vines, characterful **10**'s thatch & melon flavours are kept tangy-fresh by limy acidity. — CR

Mooiplaas Estate & Private Nature Reserve

Location/map/WO: Stellenbosch ▪ Est 1806 ▪ 1stB 1995 ▪ Tasting & sales Mon-Fri 9-4 Sat 10-2 ▪ Fee R10 ▪ Closed Easter Fri/Sun/Mon, Dec 25/26 & Jan 1 ▪ BYO picnic ▪ Walks/hikes ▪ Mountain biking ▪ 16ha Private Nature Reserve ▪ Langtafel (30 seater) luncheons or dinners every 6-8 weeks in the Manor House (a National Monument); Taste Experience presented by Dirk Roos in the 'voorkamer' (10-16 guests); booking essential ▪ Owner(s) Mooiplaas Trust ▪ Cellarmaster(s) Louis Roos (1983) ▪ Winemaker(s) Louis Roos (1983), with Matilda Viljoen (Jan 2011) ▪ Viticulturist(s) Tielman Roos (1981) ▪ 250ha/100ha (cab, ptage, chenin, sauv) ▪ 750t/8,000cs own label 57% red 41% white 2% rosé ▪ Other export brand: The Collection ▪ BWI, IPW ▪ PO Box 104 Koelenhof 7605 ▪ info@mooiplaas.co.za ▪ www.mooiplaas.co.za ▪ S 33° 51'16.3" E 018° 44'21.4" ▪ **T +27 (0)21-903-6273/4** ▪ F +27 (0)21-903-3474

Two new wines have been added to Mooiplaas' flagship range, honouring Nicolaas and Mercia Roos, who acquired the farm in 1963. Made in limited – but not entirely tiny – quantities, there's the Watershed Shiraz (12 barrels), from high-lying east-facing vineyards, and Houmoed Chenin Blanc (10 barrels). Loosely translated as 'be courageous', Houmoed refers to a 38-year-old block planted by Nicolaas. Also new is the Langtafel Taste Experience during which guests sample older vintages alongside specially selected dishes.

The Mercia Collection

★★★★ Watershed Shiraz NEW Impressive **08** debut with earthy bouquet, unevolved dark-fruit centre & rather firm tannins. Fruit intensity & acid balance show fine potential, invite further cellaring to show best.
★★★★ Rosalind Cab-led blend with cab franc & merlot. **07** exercise in restraint versus more muscular **06**. Balanced & lingering, no sharp edges, just an enjoyable - some would say old-fashioned - classic glass of SA red.
★★★★ Houmoed Chenin Blanc NEW Estate's first barrel-fermented/aged (9 months) chenin. **09** intriguing fennel, anise, salty interplay; well-judged oak, knife-like acidity cuts richness of apricot fruit.
Duel Méthode Cap Classique ★★★★ Champagne-method sparkling worth buying as much for the label as the contents. **NV** from pinot noir & chardonnay, strawberry sherbet appeal, creamy finish, tad drier than previous.

Classic range

★★★★ Cabernet Sauvignon Appealing blackcurrant/tealeaf complexity in **05** (**★★★★**). Plush fruit checked by fresh acidity, oak char slightly out of sync, so there's less elegance than in **03**; **04** (**★★★**) reviewed this edition has lovely forest floor nose but is malty, ready.

★★★★ **Chenin Blanc Bush Vine** Voluptuous & compelling **10** old-vine treasure doesn't need oak support: lengthy fermentation, lees-ageing impart super vinosity & length, 15% botrytis adds breadth & wax notes. **Cabernet Franc** ★★★★ 07's ripe black fruit seamed with variety's leafy tones, refreshing, satisfying mouthfeel. **Merlot** ★★★★ 08 no shrinking violet: bursts with morello cherry, plum & smoke; fresh, fruity, supple. **Pinotage** ★★★★ Estate's mainstay grape unoaked for early access, gains some heft from 10% oaked cab in **08**. Slips down easily with strawberry & tangerine appeal. **Shiraz** ★★★★ Previously, **05** featured ripe blueberry fruit, firm tannic structure abetted by 40% new French oak. **Sauvignon Blanc** ★★★ Flavoursome **10** has white asparagus & herbaceous bottle-age notes, tangy grapefruit acidity.

Langtafel range

> **White** ☺ ⚕ ★★★ Bottle-age & dash semillon do the business for **10** chenin/sauvignon combo. Affable, zesty & wallet-friendly, too!

Red ★★ Creamy 4-way mix, mostly merlot in **10**, uncomplicated & enjoyable. **Rosé** 🔲 ★★★ Leafy **11** from cab just a touch more sweetness than previous. — CvZ

Mooiuitsig Wine Cellars

Location: Bonnievale ▪ Map: Robertson ▪ Est 1947 ▪ Sales Mon-Thu 8-5 Fri 8-2 ▪ Tours by appt ▪ Stay-overs at De Rust Lodge info@outdoorarena.co.za; T +27 (0)23-616-2444 ▪ Owner(s) Jonker & Claassen families ▪ Winemaker(s) Nico van der Westhuizen & Jean Aubrey, with Lazarus Kholomba ▪ Viticulturist(s) Casper Matthee ▪ 150ha total ▪ 2,900t ▪ PO Box 15 Bonnievale 6730 ▪ info@mooiuitsig.co.za ▪ www.mooiuitsig.co.za ▪ S 33° 56'59.0" E 020° 2'36.1" ▪ **T +27 (0)23-616-2143** ▪ F +27 (0)23-616-2675

Founded by the Jonkers in 1947, today Mooiuitsig is one of South Africa's largest family-owned drinks wholesalers. It encompasses Mooiuitsig farm near Bonnievale with its several cellars, three depots and a distribution network, as well as a number of liquor outlets. A new low-alcohol addition to the Rusthof range is the 5L boxed Natural Sweet red.

▪ **Mooiuitzicht** *see* Mooiuitsig Wine Cellars
▪ **Moonlight Organics** *see* Stellar Winery

Moordenaarskop

Location: Somerset West ▪ Map: Helderberg ▪ WO: Stellenbosch ▪ Est 1999 ▪ 1stB 2002 ▪ Tasting, sales & cellar tours by appt ▪ Owner(s)/cellarmaster(s)/winemaker(s)/viticulturist(s) Graham Smith ▪ 0.33ha (cab) ▪ 2t/120cs own label 100% red ▪ PO Box 2889 Somerset West 7129 ▪ mwsmiths@mweb.co.za ▪ S 34° 5'55.3" E 018° 54'53.7" ▪ **T +27 (0)21-858-1202** ▪ F +27 (0)86-672-6797

Graham Smith describes the 2011 vintage as a 'calamity' for his tiny winery in Somerset West, wind, rain and hail at awkward times all but wiping out the second harvest in a row. Still, he remains chipper about the 2009 vintage and says he will continue his quest to make robust, easy-drinking cab despite setbacks.

Cabernet Sauvignon Reserve Occasional release. **Cabernet Sauvignon** ★★★ Earthy & savoury **09** still quite firm, needs more time in bottle to soften & show its potential. — IM

Môreson

Location/map: Franschhoek ▪ WO: Coastal/Franschhoek ▪ Est 1983 ▪ 1stB 1994 ▪ Tasting, sales & cellar tours daily 9.30-5 ▪ Fee R30 ▪ Closed Dec 25 ▪ Bread & Wine Restaurant daily 12-3 (see Restaurants section) & The Farm Grocer (for lighter meals) daily 9.30-4.30 ▪ Charcuterie produced by Neil Jewell ▪ Exotic Plant Company ▪ Wine blending & breadmaking ▪ Owner(s) Richard Friedman ▪ Winemaker(s) Clayton Reabow (May 2007), with Marozanne Grobbelaar (Nov 2008) ▪ Viticulturist(s) Lochner Bester ▪ 35ha/±15ha (chard, chenin, sauv) ▪ ±88t 41% red 38% white 21% MCC ▪ Euro Gap, IPW ▪ PO Box 114 Franschhoek 7690 ▪ sales@moreson.co.za ▪ www.moreson.co.za ▪ S 33° 53'11.9" E 019° 3'30.6" ▪ **T +27 (0)21-876-3055** ▪ F +27 (0)21-876-2348

'As a farm, we are a chardonnay producer,' says winemaker Clayton Reabow, who has dedicated the past four years to realigning the plantings and production to reflect this identity. With 80% of the vineyards now under chardonnay, they already have a range of award-winning méthode cap classique sparklings, from icon to everyday, as well as still wines. Some classy reds are also available at this popular tourist destination, offering a creative array of food and wine related activities to entertain everyone from casual visitors to corporate customers.

Môreson range

★★★★ **Pinotage** ✓ Pedigree of medalled **08** evident on latest **10**. Lavish dark fruit, with silky streamlined texture & firm, supple structure. Succulent & delicious. No **09**. Stellenbosch grapes.

★★★★ **Mata Mata** NEW 3-way Bordeaux blend led by cab franc, reflects house's chosen style & interest in this variety. **09** elegant & flavoursome, showing structure & poise. Will reward few years in cellar.

★★★★ **Premium Chardonnay** 🌿 Showcases power of house's chosen white variety in riper **10**. Richly textured, lime marmalade threaded with tangy acidity. Youthful, deserves cellaring. Franschhoek WO.

★★★★ **Solitaire Blanc de Blancs** ✓ Latest **NV** méthode cap classique sparkling a step up. Portion older vintages is catalyst for complexity, melds bright, vivacious citrus tone & rich, creamy lees & oak elements into elegant harmony.

Cabernet Franc ★★★★ **08** niche variety is ripe & fragrant, with bright red berries & firm structure. Youthful potential, just needs time. **Petit Verdot** Not tasted this edition, as for **Magia**, **Chenin Blanc**, **Sauvignon Blanc**, **Gala Cuvée Cape**, **One Méthode Cap Classique** (listed as 'Pinot Noir-Chardonnay MCC' last time), **Pink Brut Rosé** (previously listed as 'Brut Rosé'). Discontinued: **Cabernet Sauvignon**, **Merlot**, **Barrel Fermented Chenin Blanc**.

Miss Molly range

In My Bed Cabernet Sauvignon-Merlot not tasted, as for **Hoity Toity Chenin Blanc**, **Kitchen Thief Sauvignon Blanc** & **Méthode Cap Classique** (listed as 'Bubbly' last edition). — MW

■ **Môrewag** *see* Blomendahl Vineyards

Morgenhof Wine Estate

Location/map: Stellenbosch ▪ WO: Simonsberg–Stellenbosch/Stellenbosch ▪ Est 1692 ▪ 1stB 1984 ▪ Tasting & sales Mon-Fri 9–5.30 (Nov-Apr) & 9–4.30 (May-Oct); Sat/Sun 10–5 (Nov-Apr) & 10–3 (May-Oct) ▪ Fee R20/Morgenhof, R10/Fantail ▪ Closed Easter Fri, Dec 25 & Jan 1 ▪ Cellar tours/viewing of underground barrel cellar on request ▪ Cheese platters ▪ Morgenhof Restaurant & Coffee shop (see Restaurants section) ▪ Facilities for children ▪ Gift shop ▪ Conferences ▪ Weddings/functions ▪ Heli-pad ▪ Conservation area ▪ Morgenhof Manor House (see Accommodation section) ▪ Owner(s) Anne Cointreau ▪ Cellarmaster(s) Jacques Cilliers (Dec 2004) ▪ Viticulturist(s) Pieter Haasbroek (Apr 1998) ▪ 212ha/74ha (cabs s/f, malbec, merlot, chenin) ▪ 410t/15,000cs own label 60% red 38% white 2% rosé ▪ BWI, IPW ▪ PO Box 365 Stellenbosch 7599 ▪ info@morgenhof.com ▪ www.morgenhof.com ▪ S 33° 53'38.5" E 018° 51'39.2" ▪ **T +27 (0)21-889-5510** ▪ F +27 (0)21-889-5266

As befits a winery under French ownership since 1993 (owner Anne Cointreau is from the famous French cognac and liqueurs family), classic traditions are frequently invoked here. Such as the vineyards on the Simonsberg slopes going unirrigated, and the lack of acidification of the wines – which are generally restrained and aiming for finesse rather than showy fruitiness. More modern concerns including recognising the need for conservation – they're working on increasing the area under natural fynbos to 30 hectares. And, of course, embracing the social media: 2011 saw Morgenhof's first 'tweet-up' tasting.

Morgenhof Estate range

★★★★☆ **The Morgenhof Estate** In classic restrained, dry style, **05** (★★★★) cab-based Bordeaux blend relies on structure, not fruitiness. Very firm tannins (as with **04**) mark long, complex, but slightly hot finish.

★★★★ **Chardonnay** Last year **10** sample promised same subtlety, texture, finesse as **09**, which was showing fine creamy balance, poised acidity, subtle oak support to citrus richness; elegantly assertive.

★★★★ **Chenin Blanc** 🍴🌿 Lightly oaked **10** now bottled. soft notes of lime, citrus & honey-melon. The finish is subtle & precise, making up for the lack of intensity. 10% sauvignon for added freshness.

★★★★ **Brut Reserve** Some pleasingly developed toasty, spicy baked apple notes in **06**, tasted last year, as elegant & fresh as ever, benefitting from ageing on lees (too rare in SA). From 60:40 chard, pinot.

Cabernet Sauvignon ✓ ★★★★ Densely packed **06**, with dollop of merlot, has inviting fruit & tobacco aromas. Finishes with firm, somewhat mouth-drying tannins. **Merlot** ★★★☆ Restrained styling of **07** offers soft ripe dark berries & milk choc, but finish a little too rugged. **Merlot-Cabernet Franc** NEW ★★★ Food-friendly **08** with herbaceous, meaty aromas. In classical style, but slightly acidic, rustic finish. **Sauvignon Blanc** 🍴🌿 ★★★ **10**, tasted ex-tank last year, now perhaps fading, with crisp, delicate & simple green & tropical fruit. **Noble**

Late Harvest Await new release. **Cape Vintage** ★★★★ Last-tasted **03** had delicacy & power. Dry finish, like previous **00** (★★★★).

Fantail range

Pinotage Rosé ☺ 🍴 🖱 ★★★ Delicious, gluggable **11** fresh & nearly dry, with a zesty strawberry finish. This, **Pinotage**, white blend below WO Stbosch.

Merlot ★★★ Savoury-fruity **07** previewed last year. Herbaceous twist to full flavours; solid & firm. **Pinotage** 🍴 ★★★ Easy-drinking, juicy **09**; usual 15% merlot; light tannic grip. **Cabernet Sauvignon-Cabernet Franc** ★★ **07** now bottled, still dominated by big, furry tannins. **Chardonnay** 🍴 ★★★ Last was pleasantly insipid **08** ex-Franschhoek. **Sauvignon Blanc** 🍴 ★★ **10** last year ex tank light & simple. **Chenin Blanc-Sauvignon Blanc** 🍴 🖱 ★★ Off-dry **11** simple & soft. **Semi-Sweet** 🍴 ★★ Mild **09** from chenin not revisited. — JPf

Morgenster Estate

Location: Somerset West ▪ Map: Helderberg ▪ WO: Stellenbosch ▪ Est 1993 ▪ 1stB 1998 ▪ Tasting & sales Mon-Fri 10–5 Sat/Sun 10–4 ▪ Tasting fee R25 wine/R20 olive oil & olive products ▪ Closed Easter Fri & Dec 25 ▪ Sofia's at Morgenster (see Restaurants section) ▪ Owner(s) Giulio Bertrand ▪ Cellarmaster(s)/winemaker(s) Henry Kotzé (Oct 2009) ▪ Viticulturist(s) Bob Hobson (Aug 2008) ▪ 200ha/25ha (cabs s/f, merlot, nebbiolo, p verdot, sangio) ▪ ±120t own label 95% red 5% rosé ▪ BWI, IPW, IPW ▪ PO Box 1616 Somerset West 7129 ▪ info@morgenster.co.za ▪ www.morgenster.co.za ▪ S 34° 5' 2.9" E 018° 53' 7.8" ▪ **T +27 (0)21-852-1738** ▪ F +27 (0)21-852-1141

Morgenster was founded in 1711 by French Huguenot Jacques Malan, who named it after the morning star. Present owner, Giulio Bertrand, celebrated the tercentenary in style with several hundred guests. Since his purchase in 1992, the Italian businessman has restored the property on a grand scale, and it is now as well known for its olive oil (there are 50ha of olive groves) as its wine - both award-winners. The pair of merlot-influenced Bordeaux-style blends are still more comfortably focused than the Italian-oriented pair, which have yet to achieve consistency. The Bordeaux-style range is to be extended with a sauvignon blanc-semillon blend; we left it undisturbed in barrel as we went to press.

Morgenster Estate range

★★★★☆ **Morgenster** Youthful **09** flagship shaped by its major cab, merlot partners (also petit verdot, cab franc). Rich in sweet fruit; dense ripe tannins & oak spice, all yet to harmonise. Plenty of time on its side.

★★★★☆ **Lourens River Valley** ✓ Merlot-based **09** already showing its class. Better vintage encourages fleshier, more plush style than **08**; confident, balanced structure allows for current enjoyment & ageing. Belies its 2nd label tag.

Sauvignon Blanc-Semillon NEW 🖱 Barrel sample **11** too unformed to rate.

Italian Collection

★★★★ **Nabucco** Unshowy floral, tarry aromas true to **09**'s (★★★★) 100% nebbiolo composition. Like Tosca enjoyable younger rather than older. **08** elegant, deeper flavours.

Tosca ★★★★ Sangiovese's bright succulence lifts softish **09**. Lacks intensity of **08** (★★★★) though splashes of Bordeaux varieties add rich finish. **Caruso** 🖱 ★★★ **11** dry rosé from sangiovese with 10% cab franc; flavoursome wild strawberry tang, savoury persistence. Enjoy in freshness of youth. — AL

■ **Mori Wines** *see Casa Mori*
■ **Morkel** *see Bellevue Estate Stellenbosch*
■ **MorningSide** *see Môreson*

Morton Wines

Location/WO: Stellenbosch ▪ Est 2003 ▪ Tasting & sales by appt ▪ Owner(s) Aidan & Mandy Morton ▪ Winemaker(s) Miles Mossop ▪ Viticulturist(s) Aidan Morton ▪ 10t/700cs 100% red ▪ 5 Waterweg Stellenbosch 7600 ▪ aidan@tokara.com ▪ **T +27 (0)21-808-5972** ▪ F +27 (0)86-690-7211

Aidan Morton is viticulturist at top-rank Tokara and we've tasted three vintages made (from grapes off model vineyards, of course) with Tokara winemaker Miles Mossop. But none recently – perhaps unsurprisingly, given the day job's demands.

Shiraz ★★★★ Last was **05**; spice, choc & red fruit in harmony, savoury notes & oaky. — AL

Mostertsdrift Noble Wines

Location/map/WO: Stellenbosch ▪ Est/1stB 2001 ▪ Tasting, sales & cellar tours by appt ▪ Fee R10 ▪ Meals for groups by prior arrangement ▪ Facilities for children ▪ Conference venue ▪ Owner(s) André Mostert & Anna-Mareè Uys (Mostert) ▪ Cellarmaster(s)/winemaker(s) Anna-Mareè Uys (Jan 2001) ▪ Viticulturist(s) Nico Mostert (Jan 2001) ▪ 13ha/±8ha (cab, merlot, pinot, chard, hanepoot) ▪ ±80-100t/1,993cs own label 70% red 10% white 20% rosé + 15,000L bulk ▪ PO Box 2061 Dennesig Stellenbosch 7601 ▪ winemaker@mostertsdrift.co.za ▪ www.mostertsdrift.co.za ▪ S 33° 53' 31.7" E 018° 50' 17.6" ▪ **T +27 (0)21-889-5344** ▪ F +27 (0)86-516-1730

At this compact estate on the northern outskirts of Stellenbosch, 2012 sees the debut of Anna-Mareè Mostert-Uys' new 'baby', a Cape Blend, obviously doted upon by its mum. Like all Anna-Mareè's wines, it's made light and accessible, to be drunk early. Next project is an off-dry red.

Cabernet Sauvignon ★★★ 07 last year was more accessible than previous vintage, with nutty complexity, creamy mouthfeel. **AnéRouge ★★★** Mainly cab, rest merlot. **07**'s well-managed ripe fruit delivered balance, soft appeal. **Cape Blend** NEW 🗔 **★★★** Mainly merlot & pinotage (50/30), rest cab, **08** shows some development, good ripeness. Overtly fruity, with tangy pinotage edge. **Merlot Rosé** 🗔 **★★** Preview **10** was off-dry last time with tutti-frutti styling. **Chardonnay** 🗔 **★★☆** Pre-bottling, **10** last time charmed with peach & white flower aromas. **White Muscadel** Not tasted. — GdB

■ **Mountain Eye** *see* Kleinhoekkloof

Mountain Oaks Organic Winery

Location: Rawsonville ▪ Map: Breedekloof ▪ WO: Slanghoek ▪ Est/1stB 2003 ▪ Tasting, sales & cellar tours by appt ▪ Farm tours & talks on organic farming by appt ▪ Owner(s) Stevens family ▪ Cellarmaster(s)/winemaker(s) Christine Stevens (2003) ▪ Viticulturist(s) Christine & Mark Stevens (2000) ▪ 200ha/16ha (cabs s/f, ptage, shiraz, chard, chenin) ▪ 20-30t own label 70% red 20% white 10% rosé ▪ Debio ▪ PO Box 68 Rawsonville 6845 ▪ christine@mountainoaks.co.za, eikenbosch@iafrica.com ▪ S 33° 38' 16.1" E 019° 13' 36.0" ▪ **T +27 (0)23-344-3107** ▪ F +27 (0)86-613-6687

Christine Stevens is an author as well as a winemaker. Her second book, Harvest Diaries chronicles the organic farming lives of herself and her husband Mark. She wants to show the benefits of organics, as well as of older wines. 'Everyone wants new, new,' she sighs. The new releases (younger than usual) should certainly benefit from bottle ageing. Many of their wines are occasional releases.

Mountain Oaks Winery range

★★★★ Pinotage ✓ 10 mirrors **09** in its ripe raspberry generosity, earthy veil. Youthful grip embracing rich, juicy flavours needs time to mellow.

★★★★ Cabernet Sauvignon-Cabernet Franc 🌿 Last-tasted **07** noted as needing time to settle.

★★★★ Chardonnay Reserve 🌿 Natural ferment adds earthy subtlety to quiet apple & nut tones on **10** (★★★★). Fresh & well-textured. Give yr/18 months for oak to harmonise. Charming **09**.

★★★★ Eikenbosch White ✓ 10 (★★★★) from chenin with 37% viognier. Delicate spring apple blossom fragrance, crisp appley flavours. Unoaked, while **06** was from chenin & oaked chardonnay.

Eikenbosch Red ✓ 🌿 **★★★★** Vivid-hued **09**; youthfully firm 40/60 cab sauvignon/cab franc with sufficient ripe fruit substance for necessary ageing. **Le Jardin Rosé** 🌿 **★★★** Last was **07**. **Chenin Blanc Barrel Reserve** 🌿 No new release. **Chenin Blanc Reserve** 🌿 **★★★★** Last-tasted **05** had herbal, lavendar intrigue; fresh, supple. Oaked. **Le Jardin** 🌿 **★★★** Last was **06** white blend. — AL

Mountain Range Products

Location: Cape Town ▪ Closed to public ▪ Owner(s) Belinda Traverso, Paul Finlayson & Paul de Waal ▪ 1,000cs ▪ 41 Product Street Maitland 7405 ▪ info@mountainrange.co.za ▪ www.mountainrange.co.za ▪ **T +27 (0)21-510-2700** ▪ F +27 (0)21-511-4772

The Table Mountain-shaped glass bottles used for this Stellenbosch-sourced line-up proved an instant hit when launched several years back. Today, it's not only vinous fare that attract shoppers' attention: there's brandies and sherries, an extra virgin olive oil and a range of bottled chillies varying in strength from 1 to 10.

Table Mountain Red 🗔 **★★★** Party-starting multi-variety **NV** blend, fresh, juicy. **Table Mountain White** 🗔 **★★★** Crisp appley acidity in **NV** sauvignon-semillon combo, for summer enjoyment. Neither revisited. — DB

Mountain Ridge Wines

Location: Wolseley ▪ Map: Breedekloof ▪ WO: Breedekloof/Western Cape ▪ Est 1949 ▪ 1stB 1976 ▪ Tasting & sales Mon-Fri 8–5 ▪ Closed all pub hols ▪ BYO picnic ▪ Owner(s) 20 members ▪ Cellarmaster(s) Paul Malan (Oct 2010) ▪ Winemaker(s) Christo Stemmet (Jan 2010) ▪ Viticulturist(s) Leon Dippenaar (consultant) ▪ 477ha (cab, shiraz, chenin, cbard) ▪ 6,600t/2,500cs own label 48% red 37% white 15% rosé ▪ IPW ▪ PO Box 108 Wolseley 6830 ▪ sales@mountainridge.co.za ▪ www.mountainridge.co.za ▪ S 33° 28'42.8" E 019° 12'16.2" ▪ **T +27 (0)23-231-1070** ▪ F +27 (0)23-231-1102

Paul Malan, new cellarmaster/manager of this established Wolseley grower-owned winery, has initiated several projects, including stepped up red wine production and sharpened wine quality, efficiency, safety and quality assurance. New clients in China and Africa have been signed up in an export drive both for bottled and bulk wines.

Cabernet Sauvignon Reserve ★★★★ Fruit-forward & rounded 09, ripe plums & attractive cedar overlay from new oak. **Shiraz Reserve** ★★★★ 09 full bodied, dark berries & chocolate notes, appealing lingering pepperiness. Gear up on 07 (★★★), with spicy coffee nuance. **Shiraz Rosé** NEW 🍷 Ⓐ ★★★ 11 delicate off-dry charmer with strawberry & rosepetal nuances. **Sauvignon Blanc** 🍷 ★★★ Step-up 11 packed with tropical fruit salad & Turkish Delight aromas. Discontinued: **Malbec-Pinotage, Pinotage Rosé, Chenin Blanc, Chenin Blanc-Colombar.** — DB

Mountain River Wines

Location: Paarl ▪ WO: Western Cape/Breedekloof/Olifants River ▪ Est 1993 ▪ 1stB 1998 ▪ Closed to public ▪ Owner(s) De Villiers Brits ▪ Cellarmaster(s) De Villiers Brits, with consultants ▪ 1.2ha (shiraz) ▪ 30,000cs own label 60% red 40% white ▪ 146 Main Road Paarl 7646 ▪ dev@mountainriverwines.co.za, mattie@mountainriverwines.co.za ▪ www.mountainriverwines.co.za ▪ **T +27 (0)21-872-3245/6/7** ▪ F +27 (0)21-872-3255

Last time, owner and winemaker De Villiers Brits said he'd take his easy-drinking wines to Russia and China, and so he has. Now his sights are on growing the Paarl-based business' footprints in India and the UK. Good news, considering the distances the wines travel, is that he's looking at PET and other lightweight bottles.

Mountain River range

Pinotage ★★★ Previewed 10 powerful 'banana bread' aroma, ripe & slippery fruit with contrasting strong tannins demanding time. **Pinotage-Shiraz** Untasted. Discontinued: **Pinotage-Cabernet Sauvignon.**

Maankloof range

Chenin Blanc ☺ 🍷 ★★★ Switches from off-dry to dry in 11 preview, appealing varietal apple & thatch, zingy conclusion.

Cabernet Sauvignon 🍷 New vintage not available, as for **Sauvignon Blanc. Pinotage** ★★★ Last edition, ex-tank 10 had acetone & strawberry tones, fair grip. **Shiraz** In abeyance.

Ukuzala range

Dry Red ★★ Merlot & 3 others, 11 supple & fresh, lightish for youthful enjoyment. Tasted ex-tank, like next. **Dry White** ★★ Lemon & thatch tones on 11 slimmer's friend (low alc & sugar) from chenin & colombard.

Zaràfa range

Cabernet Sauvignon ★★ 11 berry-laden easy-drinker from Olifants River. Previewed, rating provisional, as all. **Pinotage** ★★★ 'Coffee' style 11 packed with sweet fruit but shows good grip, not overdone. **Shiraz** ★★ Appealing chocolate aroma on 11 let down by slight bitter lift. **Pinotage Rosé** Not tasted. **Sauvignon Blanc** 🍷 Ⓐ ★★ 11 not the breezy summer sipper we enjoyed last time. — CvZ

▪ **Mountain Shadows** *see* Wineways Marketing
▪ **Mountainside** *see* Ruitersvlei Wines
▪ **Mountain Stream** *see* Ashton Wynkelder

Mount Babylon Vineyards

Location: Hermanus ▪ Map: Elgin, Walker Bay & Bot River ▪ Est 2002 ▪ 1stB 2007 ▪ Tasting, sales & cellar tours by appt ▪ Cheese platters ▪ Owner(s) Johan Holtzhausen ▪ Winemaker(s) Jean-Claude Martin (2008, consultant) ▪

Viticulturist(s) Johan Pienaar (2002, consultant) ▪ 65ha/7ha (malbec, shiraz, viog) ▪ ±38t/±200cs own label 90% red 10% white ▪ PO Box 7370 Stellenbosch 7599 ▪ info@mountbabylon.co.za ▪ www.mountbabylon.co.za ▪ S 34° 19' 44.0" E 019° 19' 34.3" ▪ **T** +27 (0)21-855-2768/+27 (0)84-511-8180 ▪ F +27 (0)21-855-2768

This family business last year celebrated a decade since becoming the pioneer of grape-growing in what was later established as the Hemel-en-Aarde Ridge ward. There's innovation and originality in their wines too: an MCC blanc de noir from shiraz and a surely unique SMV blend. Now look out for another white shiraz, but without bubbles and tinged with viognier.

★★★★ **SMV** Smoky earthy aromas on last-tasted **07** (★★★★) from 80% shiraz with malbec & viognier; plush, fleshy textures, dense tannins. Oak evident but integrating. Chewy, persistent finish.

★★★★ **Pioneer Brut Reserve** Polished **07** tasted last year, a rare 100% shiraz blanc de noir MCC. Apricot-tinged, with berry hints, light-footed spice, intriguing nuttiness & herbal persistence. — MF

Mount Rozier Estate

Location: Somerset West ▪ WO: Stellenbosch ▪ Est/1stB 2011 ▪ Visits by appt ▪ Owner(s) Gabb family ▪ WIETA ▪ PO Box 3040 Somerset West 7129 ▪ wines@mountrozier.co.za ▪ www.mountrozier.co.za ▪ **T** +27 (0)21-858-1929 ▪ F +27 (0)86-613-2164

This scenic property bordering Vergelegen in the Helderberg has been purchased by Journey's End Vineyards, and now boasts conference and wedding facilities with stunning views of the Hottentots Holland Mountains. For the romantically inclined, the self-catering Peacock Cottage offers an idyllic hideway less than an hour from Cape Town. On the wine front, a new single-variety range made by Journey's End's Leon Esterhuizen is now on the scene (but not ready for review).

Single Vineyards range

★★★★ **Cabernet Sauvignon** Expressive **08** (★★★★) had creamy oak overlay to blueberry fruit; was tad sweeter & warmer (15% alc) than last-tasted **05**. This, all below, still selling.

★★★★ **Shiraz** Swashbuckler **08** savoury toned, toasty, supple; ended with lipsmacking fruit & acidity.

Merlot ★★★★ Cassis & plum on tightly knit **05**. **Sauvignon Blanc** ★★★★ Faintly mineral **08** vibrant & racy.

Mount Rozier range

Pioneer Blend ★★★★ Cab-led **05**'s fruit supported by house-style serious oaking previously. **Noble Late Harvest** ★★★★★ From semillon, 18 months French oak. Lemon custard & barley sugar on silky **08**. — CvZ

Mount Vernon Estate

Location: Paarl ▪ Map: Paarl & Wellington ▪ WO: Simonsberg-Paarl/Western Cape ▪ Est 1996 ▪ 1stB 2005 ▪ Tasting, sales & cellar tours by appt ▪ Owner(s) David & Debbie Hooper ▪ Cellarmaster(s) Debbie Hooper (Jan 2003) ▪ Winemaker(s) Debbie Hooper (Jan 2003), with Philip du Toit (Jan 2005) ▪ Viticulturist(s) Philip du Toit (Jun 1997) ▪ 110ha/27.5ha (cab, malbec, merlot, p verdot, ptage, shiraz, chard) ▪ 210-225t/1,000cs own label 80% red 15% white 5% rosé ▪ PO Box 348 Klapmuts 7625 ▪ john@mountvernon.co.za ▪ www.mountvernon.co.za ▪ S 33° 48' 57.8" E 018° 52' 51.9" ▪ **T** +27 (0)21-875-5073 ▪ F +27 (0)86-618-9821

This family winery in the Simonsberg foothills is 'busy with a major change in direction, keeping within the garagiste style'. The cellar, barrel store and warehouse have been expanded to accommodate increased production, and a tasting venue added next to the new offices.

Mount Vernon range

★★★★ **Cabernet Sauvignon** Distinctive green-leaf aromas on **08** (★★★★) mask sweet vanilla-spiced berry fruit. Quite hard tannins reflect tough vintage after riper **07**.

★★★★ **Malbec** Stylish handling of **08** shows on plump but well-rounded body, satin texture & vibrant fruitiness. Augers well for future of this variety.

Chardonnay 🍽 🎴 ★★★ Fruit on single-vineyard **10** rather overwhelmed by oak. Pleasant, food friendly, but lighter in structure.

Three Peaks range

Jean Pierre's Lunchtime Rosé NEW ☺ 🍴 🖩 ★★★ Pinotage-based maiden **11** is strawberry fruity & dry. **Sauvignon Blanc** ☺ 🍴 🖩 ★★★ Fresh & sprightly **11** shows promise. Light, likeable & unpretentious fruit-driven quaffer.

Pinotage NEW 🍴 🖩 ★★ Debutant **10** has coffee notes & angular acidity. **Cantata** ✓ 🍴 ★★★★ Pinotage-led **08** has real charm & appeal. Shows overt oakiness, nicely formed berry layers emerging. — GdB

Mulderbosch Vineyards

Location/map: Stellenbosch ▪ WO: Stellenbosch/Western Cape ▪ Est 1989 ▪ 1stB 1991 ▪ Tasting & sales Mon–Fri 9.30-4.30 Sat & pub hols 10-1 ▪ Fee R3 per wine ▪ Closed Easter Fri-Mon, Dec 25 & Jan 1 ▪ Gift shop ▪ Olive oil ▪ Conservation area ▪ Owner(s) Terroir Capital ▪ Winemaker(s) Andy Erickson (2011, consultant), with Annalie van Dyk (Jan 2009) ▪ Viticulturist(s) Werner de Villiers (Nov 2004) ▪ 80ha/45.2ha (cabs s/f, merlot, p verdot, shiraz, chenin, nouvelle, sauv, viog) ▪ 980t/±150,000cs own label 2.46% red 42.39% white 55.15% rosé + 5,000cs for clients ▪ Ranges for clients: The Wade Bales Wine Society, The Diners Club Wine Society ▪ BWI ▪ PO Box 12817 Die Boord Stellenbosch 7613 ▪ info@mulderbosch.co.za ▪ www.mulderbosch.co.za ▪ S 33° 53' 22.8" E 018° 49' 8.3" ▪ **T +27 (0)21-881-8140** ▪ F +27 (0)21-881-3514

When California-based investment company Terroir Capital, whose management includes Charles Banks, formerly co-owner of cult winery Screaming Eagle, acquired Mulderbosch in late 2010, it was a huge vote of confidence in South African wine. As part of the deal, Mulderbosch moved to the premises of what used to be sister winery Kanu on account of bigger facilities and more land, the entire property undergoing a makeover involving leading designers and engineers. Richard Kershaw, cellarmaster before the transaction, left in August last year to develop his own vineyard in Elgin but the remainder of the winemaking team stayed in place with Andy Erickson, who was Banks' winemaker at Screaming Eagle, consulting.

★★★★ **Chardonnay 09** shy nose but lots of pure juicy citrus fruit on the palate, fresh acidity, well-judged oak; great balance & long finish; not as complex as stellar **08** (★★★★★).

★★★★☆ **Chardonnay Barrel Fermented** Exhilarating **09** perhaps best of recent times, vivid, substantial but not overdone: citrus blossom, lemon-lime, yeasty aromas; palate is rich & full but balanced by tangy acidity, oak perfectly judged.

★★★★ **Small Change Chenin Blanc 09** (★★★★) even more extravagant than **08**, with high sugar (±15 g/l), 10% botrytised sauvignon. Rich, dense, with wide array of flavours including citrus, peach & apricot.

★★★★ **Sauvignon Blanc Noble Late Harvest** 2 vintages reviewed: rich **08** displays honey, herbal note, pleasing fungal flavour; concentrated & smooth with gentle acidity. More elegant **09** is lighter, fresher with some pepperiness, less obvious botrytis character; both 6 months in oak, 100% new.

Faithful Hound ★★★★★ Bordeaux-style red **09** makes stunning return to form, rich & intense but still vinous. Pure & juicy dark fruit on entry before pleasingly dry finish; modern in the best sense. **08** (★★★★), also reviewed this edition, sweet & plump with soft tannins; improvement on unbalanced **06** (★★★); **07** sold out untasted. **Cabernet Sauvignon** 🍴 ★★★★ Entirely from cab, just-dry **11** shows clean red fruit, fresh acidity, pleasant tannic grip; total production an astounding 84,000 cases. W Cape WO. **Chenin Blanc** 🍴 ★★★★ Cleverly assembled **10** displays tropical fruit, honey & hint of spice; rich & broad with gentle acidity; slightly sweetened with Noble Late Harvest. WO W Cape. **Sauvignon Blanc** 🍴 🖩 ★★★★ **11** wide range of flavour from grassy through to green melon; relatively thick textured, moderate acidity. **10** (★★★), also reviewed this edition, herbal note on otherwise neutral nose; palate is sweet & plush, acidity well concealed. WO W Cape. — CE

Mullineux Family Wines

Location: Riebeek-Kasteel ▪ Map/WO: Swartland ▪ Est 2007 ▪ 1stB 2008 ▪ Tasting, sales & tours Mon–Fri & Sun by appt Sat 10-3 ▪ Closed Easter Sun, Dec 25 & Jan 1 ▪ Owner(s) Mullineux Family Wines (Pty) Ltd ▪ Cellarmaster(s)/winemaker(s)/viticulturist(s) Chris & Andrea Mullineux (May 2007) ▪ 18ha (carignan, cinsaut, mourv, shiraz, chenin, clairette blanche, viog) ▪ 90t/4,500cs own label 50% red 40% white 10% dessert ▪ Swartland independant ▪ PO Box 369 Riebeek-Kasteel 7307 ▪ info@mullineuxwines.com ▪ www.mullineuxwines.com ▪ S 33° 23' 1.16" E 18° 53' 46.65" ▪ **T +27 (0)22-448-1183** ▪ F +27 (0)86-720-1541

Husband and wife team Chris and Andrea Mullineux are at the forefront of what's being dubbed a revolution: the rediscovery and reappraisal of the Swartland area, on the strength of a burgeoning array of definitively styled varietal bottlings and blends. Within this space Chris and Andrea are carving out enviable reputations, expanding export markets and garnering very favourable critical notices from the British wine press in particular. With fellow local agitators for artisanal winecraft, they've founded an annual wine festival, 'The Swartland Revolution', described (appreciatively) by one attendee as 'like Woodstock... but without the sex'. The emphasis at the Mullineux's (Riebeek-West) town-centre cellar is on hands-off winemaking, using the local resources of unirrigated lands and venerable old vines.

Mullineux Family Wines range

★★★★☆ **Syrah** Eagerly awaited 09 (★★★★★) (it missed our deadline last edition) rises to expectations, showing healthy ripeness of vintage. Typically understated, but enigmatic & complex. As was 08, a fine expression of artisanal winemaking, showing Swartland's great potential.

★★★★☆ **White Blend** 🔞 Carefully crafted, barrel-fermented chenin (with dashes clairette blanche, viognier) is not for casual drinking: 10 (★★★★★) demands, rewards, time & attention. Uncompromising focus & balance, with intriguing layers of texture & aroma, winding down to long, gracious finish. Older oak, as for 09.

★★★★★ **Straw Wine** 🔞 Fast attaining icon status, this label continues to set the standard for a fast growing category. From air-dried & barrel-fermented chenin. As stellar as previous vintage, sumptuous 10 shows towering sweetness, impossible concentration, yet remains elegant & balanced. Should last for decades.

Kloof Street range

★★★★ **Swartland Rouge** ✓ 'Mourvèdre-Syrah-Carignan' last edition, reflecting mourvèdre's lead in 08. 09 mainly shiraz/syrah, but remains a worthy, Med-style, fruity middleweight. Blossoms with time in glass.

★★★★ **Chenin Blanc** ✓ 🗐 🔞 Second-tier range, but still pushes the limits with smoky aromas, fullness & restrained fruit. 11 from old bushvines (Riebeek/Perdeberg) maintains high standard of maiden 10. — GdB

Muratie Wine Estate

Location/map: Stellenbosch ▪ WO: Simonsberg–Stellenbosch/Western Cape/Stellenbosch/Coastal ▪ Est 1685 ▪ 1stB ca 1920 ▪ Tasting & sales daily 10–5 ▪ Fee R20/5 wines R30/port & chocolate ▪ Closed Easter Fri, Dec 25/26 & Jan 1 ▪ Cellar tours by appt ▪ Light lunches daily 12-3 ▪ Cheese platters ▪ Conference/function venue ▪ Art gallery ▪ Guest cottage ▪ Harvest festival with live music ▪ Owner(s) Melck Family Trust ▪ Cellarmaster(s) Francois Conradie (Dec 2005) ▪ Winemaker(s) Francois Conradie (Dec 2005), Simon Zeeman (2005) ▪ Viticulturist(s) Francois Conradie (1995), assisted by Paul Wallace ▪ 110ha/42ha (cab, merlot, pinot, shiraz, chard, hanepoot, port) ▪ 300t/15,000cs own label 60% red 14% white 6% rosé 20% other ▪ BWI, IPW ▪ PO Box 133 Koelenhof 7605 ▪ info@muratie.co.za, sales@muratie.co.za ▪ www.muratie.co.za ▪ S 33° 52' 14.8" E 018° 52' 35.1" ▪ **T +27 (0)21-865-2330/2336** ▪ F +27 (0)21-865-2790

After 24 years of the Melck family 'occupation' (Rijk Melck's word), they have certainly paid their dues. With Francois Conradie now well entrenched in vineyard and cellar, it is clear that changes implemented are being successful. The range is being streamlined, with greater focus on the top shiraz and the two other flagships. Pinot noir will also be seen as a speciality - fittingly, as Muratie was the Cape pioneer of commercial pinot. Innovations include a barrel acquisition strategy and new vibrating sorting tables. A constant concern with the visitor experience keeps Muratie a must-visit farm to enjoy Cape tradition.

Apex range

★★★★ **Ronnie Melck Shiraz** Premium low-yielding grapes used for this version. Last year 08 (★★★★★) showed greater complexity & structure than previous. Bold intense aromas; core of cassis & mulberry.

Flagship range

★★★★☆ **Ansela van de Caab** Serious estate flagship. 08 combo cab, merlot, cab franc previewed last year. Forest floor intro; harnessed shy fruit on poised taut structure now unfolding.

★★★★ **Laurens Campher** NEW Interesting combo chenin, sauvignon, verdelho & dab chard. 80% new oak on well-rounded 10 still obvious. Off-dry, but the sweetness is well balanced, adding to the overall intrigue. WO Stbosch.

Fortified Wines range

★★★★ **Cape Vintage** 08 now bottled but still shy. Classic-style port from tintas barocca, roriz & francesca, dash souzão, densely packed, with brooding dark fruits, savoury liquorice ending dry & firm.

Amber Forever ★★★☆ 09 now bottled has intense sultana, developed complexity. A fortified sweet wine with true muscat d'Alexandrie character. WO W Cape. **Cape Ruby** ✓ ★★★★ Latest **NV** is delicious nutty combo with shy fruit & toffee flavours. Fiery rich intensity balanced by savoury undertone. Smooth, fresh & ready to enjoy, as was previous (★★★★). **Late Bottled Vintage** Await next.

Melck's range

Melck's White ☺ 🗎 🥂 ★★★ From sauvignon, fresh **11** tasted ex-tank a summer charmer. WO Coastal.

Melck's Red 🗎 🥂 ★★★ Mostly from cab & shiraz, lively & easy drinking **10**. WO W Cape. **Melck's Rosé** 🗎 🥂 ★★ Dry, with light red fruits. **11** from cab franc. WO W Cape.

Premium range

★★★★ **Shiraz** 09 (★★★★★) more seriously structured than **08**. Black pepper spice & exciting savouriness balanced by shy red berry notes. Palate shows off fine-tuned tannins; while well-judged 30% new oak adds to long firm finish. Needs 2 years to start showing its best.

★★★★ **Isabella Chardonnay** 🗎 🥂 Lovely yellow fruit on **10** needs some time for oak to meld. Medium-bodied, with great freshness, texture & crisp dry end. WO Stbosch.

Cabernet Sauvignon ★★★★ Dark fruit joined by tobacco whiffs & smoky overlay on brooding **08**. Firm tannic structure & a serious dry finish. **Merlot** ★★★★ Herbal lift with delicate perfume & oaky tones lead to plummy fruit on grippy & medium-bodied **08**. Lighter than **07** (★★★★). **George Paul Canitz Pinot Noir** ★★★★ Beautiful perfumed intro on **09**, step-up on **08** (★★★★). Red fruit layer over forest floor & tealeaf interest. Fine structure, with elegant tannins & a dry & fresh finale. Needs time, though. **1763 Methode Cap Classique** ★★★★ **08** with complex honey, green apple & brioche & finishing dry zing. From pinot & chard, like **07** (★★★★). Tasted last year. — JP

Mvemve Raats

Location/map/WO: Stellenbosch ▪ Est/1stB 2004 ▪ Tasting & sales by appt ▪ Fee R200 (up to 20 pax per tasting) ▪ Closed all pub hols ▪ Owner(s) Bruwer Raats & Mzokhona Mvemve ▪ Cellarmaster(s)/viticulturist(s) Bruwer Raats & Mzokhona Mvemve (Jan 2004) ▪ Winemaker(s) Bruwer Raats & Mzokhona Mvemve (Jan 2004), with Gavin Bruwer Slabbert (Feb 2010) ▪ 5t/ha ▪ 225cs own label 100% red ▪ PO Box 2068 Stellenbosch 7601 ▪ braats@mweb.co.za ▪ www.raats.co.za ▪ S 33° 58' 16.6" E 018° 44' 55.3" ▪ **T +27 (0)21-881-3078** ▪ F +27 (0)21-881-3078

Partners Bruwer Raats of Raats Family Wines and Mzokhona Mvemve classify this project as 'just two friends enjoying working together'. Considering what they've achieved since the 2004 maiden vintage, the chemistry is obviously working. Cab franc (an area of expertise for Raats) plays a big role in the 5-part Bordeaux blend, giving a different profile to that of its many competitors. Such has been the ongoing international and local acclaim, and particularly for the 2007, that De Compostella ('Field of Stars') is an apt name for this collectable wine.

★★★★☆ **De Compostella** Now bottled, **08** walks on the dark side: black fruit, liquorice & tapenade, an individual Bordeaux blend. Vintage effect, more muscular than **07**, needs longer to reach full potential. — CR

■ **My Best Friend** see Zandvliet Wine Estate & Thoroughbred Stud

My Wyn

Location/map/WO: Franschhoek ▪ Est/1stB 2001 ▪ Tasting, sales & cellar tours Mon-Fri 10-1 Oct-Apr; after hours & weekends by appt or as indicated on the gate ▪ Fee R25pp, waived on purchase ▪ Closed all pub hols ▪ Cheese platters by prior booking ▪ Owner(s) Jacoline Haasbroek ▪ Winemaker(s) Jacoline Haasbroek (2001) ▪ 4ha ▪ 550cs own label 40% red 20% white 20% port 20% MCC ▪ IPW ▪ PO Box 112 Franschhoek 7690 ▪ tastewine@telkomsa.net ▪ www.mywynfranschhoek.co.za ▪ S 33° 53' 29.3" E 019° 8' 3.6" ▪ **T +27 (0)21-876-2518, +27 (0)83-302-5556** ▪ F +27 (0)86-608-0233

Bringing pleasure to others through wine is the driving force behind Jacoline Haasbroek's tiny winery in Franschhoek. Affirmation that the owner/winemaker is on the right track regularly comes in the form of a note, usually with a photograph of a bottle of her wine gracing a table laden with food. 'Visitors who become age-long friends, from all corners of the globe, that's why wine matters.' Available, not tasted this edition, are: Cabernet Franc, Merlot, Petit Verdot, Shiraz, Sauviognier, Viognier,

My Robyn (red port), My Amber (white port) and My MCC traditional-method sparkling.

■ **Mzanzi** *see Kingsriver Estate*

Mzoli's Wines

Location: Cape Town ▪ Map: Cape Peninsula ▪ WO: Darling ▪ Meals & tasting daily 11-8 ▪ Owner(s) Mzoli Ngcawuzele ▪ NY 115 Shop No 3 Gugulethu 7750 ▪ enjoy@mzoliwine.co.za ▪ www.mzoliwine.co.za ▪ S 33° 58' 34.9" E 018° 34' 11.1" ▪ **T +27 (0)21-638-1355/+27 (0)82-487-0980**

Irrepressibly entrepreneurial Mzoli Ngcawuzele, with the Cape Wine Academy, last year staged the inaugural Gugulethu Wine Festival atop the chic Gugulethu Shopping Mall. A huge success, the event gave fresh impetus to Mzoli's campaign to establish wine as the society drink of choice in the townships. The wines listed below are house brands for his eatery, one of the hottest spots on the tourism map.

Mandisi Merlot ★★ Juicy-fruity **09** from Darling vineyards, made for the braai. **Unathi** ★★ **09** last year was a fruity, fresh red from cinsaut & ruby cab, lightly wooded. **One One Five Rosé** ★★★ Bright pink off-dry **09** had lashings of creamy strawberry fruit last edition. — GdB

■ **Nabot** *see La Motte*

Nabygelegen Private Cellar

Location: Wellington ▪ Map: Paarl & Wellington ▪ WO: Wellington/Western Cape ▪ Est 2001 ▪ 1stB 2002 ▪ Tasting, sales & cellar tours Mon-Fri 10-5 Sat 10-1 ▪ Closed all pub hols ▪ Picnics (booking essential) ▪ Tour groups ▪ Farm produce ▪ Conferences/functions ▪ Weddings ▪ Walking/hiking & mountain biking trails ▪ Self-catering luxury accommodation ▪ Owner(s) James McKenzie ▪ Cellarmaster(s) James McKenzie (Jan 2002) ▪ Winemaker(s) James McKenzie (Jan 2002) & Charles Stassen (consultant), with Maria Bosman (Jan 2002) ▪ Viticulturist(s) Johan Wiese (May 2001, consultant) ▪ 35ha/17ha (cab, merlot, p verdot, tempranillo, chenin, sauv) ▪ 120t/ 7,000cs own label 50% red 50% white ▪ PO Box 302 Wellington 7654 ▪ sales@nabygelegen.co.za ▪ www. nabygelegen.co.za ▪ S 33° 37' 54.7" E 019° 3' 51.2" ▪ **T +27 (0)21-873-7534** ▪ F +27 (0)86-561-7761

A stint as an investment banker in London gave James McKenzie a taste for fine wine and in due course he bought Nabygelegen. Recent developments include the old stables and forge being converted into a tasting room while a luxurious guesthouse was recently opened. A shaded picnic area next to the farm dam is next.

Nabygelegen Private Cellar range
★★★★☆ **1712** ✓ **07** from 50% merlot, 48% cab & petit verdot shows admirable lack of contrivance & remarkable youth: concentrated dark fruit, fresh acidity, firm but fine tannins. 22 months in oak, 30% new, a subtle presence. More like **05** than lighter **06** (★★★★).

Merlot ★★★ **07** on review was lean & tad robust, might since have mellowed. **Petit Verdot** ★★★ **08** spice & earthiness in addition to red fruit, bright acidity, fine tannins last edition. **Scaramanga** 🔲 ★★★ **10** includes 20% tempranillo to go with cab, malbec, merlot. Medium bodied with red fruit, pleasing herbal note, fresh acidity & grippy tannins. **Chenin Blanc** 🔲 🔲 ★★★ **10** has some peach flavour, appears touch insubstantial compared to better balanced previous. **Sauvignon Blanc** 🔲 🔲 ★★★ Passionfruit flavour, soft acidity on pleasant but somewhat short **11**. **Lady Anna** 🔲 🔲 ★★★ Chenin-led **10** is juicy & fresh with breakfast punch flavour profile.

Snow Mountain range
★★★★ **Syrah 09** forthcoming aromas of dark cherry, lilies; dense, concentrated, with fresh acidity, fine tannins when previewed for last edition. W Cape WOs for these.

Pinot Noir ★★★ **10** super-ripe red fruit, soft tannins, gentle acidity. **Merlot Rosé** ★★★★ Strawberry, some herbal notes on **09**. Medium body, fresh acidity & admirably dry finish. This, next, tasted for last edition. **Chardonnay** ★★★☆ Ripe citrus & some leesy character on **09**. Good fruit expression, fresh, oak well judged. — CE

Namaqua Wines

Location: Vredendal ▪ Map/WO: Olifants River ▪ Est/1stB 2002 ▪ Tasting & sales Mon-Fri 8-5 Sat 9-3 ▪ Closed Easter Fri-Mon, Ascension day & Dec 25/26 ▪ Cellar tours Mon-Fri 10 & 3, book ahead ▪ Die Keldery Restaurant Mon-Fri 8-5 Sat 9-3 Sun buffet 11-3 booking required ▪ Facilities for children ▪ Conferences ▪ Owner(s) 200 members ▪ Cellarmaster(s) Pieter Verwey & Koos Thiart ▪ Winemaker(s) Alwyn Maass, Driaan van der Merwe, Dewald

Huisamen, Johan Weideman & Reinier van Greunen ▪ Viticulturist(s) Marina Bruwer, Heine Janse van Rensburg & Nicholas Bruyns ▪ 4,990ha (cab, merlot, ptage, ruby cab, shiraz, chard, chenin, cbard, hanepoot, sauv) ▪ 112,500t/ 9.3m cs 30% red 70% white ▪ PO Box 75 Vredendal 8160 ▪ info@namaquawines.com ▪ www.namaquawines. com ▪ S 31° 42' 34.9" E 018° 30' 15.6" ▪ **T +27 (0)27-213-1080** ▪ **F** +27 (0)27-213-3476

We know them for the ubiquitous 5L casks, but keep an eye on this massive Vredendal winery's newer Spencer Bay Winemakers Reserve range, which last year won (among others) three Decanter silver medals. The winemaking team, led by Pieter Verwey and Koos Thiart, must be loving turning their hand to 'boutique' winemaking after the popular success of their high-volume offerings locally and abroad. Namaqua offers 3L and 5L bag-in-boxes, single varieties in 750ml bottles, and a méthode cap classique sparkling. Plus cellar tours, tastings and meals at stylish Die Keldery Restaurant. All boxes ticked, you might say.

Spencer Bay Winemakers Reserve range

Cabernet Sauvignon ★★★★ Inky **08** cleverly made. Warm hearted, well oaked, up a level from earthy **07** (★★★★). Tasted last year, as for all these. **Pinotage** ★★★★ After uncomplicated **07** (★★★), **08** major step up & great advertisement for the variety. Accessible, but enough padding for longer haul, zingy upbeat finish. **Shiraz** ★★★★ Smooth & rounded **08**, appealing toasty oak, smoky/savoury tinge to ripe red berry fruit. **The Blend** ★★★☆ **08** attractive five-way Bordeaux red, abundant ripe plum & prune fruit well integrated with oak. **Chardonnay** 🍷 ★★★ **10** preview plumper & riper (14.8% alc) than previous. **Sauvignon Blanc** 🍷 ★★★ Preview **10** riper feel, more tropical fruit than standard version but still zesty.

Namaqua Wines range

Cabernet Sauvignon 🍷 ★★ Stylistic goal for this range is casual easy-going enjoyment, which achieved admirably. **10** has crusty bread aroma, firm tannins. All reds lightly oaked for seasoning, structure. **Merlot** 🍷 ★★★ Preview **10** bursts with blackcurrant & mulberry but leaves impression of lightness despite 14% alc, shade less generous than previous. **Pinotage** 🍷 ★★ Old-style **10** mulberry & acetone hint, fleeting earth & plum flavours. **Shiraz** 🍷 ★★★ Step-up **10** commendably dry & very drinkable, smoky bacon & black pepper appeal. **Sauvignon Blanc** 🍷 ★★ Dusty Cape gooseberries on zesty **11**, pleasant if somewhat insubstantial. **Guinevere MCC** ★★★ Latest brut-style méthode cap classique sparkling improves on previous. **06** savoury, almost meaty notes from pinot noir (60%), lively mousse & fresh appley flavours from chardonnay. — Panel

Napier Winery

Location/WO: Wellington ▪ Map: Paarl & Wellington ▪ Est 1989 ▪ Tasting, sales & cellar tours Mon-Fri 8–5 Sat 10–3 ▪ Fee R10 ▪ Closed Easter Fri-Sun, Dec 25/26 & Jan 1 ▪ Tapas platters, preferably pre-booked ▪ Conference facilities ▪ Owner(s) Michael & Catherine Loubser ▪ Cellarmaster(s)/viticulturist(s) Leon Bester (Apr 2000) ▪ Winemaker(s) Leon Bester (Apr 2000), with Nadia Pieterse (Dec 2006) ▪ 60ha/±38ha under vine ▪ Own label 70% red 30% white ▪ Other export brand: Sir George ▪ PO Box 638 Wellington 7654 ▪ info@napierwinery.co.za ▪ www. napierwinery.co.za ▪ S 33° 38' 37.0" E 019° 2' 24.8" ▪ **T +27 (0)21-873-7829** ▪ **F** +27 (0)21-864-2728

The plan to market only single-vineyard wines is reaching fruition: St Catherine is already there, as are Greenstone and new Napier Cabernet, both due to be released as the guide went to press. Red Medallion and its barrel-selection twin Qintas (not tasted) will follow in time. The wine names come from co-owner Michael Loubser: St Catherine is a statue he saw in a small Italian village; Greenstone is the Maori name for flint, a Chenin characteristic, plus a play on the word 'steen', and Qintas is an anagram for Quality-Inspiration-Nature-Terroir-Art-Science.

Napier Winery range

★★★★ **Red Medallion** Cedar & red berries, some violets, **07** is still tightly held. 5-part Bordeaux blend, built for ageing but tannins accessible if you don't want to wait; best paired with rich dishes.

★★★★ **St Catherine** Chard with personality & taste appeal. Butterscotch vies with citrus zest, an attractive juxtaposition in **09**. Could age year or 2.

Greenstone Await next.

Lion Creek range

Cabernet Sauvignon ☺ 🍷 ★★★ Blackcurrant leaps out of **09** glass, cloaks tannins, leaving just enough grip for food, year or 2 ageing.

Cabernet-Sauvignon-Merlot NEW 🗔 ★★★ Lightly oaked **09** is appealing & approachable, offers vanilla spicing, ripe & juicy plums. **Chenin Blanc** NEW 🗔 ★★ **11** thatch & melon, nicely rounded despite low 12.5% alc. **Sauvignon Blanc-Chenin Blanc** NEW 🗔 ★★★ Fresh-fruity styling in **11**, gentle apple, leafy tones. Discontinued: **Red**, **White**. — CR

■ **Natalie** see The Natalie

■ **Nativo** see Hughes Family Wines

Natte Valleij Wines

Location/map: Stellenbosch ▪ WO: Coastal ▪ Est 1715 ▪ Tasting, sales & tours Mon-Fri 9-4 Sat by appt ▪ Closed all pub hols ▪ Facilities for children ▪ BYO picnic ▪ B&B/self-catering cottages (see Accommodation section) ▪ Owner(s) Milner family ▪ Winemaker(s) Alexander Milner (2005), with Marcus Milner (2010) ▪ 28ha total ▪ 15t/1,000cs own label 100% red ▪ PO Box 4 Klapmuts 7625 ▪ alex@boerandbrit.com ▪ www.nattevalleijwines.co.za ▪ S 33° 50' 3.6" E 018° 52' 43.2" ▪ **T +27 (0)21-875-5171**

Alexander Milner, partner with Stefan Gerber in Boer & Brit and brother of Marcus (of De Meye) is gathering his disparate parts together to the family seat at Natte Valleij. His Swallow range is now a solitary red blend, but there's a new venture with Marcus to create a Milner family brand, yet to be named. New plantings of fast-declining variety cinsaut, harvested for the first time, will hopefully aid a return to favour this underrated grape.

Swallow range

> **Swallow** ☺ ★★★ 'The Blend' last guide. Quirky 6-way blend fruit-bomb, **10** has impressive intensity, angular structure. Robust, unpolished but rich.

Discontinued: **Cabernet Sauvignon**. — GdB

■ **Natural Star** see Stellar Winery

Naughton's Flight

Location: Constantia ▪ WO: Stellenbosch/Paarl/Coastal ▪ 1stB 2003 ▪ Closed to public ▪ Owner(s) Francis Naughton ▪ Winemaker(s) Ronell Wiid (consultant) ▪ (carignan, mourv, shiraz, viog) ▪ ±15,000 btls ▪ 25 Willow Rd Constantia 7806 ▪ naughts@mweb.co.za ▪ **T +27 (0)21-794-3928** ▪ F +27 (0)21-794-3928

Francis Naughton (he owns the brand, Ronell Wiid makes the wine) has some strangely Irish good cheer brought back from a marketing trip to his native land – his Dublin importer's suggestion that perhaps the Irish will drink their way (and our way too?) out of the recession.

Shiraz ★★★★ Broad, savoury **07** ex Paarl, some stalkiness & cherry flavours. Like all except Tribua, tasted previously. **Tribua** ★★★★ Step-up **09** from shiraz & mourvèdre; viognier for fragrance. Engaging, ripe flavours: sweet fruit in modestly oaked, dry, firm package. WO Coastal. **Viognier** ★★★★ **09** offered subtle apple, apricot & spice aromas, rich satiny texture. **Délice** ★★★ **09**, from rack-dried shiraz, deliciously grapey. Sweet, clean & fresh; only 11% alc. — TJ

Nederburg Wines

Location: Paarl ▪ Map: Paarl & Wellington ▪ WO: Western Cape/Coastal/Paarl/Durbanville/Philadelphia/Groenekloof ▪ Est 1791 ▪ 1stB ca 1940 ▪ Tasting & sales Mon-Fri 8–5; Sat 10–2 (Apr-Oct) & 10–4 (Nov-Mar); Sun 11–4 (Nov-Mar) ▪ Tasting fees waived on purchases of R100+ ▪ Closed Easter Fri & Dec 25 ▪ Cellar tours Mon-Fri 10.30 & 3; Sat 11; Sun 11.30 Nov-Mar ▪ Large groups/foreign language tours by appt ▪ Visitors' centre: foundation platters in summer; soup & ciabatta in winter ▪ Historic Manor House (national monument): breakfast, lunch & dinner for groups by appt ▪ Picnic lunches Nov-Mar by appt ▪ Tour groups ▪ Gifts ▪ Conferences ▪ Museum ▪ Conservation area ▪ Owner(s) Distell ▪ Cellarmaster(s) Razvan Macici (2001) ▪ Winemaker(s) Wilhelm Pienaar (reds, 2009) & Tariro Masayiti (whites, 2006), with Samuel Viljoen (reds) & Danie Morkel (whites) ▪ Viticulturist(s) Henk van Graan & Hannes van Rensburg ▪ 1,000ha (cab, carignan, grenache, malbec, merlot, p verdot, ptage, shiraz, tannat, tempranillo, chard, riesling, sauv, sem) ▪ 17,500t/1.4m cs own label ▪ ISO 0001:2008, ISO 14001:2004, BWI, HACCP, IPW, Organic Certification (SGS) ▪ Private Bag X3006 Paarl 7620 ▪ nedwines@distell.co.za ▪ www.nederburg.co.za ▪ S 33° 43' 15.4" E 019° 0' 9.4" ▪ **T +27 (0)21-862-3104** ▪ F +27 (0)21-862-4887

Showing perfect pitch, this team led by Razvan Macici manages to sort a large range into neat market categories, capturing the styles that would interest buyers and sell at those price points, and always over-delivering on quality. Hence the decision to withdraw Cape Riesling and Premier Grand Cru, their time has passed, replaced by Pinot Grigio. The awards keep rolling in, too numerous to mention, including a number of 5 star ratings in this guide. In the ongoing quest to raise the quality bar, new varieties have been planted on an experimental basis, and in the cellar large-oak trials are taking place and carbonic maceration was used for the first time for Winemaster's Reserve Chenin. Sustainability hasn't been neglected either: all the company farms and suppliers are now IPW accredited and Nederburg has become a BWI member through the many initiatives implemented on the home farm and others.

Ingenuity range

★★★★☆ **Red** Mainly sangiovese & barbera, dab nebbiolo, **08**'s a local version of the best of Italy. Black cherries, tapenade, sweet spice, the finest prosciutto, there's heaps going on. Firmer than standout **07** (★★★★★), but no edges, & a good 10 year future.

★★★★★ **White** ⓦ Brilliant track record for this blend of 8 varieties, some oaked. Sauvignon leads in **10**, with chardonnay, semillon, but all the players have a part in this symphony of perfume & flavours. Tropical, aromatic, citrus-edged for freshness, vibrantly alive. Should age minimum 5+ years.

Manor House range

★★★★ **Cabernet Sauvignon** ✓ Fruit less expressive than previous vintages but **09** loses nothing by that, complexity remains. Dried herbs & dark spices with the trademark compact build promising a fine future. WO Paarl.

★★★★ **Shiraz** Cocoa dusting on **09** puts it into a dark savoury area, some meaty notes, all designed to please. Has nice Old World styling, with tannins giving a dry finish, ideal for food. Coastal WO, like next.

★★★★ **Sauvignon Blanc** ⓦ Minerality & touch of fynbos, always flavourful & **11** no exception, including a zesty finish which will provide some years ageing. Good match for seafood.

Winemaster's Reserve range

★★★★ **Edelrood (Cabernet Sauvignon-Merlot)** Easy to like, **09** (★★★★) offers meaty, spiced dark fruit flavours, nice generous body, for drinking sooner than **08**.

★★★★ **Special Late Harvest** ✓ ⓦ Jasmine-scented **11** shows its 25% viognier component upfront, but the real magic is in the flavours: dried peach, preserved melon, a tangy interplay between sugar & acid.

★★★★★ **Noble Late Harvest** ⓦ Cellar's expertise amply demonstrated here, their only botrytis dessert freely available. Richest of the trio, **10** (★★★★★) has 240g/l sugar enlivened by the acidity, perfectly fitting the fruit-essence flavours. A power-packed taste experience, just under **09**'s standard.

> **Riesling** ☺ ⓦ ★★★ Lovely floral, spicy notes, **11** captures the delicacy (12% alc) of this variety, offers a touch of plumping sweetness.

Cabernet Sauvignon ✓ ⓦ ★★★★ Nicely put together, pre-bottled **10** has just-crushed berries, savoury spice, but no mistaking serious intent, ageability. All these WO W Cape unless noted. **Merlot** ★★★ Lush blackcurrants & white pepper, carefully oaked (2nd/3rd fill) for gentle support, leaving **09**'s fruit to shine. WO Coastal. **Pinotage** ★★★ Wild berries & a herbal note, youthful grippy tannins, **09** would be a good match for roast lamb, cheesy pasta. **Shiraz** ✓ ⓦ ★★★★ Touch of fynbos in previewed **10**'s brambleberries, some smoky notes. Has structure for 4-5 years ageing but already drinking well. **Baronne (Cabernet Sauvignon-Shiraz)** ✓ ⓦ ★★★★ Espresso & black plums, a reflection of equal partnership in **10**, the taste appeal enhanced by plump, lively fruitiness. **Rosé** 🗏 ⓦ ★★★★ For export only. **Chardonnay** ✓ ⓦ ★★★★ Tropical with a citrus edge, **10**'s focus is on fruit purity & taste, both well catered for here. Friendly ±13% alcohol. **Chenin Blanc** ✓ ⓦ ★★★★ Limy spark to **10**, while retaining taut fruit, zesty appetite appeal. From bushvines. WO Coastal. **Pinot Grigio** NEW ✓ ⓦ ★★★★ Ex tank **11** shows green plum styling, off-dry structure converted by acidity into appetising sweet/sour flavours. **Sauvignon Blanc** ✓ ⓦ ★★★★ Passionfruit with all its tangy vibrancy, not a green note in sight, **11** offers both flavour & freshness. Discontinued: **Foundation (Sauvignon Blanc-Chardonnay)**.

Two Centuries range NEW

★★★★ **Cabernet Sauvignon** Available cellardoor only. Selection best Paarl vineyards, 2 years new French oak. **07**'s rich fruit handles such treatment, accessible, but built for the longer haul, years off its peak.

★★★★ **Sauvignon Blanc** Subtle interplay of melon & granite minerality in **09**, the age & year oaking adding to the complexity. Not showy, can underestimate it, but there's finesse, lots of class here. Coastal WO.

Private Bin range for Nederburg Auction

★★★★ **Cabernet Sauvignon Private Bin R163** Wonderfully perfumed, blackcurrants & cream, sprinkle of spice, **08** retains berry juiciness, but fine-grained tannins, (2 years new oak, as next) promise a 10 year future.

★★★★ **Merlot Private Bin R181** Iron fist in a velvet glove, **08**'s seductive ripe berries have a firm (but not harsh) wrapping of oak to give a long, illustrious life. Serious merlot, beautifully made. Durbanville WO.

★★★★ **Petit Verdot Private Bin R104** Last was **07**, black plums & beef extract, fruit good match for the firm, tannins but wine still in infancy. Would reveal its true potential over time.

★★★★☆ **Pinotage Private Bin R172** Previously, dark-toned **07** had the polished elegance the variety can deliver in careful hands; deep muscle strength from all-new barrels ensured 8+ year rewarding future.

★★★★☆ **Shiraz Private Bin R121** Plush & darkly ripe, **08** has all the classic seasoning, nutmeg & cloves, Provençal herbs one expects in the best shiraz, but is far off its peak, with much more to reveal over time. Philadelphia WO.

★★★★ **Cabernet Sauvignon-Merlot Private Bin R109** Last tasted **07** showed chocolate & cassis, with cab's 60% adding lead pencil & structure, supported by new oak. Promised to age with distinction over 10 years.

★★★★ **Cabernet Sauvignon-Shiraz Private Bin R103** Last-tasted **07** showed dense dark fruit, lots of cedar, less approachable than **04** (★★★★☆), still tightly wound, needed time for forceful tannins to meld.

★★★★ **Chardonnay Private Bin D270** ② Toasted brioche & lemon, **10** ex Paarl retains its fruit as a bold New World chardonnay where oak is an equal partner. Lovely lime-fresh finish; will give pleasure till ±2016.

★★★★☆ **Sauvignon Blanc Private Bin D215** ② Always the more tropical partner to D234, **11** (★★★★) abounds with gooseberries, passionfruit, with a mineral edge to the flavours adding interest. A bit less tension than stellar **10**.

★★★★ **Sauvignon Blanc Private Bin D234** ② The 'greener' version of the two sauvignons, courtesy of Groenekloof origin. Lime & grapefruit, **10** (★★★★☆) has more intensity than **10**, an elegant tautness that promises excellent ageing potential, 5 years or more.

★★★★★ **Sauvignon Blanc-Chardonnay Private Bin D253** ② The longer **10** (★★★★☆) is in the glass, the greater the sauvignon (70%) & chardonnay interplay; white peach, crushed almonds, but lime there throughout. Elegant & pure, less complex than **09**, but an acid seam will keep it youthful for years. Coastal WO.

★★★★ **Sauvignon Blanc-Semillon Private Bin D252** ② Cut grass & lime, **11** (★★★★☆) takes green flavours to another level, sleek & vivid, full of tension, with more mouthwatering appetite appeal than **10**. Semillon portion only apparent in the satisfying mouthfeel.

★★★★★ **Edelkeur** ② The first Cape NLH, always ex Paarl chenin. Has honeyed botrytis, but you'd think **10** was made from apricots & pineapple, such is the fruit intensity. Luscious, very sweet but acidity refreshes, adds tanginess, incredible length. Confirms brilliant trend noted in **09**. All these NLHs unoaked, available in 375ml.

★★★★☆ **Eminence NLH** ② From Paarl muscat de Frontignan, hence **10**'s (★★★★★) lovely aromatics, floral notes, exotic Asian spices. Fruit essence flavours are as seductive as always, but there's an intriguing delicacy to the richness, a finesse that comes from a reduction in sugar since **09**.

Semillon Private Bin D266 ② Await next.

Foundation range

Cabernet Sauvignon ☺ ② ★★★ Light oaking adds a meaty note to **10**'s juicy berries, no barrier to immediate enjoyment. **Merlot** ☺ ★★★ Most structured of these reds yet accessible, **10** nicely combines cassis with oak spice, has dry food-friendly finish. This & all below WO W Cape unless noted. **Shiraz** ☺ ② ★★★ **10** seduces with cappuccino perfume, flavours, smoothly rounded body. For enjoying, not ageing. **Chenin Blanc** ☺ ② ★★★ Was 'Stein' previous editions. **11** still a charmer, light (11.5% alc) & semi-sweet. **Sauvignon Blanc-Chardonnay** ☺ ② ★★★ Proven combo, **11** offers best of both worlds, sauvignon freshness & sleek lines, with the citrus flavour of chardonnay. **Lyric (Sauvignon Blanc-Chenin Blanc-Chardonnay)** ☺ ② ★★★ Aptly named, the varieties perfectly matched in **11** to deliver fruity-fresh enjoyment. Off-dry but dry enough for food.

Pinotage ② ★★★ **10**'s juicy berries given good oak foundation for few years ageing. **Duet** ★★★ 'Shiraz-Pinotage' returns to old name in **10**, remains mocha-toned, dry tannins good match for rich stews. **Shiraz-Viognier** ★★★ Mocha styling with a floral tone, **10** is juicy & appealing. **Cabernet Sauvignon-Shiraz** In abeyance. **Rosé** ② ★★ Prettily packaged **11** appeals with cranberry-toned sweetness. **Cape Riesling** ★★★ Last release, leafy **11** is a dry, light (12% alc) quaffer. Paarl WO. **Chardonnay** ② ★★★ Light oaking in **11** preview leaves tropical fruit intact. **Sauvignon Blanc** ② ★★★ Light-textured (12.5%) with a pear-fresh focus,

11 is a good seafood partner. **Chardonnay-Viognier** ★★★ Aromatic notes in 11 preview, has clean fresh drinkability. **Premier Grand Cru** ★★ Last release NV chenin/colombard mix, light & crisply dry. **Première Cuvée Brut** ★★★ Mainly crouchen in latest NV aperitif-style fizz, pear-drops & lowish 11.5% alcohol. — CR

Neethlingshof Estate

Location/map/WO: Stellenbosch • Est 1692 • 1stB 1880 • Tasting & sales Mon-Fri 9–5 (Dec/Jan 9-7); Sat/Sun 10-4 (Dec/Jan 10-6) • Fee R30pp • Closed Easter Fri & Dec 25 • Cellar tours by appt • 'Flash Food & Slow Wine' pairing R95pp - booking required • Jungle gym • Tour groups • Conference facilities • Conservation area • Annual 'Slenterfees' (Mar) • Lord Neethling Restaurant & Palm Terrace • Owner(s) Lusan Premium Wines • Cellarmaster(s) De Wet Viljoen (Jun 2003) • Winemaker(s) De Wet Viljoen (Jun 2003), with Lauren Snyman (Sep 2006) • Viticulturist(s) Hannes van Zyl (Jun 2002), with Nico Nortje • 284ha/120ha (cabs s/f, malbec, merlot, p verdot, ptage, shiraz, chard, chenin, gewürtz, riesling, sauv, viog) • 1,400t/50,000cs own label 55% red 45% white • BWI, WIETA • PO Box 104 Stellenbosch 7599 • info@neethlingshof.co.za • www.neethlingshof.co.za • S 33° 56' 28.2" E 018° 48'6.7" • **T +27 (0)21-883-8988** • F +27 (0)21-883-8941

Water resource management is one of the critical issues facing wine producers, that will require creative planning. This has been partly addressed at this historic estate near Stellenbosch town by the now complete vineyard renewal programme. This includes plantings of some of the hardier cultivars, which are producing exciting wines. They have wisely kept some old gems, like the 24 year old riesling and gewürztraminer vines, established by the legendary Günter Brözel. Being dryland vineyards, these are valuable assets.

Short Story Collection

★★★★ **The Owl Post 09** from pinotage, continues in fine form of **08**. Sumptuously styled ripe fruit but structured, with oak seamlessly integrated. Polished & ageworthy.

★★★★☆ **The Caracal** Three releases of cab-led Bordeaux blend reviewed: **06** (★★★★) riper, more robust & brash than refined, supple & juicy **07**. Latter has more cab franc which adds perfumed lift & elegance to an inherently better vintage. No **08. 09**, with merlot as understudy, most complex, structured & elegant of all. Still restrained in youth, but classically styled & ageworthy.

★★★★ **Maria** Botrytised NLH dessert from riesling, among handful in Cape. Consistently good, intense tangy lime/kumquat flavours, even in tough years. Riper **11** tad less verve than **10** (★★★★★) but still delicious!

Neethlingshof range

Sauvignon Blanc ☺ 🍴 🍷 ★★★ 11 ripe, soft tropical nuance in light & quaffable style.

Cabernet Sauvignon ★★★ 06 surly & brooding, less succulent fruit than previous. **Malbec** ✓ 🍷 ★★★★ Riper **10** has a more savoury tone. Flavoursome, light textured, supple & accessible styling. **Merlot** ★★★ Unusually meaty, earthy tone on **08**. **Pinotage** ✓ ★★★★ Cooler **07** vintage shows fresher, juicier fruit with supple structure & ageing potential. Step up on ripe & brawny **06**, with charry exit. **Shiraz** ★★★ **05** still available. Was powerful & extracted when last tasted. **Cabernet Sauvignon-Merlot** ✓ ★★★★ Cooler **09** vintage & less oak evident in fresher & brighter blend than previous. Now with more merlot, has elegant & fruit-filled balance. **Chardonnay Unwooded** 🍷 🍴 ★★★ Ripe melon & peachy-toned **11** a tad plumper, less crisp than previous. Great with creamy dishes. **Gewürztraminer** ✓ 🍷 🍴 ★★★★ Regular producer of this niche variety. **11** shows classic lichi/rosepetal in just off-dry, fresh & balanced style. For fusion food or aromatic aperitif. **Sauvignon Blanc Single Vineyard** 🍷 🍴 ★★★ Fleshier, waxy **11** has plump, food-styled succulence. Less flinty & crisp than previous. Discontinued: **Chardonnay**. — MW

Neil Ellis Meyer-Näkel

Location/WO: Stellenbosch • Est/1stB 1998 • Tasting & sales at Neil Ellis Wines • Owner(s) Neil Ellis Meyer-Näkel (Pty) Ltd • Cellarmaster(s) Neil Ellis & Werner Näkel (both 1998) • Viticulturist(s) Pieter Smit & Warren Ellis • 3,500cs own label 100% red • PO Box 917 Stellenbosch 7599 • tasting@neilellis.com • www.neilellis.com • **T +27 (0)21-887-0649** • F +27 (0)21-887-0647

A desire to expand brought pinot noir winemaker Werner Näkel (dubbed the 'king of red wine' in Germany) and one of South Africa's most respected producers, Neil Ellis, together. The wines of this small-scale but successful venture bear Neil's refined trademark, while Näkel's 'rock star' status back home helps boost exports.

★★★★ **Zwalu** 🗋 09 savoury, perfumed blend of near equal parts cab/shiraz/cab franc, restrained by firm, dry tannins, with appealing, juicy finish. Youthful & cellarworthy, now WO Stellenbosch. No 08.

Z 🗋🍷 ★★★★ The junior version of Zwalu, previewed **10** cab shows bright blackcurrant fruit & a brush of cedar. Toned & supple, with underlying seriousness. — MW

Neil Ellis Wines

Location/map: Stellenbosch ▪ WO: Stellenbosch/Swartland/Coastal/Elgin/Darling ▪ Est 1986 ▪ 1stB 1984 ▪ Tasting & sales Mon–Fri 10–4.30 Sat & pub hols 10–5 ▪ Fee R25 Premium range/R35 Vineyard Selection range ▪ Closed Easter Fri, Dec 25/26 & Jan 1 ▪ Antipasto platters in summer; soup & bread in winter ▪ Tour groups ▪ Owner(s) Neil Ellis Wines (Pty) Ltd ▪ Cellarmaster(s) Neil Ellis (1984) ▪ Winemaker(s) Reg Holder & Warren Ellis (2006) ▪ Viticulturist(s) Warren Ellis (2006) ▪ 2.5-3t/ha ▪ 50,000cs own label 50% red 50% white + 1,500cs for clients ▪ Brands for clients: Woolworths ▪ WIETA ▪ PO Box 917 Stellenbosch 7599 ▪ info@neilellis.com ▪ www.neilellis.com ▪ S 33° 55'34.92" E 018° 53'32.46" ▪ **T +27 (0)21-887-0649** ▪ F +27 (0)21-887-0647

Neil Ellis is one of the doyens of the South African wine industry, having grown from his pioneering negociant beginnings in the early 1980s to a solid, family based enterprise whose brand name is synonymous with elegance and quality. Quietly confident yet humble - a gentle giant - he's a mentor to many in the trade. The basis of Neil's success is his continuous quest to understand the vineyards and to use varieties that are 'relevant', because they are both suited to the soil and sustainable. He was the first to produce sauvignon from the now trendy Elgin and Groenekloof areas, and still continues to buy in most of his grapes from long-term contract growers. This makes son Warren, with an MSc in viticulture, a valuable Ellis team player.

Vineyard Selection range

★★★★☆ **Cabernet Sauvignon** Still-current 07 was misleadingly accessible when last tasted. Well crafted, disguising subtle power with complex layers of flavour.

★★★★★ **Grenache** Rare varietal bottling from old single-vineyard in Piekenierskloof. Fruit concentration concealed in tighter structure of cooler 09 (★★★★). Elegant but shade less engaging in youth than **08**, needs more time for pedigreed fruit to shine.

★★★★☆ **Pinotage** 09 (★★★★) shows lovely fruit purity. Unshowy but serious, with a core of sappy, savoury fruit; not quite as complex as **08**. Balanced, youthful wine deserving of cellaring.

★★★★☆ **Syrah** Complex & polished 07 still available. Showed spicy dark fruit & the trademark Ellis elegant tannins when last tasted.

★★★★☆ **Sauvignon Blanc** 🗋🖉 Refined, even in riper vintage, **10** has layers of tangy grapefruit, nectarine flavours & dusty fynbos, framed in subtly oaked structure. Good flinty length for food pairing. WO Coastal.

Premium range

★★★★ **Cabernet Sauvignon** 🗋 Cooler 09 shows leafy tone & firm cedary tannins. Still a tad austere in youth, but with cellaring, has complexity & fruit to match rating of riper & accessibly tailored **08**.

★★★★ **Shiraz** 🗋 09 from Elgin. Creamy texture, blackberry & savoury nuances last year.

★★★★ **Cabernet Sauvignon-Merlot** 🗋 09 all the components for a fine blend, just a tad disjointed in youth. Firmly structured with cassis, leather & dusty oak spice. Time will bring harmony & drinking pleasure.

★★★★ **Aenigma** 🗋 08 still current version of occasional label. Red-berried cab/merlot blend with a dusting of white pepper, from cooler Elgin grapes, not retasted.

★★★★ **Elgin Chardonnay** 🗋🖉 10 in rich yet understated style, layers of citrus peel, hazelnut & brioche flavours interwoven into subtle oaky & waxy texture. Lovely balancing acidity & food-pairing length.

★★★★ **Stellenbosch Chardonnay** 🗋🖉 11 preview too young to rate. Previous **10** ex-tank showed exhilarating vitality & appealing lemon & nutty flavours. 🗋

★★★★☆ **Groenekloof Sauvignon Blanc** 🗋🖉 Groenekloof's perfect compatibility with sauvignon clear on 11 unrated preview. Even in infancy exudes hallmark flintiness & mouthfilling array of tangy citrus, capsicum & greengage. Like **10** & previous dances with pure intensity & freshness. — MW

Nelson Wine Estate

Location/WO: Paarl ▪ Map: Paarl & Wellington ▪ Tasting & sales Mon–Fri 8–5 Sat/Sun by appt ▪ Closed all pub hols ▪ Cellar tours by appt ▪ Facilities for children ▪ Tour groups ▪ Conferences ▪ Weddings ▪ Walks/hikes ▪ Mountain biking trails ▪ Guest accommodation ▪ Owner(s) Alan Nelson ▪ Cellarmaster(s) Lisha Nelson (Nov 2007) ▪ Winemaker(s) Lisha Nelson (Nov 2007), with Solly Hendriks (Apr 2011) ▪ Viticulturist(s) Daniel Nelson ▪ 142ha/

46ha (cabs s/f, merlot, p verdot, ptage, shiraz, chard, chenin, sauv, sem) ▪ 210t/4,670cs own label 30% red 60% white 10% rosé ▪ IPW ▪ PO Box 2009 Windmeul 7630 ▪ lisha@nelsonscreek.co.za ▪ www.nelsonscreek.co.za ▪ S 33° 39'31.2" E 018° 56' 17.3" ▪ **T** +27 (0)21-869-8453 ▪ F +27 (0)21-869-8424

This horse-loving family winery in Paarl headed by advocate Alan Nelson added a new member last year - but he's a tad young to be harnessed into action. Winemaker Lisha's son, Peter-Alan, arrived around the same time as viticulturist brother Daniel delivered the 2011 harvest's first load of grapes to the cellar!

Lisha Nelson Signature Wines

★★★★☆ **Cabernet Franc** Last year we admired **08**'s delicious ripe black fruit & herbal minerality, succulence. Grip & backbone apparent on long finish. Well-judged oak - all new French for 21 months.

★★★★ **Dad's Blend** Floral blackberry & violets previously on **08** 4-way cab franc-led blend. Spicy plum & cassis in smooth, juicy mouthful, leading to complex long finish.

Nelson Estate range

★★★★ **Noble Late Harvest 08** all honeyed apricot & glucose last guide. Lively acid lead to clean finish. Balanced & rich, the naturally fermented semillon danced on stage of all-new French oak, 11 months.

Shiraz ★★★★ Spicy coconut & juicy plum, **08** smoky hint, firm dry tannin from 18 months new oak. Not retasted, like next. **Cabernet Sauvignon-Merlot** ★★★★ Deliciously lithe **08** has berry compote & cigarbox tones from 18 months new French oak. Velvety, genteel & lingering. **Rosé** 🍷 🅱 ★★★ Rhubarb tartness on dry **11**, nice taut body & zippy vitality match standard set by last **09**. **Chardonnay** 🍷 ★★★★ Previous edition we noted orange, 'rancio' & nutty butter on **09**. Creamy, with lime lift; structure from natural ferment & 11 months new French oak. **Sauvignon Blanc** 🍷 🅱 ★★★ Flinty **11** a tad sweet, misses previous' lime vibrancy. Discontinued: **Special Vintage Collection Pinotage**.

Nelson's Creek range

Shiraz 🍷 🅱 ★★★ Return to form in **10**. Rich, ripe hedgerow fruit countered by body & integrated oak. Chunky & textured. **Cabernet Sauvignon-Merlot Rosé** 🍷 Await next. **Pinotage Rosé** 🍷 🅱 ★★ Natural Sweet-style **11** with candyfloss flavour keeps up the standard. **Chenin Blanc** 🍷 🅱 ★★★ **11** maintains form with crisp appley appeal. Discontinued: **Cabernet Sauvignon, Merlot, Sauvignon Blanc**. — FM

New Beginnings Wines

Location: Cape Town ▪ WO: Paarl/Swartland ▪ Est 1996 ▪ 1stB 1999 ▪ Closed to public ▪ Owner(s) Klein Begin Farming Association ▪ Brand manager FMS Food & Beverages SA cc ▪ 13ha/10ha (cab, ptage, shiraz, chard) ▪ 10,000cs own label 70% red 25% white 5% rosé ▪ PO Box 51869 Waterfront Cape Town 8002 ▪ info@fms-wine-marketing.co.za ▪ www.fms-wine-marketing.co.za ▪ **T** +27 (0)21-426-5037 ▪ F +27 (0)21-413-0825

Living up to its name, this farmworker empowerment venture dating from the mid-1990s is making a fresh start, after the promised co-operation of an NGO collapsed. CEO Anton Blignault says the Department of Agriculture has stepped in, and plans are to focus on rehabilitation of vineyards, planting of three additional hectares, and an imminent switch to organic farming. The intention is to bottle the organic wines under a separate label.

Cabernet Sauvignon ★★★ Blackcurrant succulence on **09**, combination juicy & ripe fruit & good vintage; pleasing & easy. **Pinotage** ★★★ **09** ex Paarl step up (as most here), smooth styling & accessible juicy mulberry-perfumed fruit. Honest drinkability. **Shiraz** NEW ★★★ Forward fruit with spicy pepper tones, **09** succulent but subtle & easy drinkability. **Pinotage Rosé** 🍷 🅱 ★★ **10** light & bright summer sipper with gently dry cranberry tones. **Chardonnay** 🍷 🅱 ★★★ **10** now bottled, shows good development, delicious, balanced & crispy ripeness. — MW

- ▪ **New Cape Wines** *see* Eagle's Cliff Wines-New Cape Wines
- ▪ **New Gate** *see* Ernst Gouws & Co Wines
- ▪ **New Generation** *see* Simonsvlei International

Newton Johnson Vineyards

Location: Hermanus ▪ Map: Elgin, Walker Bay & Bot River ▪ WO: Upper Hemel-en-Aarde Valley/Elgin/Walker Bay/Overberg/Cape South Coast/Upper Hemel-en-Aarde Valley/Bot River ▪ Est 1996 ▪ 1stB 1997 ▪ Tasting & sales Mon-Fri 9–4 Sat 10–2 ▪ Closed all pub hols ▪ Heaven Restaurant Tue-Sun 9–4 ▪ Owner(s) Dave & Felicity Johnson ▪ Cellarmaster(s)/viticulturist(s) Gordon Newton Johnson (Jan 2001) ▪ Winemaker(s) Gordon Newton Johnson

(Jan 2001) & Nadia Newton Johnson (Aug 2006) ▪ 140ha/18ha (grenache, mourv, pinot, syrah, chard, sauv) ▪ 240t/10,000cs own label 50% red 50% white ▪ PO Box 225 Hermanus 7200 ▪ wine@newtonjohnson.com ▪ www.newtonjohnson.com ▪ S 34°22'9.7" E 019°15'33.3" ▪ **T +27 (0)28-312-3862** ▪ F +27 (0)86-638-9673

This archetypal family winery (two generations fully involved) is not limited by the charm that tends to accrue – it's also one whose rigorous quality across a broad spectrum is not often matched in the Cape, let alone the Hemel-en-Aarde region where they have been established longer than all save the pioneers. Thoughtful, intelligent work in vineyards and cellar (where natural processes rule: gravity rather than mechanical pumping, no yeast inoculation, for example) mean continuing learning, continuing progress – and what more can one ask? Take the Rhône-style blends (a second one now): one wonders if their rare and valuable delicacy and charm would have been possible if Gordon and Nadia NJ hadn't learnt to draw one of the Cape's unquestionably finest pinot noirs from their soil.

★★★★ **Pinot Noir** The **10** Elgin version more gutsy, earthy, acidic & powerful than the Domaine, but not lacking fresh grace, with subtle tannins & understated fruit. But not up to special **09** (★★★★★).

★★★★★ **Domaine Pinot Noir 10** like **09** a superb pure-fruited (but far from 'fruity') vintage. As usual, more brick than Elgin one's crimson. Delicate, complex perfume leads to subtle, indirect expression of lingering fruit. Supple & fine; the tannin structure almost unnoticeable - but it is deeply informing.

★★★★☆ **Full Stop Rock** Previously 'Syrah-Mourvèdre', now a drop of grenache added (it's 94% syrah), the new name with a surfing allusion. Most attractive, still-young **08**, with fine perfumed potential complexity, persistent fruit, some weight & power but fresh & even elegant. Like Grenache Blend, ex 2 H-en-A wards.

★★★★ **Grenache Blend** NEW Working name for a 2nd Rhône-inspired blend, **10** with 68% grenache + mourvèdre, syrah. Sweet, generous fruit less dense than other version; supple, silky, fresh - & very drinkable.

★★★★ **Chardonnay** This version from Kaaimansgat vineyard (WO Overberg). **09** more showy than Domaine, forthright, bright & bold in its full-flavoured appeal, touch less harmony in its succulent, tasty balance.

★★★★☆ **Domaine Chardonnay** Tough vintage shows in reduced intensity of **10** (★★★★), after fine **09**. But lingering flavour & sweet fruit there, on a structure more elegant than fat, well balanced, integrated oak.

★★★★ **Sauvignon Blanc** 🍽 🖉 Usual Elgin, H-en-A mix in grapes for **11**, with 8% oaked semillon adding to creamy, broad textural element. Green-tinged, flinty aromas lead to balanced, fresh, full-flavoured palate.

★★★★ **Resonance** Home organic sauvignon + 16% oaked Elgin semillon. **10** really charming floral, tropical fragrance - but blackcurrant notes a special delight. Balanced & silky for easy but untrivial drinking. — TJ

■ **Nicholas L Jonker** *see* Jonkheer

Nick & Forti's Wines

Location: Tulbagh ▪ Est/1stB 2004 ▪ Tasting at Saronsberg Cellar (see entry) ▪ Owner(s) Fortunato Mazzone & Saronsberg ▪ Winemaker(s) Dewaldt Heyns (2004) ▪ 2,000cs 85% red 15% white ▪ Box 25032 Monument Park Pretoria 0105 ▪ ritrovo@mweb.co.za ▪ www.saronsberg.com ▪ **T +27 (0)12-460-4367** ▪ F +27 (0)12-460-5173

Maintaining the status quo - quality food-friendly wines at decent prices - is the aim of opera-singing chef Fortunato (Forti) Mazzone for his ever-popular Pretoria restaurant, Ritrovo. Business partner, good friend and Saronsberg Cellar owner Nick van Huyssteen provides the facilities and grapes. In the pipeline is a white blend 'because I sell so much fish!'

★★★★ **Epicentre** Elegant **07** (★★★★★) previous edition showed great complexity; herbal whiffs, beef carpaccio, even violets, but core of plush red fruit & tailored tannins impressed most. Improved on **06**.

Shiraz ★★★★ Careful oaking in **07** last year gave meaty, spicy tones to plum fruit & gentle grip, promising good ageing. **Viognier** ★★★★ Peach pip & shortbread on deep palate, **09** on review had rich consistency & resonating savoury length. Rung up on **08** (★★★★), with peach & pinenut opulence. — FM

Nico van der Merwe Wines

Location/map: Stellenbosch ▪ WO: Western Cape/Stellenbosch ▪ Est/1stB 1999 ▪ Tasting by appt ▪ Owner(s) Nico & Petra van der Merwe ▪ Cellarmaster(s)/winemaker(s) Nico van der Merwe ▪ 50t/2,000cs own label 80% red 15% white 5% other + 15,000L bulk ▪ Other export brand: Mas Nicholas ▪ PO Box 12200 Stellenbosch 7613 ▪

nvdmwines@vodamail.co.za ▪ S 33° 57'48.2" E 018° 43'51.8" ▪ **T +27 (0)21-881-3063** ▪ F +27 (0)21-881-3063

The long-cherished dream of his own patch of land and winery has finally come to fruition, with the pressing of the 2011 vintage at Mas Nicolas, and Nico vdM is rightly thrilled. This veteran of 22 vintages at Saxenburg is working on tidying up after the building works, and channelling his first fully in-house vintage through the production cycle. Stylistic philosophy is centred on 'rediscovering old cultivars of the Cape, to produce unique wines'.

Nico van der Merwe Wines range

★★★★☆ **Mas Nicolas** Previously, elegant **06** had great depth & noble structure. Layers of black berry & plum fruit with tarry liquorice overtones. 50/50 cab/shiraz from same vineyards since maiden **99**.

Nicolas van der Merwe range

★★★★ **Red** Last year **06** Bordeaux-style blend showed juicier fruit profile but retained upright structure. **Syrah** ★★★★☆ Big, muscular (15.5% alc) **07** set new standard for label last edition. Larger-than-life fruit demanded attention, needed time - contrast with open-textured **06** (★★★★). **White** Await next release.

Cape Elements range

Shiraz-Cinsaut-Grenache ★★★★ New-wave blend of warm-climate varieties, **09** has malty whiff, but unfurls delightfully juicy berry flavours.

Robert Alexander range

Merlot ✓ ★★★★ Opulently concentrated fruit on **09** reflects fine vintage after softer **08** (★★★☆). Dense & finely textured, with enduring finish, belies modest pitch of range. **Shiraz** ★★★★ Hint of coriander, focused fruit, well-rounded body on **08** previously noted. **Méthode Cap Classique Brut** ★★★★ **08** chardonnay sparkling was extroverted, expressively leesy last time, lovely shortcake finish. Discontinued: **Sauvignon Blanc**. — GdB

Nico Vermeulen Wines

Location: Paarl ▪ WO: Coastal ▪ Est/1stB 2003 ▪ Closed to public ▪ Owner(s)/viticulturist(s) Nico Vermeulen ▪ Winemaker(s) Nico Vermeulen, with Judy & Izelle Vermeulen ▪ 1,500cs own label & 240,000L bulk export ▪ 3 Pieter Hugo Str Courtrai Suider-Paarl 7646 ▪ nicovermeulen@webmail.co.za ▪ **T +27 (0)21-863-2048/+27 (0)82-553-2024** ▪ F +27 (0)21-863-2048

Having worked at some top Cape cellars and most recently at Havana Hills, has stood Nico Vermeulen in good stead, he knows where the best vineyards sites are. Able to select according to his taste and vision had lead him to Durbanville, Lutzville and Elim for white varieties (vinified at Diemersdal), and a mix of warm and cool areas for red (made at Nwanedi Country Estate), for greater complexity.

★★★★☆ **The Right Red** Worth the wait for **08** (★★★★), all the shiraz boxes ticked, luscious fruit, a spice array, some scrub notes, but for earlier drinking (no hardship), less concentration than **06**. **07** skipped.

★★★★ **The Right White** ▤ Sauvignon minerality & nettles on **11** (★★★★), gentle pear flavours finishing crisply dry. Less expressive than **10**.

The Right Two Reds ★★★ Last tasted was sleek **05** merlot/cab blend with refreshing acidity & friendly tannins. **The Right Two Whites** ▤ Untasted. — CR

Niel Joubert Estate

Location/WO: Paarl ▪ Map: Paarl & Wellington ▪ Est 1898 ▪ 1stB 1996 ▪ Tasting & sales Mon-Fri 9-4 by appt ▪ Closed all pub hols ▪ Owner(s) Joubert family ▪ Cellarmaster(s) Ernst Leicht ▪ Winemaker(s) Ernst Leicht, with Niel Joubert jnr (May 2011) ▪ Viticulturist(s) Daan Joubert ▪ 1,000ha/300ha (cab, merlot, shiraz, chard, chenin, sauv) ▪ 1,953t/±80,000cs own label 1% red 50% white 49% rosé ▪ Other export brand: Hunterspeak ▪ Global Gap, IPW ▪ PO Box 17 Klapmuts 7625 ▪ wine@nieljoubert.co.za ▪ www.nieljoubert.co.za ▪ S 33° 49'54.7" E 018° 54'3.2" ▪ **T +27 (0)21-875-5936** ▪ F +27 (0)86-599-0725

The Joubert family of Klein Simonsvlei on the haunches of the Simonsberg were the only South Africans to be honoured at last year's China International show in Guangzhou, validating their prescience in looking to Asia for sales growth, and further incentivising them to act out of the box. So watch for a new white blend, billed as an antidote to the prevalent more-of-the-same market malaise.

Everything should be greener.
And everyone can drink to that.

Nedbank green Wine Awards

If you are as passionate about wine as you are about the environment, you'll be glad to know that Nedbank is committed to a sustainable future for the South African wine industry. We are actively involved in the Biodiversity & Wine Intitiative, a Green Trust project, and have a 14-year partnership with the Cape Winemakers Guild. We are continually looking for ways to protect the environment by reducing our own carbon footprint as a bank and making banking greener for our clients through initiatives such as e-statements and our Green Affinity programme. These are just some of the ways we are helping to ensure a better future for generations to come. Here's to working for a greener Earth.

MAKE THIGS HAPPEN

WWF
THE
GREEN TRUST

NEDBANK

A Member of the OLD MUTUAL Group

'Social media maven' is not a title he would use himself, but that's exactly wha
Tim Pearson is. As owner (with wife Vaughan, who took this picture) of relativ
newcomer Seven Springs Vineyards near Hermanus, UK-based Tim is expert
using Twitter, Facebook, LinkedIn and other social media to put his youn
brand – and the quality of South African wines generally – on the world map. S
effectively, he's been chosen as a case study by Prof Damien Wilson of th
Burgundy School of Business in Dijon, France.

the elegance of crystal
... is in the nose

A LIFETIME OF VALUE AND ELEGANCE

TEL: +27 (0)21 887 2173 · FAX: + 27 (0)86 524 8410
info@crystaldirect.co.za · www.crystaldirect.co.za

Quality | Bohemian Crystal | Tradition Craftsmanship

Riserva
1964

Insurance for Collectable Wines

The need for specialised insurance for collectable wines in South Africa has become increasingly vital as values rocket in complete contrast to many other assets that continue to struggle in a topsy-turvy investment world.

Aon South Africa pinpoints the wine collectables market among connoisseurs, enthusiasts, companies, auctioneers, dealers and even the occasional amateur dabbler.

"The experts in this market will tell you that selected local and international wines are enjoying good demand among discerning South Africans and that's in spite of the fact that the secondary market for investment wines in this country is still in its infancy.

"The basic message is that, among the serious collectors and other stakeholders in South Africa, wines can be a significant asset and as the size and value of those assets grows, so too does the associated risk arising from possible loss.

Insuring for these risks is all about providing cost effective, properly designed policies based on expert valuations for those who invest in, market, produce, transport or are involved in the high end of the wine market in one way or another.

"In the past, insurance of this nature tended to be placed overseas, but nowadays collectors covers are offered right here in South Africa and that obviously helps with premiums, with the insurers acknowledging the curatorship involved in such collections and pricing them accordingly on an agreed value basis, taking into account aspects such as whether sets are involved.

"The major difference when it comes to insuring wines and other collectables for that matter, is that you are dealing with appreciating rather than depreciating assets and the specialised collectable covers are formulated accordingly. In all other respects however such covers remains familiar and are premised on all risk provisions."

Contact:
0860 100 404
www.aon.co.za

Unconventional, envelope-pushing, quirky – call it what you will, but the Appelbaum family, owners of De Morgenzon estate in Stellenbosch, have taken note of research which shows that vines respond positively to harmonious sounds. Hence the Baroque music which plays 24x7 to the vines (and the wine incubating in barrel) through strategically placed speakers such as the one above co-owner **Wendy Appelbaum** and winemaker **Carl van der Merwe**. A discordant element was recently removed when members of staff voted to mute a pet irritation: the harpsichord. The vines' reaction is unrecorded.

BECAUSE *WE* THINK
OUT THE BOX
YOU GET IT
IN THE
BOX

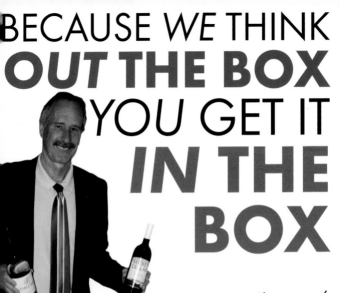

Mark Norrish

Ultra Liquors
Wine Specialist

At Ultra Liquors, we want you to enjoy the best wines South Africa has to offer.
But we also know that you can get tired of the same wine over and over again.
That's why we came up with the concept of the ULTRA WINE BOX:
you get to choose any 12 wines you like per box, from our exceptional range
– and most importantly, pay CASE LOT prices.

The ULTRA WINE BOX. **Just another way
Ultra Liquors supports the South African wine industry.
And your pocket!**

Any questions about wine? Drop me a line on
marknorrish@ultraliquors.co.za

Hailed as a landmark in regional marketing, the recently established win festival known as Swartland Revolution is both a celebration of one of Sou Africa's fastest improving wine areas and a showcase for a widening circle Swartland producers embracing a return to artisanal, natural winegrowin Photographed in Riebeek-Kasteel's town square are some of the prime move behind this internationally praised movement (clockwise from left): **Andrea** ar **Chris Mullineux** (Mullineux Family Wines), **Adi Badenhorst** (Badenhor Family Wines), **Callie Louw** (Porseleinberg), **Eben** and **Magriet Sadie** (Sad Family Wines), and **Marc Kent** (Boekenhoutskloof).

Christine-Marié range

Cabernet Sauvignon 🗎 ★★★★ Elegant **09**, blackcurrant, violet & cigarbox refinement on pre-bottling sample. Step up from last-tasted **06** (★★★★). Firm body & length from 100% new oak. Harmonious & complex. **Merlot** 🗎 ★★★★ Bold cherry & brambles, **06** dark earthy grip & concentration, big alc (15%) but soft appeal. Not retasted, like next 2 wines. **Shiraz** 🗎 ★★★★ **06** gobs of ripe black fruit, fennel & anise, warming 16.3% alc. Almond nuttiness from 100% new oak. **Chardonnay** 🗎 ★★★★ Tangerine blast on smoky vanilla **08**, lavishly oaked (18 months 2nd fill), rich & delicious. **Viognier** 🗎 ★★★★ Reported as discontinued last time, but **08** is alive & well, redolent of peaches & cream. Rounded & full, restrained but firm toasty oak from (seasoned) barrels. **Méthode Cap Classique** ★★★★ **08** sparkling last year had attractive seaweed & brioche aromas. Limestone minerality framed vibrant acidity, elegant 11% alc. **First Kiss Fortified Chenin Blanc** 🗎 ★★★★ Waxy honey & apricot, **07** last edition was sweet but balanced by limy freshness. 2 years oak, 100% new.

Niel Joubert Estate range

Sauvignon Blanc ☺🗎 ★★★ Crisp, refreshing lemongrass vibrancy to **11** preview, appealing light mineral aftertaste.

Cabernet Sauvignon 🗎 ★★★ Buchu-scented blackberry fruit, **09** gets its freshness from 50% unwooded portion; dry tannic grip at end. **Merlot** 🗎 ★★★ **09** herb & mulberry, with light oak sheen; fruit density & concentration carry to extended finish. **Pinotage** 🗎 ★★★ Light smokiness on red-berried unoaked **09**, a touch lean & inky. **Shiraz** 🗎 ★★★ Ripe cherry, plum & liquorice tones on **06**, previously tasted. A third oaked portion (15% new) gave sleek but yielding grip. **Rosé** 🗎 ★★★ Name change from 'Eerste Pluk Pinotage Rosé' though dry **11** still from pinotage, with variety's cranberry tang. **Chardonnay** 🗎 ★★ Light floral & citrus **11**, hint of oak from 3 months on staves. **Chenin Blanc** 🗎 ★★★ Pear-drop & melon friendliness on tangy, medium-bodied **11**. **Voice** 🗎 ★★★ 100% viognier. Like Christine Marié version above, not discontinued & in fact **11** is a step up from last-seen **08**, balanced sundried peach richness & acid zip. — FM

■ **Niels Verburg** *see Luddite Wines*

Nietvoorbij Wine Cellar

Location/map: Stellenbosch ▪ Est 1963 ▪ 1stB 1992 ▪ Tasting & sales Mon-Fri 9–4; phone ahead on Sat ▪ Fee R5/wine ▪ Cellar tours Fri by appt T +27 (0)21-809-3140 ▪ Closed all pub hols ▪ Conferences ▪ Owner(s) Agricultural Research Council ▪ Winemaker(s) Kajo Malek, with Craig Paulse ▪ Vineyard manager(s) Guillaume Kotzè (Apr 2002) ▪ 32ha (cabs s/f, malbec, merlot, ptage, shiraz, chard, sauv, viog) ▪ 75t/3,000cs own label 56% red 40% white 4% port ▪ Private Bag X5026 Stellenbosch 7599 ▪ winesales@arc.agric.za ▪ www.arc.agric.za ▪ S 33° 54'43.5" E 018° 51'48.9" ▪ **T +27 (0)21-809-3084/3140 ▪** F +27 (0)86-623-4014

Nietvoorbij has just appointed Kajo Malek as the new winemaker. He will now have the task of incorporating the annual research findings at the institute into the actual production of wine. The aim is to produce innovative wines, covering various styles, but with a strong focus on lifestyle-orientated and easy-drinking wines.

Nietvoorbij Wine Cellar range

Cabernet Sauvignon ★★★ Dark-fruited & toasty vanilla **05** should be drinking well now. Still selling & not revisited, as all unless noted. **Merlot** Await new, as for **Pinotage**, **Shiraz** & **Pinotage Rosé**. **Kwartet** ★★★ Cab-led 4-way Bordeaux blend, **07** cherry & pencil shaving notes from French oak. **Theart Reserve** ★★★ Second **05** Bordeaux blend on release was tad more leafy & tannic than sibling. **Chardonnay** ★★★ Lightly oaked **10** had soft pear nuance, slightly sweet farewell. **Cape Ruby** 🗎 ★ Port-style **08** from pinotage, big alc (21%) & medicinal hint. — JP

Nieuwedrift Vineyards

Location: Piketberg ▪ Map/WO: Swartland ▪ Est/1stB 2002 ▪ Tasting, sales & cellar tours Mon-Fri 9–1 & 2–6 Sat 9–2 ▪ Closed Easter Fri/Sun, Dec 25/26 & Jan 1 ▪ Meals on request; or BYO picnic ▪ Facilities for children ▪ Tour groups ▪ Conferences ▪ Owner(s) Johan Mostert ▪ Cellarmaster(s) Johan Mostert (Jan 2002) ▪ Viticulturist(s) Hugo Lambrechts ▪ 151ha/31ha (shiraz, chard, chenin, cbard) ▪ 410t total 10t/658cs own label 28% red 40% white 16% rosé 16% MCC ▪ PO Box 492 Piketberg 7320 ▪ nieuwedrift@patat.za.net ▪ S 32° 58'28.1" E 018° 45'10.6" ▪ **T +27 (0)22-913-1966/+27 (0)82-824-8104 ▪** F +27 (0)88-022-913-1966

Well worth a visit for an enthusiastic and warm Swartland welcome from owner-winemaker Johan Mostert. Of the 400 tonnes harvested only about 5 tonnes as yet make it into these select cuvées. But one senses that Johan is becoming more confident with the winemaking side of things, so perhaps this will change.

Chenin Blanc ☺ 🍷 ★★★ Fine persistent finish on **11**, follows shy stone fruit & fresh promise from nose. Essentially crisp & dry.

Shiraz ★★★★ **09** shows off Swartland plump fruit, lifted with spice & savoury tones. Palate is bright, while big 15.7% alcohol fleshes out finish. **Blanc de Noir** 🍷 ★★★ **11** fresh, zippy, light in colour & light in style, ends dry. **Méthode Cap Classique** ★★ **10** yeasty, fresh & dry. Rather simple. — JP

Nitida Cellars

Location: Durbanville ▪ Map: Durbanville, Philadelphia & Darling ▪ WO: Durbanville/Coastal ▪ Est/1stB 1995 ▪ Tasting & sales Mon–Fri 9–5 Sat 9.30–3 Sun 11-3 ▪ Closed Easter Fri, Dec 25 & Jan 1 ▪ Cassia Restaurant (see Restaurants section) ▪ Tables at Nitida T +27 (0)21-975-9537, www.tablesatnitida.co.za ▪ Conference & function venue at Cassia T +27 (0)21-976-0640 ▪ Facilities for children ▪ Mountain biking: Vellerdrome track for novice riders; part of Hillcrest/Majik forest trail (www.tygerbergmtb.co.za) ▪ Conservation area ▪ Annual festivals: Season of Sauvignon (Oct); Feast of the Grape (Mar); Soup, Sip & Bread (June) ▪ Owner(s) Bernhard & Peta Veller ▪ Cellarmaster(s) Bernhard Veller ▪ Winemaker(s) RJ Botha (2007) ▪ Viticulturist(s) Bernhard Veller & RJ Botha ▪ 35ha/16ha (cabs s/f, p verdot, riesling, sauv, sem) ▪ 150t/9,000cs own label 30% red 70% white + 1,500cs for clients ▪ Brands for clients: Woolworths ▪ PO Box 1423 Durbanville 7551 ▪ info@nitida.co.za ▪ www.nitida.co.za ▪ S 33° 50'3.8" E 018° 35'37.0" ▪ **T +27 (0)21-976-1467** ▪ F +27 (0)21-976-5631

A far cry from the run-down sheep farm engineer Bernhard Veller and wife Peta bought as somewhere to live, Nitida was awarded Top Producer at the 2009 Michelangelo Awards and Bernard has been a member of the prestigious Cape Winemakers Guild since 2005. Added to this, winemaker RJ Botha became Diners Club's 2010 Young Winemaker of the Year. On the home front, a farm garden has been established to supply the two restaurants with fresh produce, and free-range eggs will come from a social responsibility project with the farm staff. And a new wine has joined the range: 'The Matriarch' Méthode Cap Classique, so named to honour women's 'elegance, graciousness and wisdom', while the shiraz bubbly 'Matriarch in Red' celebrates women's 'strength and tenacity'.

★★★★☆ **Calligraphy** 🝆 Bordeaux blend **10** shows merlot predominance, with third cab: cassis, black cherry perfume & fleshy ripeness lead you in, but as befits a flagship, the structure is serious; savoury tannins will keep it in perfect health for years to come.

★★★★ **Weisser Riesling** 🍷 More than a whiff of the Mosel about last tasted **09**. Fragrant lime, white lily jasmine; dry, clean & pure, with great mouthfeel. Darling vines.

★★★★ **Sauvignon Blanc** 🍷 🝆 Back on form after **10** (★★★). Leafy minerality on the nose but it's **11**'s flavours where most of the action is: gooseberries & lime, lovely tangy acidity that awakens the tastebuds.

★★★★☆ **Sauvignon Blanc Club Select** 🍷 Special tank selection to highlight cool terroir. Elegant **11** fits the brief perfectly: summer meadow grasses, a lemon nuance & taut focused minerality. Good ageing potential.

★★★★☆ **Semillon** 🍷 Previously **10** had nectarine, honey, lemon & beeswax notes. Richly textured, with gentle buttery roundness, fresh tangy marmalade appeal. 50% barrel fermented.

★★★★☆ **Coronata Integration** 🍷 🝆 Complex Bordeaux-style white blend 70% sauvignon ex tank, rest older barrel semillon. Loquat & lime perfumed **10** then reveals other layers, minerality on the palate, crisp & pure; subtle oatmeal from oak. Will be even better over time.

Cabernet Sauvignon ★★★★ Last was **09**, back on track after quirky **08** (★★★). Ripe currants & peppery-leafy notes, ripe tannic grip & lingering savoury finish. WO Coastal. **Pinotage** 🍷 🝆 ★★★ Intense blueberries with a typical eucalyptus nuance, **10** is softly fleshy despite all-new oak. **Shiraz** Await next. **Chardonnay** 🍷 🝆 ★★★★ Light oaking provides gentle oatmeal, leaves **11**'s melon/tangerine fruit to shine. Freshened by limy acidity. Nudges next level. **Matriarch Méthode Cap Classique** NEW 🝆 ★★★ Champagne-method sparkling; mainly chardonnay, 30% pinot noir's influence seen in **10**'s berry aromas, hint of pink. Dry & fresh with lively mousse, an aperitif style. WO Coastal. **Matriarch in Red** ★★★ Traditional-method sparkling listed as 'Shiraz Cap Classique' last time. Plums & berries, nice fruit purity in **10**'s perfume; flavours show more fruitcake, slight smokiness. **Semillon Noble Late Harvest** Await next. Discontinued: **Coronata**. — CR

■ **Nixan Wines** see Blue Crane Vineyards

Noble Hill Wine Estate

Location: Paarl ▪ Map: Paarl & Wellington ▪ WO: Simonsberg-Paarl/Paarl/Coastal/Overberg ▪ Est/1stB 2001 ▪ Tasting & sales daily 10–5 ▪ Fee R35, waived on purchase ▪ Closed Apr 27, Jun 16 & Aug 9 ▪ Cellar tours by appt during tasting hours ▪ cosecha Restaurant (see Restaurants section) ▪ Picnic baskets ▪ Facilities for children ▪ Farm-produced extra-virgin olive oil ▪ Conservation area ▪ Owner(s) Noble Hill Trust ▪ Winemaker(s) Bernard le Roux (May 2010), with Rodney Zimba (2001) ▪ Viticulturist(s) Etienne Southey (2006) & Johan Viljoen (consultant) ▪ 50ha/30ha (cabs s/f, merlot, mourv, p verdot, syrah, sauv, viog) ▪ PO Box 111 Simondium 7670 ▪ info@noblehill.com ▪ www.noblehill.com ▪ S 33° 49' 38.0" E 018° 56' 12.1" ▪ **T +27 (0)21-874-3844**

One of the biggest innovations implemented by this (American) family-owned and -managed estate in the Simonsberg foothills is the leaf and stem water potential irrigation. 'It is a dry topic (no pun intended!),' says Kristopher Tillery, son and director, 'but has an enormous impact on the quality of grapes brought into the cellar. This cutting-edge technology allows us to control irrigation for optimal ripening of the grapes, saving vast quantities of water.' Under discussion is the planting of Rhône varieties on a newly cleared high-potential white-wine site.

Noble Hill Wines range

★★★★ **Cabernet Sauvignon** ✓ Delicious pristine blackberry fruit, forest-floor, cedar highlights to understated & elegant **08**. Firm & mouthfilling, vanilla oaky finish. A keeper.

★★★★ **Merlot** ✓ Red plums/berries & vanilla spice abound on **08**, firmly structured with precise tannin, long succulent finish. Accessible now.

★★★★ **Syrah** Very fruit-forward & bold **08** (★★★), sweet spicy dark berry fruit & a warm savoury ending. Touch overripe compared with last-tasted maiden **05**, listed as 'Shiraz'.

★★★★ **1674 Signature Blend** Bordeaux-style red shows restrained black fruit, slightly dusty but in beautiful harmony with vanilla oak. **08** is balanced, with lingering blackberry liqueur aftertaste.

★★★★ **Syrah-Mouvèdre-Viognier** NEW Intense aromas of black fruit, Rhône-style **08** is rich & deep, with delicate spice & toast. Enjoy with robust & hearty food.

★★★★ **Sauvignon Blanc** ✓ 🏅 Pungent **11**, capsicum & lemongrass aromas, full-flavoured grassy, lemony freshness, racy acidity & moderate 12.5% alc contributing to poise, length. WO Coastal.

★★★★ **Viognier** Seductive kiwi, peach & apricot on lightly oaked **09** last edition. Delicately floral, understated vanilla, refreshing & elegant farewell.

Shiraz-Mourvèdre In abeyance. **Sauvignon Blanc Reserve** NEW ✓ 🏅 ★★★★★ Hand-selected grapes from outstanding Elandskloof vineyard, intricate vinification for previewed **11**: intense but restrained greenpepper, green fig & kiwifruit array, racy but succulent & balanced freshness. Tremendous depth & aromatic complexity. Will develop well. WO Overberg.

Austin range

Occasional releases. — WB

Noble Savage

This standalone brand by Bartinney Private Cellar is aimed at 'kindred spirits, a clan bound by love of good wine, good company and living life to the full'. Previously sold only online (see www.noblesavage.co.za), it's now also available in retail in two variants, a rosy pink having joined the red. Both are very good value.

Cabernet Sauvignon Rosé NEW ☺ 🏅 ★★★ Lively, just-dry & fresh **10**, tasty tarte tatin & pomegranate, typical cab fullness & lingering flavour. WO Stellenbosch both.

Noble Savage ✓ ★★★★ Elegantly seductive cab/merlot blend, **09** step up on **08** (★★★★), ample cassis, cocoa & bramble, warm but structured, fine dry tannins & long finish. Year older French oak. — FM

Nomada Wines

Location/WO: Durbanville ▪ Est/1stB 2007 ▪ Tasting on the farm from Jan 2012 ▪ Owner(s) Riaan & Gina Oosthuizen ▪ Winemaker(s)/viticulturist(s) Riaan Oosthuizen (2007) ▪ 66ha/7ha (cabs s/f, merlot, chenin, sauv) ▪ 40t total 5t/1,000cs own label 40% red 60% white + 1,000cs for clients ▪ Brands for clients: Schaap Wines (Netherlands) ▪ PO Box 5145 Tygervalley 7536 ▪ nomadawines@gmail.com ▪ **T +27 (0)83-280-7690**

Previously nomadic vintners Riaan and Gina Oosthuizen have now established a home base on a Durbanville farm, where they are building a tasting room, to be included in the area's popular wine route. Production for their own label will always be small, but they already export to the UK, Netherlands and Finland.

★★★★ **Sauvignon Blanc** ✓ 🗎 **10** (★★★★) riper & shade off **09**. Broad, feisty grenadilla & fig flavours, with Durbanville's flinty finish.

Georgina ★★★ **09** is a brusque Bordeaux blend, boldly ripe for hearty food. **Rustica** NEW 🗎 ★★★ Lightly oaked **10** sauvignon/chenin duo is a tablemate with subtle waxy apple nuance. —MW

■ **No Name** see Pick 'n Pay
■ **Non Pareil** see L'Olivier Wine & Olive Estate
■ **Nuwehoop** see uniWines Marketing

Nuweland Wynkelder

Location: Malmesbury ▪ Map: Swartland ▪ WO: Swartland/Coastal ▪ Est 2007 ▪ 1stB 2008 ▪ Vygevallei farm stall & Nuweland wine house (R27): Tasting & sales Mon–Sat 10–6 Sun 10–4 ▪ Closed Dec 25 & Jan 1 ▪ Restaurant ▪ Facilities for children ▪ Tour groups ▪ Gifts ▪ Art ▪ Farm produce ▪ Conferences ▪ Farm/cellar (R315): Tasting, sales & cellar tours only by appt ▪ Owner(s) Juan Louw ▪ Winemaker(s)/viticulturist(s) Juan Louw (Jan 2007) ▪ 300ha/96ha (chenin) ▪ 560t/470cs own label 20% red 30% white 50% dessert + 2,700L bulk ▪ PO Box 283 Malmesbury 7299 ▪ juan@nuweland.za.net ▪ www.nuweland.za.net ▪ S 33°26′44.46″ E 018°39′1.62″ (farm), S 33° 24′03.87″ E 018° 16′41.73″ (farmstall) ▪ **T +27 (0)78-111-7913** ▪ F +27 (0)22-486-4200

The Louw family now owns the Vyge Valley Farm Stall, filled with Mariëtha Louw's gourmet preserves and other country eats, and adjacent Wine House, stocked with their own wines and those of nearby producers, on the West Coast's R27. In their Swartland cellar, hugely enthusiastic and passionate winemaking son Juan switched to whole-bunch fermentation with natural yeasts for his red wines and changed the labels to his mother tongue, Afrikaans.

★★★★ **Muscat de Alexandrie** Thought to be unique in SA: fortified dessert wine from air-dried grapes. Last year rich & very sweet but light-tripping **09** was liquid decadence: honey & floral tones, great persistence.

★★★★ **Muscat de Frontignan** Red (66%) & white muscadel in gorgeous **09**, previewed last edition. Raisins & warm honey nuances to Turkish Delight appeal. 15 months older barrels. WO Coastal.

18 Mei Grenache Noir NEW 🗎 ★★★ Picked 18 May, last Swartland grapes harvested in 2010, very late for this area. Ripe & smoky notes on **10**, firm & savoury. Previewed & showing promise, sense of excitement, as all the new wines here. **Makstok Pinotage** NEW ★★ From bushvines, brooding dark chocolate & cherries, **10** still tight, needs time. **Haasbek Tinta Barocca** NEW ★★★★ Name loosely translates as 'Gap-Toothed', a reference to 'open' structure of the 35 year old tinta bushvines i.e. not needing desuckering (shoot thinning, to promote vine balance & optimum ripening). **10** dense & peppery, earthy tones & red berried-fruit; unevolved, demands time. **Juan II** NEW 🗎 ★★★★ Bold 5-way blend mainly cab & merlot, drizzle pinotage; **10** mocha/chocolate & dark berries. 25 available cases redefines 'boutique'. **Bosstok Chenin Blanc** NEW 🗎 ★★★ From 30 year old suckered bushvines; **11** distinctly different, very ripe (±15% alc) peach/apricot, off-dry, splash sauvignon adds some freshness. **Gesuierde Sauvignon Blanc** ★★★ 'Desuckered' prefix added to **11**, paradoxically shade less appealing than previous, still fresh, crisp & summery. **Sauvignon Blanc-Chenin Blanc-Semillon** ★★★ Herbaceous notes layered with riper peach in attractive, still-selling **10**. **Straw Wine** ★★★★ Muscat d'Alexandrie raisined on straw beds 2 weeks, briefly naturally fermented, then fortified & barrel-aged. 'Hell of a job.' Last year, rich & rounded **08** preview had wonderful balanced acidity, wood provided structure, not flavour. —DB

Nuy Wine Cellar

Location/map: Worcester ▪ WO: Breedekloof/Worcester ▪ Est 1964 ▪ 1stB 1966 ▪ Tasting & sales Mon–Fri 8.30–4.30 Sat 8.30–12.30 ▪ Closed Dec 25/26 & Jan 1 ▪ BYO picnic ▪ Mountain biking ▪ Owner(s) 19 members ▪ Cellarmaster(s) Christo Pienaar (Sep 2003) ▪ Winemaker(s) Louwritz Louw (Dec 2008) ▪ Viticulturist(s) Pierre Snyman (Vinpro) ▪ 580ha (cab, merlot, muscadel, shiraz, chard, chenin, cbard, nouvelle, sauv) ▪ 12,300t/5,000cs own label ▪ PO Box 5225 Worcester 6849 ▪ wines@nuywinery.co.za ▪ www.nuywinery.co.za ▪ S 33° 39′8.7″ E 019° 38′ 30.9″ ▪ **T +27 (0)23-347-0272** ▪ F +27 (0)23-347-4994

The annual Nuy Valley Festival is getting extremely popular as people discover the wineries tucked beneath the Langeberg, cellarmaster Christo Pienaar says. To cater for demand, this muscadel specialist winery has already expanded cellar capacity from 10,000 to 12,000 tons, and there are plans to build a new tasting centre. 'At Nuy we will always strive to over-deliver on quality,' promises Christo, who sees every harvest as 'another opportunity to try and make the perfect wine'.

★★★★ **Red Muscadel** ✓ 🍽 Hugely delicious & balanced **10** preview followed by slightly syrupy **11** (★★★★). Still delightful, with grapey, fresh raisin fruit contrasting attractively with spicy spirit grip.

Rouge de Nuy ☺ 🍽 ★★★ Cherry & liquorice **10** easy-sipper is zippy & lightly oaked, punches above its price point. **Sauvignon Blanc Sparkling Vin Sec** ☺ ★★★ NV vibrant any occasion sparkling with faint sauvignon grassiness, burst of bubbly passionfruit on the tongue.

Cabernet Sauvignon 🍽 ★★ Cranberry fruit, oak grip on early-drinking, lightish (12% alc) **10**. **Barrel Selection Cabernet Sauvignon** ✓ ★★★★ Exceptional **08** a major step up on **07** (★★★) for this reserve label: dense, heady & sweet-fruited, yet with savoury finish & commendably modest 13% alc. Well-handled oak contributes fine structure & dark chocolate highlights, & platform for long fruitful ageing. **Barrel Selection Syrah** ✓ ★★★★ **08** elegant, well-crafted top-tier offering: ample smoky meat & black cherries, silky texture. Like above, one of the standout red wines of the area, especially at moderate 13% alc. **07** not reviewed, **06** (★★★) was new-oak dominated. **Shiraz** Untasted. **Chardonnay** 🍽 ★★★ Fragrant bouquet of lemon blossom, orange rind & nut, **10** pleasant if unlingering steely flavour. **Reserve Chenin Blanc** 🍽 Occasional release. **Chenin Blanc** 🍽 ★★★ Juicy **11** summer sipper, early picked for cool green-apple crispness & lowish 12% alc. **Colombar Dry** 🍽 ★★★ **11** packed with guava & bracingly fresh. **Colombar Semi-Sweet** 🍽 ★★★ 'Slightly sweet' version **11** has less intense guava than stablemate, fuller mouthfeel. **Sauvignon Blanc** 🍽 ★★★ Just-bottled (& tentatively rated) **11** takes time to open in glass to typical cut-grass & ruby grapefruit, faint sweaty undertone, tad lean. **Chant de Nuit** 🍽 ★★ Tropical-toned NV unchallenging sipper. **White Muscadel** ✓ 🍽 ★★★★ This Cape classic back on form in **07** after blip in **06** (★★★★). Irresistible winter warmer with enticing brandy-spirit & dried stonefruit intro, deliciously followed by honeyed raisins & firm, reviving acidity. Intriguing ginger nuance has one reaching for another glass. — Panel

Nwanedi Estate

Location: Paarl ▪ Map: Paarl & Wellington ▪ Est 1997 ▪ 1stB 2005 ▪ Tasting & sales Mon-Sat 10-4.30 Sun by appt & for events ▪ Closed Easter Fri & Sun, Dec 25/26, Jan 1 ▪ Fee R15 ▪ Cellar & vineyard tours by appt ▪ 12-suite Nwanedi Country Hotel ▪ Conference/wedding/function venue ▪ Restaurant ▪ Owner(s) Gavin & Jean Stork ▪ Cellarmaster(s) Gavin Stork (Apr 2004) ▪ Winemaker(s)/viticulturist(s) Nico Vermeulen (2010) ▪ 17ha (cab, mourv, shiraz, viog) ▪ 188t/2,500cs own label 100% red ▪ PO Box 955 Wellington 7654 ▪ info@nwanedi.com ▪ www.nwanedi.com ▪ S 33° 40'46.3" E 018° 58'8.1" ▪ **T** +27 (0)21-872-8723 / +27 (0)73-967-3790 / +27 **(0)83-407-4246** ▪ F +27 (0)86-618-5251 / +27 (0)86-618-5275

Veteran winemaker Nico Vermeulen not only makes Nwanedi's wine, he's occupied their cellar space as his base of operations too. So Gavin Stork's workshop and wood store has been evicted - not that he has too much time for his hobby since he and wife Jean have become hands-on hoteliers running their 4-star country hotel.

First Dawn range
Classic Shiraz (Reserved Private Bin) ★★★★ Pvsly tasted, **07** full of cinnamon, clove & choc raisins;velvety texture, firm grip ex 65% Fr oak. **Shiraz** ★★★ **08**'s choc & liquorice fruit balanced by dry roasted nuts, tannin from 18 mths Fr oak (85% new). These & those below not reassessed.

Interlude range
Chenin Blanc 🍽 Await next.

Meditation range
Cabernet Sauvignon ★★★ Pvsly tasted **08** had ample hedgerow fruit, juicy caramel spice from 18 mths Fr oak (85% new); 2007 (★★★) red fruit, leather & nice grip. — FM

▪ **Oak Lane** see Beau Joubert Vineyards & Winery
▪ **Oak Ridge** see Shoprite Checkers

Oak Valley Wines

Location/WO: Elgin ▪ Map: Elgin, Walker Bay & Bot River ▪ Est 1898 ▪ 1stB 2003 ▪ Tasting & sales Mon-Fri 9-5 Sat 10-2 (or by arrangement); Sun by appt ▪ Closed Easter Fri-Mon, Dec 25/26 & Jan 1 ▪ Walks/hikes ▪ Mountain biking trail ▪ Conservation area ▪ Self-catering cottage ▪ Owner(s) AG Rawbone-Viljoen Trust ▪ Winemaker(s) Pieter

Visser (Jun 2002) ▪ Viticulturist(s) Pieter Visser (Jun 2003), assisted by Kevin Watt (consultant) ▪ 1,786ha/48ha (cabs s/f, merlot, p verdot, pinot, shiraz, chard, sauv, sem) ▪ ±200–250t/±10,000cs own label 50% red 45% white 5% rosé ▪ Envirowines, WIETA ▪ PO Box 30 Elgin 7180 ▪ wines@oak-valley.co.za ▪ www.oakvalley.co.za ▪ S 34° 9' 24.4" E 019° 2' 55.5" ▪ T +27 (0)21-859-4110 ▪ F +27 (0)21-859-3405

This mountainside farm covers nearly 1,800 hectares, allowing room for experiments with different vineyard sites. The latest involves high density rather than altitude: a block of pinot noir planted at 10,000 vines per hectare produced its first crop in 2011. Anthony Rawbone-Viljoen reports that grape quality matched that from more conventional plantings, despite higher yields; the wine, kept separate, will be evaluated. 'An expensive experiment, the narrow rows decreeing hand labour only,' he says, 'but hopefully worthwhile.' Meanwhile, Pieter Visser's pinot is already impressive. Flowers, cattle, pigs, fynbos and mountain bike trails are other undertakings on this large-scale family farm. Son Christopher R-V, recently graduated from Adelaide University in Wine Business, is drawing up a business plan focusing on wine tourism and the possibilities for this on Oak Valley.

Oak Valley Wines range

★★★★☆ **Pinot Noir** 09 (★★★★★) echoes pinot purity of 08; great freshness & hedonistic silky undertones focus concentrated, black fruits, mushroom persistence. Oak (French, 35% new) a subtle enrichment. Delicious in youth, but no hurry to open.

★★★★ **The Oak Valley Blend** Ripe, sweet merlot spiced with cab & cab franc & whiff of French oak combine in polished 07. Firm but not harsh or inaccessible so enjoy over next 4-6 yrs.

★★★★☆ **Chardonnay** 🎖 Consistently recognisable citrus, oatmeal tones particularly expressive, persistent on 10. Edgy freshness should benefit from a year or two.

★★★★☆ **Sauvignon Blanc** 🍴 🎖 10 (★★★★) turns up the grassy dial, the greenness matched by quite feisty acid. Lees contact, 2% semillon & a tiny oaked portion may help enrich, but not in same league as 09.

★★★★☆ **The OV** 🍴 09 bounds back into form after lesser 08 (★★★★). Persuasive orange citrus, honey-rich complexity focused by precise, mineral lines. Distinctive 81/19% sauvignon/semillon partnership, compatibly oaked, balanced 13.5% alc. Lovely prospects.

Rawbones range NEW

Butchers Block 😊 🍴 ★★★ 08 merlot-cab blend with ripe fruity succulence. A modest tannic grip & a hint of oak (20% new) add form, for greater satisfaction.

Rawbones Medium-Rare ★★★ Previewed 11 from shiraz offers plentiful fresh red berries, juicily dry finish. Moderate 12.5% alcohol enhances quaffability. **Wishbone** 🍴 🎖 ★★☆ 10 sauvignon juicily fresh, its grassiness tempered by a little sweetness. — AL

Obikwa

Distell export brand, named for the indigenous Obikwa people, the front label featuring a stylised ostrich. Widely sourced, and styled for current enjoyment.

Chenin Blanc 😊 🍴 ★★★ Perky apricot & melon freshness, 11 crisp, light & fruity.

Cabernet Sauvignon 🍴 ★★★ 10 a notch up on previous. Tobacco leaf & black cherry with balance & harmony. Cocoa depth. Light, easy red for beginners. **Merlot** 🍴 ★★★ Light choc-raisin on previewed 11, soft & easy-drinking. **Pinotage** 🍴 ★★★ Light fruity raspberry on improved 10. Spicy vanilla edge & light grip from 3 months American oak. **Shiraz** ✓ 🍴 ★★★★ Ripe plum & chocolate after smoky entry, 11 good spine, spice from restrained oak (3 months). Sweetish, like most Obikwas. **Cabernet Sauvignon-Pinotage** 🍴 Not tasted. **Pinotage Rosé** 🍴 ★★★ Just 'Rosé' last time. Pinotage lends dry cranberry tang to light, fruity 11. Refreshing. **Chardonnay** 🍴 ★★★ Light citrus & honeyed blossom, 10 oak restraint creates medium body & rich, creamy mouthfeel to long conclusion. **Pinot Gris** 🍴 ★★★ Litchi & granadilla crispness, 11 preview fresh & summery. **Sauvignon Blanc** 🍴 ★★★ 11 lively lime zest & fig. Toned acidity & length. **Classic Dry White** 🍴 ★★ Tangy fig & melon, zesty acid on 11 chenin-sauvignon blend. **Moscato** NEW 🍴 ★★★ Low-alc sweet white, 11 perfumed pineapple & mango, fresh acid tang. **Cuvée Brut** 🍴 ★★ 11 crisp & cheerful light tropical chenin sparkler. Fun fizz. **Natural Sweet Red** ★★ Light sweet/sour berries on 11 low-alc 3-way blend. **Natural Sweet White** 🍴 ★★★ Light floral/grapey 11, nice acid lift to low-alc chenin, colombard, muscat mix. — Panel

■ **Oddbins** *see* Shoprite Checkers

Oewerzicht Private Cellar

Location: Greyton • Map: Southern Cape • WO: Overberg • Est/1stB 2002 • Tasting & sales Mon-Fri 8–5 Sat/Sun by appt • Guest cottages & tents • Wedding, conference & function facilities • Mountain biking/hiking trails • Owner(s)/winemaker(s)/viticulturist(s) Kootjie Viljoen • 0.5ha (cab) • 1,000cs own label 100% red • PO Box 18 Greyton 7233 • oewerzicht@telkomsa.net • S 34° 6' 14.6" E 019° 40' 7.9" • **T +27 (0)28-254-9831** • F +27 (0)28-254-9968

Making wine remains a hobby for apple and pear farmer Kootjie Viljoen. While very little remained of the small quantity of cab made in 2009, there was still some of the 2006 vintage left (available at this Greyton farm and eateries in the village); and, he says, 'I hope to make wine again this year!'

Cabernet Sauvignon ★★★ Exotically spiced & juicy 06, diamond-in-the-rough from tiny Greyton vineyard, not revisited this edition. — Panel

■ **Oggendau** *see* Eerste Hoop Wine Cellar

Old Bridge Wines

Closed to public • Owner(s) Paulinas Dal Mountain Vineyards (Pty) Ltd • 20,000cs 60% red 40% white • PO Box 557 St Francis Bay 6312 • rickety@iafrica.com • **T +27 (0)82-777-1519**

Export-focused producer and negociant sourcing wines for various brands, including private labels for specialised corporate clients. The wines include limited-edition African Gold Collection: Cabernet-Merlot, Merlot and Shiraz mainly for US, Europe and the Far East; Big Six Collection: boxed sets of Cabernet, Merlot, Pinotage, Shiraz, Chenin and Sauvignon for local game lodges/retreats and for export; and Old Bridge: Cabernet, Merlot, Pinotage, Shiraz, Chenin and Sauvignon.

■ **Old Brown** *see* Sedgwick's Old Brown Sherry

Oldenburg Vineyards

Location/map/WO: Stellenbosch • Est 1960s • 1stB 2007 • Tasting & sales Mon-Fri 10–4.30 Sat & pub hols by appt only • Fee R25 • Closed Good Fri, Dec 25/26 & Jan 1 • Refreshments for sale (cheese platters, biltong, etc.) • Owner(s) Adrian Vanderspuy • Winemaker(s) Simon Thompson (May 2004), with Philip Costandius (consultant) • Viticulturist(s) Simon Thompson (May 2004), with Paul Wallace (consultant) • 50ha/30ha (cabs s/f, merlot, syrah, chard, chenin) • 189t/2,221cs own label 66% red 34% white • PO Box 2246 Dennesig 7601 • admin@ oldenburgvineyards.com • www.oldenburgvineyards.com • S 33° 55'7.61" E 018° 56'8.75" • **T +27 (0)21-885-1618** • F +27 (0)21-885-2665

Vineyards were first planted at this magnificently sited Banghoek Valley property in the 1960s – but were sadly neglected when Adrian Vanderspuy (born on an adjacent farm, but by then living abroad) resolved 'to bring the Oldenburg vineyards back to life'. The replanted vines are managed with a combination of organic, biodynamic and 'pragmatic' means. The first releases did gratifyingly well in international and local competitions – and a new tasting room now makes the wines easier to sample and the views easier to contemplate.

★★★★ **Cabernet Sauvignon** Restrained, detailed 09 offers black fruit, almond & lead pencil aromas. With savoury fine tannins, the wine is elegant & spare, despite ripeness & the big 14.5% alcohol.

★★★★ **Chenin Blanc** NEW ▤ Medal-winning 10 takes in some chardonnay. Delicate peardrop fragrance. Thoughtful oaking (7 months, half new) gives breadth to the full palate.

Cabernet Franc ★★★★ 09 more about fine texture than taste; the fruit is faintly green-edged, with spice & oak harmoniously interwoven. **Syrah** ★★★ Raspberry & allspice notes on 09, with opulent tannins, dollops of sweet fruit; slightly hot finish though 14.5% alc down on 08's. **Chardonnay** NEW ▤ ★★★★ Beautifully polished 10. Spanspek, grapefruit aromas, creamy vanilla notes from generous French oaking (50% new) & a fresh lime finish. — MF

Old Vines Cellars

Location: Cape Town • WO: Stellenbosch/Coastal • Est/1stB 1995 • Closed to public • Owner(s) Irina von Holdt & Françoise Botha • Winemaker(s) Irina von Holdt • 15,000cs own label 40% red 60% white + 4,000cs for pvt clients ▪ 50 Liesbeek Rd Rosebank 7700 ▪ info@oldvines.co.za ▪ www.oldvines.co.za ▪ **T +27 (0)21-685-6428** ▪ F +27 (0)21-685-6446

'We are back on track and strong,' declares boutique vintner and matriarch Irina von Holdt, firmly at the helm after recently navigating some stormy (family) waters. She remains deeply passionate about wine, with the chenin flag flying top mast. Irina was the far-sighted winemaker who first championed the cause of old chenin vines, a movement now re-energised by the industry's younger guard.

Old Vines range

★★★★ **Chenin Blanc** ✓ 🗯 **10** tank sample shows lovely depth of quince & almond fruit, polished texture & balanced, pervasive acidity.

★★★★ **Vintage Brut** Unusual variety for méthode cap classique sparkling, but natural choice for arch chenin fan. **04** from bushvines, still selling. Creamy, with mineral finish when last tasted.

Baron von Holdt Latest **09** not ready. **Barrel Reserve Chenin Blanc** 🗯 **10** barrel sample too unfinished to rate. Good core of baked fruit & honey flavours that augur well for finished product. **Blue White** In abeyance.

Spring Valley range

Chenin Blanc-Sauvignon Blanc 😊 🗒 🗯 ★★★ Riper **11** preview has plump, tangy peach & glacé pineapple flavours. Appealing pocket- & palate-friendly, quaffer. All Springvalley wines WO Coastal.

Merlot NEW 🗒 ★★★ Warm-hearted **08** merlot exudes ripe & rich black cherry & marzipan. Bold & mouthfilling, for food & fireside. **Shiraz-Merlot** 🗒 🗯 Bright & piquantly juicy **11** preview is a promising Italian food partner, but still bit too youthful to rate. — MW

◼ **Old Well House** see Thorntree Wines

Olifantsberg Family Vineyards

Location: Worcester ▪ Map/WO: Breedekloof ▪ Est 2003 ▪ 1stB 2005 ▪ Tasting & sales Mon-Fri by appt ▪ Owner(s) Paul J Leeuwerik ▪ Cellarmaster(s)/winemaker/viticulturist(s) Jacques du Plessis (Nov 2009) ▪ 95ha/7ha (shiraz) ▪ 25t/700cs own label 80% red 20% white ▪ PO Box 942 Worcester 6849 ▪ duplessis.je@gmail.com ▪ www.olifantsberg.com ▪ S 33° 35' 42.76" E 019° 21' 42.39" ▪ **T +27 (0)23-342-0401** ▪ F +27 (0)23-342-8734

Aiming to grow wines that reflect not only the soils, sunshine and elevation but also the effort that's put into the vineyards, viticulturist/winemaker Jacques du Plessis keeps it simple in the cellar 'with a few experiments here and there to get good complexity'. Farming increasingly sustainably, owners Corine and Paul Leeuwerik have also identified a 70ha area for conservation.

Cabernet Sauvignon ★★★ Last year, **09** was shy & herbaceous, its subtle blackcurrant fruit hidden by taut oak tannins which may since have softened. **Shiraz** ★★★ Hot vintage **10** more robust, with Rhône-like pepperiness. **Chardonnay** NEW ★★★ **10** ripe & rich, mouthfilling food style with pithy marzipan aftertaste. — MW

Olsen Wines

Location: Paarl ▪ Map: Paarl & Wellington ▪ Est/1stB 2002 ▪ Tasting by appt only ▪ Fee R10 pp ▪ Light meals for groups of ±10 by appt only ▪ Farm-style jams ▪ Owner(s) Greg Olsen ▪ Cellarmaster(s)/viticulturist(s) Armand Botha (2000) ▪ Winemaker(s) Armand Botha (2007) ▪ 30ha ▪ 500cs 90% red 10% white ▪ Europgap registered ▪ PO Box 9052 Huguenot 7645 ▪ olsenwines@mweb.co.za ▪ S 33° 44' 4.7" E 019° 3' 5.0" ▪ **T +27 (0)21-862-3653** ▪ F +27 (0)21-862-2589

Scientist-entrepreneur Greg Olsen has orbited the earth more than 150 times and pioneered viticulture in Montana. He's also the only South African manufacturer of the inverters used to back up solar energy systems in many establishments, wineries included – the largest of which has become a tourist attraction in its own right.

Pinotage ★★★ Overtly oaky **07** showed red fruit & stern finish from all new oak when tasted previously. **Chardonnay** Await next. **Chenin Blanc** ★★★ Assertive green apple, bone-dry **08** tasted mid-09. — IM

◼ **Omalanga** see Groupe LFE South Africa

Onderkloof Vines & Wines

Location: Somerset West ▪ Map: Helderberg ▪ Est 1998 ▪ 1stB 1999 ▪ Tasting, sales & cellar tours Mon-Fri 9-5 Sat by appt ▪ Fee R20pp, waived on wine purchase of R200/more ▪ Closed all pub hols ▪ Meals/refreshments by arrangement ▪ Walks ▪ Mountain biking trail ▪ Conservation area ▪ Self-catering Cottages ▪ Owner(s) Daniël Truter & Beat Musfeld ▪ Cellarmaster(s)/winemaker(s)/viticulturist(s) Daniël Truter (Mar 1998) ▪ 64ha/15ha (cab, ptage, shiraz, chenin, chard, Muscat d'A, sauv) ▪ 60t/3,000cs own label 60% red 40% white ▪ PO Box 90 Sir Lowry's Pass 7133 ▪ wine@onderkloofwines.co.za ▪ www.onderkloofwines.co.za ▪ S 34° 6' 37.9" E 018° 53' 49.2" ▪ **T +27 (0)21-858-1538** ▪ F +27 (0)21-858-1536

Danie Truter, always positive about the SA wine industry, notes that sustainable top quality is the way forward in the wine business. To this end they have broadened their tourist appeal with the launch of three self-catering cottages, some close to nature wine walks and adrenalin boosting mountain bike trail.

Schapenberg Single Vineyard range
Cabernet Sauvignon ★★★☆ Violet-toned **06** had wild berry fruit, unkit tannins previously. Like Pinotage, Sauvignon, still selling. **Pinotage** ★★★☆ Ex low-cropped bushvines. **07** had black plum & cherry flavours. **Chardonnay** Await next, as for **Chenin Blanc**. **Sauvignon Blanc** ★★ Full-ripe **09** had melon & preserved lime, sip sitting (15% alc)!

Onderkloof range
Shiraz Await next, as for **Caernetb-Shiraz**, **Rosé** & **Floreal Blanc de Blanc**. — JP

▪ **Ondine** see Ormonde Private Cellar
▪ **One World** see Koopmanskloof Wingerde
▪ **Onyx** see Darling Cellars

Oom Tas

Distell big-volume brand depicts winefarmer 'Uncle Tas' beaming from retro label.
Oom Tas ▤ ★ Golden **NV** looks sweet but is bone-dry. Fruity chenin, cbard, hanepoot. 1,2 & 5L bottles. — Panel

▪ **Opener's** see Waterstone Wines

Opstal Estate

Location: Rawsonville ▪ Map: Breedekloof ▪ WO: Breedekloof/Slanghoek ▪ Est 1847 ▪ 1stB 1978 ▪ Tasting, sales & cellar tours Mon-Fri 9-5 Sat 10-2 Sun by appt ▪ Closed Easter Fri-Mon, Dec 25/26 & Jan 1 ▪ Restaurant Wed-Sun 9-5 ▪ Facilities for children ▪ Tour groups ▪ Gift shop ▪ Farm produce ▪ Conference facilities ▪ Conservation area ▪ Mountain biking trail ▪ Monthly music/theatre shows with dinner (Jul-Nov) ▪ Bimonthly farmers market ▪ Owner(s) Stanley Louw ▪ Cellarmaster(s) Stanley Louw (1980) ▪ Winemaker(s) Attie Louw (Sep 2010), with Jos van Wyk (Jan 2011) ▪ Viticulturist(s) Gerhard Theron (Jan 2002) ▪ 419ha/101ha (cab, ptage, shiraz, chard, chenin, Muscat d'A, sauv, sem, viog) ▪ 1,440t/6,000cs own label 20% red 65% white 10% rosé 5% desert + 25,000L bulk ▪ Other export brand: Attie's Long Shadow ▪ BWI, IPW ▪ PO Box 27 Rawsonville 6845 ▪ wine@opstal.co.za ▪ www.opstal.co.za ▪ S 33° 38' 19.8" E 019° 13' 40.8" ▪ **T +27 (0)23-344-3001** ▪ F +27 (0)23-344-3002

Joining vibrant monthly Opstal Live music weekends at the Louw family's Breedekloof estate is bimonthly Opstal Vars farmers' market, 'where fresh produce, fresh ideas and fresh people meet'. Having added 'winemaker' to his resumé, marketing-savvy young Attie Louw aims to double sales of Sixpence, its updated label 'better telling one of those stories behind a place and its people that make wine a special product'; and to 'make Opstal *the* destination in the Breedekloof'.

Opstal Estate range
Cabernet Sauvignon ★★★☆ Black-cherry-toned **06** flirted with over-ripeness when tasted, but good oaking provided structure. **Syrah-Viognier Blush** ✓ ▤ ★★★★ Previewed **11** a copper-coloured charmer, with spice, herbs & hint of apricot. 'Perfect food wine' say winemakers. **Chenin Blanc** ▤ ★★★ From two 20+ year old blocks. Last time, **09** preview burst with fresh grass & ripe green apple. **Sauvignon Blanc** ▤ ◙ ★★★ Previewed from tank, **11** fresh & zesty, lemon & lime scented. **Sauvignon Blanc Sparkling Sec** ★★★ Enjoy happy celebrations with fresh yeasty tones of carbonated **NV**. **Hanepoot** ◙ ★★★★ Big step up from last-tasted **08** (★★★), **10** shows old-vine concentration; delicious & impressive mouthful of honey, Karoo herb & dried

apricot. **Chardonnay Barrel Dessert ★★★★** Delicious & interesting **08**, revisited last year as finished wine, concentrated bright peach fruit, ends with fynbos flourish. Discontinued: **Cabernet Sauvignon-Shiraz**.

Sixpence range

Cabernet Sauvignon-Merlot NEW ▤ ▨ **★★★** Savoury spices, dark cherry notes, nice dry conclusion make **10** a great pasta partner. **Sauvignon Blanc-Semillon** NEW ▤ ▨ **★★★ 11** ideal summer lunchtime sipper, combo riper tropical fruit & shy herbal aromas. Discontinued: **Cabernet Sauvignon-Shiraz**, **Chenin Blanc-Semillon**. — DB

■ **Oracle** see Distell

Orangerie Wines

Map/WO: Swartland ▪ Est 1707 ▪ 1stB 2009 ▪ Tasting, sales & cellar tours by appt only ▪ Paardeberg Conservation Area ▪ Owner(s)/viticulturist(s) Loffie & Pieter Euvrard ▪ Winemaker(s) Pieter Euvrard (2009) ▪ 200ha/70ha (cab, malbec, merlot, ptage, shiraz, chard, chenin, sauv, viog) ▪ 15t/300cs own label 60% red 40% white ▪ PO Box 92 Malmesbury 7299 ▪ orangeriewines@yahoo.com ▪ www.orangeriewines.co.za ▪ S 33° 32′ 20.8″ E 018° 49′ 55.6″ ▪ **T +27 (0)22-482-2169** ▪ F +27 (0)22-487-3046

On one of the oldest farms on the Perdeberg slopes, Pieter Euvrard in his tiny cellar is a keen participant in the Swartland wine revolution - though most of the farm's grapes go elsewhere. Keeping intervention minimal in vineyard and cellar (natural ferment, only old oak maturation, for example) helps form the quality and great charm of his wines. Another label is promised for 2011 and, with some unusual varieties being planted, more will surely follow.

Orangerie Wines range

★★★★ White 10 chenin-led, with dabs semillon, viognier, chardonnay. In fairly oxidative, un-fruity but flavourful style popular in the area. Rich & satiny, serenely balanced. Will improve a good few years.

Red ★★★★ Sample **10** typical of new-wave Swartland reds in blend (shiraz + 17% mourvèdre) & delicious, not obviously fruity flavours; firm & fresh. **09** (★★★★) included grenache. — TJ

Orange River Wine Cellars

Location: Upington ▪ Map: Northern Cape, Free State & North West ▪ WO: Central Orange River ▪ Est 1965 ▪ 1stB 1968 ▪ Tasting & sales Mon–Fri 8–4.30 Sat 8.30–12 ▪ Fee R10/5 wines ▪ Closed all pub hols ▪ Cellar tours Mon–Fri 9, 11 & 3 (Jan–Mar) ▪ Owner(s) ±890 shareholders ▪ Cellarmaster(s) Gert Visser ▪ Cellar managers Bolla Louw (Kakamas), Chris Venter (Keimoes), Johan Esterhuizen (Upington), Johan Dippenaar (Grootdrink), Riaan Liebenberg (Groblershoop), with winemakers (in same cellar order) George Kruger/Heinrich Coetzee/Andre Smit; Rianco van Rooyen/Cobus Viviers/Mariken Jordaan; Jopie Faul/Ferdinand Laubscher/Philane Gumede; Jim de Kock/Tinus Kotze; Marco Pentz ▪ Viticulturist(s) Henning Burger (Viticultural Services Manager), with (in same cellar order) Stoney Steenkamp, Stefan Jordaan, Louwna Viviers, Stefan Louwrens, Tharien Hansen ▪ 4,200ha (ptage, ruby cab, shiraz, chard, chenin, cbard, Muscat varieties) ▪ 122,000t/20 million litres own label 20% red 40% white 20% rosé 20% ohter + 30 million litres for clients/bulk ▪ Other export labels: Island View, Gilysipao, Star Tree ▪ Ranges for customers: Country Cellars & Carnival (Spar); Seasons Collection (Liquor City) ▪ ISO 9001:2008 & 2011, WIETA, HACCP, BRC, IPW ▪ PO Box 544 Upington 8800 ▪ marketing@owk.co.za ▪ www.orangeriverwines.com ▪ S 28° 26′ 33.0″ E 021° 12′ 30.6″ ▪ **T +27 (0)54-337-8800** ▪ F +27 (0)54-332-4408

Producing an average 50 million litres of wine for its own brands and third-party clients annually, Orange River Wine Cellars (the new official name) is South Africa's largest wine producer and was able to take 2011 flood damage to the tune of 35,000 tonnes of fruit in its stride. A major feather in the cellar's cap was receiving South African Wine magazine's 2011 Best Value Cellar accolade. This, says the cellar's Rianco van Rooyen, is a result of constant investment in technology and knowledge in both cellar and vineyard, and 'proves that bigger can be better'. The drive towards quality is also evident in the flagship Reserve range - all limited-release single-vineyard wines.

Reserve range NEW

★★★★ Straw Wine √ ▨ Delicious debut! From air-dried & barrel-fermented colombard, **10** is complex, with sweet-sour twist, seductive raisiny sweetness. Excitingly different.

Merlot-Petit Verdot ★★ Near-equal blend plus splash cab, **08** is easy, appealing, with black cherry fruit. **Chenin Blanc de Barrique** ✓ 🅰 ★★★ Serious oaking (75% new wood) for **10** shows in vanilla perfume; ripe fig flavour gets limy twist from tiny portion unoaked chardonnay.

Orange River Wine Cellars range

★★★★ **White Muscadel** ✓ 🅰 Well-crafted fortified **10** is back on track after slight dip in **09** (★★★): big, ripe flavours of honey, muscat & litchi, lingering & rich.

Sparkling Brut ☺ 🅰 ★★★ **11** from chenin, exuberant peachy bubbles, attractively crisp & fresh.

Cabernet Sauvignon 🅰 ★★★ Perfect braai partner, **10** cedar & ripe mulberry fruit. **Ruby Cabernet** 🅰 ★★★ Another step up, **10** easy-drinking, with fresh cranberry flavour. **Shiraz** 🅰 ★★★ Improved **10** generous & fresh, red-berry tones, splash petit verdot adds interest. **Dry Red** NEW 🅰 ★★★ Well-made **10**, mix of 6 varieties, tastes like coffee & fresh berries. **Shiraz-Cabernet Sauvignon** 🍷 ★★ Savoury & spicy 50/50 combo, still-selling **09** unpretentious everyday quaffer. **Rosé** 🅰 ★★ Light-textured **11**, sweet raspberry toned party pleaser. **Chardonnay** 🅰 ★★★ Lightly oaked **10** pleasing lunchtime drink, with mix vanilla, lemon & lime. **Chenin Blanc** 🍷 🅰 ★★ Crisp green apples on early picked **11**. **Colombar** 🍷 🅰 ★★ Light-bodied **11**, shy guava & litchi picnic partner. **Dry White** NEW 🅰 ★★ **11** light, undemanding, with crisp citrus tail. **Sparkling Doux** 🅰 ★★ **11** cheerful & sweet bubbly for party fun. **Rosé Sparkling Wine** ★★ Refreshing sweet bubbly from chenin & pinotage, **10** is still available. **Late Harvest** 🍷 ★ Undemanding **10** from colombard, low alc, subtle sweet tropical fruit. **Nouveau Blanc Natural Sweet** 🍷 🅰 ★ From chenin, **11** preview too young to rate. **Sweet Hanepoot** 🅰 ★★★ **10** fortified dessert charms with rich raisin & honey flavours, & unusual hint of nutmeg. **Red Muscadel** 🅰 ★★★ Lovely amber-hued fortified fireside warmer, **10** all honey & raisins yet nice crisp aftertaste. **Red Jerepigo** 🅰 ★★★ Fortified dessert from ruby cab, **10** trademark raisiny taste & hints of tropical fruit. **White Jerepiko** 🅰 ★★★ Comforting full-sweet glass of fortified chenin, **10** honeyed & nutmeg dusted. **Red Port** 🅰 ★ Sweet & amenable **10** for warding off winter chills. Discontinued: **Cabernet Sauvignon-Merlot-Reserve**. —DB

■ **Oranjeland** *see* Zidela Wines
■ **Oranjerivier Wynkelders** *see* Orange River Wine Cellars

Org de Rac

Location: Piketberg ▪ Map/WO: Swartland ▪ Est 2001 ▪ 1stB 2005 ▪ Tasting, sales & tours Mon-Fri 9-5 Sat 9-1 ▪ Closed Easter Fri, Dec 25 & Jan 1 ▪ Meals/refreshments by prior arrangement; or BYO picnic ▪ Tour groups ▪ Conferences ▪ Walks/hikes ▪ Mountain biking ▪ Conservation area ▪ Game viewing ▪ Owner(s) Nico Bacon ▪ Winemaker(s) Gilmar Boshoff (Jan 2011) ▪ Viticulturist(s) Wesley du Plessis (Jun 2010) ▪ 47ha (cab, merlot, shiraz, chard) ▪ 260t/20,000cs own label 87% red 8% white 5% rosé + 8,500cs for clients ▪ Other export brand: Abbotsville ▪ Brands for clients: Imbuko Wines ▪ SGS (Organic) ▪ PO Box 268 Piketberg 7320 ▪ cellar@orgderac.co.za ▪ www.orgderac.com ▪ S 32° 57′ 44.3″ E 018° 44′ 57.4″ ▪ **T +27 (0)22-913-2397/3924** ▪ F +27 (0)22-913-3923

A diverse and fascinating farm near Piketberg where the first white wine, a chardonnay, has been made and a portion early harvested with an eye on a future MCC sparkling. This is the 'green heartbeat of the Swartland' where pips and skins are composted to be worked into the soil, wine production is entirely organic, non-organic items such as cartons, glass and plastic are recycled, and everything is focused on 'creating wines that celebrate the Swartland terroir'.

Family Reserve range

Cabernet Sauvignon 🌿 In abeyance, like **Merlot** & **Shiraz**.

Org de Rac range

★★★★ **Merlot** 🌿 Attractive **10** a big step-up & in league of **05**, succulent, layered rich dark chocolate, mulberry & cranberry. **09** also tasty if touch more herbal & savoury, dry twist in tail.

Cabernet Sauvignon 🌿 ★★★ **10** with juicy dark fruit & blackberries more appealing than somewhat austere & savoury **09** (★★). Two releases tasted, as for Merlot, Shiraz & Rosé. **Shiraz** 🌿 ★★★ **10** spicy & earthy tones, richer & more easy appeal than savoury/smoky **09** (★★★). **Rosé** 🌿 ★★★ Softly dry **10** hint mocha & ripe plum pudding; preview **11** fragrant mulberry, lively dry finish. **Chardonnay** NEW 🌿 ★★★ Fresh, scented **11**, preview shows lemon & herbal hint in friendly, lightly wooded summer quaffer. —DB

Origin Wine

Location/map: Stellenbosch ▪ WO: Western Cape/Stellenbosch ▪ Est/1stB 2002 ▪ Tasting strictly by appt ▪ Owner(s) Bernard Fontannaz ▪ MD Neville Carew ▪ Cellarmaster(s) Alain Cajeux ▪ Winemaker(s) Quintin van der Westhuizen, Seugnét Rossouw & Elisma Conradie (Sep 2010), with Ernst van Rensburg (Oct 2010) ▪ 3.5 million cs ▪ 50% red 40% white 10% rosé ▪ WIETA, Fairtrade, DLG ▪ PO Box 7177 Stellenbosch 7599 ▪ info@originwine.co. za ▪ www.originwine.co.za, www.fairhills.co.za, www.stormhoek.com, www.stormhoek.co.za ▪ S 33° 52' 39. 07" E 018° 48' 35.50" ▪ **T +27 (0)861-ORIGIN/+27 (0)21-865-8100** ▪ F +27 (0)21-865-2348

This mainly export-orientated winery's CEO, Bernard Fontannaz's energy, enthusiasm and excitement is so contagious we can't wait to taste wines from his 2012 harvest. The reason? In his quest to create a 'cherry for the top of his cake', he ended up 'baking a new cake'. Similes aside, Bordeaux legend Jacques Lurton's advice for producing a bona fide upmarket wine (see Unsung Hero below) was so practical, it made sense to apply it to the entire range. The impact on quality across the board, Fontannaz promises, will be palpable, and will go a long way towards ensuring the long-term sustainability of the brands. 'Volume matters, but I'd be kidding myself if I thought Origin could continue along that path indefinitely. No, to be sustainable, wine brands must convince consumers to pay more, to trade up. And that can only be achieved by offering more.'

Unsung Hero range NEW

Premium Red Blend ★★★★ Pricier, provisionally rated **10** preview promising mix shiraz & cab; savoury bouquet, compact cranberry centre, vanilla-sweet oak finish. Could score higher once bottled. WO Stellenbosch.

Cape Original Organic range

Shiraz-Cabernet Sauvignon ✿ ★★★ Last edition 60/40 combo **10** took step up; balanced & savoury, with faint berry fruit, vanilla overlay. 3L box.

Fairhills range

> **1962 Vineyards Selection Shiraz** NEW ☺ ★★★ **10**'s liquoricce & lilies dusted with vanilla, has poise & persistence. **Rosé** ☺ ★★★ **11** preview from merlot; appealing sunset hue, light, zesty dry berried enjoyment.

Cabernet Sauvignon-Petit Verdot ▤ ▨ ★★★ Leafy notes, liquorice & plum on medium-bodied **10**, touch less impressive than previous. **Shiraz-Merlot** ▤ ★★ Quick-quaff **11** has mulberry flavours, stalky mouthfeel. **Rosé Moscato** NEW ★★ This, Moscato, sampled from tank. Light, semi-sweet **11** mainly muscat d'Alexandrie with dash pinotage, which gives a leafy note. **1962 Vineyards Selection Chenin Blanc** NEW ▤ ▨ ★★★ **10** mid-2011 quite oaky & sweet but has nice oatmeal nuance & enlivening acidity. **Moscato** NEW ★★ Turkish Delight & ginger notes on light **11** sweet sipper. **Sauvignon Blanc** ▤ ★★★ Grass & thatch-toned **11** has same pleasant pithy texture as previous. **Semillon-Sauvignon Blanc** ▤ ★★★ Tropical **11** fresh, persistent, for early enjoyment. **Sparkling Chardonnay Brut** ▨ ★★ Charmat-method bubbly, as is next. **10** vanilla & toast flavours (from oaking of base wine), quick finish. **Sparkling Rosé Brut** ▨ ★★ Name change from 'Rosé Sparkling Wine'. **10** pretty pink colour but muted flavour, lemon/berry aftertaste.

Greenfield Organic range NEW

> **Chardonnay-Viognier** ☺ ▤ ✿ ▨ ★★★ Fruitful 80/20 combo in **10**: chardonnay's citrus character well paired with viognier's apricot, oak's vanilla.

Pinotage-Merlot ▤ ✿ ▨ ★★★ **10** intense berry melange, hint of spice on plush 60/40 mix. **Shiraz-Cabernet Sauvignon** ▤ ✿ ▨ ★★★ Uncomplicated **10**, cheery red/black fruit, tad bitter tannins. Clean but bold lines, minimalist approach deliver eye-catching labels for the new well-priced range.

Honeypot NEW

Moscato ★★ Wet earth, ripe sultana & ginger notes on unlingering **11**. **Sweet Shiraz** ★★ New bargain-priced offerings for those with a sweet tooth. **11** has pleasing tannic edge to succulent fruit. Sampled pre-bottling, like next.

Stellenbosch Drive range

Merlot-Cabernet Sauvignon ▤ ▨ ★★ **10** sweet-ripe berry fruit & strong tannins, needing time to settle. **Chardonnay** ★★★ **11** restrained, with a hint of dusty oak, shows lovely vinosity. Pre-bottling sample tasted, as for next next two. **Oaked Chenin Blanc ★★** Partly barrel-fermented **11** shows deft oaking, lots of freshness, slightly confected aroma. WO Western Cape, rest of range Stellenbosch. **Sauvignon Blanc ★★★★ 11** big step up on reticent **10 (★★)**. Forthcoming yet elegant grass, nettle, greengage notes; gravelly texture, crisp acidity & poised, dry finish.

Stormhoek range

Pinot Grigio ☺ 🍴 🔖 **★★★ 11** much improved: nuts, geranium & pear whiffs, bright acidity for summer al fresco sipping.

Cabernet Sauvignon 🔖 **★★ 10** juicy glugger with no distinguishing cab character. **Organic Merlot** NEW 🌿 **★★** Quirky curryleaf & prune nose, **11** taut tannic finish. **Pinotage** 🔖 **★★★ 10** quintessential strawberry aromas/flavours, firm tannins, slight sweetness heightens   mass appeal. **Cap'occino Coffee Pinotage** NEW **★★★ 11** appetising aromas of coffee & dark cherry, sweetness tempered by fair tannic grip, feisty acidity. Tasted pre-bottling, rating provisional, as for Merlot, Rosé, Chardonnay Pinot Grigio & Sparkling. **Rosé ★★ 11** off-dry & light, with sweet-sour flavours. **Organic Chardonnay** NEW 🌿 **★★★** Reticent **11** not as generously fruited as others in this well-priced line-up; steely acidity, light vanilla tinge. **Sauvignon Blanc** 🔖 **★★★** Freshly shelled peas, perky acidity on **11**, though lacks substance. **Chardonnay-Pinot Grigio** 🔖 **★★** Previewed **11**, 80/20 combo with lime & musk notes, slight bitter kick. **Rosé Moscato Sparkling Wine** NEW **★★ 11** light, sweet muscatty pink sparkler slips down easily. — CvZ

Ormonde Private Cellar   

Location: Darling ▪ Map: Durbanville, Philadelphia & Darling ▪ WO: Darling/Coastal ▪ 1stB 1999 ▪ Tasting & sales Mon-Fri 9–4 Sat & pub hols 9–3 ▪ Closed Easter Fri, Dec 25/26 & Jan 1 ▪ Vineyard tours by appt ▪ Picnic baskets by appt or BYO ▪ Facilities for children ▪ Walks ▪ Owner(s) Basson family ▪ Winemaker(s) Michiel du Toit ▪ Viticulturist(s) Theo Basson ▪ ±300ha (cabs s/f, merlot, mourv, p verdot, pinot, shiraz, chard, chenin, sauv, sem) ▪ 1,000t/ 35,000cs own label 40% red 60% white ▪ BWI member ▪ PO Box 201 Darling 7345 ▪ info@ormonde.co.za ▪ www. ormonde.co.za ▪ S 33° 22' 20.2"   E 018° 21' 23.6" ▪ **T +27 (0)22-492-3540** ▪ F +27 0)22-492-3470

What started out as a grape supplier to other producers has evolved into a dynamic family wine business. MD and co-owner Theo Basson believes South Africa is capable of supplying well-priced wines to the world, and sets out to prove it in his own portfolio. The premium range of mainly blends carries the property name, Ondine, and offers most of the classic grape varieties; Alexanderfontein is their big-volume range of value-for-money wines. Despite the difficult trading conditions, Theo is confident they're on the right track with their vineyards and wines. It appears so!

Ormonde range

★★★★☆ Vernon Basson Last tasted 07 **(★★★★)** combo cabs sauvignon & franc, latter's leafiness accentuated by lighter vintage; the other cab ensuring class & balance. Follows richer debut **06**, with dash merlot.

★★★★ Chardonnay Lime & oatmeal are **09**'s primary flavours but there are many nuances, including orange peel, honeycomb. Elegant, complex but unshowy, still in the prime of youth.

★★★★ Proprietor's Blend Last was top-end **09** blend sauvignon, semillon & chenin. Bellpepper & tinned pea notes, firm acidity. Creamy texture from oak & lees influence.

Theodore Eksteen ★★★☆ Nothing shy about **08** shiraz & grenache blend; ripe (15.5% alc), fruit driven, spice rich, especially aniseed, & all-new oak. Discontinued: **Sauvignon Blanc**.

Ondine range

Cabernet Sauvignon ★★★ Last edition angular **08** offered peppers & herbs, cedar & flint. Lean & bone-dry, it demanded time. **Cabernet Franc ★★★☆** Previously, **08** offered velvety ripe tannins, opulent plum & cherry fruit with variety's typical leafy notes. **Merlot ★★★** Last reviewed **08** was dusty & lean, showed hints of strawberry & prunes. Somewhat sharp & dry. **Shiraz ★★★** Previously, angular **08** showed sweet spice & toasty notes, blackcurrants & tarry smoke. Dry tannic finish. Heady 15.5% alc. **Chardonnay** 🔖 **★★★★** Richly flavoured **10** offers butterscotch & melon preserve, smoothly rounded appeal. Becomes more savoury on finish. **Chenin Blanc** 🔖 **★★★** Melon & white peach in attractive **10**, enlivened by brisk acidity. Good food match. **Sauvignon Blanc** 🔖 **★★★★** Vivid 'green' styling in **10**, asparagus & peppers, racy acidity lengthening the flavours. Could age 2-3 years. **Semillon** 🔖 **★★★★** Freshness is the key in **10**, grassy, quite sauvignon-like, with fine freshness.

Alexanderfontein range

Merlot ☺ 🍴 ★★★ Juicy, packed with berries, displaying a good oak backbone, **09** shows why merlot is so popular. **Chenin Blanc** ☺ 🍴 ★★★ Sampled from tank, **11** minerals & apples, nicely balanced with crisp acidity. Promises well.

Cabernet Sauvignon 🍴 ★★★★ Still-available **08** plush, with blackcurrant, liquorice & hint of bubblegum. Briefly oaked, very drinkable. **Shiraz** 🍴 ★★★ Black plums & smoky spice in **09**, backed by a savoury, firm structure, giving option of a few years ageing. Serve with rich food. **Chardonnay** 🍴 📖 ★★★ Subdued yellow peach on **10**, honeyed notes, crisp finish. **Sauvignon Blanc** ✓ 🍴 ★★★★ Fynbos & summer fruits vie for attention in **11**, a tightly focused, flavourful wine; good acidity helps food matching. — CR

■ **Osbloed** see Revelation Wines
■ **Osiris** see Wildekrans Wine Estate

Oubenheim Estate

Location: Vredendal ▪ Est/1stB 2002 ▪ Closed to public ▪ Owner(s) DW Viljoen & Philip Viljoen ▪ Winemaker(s) Philip Viljoen ▪ 800cs 100% red ▪ PO Box 52 Vredendal 8160 ▪ info@oubenheim.com ▪ **T +27 (0)27-213-5624/ +27 (0)83-509-9885** ▪ F +27 (0)27-213-5624

It's a decade since third-generation grape farmer Philip Viljoen started making his own single-vineyard wines, aimed at the top end of the market, at the Olifants River Valley's first wine estate. He still sells most of his crop, adding pragmatically: 'The good thing is that we have the grapes, so when the market demands more wine, we make more.'

Oude Compagnies Post Private Cellar

Location/map/WO: Tulbagh ▪ Est 1996 ▪ 1stB 2003 ▪ Tasting, sales & cellar tours by appt ▪ Walking trail (flower season Sep-Oct) ▪ Hiking trail 1-2 days (sleepover on Obiqua mountain in own tent) ▪ Mountain bike (difficult) & 15km off-road motorbike trails ▪ Owner(s) Jerry Swanepoel Family Trust ▪ Cellarmaster(s) Jerry Swanepoel ▪ Winemaker(s) Jerry Swanepoel, with Ervin Koen (Jul 2011) ▪ Viticulturist(s) Marius Robert (consultant) ▪ 235ha/ 18ha (cab, grenache, merlot, mourv, ptage, shiraz) ▪ 70t/5,000cs own label 90% red 10% rosé + 20,000L bulk ▪ Other export brand: Maison De Cygne ▪ Fairtrade ▪ PO Box 11 Tulbagh 6820 ▪ swanepoel@intekom.co.za ▪ S 33° 14'56.9" E 019° 6'49.1" ▪ **T +27 (0)23-230-1578** ▪ F +27 (0)23-230-0840

Building a hiking trail on this mountainous Tulbagh farm led owners Jerry and Henriette Swanepoel's teenage son to an exciting discovery: an ancient dwelling, and rock art near the remains of the stone structure. Both cellar and vineyards are being expanded, and a méthode cap classique sparkling will be added this year to the heretofore red-only boutique portfolio.

Compagnies Wijn range
Cabernet Sauvignon ★★★★ **08** inky succulence with cedary tannins, soft ginger nuance. Needs time. **07** (★★★★) softer, more alluring. Lithe blueberry & fynbos. Both vintages still available, neither revisited. **Merlot** ★★★★ Now bottled, **08** ample mulberry & spice on light acidic freshness & gentle tannic grip. Interesting hint of pepper. **Mourvèdre** ★★★ **09** reviewed last year had plum, cranberry & nutmeg. Juicy & ripe, just 5% new oak so a touch light despite 14.5% alc. **Pinotage** ★★★ **08** keeps up the standard of **07**. Cherry fruit with meaty tar notes, dry chalky tannin. Firm body & depth of flavour. **Pinotage Grand Reservé** Untasted. **Shiraz** ★★★☆ **08**'s ripe berry compote a step up. Well-judged density, youthful but tangy & fresh, light chalky tannin. **Caap Ensemble** ★★★ Previous were Cape Blends, various combos merlot, cab, pinotge; **09** make-up not disclosed. Flowers up first, then cocoa, turned-earth & blackcurrant. Nice. Oak just needs time to integrate. **Duet** Untasted. **Ruby Blanc** 🍴 ★★★ Dry rosé from shiraz & pinotage with raspberry sherbet appeal in quaffable **11**. — FM

Oude Denneboom

Location: Paarl ▪ Map: Paarl & Wellington ▪ WO: Voor Paardeberg/Paarl ▪ 1stB 2003 ▪ Tasting by appt ▪ 4-star self-catering cottage ▪ Private game reserve ▪ Owner(s) Niel de Waal ▪ Cellarmaster(s)/viticulturist(s) Willem de Waal ▪ 194ha/±45ha (cab, mourv, ptage, shiraz, chenin, nouvelle, viog) ▪ 400t/500cs own label 70% red 30% white ▪ Global GAP ▪ PO Box 2087 Windmeul 7630 ▪ info@oudedenneboom.co.za ▪ www.oudedenneboom.co.za ▪ S 33°37'47.28" E 018°51'55.08" ▪ **T +27 (0)21-869-8072** ▪ F +27 (0)21-853-4839

Willem de Waal reports neither change nor innovation from this peaceful haven in the Voor Paardeberg, where eland, grysbok and steenbok crop the veld surrounding the popular 4-star guest house on the property. 'Everything just continues as normal...' he says.

Black Harrier Shiraz ★★★★ 'Shiraz' pvsly, **08** higher flier than **07** (★★★★). Fleshy plum, blueberry & nutmeg spice on lissome, velvety frame. Succulent & ripe. Like others, not restasted this issue. **Eland** ★★★★ Shoulder above maiden **07** (★★★), **08**'s blend of shiraz, mourv, grenache (63/26/12) is full of cherry, blackberry & pepper. Velvety texture & superb wood integration (2 yrs older Fr/Am.). **Grysbok Chenin Blanc** 🍷 ★★★ Rich & rewarding mouthful, shows complexity. Light lily whiffs, **09** tangy grapefruit. Lively yet fat & honeyed. **Steenbok** ★★★★ Appealing combo dry leaves, peach & blossom on **09**'s viog, chenin, chard mix. Fresh acidity, leesy richness on full finish. — FM

Oude Kaap

Focused range of high-volume wines produced by DGB for export mainly to The Netherlands, Scandanavia and Germany.

Reserve Collection
Cabernet Sauvignon 🍷 ★★★ Brush of oak adds fragrance, underlines dark berry fruit on **10**. **Pinotage** 🍷 ★★★ Interesting combo pecan nut & plummy mulberry, **10** firm & food-friendly. **Shiraz** 🍷 ★★★ **10** appealing charcuterie, spicy fruit notes, balanced & rounded. **Chardonnay** ★★★ Plump **10** still selling; good varietal character, butter & coconut from light oaking. WO Western Cape both ranges. **Chenin Blanc** 🍷 ★★★ Youthful **11** preview shows creamy apple texture. Might rate higher once bottled. **Sauvignon Blanc** [NEW] 🍷 ★★★ **10** fresh, crisp & grassy picnic white.

Oude Kaap range
Cabernet Sauvignon-Merlot 🍷 ★★★ **10** juicy dark-berried duo, friendly drinkability solo or with meal. **Klassiek Rood** 🍷 ★★ Cinsaut & ruby cab **10** offers juicy plums in friendly outdoor style. **Cinsault-Ruby Cabernet** 🍷 ★★ **10** savoury red berries, rounded easy drinkability. **Blanc de Noir** 🍷 ★★★ Off-dry **11** from pinotage & shiraz, bright, tangy cranberry-toned sunset sipper. **Chenin Blanc** [NEW] 🍷 ★★ Undemanding **11** with crunchy green-apple nuances. **Klassiek Wit** 🍷 ★★ Chenin & sauvignon **11**, fresh & gentle tropical notes for easy drinking. **Elegant Wit** 🍷 ★★ Bouquet of fragrant white varieties in light, crispy semi-sweet **11**. — MW

■ **Oude Rust** *see* Mooiuitsig Wine Cellars

Oude Wellington Estate

Location: Wellington ▪ Map: Paarl & Wellington ▪ Tasting & sales daily 9-6 or by appt ▪ Closed Dec 25 ▪ Cellar tours by appt ▪ Restaurant ▪ Tour groups ▪ Facilities for children ▪ Conferences ▪ Guest house & self-catering cottage ▪ Owner(s) Rolf Schumacher ▪ Cellarmaster(s)/winemaker(s) Sydney Burke (Dec 2008) ▪ Viticulturist(s) Rolf Schumacher & Sydney Burke ▪ 31ha/13ha (cab, ruby cab, shiraz, chard) ▪ 40t/±2,500cs own label 60% red 20% white 20% rosé ▪ PO Box 622 Wellington 7654 ▪ info@kapwein.com ▪ www.kapwein.com ▪ S 33° 38' 30.38" E 019° 2' 36.12" ▪ **T** +27 (0)21-873-2262 ▪ F +27 (0)88-021-873-4639

At the gateway to the stunning Bainsway pass lies a beautiful, peaceful example of Cape Dutch architecture. Oude Wellington is a place to relax, to taste handcrafted wines and sample a little sip of their excellent brandy. The hosts focus is all about wine, food and great company.

Cabernet Sauvignon Sold out, await next. **Currant Abbey** ★ Last was friendly unwooded **09** from ruby cabernet. Still available. **Shiraz 07** available, not assessed. **Eros Potion** ★ Rustic **09**, still selling. **Chardonnay** ★★ Latest release not tasted this edition. **Dolce** ★★ Sherry-like **09** natural sweet not reviewed. Discontinued: **Vasecco, Chardonnay Barrique**. — JP

Oudtshoorn Cellar - SCV

Location: Oudtshoorn ▪ Map: Klein Karoo & Garden Route ▪ WO: Klein Karoo ▪ Est/1stB 1975 ▪ Tasting & sales at Kango Wijnhuis Mon-Fri 9-5 Sat 9-3 ▪ Fee R20 for groups of 5 or more ▪ Closed Easter Fri-Mon, Dec 25/26 & Jan 1 ▪ Book ahead for cellar tours ▪ Tour groups ▪ BYO picnic ▪ Conference facilities ▪ Owner(s) 35 members ▪ Cellarmaster(s)/winemaker(s)/viticulturist(s) Emile Schoch (2011) ▪ 200ha (merlot, muscadel, chard, cbard) ▪ 1,016t/ 5,000cs own label 16% red 84% white ▪ Other export brand: Van Hunks ▪ PO Box 46 Oudtshoorn 6620 ▪

oudtshoorn@scv.co.za ▪ www.oudtshoornwines.co.za ▪ S 33° 36' 50.0" E 022° 12' 1.1" ▪ **T +27 (0)44-272-8660** ▪ F +27 (0)44-279-1038

Shedding its old name (Kango Wines), Oudtshoorn Cellar joins Barrydale and Ladismith in the Southern Cape Vineyards portfolio, and creates 'the exciting opportunity to establish a 'truly Karoo' wine and brandy experience' for tourists on the famed Route 62. Ladismith production manager Emile Schoch comes in as head of viticulture and winemaking. Top priority is to rationalise the Oudtshoorn range and decide which cellar handles which areas of production

Rijckshof range

Hanepoot Untasted, as **Red Jerepigo**, **Gold Jerepigo** & **Vintage Port**. **Red Muscadel ★★** Latest **NV** bottling of fortified dessert not as delicate & elegant as previous. **White Muscadel ★★★** Current **NV** bottling shade off previous tiger's eye-hued fortified dessert: dried peach/apricot & orange zest, full-sweet flavours. **Ruby Port ★★** From touriga; crammed with sweet catawba grape character, shows none of port's fire & grip.

Kango range

Cabernet Sauvignon ★★ Fresh red berry melange on easy-sipping **09**. Still selling, not revisited, as for next. **Merlot ★★★** **09** vanilla overlay to plum & mulberry, grippy texture smoothed by succulent fruit. **Pinotage** Untasted, as for **Ruby cabernet**, **Shiraz**, **Cabernet Sauvignon-Merlot-Shiraz**, **Sensuality Blanc de Noir**, **Chardonnay**, **Dry White Blend** & **Morio Muscat Sparkling**. **Sauvignon Blanc** 🗏 **★★** Step-up **11** light, bright & breezy guava-toned quick-sip.

Baroness range

Sparkling Sweet Rosé Untasted. **Natural Sweet Rosé** 🗏 **★★** Lowish alc, strawberry toned, gently sweet **NV** tipple from pinotage & merlot.

Swartberg Reserve range

Pinotage New vintage not ready, as for **Shiraz** & **Chardonnay**. — Panel

◼ **Out of Africa** see African Terroir

Overgaauw Wine Estate

🍷 🎋 📷 ♿

Location/map/WO: Stellenbosch ▪ Est 1905 ▪ 1stB 1970 ▪ Tasting & sales Mon-Fri 9–5 Sat 10–3.30 (Oct-Apr) & 10–12.30 (May-Sep) ▪ Fee R10pp for groups of 6+ ▪ Closed Easter Fri-Mon, Dec 25/26 & Jan 1 ▪ Port & snack pairing R30pp, 48-hr advance booking essential ▪ BYO picnic ▪ Owner(s) Braam van Velden ▪ Winemaker(s) David van Velden (Jan 2003) ▪ Viticulturist(s) Braam & David van Velden, Vinpro ▪ 100ha/60ha (cabs s/f, merlot, ptage, touriga nacional, chard, sauv, sem, sylvaner) ▪ 60% red 40% white ▪ Other export brand: Sandrivier ▪ HACCP ▪ PO Box 3 Vlottenburg 7604 ▪ info@overgaauw.co.za ▪ www.overgaauw.co.za ▪ S 33° 56' 52.1" E 018° 47' 33.4" ▪ **T +27 (0)21-881-3815** ▪ F +27 (0)21-881-3436

The Cape's first varietal merlot; the first and only sylvaner: this family-owned winery has always been quietly innovative. Current and fourth-generation Van Velden winemaker, David, is also quietly but thoroughly sprucing up the wines. Now more modern with purer fruit, the reds in particular show greater character. We will have to wait to see how David manages his port-style wines, as Overgaauws have always been among the oldest on the market. A treat for those who haven't tasted older vintage-styles comes with the trio offered with dark chocolate, roast pecan nuts, and ginger biscuits with port-marinated blue cheese.

Overgaauw Estate range

★★★★ Cabernet Sauvignon 09 first tasted since **05** (**★★★★**). Brimful of crunchy dark, fresh berry succulence, supported by ripe, lively tannins. Very clean, long. All-new French oak spice adds extra class.

★★★★ Tria Corda Cab-based **06**, was last tasted; fresh & fine, but then needing time to harmonise.

★★★★ Cape Vintage Last was **98**, still selling. 6 traditional port varieties in structured, classic style.

Merlot ★★★★ Fruity but not simple **09**; fresh sour plum, spice flavours spruced up with well-judged oak. Good drinking now, few more yrs. First since **06**. **Touriga Nacional-Cabernet Sauvignon** 🗏 **★★★★** Just-dry **10** similar country-style blend as **09**. Extra violet, sweet dark berry attractions from 87% touriga (75% previously). **Chardonnay ★★★ 10** first since **07**. Bold lemon butter features, spiced with oak. Neither over-heavy nor complex. **Chenin Blanc** 🗏 📷 **★★★** Ripe melon& tropical tones on broad-based **11** tasted pre-bottling. Zesty & dry. **Sauvignon Blanc** 🗏 📷 **★★★** Juicy light fruit on **11** lifted by a hint of finishing sweetness. **Sylvaner** 🗏 **★★★ 10** shows usual quiet spice, apple appeal. Lightish body (just 12% alc); fruity but dry tail. No **09**.

Shepherd's Cottage range

Cabernet Sauvignon-Merlot ☺ 🗒 ★★★ Plentiful ripe fleshy dark berries on tasty, very lightly oaked **10**. Accessible but with good forming grip.

Pinotage Rosé 🗒 ★★★ Medium-bodied, dry **11** (tasted ex-tank) with attractive, persistent red fruits. **Chenin Blanc-Chardonnay** 🗒 🕸 ★★ Quietly fruity but dry **11**; juicy & with balanced zest. — AL

Overhex Wines International

Location/map: Worcester ▪ WO: Western Cape ▪ Est/1stB 2006 ▪ Tasting & sales Mon-Fri 8–5 Sat 10–4 ▪ Closed Easter Fri-Sun, Dec 25 & Jan 1 ▪ Cellar tours by appt ▪ Bistro Tue-Fri 10-5 Sat 10-4 ▪ Wine bar Fri 5-9 ▪ Facilities for children ▪ Tour groups ▪ Conferences ▪ Owner(s) G van der Wath & JC Martin ▪ Cellarmaster(s) Jandre Human (Aug 2009) ▪ Winemaker(s) Willie Malan (2002) & Ben Snyman (Dec 2010), with Zinaschke Steyn (May 2011) ▪ Viticulturist(s) Pierre Snyman (Vinpro) ▪ 7,000t ▪ own label 45% red 50% white 5% rosé ▪ ISO 22000, WIETA ▪ PO Box 139 Worcester 6849 ▪ info@overhex.com ▪ www.overhex.com ▪ S 33° 39' 28.6" E 019° 30' 55.8" ▪ **T** +27 **(0)23-347-5012** ▪ F +27 (0)23-347-1057

Emphasis on social media and cellardoor experience has seen this enterprising Worcester winery grow active on Twitter and Facebook, offer function and conference facilities, and open a family bistro with secure outdoor play area and jungle gym. On Friday evenings they open their wine bar, with music and a tapas menu to match their Balance range, marketed (along with several other own-brands) in Asia, Europe, Africa and North America.

Balance Winemakers Selection [NEW]

Merlot ☺ ★★★ Sweet berry fruit, honey & marzipan, **10** fair weight & attractive leafy conclusion. Toastiness from brief ageing in French barrels, as for all the reds in this more ambitious range. **Chardonnay** ☺ 🗒 🕸 ★★★ Easy-sipping **11** is fresh, full & rounded, elegantly oaked, ends with intriguing salty tang.

Pinotage ★★★ **10** an appealing sipper: plummy, with slight acetone zing for interest. **Shiraz** ★★★ Lifted red berry fruit, acetone sheen to easy-glugging **10**. **Chenin Blanc** 🗒 ★★★ **11** very likeable summer tipple. Guava taste, overtly fruity, slightly sweet conclusion. **Sauvignon Blanc** 🗒 🕸 ★★★ Engaging white peach-nuanced **11** needs time to open, reveals engaging apple-pith texture, long but tad thin tail.

Balance Classics

Shiraz Rosé ☺ 🗒 🕸 ★★★ Enticing strawberry scents, refreshing berry conclusion on **11**. **Sauvignon Blanc-Semillon** ☺ 🗒 ★★★ **11** more vinous & weighty than Pinot Gris-Sauvignon Blanc. Wallet-friendly everyday wine, for early enjoyment, like all these.

Reserve Cabernet Sauvignon 🗒 ★★★ Blackcurrant-laden **09** a touch coarse mid-2010. Still selling, as for **Cabernet Sauvignon-Merlot**, **Reserve Chardonnay**, **Muscat d'Alexandrie**. **Cabernet Sauvignon-Merlot** 🗒 ★★ **10** easy sherbet-toned quaffer. **Pinotage-Shiraz** 🗒 ★★ Berry jam & fruit preserve, **10** nicely rounded sipper. Like Shiraz-Merlot, lightly staved. **Shiraz-Merlot** 🗒 ★★★ **10** packed with berries, melded & soft. **Reserve Chardonnay** 🗒 ★★ Thatch & citrus, **10** good fruity centre but fleeting farewell. **Muscat d'Alexandrie** 🗒 ★★ Uncomplicated enjoyment delivered by grapey **10** semi-sweet. **Pinot Gris-Sauvignon Blanc** [NEW] 🗒 🕸 ★★ Pleasant if somewhat neutral **11** summer quaffer. **Chenin Blanc-Colombar** 🗒 ★★ Fruit-filled **11** happy marriage of chenin's apple & acidity, colombard's floral appeal. Discontinued: **Light Rosé**, **Sauvignon Blanc**, **Light White**.

Balance Sparklings

Boldly Brut Sparkling ★★★ Previously 'Vin Sec'. Appealingly dry **NV** sparkler: refreshingly foamy, lean & brief end. **Lusciously Fruity Sparkling** ★★ Aromatic **NV** bubbly lives up to its new name (previously 'Vin Doux'). Gently sweet, with hint of litchi. **Sweet Temptation Sparkling** [NEW] ★★ Sweet **NV** rosé bubbly, just 8% alc ideal for parties.

Soulo range

Cabernet Sauvignon ★★★ **09** raised the bar mid-2010 with juicy black fruit, modest 12.5% alc. Not revisited, like others in this improved range. **Pinotage** ★★★ **09** pleasantly rustic: antique furniture polish, red berry fruit, taut tannin. **Shiraz** ★★★ Characterful **09** preview needed year/2 mid-2010 for oak to knit. Should be drinking well now. **Sauvignon Blanc** ★★★ **11** textbook sauvignon: cool green fig, pear & blackcurrant notes, nice.

depth & grip. **Red Muscadel** Untasted, as for **White Muscadel**. Discontinued: **Shiraz Limited Release**, **Cabernet Sauvignon-Petit Verdot Limited Release**, **Sauvignon Blanc Limited Release**. —Panel

Overmeer Cellars

Since 1996, big-selling no-frills range by Distell. Modest alcs and 3/5L boxes for all.
Selected Red ★★★ Light berry spice on NV pinotage, ruby cab & cinsaut. **Grand Cru** ★★ Zingy kumquat preserve on dry NV chenin, cbard & cruchen mix. **Stein** ★★ Semi-sweet NV chenin/colombard pairing offers light mango & peach. **Late Harvest** ★★ Baked apple spice, sweet & simple NV equal chenin & cbard blend. —Panel

■ **Overvaal** *see Hartswater Wine Cellar*

Paarl Wine Company

Closed to public ▪ Owner(s) Izak Visagie ▪ 9 Zuidmeer Str Huguenot Paarl 7646 ▪ izak.v@pwcwines.co.za ▪ **T +27 (0)21-862-2100** ▪ F +27 (0)21-862-6400

Wine wholesalers and owners of the Cape Style bag-in-box/Purepack carton range.

Packwood Wines

Location: Knysna ▪ Map: Klein Karoo & Garden Route ▪ WO: Plettenberg Bay ▪ Est 2006 ▪ 1stB 2009 ▪ Tasting & sales Mon-Fri 11-3 ▪ Fee R15, waived if case is purchased ▪ Closed all pub hols ▪ Sales enquiries via email/sms text messages ▪ Packwood cheese lunch - book ahead ▪ Tour groups by arrangement ▪ Farm produce ▪ Walking/hiking & mountain biking trails ▪ 4-star country house plus self-catering cottages ▪ Owner(s) Peter & Vicky Gent ▪ Winemaker(s) Teddy Hall (Mar 2009, consultant) ▪ Viticulturist(s) Vicky Gent (Jan 2006) ▪ 380ha/3.5ha (pinot, chard, sauv) ▪ 5t/5,000cs own label 80% white 20% rosé ▪ PO Box 622 Knysna 6570 ▪ packwood@xnets.co.za ▪ www.packwood.co.za ▪ S 34° 0′ 18.77″ E 023° 13′ 43.33″ ▪ **T +27 (0)44-532-7614** ▪ F +27 (0)86-510-0741

Packwood lies on the outskirts of Knysna forest, 20km from popular holiday destination Plettenberg Bay. Here Peter and Vicky Gent, originally from England, offer luxury accommodation as well as maintaining a herd of dairy cows. Convinced that their location might be an exciting new terroir for wine, vineyard was planted in 2006, and top Stellenbosch winemaker Teddy Hall enlisted as consultant in 2009.

Sauvignon Blanc ★★★★ Idiosyncratic **10** shows hay on nose before rich, full palate with notes of granadilla, honey & tangy acidity. — CE

■ **Paddagang** *see Tulbagh Winery*

Painted Wolf Wines

Location: Paarl ▪ Map: Paarl & Wellington ▪ WO: Swartland/Western Cape/Paarl/Stellenbosch/Coastal ▪ Est/1stB 2007 ▪ Tasting & sales by appt Mon-Sun 10-5 ▪ Fee R25 ▪ Closed Easter Fri-Mon, Dec 25 & Jan 1 ▪ Lunch by appt (parties of 4 or less) ▪ Owner(s) Jeremy & Emma Borg, & 16 'pack members' ▪ Cellarmaster(s) Rolanie Lotz, Inge Terreblanche & Trizanne Barnard (consultants) ▪ Winemaker(s) Jeremy Borg ▪ ±65ha/40ha (grenache, merlot, mourv, ptage, shiraz, chenin, sauv, viog) ▪ 100t/15,000cs own label 75% red 20% white 5% rosé ▪ Export brand: Jemma ▪ PO Box 1489 Suider Paarl 7624 ▪ sales@paintedwolfwines.com ▪ www.paintedwolfwines.com ▪ S 33° 46′ 14.8″ E 018° 57′ 14.6″ ▪ **T +27 (0)21-863-2492**

Harmony, balance and persistence make the African Wild Dog the continent's most successful carnivorous hunter - and they're attributes 'Alpha male' Jeremy Borg seeks in these wines. A portion of the proceeds of every bottle sold now funds an Endangered Wildlife Trust research programme into these Painted Wolves. 'Alpha wine' Pictus features label art by Zimbabwean Lin Barrie, the orginal painting donated to Tusk for a charity auction in London. Joining the 16-strong pack to handle communication and sales is sister Amanda, a successful wildlife documentary filmmaker who's worked for NatGeo and Discovery channels.

'Our Pack' Varieties & Special Wines

★★★★ **Shiraz 10** matches **09**'s promise. Ample plum softness; juicy but dry ripe palate, with light tannic grip from combo French/American oak. Earthy intensity carries to long finish. WO Coastal.
Merlot ★★★ Preview tasted last edition. Blackcurrant, plum & clove, **09** dry but textured, vanilla almond note from 20% new wood, 15 months. **Guillermo Swartland Pinotage** ▤ ★★★★ Includes dashes mourvèdre &

grenache in **10**, step up on **09** (★★★). Ripe black fruit & spice, textured & round, shows elegant restraint. Well assimilated 16 months oak (French, American & Hungarian, 30% new). Like all, a preview unless noted. **Juergen Stellenbosch Pinotage** ★★★ Cranberry & herb/buchu on **10**. Medium body but chalky grip & nutty finish. Light wood sheen from 2nd fill French oak. **Pictus Red** ★★★★ Shiraz (48%) led mourvèdre & grenache in **09** blend tasted last year. Sweet ripe black fruit, pepper spice & tannic grip from 40% new oak. **Rosalind Paarl Pinotage Rosé** 🍷 ★★★ Floral red cherry tang, **11** fruity & fresh with complexity added by time on viognier lees. Light, dry, peppery finish. **Wild Yeast Barrel Fermented Chenin Blanc** NEW ★★★★ **11** a melange of sweet peach, pear & pepper. Rich, full mouthful (10.9 g/l sugar). Older French oak provides a toasty platform. WO Paarl. **Roussanne** NEW ★★★ Nectarine freshness vies with spicy vibrancy, **11** creamy texture & flavour yet also dry, rich & ripe throughout. WO Swartland. **Penny Swartland Viognier** 🍷 ★★★★ Serious intent on **11** ex Swartland single-vineyard. Creamy, spicy stonefruit richness; textured, full & poised.

Cape 'Hunting' Blends

★★★★ **Lekanyane** 🍷 Aka Jemma White. **11** follows **10** level. Vibrant chenin, viognier, verdelho (40/30/ 20) blend. Tropical pineapple & elderflower, breadth on palate from oaking (older barrels & staves). **Madach** 🍷 ★★★★ Aka Jemma Red. Shiraz & pinotage (55/32) blend in **10**. Smoky prune, liquorice & smooth body from 50/50 barrel/stave oaking.

The Den Comfort Wines

Cabernet Sauvignon 🍷 ★★★ Cocoa smoke with charry earth below, **11** ripe & approachable yet structured. Oak staved. **Pinotage** 🍷 ★★★ Raspberry & fruitcake on **11**. Rich cocoa depth & intensity. Dry texture from French/American oak, long spicy finish. **Chenin Blanc** 🍷 ★★★ Fresh melon & guava with lively lemongrass, **11** body & fullness with creamy breadth from third stave-ferment. — FM

- **Palesa** see uniWines Marketing
- **Papillon** see Van Loveren Private Cellar
- **Paradyskloof** see Vriesenhof Vineyards
- **Parker Family** see Altydgedacht Estate

Passages Wine

WO: Stellenbosch/Malmesbury ▪ 1stB 2006 ▪ Closed to public ▪ Owner(s) Ronald T Gault & Charlayne Hunter-Gault ▪ Cellarmaster(s)/winemaker(s) Ernst Gouws (2007, consultant) ▪ (cab, merlot, chard) ▪ ±5,000cs own label 70% red 30% white ▪ gaultronald@gmail.com ▪ www.passageswine.com

US citizens and now permanent residents of South Africa, Ron Gault and Charlayne Hunter-Gault came here fifteen years ago, he as the head of JP Morgan and she as a journalist, becoming the bureau chief of CNN. Lately, they've moved into the wine business, the principal market for the Passages label being their home country (Gault also a partner in premium wine brand Epicurean). The current winemaker is Ernst Gouws of Ernst Gouws & Company and grapes are sourced from around the Western Cape.

Passages range NEW

Merlot ★★★ Garnet-rimmed **08** shows mature leafy aromas with sappy dark-fruit flavours. For current enjoyment. **Cabernet Sauvignon-Merlot** ★★★ Ripe **08**, mouthfilling sweet blackcurrant fruit, plush & ready for early drinking. **Chardonnay** 🍷 ★★★★ Abundant fruit on **10**, butterscotch & vanilla layers, extra complexity from lees-ageing. Aftertaste is long & flavourful. — Panel

Paul Cluver Estate Wines

Location/WO: Elgin ▪ Map: Elgin, Walker Bay & Bot River ▪ Est 1896 ▪ 1stB 1997 ▪ Tasting & sales Mon-Fri 9-5 Sat 9-3 (Sep-Apr) 10-2 (May-Aug) ▪ Fee R25 for groups ▪ Closed Easter Fri/Sat/Sun, Dec 25/26 & Jan 1 ▪ Restaurant 'Fresh' Tue-Sat 9-3 ▪ BYO picnic ▪ Conservation area (part of UNESCO Heritage Site Kogelberg Biosphere) ▪ Mountain biking track open to public, fee payable ▪ Open air amphitheatre hosting concerts Dec-Mar ▪ Owner(s) Cluver family ▪ Cellarmaster(s) Andries Burger (Nov 1996) ▪ Winemaker(s) Andries Burger (Nov 1996), with Nina Swiegelaar (Jan 2010) ▪ Viticulturist(s) Craig Harris (Jan 2010) & Kevin Watt (Mar 2005, consultant) ▪ 2,400ha/ 90ha (pinot, chard, gewürz, riesling, sauv) ▪ 300t/20,000cs own label 20% red 80% white ▪ Brands for clients: Woolworths ▪ BWI Champion ▪ PO Box 48 Grabouw 7160 ▪ info@cluver.com ▪ www.cluver.com ▪ S 34° 10'6.2" E 019° 5'8.1" ▪ **T +27 (0)21-844-0605** ▪ F +27 (0)21-844-0150

'Understated and elegant – complexity that develops with age,' is how Andries Burger describes his wine style. Unwittingly, so too the ethos of this timeless, classy Elgin spread. The Cluvers have been here since 1896, with former neurosurgeon Paul Cluver pioneering commercial wine farming a hundred years later. Wine is but part of a holistic operation, amongst apples, pears, a Hereford stud and eco-tourism, and half of the 2,400ha estate – part of the Kogelberg Biosphere, a UNESCO World Heritage Site – has been given over to conservation. Family-owned and -run, four of five current-generation siblings as well as brother-in-law Burger work here, with a 'family' of support staff from vineyard to tasting room. Although relatively new to the local wine firmament, it's already amongst the pantheon.

★★★★ **Pinot Noir** 🍽 🍷 Refined & serious, radiant **10** has medium-weight mineral centre with succulent cherry fruit & tangy, structured texture. 11 months 20% new wood fully absorbed into the structure.

★★★★★ **Seven Flags Pinot Noir** Scintillating barrel selection of single clone from farm's best site. **09** has all the nuance of fine pinot; beguiling clay-earth aromas, red-berry fruit woven into polished, elegant package – power in the gentlest form! 'Burgundian everything' - clones, yeasts, oak (11 months, 25% new).

★★★★☆ **CWG Auction Reserve Pinot Noir** NEW 🍷 Selected grapes of three clones ex highest vineyard, just 40 cases for 2011 auction debut. **10** leaps from the glass with alluring cherry & spice from 11 months oak, 20% new. Follows with astounding texture, bold fruit & full grip of powdery tannins. Very fine layered finish.

★★★★☆ **CWG Auction Reserve Wagon Trail Chardonnay** From oldest vineyard (23 years), **09** a study in restraint last edition: elegant mineral & lime notes to creamy texture, long finish.

★★★★☆ **Chardonnay** 🍽 🍷 **10** a sleeper: toned lemon & lime fruit nurtured by fine oak in youth, will unfurl in polished, chic splendour given year or two. Wild yeast ferment in French barrels, 45% new.

★★★★☆ **Gewürztraminer** ✓ 🍽 🍷 Semi-dry version, a Cape benchmark. **10** (★★★★) delicate litchi notes, super sugar/acid balance with grip for food, but not as complex as **09**, a 'Turkish Delight'!

★★★★ **Riesling** ✓ 🍽 🍷 'Weisser Riesling' previous editions. **10** orange-peel aroma, white pepper facet to 'wet pebble' minerality. Technically semi-sweet (12.4 g/l sugar) but ably freshened by tingling acidity.

★★★★ **Close Encounter Riesling** 🍷 With 'Weisser Riesling' suffix previously. Sweeter than above (35 g/l sugar; 9.8% alc), in 'German Auslese' style. **10** open, floral ginger & lime fruit, lovely fresh finish.

★★★★ **Sauvignon Blanc** ✓ 🍽 🍷 **10** bristles in cellar's cool, grassy styling; edgy capsicum & minerality leavened - just - by leesy width & 8% plumping wooded semillon.

★★★★☆ **Noble Late Harvest** ✓ 🍷 Superb riesling botrytised dessert listed with 'Weisser Riesling' prefix previous editions. Shimmering old-gold hue leads out near-unctuous apricot ripeness stunningly cut by tangy lime fruit, a stony minerality in long electric finish. Brilliant balance, **10** a thing of beauty. — DS

■ **Paul de Villiers** see Landskroon Wines

■ **Paulina's Reserve** see Rickety Bridge Winery

Paul Wallace Wines

Location/WO: Elgin ▪ Est/1stB 2004 ▪ Closed to public ▪ Owner(s)/viticulturist(s) Paul Wallace ▪ Winemaker(s) Paul Wallace, with Justin Hoy ▪ 25ha/10.5ha (malbec, pinot, sauv) ▪ 70t/95cs own label 100% red ▪ BWI, IPW ▪ PO Box 141 Elgin 7180 ▪ wallovale@mweb.co.za ▪ www.wallovale.co.za ▪ **T +27 (0)21-848-9744/+27 (0)83-255-1884/+27 (0)82-572-1406** ▪ F +27 (0)86-646-3694

After establishing vineyards on their Elgin property in 2004, the Wallaces have now released their first wine from this homegrown fruit. With the natural freshness associated with Elgin, its pure fruit and drinkability, it should prove popular. A further five hectares remain to be planted; with what is still under consideration. 'I'm thinking of trying a variety not yet found in South Africa,' says Paul Wallace

★★★★ **Malbec** ✓ **08** first from home vineyards. Brimming with bright red cherry fruit; minerally freshness, succulent tannin in support. Well-judged oak (33% new) adds dimension. — AL

Pax Verbatim Vineyards

Location: Somerset West ▪ WO: Western Cape ▪ Est 2003 ▪ Closed to public ▪ Owner(s) Richard Hilton ▪ Cellarmaster(s)/winemaker(s) Richard Hilton (2003) ▪ Viticulturist(s) Tjuks Roos & Richard Rose (consultants) ▪ (syrah, viog) ▪ 12-14t/800cs own label 35% red 65% white ▪ richard@paxverbatim.co.za ▪ www.paxverbatim.co.za ▪ **T +27 (0)21-855-5244** ▪ F +27 (0)86-618-4089

According to Richard Hilton wine is important because 'it is biblical, convivial, plea-surable, health-giving, and dates back to the birth of civilised man.' Clearly no lack of inspiration here. The motto is to use fruit that is farmed as organically as possible and in winemaking to allow the grapes to express a sense of place.

★★★★ **Blazing Hill Syrah** From Helderberg vineyard, **09** in riper, more dark-fruited mould than restrained **08**. Dense palate expresses richer style with complex savoury undertone. Nicely dry to end.

★★★★ **Rockwater Fountain Viognier ✓ ▤** **10** again in fine focused & mineral mould; pretty floral notes with restrained citrus fruit leading to subtle, lingering end. Mix Elgin & Helderberg fruit, 10% brush of oak. — JP

■ **Peacock Ridge** see Waterkloof
■ **Pearlstone** see Rhebokskloof Wine Estate

Pearly Bay

KWV range where the well assembled wines are as unpretentious as their names. To drink, preferably well chilled, rather than to ponder over. Main markets are Scandi-navia, Denmark, USA and Asia, as well as back home.

Cape Red ▤ ★★ Light, smooth fruit; dryish tannin tail. **NV**, WO W Cape, as for all. **Cape Sweet Rosé ▤** ★★ Light & fresh with sweet muscat fruit. **Cape Rosé ▤** ★★ Tangy cranberries, fresh & fruitily sweet. **Cape White ▤** ★★ Gently fruity & dry. **Cape Sweet White ▤** ★★ Light, fresh with sweet grapey flavours. **Celebration White** ★★ Perfumed, fruity & sweet fizz. This & Rosé below have low 8% alc. **Celebration Sparkling Rosé** ★★ Coppery-tinged; quiet flavour & fizz. — AL

■ **Pecan Stream** see Waterford Estate
■ **Pella** see Super Single Vineyards
■ **Pepin Condé** see Stark-Condé Wines

Perdeberg Winery

Location/WO: Paarl ▪ Map: Paarl & Wellington ▪ Est 1941 ▪ 1stB 1942 ▪ Tasting & sales Mon-Fri 8–5 Sat 9.30–2 ▪ Closed Easter Fri-Mon, Dec 25/26 & Jan 1 ▪ Cellar tours Mon-Fri by appt ▪ Meals, pre-booked week in advance, for groups of 10 or more ▪ BYO picnic ▪ Annual October Festival ▪ Owner(s) 30 members ▪ Cellarmaster(s) Albertus Louw (Oct 2008) ▪ Winemaker(s) Riaan Möller (Dec 2006) & Carla Herbst (Jun 2008) ▪ Viticulturist(s) Jaco Engelbrecht (Nov 2011) ▪ 6,000ha/2,076ha (cab, cincaut, merlot, ptage, shiraz, chard, chenin, sauv) ▪ 18,000t/150,000cs own label 60% red 40% white ▪ BWI, HACCP, IPW, WIETA ▪ PO Box 214 Paarl 7620 ▪ info@perdeberg.co.za ▪ www.perdeberg.co.za ▪ S 33° 39' 30.00" E 018° 49' 37.00" ▪ **T +27 (0)21-869-8244** ▪ F +27 (0)21-869-8245

With the rare distinction for a large producer that all its wines are certified, Perdeberg is eons away from the cooperative that bottled very few of its wines a few short years ago. Its big portfolio includes David Frost Signature, Waka Waka, SAAM and Bottelary (all separately listed), the first in partnership with the renowned golfer, the next two with retailers in the UK and Germany respectively. Not that the Perdeberg wines have been neglected in this expansion, a Weisser Riesling Natural Sweet and Méthode Cap Classique have been added to the range.

Flagship Collection

★★★★ **Rex Equus Chenin Blanc** Previously, parading melon & pineapple preserve, **08** was full-bodied, sinuous, with a fine bead of acid giving length. Barrel fermented/aged.

Rex Equus Cabernet Sauvignon ★★★★ Vineyard selection, shifts cellar's trademark drinkability into another class, as all these. Last-tasted **07** had cedar-dusted full-ripe plums. **Rex Equus Shiraz** ★★★★ Scented with Belgian chocolate & venison carpaccio, still-available **07** too appealing to age. Discontinued: **Rex Equus Sauvignon Blanc**.

Reserve range

★★★★ **Pinotage ✓ ▤ ▨** From old bushvines. Fruit just one of **10**'s attractions: crushed berry vibrancy supported by balanced oaking for spicing, structure, length and 3-4 years ageing.

★★★★ **Chenin Blanc ✓ ▤ ▨** Perfect balance of fruit, oak & acidity in **10**; tropical fruit & shortbread, with an intriguing edge of ginger.

★★★★ **Sauvignon Blanc ✓ ▤ ▨** Nice contrasts in **10**, tropical aromas reflect ripeness but sauvignon leafiness is not sacrificed, comes through in the flavours, acid-spiked finish.

★★★★ **Chardonnay-Viognier** ✓ 🍷 🏵 Peach with a nutty overlay, **10** loses none of this blend's trademark boldness nor tangy taste appeal. Just off-dry. Year in barrels, third new.

★★★★ **Méthode Cap Classique Brut** NEW ✓ Classy bottle-fermented bubbly from chardonnay, **09** makes an admirable debut. Citrus zest & brioche perfume, flavours & an extended, vibrant finish.

★★★★☆ **Weisser Riesling** NEW ✓🏵 Natural Sweet with a touch of oak, gorgeous **10** is a powerhouse of flavours. Pure pineapple essence, tangy & irresistible. Full sweetness (133g/l) tempered by limy acidity, giving ultra-long finish. From Durbanville grapes. In 500ml.

Shiraz ✓ ★★★★ Black plums, campfire smoke, dried herbs, **09** ticks all the boxes, including soft, full-bodied appeal. To enjoy, not age. Discontinued: **Chenin Blanc-Sauvignon Blanc-Semillon**.

Simply Delicious range

Cabernet Sauvignon ☺🍷🏵 ★★★ Juicy, lively **10** is packed with berries, oak savouriness adds more interest. Enjoy rather than age. **Merlot** ☺🍷🏵 ★★★ Plush berries, lovely fleshy roundness to **10**, lightly oaked, as rest of these reds, & designed to please. **Shiraz** ☺🍷🏵 ★★★ Smoky hedgerow berries, soft luscious texture, **10** is oh so easy to drink.

Pinotage 🍷🏵 ★★★ Trademark blueberries in a juicy package, **10** has a firm backbone, dry finish, good match for rich dishes. **Cabernet Sauvignon-Merlot** 🍷🏵 ★★★ **10** savoury overlay to fruit, juiciness offsets tannins. **Rosé** 🍷 ★★★ Last was strawberry-scented **09**, crisp & dry. **Chenin Blanc** 🍷🏵 ★★★ Passionfruit & apple in **11**, crisp, lively freshness. **Sauvignon Blanc** 🍷🏵 ★★★ Minerality abounds in **11**, clean & focused, no pretensions. **Soft Smooth Red** 🍷🏵 ★★★ **10** berry compote from 3-way mix. Off-dry, lightly oaked. This range previously listed as 'Value for Money'. — CR

Peter Bayly Wines

Location: Calitzdorp ▪ Map: Klein Karoo & Garden Route ▪ WO: Klein Karoo ▪ Est 2002 ▪ 1stB 2004 ▪ Tasting, sales & tours by appt ▪ Owner(s) Peter & Yvonne Bayly ▪ Winemaker(s)/viticulturist(s) Peter Bayly ▪ 6.6ha/1.2ha (tinta, touriga, souzão) ▪ ±8t/±660cs own label ▪ PO Box 187 Calitzdorp 6660 ▪ info@baylys.co.za ▪ S 33° 29'43.2" E 021° 41'56.0" ▪ **T +27 (0)44-213-3702** ▪ F +27 (0)86-513-2727

A favourable response to the maiden vintage (2009) of Peter Bayly III, their unfortified blend of Portuguese varieties, has spurred Calitzdorp boutique vintners Peter and Yvonne Bayly to increase production. This will happen on solar power and without recourse to the national grid; a water-driven turbine generator in the river is being considered for top-up.

Peter Bayly range

★★★★ **Cape Vintage Port** Touriga, tinta & souzão, foot-trodden by family & friends. Accessible **07** still selling, last year was rich & opulent but not too sweet, showed good maturation potential.

III ★★★ Rustic charmer from old-oak-matured touriga with dashes tinta & souzão. **10** ultra ripe & dark, suffused with chocolate flavour. **Cape White Port** ★★ Still available **NV** dry & fiery sipper from chenin, with sherry-like apple notes. — Panel

Peter Falke Wines

Location/map/WO: Stellenbosch ▪ 1stB 2003 ▪ Tasting & sales Tue-Sun 11-7 Mon by appt ▪ Fee R40 ▪ Closed Easter Fri, Dec 25/26 & Jan 1 ▪ Cellar tours by appt 11-4 ▪ Cheese platters & refreshments ▪ Owner(s) Franz-Peter Falke ▪ Winemaker(s) Tertius Naudé (Aug 2005) ▪ Viticulturist(s) Werner Schrenk (Jan 2009) ▪ 20ha/±6ha (cab, shiraz) ▪ 100t/6,000cs own label 65% red 25% white 10% rosé ▪ PO Box 12605 Stellenbosch 7599 ▪ info@ peterfalkewines.co.za ▪ www.peterfalkewines.co.za ▪ S 34° 0'2.1" E 018° 50'19.3" ▪ **T +27 (0)21-881-3677** ▪ F +27 (0)21-881-3667

Owned by Germany-based sports-footwear king Franz-Peter Falke, this small property is still buying in grapes for the wine range but replanting of the old uprooted vineyards with cab and shiraz has taken place. In the pipeline is a pinot noir and méthode cap classique sparkling. Boasting one of the most original and modern tasting rooms in the winelands, set in the Cape Dutch homestead, it was created to incorporate all five senses, sight, sound, touch, smell and taste.

Signature range

★★★★ **The Blend** Name change from 'Red'. Cab franc & merlot domination gives **08** fleshy succulence, nice grassy tones to the berry mix. Careful oaking, 50% new, has smooth, supple effect.

Syrah ★★★★ New World style, intensely fruity, luscious, with smooth drinkability. Tannins in **07** are a well-covered backbone. **Sauvignon Blanc** ★★★★ Unusually, fermented in new oak (including 20% acacia!) with natural yeasts. From barrel, **10** has savoury oatmeal overlay, brisk acidity. Discontinued: **Cabernet Sauvignon**.

PF range

Cabernet Sauvignon ★★★ Dusty blackcurrants lead you in but **08**'s tannins still brusque, need year or two to integrate, soften. **Blanc de Noir** Current **11** untasted. **Sauvignon Blanc** ★★★ Crunchy pears & lime, **10** is an ideal summer wine, offers crisply dry enjoyment. — CR

■ **Peter Veldsman** see Asara Wine Estate & Hotel
■ **Petit** see Ken Forrester Wines

Pfeifer's Boutique Wines

Location: Somerset West ▪ Map: Helderberg ▪ Est 2000 ▪ 1stB 2003 ▪ Tasting & sales by appt ▪ Closed Easter Fri/Sun, Dec 25 & Jan 1 ▪ Owner(s) René Hans & Maya Pfeifer ▪ Winemaker(s)/viticulturist(s) Pascal Pfeifer (Jun 2006) ▪ 1.675ha/1.4ha (shiraz) ▪ 14–16t/±75cs own label 100% red ▪ IPW member ▪ PO Box 5238 Helderberg 7135 ▪ enquiries@pfeifersvineyard.co.za ▪ www.pfeifersvineyard.co.za ▪ S 34° 01' 10.98" E 018° 47' 17.06" ▪ **T +27 (0)21-842-3396** ▪ F +27 (0)21-842-3396

Only a tiny portion of this considerable IPW-certified farm is given over to grapes, and a minuscule portion of those is chanelled into the the Caelum (heavenly) Syrah. Most of the fruit is sold off to other wine producers, some in the immediate area, others as far away as Greyton and Cape Agulhas.

Pfeifer's Boutique Wines range

Caelum Syrah ★★★ Last-tasted **07** had strict tannins but lively fruit. Discontinued: **Que Syrah**. — AL

■ **Phambili** see Wellington Wines
■ **Philip Jonker** see Weltevrede Estate

Philip Jordaan Wines

WO: Western Cape ▪ Est/1stB 1998 ▪ Wine orders taken by The Wine Call Centre, Paarl T 086-174-4447 F 021-870-1139 ▪ Tasting & tours by appt at Hex River Crossing T 023-354-8708 or email leon@vinpro.co.za ▪ Owner(s) Philip Jordaan & Leon Dippenaar ▪ Cellarmaster(s)/winemaker(s) Philip Jordaan ▪ Viticulturist(s) Leon Dippenaar ▪ PO Box 7198 Noorder Paarl 7623 / PO Box 1 Hex River 6855 ▪ daneel@wineorders.co.za ▪ www.auctioncrossing.co.za ▪ **T +27 (0)86-174-4447 / +27 (0)23-354-8708** ▪ F +27 (0)21-870-1139 / +27 (0)23-354-8604

With recent cabernet franc vintages ageing in barrel, and the current release selling out fast, the sauvignon is likely to be the only wine available for much of this year. This recurring dearth has stimulated Philip Jordaan's thoughts of extending his range – in partnership with Hex River Crossing Cellar.

Limited Edition Cabernet Franc ★★★★ Elegant, supple & mature **06** with savoury, lean red fruit. Frequent Wine of the Month Club 'Most unusual red' choice. **Sauvignon Blanc** 📖 ★★★ Stylishly packaged, **10** tasted last year was fresh, fruity summer sipper with pleasantly stony finish. — IM

Phizante Kraal

Location/WO: Durbanville ▪ Map: Durbanville, Philadelphia & Darling ▪ 1stB 2005 ▪ Tasting & sales Mon-Fri 9-4 Sat 10-2 ▪ Fee R15 ▪ Farm produce ▪ Owner(s) André & Ronelle Brink ▪ Winemaker(s) André Brink (Jan 2005, Diemersdal) ▪ Viticulturist(s) André Brink ▪ 50ha (cab, shiraz, chenin, sauv) ▪ 1,000cs own label ▪ PO Box 8 Durbanville 7551 ▪ ronelle@phesantekraal.co.za ▪ www.phizantekraal.co.za ▪ S 33° 47' 7.66" E 018° 40' 15.6" ▪ **T +27 (0)21-976-2114** ▪ F +27 (0)21-976-2113

Dating back to 1698 and in the family since 1897, this historic farm's grapes were sold off until André and Ronelle Brink's passion to make their own wine overwhelmed them. 'But we still only bottle 10% of the harvest under our own name, giving our wines a feeling of exclusivity because they aren't available everywhere.'

Diemersdal's Thys Louw makes them: 'Our families have been friends for many generations and he was therefore the obvious choice.'

★★★★ **Sauvignon Blanc** ✓ 🍷 Pungent **11** waves Durbanville flag with dusty, gooseberry & herbal nuances; good concentration & lengthy flavour.

Cabernet Sauvignon ★★★ Cheery **08** berries & spice, tad rustic & fleeting. **Shiraz** ★★★★ **08** very appealing special occasion sipper with rich, vibrant red fruit, harmonious oak touches. — Panel

PicardiRebel

Est 1994 ▪ PO Box 1868 Cape Town 8000 ▪ **T** +27 (0)21-469-3300 ▪ **F** +27 (0)21-469-3434

Drinks retail chain Picardi Rebel's Colin Frith says the situation this year is much as last – consumers are still forsaking big-name wine brands for value-for-money, like Picardi's house ranges Hippo Creek, Naked Truth and Coast Merlot. With big estates releasing stock in search of much-needed liquidity, there' plenty to choose from. Focused in-store activity is helping consumers navigate the less familiar territory.

Pick 'n Pay

WO: Swartland ▪ Enquiries Neil Cooke ▪ Pick n Pay Corporate Brands PO Box 908 Bedfordview 2008 ▪ ncooke@ pnp.co.za ▪ www.picknpay.co.za ▪ **T** +27 (0)11-856-7000 ▪ **F** +27 (0)86-616-5949

Last year, this national retail chain of supermarkets launched a range of bottled house wines, developed by senior buyer Neil Cooke and Suzanne van Dyk, brand development manager at Swartland Winery. Pitched as an 'everyday, well-priced quality range offering great value for money', it encompasses nine popular styles, and complements the 'No Name' house range from Robertson Winery.

Pick 'n Pay range NEW

Cabernet Sauvignon ☺ 🍷 📖 ★★★ **10** for early enjoyment, soft & rounded blackcurrant fruit flavours. **Pinotage** ☺ 🍷 📖 ★★★ Variety's typical banana & strawberry, **10** juicy & satisfying, enough substance to match braaied meats. **Chardonnay** ☺ 🍷 📖 ★★★ Tropical & citrus-toned **11** is fruity & medium bodied, lightly oaked for easy/early enjoyment. **Chenin Blanc** ☺ 🍷 📖 ★★★ Spicy **11** bursts with flavour, brisk & dry for summertime sipping. From Swartland Winery, as all the range.

Merlot 🍷 📖 ★★ **10** jammy & sweetish. **Shiraz** 🍷 📖 ★★★ **10**'s tart red berry acidity enlivens its sweet ripeness. **Rosé** 🍷 ★★ Light, sweet berry-fruited **NV** pink from pinotage. **Sauvignon Blanc** 🍷 📖 ★★★ Lunchtime companion **11** brisk, engaging capsicum & grass mouthful. **Late Harvest** 🍷 ★★★ Chenin & colombard in equal **NV** partnership. Faint floral notes, pleasantly sweetish tail.

No Name range

Dry Red ★★ Berry-toned everyday red, lightly chill in summer for extra enjoyment. **NV**. Available in various boxed formats, as for all below. **Semi-Sweet Rosé** ★★ Colombard, chenin & ruby cab in gently sweet **NV** combo. **Dry White** ★★ Trio white varieties deliver unpretentious, zesty enjoyment. **NV. Extra Light Dry White** ★ Low-alc colombard/chenin mix, **NV**, with faint guava whiffs. **Selected Stein** ★★ Semi-sweet & light (10.5% alc) **NV** al fresco companion. **Johannisberger White** ★★ Spice highlights on light, sweet grapey **NV** quick-sip. **Late Harvest** ★★ Uncomplicated, light picnic stalwart. **NV** colombard & chenin. **Johannisberger Red** ★ Light juicy appeal, slight tannic tug courtesy ruby cab. **NV**. All these from Robertson Winery. — Panel

Pick's Pick

WO: Stellenbosch/Western Cape/Elgin ▪ Owner(s) Alan Pick ▪ Shop 30 Nelson Mandela Square Sandton 2196 ▪ thebuttershop@mweb.co.za ▪ **T** +27 (0)11-784-8676/7 ▪ **F** +27 (0)11-784-8674

Owner Alan Pick keeps adding to this range, only using wines from his winemaker friends and all designed to match the food at Butcher Shop & Grill in Sandton. Competitively priced in these economic times and available for takeaway sale from the cellar, this exclusive range is offered in addition to an extensive winelist. Alan knows how to keep the patrons happy.

★★★★ **Cabernet Sauvignon** Rich blackcurrant & cigarbox styling on last-tasted **09**, Diemersdal's textbook cab. Celebrated fruit, had verve & juiciness, enough tannin grip for definition, few years cellaring.

★★★★ **Merlot** 🗄 Mocha chocolate, plummy notes in **08** (★★★★) ex Jordan, but sterner, more savoury than **07**; developing, not for keeping. 18 months French barriques, 80% new.

★★★★☆ **Pinotage 09** from Beyerskloof is typically expressive & forthright, showing vintage's sublime ripeness, high-toned wild berry fruit & boldly full body.

★★★★ **Cabernet Sauvignon-Shiraz-Merlot** 🗄 **10**'s savoury tone inherently food compatible, so this polished, juicy red from Guardian Peak is a good choice by the restaurant. Easy solo drinker, too, thanks to not-quite-dry styling. WO W Cape.

★★★★ **Sauvignon Blanc** 🗄 🍇 Lemongrass & crushed fig leaves, Jordan's **11** tank sample has less vibrancy, tension than thrilling **10** (★★★★★) but remains sleekly delicious.

★★★★ **Late Bottled Vintage** Last-tried **02** from leading port house JP Bredell had ripe, accessible fruit, measured structure, long spicy finish.

Cabernet Sauvignon NEW ★★★★ Red berries & a grassy note, befitting Paul Cluver's Elgin terroir, nicely rounded **09** has a serious side, enough tannin to age. **Protea Merlot** ★★★★ Previously dark choc perfume on **08** gave way to palate's berries, freshness, good tannin grip for food. Ex Rupert Wines, as for other Protea. **Shiraz** 🗄 ★★★★ **10** 2nd Guardian Peak red in line-up. Seductive vanilla & clove, full body & velvet texture courtesy of a little bit of sugar. **Shiraz** NEW 🗄 ★★★★ **07**, with dash mourvèdre, juicy red & black fruit, a grind of pepper, fresh & soft mouthful. By Zevenwacht. **Syrah-Mourvèdre-Viognier** 🗄 ★★★★ Fruit the hero in last-tasted **08** from Boekenhoutskloof. Plum coulis intensity, depth & succulence, smoky, spicy notes. **The Blend** NEW 🗄 ★★★★ Neil Ellis'**09** cab/shiraz blend (dash other varieties) is smoky, tasty & generous, with smoothly succulent dark fruit. WO W Cape. **Rosé** NEW 🗄 🍇 ★★★ Merlot blend ex Jordan, **11** sample is cranberry scented, light textured & zesty. Works both as an aperitif & with food. **Chardonnay** 🗄 ★★★ Lees-ageing adds richness to white peach, citrus flavours on stylish **10** from The Winery of Good Hope. Has sufficient zesty acidity, minerality to deliver mealtime satisfaction. **Protea Sauvignon Blanc** ★★★★ Last time, zesty tropical & gooseberry tones & a mineral flick in **09**'s tail reflected 2 fruit sources, one cooler. **Cape White Blend** 🗄 ★★★★ Last **09** chenin-viognier-chardonnay by Teddy Hall had intriguing perfume, flavours: olive oil, jasmine woven through appley fruit. Portion oaked. More delicious than **06** (★★★★). — CR

■ **PieQue Select Wines** see Linton Park Wines
■ **Pierneef Collection** see La Motte
■ **Pierre Jourdan** see Haute Cabrière
■ **Pikkewyn** see Groupe LFE South Africa
■ **Pinecrest/Pinehurst** see Môreson
■ **PK Morkel** see Bellevue Estate Stellenbosch

Place in the Sun   NEW

Location: Stellenbosch ▪ WO: Stellenbosch/Western Cape ▪ Est/1stB 2010 ▪ Closed to public ▪ Owner(s) Distell ▪ Cellarmaster(s)/winemaker(s) Deon Boshoff (2010) ▪ Viticulturist(s) Annelie Viljoen (2010) ▪ 1,000t ▪ ISO 9001 & ISO 14001 (pending), Fairtrade, IPW ▪ PO Box 184 Stellenbosch 7599 ▪ dboshoff@distell.co.za ▪ www.placeinthesun.co.za ▪ T +27 (0)21-809-7000

For winemaker Deon Boshoff, this new range from wine giant Distell brings his career full circle. The son of farmworkers, he received a scholarship to study winemaking, and now this Fairtrade label ensures that money is channelled back into community projects and bursaries similar to the one which gave him his start. Deon believes that empowered workers produce superior grapes, and says his aim is to make affordable wines enjoyable by all.

Cabernet Sauvignon 🗄 🍇 ★★★ Shows something of variety's sterner side in food-styled **10**. **Merlot** 🗄 🍇 ★★ Intense mocha aromas & perky acidity on **10** informal occasions red. **Shiraz** 🗄 🍇 ★★★ Full-flavoured, ripe, ultra-juicy **10** is disconcertingly easy to drink! **Sauvignon Blanc** 🗄 🍇 ★★★ Fresh, fruity **11** nicely flavoured & balanced for summer sipping. W Cape WO. — Panel

Plaisir de Merle

Location: Paarl ▪ Map: Franschhoek ▪ WO: Simonsberg-Paarl/Western Cape ▪ Est 1993 ▪ 1stB 1994 ▪ Tasting, sales & cellar tours Mon-Fri 9-5 Sat 10-4 (Nov-Mar) & 10-2 (Apr-Oct) Sun by special request for groups of 15+ ▪ Fee R20 std tasting/R50 flavour sensation: fudge-exclusive & blind tasting ▪ Closed Easter Fri/Sun & Dec 25 ▪ Croissant & cold meat platter with glass of wine R65, available during trading hours ▪ Facilities for children ▪ Gifts ▪ Conservation area ▪ Manor House (sleeps 8) can be booked for functions, conferences & weddings ▪ Owner(s) Distell ▪

Cellarmaster(s) Niel Bester (1993) ▪ Viticulturist(s) Hannes van Rensburg & Freddie le Roux (both 1993) ▪ 974ha/
400ha (cabs s/f, malbec, merlot, p verdot, shiraz, chard, sauv) ▪ 800t/40,000cs own label 80% red 20% white ▪
ISO 9001:2008, ISO 14001:2004, BRC, BWI, SGS ▪ PO Box 121 Simondium 7670 ▪ plaisirdemerle@capelegends.
co.za ▪ www.plaisirdemerle.co.za ▪ S 33° 51' 0.0" E 018° 56' 36.2" ▪ **T +27 (0)21-874-1071** ▪ F +27 (0)21-
874-1689

The idea shocked guests at the opening of the new cellar on 1st December 1993, but
once they'd tasted the infant 1993 Cabernet Sauvignon, all agreed how drinkable it
was. From the start, the goal of winemaker Neil Bester and the then-consultant,
Château Margaux director Paul Pontallier, was 'a top quality red of power and softness, with drinkability yet depth'. After all these years, Bester is still in charge, having successfully honed the whole range in this style.

★★★★ **Cabernet Sauvignon** The original drinkable-on-release cab (**93**) remains true to type with **08**.
Splashes merlot, shiraz, petit verdot expand aromatics, increase flesh. Winningly fresh & delicious.

★★★★☆ **Cabernet Franc** From a single vineyard, spicy, fragrant & leafy **07** is supple & rich. New-oaked,
savoury **06** also available, but **08** sold out. No **09**.

★★★★ **Malbec** Less overt than many, **08** last year had sweet fruit, soft tannins, richly balance. No **09**.

★★★★ **Shiraz** Rather more noticeable than usual oak (some American) on **09**, otherwise shows usual affable light touch, spice, red fruit purity with poised, savoury length.

★★★★ **Grand Plaisir** When **07** reviewed mid-2010 we noted powerful new-oak aromas, forceful, well-
fuited palate, slightly drying end. Cab-led sextet; 15% shiraz plus Bordeaux varieties.

★★★★ **Chardonnay** ✓ Satisfyingly familiar lime lightly brushed with toasty oak greet on **10**. Lively but
with sufficient balancing substance. Well judged from lesser vintage.

★★★★ **Sauvignon Blanc** 🗐 🕮 Introductory sauvage aromas gain elegance, sophistication from gentle,
leesy breadth on **11**. Focused, pure with concluding flourish of vitality adding delicious length. WO W Cape.

Merlot ★★★★ Pleasant crushed velvet texture, integrated tannins, oak enhance overall harmony on **09**. Fruit,
though ripe, needs 2/3 yrs to fully blossom. — AL

■ **Poker Hill** *see* Somersbosch Wines
■ **Polkadraai Road** *see* Beau Joubert Vineyards & Winery
■ **Polo Club** *see* Val de Vie Wines

Pongrácz

SA's highest volume bottle-fermented range has driven the marketing of this category locally, paying fitting homage to aristocratic Hungarian army officer
Desiderius Pongracz, who was for many years Bergkelder's viticulturist. Its mandate
to deliver thousands of pallets of easy, reliable, MCC to African markets is only made
possible by parent Distell's distribution strengths.

Desiderius ★★★★ Persistent, harmonious & fresh **03** MCCsteps-up in quality from **02** (★★★☆), showing
yeasty complexity & creamy texture. Delivers what standard Brut did a decade ago. 60:40 blend chardonnay,
pinot; next 2 reverse these proportions. **Pongrácz Brut** ★★★ Popular NV blend a usefully reliable MCC. Offers
sweetly pleasant fruity entry, which is quick to fade. **Rosé** ★★★ Strawberry pink NV MCC fresh with pleasantly
frothy mousse & slightly stern, brisk finish. These last two also in 375ml bottles. — IM

■ **Porcelain Mountain** *see* Porseleinberg
■ **Porcupine Ridge** *see* Boekenhoutskloof Winery

Porseleinberg   🔖 NEW

Location: Malmesbury ▪ WO: Swartland ▪ Est 2009 ▪ 1stB 2011 ▪ Closed to public ▪ Owner(s) Boekenhoutskloof
Winery Pty Ltd ▪ Winemaker(s)/viticulturist(s) Callie Louw (Jun 2009) ▪ 85ha/15ha (shiraz) ▪ 6t/300cs own label
100% red ▪ Organic EU Control Union ▪ PO Box 433 Franschhoek 7690 ▪ callie@porcelainmountain.com ▪ **T +27
(0)79-884-2309** ▪ F +27 (0)86-566-9332

Callie Louw has free rein in these (now) Boekenhoutskloof-owned vineyards, where
star winemaker Eben Sadie famously sourced grapes for his first Columella. Inspired
by biodynamic Frenchman Gérard Gauby, Callie says: 'The main focus is to make the
wine in the vineyard. We farm organically and have plans in place to make the farm
a sustainable unit.' In an old (insulated) shed, whole grape bunches are simply given

'a light foot stomp' and 'a bit of sulphur'. Judging from the promising debut below, less really *is* more.

★★★★ **Porseleinberg** ❀ 100% shiraz, superb **10** mid-2011 is a velvet hand in an iron glove: beautifully ripe, lavender scented fruit tightly gripped by fine, dry tannin, demanding patience or vigorous aeration. — Panel

■ **Porter Mill Station** see Tulbagh Winery
■ **Porterville Cellars** see Tulbagh Winery

Post House Vineyards

Location: Somerset West ▪ Map: Helderberg ▪ WO: Stellenbosch ▪ Est/1stB 1997 ▪ Tasting, sales & cellar tours Mon-Fri 9-5 Sat 9.30-12.30 ▪ Fee R25 ▪ Closed all pub hols ▪ BYO picnic ▪ Guesthouse ▪ Owner(s) Nicholas Gebers ▪ Cellarmaster(s) Nick Gebers ▪ Winemaker(s) Nick Gebers, with Pippa Orpen ▪ 70ha/39ha (cab, merlot, p verdot, ptage, shiraz, chenin, sauv) ▪ 200t/8,000cs own label 65% red 35% white ▪ PO Box 5635 Helderberg 7135 ▪ info@posthousewines.co.za ▪ www.posthousewines.co.za ▪ S 34° 1'8.1" E 018° 48'41.6" ▪ **T +27 (0)21-842-2409** ▪ F +27 (0)21-842-2409

It's been a time of consolidation, says Nick Gebers, owner/winemaker at this Helderberg property. 'After introducing four labels over the last few years, we have focused on growing the current labels and improving the quality of the wine through better vineyard management.' But the future has not been neglected, he adds: 'Extensions to the winery are still planned, for a new production room.'

★★★★☆ **Cabernet Sauvignon** ✓ Full-bodied **08** (★★★★) less impressive than **07**; with cassis, cigarbox & earthy herbal notes, firm dry grip. Still tight, needs time to show true potential.

★★★★ **Merlot** ✓ **08** much like previous: with plentiful raspberry, fynbos & mint choc. Full & balanced, elegant, with rich savoury conclusion. For the long haul.

★★★★ **Shiraz** ✓ Rich & powerful black berry, spice & floral tones, balanced **08** has firm grip, with a lingering warm, savoury end. A keeper, but a tad off **07** (★★★★★).

★★★★ **Missing Virgin** Powerful (15.5% alc) blend pinotage & petit verdot. **09** shows seductive dark sweet plums, spice. Noticable grip on warm conclusion suggests it needs time to mellow.

★★★★☆ **Penny Black** ✓ Floral notes, spice-cake & fynbos abound on powerful **08** blend led by shiraz & merlot. Mouthfilling, concentrated dark fruit leads to solid finish lifted by touch of chenin. Should improve for 8+yrs. For a hearty meat dish.

★★★★☆ **Chenin Blanc** ✓ Multi-dimensional, rich & toasty, with tropical fruit, citrus & crème caramel flavours on **10** as on previous. Dense & concentrated fruit supported by sweet vanilla oak, extra complexity from lees-ageing. Should reward ageing 5+ yrs.

★★★★☆ **Treskilling Yellow** Thrilling **08** NLH from chenin tasted last year. Rich peach, apricot & spice in full harmony, before bright zesty tail leaves lingering richness.

Blueish White ☺ ★★★ **10** blends sauvignon & chenin blend for early enjoyment; upfront tropical, citrus & grassy aromas; dry tangy finish.

Blueish Black ✓ ★★★★ Dependable shiraz- & pinotage-led **09** blend delights as usual with blackberries, spice & floral notes, friendly tannins. **Sauvignon Blanc** ★★★★ **09** pungent green fruit & gooseberry, good acid structure, mineral undertone. Tasted last edition. — WB

■ **Pride of Africa** see Groupe LFE South Africa
■ **Princess** see Alluvia Winery & Private Residence Club
■ **Private Collection** see Saxenburg

Prospect1870

Location: Ashton ▪ Est 1990 ▪ 1stB 1998 ▪ Closed to public (tasting at The Wine Boutique, Main Rd, Ashton) ▪ Owner(s) De Wet Family ▪ Winemaker(s) Chris de Wet ▪ 35ha (cab, merlot, ptage, shiraz, chard, sauv, viog) ▪ 500cs ▪ PO Box 141 Ashton 6715 ▪ chris@prospectvineyards.co.za ▪ www.prospectwines.co.za ▪ **T +27 (0)82-878-2884** ▪ F +27 (0)86-513-1999

Chris de Wet, vinifying limited quantities from grapes sharing space with fruit on the Ashton family farm, has released his first white, a 2011 viognier. This variety also features (with shiraz) in the 2010 Leatherwood blend, released at the end of last year along with the 2010 Cab. A promising 2010 Prospect 'estate blend' will be bottled this year.

Prospect1870 range

★★★★ **Prospect** Classy **06** was succeeded by **NV** (★★★). Rich, purposeful 15% alc kick, 21 mths Fr oak, 100% new. Not revisited.

Leatherwood range

Cabernet Sauvignon Latest vintages of this, **Shiraz-Viognier** & **Viognier**, not ready at press time. —Panel

■ **Protea** see Anthonij Rupert Wines
■ **Provenance** see Saronsberg
■ **Provin** see Douglas Wine Cellar
■ **Provoyeur** see Bellevue Estate Stellenbosch

Pulpit Rock Winery

Location: Riebeek West ▪ Map/WO: Swartland ▪ Est 2003 ▪ 1stB 2004 ▪ Tasting & sales Mon-Fri 8.30–5 Sat 10–2 ▪ Closed Easter Fri-Sun, Dec 25/26 & Jan 1 ▪ Cellar tours by appt ▪ BYO picnic ▪ Walking/hiking & mountain biking trails ▪ Annual olive festival (May) ▪ Restaurant T +27 (0)22-461-2030 ▪ Self-catering accommodation ▪ Owner(s) Brinkshof Wines (Pty) Ltd ▪ Winemaker(s) Jaco van der Merwe (Oct 2008) ▪ Viticulturist(s) Marco Roux (Dec 2008, consultant) ▪ 600ha/450ha (ptage, shiraz, chard, chenin) ▪ 650t/15,000cs own label 70% red 29% white 1% rosé + 200,000L bulk ▪ Other export brand: Cape Tranquility ▪ PO Box 1 Riebeek West 7306 ▪ info@ pulpitrock.co.za ▪ www.pulpitrock.co.za ▪ S 33° 20'47.4" E 018° 51'14.1" ▪ **T +27 (0)22-461-2025** ▪ F +27 (0)22-461-2028

The Brink family have been farming in the Riebeek West area for decades and currently oversee a huge 400ha of vineyard. Own-label wine however is a fairly recent development, a 1000-ton capacity cellar coming on line in time for the 2004 harvest. Wine, after all, is an advertisement for 'country, region and town'.

Reserve range NEW

★★★★ **Pinotage** ✓ Well put together **09** shows red fruit, vanilla, spice: medium bodied but good flavour intensity before long, dry finish. 16 months in French oak, 80% new.

★★★★ **Chardonnay** ✓ Pure & focused **09**, citrus, peach, vanilla & spice; medium body with good fruit definition, well-judged oak, bright acidity.

Cabernet Sauvignon ★★★ Pleasant, undemanding **09** is medium bodied with plenty of red & black fruit, fine tannins. **Merlot** ★★★ **09** juicy dark fruit, fresh acidity, pleasing tannic grip makes for well-balanced, appealing proposition. **Shiraz** ★★★ **09** has dark fruit, fresh acidity, fine tannins but doesn't shout the variety.

Premium range

Cabernet Sauvignon ★★★★ **05** showed rich plum-like fruit, firm tannins, offered good future when tasted previously. **3PR** ★★★ Simple but comforting fortified **08** from pinotage had baked red fruit, soft acidity & little tannic grip last edition. Discontinued: **Merlot, Pinotage, Shiraz, Chardonnay**.

Brink Family range

Chardonnay ☺ 🍷 📖 ★★★ **11** immensely likeable, with oodles of citrus & peach, bright acidity.

Cabernet Sauvignon ★★★ Clean dark fruit on well-made but light-bodied, straightforward **09**. **Merlot** ★★ **10** is earthy, tart, puckering. **Pinotage** ★★★ Uncomplicated **08** showed dark cherry, bright acidity, firm tannins last edition. **Shiraz** ★★★ Red & black fruit on **09**. No great complexity but well balanced, appealing. **Rosé** NEW 📖 🍷 ★★ Very ripe **NV** (**11**) from pinotage is overtly sweet, lacks nuance. **Chenin Blanc** 📖 🍷 ★★★ Rustic **11** has peach flavour of previous but misses its zing, smooth drinkability. Discontinued: **Sauvignon Blanc**. —CE

■ **Pure African** see Bellevue Estate Stellenbosch

Quando Vineyards & Winery

Location: Bonnievale ▪ Map/WO: Robertson ▪ Est/1stB 2001 ▪ Tasting & sales by appt ▪ Closed all pub hols ▪ Owner(s) F M Bruwer cc ▪ Cellarmaster(s)/winemaker(s) Fanus Bruwer (Jan 1991) ▪ Viticulturist(s) Martin Bruwer (Jan 1991) ▪ 190ha/80ha (chenin, sauv) ▪ 2,500cs own label 10% red 90% white ▪ PO Box 82 Bonnievale 6730 ▪ info@quando.co.za ▪ www.quando.co.za ▪ S 33° 56'9.6" E 020° 1'28.8" ▪ **T +27 (0)23-616-2752** ▪ F +27 (0)23-616-2752

As Robertson boutique label Quando enters its 2nd decade, owners and brothers Fanus and Martin Bruwer are more convinced than ever that wine is made in the vineyard: 'We are just fermentation jockeys in the cellar.' Hence thoroughly researched new sites, new clones and – after a 'viticultural holiday' to New Zealand – new pruning techniques.

★★★★ **Sauvignon Blanc** 🍃 📖 Faint grass whiffs on green, mineral **11** (★★★), lovely weight on the palate but somewhat less fruit-filled & engaging than **10**.

★★★★ **Chenin Blanc-Viognier** ✓ 📖 📖 Creative & delicious unwooded **11** gets spicy pineapple, thatch & vibrant freshness from chenin (ex 30 year old vines), opulence from 23% viognier, & weight from lees-ageing.

Pinot Noir 📖 ★★ Soft red-berry-fruited **09** still selling. — Panel

■ **Queen** *see Alluvia Winery & Private Residence Club*

Quest Wines

Location: Worcester ▪ WO: Western Cape ▪ Est 2006 ▪ 1stB 2010 ▪ Closed to public ▪ Owner(s) Anja van Rijswijk & Hendrik Myburgh ▪ Cellarmaster(s)/winemaker(s) Hendrik Myburgh (2006) ▪ 1,000cs own label 100% red ▪ 12 Otto du Plessis Street Worcester 6850 ▪ admin@questwines.co.za ▪ www.questwines.co.za ▪ **T +27 (0)23-342-5856** ▪ F +27 (0)23-342-5856

Co-owner Hendrik Myburgh has transitioned from buying in wine to making it himself, and is delighted with the results. He's now focused on marketing and distributing the 2010 vintage, and improving barrel maturation facilities for the 'promising' 2011 reds. Unexpected demand for his larger-format 3L and 5L 'special occasion wines' means he's (not unhappily) having to bottle on a larger scale.

Cape Roots range

Merlot ☺ 📖 ★★★ Cheerful, light, well-formed **10** picnic sipper with hint of liquorice.

Cabernet Sauvignon 📖 ★★ **10** fruity, uncomplicated & quaffable. — Panel

Quinta do Sul

Location: Calitzdorp ▪ Map: Klein Karoo & Garden Route ▪ WO: Klein Karoo ▪ Est 2005 ▪ 1stB 2008 ▪ Visits by appt ▪ Owner(s) Alwyn & Louw Liebenberg, Beulah Grobbelaar ▪ Cellarmaster(s)/winemaker(s) Alwyn Liebenberg (Jun 2005) ▪ 10ha/2.5ha (tannat, tinta amerela, tinta barocca, tinta roriz, touriga nacional, shiraz, souzão) ▪ 5t/290cs own label ▪ 3 Rawson Street Montagu 6720 ▪ alwyn@thegoosewines.com ▪ www.quintadosul.co.za ▪ **T +27 (0)82-610-2279**

Vinification of the port produced by Alwyn Liebenberg on this small family-owned Calitzdorp farm remains the same: blending from seven grape varieties follows what the vineyard offers in a given season, and fermentation is in shallow, open tanks with the alcohol added bit by bit. What's new is the distribution model: The Goose Wines has taken on Quinta do Sul, now the owner of several awards, including a top spot at last year's Classic Trophy show. 'An accolade for our first vintage!'

★★★★ **Vintage Port** Traditional port grapes plus shiraz, tannat. Very ripe & fruit-sweet **09**, plummy, plump & pliable; more Ruby in style with less spirit attack, tannic grip than Vintage. Delicious & distinctive. — CvZ

Quoin Rock Winery

Location: Stellenbosch/Elim ▪ Map: Stellenbosch ▪ WO: Simonsberg–Stellenbosch/Western Cape/Cape Agulhas ▪ Est 1998 ▪ 1stB 2001 ▪ Stellenbosch: Tasting & sales daily 9–5 ▪ Fee R20 ▪ Closed Easter Fri/Sun, Dec 25/26 & Jan 1 ▪ Cheese platters ▪ Cape Agulhas: Tasting by appt T 028-482-1619 ▪ Owner(s) to be advised ▪ Winemaker(s) Narina Cloete (Jun 2010) ▪ Viticulturist(s) Louis Buys (Dec 2007) ▪ 3,200ha/71ha (cabs s/f, merlot, pinot, shiraz, chard, sauv) ▪ 200t/11,000cs own label 55% red 35% white 7% MCC 3% dessert ▪ PO Box 1193 Stellenbosch 7599 ▪ tasting@quoinrock.co.za ▪ www.quoinrock.com ▪ S 33° 52' 42.5" E 018° 52' 2.3" (Stb) S 34° 31' 42.62" E 019° 49' 57.36" (CA) ▪ **T +27 (0)21-888-4740** ▪ F +27 (0)21-888-4744

Having a range created from such diverse home-owned vineyards could appear schizophrenic but it makes total sense when you taste the wines. Cool-climate intensity in the coast-proximity whites (pinot noir has also been planted there) and warmer fruit expression in the rest: their quality links them. With the exception of

Oculus, named after a design feature in the cellar, the distinctive names are ships which sank off Cape Agulhas, another link back to that area. To possibly come within the currency of the Guide, is the creation of a stage over the stream so that visitors can picnic in the natural amphitheatre overlooking it, while watching live performers. The 'cave', Quoin Rock's second, deeper and medieval-atmosphere cellar will also be opened for functions.

Quoin Rock range

★★★★☆ **Simonsberg Syrah** Last edition youthful **08** was refined, had pure red fruit & violets, with tinge of lovely floral-herbaceous fragrance. Melting but forceful tannins. Deserved 5+ years.

★★★★ **The Centaur** NEW Great care in shiraz-led **09**: whole-berry natural ferment, long skin contact, new oak maturation, result is crimson-hued brambleberries & black pepper, fine-grained tannins. Drink till ±2020.

★★★★ **The Mendi** Previously listed as 'Simonsberg Estate'. Cab & shiraz comprise 80%. Opulent dark fruit in **07**, offset by firm dry tannins, which add a savoury seam to the flavours. One to age 7+ years.

★★★★ **Cape Agulhas Chardonnay** Supremely elegant, with cool-climate styling, **08** shows no ageing, is silky, lime-toned. Year barrel ferment/matured treatment enriches the palate, gives an almond overlay.

★★★★★ **The Nicobar Sauvignon Blanc** Distinctive sauvignon only from best years. Superb **09** (★★★★★) drier than **07**, 25% new oak detectable only in breadth, depth. Exquisite balance, subtle emergent complexity. Natural yeasts.

★★★★ **Cape Agulhas Sauvignon Blanc 09** (★★★★★) last year had splendid balance; more integrated acidity than **07**. Notably green character, but invoked tropical & earthy support for delicious, serious depth.

★★★★ **Simonsberg Oculus** Previously, 15% viognier added texture & subtle peach to the sauvignon of serious, handsome **07**. Was subdued, brooding, acidic; portion new oak more obvious than previously.

★★★★ **Cape Agulhas Cap Classique** Pink-tinged gold of last chardonnay/pinot noir **NV** traditional-method sparling reflected its subtle berry loveliness; fresh, elegant & dry, hinted at promising development.

★★★★ **Simonsberg Vine Dried Sauvignon Blanc** Previously, there was more intensity on splendid, old-gold **09** (★★★★★) than lighter **08**. Rich, big (14.5% alc) & clean, with near-dry marmalade finish.

Merlot ★★★★ Plums & dark berries show **09**'s ripeness, well anchored by youthfully firm tannins. Finishes dry & savoury. WO W Cape. — CR

Raats Family Wines

Location/map: Stellenbosch ▪ WO: Stellenbosch/Coastal ▪ Est/1stB 2000 ▪ Tasting & sales Mon-Fri by appt ▪ Fee R200 (up to 20 pax per tasting) ▪ Closed all pub hols ▪ Owner(s) Bruwer Raats ▪ Cellarmaster(s)/viticulturist(s) Bruwer Raats (Jan 2000) ▪ Winemaker(s) Bruwer Raats (Jan 2000), with Gavin Bruwer Slabbert (Feb 2010) ▪ 25ha (cab f, chenin) ▪ 120t/9,000cs own label 15% red 85% white ▪ PO Box 2068 Stellenbosch 7601 ▪ braats@mweb.co.za ▪ www.raats.co.za ▪ S 33° 58'16.6" E 018° 44'55.3" ▪ **T +27 (0)21-881-3078** ▪ F +27 (0)21-881-3078

Choosing to specialise in chenin and cab franc set winemaker/viticulturist Bruwer Raats on a quest to understand what best suits them - old vines (the oldest is 67 years) and a combination of soils for chenin. The secret of his success with cab franc is that it is only grown on decomposed dolomite granite in his and his suppliers' vineyards. This gives 'a great acidity and freshness to the wine and adds minerality to the finish'. Add to that the unirrigated vines being 18-23 years old and the wine being unfined, unfiltered. Raats bravely and publicly benchmarks his wines against the best in the world (including Bordeaux legend Cheval Blanc).

Raats Family Wines range

★★★★☆ **Cabernet Franc** Tobacco leaf & black cherry, handsome **09** has an intriguing baked earth note & mineral finish adding to its attraction, individuality. Built for a distinguished 8+ year future, youthful tannins are accessible but firm, will integrate over time.

Chenin Blanc 🍴 Await next.

Original range

Red Blend 🍴 ★★★ Revisited cab franc-led **09** is fruit-focused, ripe mulberries supported by fine-grained oak needing a year/2 to soften. **Chenin Blanc** ✓ 🍴 ⬙ ★★★★ From 35+ year old vines. Tropical-toned unoaked **11** has an appealing waxy note, softly rounded body & good drinkability. — CR

▪ **Racetrack** see Damaraklooof
▪ **Radford Dale** see The Winery of Good Hope
▪ **Rainbow Nation Wines** see Catch Of The Day

Rainbow's End Wine Estate

Location/map: Stellenbosch ▪ WO: Banghoek ▪ Est 1978 ▪ 1stB 2002 ▪ Tasting, sales & tours by appt ▪ Fee R25, waived on purchase of 4+ btls ▪ Closed Dec 25 & Jan 1 ▪ Sales also via website, delivery free of charge ▪ BYO picnic ▪ Conservation area ▪ 4x4 trail ▪ Owner(s) Malan family ▪ Cellarmaster(s) Anton Malan (Nov 2000) ▪ Winemaker(s) Anton Malan (Nov 2000) & Francois Malan (Jan 2005) ▪ Viticulturist(s) Francois Malan (Jan 2005) ▪ 52ha/21.6ha (cabs s/f, malbec, merlot, p verdot, shiraz) ▪ 120t/4,100cs own label 90% red 10% rosé ▪ IPW, GlobalGap (CMI) ▪ PO Box 2253 Dennesig 7601 ▪ info@rainbowsend.co.za ▪ www.rainbowsend.co.za ▪ S 33° 56' 25.8" E 018° 56' 42.6" ▪ T +27 (0)21-885-1719/+27 (0)83-411-0170/+27 (0)82-404-1085 ▪ F +27 (0)21-885-1722

Winemaking facilities have been expanded at the Malan family's quiet corner at the very top of the Banghoek Valley. 'Demand has seen production increase from 2300 to 4100 cases,' says son Anton happily. 'Exports to Switzerland and Singapore have taken off. Our Shiraz 2008 won gold at the Wine Style Asia Awards.'

★★★★ **Cabernet Sauvignon** √ ☒ 10's deep cassis & earthy herbal notes mingle with sweet oak flavours, leading to a lively, juicy finish. With firm structure to age. Touch of last-tasted **08** (★★★★☆)

★★★★ **Cabernet Franc** √ ☒ 10 shows full ripeness, with earthy, peppery, cassis & mint choc flavours. Full-bodied with a firm oaky grip & blackberry tang.

★★★★ **Limited Release Cabernet Franc** ☒ Milk choc & bright, fresh cherries on 10. Firmly structured with mouthfilling, juicy fruit & a lingering spicy herbal conclusion. Time should reveal more qualities.

★★★★ **Merlot** √ ☒ 10 is full-bodied with earthy rich plumcake & spice. Ripe & serious with a silky mouthfeel & firm grip as the flavours linger on & on. Will reward a few years in bottle.

★★★★ **Shiraz** √ ☒ 10 from single vineyard is a tad off the pace of **08** (★★★★☆). Inky purple, spicy plum & mulberry; elegant & fresh with a firm finish. A keeper. — WB

Raka

Location: Stanford ▪ Map: Elgin, Walker Bay & Bot River ▪ WO: Klein River/Western Cape/Coastal ▪ Est/1stB 2002 ▪ Tasting & sales Mon–Fri 9–5 Sat 10–3 ▪ Tasting fee: 6 wines on daily tasting list free, other wines R10/wine ▪ Closed Easter Fri & Dec 25 ▪ Cellar tours & large groups by appt ▪ BYO picnic ▪ Conservation area ▪ Owner(s) Piet Dreyer ▪ Winemaker(s) Josef Dreyer (Jan 2007) ▪ Viticulturist(s) Pieter Dreyer (Jan 2007) ▪ 760ha/62ha (5 Bdx, mourv, ptage, sangio, shiraz, sauv, viog) ▪ 350t/15,000cs own label 75% red 17% white 8% rosé ▪ BWI, IPW ▪ PO Box 124 Caledon 7230 ▪ info@rakawine.co.za ▪ www.rakawine.co.za ▪ S 34° 23'56.1" E 019° 37'26.7" ▪ T +27 (0)28-341-0676 ▪ F +27 (0)86-606-5462

Dryer daughter Jorika has returned to the family farm to head up marketing - having an immediate impact by ensuring that Biodiversity & Wine Initiative status was acquired. Raka can celebrate the 10th anniversary of their first bottling proud of what has been achieved. They continue to strive to be abreast of the latest technological advances, while not neglecting tradition. The latter element now enhanced by 20 Hereford cattle to help with weed control in winter. The wines offer good value and quality, and are made in a modern, easy style that keeps customers in numerous countries coming back for more.

★★★★ **Cabernet Sauvignon** 09 still shy, with trademark ripe dark berry fruit, gentle oak overlay leading to lush, juicy palate with good vibrancy & a soft tannin structure.

★★★★ **Malbec** 09 starts very shy (some cellar time wanted?). Fine lavender & sea breeze notes lead to firm but fine tannin structure & good mouthfeel.

★★★★ **Barrel Select Merlot** Oak dominates on 09 (★★★); light on fruit, with a rather lean profile coming across as quite austere. Not as balanced as rich 08.

★★★★ **Mourvèdre** NEW √ Varietal meaty, coriander spice intro on fine debut 09. Palate continues with savoury rather than fruity flavours. Good acidity rounds out complex food-friendly composition.

★★★★☆ **Biography Shiraz** √ 09 continues flagship role, but in more elegant mould, with shy red fruits, white pepper spice & a hint of sea breeze. Cool, fresh palate follows with delicate fine, lingering tannins. Judicious oaking (just 25% new barrels for a year) adds to well-balanced whole.

★★★★ **Figurehead Cape Blend** √ 08 usual recipe of 5 Bordeaux red varieties plus pinotage. Dark fruits, good ripeness leads to complex palate with spice & herbal notes adding interest to soft profile.

Spliced 😊 🍽 ★★★ Friendly tying together of merlot & ruby cab with a strand of cab; **09** has lovely dark fruit, subtle spice with dry & tangy grip. **Rosé** 😊 🍽 ★★★ **10** combo Bordeaux varieties plus shiraz. Complex, fragrant nose with dry, firm & savoury end.

Cabernet Franc ★★★★ **08** last year showed variety's perfume & lithe harmonious palate; more concentration than **07** (★★★★). **Petit Verdot** ✓ ★★★★ Brooding dark cherry & cassis with great fruit purity. **09** more confident than **08** (★★★★). Rich, with complex savoury support & refreshing acidity. **Pinotage** ★★★★ Good oak balance supports ripe perfumed fruit concentration. **10** is slow to open up to compact layers & savoury edge. With some Franschhoek grapes. **Sangiovese** ★★★ Tart cherry, lighter with firm dry tannins; focused **09** has a lingering savoury note begging for food. **Quinary** ★★★★ Herbaceous note with ripe fruit profile on mature **07** five-way Bordeaux blend. **Chenin Blanc** 🍽 ★★★ Citrus & oak aromas seduce on accomplished **10**. Confident & rounded; lovely texture & good balance. Paarl grapes. **Sauvignon Blanc** 🍽 ★★★★ **10**'s shy tropical fruit has fragrant lift; in lighter idiom with soft acidity. Delicate **11** ex-tank even shyer, with poised, subtly textured finish. **Shannonea** 🍽 ★★★★ Food-friendly **09** last year had good mineral grip. WO W Cape. — JP

Rall Wines

Location: Stellenbosch ▪ WO: Swartland/Coastal ▪ Est/1stB 2008 ▪ Tasting, sales & cellar tours by appt ▪ Owner(s)/winemaker(s)/viticulturist(s) Donovan Rall ▪ 10t/500cs own label 50% red 50% white ▪ info@rallwines.co.za ▪ www.rallwines.co.za ▪ **T +27 (0)72-182-7571**

Donovan Rall wishes to produce wines that are truly unique. We think he has certainly achieved this, and even more remarkable is that it has happened so fast - this is only the third vintage of the fine Rall white blend. His constant seeking out of older vineyards, added to his focused approach, should ensure that those who tip him as a real star of the future will not be disappointed.

★★★★ **Rall Red** Tiny production of handcrafted **09** from mostly shiraz with splashes carignan & grenache, ex Swartland. Smartly combines all components to express delicate perfume & fine fruit tannins.

★★★★★ **Rall White 10** (★★★★★) continues excellent track record. Blend of mostly chenin & chard, plus verdelho & viognier (like **09**), off Swartland & Stellenbosch vineyards. Gentle overlay from older oak barrels introduces exotic fruits woven together by acid, with fleshy feel. — JP

▪ **Raoul's** *see* Beaumont Wines
▪ **Ready Steady** *see* Southern Sky Wines
▪ **Rebourne Fairtrade** *see* Imbuko Wines
▪ **Red Gold** *see* Bushmanspad Estate

Red Tape   NEW

Location: Somerset West ▪ WO: Elgin ▪ Est 2007 ▪ 1stB 2008 ▪ Sales by prior arrangement ▪ Owner(s) Tanja Beutler ▪ 250cs own label 100% red ▪ PO Box 804 Somerset Mall 7137 ▪ tanja@hiddengems.co.za ▪ **T +27 (0)21-855-4275** ▪ F +27 (0)86-612-6118

Economic recession is another way of saying 'opportunity' for dynamic wine marketer and garagiste winemaker (at Topaz Wine) Tanja Beutler. Her new brand is a cheeky sideswipe at the myriad rules and regulations dogging everyday life – the intention being that a glass of her merlot will help ease all bureaucratic headaches.

★★★★☆ **Merlot** Classic **09** from Elgin is savoury & elegant with lovely intense heart of red berries. Vibrant & youthful, fine integrated tannin structure. Perfect for food (& easing bureaucratic headaches). — Panel

Reginald James   NEW

Location/WO: Durbanville ▪ Est/1stB 2011 ▪ Closed to public ▪ Owner(s) RJ Botha & Bernhard Veller ▪ Winemaker(s)/viticulturist(s) RJ Botha (Feb 2011) ▪ 3t/140cs own label 100% white ▪ rj@nitida.co.za ▪ **T +27 (0)83-560-3419** ▪ F +27 (0)21-976-1467

Winning Diners Club Young Winemaker of the Year in 2010 was a turning point for Nitida winemaker RJ Botha. It spurred him on to take what will hopefully be the first step on the ladder to solo success by launching his own wine label. RJ is warm in his praise for Nitida owner Bernhard Veller, whom he credits with mentoring him straight out of university, and believes that with his help, he can create a truly world-class brand.

★★★★ **Sublime** ✓ 🖹 Excellent Bordeaux-inspired white blend, **11** unwooded sauvignon (70%) with heft from oaked semillon. Fresh & mouthwatering now, sublimer pleasures promised with time. — Panel

◼ **Releaf Organic** *see* Imbuko Wines

Remhoogte Wine Estate

Location/map: Stellenbosch ▪ WO: Simonsberg–Stellenbosch/Stellenbosch ▪ Est 1994 ▪ 1stB 1995 ▪ Tasting & sales Mon-Fri 9–4.30 Sat 10-4 summer & 10-1 winter ▪ Fee R20 ▪ Closed Easter Fri-Sun, Dec 25/26 & Jan 1 ▪ Cellar tours by appt ▪ Picnic baskets - booking required ▪ Walking/hiking trails ▪ Game ▪ Guest cottage ▪ Owner(s) Murray Boustred Trust ▪ Cellarmaster(s) Chris Boustred (Jan 2011) ▪ Winemaker(s)/viticulturist(s) Chris Boustred (Jan 2007) ▪ 55ha/30ha (cab, merlot, ptage, shiraz, chenin) ▪ 170t/6,000cs own label 80% red 20% white + 40,000L bulk ▪ BWI, IPW ▪ PO Box 2032 Dennesig 7601 ▪ info@remhoogte.co.za ▪ www.remhoogte.co.za ▪ S 33° 53'4.2" E 018° 51'4.6" ▪ **T +27 (0)21-889-5005** ▪ F +27 (0)21-889-6907

Wildlife is a pervasive theme at this Stellenbosch property owned by the Boustred family. Labels feature a crest with prancing zebras, there's self-catering accommodation in the form of Zebra Cottage and picnics can be arranged overlooking a game camp stocked with springbok, wildebeest and, yes, zebra.

★★★★☆ **Merlot Reserve** 07 still selling mid-2011. Impresses with huge concentration while remaining balanced, fresh.

★★★★ **Estate Blend** Powerful 07 (★★★★) even more demanding than bold **06**. Merlot, shiraz, cab, pinotage deliver plush black fruit concentration, well-rounded mouthfeel; tannins a satisfyingly dry conclusion.

★★★★☆ **Honeybunch Reserve Chenin Blanc** NEW 🖹 Barrel fermented/aged **10** from venerable single-vineyard: has admirable flavour intensity & freshness; peach, yellow apple, honeysuckle & spice complexity.

Cabernet Sauvignon ★★★ Last edition **08** was medium bodied, with cassis, fresh acidity & austere end. **Merlot** ★★★★ Plush **09** is rich & full with ripe red fruit, smooth texture before slightly 'hot' finish. **Pinotage** ★★★ Ultra-ripe fruit on previously tasted **09** made for huge concentration but generous tannins & soft acidity. **Valentino Shiraz** NEW ★★ Wild yeast fermented **09** a serious attempt: opaque, big grape tannins cosseted by vanilla oak spicing, lengthy dry finish. **Aigle Noir** ✓ ★★★★ Savoury **09** from merlot, shiraz, cab, pinotage. Attractive herbal edge to red fruit, medium bodied & poised. **Chenin Blanc** ✓ 🖹 ★★★★ Peachy **10** revisited as finished wine, shows good fruit concentration, bright acidity; has additional complexity from portion oak fermented/lees ageing & well-concealed 7g/l residual sugar. WO Stellenbosch. Discontinued: **Bonne Nouvelle**. — CE

Re'Mogo Wines

Location/map: Stellenbosch ▪ Est 2004 ▪ Tasting & sales Mon-Fri & pub hols 9-3 Sat 9-12 ▪ Owner(s) Re'Mogo Holdings (Pty) Ltd ▪ Cellarmaster(s)/winemaker(s) Louwtjie Vlok ▪ 50% red 50% white ▪ Khayamnandi Tourism Centre PO Box 7462 Stellenbosch 7599 ▪ remogo.holdings@gmail.com ▪ www.remogo.co.za ▪ S 33°55'9.47" E 018°51'7.90" ▪ **T +27 (0)82-638-6774, +27 (0)82-253-5126, +27 (0)72-030-5317** ▪ F +27 (0)86-610-7047

A mentoring programme sponsored by the Netherlands government has given Thamsanqa Hombana, international business manager of this Stellenbosch-based empowerment venture, the opportunity to show Re'Mogo's wines at three different international shows a year. At home, an agreement between Fairtrade South Africa and retail giant Pick 'n Pay to prioritise Fairtrade products, prompted Thamsanqa to engage in talks with the nation-wide chain about a listing.

Chenin Blanc ☺ 🖹 ★★★ Attractive combo honey & ripe apple, **10** was soft, fleshy & balanced. **Sauvignon Blanc** ☺ 🖹 ★★★ **10** was fruity, light style with herbal edge.

Cabernet Sauvignon 🖹 ★★★ Fruity, dark cherry **09** had fresh acidity to cut tarry oak. **Pinotage** 🖹 ★★★ Vibrant red fruit combined with soft vanilla in **09**, juicy yet firm end. **Pinotage Rosé** 🖹 ★★ Red-fruited dry **10** needed to settle. All except Chenin were tasted as samples, none re-tasted this edition. — IM

◼ **Renosterbos** *see* Hofstraat Kelder

Restless River

Location: Hermanus • Map: Elgin, Walker Bay & Bot River • WO: Upper Hemel-en-Aarde Valley/Elgin/Coastal • Est 1999 • 1stB 2005 • Tasting, sales & tours by Mon-Sun by appt • Closed pub hols • Charcuterie, cheese platters & refreshments - booking essential • BYO picnic • Owner(s) Craig & Anne Wessels • Winemaker(s) Craig Wessels (Jan 2005) • Viticulturist(s) Anne Wessels (Nov 2004) & Craig Wessels • 20ha/6ha (cab, chard) • 10t/100cs own label 70% red 30% white • PO Box 1739 Hermanus 7200 • anne@restlessriver.com • www.restlessriver.com • S 34° 21'26.11" E 19° 16'32.80" • T +27 (0)28-313-2881, +27 (0)82-650-3544 • F +27 (0)21-448-7487

Wine has long been a 'religion' for Craig Wessels, so buying a tiny patch of land in Upper Hemel-en-Aarde Valley in 2004 was the proverbial dream come true for him and wife Anne. Together, they make tiny amounts of wine from some of the oldest cab and chardonnay vines in the area, encouraging the grapes to express their own distinctive characteristics. Next challenge: stop the baboons and Kwezi the dog from eating all the grapes first.

★★★★ **Chardonnay** No spring chick, yet sense of unrealised promise about **08** invites further cellaring. Barrel-fermentation imparts nutty oak, balanced by intense blossomy citrus flavours. Some Elgin fruit.
Cabernet Sauvignon ★★★ **08** is modern, overtly fruity yet tips a beret to Old World with herbal nuance to blackcurrant tone. Fine balance, smooth finish, promising debut. —Panel

Retief Wines

Location/WO: Paarl • Map: Paarl & Wellington • Est 1747 • 1stB 2004 • Tasting & sales Mon-Fri 10-5 Sat/Sun by appt • Closed all pub hols • Owner(s) Pearl Mountain Wines (Pty) Ltd • Winemaker(s) Robert Frater (2004, De Zoete Inval) • Viticulturist(s) Graham Retief • 10.08ha (cab, merlot, shiraz, chard) • 67t/7,500 litres 100% red • PO Box 709 Northern Paarl 7623 • retief@new.co.za • S 33° 41'44.4" E 018° 57'11.1" • T 021-872-9088 • F 021-872-9983

Winemaking is still a sideline at this Paarl table-grape farm located on the old wagon trail which once linked Cape Town to the hinterland. However, plans are afoot to build restaurant, function venue and cellar facilities by 2014.

Above the Mist range
Cabernet Sauvignon ★★★ Honest, well-oaked **07**, cassis & cedar. Tasted previously, as all. **Merlot** ★★★ Whiffs coffee & chocolate on fleshy **07**.

Retief range
Wagon Trail ★★★ **05** shiraz/merlot blend well balanced, lively. **Above the Mist** ★★★ Spicy merlot-led blend, **05** firm but juicy. **Yes It's Red** ★★ Last tasted was strawberry-ripe **07** with 15% alc. —CvZ

Revelation Wines

Location: Somerset West • Map: Helderberg • WO: Stellenbosch • Est 2009 • 1stB 2010 • Tasting, sales & cellar tours daily - please call ahead • Tasting fee R20, refundable on purchase • Owner(s) Bertus van Niekerk & Selma Albasini • Cellarmaster(s) Bertus van Niekerk (Jan 2010) • Winemaker(s) Bertus van Niekerk (Jan 2010), with Selma Albasini (2010) & Hendrik van Niekerk (2011) • 100cs own label 50% red 50% white • 33 Eagle Crescent Somerset West 7130 • bertus@zarevelation.com • www.zarevelation.com, www.osbloed.com • S 34° 5'26.22" E 018° 51'55.87" • T +27 (0)83-400-2999

Former clergyman Bertus van Niekerk says it was inevitable that he would eventually make his own wine. 'I think of wine as a divine gift, a noble commodity that enriches life and the experience of it on almost every level of existence.' So in 2010 he made two barrels with artist wife Selma Albasini in their suburban garage, doubling production in 2011, son Hendrik also involved. 'Our facility is humble, but we lend stature to it with undiluted joie de vivre.'

Revelation range
Cabernet Sauvignon ★★★ From Helderberg grapes, classic blackcurrant fruit profile, **10** preview is forthcoming, rounded, highly drinkable, well-judged oak grip to finish. **Cinsaut** ★★★☆ Template for the variety: **11** preview light & delicate flowers & red berries, juicy ripe fruit balanced by downy tannins. 40 year old Muldersvlei bushvines. **Chardonnay** ★★★ Barrel-fermented **10** preview is clean & vibrant, shows lees-age complexity in lightly oxidative style. Bodes well for future. Faure grapes. **Riesling** ★★★ Not your common or Mosel riesling:

previewed **11** from Elgin is barrel-aged, with 15% botrytis & dash chardonnay adding broad honey, lemon & biscuit tones. Delightfully quirky.

Osbloed range

Osbloed ★★★ 'Ox blood', colloquial Afrikaans for robust red. **09** shiraz, cab is in fact quite genteel, well structured, hits the easy-drinking mark with juicy, spicy dark berries & ripe tannins. — Panel

Reyneke Wines

Location/map: Stellenbosch ▪ WO: Stellenbosch/Coastal ▪ Est 1863 ▪ 1stB 1998 ▪ Tasting, sales & cellar tours Mon-Fri 10-5 Sat 10-1 pub hols by appt ▪ BYO picnic ▪ Paintings by Mila Posthumus on display ▪ Owner(s) Reyneke Wines (Pty) Ltd ▪ Cellarmaster(s) Rudiger Gretschel ▪ Winemaker(s) Rudiger Gretschel & Joan Heatlie, with Ryan Mostert (Jan 2011) ▪ Viticulturist(s) Johan Reyneke & Joan Heatlie ▪ 40ha/32ha (cabs s/f, merlot, ptage, syrah, chenin, sauv) ▪ 140t/10,000cs own label 70% red 30% white & 1,000cs for clients ▪ Brands for clients: Woolworths ▪ BDOCA (Organic), Debio Norway (Organic), Demeter (biodynamic), FFF (Woolworths), IPW, WIETA ▪ PO Box 61 Vlottenburg 7604 ▪ wine@reynekewines.co.za ▪ www.reynekewines.co.za ▪ S 33° 57' 27.7" E 018° 45' 7.0" ▪ **T** +27 (0)21-881-3517/3451 ▪ F +27 (0)21-881-3285

'We believe that there is no greatness without goodness.' This is the motto of the only certified biodynamic producer in South Africa. A new Organic range has been added, with two wines made from grapes sourced from other organic producers. The established top tier Biodynamic range will always be produced exclusively from Johan Reyneke's lovingly cared for vines. Success has followed dedication, with the Reyneke wines triumphing at last year's Nedbank Green Awards as well as receiving great reviews on their first entry into the USA market. Just reward for this leader in organic and sustainable farming - and maker of very fine wines.

Biodynamic range

★★★★ Pinotage ⚘ ⚲ Latest **10** has perfume abundance, lavender whiffs over sweet fruit promise. Brooding rich palate follows with fine acid & tannin balance for bright & fresh end. **09** skipped.

★★★★☆ Reserve Red ⚘ **09** has a stunning nose of coriander, white pepper & dry spices. The bold palate shows off plush shiraz spice & vibrant fruit, while dash cab adds to fine structure. All elements harmoniously poised to evolve over next 10 years or so.

★★★★ Cornerstone ⚘ **09** not as poised as **08** (★★★★☆). Savoury undertone woven into mix dark berry with serious tannins begging food & some time to settle. From cab with support from shiraz & merlot.

★★★★ Chenin Blanc ⚘ ⚲ **10** from ultra-low-yielding vineyards expresses typical chenin tinned apple & mineral notes. Vinous with ripe sweet stonefruit, ending dry. Broadened by old-oak barrelling.

★★★★☆ Reserve White ⚘ ⚲ Subtle oak aromas, lime & fynbos introduce fresh & pure **10**. The palate is pure class with a precise & focused end that lingers to a perfectly dry conclusion. This is an excellent example of balance. Needs 6 months to settle.

★★★★☆ Sauvignon Blanc ⚘ ⚲ **10** (★★★★) has softer palate texture with prominent acid, while fine **11** is all about balanced tension between fruit weight, taut acid & fine lingering minerality. Both barrel fermented in older oak adding nuance to structure.

Organic range NEW

★★★★ Chenin Blanc-Chardonnay-Sauvignon Blanc ✓ ▤ ⚘ ⚲ Attractive oaky notes promise to settle on **10** with 65% chenin. Ripe fruit aromas, viscous, rounded palate with layered citrus & stonefruit complexity. Good freshness, moderate 13% alc.

Shiraz ✓ ▤ ⚘ **★★★★** Savoury elements dominate on **09** with ripe firm tannins requiring time to settle. Ripe fruit balanced by integrated oak. These both WO Coastal. — JP

Rhebokskloof Wine Estate

Location: Paarl ▪ Map: Paarl & Wellington ▪ WO: Paarl/Coastal ▪ 1stB 1975 ▪ Tasting & sales Mon-Fri 9-5 Sat/Sun 10-3 ▪ Fee R15/5 wines ▪ Cellar tours by appt ▪ Rhebokskloof Restaurant open daily for b'fast & lunch, dinner Tue-Sat ▪ Facilities for children ▪ Tour groups ▪ Gifts ▪ Weddings, functions & conferences ▪ Walks/hikes ▪ Live concerts ▪ Luxury tented camps ▪ Owner(s) Siebrits & Albie Laker, ASLA Group ▪ Cellarmaster(s)/winemaker(s) Rolanie Lotz (Jan 2007) ▪ Viticulturist(s) Karin Louw (Jan 2007) ▪ 180ha/21.5ha (shiraz, chard) ▪ 152t/12,000cs own label 80% red 15% white 5% rosé + 1,500cs for clients ▪ PO Box 2637 Paarl 7620 ▪ info@rhebokskloof.co.za ▪ www.rhebokskloof.co.za ▪ S 33° 41' 6.1" E 018° 55' 56.6" ▪ **T** +27 (0)21-869-8386 ▪ F +27 (0)21-869-8386

It is possible that in 1797, while his home was being built, Rhebokskloof founder Petrus van der Merwe slept in a tent on the farm. It's a 'dead cert' he wouldn't have had the conveniences current-day guests enjoy when they check into the new tented camp beside the vineyards. Available for pre-booked groups, it comprises luxury sleeping and ablution facilities as well as a dining and dance area so guests can eat, sleep and kick up their heels alongside the vines.

Mountain Vineyards Reserve range

★★★★ **Black Marble Hill Syrah** Reined-in tannins, olive tones to black-fruited flagship red in **08**. Restrained & more elegant than **06** (★★★★), similar composure, berry & scrub notes as **07**.
Sandstone Grove Chardonnay ★★★★ Gentle citrus, nutty highlights from partial barrel fermentation/ageing last time on well-flavoured, textured **07**.

Rhebokskloof range

Pinotage ✍ ★★★★ **10** more affable & fruity, less reliant on wood than several other reds from this stable. Has concentration, structure to possibly score higher given year/2. **Shiraz** ★★★ Enticing cranberry, lily whiffs allude to satisfying sipper but **09** stumbles at the tannin hurdle, is very firm & sappy. **Mourvèdre-Shiraz-Grenache** ★★★★ Well-balanced **08** happy marriage 52% mourvèdre, nearly equal dollops shiraz, grenache. Dark plums laced with anise & tarry oak. This, Viognier & sparkling below not retasted. **Chardonnay** ✍ ★★★ Toasted nut courtesy smart oaking (year, 30% new), wildflower scents, smooth vanilla-lemon flavours hit all the right drinkability buttons in **10**. **Viognier** ★★★ Bitter lift on finish previously detracted from pleasing peachiness, lightness of **08**. **Chardonnay Méthode Cap Classique** ★★★★ Inviting toffee apple & toasty brioche, fine mousse & creamy finish lift the bar in **07** champagne-method sparkling; pleasing celebration package. **Tamay Sparkling** ★★ Hint viognier adds perfume to chardonnay-led combo in **08**, softly sweet & frothy.

Pearlstone range

Cabernet Sauvignon-Merlot ☺🏱 ★★★ Fair grip but cab-led mix bursts with generous fruit in **09** well-knit mealtime companion.

Pinotage 🏱 ★★★ Strawberries & cream **09** crafted for early enjoyment with supple tannin & sweet fruit. This competitively-priced range mainly for consumption at the estate's restaurant & function venue. All WO Coastal, unless stated; reds lightly oaked. **Shiraz** 🏱 ★★ Medicinal scent on **09** mutes red berry/plum fruit; like big brother, also tad extracted. Only this, Cab-Merlot & Sauvignon tasted for this edition. **Merlot Rosé** 🏱 ★★ Coral pink **10** boiled sweets, fresh acidity, gently sweet. WO Paarl, as is Chenin. **Chenin Blanc** 🏱 ★★★ Light-footed (12.4% alc) **10** nicely textured, persistent pithy end. **Sauvignon Blanc** 🏱 ★★★ Green apple & grass-nuanced **11** perky acidity, brief farewell; cheerful pick-me-up. **Sparkling Rosé** ★★★ Drop shiraz provides rosy glow to viognier-led carbonated **NV** sparkler, with chardonnay. — CvZ

■ **Rhinofields Reserve** see Durbanville Hills
■ **Richeneau** see High Constantia Wine Cellar

Rickety Bridge Winery

Location/map: Franschhoek ▪ WO: Western Cape/Franschhoek/Coastal/Paarl ▪ Est 1990 ▪ Tasting, sales & cellar tours Mon-Sat 9-7 (Dec-Mar) & 9-5 (Apr-Nov) Sun 10-5 ▪ Closed Dec 25 & Jan 1 ▪ Fee R20, waived on purchase ▪ Restaurant Mon-Sun 11-4 (see Restaurants section) ▪ Facilities for children ▪ Gift shop ▪ Farm produce ▪ Conferences ▪ Weddings ▪ 4-star guest house (see Accommodation section) ▪ Owner(s) DS Sarnia (Pty) Ltd ▪ Cellarmaster(s) Wynand Grobler (Nov 2007) ▪ Winemaker(s) Wynand Grobler (Nov 2007), with Danie de Bruyn (Jan 2011) ▪ 91ha/39ha (cab, merlot, shiraz, chard, chenin, sauv, sem) ▪ 160t/10,000cs own label 45% red 45% white 10% rosé ▪ PO Box 455 Franschhoek 7690 ▪ info@ricketybridge.com ▪ www.ricketybridge.com ▪ S 33° 53'58.5" E 019° 5'27.6" ▪ **T +27 (0)21-876-2129** ▪ F +27 (0)21-876-3486

Grapes for this upmarket wine and lifestyle estate in Franschhoek are sourced widely, from Koekenaap to Elgin, but the wine team is especially proud that local fruit was the power behind two significant recent garlands: Decanter gold and a Top 100 spot. The latter went to their flagship red, The Bridge, made from a once 'shabby bushvine cabernet vineyard' whose potential was recognised and nurtured by cellarmaster Wynand Grobler, in what he counts as a career highlight.

Icon Wines

★★★★☆ **The Bridge** 100% cab in tasteful - & tasty - package, from own bushvine single-vineyard. Elegant **08** showed stunning integration of cool blackcurrant fruit & fine wood tannin when last tasted.

Paulina's Reserve range

★★★★ **Cabernet Sauvignon** Just 'Paulina's Reserve' previous editions. Elegantly dry **08**, super blackcurrant fruit, approachable now with plenty in store for those who wait. No **07**.

★★★★ **Sauvignon Blanc** ✓ 🍷 Higher general rating for this improved label. **10**, with small barrel-fermented portion, fuller than **09**, interesting gooseberry flavours, unaggressively fresh.

Chenin Blanc ✓ 🍷 ★★★★ Nutty **10** broad of beam, soft apple pie & custard flavours firmed by fresh acidity. WO Western Cape, as for Sauvignon. **Semillon** 🍷 ★★★★ A 'graduate' of the RB range in new finery, **08** mellow lanolin textures, subtle oak (year, 20% new) & relative age add to laid-back allure.

Rickety Bridge range

★★★★ **Shiraz** ✓ **09** packed with juicy fruit, supple tannins support mulberry flavours. Less spicy than **08**, also from Coastal vines.

Rosé ☺ 🍷 ★★★ **11** ex-tank bursts with strawberries, really tangy dry tail. WO Western Cape.

Merlot ✓ ★★★☆ **08** clean-cut floral features & gentle mouthfeel stiffened by 14.5% alc & wood tannin. WO Paarl. **Pinotage** ★★★ Powerful **09**, spicy plum fruit wrapped in stern tannins. WO Western Cape. **The Foundation Stone** ★★★★ Shiraz & 4 other mainly southern Mediterranean varieties; previewed **10** sunny fruit flavours but rather severe youthful tannins, needing time. WO Coastal. **Chardonnay** 🍷 ★★★ Upholstered **10**, ripe hazelnut & caramel tones invigorated by crisp citrus fruit. **Chenin Blanc** 🍷 **11** preview too unformed to rate, but seems fruitier than **10**. This & next WO Western Cape. **Sauvignon Blanc** 🍷 ★★★ Clean & dry **11**, tropical hints poke through yeast character of preview mid-2011. **Natural Sweet Chenin Blanc** 🍷 ★★★ Near-ochrehued **10** has a swashbuckling full-sweet finish. Only seasoned oak. — DS

Rico Suter Private Cellar

Location: Worcester ▪ Map/WO: Breedekloof ▪ Est/1stB 2004 ▪ Tasting, sales & tours by appt ▪ Cheese platters & homemade bread ▪ Tour groups ▪ Olive oil & table olives ▪ BYO picnic ▪ Walking/hiking & mountain biking trails ▪ Bird watching ▪ Guesthouse (bookings: erika@ricosuterwines.com) ▪ Owner(s) Suter Family Trust ▪ Cellarmaster(s) Rico Suter, advised by Carlo Suter ▪ Winemaker(s) Rico Suter ▪ Viticulturist(s) Bruno Suter (2004) ▪ 750ha/45ha (cab, cinsaut, p verdot, ptage, shiraz, sauv, viog) ▪ 8-15t/ha 8,850L own label 95% red 5% white + 22,000L for Overhex Private Cellar ▪ PO Box 38 Breervier 6858 ▪ ricosuterwines@breede.co.za ▪ S 33° 31'39.00" E 019° 15'13.00" ▪ **T +27 (0)23-355-1822** ▪ F +27 (0)86-642-6591

Visitors at this Breedekloof estate enjoy a range of mainly red wines, tasted in the company of many other guests – of the feathered kind: bird sightings over the past year include fish eagles and secretary birds. Co-owner Rico Suter believes their presence is a reflection of his family's 'almost-organic' approach to winegrowing.

★★★★ **L'Amitié** Individual & complex **06** combo cinsaut, shiraz, petit verdot, viognier. Silky mouthfeel, floral notes, emphatic dry exit.

★★★★ **Cabernet Sauvignon-Syrah** **06** earthy wafts, ripe black berries, soft & seductively juicy centre contrasts with elegant dry end.

Cabernet Sauvignon ★★★ **05** succulent & plummy, with savoury flavours. Only Pinotage tasted this edition, others previously. **Petit Verdot** ★★★★ **04** broad shouldered, with savoury tones & chocolate/mocha overlay. Good tannic support, provides backbone for ageing. **Pinotage** ★★★ **08** big & savoury, with cedar & liquorice, layers of plums & red berries add balance. **Syrah** Await next, as for **Cabernet Sauvignon-Petit Verdot, Sauvignon Blanc, Viognier-Chenin Blanc**. — DB

Ridgeback

Location: Paarl ▪ Map: Paarl & Wellington ▪ WO: Paarl/Western Cape ▪ Est 1997 ▪ 1stB 2001 ▪ Tasting & sales Mon-Sat 10-5 (peak season) & 10-4 (winter months) Sun 10-4 ▪ Fee R15/5 wines, R25/10 wines ▪ Closed Easter Fri, Dec 25 & Jan 1 ▪ Cellar tours by appt ▪ The Deck Restaurant, open Mon-Sun 10-3 ▪ 4-star/5-room Ridgeback Guest House & 1 self-catering cottage ▪ Walking/hiking trails ▪ Owner(s) Kilimanjaro Investments ▪ Cellarmaster(s)/winemaker(s) Toit Wessels (Jan 2007) ▪ Viticulturist(s) Toit Wessels (Mar 2000) ▪ 65ha/35ha (cabs s/f, grenache, mourv, shiraz, sauv, viog) ▪ 225t/15,000cs own label 60% red 35% white 5% rosé ▪ PO Box 2076 Windmeul Paarl

7630 ▪ tasting@ridgeback.co.za ▪ www.ridgebackwines.co.za ▪ S 33° 40′ 24.9″ E 018° 54′ 53.5″ ▪ **T +27 (0)21-869-8068** ▪ F +27 (0)21-869-8146

The winemaking and marketing teams at this Paarl property are showing the tenacity their eponymous canine friends are lauded for. 'We're not waiting for the light at the end of the tunnel', they say, referring to the general economic malaise and unhelpful currency fluctuations; 'We're creating our own light, right here in it!' Good fruit from their meticulously kept vineyards is a good start, allowing wines of balance and restraint to emerge without the need for manipulation.

Ridgeback Wines range

★★★★ **Cabernet Franc** ✓ Pepper spice & leafiness accentuate herbal edge in elegant **08** blend. Savoury acidity & well-judged oaking enhance satisfyingly ripe, succulent core of pure red fruit.

★★★★ **Shiraz** Trimly elegant **07**'s cherry, spice & smoky aromas led to full-flavoured but restrained palate tasted last yr, with tannic underpinning. WO W Cape.

★★★★ **Journey** Merlot, cab franc blend, splash cab in fine **06** tasted mid-10. Plenty fruit lurking in slightly sombre, vinous & oaky shell, needed few years. Smooth tannic firmness, lovely light elegance.

★★★★ **Chenin Blanc** NEW ✓ Barrel-fermented **10** benefits from year in bottle. Just off-dry - rich, robust & harmoniously constructed, with fine minerality & texture.

Sauvignon Blanc ☺ ▤ ★★★ Lipsmackingly fresh, textured **11** both herbal & tropical in style. Sufficiently light for lunchtime enjoyment. **Vansha White** ☺ ▤ ★★★ Paarl-Darling **11** blend sauvignon, chenin, viognier is cheerful, pithily structured & spicy with no shortage of flavour.

Cabernet Sauvignon ★★★ Classic signals in **08** imply seriousness, but flavours charmingly fleshy & accessible, well-integrated tannins underpin. **Merlot** ★★★ Usual herbaceous edge to plummy **08** tasted last yr, oak added to savoury element, a touch lean, but good firm finish. **Vansha Cabernet Sauvignon-Merlot** ▤ ★★★ Unpretentious & tasty **09** tasted mid-10. Was pleasingly poised between serious & easy pleasures. **Vansha SGMV** ▤ ★★★ Savoury, unpretentious shiraz-led **10** blend delivers plenty dense fruit, though chunky tannins still need to settle. **His Master's Choice** ★★★ tasted mid-09, ripe shiraz & Coastal mourvèdre; floral hints to sweet fruit, but elegance nudged tannic leanness. **Shiraz Rosé** ▤ ★★ Fresh appeal in simple, earthy **11** with splash viognier. **Viognier** ★★★ Aromatic, oaked & spicily dry **10** not overblown. Rich, but restrained by pithy stone fruit & refreshing finish. **Natural Sweet Viognier** ★★★ **10** tasted last year a big jump from unctuous previous **06** (★★★). Was delicately delicious & sweet, with a touch of oak. **Cape Ruby** ★★★ Flavoursome, uncomplex **09** from shiraz, with mild tannins & fresh conclusion tasted last edition. — IM

Ridgemor Farm   🍴 🎪 ⛳ 📷

Location: Somerset West ▪ Map: Helderberg ▪ WO: Stellenbosch ▪ Est 2003 ▪ 1stB 2005 ▪ Tasting & sales Mon-Fri 10-4; weekends at driving range 10-4 ▪ Fee R30pp ▪ Closed all pub hols & Dec 24 to Jan 1 ▪ Ridgemor Villa Guesthouse ▪ Weddings/functions ▪ Conferences ▪ Golf ▪ Fishing ▪ Walks/hikes ▪ BYO picnic ▪ Quad biking ▪ Owner(s) Veronique Barge ▪ Winemaker(s) Johan Joubert ▪ Viticulturist(s) Berto van der Westhuizen ▪ 101ha/±32ha (cab f, pinot, sangio, shiraz, chenin, sauv) ▪ 210t 77% red 12% white 11% rosé ▪ PO Box 3625 Somerset West 7129 ▪ info@ridgemorwines.com ▪ www.ridgemorwines.com ▪ S 34° 2′ 39.3″ E 018° 46′ 25.4″ ▪ **T +27 (0)21-842-2255** ▪ F +27 (0)21-842-3393

This venerable property was originally a tobacco and cattle spread, but its auspicious location on a ridge overlooking False Bay prompted its conversion into a wine farm. It was acquired in 2003 by a Dutch family and redeveloped, and current owner Veronique Barge presides over an estate with many activities and amentities, not least a 'must-have' wedding venue set in a newly refurbished barn.

Cuvée Twister Cabernet Franc ★★★ **05**'s firm tannins were cushioned by some sweetness when reviewed, should since have mellowed. This, Chenin Reserve, still selling, not revisited. **Cuvée Quint Shiraz** ★★★ Clean leather & forest floor on traditionally styled **05**, not for further keeping. **Shiraz-Cabernet Franc** In abeyance, as is **Pinot Noir-Shiraz-Cabernet Franc**. **Chenin Blanc Reserve** ★★★ Wooded **07** quiet, gently off-dry. **Sauvignon Blanc** NEW ▤ ★★★ One of the older sauvignons entered for tasting, still very much alive. **09** white asparagus & honeyed bottle age. **Chenin Blanc-Viognier 08** selling, but not tasted. Discontinued: **Cuvée Lynette Pinot Noir, Cuvée Terry Lynn Shiraz Rosé, Cuvée Blondie**. — CvZ

Riebeek Cellars

Location: Riebeek-Kasteel ▪ Map/WO: Swartland ▪ Est 1941 ▪ Tasting and sales Mon-Fri 9-5 Sat 9-4 Sun 10.30-4 (wine boutique) ▪ Fee R10 ▪ Closed Easter Fri, Dec 25 and Jan 1 ▪ Cellar tours by appt ▪ BYO picnic ▪ Owner(s) ±40 shareholders ▪ Cellarmaster(s) Zakkie Bester (Dec 1999) ▪ Winemaker(s) Eric Saayman and Alecia Boshoff (Jan 1997/Dec 2004), with JM Craffordt (Dec 2009) ▪ Viticulturist(s) Hanno van Schalkwyk (Sep 2000) ▪ 1,200ha (cab, carignan, merlot, mourv, ptage, shiraz, tinta amerela, chard, chenin, sauv, viog) ▪ 17,000t/150,000cs own label 50% red 40% white 10% rosé and ±40,000cs for clients ▪ Brands for clients: Broken Rock, Rocheburg, Royal, Steenbok ▪ BWI, Fairtrade, HACCP, WIETA ▪ PO Box 13 Riebeek-Kasteel 7307 ▪ info@riebeekcellars.co.za ▪ www.riebeekcellars.com ▪ S 33° 22' 58.0" E 018° 54' 54.5" ▪ **T +27 (0)22-448-1213** ▪ F +27 (0)22-448-1281

The premium Kasteelberg label, produced in small quantities, is proving to be a great success. The 2011 Viognier (we look forward to trying it next year) became the first example of this variety to win the coveted General Jan Smuts Young Wine Show Trophy - no mean feat in a fiercely contested competition. At this large Swartland producer the focus is on viticulture, as the view is taken that only quality fruit can be transformed into quality wines. The Riebeek valley boasts great potential and, under the guiding hand of cellar master Zakkie Bester, this winery looks set to reach their goals.

Riebeek Collection

Pinotage ☺ 🍷 📷 ★★★ Shy smoky intro hides typical banana and red berry pizazz. Lively palate follows with **10** showing deft balance of oak sweetness. **Cape Ruby Port** ☺ ★★★ Friendly fruity fireside companion has gentle toffee notes follow to lingering, fiery end. Tasty **NV** mostly touriga nacional.

Cabernet Sauvignon 🍷 📷 ★★★ Juicy **10** has region's dark berry ripeness and oak-sweet end. **Merlot** 🍷 📷 ★★★ **10** is similar vein to cab above with ripe fruit and sweet oak combo. **Shiraz** 🍷 📷 ★★★ **10** disjointed savoury fruit combo. **Cabernet Sauvignon-Merlot** 🍷 ★★★ Pretty berry fruited **09**, tasted last ed and still selling. **Shiraz-Cinsaut** 🍷 ★★ Last was **09** red-fruited unwooded sipper, still available. **Pinotage Rosé** 🍷 ★★ **10** berry delight, still selling. **Chardonnay** 🍷 ★★★ **09** tasted last edition, still selling. **Chenin Blanc** 🍷 📷 ★★★ Zippy acid and fleshy tropical appeal on lightish **11**. **Sauvignon Blanc** 🍷 ★★★ Very ripe tropical style, **11** balanced with simple austerity. **Viognier** 🍷 ★★ Floral **09** simple and fruity last tasted. **Montino Petillant Light** 🍷 ★★ Semi-sweet, grapey **NV** white fizz. **Montino Petillant Natural Sweet Rose** 🍷 ★★ NV, perfumed sweet and light, fizz. **Pieter Cruythoff Brut** ★★★ Fruity and crisp **NV** sparkling from chard and pinot. **Cape Vintage Port** ★★★★ Last tasted was decadently smooth, rich, fruitcakey **05**. Discontinued: **Late Harvest**.

Kasteelberg range

Viognier ★★★★ **10** in bold Swartland idiom. Has fragrant intensity, hinting at complex rich flavours but oak and sugar a tad overwhelming. **Kasteelberg MCC** ★★★ Last was **NV** sparkler from pinots blanc and noir with green apple zip and baked bread richness. Still available.

A Few Good Men range

Cabernet Sauvignon 🍷 ★★★ In sweeter vein with rich brooding cassis, ripe rounded palate, **09** has pleasant savoury thread to counter plush character. **Merlot** 🍷 ★★★ Attractive berry and toasty notes mingle on fruity **09**. **Pinotage** ★★★★ Same vintage still selling, last was juicy **09** with coffee notes and ripe berry richness. **Shiraz** ✓ 🍷 ★★★★ Lovely red berry lift to dark fruit ripeness combines well with smoke and savoury elements. Oaking nicely done on **09**. **Chardonnay** ★★★★ Sumptuous **09** tasted last still available. — JP

■ **Riebeek Retail Brands** see Riebeek Cellars
■ **Rietrivier** see Montagu Wine and Spirits Co

Rietvallei Wine Estate

Location/map: Robertson ▪ WO: Robertson/Western Cape ▪ Est 1864 ▪ 1stB 1975 ▪ Tasting and sales Mon-Fri 8.30-5 Sat 10-2 ▪ R10pp for groups of 15+ ▪ Closed Easter Fri/Sun, Dec 25 and Jan 1 ▪ Cellar tours by appt ▪ Cheese platters, book ahead for groups of 6+ ▪ Farm produce ▪ Conservation area ▪ Owner(s)/winemaker(s) Johnny Burger ▪ Cellarmaster(s) Kobus Burger (2003) ▪ 350ha/180ha (cab, red muscadel, shiraz, chard, sauv) ▪ 2,000t/50,000cs own label 40% red 45% white 10% rosé 5% fortified + 1,000,000 litre in bulk ▪ Other export brands: Stonedale, Wild Rush ▪ PO Box 386 Robertson 6705 ▪ info@rietvallei.co.za ▪ www.rietvallei.co.za ▪ S 33° 49' 25.7" E 019° 58' 39.4" ▪ **T +27 (0)23-626-3596** ▪ F +27 (0)23-626-4514

Fortunate enough to harvest from some vines planted over a century ago by the second generation here, incumbent winemaker Kobus Burger last year was further blessed with twin sons Johnny and Austin. Despite a small dip in tonnage and own-brand bottlings in 2011, Rietvallei continues to meet export demand across Western and Eastern Europe, Scandinavia, the UK, US, Asia and Australia. No doubt the new generation will be equally comfortable covering all the bases, from premium to pocket-pleasing entry level.

Special Select range

★★★★ **Esteanna** Last edition, cab-based **08** with cab franc & petit verdot had brooding blackcurrant, ripe plum & tobacco aromas/flavours, good new oak-assisted structure for ageability.

★★★★★ **Muscadel 1908** Centenary single-vineyard **08** fortified dessert previously was packed with raisins, candied cherry, fruitcake & nuttiness. Clean spicy lift & brilliant balanced, rich sweetness subtly delivered. **Shiraz** ★★★ Now bottled, **08** shows Aussie-like eucalyptus overlay to redcurrant fruit, meaty nuances, more obvious oak (85% new) than previous. **Juanita Cabernet Sauvignon Rosé** 🍾 ★★ Previously 'Juanita Rosé'. Stewed berries & plum delight on dry, savoury **11**. **Chardonnay** 🍾 ★★★★ Revisited as finished wine, citrus & stonefruit-toned **10** lives up to promise shown last edition: new oak well integrated, adding spice, roundness & weight. Now flying Business Class with KLM. **Sauvignon Blanc** 🍾 ★★★★ Ebullient **10**, now bottled, brims with white asparagus & tinned pea; lime-zest acidity adds bounce to otherwise weighty palate, extends the finish. For current enjoyment. W Cape WO. Discontinued: **Viognier**.

Classic Estate range

Natural Chardonnay 😊 🍾 ★★★ Unwooded **11** is pleasantly full bodied & well toned thanks to brisk lemon acidity, vibrant pear/white peach flavour.

Cabernet Sauvignon 🍾 ★★★ **09**, previewed last time, still youthfully fruity, shows a stalky hint in quick finish. **Shiraz-Petit Verdot-Viognier** ★★★★ Still-selling **09**'s 75% shiraz contributed pepperiness, the viognier peachy fruit, & the petit verdot savoury notes & structure. **Chenin Blanc** 🍾 ★★ Understated **11** perfect summer white: lightish, with cool green fruit, perky tail. **Sauvignon Blanc** 🍾 ★★★ Asparagus & dust on expressive quick sip **11**. **Red Muscadel** ★★★ Amber **10** fortified dessert billows berries & raisins; unctuous & lengthy flavours are exotically seasoned with Indian spices.

John B range

Cabernet Sauvignon-Tinta Barocca 🍾 ★★★ **10** harmonious & spicy mix, with cab's structure. All these still selling. **Cabernet Sauvignon-Merlot Rosé** 🍾 🍾 ★★ Dry **10** pretty & light. **Riesling** 🍾 🍾 ★★★ Semi-sweet **10** lowish alc for picnic/party fun. **Sauvignon Blanc-Colombar** 🍾 🍾 ★★★ **10** all summery charm. Just-dry, low alc, nice crisp acid bite. — Panel

■ **Rijckholt** *see* Zandvliet Wine Estate & Thoroughbred Stud
■ **Rijckshof** *see* Oudtshoorn Cellar - SCV

Rijk's Estate

Location/map/WO: Tulbagh ▪ Est/1stB 2007 ▪ Tasting, sales & tours by appt only ▪ Fee R10/wine ▪ Owner(s) Neville Dorrington ▪ Winemaker(s) Pierre Wahl (Jan 2007), with Lukas van Loggerenberg (Jan 2010) ▪ Vineyard manager(s) Boet Eddy ▪ 40ha/14.4ha (carignan, grenache noir, mourv, ptage, shiraz, tinta amarela, viog) ▪ ±60t/4,000cs own label 100% red ▪ PO Box 400 Tulbagh 6820 ▪ wine@rijks.co.za ▪ www.rijksestate.co.za ▪ S 33° 16'1.5" E 019° 8'42.0" ▪ **T +27 (0)23-230-1622** ▪ F +27 (0)23-230-1650

The main aim of Rijk's Estate (sibling of Rijk's Private Cellar) is to showcase the Tulbagh Valley's red-wine potential in the most natural and elegant bottlings. To this end the best-quality grapes from top-performing blocks are selected. A further barrel selection is then made to ensure the finest quality in the bottle.

★★★★ **Shiraz** Very ripe **07**, hints of baked fruit, but last edition retained elegance courtesy crisp acidity, savoury oak & floral element from dash viognier; ±15% alc obvious but not a detraction.

★★★★ **The Master** Shiraz-led (50%) **07**, dollops mourvèdre, pinotage. Opulent dark berry fruit, full body, with new oak masking warming effects of ±15% alc. Tight tannin noted last year may have relaxed. — WB

Rijk's Private Cellar

Location/map: Tulbagh ▪ WO: Tulbagh/Coastal ▪ Est 1996 ▪ 1stB 2000 ▪ Tasting & sales Mon-Fri 10–4 Sat 10–2 ▪ Fee R10/wine, waived on purchase ▪ Closed Easter Fri-Mon, Dec 25 & Jan 1 ▪ Cellar tours by appt ▪ Rijk's Guest House ▪ Conferences ▪ Owner(s) Neville Dorrington ▪ Winemaker(s) Pierre Wahl (Jan 2002), with Lukas van Loggerenberg (Jan 2010) ▪ Viticulturist(s) Boet Eddy (Jun 1996) ▪ 135ha/22ha (ptage, shiraz, chenin) ▪ 140t/15,000cs own label 65% red 35% white ▪ IPW ▪ PO Box 400 Tulbagh 6820 ▪ wine@rijks.co.za ▪ www.rijks.co.za ▪ S 33° 16'1.5" E 019° 8'42.0" ▪ **T +27 (0)23-230-1622** ▪ F +27 (0)23-230-1650

The past year was one of consolidation for this boutique Tulbagh cellar, as the focus began shifting to producing wines only from what are considered the best-suited varieties: chenin, pinotage and shiraz. Some 10ha were replanted accordingly, says Pierre Wahl, who marks a decade in the Rijk's cellar this year. A new label, 'Touch of Oak', is being introduced - lightly oaked, fruit-driven wines. These will form part of a trio of bottlings of each variety, along with a more serious style and finally a reserve, which is a special selection of grapes and barrels. New export markets in the UK and US have been established, joining existing Sweden, The Netherlands and Luxembourg.

★★★★ **Pinotage** 07's juicy plum/mulberry & spice notes, firm tannins ably support the rich, concentrated berries, leading to lingering savoury conclusion.

★★★★☆ **Pinotage Reserve** Espresso-spiked plum notes, 07 (★★★★) savoury, spicy & silky, with super fruit purity & grip. Like 06, full-bodied with an enduring spicy aftertaste, shade less elegant.

★★★★ **Pinotage with Touch of Oak** 10 plum cake & spice nuances, lipsmacking acidity; gently oaked, letting the berry fruit shine. For early enjoyment.

★★★★ **Shiraz** 06 (★★★★) off the pace of showstopping 05. Bullish & bold, with sweet-ripe dark berries & spice cake. Full-bodied, rich mouthfeel with a warm, spicy finish. Lacks grip & finesse of previous.

★★★★ **Bravado** 04 a compelling shiraz/pinotage-led blend. Opulent yet elegant, with concentrated black berry & spice, balanced & moreish. Drink now.

★★★★☆ **Chardonnay Reserve** Sumptuous 07 last year exuded apple & citrus complexity, delivered depth & richness. Despite its intensity, showed assured balance.

★★★★ **Chenin Blanc** Vibrant tropical notes & creaminess on 08 last edition, balanced by well-judged oak. Delicious, with structure to improve year/2. WO Coastal.

★★★★☆ **Chenin Blanc with Touch of Oak** 🔖 10 (★★★★) touch off complexity of flamboyant 09, crisp apple & citrus flavours, lipsmacking texture with hint of oak. For early drinking.

★★★★ **Chenin Blanc Reserve** 08's (★★★★★) elegant & fine expression of Tulbagh fruit, & step up from 07. Mouthfilling honey, candied lime & butterscotch, creamy persistence. Has developed well, with all elements in place.

Shiraz with Touch of Oak NEW ★★★ 09's soft, juicy, spicy. Gluggable, well made with mouthfilling dark berry fruit - a crowd pleaser. Enjoy soon. **The Crossing** ★★★★ 06 trumps 05 (★★★★), shows warm spice, floral lift, leathery/peppery shiraz & mourvèdre fruit. Slick & smooth, for current drinking. **Chardonnay** ★★★★ 07 barrel-fermented version vast improvement on 06 (★★★). Rich, bold & engaging; concentrated candied lemon & butter flavours, creamy texture & velvety vanilla fun. Yum! **Fascination** ★★★★ Semillon/sauvignon combo 08 richer, more complex than 07 (★★★★) last edition. Tropical fruit, creamy mouthfeel & vanilla nuance. WO Coastal. Discontinued: **Cabernet Sauvignon, Merlot, Cabernet Sauvignon-Merlot, Iceberg Red, Sauvignon Blanc, Semillon, Iceberg White.** — WB

Rivendell

NEW

Location: Bot River ▪ Map: Elgin, Walker Bay & Bot River ▪ WO: Walker Bay ▪ Est 2008 ▪ 1stB 2011 ▪ Tasting & sales daily 8–5 ▪ Closed Jan 1 ▪ Bistro open daily 8-5; also available for small functions ▪ Facilities for children ▪ Tour groups ▪ Conferences ▪ Walks/hikes ▪ Owner(s) Whales & Castle Investments (Pty) Ltd, with shareholders Heimo & Maria Thalhammer ▪ Farm Manager Brandon Scorgie (2008, consultant) ▪ Winemaker(s) Kobie Viljoen (Mar 2010, Gabriëlskloof) ▪ Viticulturist(s) Schalk du Toit (Mar 2008, consultant) ▪ ±8ha/±4ha (shiraz, sauv) ▪ 32t/500cs own label 33% red 67% white ▪ PO Box 181 Onrusrivier 7201 ▪ office@rivendell-estate.co.za ▪ www.rivendell.com ▪ S 34°18'5.22" E 019° 8'32.23" ▪ **T +27 (0)28-284-9185** ▪ F +27 (0)28-284-9597

Having fallen in love with the Bot River Valley, Heimo Thalhammer has revived a winemaking tradition founded by his Slovene great-grandparents in the twilight years of the Austro-Hungarian empire. A couple of hectares each of sauvignon and shiraz in the shade of the Kogelberg have produced their maiden vintage, vinified by Kobie Viljoen at Gabriëlskloof. On the R43 between Bot River and Hermanus, part of the world-renowned Whale Route, Rivendell's tasting room and bistro may soon be extended to include self-catering accommodation.

Sauvignon Blanc 🍷 📖 ★★★☆ Junior vines (2008) do sterling work in **11** preview: appealing, fresh, aromatic, typical if understated sauvignon flavours, & a mineral note which augurs well for this label's future. — Panel

■ **River Garden** *see* Lournesford Wine Estate
■ **River Grandeur** *see* Viljoensdrift Wines & Cruises
■ **River's Edge** *see* Weltevrede Estate
■ **Robert Alexander** *see* Nico van der Merwe Wines

Robertson Wide River Export Company

PO Box 441 Stellenbosch 7599 ▪ niccic@vinimark.co.za ▪ **T** +27 **(0)21-883-8043/4** ▪ F +27 (0)21-886-4708

Joint venture between Robertson Winery and Vinimark, handling all Robertson Winery exports under brand names such as Robertson Winery, Kaapdal, Kleindal, Silversands and Veldt.

Robertson Winery

Location/map/WO: Robertson ▪ Est 1941 ▪ 1stB 1987 ▪ Tasting & sales Mon-Thu 8–5 Fri 8–5.30 Sat/Sun 9–3 ▪ Closed Easter Fri, Dec 25 & Jan 1 ▪ Cellar tours by appt ▪ Conference facilities ▪ Small wine museum ▪ Owner(s) 43 members ▪ Cellarmaster(s) Bowen Botha (Jan 1982) ▪ Winemaker(s) Lolly Louwrens, Francois Weich & Jacques Roux (May 1995/Sep 1997/Jan 2000) ▪ Viticulturist(s) Briaan Stipp (May 2005) ▪ 2,100ha (cab, shiraz, chard, chenin, sauv) ▪ 30,400t ±11.3m L for clients ▪ ISO 22000, WIETA ▪ PO Box 37 Robertson 6705 ▪ info@robertsonwine.co.za ▪ www.robertsonwinery.co.za ▪ S 33° 48'36.8" E 019° 52'51.4" ▪ **T** +27 **(0)23-626-3059** ▪ F +27 (0)23-626-2926

Despite handling over 2,000 tons of grapes, making over 10-million litres of wine and exporting to 40 countries, this winery is built on close ties with its 40+ grower families. Progressive thinking balances viticultural dedication with savvy marketing and a strong social upliftment ethic, embodied by the Constitution Road Wine Growers company for employees. This spells versatility: perennially acclaimed vineyard selection wines, an array of varietal wines under screwcap, and several single-varietal and blended options in re-jigged flexible packaging. Ever on the update, 'RW' has introduced a pinot grigio and a 'light' merlot. Says marketing man Geoff Harvey: 'The former is accessible and taking the world by storm; the latter taps into growing red-wine consumption and the trend, with our stricter drinking-and-driving laws, to lower-alcohol wines that taste good.'

Constitution Road range

★★★★☆ **No. 1 Constitution Road Shiraz** ✓ Serious flagship single-vineyard red is lavishly oaked, generous & bold in violet-toned **08**. Clean leather, mulberry bouquet leads to dark-fruit heart, endless savoury conclusion. Like **07** (★★★★), shows warming 15% alc, but more akin to standout **06** in terms of structure & focus.

Vineyard Selections

★★★★ **Prospect Hill Cabernet Sauvignon** ✓ Ex-barrel **08** billows lanolin, violets, blackcurrant, milk chocolate; palate as layered, mouthfilling & enduring. As curvy as plush **07**. All reds in range 2+ years in oak.

★★★★ **Phanto Ridge Pinotage** ✓ Earth, dark chocolate & wildflowers characterise **09** preview. Rounded tannins & juicy centre augur well for future development once bottled. Similar spice highlights as fruity **07**.

★★★★ **Kings River Chardonnay** ✓ 🍷 Showy barrel-fermented **10** preview, butterscotch, lemon & lime marmalade, creamy vanilla-lime finish. Seems set to follow in footsteps of **09** once bottled.

★★★★ **Retreat Sauvignon Blanc** ✓ 📖 Fig & passionfruit on racy **10**, similar to well-defined **09**, has similarly silky tail from extended lees-ageing. Preview **11** youthful, heading in same direction.

Wolfkloof Shiraz ★★★★ Savoury **08** tasted from barrel: prosciutto & tobacco, firm tannins & drying finish. Nudges next level, unlike ultra-ripe **07**. Discontinued: **Almond Grove Weisser Riesling Noble Late Harvest**.

Winery range

Pinot Noir ☺ 🗎 🅿 **★★★** Unoaked **11** showcases appealing strawberry aromas/flavours, gentle spice; commendably moderate ±13% alc, savoury finish. **Cabernet Sauvignon-Shiraz** ☺ 🗎 🅿 **★★★** Easy-sipping **10** appealing mix of cab's blackberry & shiraz's spice, dusted with cinnamon. **Chardonnay** ☺ 🗎 🅿 **★★★** Suggestion of vanilla & baked apple pie on welcoming **10**, just enough acidity for elegance & freshness. **Chenin Blanc** ☺ 🗎 🅿 **★★★** Ideal al fresco white, **11** is flavourful, not too dry or alcoholic, charming fruit salad aftertaste. **Sauvignon Blanc** ☺ 🗎 🅿 **★★★** Spread of picking dates yields a fairly complex spectrum of fruits in bouncy **11** tipple.

Cabernet Sauvignon 🗎 🅿 **★★★** Dusty blackberries & controlled tannins on **10**, plumped by spoon sugar. All reds briefly wooded unless noted. **Merlot** 🗎 🅿 **★★ 11** lightly fruited & drying, mere suggestion of choc-mocha. **Pinotage** 🗎 🅿 **★★ 10** had gruffer tannins than others in range mid-2010. Still selling & not revisited. **Ruby Cabernet** 🗎 **★★★ 11** nothing fancy, just an honest, fruity, unoaked dry red to drink while making supper. **Shiraz** ✓ 🅿 **★★★★ 10** perfect braai red: meaty (& dark berry) flavours already included, nice & smooth, spicing from 6 months oak adding a touch of class. **Pinot Grigio** NEW **★★★** Promising **11**, sampled from tank, is delicate & dry, shows a herbal touch to floral & musky perfumes. **Viognier** 🗎 🅿 **★★★** Team knows how to handle this high-maintenance variety; **10** savoury & spicy, good peachy varietal character, lees-ageing adds substance. **Beaukett** 🗎 🅿 **★★★ 11** affable & unassuming off-dry mix muscadel & colombard. **Gewürztraminer Special Late Harvest** ✓ 🗎 **★★★★** Classic litchi & Turkish Delight, **09** last time was light bodied but rich thanks to touch botrytis. **Muscadel** Await new. **Port** New vintage not available.

Chapel range

Red ★★ Easy-going anytime companion from ruby cab. These all NV & for early drinking. Available in 500ml, 750ml & 1.5L. **White ★★** Tropical marriage colombard & chenin for long, lazy summer days. **Semi-Sweet ★★** Juicy & fresh white crowd-pleaser. **Rosé ★** Ultra-light sweet pink, only ±7% alc.

Natural Sweet range

Red ★ Country-style quaffer from ruby cab. All in range NV & full-sweet, less than 8% alc. Also available in 3L. **Rosé ★★** Sweet, pretty & pink, dash muscadel adds the musky/grapey allure. **White ★★** Floral & soft, glides down easily.

Two-Litre Certified Cultivar Cask range

Chardonnay ☺ **★★★** Luscious **10** appears to have been made in a French bakery: vanilla-infused, cinnamon-dusted apple tart. Sip slowly without the guilt! **Chenin Blanc** ☺ **★★★ 11** lunchtime pick-me-up with lightish alc, fresh green-apple dash. **Sauvignon Blanc** ☺ **★★★** Herb-seamed tropical flavour in gentle **11** delight.

Cabernet Sauvignon ★★★ Balanced tannins & dusty black fruit, **10** for solo sipping or mealtime enjoyment. **Merlot ★★** Choc-sprinkled **11** lightly fruited & firm, natural food partner. **Ruby Cabernet ★★★** Unwooded & unpretentious **11** red with clean & pure strawberry flavours. **Shiraz** ✓ **★★★★** Ebullient **10**, smooth & full; berries, meat & spice say 'braai mate deluxe'.

Three-Litre Cultivar Slimline range

Cabernet Sauvignon 11 vintage of this, **Shiraz**, **Chardonnay** selling but not tasted. **Merlot ★ 11** tank sample is chocolate-toned, ultra-dry. **Sauvignon Blanc ★** Greenpepper notes & crisp acidity on **11**. **Sauvignon Blanc Extra Light ★★ 10** softly grassy when last visited.

Three-Litre Blended range

Smooth Dry Red ★★ Exactly as advertised: smooth, dry, red. NV, as all these. **Crisp Dry White ★★** Unpretentious & summery patio wine. **Extra Light ★** Low-alc white, dry guava-toned fun. **Johannisberger Semi-Sweet White ★★** Semi-sweet & perfumed quaffer. **Natural Sweet Red (Slimline Packed) ★** Ruby cab made sweet 'n simple for effortless tippling. **Natural Sweet Rosé (Slimline Packed) ★★** Pretty pink party wine. **Johannisberger Semi-Sweet Red ★** Unexpected tannin nibble prevents ruby cab from being cloying.

Combibloc range

Smooth Dry Red ★★ Light & easy for quaffing fun. **Crisp Dry White ★★** Trio white varieties hit right drinkability note. **Crisp Extra Light ★** Off-dry but crisp, with low 10% alc. **Selected Stein ★★** Light (10.5% alc) & semi-sweet. **Fruity Late Harvest ★★** Spicy lunchtime al fresco white. **Natural Sweet Rosé ★★** Deep pink & packed with cranberries. **Natural Sweet White ★★** Low alc grapey-sweet tipple. **Smooth Sweet Red ★** Not as sweet as name suggests, but certainly smooth. This, all above, NV.

Light Cultivar range

Merlot NEW ★ 11 tank sample ultra-dry, sprinkled with choc. Low alc (±9%) for all these. **Pinotage Rosé** 🍴 📷 ★ Effusive boiled sweets character in 11, serve well chilled. **Chenin Blanc** 🍴 📷 ★★ For sushi, say the winemakers: 11 certainly perky enough to match the richness of salmon roses. **Sauvignon Blanc** 🍴 📷 ★ 11 low alc slimmer's friend.

Vendange Sparkling Wines

Vin Rouge ☺ ★★★ Refreshing & vivacious, with low 7.5% alc. NV carbonated sparkling crafted for every-day enjoyment, as are all these.

Brut ★★★ Zingy dry sparkler infused with Granny Smith apples. **Vin Blanc** ★★★ Semi-sweet, low-alc bubbly with spicy appeal. **Rosé** ★★★ Deep pink, low-alc grapey fizz. — Panel

---

Robert Stanford Estate

Map: Elgin, Walker Bay & Bot River ▪ WO: Walker Bay ▪ Est 1855 ▪ 1stB 2008 ▪ Tasting & sales daily 9-5 ▪ Closed Dec 25 & Jan 1 ▪ Madre's Kitchen Thu-Mon 8-4 ▪ Facilities for children ▪ Gift shop ▪ Farm produce ▪ Walking/hiking & mountain biking trails ▪ Conservation area ▪ Distillery (grappa & fruit spirits) ▪ Glass workshop ▪ Tram tours through vineyards ▪ Owner(s) Kleinrivier Beleggings (Pty) Ltd ▪ Cellarmaster(s)/winemaker(s) Johan Joubert (Sep 2007, Kleine Zalze) ▪ Viticulturist(s) Jan Malan (Jan 2003) ▪ 176ha/68ha (pinot, shiraz, chard, sauv, sem) ▪ 370t/1,200cs own label 40% red 30% white 15% rosé 15% MCC ▪ BWI Champion ▪ wines@robertstanfordestate.co.za ▪ www.robertstanfordestate.co.za ▪ S 34° 25'49.41"E 019° 27'49.98" ▪ T +27 (0)28-341-0441 ▪ F +27 (0)86-655-6944

'People who would have driven by in the past, are now turning in,' says Jan Malan, driving force behind the rejuvenation of one of Walker Bay's original farms. In a few short years the diverse offering (wine, distillery, deli, tram tours, glassworks) has grown, as have retail and restaurant listings with a new national distributor. Harvest festivals, seasonal soirées and wine club functions are also in the works.

Sir Robert Stanford Estate range

★★★★☆ **The Hansom** Understated & elegant, stylishly presented cab-led 09 offered concentrated black-currant fruit last edition, so well crafted that substantial alc & smidgen sugar didn't jar.

★★★★ **Chenin Blanc** NEW ✓ Dusty notes on chic 10 oak-fermented chenin that avoids being big & ripe, its tropical melon flavours offered by fine acidity, wood in unobtrusive support.

★★★★ **Sauvignon Blanc** ✓ 10 (★★★★) brisk acidity a counterpoint to ripe fig profile, persistent flavour, but one step behind cool, calm & collected 09 with its delicious mineral conclusion.

Rosé NEW ★★★ Strawberry tones to light, brisk, semi-dry 10. — DS

■ **Robin Hood Legendary Wine Series** *see* Arumdale Cool Climate Wines
■ **Rockfield** *see* Du Preez Estate

Romond Vineyards

Location: Somerset West ▪ Map: Helderberg ▪ WO: Stellenbosch ▪ Est 1993 ▪ 1stB 2003 ▪ Tasting, sales & tours by appt Mon-Sat 10-5.30 Sun 11-5.30 ▪ Fee R25, waived on purchase ▪ Closed Easter Fri-Sun, Dec 25/26 & Jan 1 ▪ Olive oil ▪ The Vintner's Loft self-catering apartment ▪ Owner(s) André & Rhona Liebenberg ▪ Winemaker(s) André Liebenberg ▪ Viticulturist(s) Francois Hanekom (May 2007, consultant) ▪ 11.5ha/9.5ha (cabs s/f, merlot, ptage) ▪ PO Box 5634 Helderberg 7135 ▪ info@romond.co.za ▪ www.romondvineyards.co.za ▪ S 34° 1'58.6" E 018° 49'56.1" ▪ T +27 (0)21-855-4566 ▪ F +27 (0)21-855-0428

'Our end of harvest celebration saw an empty table as our guests helped fight the devastating fire that raged on the Helderberg that day,' recounts boutique vintner André Liebenberg. 'The cellar and vineyard were thankfully spared, but future fire risk induced me to fell a mixed forest. This has exposed a prime slope, ready for development — perhaps for more of my beloved cab franc.'

Pinotage ★★★★ 09, now bottled, is fruity but serious, with pure ripe dark berries, plums & leafy notes. Balanced & juicy, with delicious grip to finish. **Rebus** ★★★★ Quality of the grapes reflected last year in full-bodied, concentrated tones of 07 cab franc/cab blend, showed more finesse & class than last-reviewed 03 (★★★). **Impromptu** ★★★★ Ever-improving dry rosé from merlot. 10 more complex & vibrant, mouthfilling ripe cherries, rosepetal & spice. Long spicy finish cries out for food. — WB

Roodeberg

Something of a South African tradition, this KWV brand is now modelled on a fresher, purer-fruited style, reflecting the international trend to wines with less oak and more finesse. Well received by new local wine drinkers, it has also attracted positive comments in Sweden and Canada.

Roodeberg Red ✓ ★★★★ Upward quality/style curve continues with this local favourite. Freshness, purer red fruit, spice main benefits on **09** cab-based blend. **Roodeberg White** 📖 ★★★ Hints spice, wild herbs, minerals add interest to **10** juicy sextet based on chenin & chardonnay. Drops 'Blend' from name. — AL

Roodezandt Wines

Location/map/WO: Robertson ▪ Est 1953 ▪ Tasting & sales Mon-Fri 8-5 ▪ Cellar tours by appt Mon-Fri 8-12 & 2-5 ▪ Closed all pub hols ▪ Sales (at cellar price) also from La Verne Wine Boutique Mon-Thu 9-5.30 Fri 9-6 Sat 9-5 ▪ Facilities for children ▪ Owner(s) 60 members ▪ Cellarmaster(s) Christie Steytler (May 1980) ▪ Winemaker(s) Ferdi Coetzee (2009), with Tiaan Blom (Oct 2005) ▪ Viticulturist(s) Jaco Lategan (Dec 2006) ▪ 1,600ha (cab, merlot, ptage, ruby cab, shiraz, chard, chenin, cbard, sauv) ▪ 27,000t/21m L bulk ▪ BSCI, HACCP ▪ PO Box 164 Robertson 6705 ▪ info@roodezandt.co.za ▪ www.roodezandt.co.za ▪ S 33° 48'33.2" E 019° 52'47.3" ▪ **T +27 (0)23-626-1160** ▪ F +27 (0)23-626-5074

This Robertson 'specialist production house' aims to be 'the preferred long-term bulk wine supplier to selected major brand owners worldwide', the core business being 'tailor-made bulk'. Don't think of Roodezandt as just a faceless corporate, though: visitors remain welcome for tastings and tours (see above), and the own-brand wines are also available for sale at La Verne Wine Boutique across the street.

Balthazar range

★★★★ **Cap Classique Brut** Ambitious top-label champagne-method sparkling, NV (**07**) from chardonnay, 2 years on lees. Elegant & accomplished; lovely shortbread nose, lemon-marmalade finish last year.
Classic Cabernet Sauvignon ★★★★ Soft & integrated **05** had hint of dates & scented fynbos last edition; noted then for early drinking.

Roodezandt range

Sauvignon Blanc ☺ ★★★ Easy-drinking **11**, soft gooseberry & cut-grass mouthful.

Cabernet Sauvignon ★★ Leafy **10** lacks fruit to soak up firm oak tannins. Needs food. **Syrah** ★★★ Step-up **10** pleasing red berry aromas & flavours, refreshing acidity for casual sipping. **Special Late Harvest** 📖 ★★★ From chenin & muscadel, floral **11** fresh & fruity; good match for Thai & other spicy food. **Red Muscadel** 📖 ★★★★ Seductive apricot-toned **10**'s grapey sweetness well balanced by firm acidity; for fireside conversations.

Keizer's Creek range

The Red 📖 ★★ Unwooded entry-level NV blend with baked berry fruit. **The White** Not tasted. — Panel

Rooiberg Winery

Location/map/WO: Robertson ▪ Est 1964 ▪ 1stB 1974 ▪ Tasting & sales Mon-Fri 8-5.30 Sat 9-3 ▪ Fee R10pp for tour groups ▪ Closed Easter Fri, Dec 25 & Jan 1 ▪ Bodega de Vinho Restaurant & Bakery Mon-Fri 8-5.30 Sat 9-3 ▪ BYO picnic ▪ Facilities for children ▪ Tour groups ▪ Gift shop ▪ Rooiberg Conservancy ▪ Owner(s) 30 members ▪ Cellarmaster(s) André van Dyk (Oct 2002) ▪ Winemaker(s) André Scriven (Jan 2008), with Johan Gerber (Jun 2011) ▪ Viticulturist(s) Hennie Visser (2007, Vinpro consultant) ▪ 7,500ha/667ha (cab, merlot, ptage, ruby cab, shiraz, chard, chenin, cbard, sauv) ▪ 10,000t/175,000cs own label 40% red 60% white ▪ Export brands: African Dawn, Amandalia, Cape Avocet, Goeie Tye, Table View, Tembana Valley, Zebra Collection ▪ Brands for clients: AlexKia, Cape Dreams, Ferling Noble, Woolworths ▪ ISO 9001:2000, BWI, HACCP, IPW, SGS Organic ▪ PO Box 358 Robertson 6705 ▪ info@rooiberg.co.za ▪ www.rooiberg.co.za ▪ S 33° 46'35.3" E 019° 45'42.9" ▪ **T +27 (0)23-626-1663** ▪ F +27 (0)23-626-3295

'We are market- rather than production-driven,' says CEO Johan du Preez, explaining that the proposal to the Robertson area grower-owners to convert from a co-operative into a private company will allow Rooiberg to service existing and new markets better by expanding 'already famous brands' and further improving value for money. 'The consumer is king (if he takes the trouble to shop around) so we embrace a policy of oversupply in quality.' Despite expanding into China, Russia and the US the past year, the focus is also local: 'To convince traditional beer and spirit drinkers that a good wine brand evokes good feelings, and feelings drive action.'

Reserve range

Cabernet Sauvignon 🦿 ★★★★ Smoke & clean leather appeal, **10** tighter & more restrained than Pinotage, Shiraz, deserves year/2 to unfurl. Steady improvement shown in this boutique range - only 250-500 cases available. **Merlot** 🦿 ★★★ New French oak adds vanilla sweetness, plumps out herb-toned, savoury **10**. **Pinotage** ✓ 🦿 ★★★★ Focus, depth & concentration on step-up **10**. Packed with mulberries, less reliant on oak than Shiraz. Like **09** (★★★★), enough sweet fruit to drink young & improve 3+ years. **Shiraz** ✓ 🦿 ★★★★ **10** raises the bar on admirable **09** (★★★★): brooding savoury bacon aromas, vibrant, refreshing, despite intense fruit concentration. Currently trading off oak (100% new, like all reds), needs year/2 to meld, gain more complexity. **Chardonnay** 🦿 ★★★ Lime & lemon, tropical overlay to oak-tinged **10**. Medium body, creamy tail.

Rooiberg range

Merlot ☺🦿 ★★★ Coriander & fenugreek, meaty notes on fresh & commendably dry **10**. Lightly oaked, as most reds in range. **Mountain Red** ☺🦿 ★★★ Previously 'Selected Red'. Quintet fruity varieties make for juicy, uncomplicated enjoyment in bottled **10** & previewed **11**. **Pinotage Rosé** ☺🦿 ★★★ Slightly sweet flick in tail of candyfloss & strawberry **11**, hits the drinkability spot. **Red Natural Sweet** ☺🦿 ★★★ Characterful & silky **11**, beguiling chocolate-nuanced sweetness checked by friendly tannic nip; really well made. **Red Muscadel** ☺🦿 ★★★ Previewed **10** fortified's super-sweetness lifted by pleasantly fiery finish, ideal winter warmer.

Cabernet Sauvignon 🦿 ★★ Vanilla seam, herbal sprinkling on firm **10** quick-sip. **Pinotage** 🦿 ★★★ Mulberry-infused **10** smooth & supple; enjoy lightly chilled in summer. **Shiraz** 🦿 ★★★ Dusty oak, red fruit & floral wafts on **10**, fairly firm finish for food. **Cabernet Sauvignon-Merlot (Roodewyn)** 🦿 ★★ Easy-drinking **10** starting to tire, enjoy soon. **Chardonnay** 🦿 ★★ Slightly warming, **11** not quite in league of previous. Lightly oaked for sipping on the Breede River. **Chenin Blanc** 🦿 ★★★ Bubblegum fragrance on quiet **11**. Crisp, with lightish 12.5% alc for lunchtime imbibing, as next. **Cape White (Colombar)** 🦿 ★★ Gently sweet preview **11** bursts with guava. **Sauvignon Blanc** 🦿 ★★ Intriguing white pepper hint on forthcoming **11**, brisk acidity softened by smidgen sugar. **Chenin Blanc-Sauvignon Blanc** 🦿 ★★★ Zingy **11** preview pineapple, grass & thatch complexity, slips down easily. Rating provisional, should score higher once settled. **Brut Sparkling** ★★ Fizzy Granny Smith apple appeal, bit of grip for food partnering. **NV. Vin Doux Sparkling** ★★ Vivacious **NV** with explosive bubbles, grapey sweetness from muscadel. **Flamingo Sparkling** ★★ Refreshing rosé bubbly from red muscadel, muted berries, brief farewell. **NV. Rosé Natural Sweet** 🦿 ★★ Tealeaf-scented **11** sweetie from red muscadel. **Blanc Natural Sweet** 🍴🦿 ★★ Matchstick whiff on grapey **11**. **Cape Vintage** ★★★★ 'Vintage Port' previously. **07** from pinotage delicious Xmas cake flavours, good tannin grip. — Panel

Rosendal Winery   🍴🏠📷♿

Location/map: Robertson ▪ 1stB 2003 ▪ Tasting, sales & cellar tours Mon-Sat 8-5 Sun 9-1 ▪ Fee only charged for groups of 10+ ▪ Restaurant & Guesthouse (see Restaurants & Accommodation sections) ▪ Spa & wellness wentre ▪ Conferences ▪ Owner(s) Geir Tellefsen & Sissel Anderssen ▪ Cellarmaster(s)/winemaker(s) Philip Costandius (2008, consultant) ▪ 18ha ▪ 80% red 15% white 5% rosé ▪ PO Box 3 Suite 128 Roggebaai 8012 ▪ info@rosendalwinery.com ▪ www.rosendalwinery.com ▪ S 33° 48'7.8" E 019° 59'19.0" ▪ **T +27 (0)21-424-4498 / +27 (0)23-626-1570 (farm)** ▪ F +27 (0)21-424-1570

This luxury guesthouse and wellness spa near Robertson is now starting to make waves with its wines, with exports to Africa and Europe well underway. Cellarmaster Philip Costandius sources high-quality grapes, mostly red, from a variety of areas, and the wines are proving popular, particularly as personalised gifts for businesses.

Reserve Limited range

★★★★ **Black Eagle** Substantial flagship **04** last edition was a smooth mix of shiraz, cab & merlot. **Merlot** ★★★★ When last tasted, elegant **03** had the structure to cellar longer. **Wild Blue Yonder** Sold out, await new. **Red Rock** NEW **06** not rated.

Barony range

Candelabra Shiraz NEW ★★★ Smoky bacon, red berries & spice on firm & tight **09**, will benefit from hour/2 decanting or further ageing. **Sophie** ★★★★ Previously reviewed **06** Bordeaux-style red was leafy, dash pinotage added mulberry fruit to counter robust tannins. **Cecile Sauvignon Blanc** ★★★☆ Crisply fruity **09** had ripe granadilla & leesy fatness, was well formed last year.

Hilltop range
Cabernet Sauvignon Reserve NEW ★★★ Shy, food-styled **09** shows light fruit, firm acidity & chalky tannins.
Merlot ★★★☆ From Wellington, **09** last time tad rustic but offered solid black-fruit flavours & friendly tannins.
Sauvignon Blanc ★★★ Lime & gooseberry fruit, soft acid on **10**, fair length for relaxed sipping. —Panel

Ross Gower Wines

Location/WO: Elgin • Map: Elgin, Walker Bay & Bot River • Est 2003 • 1stB 2004 • Tasting, sales & tours by appt • Meals & picnic baskets by arrangement • Glen Stuart self-catering cottages • Conservation area • Owner(s) Gower family • Winemaker(s) Robert Gower (2004) & James Gower (2007) • Viticulturist(s) Robert Gower • 83ha/±7ha (shiraz, sauv) • 10,000cs own label 40% red 45% white 15% MCC • PO Box 161 Elgin 7180 • info@rossgowerwines.co.za • www.rossgowerwines.co.za • S 34° 14'17.7" E 019° 7'3.7" • **T +27 (0)21-844-0197** • F +27 (0)86-611-2179

Happier times have followed the sad passing of gregarious winemaker and co-founder, Ross Gower, with the celebration of son Robbie's wedding on the Elgin family farm. He and brother James, with ever-supportive mother Sally, continue Ross' legacy, drawing strength from his well-rounded winemaking style and their own harvest experiences abroad. The successful Valley Road Vintners range is sold only in restaurants, while the bottle-aged 'family' range below, with commendably moderate alcohol, shows typical Elgin elegance.

★★★★ **Sauvignon Blanc** 🔲 Previously tasted **09** (★★★★) was pleasingly textured & elegant, with green fig & nettle aromas, but shade off **08**.
Cabernet Sauvignon 🔲 ★★★☆ Newer vintage still maturing, as for Merlot. **07** showed brooding cassis & liquorice with a tinge of greenpepper & firm structure. **Merlot** 🔲 Await new release. **Shiraz** 🔲 ★★★☆ **08** combines savoury white pepper nuance & red berry juiciness. Riper tone than previous, in supple & accessible styling. **Rosé** 🔲 ★★★ **10** all but sold out. **11** is light & savoury with low ±10% alc, from cab/shiraz. Tart, tannic twist suits al fresco fare. **Rhine Riesling** 🔲 ★★★★ Perfumed **10** is crisply off-dry, genteel, shows varietal's delicate sweet/sour balance & potential to develop. **Pinot Noir Brut** ★★★☆ Fruity champagne-method sparkling **08** exudes cranberry flavours with savoury tannin undertone. Dapper & appealing aperitif or food partner. —MW

▮ **Rotsvast** see Baarsma Wine Group
▮ **Route 303** see Ultra Liquors
▮ **Royle** see Arra Vineyards

Rozendal

Location/map: Stellenbosch • 1stB 1983 • Tasting, sales & tours by appt • Luxury auberge with restaurant & amenities • Owner(s) Kurt & Lyne Ammann • Winemaker(s) Kurt Ammann • 6ha (cabs s/f, merlot) • 100% red • PO Box 160 Stellenbosch 7599 • rozendal@mweb.co.za • www.rozendal.co.za, www.rozendalvinegar.co.za • S 33° 55'51.9" E 018° 53'47.4" • **T +27 (0)21-809-2600, +27 (0)21-887-5612** • F +27 (0)86-612-9046

Rozendal no longer harvests its six-hectare vineyard except to make a 'Bordeaux blend' for its awarding-winning balsamic vinegars (another New York medal last year). However, vintages dating back as far as the superlative 1983 are still available from the Stellenbosch farm and its upmarket auberge.

▮ **Rozier Bay/Reef** see Mount Rozier Estate

Rudera Wines

Location: Stellenbosch • WO: Stellenbosch/Walker Bay/Elgin • Est 1999 • 1stB 2000 • Tasting, sales & cellar tours Mon-Fri 11-4 Sat/Sun by appt • Fee R30 • Closed all pub hols • Conference facilities • Owner(s) Rudera Wines CC • Cellarmaster(s) Chris Keet • Winemaker(s) Adele Swart (Jan 2011), with Andre Roux (Apr 2011) • Viticulturist(s) Andre Roux (Apr 2011) • 15ha/10ha (cab, shiraz, chenin) • ±100t/5,000cs own label 40% red 60% • IPW • 14 Napier Street Paarl 7646 • info@rudera.co.za • www.rudera.co.za • **T +27 (0)21-852-1380 (Office), +27 (0)21-871-1749 (Cellar)** • F +27 (0)21-852-1380

Eleven years in the making and the Rudera dream has finally found a home: wines can now be tasted on the breathtaking D'Olyfboom Estate in historic Paarl. The fully renovated 300-year old cellar is winemaking HQ for the new team headed by Chris Keet as cellar master, leading the winemaker-viticulturist duo of Adele Swart and Andre Roux. The philosophy is to let the vineyards do the talking, so the focus is on terroir and special vineyards to show off unique wine personalities. Things are done as naturally as possible, to ensure that these wines remain characterful and true to their origin and individuality.

★★★★ Cabernet Sauvignon 09 sample ex barrel, has all the hallmarks of higher honours. Currently quite shy with brooding dark fruit & dense compact palate. Masculine tannins especially need time to meld.

★★★★☆ Platinum Cabernet Sauvignon Same vintage still selling, but name change from 'Platinum Red'. Last was intense & concentrated **07** with finely managed velvety tannins & persistent spicy finish.

★★★★ Syrah Now bottled, **09** more composed, still shy with oak quite prominent, but begs for time to evolve. Lovely savoury palate with cherry freshness ends firm & ultra-dry. WO Walker Bay.

★★★★ De Tradisie Chenin Blanc 09 tasted last year concentrated & persistent, with crisp, dry & food-friendly structure. Includes some Elgin grapes.

★★★★☆ Robusto Chenin Blanc 09 (★★★★) now bottled displays citrus combo with toasty oak aromas. In drier style than previous **08** with bright cleansing acid cutting barrel fatness in support of balanced clear fruit.

★★★★☆ Chenin Blanc Noble Late Harvest From chenin, **08** great exposition of style with fine honey blossom, apricot & distinct earthy tones. The palate is wonderfully complex with perfect balance between sweetness & acid. Some new oak aids complexity & is well integrated.

Platinum Chenin Blanc ★★★★ Tasted last year as 'Platinum White,' **09** from low-yielding Elgin chenin had smoky lime-apricot notes, taut flinty palate & good length. — JP

Rudi Schultz Wines

Location/WO: Stellenbosch ▪ Est 2002 ▪ Tasting by appt ▪ Closed all pub hols ▪ Owner(s) Rudi Schultz ▪ Cellar-master(s)/winemaker(s) Rudi Schultz (Jan 2002) ▪ Viticulturist(s) Dirkie Morkel (consultant) ▪ 10t/800cs own label 100% red ▪ 8 Fraser Road Somerset West 7130 ▪ rudi@thelema.co.za ▪ **T +27 (0)82-928-1841** ▪ F +27 (0)21-885-1800

Rudi Schultz looks back with most pride, he says, at his 11 vintages making wine at Thelema. He's been making his elegant own-label wine (from vines in Stellenbosch's Bottelary Hills) for nearly as long, and with as much acclaim. The Reserve is made only in outstanding years and unfortunately in tiny quantities: a mere 167 magnums of the splendid 2009.

★★★★☆ Syrah ✓ Serious but delicious even in youth. **08** was grander than **09** (★★★★) - but this also in generous style, well structured. Lovely texture & enough intensity for lingering pleasure.

★★★★☆ Reserve Syrah Only in great years - last was **05**. **09** deeper, richer colour than standard version; finer, more complex aromas & flavours. In warm, ripe style with velvety texture; subtle & unshowy, with depth & persistence. Integrated all-new oak (15% for standard version). Will grow over 5-10 years.

Viognier Await next release. — TJ

Ruitersvlei Wines

Location/WO: Paarl ▪ Map: Paarl & Wellington ▪ Est 1692 ▪ 1stB 1995 ▪ Tasting & sales by appt ▪ Owner(s) JA Faure ▪ Winemaker(s) Jurgen Siebritz, with Louis van Zyl (Jun 2007/Mar 2008, consultants) ▪ Viticulturist(s) Kobus Mostert (Nov 2001, consultant) ▪ 580ha/248ha (cab, ptage, shiraz, chard, chenin, sauv) ▪ 750t/50,000cs own label 70% red 30% white; 700cs for clients ▪ Brands for clients: Vaughan Johnson Wine Shop ▪ IPW ▪ PO Box 532 Suider-Paarl 7624 ▪ marketing@ruitersvlei.co.za ▪ S 33° 45' 10.8" E 018° 54' 28.0" ▪ **T +27 (0)21-863-1517** ▪ F +27 (0)21-863-1443

Production continues for their own and customer labels, but planning is on hold at this Suider Paarl estate while sale negotiations are under way. In the meantime, the tasting room remains open for visitors.

Ruitersvlei range

Chenin Blanc ☺ 🍷 ★★★ **11** tank sample (as next), shows improvement from last time. Riper, softer acidity, better drinkability. **Sauvignon Blanc** ☺ 🍷 ★★★ **11** poolsider is crisp & enticingly fruity.

Cabernet Sauvignon 🍷 ★★★ Now bottled, **09** shows ripeness & chalky tannins, fruit has evolved & opened. **Pinotage** 🍷 ★★★ Varietal character centre-stage on **08**, last year was spicy, juicy, firmly tannic. **Shiraz** 🍷 ★★ Pleasant but lightweight **08** showed jammy fruit previously. **Private Collection** Untasted.

Mountainside range

Red ☺ 🍷 ★★★ Star of this budget-friendly range, **10** is quaffably fruity, juicy & affable.

White 🍷 ★★ **10** is fresh, fruity & eminently quaffable. — GdB

Rupert & Rothschild Vignerons

Location: Paarl • Map: Paarl & Wellington • WO: Western Cape • Est 1997 • 1stB 1998 • Tasting, sales & cellar tours Mon-Fri 9-4.30 Sat (Nov-Feb) 9-4.30 • Fee R5/wine • Closed Ash Wed, Easter Fri-Mon, Dec 25 & Jan 1 • Owner(s) Rupert family & Baron Benjamin de Rothschild • Cellarmaster(s) Schalk-Willem Joubert (Jun 1997) • Winemaker(s) Yvonne Lester (Sep 2001), with Clive Radloff (Jun 1997) • Viticulturist(s) Renier Theron (Oct 2003) • 90ha (cabs s/f, merlot) • 900t/60,000cs own label 93% red 7% white • ISO 14001, HACCP, IPW • PO Box 412 Franschhoek Valley 7690 • info@rupert-rothschildvignerons.com • www.rupert-rothschildvignerons.com • S 33° 50'14.5" E 018° 56'51.1" • **T +27 (0)21-874-1648** • F +27 (0)21-874-1802

Anton Rupert purchased this Simonsberg farm in 1986 as part of his vision to see the Cape ranked with the best winelands in the world and not 'full of houses'. His partnership with Baron Edmond de Rothschild, owner of Château Clarke in Bordeaux, was forged in 1997. The wine team too are long-term partners here: 'A huge privilege to be in the same cellar for so long,' says winemaker Yvonne Lester. 'We now thoroughly understand the vineyards - for instance, Stellenbosch fruit provides fresh fruit flavours, elegance, while structure and depth come from Darling; also what works in the cellar and fits our wine style. Making only three wines allows for attention to finer details, so we're never bored!'

★★★★☆ **Baron Edmond 09** reflects class of vintage; wealth of ripe aromas, rich texture embraced in youth by cab's stern tannins. Moderate 13.5% alc, freshness, well-absorbed all-new oak additional refinements. Cab-based as usual, with 30% merlot. **08** sold out untasted by us.

★★★★ **Classique** Multi-sourced **09** cab-merlot with similar savoury, smoky restraint as **08**. Succulent, very firm tannins need year/2 to resolve with fresh, sweet flesh. Admirably modest oak, alc.

★★★★ **Baroness Nadine** Consistent style, quality. **09**'s cooler citrus tones, bracing freshness toned by creamy texture from 80% barrel ferment, a third of the barrels new. Will reward few years ageing. — AL

■ **Rupert Wines** see Anthonij Rupert Wines

Russo Family Vintners

Map: Durbanville, Philadelphia & Darling • Est 2004 • 1stB 2007 • Tasting, sales & tours Mon-Fri 9-4 Sat by appt • Closed all pub hols • Owner(s) Henk & Terèsa Rossouw • Winemaker(s) Terèsa Rossouw (2007) • 6.5ha/4ha (cabs s/f, malbec, merlot, p verdot) • 35t/400cs own label 100% red • PO Box 4402 Tyger Valley 7536 • teresa@russowines.co.za • www.russowines.co.za • S 33° 48'37.9" E 018° 37'04.3" • **T +27 (0)21-979-1960** • F +27 (0)21-979-1996

Small scale and focussed is the way that wine is crafted here. Only the best, but traditional equipment is used, while having only one wine ensures that all passion, care and applied labour go into it. With the Malbec vineyard now ready we look forward to a five way Bordeaux from Terèsa and Henk Rossouw soon.

★★★★ **Russo** Same vintage still selling. Last was elegant & restrained **07**. — JP

Rustenberg Wines

Location/map: Stellenbosch • WO: Simonsberg-Stellenbosch/Stellenbosch/Coastal/Western Cape • Est 1682 • 1stB 1892 • Tasting & sales Mon-Fri 9–4.30 Sat 10–1.30 • Closed Easter Fri/Sun, Dec 25 & Jan 1 • Gift shop • Garden

▪ Owner(s) Simon Barlow ▪ Cellarmaster(s) Randolph Christians (Sep 2007) ▪ Winemaker(s) Randolph Christians (Sep 2007), with Gareth le Grange (2003) ▪ Viticulturist(s) Nico Walters (1999) ▪ 1,200ha/±154ha (cab, grenache, malbec, merlot, mourv, shiraz, chard, rouss, sauv) ▪ ±942t/70,000cs own label 56% red 42% white 2% other ▪ BWI, IPW ▪ PO Box 33 Stellenbosch 7599 ▪ wine@rustenberg.co.za ▪ www.rustenberg.co.za ▪ S 33° 53′44. 8″ E 018° 53′33.6″ ▪ **T** +27 **(0)21-809-1200** ▪ F +27 (0)21-809-1219

This year this iconic Stellenbosch estate on the rich red slopes of the Simonsberg celebrates 70 years of Barlow ownership - though current MD, Simon Barlow, sees himself more as a caretaker of the land than owner. 'Our new wines have been launched and immediately attained great listings, especially in the UK' says Dave Hutton, marketing manager. 'For the next year we will focus on satisfying the growing demand in wine tourism.' To this end a delicatessen and conference venue are planned. Rustenberg is also hosting the first Mountain Warrior Trail Run through the Stellenbosch mountains. In the vineyards, sustainable agriculture is a priority, and a leading role in the Greater Simonsberg Conservancy continues.

Site Specific range

★★★★☆ **Peter Barlow** 100% cab from Rustenberg's finest red vineyard. Cassis- & herb-laden **08** with restrained power & regal bearing. Gorgeous fruit still masked by polished oak. Should reward 5+ yrs ageing.

★★★★☆ **Syrah** Concentrated blackberry, cinnamon, game, violets on vibrant **09** followed by rich & plush spice-cake, stylish oak with terrific balance. Vivacious & seamless.

★★★★☆ **Five Soldiers** Multi-dimensional **09** displays citrus zest, apple blossom, lime & nut oil; complex, & elegant fruit flavours harmonise with subtle nuttiness & creamy texture. Keep 8+ yrs.

Regional range

★★★★☆ **John X Merriman** Classically styled five-way Bordeaux blend. **09** makes a statement with layers cassis, lead pencil, sweet tobacco; persistent mineral end. Powerful yet refined. For 8+ yrs hence.

★★★★ **RM Nicholson** ✓ 🍷 Ex-barrel **10**'s blackcurrants spiced by dried herbs, fynbos. Cab/shiraz/merlot-led blend with pure fruit & hints of oaky vanilla on the conclusion. Balanced, firm & rich.

★★★★ **Chardonnay** ✓ 🍷 🏵 As before, melon, apricot & apple flavours in **10**, complemented by creamy oak. Serious yet delicate with concentrated lemon centre and fine minerality.

★★★★ **Roussanne** 🍷 🏵 **11** preview back on form after uncomplex **10** (★★★★). Balanced & complex sweet peach, white flowers & apple flavours, with vanilla overtones. Creamy mouthfeel.

★★★★ **Sauvignon Blanc** ✓ 🍷 🏵 **11** preview shows lemongrass, pear & herbal aromas. Bright & focused, full-flavoured with a grassy, lemony bite; drop semillon for weight, portion Elgin fruit.

★★★★ **Schoongezicht White** ✓ 🍷 🏵 Previously 'WWT'. Tropical fruit, white blossoms on ex-tank unoaked **11** from semillon, viognier, grenache, roussanne. Full-bodied, complex & mouthfilling, with a delightful lemon twang.

★★★★☆ **Straw Wine** Pure melon, ripe peach & white flowers on **10** from air-dried viognier chenin, crouchen. Bright, rich & elegant fruit with ample streaks of fresh lemon zesty acidity. WO Coastal, as is next white.

Merlot NEW ✓ 🍷 🏵 ★★★★ **10** preview with bright red fruit, lavender & vanilla wafts. Poised & well-structured, with a delicious concluding fruit acid grip. **Unwooded Chardonnay** 🍷 🏵 ★★★★ Adds 'Unwooded' to name. Well-balanced **11** preview has fresh citrus & apple notes, lemon cream finish. — WB

Rust en Vrede Estate

Location/map/WO: Stellenbosch ▪ Est 1694 ▪ 1stB 1979 ▪ Tasting, sales & cellar tours Mon-Sat 9-5 ▪ Fee R40/4 wines & R70/6 wines, waived on purchase ▪ Closed Easter Fri/Sun, Dec 25 & Jan 1 ▪ Rust en Vrede Restaurant (see Restaurants section) ▪ Gift shop ▪ Owner(s) Jean Engelbrecht ▪ Cellarmaster(s) Coenie Snyman (Dec 2006) ▪ Winemaker(s) Coenie Snyman (Dec 2006), with Schalk Opperman (Dec 2006) ▪ Viticulturist(s) Dirkie Mouton (Jun 2010) ▪ 50ha/45ha (cab, merlot, shiraz) ▪ ±300t/20,000cs own label 100% red ▪ IPW ▪ PO Box 473 Stellenbosch 7599 ▪ info@rustenrede.com ▪ www.rustenvrede.com ▪ S 33° 59′54.0″ E 018° 51′22.5″ ▪ **T** +27 **(0)21-881-3881** ▪ F +27 (0)21-881-3000

This grand Stellenbosch estate, while expressing its pride in its splendid past through the restoration of its historic buildings and the name of its most expensive wine, has its focus firmly on the present (and the future: winemaker Coenie Snyman is working on a 15-year plan to 'improve quality & style'). And also a focus, perhaps, on the United States, where owner Jean Engelbrecht has had great marketing success, and where many clearly appreciate the rich, ultra-ripe, oaky plushness, with a hint of sweetness, expressed in the Rust en Vrede reds (red wine has long ruled here): wines undoubtedly not for the faint of heart!

★★★★ **Cabernet Sauvignon 08** (★★★★) big-framed, gawky, without the lush handsomeness of **07**. Flattened by 18 months in all-new Fr oak, 15% alcohol. A little sugar adds to the richness.

★★★★ **Merlot 10** has mulberry & greengage plum notes, sweet-centred, fresh and slightly edgy. Nicely forward, with fruit purity, not evidently oaky. Driest of the range & a rare venture below 15% alc.

★★★★ **Shiraz 08** (★★★★) overdone in less fruit-rich vintage: big 15.3% alc, all-new oak (French/US mix). Dusty kirsch notes, faded spice. Lacks the intensity of **07**.

★★★★☆ **Single Vineyard Syrah 09** (★★★★) dollops of red fruit, mega-ripe though still fresh enough. Invasion of flavour (berry not spice), texture, huge 15.5% alcohol. Sweetness of mostly US new oak abetted by few grams sugar. **08** promised more savoury focus.

★★★★☆ **1694 Classification** Pricey shiraz-cab blend honouring date property was granted. Massive & unabashed **09**, with dense raisiny fruit, weighty & plush. Tobacco & wood-shaving whiffs (customary new oak, mostly French here), sumptuous textures, fruit & generous alcohol.

★★★★☆ **Estate** Previously 'Estate Wine'. **08** (★★★★) cab-led blend with shiraz & a little merlot. Accessible & showy, with nutty, berry notes, sweet vanilla whiffs. Fresh, savoury despite big alcohol & evident oak. Like **07**, should keep good few years. — MF

■ **Rusthof** *see* Mooiuitsig Wine Cellars

Rusticus Vintage Cellar

Location/map: Robertson ▪ WO: Western Cape/Robertson ▪ Est/1stB 2001 ▪ Tasting, sales & cellar tours Mon-Fri 10-4 Sat 10-2 & by appt after 2 ▪ Fee R20pp incl cellar tour, refunded on any purchase ▪ Closed all pub hols ▪ Facilities for children ▪ Tour groups ▪ BYO picnic, on provision a bottle of Rusticus wine is purchased ▪ Conferences ▪ Birding walk ▪ 4x4 trail ▪ Pat Busch Private Nature Reserve (2,000ha), www.patbusch.co.za, with self-catering cottages & guest houses - up to 45 guests (see Accommodation section) ▪ Annual Wacky Wine; Slow Wine on the River; Hands on Harvest Festivals ▪ Owner(s) Stephan & Lindi Busch ▪ Cellarmaster(s)/winemaker(s)/viticulturist(s) Stephan Busch (2004) ▪ 228ha/15ha (cab, merlot, ptage, shiraz, chenin, cbard, viog) ▪ 150t total; 5-15t/1-2,000cs own label 50% red 50% white ▪ PO Box 805 Robertson 6705 ▪ info@rusticus.co.za ▪ www.rusticus.co.za ▪ S 33° 48'18.4" E 019° 59'2.8" ▪ **T +27 (0)23-626-2033** ▪ F +27 (0)86-573-2156

There are plenty of good reasons to visit this boutique wine cellar, not least being the fabulous game drives and walks available on the family-owned reserve. When it comes to winemaking, Stephan Busch opts for minimal intervention without short cuts, and believes his 'Swansong' wine illustrates this point perfectly.

★★★★ **Swansong SMV** Rhône-like **10** opaque & densely fruited, with coriander & scrub, some lift & savoury finish. Fine, not contrived; older oak, so shiraz/mourvèdre/viognier combo shines. 10% Paarl grapes.

★★★★ **Tilled Earth** Previously **08** juicy berry mix of merlot, cab & shiraz (42/37/21), fleshy but firm & satisfying sipper. Not revisited, as for Odyssey & Viognier.

Merlot Wild Ferment Untasted, like **Pinot Noir**. **Odyssey** ★★★ **08** cab-led blend with merlot. Previously, intense black fruit/choc-mocha richness melded well with spicy centre & moderate alc. **Viognier** ★★★★ Nutty peach & stonefruit **09** preview in oxidative style last time. Smoky, rich but restrained. Robertson WO. Discontinued: **Cabernet Sauvignon Limited Release**, **Pinotage**, **Shiraz Limited Release**, **Shiraz**. — Panel

Saam Mountain Vineyards

Location/WO: Paarl ▪ Est/1stB 2007 ▪ Tasting at Perdeberg Winery ▪ Owner(s) Bibendum Wine Limited & Perdeberg Winery ▪ Cellarmaster(s) Albertus Louw (Oct 2008) ▪ Winemaker(s) Riaan Möller (Dec 2006) & Carla Herbst (Jun 2008) ▪ Viticulturist(s) Jaco Engelbrecht (Nov 2011) ▪ 6,000t/50,000cs own label 80% red 20% white ▪ PO Box 214 Paarl 7620 ▪ kirstie@saam-mountain.com ▪ www.saam-mountain.com ▪ **T +27 (0)21-869-8244** ▪ F +27 (0)21-869-8245

SAAM, meaning 'Together', is one of Perdeberg Winery's joint ventures, here between London retailer Bibendum Wine Ltd and some of Perdeberg's 30 grape suppliers. Current range consolidation is part of brand strategy, which includes plans to expand beyond the UK, including South Africa, where the wines will shortly be appearing on shelves.

Saam Single Vineyard Selection

★★★★☆ **Middelburg Chenin Blanc** 🍷 🖥 From Perdeberg vineyard. Savoury **10** (★★★☆) comes down a notch from impressive **09**, oaking still a dominant factor, needs time to meld with fruit.

Koopmanskraal Shiraz Last was **06**, awaiting next. **Heldersig Shiraz-Viognier** 🍷 Await new vintage. **Phisantekraal Sauvignon Blanc** 🍷 New bottling not ready. Discontinued: **Eensaamheid Pinotage**, **Heldersig Pinotage-Viognier**.

Saam Quality range

Cabernet Sauvignon 😊 🍷 🖥 ★★★ Luscious berries in **10**, light oak giving savoury seam, palate grip.
Shiraz 😊 🍷 🖥 ★★★ Savoury, smoky overlay to **10**'s piquant berries, appealing fruity plumpness.

Pinotage 🍷 🖥 ★★★ Juicy blueberries lightly oaked, **10** finishes dry enough for food compatibility. **Chenin Blanc** ✓ 🍷 🖥 ★★★★ Distinctive thatch & red-apple styling in **10**, brightened by racy acidity. Has ability to age a few years. **Sauvignon Blanc** 🍷 🖥 ★★ **10** asparagus flavours, lightish (12% alc) & ultra-fresh. — CR

Sadie Family Wines

Location: Malmesbury ▪ Map/WO: Swartland ▪ Est 1999 ▪ 1stB 2000 ▪ Tasting by appt ▪ Owner(s) The Sadie Family (Pty) Ltd ▪ Winemaker(s)/viticulturist(s) Eben Sadie (1999) ▪ 17ha (grenache, mourv, syrah, chenin, clairette, palomino, rouss, viog) ▪ 28t/1,600cs own label 50% red 50% white ▪ PO Box 1019 Malmesbury 7299 ▪ office@ thesadiefamily.com ▪ S 33° 31'31.0" E 018° 48'18.1" ▪ T +27 (0)22-482-3138 ▪ F +27 (0)86-692-2852

There can be no review of this cellar or its wines without Eben Sadie, because he's at the core of it, the winemaker, viticulturist, strategist, salesman. Anyone who has ever heard him speak will confirm that he's a super salesman, whether it's an idea, an area, a variety or a winemaking style. But the reason for Sadie Family's wine success lies much deeper, because he is also an artist. He has gone beyond the technical or practical skills needed to make good wine, he instinctively knows when to let nature take its course, when less is more, and he takes risks in this regard, so much does he believe in his vision. Fortunately for us, most of his risks pay off and we see one of the country's trailblazers inspire others around him. The annual Swartland Revolution is a great way of seeing the result.

★★★★★ **Columella** Mainly shiraz, with mourvèdre & grenache, which Eben Sadie believes best match the Swartland. That's what **09** shows: ripe dark fruit & scrub, savoury spice interwoven through the perfume, flavours, & not least, supple tannins. Nothing showy, just perfect harmony. Follows sensual **08** (★★★★☆).

★★★★★ **Palladius** Unfined/filtered, 18 months lees-ageing. **10** (★★★★☆) blend 8 mainly Rhône whites, unspecified combo but who cares? It's what's in the glass that counts & that's masterly. Melon & kumquat, crushed almonds, a mineral core. Smooth, curvaceous & a very long finish. Follows stellar **09**. — CR

Saltare

Location: Stellenbosch ▪ WO: Swartland ▪ 1stB 2005 ▪ Closed to public ▪ Owner(s) Christoff & Carla Pauw ▪ Cellarmaster(s)/winemaker(s) Carla Pauw (2005) ▪ 11t/830cs own label 15% red 15% white 70% MCC ▪ PO Box 2290 Dennesig Stellenbosch 7601 ▪ info@saltare.co.za ▪ www.saltare.co.za ▪ T +27 (0)21-883-9568 ▪ F +27 (0)86-021-883-9568

Saltare, means to dance, and the talented young owners of this micro scale winery, have some underprivileged youth, doing just that, through their support of the Ikapa Dance Theatre. Carla & Christoff are inspired by food, wine and educational travel, especially to biodynamic producers and the Champagne region. No surprise that a new Brut Rose is imminent.

Syrah ★★★★ Fast-forward to **07** after **04**. Stewed prune & spicy tobacco in densely woven, ultra-ripe style from Swartland grapes. **Specialis 08** still incubating at press time. **Chenin Blanc** ★★★★ From old Swartland vines, **09** still selling. Last edition showed ripe quince & honey flavours. **Méthode Cap Cassique Brut Reserve** ★★★ Food-styled **07** traditional-method sparkling still available. Shares W Cape WO, chardonnay/pinot blend & ultra-dry styling with **NV** version below. **Méthode Cap Cassique Brut Nature** ★★★★ No sulphur/sugar added, hence 'Brut Nature' suffix this edition. **NV** fruitier & creamier than 'brut' branding suggests, appealing brioche & hazelnut tone. — MW

Sanctum Wines

Location: Elgin • WO: Overberg • Est/1stB 2002 • Closed to public • Owner(s) Mike & Alice Dobrovic • Winemaker(s) Mike Dobrovic • 3.2t/240cs 100% red • PO Box 110 Grabouw 7160 • sanctumwines@gmail.com, alice@breede.co.za • **T +27 (0)21-849-8504** • F +27 (0)21-849-8504

The wines of Sanctum used to be made from bought-in grapes but finally have a home, Mike and Alice Dobrovic having acquired property in Elgin, where they farm apples and grapes. Mike, who spent many years as winemaker for Mulderbosch, is set to be based here permanently in an apartment with 'stunning views'.

★★★★☆ **Shiraz 07** very elegant with flavours of cherry, raspberry & piercing pepper. 18 months all-new oak. Stanford vineyards. Still selling mid-2011, not retasted. — CE

Santa Cecilia

Map: Swartland • Est/1stB 2008 • Tasting facility in The Wine Kollective: Mon-Sat 10-5 Sun 10-3 • Closed Easter Fri, Dec 25 & Jan 1 • Gifts • Farm produce • Bar Bar Black Sheep Restaurant adjacent to tasting facility • Overnight facility 'The Santa Cecilia Boudoir' • Owner(s) Anton Espost & Thys Greeff • Winemaker(s) Anton Espost, Thys Greeff & Hugo Basson (2008, Annex Kloof) • Viticulturist(s) Thys Greeff (Feb 2008), Outback Viticulture • 1,000cs own label 30% red 70% white • PO Box 61 Riebeek-Kasteel 7307 • espost@telkomsa.net • S 33° 23' 1.48" E 018° 53' 46.54" • **T +27 (0)22-448-1008/+27 (0)82-776-9366**

'We do our own thing,' says co-winemaker Anton Espost. 'We're so small that market trends can totally be ignored.' But the popularity of Santa Cecilia wines made using minimal interference or 'Inner Peasant Winemaking (IPW) rules' has warranted expansion into a new cellar 'under an oak tree' in central Riebeek-Kasteel. 'The barrels share space with curing salamis, chorizos, olives and capers. We are still debating whether a small porn collection is an appropriate requirement!'

Sarah's Creek

[NEW]

Closed to public • Owner(s) Dirk C Malherbe • Winemaker(s) Marga Malherbe • 20ha (cab, merlot, sauv) • PO Box 6531 Welgemoed 7538 • info@sarahscreek.co.za • www.sarahscreek.co.za • **T +27 (0)84-941-2526**

Situated on the slopes of the Langeberg Mountains, this family-owned Robertson estate is now in the hands of 12th generation offspring, Dirk Malherbe. Named for an earlier family member who dawdled on her way to school, distracted by the beautiful surroundings, today the farm tries to embody her simplicity and enthusiasm in their handcrafted wines. Plans are afoot to restore the original wine cellar, where winemaker Marga Malherbe will continue combining traditional practices and modern technology.

Saronsberg

Location/map: Tulbagh • WO: Tulbagh/Coastal • Est 2002 • 1stB 2004 • Tasting & sales Mon-Fri 8-5 Sat 10-2 • Fee R25pp • Closed Easter Fri/Sun, Ascension day, Dec 25 & Jan 1 • Cellar tours by appt • Olive oil • BYO picnic • Art works & sculptures on display • Christmas in Winter Tulbagh Festival (Jun) • Owner(s) Saronsberg Cellar (Pty) Ltd • Cellarmaster(s) Dewaldt Heyns (2003) • Winemaker(s) Dewaldt Heyns (2002), with Jolandie van der Westhuizen (2011) • Viticulturist(s) Dewaldt Heyns • 500ha/50ha (shiraz) • 320t own label 70% red 30% white • WIETA • PO Box 361 Tulbagh 6820 • info@saronsberg.com • www.saronsberg.com • S 33° 14'48.2" E 019° 7'2.0" • **T +27 (0)23-230-0707** • F +27 (0)23-230-0709

Owner Nick van Huyssteen and cellarmaster Dewaldt Heyns clock up a decade-long association this year. From start-up in 2002, Saronsberg is now one of the country's undoubted shiraz specialists and has contributed to the continually improving regard for Tulbagh as a fine-wine area. The duo clearly don't believe in rushing things, even when adding new wines to the line-up. Their Brut Méthode Cap Classique sparking joined the range after a leisurely 32 months on the lees! The bubbly was used to celebrate Saronsberg hosting two stages of the world famous mountain bike challenge, the Cape Epic, last year (and all the attendant media coverage, since it was televised for the first time), and their success in having five wines chosen for the inaugural Top 100 competition.

Saronsberg range

★★★★ **Shiraz** Worthy successor to acclaimed **08**, **09** shows leashed power, juicy black fruit with earthy cocoa nuance, depth & density. Approachable but with structure to last 6+ years.

★★★★☆ **Seismic 08** continues starry trajectory of cab (72%), merlot, petit verdot & malbec blend. Ripe, rich blueberry & fruitcake with earthy density. Muscle from 20 months French oak, 100% new, but accessible now. Fine tannin for good ageing. WO Coastal.

★★★★☆ **Full Circle** Shiraz-led Rhône blend with grenache, mourvèdre, viognier. **09** keeps bold smoky bramble richness of previous. Layers of sweet ripe fruit, spice & integrated wood. 19 months new French oak adds elegance, tone & ageability. Drinks well but can go for years.

★★★★ **Viognier** Rich **10** offers dried apple & peach freshness integrated with creamy toast notes from year older oak. 15% naturally fermented. Nuanced, structured & serious. Long finish.

★★★★ **Sauvignon Blanc Straw Wine** Previously tasted **06** had molten pineapple & honeycomb, rich sweetness. The 22 months barrel fermentation/maturation gave a shortbread seasoning, hidden strength.

Brut Méthode Cap Classique NEW ★★★★ Brioche & 'oystershell' on **07** sparkling, 32 months lees-aged. Lime chalkiness adds texture to crisp, zesty 100% chardonnay bubbly.

Provenance range

★★★★ **Shiraz** 2009's sultry plushness retains standard of **08**. Bold, savoury yet soft. 21 months in a third new French oak provides silky tannin platform. Fruit core maintains the harmony. WO Coastal, like next.

★★★★ **Rooi** Top-notch Bordeaux red, **10** over-delivers, like **09**. Packed with blackcurrant, cocoa & char; plush texture masks brooding intensity, smoothly compelling, beautifully integrated & supple. Will age well.

Shiraz Rosé ★★★ Light & fresh **11**, pomegranate zip & dryness, amiable quaffer. **Sauvignon Blanc** 🔖 ★★★★ Bold fig nose & tangy lime zest palate, **11** sampled from tank. 6 months lees-ageing & 10% semillon flesh out mouthfeel & body. — FM

Sauvignon.Com

Location: Durbanville ▪ WO: Coastal ▪ Est/1stB 2010 ▪ Closed to public ▪ Owner(s) Thys & Tienie Louw ▪ Winemaker(s) Thys Louw & Mari van der Merwe (both Jan 2010) ▪ Viticulturist(s) Div van Niekerk (Jan 2010) ▪ 200t/30,000cs own label 100% white ▪ PO Box 27 Durbanville 7551 ▪ info@sauvignon.com ▪ www.sauvignon.com ▪ **T** +27 (0)82-442-1317 ▪ F +27 (0)21-979-1802

Ironically co-owner Thys Louw has yet to give his Internet-inspired brand its 'virtual home' (especially now he's added the domain sauvignonblanc.com to the already owned sauvignon.com). But, if he didn't get to build a website last year, it's because he was building sales, including 30,000 cases to a major UK supermarket, launching a Cab (which missed our deadline), and making wine at Durbanville family estate, Diemersdal.

Sauvignon Blanc ☺ 🔖 🍷 ★★★ Characterful **11** ready for summertime fun: playful mix cool grassy & warmer tropical fruit, crunchy acidity; just 'chill'. WO Coastal. — CvZ

Savanha

Vinified by Stellenbosch-based Spier, Savanha wines celebrate the vibrant energy of the South African Sun in a fun, relaxed and social way. The Savanha Sun range, known for its richness of colour and flavour, speaks of abundant sunshine and lazy summer days. Savanha Special Reserve, Savanha Naledi and Savanha Frieda's Vine (a Fairtrade offering) are available in export markets only. See Spier entry for tasting/sales details.

Naledi range

★★★★ **Cabernet Sauvignon** Restraint the hallmark of savoury **09**. Tobacco, clean leather top notes to ample fruit, reined in by firm tannins, judicious oak. Drinks well now. WO Coastal, as all unless noted.

★★★★ **Merlot 09** back on track after last **07** (★★★★). Creamy plum fruit enlivened by zesty acidity, structured by taut tannins. Good now but will improve with few years ageing.

★★★★ **Pinotage 09** (★★★★) similar to demure **08**: lavender & smoke, strawberry & vanilla oak; malleable tannins, 15% alc adding viscosity, warmth to tail. WO Paarl.

Chardonnay ★★★★ Barrel-fermented **10** nudges next level. Butterscotch & toffee, lemon wafts; bright acidity lifts oak sweetness on palate, extends farewell. — CvZ

■ SAVISA *see African Terroir*

Saxenburg

Location/map/WO: Stellenbosch ▪ Est 1693 ▪ 1stB 1990 ▪ Tasting & sales Mon-Fri 9–5 Sat/Sun 10-4 ▪ Fee R15 ▪ Closed Easter Fri & Dec 25 ▪ Cheese platters ▪ Gifts ▪ BYO picnic ▪ Conservation area ▪ Game park ▪ Guest House ▪ Owner(s) Adrian & Birgit Bührer ▪ Cellarmaster(s) Nico van der Merwe (Nov 1990) ▪ Winemaker(s) Nico van der Merwe (Nov 1990), with Edwin Grace (Jan 2005) ▪ Viticulturist(s) Donovan Diedericks (Apr 2008) ▪ 195ha/85ha (cabs s/f, malbec, merlot, ptage, shiraz, chard, chenin, sauv, viog) ▪ 650t/50,000cs own label 78% red 20% white 2% rosé ▪ Other export brands: Bosman's Hill, Gwendolyn ▪ PO Box 171 Kuils River 7580 ▪ info@saxenburg.co.za ▪ www.saxenburg.co.za ▪ S 33° 56′47.9″ E 018° 43′9.4″ ▪ **T +27 (0)21-903-6113**

The high flying aristocrat of the Polkadraai hills maintains impressive standards year after year, under the guidance of veteran cellarmaster Nico van der Merwe, who has made every vintage since their inception in 1990. In the past year the white wine cellar has been expanded, and the vineyards are in the first stages of a major make-over, with new varieties pinot noir and semillon being added to the fold. Drip irrigation systems are being installed to optimised water resources, part of a conscious effort to respect the environment. Although the estate's ethos is based on tradition, the next generation of owners, Fiona and Vincent Bührer, are bringing dynamic new ideas into the mix.

Saxenburg Limited Release

★★★★★ **Shiraz Select** Stunning depth & complexity of **07** maintains lofty standards of **05** & **06**. Beautifully judged weight & structure underscore rich, complex fruit in a dry, intense package. Evolved & integrated now, but shows ageing potential.

Private Collection

★★★★☆ **Cabernet Sauvignon 08** maintains superior standard of range. Supple, plush & stately, showing fine craftsmanship. Taut & tarry, black & herbaceous, in classic Bordeaux style. Eminently satisfying special occasion treat.

★★★★☆ **Merlot** Plush, aristocratic interpretation of variety, **08** offers layers of complex black fruit with real backbone. Deserving of its place in this esteemed range, should get even better with time in bottle.

★★★★ **Shiraz** Overtly hefty, concentrated **08** (★★★★★) still reveals charming floral scents, wild scrub & peppery spices, after meaty, sombre **07**. Finely crafted & complex, with thickly textured tannins, promises years of development in bottle.

★★★★☆ **Chardonnay ✓** Luscious heavyweight, yet noble & elegant. **10** copes ably with judicious oaking (8 months French, only 5% new), to present subtle buttery citrus layers. Fine, gimmick-free varietal expression.

★★★★ **Sauvignon Blanc ✓** 🔲 Intense, concentrated aromas, lovely balance on **11** (★★★★★) underscore class & versatility of this producer at top level. A step up on already impressive **10**, expressing very special fruit perfectly ripened & deftly elevated.

Pinotage ★★★★ Exaggerated varietal character on **08** tasted last year not to every taste. **Le Phantom Brut Cap Classique** ★★★★ Mainly chardonnay, **NV (08)** sparkler was focused, lean & refreshing when tasted.

Guinea Fowl range

Red ✓ 🔲 ★★★★ 2nd-tier merlot/cab blend, **09** shows more weight & intensity than not-so-grand 'Grand Vin'. Time in barrel & splash shiraz fill out body. **Rosé** 🔲 ★★★ Sweetly spicy, **11** with tart strawberry fruit, tiny hint of sugar. Previewed, like next. **White** 🔲 ★★★ Consistently pleasant unwooded chenin-viognier. **11** has lots of character & ripe fruity flavour.

Concept range

Grand Vin Blanc ☺ 🔲 ★★★ Laudable entry-level **NV** sauvignon-chenin blend for unserious occasions. Tank sample has generous fruit, gentle acidity.

Grand Vin Rouge 🔲 ★★★ Fresh & fruity, unpretentious **NV** Bordeaux-style red. — GdB

Scali

Location: Paarl ▪ Map: Paarl & Wellington ▪ WO: Voor Paardeberg ▪ Est/1stB 1999 ▪ Tasting, sales & cellar tours Mon-Sat by appt ▪ Closed all pub hols ▪ B&B ▪ Owner(s) Willie & Tania de Waal ▪ Cellarmaster(s)/winemaker(s) Willie & Tania de Waal (Aug 1999) ▪ Viticulturist(s) Willie de Waal (Feb 1991) ▪ 270ha/70ha (cab, merlot, ptage, syrah, chard, chenin, rouss, sauv, viog) ▪ 30t/2,000cs own label 67% red 33% white ▪ BDOCA (vyds certified organic) ▪ PO Box 7143 Noorder-Paarl 7620 ▪ info@scali.co.za ▪ www.scali.co.za ▪ S 33° 36'70.6" E 018° 51'49.5" ▪ T +27 (0)21-869-8340 ▪ F +27 (0)21-869-8383

Scali is finally certified organic, owner-winemaker Willie de Waal relating that the conversion process took its toll on production but this now having stabilised. When he speaks of 'preserving the land for future generations', he means it – he and his wife Tania becoming parents of their fifth child in 2010. 'A lively team. Just watch the extra dimension they'll bring to Scali wines in future!'

★★★★ **Pinotage** Engagingly artless 08 shows red cherry, some earthiness; good fruit concentration, fresh acidity & densely packed tannins; year French oak, 20% new, an unobtrusive scaffolding.

★★★★ **Syrah** Noble, serious 08 (★★★★★) has real sense of place. Red berries, fynbos aromas; perfectly delineated, concentrated fruit, fresh acidity & fine spicy tannins; only 20% new oak (2 years French) attuned to De Waals' goal of fruit (not oak) expression, as was slightly higher 30% for 07.

★★★★☆ **Blanc** Intellectually demanding 09 from 50% chenin, 20% chardonnay, rest roussanne, sauvignon, viognier; year older oak. Hugely complex with great breadth & depth of flavour: apple, green melon, peach, apricot, nuts, spice; weightless intensity before super-dry finish. — CE

■ **Scarlett Organic** *see* Seven Sisters

Schalk Burger & Sons Wine Cellar

Location/WO: Wellington ▪ Map: Paarl & Wellington ▪ Est/1stB 2005 ▪ Tasting, sales & cellar tours Mon-Fri 9–5 Sat 9–2 ▪ Fee R15 ▪ Closed Dec 25 & Jan 1 ▪ Tour groups ▪ Gifts ▪ BYO picnic ▪ Conferences ▪ Welbedacht Cricket Oval ▪ Owner(s) Schalk Burger Family Trust ▪ Winemaker(s) Jacques Wentzel (Jul 2007, consultant) ▪ Viticulturist(s) Tony Julies (Jan 2007, consultant) ▪ 140ha/130ha (19 varieties r/w) ▪ 1,100t 75% red 20% white 5% rosé ▪ PO Box 51 Wellington 7654 ▪ tiaan@welbedacht.co.za, www.meerkatwines.co.za, www.schalkburgerandsons.co.za ▪ S 33° 34'39.8" E 019° 1'12.8" ▪ T +27 (0)21-873-1877 ▪ F +27 (0)86-669-5641

Long-gestated méthode cap classique bubbles were broached for two Burger weddings. Springbok flank Schalk jnr tied the knot a month before sister, Rene. And exceedingly social they were too - much like the meerkat gatherings which paterfamilias and label-copywriter Schalk snr lauds on their wines' back tags. He quips that mates from his own Springbok rugby playing days always need to have the furry critters' fondness for company explained. 'Gregarious' is a big word for a rugby player...' A child of the African soil, he and marketing director son Tiaan dream that many generations of Burgers continue to farm this Wellington land.

Proprietors Reserve range

★★★★ **No.6** Striking shiraz-led 6-way mix. 06 (★★★★☆) plush fruitcake & plum spice, big & bold but harmonious, lithe as a flank brushing off a tackler. 2 years older French oak. Step up on 05.

★★★★ **Myra** Last tasted was barrel fermented/aged viognier, chenin, chardonnay blend. 07 oxidative styling, rich & satiny.

Welbedacht range

★★★★ **Cabernet Sauvignon Barrique Select** ✓ Stylish 08, structured & concentrated from 2 years 50% new oak, offers ample cranberry & fynbos in rich, dry body. Maintains refined & supple standard of 07.

★★★★ **Merlot Barrique Select** ✓ 08 matches 07's promise. Ripe mulberry & cocoa depth. Soft texture yet firm structure from 2 years French oak, 15% new. Stylish & refined. Lengthy too.

★★★★ **Syrah** ✓ 🖽 Plush fruit vies with fresh acid in 08, made for long haul. Nuanced, deep, smoky & spicy with dry tannin & solid centre. Follows improved 07 in terms of concentration, length.

★★★★ **Cricket Pitch** 08 hit for 4! Striking cassis & cigar spice on rich, soft palate. Harmony of fruit, acid & wood. Gentle but structured blend of cab, merlot & cab franc. Lesser 07 (★★★★) preview needed time.

★★★★ **Hat Trick** Textured length previously on three-way Cape Blend, pinotage (50%) with shiraz, merlot. 07 had blueberry, plum & nutmeg spice. Juicy & rounded.

Pinotage ★★★★ Black cherry & cinnamon on dense, dark yet yielding 09 preview. Dry integrated tannin from 18 months French oak. **Chardonnay Barrel Fermented** 🖽 ★★★★ 09 keeps the standard. Creamy orange blossom & marmalade on broad palate. Juicy & fresh from natural fermentation. **Chenin Blanc Barrel Fermented** 🖽 ★★★ Rich tarte tatin on previewed 09, ample width on palate & finish. Wood a bit prominent, needs time to settle. **Sauvignon Blanc** 🖽 🌿 ★★★ Widescreen lemon zest, passionfruit & gravel flavour spectrum in 11, typically perky acidity makes for juicy refreshment.

Meerkat range

Pinotage 🗎 ★★★ Tangy red & black fruit on **09** last time, light oak char. **Burrow Blend** 🗎 ★★★ Incense & cassis on soft **08** 4-way merlot-led blend tasted previously. **Pinotage Rosé** 🗎 ★★★ Last time, **10** was all overt fruit & cranberry dryness. **Chenin Blanc** 🗎 🍸 ★★★ Ripe melon & crisp apple, **11** light refreshing appeal. **Sun Angel Semi-Sweet** ★★★ Sweetly charming **08** chenin & hanepoot tasted previously. — FM

Schalkenbosch Wines

Location/map: Tulbagh ▪ WO: Tulbagh/Western Cape ▪ Est 1792 ▪ 1stB 2002 ▪ Tasting, sales & tours by appt ▪ Closed all pub hols ▪ Tour groups ▪ Walking/hiking & mountain biking trails ▪ Conservation area ▪ Self-catering cottages ▪ Owner(s) Platinum Mile Investments ▪ Cellarmaster(s)/winemaker(s) Gielie Beukes (Jun 2010) ▪ Viticulturist(s) Johan Wiese & Andrew Teubes ▪ 1,800ha/37ha (cab, shiraz) ▪ 140t/10,000cs 80% red 18% white 2% rosé ▪ BWI champion ▪ PO Box 95 Tulbagh 6820 ▪ info@schalkenbosch.co.za ▪ www.schalkenbosch.co.za ▪ S 33° 18'49.7" E 019° 11'59.9" ▪ **T +27 (0)23-230-0654/1488** ▪ F +27 (0)86-519-2605/+27 (0)86-654-8209

Sprawling above Tulbagh and into the Witzenberg mountains, this 1,800ha Biodiversity & Wine Initiative Champion property is revitalising the region's environment, with fauna rehabilitation, alien vegetation clearing and water management programmes already in place. New winemaker Gielie Beukes is upbeat about their first méthode cap classique sparkling, three years in the making.

Schalkenbosch range

★★★★ **Stratus** ✓ Elegant & characterful shiraz blend (WO W Cape), **07** flagship label offers intense, complex berry fruit, silky texture. Underlines estate's affinity with Rhône style.

Cuvée Brut Cap Classique NEW! ★★★★ New limited-release traditional-method sparkling from pinot noir & chardonnay, **07** is resolutely dry, austere, lean & refreshing.

Edenhof range

Shiraz ☺ ★★★ Uncomplicated, balanced middleweight, **09** offers dry, dark, fruity core with hints of spiciness. **Sauvignon Blanc** ☺ 🗎 🍸 ★★★ Previewed **11** is light & refreshing, with honest fruit.

Cabernet Sauvignon ✓ ★★★★ Carefully-crafted, great value, as for rest of this middle range, **09** benefits from fine vintage. Classically dry, lithe & elegant. **Pinotage** ★★★ **09** shows generous body & plummy fruit, let down by rustic notes. **Cabernet Sauvignon-Merlot** ★★★ Ripe, softly fruity **09** over-delivers. Lighter bodied, quaffable, somewhat brief finish. **Glen Rosa** ✓ ★★★★ Eminently dry **09** Bordeaux-style blend is lean but elegant, with restrained dark fruit & thick tannins. **Bin 409** ✓ ★★★★ A worthy understudy to Stratus, **09** shows similar fruit & structure profiles. Charming, affordable everyday quaffing. **Chardonnay** 🗎 ★★ Unwooded **09** quaffer has modest but pleasant fruitiness. This & next not revisited. **Viognier** 🗎 🍸 ★★★ Spicy peach fruit & atypically bracing acidity on **10**. **Blanc de Blanc** 🗎 🍸 ★★ Previewed **11** less fruity than previous, tartly acidic. Discontinued: **Cabernet Sauvignon-Shiraz**.

Isis range

Dry Red 🗎 🍸 ★★★ Decently concentrated entry-level pocket-pleaser, previewed **10** a bit gawky, needs time to settle. **Rosé** 🗎 🍸 ★★★ Dry **10** from shiraz was fuller, meatier than previous. Not revisited. **Dry White** 🗎 🍸 ★★ Pungent but fruity tank sample **11**, pleasant quaffer. 1L bottle, as for Red. — GdB

▪ **Scholtzenhof** see Ken Forrester Wines

Schonenberg Wines

Location: Stellenbosch ▪ Est 2005 ▪ 1stB 2006 ▪ Tasting by appt ▪ Owner(s) Jaco & Yolande Marais ▪ Winemaker(s) Jaco & Yolande Marais (2005) ▪ Viticulturist(s) Jaco Marais (2005) ▪ European ISO 65 organic certification ▪ Suite 13 Private Bag X3019 Paarl 7620 ▪ info@schonenbergwines.co.za ▪ www.schonenbergwines.co.za ▪ **T +27 (0)74-100-9769** ▪ F +27 (0)86-651-2485

Organically produced wines are a passion for Jaco and Yolande Marais. Shiraz has been successful in the past, whilst they stay actively involved with the constant promotion of the certification process. No wine to taste this time, but we look forward to their next instalment of sustainable labours.

Schonenberg Wines range

★★★★ **Syrah** 🌿 Ripe-styled **07** (★★★★) still available.

Pinotage ☸ ★★★★ Aromatic **07** last tasted still selling at time of going to press. **Cape Blend** ☸ ★★★★ **06** from syrah & pinotage last edition & still selling.

Walking The Path range

Springdoring Steen ★★★ Eccentric & oxidative **10** from chenin, last reviewed; still available. — JP

■ **Schoone Gevel** *see La Motte*

■ **Schultz Family** *see Rudi Schultz Wines*

Seal Breeze Wines

Location: Lutzville ▪ Map: Olifants River ▪ WO: Lutzville Valley ▪ Est 2004 ▪ 1stB 2005 ▪ Tasting, sales & cellar tours Mon-Fri 9-4 Sat 9–12 ▪ Closed Easter Fri-Mon, Ascension Day, Dec 25 & Jan 1 ▪ Meals/refreshments by prior arrangement ▪ Facilities for children ▪ Tour groups ▪ BYO picnic ▪ Owner(s) John & Joan Wiggins ▪ Cellarmaster(s) Joan Wiggins (Feb 2004) ▪ Winemaker(s) Joan Wiggins (Feb 2004), with Toy Brand (Feb 2006) ▪ Viticulturist(s) Joan Wiggins ▪ ±92ha/±70ha (cab, merlot, shiraz, chenin, cbard, hanepoot, sauv) ▪ 1,200t/780cs own label ▪ PO Box 33 Lutzville 8165 ▪ jwiggins@kingsley.co.za ▪ www.sealbreezewine.co.za ▪ S 31° 34'50.1" E 018° 19'9.8" ▪ **T +27 (0)84-505-1991** ▪ F +27 (0)27-217-1458

Joan Wiggins' West Coast winery is an annual stop-off for Journey of Hope, an organisation for survivors of breast cancer. Every year a hardy band of travellers rough it under canvas and rise early to pick and stomp enough grapes for the 2,000 bottles Joan donates to the cause.

Cabernet Sauvignon ☸ **10** too young, unknint to rate. **09** (★★★★) went up a notch mid-2010; had generous but balanced alc, fine tannin structure. **Merlot** ☸ ★★★ Charry oak seasoning to prune & date aromas, pre-bottling **10** lovely if unconcentrated milk chocolate flavours, warm aftertaste. **Shiraz** ★★★ Appealing meaty aroma & dusty overlay, **10** tannins still quite gruff, allow time to soften. **Sauvignon Blanc** ★★★ **11** ripe lemon & passionfruit, engaging if unlingering fruity mouthful. Very youthful, could score higher given time to settle in bottle, as for all these. Discontinued: **Sweet Hanepoot.** — Panel

■ **Season's Collection** *see Orange River Wine Cellars*

Secateurs

Location: Malmesbury ▪ WO: Swartland/Coastal ▪ Est/1stB 2009 ▪ Tasting by appt at Badenhorst Family Wines ▪ Owner(s) The Badenhorst Family ▪ Winemaker(s) Adi Badenhorst, with Jasper Wickens (2008) ▪ Viticulturist(s) Pierre Rossouw (consultant) ▪ 60ha/23ha (cinsaut, grenache, shiraz, chard, chenin, rouss) ▪ 1,800cs own label 60% red 40% white ▪ PO Box 1177 Malmesbury 7299 ▪ adi@iafrica.com ▪ www.aabadenhorst.com ▪ **T +27 (0)82-373-5038** ▪ F +27 (0)21-794-5196

Though listed separately from their Badenhorst Family Wines siblings, these characterful and well-priced wines are also grown by cousins Adi and Hein Badenhorst at their Kalmoesfontein farm in the Swartland's Siebritskloof. (Some grapes supplied by a neighbour.) Though these are the 'easy-drinkers' in the Badenhorst portfolio, their combination of old dryland bushvine fruit quality, minimalist winemaking and delightful beyond-retro labels make them truly special - and worthy of the rave reviews they get around the world.

Rosé ☺ 🍷 ☸ ★★★ Perky pink from cinsaut, shiraz & grenache, **11** snappy & dry, perfect with cured meats.

Red Blend ✓ 🍷 ★★★★ Shiraz leads 7 blend partners, aged both old vats & concrete tanks. Spicy centre of **10** lifts ripe mulberry fruit in fresh, firm mouthful. WO Coastal. **Chenin Blanc** ✓ 🍷 ★★★★ **11** ripe & full, packed with savoury flavour & a mineral texture that makes it really good with food. Old vines, each new day's harvest added to fermentation over 3 weeks. — DS

■ **Secret Cellar** *see Ultra Liquors*

Sedgwick's Old Brown Sherry

Venerable Distell brand (1886), blend of jerepiko and dry sherry, in 750ml, 1L & 2L.

Sedgwick's Old Brown Sherry 🍷 ★★ Nuts, caramel & sweet toffee on sweet, creamy **NV** sipper. — Panel

Seidelberg Wine Estate

Location/WO: Paarl ▪ Map: Paarl & Wellington ▪ Est 1692 ▪ 1stB 1989 ▪ Tasting & sales Sun-Thu 9-5 Fri/Sat 9-6 ▪ Fee R20pp ▪ Closed Easter Fri, Dec 25 & Jan 1 ▪ Tour groups by appt ▪ Red Hot Glass studio ▪ Owner(s) De Leuwen Jagt Wine Company ▪ Cellarmaster(s) Alicia Rechner (Dec 2009) ▪ Winemaker(s) Paarl/Darling ▪ 410ha/100ha (cabs s/f, malbec merlot, mourv, ptage, red muscadel, shiraz, chard, chenin, sauv, viog) ▪ ±700t/50,000cs 70% red 20% white 10% rosé ▪ BWI ▪ PO Box 505 Suider-Paarl 7624 ▪ info@seidelberg.co.za ▪ www.seidelberg.co.za ▪ S 33° 45' 50.5" E 018° 55' 9.7" ▪ **T +27 (0)21-863-5200** ▪ F +27 (0)21-863-3797

Change of ownership at this this historic Paarl property: it is now owned by De Leuwen Jagt Wine company, with Alicia Rechner making the wines. The estate will become the tasting venue for Spice Route wines and home to the Spice Route Restaurant. The popular De Leuwen Jagt and Seidelberg wines will still be produced, and the Red Hot Glass studio will remain an attraction.

Seidelberg range

Cabernet Sauvignon ★★★★ Classic cassis, tomato & violet restraint on **09**. Dry oak platform adds structure. Good concentration & length. **Merlot NEW** ▨ **★★★★** Vibrant ripe mulberry & cocoa to **10**. Yielding plushness to body with some depth & dry tannin appeal. Good length. **Pinotage ★★★** Spicy oak dominates **09**'s ripe black fruit succulence. Truffly earthiness adds interesting dimension to medium body. **Chardonnay** 🍴 ▨ **★★★★** Interplay of lime zest & vanilla smoke on smart **10**. Gentle sheen of oak adds structure, panache. Long creamy almond tail. **Sauvignon Blanc** 🍴 ▨ **★★★** Rounded fullness to **11**. Typical lemongrass & straw liven fresh, zesty mouthful. Fruit ex Darling & Paarl.

De Leuwen Jagt range

Cabernet Sauvignon ▨ **★★★** Tobacco leaf overlay on **10** berry backdrop. Soft, gentle & restrained. Light concentration & body. Great Cab for novices. **Pinotage** ▨ **★★★** Coffee whiffs, cocoa & black berry fruit on **10**. Juicy simplicity personified. Light, clean & approachable. Touch short. **Shiraz** ▨ **★★★ 10** step up on pvs. Plum spice & earthy depth on soft textured mouthful. Appealing & uncomplicated. Medium length. **Leuwenrood** 🍴 ▨ **★★★ 10** preview a vibrant step up on previous, spicy plum in merlot, cab franc, malbec mix. Juicy & delicious, with some depth. **Rosé** 🍴 ▨ **★★★ 11** lovely muscat aroma & off-dry cherry/berry flavours, notch up on previous. Tangy, juicy & tasty. **Leuwenblanc** 🍴 ▨ **★★★★ 11** is all fig, gooseberry & herbs from sauvignon, chenin & nouvelle. Nice acid zip & structure. **Nuance** 🍴 ▨ **★★★** Light off-dry white, **11** pepper, nettle & flowers, easy grapey enjoyment. **Muscadel ★★★★** Rich. raisined, balanced muscat sweetness on last **09**. — FM

■ **Semara** see Wine-of-the-Month Club
■ **Senso** see Flavors of Wine
■ **Sentinel** see Wine-of-the-Month Club

Sequillo Cellars

Map/WO: Swartland ▪ Est/1stB 2003 ▪ Tasting & sales Mon-Fri by appt ▪ Closed all pub hols ▪ Owner(s) Eben Sadie & Cornel Spies ▪ Cellarmaster(s)/winemaker(s) Eben Sadie (Jan 2003) ▪ 20ha (grenache, mourv, syrah, chenin, clairette, rouss, viog) ▪ 45t/3,000cs own label 50% red 50% white ▪ PO Box 1019 Malmesbury 7299 ▪ info@sequillo.com ▪ www.sequillo.com ▪ S 33° 31' 31.0" E 018° 48' 18.1" ▪ **T +27 (0)22-482-3138** ▪ F +27 (0)86-692-2852

The brand name Sequillo ('an arid, dry place of great purity') and the 'doodling' pencil lines used in its logo are clues to the underlying philosophy: identifying and vinifying unique Swartland parcels, constantly experimenting and, without compromising quality, 'having fun'. But the brand's creator being Eben Sadie, among South Africa's top winegrowers and a pioneer of the Swartland revival, a possible downside was always going to be that Sequillo would play Cinderella to the renowned Sadie Family Wines bottlings. So, to better differentiate and re-energise Sequillo, Eben (with business partner Cornel Spies) has changed, well... everything. 'Except the staff.' Restrategised vineyard selection and vinification now aim for 'more fruit, more freshness'. The labels, too, are changing each year 'because our wines change every year'.

★★★★☆ Sequillo Red Swartland rendition of pure, spicy, sun-drenched Mediterranean-fruit, with mineral finesse. **09** apparently light, deceptively easy, but with attitude. Will mature with grace.

★★★★☆ **Sequillo White** ✓ Layers of complex flavours interleaved with mineral texture - no obvious fruitiness - a taste experience rather than mere libation. **10** fresher, perhaps, in new styling courtesy traditional palo
mino & clairette in eclectic blend, a satisfying alternative to many squeaky clean, stark dry whites. — DS

■ **Sereia** *see* Anatu Wines

Ses'Fikile

Location/WO: Paarl ▪ Est 2004 ▪ 1stB 2006 ▪ Closed to public ▪ Owner(s) Indlezane Investments ▪ Cellarmaster(s)
Danie Marais (Windmeul Cellar) ▪ Winemaker(s) Francois van Niekerk (Windmeul Cellar) ▪ Viticulturist(s) Anton
Laas (Windmeul Cellar) ▪ 5,500cs own label 70% red 30% white ▪ PO Box 38055 Pinelands 7430 ▪ sesfikile@
gmail.com

Ses'Fikile means 'we have arrived, in style' and so have ex-teacher vintners, Jacky
Mayo, Nondumiso Pikashe and Nomvuyo Xaliphi. Market opportunities in Germany
and The Netherlands have been established, and the wines are styled in conjunction
with supplier Windmeul Cellar to suit particular customer specs.

Rainsong range

Pinotage 🔲 ★★★ Range name change from 'Ses'Fikile' last time. Soft & juicy **09**, medium-bodied with touch
of oak spice. Food friendly & yummy! **Shiraz** Await new vintage, as for **Cabernet Sauvignon-Merlot**. **Chenin Blanc** 🔲 ★★★ Juicy, sweet ripe apples on unoaked **11**. Cheerful summer tipple. — WB

Seven Oaks

Location: Worcester ▪ Map: Breedekloof ▪ WO: Breedekloof/Western Cape/Robertson ▪ Est 2003 ▪ 1stB 2004 ▪
Tasting by appt ▪ Owner(s) Patrick & Jacqui Pols ▪ Cellarmaster(s) Bennie Wannenburg (May 2010,
Waboomsrivier) ▪ Winemaker(s) Bennie Wannenburg, with Wim Viljoen (both May 2010, Waboomsrivier) ▪ Viti-
culturist(s) Pierre Snyman (2003, consultant) ▪ 62ha/42ha (cinsaut, ptage, ruby cab, shiraz, chard, chenin, chard,
sauv) ▪ 345t/2,000cs own label 50% red 45% white 5% rosé ▪ Customer brand: Villa Verde ▪ PO Box 11 Breerivier
6858 ▪ jacqui@sevenoaks.co.za ▪ www.sevenoaks.co.za ▪ **T +27 (0)83-639-0405** ▪ F +27 (0)86-617-8102

Owners Patrick and Jacqui Pols have moved vinfication of their boutique wine brand
to down-the-road Waboomsriver Cellar and, at press time, planned to bottle a
pinotage under their 6+1 label and plant ruby cab. Proceeds from the 'Under the
Tanks' music concerts they host during the Breedekloof's annual Soetes & Sop festival go to a local school.

Sauvignon Blanc ☺ 🔲 📖 ★★★ Zingy lemon, lime & fig, **11** nice length & flinty tail.

Padre Rednose Merlot-Cabernet-Sauvignon 🌿 ★★★ Blueberry & caramel toffee galore, **06** soft &
approachable, with warm feel. Robertson WO. **Cabernet Sauvignon-Shiraz** 🔲 ★★★ Jumps couple of vintages but ratchets up quality in **09**, lightly wooded 60/40 blend with peppery plum bite. **6+1 Cabernet Sauvignon-Shiraz** Await new vintage. **Pinotage Rosé** 🔲 📖 ★★★ **10** semi-sweet cherry, berry quaffer with light
acid lift. WO W Cape, as for Semi Sweet. **Chenin Blanc** 🔲 📖 ★★★ Zesty, tropical & straightforward **11**. **Chenin Blanc Semi Sweet** 🔲 📖 ★★★ Guava & ripe melon, sweetness downplayed on **10** quaffer. — FM

Seven Sisters

Location/map: Stellenbosch ▪ WO: Western Cape ▪ Tasting & sales: phone ahead ▪ Owner(s) African Roots Wine ▪
Winemaker(s) Andries Blake ▪ PO Box 4560 Tygervalley 7536 ▪ vivian@africanrootswines.com ▪ www.
sevensisters.co.za ▪ S 33° 59' 23.41" E 018° 46' 34.35" ▪ **T +27 (0)21-982-2200** ▪ F +27 (0)21-982-7428

Seven sisters, seven fun wines! The wines echo the enthusiasm of these partners
with each wine delivering a wonderful element of unique vibrancy. This successful
brand ultimately aims to please, to keep wine-drinking fun and especially to be
enjoyed where friends and family gather.

Cabernet Sauvignon Carol ☺ 🔲 📖 ★★★ Tarry, smoky complexity leads to supple & ripe red berry palate. **10** fresh & easy with lingering cherry end. **Chenin Blanc Yolanda** ☺ 🔲 📖 ★★★ Crisp promise with
delicate apple blossom, clean and steely entry. **11** ends light & dry. **Sauvignon Blanc Vivian** ☺ 🔲 📖
★★★ Grassy style with good focus, crisp, light & dry. **11** leaves clean refreshing impression, ideal for sum-

mery delight. **Sweet Rosé Twena** ☺ 🍷 ★★★ Happy, vibrant & fruity **11** offers satisfying semi-sweet profile with perfume & tasty end. Light rose in colour.

Merlot June ★★ Earthy **11** ex-tank needs to settle. **Pinotage-Shiraz Dawn** 🌐 ★★ Vanilla & dark berry appeal on edgy **10**. **Bukettraube Odelia** 🍷 ★★★ Delicate aromas, cherry & gently spiced **11** has semi-sweet end. —JP

Seven Springs Vineyards

Location: Hermanus ▪ WO: Overberg ▪ Est 2007 ▪ 1stB 2010 ▪ Closed to public ▪ Owner(s) Tim & Vaughan Pearson ▪ Winemaker(s) Riana van der Merwe (Nov 2009) ▪ Viticulturist(s) Peter Davison (Jul 2007, consultant) ▪ 12ha/ ±8ha (pinot, syrah, chard, sauv) ▪ ±33t/2,400cs own label 60% red 40% white ▪ Private Bag X15 Suite 162 Hermanus 7200 ▪ info@7springs.co.za ▪ www.7springs.co.za ▪ **T** +27 (0)82-487-7572; **UK** +44 1789740502 ▪ F +27 (0)86-571-0623

Clocking up maximum digital mileage is UK co-owner Tim Pearson, who uses social media so effectively to spread the word about this relatively new winery near Hermanus that he was picked as a case study by Prof Damien Wilson of the Burgundy School of Business. There's lots to Twitter and Facebook about: the maiden sauvignon launched to international critical acclaim, the first harvest of pinot noir, and new chardonnay and syrah still in the wings at press time.

Seven Springs Vineyards range NEW

Syrah 🍷 Unrated pre-bottling sample **10** still incubating but promises well: aromatic, soft, red cherry & liquorice, pleasant charry oak flavours. **Chardonnay** ★★★★ Full-flavoured **10**, lemon-butter aromas, rounded but intense lime & oak flavours, tangy finish - seems tailor made for crayfish on the braai. **Chardonnay Unwooded** 🍷 ★★★ Fruity preview **11** appealing combo of lightness, good varietal character & ripe flavours (pear & melon). Lovely this summer & possibly next 2 or 3. **Sauvignon Blanc** 🍷 ★★★★ Youthful (& tentatively rated) preview **11** bright, crisp & aromatic, good concentration of lemon & passionfruit, & a distinct & unusual flowery scent. Real charmer. —Panel

Seven Steps Wines

Location: Cape Town ▪ WO: Western Cape/Elgin ▪ Est/1stB 2009 ▪ Tasting by appt only ▪ Owner(s) Travis Braithwaite & Pragasen Ramiah ▪ Cellarmaster(s)/winemaker(s) Travis Braithwaite ▪ (shiraz, sauv) ▪ 800cs own label 30% red 70% white ▪ PO Box 981 Sea Point Cape Town 8060 ▪ info@sevenstepswines.com ▪ www.sevenstepswines.com ▪ **T** +27 (0)82-368-5270 ▪ F +27 (0)86-625-0109

A brand created by Pragasen Ramiah and Travis Braithwaite, sourced from different parts of the winelands. The evocative name refers to District Six in Cape Town, because the brand was intended to be 'a memory that lives in the hearts of all those that lived, loved, played and worked in District Six... and celebrates a lifestyle that defines South Africa... whose people are full of heart'.

Syrah ★★★★ last was showy **08**; rose geranium scent, meaty hint, sweet-fruited with charry oak, smoothed by few grams sugar. **Sauvignon Blanc** ✓ ★★★★ Passionfruit with attractive leafy/herbal nuances, **10** has tangy appetite appeal where fruit & acid are in perfect sync. —CR

Shannon Vineyards

Location/WO: Elgin ▪ Map: Elgin, Walker Bay & Bot River ▪ Est 2000 ▪ 1stB 2003 ▪ Tasting by appt ▪ Owner(s) Stuart & James Downes ▪ Winemaker(s) Gordon Newton Johnson & Nadia Newton Johnson ▪ Viticulturist(s) Kevin Watt (consultant) ▪ 75ha/15.5ha (merlot, pinot, sauv, sem, viog) ▪ 100t/3,000cs own label 66% red 34% white ▪ BWI, Global GAP, IPW, Tesco's Natures Choice ▪ PO Box 20 Elgin 7180 ▪ james@shannonwines.com ▪ www.shannonwines.com ▪ S 34° 11'3.9" E 018° 59'3.6" ▪ **T** +27 (0)21-859-2491 ▪ F +27 (0)21-859-5389

'We grow wines to express, not impress,' James Downes says of this winery he co-owns with his Chile-based brother, Stuart. It is precisely through their individual expression that they are impressing far and wide; the 2008 Mount Bullet fetched R6500 a bottle on an auction in Denver, US. If this has set a benchmark for SA merlot, the rest of the range (made by Nadia and Gordon Newton Johnson in their Hemel-en-Aarde cellar), is working toward similar distinction. Special attention is being paid to toasting of the oak barrels for the pinot to ensure the fruit and all-important texture take centre stage.

★★★★☆ **Mount Bullet** Thoroughly fine & compelling 09 follows exceptional 08 (★★★★★). Tantalises with its elusive perfume, freshness & silky tannins. But there's no lack of substance in its rich savoury flavours. Lovely now & for yrs to come.

★★★★☆ **Rockview Ridge Pinot Noir** Previously 'Rocklands'. Annual improvements, especially in oaking regime, see smoky oak nuances more in tune with perfumed red cherries on 09. Silky texture, fresh core & fine, framing tannins augur well for future.

★★★★☆ **Sanctuary Peak Sauvignon Blanc** 🖥 🕸 Used to bear just variety name. 10 cool, pure impression but oaked semillon (12%) greater influence on aromatics, mouthfeel than on 09. Weighty with balanced minerally lift & long, savoury tail.

Macushla Pinot Noir Noble Late Harvest Await next. — AL

■ **Shepherd's Cottage** see Overgaauw Wine Estate

Ship Sherry

Jerepiko-style sweet fortified from two muscats, chenin and dry sherry, by Distell.

Ship Sherry 🖥 ★★ Sweet malty toffee, sultana & almond on spirited, creamy NV. — Panel

Shoprite Checkers

Enquiries: Stephanus Eksteen ▪ 40,000cs own labels 50% red 45% white 5% rosé ▪ PO Box 215 Brackenfell 7561 ▪ seksteen@shoprite.co.za ▪ www.shoprite.co.za ▪ **T +27 (0)21-980-4000** ▪ F +27 (0)21-980-4421

'People have faith in the brand,' says wine buyer Stephanus Eksteen of this national supermarket chain's popular in-house Oddbins range, 'so we dabble a bit here and there, and get them to try more unusual varieties, like riesling, grenache and mourvèdre.' The Oak Ridge range is on hold for the moment.

■ **Short Story** see Neethlingshof Estate
■ **Shosholoza** see Catch Of The Day
■ **Signal Cannon** see Vondeling

Signal Gun Wines

Location/WO: Durbanville ▪ Map: Durbanville, Philadelphia & Darling ▪ Est/1stB 2006 ▪ Tasting & sales Tue-Fri 10-4 Sat 10-3 ▪ Fee R15 ▪ Closed Easter Fri, Dec 25 & Jan 1 ▪ Light meals & refreshments at The Winebar & Bistro Tue-Fri 10-10 Sat 9-10 Sun 9-4 ▪ Conference facilities ▪ Conservation area ▪ Owner(s) WRM de Wit ▪ Cellarmaster(s)/winemaker(s) MJ de Wit (Jan 2006) ▪ Viticulturist(s) MJ de Wit (Jan 2001) ▪ 210ha/100ha (cab, merlot, ptage, shiraz, chard, sauv) ▪ 12t/400cs own label 50% red 50% white ▪ PO Box 2359 Durbanville 7551 ▪ signalgun@hoogeberg.com ▪ www.signalgun.co.za ▪ S 33° 49'13.26" E 018° 36'40.32" ▪ **T +27 (0)21-976-1957** ▪ F +27 (0)21-975-0648

Modern-day wine-making at the old Hooggelegen farm in Durbanville began as MJ de Wit's hobby in 2006. Substantial viticulture here was well established, however, and the farm has been in the family for a long time (MJ's father, Wouter, is the fifth-generation owner and grape grower), so tradition is likely to be a strength.

★★★★ **Shiraz** 🖥 Last tasted was restrained, harmonious & savoury-tailed 07 with well-knit tannins.
Sauvignon Blanc 🖥 ★★★★ Last year, 10 a nice fruity & zesty mouthful. — TJ

Signal Hill Wines

Location: Cape Town ▪ Map: Cape Peninsula ▪ WO: Piekenierskloof/Western Cape/Simonsberg-Paarl/Stellenbosch/Cape Town ▪ 1stB 1997 ▪ Tasting, sales & cellar tours Mon-Fri 11-7 Sat 12-5 ▪ Fee R40pp, waived on purchase ▪ Closed all pub hols ▪ Cheese platters, sushi, sirloin & tapas during open hours ▪ Owner(s) Kyle Zulch & Jean-Vincent Ridon ▪ Cellarmaster(s) Kyle Zulch, Jean-Vincent Ridon ▪ Winemaker(s) Kyle Zulch, Jean-Vincent Ridon & Laurence Buthelezi ▪ Viticulturist(s) Kyle Zulch ▪ 4ha (cab f, mourv, pinot, syrah, crouchen) ▪ 75% red 20% white 5% rosé ▪ Heritage Square 100 Shortmarket Street Cape Town 8001 ▪ info@winery.co.za ▪ www.winery.co.za ▪ S 33° 55'15.06" E 018° 25'5.54" ▪ **T +27 (0)21-424-5820** ▪ F +27 (0)21-422-5238

It took a Frenchman, Jean-Vincent Ridon, to establish the country's only city-centre winery, in the heart of Cape Town. Further, he and winery partner (since 2010) Kyle Zulch make, amongst others, wines from three city vineyards. The fourth citified wine can hardly be said to have a vineyard origin. In 2011 they harvested grapes from a single vine (about 20 bottles' worth) – but it is, says J-V, 'the oldest known fruit-bearing vine of the southern hemisphere'. The question remains, what cultivar is it? Chenin? Or perhaps crouchen blanc? All the wines listed below, except for Olympia, were tasted for previous editions.

Signal Hill range

★★★★ **Malbec 05** vanilla-edged blood-iron notes; full-bodied, concentrated, fresh.

★★★★☆ **Camps Bay Vineyard** Just one barrel from **09** maiden harvest off city/near-beachside vyd. Glorious fruity aromas lead to fresh delightful flavours. Firm structure, & lingering dry finish.

★★★★ **Petit Verdot** Sharp **04** (★★★★) needed food to show best. **03** more seductive.

★★★★☆ **Clos d'Oranje** From tiny, ungrafted shiraz vineyard near central Cape Town. **06** (★★★★★) bigger, bolder than maiden **05**. Spicy vibrancy beneath fine structure. Like all these, made to partner food.

★★★★ **Grenache Blanc** Scintillating **08**; subtle scents; silky, & savoury mineral core. Used oak.

★★★★ **MCC Pinot Noir 06** disgorged on demand at winery. Quiet mousse, but lovely mature aromas. Shows benefit of 4 yrs on lees, dryness of no dosage. No sulphur added.

★★★★★ **Empereur Rouge** Delicious, ultra-sweet, warm & raisiny **06** from cab.

★★★★ **Crème de Tête Muscat d'Alexandrie NLH** Last tasted was hedonistic **03**.

★★★★★ **Eszencia** Magnificent **NV** (**02**), probably a one-off, sweet & rich, electrified by nervy acidity.

★★★★ **Mathilde Aszú 6 Puttonyos** Last **02** Tokaji lookalike from botrytised furmint & sauvignon.

★★★★ **Vin de l'Empereur** Vivid **05** last-tasted botrytised dessert from muscat d'Alexandrie.

Olympia Cabernet Franc ★★★ Attractive aromas on mature-looking **08**. Light-centred, with just a little fruit concentration & a rather uneasy structure. **Grenache Noir** ★★★★ Modestly oaked **07** with pleasing vinosity; spicy, savoury & dry. **Pinot Noir** ★★★★ Cherry, forest floor concentration in supple **07**. **Syrah** ★★★★ Fresh & fleshy **06**. **The Threesome** ★★★★ **NV** blend (2006-08) cab, shiraz, merlot. Rich fruitcake, spice notes on firm, full-bodied, full-flavoured palate with herbal edge. **Rosé de Saignée** ★★★★ **06** savoury vinosity & rounded dryness. **Straw Wine** ★★★★ None since **01**.

Buthelezi range

Tutuka Syrah ★★★ Winemaker Laurence Buthelezi's own-label. Last tasted was **04**. — TJ

■ **Signatures of Doolhof** see Doolhof Wine Estate

Sijnn

WO: Malgas/Swellendam ▪ Est 2003 ▪ 1stB 2007 ▪ Tasting & sales at De Trafford Wines Fri & Sat 10-1 ▪ Closed all pub hols ▪ Owner(s) David & Rita Trafford, Simon Farr, Quentin Hurt ▪ Winemaker(s) David Trafford, with Waldo van Zyl (May 2011) ▪ Viticulturist(s) Schalk du Toit (2002, consultant) ▪ 125ha/16ha (cab, mourv, shiraz, touriga nacional, trincadeira, chenin, rouss, viog) ▪ 36t/1,900cs own label 83% red 10% white 7% rosé ▪ PO Box 495 Stellenbosch 7599 ▪ info@sijnn.co.za ▪ www.sijnn.co.za ▪ **T** +27 (0)21-880-1611 ▪ F +27 (0)21-880-1611

A truly original project, vineyards set in an area better known as a fisherman's paradise (co-owner David Trafford has a holiday home here), and then not only to plant varieties used to warmer conditions, but also lesser-known ones like trincadeira. But this risk has paid off, there are good ratings internationally from Jancis Robinson, Stephen Tanzer and Wine Spectator; exports are growing; and Malgas has been proclaimed a wine ward. Plantings of other Portuguese and Rhône varieties are planned to blend into the current range, and who knows, maybe create something else original?

★★★★ **Sijnn** Shiraz/mourvèdre with dabs touriga, trincadeira & cab, **09** has smoky dark fruit, black pepper; herbal notes give a piquant lift. Fresh & lively but can age, drink now till ±2016.

★★★★ **White** Close to half each chenin & viognier, **10** naturally fermented in small French oak is rich & showy; dried peach & melon preserve against a savoury backdrop that tames it for food.

Rosé ★★★★ Savoury **10**'s morello cherries & tealeaf come from natural ferment in oak & blend trincadeira, mourvèdre & shiraz. Discontinued: **Cabernet Sauvignon**, **Mourvèdre**, **Trincadeira**, **Malgas**. — CR

■ **Silverhurst** see High Constantia Wine Cellar

■ **Silver Myn** *see Zorgvliet Wines*
■ **Silversands** *see Robertson Wide River Export Company*

Silverthorn Wines

WO: Robertson ▪ Est 1998 ▪ 1stB 2004 ▪ Closed to public ▪ Owner(s) Silverthorn Wines (Pty) Ltd ▪ Cellarmaster(s), winemaker(s)/viticulturist(s) John Loubser (1998) ▪ 10.5ha/4ha (cab, shiraz, chard) ▪ 50t/750cs own label 66% white 34% rosé ▪ IPW ▪ PO Box 381 Robertson 6705 ▪ john@silverthornwines.co.za ▪ www.silverthornwines.co za ▪ **T +27 (0)21-712-7239** ▪ F +27 (0)21-712-7239

Investment by wine-loving bankers in Karen and John Loubser's project (he's also GM and cellarmaster at Steenberg) has meant they've been able to increase production of their two bubblies, and also to make 'a special cuvée'. The classic pinot-chardonnay blend is as yet still serving its three years on its fermentation lees; watch for it towards the end of 2012.

★★★★ **The Green Man Blanc de Blancs** Surprisingly honeyed 08, with creamy, biscuity flavours, grapefruit & lime whiffs, some barrel notes (though only older oak used) evident in evolved leesy style.

★★★★ **Genie Rosé Brut** An unusual (& successful) MCC now solely from shiraz. Lean, elegant & dry 08 with spicy, raspberry notes. Way off its peak despite 30 months spent on the fermentation lees. — MF

■ **Simonay** *see Simonsvlei International*
■ **Simonsbosch** *see Koelenhof Winery*

Simonsig Landgoed

Location/map: Stellenbosch ▪ WO: Stellenbosch/Western Cape ▪ Est 1953 ▪ 1stB 1968 ▪ Tasting & sales Mon-Fri 8 30-5 Sat 8.30-4 Sun 11-3 ▪ Fee R25pp (incl glass) ▪ Closed Easter Fri/Sun, Dec 25 & Jan 1 ▪ Cellar tours daily at 11 & 3 (booking advised) ▪ Cuvée Restaurant *see Restaurants section* ▪ Facilities for children ▪ Tour groups ▪ Gifts ▪ Farm produce ▪ Conferences ▪ 4x4 Landrover experience ▪ Labyrinth vineyard ▪ Owner(s) Pieter, Francois & Johan Malan ▪ Cellarmaster(s) Johan Malan (1981) ▪ Winemaker(s) Debbie Thompson (Nov 1999) & Hannes Meyer (Ju 2009), with Juan Carstens (Jan 2011) ▪ Viticulturist(s) Francois Malan (Jan 1981) & Tommie Corbett (Nov 2008), with Johan Pienaar & Conrad Schutte (Vinpro) ▪ 300ha/210ha (cab, merlot, ptage, pinot, shiraz, chard, chenin, sauv) ▪ ±2,872t/±170,000cs own label 33% red 47% white 18% MCC & ±18,500cs for clients ▪ Brands for clients: Champany Inn, Nandi Zulu, Malan Reeks, Rouana, The Warhorse, Wine of the Month Club, Woolworths ▪ HACCP 2009, BWI, SANAS ▪ PO Box 6 Koelenhof 7605 ▪ wine@simonsig.co.za ▪ www.simonsig.co. za ▪ S 33° 52' 12.1" E 018° 49' 31.7" ▪ **T +27 (0)21-888-4900** ▪ F +27 (0)21-888-4909

Timely innovation has always been part of the strategy at this well established, large family estate. The 40th anniversary of the Cape's first champagne-method sparkling wine was celebrated in 2011. Kaapse Vonkel (in chic new guise) still thrives, joined now by others, including Cuvée Royale, one of the Cape's finest bubblies, and (for Woolworths) an excellent sparkling Rosé with no added sulphur. But not all necessary change is cheerful: while new wines have recently arrived (like a straw wine and the coffee-style SMV), one of the Cape's longest-serving labels, the sweet Franciskaner, has gone. Another long-server, the Chenin, happily remains as a brilliant bargain. The estate's reds are another grand focus: big, bold modern wines, contrasting powerfully with the delicacy of the sparklers.

★★★★☆ **Redhill Pinotage** 09 (★★★★) has lovely fruit flavour underpinning the all-new oak (the other way round might be preferable!). Powerful, thickly textured & well-built, the noticeable fruit sweetness a little awkwardly at odds with these aspects & some drying tannins. Less suave than 08.

★★★★☆ **Merindol Syrah** Approaches elegance more than others in range - less alcohol & obvious oak (though all-new) & extraction, allowing more expressive fruit. 08 smartly balances fruit & spice with firm structure. A touch drying on finish, but still a long way to go.

★★★★☆ **Tiara** Cab-based Bordeaux-style blend. 08 (★★★★) takes further 07's drift from traditional restraint to tannic, extracted, slightly sweet power - but plenty of juicy flavour to balance all that.

★★★★ **Frans Malan Cape Blend** As usual, the sweet warmth of pinotage (73%) pleasingly complemented by brighter cab & merlot. Loads of succulent fruitiness on 08 well supported by strong infrastructure.

★★★★ **Aurum Chardonnay** Still-available 07 (previously listed as 'Chardonnay Reserve'), barrel selection from best vineyards, tight in youth, should be showing best now & for next yr/2. 08 sold out.

★★★★ **Chenin Avec Chêne** Last year, previewed **09** showed as less bold than **08**; subtle fruit intensity, light oak accenting thatchy minerality. Rich & supple, a little sugar balanced by fresh acid.

★★★★☆ **Cuvée Royale** MCC sparkling mostly ex-chardonnay, ±5 years on yeast sediment in bottle adding complexity, character. Finest of the bubblies here. Last year, **05** offered mature complexity & freshness.

★★★★ **Kaapse Vonkel Brut 09** edition of venerable label showing better than previous - more development adding brioche notes to fresh apple. Not deep or complex, but fresh & balanced.

★★★★ **Kaapse Vonkel Brut Rosé** Méthode cap classique sparkling, **09** (★★★★) has, at 80%, more pinotage than usual, with pinots noir & meunier. Fruity & bright, though a touch less deliciously developed than **08**, & less refined than 'blanc' partner.

★★★★ **Vin de Liza** 🈯 Varieties dropped from name, but still a Noble Late Harvest from sauvignon & semillon. After simple **09** (★★★★), **10** satisfies with silky, gently unctuous (perhaps too soft) charm.

Chenin Blanc ☺ 🍴 🈯 ★★★ A great Cape tradition for 40+ years. **11** as charming as ever (& as respectworthy - it will age a good few years). Just off-dry, fruity & fresh.

Labyrinth Cabernet Sauvignon ★★★ Ripe, flavoursome sample **08** rather more light-centred than serious **07**, but also sweet fruit & firm, dry structure. **Pinotage** ★★★ Big but unoaked **08** has sweet-fruited & unpretentious charm, & a rather heavy texture. **Mr Borio's Shiraz** ★★★ Easy-drinking but not frivolous **09** less showy than previous. Solid, even powerful structure, with savoury, lightish but ripe fruit. **Adelberg** 🍴 🈯 ★★ Soft, easy-going **10** cab-merlot, lightly wooded & just off-dry. **The SMV** 🍴 ★★★ Just a smidgen viognier with the shiraz & mourvèdre of **09**. Continues soft, off-dry, coffee-redolent style of previous. **Cabernet Sauvignon-Shiraz** 🍴 ★★★ **10** more structured & satisfying than **09**. Just-dry, savoury & pleasant. **Chardonnay** 🍴 ★★★ Gently rich **10** nearly as thoroughly pleasing as **09** - just a little lighter, less concentrated & rather oakier. **Gewürztraminer** 🍴 🈯 ★★★ **11** Special Late Harvest takes in 15% morio muscat. Sweet, with a rather coarse floral-fruity-cosmetic prettiness. **Sunbird Sauvignon Blanc** 🍴 🈯 ★★★☆ Forceful but unaggressive **11**, packed with flavour as ever, happily straddling the grassy-tropical split. Widely sourced grapes. **Adelblanc** 🈯 ★★★ Last year, **10** sauvignon-based blend with semillon showed full, ripe & cheerfully zesty. **Encore Vin Sec** ★★★★ **07** chardonnay-based MCC sparkling last year showed just-off-dry, earthy-appley charm. **Straw Wine** NEW ★★★★ Grapey & floral perfumed aromas resolve to a lovely, rather elegant (though simple) dried-pear finish on **09**, from sun-dried grapes. Discontinued: **Viognier Sur Lie en Barrique, Franciskaner.** — TJ

Simonsvlei International

🍴🥂🎋📷🎎&

Location: Paarl ▪ Map: Paarl & Wellington ▪ WO: Western Cape/Coastal ▪ Est/1stB 1945 ▪ Tasting & sales Mon-Fri 8–5 Sat 8.30–4.30 Sun 11–3 ▪ Fee R20pp ▪ Closed Dec 25 ▪ Snacks & cooldrinks served during opening hours; or BYO picnic ▪ Playground for children ▪ Gift shop ▪ Conference/function venue (80 pax) incl. equipment, breakaway areas, lunches, etc. ▪ Conservation area ▪ Owner(s) 65 shareholders ▪ Cellarmaster(s) Francois van Zyl (Nov 2000) ▪ Winemaker(s) Ryan Puttick (Nov 2010), with Christine Jones (Jun 2010) ▪ Viticulturist(s) Ryan Puttick (Nov 2010) & Francois van Zyl (Nov 2000) ▪ 1158ha (shiraz, chenin) ▪ 7,400t 48.5% red 48.5% white 2% rosé 1% other ▪ Brands for clients: Kelvin Grove, Ocean Basket, Woolworths ▪ ISO 9001:2008, BWI, Fairtrade, HACCP, IPW ▪ PO Box 584 Suider-Paarl 7624 ▪ info@simonsvlei.co.za ▪ www.simonsvlei.com ▪ S 33° 47'24.9" E 018° 55'49.1" ▪ T +27 (0)21-863-3040 ▪ F +27 (0)21-863-1240

Standing proud beside the Old Paarl Road since 1947, this noteworthy producer of good-value wines never stops looking for new directions. Winemaker (since 2010) Ryan Puttick says the team are out-of-the-box thinkers when it comes to wine, citing their New Generation range as evidence. Moving beyond the trendy coffee-infused pinotage already pervading the market, a vanilla toffee-flavoured shiraz in a chunky, heavyweight bottle has made its appearance. At the serious end of the extensive array is the vineyard-selection South Atlantic series, expressing unique viticultural sites.

Hercules Paragon range

Cabernet Sauvignon ★★★★ Flagship range, featuring occasional bottlings. **08**, first tasted since **05** (★★★★), is medium bodied, elegant fruit profile let down by big oak vanilla. **Shiraz** Await next. **SMCV** ★★★★ Shiraz-led blend, maiden **08** previously had appealing fruity lift from dashes mourvèdre, cinsaut, viognier. **Sauvignon Blanc** NEW 🍴 ★★★★ Heady, pungent aromatics on substantial **09** reflect age development. Exaggerated asparagus character mars otherwise fine effort.

South Atlantic range

Shiraz ★★★★ Range not revisited this ed. Maiden **08** had smoky mantle with meaty, pepper-spicy fruit. Coastal WO, as for all following. **Shiraz-Cabernet Sauvignon ★★★★** Stylish **08** showed solid fruit core with silky tannins last edition, with dark berries, damson & sour cherries. **Chardonnay** 🥂 **★★** Wooded **09** rather bland, spirity. **Sauvignon Blanc** 🥂 **★★★ 10** from Durbanville fruit had peardrop & apple flavours with grassy finish.

New Generation range NEW

Ja-Mocha ✓ **★★★★** Moves here from from Hercules range. From pinotage, not as expressively 'coffee' as expected; well-rounded, wild-berry **10** has appeal without gimmicky flavouring. **Toffee Chunk ★★★★** Debut **10** from shiraz is well constructed but lopsided, with charred wood & minty vanilla notes.

Premier range

> **Shiraz Rosé** ☺🥂🦚 **★★★** Consistently wholesome & satisfying, **11** is dry, with ripe berry notes. Everyday sundowner. **Chardonnay** ☺🥂 **★★★** More overt oak on **10**, but retains supple elegance & balance, with gentle twist of lemon on finish.

Cabernet Sauvignon 🥂 **★★★** Juicy, fruity **08** had soft ripe tannins, pleasing tarry core last time. **Pinotage** 🥂 **★★★ 09** last time was softer, more refined than previous, with appealing ripe red berry fruit, smooth tannins. **Shiraz** ✓ 🥂 **★★★★ 09** is juicy, fresh & fruity, with hint of serious intent. Upper-middle range still presents great value without frills. **Cabernet Sauvignon-Merlot** 🥂 **★★ 10** rather gawky structure, sweet edge & bitter tannins. This & next 3 tasted last time. **Rosé** In abeyance. **Bukettraube ★★★** Floral scents & cloves noted on semi-sweet **10**. **Chenin Blanc** ✓ 🥂 **★★★★** Ripe & vibrant **10** burst forth with pineapple & melon fruit on review. **Sauvignon Blanc** 🥂 **★★★** Nettles & dusty pebbles on fresh, vibrant **10**, previously was light bodied, but focused & elegant. **Humbro Hanepoot** 🥂 **★★★** Reliable **NV** super-sweet winter warmer, rich raisin-muscat fruit, lingering spirity finish. **Humbro Red Jerepiko** 🥂 **★★★** Quintessential Cape indulgence, sweet & sticky **NV** fortified dessert, spicy baked fruit & nutty finish.

Lifestyle range

> **Cabernet Sauvignon** ☺🥂 **★★☆** Undemanding, pleasantly smooth **09** has honest berry fruitiness. **Merlot** ☺🥂 **★★★** Perfect drinking for the price-conscious. **10** is sound, appealing, no-frills value. **Pinotage** ☺🥂 **★★★** Honest, fruity, unwooded **09** shows typical acetone-berry profile.

Shiraz ★★★ 09 previously had rich plum-pudding fruit, peppery spices. Over-achiever at the price. **Sweet Shiraz** NEW 🥂 **★★ 10** quirky, light, sweet & nutty. **Charming Red** 🥂 **★★ NV** simple, fruity, semi-sweet. This & next 5 previously tasted. **Simonsrood ★★★** Honest, fruity **NV** 4-way blend. **Blanc de Blanc ★★ NV** from chenin, lightish, cheerful & easy-drinking. **Sweet Chenin Blanc** NEW 🥂 **★★ 10** shows vibrant melon fruit with tangy finish. **Stein ★★** Thinnish off-dry **NV** chenin. **Simonsblanc ★★** Stalwart poolsider, **NV** from chenin & sauvignon, fruity, off-dry. **Natural Sweet Rosé ★★** Extra-light, sweetly juicy **NV** from chenin with dash pinotage. 1.5L bottles only. Discontinued: **Chenin Blanc Sparkling Wine, Sweet Rosé Sparkling Wine.**

Eco Glass Lifestyle range NEW

Cabernet Sauvignon 🥂 **★★** Entry-level, fresh & off-dry **09**. This & next: new range of PET (plastic)-packaged anytime quaffers. **Chenin Blanc** 🥂 **★★** Light & fruity **11** ideal picnic wine in shatterproof PET bottle.

Simonay range

Classic Red, Blanc de Blanc, Natural Sweet Rosé, Stein & Late Harvest in 5L boxes, untasted. — GdB

■ **Simply Red/White** see PicardiRebel

Sir Lambert Wines

Location/WO: Lamberts Bay ▪ Map: Olifants River ▪ Est 2004 ▪ 1stB 2007 ▪ Tasting Mon-Fri 9-5 Sat 9-3 at Diemersdal or by appt in Lamberts Bay ▪ Closed Easter Fri/Sun, Dec 25 & Jan 1 ▪ BYO picnic ▪ Xamarin Guest House & Restaurant ▪ Conference & function venue (up to 250 people) ▪ Game drives ▪ Golf course ▪ Tour groups ▪ Conservation area ▪ 4x4 trail ▪ Facilities for children ▪ Owner(s) John Hayes, Johan Teubes & Thys Louw ▪ Winemaker(s) Thys Louw & Mari van der Merwe ▪ Viticulturist(s) Johan Teubes (2004) ▪ 10ha (shiraz, sauv) ▪ 60t/ 3,000cs 10% red 90% white ▪ PO Box 27 Durbanville 7551 ▪ info@sirlambert.co.za ▪ www.sirlambert.co.za ▪ S 32°55'52.40" E 018° 18' 19.50" ▪ **T** +27 (0)21-976-3361 ▪ F +27 (0)21-979-1802

This joint venture between Diemersdal Estate and West Coast partners is attracting considerable interest overseas, particularly in the US and Sweden, with five-sixths of production going abroad. 'Customers in these markets,' says Diemersdal winemaker Thys Louw, 'share our wine philosophy, simply encapsulated by American author Clifton Fadiman: 'If food is the body of good living, wine is its soul'.'

★★★★ **Sauvignon Blanc** 🍷 🏵 Maritime influence evident in **11**'s cool green aromas, zingy acidity, 'oystershell' minerality in the aftertaste. Satisfying, if shade more measured, less showy than **10**.

The Admiral's Shiraz ★★★★ 1st WO Lamberts Bay shiraz last edition was peppery, leathery, **09** had well-rounded mouthfeel, showed potential despite slightly warm tail. — CvZ

■ **Sir Robert Stanford** *see Robert Stanford Estate*

Six Hats   NEW

Location: Citrusdal ▪ WO: Western Cape ▪ Est/1stB 2007 ▪ Closed to public ▪ Owner(s) Charles Back, Mike Paul & other grape farm owners ▪ Cellarmaster(s) Jaco Brand (Nov 2009) ▪ Winemaker(s) Jaco Brand, with Andries de Klerk (both Nov 2009) ▪ Viticulturist(s) Charl du Plessis (Nov 2009) ▪ 550ha (cab, grenache, ptage, pinot grigio shiraz, chard, chenin, sauv, viog) ▪ 5,000t/25,000cs own label 50% red 45% white 5% rosé + 100,000cs for clients ▪ Export label: Six Hats Fairtrade Wines ▪ Brands for clients: Asda, Co-op, Fairtrade Original, M&S, Sainsbury's ▪ HACCP 2004, WIETA, Fairtrade ▪ PO Box 41 Citrusdal 7340 ▪ info@citrusdalwines.co.za ▪ www.citrusdalwines.co.za ▪ **T +27 (0)22-921-2233** ▪ F +27 (0)22-921-3937

An initiative spearheaded by Fairview's Charles Back, the Six Hats Fairtrade wine range is built on a conscious awareness of the roles and responsibilities of all parties involved in progressive and equitable wine farming. Six principles - partnership, potential, change, equity, dignity and sustainability - guide the collaborations, and the positive results are already evident on the participating farms in Malmesbury and Piekenierskloof. On a purely monetary level, minimum prices are set for grapes, and a percentage of sales revenue is ploughed back into community upliftment projects.

Six Hats Fairtrade range

Shiraz 😊 🍷 ★★★ Easy & fruity **09** with savoury spice, dark berries in balance with firm oak. Fun to drink, as most here. **Chardonnay** 😊 🍷 🏵 ★★★ Loads of citrus, apple & melon flavours, barrel-fermentation gives a sweet vanilla overlay to smooth **11**. **Chenin Blanc** 😊 🍷 🏵 ★★★ Tropical fruit flavours on easy-drinking **11** picnic white. **Sauvignon Blanc** 😊 🍷 🏵 ★★★ Green & grassy **11** is fresh with a lingering zesty finish. Perfect for summer. **Viognier** 😊 🍷 🏵 ★★★ Ebullient apricot & floral notes, **11** fresh & lingering, not for keeping.

Cabernet Sauvignon 🍷 ★★★ **09**'s black fruit masked by oak mid-2011, bit terse on finish. May harmonise given time. **Grenache** ✓ ★★★★ Candied strawberry on **09**. Fresh, with lovely earthiness - balanced & harmonious. Stock up! **Pinotage** ✓ 🍷 ★★★★ Cheerful **09**, smooth vanilla oak on juicy plums. Fresh & delicious. **Pinotage Rosé** 🍷 🏵 ★★ Fruity & light, **11** easy summer sipper. — Panel

■ **Sixpence** *see Opstal Estate*
■ **1685** *see Boschendal Wines*
■ **Sixty 40** *see Boland Kelder*

Sizanani Wines

Location: Stellenbosch ▪ WO: Western Cape ▪ Est 2005 ▪ 1stB 2006 ▪ Tasting & sales at Bellevue Estate Stellenbosch ▪ Owner(s) Stellenbosch Wine and Logistics (Pty) Ltd ▪ Winemaker(s) Wilhelm Kritzinger & Anneke Potgieter (both 2005, Bellevue) ▪ Viticulturist(s) Dirkie Morkel (Feb 2005, Bellevue) ▪ 2,000cs own label 40% red 40% white 20% rosé ▪ PO Box 33 Koelenhof 7605 ▪ info@sizanani-wines.co.za ▪ www.sizanani-wines.co.za ▪ **T +27 (0)21-865-2055** ▪ F +27 (0)21-865-2899

The employees of Stellenbosch estate Bellevue previously had a minority stake in the Sizanani brand but full ownership was transferred to them last year. 'It used to be just another day in the vineyards for the workers, but now they have real control over their future and that of their children,' says Randall Piceur, managing director of the holding company. UK retailer Marks & Spencer snapped up a container of wine almost immediately, so a bright start for the solo endeavour.

★★★★ **Sauvignon Blanc** NEW ✓ 📖 😊 Shy nose but good fruit definition on **11**. Range of flavour from greenpepper through lime & vibrant acidity, pleasingly dry finish.

Pinotage ★★ Red cherry & vague coffee note on nose & palate of light **08**. **Red Blend** Untasted. **Cabernet Franc Rosé** 📖 😊 ★★★ Previewed **11** intense red fruit, purity & freshness make for very appealing proposition. **Chenin Blanc** 📖 😊 ★★★ **11** guava & melon flavours, light & straightforward. — CE

Skilpadvlei Wines

Location/map/WO: Stellenbosch ▪ Est 2004 ▪ 1stB 2001 ▪ Tasting & sales Mon-Sat 8-5 Sun 8-4 ▪ Fee R15 ▪ Closed Dec 25/26 & Jan 1 ▪ Restaurant Mon 8-5 Tue-Sat 8-late Sun 8-4 ▪ Facilities for children ▪ Conferences ▪ Weddings & functions ▪ B&B guesthouse & self-catering cottages ▪ Owner(s) WD Joubert ▪ Cellarmaster(s) Koewie du Toit (consultant) ▪ Viticulturist(s) Johan Pienaar & Eben Archer (consultants) ▪ 78ha/55ha (cab, merlot, ptage, shiraz, chenin, sauv) ▪ 652t/6,000cs own label 80% red 20% white ▪ PO Box 17 Vlottenburg 7604 ▪ info@skilpadvlei.co. za ▪ www.skilpadvlei.co.za ▪ S 33° 57' 31.5" E 018° 45' 52.4" ▪ **T +27 (0)21-881-3237** ▪ F +27 (0)21-881-3538

At this popular tortoise-themed wine and lifestyle venue on the M12 into Stellenbosch, they've added more B&B rooms, extended restaurant space, and upgraded facilities for tastings, weddings, functions and conferences. 'Affordable quality' is a mantra all visitors will applaud.

ML Joubert ★★★ The flagship, from cab & merlot. **07** blackcurrant & violet, light tannic grip from 18 months in oak, mostly new, rich cocoa finish. **Skilpaddop Dry Red** 📖 ★ **09** edgy & herbal near-equal mix merlot & pinotage. & following, not retasted. **Cabernet Sauvignon-Shiraz** ★★★ Dollop shiraz (25%) adds flesh to green-toned **08**, has firm cab handshake. **Chenin Blanc** 📖 ★★ Figgy **11** a light & crisp quaffer. **Sauvignon Blanc** 📖 ★★ Gooseberry lightness to **11**, tangy summertime sipper. Discontinued: **Skilpaddop Rosé, Skilpaddop Dry White.** — FM

■ **Skoon Vallei** *see* Eerste Hoop Wine Cellar

Slaley

Location/map: Stellenbosch ▪ WO: Simonsberg–Stellenbosch ▪ Est 1957 ▪ 1stB 1997 ▪ Tasting & sales Mon-Sat 10-4 ▪ Fee R20, waived on purchase ▪ Closed Easter Fri, Dec 25/26 & Jan 1 ▪ Cellar tours by appt ▪ Light meals during tasting hours ▪ Farm produce ▪ Conference facility with AV capacity ▪ Owner(s) Hunting family ▪ Winemaker(s) Marius Malan (Oct 2005, consultant), with Tremayne Smith (Jun 2011) ▪ Viticulturist(s) Jaco Mouton (Jun 1999, consultant) ▪ 240ha/51ha (cab, merlot, ptage, shiraz, chard, sauv) ▪ 320t/12-15,000cs own label 90% red 9% white 1% rosé ▪ IPW ▪ PO Box 119 Koelenhof 7605 ▪ info@slaley.co.za ▪ www.slaley.co.za ▪ S 33° 51' 53.7" E 18° 50' 51.1" ▪ **T +27 (0)21-865-2123** ▪ F +27 (0)86-529-2347

The wry reporting of a 'fire in the tasting room which precipitated a minor revolution in decor' doesn't quite capture the drama, because the roof was badly burnt when the fireplace flue caught alight, necessitating the temporary relocation of visitor tastings outside or to the cellar. All now rebuilt and it's business as usual. A little known fact is that one of the oldest pinotage bushvine blocks in the industry is here, planted in 1954 and named the 'Slaley clone'. The grapes are used in Slaley Pinotage.

Hunting Family range

★★★★ **Merlot** Last was **04** (★★★★) ripe prunes & plums, with firm tannins which may since have softened. Not as elegant as **02**.

★★★★ **Shiraz** Previously tasted **04**, combo ripe dark berries & earthy, smoky & gamey nuances; subtler oaking than earlier vintages; long savoury finish.

★★★★ **Reserve Noble Late Harvest Chardonnay** Last was **07**, decadent & irresistible, concentrated honey/raisin character (from vine-dried grapes) perfect match for strong cheeses.

Pinotage ★★★★ Last edition **06** showed good pinotage tarry & smoky flavours but needed time to settle. **Cabernet Sauvignon-Merlot** ★★★ Previously **07** equal blend had ripe fruit with tar, liquorice & nettle hints. Heady 15% alc needed time to integrate. **Chardonnay** 😊 ★★★★ Lacking the fruit of **09** (★★★★), barrel-fermented **10** has an attractive citrus & mineral profile, restrained slate-dry finish.

Broken Stone range

Cabernet Sauvignon ★★★ Last edition **04** had black berry, blackcurrant & plum, earthy dry finish. **Pinotage** ✓ ★★★★ A huge leap from **03** (★★★), **04** worth the wait. Smoothly polished creamy mulberries, succulence of the variety adding to the pleasure. Drink now till ±2016. **Shiraz ★★★★** Last-tasted spicy & peppery **06** had good fruit expression, savoury scrub & mineral hints, elegant dry finish. **Cabernet Sauvignon-Shiraz √ ★★★★** Lots going on in **06**, smoked meat, liberally sprinkled dried herbs, firm tannin backbone cloaked by the berry fruit. **Sauvignon Blanc ★★★** Last was **09**, ripe fig & savoury nuances, firm acidity.

Social range

Lindsay's Whimsy Cape Blend 🗎 ▨ ★★★ Smoky hedgerow fruit, **10** charms with its gutsy rusticity. Equal pinotage & merlot, splash cab. **Lindsay's Whimsy Rosé 🗎 ▨ ★★★** Dry **10** from shiraz is light-hearted (12. 9% alc) summer fare. — CR

Slanghoek Winery

Location: Rawsonville • Map: Breedekloof • WO: Slanghoek • Est 1951 • 1stB 1970 • Tasting & sales Mon-Fri 8–5 Sat 10–1 • Closed Easter Fri/Sun, Dec 25 & Jan 1 • Cellar tours by appt • Picnic baskets, booking required • Slanghoek MTB Route, fee R20: 13km ride with optional extra, more challenging 4km • Owner(s) 25 producers • Cellarmaster(s) Pieter Carstens (Aug 2002) • Winemaker(s) Nico Grundling & Paul Burger (Dec 2002/Dec 2008), with Jacques de Goede & Jaco Theron (Dec 2001/Oct 2007) • Viticulturist(s) Callie Coetzee (Nov 2010) • 1,830ha • 30,000t/40,000cs own label 25% red 55% white 10% rosé 10% fortified • Other export brand: Zonneweelde • ISO 22000, BWI, IPW • PO Box 75 Rawsonville 6845 • info@slanghoek.co.za • www.slanghoek.co.za • S 33° 39'1. 1" E 019° 13'49.0" • **T +27 (0)23-344-3026** • F +27 (0)23-344-3157

Majestic mountain vistas are enough reason to visit the Slanghoek Valley, but this get-up-and-go grower-owned winery at its heart offers many additional enticements: summer picnics, harvest vineyard tours, winter soup-and-sweet-wine evenings and, a perennial favourite, Blend & Bottle sessions during which participants create their own unique blends.

Private Selection

★★★★ Noble Late Harvest Honey & nougat nuanced **07** has improved in bottle: more complex, well-knit, though lacks weight, vibrancy of previous. Mainly chenin, dash muscat d'Alexandrie; 9 months French oak.

> **Cabernet Sauvignon** ☺ **★★★ 09** sleek blackberry sipper with medium body (13% alc) & touch new oak adding spice appeal (as for all reds in range; these mostly more characterful than the dry whites). **Pinotage** ☺ 🗎 **★★★** Quintessential strawberry, faint bitter lift on **08**; pleasing balance & length. **Shiraz** ☺ **★★★** Medium-bodied **08** generously flavoured & oaked. **Camerca** ☺ 🗎 **★★★ 09** repeats successful recipe 50/ 45 cab/merlot, dash cab franc. Restrained but still generous, engaging. **Special Late Harvest** ☺ 🗎 ▨ **★★★ 11** from hanepoot; balanced package of coconut, muscat & melon.

Merlot 🗎 ★★★ 09 very ripe & juicy, more complex oak highlights than last vintage. **Chardonnay 🗎 ▨ ★★★** Previewed **11** carbon copy of **10**: delicate oak, good weight. This, other dry whites, need more varietal expression to rate higher. **Chenin Blanc 🗎 ▨ ★★** Zesty & light **11** back on track after dip in **10**. **Sauvignon Blanc 🗎 ▨ ★★★** Faint white peach & grass bouquet, gravelly aftertaste on **11**. **Crème de Chenin √ ★★★★ 10** Natural Sweet has dried apricots, peaches & bitter almond notes from small portion botrytis, gentle sweetness enlivened by lime tang. Nudges higher rating, worth seeking out. **Cuvée Brut ★★** Dry sparkling has sherbet & apple notes courtesy chardonnay portion (with chenin & colombard) in latest **NV** bottling. **Vin Doux ★★★** Exuberant & perfumed sweet **NV** bubbly; enjoy chilled. **Sweet Hanepoot √ ★★★★** Previewed fortified dessert takes provisional step up in **11** with rose/watermelon freshness, integrated spirit. Deliciously slippery. **Red Muscadel √ ▨ ★★★★** Cherry-toned **11** has spirity succulence for fireside appeal; shorter, less complex than last-tasted **09** (**★★★★**). **10** sold out untasted. **Red Jerepiko ▨ ★★★★ 11** fortified dessert from pinotage; luscious, with seemingly dry tealeaf finish. **Cape Ruby** Port-style **11** preview too unformed to rate; warming fortification tamed by lashings touriga black-fruit flavour.

Vinay range

> **Crispy White** ☺ **★★★** Fruitful mix sauvignon, chenin, colombard; zippy acidity cuts dollop sugar.

Red ★★ Cheerful melange pinotage, malbec & petit verdot. **Rosé ★★** Semi-sweet, low-alc anytime sipper from muscadel. 1L bottle, like White. **NV**, as all. — CvZ

Slowine

Location/map: Villiersdorp ▪ WO: Western Cape/Overberg ▪ Est/1stB 2005 ▪ Tasting & sales Mon-Fri 8-5 Sat 9-1 ▪ Fee R10 for groups of 7+ ▪ Closed Easter Fri-Mon & Dec 25/26 ▪ Kelkiewyn Restaurant/Farm Stall T +27 (0)28-840-0900 Mon-Fri 8-5 Sat/Sun & pub hols 8-3 ▪ Farm produce ▪ Walking/hiking, mountain biking & 4x4 trails ▪ Tractor museum open on request ▪ Owner(s) Villiersdorp Cellar ▪ Shareholders Beaumont Wines & Luddite Wines ▪ Cellarmaster(s) Flip Smith (Jan 2011) ▪ Winemaker(s) Technical team: Sebastian Beaumont, Niels Verburg & Flip Smith ▪ Production Flip Smith, with André Bruyns (Dec 2009) ▪ Viticulturist(s) André Bruyns (Dec 2009) ▪ 300ha (merlot, chenin, sauv) ▪ 3,600t/20,000cs own label 40% red 40% white 20% rosé ▪ BWI, IPW ▪ PO Box 14 Villiersdorp 6848 ▪ marketing@slowine.co.za ▪ www.slowine.co.za ▪ S 33° 59' 11.2" E 019° 17' 48.5" ▪ **T +27 (0)28-840-1120** ▪ F +27 (0)028-840-1833

For a brand which celebrates an unhurried approach, developments take place rather swiftly. Under aegis of owner Villiersdorp Cellar and shareholder wineries Luddite and Beaumont, since last edition Flip Smith was appointed winemaker, the marketing function expanded and packaging given a facelift. The Geometric Tortoise, featured on the labels, continues to benefit from a portion of sales.

Slowine range

Cabernet Sauvignon ☺☐◎ **★★★ 10** sweet vanilla, chunky plum fruit, balanced for easy quaffability. **Merlot** ☺☐ **★★★ 09** more substance than last. Bright, juicy berries with good chewy tannins. **Rosé** ☺ ☐◎ **★★★** Dry charmer from pinotage. **11** candyfloss & punnet of ripe red berries. **Chenin Blanc** ☺☐ ◎ **★★★** Previewed **11** vibrant, brims with white peach & crisp apple, floral nuance in aftertaste. **Sauvignon Blanc** ☺☐◎ **★★★** Stock up for summer! Ex tank **11** bright & zesty, with lemon & Granny Smith apple. **Chenin Blanc-Sauvignon Blanc** ☺☐◎ **★★★** Pre-bottling, **11** slight hints of blossom & grass, pleasing balance, zesty lemony conclusion. Lipsmacking!

Shiraz ☐ **★★★** Easy sipper **09** trumps previous with brooding dark berries & white pepper. — WB

- **Smook Wines** *see* Anthony Smook Wines
- **Snow Mountain** *see* Nabygelegen Private Cellar
- **Social** *see* Slaley
- **Soek Die Geluk** *see* Goedvertwacht Wine Estate
- **Soet Izak** *see* Jason's Hill Private Cellar

SoetKaroo Wine Estate

Location: Prince Albert ▪ Map: Klein Karoo & Garden Route ▪ WO: Western Cape ▪ Est 2000 ▪ 1stB 2004 ▪ Tasting & sales Mon-Sat 9-1; afternoons by appt ▪ Closed Dec 25 ▪ Owner(s) Herman & Susan Perold ▪ Cellarmaster(s)/winemaker(s) Susan Perold (Jan 2007) ▪ Vineyard manager(s) Herman Perold ▪ 2t ▪ 56 Church Str Prince Albert 6930 ▪ perold@netactive.co.za ▪ www.soetkaroo.co.za ▪ S 33° 13' 21.9" E 022° 1' 48.0" ▪ **T +27 (0)23-541-1768** ▪ F +27 (0)86-524-3801

2011 highlights for vintner Susan Perold included a Terroir Award for her rare Red Muscat d'Alexandrie. A self-proclaimed traditionalist, she keeps things simple in her tiny Prince Albert hamlet cellar, aiming for dessert wines 'lighter, fruitier, less sweet and true to the flavour and character of each variety'. Her answer to our stock question - Any particularly old, unique or unusual blocks on your estate? - is vintage Susan: 'Herman Perold' - her vineyardist husband!

★★★★ Touriga Nacional Classic port grape purposely lighter styled (±18% alc); **09** perfectly balanced; **10** (★★) tad sugary, oxidative, less impressive. Also available in limited 500ml presentation packages.

Red Muscat d'Alexandrie ★★★ Fortified dessert from unusual red hanepoot, smidgen (red) muscadel. **10** red berry & savoury flavours, alc shade more obvious than usual. **Petit Verdot** In abeyance. Discontinued: **Touriga Nacional-Petit Verdot.** — Panel

- **Sojourn** *see* Elberti Wines
- **Solms-Astor** *see* Solms-Delta

Solms-Delta

Location/map: Franschhoek ▪ WO: Western Cape/Coastal ▪ Est 1690 ▪ 1stB 2004 ▪ Tasting & sales daily 9–5 ▪ Fee R10pp ▪ Closed Dec 25 & Jan 1 ▪ Cellar tours by appt ▪ Fyndraai Restaurant (see Restaurants section) ▪ Walking/hiking trails ▪ Conservation area ▪ Museum van de Caab & archaeological sites ▪ Harvest festival (Mar) ▪ Summer music concerts ▪ Delta draf (Apr) ▪ Owner(s) Solms & Astor families and Workers' Trust ▪ Cellarmaster(s) Fanie Karolus (Jan 2007) ▪ Winemaker(s) Hilko Hegewisch (Mar 2003, consultant), with Maria Botha (May 2011) ▪ Viticulturist(s) Rosa Kruger (Jul 2011, consultant) ▪ 78ha/30ha (grenache n/b, mourv, shiraz, chenin, Muscat d'A, Muscat de F, sem, viog) ▪ 220t/25,000cs own label 30% red 13% white 8% rosé 49% other ▪ IPW ▪ PO Box 123 Groot Drakenstein 7680 ▪ info@solms-delta.co.za ▪ www.solms-delta.co.za ▪ S 33° 51'51.0" E 018° 59'23.8" ▪ **T +27 (0)21-874-3937** ▪ F +27 (0)21-874-1852

In answer to our stock question, Why does wine matter?, co-owner and neuroscientist Mark Solms says: 'It is, and has been for centuries, the cornerstone of economic and social life for thousands of people in the Cape. Its future role can be shaped by what transpires today.' Which is partly why farmworkers are equal shareholders with the Solms and Astor families in this remarkable winery, whose painstakingly researched backstory is both a fascinating record spanning millennia and a template for modern-day multiculturalism. Some 30,000 visitors make their way through the museum, tasting room, indigenous culinary garden and restaurant each year; the wines receive critical acclaim worldwide; and production is set to double. Coming on board to ensure ongoing business, social and environmental sustainability are assistant winemaker Maria Botha, CEO Craig MacGillivray, sales supremo Claire Wright and viticulture guru Rosa Kruger.

Solms-Delta range

★★★★☆ **Africana** From desiccated shiraz - a style specialised in here. Tasted last year, silky, smooth & fresh **08** showed a vibrant acidity & a sweet-sour finish - the residual sugar imperceptible.

★★★★ **Hiervandaan** Last tasted was spicy & feisty **07**. Shiraz-based + 4 other Rhône varieties.

★★★★ **Lekkerwijn** 🌿 Healthy dollop shiraz (+ usual grenache, mourvèdre, viognier) & a bit less sugar (it's now officially dry) distinguish carefree **10** from **09**. Full-fruited, with an emphatic farewell.

★★★★☆ **Amalie** ✓ 🌿 Characterful Rhône-style white blend, **10** adds 33% roussanne to usual viognier, grenache blanc (vine-dried). Seductive jasmine, ginger & some viognier meatiness; rounded, rich body corseted by lively acidity, so aftertaste is crisp & fresh. WO Coastal.

★★★★ **Koloni** 🌿 **10** semi-dry blend vine-dried muscats d'Alexandrie & de Frontignan, lovely Turkish Delight perfume & zingy freshness ensuring food compatibility. Last **07** (★★★★☆) mostly riesling & muscat.

Gemoedsrus Await new vintage.

Solms-Astor

Cape Jazz Shiraz ☺ ★★★ Personality- & fun-laden spritzy red fizz. Latest **NV** is light, off-dry, perky & gently grippy.

Langarm 🌿 ★★★★ 'Sock hop' dance style alluded to in name reflects in exuberant fruitiness of **10**, suave combo shiraz, pinotage, tannat, mourvèdre. **Vastrap** 📖 ★★★ **10** a smoky, attractive but austere blend chenin, semillon & riesling. Demands food. — CvZ

Solo Wines

Location: Stellenbosch ▪ WO: Western Cape/Stellenbosch ▪ Est/1stB 2009 ▪ Closed to public ▪ Wine sales by appt or telephonically ▪ Owner(s)/winemaker(s) Philip Costandius ▪ 50% red 50% white ▪ PO Box 241 Stellenbosch 7599 ▪ wine@solowines.com ▪ www.solowines.com ▪ **T +27 (0)21-881-3200** ▪ F +27 (0)21-881-3200

Adding a new string to his bow in the fourth year of flying solo, owner/winemaker Philip Costandius is harnessing his vast experience to present weekend entry-level winemaking courses. A fan of elegance and 'modern classic' styling, the Cape Winemakers Guild member steers clear of 'brash and overbearing' winemaking.

Syrah ★★★★ Now bottled, **09**'s spicy ripe black fruit & plums balance chalky texture with dry tannin from 18 months in 2nd fill oak. **CWG Auction Reserve The Guildsman** ★★★★ Cab-led 6-way blend. Harmonious & rounded **09** a notch up on last-tasted **07** (★★★★); spicy black cherry, integrated oak (2nd fill French, 2 years), enduring richly fruited finish. **Viognier** ★★★★ **10** spicy restraint & elegance. Juicy honey & quince tang, light wood sheen from 15% oak for 6 months. Not overblown. — FM

Somerbosch Wines

Location/WO: Stellenbosch ▪ Map: Helderberg ▪ Est 1950 ▪ 1stB 1995 ▪ Tasting & sales daily 9-5 ▪ Fee R20/6 wines, waived on purchase of any 3 btls; R40pp/ice cream & red wine tasting ▪ Closed Dec 25 & Jan 1 ▪ Cellar tours by appt ▪ Somerbosch Bistro: breakfast & lunch daily ▪ Facilities for children ▪ Farm produce ▪ Conferences ▪ Owner(s) Somerbosch Wines cc ▪ Cellarmaster(s)/winemaker(s)/viticulturist(s) Marius & Japie Roux (both 1995) ▪ 55ha/43ha (cab, merlot, shiraz, sauv) ▪ 350t 55% red 45% white ▪ PO Box 12181 Die Boord 7613 ▪ enquiries@ somerbosch.co.za, sales@somerbosch.co.za ▪ www.somerbosch.co.za ▪ S 34° 0' 28.6" E 018° 49' 6.9" ▪ **T +27 (0)21-855-3615** ▪ F +27 (0)21-855-4457

'We like customers to have as much fun drinking our wines as we have making them,' say brothers Japie and Marius Roux, explaining innovations like the red-wine ice cream tastings at their family-friendly farm. They recently bought four 2,500l tanks to focus on making smaller quantities of high-quality wines.

Somerbosch range

★★★★ **Kylix** ▤ Higher general rating for this amply bottle-aged red blend, **04** from cab, shiraz, merlot. Vivid fruit & minerals, solid oaking structures ripe flavours, as does ample freshness.

Cabernet Sauvignon ▤ ★★★ Elegantly styled, fresh & firm **08** shows streamlined tannins & acidity. **Merlot** ★★ Previously tasted **07** had meaty savouriness with stern acidity. **Pinotage** ★★★ Uncomplicated meaty, vanilla **09** for everyday drinking. **Shiraz** ★★★ Refreshing acidity of spicy **08** gives sweet-sour profile. **Chardonnay** ▤ ★★★ Still-selling **10** melon & sweet baked-apple flavours. **Chenin Blanc** ▤ Await new vintage. **Sauvignon Blanc** ▤ ★★★ Crisply fruity **11** has zippy freshness. Everyday quaffer. **Méthode Cap Classique Brut** Await new. **Late Bottled Vintage Port** ★★★ **06** from cab, warming fireside sipper tasted for previous edition. Discontinued: **Chenin Blanc Natural Sweet Limited Release**.

Poker Hill range

Shiraz-Merlot ▤ ★★ New bottling not ready, as for **Semillon-Chenin Blanc**. — IM

▪ **Somerlust** *see* Viljoensdrift Wines & Cruises
▪ **Sonata** *see* Waterstone Wines
▪ **Songloed** *see* Groupe LFE South Africa
▪ **Sonop Organic** *see* African Terroir

Sophie   NEW

Location/WO: Elgin ▪ Est/1stB 2009 ▪ Closed to public ▪ Owner(s) Andrew Gunn ▪ Cellarmaster(s) Werner Muller (May 2011) ▪ (cab, merlot, shiraz, sauv) ▪ 150t/10,000cs own label 10% red 85% white 5% rosé ▪ PO Box 527 Grabouw 7160 ▪ orders@sophie.co.za ▪ www.sophie.co.za ▪ **T +27 (0)28-284-9678** ▪ F +27 (0)28-284-9078

These wines with their catchy branding are made at Iona Vineyards in Elgin using grapes from selected producers in the valley, as well as wines surplus to the winery's requirements, with 'no compromise, no matter what the price point' according to owner Andrew Gunn. The range amusingly includes 'the most famous woman to never exist', Sophie Te'blanche, a name which stemmed from the vineyard workers' mispronunciation of sauvignon blanc.

Le Rouge ✓ ▤ ★★★★ Appetising, smoky **08** Bordeaux-shiraz red is fresh & vibrant, with harmonious fruit & oak. **Rose** ✓ ▤ ★★★★ **10** rosé from cab is dry & well structured, lipsmacking red-fruit flavours & lingering berry finish. **Te'blanche** ✓ ▤ ▨ ★★★★ Delicious, balanced **11** is light & fresh with zingy acidity, rounded mouthfeel & mineral finish. Over-delivers on price. — Panel

▪ **Sopiensklip** *see* Springfontein Wine Estate
▪ **Soulo** *see* Overhex Wines International
▪ **South Africa** *see* Wineways Marketing
▪ **South African Soul** *see* Belbon Hills Private Cellar
▪ **South Atlantic** *see* Simonsvlei International
▪ **Southern Cape Vineyards** *see* Barrydale Cellar - SCV

Southern Right

Location: Hermanus ▪ Map: Elgin, Walker Bay & Bot River ▪ WO: Hemel-en-Aarde Valley/Walker Bay ▪ Est 1994 ▪ 1stB 1995 ▪ Tasting, sales & cellar tours Mon-Fri 9-5 Sat 9-1 ▪ Closed Easter Fri/Mon, Dec 25/26 & Jan 1 ▪ Fynbos reserve, renosterveld reserve & 3 wetlands ▪ Quad bike route ▪ Owner(s) Mark Willcox, Mikki Xayiya & Anthony Hamilton Russell ▪ Winemaker(s) Hannes Storm (2004) ▪ Viticulturist(s) Johan Montgomery (2005) ▪ 447ha/ ±36ha (ptage, sauv) ▪ 225-280t/15-20,000cs own label 20% red 80% white ▪ PO Box 158 Hermanus 7200 ▪ hrv@hermanus.co.za ▪ S 34° 24'3.2" E 019° 13'0.4" ▪ **T +27 (0)28-312-3595** ▪ F +27 (0)28-312-1797

For co-owner Anthony Hamilton Russell, buying this large Hemel-en-Aarde Valley property in 2006 as a permanent home for Southern Right is a highlight of his involvement with this label. A home, too, for nature: the Table Mountain Sandstone Fynbos reserve is now almost free of aliens. Clearing the two renosterveld reserves and the banks of the Onrus River are focuses this year. There's also commitment, of course, to the two preferred grape varieties. Five clones and 17 individual blocks allow the creation of a complex sauvignon; eschewing American oak, and striving for restraint and minerality, result in a pinotage after the owner's heart.

★★★★☆ **Pinotage** ✓ Always an accomplished expression of the variety, with well-judged oak (just 30% new), precision & poise. Measured & finely textured **10** has, despite dashes of 5 other varieties, quintessential strawberry & earth tones. Like the wine below, will reward a few years ageing.

★★★★☆ **Sauvignon Blanc** ✓ Flamboyant **11** in similar vein to striking **10**; as intensely redolent of capsicum & cut grass, equally 'maritime' & flinty. Flavoursome, with persistent lemony finish helped by a smidgen of semillon. From estate & bought-in Walker Bay fruit. — CvZ

Southern Sky Wines

Location: Paarl ▪ Map: Paarl & Wellington ▪ Est/1stB 2002 ▪ Tasting & sales by appt ▪ Owner(s) Andrew Milne ▪ Winemaker(s) Andrew Milne (Jan 2003) ▪ 10,000cs own label 95% red 5% white ▪ Export brands: Almara, Les Fleurs, Marimba, Ready Steady, Rowlands, Tara Hill ▪ PO Box 1312 Paarl 7624 ▪ andrew@ssw.co.za ▪ www.ssw. co.za ▪ S 33° 45'8.9" E 018° 57'43.7" ▪ **T +27 (0)21-863-4440** ▪ F +27 (0)21-863-0444

Asian markets can't get enough of Paarl-based negociant Andrew Milne's Almara, Les Fleurs, Marimba, Ready Steady, Rowlands and Tara Hill wines. China, Malaysia and now Vietnam like the taste - and Andrew says sales in Gauteng are showing good growth too. Unlike many other proud parents, he's resisted the temptation to name a wine after his first-born child...

South Hill Vineyards

Location/WO: Elgin ▪ Map: Elgin, Walker Bay & Bot River ▪ Est 2001 ▪ 1stB 2006 ▪ Tasting Mon-Fri 9-5 Sat/Sun 10-4 ▪ Original artworks (Red Gallery) ▪ Guesthouse (see Accommodation section) ▪ Function venue for conferences & weddings ▪ Conservation area ▪ Owner(s) South Hill Vineyards (Pty) Ltd ▪ Winemaker(s) Sean Skibbe (Jun 2005) ▪ Viticulturist(s) Andrew Teubes (Mar 2006, consultant) ▪ 57ha/28ha (cab, pinot, shiraz, chard, riesling, sauv, sem, viog) ▪ 130t/3,500cs own label 20% red 80% white ▪ PO Box 120 Elgin 7180 ▪ info@southhill.co.za ▪ www.southhill.co.za ▪ S 34° 13'59.5" E 019° 6'44.3" ▪ **T +27 (0)21-844-0888** ▪ F +27 (0)21-844-0959

This was a neglected apple and pear farm little more than a decade ago, but South Hill is now helping to demolish the idea that the only red wine in which the Elgin Valley can excel is pinot noir. The cab planted on their warmer north-facing slopes (sauvignon facing south) is an undoubted, elegant success.

★★★★☆ **Cabernet Sauvignon** ✓ 📖 Intense & nuanced **09** with sweet cherry notes, continues elegant styling. Oak (10% new) thoughtfully handled. Fresh but not green, savoury but not simple, ripe but not fat.

Cabernet Sauvignon Rosé 📖 Await next vintage. **Sauvignon Blanc** ✓ 📖 ★★★★ Fresh herbaceous **10** light & elegant though less expressive, intense, than standout nettly **09** (★★★★). — MF

■ **Spencer Bay** see Namaqua Wines

Spice Route Winery

Location: Swartland ▪ Map: Paarl & Wellington ▪ WO: Swartland/Darling ▪ Est/1stB 1998 ▪ Closed Easter Fri, Dec 25 & Jan 1 ▪ Restaurant ▪ Tour groups by appt ▪ Glass blowing factory & gift shop ▪ Farm produce ▪ Owner(s) Charles Back ▪ Winemaker(s) Charl du Plessis (Dec 2001), with Licia Solomons (Jan 2006) ▪ 400ha/115ha (cab, grenache, merlot, mourv, ptage, shiraz, chenin, sauv, viog) ▪ 900t 60% red 40% white ▪ IPW ▪ PO Box 583 Suider-Paarl 7624 ▪ spiceroute@iafrica.com ▪ www.spiceroutewines.co.za ▪ S 33° 45'50.5" E 018° 55'9.7" ▪ **T +27 (0)21-863-5200** ▪ F +27 (0)21-863-3797

This large winery and farm, owned by Charles Back of Fairview fame, pioneered the modern 'rediscovery' of the Swartland region, though its approach often differs from that taken by most of the Young(ish) Guard that inherited and furthered the revolution: as in the use of new oak, and the lavish styling and extreme ripeness characteristic of Charl du Plessis's Spice Route reds. Back's pioneering ways continue, however. For example, the petite sirah and tannat grapes that make their way into Malabar come from the Cape's maiden vineyards of these varieties. Spice Route's tasting room in Paarl has, incidentally, moved from Fairview to next-door Seidelberg.

★★★★ **Pinotage** ✓ Consistent & appealing - **09** with usual seductive logan/blackberry note, firm but unobtrusive structure, subtle oaking, leaving pure, fresh fruit. Few years in bottle will do only good.

★★★★ **Flagship Syrah** **08** continues fairly restrained mode, but still very ripe, & rather delicious even in youth. Powerful, but suaver than Shiraz: silkier, less abrasive. Oaky, but balanced by fruit.

★★★★ **Shiraz** Sweet-fruited, ripe, full-flavoured, full-throttle... **09** has full everything, really - it's a big, rich, oaky, assertive wine, with its own sort of balance & successful within its chosen style.

★★★★☆ **Malabar 07** (★★★★) half shiraz, 4 others in support. After excellent **06**, this shows opululence become over-ripe, with raisiny, porty character & soft sweetness but no depth. Drink soon.

★★★★☆ **Chenin Blanc** 🍸 🖉 Lightly oaked **10** happily repeats **09**'s clean, intense & delicious formula. Same good balance, lingering lemony finish; same prospects for beneficial year/2 in bottle.

★★★★☆ **Sauvignon Blanc** 🍸 🖉 **11** (★★★★) from Darling vineyards as always, but less flamboyant in its attractive mix of green & tropical styles than **10**. Restrained acidity, refined & very enjoyable.

Mourvèdre ★★★★ **09** tighter than **08**; similar interesting aroma/flavour profile. Not fruity, but well balanced, with sturdy, rustic charm. **Chakalaka** ★★★★ **09** has travelled well since sampled last year. Easy, delicious drinking, but built firmly enough. Typically ripe, a little sweet. **Viognier** 🍸 🖉 ★★★ Muted aromas, flavours on **10** - unusual for a ripe version of this flamboyant grape. Decent but dull. — TJ

Spier

Location/map: Stellenbosch ▪ WO: Coastal/Western Cape/Stellenbosch/Olifants River/Paarl ▪ Est 1692 ▪ 1stB 1770 ▪ Tasting 10-4.30 & sales 9-5 daily ▪ Fee R35, R100 for personal one on one tasting ▪ Facilities for children ▪ Tour groups ▪ Gift shop ▪ Farm produce ▪ Conferences ▪ Manor House museum & The Heritage Walk ▪ Conservation area ▪ 4-star Hotel & Spa ▪ Eight Restaurant & Spier Hotel Restaurant (see Restaurants section) ▪ Owner(s) Spier ▪ Cellarmaster(s) Frans Smit (Dec 1995) ▪ Winemaker(s) Johan Jordaan (reds, Jul 2007) & Jacques Erasmus (whites, Apr 2007), with Tania Kleintjies, Godfrey Singo & Anthony Kock (2007/2008/2009) ▪ Viticulturist(s) Johann Smit (Dec 1999) ▪ 850ha/193ha (barbera, cabs s/f, malbec, merlot, mourv, p verdot, ptage, shiraz, chard, chenin, sauv, sem, viog) ▪ 3,340t/±1.1m cs own label 65% red 31% white 3% rosé 1% MCC ▪ ISO 22000:2007, BWI, Fairtrade, IPW, Organic, WIETA ▪ PO Box 99 Lynedoch 7603 ▪ info@spier.co.za ▪ www.spier.co.za ▪ S 33° 58' 24.0" E 018° 46' 58.9" ▪ **T +27 (0)21-809-1143/6 (wine centre)** ▪ F +27 (0)21-809-1144

In the iconic 'green' anthem by Joni Mitchell, they paved paradise and put up a parking lot. At this Stellenbosch property, where change is in the air, they're doing the opposite: ripping up a parking lot to plant a vineyard. The intention is to endorse the high-quality Spier wines, and create a more definite wine-as-a-lifestyle destination. So, tasting and restaurant facilities are being revamped to put the focus back on wine, provenance and heritage. There's also a heritage walk through the manor house, part of the vineyards and past several of the phenomenal 21 Cape Dutch gables on the property. These are the inspiration behind the newest range to join the line-up.

Frans K. Smit range

★★★★★ **Frans K. Smit** Limited-release flagship named for cellarmaster; varieties differ each vintage. **07** (★★★★★) loses shiraz, ups cab & malbec ('best vintage ever for malbec'). Lavishly oaked (30 months new) & fruit-filled yet savoury & well composed. For ageing many years, like dense & dark **06**.

21 Gables range NEW

★★★★ **Pinotage** Lush **09** has fruit concentration, depth, to parry strong oak (70% new, mainly French); substantial & pleasing, structure to improve good few years. WO Stellenbosch.

★★★★☆ **Chenin Blanc** 🍷📖 Heady apple & apricot, cinnamon & vanilla on intense, partially barrel-fermented **10**; includes large portion dryland fruit from venerable vineyards in Durbanville. Dry & savoury, with obvious but not unattractive tannin & some sweetness.

Creative Block range

★★★★ **5** Raspberry & blackberry under sweet vanilla oak in voluptuous **09** cab-led Bordeaux blend. Higher portion malbec (12%) than **08** contributes tad tannin, ageability. Named for number of varieties in blend.

★★★★ **3** Scrub & lily nuances on polished **09** shiraz, mourvèdre, viognier combo. Firm but balanced structure, less concentrated than red stablemate but no less impressive. Similar to juicy, approachable **08**.

★★★★ **2** ✓ 📖 **11** accomplished sauvignon/semillon mix with former's gooseberry & asparagus, latter's lanolin. Satisfying grip ex 5 months lees-ageing; unoaked versus **10**'s 5% barrel-fermented portion.

8 NEW 📖 ★★★☆ Cape Blend from Paarl Fairtrade farm. Drop viognier plus 7 red varieties; pinotage the star (30%) in **10**. Dried grass, fynbos & smoked meat notes, very dry 'woody' tannins. Big alc well hidden, smooth & long. For earlier drinking, but in many ways more satisfying than its 'big brothers'.

Vintage Selection

★★★★ **Pinot Noir** NEW From Elgin fruit. Leafy pomegranate-toned **09** delightfully delicate yet with sufficient grip, succulence for ageing few years.

Cabernet Sauvignon Bottled on demand, mainly for export, not tasted, as for **Pinotage, Shiraz** & **Sauvignon Blanc**.

Signature range

> **Cabernet Sauvignon** ☺📖📖 ★★★ Soft & approachable **10** for everyday imbibing; lightly oaked, tad confected plum character. **Merlot** ☺📖📖 ★★★ **10** quintessential merlot with dark plummy fruit, hint sappy tannins, juicy finish. Slips down easily. WO W Cape for this range. **Rosé** ☺📖📖 ★★★ Boiled sweets on wallet-pleasing **11** from shiraz accentuated by tealeaf whiffs, food-friendly astringency. Lipsmacking. **Chardonnay** ☺📖 ★★★ Lemon & lime tickled **11** lovely vinosity & length, weight, from 5% barrel-fermented portion. Deft green herb touch, few grams sugar for extra appeal. **Sauvignon Blanc** ☺📖📖 ★★★ Step-up **11** is vibrant, with good varietal character. Shows that, like all here, quality can be delivered in large volumes.

Pinotage 📖📖 ★★★ Hint raisins on uncomplex **10**, gentle strawberry-sweet sipper designed to win friends easily. **Shiraz** ✓ 📖📖 ★★★★ Attractive fynbos fragrance on supple & generous **10**. Carefully crafted for early enjoyment. Excellent value. **Chenin Blanc** 📖 ★★★ Thatch & floral **11** pleasing Granny Smith apple bite, brisk flick in tail.

Methodé Cap Classique range NEW

★★★★ **Méthode Cap Classique** ✓ Engaging & well-priced champagne-method sparkling. Myriad tiny creamy bubbles on seabreeze-fresh **09** chardonnay/pinot mix (71/29). Tight, mineral finish, needs bottle-ageing to gain complexity. **08** pleasing marriage Granny Smith apple & toastiness; lighter body from 100% chardonnay. Gorgeous filigree label on **07**, attractive bruised apple bottle-age, weightier than younger vintages courtesy higher portion pinot noir (39%). WO Stellenbosch.

Organic range NEW

Cabernet Sauvignon 🌿 ★★★ **10**'s ripe almost jammy fruit dusted with spice; very sippable & packed with flavour, amicable tannic tug. WO Olifants River. **Sauvignon Blanc** 📖 🌿📖 ★★★ Faint blackcurrant & grassy notes, **10** engaging pithy texture, slight fruit-sweet edge. These both in recycled glass bottles, labels printed on recycled paper, sealed with cork & beeswax.

CWG Auction Reserve range

★★★★☆ **Merlot** Lots of toasty coconut oak seasoning on sugar plum & blackberry laden 09 (★★★★) from single-vineyard on (Stellenbosch) home farm. Unlike plush 08, which had presence but didn't demand centre stage, this boldly oaked & needs more than year/2 to knit.

★★★★ **Pinotage** NEW Opaque 09 an extrovert: there's characteristic banana & strawberry, obvious oak spiciness & tannin grip from 24 months 100% new oak. Despite being better integrated than stablemate, still too brusque to broach; wait 3+ years. WO Stellenbosch.

Private Collection

This super-premium range comprising single-variety wines only for export; latest vintages not reviewed. — CvZ

Spioenkop Wines

Location: Elgin ▪ Map: Elgin, Walker Bay & Bot River ▪ WO: Western Cape/Elgin/Walker Bay ▪ Est 2008 ▪ 1stB 2010 ▪ Tasting, sales & cellar tours Tue-Fri 10.30-3.30 Sat/Sun by appt ▪ Fee R20, waived on purchase (case of wine) ▪ Closed all pub hols ▪ Facilities for children ▪ BYO picnic ▪ Walking/hiking trails ▪ Conservation area ▪ Weddings/functions ▪ Self-catering cottage ▪ Owner(s) Valuline 119 (Pty) Ltd, 4 shareholders ▪ Cellarmaster(s)/winemaker(s)/viticulturist(s) Koen Roose-Vandenbroucke (2008) ▪ ±47ha/10ha (ptage, pinot, riesling, chenin, sauv) ▪ 40t/2,500cs own label 20% red 80% white ▪ PO Box 340 Grabouw 7160 ▪ info@spioenkopwines.co.za ▪ www.spioenkopwines.co.za ▪ S 34° 14' 14" E 019° 3' 50" ▪ **T +27 (0)21-859-1458**

Koen and Lore Roose, importers of South African wine into Belgium for over a decade, acquired land in Elgin in 2005 intent on making their own wine. Koen, who revels in being known as 'that crazy Belgian guy' wants to make wines which will be considered in the same company as Petrus and Opus One, that is wines which provide a 'unique wow feeling'.

1900 range

★★★★☆ **Pinotage** NEW 10 displays dark cherry, violets & spice; medium body with perfectly delineated fruit, fresh acidity & fine tannins; supportive 10 months in 300L French oak, 47% new. Mainly Simonsberg/Stellenbosch grapes, 5% Elgin.

★★★★ **Sauvignon Blanc Barrel Selection** NEW 10 apple & subtle herbal note; good weight; poise & finesse from soft but sufficient acidity; 10 months used oak gives structure, not wood flavour. WO Walker Bay.

Sauvignon Blanc 🖉 Previewed 11 passionfruit & yellow apple flavour, moderate acidity. Too unformed to rate, shows same youthful tautness as elegant & thrilling 10 (★★★★), deserves time to unleash full potential.

Spioenkop Wines range

Riesling NEW 🖉 Clean-as-a-whistle 11 shows lime, green apple flavour & bracing acidity. Extremely youthful & unevolved mid-2011 (& hence unrated), should reward a good few years of bottle maturation. WO Elgin. **Sauvignon Blanc** 🖉 Elegant 11 unrated preview has lime, subtle herbal flavours, moderate acidity before long, savoury finish. Seems better balanced, less austere than 10 (★★★★). Elgin grapes. — CE

■ **Splattered Toad** see Cape Point Vineyards
■ **Splendour** see Villiersdorp Cellar

Spookfontein Wines

Location: Hermanus ▪ Map: Elgin, Walker Bay & Bot River ▪ WO: Upper Hemel-en-Aarde Valley ▪ Est 2000 ▪ 1stB 2004 ▪ Tasting, sales & cellar tours by appt ▪ Two self-catering guest cottages ▪ Conservation area ▪ Owner(s) Spookfontein cc (Mike Davis) ▪ Winemaker(s) Craig Sheard (Feb 2006, consultant) ▪ Viticulturist(s) Andries Gotze (Jan 2009, consultant) ▪ 313ha/±12ha (cabs s&f, merlot, pinot) ▪ 50t/1,000cs own label 100% red ▪ PO Box 12031 Mill Street Cape Town 8010 ▪ cjswine@hotmail.com ▪ S 34° 21' 19.5" E 019° 17' 20.8" ▪ **T 082-265-1071**

Despite a disastrous 2010 harvest during which this Upper Hemel-en-Aarde Valley property lost 80% of its crop, owner Mike Davis and winemaker Craig Sheard didn't abandon their bid to become the first – if the plan comes together – organically certified winery in the Overberg. Fortunately, 2011 was a great if low yielding year, so at least there'll be something in bottle with which to celebrate when they do!

Cabernet Sauvignon ★★★★ Lean but well-knit 07, savoury, with walnut & cigarbox complexity. Not revisited, as all. **Cabernet Franc** ★★★★ Plush fruit (ex 13% cab) on 07, youthfully taut tannins may since have yielded. **Merlot** ★★★ Floral & high-toned 07's 14% alc & 25% new oak too robust for fruit on review, may since have assimilated. **Pinot Noir** ★★★ **08** from young single-vineyard, fresh raspberry & earthy allure. Label should gain complexity, depth as vines mature. **Phantom** ★★★★ Cab, merlot, cab franc marriage (50/30/20) in poised **07**, minty nuances, elegant oaking, 25% new. **Rosé** ★★★ Light, dry & berried **08** from merlot. — CvZ

Springfield Estate

Location/map/WO: Robertson ▪ Est/1stB 1995 ▪ Tasting & sales Mon-Fri 8–5 Sat 9–4 ▪ Closed Easter Fri/Sun, Dec 25 & Jan 1 ▪ Cellar tours by appt ▪ BYO picnic ▪ Owner(s) Bruwer family ▪ Cellarmaster(s)/viticulturist(s) Abrie Bruwer ▪ Winemaker(s) Abrie Bruwer, with Johan van Zyl ▪ 150ha (cabs s/f, merlot, p verdot, chard, sauv) ▪ IPW ▪ PO Box 770 Robertson 6705 ▪ admin@springfieldestate.com ▪ www.springfieldestate.com ▪ S 33° 50′ 12.1″ E 019° 54′ 54.0″ ▪ **T +27 (0)23-626-3661** ▪ F +27 (0)23-626-3664

The chardonnays are perhaps the standout wines at this highly respected, well-established family estate. There are two marvellously different characterful versions grown on the farm's lime-rich soils, one of them the acme of risky natural winemaking and both offering the bonus to winelovers of being released after the crudeness of youth has started developing into something really good. But some aficionados swear by the sauvignons instead – or as well. (How does Abrie Bruwer magic these wines, with their moderate alcohol levels, out of Robertson? Through patient, clever work in both vineyards and cellar, of course.) And then there are the reds that are so far from negligible. 'True gems of tradition,' Abrie and sister Jeanette Bruwer claim of their wines, with some justice.

★★★★☆ **Méthode Ancienne Cabernet Sauvignon** Naturally fermented, unfined & unfiltered as usual, **04** tasted last year was alive & intense; fresh cedary cassis notes; fine, insistent dry grip.

★★★★ **The Work of Time** Fine leafy, spicy aromas on **04** (★★★★★) last year. Cab franc-led (45%), with cab, merlot, petit verdot). Classically dry, fresh; richly layered. Best after 4+ years. **03** merlot-driven.

★★★★☆ **Méthode Ancienne Chardonnay** Not your standard chard in the naturalness of its making or its interest. Plus something lively & exciting (&, wonderfully, a touch funky) obvious on **09** from first sniff to lingering finish. Not fruity, but full, ripe flavours absorb the all-new oaking; lightly rich, substantial, balanced.

★★★★ **Wild Yeast Chardonnay** ✓ Earthy & oatmeal touches to ripe, flavourful **09** - more obvious sweet, delicious fruit, & a little less light-footed though with good acidity, than version above. To seriously enjoy.

★★★★ **Life From Stone Sauvignon Blanc** 🖩 Showy green pungency on **11** (★★★★), with sweaty undertones - a touch less fresh than **10**. Lots of green-tinged fruit, ending with slightly sour boiled-sweet note.

★★★★ **Special Cuvée Sauvignon Blanc** ✓ 🖩 Gentler, riper-fruited than above, **11** hints at perfumed peach: Weightier, silkier too, yet fresher. Both these with moderate 12.5% alcohol, bone-dry.

Whole Berry Cabernet Sauvignon ★★★ Appealing spicy fruitiness on **09**, with herbal & vanilla notes. Easy-going, round & soft, but marred by some bitterness. **Pinot Noir** ★★★★ **07** tasted last year was ripe & silky, with fine acid to freshen & lengthen succulent sweet fruit. — TJ

Springfontein Wine Estate

Location: Stanford ▪ Map: Elgin, Walker Bay & Bot River ▪ WO: Walker Bay ▪ Est 1996 ▪ 1stB 2004 ▪ Tasting, sales & cellar tours Mon-Fri 10-4 Sat by appt 10-2 ▪ Closed Easter Fri/Sun, Dec 25/26 & Jan 1 ▪ Tour groups ▪ Farm produce ▪ BYO picnic ▪ Walking/hiking trail ▪ 3 self-catering cottages ▪ Owner(s) Weber family & friends ▪ Cellarmaster(s) Christo Versfeld (Dec 2006) ▪ Winemaker(s) Christo Versfeld (Dec 2006), with Charlton Pietersen (Oct 2009) ▪ Viticulturist(s) Andre du Toit ▪ 500ha/25ha (cab, ptage, chenin) ▪ 145t/10,000cs own label 80% red 18% white 2% rosé ▪ PO Box 71 Stanford 7210 ▪ marketing@springfontein.co.za, info@springfontein.co.za ▪ www.springfontein.co.za ▪ S 34° 25′ 38.5″ E 019° 24′ 32.7″ ▪ **T +27 (0)28-341-0651 / +27 (0)72-371-7546** ▪ F +27 (0)28-341-0112

Developing people is part of the mantra at this German-owned Stanford boutique winery and vineyard, and they embraced the local community by sponsoring the inaugural Penguin Plunge to raise funds for those in need. Participants happily parted with good cash to jump into the icy Klein River in the middle of winter for the simple reward of doing good, and a glass of spicy Springfontein Glühwein! A restaurant is planned to enhance the visitor's – somewhat warmer – experience.

Single Vineyard range

★★★★ **Jonathan's Ridge Pinotage** Refined pinot noir-like grace to sweetly fruited **09**, generous (mostly new) wooding unobtrusive. For winter log fires & oxtail.

★★★★ **Jil's Dune Chenin Blanc** Single-vineyard given Full Monty treatment, but billowing **10** (★★★☆) doesn't quite truss up the tropical ripeness, opulent oak & not-quite-dry finish, unlike the less obvious **09**.

Estate Wine range

★★★★ **Terroir Selection Cabernet Sauvignon** [NEW] ✓ Compelling **08** proffers toned red-berry features in clean - not lightweight - style, with enough grip for seriousness.

★★★★ **Red** Stylish **07** showed refinement last year, the substantial new oak well melded.

★★★★ **Terroir Selection Chenin Blanc** 🖉 Expressive summer fruit-salad styling, but more urbane than cellarmate; sweetly-wooded **10** (★★★★) a yard short of the balance of **09**.

Terroir Selection Pinotage ★★★★ Trenchant **08** offers sweet plum flavour; no longer new wood, but with a 15% alc bang! **Ulumbaza** ★★★★ Shiraz led mourvèdre in **07**'s spicy pears-in-red-wine styling previously. **CY01 Chardonnay** ★★★ **08** was full of oak-enhanced nutty tones when last tasted. **Terroir Selection Sauvignon Blanc** [NEW] 🖉 ★★★ Retiring, tropical-style **10**, fleshy melon fruit spruced up with fresh acid seam. **White** ★★★★ Sauvignon's penetrating intensity was leavened in **09** by pithy semillon fruit & just enough wood when last reviewed. **Ikhalezi Noble Late Harvest 07** not yet ready.

Sopiensklip range

Pink [NEW] ☺🍴🖉 ★★★ Rosé from mourvèdre, Disney pink **10** packed with perky cherry charm, fresh & dry. **White** ☺🍴🖉 ★★★ Unoaked semillon/chardonnay medley fuller in **10**, more earthy than fruity, no less appealing.

Red ★★★ Merlot & pinotage-led **08** brimmed with plum fruit & soft, gluggable charm last year. — DS

Spring Grove Wines

Location/map/WO: Stellenbosch ▪ 1stB 2005 ▪ Tasting & sales by appt ▪ Owner(s) Parodi family ▪ Winemaker(s) Neil Moorhouse (2005) ▪ Viticulturist(s) Hannes Jansen van Vuuren (Mar 2008) ▪ 10ha/6.4ha (sangio, shiraz, pinot gris, sauv, viog) ▪ 41t/25,200L bulk ▪ PO Box 670 Vereeniging 1930 ▪ hannes@zorgvliet.com ▪ S 33° 54' 46. 50" E 018° 56' 13.6" ▪ **T +27 (0)82-856-8717** ▪ F +27 (0)86-697-3938

Formerly part of neighbouring Zorgvliet and with its wines still made there, regenerated Spring Grove's young sangiovese and pinot gris vines hint at the Italian extraction of its Parodi family owners. With half an eye on nearby L'Ormarins/Anthonij Rupert Wines' success with the varieties, viticulturist Hannes Jansen van Vuuren is upbeat about their potential on Spring Grove's particular combination of altitude and soil, even in advance of the first pinot gris harvest.

★★★★ **Sauvignon Blanc** ✓ 🍴 Harmonious sample **11** (★★★★) fresh & enticing with lovely zesty mineral finish, though not as gutsy as **10**.

Shiraz ✓ 🍴 ★★★★ Barrel sample **09**'s succulent fruitiness underlined by savoury, spicy tannins offering pleasing balance & some seriousness. **Viognier** ★★ **10** forthcoming & bold tasted last year. — IM

■ **Springtree** see Fish Hoek Wines
■ **Spring Valley** see Old Vines Cellars
■ **Spruitdrift** see Namaqua Wines
■ **Stablemate** see Excelsior Estate

Stanford Hills Winery

Location: Stanford ▪ Map: Elgin, Walker Bay & Bot River ▪ WO: Walker Bay ▪ Est 1856 ▪ 1stB 2002 ▪ Tasting, sales & tours Mon–Fri 8–5 Sat 10–1 ▪ Closed all pub hols ▪ Grappa, olive oil, preserves ▪ BYO picnic ▪ Hiking/mountain biking trails ▪ 3 self-catering Cottages ▪ Owner(s) Stanford Hills Estate (Pty) Ltd ▪ Cellarmaster(s)/winemaker(s) Peter Kastner (Apr 2005) ▪ Viticulturist(s) Niel Otto (Aug 2007, consultant) ▪ 131ha/12ha (ptage, shiraz, chard, sauv) ▪ 60t/2,000cs own label 66% red 34% white ▪ PO Box 1052 Stanford 7210 ▪ info@stanfordhills.co.za ▪ www.stanfordhills.co.za ▪ S 34° 25'21.4" E 019° 28'25.7" ▪ **T +27 (0)28-341-0841** ▪ F +27 (0)28-341-0286

They're celebrating their first shiraz harvest at these isolated vineyards outside Stanford - and it's quality in the vineyards, and bringing out their character that Peter Kastner says he aims at. Visitors no longer need to make appointments to taste the wines – most will be particularly pleased with the Pinotage.

★★★★ **Jacksons Pinotage** 09 fulfills promise of preview last year. Grown in stature & seriousness, but still bright, clean, sweet fruit leading to dry finish. Lightly rich, with good supportive oaking.

Jacksons Chardonnay ★★ Unbottled sample 09 tasted last year. Retasted, now shows balance & flavour but oxidative character problematically pronounced. **Jacksons Sauvignon Blanc** 🗎 ★★★ 10 noted last edition as not deep, but balanced, unshowy & interesting. — TJ

Star Hill

Location/WO: Montagu ▪ Map: Klein Karoo & Garden Route ▪ Est 2005 ▪ 1stB 2009 ▪ Tasting & sales Mon-Fri 9-4 Sat/Sun 9-3 ▪ Closed Dec 25 ▪ Cellar tours by appt ▪ The Trading Post farm stall & restaurant ▪ Facilities for children ▪ Gifts ▪ Farm produce ▪ Conference facilities on Killarney farm ▪ Walks/hikes ▪ Mountain biking ▪ Akkerboom self-catering cottages (www.akkerboomcountrycottages.com) ▪ Owner(s) Grant Hatch & Christopher Palmer Tomkinson ▪ Winemaker(s) Lourens van der Westhuizen (consultant) ▪ Viticulturist(s) Lourens van der Westhuizen & Leander Gagiano (consultants) ▪ 15ha (shiraz, chenin, sauv, viog) ▪ 500cs own label 60% red 40% white ▪ PO Box 342 Montagu 6720 ▪ starhill@tradouw.co.za ▪ www.starhillwines.com ▪ S 33° 54' 46.86" E 020° 29'32.31" ▪ **T +27 (0)28-572-1610** ▪ F +27 (0)28-572-1644

Christopher Palmer-Tomkinson and Grant Hatch, who own this farm in the Tradouw Highlands, have a common goal: producing great wines at altitude. They 'struck gold', they say, when they found winemaker Lourens van der Westhuizen (cellarmaster/co-owner of Arendsig), who shares their philosophy of making wines that fully express this unique winegrowing site.

★★★★ **Shiraz** Single-vineyard 09 elegant & complex expression of the variety: pepper/spice highlights to blackberry, rounded mouthfeel. Still selling, as for Viognier.

Chenin Blanc Wild Yeast NEW ★★★★ Persistent & engaging 10, older oak matured, fresh acidity well balanced by juicy green & yellow apple fruit. Nudges next level. **Viognier** ★★★★ Substantial alc, softening dab sugar well disguised by 09's energetic lime freshness, achieved through different picking dates. — Panel

Stark-Condé Wines

Location/map: Stellenbosch ▪ WO: Stellenbosch/Jonkershoek Valley/Elgin ▪ Est/1stB 1998 ▪ Tasting & sales Mon-Sun 10-4 ▪ Fee R30 pp ▪ Closed Easter Fri, Dec 25 & Jan 1 ▪ Postcard Café open daily 9.30-4 for light meals, coffee & cake ▪ Owner(s) Jonkershoek Cellars (Pty) Ltd ▪ Cellarmaster(s)/winemaker(s) José Conde (1998) ▪ Viticulturist(s) Pieter Smit (1998, consultant) ▪ 250ha/40ha (cabs s/f, merlot, p verdot, shiraz) ▪ 100t/6,000cs own label 80% red 20% white ▪ PO Box 389 Stellenbosch 7599 ▪ info@stark-conde.co.za ▪ www.stark-conde.co.za, www.postcardcafe.co.za ▪ S 33° 57' 15.81"E 018° 54' 34.96" ▪ **T +27 (0)21-861-7700 / +27 (0)21-887-3665** ▪ F +27 (0)21-887-4340

It's a story of returning to roots. After global travels and living in Japan for more than two decades, Hans-Peter Schröder relocated to Stellenbosch and bought Oude Nektar estate in Jonkershoek Valley in the late 80s. He was later joined by son-in-law José Conde, a native of Kansas City. The early vintages of Stark Wines (named for Schröder matriarch, Francesca) and then Stark-Condé Wines were predominantly exported. Now, with the success of Postcard Café – where Marie Conde conjures up (among other delights) Japanese-style iced coffee – and the uniquely beautiful tasting room, one fifth of production is sold off the farm and South Africa is the largest market. Grapes from other cool areas complement the home-vine bottlings in the Pepin Condé range.

Three Pines range

★★★★☆ **Cabernet Sauvignon** Extraordinary grace defines house-style; 09 (★★★★★) stamped with finesse reflecting the fine single-vineyard soil of origin. Perfectly ripe fruit & cosseting structure yield a rare combination of delicacy & power. Unfined/filtered; dabs merlot, petit verdot as in 08. WO Jonkershoek for this duo.

★★★★★ **Syrah** Crafted from highest home-vineyard revered for elegance; 09 seductive berry flesh in pliable parcel, truly delectable. Many strings to this bow: portion whole-berry ferment, combo wild & commercial yeasts (local & Rhône), mix of oak. Like 08, not to be hurried.

Stark-Condé range

★★★★ **Cabernet Sauvignon** Home-farm's four best cab blocks, joined by best merlot & cab franc (& splash petit verdot), 09 spotlights the red berry refinement that is Jonkershoek. As stylish as 08.

★★★★ **Syrah** Striking white pepper spice & purple fruit grounded by tannic grip, **09** excellent gutsy style, less ethereal than Three Pines version, no less enjoyable.

Pepin Condé range

★★★★ **Chenin Blanc** ✓ 🍷🏵 Fabulous **10** melds melon fruit with rich vinosity, ending firm & fresh. Super balance of components. Wild yeasts & 40% cask-fermented, 5% new.

★★★★ **Sauvignon Blanc** ✓ 🍷🏵 The antithesis of 'green' styling. **10** (★★★★) fleshes out natural acidity with lees & (older) oak richness, less complex than intriguing **09**. WO Elgin.

Cabernet Sauvignon ✓ 🍷 ★★★★ **09**'s plush dark fruit guided by firm yet yielding tannic structure. Gear up on **08** (★★★★), very attractive now & for few years. **Pinot Noir** NEW 🍷🏵 ★★★★ 2t/ha yielded mere 150 cases of **10**; elegant, cherry charm to earthy grip, easy now but will reward patience. WO Elgin. —DS

◼ **Starlette** *see* Allée Bleue Wines
◼ **Star Tree** *see* Orange River Wine Cellars

Steenberg Vineyards

Location: Constantia ▪ Map: Cape Peninsula ▪ WO: Western Cape/Coastal/Constantia ▪ Est 1990 ▪ 1stB 1996 ▪ Tasting & sales Mon–Fri 9–6 Sat/Sun 10–6 ▪ Fee R50 for flagship range, waived on purchase ▪ Closed Easter Fri & Dec 25 ▪ Cellar tours 11 & 3 daily ▪ Bistro Sixteen82 winery restaurant; Catharina's at Steenberg (see Restaurants section for both) ▪ 5-star Steenberg Hotel & Spa; conferences; world-class golf course, walking trail ▪ Extensive merchandising area ▪ Annual festivals: Constantia Fresh (Feb), Spring it on Constantia (end Oct) ▪ Conservation area ▪ Owner(s) Graham Beck Enterprises ▪ Winemaker(s) JD Pretorius (Mar 2009) ▪ Vineyard manager(s) Johann de Swardt ▪ 90ha/60ha (merlot, sauv) ▪ 312t/35,000cs own label 40% red 60% white ▪ WIETA ▪ PO Box 224 Steenberg 7947 ▪ info@steenbrg.co.za ▪ www.steenberg-vineyards.co.za ▪ S 34° 4' 17.0" E 018° 25' 31.1" ▪ **T +27 (0)21-713-2211** ▪ F +27 (0)21-713-2201

Steenberg has built its reputation on sauvignon and semillon, and offers no fewer than eight styles, alone or in combination, ranging from the pleasurably unpretentious to the magisterial. Winemaker JD Pretorius has the choice of fruit from his own vineyards and other prime sites in Darling and Durbanville, but his abiding passion is getting the unique character of the winery's 22-year-old Reserve Sauvignon vineyard into bottle and winning the variety still greater critical acclaim. Ongoing efforts in the tasting centre have also been rewarded, with a programme exploring new food and wine pairing options helping win Steenberg the Great Wine Capitals Best of Wine Tourism global award for Best Wine Services.

Steenberg Vineyards range

★★★★ **Merlot** Familiar eucalypt character & ripe plummy **09** fruit enveloped in smoky oak, currently masking fruit richness but sufficiently concentrated to endure firm though supple tannins. WO Constantia, as are next two, Sauvignon Blanc & Semillon.

★★★★ **Nebbiolo** Thoroughly appetising rendition of Piedmont variety in excellent **09** (★★★★★) step-up from **08**. No new oak to augment already firm, lithe grape tannins which with fine natural acidity ably frame gorgeously rich & savoury flavours.

★★★★ **Shiraz** Nod to Rhône in expressive, youthful **09** (★★★★★) with more vivid red fruit than **08**. Earthy minerality & line of fine acidity throughout, with beautifully integrated, textured tannins underpinning convincingly savoury finish.

★★★★☆ **Catharina** 'Best of vintage' barrel selection. Tasted mid-09, **07** cab & merlot, some cab franc. Elegant yet perfumed & hedonistic too. As always, will reward further cellaring.

★★★★ **Sauvignon Blanc** Fresh, perky **11** spent extended time on lees, adding textured appeal to precisely focused minerally style, with mouthwatering finish. Several pickings ensure range of aromas & flavours.

★★★★★ **Sauvignon Blanc Reserve** Sleek herbaceous **10** tasted last year had lees-induced weight & great concentration. Zingy acidity & piercing minerality provided precise focus & freshness.

★★★★☆ **Semillon** Utterly satisfying, weighty **10** back on form after lighter **09** (★★★★) with rich nuttiness from barrel & time on lees. Perfect harmony between oak & fruit, with sublime texture, deliciously rich fruit flavours & pithy, minerally finish.

★★★★★ **Magna Carta** Astonishing **10** (★★★★★☆) barrel-fermented sauvignon-semillon blend deserving of reputation & price. Pristine (as we remarked of **09** too), layered herbaceous fruit with semillon's weighty, textured richness to match steely acidity & stony minerality which will need time to yield.

★★★★☆ **Sauvignon Blanc-Semillon** 08 with 66% new-oaked semillon mid-09 showed complex flavours & creamy oak. Delicious but needed touch more verve. Occasional bottling.

★★★★★ **CWG Auction Reserve The Magus** Precise, linear **10** exhibits considerable depth & concentration. Older barrels add dimension & breadth to piercing minerality, steeliness & focused herbaceousness. Needs time to unfurl. As for Magna Carta, a blend own, Darling & Durbanville grapes.

★★★★ **1682 Chardonnay** Dab pinot in pleasingly rich, harmonious **10** MCC from Robertson vyds. More than year on lees and reserve wine component succeeds in adding breadth and mouthfilling deliciousness.

★★★★ **1682 Pinot Noir** Fragrant, austere & focused **08** MCC made in attractive rosé style flaunts fine, persistent bubbles. Firm pinot backbone masks fruit, showing less depth & complexity than **07** (★★★★★). WO W Cape.

HMS Echo NEW 🍷 ★★★★ Merlot-led **09** inter-regional mix, with cab franc & cab sees older barrels for accessibility & freshness; good everyday drinking. **HMS Sphynx Chardonnay** ★★★★ Tropical blend own/Robertson grapes delightfully fresh & rich **11**. Luxuriously integrated oak adds weight & breadth. **HMS Rattlesnake Sauvignon Blanc** ★★★★ Poised, vibrant **11** blend own & Darling, Durbanville fruit has dash semillon & barrel portion for weight & texture.

Klein Steenberg range

Cabernet Sauvignon NEW Accessible **10**'s juicy fruit makes easy, everyday quaffing. This, following, WO W Cape. **Sauvignon Blanc** 🍷 ★★★ **11** blend appetisingly fresh & simple for light lunchtime sipping. WO W Cape for both. Discontinued: **Red**, **Rosé**. — IM

■ **Steenhuis** *see* Wine-of-the-Month Club

Stellar Winery

Location: Klawer ▪ Map: Olifants River ▪ WO: Western Cape ▪ Est 2000 ▪ 1stB 2001 ▪ Tasting & sales Mon–Fri 8–5 ▪ Closed most pub hols ▪ Cellar tours by appt ▪ BYO picnic ▪ Owner(s) Rossouw family, Stellar Empowerment Trust & others ▪ Cellarmaster(s) Berty Jones (Oct 2008) ▪ Winemaker(s) Klaas Coetzee (Aug 2010) & Mauritius Naude ▪ Viticulturist(s) Elizabeth Cloete (2011) ▪ ±68ha/Stellar Farming & ±149ha/Independant organic producers (cab, merlot, ptage, ruby cab, shiraz, chenin, chard, muscat d'A, sauv) ▪ 11,900t ▪ Other export brands: African Star, Firefly, Ithemba, Moonlight Organics, Natural Star, Running Duck, Sunshine Organics, Ubuntu ▪ Brands for clients: Ilula Gepa, La Place, Usapho ▪ Control Union (organic certification), Fairtrade ▪ PO Box 4 Klawer 8145 ▪ info@stellarorganics.com ▪ www.stellarorganics.com ▪ S 31° 53′ 13.7″ E 018° 37′ 53.0″ ▪ **T +27 (0)27-216-1310** ▪ F +27 (0)86-635-1968

The exciting news from this large organic wine producer is that the newly fitted-out Vredendal cellar, which has come on-stream the past year, has freed up space in their other cellar at Trawal. Why is this so exciting? Because it finally enables them to produce a significant quantity of their boutique 'No Sulphur-Added' range – something they've been striving after for some time. Winemaker Klaas Coetzee remains committed to interfering as little as possible in the winemaking process as he tries to reflect terroir in every bottle, and strongly believes his wines are good for your health – in moderation of course.

Stellar Organics range

Cabernet Sauvignon 🍷 ❀ 🌿 ★★★ Friendly **11**, succulent dark-berried centre, measured grippy mouthfeel. Quality characterises this steadily improving & wallet-friendly range. **Merlot** 🍷 ❀ 🌿 ★★★ Blackberries & milk chocolate on chewy **11**, cheery pasta companion. **Pinotage** 🍷 ❀ 🌿 ★★★ Foursquare **11**, high-toned cherry fruit, for fans of old-style pinotage. **Shiraz** 🍷 ❀ 🌿 ★★★★ **11** standout in line-up: white pepper whiffs, spice & generous red fruit, characterful, satisfying. **Rosé** 🍷 ❀ 🌿 ★★★ 'Shiraz Rosé' last time. Sunset-hued **11** delightfully sweet & sour, juicy centre & dry conclusion. **Chardonnay** 🍷 ❀ 🌿 ★★★ Last edition, affable **10** brushed by vanilla & coconut, balanced despite slight sweet touch. **Chenin Blanc** 🍷 ❀ 🌿 ★★ Step-up **11** reflects easier vintage in Olifants; baked apple flavour offer satisfying summer sipping. **Sauvignon Blanc** 🍷 ❀ 🌿 ★★★ **11**'s grassy & herbal notes, crisp acidity make for easy drinking. **Sauvignon Blanc Reserve** ❀ 🌿 ★★★★ **09** reflects excellent sauvignon vintage: tinned asparagus & lanolin bottle-age, restrained & mouthfilling, zesty grapefruit farewell. **Semillon Reserve** NEW ★★★★ Like Sauvignon Reserve, a preview; mirrors the standout vintage. **09** toasted almond & wax, honey-nougat; vivacious palate packed with lemon, engaging pithy twist. **Colombard-Sauvignon Blanc** 🍷 ❀ 🌿 ★★ Anytime sipper **11**, muted guava, gentle waxy tones. **Chenin Blanc-Sauvignon Blanc** 🍷 ❀ 🌿 ★★★ Friendly **11** ripe & tropical, with chenin's dried hay nuance.

Stellar Organics No-Sulphur-Added

Cabernet Sauvignon 🍷 ☀ 🖾 ★★ From a fairly easy vintage here, rustic **11** under-delivers: yeasty whiffs to shy cassis. **Merlot** 🍷 ☀ 🖾 ★★★ Dark berries & ink, chocolate on **11**, slips down easily with bright fruit, supple tannin. **Shiraz** 🍷 ☀ 🖾 ★★ **11** undemanding spicy red-fruit quaffer.

Live-A-Little range

Really Ravishing Red 🍷 ☀ ★★ Like the figure on the label, slightly plump but such fun! Comfortable **NV** sipper, as all these. **Rather Revealing Rosé** 🍷 ☀ ★★★ Faint cranberry aroma, tangy & dry with plenty of unpretentious appeal. **Wildly Wicked White** 🍷 ☀ ★★ Fragrant jasmine, kiwi & Turkish Delight flavours: lives up to its name. **Slightly Sweet & Shameless** 🍷 ☀ ★★ Spicy scent, litchi & melon taste, sweet goodbye.

Heaven on Earth range

★★★★ **Natural Sweet** ☀ Honey-sweet **NV** dessert from muscat d'Alexandrie, partially dried on straw & rooibos, fermented in seasoned barrels. Marmalade aromas, delicious muscat flavours last year. — Panel

■ **Stellcape Vineyards** see StellenRust

Stellekaya Winery

Location/map: Stellenbosch ▪ WO: Stellenbosch/Paarl ▪ Est 1998 ▪ 1stB 1999 ▪ Tasting, sales & cellar tours Mon-Fri 10-4 ▪ Fee R50 ▪ Closed all pub hols; Dec 16 to Jan 2/3 ▪ Private luncheon & wine tasting with winemaker by arrangement (up to 6 pax) ▪ Owner(s) Dave & Jane Lello ▪ Winemaker(s) Ntsiki Biyela (Feb 2004) ▪ Viticulturist(s) Paul Wallace (Jan 2005, consultant) ▪ 23ha/15ha (cab) ▪ 6,000cs own label 100% red ▪ Brands for clients: Amadoda Braai Restaurant, Exact Africa, The Grand Beach Café ▪ IPW ▪ PO Box 12426 Die Boord Stellenbosch 7613 ▪ info@stellekaya.co.za ▪ www.stellekaya.co.za ▪ S 33° 56′ 27.6″ E 018° 50′ 47.3″ ▪ **T +27 (0)21-883-3873** ▪ F +27 (0)21-883-2536

Mainly red wines are produced here, blends and single varieties, to which pinotage was added last year. The exception is an everyday white to meet consumer demand. The other way visitors are being catered for are two wine clubs: Zodiac, which offers wine discounts, and the more popular Aquarius - founder members assist winemaker Ntsiki Biyela in blending four wines, the two best of which are then bottled and sold exclusively to members in the Cape and Gauteng.

Premium range

★★★★ **Merlot** ✓ Such power in the berry, mint crisp flavours, one almost forgets how well made **08** is. Oak is in careful support, mainly older barrels, to retain the supple sleekness, fruit focus.

★★★★ **Shiraz** ✓ Luscious red berries are **08**'s platform for spice array, vanilla, black pepper, cinnamon, but a wilder scrub note creeps into the palate, adding to the complexity. Ripe & ready.

★★★★ **Orion** Flagship, cab-led Bordeaux blend. Impressive blackcurrant intensity, lithe polished tannins from 22 months new French oak, **07** is already delicious but will reward futher 6+ years cellaring.

Cabernet Sauvignon ★★★★ Cappuccino & ripe plums, **08** captures your attention but best is still to come - has 7+ year future, needs year or 2 to meld. **Pinotage** NEW ✓ 🍷 ★★★★ Hedgerow fruit & fynbos, **08** shows the trademark succulence that make pinotage so enjoyable to drink. Ideal venison match. **Cape Cross** ★★★★ Cab domination shows in **08**'s lush blackcurrant, matches dry tannins but even better in a year. **07** sold out untasted. Creamy berries, hint of cloves, merlot-led **06** is drinking well. **Hercules** ★★★★ **08** half sangiovese, rest cab, merlot. Black cherry compote & ginger biscuit, juicy, lively; dry food-friendly finish.

Boschetto range

Red ☺ 🍷 ★★★ Mainly cab in appealing **09** with 3 partners; vibrant blackcurrants juicy counterpoint to oaking. For food or drink solo.

White 🍷 🖾 ★★★ Quaffer from chenin, **10** has pear flavours, nice freshness. — CR

■ **Stellenbosch Drive** see Origin Wine

Stellenbosch Hills Wines

Location/map: Stellenbosch ▪ WO: Polkadraai Hills/Stellenbosch ▪ Est 1945 ▪ 1stB 1972 ▪ Tasting & sales Mon-Fri 8-5 Sat & pub hols 10-3 ▪ Fee R10; R40 wine, biltong & droëwors tasting ▪ Closed Easter Fri, Dec 25 & Jan 1 ▪ The Tank art gallery ▪ Owner(s) 16 members ▪ Cellarmaster(s) PG Slabbert (Jan 1997) ▪ Winemaker(s) Juan Slabbert (Jan 2009) ▪ Viticulturist(s) Johan Pienaar & Eben Archer (consultants) ▪ 715ha (cab, merlot, ptage, shiraz, chard, chenin, muscat de Hambourg, sauv) ▪ 8,000t/10,000cs own label 68% red 30% white 2% other ▪ IPW ▪ PO Box 40 Vlottenburg 7604 ▪ info@stellenbosch-hills.co.za ▪ www.stellenbosch-hills.co.za ▪ S 33° 57′ 38.2″ E 018° 48′ 1.8″ ▪ **T +27 (0)21-881-3828** ▪ F +27 (0)21-881-3357

The name dates back only to 2003, but the winery (drawing on 16 farmers) evolved from Vlottenburg Co-op, founded nearly 60 years earlier. For wine and chocolate pairing go elsewhere, for at Stellenbosch Hills the offering is dried meats: 'an improved biltong and droëwors adventure', no less. It is, says cellarmaster PG Slabbert, 'a logical and lekker local match'!

Stellenbosch Hills Wines range

★★★★ **1707 Reserve Red** 'Red' joins name. 08 (★★★★) from shiraz plus Bordeaux grapes. Last year, cranberry fruit dominated by sweet toasty oak. Fine tannins add to soft mouthfeel. 07 more harmonious.

Cabernet Sauvignon 🗔 ★★★ Fruit aromas on 08 lead on to firm, plush but unbalanced palate (4g/l sugar stands out). This & all wines in the range except Merlot, tasted for previous editions. **Merlot** 🗔 ★★★ Food-friendly 08 displaying mocha & blackberry notes. Fresh & pleasant, but straightforward. **Pinotage** 🗔 ★★★ Interesting red & black berries & liquorice note on 08, some sugar sweetness jarring palate. **Shiraz** 🗔 Await next. **Chardonnay** 🗔 ★★★★ Impressive 08 with good oak influence & a savoury flavour intensity. **Chenin Blanc** 🗔 ★★ Just-dry 10 tasted ex tank. **Sauvignon Blanc** 🗔 ★★★ Pleasant, greenish & very zesty 10 preview. **1707 Reserve White** ★★★★ Opulent 09 chardonnay with semillon & viognier. All-new oak drives intensely flavoured, ultra-rich but dry palate. **Muscat de Hambourg** ★★ Easy-going jerepigo-style NV.

Polkadraai range

Pinotage-Merlot 🗔 ★★ Awkward, oaky 09 last year. **Chenin Blanc-Sauvignon Blanc** 🗔 ★★ Easy, just-dry 11; lemon-twist finish. **Pinot Noir Rosé Sparkling** ★★ Previously 'Rosé'. Sweet, simple 10 bubbly. —JPf

Stellenbosch Ridge [NEW]

Location/WO: Stellenbosch ▪ Est 2004 ▪ 1stB 2005 ▪ Closed to public ▪ Owner(s) Jean Engelbrecht ▪ Winemaker(s) Coenie Snyman (Jan 2005), with Schalk Opperman (Jan 2005) ▪ Viticulturist(s) Dirkie Mouton (Jan 2010) ▪ 7t/ 600cs own label 100% red ▪ IPW ▪ PO Box 473 Stellenbosch 7599 ▪ info@rustenvrede.com ▪ www. stellenboschridge.com ▪ **T +27 (0)21-881-3881** ▪ F +27 (0)21-881-3000

The 2009 vintage of Stellenbosch Ridge introduces an exciting new premium brand by Rust en Vrede owner Jean Engelbrecht and winemaker Coenie Snyman. Made from selected grapes mainly from the Helderberg and Simonsberg, the Bordeaux-style blend has allowed both to explore beyond the estate's vineyards. Vinified, off and on, from 2005, and currently at just 600 cases (with some already going to Belgium and Switzerland), the brand may expand to include different varieties, wines and sites, and eventually find its own home.

★★★★☆ **Stellenbosch Ridge** Serious 09 Bordeaux style blend, cab (63%), merlot, petit verdot, malbec, is dark & rich. Full bodied, with fruit & oak (40% new) in harmony, 15% alc well hidden. For the long haul. —Panel

Stellenbosch University Welgevallen Cellar

Location/map: Stellenbosch ▪ WO: Stellenbosch/Elgin ▪ Est 2001 ▪ 1stB 2009 ▪ Tasting Mon-Fri 9-4 Sat by appt ▪ Fee R10pp ▪ Closed all pub hols & Dec 25 to Jan 10 ▪ Owner(s) Stellenbosch University ▪ Cellarmaster(s)/ winemaker(s) Riaan Wassüng (Jan 2004) ▪ Viticulturist(s) Vaatjie Jacobs (Jan 1973) ▪ 11ha/10ha (cab, ptage, shiraz, chard, sauv) ▪ 2,300cs own label 68% red 32% white ▪ Department of Viticulture & Oenology Private Bag X1 Matieland 7602 ▪ winesales@sun.ac.za, rfw@sun.ac.za ▪ http://academic.sun.ac.za/viti_oenol ▪ S 33° 56′ 22. 75″ E 018° 52′ 1.01″ ▪ **T +27 (0)21-808-2925** ▪ F +27 (0)21-808-4781

Pinotage was created when Prof Abraham Perold of Stellenbosch University's oenology faculty crossed hermitage (cinsaut) and pinot noir in the 1920s. The first seedlings were planted adjacent to the cellar, inspiring the current student winemakers to 'extend our historical connection with this by producing even better pinotage wines'. They also plan to become part of the Stellenbosch Walking Route, and expand their repertoire with a shiraz and méthode cap classique sparkling.

Die Laan range

Rector's Reserve Pinotage Occasional release. **Pinotage** ★★★☆ Abundant mocha & smoked meat in 09 rendition of fashionable style. Plush fruit checked by firm tannins & well-judged acidity. **Cape Blend** ★★★★

Harmonious, seamlessly oaked **09** blend cab & pinotage, splash petit verdot. Appetisingly fresh, with savoury spiciness. **Viognier** 🍷 ★★★ Typical floral/peachy scented **10**, restrained & crisply dry. Satisfying texture, ample freshness.

Maties range

Dry Red ★★ Big, satisfying, meaty **NV** blend of a miscellany of vintages & varieties tasted previous edition. —IM

Stellenbosch Wine & Country Estate

Location: Stellenbosch ▪ Est 2004 ▪ 1stB 2005 ▪ Closed to public ▪ Owner(s) Stellenbosch Wine & Country Estate (Pty) Ltd ▪ Winemaker(s)/viticulturist(s) Wynand Pienaar (Feb 2004) ▪ 29.8ha (cinsaut, ptage, shiraz, chenin) ▪ 31t/1,450cs 80% red 20% white ▪ PO Box 158 Elsenburg 7607 ▪ wynlpers@iafrica.com ▪ **T +27 (0)83-305-7332** ▪ F +27 (0)21-982-7925

The go-ahead for further development finally granted, it was time to plan and build at this residential and wine estate, which lies to the west of Stellenbosch. In the meantime, the vineyards have been rented out. 'But we will take back our existing vineyards and plant new ones in the near future,' assures consultant winemaker Wynand Pienaar.

Stellendrift - SHZ Cilliers/Kuün Wyne

Location/map/WO: Stellenbosch ▪ Est 1995 ▪ 1stB 1996 ▪ Tasting & cellar tours by appt ▪ Owner(s) Fanie Cilliers (SHZ Cilliers/Kuün Wines) ▪ Cellarmaster(s)/winemaker(s)/viticulturist(s) Fanie Cilliers (Nov 1995) ▪ 5,800cs own label 90% red 10% white ▪ PO Box 6340 Uniedal 7612 ▪ fcilliers@vodamail.co.za ▪ www.stellendrift.co.za ▪ S 33° 58' 54.92" E 018° 46' 15.91" ▪ **T +27 (0)21-887-6561** ▪ F +27 (0)21-887-6561

Stellenbosch-based small-scale producer Fanie Cilliers has been busy bottling wines under both his regular and occasional labels. Close to his heart is Jako's Pinotage-Cabernet, in honour of his late brother, a pinotage pioneer whom he credits with grafting the first pinotage vines in the Breede River Valley in 1968.

Stellendrift range

Reserve Cabernet Sauvignon Await next vintage, as for **Merlot**. **Kruispad Pinotage** 🍷 ★★★ Tasted previously, **05** earthy & herbal, with integrated alc & firm tannins which should have softened by now. **VOC Syrah** ★★★ **05** last year showed characteristic earthy, leathery notes, some dark berries in the background. Paarl grapes. **Merlot-Cabernet Sauvignon Blitz** Await new release. **Cape Huguenot Merlot-Pinotage** ★★★ Merlot-led **05**, pasta partner with mocha & plum flavours previous edition. **Giant Sauvignon Blanc** 🍷 ★★★★ Named after Giant/King Protea, South Africa's national flower. Well-balanced debut **09** last year appealed with kiwi, ripe fig & gooseberry. **Cape White Savour** Unrated in our previous guide, **07** mainly sauvignon, dash chenin, unwooded.

Cilliers Cellars range

De Reijgersdaal Cabernet Sauvignon This & **Elizabeth Couvret Merlot** not tasted. **Jacko's Pinotage-Cabernet Sauvignon** NEW ★★ **05** no spring chicken yet still juicy & accessible, toffee scent & sweet berry taste.

De Oude Opstal range

Cabernet Sauvignon Reserve ★★★ Blackberry & dried fruit on earthy **05**, oak was still obvious mid-2010. **Merlot-Cabernet Sauvignon** ★★★ Last edition **04** was leaner, with herbal notes, best enjoyed soon. — DB

StellenRust

Location/map/WO: Stellenbosch ▪ Est/1stB 1928 ▪ Tasting & sales Mon-Fri 10–5 Sat 10–3 ▪ Fee R20 incl appetisers ▪ Bottelary property: tasting by appt only ▪ Closed Ash Wed, Easter Fri-Mon, Ascension day, Dec 25/26 & Jan 1 ▪ Cellar tours by appt ▪ Farm-style platters & pre-arranged lunches/dinners ▪ BYO picnic ▪ Tour groups ▪ Grape 'stompings' ▪ Gifts ▪ Conferences ▪ Weddings/functions (300+ pax) ▪ Walking/hiking & mountain biking trails ▪ Art exhibition ▪ Owner(s) StellenRust Family Trust ▪ Cellarmaster(s) Tertius Boshoff (Jan 2004) ▪ Winemaker(s) Tertius Boshoff (Jan 2004), with Robert Lennox (Jun 2011) ▪ Viticulturist(s) Kobie van der Westhuizen (Jan 2000) ▪ 500ha/250ha (cab, cincaut, merlot, ptage, shiraz, chard, chenin, Muscat d'A, sauv) ▪ 1,700t/150,000cs own label 69% red 30% white 1% rosé + 20,000cs for clients ▪ Other export brands: Steenrust, STELL, StellCape, Steynsrust ▪ Brands for clients: Amera, Embrace, Sabi Sabi private game lodge ▪ HACCP 2005, Fairtrade ▪ PO Box 26

Koelenhof 7605 ▪ info@stellenrust.co.za ▪ www.stellenrust.co.za ▪ S 33° 59′ 18.0″ E 018° 50′ 57.9″ (Hberg) S 33° 51′ 44.41″ E 018° 46′ 34.11″ (Btlry) ▪ **T +27 (0)21-880-2283** ▪ F +27 (0)21-880-2284

Take one of the largest family-run farms in Stellenbosch's acclaimed 'Golden Triangle', two energetic young wine enthusiasts (one a dentist and the other an accountant by qualification), a newly expanded 2,000t cellar, and you have the recipe for a very successful winery. Not that the formula remains constant, as winemaker Tertius Boshoff and viticulturist Kobie van der Westhuizen consider diversity and flexibility keys to their success. With 250ha under vines there is plenty of scope for creativity and growth, equally bestowed on their social responsibility, sound labour and environmentally sustainable practices.

Super Premium range

★★★★ **Peppergrinder's Shiraz** Single-vineyard 08 (★★★★) more harmonious & flavoursome than premium shiraz below. Robust style with riper, savoury, fynbos tone but a shade off elegant & restrained 07.

★★★★ **Timeless** ✓ 08 has more cabernet in the 3-way Bordeaux blend than usual. Tad more restrained & sombre, with less fruit intensity than 07. Still quietly confident & ageworthy, with good structure.

★★★★ **Barrel Fermented Chardonnay** ✓ 🏵 Cool, high-lying limestone soils impart a minerality to 10 (★★★★★) that focuses tangy marmalade & toasted nut flavours. Natural ferment & oak add richness but retains elegant restraint, verve & length. Step up on 09.

★★★★☆ **'46' Barrel Fermented Chenin Blanc** ✓ 🏵 Pedigree of low-yielding (2t!) 46 year old single vineyard shows, even in riper vintage. Naturally fermented 10 echoes the tangy, botrytis-tinged quince & honey flavours found in 09 (★★★★★). Just off-dry, balanced & delicious now, but also ageworthy.

★★★★ **Chenin d'Muscat Noble Late Harvest** Old chenin & muscat vineyards (together a 100 years old!) yield a light & vivacious elixir in 09 from mere 1t of grapes. Gentle apricot, almond & hint of perfume, subtly oaked. Delightful!

Cornerstone Pinotage NEW ★★★★ Low-yielding old vines show up variety's pinot noir parentage in youthful & tightly structured 08, with piquant cherry & perfumed tone. More elegant than premium version. **JJ Handmade Reserve** NEW ★★★★ Pinotage dominates 08's 4-way Cape/Bordeaux blend. Bold, ripe & juicy, with firm underlying structure. One for the table & cellar.

Premium range

Sauvignon Blanc ☺ 🍽 🏵 ★★★ 11 crisp & light, green apple tone & flinty farewell. Zesty food style with friendly 12% alc.

Cabernet Sauvignon ✓ 🍽 ★★★★ 09 tightly knit in cool vintage, shows blackcurrant & cedar in juicy restraint. Quality in place, just youthful, needs time. **Merlot** NEW 🍽 ★★★ Piquant but bright 09 shows youthful restraint. Juicy, red berry core sheathed in chalky tannins, will blossom with time. **Pinotage** 🍽 🏵 ★★★ Rustic & ripe 10 is a tad warm, with sour plum tone. Needs food. **Shiraz** 🍽 ★★★ Tight 09 gruff in youth with scrub & liquorice tone. **Simplicity** ✓ 🍽 ★★★★ 09 merlot leads shiraz & cab in accomplished blend. Flavoursome & ageable, with firm, supple tone. **Chardonnay** ✓ 🍽 🏵 ★★★★ 11 balanced & flavoursome pear & lemongrass with tangy twist. Delightful solo or with seafood. **Chenin Blanc** ✓ 🍽 🏵 ★★★★ Ripe & crisp 11 shows fresh balance & drinkability; appealing lees & botrytis nuances enriche apple flavours.

Kleine Rust range

Pinotage Rosé ☺ 🍽 🏵 ★★★ Just 'Rosé' last time. 11 is for sunset sipping. Crisply ripe, red berried appeal. **White** ☺ 🍽 🏵 ★★★ 11's chenin/sauvignon duo has fresh, juicy apple drinkability. **Semi-Sweet** NEW ☺ 🍽 🏵 ★★★ Dainty, perfumed & light 11 from chenin, sauvignon & muscat.

Red 🍽 🏵 ★★★ 10 mostly pinotage & shiraz. Friendly, savoury & mocha toned, for everyday enjoyment. — MW

Stellenzicht Vineyards

Location/map/WO: Stellenbosch ▪ Est 1982 ▪ 1stB 1989 ▪ Tasting & sales Mon-Fri 9–5 Sat/Sun 10–4 ▪ Fee R25, waived on purchase ▪ Closed Easter Fri, Dec 25 & Jan 1 ▪ Cellar tours by appt ▪ Owner(s) Lusan Premium Wines ▪ Winemaker(s) Guy Webber (Oct 1998), with Nataleé Both (Aug 2010) ▪ Viticulturist(s) Johan Mong (Apr 2007) ▪ 228ha/99ha (cab, merlot, ptage, shiraz) ▪ 795t/20,000cs own label 85% red 15% white ▪ BRC, HACCP ▪ PO Box 104 Stellenbosch 7599 ▪ info@stellenzicht.co.za ▪ www.stellenzicht.co.za ▪ S 33° 59′ 50.0″ E 018° 51′ 59.8″ ▪ **T +27 (0)21-880-1103** ▪ F +27 (0)21-880-1107

There are few as unassuming in the winelands as Stellenzicht cellarmaster Guy Webber. Asked what his biggest career success is to date, he replies 'Every opened bottle is a highlight'. His wines, however, make more of a statement, the Syrah in particular a South African benchmark. New to the range are a Chardonnay and Petit Verdot made in experimental fashion with 'no added sulphites'. Such wines can be considered a more authentic product, a significant part of human intervention removed from the winemaking process although it has to be said the two Stellenzicht examples have a somewhat unusual flavour profile. 'It's not by mistake but by design that the wines taste the way they do,' says Webber. 'They're definitely not mainstream.'

Stellenzicht Specialities range

★★★★☆ **Syrah** Blockbuster in the best sense, **05** intense dark fruit, spice, charry oak (20 months, 90% new) & ±16% alc not out of place. Still selling mid-2011.

★★★★ **Semillon Reserve** Boldly envisioned **09** (★★★★☆) is complex, rich & full; shows citrus, bruised apple, wet wool, honey & spice; big but perfectly balanced, oak apparent but an embellishment rather than a distraction & a long, savoury finish. Better resolved than **08**.

Rhapsody ★★★★ **07** from pinotage & shiraz. Big & bold with strawberry & spice flavours when last tasted. More confident & stylish than **06** (★★★★). These previously listed under 'Stellenzicht Vineyards range'.

Cellarmaster's Release range

★★★★ **Shiraz** Last edition **07** (★★★) showed ripe dark fruit & heavy vanilla. First release since **04**.

Petit Verdot No Added Sulphites NEW ★★★ **08** has great curiosity value with dark fruit, chocolate, spice & not off-putting meaty note. **Chardonnay No Added Sulphites** NEW 🔲 ★★★ Fascinating **10** has hint of citrus alongside yeasty, almost malty tones; fresh acidity lends verve. Discontinued: **Cabernet Sauvignon**, **Pinotage**.

Golden Triangle range

★★★★☆ **Pinotage** Carefully conceived **09** is medium bodied, juicy & fresh; intense red cherry & spice flavours before long, dry finish; 22 months in oak from a variety of sources, 25% new.

Cabernet Sauvignon ★★ Lean **06** shows red fruit, herbal note. **Merlot** ★★★ Paint-by-numbers **08** is smooth, with ripe dark fruit & chocolate. **Shiraz** ★★★★ **08** closed, tightly packed mid-2011, hint of red & black fruit, some spice - should benefit from time in bottle. **Chardonnay** ★★★★ Citrus & baked bread note on rich, full **08** last time. **Sauvignon Blanc** 🔲 ★★★ Straightforward **11** preview, juicy pineapple, gentle acidity. — CE

Sterhuis

Location/map: Stellenbosch ▪ WO: Bottelary ▪ Est 1980 ▪ 1stB 2002 ▪ Tasting, sales & cellar tours by appt ▪ Closed Christian holidays ▪ Facilities for children ▪ Conservation area ▪ Owner(s) Kruger family ▪ Winemaker(s) Johan Kruger ▪ Vineyard manager(s) Jaco Mouton ▪ 100ha/48ha under vine ▪ 300t/6,000cs own label 25% red 75% white ▪ PO Box 131 Koelenhof 7605 ▪ johan@sterhuis.co.za ▪ www.sterhuis.co.za ▪ S 33° 54'43.1" E 018° 46'4.2" ▪ T +27 (0)83-411-0757 ▪ F +27 (0)21-906-1195

Two new labels on the portfolio of this Bottelary family farm (though Johan Kruger makes the wines elsewhere). Times are tough at the top end, says Johan, and these are 'inspired by the recession' – more affordable versions of Sterhuis. In the vineyards, farming moves in an ever more sustainable direction. Here Kruger senior, André (a lawyer by day), is more involved, though his love of gardening has also resulted in a study into fynbos and a passion for pincushion proteas.

★★★★ **Cabernet Sauvignon** Gd varietal character, pure freshness & quiet authority on last-tasted **07**. Gently sweet-fruited, but with strong, lean muscularity & earthy tang. All in balance.

★★★★☆ **Sterhuis Astra Red** Tasted last year, **06** (★★★★☆) from 70/30 cab & merlot had more herbaceous tones than plummy **05**, on lean side, with moderate fruit, but pleasing notes cedar, tobacco.

★★★★ **Chardonnay Barrel Selection 09** adds nutty oak note to full, lingering lime, grapefruit character. Finely textured & well balanced - piquant acidity coping with a touch of sweetness. Not retasted.

★★★★ **Chenin Blanc** From 41 year old vines, **09** (★★★★) rather subdued, but round & richly textured. Tasted last year, it looked as though it might offer more with time. Like **08**, only older oak used.

★★★★ **Sauvignon Blanc** Bone-dry & fresh, but citrus-rich **10** has an almost velvety softness, helped by a portion fermented naturally in older wood. Certainly less aggressive than many, & very drinkable.

★★★★☆ **Astra White 08**'s aromas last year suggested peachy viognier as well as oak - but no, equal blend sauvignon, chardonnay, chenin. Lime, lemongrass on balanced, lingering fresh palate.

★★★★ **Blanc de Blancs Méthode Cap Classique** ✓ **08** sparkling from chardonnay, seriously dry, elegant & forceful; like previous, with developed yeasty notes to its fresh apple & citrus. Good to look at too: gleaming gold in its clear bottle.

Merlot-Cabernet Sauvignon NEW ☺ 🍽 ★★★ Easy-going, approachable but untrivial **08**, its ripe fruit unobscured by modest oaking. **Chenin Blanc-Viognier** ☺ 🍽 ★★★ Subtle, attractive aromas on **11** advertise the 30% viognier component. Gentle, soft & dry, with a finishing hard bite.

Merlot ★★★★ **08** in serious, even austerely elegant style, properly dry, with a slight herbal note to its red fruit. **Unwooded Chardonnay** NEW ✓ 🍽 ★★★★ An unshowy & pleasure-giving example of this style. Nothing overdone in **11**: fresh, medium-bodied & dry, with lingering flavours. **Viognier** ★★★★ Last edition, **09** showed understated peachy notes; pleasant but not much concentration. — TJ

Stettyn Cellar

Location: Villiersdorp ▪ Map: Worcester ▪ WO: Worcester/Western Cape ▪ Est 1964 ▪ 1stB 1984 ▪ Tasting & sales Mon-Thu 8-5 Fri 8-4.30 Sat (Oct-Mar) 10-1 ▪ Closed all pub hols ▪ Cellar tours from 1.30-4 by appt ▪ Lunch by arrangement (24 hrs in advance); or BYO picnic ▪ Facilities for children ▪ Vineyard tours R200pp ▪ Stettyn music evenings (±Oct) ▪ Owner(s) 4 major producers (3 family owned) ▪ Cellarmaster(s) Albie Treurnicht (Nov 2000) ▪ Winemaker(s) Albie Treurnicht (Nov 2000), with Jean-Prieur du Plessis (Oct 2007) ▪ Viticulturist(s) Pierre Snyman (Vinpro) ▪ 365ha (cab, merlot, ptage, shiraz, chard, chenin, sauv) ▪ 5,600t/3,400cs own label 25% red 75% white + 5.1m L bulk ▪ Brands for clients: FirstCape ▪ ARA, HACCP, WIETA ▪ PO Box 1520 Worcester 6849 ▪ stettyncellar@ breede.co.za ▪ www.stettyncellar.co.za ▪ S 33° 52' 14.8" E 019° 22' 2.3" ▪ **T +27 (0)23-340-4220** ▪ F +27 (0)23-340-4220

Situated scenically in the Klein Drakenstein foothills north of Villiersdorp, Stettyn takes its name from the former Prussian city Stettin, now Szczecin. A speciality, Vin de Paille, was set to return in late 2011 to the stable of an operation that has enjoyed considerable success abroad thanks to its partnership with export phenomenon FirstCape. 'Evening under the Stars', featuring a guest live performer, is set to become an annual attraction.

Signature Reserve range

Shiraz-Cabernet Sauvignon ✓ ★★★★ **09** opaque & brooding, with cab's leafy notes, shiraz's supple mouthfeel. Pleasantly rounded for drinkability. WO W Cape. Discontinued: **Cabernet Sauvignon**, **Shiraz**.

Millstone range

Stone Red 🍽 ★★★ Previously tasted **08** a winter-warming combo mainly cab; had exotic spicing from 13% souzão. Still selling, as next. **Shiraz Rosé** 🍽 🎨 ★★★ Bursting with berries last edition, **10** was off-dry but no pushover courtesy nudge tannin. **Chenin Blanc** 🍽 🎨 ★★★ Slightly sweaty **11** more pungent than most examples; has engaging pithy wag in tail but is lean. **Sauvignon Blanc** 🍽 🎨 ★★★ **11** understated mowngrass flavour, lovely presence, measured acidity. Discontinued: **Merlot**. — Panel

▪ **Steytler** see Kaapzicht Wine Estate
▪ **Stilfontein** see Eerste Hoop Wine Cellar

Stoep

Est/1stB 2001 ▪ Tasting, sales & tours by appt ▪ Owner(s) Zelpy 1023 (Pty) Ltd: 3 shareholders Gerrit Mars (SA), Sven Haefner (Swiss) & Daniel Hofer (Swiss) ▪ Cellarmaster(s)/winemaker(s) André Liebenberg (Romond) & Gerrit Mars ▪ 50% red 50% white ▪ Export brands: Stoep, Stoepwijn ▪ gerritmars@mweb.co.za ▪ **T +27 (0)82-352-5583**

'It's planet-hopping,' jokes Gerrit Mars in response to last year's reference to his globe-trotting lifestyle. Reds, made by André Liebenberg of Romond, were maturing in barrel, as was a chardonnay, vinified by Meyer Joubert of Joubert-Tradauw Private Cellar. This year, a slower pace will allow him to be more hands-on when it comes to this boutique brand.

Merlot Await next. **Shiraz** Await next. **Chardonnay** NEW Missed our deadline. **Sauvignon Blanc** Await next. Discontinued: **Chenin Blanc**. —

■ **Stonechurch** *see* Baarsma Wine Group
■ **Stonedale** *see* Rietvallei Wine Estate

Stonehill

Location/map/WO: Stellenbosch ▪ Est 1990 ▪ 1stB 2003 ▪ Tasting by appt ▪ Owner(s)/vineyard manager(s) Lorna Hughes ▪ Winemaker(s) Mark Carmichael-Green ▪ 4ha/3.2ha (cab, shiraz) ▪ 100% red ▪ PO Box 612 Stellenbosch 7599 ▪ lhughes@telkomsa.net, lorna@stonehillwines.co.za ▪ www.stonehillwines.co.za ▪ S 33° 54'4.8" E 018° 48'56.4" ▪ **T +27 (0)73-420-3300** ▪ **F** +27 (0)21-865-2740

Hiring a truck instead of her smaller farm pickup to deliver wine to the shipper's warehouse was a highlight of the past year for owner/viticulturist Lorna Hughes whose exports have doubled. She's now studying dog behaviour in her spare time. 'Bristle drove me to it!' she says of the much-loved pooch depicted on her labels.

Bristle Red ☺ ★★★ Modestly oaked, juicy 08 nicely structured & balanced cab-shiraz blend. Accessible, offering early drinkability. **Dry Cabernet Sauvignon Rosé** ☺ 🍽 ★★★ Appetisingly fresh, oaked 09 better for extra year in bottle. Satisfyingly dry, & weighty. For spicy food!

Bristle White 🍽 🏵 ★★★ 100% viognier, fermented in unusual combo Hungarian, Romanian & French oak 10 richly tropical & floral but not lacking freshness. Discontinued: **Four Barrels Cabernet Sauvignon**. — IM

Stone Ridge Wines

Location/WO: Paarl ▪ Map: Paarl & Wellington ▪ Est 2002 ▪ 1stB 2003 ▪ Tasting by appt only ▪ Winemaker(s) Bertus Fourie (consultant, Jan 2010) ▪ Viticulturist(s) Jan Eksteen (2002) ▪ 1,100ha/175ha (cab, ptage, shiraz chenin, sauv) ▪ 20t/1,200cs own label 30% red 70% white ▪ PO Box 7046 Northern Paarl 7623 ▪ stoneridge@uitkijk.co.za ▪ **T +27 (0)82-324-8372** ▪ **F** +27 (0)21-869-8071

New packaging is on the cards for this Voor Paardeberg property to mark the launch of its flagship red, a shiraz. They're also handing over distribution to a specialist to free up time to spend in the vineyards 'getting the basics right', the only way to ensure wines express their terroir.

Eksteen Family Vineyards Reserve range

★★★★☆ **Chenin Blanc 'Bush Vine 1977'** 🍽 Last edition, tropical notes, citrus & pear on 10 ex bushvine vineyard. Lees contact & sensitive oaking added complexity & depth to candied orange peel conclusion.
Shiraz NEW ★★★★ Barrel sample (rating provisional) 10 from Paarl single-vineyard is ripe & smooth, with well-hidden 14.5% alc, integrated tannins. Black plum & pepper appeal.

Stone Ridge range

Shiraz ★★★ Lily-perfumed 09 had supple tannins, juicy fruit centre mid-2001, was refreshing & interesting **Sauvignon Blanc** 🍽 ★★★★ 09 previously nicely balanced & perfumed with gooseberry, whiff of vanilla courtesy small oak-fermented portion. 10 (★★★) was less fruity, slimmer. — CvZ

Stonewall Wines

Location: Somerset West ▪ Map: Helderberg ▪ WO: Stellenbosch ▪ Est 1828 ▪ 1stB 1997 ▪ Tasting & sales by appt Mon-Fri 10-5 Sat 10-1 ▪ Closed Easter Fri-Sun, Dec 25/26 & Jan 1 ▪ Refreshments by appt ▪ Helderberg Wine Festival ▪ Owner(s) De Waal Koch ▪ Cellarmaster(s) Ronell Wiid (Jan 2000, consultant) ▪ Winemaker(s) De Waal Koch (Jan 2000) ▪ Viticulturist(s) De Waal Koch (Jun 1984) ▪ 90ha/70ha (cabs s/f, merlot, ptage, shiraz, chard, pinot gris, sauv) ▪ 300t/2,000cs own label 80% red 20% white ▪ PO Box 5145 Helderberg 7135 ▪ stonewall@mweb.co.za ▪ S 34° 1'59.0" E 018° 49'14.6" ▪ **T +27 (0)21-855-3675** ▪ **F** +27 (0)21-855-2206

Wine production behind the landmark white wall enclosing this family Helderberg winery is becoming more and more environmentally friendly. 'And that's a positive thing,' says owner De Waal Koch. 'We concentrate on making classic wine styles, no shortcuts.'

Cabernet Sauvignon ★★★★ 08 upfront earthy dark berry fruit is still masked by oak & firm acid, needs time for integration. **Rubér** ★★★★ Changing Bordeaux blend; merlot-led 08 is austere & very dry with dusty hedgerow fruit & firm lifting grip on finish. Needs food. **Chardonnay** √ 🏵 ★★★★ 10 easy-sipper; firm oak nudges ripe, concentrated spicy fruit in zesty palate. **Vale Felice ★★★** Fortified merlot. **08** offers sweet spicecake with plum nuances, all in a rather spirity grip. — WB

StoneyCroft

Location/map/WO: Stellenbosch ▪ Est 2000 ▪ 1stB 2001 ▪ Tasting by appt ▪ Owner(s) John & Margie Stone ▪ Winemaker(s) Danie Steytler (2001), with Danie Steytler Jnr (both Kaapzicht) ▪ Viticulturist(s) Gary Probert (Jan 2010, consultant) ▪ 4ha/3.5ha (cab, shiraz) ▪ 20t/1,500cs own label 100% red ▪ PO Box 239 Koelenhof 7605 ▪ margie@stoneycroft.co.za, john@stoneycroft.co.za ▪ www.stoneycroft.co.za ▪ S 33° 53′24.41″ E 018° 48′19.78″ ▪ **T +27 (0)21-865-2301** ▪ F +27 (0)21-865-2360

Stellenbosch boutique vintners John and Margie Stone have planted 1.7ha of cabernet and expect the first vintage to be 2014. A varietal Cabernet and a Cabernet-Shiraz blend will then join their successful Shiraz. Increasingly popular music soirées afford wine and music lovers the opportunity to enjoy the view of the Bottelary Hills vineyards and Table Mountain.

★★★★ Shiraz 07 still tightly bound but balanced, savoury tones with sweet-sour brightness & good core of fruit. Alc (14.5%) not evident. — MW

Stony Brook

Location/map: Franschhoek ▪ WO: Franschhoek/Elgin ▪ Est 1995 ▪ 1stB 1996 ▪ Tasting & sales Mon-Fri 10–5 (Oct-Apr) & 10–4 (May-Sep); Sat 10–1 ▪ Fee R25 ▪ Closed all pub hols ▪ Self-catering cottages ▪ Owner(s) Nigel & Joy McNaught ▪ Cellarmaster(s) Nigel McNaught (1995) ▪ Winemaker(s) Nigel McNaught (1995), with Michael Blaauw (Jan 2008) ▪ Viticulturist(s) Paul Wallace (consultant) ▪ 23ha/14ha (cab, malbec, merlot, mourv, p verdot, pinot, shiraz, tempranillo, chard, sem, viog) ▪ 80t/5,000cs own label 56% red 40% white 4% rosé + 700cs for clients ▪ Brands for clients: Elgin Grove, Klein Dassenberg ▪ ISO 14001:2003 ▪ PO Box 22 Franschhoek 7690 ▪ info@ stonybrook.co.za ▪ www.stonybrook.co.za ▪ S 33° 56′28.7″ E 019° 7′4.1″ ▪ **T +27 (0)21-876-2182** ▪ F +27 (0)86-664-2794

There's a saying in the wine industry that to make a small fortune you must start with a big one. Big profits also occur, of course, but the McNaughts are delighted to report 'Break-even at 13 years! Suddenly the night time stresses faded.' Further relief for this family-owned property has come with the arrival of son Craig, whose Jack-of-all-trades job will include cellar and tasting-room assistant as well as head of marketing.

★★★★☆ Syrah Last tasted **06** (★★★★) dense, with dry tannins, glowing alc on finish; **04** more elegant.
★★★★☆ Ghost Gum Mainly cab from single vineyard; splash merlot for extra breadth. **07** still oak-veiled. Suggestion of sweet fruit, clipped by alcohol glow in tail. Lacks depth of **06** (★★★★★).
★★★★ The Max Bold, cab-led blend with merlot. **08** showing some evolution in its meaty merlot tones & flesh but its structure & balance allow for beneficial year/2 ageing.
★★★★ SMV 07 quite grippy, unsettled tasted last year. Enough silky substance in its shiraz, mourvèdre, viognier make-up to benefit from year or 2 & mask the 15% alc.
★★★★ Snow Gum 07 first since **04**. Country-style malbec/mourvèdre blend. Very tasty minerally, earthy tones matched by hearty tannins.
★★★★ Semillon Reserve Last-tasted aromatic **08** (★★★★★) finer than **06**; needing time to show best.
★★★★ The 'J' 🍃 Noted last yr, oaked **09** (★★★★☆) from viognier, semillon, sauvignon showed subtle intrigue; apricot, earthy whiffs; concentrated & persistent. Barely off-dry. **08** (★★★★).
★★★★ The Lyle Elegant **06** MCC from chardonnay, pinot still selling. Toasty, nutty shell, massively spritzy mousse. Should age well ±5 yrs. 34 months on lees. WO Coastal.
★★★★ V on A Honey-gold Natural Sweet from viognier. Luscious, tangy & moreish. **09** (★★★★☆) tasted last year ex-barrel was first since **06**.
Merlot NEW **★★★** Fresh & juicy **08** with straightforward red plum flavours & structure favouring early drinking. **Mourvèdre** NEW **★★★★** Pleasantly robust. Mint & gamey notes on **08** paced by rumble of rounded tannin. Hearty fare recommended. **Shiraz** 🍃 **★★★★** Dark spice on **07** muted by full ripeness. Soft with finishing sweetness to temper alc glow. **06** (★★★★) fine & concentrated. **Camissa** 🍃 **★★★★** Almost liqueur-like perfume on **08** (no **07**). Sweet fruit too from cab/merlot mix held by frisson of dry tannin. **Rosé** 🍃 **★★★** Rejoins range with food-friendly **10** from merlot. Savoury, convincing mouthful with lift of wild strawberries. Long & dry. **Rose de Vert ★★★★** Oaked, sweet, full-flavoured **07** from red semillon still selling. Previous was **98** (★★★). **Heart Of**

The Lees Sauvignon Blanc ✓ ★★★★ Unshowy **09** shows cool lines of Elgin; lees, natural ferment in barrel add to textural interest, restrained complexity, lengthy finish. Up on **08** (★★★★). **Sauvignon Blanc** 🗋 ★★★ **10** quiet tropical tones just holding out over creeping age. WO Elgin — AL

■ **Stormhoek** *see* Origin Wine

Stoumann's Wines

Location: Vredendal ▪ Map: Olifants River ▪ Est/1stB 2008 ▪ Tasting, sales & cellar tours Mon-Fri 8-5 Sat by appt ▪ Closed all pub hols ▪ Cheese platters/meals/braai available on request ▪ Tour groups ▪ Farm produce ▪ Conferences ▪ Owner(s) Napoleon Stoumann ▪ Cellarmaster(s)/winemaker(s) Erik Schlünz (Dec 2007) ▪ Viticulturist(s) Jeff Joubert (Jan 2008, consultant) ▪ 120ha/100ha (cab, merlot, muscadel r/w, ptage, ruby cab, shiraz, chard, chenin, cbard, hanepoot) ▪ 1,040t/2,000cs own label 50% red 40% white 10% rosé + 800,000L bulk ▪ IPW ▪ PO Box 307 Vredendal 8160 ▪ eschlunz@cybersmart.co.za ▪ www.stoumanns.co.za ▪ S 31° 41′ 20.5″ E 018° 30′ 23.3″ ▪ **T +27 (0)27-213-2323/+27 (0)83-633-0580** ▪ F +27 (0)27-213-1448

Last year, record yields fitted perfectly with a drive to increase exports of the Stoumann's range, made to be 'enjoyable, easy-drinking wines of high quality'. Cellarmaster Erik Schlünz subscribes to a traditional, unhurried winemaking philosophy at this family-owned Vredendal winery. New vintages of their Cabernet, Shiraz, Vin de la Tortue, Rosé Perlé, Chardonnay, Chenin Blanc, Sauvignon Blanc, Hanepoot Jerepigo and Red Jerepigo not ready at press time.

■ **Stout Izak** *see* Jason's Hill Private Cellar

Strandveld Wines

Location/WO: Elim ▪ Map: Southern Cape ▪ Est 2002 ▪ 1stB 2003 ▪ Tasting, sales & cellar tours Mon-Thu 8-5 Fri 8-4 Sat 10-3 ▪ Closed Easter Fri & Dec 25 ▪ Farm produce ▪ BYO picnic ▪ Walks/hikes ▪ Mountain biking ▪ Conservation area ▪ Two self-catering cottages ▪ Owner(s) Strandveld Vineyards & Rietfontein Trust ▪ Winemaker(s) Conrad Vlok (Dec 2004) ▪ Viticulturist(s) Tienie Wentzel (Oct 2009) ▪ 850ha/70ha (pinot, shiraz, sauv, sem) ▪ 246t/ 12,000cs own label 43% red 57% white ▪ BWI ▪ PO Box 1020 Bredasdorp 7280 ▪ info@strandveld.co.za ▪ www. strandveld.co.za ▪ S 34° 39′ 59.2″ E 019° 47′ 26.8″ ▪ **T +27 (0)28-482-1902** ▪ F +27 (0)28-482-1906

Marketing man Danie Pretorius believes 'a glass of wine allows you to experience the soul of a place without your being physically there', so it's serendipitous that winemaker Conrad Vlok's bottlings so vividly convey the cool maritime essence of the vast, windswept Agulhas plain. The new pinot noir honours an 18th-century Swedish traveller who wrote eloquently about Elim's flora and indigenous people. Vineyard expansion (more pinot, sauvignon and 10ha for Franschhoek top-ranker La Motte) is guided by their participation in the Nuwejaars Wetland Special Management Area, a pioneering eco project.

Strandveld Wines range

★★★★ **Anders Sparrman Pinot Noir** NEW Limited release (221 cases) **09**, less immediately showy than sibling below, though greater oak influence (40% new) & richer fruit. Needs time to knit & fill out, fine potential.

★★★★☆ **Syrah** Dashes grenache & viognier, longer period in higher proportion new oak than Shiraz below. **09** quiet but not sombre, taut but not ungenerous despite the cooler vintage. Like **08**, pepper/scrub nod to the Rhône.

★★★★☆ **Sauvignon Blanc** ✓ 🍾 Always one of the area's most accomplished, from a single-vineyard; **10** (★★★★★) standout in a difficult vintage (though perhaps for earlier enjoyment than stellar **09**). Khaki bush & wet stone highlights to cool green aromas, satisfying weight & freshness without excessive acidity.

★★★★☆ **Adamastor** ✓ 🍾 Impressive Bordeaux-style white flagship, masterly blend semillon & sauvignon (57/43), tad new wood in **10**; waxy lemon tones, restrained oak seasoning & peppery finish. Obvious marine influence in cool, restrained tone, also evident in rich & regal **09** (★★★★★).

First Sighting range

★★★★ **Shiraz** 🗋 Forthcoming & slightly wild **09** (★★★★☆) unrestrained red fruit, lashings acidity for zesty appeal. **08** was more floral & ageworthy.

Pinot Noir 🗋 ★★★★ Smoke & tar overlay to distinctive pinot cherry/raspberry notes, **09** less depth & intensity than senior version, a little sappy & angular courtesy cool vintage. Drink while the other matures. **Sauvignon**

Blanc ✓ 🗐 🏵 ★★★★ Dollop semillon adds weight, gentle waxy tone to **10**; drop nouvelle boosts zingy appeal. For earlier drinking than stablemate. Discontinued: **Chardonnay-Semillon-Viognier.** — Panel

- ▪ **Strelizia** *see Blue Crane Vineyards*
- ▪ **String of Pearls** *see Francois La Garde*
- ▪ **Stumble Vineyards** *see Flagstone Winery*
- ▪ **Suikerbosch** *see Zidela Wines*
- ▪ **Suikerbossie Ek Wil Jou Hê** *see Boer & Brit*

Sumaridge Wines

Location: Hermanus ▪ Map: Elgin, Walker Bay & Bot River ▪ WO: Upper Hemel-en-Aarde Valley ▪ Est 1997 ▪ 1stB 2000 ▪ Tasting & sales daily 10-3 ▪ Fee R25 for groups of 6+, waived on purchase ▪ Closed Easter Fri/Sun, Dec 25/ 26 & Jan 1 ▪ Tasting platter options plus kiddies platter, also available (Aug-May) as picnic ▪ Facilities for children ▪ Tour groups ▪ Conferences ▪ Weddings/functions ▪ Luxury Guesthouse ▪ Conservation area ▪ Extensive nature trails ▪ Mountain biking ▪ Bas & fly fishing by arrangement ▪ Owner(s) Simon & Holly Turner ▪ Cellarmaster(s)/ vineyard manager(s) Gavin Patterson (Jun 2005) ▪ Winemaker(s) Gavin Patterson (Jun 2005), with Reginald Maphumulo (Jun 2011) ▪ 210ha/42ha (cab f, malbec, merlot, ptage, pinot, syrah, chard, sauv, sem, viog) ▪ 150t/ 8,000cs own label 45% red 50% white 5% rosé & 25,000L bulk + 50,000L for other brands ▪ IPW ▪ PO Box 1413 Hermanus 7200 ▪ info@sumaridge.co.za ▪ www.sumaridge.co.za ▪ S 34° 22′ 1.6″ E 019° 15′ 18.6″ ▪ **T +27 (0)28-312-1097** ▪ F +27 (0)86-623-4248

Goals are all long-term here. 'We take a holistic view ensuring all aspects of the business are in symbiosis with the land' explains cellarmaster Gavin Patterson. 'To us it's more important than being organic/biodynamic/sustainable etc.' Increasing planting density from 4000 to 8000 vines per hectare, to generate greater inter-vine competition and efficiency of land use is one such symbiotic innovation.

★★★★ **Pinot Noir** 🏵 Elegant, perfumed **10** already drinkable. Great freshness but also supple & silky with charming, poised cherry, forest floor features. Best enjoyed over next 2 or 3 years.

★★★★ **Epitome** Vivid shiraz spice noted last year on **08**, with richness of 30/10% pinotage/merlot.

★★★★ **Sauvignon Blanc** 🗐 🏵 Cool-climate tang rather too bracing in **10 (★★★★)**. The modesty of the citrus, greengage flavours suggests earlier drinking than for pure, deep **09**.

Merlot ★★★★ **09** sample reveals deep, subtle perfume, suave velvety texture, fine grip & freshness. Rich & flavoursome without being overly fruity or heavy. Provisional rating. **08** needed year/2 to calm. **Merlot Rosé** 🗐 ★★ Substantial **10** firmed by a touch of tannin. Plentiful bright fruit & flame-licked colour add to appeal. Dry & food-friendly. **Chardonnay** 🗐 🏵 ★★★★ Ex-barrel, satisfying **10** shows pure limey, spicy features. Elegant, creamy texture with cleansing acid thread. Like **09**, fermented & aged in 30% new oak. **Maritimus** 🗐 🏵 ★★★★ Sample **10** from 65% sauvignon, with oaked chardonnay, semillon & a drop of viognier. Quietly vinous; should fill out in yr/2. Follows step-up **09 (★★★★)**. — AL

Summerhill Wines

Location/map/WO: Stellenbosch ▪ 1stB 2008 ▪ Tasting & sales Mon-Thu 9-4.30 Fri 9-2 ▪ Closed all pub hols ▪ Dorpstraat Restaurant Theatre open for lunch & dinner Tue-Sat 11-10; live performances evenings 8.30-10 - bookings T +27 (0)21-889-9158 or info@dorpstraat.co.za ▪ Tour groups (120 pax) ▪ Owner(s) Summerhill Wines cc, Charles R Hunting ▪ Winemaker(s) Hannes Meyer (white, Simonsig) & Anri Beyers (red, Beyerskloof) ▪ Viticulturist(s) Paul Wallace (consultant) ▪ 15ha/3.5ha (merlot, shiraz, chenin) ▪ 24t/1,250cs own label 40% red 60% white ▪ PO Box 12448 Die Board 7613 ▪ charles@summerhillwines.co.za, manager@summerhillwines.co.za, reception@summerhillwines.co.za ▪ www.summerhillwines.co.za ▪ S 33° 52′ 57.71″ E 018° 50′ 49.39″ ▪ **T +27 (0)21-889-5015** ▪ F +27 (0)86-621-8047

Having thought out the box and facilitated the move of Dorpstraat Restaurant Theatre from Stellenbosch town to their estate nearby, Charles Hunting and team can offer an unusual and increasingly popular cellardoor experience: winetasting, light lunch or dinner plus an ever-changing programme of live shows.

Chenin Blanc ☺ 🗐 🏵 ★★★ Bang for your buck, like previous, sunny **11** gushes fruit & flicks a not-quite-dry tail.

Shiraz-Merlot 🗐 ★★ Chunky, berried **09**, last year had a spicy overlay from oak staving. — DS

Sumsaré Wines

Location/map/WO: Robertson ▪ Est 2008 ▪ 1stB 2007 ▪ Tasting, sales & tours by appt Mon–Fri 9–5 Sat 9–1 ▪ Closed Easter Fri–Mon, May 13, Pentecost, Dec 25/26 & Jan 1 ▪ Tour groups ▪ Facilities for children ▪ Farm produce ▪ BYO picnic ▪ Museum ▪ Owner(s) Francèl Rabie, Daniël Johannes Erasmus, Danielle Erasmus & Janine Joubert ▪ Winemaker(s) Jacques Roux (Robertson Winery) ▪ Viticulturist(s) Briaan Stipp (Robertson Winery) ▪ 450ha/40ha (cab, ruby cab, shiraz, chard, chenin, cbard, muscadel w) ▪ 700t/±130cs own label 100% red ▪ PO Box 402 Robertson 6705 ▪ sumsare.wines@barvallei.co.za ▪ www.sumsarewines.co.za ▪ S 33° 54' 14.66" E 019° 40' 4.75" ▪ **T +27 (0)23-626-2152, +27 (0)82-221-6653** ▪ F +27 (0)86-696-4007

Last year, while still a final-year student of viticulture and oenology at Stellenbosch University, Johannes Erasmus made his first wines for the family's boutique wine brand (their surname spelt backwards). A sauvignon and a lightly wooded chardonnay (untasted by us), made with the guidance of Lourens van der Westhuizen of Arendsig, join the shiraz made at nearby Robertson Winery, to which they deliver most of the grapes from their farm, Wandsbeck.

Limited Release Shiraz ★★★ Last edition we noted fans of wood will love **07**, powerfully scented with sweet oak (33% new), spiced with dark berries & for early enjoyment. **Sauvignon Blanc** NEW ★★ 'Intensive manual labour' went into **11**, shy but quaffable, plenty of juicy fruit makes appealing mouthful. —Panel

Super Single Vineyards

Location: Stellenbosch ▪ WO: Stellenbosch/Sutherland-Karoo ▪ Est/1stB 2004 ▪ Closed to public ▪ Owner(s)/viticulturist(s) Daniël de Waal ▪ Winemaker(s) Daniël de Waal, with Kyle Zulch ▪ 60ha Canettevallei Farm ▪ (cab, nebbiolo, p verdot, pinot, shiraz, tempranillo, riesling) ▪ 1,000cs 80% red 20% white ▪ PO Box 89 Vlottenburg 7604 ▪ pella@adept.co.za ▪ www.supersinglevineyards.co.za ▪ **T +27 (0)72-200-5552 (Daniël de Waal) / +27 (0)82-556-0205 (Kyle Zulch)** ▪ F +27 (0)21-881-3026

Daniël and Ingrid de Waal's venture has grown exponentially, both in range and volume. The Pella brand, symbolically referring to a gathering place, now represents one range. This year sees the launch of a pinotage from an ancient vineyard on their property, Canettevallei, and the first Sutherland-sourced shiraz from 1,500m high Karoo vineyards. Back home, the parallel lavender farming enterprise produces essential oils and locally handmade aromatic products.

Pella Coastal Wines range

★★★★ **Cabernet Sauvignon** Back-to-back vintages show evolution of earthy, intense, dry style. **07** is more approachable, **08** (★★★★★) with dollop of malbec press-wine, more tarry & focused. Both from Stellenbosch fruit, both luscious & classy. For keeping.

★★★★ **Thomas Se Dolland Pinotage** NEW Tiny production from 60+ year old Stellenbosch dryland vineyard, maiden **08** is dense & concentrated. Seriously conceived & handled, will reward long cellaring.

★★★★ **The Vanilla** Nearly pure **10** chenin replaces previous 4-way blend, but retains intense ripe fruit & waxy overlay. From 38 year old Stellenbosch vineyard. Eponymous vanilla notes deftly integrated.

Sutherland Continental Wines

★★★★ **Mount Sutherland Syrah** Just 'Syrah' when previewed last time, **09** has since improved. Maiden crop off Sutherland vines, explores cool-climate potential. Rhône-like pepperiness, elegance & length. — GdB

■ **Sutherland** see Thelema Mountain Vineyards
■ **Sutherland Continental** see Super Single Vineyards
■ **Swallow** see Natte Valleij Wines
■ **Swartberg Reserve** see Oudtshoorn Cellar - SCV

Swartland Winery

Location: Malmesbury ▪ Map/WO: Swartland ▪ Est/1stB 1948 ▪ Tasting & sales Mon–Fri 8–5 Sat 9–2 ▪ Closed Mar 21, Easter Fri/Sun, Dec 25/26 & Jan 1 ▪ Facilities for children ▪ Tour groups ▪ Farm produce ▪ Owner(s) 60 producers ▪ Cellarmaster(s) Andries Blake (Dec 1995) ▪ Winemaker(s) Andries Eygelaar, Sean Nieuwoudt & Corrien Geleijnse (Jan 2000/Jan 2004/Jan 2006) ▪ Viticulturist(s) Claude Uren (Nov 2010) ▪ 2,689ha (cab, malbec, merlot, ptage, shiraz, chard, chenin, sauv) ▪ 20,000t 55% white 38% red 5% rosé 2% sparkling ▪ Brands for clients: Pick 'n

Pay, Woolworths ▪ BRC, IFS, IPW, WIETA ▪ PO Box 95 Malmesbury 7299 ▪ suzanne@swwines.co.za ▪ www.swwines.co.za ▪ S 33° 27' 12.7" E 018° 45' 17.7" ▪ **T +27 (0)22-482-1134** ▪ F +27 (0)22-482-1750

Export markets are becoming a key focus, and with a strong and diversified export portfolio ranging from the Seychelles to Cyprus, this large producer has taken to the 'My Swartland' motto. Setting this region apart is the predominance of bushvines (rather than growing on trellises), and with much of the fruit in the region also cultivated without irrigation, this follows directly on the 'Small berries – big taste' campaign. Dryland farming gives vines that produce small berries with concentrated flavour. With this in mind, the top tier Idelia and Indalo ranges have been combined and renamed - now proudly waving the flag.

Swartland Bushvine range

★★★★ **Shiraz** 🌐 Ex-barrel **10**, so provisional rating. Good regional expression, with vibrant red & dark berries, pepper spice following to juicy composed palate. Ends dry, with supportive oak.

★★★★ **Idelia** The blend made-up for **08** a cellar secret, as before. Attractive upfront dark fruited charm, leads to balanced, ripe & rich style; highish alcohol has vibrant acidity in support.

Cabernet Sauvignon 🌐 ★★★★ Sampled **10** has complex intro of black berry, graphite & earth components. Richly textured in unashamedly New World idiom. **Pinotage** 🌐 ★★★★ Big, ripe fruit abounding from **10** ex-barrel. Luscious weight continues to sweet impression on the finish. **Chenin Blanc** 🌐 ★★★ Oak needs to be more integrated on sampled **11**, but attractive fruit on medium body. Perhaps higher rating once settled. **Sauvignon Blanc** ★★★★ **10** sampled last year, with intense tropicality & well balanced acid.

Swartland range

★★★★ **Red Jerepigo** ✓ 🍷 Toffee, rich raisins & brooding dark fruits with smoky overlay leading to complex palate of cold coffee, with lingering nutty end. Latest NV from pinotage.

Cabernet Sauvignon ☺🌐 ★★★ Herbal edge on **10** complements tobacco & cassis, with rounded fruity palate & soft tannins to end. For early drinking. **Pinotage** ☺🍷🌐 ★★★ Typical banana loaf, red berry aromas lead to bright cherry juiciness. **10** has grippy, serious send-off. **Shiraz** ☺🍷 ★★★ **10** has lifted red berry foil to sweet ripeness. **Dry Red** ☺🍷 ★★★ Ideal braai partner. Has good earthy/fruit flavour combo. **NV. Chardonnay** ☺🍷🌐 ★★★ Lightly chipped **11**, in fresh fruit-forward approach; tropical & citrus nose leads to rounded, medium-bodied finish. **Chenin Blanc** ☺🍷🌐 ★★★ Beautiful perfumed intro to sampled **11**. Flavours offer fruity combination with spice, ending fresh & dry. **Sauvignon Blanc** ☺🍷🌐 ★★★ Tropical, fresh & dry **11** tasted ex-tank; for early drinking.

Merlot 🍷🌐 ★★ Jammy sweetish **10**. **Tinta Barocca** 🍷🌐 ★★★ Oaky overlay on **10** follows to appealing ripe-fruited palate. **Merlot-Shiraz** 🍷🌐 ★★ **10** has soft, fruity appeal. **Blanc de Noir** 🍷🌐 ★★★ Delicate strawberry perfume on **11** in light & fruity style. **Bukettraube** 🍷🌐 ★★★ Gently sweet **11** has light spice & rounded palate. **Cuvée Brut** ★★★ Latest NV bubbly; summery & light crispness from sauvignon. **Demi Sec** ★★ Fruity & sweet NV bubbly. **Hanepoot** ✓🍷 ★★★★ White chocolate, sultana richness promised on NV fortified sweetie. Richly viscous yet balanced palate. Good typicity. **White Jerepigo** 🍷 ★★★ NV fortified from chenin, with grapey, vanilla notes. Easy winter drink. **Port** 🍷 ★★★ Easy fruit-forward NV combo tinta barocca & shiraz. **Vintage Port** ★★★★ Step up in **07** with greater complexity than **06** & dry-seeming finish. Layered flavours of savoury liquorice, brooding fruit & nutty rich texture, harnessed by well judged oak & fortification. Discontinued: **Shiraz-Malbec**, **Grand Cru**.

D'Vine NEW

Cabernet Sauvignon-Merlot 🍷 ★★ Tutti-frutti NV party red. **Rosé** 🍷 ★★ NV from pinotage; sweet berry juice. **Sauvignon Blanc-Chenin Blanc** 🍷 ★★ Simple off-dry NV blend. — JP

■ **Sweet Dreams** see Groupe LFE South Africa

SylvanVale Vineyards

Location/map: Stellenbosch ▪ WO: Devon Valley ▪ Est 1997 ▪ 1stB 1998 ▪ Tasting & sales daily 11–7 ▪ Fee R25 ▪ Open pub hols ▪ Flavours Restaurant: 120 seater (see Restaurants section); Vineyard Terrace; Cedarwood Bar & Lounge ▪ The Devon Valley Hotel: 50 rooms (see Accommodation section) ▪ Facilities for children ▪ Tour groups ▪ Conferences ▪ 6 Banqueting venues (max capacity 98 pax) ▪ Walking/hiking trails ▪ Owner(s) Louis Group Hotels, Spas & Vineyards ▪ Winemaker(s) Mark Carmichael-Green (Sep 2003, consultant) ▪ Viticulturist(s) Lorna Hughes (1997, consultant) ▪ 8ha/4.3ha (cab, ptage, chenin) ▪ 6t/525cs own label 100% rosé ▪ PO Box 68 Stellenbosch

7599 • info@sylvanvale.com • www.sylvanvale.com • S 33°54'12.5" E 018°48'57.7" • T +27 (0)21-865-2012 • F +27 (0)21-865-2610

These Devon Valley vineyards produce just enough for corporate owner Louis Group's three South African hotels, and limited exports to the group's overseas facilities. Last year (after our deadline) a Ghost Tree Sauvignon joined the portfolio, and the pinotage and chenin vines - the latter possibly the oldest in Stellenbosch - were ploughed up and replanted.

★★★★ **Pinotage Reserve** Suitably mature, sweetish, violet-scented 05, bold flavours ready to be enjoyed now. Oak maturation structures richly lush fruit flavours.

Rosé ☺ 🍽 ★★★ Name changed from 'Dry Cabernet Sauvignon Rosé' yet previewed 11 is still from cab, still dry. Fresh & delicious berry compôte taste, weight & dimension from brief barrel-ageing.

Cabernet Sauvignon ★★★☆ Accessible, refreshing 05 offers juicy fruit & sufficient structure (from mostly new oak) for seriousness in style & ageability. **Ghost Tree Pinotage** Await new vintage, as for **Shiraz**, **Devon Valley Red** & **Old Vine Chenin Blanc. Family Reserve** ★★★★ Firm cab & spicy shiraz harmonise well with pinotage juiciness, 05 steps up from 04 (★★★★). Ready to drink. Oak, mostly new, complements sweet black cherry flavours. — IM

■ **Table Bay** see Ultra Liquors
■ **Table Mountain** see Distell
■ **Table View** see Rooiberg Winery

Tall Horse

Cheerful labels and easy, fruit-forward style of this giraffe-themed DGB brand have clearly captured consumer tastes locally and overseas, where volumes are growing. Website www.tallhorsewines.com continues the quirky brand persona.

Tamboerskloof Wine

Location/map/WO: Stellenbosch • Est 2000 • 1stB 2002 • Tasting, sales & cellar tours Mon-Fri 9-4.30 • Fee R20, waived on purchase • Closed all pub hols • Owner(s) Gerard de Villiers • Winemaker(s) Gunter Schultz (Sep 2007), with Julio Engelbrecht (Jan 2008) • Viticulturist(s) Gunter Schultz (Sep 2007) • 22ha/10ha (mourv, shiraz, rouss, viog) • 70t/5,000cs own label 87% red 8% white 5% rosé • BWI, IPW • PO Box 12584 Die Boord 7613 • admin@kleinood.com • www.kleinood.com • S 33°59'42.6" E 018°52'14.8" • T +27 (0)21-880-2527 • F +27 (0)21-880-2884

Less truly is more, believe owner Gerard de Villiers and winemaker Gunter Schultz, the duo behind this focused Helderberg boutique winery previously listed as 'Kleinood'. Less intervention in the vineyards, allowing wild yeast spontaneity in the cellar, and less new wood on the wine during maturation. Roussanne was planted last year and an extra virgin olive oil, De Boerin, introduced.

★★★★☆ **Syrah** Only estate fruit for 1st time in 07, tasted last year. Dashes mourvèdre & viognier aid signature perfume appeal: berries, white pepper & attractive 'wild' element. Palate savoury, with bright fruity centre, accessible but will keep well.

★★★★ **Viognier** 🌱 One of Cape's best, natural ferment & lees-ageing add structure to succulent fruit, so no blowsiness. 11 nectarine & stonefruit, nice white pepper twist on broad palate. 30% older-oaked. — FM

Tanagra Private Cellar

Location/WO: McGregor • Map: Robertson • Est/1stB 2003 • Tasting, sales & cellar tours daily by appt • Wine- & grappa tasting with lunch (min 4 persons) to be pre-booked • Farm produce • Boutique distillery (European style Grappa & Eau de Vie) • Luxury farm accommodation in 5 cottages (self-catering/B&B) • Adjoining Vrolijkheid Nature Reserve, ideal for hiking, mountain-biking & birding with direct access from farm • Owner(s) Robert & Anette Rosenbach • Cellarmaster(s) Robert Rosenbach & John Hargreaves (consultant) • Winemaker(s) John Hargreaves & Andreas Barth (consultants) • Viticulturist(s) Jaco Lategan (McGregor Winery) • 78ha/12.5ha (cabs s/f, merlot, ptage, shiraz, cbard) • 114t/250cs own label 80% red 20% rosé • IPW • PO Box 92 McGregor 6708 • tanagra@tanagra-wines.co.za • www.tanagra-wines.co.za • S 33°55'29.6" E 019°52'15.9" • T +27 (0)23-625-1780 • F +27 (0)23-625-1847

'Life's too short to drink bad wine,' say German owners Anette and Robert Rosenbach, now in their third year at this boutique winery, eau de vie distillery and guest house near McGregor. 'So making good wine is an obligation!' After linguist Anette's discovery that the name 'Tanagra' comes from the Khoisan for 'main shade', the new label depicts the giant wild fig sheltering the historic homestead.

Cabernet Sauvignon ★★★ 07 big & bold, with earthy dark-berried tones, firm tannin base. Like John's Medley & Carah, still selling. **Merlot** This, **Shiraz** & **Felicity** untasted; await next. **John's Medley** ★★★ Dark chocolate & ripe plum on 07 merlot (80%) & cab franc combo. **Carah** ★★★ Mainly shiraz with dashes cab & merlot, 06 very ripe & plumped by sugar. **Heavenly Chaos** NEW ★ Two vintages tasted: merlot (75%) & cab in 06, whole berry & wild yeast fermented; quartet fruity varieties in 10. Both will have their adherents. Discontinued: **Devine Order Cape Dry White**. — Panel

Tanzanite Wines

Location: Worcester ▪ Est 2006 ▪ Tasting Mon-Sat by appt ▪ Owner(s) Wentzel & Melanie van der Merwe ▪ Cellarmaster(s) Melanie van der Merwe (Apr 2006) ▪ 400cs own label ▪ PO Box 5102 Worcester 6850 ▪ melanie@tanzanitewines.co.za ▪ www.tanzanitewines.co.za ▪ **T +27 (0)23-347-0018** ▪ F +27 (0)86-694-0654

Boutique méthode cap classique specialist Melanie van der Merwe is happy and privileged to be able to handcraft small parcels of sparkling 'exactly as I want them', and have time with young daughters Mari and Hane. They're already learning the art, and doubtless they'll be involved with the magnums and vintaged bottlings amongst the 'few cards' up mom's sleeve.

★★★★ **Méthode Cap Classique** Luxurious handcrafted sparkling from mainly chardonnay, with the variety's elegance in the vanguard. **NV**, 30 months on lees, it's for contemplation as well as celebration.

★★★★ **Méthode Cap Classique Brut Rosé** More demure, less opulent than cellarmate, grip of dominant pinot noir (60%) adds texture to lengthy finish. **NV**, degorged late 2010. — DS

■ **Tara Hill** see Southern Sky Wines

Tassenberg

Enduring light dry red affectionately known as 'Tassies'. Launched 1936, blend has varied over the years but not the affable persona. 750ml, 2L & 5L. By Distell.

Tassenberg 🗐 ★★★ Effortless unwooded cab & cinsaut, spicy plum & gentle herbal grip. **NV**. — Panel

Taverna Rouge

Big-selling, off-dry, budget-priced red blend by Distell; available in 750ml and 2L.

Taverna Rouge 🗐 ★★ Berry simplicity to **NV** quaffer, mild mix cab, ruby cab & cinsaut. — Panel

TCB Wines

Location: Rawsonville ▪ Map: Breedekloof ▪ WO: Western Cape ▪ Est 2002 ▪ 1stB 2008 ▪ Tasting, sales & cellar tours Mon-Fri 8-5 ▪ Fee R10pp ▪ Closed all pub hols ▪ Tour groups ▪ BYO picnic ▪ Conferences ▪ Self-catering units ▪ Owner(s) TC Botha ▪ Cellarmaster(s) TC Botha & Christo Basson ▪ Winemaker(s) Christo Basson (Oct 2008) ▪ Viticulturist(s) Johan Slabber (Feb 1999) ▪ 90ha (cab, merlot, ptage, chenin cbard, nouvelle, sauv, sem) ▪ 1,800t/300cs own label 50% red 50% white + 100cs for clients ▪ IPW ▪ PO Box 56 Rawsonville 6845 ▪ basson.christo8@gmail.com ▪ **T +27 (0)23-349-1748** ▪ F +27 (0)23-349-1325

The sixth TC Botha to farm the Rawsonville family property aims to provide quality, good-value wines, with more making their debut this year. Visitors are invited to book into self-catering cottages while enjoying the views of the vineyards and snow-blanketed Sneeukoppie Mountain. Exports to the US, UK and Germany.

Cape Sparrow Selection

Classic Red ☺ ★★★ Appeared as **NV** preview under 'Swallow Collection' branding last time, now bottled. Well-made, cheerful 10, soft, light & fruity 4-way blend for early pleasure. **Sauvignon Blanc** NEW ☺ ★★★ Fresh & fruity 11 summer sipper. — WB

Teddy Hall Wines

Location: Somerset West ▪ WO: Stellenbosch ▪ Closed to public ▪ Owner(s)/cellarmaster(s)/winemaker(s)/viti-culturist(s) Teddy Hall ▪ PO Box 2868 Somerset West 7129 ▪ teddy@teddyhallwines.com ▪ www.teddyhallwines.com ▪ **T** +27 **(0)83-461-8111** ▪ F +27 (0)86-504-8178

Jan Blanx, a rebellious soldier in the time of Jan van Riebeeck. Sybrand Mankadan, a bibulous theologist. Dr Jan Cats, a doctor whose surgery was all too close to the mortuary. Hercùles van Loon, a lovelorn pastor who died by his own hand. These are the names of figures in Stellenbosch history which now adorn the wines of accomplished Teddy Hall. 'I don't own a farm or homestead but I'm committed to Stellenbosch and hence why I've embraced these characters,' he says. 'They weren't the most pious and hopefully they lend an edge which defines the brand.'

Premium range

★★★★☆ **Hercùles van Loon Cabernet Sauvignon** NEW **08** is everything cab should be: aromas of cassis & cedar (from 100% new French oak) before a palate which shows concentrated, optimally ripe fruit, fresh acidity & firm but fine tannins; great balance & length.

★★★★ **Syrah Reserve** Plump & succulent, bright red fruit, fine pepper & clove spice on attractive, ageworthy **08** when last tasted.

★★★★☆ **Dr Jan Cats Chenin Blanc Reserve** 'Chenin Blanc Reserve' previously. At cutting edge of what can be done with chenin, **10** perfectly proportioned but closed mid-2011. Honeysuckle, peach aromas; pure & focused with great line of acidity, before savoury, almost saline finish. Will benefit from time in bottle.

Sybrand Mankadan Chenin Blanc NEW 🔲 ★★★★ Subtle **10** shows flavours of citrus, peach & some spice, tangy acidity; 5% barrel-fermented portion rounds out palate. **Jan Blanx Super White Cuvée** NEW 🔲 ★★★ **NV** is sauvignon-led but includes dashes semillon, chenin. Super-grassy but also hint of lime, bracing acidity. **Blanc de Blancs Méthode Cap Classique** ★★★★ Champagne-method sparkling from chardonnay, retasted **05** is rich & full with developed character; baked bread, yeasty notes, creamy mousse, gentle acidity. Drink up.

Moments Collection

Winter Moments Shiraz-Cabernet Sauvignon 🔲 ★★★ Seductive red-black fruit notes, slight pepperiness on **09**. Well-managed tannins, juicy, uncomplicated when last tasted. **Summer Moments Chenin Blanc** 🔲 ★★★ **10** delivers yellow fruit, honey, spice & some leesy character. Rich & full, moderate acidity, savoury finish.

Sgt Pepper range NEW

Sgt Pepper 🔲 ★★★ Shiraz-led blend **09** shows ripe berry fruit, not nearly as piquant as name implies. — CE

■ **Tembana Valley** *see Rooiberg Winery*

Tempel Wines

Location: Paarl ▪ Map: Paarl & Wellington ▪ Est 2000 ▪ 1stB 2003 ▪ Tasting, sales & cellar tours by appt ▪ Fee R25 ▪ Guest Lodge (B&B), 5 cottages ▪ Owner(s)/winemaker(s) Alf Ljungqvist ▪ 6ha/4.2ha (ptage) ▪ 18t/900cs own label 85% red 15% white ▪ PO Box 7295 Noorder-Paarl 7623 ▪ sales@tempelwines.co.za ▪ www.tempelwines.co.za ▪ S 33° 40' 34.0" E 018° 58' 32.2" ▪ **T** +27 **(0)21-872-4065** ▪ F +27 (0)21-872-3883

Alf Ljungqvist, Swedish owner of this Paarl boutique pinotage specialist, decided to extend the maturation of his Bush Vine Reserve to 24 months, resulting in what he terms 'an empty year' for Tempel this edition. Even the Innocence blanc de noir featured last time was snapped up 'in a flash', so nothing for us to do but encourage fans to check with the estate about release dates for the new vintages.

■ **Terra Del Capo** *see Anthonij Rupert Wines*
■ **Terra Madre** *see High Constantia Wine Cellar*

Teubes Family Wines

Location: Vredendal ▪ Map: Olifants River ▪ Est 2010 ▪ 1stB 2011 ▪ Tasting & sales Mon–Fri 8.30–5.30 Sat 8.30–4.30 Sun 9–12 ▪ Fee R15 ▪ Closed Easter Sat/Sun, Dec 25 & Jan 1 ▪ Cellar tours by appt ▪ Tour groups (up to 40 pax) ▪ Farm produce ▪ BYO picnic ▪ Conferences ▪ Walks/hikes ▪ Bergkraal 4x4 trail ▪ Mountain biking ▪ Conservation area ▪ Guest cottages ▪ Owner(s) Johan & Ella Teubes ▪ Cellarmaster(s) Sybrand Teubes ▪ Winemaker(s) Sybrand Teubes & Lorraine Geldenhuys (consultant) ▪ Viticulturist(s) Johan Teubes ▪ (cab, ptage, shiraz, chard, sauv) ▪ 160t/1,500cs own label 53% red 47% white + 3,000cs for clients & 75,000L bulk ▪ PO Box 791 Vredendal 8160 ▪

ella@teubeswines.co.za ▪ www.teubeswines.co.za ▪ S 31° 43′ 19.1″ E 018° 30′ 14.5″ ▪ **T +27 (0)27-213-2377**
▪ F +27 (0)27-213-3773

Well-known Cape viticulturist Johan Teubes, guest cottage hostess and hiking guide
wife Ella, and winemaker son Sybrand last year celebrated the Olifants River's 'first
modern boutique winery' on Houmoed farm, completed in a record 22 days while
their 2011 Pinotage cooled its feet awaiting processing. The first on-site bottling was
the new Malkopbaai Sauvignon. This will be their specialist variety, nurtured to
express the distinctiveness of local Lamberts Bay and other cool-climate sites in the
region.

Pinotage New vintage not available at print time; nor were maiden **Cabernet Sauvignon** & **Shiraz**. **Chardonnay ★★★★** Previously, 08 had struck match whiff to peaches & cream palate. Still selling. **Malkopbaai Sauvignon Blanc** NEW **★★★★** Zesty 11 cool & grassy with flinty note, melon flavour. Nudges next level. Their separately listed joint-venture sauvignon (and shiraz), Sir Lambert, also available ex tasting room. — Panel

Thabani Wines

Location: Cape Town ▪ Closed to public ▪ Owner(s) Jabulani Ntshangase ▪ PO Box 1381 Stellenbosch 7599 ▪
thabani@iafrica.com ▪ www.thabani.co.za ▪ **T +27 (0)21-412-9302** ▪ F +27 (0)86-648-3676

Jabulani Ntshangase continues his participation in the wine business from his shop,
Grand World of Wines at the Westin Grand Hotel on Cape Town's foreshore, where
you can enquire about his mainly restaurant-listed Thabani wines. Thabani is Nguni
for joyful, and that's just how his role as mentor to young black winemaking talent
leaves him feeling.

Thandi Wines

Map: Elgin, Walker Bay & Bot River ▪ WO: Western Cape/Elgin/Stellenbosch ▪ Est 1995 ▪ Tasting & sales daily 7.
30-5 ▪ Fee R15pp ▪ Closed Dec 25 & Jan 1 ▪ Restaurant: T +27 (0)21-844-0343 open daily 7.30-5 ▪ Facilities for
children ▪ Tour groups ▪ BYO picnic ▪ Hiking/mountain biking trails ▪ Owner(s) Thandi Wines (Pty) Ltd ▪ Cellarmaster(s)/winemaker(s) Nicky Versfeld (Oct 2009, consultant) ▪ Fairtrade ▪ PO Box 597 Stellenbosch 7599 ▪
vernon@thandiwines.co.za ▪ www.thandiwines.com ▪ **T +27 (0)21-844-0247/+27 (0)21-844-0041** ▪
F +27 (0)86-561-0152

This empowerment company, more than half-owned by 250 farmworker families,
produced the world's first Fairtrade-accredited wine label. Profits go towards upliftment initiatives but, as noted before, the wines need no political 'feelgood' gloss to
make them taste good - though this year the reds impressed more.

Thandi Single Varietal range

Cabernet Sauvignon ▤ **★★★** Overt, ripe, sweet fruitiness on 08, but firm & dry. All the still wines in this range tasted previously. **Pinot Noir ★★★★** 07's cherry fruit & balanced freshness promised charming early drinking. WO Elgin. **Shiraz Rosé** ▤ ▨ **★★** Last year, just-dry & just-fruity 10 was light & fleeting. **Chardonnay** ▤ ▨ **★★★★** Quiet, attractive citrus aromas & flavours on easy-going but serious 10. **Sauvignon Blanc** ▤ ▨ **★★★★** 10's showy aromas led to mouthful of succulence & tropical flavour. **Shiraz Rosé Sparkling** NEW ▨ **★★** Sweet 11 with light fruit & spice amongst the bubbles.

Thandi Dual Varietal range

Cabernet Sauvignon-Merlot ☺ ▤ ▨ **★★★** Unpretentious & thoroughly tasty 10, unoaked to keep the flavours pure, a little structure to hold them in place. **Shiraz-Cabernet Sauvignon** ☺ ▤ ▨ **★★★** This 10 perhaps the more exciting of the two reds, packed with flavour. Neither one is bone-dry, but this adds to the fruit impact. **Chardonnay-Chenin Blanc** ☺ ▤ ▨ **★★★** Inviting, attractive 11 is deft, fresh & easy-drinking. The chardonnay was oak-aged. These whites have welcome modest alc levels. **Sauvignon Blanc-Semillon** ☺ ▤ ▨ **★★★** Less seductive than previous vintage but pleasant, 11 has light flavours, shows some sweetness. Most Thandi wines ex-Stellenbosch, but WO W Cape. — TJ

■ **The Auction Crossing** *see* Hex River Crossing Private Cellar

The Bernard Series

Grapes sourced from an organically certified vineyard, utilised for the first time this year, show their impressive quality in the Basket Press Syrah. The maverick winemaker, Bernard Podlashuk, after whom this premium DGB-owned Bellingham range is named, would certainly have approved, considering that he was first to produce a shiraz in this country.

★★★★☆ **Bush Vine Pinotage** New Darling grape source & cooler vintage impart piquancy to savoury **09** (★★★), with toasty dry finish. Lacks gravitas, fruit & elegance of **07** from Stellenbosch grapes. No **08**.

★★★★ **Basket Press Syrah ✓ 09** has a dash of malbec, & a core of dark fruit, cedar & leather tightly woven into firmer tannin structure & oak. Will reward ageing. WO Coastal. **08** skipped.

★★★★ **Small Barrel SMV** Elegant **07** still current. When last tasted, was lighter styled & savoury. WO Paarl.

★★★★ **Old Vine Chenin Blanc** 🍽 🖐 Riper, plumper **10** (★★★★) is subtly oaked, with quince & almond flavours. Lacks vibrancy & freshness of **09**, a trend evident in most of these whites. WO Coastal, as for Viognier.

★★★★ **Whole Bunch Roussanne** 🍽 🖐 Rare-in-Cape Rhône white grape, reticent in **10** (★★★★), gently aromatic, with silky texture. Less tangy than **09**, still appealing. WO Paarl, as Grenache Blanc-Viognier.

★★★★ **Hand Picked Viognier** 🍽 🖐 **10** (★★★) lacks fruit & tanginess evident in **09**, quieter, demure, gentle acidity & aromatic chamomile tone.

Whole Bunch Grenache Blanc-Viognier NEW 🍽 🖐 ★★★★ Grenache blanc dominates understated & earthy **10** blend from Paarl grapes. Subtle waxy lanolin & freshening citrus lift. Graceful table mate. — MW

The Berrio Wines

Location: Elim ▪ Map: Southern Cape ▪ WO: Elim/Western Cape ▪ Est 1997 ▪ 1stB 2002 ▪ Tasting & sales Mon-Fri 9-4.30 Sat 10-3 (booking essential) ▪ Closed Easter Fri/Sun, Dec 25/26 & Jan 1 ▪ Snack/lunch platters by prior booking; or BYO picnic ▪ Owner(s) Francis Pratt ▪ Cellarmaster(s) Francis Pratt (Feb 2009) ▪ Viticulturist(s) Andrew Teubes (Jan 2006, consultant) ▪ 2,276ha/38ha (cabs s/f, malbec, merlot, p verdot, pinot, syrah, sauv, sem, viog) ▪ ±40t/17,170cs own label 20% red 80% white ▪ Fairtrade ▪ PO Box 622 Bredasdorp 7280 ▪ wine@theberrio.co.za ▪ www.theberrio.co.za ▪ S 34° 37' 17.0" E 019° 48' 32.3" ▪ T +27 (0)28-482-1880 ▪ F +27 (0)86-603-2894

Given that the highlight of his overseas travels was drinking a 1917 riesling, it's little wonder that Francis Pratt aspires to produce ageworthy white wines on his farm in cool, southerly Elim. 'So far, they've proved their ability to be drunk over five years.' Red-wine wise, the coming year will see the launch of a Syrah, Pinot Noir and Bordeaux-style blend, all farmed organically as far as possible. 'The establishment of the Nuwejaars Wetland Special Management Area has created a new attitude towards nature.' Besides, getting things right in the vineyard means 'no unnecessary corrections' in the cellar.

★★★★ **Cabernet Sauvignon** 🍽 First since **06, 09** (★★★★) surprisingly succulent for cool vintage. Touch herbaceous, but well padded with fruit, sweet vanilla from portion American oak. Some Stellenbosch grapes.

★★★★☆ **Sauvignon Blanc ✓** 🍽 🖐 Previous vintages have blazed a trail for this windswept area, still refined, incredibly complex 5+ years on. **10** (★★★★) same taut, mineral qualities in slightly lower register, lovely nectarine & greengage perfumes. Misses exquisite layering of **09** (★★★★★), sophistication of **08**.

★★★★☆ **The Weathergirl ✓** 🍽 🖐 Aptly named white blend, given marginal Elim climate. No oak embellishment for these, just pristine sauvignon (70%) & semillon fruit in **10**, grassy, athletically lean, youthfully reserved but beautifully built & weighted to improve good few years. — Panel

🔲 **The Blends** see Bellingham
🔲 **The Cheviot Winery** see Cheviot Winery
🔲 **The Cirrus Wine Company** see Cirrus Wine Company

The Company of Wine People

Location/map: Stellenbosch ▪ Est 2004 ▪ Tasting & sales Mon-Fri 9-5.30 Sat 9-5 Sun 10-4 ▪ Fee R10pp ▪ Closed Easter Fri, Dec 25 & Jan 1 ▪ The Duck Pond Restaurant (see Restaurants section) ▪ Facilities for children ▪ Owner(s) 200+ shareholders ▪ Winemaker(s) Abraham de Villiers (Jan 2005), Bernard Claassen (2004) & Stephan Smit ▪ Viticulturist(s) Francois de Villiers ▪ ISO 9001, BRC, Fairtrade, IFS, IPW, SANS 1841, WIETA, Woolworths ▪ PO Box

465 Stellenbosch 7599 ▪ info@thecompanyofwinepeople.co.za ▪ www.thecompanyofwinepeople.co.za ▪ S 33° 59'25.8" E 018° 46'2.5" ▪ **T +27 (0)21-881-3870** ▪ F +27 (0)21-881-3102

As if its Arniston Bay 'lifestyle' label doesn't already conjure up images of sunshine and sea, brand owner and major industry player The Company of Wine People is launching a Winemakers Retreat range under the brand (which also boasts new packaging, including plastic/PET bottles where appropriate). Not that one can imagine winemakers Abraham de Villiers, Bernard Claassen and Stephan Smit having much free time, given they're also responsible for separately listed Kumkani, Versus and Welmoed. All well known in Europe, the US and Asia, the brand to 'visit' is Welmoed with its Duck Pond Restaurant.

▪ **The Den** *see Painted Wolf Wines*
▪ **The Diamond Collection** *see Lutzville Cape Diamond Vineyards*
▪ **The Diners Club Wine Society** *see Mulderbosch Vineyards*

The Drift Farm   NEW

WO: Western Cape ▪ 1stB 2005 ▪ Wine sales Mon-Fri 8.30-4 ▪ Owner(s) Jack family ▪ Winemaker(s) Bruce Jack & Trizanne Barnard ▪ Viticulturist(s) Chris Keets (consultant) ▪ 204ha/12ha (barbera, malbec, pinot, shiraz, tannat, tinta barocca, touriga franca, touriga nacional, chard) ▪ WIETA ▪ PO Box 55 Napier 7270 ▪ info@thedrift.co.za ▪ www.thedrift.co.za ▪ **T +27 (0)86-150-2025** ▪ F +27 (0)86-583-7456

Built on organic principles, the Jack family's small farm produces award-winning vegetables, herbs and olives, but the highlight for Bruce Jack (of Flagstone and Kumala fame) has been teaming up with Trizanne Barnard (as Trizanne Signature Wines) to make wines from this 'little piece of heaven' in the Overberg.

★★★★ **Bowwood Cabernet Sauvignon-Merlot** Previously listed under Bowwood. Classic Bordeaux style, **05** sumptuous blackcurrant & leafy tobacco; well developed, drinking very well now. Agter Paarl grapes.

★★★★ **Riesling** 🥂 Off cool Swartberg vines, **08** shows some development though still lively, fruity & a good expression of the variety. Lightish alc (±11%) perfect for lunchtime.

Year of the Rooster Rosé 🥂 ★★★★ Preview **11** from port grape touriga franca has plenty red fruit character: dry & serious with good structure, boding well. — Panel

▪ **Theewaterskloof Cellars** *see Villiersdorp Cellar*

The Foundry

Location/map: Stellenbosch ▪ WO: Stellenbosch/Coastal ▪ Est 2000 ▪ 1stB 2001 ▪ Tasting, sales & cellar tours by appt ▪ Closed all pub hols ▪ Owner(s) Chris Williams & James Reid ▪ Cellarmaster(s)/winemaker(s) Chris Williams (Nov 2000) ▪ Viticulturist(s) Chris Williams (Nov 2000), with growers ▪ 11ha (grenache, syrah, viog, rouss) ▪ ±30t/2,000cs own label 40% red 60% white ▪ PO Box 12423 Die Boord 7613 ▪ thefoundry@mweb.co.za ▪ www.thefoundry.co.za ▪ S 34° 1'1.7" E 018° 45'24.7" ▪ **T +27 (0)82-577-0491** ▪ F +27 (0)21-843-3274

Now in its second decade, the collaboration between Meerlust cellarmaster Chris Williams and James Reid (latterly owner of a Voor Paardeberg farm and cellar) was buoyed by the success of their maiden Grenache Blanc (including this guide's five star garland last edition). Consistent with their Rhône orientation, they're now launching a standalone Roussanne, a scarce-in-the-Cape variety Chris believes is well suited to its Mediterranean climate and granitic soils. The goal remains 'interesting and authentic wines' with 'dedication to terroir-driven styles'.

★★★★☆ **Syrah** Classy **07**, very smooth & polished, bridges the spicy/fruity style divide, melds best of both in harmonious rendition.

★★★★★ **Grenache Blanc** ✓ **10** (★★★★☆) ample, more generous, modestly less thrilling than perfectly crafted **09** debut. Both are pure-fruited, with clean minerality; latest has enriching 5.3g/l residual sugar. Barrel-fermented, like all the whites. WO Coastal.

★★★★ **Viognier** Luxurious **09**, full & peachy; beautifully balanced: achieves difficult (in Cape) feat of pure, ripe fruit flavour without big alc or cloying sweetness.

Roussanne NEW ★★★★ Perfumed, delicately floral **10**, 'pebbly' minerality in the stonefruit flavours, bracing freshness in the just-dry tail. — DS

▪ **The Goats do Roam Wine Company** *see Goats do Roam Wine Company*

The Goose Wines

Location: George ▪ Map: Klein Karoo & Garden Route ▪ WO: Upper Langkloof ▪ Est 2005 ▪ Tasting & sales by appt ▪ Meals/refreshments by appt ▪ Guesthouse ▪ Owner(s) Retief Goosen & Werner Roux ▪ Cellarmaster(s)/winemaker(s) Alwyn Liebenberg (Jan 2007) ▪ Viticulturist(s) Bennie Botha (Jan 2009) ▪ 500ha/21ha (cab, shiraz, sauv) ▪ 120t/9,333cs own label 66% red 34% white + 70cs for clients ▪ Brands for clients: Reuben's (Franschhoek + Robertson) ▪ HACCP ▪ PO Box 10 Oudtshoorn 6620 ▪ info@thegoosewines.com ▪ www.thegoosewines.com ▪ S 33° 48' 53.5" E 022° 34' 23.4" ▪ **T +27 (0)83-787-3000** ▪ F +27 (0)86-540-8077

Expect to hear more about - and from - this winery, part-owned by renowned golfer Retief 'The Goose' Goosen, in the cool Upper Langkloof wine ward. Farm events, a wine club, expanded online activity and sponsorships are planned, along with wider local distribution and a drive into the US, China and other export markets. A 187ml bottling of The Gander wines for SAA attracted a degree of interest that encourages them 'to continue to market these small bottles aggressively' and consider bottling the flagships in the convenient and affordable format as well.

The Goose range

★★★★ **Expression** Previewed previously, bottled **08** elegant shiraz (67%) & cab from one of SA's highest sites. Appealing herbal edges to juicy centre, fine & lengthy tannins. Gear up on taut **07** (★★★), tasted out of vintage sequence.

Sauvignon Blanc ★★★★ Rich & ripe **10** offers passionfruit & green melon. Bright & flavoursome mouthful for solo sipping or seafood, but shade off subtle & persistent **09** (★★★★).

The Gander range

Shiraz ★★★ Still-selling **09** previously infused with berries, splash viognier gave floral lightness. **Sauvignon Blanc** 🍽 ★★★ Step up for now-bottled **10**, with 40% Devon Valley grapes. Lean & austere but with engaging lime fruit, modest 13% alc ideal for al fresco enjoyment. — Panel

The Grape Grinder [NEW]

Location: Paarl ▪ WO: Western Cape ▪ Est/1stB 2010 ▪ Closed to public ▪ Owner(s) Oliver Kirsten & Johan du Toit ▪ Cellarmaster(s)/winemaker(s) Richard Rowe (Dec 2010, consultant) ▪ 15,000cs own label 100% red ▪ ISO 2009, BRC, WIETA ▪ PO Box 606 Paarl 7624 ▪ oliver@grapegrinder.com ▪ www.grapegrinder.com ▪ **T +27 (0)21-863-3943** ▪ F +27 (0)86-588-4338

The Grape Grinder was established in late 2010 in Paarl by Johan du Toit and Oliver Kirsten, originally behind the funky Juno Wine Company initiative. They pinpointed the North American and Scandinavian markets as particularly responsive to innovation in wine coupled with strong branding, and came up with The Grinder Pinotage (unashamedly in the modish 'coffee' style). Early indications are that the new wine is going down a storm. Albeit limitedly, also available locally.

Pinotage 😊 🍽 🖼 ★★★ Attention-grabbing contemporary packaging; big, almost sumptuous espresso-in-a-glass styling, easy to drink, fair priced - **10** ticks all consumer boxes. — Panel

■ **The Greenhouse** *see* Bon Cap Organic Winery

The High Road

Location/map/WO: Stellenbosch ▪ Est/1stB 2003 ▪ Tasting & sales by appt ▪ Closed all pub hols ▪ Boardroom facilities ▪ Owner(s) Les Sweidan & Mike Church ▪ Winemaker(s) Mark Carmichael-Green (2004, consultant) ▪ Viticulturist(s) Paul Wallace (2004, consultant) ▪ 26t/2,000cs own label 100% red ▪ PO Box 4721 Cape Town 8000 ▪ www.thehighroad.co.za ▪ S 33° 56' 27.1" E 018° 50' 49.1" ▪ **T +27 (0)21-425-4209** ▪ F +27 (0)21-886-4288

This small specialist winery (sourcing grapes from 'the high slopes of the Golden Triangle in Stellenbosch') has done well in competitions with its Bordeaux blends – joined this year by a more ambitious barrel selection label. Another grape variety comes into play from the 2010 vintage, 'but at this stage we can't say too much'.

★★★★ **Director's Reserve** [NEW] Classic, youthful **08** from 60% cab plus equal merlot, cab franc. Plush & luminous, its bright blackcurrant fruit interwoven with vanilla spice from the all-new oak. Evenly, richly textured.

Classique ★★★★ Refreshingly herbal **08** from equal cab & merlot, some cab franc. Fine tannins, persistent flavours but no complexity. **Reserve ★★★★** Same varieties, with more cab. Robust & grippy **08**, tannic & savoury, showing evidence of all-new oak (but well integrated). —MF

The House of GM&Ahrens

Map: Franschhoek ▪ Est 2007 ▪ 1stB 2008 ▪ Tasting, sales & cellar tours by appt ▪ Closed all pub hols ▪ Meals/refreshments by appt ▪ Owner(s) Albert Ahrens & Gerrit Maritz ▪ Cellarmaster(s)/viticulturist(s) Albert Ahrens (Jan 2007) ▪ 7t/250cs own label 100% MCC ▪ P O Box 5619 Helderberg 7135 ▪ info@gmahrens.com ▪ www.gmahrens.com ▪ S 33° 54′ 14″ E 019° 07′ 08″ ▪ **T +27 (0)79-196-6887**

When winemaker Albert Ahrens and lawyer Gerrit Maritz met for the first time during the 2006 harvest, they quickly realised they shared a passion for bubbly. 'We impulsively decided to make our own méthode cap classique and duly produced 600 bottles the following harvest.' Sourcing the best possible grapes, they still work with small quantities but production has increased to the extent that they have established this boutique bubbly house in Franschhoek. Tasting and sales of the wines, unready for review, is by appointment.

The House of JC le Roux

Location/map: Stellenbosch ▪ WO: Western Cape ▪ 1stB 1983 ▪ Tasting & sales Mon-Fri 8–5 Sat 10–4 Sun (Oct-Apr only) 10–4 ▪ Fee R20-R55 ▪ Tour & AV show complimentary, Mon-Fri 10, 11.30 & 3 Sat 10 & 12 Sun (Oct-Apr only) 10 & 12 ▪ Closed Easter Fri & Dec 25 ▪ Tour groups ▪ Gifts ▪ Seasons restaurant ▪ Owner(s) Distell ▪ Cellarmaster(s) Elunda Basson ▪ Winemaker(s) Elunda Basson (2007), with Hentie Germishuys (Oct 2002) ▪ Farm manager Willem Laubscher ▪ Viticulturist(s) Bennie Liebenberg (Jan 2000) ▪ 27ha own vyds ▪ 20% red 80% white ▪ ISO 9200 certified ▪ PO Box 184 Stellenbosch 7599 ▪ info@jcleroux.co.za ▪ www.jcleroux.co.za ▪ S 33° 54′ 16.6″ E 018° 48′ 37.4″ ▪ **T +27 (0)21-865-8200** ▪ F +27 (0)21-865-2586/+27 (0)21-865-2585

The place of JC le Roux in local affections is undimmed, according to the 2011 Media 24 TGI ICON brand survey, which found it 'the country's top alcoholic wine brand' in a consumer poll to determine which brands are used and loved by South Africans 'irrespective of age, income, race or language'. A non-vintage Brut is a new addition to the range. 'A non-vintage blend of classic varieties is generally considered the foundation of French champagne', says winemaker Elunda Basson, 'but JC le Roux's existing MCC range comprises predominantly single cultivar, vintage offerings. We simply had to make a more accessible non-vintage Brut for everyday enjoyment.'

Méthode Cap Classique range

★★★★ Scintilla Previously tasted yeasty **02** MCC sparkling blend chardonnay & pinot noir maintains extraordinary freshness, emphasized by bone-dry, lemon & mineral finish. No **01** made.

La Vallée ★★★ Off-dry **NV**; subtle nutmeg & ripe pear; good partner for spicy food. Like Rosé version, tasted last year; both mostly pinot. **Pinot Noir ★★★★** Steely **08** vinified pale & notably dry. Fresh, lean & steely style with enduring finish. **Brut NEW ✓ ★★★★** Charming, harmonious **NV** shows yeasty brioche aromas & desirable creamy richness. **Pinot Noir Rosé ★★★** Delicate pink **08** has developed, yeasty aromas. Fresh & subtly fruity, with decent structure, breadth & focus. **La Vallée Rosé ★★★★** Pretty onion-skin **NV**. Raspberry fruitiness in off-dry but refreshing style.

Sparkling range

Sauvignon Blanc ☺ ★★★ Fresh carbonated **11** sparkler delivers plenty appeal & cheer. Although dry, abundant fruit gives sweet impression.

Le Domaine ★★ Spicy, sweet **NV** blend sauvignon, chenin, muscat. This & next 2 tasted last edition. **La Fleurette ★★** Cloying sweetness in floral **NV**. **La Chanson ★★** Simple, sweet, light red **NV** sparkler. —IM

▪ **The House of Krone** see Twee Jonge Gezellen Estate-The House of Krone
▪ **The House of Mandela** see House of Mandela
▪ **The Juno Wine Company** see Juno Wine Company
▪ **The Legends** see Bellingham

Thelema Mountain Vineyards ⬍ 🌲 ♿

Location/map: Stellenbosch ▪ WO: Stellenbosch/Elgin/Western Cape ▪ Est 1983 ▪ 1stB 1988 ▪ Tasting & sales Mon-Fri 9–5 Sat 10–3 ▪ Fee R25/6 wines, waived on purchase ▪ Closed all pub hols ▪ BYO picnic ▪ Owner(s) McLean & Webb Family Trusts ▪ Cellarmaster(s) Gyles Webb (1983) ▪ Winemaker(s) Rudi Schultz (Dec 2000), with Duncan Clarke (Jan 2009) ▪ Viticulturist(s) Talitha Venter (Jan 2010) ▪ 250ha/95ha (cab, grenache, merlot, p verdot, pinot, shiraz, chard, muscat d'F, riesling, rouss, sauv, viog) ▪ 850t/50,000cs own label 40% red 60% white ▪ PO Box 2234 Dennesig Stellenbosch 7601 ▪ wines@thelema.co.za ▪ www.thelema.co.za ▪ S 33° 54' 30.0" E 018° 55' 23.4" ▪ **T +27 (0)21-885-1924** ▪ F +27 (0)21-885-1800

This fine family winery on the now more crowded crest of the Helshoogte pass outside Stellenbosch was a fore-runner of the 1990s revolution in Cape winemaking. The ripe, pure-fruited wines (first bottled vintage 1988) were a revelation to many then – it took longer to understand that the classically firm structure Gyles Webb insisted upon would ensure their ageability. Rudi Schultz has been working alongside him in the cellar for over a decade now, and the modern-classic approach continues, as does the reputation for excellence. There's ripeness, power, and a generous use of oak, but they typically eschew showy flamboyance, and (with a few deliberate exceptions) the wines are always properly dry. Thelema's Elgin outpost is so far a touch less successful, but these are early days.

Thelema range

★★★★☆ **Cabernet Sauvignon** Last edition, finely poised **08** showed power & appetising refinement; restrained sweet berry fruit well supported by oak; dry, focused finish. More harmony in 5+ years.

★★★★☆ **The Mint Cabernet Sauvignon** Name-giving herbaceous note prominent but in harmony with serious fruit on big, impressive **09**, whose power doesn't preclude charm. Strongly built, with 10 years to go – still very youthful.

★★★★ **Merlot** 09 (★★★★) less harmonious than **08**. Plummy ripeness combines with merlot's herbal notes. Milk chocolate a continuing theme. Powerful but streamlined.

★★★★☆ **Merlot Reserve** Always one of the Cape's best, as with fine **09** which leaps majestically ahead of standard version - lacking its green note. Typical Thelema power, but plenty of flesh & rounded charm, fresh & flavourful, with long succulently dry finish.

★★★★ **Shiraz** 08 with maybe not quite the refinement & elegance of previous, but still very appealing & flavourful. Oak apparent in youth, but might integrate; solid, chewy & tasty.

★★★★☆ **Rabelais** Pricey, flamboyant 80:20 cab, merlot selected from new-oak barrels. Dark chocolate & blackcurrant revel in **07**'s fine ripe structure. Tasted last year, prominent spicy oak added sweetness to finish.

★★★★ **Chardonnay** 🍸 🍃 Reliable quality on **10**. Refreshing, lipsmacking & (like all Thelema wines) properly dry, with integrated oak complementing citrus flavours. A touch leaner, more elegant than Ed's.

★★★★ **Ed's Reserve Chardonnay** 🍃 Jump from **07** to **10** - single-clone vineyard still giving overt muscat notes. Elegant silkiness, in richer & fuller style than standard version, well trimmed by fine acidity.

★★★★ **Sauvignon Blanc** 🍸 🍃 Tasted pre-bottling, as usual. **11** less showily exuberant than previous, but deft, focused & smart, combining fruitfulness (mostly citrus) with elegant green cut.

> **Muscat de Frontignan** 😊 🍸 🍃 ★★★ Generous as always with its grapey scents, tasty **11** has an undeniable winning & easy just-off-dry charm.

Mountain Red 🍸 ★★★ **08** another friendly but not trivial shiraz-based blend, with ripe fruit & a good structure. Ready for drinking. WO W Cape. **Riesling** 🍸 🍃 ★★★ **10** drops 'Rhine' prefix. Not up to usual standard: pleasant, with balanced sweet touch & limy freshness, but early terpene notes & a bit insipid. **Rhine Riesling Late Harvest** ★★★★ Sweetly delicious **08** (to be thrilling would require more acidity in the balance), uncloying, dry-seeming end, thanks to clean, elegant lightness. **Vin de Hel Muscat Late Harvest** NEW ★★★★ **08** seems sweeter than Riesling version, but less so in fact, & less refined. Forthcoming grapey, scented pleasures; tasty but simple. Discontinued: **Muscadel**.

Sutherland range

★★★★ **Chardonnay** 🍸 🍃 Drops 'Wooded' from name with **10** (★★★★). Paler colour than the Stellenbosch versions, & generally paler flavours, aromas too; green limyness thinner than in **09**.

★★★★ **Sauvignon Blanc** 🍸 🍃 Enticing & incisive **11**, with its tropical fruit & citrus perhaps more forthcoming than **10**'s. Pleasingly balanced, nice breadth & weight. Sampled pre-bottling.

★★★★ **Roussanne-Viognier** 🟦 We last year promised complexity in year/2 for maiden **09**; viognier reticent at first amidst aromas thatch, fennel, but showed peachily on lightly oaked, refined palate.

Pinot Noir 🔖 ★★★ More toasty oak on **10** than previous, with similarly light-fruited, modest structure. Pleasant, easy drinking. **Shiraz** ★★★ Like next wine, tasted last year. Ripeness & power combine with herbal tang & lots of new oak influence on **08**. **Cabernet Sauvignon-Petit Verdot** ★★★ Quietly pleasant aromas, sweet pastille flavours on light-fleshed, bitter-edged **08**. Just the alc is big! **Rhine Riesling** 🟦 ★★★★ Last year, **09** showed a little richer, prettier than Stellenbosch cousin, but also a steelier core & fine grapefruit finish. Discontinued: **Chardonnay Unwooded**, **Viognier**. — TJ

■ **The Lighthouse Collection** see Arniston Bay
■ **The Marais Family** see Wonderfontein

The Mason's Winery

Location: Paarl ▪ Map: Paarl & Wellington ▪ Est/1stB 2001 ▪ Tasting & sales by appt ▪ Restaurant 'Proviant' adjacent to cellar ▪ Owner(s) Mason's Hill Wines (Pty) Ltd ▪ Cellarmaster(s)/winemaker(s)/viticulturist(s) Derek Clift (2001) ▪ 45ha/4ha (shiraz) ▪ 15t/5,000cs own label 100% red ▪ PO Box 515 Suider-Paarl 7624 ▪ masons@cliftgranite.co.za ▪ www.cliftgranite.co.za ▪ S 33° 45' 20.5" E 018° 57' 42.6" ▪ **T +27 (0)83-228-7855** ▪ F +27 (0)21-863-1601

Derek Clift is sticking to his guns, aiming to produce wines for the discerning drinker, wines that are age worthy and massive. This Shiraz specialist is looking to release two 2007 vintages soon. The one possibly to be called 'Voeltjiesgat' will be from a special single block.

★★★★ **Mason's Shiraz** Await next release. Previous **05** (★★★) showed more maturity than expected, was not as rich as standout **04**.

Klipkapper Chenin Blanc ★★★ **11** resting in barrel. — JP

Thembi & Co

Location/WO: Paarl ▪ Map: Paarl & Wellington ▪ Est/1stB 2009 ▪ Tasting & sales Mon-Fri 8-5 Sat 9-1 ▪ Closed Easter Fri-Sun, Ascension day, Sep 24, Dec 25/26 & Jan 1 ▪ Cellar tours on request ▪ Owner(s) Thembi Tobie ▪ Cellarmaster(s)/winemaker(s) Heidi Dietstein (Mar 2010, Boland Kelder) ▪ Viticulturist(s) Jurie Germishuys (Jul 2009, Boland Kelder) ▪ (merlot, shiraz, chenin, sauv) ▪ 50% red 50% white ▪ PO Box 3511 Paarl 7620 ▪ thembi@thembiwines.co.za ▪ www.thembiwines.co.za ▪ S 33° 41' 19.6" E 018° 57' 20.1" ▪ **T +27 (0)21-862-6190/ +27 (0)83-277-5117** ▪ F +27 (0)21-862-5379

The 'sold out' signs going up on her chenin was a highlight of the past year for wine entrepreneur Thembi Tobie. The fruit of the vine used to be forbidden, but this only spurred her into learning more. She's become part of Boland Kelder's social responsibility and empowerment initiative and - no shrinking violet - she engages with growers and winemakers alike.

Thembi range

Merlot 🟦 ★★★ Gentle mulberry on medium-bodied **09**, uncomplicated & easy. **Shiraz** 🟦 ★★★ Slightly meaty **09** is appealing if a touch light-footed compared with previous, not as lingering. **Chenin Blanc** 🟦 ★★★ Approachable **11**, zesty lemon & kiwi appeal. **Sauvignon Blanc** 🟦 ★★★ Lively gooseberry & fig on uncomplicated **11** quaffer. — FM

The Natalie

Building on a long relationship with Alan Pick, Etienne le Riche produced this wine for The Butcher Shop and Grill. See Pick's Pick for contact details.

Natalie range

The Natalie ★★★★ Sister to Le Riche Cabernet Merlot, with cabernet franc & petit verdot. **09** in similar style with dark fruits, slightly more prominent oaking & firm long finish. Very dry. Named after Alan Pick's daughter. — JP

The Parlotones

Location: Stellenbosch ▪ WO: Coastal/Western Cape ▪ Est/1stB 2009 ▪ Closed to public ▪ Owner(s) The Parlotones & Hands on Wine (Pty) Ltd ▪ Winemaker(s) Hugo Truter & Pieter-Niel Rossouw, advised by Pieter Walser & Allan Mullins ▪ Hands on Wine Private Bag X5061 Stellenbosch 7599 ▪ team@handsonwine.net ▪ www.theparlotoneswine.net ▪ **T** +27 (0)82-375-3048 ▪ F +27 (0)86-218-5993

Interest in this growing range - a joint venture between the eponymous South African indie-rock band and Hands on Wine, available solely through Woolworths - is no longer limited to locals: Sweden and the US want the wines too. Distinctively mascaraed lead singer Kahn Morbee says the maiden rosé is like lying in strawberry fields in a pale pink sunset, tasting raspberries and melted marshmallows.

Giant Mistake 🔲 ★★★ Light, easy 5-way cab-led blend. **09** soft approachable fruitcake spice, some grip & succulence. A red for beginners. **We Call This Dancing** **NEW** 🔲 🖾 ★★★ Maiden rosé has light raspberry, candy charm, **10** dry, crisp & fresh. WO W Cape. **Push me to the Floor** 🔲 🖾 ★★★★ Chenin-led white blend still available, **10** ripe & balanced, perfume from gewürztraminer & viognier. — FM

▪ **The Pavillion** *see* Boschendal Wines
▪ **The Reef** *see* Arniston Bay
▪ **The Rhino** *see* Linton Park Wines
▪ **The Ruins** *see* Bon Cap Organic Winery
▪ **The Sadie Family** *see* Sadie Family Wines

The Saints

Unpretentious and affordable range of 'weekday wines' by DGB, also available in 1.5L magnums.

St Raphael ★★ Rounded drinkability from berry-toned sipper. WO W Cape & not revisited, as for all. **St Vincent** ★★★ Brisk & fruity **NV** sauvignon, chenin & colombard party starter. **St Morand** ★★ Semi-sweet **NV** white wallet pleaser. **St Celine** ★ Natural Sweet, like next two; sugary, needs a bit more freshness. **NV**. **St Claire** ★★ Sunny, strawberry-fresh lunchtime tipple with low ±8% alc. **NV**. **St Anna** ★★ Light (±8% alc), spicy & appealing **NV**. — MW

▪ **The Shore** *see* Arniston Bay
▪ **The Spice Route Winery** *see* Spice Route Winery
▪ **The Springtree Wine Company** *see* Fish Hoek Wines
▪ **The Strata Series** *see* Flagstone Winery

The Three Foxes

WO: Groenekloof/Swartland ▪ Est/1stB 2004 ▪ Tasting by appt at Mullineux Wines ▪ Owner(s) Pascal Schildt, Olivier Schildt & Chris Mullineux ▪ Winemaker(s)/viticulturist(s) Chris Mullineux (Jan 2004) ▪ 1.2ha (syrah, chenin, clairette) ▪ 6t/400cs own label 80% red 20% white ▪ PO Box 369 Riebeek-Kasteel 7307 ▪ info@the-three-foxes.com ▪ www.the-three-foxes.com ▪ **T** +27 (0)82-333-6888 ▪ F +27 (0)82-121-333-6888

These foxes comprise the Schildt brothers, Pascal and Olivier and Riebeek-Kasteel-based winemaker, Chris Mullineux. Their mission statement is to vinify distinctive parcels of grapes to produce wines that appeal to their personal taste, without commercial considerations getting in the way. The search and choice of fruit remains nomadic, with no particular prescripts; next in line is a 2011 mourvèdre. Production is garagiste in scale, but depends very much on what's available.

★★★★ **Sangiovese** Ex Groenekloof single-vineyard, **08** previously showed Xmas cake, ginger & iodine nuances. Judiciously oaked, supple yet structured.

★★★★ **Castillo Syrah** Fragrantly herbaceous **09** from Swartland vines is elegantly weighted, juicy & complex. Unshowy but focused, unfurling over time in glass. Will benefit from cellaring. — GdB

▪ **The Tin Mine** *see* Zevenwacht

The Township Winery

Location: Paarl ▪ WO: Western Cape ▪ Est 2009 ▪ 1stB 2010 ▪ Closed to public ▪ Owner(s) The Township Winery cc ▪ Cellarmaster(s) Wilhelm van Rooyen (Oct 2009, consultant) ▪ 400cs own label100% white ▪ PO Box 63 Philippi 7781 ▪ kate@jambela.co.za ▪ **T +27 (0)21-371-6083** ▪ F +27 (0)21-371-6083

Previously listed as 'Dido', The Township Winery is the tale of housing developer Kate Jambela's journey into wine, demystifying it and using it as a tool for empowerment for the women of Langa, Gugulethu and Philippi. Facilitated by wine entrepreneur Graham Knox, the 'urban winery' project seeks to bridge the 'wide but also very deep' divide between land owners who can afford to plant grapes for wine and the majority of the population. Grapes are currently sourced from various regions, but vineyards within and adjacent to the townships are planned.

The Township Winery range

Philippi Sauvignon Blanc ▣ ▨ ★★★★ Big-boned, generous **10** revisited mid-2011, overtly grassy with potent asparagus whiff. Style may not appeal to all.

Dido range

★★★★ **Cabernet Sauvignon** Drink-now **04** impressed last year with brooding black fruit & tealeaf herbaceousness. Wellington grapes, as all unless noted. Not retasted, as next 4.
Hamilcar Merlot Await next. **Pinotage** ▣ ★★★ **09** was fresh, youthful, with vibrant berry fruit, restrained tannins. Some Darling vines. **Shiraz** Untasted. **The Storm Mourvèdre-Shiraz** ▣ ★★★ Light-bodied **09** showed feisty cherry fruit, hints of pepper & spices. **Pinot Grigio** ✓ ▣ ▨ ★★★★ Charming, smoothly rounded body, **10** couches beeswax & stonefruit notes. Forthright & elegant. WO W Cape. **Sauvignon Blanc** ▣ ★★★ **09** from Durbanville grapes was lean & steely last edition, with restrained gooseberry flavour. — GdB

Theuniskraal Estate

Location/map/WO: Tulbagh ▪ Est 1705 ▪ 1stB 1947 ▪ Tasting & sales Mon-Fri 9–12 & 1–4 Sat 10–1 ▪ Closed Easter Sat/Sun, Dec 25 & Jan 1 ▪ Owner(s)/viticulturist(s) Jordaan brothers ▪ Cellarmaster(s)/winemaker(s) Andries Jordaan (1991) ▪ 140ha total ▪ BWI ▪ PO Box 34 Tulbagh 6820 ▪ tkraal@lando.co.za ▪ www.theuniskraal.co.za ▪ S 33° 13'41.3" E 019° 8'7.1" ▪ **T +27 (0)23-230-0687/89** ▪ F +27 (0)23-230-2284

Winemaker Andries Jordaan, 4th generation of this family-owned Tulbagh Estate, says of his frequently best-value-awarded wines: 'I think it is important that your style of winemaking fits the demand of your potential market' and then to deliver this consistently. The ageless Cape Riesling brand, now 63 years young, bears out this philosophy.

Prestige ☺ ▨ ★★★ Uncomplicated, juicy ruby cab-based blend, **10** ripe & bright. **Cape Riesling** ☺ ▨ ★★★ Evergreen Cape standard, **11** as always fresh, light & dependable. May it never fall to fashion. **Semillon-Chardonnay** ☺ ▨ ★★★ **11** near-equal unwooded blend with surprising roundness & fruity satisfaction. Lingers pleasantly. **Bouquet Blanc** ☺ ▨ ★★★ Natural Sweet-style **11** preview bursting with sweet muscat & gewürztraminer spiciness.

Rosé ▨ ★★ Muscat & shiraz in **10** make odd bedfellows. Sweetish, light & plummy. — GdB

■ **The Village Walk** see Franschhoek Cellar
■ **The Wade Bales Wine Society** see Mulderbosch Vineyards

The Wine Fusion

Location: Wellington ▪ WO: Western Cape/Wellington/Coastal ▪ Est 2007 ▪ Closed to public ▪ Cellarmaster(s) Graham Knox (Dec 2007) ▪ Winemaker(s) Wilhelm van Rooyen (Oct 2009) ▪ 1.5m litres bulk 60% red 40% white ▪ c/o Wine Masterpieces Pty Ltd PO Box 1209 Wellington 7654 ▪ graham@thewinefusion.com ▪ **T +27 (0)21-447-4476** ▪ F +27 (0)21-447-4476

In an effort to break the 'stranglehold that the packaging companies have on locally bottled South African wine', Wellington-based wine entrepreneur Graham Knox has teamed up with hand-picked local winemakers and UK-based Wine Fusion, exporting small volumes of high-quality, custom-made bulk wine for bottling and distribution there, retailing in the £7-£13 bracket. Small quantities will be available locally.

★★★★ **The First Chapter** 🗋 Fruity/leathery intro to **10** shiraz, viognier blend, followed by rush of sweet black cherry & plum to an appealing savoury conclusion.

Two Blocks 🗋 ★★★★ 100% cab, with the grape's green leafiness & blackcurrant, hint of pencil shaving from laudably understated oak. **10** fruit driven but serious & elegant. WO Coastal. **The Grid Pinotage** 🗋 ★★★☆ From a Wellington single-vineyard comes juicy & generous **10**, ripe & round, rather tasty spicy plum pudding flavour. **Pin Zin** 🗋 ★★★ Rare but happy pinotage & zinfandel liaison, **10** oozes dark wild berry & pepper. Medium body, attractively tart & savoury food wine. WO Wellington. **The Long Lunch** 🗋 ★★★ Nods to Côtes du Rhône in light, fresh & spicy **10** blend headed by cinsaut & mourvèdre, with nutty cherry scents. **Incognico White** 🗋 ★★★★ 'Incognico' here is black grape shiraz, vinified as a white with floral viognier. Vibrant **10** is juicy-fruity & tangy-fresh. — Panel

---

The Winery of Good Hope

Location: Somerset West ▪ Map: Helderberg ▪ WO: Stellenbosch/Swartland/Western Cape/Elgin/Stellenbosch ▪ Est/1stB 1998 ▪ Tasting & sales Mon-Fri 9-5 by appt ▪ Closed all pub hols ▪ Owner(s) Alex Dale, Andrew Openshaw, Yalumba, Edouard Labeye, Cliff Roberson, Ben Radford, Heather Whitman ▪ Cellarmaster(s) Edouard Labeye (1998) ▪ Winemaker(s) Jacques de Klerk (Oct 2009), with Tubby May (2002) ▪ Viticulturist(s) Edouard Labeye & Jacques de Klerk ▪ ±100ha (cab, merlot, pinot, shiraz, chard, chenin, viog) ▪ 500t/40,000cs own label 50% red 50% white ▪ Brands for clients: Pick's Pick ▪ BEE, IPW, WIETA ▪ Postnet Suite 124 Private Bag X15 Somerset West 7129 ▪ thewineryofgoodhope@thewineryofgoodhope.co.za ▪ www.thewineryofgoodhope.com ▪ S 34° 0' 57.5" E 018° 49' 2.6" ▪ **T +27 (0)21-855-5528** ▪ F +27 (0)21-855-5529

For MD Alex Dale, a natural approach to wine will inevitably feature more strongly as he steers the winery into the future. 'I'm intent on making wines naturally, with balance, freshness and subtlety. I want clear water between Good Hope and brash, overtly commercial styles that are currently popular.' Three major accreditations and audits in the past year reflect Alex's philosophy of keeping ethics, environment and community firmly in his sights. The Land of Hope Trust underwrites the winery's workers and their dependents' educational aspirations, while water waste management and environmental impact programmes enhance the concern's green credentials. Despite economic recession, further plantings and cellar and equipment upgrading continue.

Radford Dale range

★★★★☆ **Merlot** ✓ 🗋 Eucalyptus edge to rich & ripe but restrained **09**. Supple, bright fruit flavoured core revealed within beautifully integrated, spicy oak. Touch minerality enhances firmly savoury, dense finish.

★★★★☆ **Freedom Pinot Noir** 🗋 Alluring, expressive, complex **10** from Elgin grapes, with finesse, elegance & earthiness typical of this cooler area. Fruit, oak in poised balance, finishes with mineral freshness.

★★★★☆ **Shiraz** ✓ 🗋 Astonishingly aromatic & flavoursome **09** has lovely fruit & spice definition. Skilfully constructed, with sumptuous ripeness checked by savoury grip of seamless oaking. Satisfyingly complex.

★★★★ **Gravity** 🗋 Dense, suave textured **08** blend shiraz (for spice), merlot (flesh) & cab (structure) is usual polished, balanced self. Meticulously vinified using gravity-assisted techniques for soft, plush flavours.

★★★★ **Shiraz-Merlot** Spicy appeal in **09** (★★★★) lacks freshness & focus of **08**. Very ripe, soft red fruit a little intimidated by firm tannins.

★★★★☆ **Chardonnay** 🗋 Classic-styled **10** lighter than previous but still with lovely weight & richness. Layers of fresh flavour supported by stylish oaking & backbone of savoury acidity & stony minerality.

★★★★☆ **Renaissance Chenin Blanc** NEW 🗋 **10** actually 2nd bottling, after experimental **09** from old chenin vineyards. Intense, generously textured, complex with a fresh citrus twist & superbly integrated oak. Long finish delivers lemon pithiness & minerality. Top wine of the 4 chenin bottlings across ranges.

★★★★☆ **Viognier** 🗋 📷 Overtly smoky, spicy aromas on **10** (★★★★), fermented dry in barrel. Oak influence more dominant than **09**, & perhaps too much for fruit, though fine acidity carries the flinty finish.

★★★★☆ **Vine Dried Viognier** 🗋 Bronze tinged **10** shows exceedingly complex aromas, seems sweeter, more unctuous than declared 130 grams sugar (half that of previous vintage). But peachy viognier sweetness checked by sufficient savoury acidity.

Shiraz-Viognier 🗋 In abeyance.

Land of Hope range

★★★★☆ **Cabernet Sauvignon** 🗋 Structured, youthful **09** needs time to reveal oak-woven layers. From single vineyard in elegant style with tannin & acidity tightly wound around dense, plush & expressive fruit core.

★★★★ **Chenin Blanc** 🔲 Delicious, charming, just-dry **10**, generously textured from oaking & lees contact. Vibrant, full flavours from single vineyard bushvines. Seductive fruit flavours lighter than **09**'s (★★★★☆).

Black Rock range

★★★★☆ **Red Blend** 🔲 Herbs & bush-scrub spiciness in individual & complex **08** (★★★★) shiraz-led blend with carignan, grenache & mourvèdre. Less concentrated than **07** but compelling & harmonious.

★★★★ **White Blend** 🔲 Confident, fragrant chenin-based **09** with chardonnay, clairette, viognier; spicily sweet & rich stonefruits supported by seamless oaking & balanced by pithiness. These WO Swartland.

Vinum range

★★★★ **Cabernet Sauvignon** ✓🔲🦋 Perfumed **10** abundant pure fruit currently masked by tight, spicy oak tannins, unusual for this accessible range. No less tasty & plush, with appealing minerality carrying finish.

★★★★ **Chenin Blanc** ✓🔲 Lovely **10** exhibits charm & confidence, though lacks depth of **09** (★★★★☆). Oak & lees contact broadens stone fruit flavours, while acidity focuses finish, ensuring flawless balance.

The Winery of Good Hope range

Unoaked Chardonnay 😊🔲 ★★★ Charming, easy drinking but classy & perkily fresh **11**. Lees contact adds richness & breadth. WP W Cape, as for Pinot Noir below.

Pinot Noir Reserve 🔲 ★★★★ **10** juicy & elegant, with bright cherry fruit & touch of earthiness. Tannins not as integrated as **09** (★★★★); but very drinkable. **Bush Vine Pinotage** 🔲🦋 ★★★★ Overt mocha & spiciness in **10**, from older, low yielding vines. Usual succulent fruitiness with attractively savoury finish. **Mountainside Shiraz** ✓🔲 ★★★★ Juicy, stylishly balanced, very drinkable **10** has accessible, freshly ripe fruit flavours, with spicy grip to finish. **The Beautiful Game Shiraz** 🔲 In abeyance. **Oceanside Cabernet Sauvignon-Merlot** ✓🔲 ★★★★ Pure-fruited, vibrant, supple **10** blend. May lack power of **09** (★★★★) but still classic, without being too serious. **Granite Ridge Reserve** ★★★★ **08** shiraz-led blend last year showed aromatic complexity; harmonious & framed by oak. First since charming **06** (★★★). **Bush Vine Chenin Blanc** ✓🔲 ★★★★ Pocket-friendly **10** over-delivers on quality with expressive flavours, length, concentration & freshness. Discontinued: **Chenin Blanc-Chardonnay-Viognier**. — IM

🔳 **The Wolftrap** *see Boekenhoutskloof Winery*
🔳 **Thierry & Guy** *see Fat Bastard*
🔳 **33 Degrees South** *see Wellington Wines*

Thokozani Wines

Map: Paarl & Wellington ▪ WO: Wellington ▪ Est/1stB 2005 ▪ Tasting & sales daily 10-5 ▪ Fee R15 ▪ Closed Dec 25 ▪ Cellar tours by appt ▪ Seasons Restaurant (see Restaurants section) ▪ Tour groups ▪ Conferences ▪ Walking/hiking & mountain biking trails ▪ Thokozani Cottages ▪ Owner(s) Diemersfontein employees, external investors & Diemersfontein Wines ▪ Cellarmaster(s) Brett Rightford (Nov 2005) ▪ Winemaker(s) Francois Roode (Sep 2003) ▪ Viticulturist(s) Waldo Kellerman (Aug 2007) ▪ 180ha/60ha (cabs s/f, grenache, malbec, mourv, p verdot, ptage, roobernet, shiraz, chenin, viog) ▪ 60t/4,000L own label 40% red 40% white 20% rosé ▪ WIETA ▪ PO Box 41 Wellington 7654 ▪ info@thokozani.co.za ▪ www.thokozani.co.za ▪ S 33° 39'41.1" E 019° 0'31.1" ▪ **T +27 (0)21-864-5050** ▪ F +27 (0)21-864-2095

The black economic empowerment (BEE) offshoot of Diemersfontein Wine & Country Estate, Thokozani ('Celebration') was established in 2005 with the aim of turning farmworkers into shareholders. It's proved to be one of the most successful ventures of its kind, becoming firmly established and marketing its wine in the US, Europe and Botswana. Additional sustainable income is supplied by four cottages on the estate, for guests holidaying or using the conference facilities.

★★★★ **CCV** ✓🔲 Name changes according to blend proportions: delicious **10** mainly chenin, dollops chard, viognier, unwooded; citrus aromas, round & creamy body from lees-ageing, lingering floral aftertaste. Yum!

Rosé 😊🔲 ★★★ Summer sipper from shiraz, pinotage & mourvèdre, off-dry & cheerful **11** preview.

SMV ✓ ★★★★ Shiraz, mourvèdre & viognier, **10** similar bold black berry fruit, smoke & dark chocolate as previous, on firm, food-friendly oak foundation. For early drinking, as all these. — WB

🔳 **Thomas Kipling** *see Bovlei Cellar*

Thorntree Wines

Est/1stB 2001 ▪ Closed to public ▪ Owner(s)/winemaker(s) André Badenhorst ▪ 50,000cs 50% red 50% white ▪ Suite 310 Private Bag X16 Constantia 7848 ▪ andrebad@iafrica.com ▪ www.thorntreewines.co.za ▪ **T +27 (0)21-786-2487** ▪ F +27 (0)21-786-1476

André Badenhorst and UK investor Edwin Doran are now the proud owners of Far Horizons farm and its brand, Horse Mountain Wines, in Voor Paardeberg. Badenhorst's Thorntree label, now part of the Horse Mountain stable, has built a strong following in several countries and they were considering marketing them locally, too.

- **Three Peaks** *see* Mount Vernon Estate
- **Three Pines** *see* Stark-Condé Wines
- **Three Rivers** *see* Bon Courage Estate

Thunderchild

NEW

Location/WO: Robertson ▪ Est 2003 ▪ 1stB 2008 ▪ Wines available from Rooiberg Winery, Ashton Cellar, Robertson Winery, Ashton Wine Boutique, Affie Plaas Farmstall, Platform 62, Tanagra Winery, De Wetshof Winery & La Verne Wine Boutique - see individual cellars for opening times ▪ Owner(s) Thunderchild Wingerd Trust ▪ Cellarmaster(s) Various Robertson winegrowers ▪ 5ha (cabs s/f, merlot) ▪ PO Box 770 Robertson 6705 ▪ info@thunderchild.co.za ▪ www.thunderchild.co.za ▪ **T +27 (0)23-626-3661** ▪ F +27 (0)23-626-3664

Next to the Herberg Children's Home in Robertson is a 5ha spread that for years had been an ageing apricot orchard. In 2002, friends of the home suggested the site be replanted with vines. The local imagination was fired, and contributions poured in, from fertiliser and plant material to trellising and financial aid. Red varieties were planted in 2003 and local viticultural expertise and cellar facilities were donated. After a year in French oak, and a further year in bottle, the maiden blend came to the market in honour of, and for the benefit of, the 122 children who see the vineyard every day from the home alongside.

Thunderchild ✓ ★★★★ Boldly flavoured Bordeaux blend, 37% each cab franc & merlot, rest cab. **08** mulberry compote, chocolate swirl, pepper twist & amenable tannins to cellar or enjoy now with hearty fare. — Panel

Tierhoek

Location: Citrusdal ▪ Map: Olifants River ▪ WO: Piekenierskloof ▪ Est 2001 ▪ 1stB 2003 ▪ Tasting, sales & cellar tours Mon-Fri 8.30-4.30 Sat by appt ▪ Fee R20, waived on purchase ▪ Closed all pub hols ▪ BYO picnic ▪ Walks/hikes ▪ Conservation area ▪ Guesthouse (sleeps 9) ▪ Owner(s) Shelley Sandell ▪ Cellarmaster(s) Roger Burton (Oct 2006) ▪ Winemaker(s) Basie Snyers (assistant, Oct 2006) ▪ Viticulturist(s) Ryno Kellerman (Aug 2006), advised by Johan Viljoen ▪ 700ha/16ha (grenache, shiraz, chenin, sauv) ▪ 60t/3,000cs own label 30% red 70% white ▪ PO Box 53372 Kenilworth 7745 ▪ admin@tierhoek.com ▪ www.tierhoek.com ▪ S 32°23'27.49" E 018°51'24.14" ▪ **T +27 (0)21-674-3041** ▪ F +27 (0)21-674-3041

With the help of winemaker Roger Burton, Shelley Sandell is keeping late husband Tony's dream alive near the top of Piekenierskloof Pass. Tony had moved gigantic boulders to add 16 ha of vineyard to the 60 year-old ungrafted grenache and 40 year-old chenin vines already there when they bought the farm in 2001. Recent high spots include admission to the International Grenache Symposium and having their 2009 vintage voted 2nd best SA Chenin in Decanter magazine.

Tierhoek range

★★★★ **Grenache** Barely detectable oaking on pale, sweet-fruited **09** with dollop shiraz to spice generous, supple fruit. Warm finish not out of synch with generous style.

★★★★ **Grenache Syrah** NEW Wild berry & scrub aromas on **09** blend, leading to enticing, abundant rich & spicy flavours. Youthful & generous, with sufficient tannin & firm acidity to contain ripeness.

★★★★ **Chenin Blanc** ✓ Preview off-dry **10** gorgeously rich & soft with layers of beguiling fruitiness before variety's steely acidity unsheathed to sculpt long, focused, flavoursome finish.

★★★★ **Sauvignon Blanc** ✓ Incredibly fresh, complex, minerally **11** (★★★★★) has layered, textured depth & impressive, unfurling flinty length. More poise & generosity than **10**. Preview, so rating provisional.

★★★★ **Straw Wine** Delightful **06**'s 'air-dried' chenin displayed rich honeyed flavours when tasted mid-09, spiced by time in oak. Fresh, savoury acidity balanced unctuous sweetness.

Discontinued: **Shiraz**.

Piekenierskloof range

★★★★ **Piekenier's Sauvignon Blanc** NEW ✓ Fine, bone-dry & minerally **10** over-delivers on quality, with steely precision & long, flinty finish. Will unfold with further time in bottle.

White ★★★★ Structured sauvignon, chardonnay **10** blend tasted last year; emphatic cool-climate acidity. Discontinued: **Red**. — IM

- ■ **Timbili** *see* Ernst Gouws & Co Wines
- ■ **Tin Mine** *see* Zevenwacht
- ■ **Title Deed** *see* Croydon Vineyard Residential Estate
- ■ **TJ** *see* Twee Jonge Gezellen Estate-The House of Krone

TMV Wines

WO: Tulbagh/Coastal/Western Cape ▪ Est 1999 ▪ 1stB 2004 ▪ Closed to public ▪ Owner(s) Jason Scott & George Austin ▪ Winemaker(s) Rebecca Tanner (Jul 2009) ▪ ±500cs own label 50% red 45% white 5% sweet wine + 800cs for Woolworths ▪ PO Box 19 Tulbagh 6820 ▪ tmvwines@gmail.com ▪ **T +27 (0)82-897-2272** ▪ F +27 (0)82-897-2272

This was the name of the range of bought-in wines at Tulbagh Mountain Vineyards. But when Jason and Jennifer Scott and George Austin sold that farm, they cannily retained this brand – and the excellent wines bearing it. No new vintages (though the fourth edition of the splendid Vin Pi is bottled and waiting its turn); the notes below are from previous editions.

★★★★☆ **Swartland Syrah** 🗐 Delicious **07**, with fleshy succulence; subtle tannin & oaking.

★★★★ **Mourvèdre-Cinsault 06** one-off, previously noted for iron & spice tones, warmingly long. W Cape.

★★★★☆ **White** Earth & minerals with riper spicy flavours on oaked **09** chenin-led quintet. Natural ferment lessens varietal dominance, adds intricacy. Soft but well structured, persistent. WO Coastal.

★★★★☆ **Vin Pi Three** Gorgeous **NV** sticky from air-dried Swartland chenin, solera-aged. 3rd edition, with lifted honey, lingering toffee, apricot. Fine acidity prevents cloy (despite 300g/l sugar!). — AL

Tokara

Location/map: Stellenbosch ▪ WO: Stellenbosch/Walker Bay/Western Cape/Elgin ▪ 1stB 2001 ▪ Tasting & sales Mon-Fri 9–5 Sat/Sun 10–3 ▪ Closed Easter Fri/Mon & Dec 25 ▪ Tokara Restaurant Tue-Sun lunch 12.30-2.30 dinner 7-9.30 ▪ Delicatessen Tue-Sun 10-4 ▪ Facilities for children ▪ Gift shop ▪ Art exhibitions ▪ Owner(s) GT & Anne-Marie Ferreira ▪ Winemaker(s) Miles Mossop (Jan 2000), with Dumisani Mathonsi (Jan 2004) ▪ Viticulturist(s) Aidan Morton (Nov 2000) ▪ 104ha (cabs s/f, grenache, malbec, merlot, mourv, p verdot, ptage, shiraz, chard, chenin, sauv, sem) ▪ 705t/50,000cs own label 40% red 59% white 1% rosé ▪ PO Box 662 Stellenbosch 7599 ▪ wine@tokara.com ▪ www.tokara.com ▪ S 33° 55' 2.9" E 018° 55' 13.7" ▪ **T +27 (0)21-808-5900** ▪ F +27 (0)21-808-5911

For half a decade this Guide's entry for banker GT Ferriera's grand project just outside Stellenbosch town carried, essentially, the plaintive indication: 'Nothing yet - see Zondernaam'. Under the latter name a few wines were released, until in 2006: 'The wait is over', and we listed (in red ink) four Tokara wines. Since when the range has grown greatly, as has the prestige accruing to the winery (and its winemaker since the start, Miles Mossop). Vineyard size too has grown, at home and on newer Tokara properties in the Hemel-en-Aarde area and in Elgin. These bring further interest and breadth to the collection of modern classics made here: refined, restrained but fruit-filled, approachable wines. But, as if declaring definitive maturity for the project, that old Zondernaam label is disappearing.

Reserve Collection

★★★★☆ **Cabernet Sauvignon 02** (★★★★), with cab & petit verdot portions, fine effort in poor vintage but not up with **01**. Lightish, clean & classic in its elegant balance, but fairly simple. Drink soon.

★★★★☆ **Director's Reserve Red** Cab-based with 4 other varieties. Youthful **08** in modern style, with lots of ripe, sweet fruit & obvious oak, but all expressed with refinement & restraint. Under suave, smooth silkiness ripples a serious muscularity - acidity, superfine tannins. Give 3+ years.

★★★★ **Stellenbosch Chardonnay** 🗔 After step-up **09** (★★★★★), **10** leaner, with subtle aromas & flavours & well-integrated oak. Plenty of limy-lemon acidity in its make-up.

★★★★ **Walker Bay Chardonnay** More expressive than Stellenbosch version in **10**, gentler & more delicate, with charming light delicacy, harmonious balance, & lingering flavours.

★★★★☆ **Walker Bay Sauvignon Blanc** 🗁 **10** (★★★★) lighter & leaner than **09**, with a strong green bite to finish. But good balance not in question, nor the interesting & lingering aromas, flavours.

★★★★☆ **Elgin Sauvignon Blanc** 🗔 🗁 Coolly refined **10** riper & broader than Walker Bay version, nicely combining the greener asparagus notes with citrus & tropical fruit. Subtle intensity, with a thrilling acidity that adds tension but doesn't dominate.

★★★★★ **Director's Reserve White** 🗔 **10** same 70/30 sauvignon/semillon blend as brilliant **09**, though semillon's lemon-cream notes dominant in youth - along with oak notes yet to fully integrate. Racy & elegant, but forceful & subtly flavourful. Should benefit from 5+ years in bottle.

★★★★☆ **Noble Late Harvest** Red-gold **10** perhaps richer than **09**, but more delicate than many examples. The range of flavours (find honey, marmalade, sultana, apricot and more!) packed tightly in clean, fresh whole. WO Western Cape.

Pinotage Await new vintage.

Tokara range

★★★★ **Shiraz** 🗔 **09** well-knit, with pleasing range of notes from perfumed blackcurrant to dry herbalness. Good, firm structure, just a bit drying on the finish. Should benefit from few years in bottle.

★★★★ **Sauvignon Blanc** ✓ 🗔 🗁 **10** as fine a bargain as usual. It has weight as well as characterful flavour (nothing too showy, though), but is mostly about crisp, suave precision.

Cabernet Sauvignon 🗔 ★★★★ Seriously made & rather delicious **09** with usual dollops other Bordeaux varieties. Subtly oaked. Drinkable now but no hurry. **Grenache Rosé** 🗔 🗁 ★★★ Bone-dry & fresh **11**, the spicy, fruity charm well controlled & unfrivolous. WO Walker Bay. **Chardonnay** ✓ 🗔 🗁 ★★★★ Uncomplicated, lightish but lively & appealing **10**. Lemony fruit & a touch of richness in its good balance. WO Western Cape, as for Sauvignon. **Noble Late Harvest** Occasional release. — TJ

■ **Tokolosh** see Klein Parys Vineyards
■ **Tooverberg** see Klein Parys Vineyards

Topaz Wine

Location/map/WO: Stellenbosch ▪ Est 2000 ▪ 1stB 2001 ▪ Tasting & sales by prior arrangement ▪ Wines also available at cellardoor prices from Vineyard Connection ▪ Owner(s) Topaz Wine Company (Pty) Ltd, shareholders Clive Torr, Tanja Beutler, Anthony Hill & Christopher Cosgrove ▪ Cellarmaster(s) Clive Torr (May 2000) ▪ Winemaker(s) Clive Torr, with Tanja Beutler (both May 2000) ▪ 0.04ha (pinot) ▪ 3t/875cs own label 80% red 20% white ▪ IPW ▪ PO Box 804 Somerset Mall 7137 ▪ tanja@topazwines.co.za ▪ www.topazwines.co.za ▪ S 33° 50' 55.67" E 018° 51' 26.19" ▪ **T +27 (0)21-855-4275** ▪ F +27 (0)86-612-6118

Buying in most of their fruit (except for the decade-old half-hectare in the garden) allows original SA garagistes Clive Torr and Tanja Beutler (and a couple of new shareholders) the freedom to experiment with various styles, varieties and blends, as the name of their latest offering, recession-beating Custom Crush, suggests.

★★★★ **Pinot Noir** Previously tasted **08** elegant yet lively, concentrated varietal farmyard character. Accessible in youth, but firm structure & minerality suggested promising future. Elgin vines.

★★★★ **Syrah** Last tasted was elegant, smoothly textured & fine-tannined **07**.

★★★★ **Custom Crush** NEW ✓ Fresh, complex, herbal **08** equal blend cab & cab franc with well integrated oaking. Joyful & inviting, a wine to tuck into at the price, delivering the smile promised on the label.

★★★★ **Viognier** Oaked, off-dry **09**. Rich, concentrated flavours gave hedonistic pleasure last year.

Chardonnay Await next. — IM

Topiary Wines

Location/map/WO: Franschhoek ▪ Est 2005 ▪ 1stB 2006 ▪ Tasting, sales & tours Mon-Fri 11-5 Sat (summer only) 10-4 ▪ Closed Easter Sun, Dec 25/26 & Jan 1 ▪ Meals/refreshments on special request; or BYO picnic ▪ Small tour

groups ▪ 1.7km Fynbos hiking trail ▪ Conservation area ▪ Owner(s) Roy & Hilary Andrews ▪ Cellarmaster(s) Mark Carmichael-Green (Nov 2010, consultant) ▪ Winemaker(s) Mark Carmichael-Green (Nov 2010, consultant), with JM Basson (Nov 2010, consultant) ▪ Viticulturist(s) Malcolm Pemberton (Jan 2005), with Paul Wallace (consultant) ▪ 63ha/20ha (cab, shiraz, chard, chenin) ▪ 50t/1,980cs own label 72% red 15% rosé 13% MCC + 13,350L bulk ▪ IPW ▪ PO Box 108 La Motte 7691 ▪ topiarysales@telkomsa.net ▪ www.topiarywines.com ▪ S 33° 51'52.2" E 019° 2'39.0" ▪ **T** +27 (0)21-867-0258 ▪ **F** +27 (0)86-750-1742

The name for this Franschhoek property comes from farm manager Malcolm Pemberton's hobby, amply displayed in the sculpted garden. A young operation by industry standards, they accidently discovered a treasure: the highly rated Blanc de Blancs méthode cap classique sparkling was initially conceived as a vehicle for early harvested grapes from a young chardonnay vineyard. With two 5 star ratings in succession, they're reassessing and further chardonnay plantings are planned.

★★★★ **Cabernet Sauvignon** ✓ Seductive perfume array - black plum, scrub, sweet spice - but the palate is the main attraction: fruit rich, lush, smooth textured. **08** ready now, can keep a few years.

★★★★ **Shiraz** ✓ Tar & wild berries in **08**, follows in **07**'s footsteps with its succulence & silky smooth body. Drinking so well, hard to resist or cellar.

★★★★ **Rosé** 🗏 Last edition just-dry **09** (★★★★) from cab & shiraz was for al fresco sipping. Not as convincing as **08**.

★★★★ **Blanc de Blancs Brut** ✓ Toned, polished méthode cap classique sparkling from chardonnay, **09** showcases the variety's citrus zest & leafy freshness. 18 months on lees gives creamy biscuit balance to the racy acidity. Confirms complex **08** was not a one-off achievement of excellence.

Cabernet Sauvignon-Shiraz ★★★★ Despite 54% cab, **07** has the dark fruit, gamey profile of shiraz. Underpinned by firm tannins, will keep 3-5 years. — CR

▪ **Tormentoso** *see* MAN Vintners
▪ **Tortoise Mountain** *see* Saam Mountain Vineyards
▪ **Totus** *see* Trajan Wines
▪ **Towerkop** *see* Ladismith Cellar - SCV
▪ **Township Winery** *see* The Township Winery

Trajan Wines

Location: Stellenbosch ▪ WO: Coastal/Western Cape ▪ Est 2005 ▪ 1stB 2008 ▪ Closed to public ▪ Owner(s) Mark van Schalkwyk & Constant Visser ▪ Winemaker(s) Mark van Schalkwyk (Sep 2005) ▪ Viticulturist(s) Outback Viticulture ▪ 2,500cs own label 70% red 30% white ▪ PO Box 1498 Stellenbosch 7599 ▪ info@trajanwines.co.za ▪ www.trajanwines.co.za ▪ **T** +27 (0)83-505-2681 ▪ **F** +27 (0)86-299-4281

Trajan was founded to export bulk wine, but the emphasis has shifted to higher quality and the local market. A stylish chenin has been added to the top-tier Totus Premium range and now a mid-priced line-up is planned. Funding continues for community projects: a farmworkers' crèche and day-care centre, and the Missing Children South Africa Foundation.

Totus Premium range
Cabernet Sauvignon 🗏 ★★★★ Bright, sweet blackcurrant tones in light-textured **08**, firm tannin frame. This & next 2 tasted last year. **Pinotage** 🗏 ★★★ **08** was balanced & easy-drinking last time, structured to highlight gentle raspberry juiciness, finished with pleasant bitter nip. **Shiraz-Mourvèdre** 🗏 ★★★★ Appealing **08** partnership mid-2010 was full of spicy warmth, gamey red fruit extras. Well structured without heaviness. **Chenin Blanc** NEW 🗏 🥂 ★★★★ Appealing **10** shows lovely sunny ripeness, deftly handled oaking lends body & form without dominating. **Sauvignon Blanc** ✓ 🗏 🥂 ★★★★ Classy, nicely balanced **11**, typical Durbanville fruit character, ripe & supple, with leesy weight & crisp acidity. WO W Cape. — GdB

▪ **Transkaroo-Bring My Huis Toe/Take Me Home** *see* Boer & Brit
▪ **Travino** *see* Klawer Wine Cellars

Tread Lightly by Backsberg

Location: Paarl ▪ WO: Western Cape ▪ Est/1stB 2010 ▪ Tasting & sales at Backsberg Mon-Fri 8-5 Sat 9.30-4.30 Sun 10.30-4.30 ▪ Fee R15 ▪ Open 365 days a year ▪ Cellar tours by appt ▪ Backsberg Restaurant (see Restaurants section) ▪ Tour groups ▪ Gift shop ▪ Figs & preserves for sale ▪ BYO picnic ▪ Conferences ▪ Weddings & functions ▪ Conservation area ▪ Sunday picnic concerts (Dec-Jan) ▪ Owner(s) Michael Back ▪ Winemaker(s) Guillaume Nell (Jan 2008) ▪ Viticulturist(s) Clive Trent (Jul 1992) ▪ (cab, merlot, shiraz, chard) ▪ PO Box 537 Suider-Paarl 7624 ▪ info@ treadlightly.co.za ▪ www.treadlightly.co.za ▪ S33° 49'42.9" E018° 54'56.9" ▪ **T +27 (0)21-875-5141** ▪ F +27 (0)21-875-5144

The creation of family-owned and -run Backsberg, this first certified South African wine in lightweight and shatterproof PET (plastic) bottles has proved a particular hit with concertgoers, picnickers and hikers - and so has the wine inside. An easy-drinking chenin has been added to the line-up, and the Back family are confident the popularity of this alternative packaging will continue to grow.

Tread Lightly range

Chenin Blanc NEW ☺ 🍷 ★★★ Fruity & juicy **11**, crisp apple & lemon flavours. Fresh & summery.

Merlot 🍷 ★★★★ Ripe vanilla-soaked plums & spice, **08** is easy to drink, with subtle oak influence. Not retasted, as for next. **Sauvignon Blanc** 🍷 ★★★ Greenpepper & gooseberry billowed from **10**, fresh & crisp when tasted last time. — WB

■ **Tribal** *see African Terroir*
■ **Tricolore** *see Weltevrede Estate*

Trizanne Signature Wines

Location: Somerset West ▪ WO: Elim/Swartland ▪ Est 2008 ▪ 1stB 2009 ▪ Closed to public ▪ Wine sales via website ▪ Owner(s)/winemaker(s) Trizanne Barnard ▪ 12t/650cs own label 40% red 60% white ▪ Postnet Suite 407 Private Bag X15 Somerset West 7129 ▪ info@trizanne.co.za ▪ www.trizanne.co.za ▪ **T +27 (0)21-789-2185/+27 (0)82-383-6664** ▪ F +27 (0)86-669-0913

'Signature' as a title for Trizanne Barnard's wine range - and it has become a range - is not some marketing hype but a serious quest to put her stamp on carefully sourced grapes from different terroirs. There can be no greater contrast than the sleek classical Sauvignon-Semillon from Elim and the dark Swartland wildness of the Shiraz, except for the polish she has given both. There is a third wine on the way, small volume and just for export, unrevealed at time of going to press.

★★★★ **Syrah** NEW ✓ **09** is 86% shiraz, plus splashes mourvèdre, grenache & carignan, which Trizanne B's careful touch converts to a sleek, scrub-toned thing of beauty, full of interest. WO Swartland.

★★★★ **Sauvignon Blanc-Semillon** 🍷 🌿 Passionfruit attests to ripeness of Elim grapes but no mistaking **10**'s taut intensity, limy minerality. Slight oak infusion from barrelled semillon. 4+ years ahead. — CR

Truter Family Wines   NEW

WO: Coastal ▪ Est 2008 ▪ 1stB 2010 ▪ Closed to public ▪ Owner(s) Hugo & Celeste Truter ▪ Winemaker(s) Hugo Truter ▪ 250cs own label 100% white ▪ hugo@truterfamilywines.co.za ▪ www.truterfamilywines.co.za ▪ **T +27 (0)83-639-6288**

Hugo Truter is cellarmaster at a large Wellington cellar while his wife Celeste is also a trained winemaker. 'With two winemakers living under the same roof, it was inevitable that we'd end up with our own label.' Only one wine to date: Agaat Christina, Agaat (Afrikaans for the semi-precious gemstone agate) being the stone associated with Gemini, the star sign of their twin sons, while Christina was the name of Hugo's grandmother.

★★★★ **Agaat Christina** ✓ 🍷 Sauvignon, nouvelle-led **10** attractive & nuanced bouquet of fresh grass, peach & capsicum, sweet-sour tropical fruit flavour balanced by lively acidity. — Panel

TTT Cellar

Location/WO: Calitzdorp ▪ Map: Klein Karoo & Garden Route ▪ 1stB 2003 ▪ Tasting, sales & tours Mon-Fri 8-4 Sat 8-2 Sun by appt ▪ Closed Easter Fri-Mon, Apr 27, May 1, Dec 25 & Jan 1 ▪ Honey & olive oil ▪ BYO picnic ▪ Owner(s) Ashley & Pat Mason ▪ Cellarmaster(s)/viticulturist(s) Ashley Mason ▪ Winemaker(s) Ashley Mason, with Johan Julies ▪ 0.5ha (souzão, tinta barocca, touriga nacional, hanepoot) ▪ 4t/300cs own label 100% red ▪ PO Box 7067 Newton Park 6055 ▪ tttcellars@iafrica.com ▪ S 33° 31' 50.94" E 021° 41' 44.88" ▪ **T +27 (0)44-213-3114** ▪ F +27 (0)44-213-3114

Ashley 'Sparks' Mason runs an electrical contracting business in Port Elizabeth, but a hobby that's taking up ever more space in his life is winemaking on the Calitzdorp farm he owns with wife Pat. Daughters Debbie and Talana contribute cross-stitch pictures for sale in the tasting area, along with honey, olive oil and knitted scarves.

LTD ★★ Previously listed as 'Petit Verdot'. Last year's preview revisited, **10** beginning to tire, needs drinking soon. **Shiraz** Untasted. **Hilltop Blend** ★★★ Still-selling **07**, from port grapes, was lightly oaked & carefree previously. **Rosé** Await next. **Chenin Blanc** NEW ★★★ **11** fairly neutral, doesn't linger. **Muscat d'Brigne** NEW **11** mix mainly chenin & white muscat de Frontignan (unfortified), too unformed to rate. **Hanepoot** ★★★★ Previous edition, fragrant **08** fortified dessert took big step up from last **05** (★★★). Rich but uncloying, extravagantly flavoured. **Red Muscadel** NEW ★★ Red-berry-infused **10** fortified dessert in lighter style, with low (15%) alc. **Cape Ruby** ★★ Port-style **NV** from 50/50 touriga & tinta. Dried herbs & dark fruit, very dry. **Cape Vintage** ★★★ Last edition **09** had underlying Xmas cake, redcurrant notes, sweet & fiery tail but lacked grip. **Cape White** Port-style fortified from chenin, **NV**. Now bottled, past best. Discontinued: **Cabernet Sauvignon**. — Panel

Tukulu

Location: Darling ▪ WO: Groenekloof ▪ Est 1998 ▪ 1stB 1999 ▪ Tasting by appt at Trinity Lodge in Darling ▪ Owner(s) Distell, Leopont 98 Properties, Maluti Groenekloof Community Trust, a group of Gauteng based black businessmen ▪ Winemaker(s) Samuel Viljoen (Sep 2007) ▪ Viticulturist(s) Hannes van Rensburg (1998) ▪ 975ha/382ha under vine ▪ 73% red 27% white ▪ BWI, Fairtrade, SGS Lacon, WIETA ▪ PO Box 184 Stellenbosch 7599 ▪ tukulu@capelegends.co.za ▪ www.tukulu.co.za ▪ **T +27 (0)21-809-8330** ▪ F +27 (0)21-882-9575

One of the partners in this joint venture is a consortium of black taveners who are promoting a culture of wine in the 'townships', where beer is the traditional drink. Their task has been helped through the setting up of the Soweto Wine Festival and the newer Gugulethu Wine Festival, at both of which Tukulu participated. 'The chenin blanc and pinotage were particularly well-liked at both,' says Gwen Job, Tukulu Brand Manager.

Fairtrade Cabernet Sauvignon ☺ 🍽 🌿 ★★★ **10** in ready-to-drink style. Soft, mouthful crushed blackberries; minimal tannin resistance. **Fairtrade Chenin Blanc** ☺ 🍽 🌿 ★★★ Floral, honey fragrance, dainty & sprightly fruity acid attractions on medium-bodied, dry **11**. Adds 'Fairtrade' to name. This & all following wines sampled ex-tank.

Papkuilsfontein Pinotage ★★★☆ Previously just 'Pinotage'. Pure ripe raspberry notes on modern **09**. Juicy, smooth & fresh with nip framing tannin. **Fairtrade Unwooded Syrah** 🍽 🌿 ★★★ Smoky, dark berry aromatic intensity; contrasting juicy, easy-going flavours, supple tannins on **10**. **Organic Chardonnay** 🍽 🌿 🌿 ★★★★ **11** shows promise. Inviting lemon butter aromas, brisk citrusy flavours balanced but yet to integrate. May rate higher once bottled. No **09**, **10**. **Fairtrade Sauvignon Blanc** 🍽 🌿 ★★★ Lush pineapple aromas on **11**. Zesty with sweet-fruited finish. Discontinued: **Organic Sangiovese**, **Shiraz**, **Viognier**. — AL

■ **Tulbagh Mountain Vineyards** see Fable

Tulbagh Winery

Location: Tulbagh/Porterville ▪ Map: Tulbagh ▪ WO: Tulbagh/Coastal ▪ Est 1906/2006 ▪ 1stB 1910 ▪ Tulbagh Cellar: Tasting & sales Mon-Fri 8–5 Sat & pub hols 9–1 Sun at Paddagang Wine Shop 11–3 ▪ Porterville Cellar: Tasting & sales Mon-Fri 8–5 ▪ Closed Easter Fri-Sun & Dec 25/26 ▪ Cellar tours by appt ▪ Gifts ▪ Farm produce ▪ BYO picnic ▪ Conferences ▪ Walks/hikes ▪ Mountain biking in the area ▪ Owner(s) 86 members ▪ Cellarmaster(s) Production Manager Naude Bruwer (Jan 2010) ▪ Winemaker(s) Porterville: John King, with Paul Jordaan (Feb 2010/Apr 2010); Tulbagh: Helena Neethling, with Anmar Roberts (Jun 2010/Mar 2010) ▪ Viticulturist(s) Hugo Lambrechts (Oct 2007) ▪ 1,230ha (cab, merlot, ptage, shiraz, chenin, chard, sauv) ▪ 11,823t/50,000cs own label 60% red 35% white 5% rosé & 8m L bulk + 20,000cs for clients ▪ Brands for clients: Grimont (Germany), Millberg (UK/France) ▪ IPW ▪ PO Box 85 Tulbagh 6820; PO Box 52 Porterville 6810 ▪ info@tulbaghwine.co.za ▪ www.tulbaghwine.co.za ▪ S 33° 15' 8.8" E 019° 8' 36.5" ▪ **T +27 (0)23-230-1001 (Tulbagh); +27 (0)22-931-2170 (Porterville)** ▪ F +27 (0)23-230-1358; +27 (0)22-931-2171

With a new team at the helm since 2009, it is clear that their changes have successfully been implemented to improve quality, especially on the Klein Tulbagh wines. The product range has been streamlined and is more precisely focused to cater for the specific needs of the 14 export markets. To keep it all exciting they have added the interesting Pinotage Doux Sparkling and the quirky Sauvignon, which blends cabernet sauvignon and sauvignon blanc).

Klein Tulbagh Reserve range

Cabernet Sauvignon ★★★ 10 sample promises oak-driven choc-mocha notes with ripe cherry support, richer than previous **05**. **Merlot ★★★ 04** showed developed, earthy notes harmonised by delicate cherry fruit. Tasted last year, like next wine. **Pinotage ★★★★ 08** had youthful vibrancy, refreshing red fruits & dry finish. **Shiraz** ◙ **★★★** Jump from **04** to **10** sample with bold fruit, 15.4% alc, obvious oak in modern idiom. **Vintage Port ★★★** Last tasted **02** from pinotage had old-style lower alc, high sweetness .

Porter Mill Station range

Cabernet Sauvignon ★★ As for below these for export, not reassessed. Ripe prune on **06**, hint austerity relieved by lingering fruit flavours. **Pinotage ★★★ 06** was well balanced with fine tannins & dry end. **Shiraz ★★★** Oaky, lean & savoury **06**. **Chenin Blanc ★★★** Confectionary aromas & perky freshness on food-friendly **07**. **Sauvignon Blanc ★★** Ripe fruit on light, dry **09**.

Tulbagh range

> **Pinotage** ☺ ▤ ◙ **★★★** Dark fruit bellows from juicy, yet dry-ending **10** pre-bottling sample. **Chardonnay** ☺ ▤ ◙ **★★★** Fresh, unwooded **11** is dry, for summery refreshment. **Chenin Blanc** ☺ ▤ ◙ **★★★** Stone fruit & apple freshness combine on balanced, fruity & dry **11**. Step up from delicate **10**.

Cabernet Sauvignon ▤ ◙ **★★ 10** has slight herbal astringency. **Merlot** ▤ ◙ **★★** Attractive choc-mint nose on **10** has awkward tannins to end. **Shiraz** ▤ ◙ **★★★** Previewed **10** is full-fruited, with very attractive & sumptuous berry deliciousness on the palate. Ends with powerful punch. **Shiraz-Pinotage** ▤ ◙ **★★** Coffee aromas, juicy sweetness on off-dry **11**. WO Coastal. **Rosé** ▤ ◙ **★★** Semi-sweet & light **11** has typical pinotage redfruit appeal. **Sauvignon Blanc** ▤ ◙ **★★★ 11** has just 10.5% alc, crisp acid & ends dry. **Colombard-Chenin Blanc** ▤ ◙ **★★ 11** 60/40 combo in fruity off-dry mould. **Sparkling Pinotage Doux** NEW ◙ **★★★** Interesting debut **10** sparkling & sweet, has firm end. WO Coastal. **Sauvignon** NEW ▤ ◙ **★★** Easy off-dry red **10**, 70/30 combo cab & sauvignon blanc. **Port ★★** Oxidative **07** with toffee sweetness.

Paddagang range

Paddapoot Hanepoot ★★ Sold out, await new. **Brulpadda ★★★** Pinotage/ruby cab combo on sweet **NV** fortified. — JP

■ **Tullie Family Vineyards** see Lanner Hill
■ **Tumara** see Bellevue Estate Stellenbosch

Twee Jonge Gezellen Estate-The House of Krone   🍴🍷📷

Location/map: Tulbagh ▪ WO: Western Cape/Tulbagh ▪ Est 1710 ▪ 1stB 1937 ▪ Tasting & sales Mon-Fri 9–4 Sat & pub hols 10-2 ▪ No charge for casual tasting; formal tasting + large groups: fee on request ▪ Cellar tours Mon-Fri 11 & 3; Sat & pub hols 11 ▪ Closed Easter Fri-Mon, May 1, Dec 25/26 & Jan 1 ▪ Annual festivals: Christmas in Winter (Jun) & Summer Elegance (Dec) ▪ Owner(s)/cellarmaster(s) Nicky Krone ▪ Winemaker(s) Matthew Krone, with Stephan de Beer ▪ Viticulturist(s) Nicky & Matthew Krone ▪ 550ha/100ha (pinot, shiraz, chard) ▪ 5% red 80% white 15% rosé ▪ PO Box 16 Tulbagh 6820 ▪ tjg@mweb.co.za ▪ www.houseofkrone.co.za ▪ S 33° 14'18.1" E 019° 6'51.8" ▪ **T** +27 (0)23-230-0680 ▪ F +27 (0)23-230-0686

Nicky Krone dreamed of making a South African equivalent of champagne back in 1969; he had all the equipment. What would have been a ground-breaking wine had to be postponed because of the ground breaking – the 1969 earthquake. It took until 1987 for the first Krone Borealis (named for the Corona Borealis constellation, the golden crown Bacchus threw into the heavens to prove his love of Ariadne, and a play on 'Krone') to be made and another three years before it was launched. More recently the range has been increasingly trimmed, and Mary and Nicky Krone's favourite wine style has become their focus of attention.

Krone range

★★★★ Borealis Brut Fresh & refreshing 50/50 chardonnay, pinot noir blend. **08** distinguished by its bruised apple features, lively creamy mousse & truly 'brut' conclusion. Elegant, as was **07** (**★★★★★**).

★★★★☆ Nicolas Charles Krone Marque 1 NV multi-vintage MCC (**01, 02, 03**). With extra lees contact, we noted greater toasty, creamily rich distinction last year. Vibrates with life & class. 50/50 pinot/chard.

★★★★ **Rosé Cuvée Brut** Previously tasted, salmon-hued **05** showed bracing briskness to complement food or sip solo. Mirrors **02** predecessor.

TJ range
Discontinued: **Light**. — AL

- Twin's Peak *see Lateganskop Winery*
- Two Centuries *see Nederburg Wines*
- Two Cubs *see Knorhoek Wines*

Two Oceans

Location: Stellenbosch ▪ WO: Western Cape ▪ Tasting & sales at Bergkelder ▪ Owner(s) Distell ▪ Cellarmaster(s) Deon Boshoff & Andrea Freeborough ▪ Winemaker(s) Justin Corrans, Peter Badenhorst, Bonny van Niekerk, Elize Coetzee ▪ Viticulturist(s) Bennie Liebenberg, Annelie Viljoen ▪ Distell PO Box 184 Stellenbosch 7599 ▪ info@distell. co.za ▪ www.twooceanswines.co.za ▪ T +27 (0)21-809-7000

Awards and accolades continue to roll in for this good-value Distell brand, which offers easy-drinking reliability. A new partnership sees Two Oceans supporting the WWF Southern African Sustainable Seafood Initiative (SASSI) by funding wallet-sized cards indicating the best seafood choices from a sustainability point of view. The intention is to team up with similar initiatives around the world, reinforcing the link between maritime influences on the wine and the wine itself. Lighter-weight bottles further underline the commitment to eco-improvement.

Shiraz Rosé ☺ ★★★ **11** a light, off-dry candyfloss & berry patio pleaser. **Chardonnay** ☺ ★★★ Delicious tangerine & cream on light platform of oak, **10** integrated, rounded & long.

Pinot Noir ✓ ★★★★ Delicate nuanced chalky cranberry on previewed **11**, fungal notes develop in the glass, merge with smoky char & good grip. Integrated lithe elegance. Fine effort, bargain priced, nudges next level. **Pinotage** ★★ Cherry smoke on **10**, medium body with dab sugar, as all the reds. **Shiraz** ★★★ Plum, cocoa & pepper, **10** densely textured, gentle grip from 3 months new French oak. Mouthfilling, long spicy finish. **Cabernet Sauvignon-Merlot** ★★★ Faint herbal edge to mulberry fruit, **11** pleasant, light bodied & somewhat less intense/vibrant than previous. **Soft & Fruity Red** 🗎 ★★ Ample berry fruit, liquorice twist, **10** straightforward easy-drinker. **Shiraz-Cabernet Sauvignon** ★★★ Light plum pudding, spice & pepper; soft, mouthfilling & harmonious. **10** gentle oaking, French chips used. Long tail. **Merlot-Shiraz** ★★★ Easy-drinking **09** offers spicy plum & cherry lightness. **Pinot Grigio** 🗎 ★★ **11** has green apricot tang & light delicacy, though doesn't linger. **Sauvignon Blanc** 🗎 🖾 ★★★ Green apple crispness to **11**, white pepper finish. **Semillon-Chardonnay** ★★ 70/30 mix in dryish **10**, nettle & cream, soft oak sheen. **Chenin Blanc-Sauvignon Blanc** 🗎 ★★★ Chenin's passionfruit tang leads zesty **11** summer refresher. **Fresh & Fruity White** 🗎 ★★ Fresh guava & lemon on **11**, more satisfying than simple & light **10** (★★). — Panel

- Two Tunns *see Valley Vineyards Wine Company*
- Tygerberg *see Altydgedacht Estate*
- Uiterwyk Estate *see DeWaal Wines*

Uitkyk Estate

Location/map: Stellenbosch ▪ WO: Simonsberg–Stellenbosch ▪ Est 1712 ▪ 1stB 1957 ▪ Tasting, sales & cellar tours Mon-Fri 9–5 Sat/Sun 10–4 ▪ Fee R15/5 wines ▪ Closed Easter Fri & Dec 25 ▪ Facilities for children ▪ Tour groups ▪ BYO picnic; or order 24hrs in advance ▪ Conferences ▪ Conservation area ▪ 4x4 trail ▪ Manor House museum ▪ Owner(s) Lusan Premium Wines ▪ Cellarmaster(s) Estelle Lourens (Oct 2000) ▪ Winemaker(s) Estelle Lourens (Oct 2000), with Ian Wolmarans (Jul 2011) ▪ 591ha/140ha (cab, shiraz, chard, pinot grigio, sauv) ▪ 772t/9,200cs 55% red 45% white (Uitkyk) & 35,500cs 53% red 45% white 2% rosé (Flat Roof Manor) ▪ BWI champion ▪ PO Box 104 Stellenbosch 7599 ▪ svanheerden@distell.co.za, cevangraan@distell.co.za ▪ www.uitkyk.co.za ▪ S 33° 51'24.8" E 018° 51'50.7" ▪ T +27 (0)21-884-4416 ▪ F +27 (0)21-884-4717

This is a historic property with a homestead in the neoclassical style and thought to be the work of famed French designer Louis Michel Thibault. Winemaking focuses, they say here, on harnessing what nature has to offer. With a view to the future, work has begun on a MCC for release in perhaps a few years.

★★★★ **Carlonet** Mostly cab (a smidgen of shiraz), the latest of this historic label not up to standard of **07**. **08** (★★★★) has sweetness – from oaking & high 14.9% alc – over green notes.

Shiraz Reserve Await next. **Cabernet Sauvignon-Shiraz** ★★★★ Soft & satisfying **07**, had expressive liquorice & cold coffee notes last edition. **Chardonnay** ✓ 🈂 ★★★★ **10** has rich rounded fruit, with satisfying oak aromas. Fruit & oak sweetness countered by balanced dry end. **Sauvignon Blanc** 🍴 🈂 ★★★ Tank sample of **11** in usual crisp grassy style with floral overtones. A zesty acidity & dry finish adds focus. — JP

▪ **Uitvlucht** *see* Montagu Wine & Spirits Co

▪ **Ukuzala** *see* Mountain River Wines

Ultra Liquors

Location: Cape Town ▪ WO: Western Cape/Coastal/Darling ▪ Owner(s) Colin Robinson ▪ Winemaker(s) various winemakers ▪ 426 Main Rd Wynberg Cape Town 7824 ▪ marknorrish@ultraliquors.co.za, dale@tablebayinternational.co.za ▪ **T** +27 (0)21-797-4341 ▪ F +27 (0)21-797-4351

This nationwide drinks retailer sources its own-brand wines under the intrepid leadership of Mark Norrish, pitching them at remarkable prices for the quality. The corporate emphasis is on knowledgeable service, and staff is encouraged to complete Cape Wine Academy courses, which, Mark believes, 'provides our customers with a richer and more satisfying shopping experience'.

Table Bay range

Cabernet Sauvignon ★★★★ **07** & **08**, previously reviewed, both took step up with similar characteristics: toasty vanilla, mocha-tinged black cherries. **Merlot** ★★★ Meaty, savoury **08** shows ripe berry fruit. Juicy, smooth. WO Darling. **Shiraz** ★★★ **08** upped the quality last year with spicy leather nuance, ripe berries, lingering juicy finish. **Starboard Red** ★★ Lean, nutty **NV** 4-way blend with hint of jammy red berries. **Spinnaker White** ★★★ **NV** sauvignon-chenin blend with waxy-nutty oxidative notes. **Chenin Blanc** ★★★ Opulent ripe tropical fruit on **11** tank sample is backed by crisp acidity, tangy finish. Shows promise. WO Coastal. **Sauvignon Blanc** ✓ ★★★★ Generous grassy nose on Darling-sourced **11** follows to appealing salty-mineral, lean palate. **Méthode Cap Classique** ✓ ★★★★ **NV** traditional-method bubbly from Robertson chardonnay & pinot noir. Invitingly crisp & fresh, baked apples & cinnamon lifted by lees richness. Discontinued: **Chardonnay**.

Monfort range NEW

Cape Tawny ★★★ Oxidative **NV** toffee-raisin fortified dessert offering from Bonnievale. Has typical spirit grip & unctuous dried fruit flavours.

Secret Cellar range

Cabernet Sauvignon Reserve NEW ☺ ★★★ Competent, middleweight **07** shows evolution, elegant blackcurrant fruit beginning decline. For current enjoyment. **Shiraz Reserve** NEW ☺ ★★★ **07** shows development, but also finesse. Stately oak a tad rich for juicy berry fruit. Drink-now bargain.

Cabernet Sauvignon Selection 633 ★★★ **06** last year tempted with savoury/meaty notes to plush dark berry medley, cranberry twist. **Shiraz Selection 480** ★★★ **04** was more sedate than 275 stablemate, meaty edge to luscious berry fruit. Not revisited, as next 3. **Shiraz Selection 275** ★★★ **05** was big & warming with mulberry & black pepper heart. **Classic Red Selection 220** ★★★ **NV** combo cabs sauvignon & franc last time had plump fruit centre, soft finish. **Cabernet Franc-Petit Verdot Selection 299** Untasted. — GdB

▪ **Umfiki** *see* Goudini Wines

Umkhulu Wines

Location: Franschhoek ▪ Est/1stB 2000 ▪ Closed to public ▪ Owner(s) Fiona Phillips ▪ Winemaker(s) Wilhelm Kritzinger ▪ 10,000cs 100% red ▪ PO Box 132 Simondium 7670 ▪ info@umkhulu.co.za ▪ www.umkhulu.com ▪ **T** +27 (0)21-876-2649 ▪ F +27 (0)21-876-2649

As with all export brands over the past year, it's been a tough one for Umkhulu, the strong Rand a significant factor in this regard. But Fiona Phillips' Umkhulu brand, part of the Cybercellar stable, is still listed with some of the big guns in America, including the cruise line Holland America.

★★★★☆ **Pinotage** Firmish tannins add texture to modern **04**'s slightly sweet fruit. This & all below tasted pvs editions, not revisited. The reds mostly ±yr oak, 25-50% new.

★★★★ **Tian** Cabernet-led Bordeaux blend. Shy **03** (★★★★) light textured; **02** was dense, tad extracted. **Malbec** ★★★★ **05**'s exuberent mulberry fruit reined in by stern tannins. **Shiraz** ★★★★ **04** straightforward & rich. **Ubuntu** ★★★★ Three-way 'Cape blend'pinotage, merlot, petit verdot in pliable **05**. **Akira** ★★★★ Elegant yet generous **03** mixed cabernet, petit verdot & pinotage. **Njalo** ★★★ Few years ago **05**'s tannins needed time or food. Combo merlot, shiraz,pinotage. —

United Nations of Wine

Location: Sandton ▪ Est/1stB 2005 ▪ Closed to public ▪ Owner(s) Dogwood Trust ▪ Cellarmaster(s)/winemaker(s) David John Bate (Jun 2005) ▪ 20,000cs own label 30% red 70% white ▪ 8 Royal Ascot Lane Sandown Sandton 2196 ▪ info@unitednationsofwine.com ▪ www.unitednationsofwine.com ▪ T +27 (0)11-884-3304 ▪ F +27 (0)11-883-0426

Export-orientated United Nations of Wine has expanded into Asia with new representation in Hong Kong and Singapore, and secured national distribution in Canada for what cellarmaster David John Bate calls their 'high quality, affordable wines', citing the carbon neutral Frisky Zebras Shiraz and Sauvignon Blanc as examples of wines that are '100% earth-friendly by nature'.

Dusty Rhino

Black Rhino Limited Release Shiraz 🖿 ★★ Dusty oak overlay on red plum fruit. This range, G Spot, Luscious Hippos & most in the Frisky Zebra line-up still selling, not revisited. All **NV**. **White Rhino Limited Release Chenin Blanc** 🖿 ★★ Tropical-toned & zesty, best enjoyed soon.

Frisky Zebras

Captivating Cabernet Sauvignon 🖿 ★★ Sweet & sour sipper. **Mystic Merlot** 🖿 ★★ Plummy, fresh & quick finishing. **Seductive Shiraz** 🖿 ★★ Brisk & uncomplicated, oak doesn't compromise glugability. New bottling tasted, as for **Sensuous Sauvignon. Succulent Chardonnay** 🖿 ★★★ Step up last edition with vivid lemon flavours, good weight. **Sultry Chenin Blanc** 🖿 ★★★ Herb garden notes, fine flavour. **Sensuous Sauvignon Blanc** 🖿 ★★ Faint notes of gooseberry & peardrops. Previous bottling Canada's Best Wine Under $25.

G Spot

Sinful Shiraz 🖿 ★★ Woody character dominated quiet fruit when last tasted. **Smouldering Sauvignon Blanc** 🖿 ★ Tart & lemony, to whet the appetite.

Harmony Tree range NEW

Shiraz ☺ ★★★ Lightly oaked new addition goes straight to the top of the class. Quite firm, but enough fruity flavour for immediate enjoyment.

Luscious Hippos

Red Hippo Limited Release Pinotage 🖿 ★★ Strawberry-fruited easy swig. **Golden Hippo Limited Release Chardonnay** ★★ Shy & unoaked, with hippo-like girth. — CvZ

uniWines Marketing 🍷🍴🎪🏠📷🎿&

Location: Rawsonville ▪ Map/WO: Breedekloof ▪ Est/1stB 2007 ▪ Tasting & sales Mon-Fri 8–5 Sat 10–2 ▪ Closed Mar 21, Easter Fri-Mon, Apr 27, Jun 16, Dec 25 & Jan 1 ▪ Cellar tours Mon-Fri ▪ BYO picnic ▪ Children welcome ▪ Soetes and soup festival ▪ Breedekloof outdoor festival ▪ Cheese platters by prior arrangement ▪ Conference facilities ▪ Tour groups ▪ Owner(s) 50 shareholders ▪ Cellarmaster(s) Nicolaas Rust (Mar 2008) ▪ Winemaker(s) WS Visagie (Nov 2010), Hattigh de Villiers (Sep 2010), Charl Myburgh (Dec 2007), Schalk van der Merwe (Dec 2007), Christo Smit (Jan 2001) & Marie Stofberg (Nov 2008) ▪ Viticulturist(s) Gert Engelbrecht (Aug 2009) ▪ 6,000ha/2,050ha (cab, cinsaut, merlot, ptage, shiraz, chard, chenin, cbard, sauv) ▪ 36,200t/100,000cs own label 50% red 50% white + 50,000cs for clients ▪ Brands for clients: Cape Promise ▪ ISO 22000:2008, BWI, Fairtrade, IPW, WIETA ▪ PO Box 174 Rawsonville 6845 ▪ info@uniwines.co.za ▪ www.uniwines.co.za, www.grooteiland.co.za ▪ S 33°43'16.7" E 019°21'0.0" ▪ T +27 (0)23-349-1110 ▪ F +27 (0)23-349-1980

This dynamic amalgamation of diverse producers and brands operates from 3 big cellars in the Breedekloof district, Daschbosch, Groot Eiland and Nuwehoop. They produce wine in large volumes, destined mostly for European markets, including Fairtrade products. Now they've engaged consultants to consolidate and stratify their products into more comprehensible, price-pitch targeted ranges. They hope to launch their new image early this year, with an 'iconic' brand to follow soon.

Daschbosch range

★★★★ **Nectar de Provision White** Complex & appealing fortified **NV** from colombard, pungent ripe figs, honey nuances, underlying minerality.

Nectar de Provision Red ★★★ This & White above are local versions of Cognac's classic aperitif, Pineau des Charentes. Red variant from merlot, with nutty raisin aromas. **NV**. Neither revisited.

Ankerman range NEW

Cabernet Sauvignon-Merlot ☺ ▤ **★★★** Previewed **10** is fresh, juicy & light bodied. **Chenin Blanc-Chardonnay** ☺ ▤ **★★★** Previewed **11** is a cheerful, deftly handled anytime blend.

Groot Eiland range

Shiraz ☺ **★★★ 09** is nutty, light, juicy-fruity. Pleasant everyday tipple. **Shiraz Rosé** NEW ☺ ▤ **★★★** Strawberry delight, **11** presents sweet fruit parfait in a glass. Ripe & appealing cooler for frivolous fun days. **Sauvignon Blanc** ☺ ▤ ▨ **★★★** Fresh, crisp **11** shows generous, sweetish fruit with well-focused aromatic edge. Ripe & sunny.

Cabernet Sauvignon ★★★ 09 shows promising black fruit, but lean body fades quickly. **Merlot ★★☆** Sweet, minty fruit with softly textured tannins, **09** fades to lean, brief finish. **Pinotage ★★★** Juicy & ripe **09** had supple tannins last edition, ideal for pasta partnering. **Reserve Shiraz-Pinotage ✓ ★★★★** Stylish top-of-range Cape Blend, shows balance & finely shaped fruit. **09** expresses ripe vintage. Red meat companion. **Chardonnay ★☆** Understated fruit previously on **09**. **Chenin Blanc** ▤ ▨ **★★** Whiffs of apple on unassuming & crisp **10**. This & next tasted last yr. **Brut Sparkling Rosé ★★** Pretty pink **NV**, dry strawberry-spiked sparkler from pinotage. Discontinued: **Brut Sparkling**.

Meander range

Merlot-Shiraz NEW ☺ ▤ ▨ **★★★** Unfussy, fruity **10** is quaffable at impressive price pitch. **Chenin Blanc-Colombar** NEW ☺ ▤ ▨ **★★★ 11** preview an appealing, fruity, pocket-friendly newcomer.

Palesa Fairtrade range

Merlot ☺ ▤ **★★★** Firmer tannin grip on **10**, with pleasant juicy berry fruit. Ripe & friendly quaffer. **Pinotage** ☺ ▤ **★★★** Typical varietal wild fruit & acetone on **10**, nicely tempered with ripeness & gentle oak. **Chenin Blanc** ☺ ▤ **★★★** Fresh & enticingly tropical **11** brims with fruit. Rounded body, gentle acid. Summer delight.

Sauvignon Blanc ▤ **★★★ 10** last edition: tangy apple twist with herbaceous edge. — GdB

▪ **Unplugged 62** *see* Joubert-Tradauw Private Cellar
▪ **Unsung Hero** *see* Origin Wine
▪ **Upington** *see* Orange River Wine Cellars

Upland Organic Estate

Location/WO: Wellington ▪ Map: Paarl & Wellington ▪ Est 1990 ▪ 1stB 1996 ▪ Tasting, sales & tours by appt ▪ Self-catering cottages ▪ Distillery: brandy & grappa ▪ Organic olives, olive oil, dried fruit & nuts ▪ Craft workshop ▪ Owner(s) Edmund & Elsie Oettlé ▪ Cellarmaster(s)/winemaker(s)/viticulturist(s) Edmund Oettlé ▪ 46ha/1500cs (cab, chenin, cbard, crouchen) ▪ 10t/600cs own label 100% red ▪ Debio Organic Certification ▪ PO Box 152 Wellington 7654 ▪ info@organicwine.co.za ▪ www.organicwine.co.za ▪ S 33° 40′ 19.9″ E 019° 2′ 40.0″ ▪ **T +27 (0)82-731-4774** ▪ F +27 (0)21-873-5724

Wellington owner/winemaker (and part-time veterinarian) Edmund Oettlé has been tackling the problem of making sulphur-free yet full-bodied, long-lasting wines on his organic farm for several years. His Guinevere port was a first step; with his upcoming 09 Cab he believes he's cracked the unfortified category. 'South Africa's first?' he wonders, hoping to continue with preservative-free wines – 'if the market is ready for them'.

Cabernet Sauvignon ❀ **★★★** Juicy drinkability in **08**, succulent blackcurrant taste underpinned by supportive structure. Moderate 13% alcohol. **Guinevere Cape Ruby** ❀ **★★★** Unusual **06** fortified dessert from cab, bottled with near-zero sulphur. Interesting orange/blueberry combo when last tasted, quite fiery aftertaste. — MW

Usana

Location/map: Stellenbosch ▪ WO: Stellenbosch/Western Cape ▪ Est/1stB 2003 ▪ Tasting & sales by appt ▪ Owner(s) JP & Pierre Winshaw ▪ Winemaker(s) Clinton le Sueur (2010, consultant) ▪ Viticulturist(s) Deon Joubert, Nikki Joubert & Henry Kotze (consultant) ▪ 300ha/60ha (cabs s/f, merlot, chard, pinot gris, sauv) ▪ 29t/2,000cs own label 15% red 85% white ▪ PO Box 68 Lynedoch 7603 ▪ jp@usanawines.co.za, pierre@usanawines.co.za ▪ www.usanawines.co.za ▪ S 33° 56′ 29.7″   E 018° 46′ 16.3″ ▪ **T +27 (0)83-650-9528**

Brothers JP and Pierre Winshaw are determined to make their own mark in the industry in which their grandfathers excelled. Bill Winshaw started Stellenbosch Farmers Winery (now Distell) while Deon Joubert was an influential grape grower in Stellenbosch. 'Big shoes,' they say while hatching plans to open a tasting room and investigating how to incorporate their other business – grass-fed beef.

★★★★ **The Fox** Last time **07** (★★★) shifted stylistic gear to 100% cab (previously a blend); offered cassis & spicy cedar (from year French oak), dry tannins but less concentration, for earlier enjoyment than robust **06**.

★★★★ **Sauvignon Blanc** ✓ 🍴 Aromatic, complex **11** preview flavoursome & mouthfilling, savoury seam to passionfruit flavour. From Stellenbosch & Elgin vines.

Pinot Gris NEW 🍴 ★★☆ Bone-dry **11** understated but crisp 'anything but chardonnay' alternative. Discontinued: **Nectar**. — CvZ

Uva Mira Vineyards

Location/map/WO: Stellenbosch ▪ Est 1997 ▪ 1stB 1998 ▪ Tasting & sales Mon-Fri 9-5 Sat/Sun 10-4 ▪ Fee R20-R40 ▪ Closed Easter Fri, Dec 25 & Jan 1 ▪ Cheese platters & savoury meat platters ▪ Tour groups ▪ Farm produce ▪ Conservation area ▪ Owner(s) Denise Weedon ▪ Winemaker(s) Matthew van Heerden (May 2003), with Desmond Solomons (Nov 2004) ▪ Viticulturist(s) Matthew van Heerden (May 2003) ▪ 140ha/30ha (cabs s/f, merlot, shiraz, chard, sauv) ▪ 100t/7,000cs own label 60% red 40% white ▪ IPW ▪ PO Box 1511 Stellenbosch 7599 ▪ info@ uvamira.co.za ▪ www.uvamira.co.za ▪ S 34° 1′ 31.3″   E 018° 51′ 26.1″ ▪ **T +27 (0)21-880-1683** ▪ F +27 (0)21-880-1682

With all their vineyards having reached double digit figures (the oldest 22 years, the youngest 10 years), the experienced team at this high-lying winery can see the benefits of the micro-managing systems and flavour-mapping they have introduced. These enable identification of the slightest differences in the grapes from a specific spot within a vineyard. 'This allows us to take advantage of vineyard variation to achieve specific wine flavours and our winemaking goals,' says Matthew van Heerden. In other words, as little as possible is left to chance. The range does evince a sense of confidence and completeness.

Vineyard Selection

★★★★ **Syrah** Vivid spice, minerals last year suggested cool terroir on **08**, but opulent red fruit, ripe tannins.

★★★★☆ **Red Blend** Layered brilliance, complex aromas & classy oak attractions on **07**. Fresh, deep flavours beautifully balanced with cab-focused structure. Merlot, cab franc, shiraz add savoury conclusion.

★★★★☆ **Single Vineyard Chardonnay** Always classy & modern. Complex limey, oatmeal on **10**, gentle creamy texture offset by lively mineral core. Sensitively handled in lighter vintage. Drinks well now & for few yrs.

Cellar Selection

★★★★ **Sauvignon Blanc** 🍴 **10** preview showed generous flavours. Bracing minerality; tangily dry, long.

Merlot-Cabernet Sauvignon ★★★★ Accessible, well structured **07** showed opulent yet fresh dark fruit last yr. 82/18 blend. — AL

Vaalvlei Wines

NEW

Map: Elgin, Walker Bay & Bot River ▪ WO: Walker Bay ▪ Est 2005 ▪ 1stB 2008 ▪ Tasting & sales Mon-Sat 11-5 by appt ▪ Closed Easter Fri & Dec 25 ▪ Self-catering cottages ▪ Fly-fishing ▪ Owner(s) Terblanche family ▪ Cellarmaster(s)/viticulturist(s) Naas Terblanche (Mar 2005) ▪ Winemaker(s) Naas Terblanche (Mar 2005) & Josef Dreyer (Aug 2005, Raka), advised by Charl van Teijlingen CWM (Mar 2008) ▪ 50ha/3ha (shiraz, sauv) ▪ 19t/325cs own label 40% red 60% white ▪ PO Box 92 Stanford 7210 ▪ info@vaalvlei.co.za ▪ www.vaalvlei.co.za ▪ S 34° 26′ 56.11″ E 019° 33′ 07.05″ ▪ **T +27 (0)28-341-0170/+27 (0)72-782-3431**

The Terblanche family's micro cellar near Stanford on the Cape's south coast is fully equipped for handcrafting wine, and 'our whole family' contributes to and encourages the collective winemaking effort, aided by Cape Wine Master Charl van Teijlingen and Raka winemaker Josef Dreyer. Naas Terblanche and his clan are aware of the area's tourist appeal, and offer fly-fishing and self-catering cottages.

Shiraz Reserve ★★★ Big & bold, sweet-fruited, spicy **10** ends with a warm hug of vanilla. **Shiraz** ★★★ Concentrated spicy black fruit, **10**'s 16% alc not for the faint of heart. **Sauvignon Blanc** 🍷 ★★★ 2 vintages reviewed: drink-soon **10** dry, grassy & quite developed; **11** (★★★) medium bodied & fruity, ends with a fresh greenpeppery flourish. — Panel

Val de Vie Wines

Location: Paarl ▪ Map: Paarl & Wellington ▪ WO: Coastal/Western Cape ▪ Est 2003 ▪ 1stB 2004 ▪ Tasting & sales Mon-Fri 8-5 Sat/Sun & pub hols 10-4 ▪ Cellar tours by appt ▪ Closed Easter Fri, Dec 25 & Jan 1 ▪ Platters by prior arrangement ▪ Conservation area ▪ Owner(s) Val de Vie Wines (Pty) Ltd ▪ Vineyard manager(s) Heinie Nel ▪ 24ha (carignan, cinsaut, grenache n/b, marsanne, mourv, rouss, shiraz, clairette, viog) ▪ 75t/4,250cs own label 60% red 40% white ▪ PO Box 6223 Paarl 7620 ▪ wine@valdevie.co.za ▪ www.valdevie.co.za ▪ S 33°48'15.0" E 018°58' 4.0" ▪ T +27 (0)21-863-6161 ▪ F +27 (0)21-863-2741

More botox than facelift is how winemaker Harold Versfeld describes the tweaking of the wine range from this upmarket wine, polo and lifestyle estate near Paarl. And on the subject of the body beautiful: Olympic gold medallist Ryk Neethling added a splash with an eponymous wine, Rhône-styled of course, like most of the other wines in the lineup. Versfeld reports that grapes are still bought in, mainly from the Swartland as the home-vines are still too young. 'But we harvested some grenache blanc and clairette blanche from Val de Vie in 2011 which was a real thrill.'

Val de Vie range

★★★★ **Shiraz** 08's smoky mulberry & plum appeal follows similar 07. Rounded yet muscled & firm. Dark char depth & density. Oak shows restraint, 70% new for 11 months. Long finish.

★★★★ **Ryk Neethling** NEW 09 as toned as the swimmer's body. Savoury rich black fruit from shiraz, dabs carignan, mourvèdre, grenache & cinsaut. Refined textured appeal, fine dry tannin & long silky finish.

★★★★☆ **Val de Vie** Premium-priced flagship, mainly mourvèdre (50%), shiraz & dabs grenache, carignan & cinsaut. 07 last year ripe & concentrated yet elegant, 80% new wood already assimilated.

★★★★ **GVC** 🍷 Graceful 08 blend of grenache blanc (50%), viognier & clairette blanche. Vanilla (from 100% new oak, 7 months on lees) layered with citrus & stonefruit freshness. Not revisited.

Discontinued: **Mourvèdre, Shiraz-Mourvèdre**.

Polo Club range

Red 🍷 ★★★★ Last-tasted 07 mimicked flagship: succulent & spicy, with tarry notes partly from 16 months oak, 50% new. **Chardonnay** NEW 🍷 ★★★ Refreshing tang of citrus & marmalade a counterfoil to medium bodied 09's brûlée richness. Subtle platform of oak, just 5% new. **Filly** NEW 🍷 ★★★ 10 lively sauvignon-led blend, light apple & grass, (legally) de-alcoholised to 10.5%. Discontinued: **White**. — FM

Val du Charron

Location: Wellington ▪ Map: Paarl & Wellington ▪ WO: Western Cape ▪ Est 2007 ▪ 1stB 2009 ▪ Tasting daily 10-4 ▪ Sales Mon-Fri 8-5 ▪ Cellar tours during tasting hours ▪ Breakfast & lunch daily; dinner by appt ▪ Tour groups ▪ Conference/function facility (100 pax) ▪ Walking/hiking & mountain biking trails ▪ 4-star Guesthouse: stay@ vdcwines.com (see Accommodation section) ▪ Owner(s) Val du Charron Wines (Pty) Ltd ▪ Winemaker(s) Bertus Fourie (Apr 2010, consultant) ▪ Viticulturist(s) Heinie Nel (Apr 2010, consultant) ▪ 43ha/21ha (cab, ptage, shiraz, chard, chenin) ▪ ±30t/±583cs own label 80% red 20% white ▪ Other export brands: Good Girl, Wild Girl ▪ IPW ▪ PO Box 890 Wellington 7654 ▪ ce@vdcwines.com ▪ www.vdcwines.com ▪ S 33° 37' 28.14" E 019° 2' 55.32" ▪ T +27 (0)21-873-1256 ▪ F +27 (0)86-509-4865

With Bertus Fourie as the ideal consultant both for his skills and knowledge of local conditions, things are progressing at this Wellington cellar. A state-of-the-art press has been installed as part of the cellar upgrade, and the new tasting venue is operational. Blends are the way forward, all with evocative and apt names from local history. Erasmus was the farm's first owner; Black Countess was a slave's daughter who married the Earl of Stamford, and Four White Legs refers to an exception to the

Bain's Pass toll, if the horse had this feature. On the cards are another white blend and a Bordeaux blend, to be released this year.

Erasmus NEW ★★★★ Mainly cab in 09, but pinotage, merlot & malbec add mint & buchu tones to blackcurrant flavours. Ready, can age a few years. **Black Countess** NEW ★★★★ Shiraz, touches viognier & carignan, **10** lives up to name: black fruit compote, oak a hidden strength. Made to enjoy now. **Four White Legs** NEW ★★★★ Chenin, sauvignon, with dabs viognier & semillon, hence name. Carefully oaked **11** tastes of fresh red apples, crisp & juicy, full bodied. Discontinued: **Chenin Blanc**. — CR

Valley Green Winery NEW

Location/WO: Elgin ▪ Map: Elgin, Walker Bay & Bot River ▪ Est/1stB 2011 ▪ Tasting & sales Mon-Fri 9-5 Sat/Sun/ after hours by appt only ▪ Fee R10 for groups of 10+ ▪ Closed Easter Fri-Mon & Dec 25 ▪ Cellar tours by appt ▪ BYO picnic ▪ Light lunches, buffet lunches & picnics by appt ▪ Owner(s) Malcolm J Dicey ▪ Cellarmaster(s) Catherine Marshall (Jan 2011, consultant) ▪ Winemaker(s) Catherine Marshall (Jan 2011, consultant), with Shaun Fortuin (Jan 2011, consultant) ▪ Viticulturist(s) Johan Viljoen (Jan 2011, consultant) ▪ 72ha/20ha ▪ 150t mostly sold to other cellars, own label 50% red 50% white ▪ WIETA, IPW ▪ PO Box 36 Elgin 7680 ▪ info@valleygreen.co.za, elzaan@valleygreen.co.za ▪ S 34° 12′ 12.07″ E 19° 02′ 35.10″ ▪ **T +27 (0)21-848-9770** ▪ F +27 (0)86-718-2203

'Wine is the perfect ending to any day,' says owner Malcolm Dicey, entering the market with a sauvignon made from premium grapes previously sold to 'top producers'. He's upgrading his vineyards using environmentally sustainable techniques, and increasing production facilities to expand the range. 'Elegant and balanced wines that reflect our sites' is the philosophy.

Hannay Wines range
Sauvignon Blanc 🍾 ★★★ Lovely wine to end any day: smooth & fresh, lively gooseberry & cut grass flavours, **11** satisfying glassful. — Panel

■ **Valley Road Vintners** *see* Ross Gower Wines

Valley Vineyards Wine Company

Location: Riebeek-Kasteel ▪ WO: Swartland ▪ Est/1stB 2009 ▪ Closed to public ▪ Owner(s) Richard Addison & Richard James ▪ ±50,000cs own label 40% red 40% white 15% rosé 5% other ▪ Other export brand: Two Tunns ▪ PO Box 2175 Riebeek-Kasteel 7307 ▪ raddison@valleyvineyardswine.com ▪ www.valleyvineyardswine.com ▪ **T +27 (0)79-174-2801**

Riebeek Cellars is their local winemaking partner, the Swartland their focus, the world their market, but the two Richards (Addison, the owner and James, the sales director of this UK merchant house) have prioritised Europe and North America. The latter has seen major growth, reports Richard A, who's working with an in-house designer to create innovative packaging for a changing market.

24 Rivers range NEW
Merlot 🍾 ★★★ Understated **10** is juicy & light with fresh acidity. **Chardonnay** 🍾 ★★ Light lemon fruit on straightforward unwooded **10**. **Chenin Blanc** 🍾 ★★★ **10** ripe tropical fruit, gentle & crisp. **Sauvignon Blanc** 🍾 ★★ Light-hearted **10** is pleasantly tart with hints of greengage.

Mischief Maker range NEW
Cabernet Sauvignon 🍾 ★★★ Leafy, spicy **10** with appealing varietal character on light, compact body. **Merlot** 🍾 ★★★ Raspberry cordial on juicy, light **10** with brief racy finish. **Pinotage** 🍾 ★★★ Ribena & cherry, **10** sweet & juicy, pleasant quaffing. **Chardonnay** 🍾 ★★ Cheerful & plump **10**, ripe pear & lemon untrammelled by oak. **Chenin Blanc** 🍾 ★★★ Gently crisp **10**, ripe apple & almond, warm finish. **Sauvignon Blanc** 🍾 📖 ★★ **10** sipper is light in alc (±11%) for summer fun.

Post Tree range NEW
Shiraz-Cinsaut 🍾 📖 ★★★ Coffee & sweet smoky berry fruit make **10** amenable braai mate. **Chenin Blanc** 🍾 ★★★ Light, fresh **10**, flowers & green fruit to take to book club.

The Royal range NEW

> **Shiraz-Cabernet Sauvignon** ☺ 🍽 ★★★ Appealing & well-formed **09**, juicy-fruity, with spicy cherry jam flavours.

Chenin Blanc 🍽 ★★★ Fresh & fruity, light & easy **09** with hint of white nuts. — Panel

■ **Van Hunks** *see* Oudtshoorn Cellar - SCV

Van Loveren Private Cellar

Location/map: Robertson ▪ WO: Robertson/Western Cape ▪ Est 1937 ▪ 1stB 1980 ▪ Tasting & sales Mon-Fri 8.30-5 Sat 9.30-1 ▪ Closed Easter Fri/Sun, Dec 25 & Jan 1 ▪ Cellar tours by appt ▪ Cheese platters; regional tasting platter (dried fruit & nuts paired with 4 wines) ▪ Walking/hiking & mountain biking trails ▪ Self-catering farm cottage ▪ Owner(s) Nico, Wynand, Phillip, Hennie, Bussell & Neil Retief ▪ Cellarmaster(s) Bussell Retief ▪ Winemaker(s) Danelle van Rensburg (Jan 2007) ▪ Viticulturist(s) Neil & Hennie Retief ▪ 400ha (cab, merlot, ptage, pinot, shiraz, chard, chenin, cbard, sauv) ▪ 5,000t/1,000,000cs own label 33% red 33% white 34% rosé ▪ Brands for clients: Makro, Woolworths ▪ BWI, Fairtrade, IPW ▪ PO Box 19 Klaasvoogds 6707 ▪ info@vanloveren.co.za ▪ www. vanloveren.co.za ▪ S 33° 52' 31.3" E 020° 0' 9.1" ▪ **T +27 (0)23-615-1505** ▪ F +27 (0)23-615-1336

'The acme of my career,' says cellarmaster Bussell Retief wryly, 'is dealing with five family members, each of whom contributes to the success of our brand, and that at a time when the industry's struggling!' The five are CEO Phillip, viti men Neil and Hennie, and Van Loveren founder brothers of the previous generation, Wynand and Nico, who occasionally become involved in winemaking and construction on the iconic Robertson estate. There'll be some of the latter soon, with extensions to the sales/tasting area planned. Recent news is of the purchase of three farms, where there have been 25ha of new plantings of virtually every popular variety.

Christina Van Loveren Limited Release range

★★★★ **Shiraz** ✓ Revisited as finished wine, **09** affirms its pedigree: luscious dark fruit/chocolate highlighted by herbs & spice; velvet palate given form by firm tannins. Will reward cellaring.

★★★★ **Chardonnay** ✓ 🍽 10's (★★★★) vanilla & shortbread enlivened by zesty acidity, generous grapefruit flourish; commendably delivers all this without overt sweetness or big alc. **09** was more powerful.

★★★★ **Sauvignon Blanc** ✓ 🍽 🍽 Darling grapes in melon & pineapple-nuanced **11**. Intensely flavoured & smooth, with lipsmacking acidity. Like lime & herb **10**, has great persistence. WO W Cape.

★★★★ **Rhine Riesling Noble Late Harvest** NEW Delicate, poised botrytised dessert, **08** tiger's eye hue, marmalade & ginger richness lifted by zingy acidity; wonderful presence delivered with less than 11% alc.

Cabernet Sauvignon 🍽 ★★★★ Ex-barrel **10** delivers vibrant fruit on firm tannin base, savoury tones to earthy mulberry aromas/flavours. Structured for 3+ years ageing. **Méthode Cap Classique Brut** ★★★★ NV (08) champagne-method sparkling from chardonnay (86%) & pinot noir, attractive shortcake & lemon, bouncy bubbles & dry finish make for a refreshing celebrator.

Van Loveren range

★★★★ **Red Muscadel** ✓ 🍽 Red fruit pastille **11** in footsteps of raisiny **08**: mouthcoating sweetness, uncloying, wonderfully persistent flavours.

> **African Java Pinotage** ☺ 🍽 ★★★ Just 'Pinotage' last time. **11** now fashionably & unashamedly 'café au lait' styled, complete with creamy texture & cube sugar; remains perky though. **River Red** ☺ 🍽 🍽 ★★★ **11** crowd-pleasing unwooded combo ruby cab (60%), merlot, shiraz. Delightfully drinkable. **Blanc de Noir Red Muscadel** ☺ 🍽 ★★★ Aka 'Blush'. Unfortified semi-sweet **11**, appealing sweetpea fragrance, honey flavours; lovely pick-me-up. **Neil's Pick Colombar** ☺ 🍽 🍽 ★★★ Tropical guava, mouthfilling fruit, lowish 12% alc: **11** perfect off-dry picnic libation. **Gewürztraminer Special Late Harvest** ☺ 🍽 🍽 ★★★ Good all-rounder: **11** loads of pretty gewürztraminer litchi, barley sugar & rosepetal, plus substantial surprisingly dry flavour for this style.

Merlot 🍽 ★★★ **11** bursts with sour cherries & plums, affable tannins for quaffing fun. **Cramond Cabernet Sauvignon-Merlot** NEW 🍽 ★★★ **09** unpretentious Bordeaux blend with merlot's plums, cab's backbone. **Cabernet Sauvignon-Shiraz** 🍽 ★★★ Toasty oak seasoning ex staves in **10**, berry fruit infused with fynbos. **Blanc de Noir Shiraz** 🍽 ★★★ Copper coloured **11**, spicy aroma, light & understated, ends dry. **Cape Riesling** 🍽 Await next. **Chardonnay** 🍽 🍽 ★★★ Apple pie **11** faintest suggestion of oak, softly rounded & gently long. **Pinot Grigio** 🍽 🍽 ★★ Still one of few varietal bottlings in SA. Green herb tinged **11**, markedly dry & crisp mealtime companion. **Sauvignon Blanc** 🗐 🔯 ★★★ Grass & greenpepper in 11, engaging pithy conclusion. **Cramond Sauvignon Blanc-Chardonnay** 🗐 🔯 ★★★ Warm bread hint, pineapple tang, somewhat abrupt end to 11 flavour. 80% sauvignon. **Blanc de Blanc** 🗐 🔯 ★★ Blend changes to chenin & semillon in 11, light-bodied party sipper. Also in 500ml. **Vino Blanc** ★★ Dry NV merges chenin & semillon; for early drinking. In 500ml. **Cape Ruby** ★★★★ 'Ruby Port' last time. Rainy day warmer from touriga much drier than previous, still very drinkable. Dark chocolate & plum pudding delight. **NV.** Discontinued: **Colombar-Chardonnay**.

Four Cousins range

Dry Red ★★★ Dusty plum, silky & unoaked for immediate enjoyment. 1,5L only. **NV**, as for all. Highest alc of these (14%; rest 12.5%-7.5%). **Dry White** 🗐 ★★ Guava, pineapple on refreshing zippy glassful of colombard & sauvignon. **Extra Light White** 🗐 ★★ Slimmer's friend from semillon & fernão pires; Weigh-Less endorsed. **Natural Sweet Red** ★★ Soft & sweet marriage red varieties & grape juice. 750ml & 1.5L, as for next & Natural Sweet White. **Natural Sweet Rosé** ★★★ Appealing midday tipple with jasmine high notes; red muscadel & grape juice. **Light Natural Sweet Rosé** 🗐 ★★ Pretty rose pink, cranberry zing. **Natural Sweet White** 🗐 ★★ Blend of white muscadel & grape juice; scented grapey fun.

Five's Reserve range

Cabernet Sauvignon 🔯 ★★★ 10 easy-going, red berry toned. Now all cab, previous had dollop merlot, hence name change. **Pinotage** 🔯 ★★★ Step-up for blueberry-chocolate & spiced 10, genteel tannins. These Fairtrade certified; grapes from Van Loveren's black economic empowerment partner's vineyards. **Merlot Rosé** 🗐 🔯 ★★★ Dry impression on 11 despite dash sugar, perfect with sunsets. **Chenin Blanc** 🗐 🔯 ★★★ Leafy 11 ultra-dry, with green-apple acid nip in tail.

Papillon Sparkling range

Brut ★★★ From colombard & sauvignon; ebullient extra-dry style, frisky mouthfeel, lemon farewell. **NV**, as all. **Demi-Sec** ★★ Celebratory semi-sweet fizz from white muscadel, jasmine infused sweet-sour appeal. **Vin Doux** ★★ Frothy red muscadel for the sweet-toothed.

Four Cousins Sparkling range

Sauvignon Blanc Brut ★★★ Quietly delicious, bone-dry, perfect for oysters. Previously vintage dated, now **NV**, as for all. Others in range sweetened with 40% grape juice. **White** ★★ Grapey, lightly spiced sparkler; bubbles add lift & vibrancy to white muscadel. This, both following, light alcs. **Blush** ★★★ Copper hue, exuberant mousse, creamy aftertaste. **Red** ★★ Cheerful sweet from ruby cab. Discontinued: **Méthode Cap Classique Brut**.

Wolverine Creek Limited Release range

Now discontinued. — Panel

■ **Vansha** *see* Ridgeback
■ **Van Zijls Family Vintners** *see* Imbuko Wines

Van Zylshof Estate

Location: Bonnievale ▪ Map/WO: Robertson ▪ Est 1940 ▪ 1stB 1994 ▪ Tasting & sales Mon-Fri 9-5 Sat 9-1 ▪ Closed Easter Fri, Ascension day, Dec 25 & Jan 1 ▪ Cellar tours by appt ▪ Owner(s) Van Zylshof Trust ▪ Cellarmaster(s)/winemaker(s)/viticulturist(s) Andri van Zyl (Mar 1993) ▪ 37ha/42ha ▪ 450t/±4,000cs own label 15% red 80% white 5% rosé ▪ PO Box 64 Bonnievale 6730 ▪ vanzylshof@lando.co.za ▪ www.vanzylshof.co.za ▪ S 33° 56' 18.5" E 020° 6' 23.4" ▪ **T +27 (0)23-616-2401** ▪ F +27 (0)23-616-3503

This third-generation Bonnievale farm is run along the same lines as family estates in France. 'Different generations manage all aspects of operation – from day-to-day tending of the vines to marketing.' Cellarmaster Andri van Zyl believes the result is consistent quality: 'Wines that make you want to come back for more.'

Chenin Blanc ☺ 🗐 ★★★ Tropical fruit salad appeal on zesty 11, pineapple tang in tail. Would enliven any occasion. Previewed, as next. **Sauvignon Blanc** ☺ 🗐 ★★★ Step-up 11 shows class in careful acid management, mineral seam. Like Chenin, lightish alc for lunchtime enjoyment.

Cabernet Sauvignon-Merlot 🗐 ★★★ Preview 10 youthful, wallet-pleasing braai companion: dark fruit & spicy chocolate, easy grip. **Rosé** NEW 🗐 ★★★ 11 food-friendly pink from merlot, cheerful & juicy, dry spicy conclusion. **Chardonnay** 🗐 ★★★ Citrus fruit masked mid-2011 by vanilla & 'pine needle' oak notes on 10. **Chardonnay Riverain** ✓ 🗐 ★★★★ Standout vintage for this unwooded version: 11 complex, layered with lime peel, white flowers, refreshed with zingy acidity. Could convert the ABC - 'Anything But Chardonnay' - crowd. **09** (★★★★) too was irresistible; **10** sold out untasted. — Panel

Vaughan Johnson's Wine & Cigar Shop

Location: Cape Town ▪ Map: Cape Peninsula ▪ Est/1stB 1985 ▪ Sales Mon-Fri 9–6 Sat 9–5 Sun 10–5 ▪ Open pub hols ▪ Gifts, souvenirs, spirits & beer available ▪ Owner(s) Vaughan Johnson ▪ PO Box 50012 Waterfront 8002 ▪ vjohnson@mweb.co.za ▪ www.vaughanjohnson.co.za ▪ S 33° 54' 19.15" E 018° 25' 10.68" ▪ **T +27 (0)21-419-2121** ▪ F +27 (0)86-509-6401

Word from our man in the retail industry (his bustling wine shop a landmark on Cape Town's V&A Waterfront) is that the market remains tough, with all sectors trading down. In the face of bewildering choices, Vaughan feels the value he can add is honest, reliable advice and information. His bespoke range of good-value wines, sourced mainly from the Paarl area, is reviewed again after an absence, and still features in the bargain stakes.

Vaughan Johnson range

Good Everyday Cape Red 🖿 ★★★ Juicy berry fruit with hint of smokiness on likeable **NV**. This & next 3 from Paarl. **Good Everyday Cape White** 🖿 ★★ True to name, fresh & fruity **NV** is quintessential quaffing.

Waterfront Collection

Captain's Claret ☺ 🖿 ★★★ Ripe, spicy plum fruit & good body on **09**. **Great White** ☺ 🖿 ★★★ **11** dependable easy-priced, easy-drinking blend. — GdB

▪ **Veelplesier** *see* Baarsma Wine Group

Veenwouden Private Cellar

Location/WO: Paarl ▪ Map: Paarl & Wellington ▪ Est 1989 ▪ 1stB 1993 ▪ Tasting, sales & cellar tours by appt ▪ Fee R100 if no purchase made ▪ Owner(s) The Van Der Walt Trust ▪ Cellarmaster(s) Marcel van der Walt ▪ Winemaker(s) Marcel van der Walt, with Faried Williams ▪ Viticulturist(s) Marcel van der Walt, with Sias Louw ▪ 14ha/12.5ha (cabs s/f, malbec, merlot, p verdot) ▪ ±100t/5,500cs own label 90% red 10% white ▪ PO Box 7086 Northern Paarl 7623 ▪ admin@veenwouden.com ▪ www.veenwouden.com ▪ S 33° 41' 7.0" E 018° 57' 52.4" ▪ **T +27 (0)21-872-6806** ▪ F +27 (0)21-872-1384

When this Paarl farm turned to wine in 1989, its location wasn't regarded as likely to produce premium quality. In fact, Ebenaezer, its previous name, had been planted to table grapes. But the late Deon van der Walt believed its rich, ferrous clay subsoils resembled most closely those in Pomerol (where his favourite wines came from), and thought its climate comparable with California's. After the maiden 1993 vintage, ex-golfing pro Marcel van der Walt, Deon's brother, took over winemaking duties and has guided the flagship reds into the modern idiom of softer tannins, less new oak and earlier drinkability but still with the structure to age. If this undeveloped spot between Paarl and Wellington once seemed an unusual choice, it has been vindicated by the quality of the wines.

Premium Collection

Chardonnay Await next - no longer called 'Special Reserve'.

Reserve Collection

★★★★☆ **Merlot Reserve** 09 (★★★★) ripe but unshowy chocolate aromas, some oak toast too. Pleasantly fresh, light-textured fruit with softish tannin. Best over next 5-6 years. **08** sold out; **07** showed polish, class.

★★★★ **Syrah** 08 noted last yr as youthfully approachable. Light red fruits, spice, tempered tannins & careful oaking in tune with less concentrated vintage.

★★★★ **Classic** Good **07** has restrained presence. Cabernet's fresh blackberry scents, structure fleshed out by merlot, malbec; cabernet franc adds spice. Harmonious now or keep 4-6 yrs. Beautifully built **06** (★★★★★).

Vivat Bacchus Collection

Red ★★★★ 10 merlot, syrah blend; velvety smooth with rich dark berries, chocolatey tones. As approachable as previously tasted **08** (**09** sold out). **Chenin Blanc** 🔖 **★★★ 11** from 100% unoaked chenin. Easy but not simple; attractive tropical flavours, plump & juicy with tangy fruity acid tail. **10** sold out untasted. — AL

◼ **Veldt** *see Robertson Wide River Export Company*

Vendôme

Location/WO: Paarl ▪ Map: Paarl & Wellington ▪ Est 1692 ▪ 1stB 1999 ▪ Tasting & sales by appt ▪ Fee R5, refunded on purchase ▪ Closed all pub hols ▪ Conferences/functions for up to 60 ▪ Owner(s) Jannie le Roux snr ▪ Winemaker(s) Jannie le Roux jnr ▪ Viticulturist(s) Jannie le Roux snr & jnr ▪ 40ha (cabs s/f, merlot, shiraz, chard, chenin, cbard, sauv, sem) ▪ 10t/550cs own label 70% red 30% white ▪ PO Box 36 Paarl 7645 ▪ lerouxjg@icon.co.za ▪ www.vendome.co.za ▪ S 33° 45′27.8″ E 018° 58′42.4″ ▪ **T +27 (0)21-863-3905** ▪ F +27 (0)21-863-0094

Named for a commune in central France, Vendôme has been farmed by the Le Roux family for 10 generations. Huguenot descendants Jannie le Roux snr and jnr handcraft their wines in the time-honoured manner. Like many French wineries, their charming riverside property is (now) open only by prior appointment. Less traditional are the conference and function facilities still offered by arrangement.

Classique ★★★★ Brooding **04** combo merlot & two cabs attractively rustic, dense plum centre last edition. Not revisited, as all. **Merlot-Cabernet Sauvignon ★★★** Leather, malt & prune **04** also merlot-led (60%) but in older style than flagship. **Sans Barrique ★★★★ 09** unoaked semillon/sauvignon blend (61/39) raised the bar on last-tasted **06** (**★★★★**). Rounded & rich courtesy 6 months lees-ageing, buoyed by freshening acidity. — CvZ

◼ **Vera Cruz Estate** *see Delheim Wines*

Vergelegen Wines

Location: Somerset West ▪ Map: Helderberg ▪ WO: Stellenbosch/Coastal/Western Cape ▪ Est 1987 ▪ 1stB 1991 ▪ Tasting & sales daily 9.30–4 ▪ Cellar tours daily at 10.30, 11.30 & 3 (Nov-Apr); 11.30 & 3 (May-Oct) ▪ Tasting R30/ 6 wines (excl Vergelegen Red and White), R10 each for flagship wines; Cellar tour R20pp incl. tasting of 4 premium range wines ▪ Closed Easter Fri, May 1 & Dec 25 ▪ The Vergelegen Restaurant, Camphor Forest Picnic & Rose Terrace Bistro (see Restaurants section) ▪ Facilities for children ▪ Gift shop ▪ Historic Cape Dutch homestead; library; exhibition corridor ▪ 300 year old camphor trees (proclaimed as National Monuments in 1942) ▪ Conservation area ▪ RMB Starlight Classics (held annually); Camellia Garden of Excellence; programme of events on website ▪ Owner(s) Anglo American plc ▪ Winemaker(s) André van Rensburg (Jan 1998) ▪ Viticulturist(s) Niel Rossouw (Apr 1995) & Dwayne Lottering (Nov 2003) ▪ 3,500ha/158ha (cab, merlot, sauv) ▪ 680t/63,000cs own label 58% red 42% white ▪ ISO 9001, ISO 14001, OSHAS 18000, BWI champion, WIETA ▪ PO Box 17 Somerset West 7129 ▪ vergelegen@vergelegen.co.za ▪ www.vergelegen.co.za ▪ S 34° 4′37.0″ E 018° 53′30.6″ ▪ **T +27 (0)21-847-1334** ▪ F +27 (0)21-847-1608

For winemaker André van Rensburg, who after 14 years still regards working on Vergelegen as the world's greatest wine privilege, wine matters because it is a summary of values which, though old fashioned, still matter. 'Wine is a beacon of hope and civilisation in a world becoming more barbaric, selfish and destructive." What also matters is consistent improvement. Here, the virus eradication project led by Prof Gerhard Pietersen has been so successful it is being emulated in New Zealand and Israel, and Van Rensburg will be collaborating with sibling company Anglo Platinum to determine if the precious metal can be used to remove that nemesis, oxygen, from wine.

Flagship range

★★★★☆ Vergelegen Red Masterly flagship **06**, mainly cab (90%) dashes merlot, cab franc; measured tannic grip cossets plush & still youthful fruit, fine & dry. Like handsome **05** (**★★★★★**), should continue to improve good few years.

★★★★☆ Vergelegen V 07 should be broached only in 3+ years; not that it's unknit, because it's so classically structured with authoritative tannins, lush fruit, firm acidity, it couldn't possibly share its charms so young. Same varieties as above, similar proportions.

★★★★☆ **Vergelegen White** Pioneering & still standout semillon-sauvignon blend, with some barrel fermentation/ageing. Unlike introverted **09** (65% sauvignon), **10** has 59% semillon. Reminiscent of Graves (Bordeaux), flint overlain with white peach, delicate 'wet stone' minerality.

Reserve range

★★★★☆ **Cabernet Sauvignon** Poised **07** (★★★★) seductive savoury richness, firm tannins; not as concentrated as **06**, vintage possibly playing a role, but still elegant & understated. Dashes petit verdot, cabernet franc, merlot.

★★★★☆ **Merlot** Ripe & lavishly oaked but so very well judged & accomplished, **08** a study in finessed fruit & complexity: plum, blackberry, fenugreek & dust; mimics distinguished, dark-berried **07**.

★★★★☆ **Shiraz** **07** riper style but gently handled/oaked to maximise bright red fruit & spice, supple texture. Shade off silky **06** (★★★★★). This, next, not revisited.

★★★★ **Cabernet Franc-Merlot** Quietly persuasive **06** (★★★★★) sold out; bold **05** still selling.

★★★★☆ **Chardonnay Reserve** Magnificent **10** signature citrus grip/creamy tension, fennel notes to oatmeal & nut base, refined savoury conclusion. Like riveting **09**, worth ageing 5+ years.

★★★★☆ **Sauvignon Blanc Reserve** Aficionados know this S African flag bearer as 'Schaapenberg', a reference to the 23 year old source vineyard. **11** reserved & very tight with 'oystershell' minerality & greengage vivacity waiting to fully unfold.

★★★★ **Semillon** Last time fruitier **08** heralded departure from previous more savoury & oxidative versions.

Discontinued: **Weisser Riesling Noble Late Harvest**.

Premium range

★★★★ **Shiraz** NEW Unusually for this range, only own grapes: '**08** is 99% fruit originally destined for the Reserve; that's how strict our criteria are.' Joie de vivre contained by dense tannins.

★★★★ **Cabernet Sauvignon-Merlot** Fragrant **07** has splashes cab franc, petit verdot; same lithe feel as **08**, which more spiced with cab franc. Only Chardonnay, Shiraz tasted for this edition.

★★★★ **Chardonnay** Partially oaked version, fruit from Darling, Elgin, Walker Bay & home vineyards. Lemongrass-toned **10** calm, collected, as seamless as elegant **09**.

★★★★ **Sauvignon Blanc** **10** headily pure aromas, steely clean feel fleshed with lees-ageing & dash semillon, bracing farewell.

Vin de Florence ★★★★ Off-dry **09** gently spicy sipper. WO W Cape. — CvZ

Vergenoegd Wine Estate

Location/map: Stellenbosch • WO: Stellenbosch/Western Cape • Est 1696 • 1stB 1972 • Tasting & sales Mon-Fri 9–5 Sat/Sun 9.30–4 • Fee R15 • Closed Easter Fri, Dec 25 & Jan 1 • Cellar tours by appt • Facilities for children • Tour groups • Wine related gifts • Fresh duck eggs in spring • 6 boule courts • Guided historical walks & duck tours by appt • Conservation area • Pomegranate Restaurant open for lunch Tue-Sat, dinner by appt • Owner(s) Vergenoegd Trust • Cellarmaster(s) John Faure (Nov 1983) • Winemaker(s) Marlize Jacobs (Dec 2007) • Viticulturist(s) Marlize Jacobs (Dec 2007), advised by Drikus van der Westhuizen (2004) • 300ha/±72ha (cabs s/f, malbec, merlot, p verdot, shiraz, tinta barocca, touriga nacional) • 500t 94% red 3% white 3% rosé • BWI, IPW • PO Box 1 Faure 7131 • info@vergenoegd.co.za • www.vergenoegd.co.za • S 34° 2' 2.8" E 018° 44' 20.1" • **T +27 (0)21-843-3248** • F +27 (0)21-843-3118

John Faure has been making classic-styled wines at this family farm for about as long as a few hotshot young Cape winemakers have been alive. The 500 Runner Ducks (as celebrated in one of the wine ranges) took responsibility for snail management in the vineyards rather more recently, contributing to the estate's non-invasive farming practices. The lineage of the bird population encouraged by the preservation of renosterveld and wetlands is even more ancient than that of the Faures, however – the family have been at Vergenoegd only since the 1820s.

Vintage Collection

★★★★ **Cabernet Sauvignon** **04** has estate's signature restraint, with cedar spice ex intricate oaking.

★★★★ **Shiraz** **04** sappy red fruit with house's savoury finish.

★★★★☆ **Vergenoegd** Bordeaux blend **04** succulent, accessible yet cellarworthy.

Merlot ★★★★ Blackcurrant & leafy notes to food-friendly & firm **04**. **Terrace Bay** ★★★★ Blend of 5 red varieties. **04** less serious than previous, but big 14.5% alc in balance. All in this range still selling, none retasted.

Standard range

★★★★ **Cabernet Sauvignon** Hint of shiraz in **05** adds spice & leather tones; cedar from 2 years oak.

★★★★ **Merlot** ✓ Ripe but fresh, classic-style **06**, with drops cab franc & touriga, offers graphite, choc & plum. Fine tannin structure & intelligent oaking. Only wine in range tasted this year.

★★★★ **Shiraz 05** a wine to keep, with harmonious oaking, & a lingering pruney finish.

★★★★ **Vergenoegd** Bordeaux-style **05**, with plenty of fruit & good structural support.

Terrace Bay ★★★ **05** a ripe-fruited 5-way red blend. **Old Cape Colony Vintage Port** ★★★★ Mouthfilling, subtly balanced **04** from touriga & tinta with layers nuts & spice.

Runner Duck range

Red ☺ 🍷 ★★★ Powerful, just-dry **09** blend touriga, malbec, cab franc now bottled. Robust, spicy & meaty, with floral tones & rounded tannin. **Rosé** ☺ 🍷 ★★★ Soft, bone-dry, full-bodied malbec-led **11** sample (merlot & cab franc support), with anise-spiced plum flavours.

White NEW 🍷 🍷 ★★★ Fresh & zesty **11** from tropical-toned sauvignon & 15% colombard. WO W Cape.

Limited Edition range NEW

Cabernet Franc ★★★★ Heady, super-ripe **09** made in tiny volumes, with notes of tobacco, leather, spiced plums. Light oaking. Warming 15% alc. **Tawny Port** ★★★ Sweetly rich & rustic once-off **99** from tinta barocca; nuts, brandy-macerated black fruit & sage. Acid a little out of sync. — JPf

Verlieft Wines

Location: Stellenbosch • Est 2010 • Tasting & sales by appt • Closed Easter Fri-Mon, Dec 25/26 & Jan 1 • Owner(s) Roos & Co. Wines • Cellarmaster(s) Dirk Roos • PO Box 104 Koelenhof 7605 • dirk@verlieftwines.com • www.verlieftwines.com • **T +27 (0)82-904-6886**

There's style innovation here: owner Dirk Roos is marketing 'earth-conscious wines' and a New York artist, Jason Oliva, has been engaged to design the artwork for the labels. For all that, there's tradition too: grapes are hand-harvested from environment-friendly grapes, bottles are labelled by hand using a letter-press for printing, each bottle numbered and signed with a certificate of authenticity. First up for the Roos touch, a single-barrel cab-shiraz 2005 blend.

Versailles

Location/WO: Wellington • Map: Paarl & Wellington • Est/1stB 2004 • Tasting, sales & tours by appt • Conservation area • Owner(s) Annareen de Reuck (Malan) • Winemaker(s) Loftie Ellis • Vineyard manager(s) M Joseph • 100ha (cab, merlot, shiraz, chenin) • ±1,200t • PO Box 597 Wellington 7654 • adereuck@ezinet.co.za, orders@versailleswines.co.za • www.versailles.co.za • S 33° 37′ 34.98″ E 018° 59′ 37.11″ • **T +27 (0)21-873-2618/ +27 (0)82-898-9314** • F +27 (0)21-873-2618/+27 (0)21-873-2608

The wine gene is strong in the Malan family, with male heirs having helped establish three major cooperative cellars in the Wellington area. However, when wine was made in the original cellar on the home-farm for the first time in 100 years, it was by Annareen, the first female to take the helm of the clan's operation.

Shiraz ★★★ Uncomplicated & zesty **05** for early enjoyment, should be broached soon. Not revisited, as all. **Cabernet Sauvignon-Merlot** ★★★ **09** pocket pleaser has plummy fruit centre, friendly tannins. **Chenin Blanc** ★★ Still-selling apple-toned **10** promises carefree al fresco dining with moderate 12.6% alc. **Sauvignon Blanc** ★★★ Capsicum nuance, sweaty whiff on **09**; brisk, with satisfying weight. — CvZ

Versus

Innovative and unconventional packaging has always been a feature of this range of easy-drinkers from The Company of Wine People, and last year the distinctive diamond-shaped label was given added colour as well as catchy taste descriptors. The back label now has a QR code for immediate web access, and there's more techno-savviness in the brand's blog, Facebook and Twitter presence.

Versus Original range

Simply Rocking Red 🍷 🔲 ★★★ 'Red' last time. **11** smooth & savoury, with balanced gentle structure. Unwooded. **Dry Rosé** 🍷 🔲 ★★★ 'Rosé' previously. Previewed **11** light-bodied al fresco pink, savoury berry flavours. **Simply Wicked White** 🍷 🔲 ★★ Name changed from 'White'. Crisp & fresh **11**, bursting with summer appeal. Western Cape WO for this range & next.

Versus Naturally Sweet range

Red 🍷 ★ Sweetly spicy, light & genial quaffing wine. **NV**, as for all these. **Rosé** 🍷 ★★ Light & crisp, strawberry sweetness for easy drinking. **White** 🍷 🔲 ★★ Soft & charming low-alcohol sweetness. — MW

◼ **Vertex Reserve** see Bonnievale Cellar
◼ **Vierfontein** see Dâbar

Vilafonté

Location/map: Stellenbosch ▪ WO: Paarl ▪ Est 1996 ▪ 1stB 2003 ▪ Tasting, sales & tours by appt ▪ Owner(s) Mike Ratcliffe, Zelma Long & Phil Freese ▪ Winemaker(s) Zelma Long, Martin Smith (May 2010) ▪ Viticulturist(s) Phil Freese (1996), Edward Pietersen (2007) ▪ 17ha (cabs s/f, malbec, merlot) ▪ 60t/1,595cs own label 100% red ▪ Unit 7C Lower Dorp Street Bosman's Crossing Stellenbosch 7600 ▪ info@vilafonte.com ▪ www.vilafonte.com, www.vilafonte.blogspot.com ▪ S 33° 56′ 26.8″ E 018° 50′ 49.8″ ▪ **T +27 (0)21-886-4083** ▪ F +27 (0)21-883-8231

With Martin Smith the resident winemaker, the eminent American owners (along with Warwick's Mike Ratcliffe) ultimately control production here. Phil Freese, consultant to some of California's grandest names as well as illustrious Cape ones, designed and directs the vineyards on the Paarl side of the Simonsberg. Also a frequent visitor is Zelma Long, whose international acclaim as a winemaker would be impossible to convey briefly. Vilafonté calls itself 'the first winery in South Africa to be focused on producing wine specifically for the US market' – something probably discernible in their ripe-fruited, plush, luxuriously oaked expression of local conditions. In 2012, Vilafonté expects more than half of their sales to be made through 'the growing network of wine aficionados' in their Wine Club.

★★★★☆ **Series C** Standout, succulent Bordeaux blend, with amply oaked super-ripe fruit a hallmark, always cab-dominated. Two tasted. **09** (54% plus merlot, cab franc, malbec) rich, textured & spicy, the cab franc adding lift. **08** (★★★★) less persistent, despite higher (66%) cab (no cab franc); slightly less new oak.

★★★★☆ **Series M** Spicy, cedarwood, tealeaf aromas on **09** where the oak is evident but integrating. Here perfume, not texture, is the keynote. Previous **07** was near-equal blend cab, merlot, malbec, but here the juicy fruity malbec dominates with 46%; tiny drop cab franc. Lighter oaking (60% new) than Series C. — MF

Viljoensdrift Wines & Cruises

Location/map/WO: Robertson ▪ Est/1stB 1998 ▪ Tasting & sales at Riverside venue Mon-Fri 9–5 Sat & 1st Sun/ mnth 10-3 ▪ Closed Easter Fri, Dec 25, Jan 1 ▪ Deli - create your own picnic ▪ Facilities for children ▪ Tour groups ▪ Gift shop ▪ Conferences ▪ Robertson Wacky Wine/Wine on River/Slow weekend ▪ Self-catering cottage in Montagu ▪ Owner(s) Fred & Manie Viljoen ▪ Cellarmaster(s) Fred Viljoen (1998) ▪ Winemaker(s) Fred Viljoen, with Zonia Lategan ▪ Viticulturist(s) Manie Viljoen (1998) ▪ 240ha/120ha (cab, ptage, shiraz, chard, chenin, sauv) ▪ 200t/±80,000cs own label 55% red 40% white 4% rosé 1% ports + 15,000L for clients ▪ Other export brands: Driftwood, Elandsberg ▪ BWI, IPW, IPW ▪ PO Box 653 Robertson 6705 ▪ wines@viljoensdrift.co.za ▪ www.viljoensdrift. co.za ▪ S 33° 52′ 8.4″ E 019° 59′ 13.6″ ▪ **T +27 (0)23-615-1901 (cellar); +27 (0)23-615-1017 (tasting/cruises)** ▪ F +27 (0)23-615-3417

This convivial family winery on the Breede River certainly has the recipe to draw the tourist crowds for a fun, relaxing day's wine tasting. Their range of approachable, generally flavoursome and always affordable wines can be enjoyed on a river boat cruise, at facilities on the bank, or during any of several local wine festivals.

River Grandeur range

Cabernet Sauvignon ★★★★ Savoury & long **09** 'oystershell/graphite' minerality, nice herbaceous lift. Standout for the region, nudges next level. **Merlot** ★★★★ **09**'s spicy red berries with smoky oak veneer, bright acidity tweaking 15% alc into harmony. Not retasted. **Pinotage** 🔲 ★★★ **10** familiar sweet mulberry fruit & big body; shade more robust than previous though, so better with food than solo. **Shiraz** ★★★ **08** clean leather & rich savoury fruit, succulent tannin. Tasty but seems to be evolving quickly, drink soon. **Cape Blend ★★★ 10** bursts with berries, shows youthfully firm tannin & acidity, allow year/2 to settle & show better. **Chardonnay** 🍷 🄡 **★★★** Acacia & nuts on **11**, considered & balanced lemon & lime palate, commendable example of variety. **Chenin Blanc** 🍷 Await new. **Sauvignon Blanc** 🍷 🄡 **★★★** Dust & perfume, some green aromas & flavours on fresh **11**; lemon acidity, light 12% alc ideal for summer.

Viljoensdrift range

Serenity Await new. **Rosé** 🍷 **★★★** Pale coral pink **11** delicately perfumed, vinous but lightly flavoured & dry. **Villion ★★★** Last was **06** from chardonnay, latest méthode cap classique sparkling is **NV**, with deepish yellow hue showing bottle-age, a seabreeze note, nut & honey, toasty rich palate. **Cape Vintage Reserve ★★** Oxidative & savoury port-style fortified, **08** big & boldly flavoured, sweetish finish. Discontinued: **Wine on the Water Sweet Rosé**. — Panel

■ **Village Collection** *see* Tulbagh Winery
■ **Villa San Giovanni** *see* Zandvliet Wine Estate & Thoroughbred Stud
■ **Villa Verde** *see* Seven Oaks

Villiera Wines

Location/map: Stellenbosch ▪ WO: Stellenbosch/Western Cape ▪ Est/1stB 1983 ▪ Tasting, sales & cellar tours Mon-Fri 9-5 Sat 9-3 ▪ Closed Easter Fri, Dec 25 & Jan 1 ▪ Dalewood cheese platters & soft drinks; or BYO picnic ▪ Conference venue (up to 40 pax) ▪ Wildlife Sanctuary ▪ Game drives & birding R150pp (R75 for children under 15) incl tasting & self-guided tour of cellar, book ahead ▪ Owner(s) Grier family ▪ Cellarmaster(s) Jeff Grier (1983) ▪ Winemaker(s) Christiaan Visser (Dec 2008) ▪ Viticulturist(s) Simon Grier ▪ 400ha/210ha (cab, merlot, ptage, pinot, shiraz, chard, chenin, sauv) ▪ 1,800t/60,000cs own label 24% red 37% white 3% rosé 36% MCC; 14,000cs for Marks & Spencers & 21,000cs for Woolworths ▪ Other export brand: Groot Geluk (Belgium) ▪ HACCP, WIETA ▪ PO Box 66 Koelenhof 7605 ▪ wine@villiera.com ▪ www.villiera.com ▪ S 33° 50' 14.4" E 018° 47' 34.4" ▪ **T +27 (0)21-865-2002/3** ▪ F +27 (0)21-865-2314

Doing the right thing by the environment and in terms of social upliftment and business relationships has always been an important aspect of this family-owned farm, and has earned the respect of peers and associates over time. Combined financial and environmental reasons have seen the installation of SA's largest roof-mounted PV solar panel array – a draw in its own right – while the 220ha Villiera Wildlife Sanctuary offers visitors on the new game drives guaranteed sightings of a fantastic variety of wildlife. On the wine-making side, quality big-name clients like Woolworths and M&S keep the family on their toes and their name synonymous with good value. Bubbly accounts for more than a third of production and innovations in the pipeline include a sulphur-free white and red.

Cellar Door range

★★★★ Rhine Riesling Noble Late Harvest Last-tasted **05** showed lingering flavours; finely rich. 500ml.

Villiera Wines range

★★★★ Shiraz ✓ Previously rated **08** cemented advance of **05** (no **06**, **07**). Peppery spice to mulberry fruit, good grip yet accessible. Great value.

★★★★ Monro Merlot-based **06** (★★★★) with cab, dash of cab franc less concentrated than **05**. Elegant style, positive entry sends all the right signals. Judiciously oaked, light, spicy finish.

★★★★ Traditional Barrel Fermented Chenin Blanc ✓ 🄡 Gold-tinged **10** has complexity, depth, breadth ensured by low yields, barrel fermentation & touch botrytis. Long finish, rich (just-dry) but not cloying.

★★★★ Traditional Bush Vine Sauvignon Blanc 🄡 Low-yielding old vineyard pruned to ensure herbaceous style. **11** (★★★★) less complexity, depth than **10**.

★★★★☆ Brut Natural No sulphur or dosage in refined, bone-dry **08** (★★★★) from chardonnay. Appealing creamy texture, though not as complex as **07**.

★★★★★ Monro Brut ✓ Limpid gold **06** equal blend chardonnay-pinot noir, luxuriously enriched by oak & 5 yrs lees maturation. Ultra classy, layered, rich & complex. Ticks boxes for balance, length, creamy refinement.

★★★★ Tradition Brut Popular celebratory tipple. Latest **NV** (★★★★) simpler than previous, but perfectly balanced, full-fruited, rich & sufficiently weighty.

★★★★☆ Reserve Brut Rosé Tasted last year **00** 'a unique one-off' in magnum, 52% pinotage & pinot-led, nine years sur lie! Onion-skin allure, rich texture with black-grape weight, was amazingly fresh.

★★★★☆ **Inspiration** 🄡 Botrytised chenin, riesling dessert style previewed last year. Bronze **10** now shows unctuous dried fruit flavours with citrus twist. Delightful fresh acidity ably controls richness.

> **Chenin Blanc** ☺🄡 ★★★ Pre-bottling **11** charmingly pleasant & tastily fruity. **Gewürztraminer** ☺🄡 ★★★ Off-dry spicy preview **11**: Turkish Delight notes, zesty acidity. **Sauvignon Blanc** ☺🄡🄡 ★★★ **11** delivers abundant tropical flavours for everyday drinking. WO W Cape.

Cabernet Sauvignon ★★★★ Classic expression, signature restraint; **08** tasted previously upped ante on **07** (★★★★), brimming with fruit, textured tannins. **Merlot** ✓ ★★★★ Smoky plum **09** lively & refreshing, fairly light & perfectly accessible for early drinking. **Pinotage** ★★★ Popular mocha-laced **09** has simple, easy flavours & appetising sour cherry finish. **Rhine Riesling** ★★★★ Last tasted was ethereal, spicy, off-dry **09**. **Brut Special Dosage** ★★★★ Attractive NV sparkler slightly sweeter than Tradition, softens & adds richness, for those who find Brut a little too dry. **Tradition Rosé Brut** ★★★★ Mouthfillingly fruity NV has firm structure & earthiness. 63% pinotage (with chard & pinot) lends 'wild', savoury finish. **Fired Earth** ★★★★ LBV-style port. Last tasted was rather spiritous but flavourful **04** from touriga, shiraz & pinotage.

Down to Earth range

> **Red** ☺🄡 ★★★ Deliciously savoury **10** blend touriga, shiraz, attractively rustic style for pizza & pasta. **White** ☺🍴🄡 ★★★ Sauvignon-semillon **11** blend a nattily labelled everyday wine; fresh, crisp & dry with spicy hint. — IM

Villiersdorp Cellar

Location/map: Villiersdorp ▪ WO: Western Cape ▪ Est 1922 ▪ 1stB 1974 ▪ Tasting & sales Mon-Fri 8-5 Sat 9-1 ▪ Fee R10 for groups of 7+ ▪ Closed Easter Fri-Mon & Dec 25/26 ▪ Kelkiewyn Restaurant/Farm Stall T +27 (0)28-840-0900 Mon-Fri 8-5 Sat/Sun & pub hols 8-3 ▪ Farm produce ▪ Walking/hiking, mountain biking & 4x4 trails ▪ Tractor museum open on request ▪ Owner(s) 40 growers ▪ Cellarmaster(s) Flip Smith (Jan 2011) ▪ Winemaker(s) Flip Smith (Jan 2011), with André Bruyns (Dec 2009) ▪ Viticulturist(s) André Bruyns (Dec 2009) ▪ 300ha (merlot, chenin, sauv) ▪ 3,600t/9,500cs own label 30% red 30% white 30% rosé 10% fortified ▪ BWI, IPW ▪ PO Box 14 Villiersdorp 6848 ▪ marketing@slowine.co.za ▪ www.villiersdorpcellar.co.za ▪ S 33° 59' 11.2" E 019° 17' 48.5" ▪ **T +27 (0)28-840-1120** ▪ F +27 (0)28-840-1833

Villiersdorp Cellar is situated in Villiersdorp village near the Theewaterskloof Dam, hence the grower-owned winery's punningly named Dam Good range. Travel down the main street to the tasting room, deli and restaurant, and you'll find not only Dam Good wine but also special bottlings of *moskonfyt* (unctuous must jam), the cellar's calling card since inception in 1922. Also on the premises is South Africa's only private tractor museum, each machine in perfect working order.

Dam Good range

> **White** ☺🍴🄡 ★★★ Thai-food-friendly **11**, ex tank cheerful fragrant fruit (mainly chenin), ends with lemon flick. As the range name says... **Rosé** ☺🍴🄡 ★★★ Pretty pink Natural Sweet **11** with pinotage's Turkish Delight & strawberry tones, silky texture. Serve chilled with curry.

Red 🍴🄡 ★★★ Previewed **10** merlot/shiraz perfect cheer for cold, rainy days. Dark fruit, soft spice, pleasant grip of tannin.

Villiersdorp Cellar range

Hanepoot Jerepiko ✓ 🄡 ★★★★ Fortified dessert aka 'Treintjiewyn'. Orange rind & watermelon nuances to sunshine-sweet **11** preview. Slippery, luscious, long, with balanced alc. **Cape Ruby** 🄡 ★★ Ex tank, unwooded **11** more like high-alc red than traditional port style. Light-hearted & sweet. — WB

■　**Vinay** *see* Slanghoek Winery
■　**Vin d'Ester** *see* Linton Park Wines

Vinimark

Closed to public ▪ Directors Tim Rands, Cindy Jordaan, Geoff Harvey & Gys Naudé ▪ Exports: Geoff Harvey ▪ geoff@vinimark.co.za ▪ PO Box 441 Stellenbosch 7599 ▪ www.vinimark.co.za ▪ **T +27 (0)21-883-8043/4** ▪ F +27 (0)21-886-4708

Wine merchants marketing, selling and distributing various ranges with local partners, including Robertson Winery, Kleindal, Long Beach and Silversands, some listed separately.

■ **Vin Maison** *see* Maison

Vins d'Orrance

Location: Constantia ▪ WO: Western Cape ▪ Est/1stB 2000 ▪ Tastings by appt ▪ Owner(s) Christophe & Sabrina Durand ▪ Cellarmaster(s)/winemaker(s) Christophe Durand ▪ 11ha ▪ 24t/1,500cs ▪ PO Box 23923 Claremont 7735 ▪ christophe@vinsdorrance.co.za ▪ www.vinsdorrance.co.za ▪ **T** +27 (0)21-683-7479 ▪ F +27 (0)21-683-7489

Excellent Wine Spectator ratings, a listing at Monte Carlo's illustrious Louis XV Hôtel de Paris and being served at the wedding of Monaco's Prince Albert II have recently rewarded the stylish-yet-classical winemaking approach of forward-thinking Frenchman Christophe Durand, who, with Gallic panache, dedicates his wines to the women in his life: daughters Ameena and Anais, and partner Sabrina.

★★★★☆ **Syrah Cuvée Ameena** Vivid red fruit & garrigue spiciness ensure elegant Rhône styling in **09** blend Elgin, Perdeberg fruit. Half-new oak discernible but well-judged, supporting the supple tannins & complex flavours, all wound together by bright, savoury acidity.

★★★★ **Chardonnay Cuvée Anaïs** Stylish, elegant **10** has Elgin minerality (also Franschhoek grapes), steely freshness. Also creaminess, fresh lime thread & judicious oaking. Youthful shyness will unfold.

★★★★ **Kama** Concentration & complexity of barrel-fermented **10** (★★★★★) chenin fulfils meaning of its Sanskrit name ('sensual pleasure'), capturing fruity purity & seductive rich texture of old vines in Perdeberg. Step-up from **09** with appetising acidity & cleansing pithiness. — IM

■ **Vinum** *see* The Winery of Good Hope
■ **Vior** *see* Malanot Wines

Virgin Earth

Location: Riversdale ▪ WO: Langeberg-Garcia/Philadelphia/Coastal/Overberg ▪ Est 2002 ▪ 1stB 2003 ▪ Closed to public ▪ Owner(s) Kobus du Plessis ▪ Winemaker(s) Piet Kleinhans (Sep 2008) & Joseph Gertse (Jan 2000) ▪ Viticulturist(s) Rudi Benn (Jan 2001) & Hendrik Otto (2004) ▪ 13,000ha/21ha (cabs s/f, merlot, p verdot, shiraz, sauv, sem, verdelho, viog) ▪ 35,000cs own label 40% red 45% white 15% rosé ▪ WIETA ▪ Postnet Suite #57 Private Bag X18 Milnerton 7435 ▪ sales@havanahills.co.za ▪ www.havanahills.co.za ▪ **T** +27 (0)21-972-1110 ▪ F +27 (0)21-972-1105

This large game and wine farm is owned by Kobus du Plessis of Havana Hills, whose winemaking and viticultural team happily do stints out here in the Klein Karoo. Pinot noir joins the range for stylistic reasons, despite its Philadelphia origin, because the delicacy and lower alcohol fit in with the restraint evident in recent Virgin Earth releases. Next on the agenda are organic certification, and Fairtrade, WIETA and IPW affiliation.

★★★★ **Pinot Noir** Previously listed & reviewed under Havana Hills. Red berries & undergrowth nuances, **09** is tightly focused reflection of cool-climate terroir. Pure, elegant & classic. WO Philadelphia.

★★★★ **High 5ive** Still available, **07** Bordeaux blend, third shiraz, celebrates red fruit, savoury nuances tantalise. Polished lines, dab sugar adds weight. Already seductive, could age 5+ years.

★★★★ **Noble Late Harvest** From semillon, last **08** ticked all the boxes: deeply rich & full flavoured; apricot, pineapple, good length. Deliciously easy to drink. 30% in seasoned barrels. 500ml.

Pinotage ★★ Previously, trim (12.8% alc) **08** had plums, ripe tannins. **Lost Barrel Shiraz** ★★★ Last was **07**, with smoky dark fruit, plump, & nice tannin grip. Designed to please now & next few years. Overberg WO. **Chenin Blanc** 🍽 ★★★★ Thatch & bruised apple in last-tasted **10**, off-dry but acidity provided balance, touch of oak complexity. Coastal WO. **Pepper Tree Sauvignon Blanc** 🍽 ★★★★ Fynbos & lemon zest, plumped up by dab sugar, **11** is individual & friendly, with just 12% alc. **Succulent** ★★★★ Wooded off-dry semillon, viognier blend. Last year **10** had waxy melon styling, full-bodied yet retained freshness. Already delicious, could age few years. Improved on aptly named **08** (★★★★). **Viognier MCC** ★★★ Bubbles enhancing peachiness, **08** last edition was not your usual méthode cap classique style. Flavourful enough for creative food pairing. Discontinued: **Virgin Earth Reserve**. — CR

Virginia

For over 40 years, a consistent semi-sweet white, widely sourced, by Distell.

Virginia ★★ Mango & melon semi-sweet **NV** chenin/colombard mix. 2 & 5L packs. — Panel

■ **Vivat Bacchus** *see Veenwouden Private Cellar*

Vleiland Wines

Location: Vredendal ▪ Map/WO: Olifants River ▪ Est 2004 ▪ 1stB 2005 ▪ Tasting & sales by appt Mon-Fri 8-5 Sat 8-12 ▪ Closed Easter Fri-Mon, Dec 25 & Jan 1 ▪ BYO picnic ▪ Farm produce ▪ Walks/hikes ▪ 4x4 & mountain bike trails ▪ Owner(s) Nico Laubscher snr, Alette Laubscher, Nico Laubscher jnr ▪ Winemaker(s)/viticulturist(s) Nico Laubscher ▪ 48ha (cab, ptage, shiraz, chenin, cbard, sauv) ▪ 790t/280cs own label 100% red ▪ PO Box 627 Vredendal 8160 ▪ alzanne@nashuaisp.co.za ▪ S 31° 44'42.24" E 018° 32'8.16" ▪ **T** +27 (0)27-213-2525/+27 (0)82-905-1640 ▪ F +27 (0)27-213-2825

Nico Laubscher jnr again vinified just 5 barrels of cab and 5 of shiraz in 2011. He'd love to pay more attention to the wine side of the business, he says, but growing cucumbers and grapes, which also supply Namaqua Wines, and setting up an empowerment project keep him on the hop at the Vredendal family spread.

Two of the Best ★★ Last year switched to 3-way blend shiraz (45%), cab & pinotage in sunny **09**. — Panel

Vondeling

Location: Paarl ▪ Map: Paarl & Wellington ▪ WO: Voor Paardeberg ▪ Est 2001 ▪ 1stB 2005 ▪ Tasting, sales & tours by appt ▪ Owner(s) Armajaro Holdings UK ▪ Cellarmaster(s) Matthew Copeland (Jul 2007) ▪ Winemaker(s) Matthew Copeland (Jul 2007), with William Mofokeng (Jan 2005) ▪ Viticulturist(s) Julian Johnsen (Aug 2000) ▪ 467ha/40ha (cabs s/f, carignan, grenache r/w, malbec, merlot, mourv, p verdot, shiraz, chard, chenin, Muscat de F, sauv, viog) ▪ 250t/150,000cs own label 48% red 49% white 3% rosé ▪ Other export brand: Signal Cannon ▪ PO Box 57 Wellington 7654 ▪ admin@vondelingwines.co.za ▪ www.vondelingwines.co.za ▪ S 33° 35'45.7" E 018° 51'6.4" ▪ **T** +27 (0)21-869-8595 ▪ F +27 (0)21-869-8219

This British-owned Voor Paardeberg winery has been pretty low key in the 11 years since it was first purchased. No longer. A marketing team is now in place, production will move across the road to the erstwhile David Frost cellar once the purchase is approved, and then there'll be a tasting room and bigger cellar. And there are hints that a boutique hotel and restaurant might be on the cards.

★★★★ **Sauvignon Blanc** 🍷 🌿 Vibrant hit of lemon & grass, **11** maintains tone of **10** in its flinty minerality & succulence. Long finish.

★★★★ **Babiana** 🍷 🌿 Well-crafted 4-way chenin-led blend, naturally fermented & no added acid. Complex **09** lime marmalade fullness, body & breadth yet dances lightly on oak stage.

★★★★ **Petit Blanc** 🍷 🌿 **11** (★★★) fig & pear on easy-drinking mix of chenin, viognier & chardonnay. Tangy & fresh but less impressive than vibrant **10**.

Erica Shiraz ✓ ★★★★ **08** repeats dashed of grenache, carignan, mourvèdre used in **07** (★★★) to better effect. Dense, rich mouthful of earthy beetroot & plum spice. Dark intensity balanced by fruit purity & third new oak. Lengthy. **Baldrick Shiraz** 🍷 🌿 ★★★ Plush **10** is savoury & spicy with chunky body. Less sleek than previous but serious nonetheless. Dabs mourvèdre & viognier. **Cabernet Sauvignon-Merlot** ✓ ★★★★ **07** a notch up on **06** (★★★★). More rounded, nuanced black fruit & cigar spice. Svelte & sexy. Lovely depth & softness. **Petit Rouge** 🍷 🌿 ★★★ **10** continues **09** appeal. Plum & berry from 60/40 merlot/cab mix, pepper twist on gently rounded body. **Chardonnay** 🍷 ★★★★ Elegantly restrained **09** keeps the serious intent. Orange blossom mingles with vanilla & honey from oak (33% new). **Sweet Carolyn** ★★★★ Excellent muscat-led straw wine. Last reviewed **06** an apricot & honey indulgence, bright limy acidity & pithy flick in tail. Delicious! **05** (★★) noted previously as funky. — FM

Von Ortloff

Location: Franschhoek ▪ Est 1992 ▪ 1stB 1994 ▪ Closed to public ▪ Owner(s) Evi & Georg Schlichtmann ▪ Cellarmaster(s)/winemaker(s)/viticulturist(s) Evi & Georg Schlichtmann (1992) ▪ 34.5ha/8ha (shiraz, chard, sauv) ▪ 50t/1,800cs own label 75% red 25% white ▪ PO Box 341 Franschhoek 7690 ▪ vonortloff@mweb.co.za ▪ **T** (0)21-876-3432 ▪ F +27 (0)21-876-4313

This Franschhoek property is a far cry from Georg and Evi Schlichtmann's former lives in Germany, he as a Munich-based BMW executive, she as an architect. Something of that came with them, because the wines have numbers, similar to the car series concept, and the packaging is sleekly modern. For the rest, Evi took over the viticulturist role and will oversee replanting of cab and merlot, while Georg is the winemaker. Most of their sales are to private clients, the majority overseas, but locals can enjoy the wines in Franschhoek restaurants.

★★★★ **No. 1 Syrah** Hedgerow berries with asphalt, scrub nuances, last tasted **08** offered complexity & flavours more Old World than New. Polished, refined tannins. WO Coastal.

★★★★ **Cabernet Sauvignon-Merlot** Creamy cassis, vanilla, other spicing, but **05** year ago was an iron fist in a velvet glove, the firm tannins seaming the fruit, providing an 8+ year rewarding future.

★★★★☆ **Quintessence** Last was **05**, blend cab, merlot with serious oaking (22 months French barriques, 50% new), handled with aplomb. Red berries & chocolate, cigarbox, extra bottle-age aided current enjoyment. Drink till 2020.

★★★★ **Chardonnay** Citrus peel & roast nuts, oak a big presence in bold **08** last edition, but the savoury/tobacco finish made a marvellous food match. Fermented/year new barriques.

No. 7 Await next. **No. 5** ★★★★ Sauvignon with grassy, fynbos nuances, **10** last year was trim, taut & athletic, crackled with freshness. — CR

▪ **Voorspoed** *see* Baarsma Wine Group

Vrede en Lust Wine Farm

Location: Paarl ▪ Map: Paarl & Wellington ▪ Est 1688 ▪ 1stB 2002 ▪ Tasting & sales daily 10–5 (tasting room closed on Mon from 1 Jun to 31 Aug) ▪ Closed Good Fri & Dec 25 ▪ Tours 10–4 by appt ▪ Cotage Fromage Deli & Restaurant ▪ Guest accommodation in three deluxe suites & Manor House ▪ Tour groups by appt ▪ Conferences & functions ▪ Play area for children ▪ Petanque courts ▪ Owner(s) Buys family ▪ Winemaker(s) Susan Erasmus (2006), with Ansoné Fourie (2009) ▪ Viticulturist(s) Etienne Buys (Jun 1998) ▪ 340ha total ▪ Vrede en Lust: 35ha (cab, grenache, malbec, merlot, p verdot, shiraz, chard); Casey's Ridge, Elgin: 48ha (cab f, shiraz, chard, chenin, pinot g, sauv, sem, viog); Ricton: 42ha (cab, cinsaut, mourv, ptage, shiraz, chard) ▪ 680t/20,000cs own label ▪ WIETA member ▪ PO Box 171 Groot Drakenstein 7680 ▪ info@vnl.co.za ▪ www.vnl.co.za ▪ S 33° 50' 15.9" E 018° 57' 13.4" ▪ **T +27 (0)21-874-1611** ▪ F +27 (0)21-874-1859

This polished property elegantly reflects its three-century history, while constantly innovating and keeping up with trends. The cellar has been expanded and upgraded to accommodate increased tonnage from the Buys family's farms in Elgin and nearer-by in the Simonsberg foothills, and winemaker Susan Erasmus is delighted with the quality of the whites and the promise of the shiraz. Also highly rated is the new automatic grape sorter, which has been 'bliss to work with'.

Vredenheim Wines

Location/map/WO: Stellenbosch ▪ Tasting & sales Mon-Fri 9–4.45 Sat 10–4.45 (summer) &10–3 (winter) Sun 11–3 ▪ Closed Easter Fri, Dec 25/26 & Jan 1 ▪ Barrique Restaurant, T +27 (0)21-881-3001 ▪ Hudson's Coffee Shop, T +27 (0)21-881-3590 ▪ Conferences/functions ▪ Vredenheim Angus Stud ▪ Jaguar cars for hire ▪ Curio shop ▪ Guesthouse ▪ Owner(s) Bezuidenhout family ▪ Winemaker(s) Kowie du Toit ▪ Viticulturist(s) Kalie Kirsten ▪ 80ha under vine ▪ 10,000cs own label 60% red 40% white ▪ PO Box 369 Stellenbosch 7599 ▪ wine@vredenheim.co.za ▪ www.vredenheim.co.za ▪ S 33° 57' 38.2" E 018° 48' 29.4" ▪ **T +27 (0)21-881-3637** ▪ F +27 (0)21-881-3296

Never a dull moment on this Stellenbosch estate, home of the Bezuidenhout family. Wine, food, accommodation, curios, nursery and astounding gardens are all part of the fun. And for petrolheads, Jaguars for hire. Plus the wine-loving businessperson's ideal: a conference venue in the cellar.

Merlot ☺ ▤ ★★★ Plum, chocolate & oaky whiffs on **09**. **Vredenvonkel** ☺ ★★★ Light-bodied **NV** pink sparkler to get the party started.

Pinotage ▤ ★★ Strawberry, smoky aromas on sweetish **08**. Not retasted, as for most below. **Shiraz** ▤ ★★★ Lightish **08** vibrant & spicy. **Reserve** NEW ✓ ▤ ★★★★ **08** from shiraz & cab is juicy, smooth & spicy, sweet fruit & soft tannins, lovely balance. **Rosé** ★★ Earthy **NV** semi-sweet from shiraz, zesty, more vinous than fruity.

Sauvignon Blanc 🔲 ★★★ Bright & zingy kiwi & passionfruit on dry, crisp **11**. **Angel's Natural Sweet** 🔲 ★★ Softly sweet **NV** offering from viognier. Discontinued: **Cabernet Sauvignon**, **CJB Reserve**. — WB

Vredevol Private Wine Cellar

Location: Stellenbosch ▪ WO: Walker Bay ▪ Est 2010 ▪ 1stB 2008 ▪ Closed to public ▪ Owner(s) Johan & Anne-Mar le Hanie ▪ Cellarmaster(s)/winemaker(s) Johan van Wyk (Jul 2010) ▪ 30ha ▪ 500cs own label 50% red 50% white ▪ PO Box 12695 Die Board 7613 ▪ vredevol.wines@vodamail.co.za ▪ **T +27 (0)21-887-1277** ▪ F +27 (0)21-887-1288

'We had too much going on the past year, including building of the new cellar, so no new releases,' says co-owner Johan le Hanie. 'But that is about to change.' Plans include a possible Out-of-Region brand pinot/chardonnay blend and a shiraz favourite of winemaker Johan van Wyk.

Bordeaux Blend ★★★★ Dense core of dark berries on **08** cab-led blend last year, tannins should be more approachable now. — WB

Vriesenhof Vineyards

Location/map: Stellenbosch ▪ WO: Stellenbosch/Piekenierskloof ▪ Est 1980 ▪ 1stB 1981 ▪ Tasting & sales Mon-Thu 10-4 Fri 10-3.30 Sat by appt ▪ Fee R25 ▪ Closed all pub hols ▪ Cellar tours by appt ▪ Meals/refreshments by appt ▪ Owner(s) Landgoed Vriesenhof (Pty) Ltd ▪ Cellarmaster(s) Jan Coetzee ▪ Winemaker(s) Nicky Claasens (2008), with Richard Phillips (2001) ▪ Viticulturist(s) Coetzee Ehlers ▪ 60ha/45ha (cabs s/f, merlot, pinot, ptage, chard) ▪ 300t/17,000cs own label 90% red 10% white ▪ PO Box 155 Stellenbosch 7599 ▪ info@vriesenhof.co.za ▪ www.vriesenhof.co.za ▪ S 33° 58' 16.7" E 018° 52' 2.8" ▪ **T +27 (0)21-880-0284** ▪ F +27 (0)21-880-1503

Vriesenhof's style is resolutely traditional – the wines are properly dry, flavour is there aplenty but the fruit is neither 'up-front' nor hidden by lashings of new oak. This also applies to the Paradyskloof range, designed for easier, less pricey drinking, which is taken seriously and not dumbed-down. But change happens even in Jan Coetzee's Stellenbosch Paradyskloof paradise: modern fermentation methods, for example, and now extensive new plantings in the Talana Hill section, introducing new soil types, clonal variations and even new varieties. These, they say, 'will shift the focus of our wines in a new direction' – not too far, we trust.

Vriesenhof range

★★★★ **Cabernet Sauvignon** Traditional in its dryness, lack of upfront fruitiness, & strong build. **06** (no **05**) a touch austere, with slightly drying tannic finish, but satisfying & ready. Only in magnums.

★★★★ **Grenache** Perhaps the tastiest in the range, though serious, **09** has sweet red & black fruit packed round a strong core. Will grow over few years; decant in youth. Magnums only. Ex Piekenierskloof.

★★★★ **Pinot Noir 08** (★★★★★) like **07** needed time for tannins to soften, tasted last yr. Initially sombre, opened up to show great balance: lightness, freshness with depth, silkiness.

★★★★ **Kallista 05** usual blend merlot, cabs sauvignon & franc. Last year showed big tannins (perhaps from 3 years in older oak barrels) & moderate substance. Best opened in next few years.

★★★★☆ **Chardonnay** After splendid **09**, lesser vintage shows in **10** (★★★★). But again classically styled & fine: steely, dry & elegant, with refined lemon & lime character, supported by moderate oaking.

Pinotage NEW ★★★★ **06** shows some animal notes & awkwardness. **07** (★★★★) cleaner, more sweet fruit intensity; also a rather heavy feeling to it. House-style dry finish. Discontinued: **Enthopio**.

Paradyskloof range

Cabernet Sauvignon NEW ★★★ Simple & eminently drinkable version: **09** with sweet, light fruit, modest structure. **Pinot Noir** ★★★ Lightly built **10** shows a little toasty oak (though none was new), with sweet red berry/cherry fruit. Good drinking now. **Pinotage** ★★★ Clean varietal aromas on **09** - simpler, less oak than on senior version. Sweet fruit, but a lot of tannin & acid too. **Chardonnay** ★★★ **10** in same classic mould as Vriesenhof version, but a little lighter-fruited & easier. Pleasing, well balanced. **Muscat d'Alexandrie** ★★★ Light, bright & not too sweet **08** from rather rare red hanepoot - 50 yr old vines. Tawny-coloured; just 15% alc. Discontinued: **Cabernet Sauvignon-Merlot**. — TJ

Vruchtbaar Boutique Winery

Location/map/WO: Robertson ▪ Est/1stB 2001 ▪ Tasting, sales & cellar tours Mon-Sat by appt ▪ Closed all pub hols ▪ Owner(s) Alwyn & Francois Bruwer ▪ Cellarmaster(s)/winemaker(s) Francois Bruwer ▪ Viticulturist(s) Briaan Stipp (consultant) ▪ 35ha (cab, merlot, ptage, ruby cab, chard, chenin, sauv) ▪ 400t/±437cs own label 62% red 38% white ▪ PO Box 872 Robertson 6705 ▪ vruchtbaar@mweb.co.za ▪ S 33° 48′ 17.7″ E 019° 51′ 43.6″ ▪ **T +27 (0)82-739-5553/+27 (0)82-335-1152** ▪ F +27 (0)23-626-2334

Cellarmaster Francois Bruwer is emphatic about keeping the winemaking style at his family's boutique winery near Robertson 'as primitive as possible'. 'The old people could make wine with limited equipment,' he says, 'and I try to follow in their footsteps.' They've bottled their first pinotage under the label Picasso, and changed the Island Red blend to 50/50 cab/pinotage.

★★★★ **Cabernet Sauvignon** Concentrated 08 preview fruit-filled sipper with modern styling. Dense & lingering, with tannins giving form. Rating provisional. Last 06 was integrated, polished & harmonious.

★★★★ **Chenin Blanc Limited Edition** In contrast to sinuous 08, bold 09 (★★★★) not for the faint-hearted: mid-2010 had ripe tropical tones lashed with buttery oak, active 15% alc.

Island Red ☺ ★★★ Happy **NV** marriage cab & pinotage, bright & refreshing, light tannin for everyday enjoyment.

Pinotage ★★★ Quintessential banana/strawberry characters on 09, revisited as bottled wine. Dense, ripe, certainly delivers power but with noticeable sweetness. **Chardonnay** ★★★★ Cordial-like 09 slipped down easily last edition, with orange & tangerine aromas/flavours, off-dry but (just) balanced by acidity, touch tannin. **Chenin Blanc Unwooded** NEW ★★★ Previewed 11 nutty & fruity, satisfying weight & vinosity. **Noble Late Harvest** Untasted. — Panel

Vukani Wines

Location: Plettenberg Bay ▪ Est 2005 ▪ Tasting & sales daily 10-5.30 ▪ Fee R30 ▪ Owner(s) Peter & Caroline Thorpe ▪ Cellarmaster(s)/winemaker(s) Anton Smal ▪ Viticulturist(s) Peter Thorpe ▪ ±1,400cs own label 56% red 44% white ▪ PO Box 1606 Plettenberg Bay 6600 ▪ peter@vukaniwines.com, danny@bramonwines.co.za ▪ www.bramonwines.co.za ▪ S 33° 57′ 25.0″ E 023° 28′ 50.8″ ▪ **T +27 (0)44-534-8007** ▪ F +27 (0)44-534-8007

This BEE project was the brainchild of the owners and Johnathan Kamkam, at that time an employee at the Bramon farm in Plettenberg Bay. Originally intended to serve the onsite restaurant, such has been its success, he now markets the wine independently to retailers throughout the country and beyond.

Cabernet Sauvignon ★★★ No re-tasted this edition, as for all below. Tasty 04 melange spice & fruit, smoothly meshed, savoury finish. **Pinotage** ★★★ Mouthwatering acidity curbed 09's sweetness. **Shiraz Rosé** ★★★ Pleasing dry, spicy 09's juiciness balanced by invigorating acidity. Robertson vines. **Chenin Blanc** ★★★ Pale gold 09 offered plenty flavour. Lees & oak provided character & breadth. WO Stellenbosch. **Sauvignon Blanc** ★★★ Shy 09 showed brisk green apple flavours. — IM

Vuurberg

Location/map: Stellenbosch ▪ WO: Stellenbosch/Western Cape ▪ Tasting, sales & tours by appt ▪ Closed all pub hols ▪ Owner(s)/cellarmaster(s) Sebastiaan Klaassen ▪ Winemaker(s) Donovan Rall (Oct 2010) ▪ 8ha (cabs s/f, malbec, merlot, p verdot, viog) ▪ 2,000cs own label 50% red 50% white ▪ PO Box 449 Stellenbosch 7599 ▪ vuurberg@mac.com ▪ www.vuurberg.com ▪ S 33° 54′ 28.9″ E 018° 56′ 52.7″ ▪ **T +27 (0)82-387-6235**

Ebullient Netherlander Sebastiaan Klaassen has handed over winemaking duties to Donovan Rall at his boutique farm and winery in the spectacular Banhoek Valley just outside Stellenbosch. Rall's impressive Swartland experience should only confirm the styling of the white blend, and he firmly intends 'to keep making wine in the traditional way and to keep things simple in the cellar'.

Vuurberg Reserve ★★★★ 09 from half petit verdot plus cab, merlot, malbec - a really tasty ensemble. Bit less woody on 08, but also big, bold. **White** ▤ ★★★★ Some Swartland grapes in 10: chenin, viognier & 3 others. Easy-going, flavourful burly charm, with a sweet note & piquant oaky edge. — TJ

 W see Whalehaven Wines

Waboomsrivier Wine Cellar

Location: Worcester ▪ Map/WO: Breedekloof ▪ Est 1949 ▪ Tasting & sales Mon-Fri 8-5 ▪ Closed all pub hols ▪ Cellar tours by appt during harvest ▪ Soetes & Soup festival; Outdoor festival ▪ Cellarmaster(s) Bennie Wannenburg (Sep 2005) ▪ Winemaker(s) Wim Viljoen (Sep 1991), with Gustav Fouché (Jan 2011) ▪ Viticulturist(s) Pierre Snyman (Vinpro) ▪ ±1106ha (cab, ptage, chenin, cbard) ▪ 15,799t/6,000L 5% red 95% white ▪ ISO 22000:2011 ▪ PO Box 24 Breërivier 6858 ▪ sales@wabooms.co.za ▪ www.waboomsrivier.com ▪ S 33°31'43.08" E 019°12'35.24" **T +27 (0)23-355-1730** ▪ F +27 (0)23-355-1731

Two 'firsts' last year for this grower-owned Breedekloof winery, now a limited liability company: it was the first vintage for assistant winemaker Gustav Fouché, ex Delheim, and year one as holder of BRC/ISO 22000 certification, sought in response to client demand and awarded after five years of work.

Wagenboom range NEW

Hanepoot ☺ ★★★ Fortified **08** is grapey & fresh with pleasant lick of fire in the conclusion. Serve well chilled.

Pinotage ★★ Juicy, plummy **09** everyday red with zippy finish. **Chenin Blanc** 🍴 🥂 ★★ Tropical fruit flavours, **11** light easy sipper. **Sauvignon Blanc** 🍴 🥂 ★★ Crisp, early-picked **11** for current enjoyment. —Panel

Waka Waka Wines NEW

WO: Paarl ▪ Est 2011 ▪ 1stB 2010 ▪ Closed to public ▪ Owner(s) REH Kendermann & Perdeberg Winery ▪ Cellarmaster(s) Albertus Louw (Oct 2008) ▪ Winemaker(s) Riaan Möller (Dec 2006) & Carla Herbst (Jun 2008) ▪ Viticulturist(s) Jaco Engelbrecht (Nov 2011) ▪ PO Box 214 Paarl 7620 ▪ info@perdeberg.co.za ▪ www.perdeberg.co.za **T +27 (0)21-869-8244** ▪ F +27 (0)21-869-8245

Produced by Perdeberg Winery, this is a new global value-for-money brand developed in partnership with REH Kendermann in Germany. The name is already an advantage and would have instant recognition (with a smile?) amongst soccer fans because it was the 2010's FIFA World Cup anthem in South Africa, performed by Shakira and Freshlyground, with enthusiastic sing-alongs by stadium audiences. The fans won't be disappointed in the wines, taste appeal is paramount.

Shiraz-Cabernet Sauvignon 🥂 ★★★ Good mix red berries & structure in **10**, easy drinking. **Sauvignon Blanc-Chenin Blanc** 🥂 ★★★ From bushvines, **10** shows gooseberries, some tropical notes & good body from moderate alcohol (12.8%). —CR

▪ **Walker Bay Vineyards** *see* Birkenhead Estate & Brewery
▪ **Walking The Path** *see* Schonenberg Wines
▪ **Wamakersvallei Winery** *see* Wellington Wines

Wandsbeck Wyne Koöp Bpk

Location/map: Robertson ▪ WO: Robertson/Worcester ▪ Est 1965 ▪ 1stB 1986 ▪ Tasting & sales Mon-Fri 8-5 Sat, Sun by appt ▪ Closed all pub hols ▪ Cellar tours by appt ▪ Owner(s) 19 members ▪ Cellarmaster(s) Jacques du Toi (Jun 2008) ▪ Winemaker(s) Adriaan Foot (Jan 2009) ▪ Viticulturist(s) Briaan Stipp (consultant) ▪ 8,777ha/516ha (cab, cinsaut, merlot, ruby cab, shiraz, chenin, chard, cbard, sauv) ▪ 7,000t/2,000cs own label 43% red 29% white 14% rosé 14% other + 600,000L bulk ▪ Brands for clients: Grysberg, Smokey Mountain ▪ IPW ▪ PO Box 267 Robertson 6705 ▪ wandsbeck@breede.co.za ▪ www.wandsbeckwyne.co.za ▪ S 33° 55' 60.0" E 019° 36' 34.4" **T +27 (0)23-626-1103** ▪ F +27 (0)23-626-3329

The emphasis at this Robertson cellar has been on marketing since winemaker Adriaan Foot's wife Lara took up the position. Their new Revelation label depicts the scenic Agterkliphoogte Valley and includes a white blend, with a red to follow; a spruce-up of the premises and distribution are also receiving attention.

Wandsbeck range

Revelation White NEW ☺ 🍴 🥂 ★★★ Crisp & lightish **11** chenin/chard combo brims with character: pineapple, lemon, thatch. For early enjoyment.

Cabernet Sauvignon ★★★ Nutty/vanilla overlay on sweet plums of friendly **09**. Still selling, as for Ruby Cabernet-Shiraz, Symphony of Rose & Red Muscadel. **Merlot** NEW 🍽 🖼 ★★★ **10** juicy & bold, gentle tannins for accessibility, warm flush from 14.5% alc. Also in 1.5L for extra fun. **Shiraz** Await new. **Ruby Cabernet-Shiraz** ★★★ Warm hay & plums on unwooded **08** pizza pal. **Symphony of Rosé** 🍽 🖼 ★★ Pretty Natural Sweet-style perlé pink from shiraz, **10** all cranberries & good cheer. **Sauvignon Blanc** 🍽 🖼 ★★★ Reticent **11** relatively neutral yet fresh & bone-dry. **Red Muscadel** ★★★ Honeyed **08** blue cheese companion. WO Worcester. Discontinued: **Chenin Blanc, Colombar**. — Panel

Warwick Estate

Location/map: Stellenbosch ▪ WO: Stellenbosch/Western Cape ▪ Est 1964 ▪ 1stB 1983 ▪ Tasting & sales daily 10–5 ▪ Fee R25pp ▪ Closed all pub hols ▪ Cellar tours by appt ▪ Gourmet picnics in summer; Tapas inspired winter menu ▪ Facilities for children ▪ Gifts ▪ Conference facilities ▪ Conservation area ▪ Owner(s) Ratcliffe family ▪ Winemaker(s) Nic van Aarde (May 2011) ▪ Viticulturist(s) Ronald Spies (Nov 2001) ▪ 110ha/60ha (cabs s/f, merlot, ptage, shiraz, chard, sauv) ▪ 300t/29,595cs own label 60% red 40% white ▪ BWI, WIETA ▪ PO Box 2 Elsenburg 7607 ▪ info@warwickwine.com ▪ www.warwickwine.com ▪ S 33° 50′ 26.6″ E 018° 51′ 51.0″ ▪ **T +27 (0)21-884-4410** ▪ F +27 (0)21-884-4025

It seems that Stellenbosch family estate Warwick is on a roll. The accolades keep pouring in, most recently two tourism ones: the Great Wine Capitals of the World 'Innovation in Tourism' award, and being ranked the No 1 wine destination in Stellenbosch on the world's biggest travel website, Tripadvisor.com. Nor did famous personalities pass them by: on her recent South African visit, Michelle Obama as America's First Lady was presented with the eponymous Warwick wine by the American consul general, and in the new James Bond novel, Bond in Cape Town seduces the heroine with a vintage bottle of Warwick's Three Cape Ladies (he 'knew its reputation'). And the same wine continues its ratings track record, with a 6th 90+ score in Wine Spectator.

★★★★ **The First Lady Cabernet Sauvignon** ✓ For earlier drinking, hence part Robertson fruit, older barrels & shorter oaking. But **09** gives full value, opulent fruit, cedar/savoury spicing, friendly dry finish. Less gravitas than **08** (★★★★★).

★★★★☆ **Cabernet Franc** Improving on the high standard set by **07** & previous vintages, **08** (★★★★★) is layered, complex, a template for the variety. Masterly oaking adds cigarbox note. Herbaceous, yet with ripe mulberries, its succulence tempered by fine-grained tannins. Gorgeous, drink till ±2020.

★★★★ **Old Bush Vines Pinotage** 🖼 Blueberries, black pepper, modern style **09** has married good oaking to the plush fruit to give balance & flavour complexity. For drinking earlier than fine **08** (★★★★★).

★★★★ **The Black Lady Syrah** Original take on shiraz, **07**'s fruit core is black cherries, piquant berries, but the overriding style is savoury: burnt match, mineral, cigarbox. Needs rich food. **06** (★★★★★) more showy.

★★★★☆ **Trilogy (Estate Reserve)** Bordeaux blend & flagship, **08** treads that fine line between accessibility & structure. Cassis & tobacco, white pepper & polished tannins all give immediate pleasure, but the best is yet to come, drink till ±2020.

★★★★ **Three Cape Ladies** Equal pinotage, cab & shiraz in **08** makes for a flavour-packed blend; smoky notes in the dark berries, pinotage's trademark succulence given focus, structure by cab, 32 months oaking. Less fine than great vintage **07** (★★★★★).

★★★★ **Chardonnay** 🖼 Hazelnuts & citrus rind, **10** is silk textured & full flavoured, this lady has curves in all the right places. Delicious now, drink till ±2015.

★★★★ **Professor Black Sauvignon Blanc** 🍽 🖼 After austere **09**, extroverted last **10** (★★★★★) had concentrated peach, exotic stonefruit & fragrant nectarine. Poised, self-assured, with firm acidity. — CR

Waterford Estate

Location/map: Stellenbosch ▪ WO: Stellenbosch/Elgin/Western Cape ▪ Est/1stB 1998 ▪ Tasting, sales & cellar tours Mon-Fri 9–5 Sat 10–5 ▪ Tasting fees: R40/standard; R65/chocolate; R50/The Jem (current vintage only); R120/romantic (bubbly & chocolate); R200/reserve; R550/wine drive; pre-booking essential ▪ Closed Easter Fri, Dec 25 & Jan 1 ▪ Tea/coffee/soft drinks & chocolates ▪ 14ha BWI conserved land ▪ Owner(s) Jeremy & Leigh Ord, Kevin Arnold ▪ Cellarmaster(s) Kevin Arnold (1998) ▪ Winemaker(s) Francois Haasbroek (2005), with Mark le Roux (Jul 2009) ▪ Viticulturist(s) Lombard Loubser (Oct 2003) ▪ 120ha/60ha (barbera, cab, sangio, shiraz, tempranillo, chard, sauv) ▪ 503t/40,000cs own label 51% red 45% white 3% rosé 1% other ▪ PO Box 635

Stellenbosch 7599 ▪ info@waterfordestate.co.za ▪ www.waterfordestate.co.za ▪ S 33° 59' 44" E 018° 52' 12.0" ▪
T +27 (0)21-880-0496 ▪ F +27 (0)21-880-1007

Over recent years, this stylish Helderberg winery has been increasingly advancing
claims to be placed amongst the country's leading producers. Not only is The Jem
(named for owner Jeremy Ord) one of the most convincing of the super-expensive
local reds, but the range shows an impressive depth. Increasingly the wines, with
part-owner Kevin Arnold as cellarmaster, rely on elegance and restraint for impact;
the combination of this with clearly expressed ripe-fruitedness, marks them as balanced between classic and modern in style. The new Library Collection of small parcels of mature wines (mostly one-offs) reveals some of the thought, work and
experimentation behind Waterford's success. 'They are pets!' says winemaker
Francois Haasbroek. 'We pretty much use the Collection as an experimental platform to play with alternatives.' With some success, it seems.

Waterford Estate range

★★★★☆ **Cabernet Sauvignon ✓** First-class example of modern but classically reminiscent cab. **08** ripe &
flavourful, but fruit disciplined by firm structure & moderate oaking, leading to strong dry finish. Should benefit
from 5+ years in bottle.

★★★★☆ **Kevin Arnold Shiraz 08** tasted last year continues shift to more suppleness, elegance. Focus on
core textural richness, savoury flavours & length. Oak, none new, gives unobtrusive support.

★★★★☆ **The Jem 07** cab-led varietal septet, last year showed more complex flavour than previous, & both
plush texture & freshness. Focused by integrated tannin, polished by oak. No **08** - not up to high standard.

★★★★☆ **Reserve Chardonnay** Fine **10** lovelier, creamier, silkier than standard version (with 100% new
oak instead of 35%, but supportive & integrated). Harmonious, light-feeling & genuinely elegant, with flavours
echoing (even multiplying & expanding) on long finish. Should improve good few years.

★★★★☆ **Chardonnay 10** (★★★★) vital & fresh like **09**, but a touch less impressive. Like senior partner
unflashily refined, with restrained oak influence, & enough fruit for lingering satisfaction.

★★★★ **Sauvignon Blanc** Like **09**, particularly good **10** (★★★★★) not overtly fruity; citric minerality with
usual - but subtly expressed - spectrum of flavours. Good balance, fresh & lightly rich.

Rose Mary ★★★ Fruitily dry, lightish, charming & delicate **10** rosé from 5 varieties, tasted last year.

Library Collection NEW

★★★★ **Edition BB** Name denotes 5-way, cabernet-based Bordeaux blend. Modern-style **04** in its attractively mature prime, with plentiful sweet fruit - though tannins still forceful in overall easy harmony.

★★★★ **Edition CSS** Combo cabernet, sangiovese, shiraz works oddly & interestingly well! Youthful **08** dry
& succulently savoury; fresh red fruit packed on firm structure. Italianesque finish of sour cherries.

★★★★ **Edition SBS 07** blend sauvignon, semillon - the latter's lanolin & lemon prominent, but the flavours
showing maturity. Soft, lingering, well balanced. For pleasurable drinking soonish.

★★★★☆ **Edition VSBC 07** another twist on white blend: viognier plus sauvignon, chenin, well complemented by toasty oak. Mature, probably at its peak. Delicious, silkily textured, lingering.

Edition MB ★★★★ Shiraz-based 'Mediterranean blend'. **04** shows marked ripeness on aromas, flavours - tasty,
but slightly unharmonious with dry tannic presence.

Waterford range

★★★★ **Heatherleigh Family Reserve** Made in solera system (vintages added to ongoing blend), so **NV**
Oaked. Latest from muscat & chenin lovely as ever, delicate perfume & clean, fresh, not-too-sweet satisfaction.

★★★★ **Sauvignon Blanc** 📖 Preview of **11** (★★★★) Elgin version flavourful but less substantial, complex, finely balanced than current Estate one. Bracing, as was **10**, but more aggressive acidic whack.

Pinot Noir ★★★★ Toasty oak touch works well with Elgin's characteristic berry fruit delicacy on **10**. Unassuming, but with the genuine charm that this variety can show.

Pecan Stream range

Chenin Blanc ☺ 📖 **★★★** Refreshing but full & fat **11** shows peachy viognier addition in aromas, flavour.
Light oaking adds breadth. Nicely dry. These all WO W Cape. **Pebble Hill** ☺ 📖 **★★★** Blend shiraz & 4 others. Chunkily built but not too powerful **09** preview is ripely fruity, with easy appeal.

Sauvignon Blanc 📖 **★★★** Pre-bottling, **11** light & easy, with usual tropicality & a citrus bite. — TJ

■ **Waterfront Collection** *see Vaughan Johnson's Wine & Cigar Shop*

Waterhof *see* Waterstone Wines

Waterkloof

Location: Somerset West ▪ Map: Helderberg ▪ WO: Stellenbosch ▪ Est 2004 ▪ 1stB 2005 ▪ Tasting & sales daily 10-5 ▪ Fee R30/6 wines ▪ Closed Easter Fri, Dec 25 & Jan 1 ▪ Cellar tours by appt ▪ The Restaurant at Waterkloof T +27 (0)21-858-1491 (see Restaurants section) ▪ Walking/hiking trails ▪ Conservation area ▪ Art collection on display ▪ Tutored horse riding tours with ploughman's platter & wine tasting ▪ Owner(s) Paul Boutinot ▪ Cellarmaster(s) Werner Engelbrecht (Jun 2004) ▪ Winemaker(s) Werner Engelbrecht (Jun 2004), with Nadia Barnard (Dec 2008) ▪ Viticulturist(s) Christiaan Loots (Jan 2010), advised by Werner Engelbrecht ▪ 120ha/52ha (cabs s/f, grenache, merlot, mourv, shiraz, chard, chenin, sauv, sem, viog) ▪ 450t/10,000cs own label 50% red 45% white 5% rosé ▪ BWI champion ▪ PO Box 2093 Somerset West 7129 ▪ info@waterkloofwines.co.za ▪ www.waterkloofwines.co.za ▪ S 34° 5′ 55.4″ E 018° 53′ 22.8″ ▪ **T +27 (0)21-858-1292** ▪ F +27 (0)21-858-1293

'Circle of life' is not just a clever name for some typically elegant, deliciously unassertive wines from this Schapenberg winery. The concept is central to the hugely ambitious project of Paul Boutinot, the British wine importer. Compost, for example, is made from restaurant waste, grapeskins and other winery residues, vineyard weeds and cuttings – and returned to the soil. In the vineyards they've moved beyond organic farming to embrace the esoteric practices of biodynamics. Two cows, 120 chickens and 130 sheep are now helping the process, and a nursery has been established to grow the plants used in biodynamic preparations. In the cellar, Werner Engelbrecht aims to encourage Waterkloof - the land, the circle of life here - to express itself, by following 'a natural and traditional approach'.

Waterkloof range

★★★★ **Circle of Life Red** 09 is 80% merlot & shiraz, plus 4 others. Touch more elegant than 08, but also sophisticated easy-going. Deep & subtle & delicious too, for early unfrivolous pleasure.

★★★★☆ **Sauvignon Blanc** 🛇 10 more open & expressive in youth than 09, with flavours expanding & proliferating as they linger. Some invisible sugar softens acidity, adds mouthfilling breadth. Takes Circumstance version to higher level of intensity and interest.

Circle of Life White 🛇 ★★★★ 10, like 09 (★★★★) blends 60% sauvignon with chenin, semillon; has similar lime & peach notes, but better balance, more intense, showing sugar less.

Circumstance range

★★★★☆ **Syrah** The star of the range. Ripe aromas on 09, with subtle fruit plus overtones of lilies & fresh herbs; a fine dark chocolate note on lingering conclusion. Flowing, supple, unobtrusively structured. Properly dry, but a fruit sweetness the only unclassical note. Delicious now & for good few years.

★★★★ **Chardonnay** 🛒 Touch more restrained, finer than previous, 09 also shows less oak (though 70% new barrels). Light-feeling moderate alcohol (12.5%), dry, crisp & fresh. Smart but unshowy.

★★★★ **Sauvignon Blanc** 🛒 🛇 Incipient complexity on 11, with aromas & flavours from peach & pear to a fennel hint - happily evading stereotypes. Intense, powerful; richness balanced by a big savoury acidity.

★★★★ **Viognier** 🛒 🛇 Refined (much less ripe) 10 back to the mark after clumsy 09 (★★★). Some might find its typical floral peachiness a touch dilute rather than elegant; others will relish the lightness!

Cabernet Sauvignon ★★★ 09 quietly serious, more savoury than fruity, but a sweetly ripe element too. Lightly oaky, fairly chunky, highly drinkable. **Merlot** ★★★★ Herbal element jostles 09's red fruit. Soft texture, but a grippy, slightly fiery, powerful finish. **Cape Coral Mourvèdre** 🛒 ★★★ Dry, elegantly unfruity 11 rosé as understated as its pale onionskin colour. Round, balanced; a little finishing bite. **Chenin Blanc** 🛒 ★★★★ As for 08, the oaking stands out on 09's intense flavours ripe apple, thatch, dried pineapple. Rich & not quite harmonious.

Peacock Ridge range

Merlot ★★★★ Ripe 08 tasted last year had herbal twist concluding friendly, light-fruited palate. **Sauvignon Blanc** 🛒 🛇 ★★★★ An earthy tug to the citrus-dominant fruit on 11, avoiding usual green/tropical Cape style. Big but unaggressive acidity. — TJ

Waterstone Wines

Location: Somerset West ▪ Map: Helderberg ▪ WO: Western Cape/Stellenbosch/Coastal ▪ Est/1stB 2007 ▪ Tasting, sales & cellar tours by appt ▪ Closed all pub hols & Dec 15-Jan 3 ▪ Tour groups ▪ Self-catering accommodation ▪

Owner(s) Pim de Lijster & Reino Kruger ▪ Cellarmaster(s)/winemaker(s) Andries de Klerk (Oct 2010) ▪ 41ha (cab, merlot, ptage, shiraz, chard, chenin, sauv) ▪ 40,000cs own label 65% red 35% white ▪ Other export brand Compadre ▪ PO Box 1560 Somerset West 7129 ▪ info@waterstonewines.co.za ▪ www.waterstonewines.co.za ▪ S 34° 2'0.3" E 018° 48'34.8" ▪ **T +27 (0)21-842-2942** ▪ F +27 (0)86-505-8691

Aiming for consistency at affordable prices in the 3-million litres it produces each year, this Helderberg-based winery relies heavily on its experienced winemaking team (an impressive 30 vintages between them) to deliver. And they certainly do, with more than 10 awards across the various tiers, mostly aimed at international markets, Waterstone last year was rated as one of South Africa's top three 'good value' brands by Wine magazine.

Waterhof range

Cabernet Sauvignon Reserve ★★★ 08 has sweet fruit & vanilla oak notes, bitter cherry astringency, needs more time to mellow. **Shiraz Reserve ★★★ 07** quite harks back to Old Cape with sweet-sour flavours, but shows good length & balance. **Chardonnay Reserve ★★★★** Last edition, lightly oaked **08** was poised & lively, had lime & vanilla appeal. **Sauvignon Blanc Reserve ★★★★ 10** stand-out in range showing best varietal character & balance at commendably moderate alc. Restrained tropical bouquet, lengthy grassy flavour. Stellenbosch WOs for these.

Africa range

Bomvu 🔲 **★★ 08** lively cab & shiraz mix, lightly oaked. This, next, not revisited. Both WO Coastal. **Ifulu** 🔲 **★★★ 09** easy-sipping papaya/cut grass combo, mostly chenin.

Africa Five range

> **Cape Premier Red** NEW ☺ **★★★** Mostly pinotage, with shiraz & cab, drop merlot. Layers strawberry, banana & spice, tasty & ready to enjoy. **06** ends dry, unlike other reds in this entry-level range. **Sauvignon Blanc** NEW ☺ 🔲 **★★★ 11** stand-out white in range, uncomplex but unmistakably sauvignon.

Cabernet Sauvignon ★★ Savoury **10** is fleshy, with obvious 14.5% alc. Lightly oak-staved, like most Waterstone reds. **Merlot ★★★ 10** faintly creamy/plummy. As for Cab, Pinotage, Shiraz, gets crowd appeal from dollop sugar. **Pinotage ★★** Generous fruit flavour of **10** seamed with bitterness. **Shiraz** 🔲 **★★★** Like previous bottling, lily-scented **10** is friendly & sippable. **Cabernet Sauvignon-Shiraz ★★** Prunes & hint malt on zesty **08**, for drinking soon. **Chardonnay ★★ 10** pleasant quaffer though, unlike previous, has no varietal character. **Chenin Blanc ★★** Thatch & peardrop nuances, **11**, soft pithy grip. WO Stellenbosch, as for Cape Premier Red & Sauvignon. Discontinued: **Bordeaux Blend**.

African Lizard

Cabernet Sauvignon ★★ 08's firm tannins padded by hint sugar. This, Shiraz still selling, not revisited. **Shiraz ★★** Previous edition, NV had dusty overlay to tutti-frutti aromas/flavours. **Cape Premier Red Blend** Await next, as for **Chardonnay** & **Chenin**.

Cape Discovery range NEW

Cabernet Sauvignon ★★ Solid fruit centre, firm tannin on **10** quick-quaff. **Chardonnay ★★** Lemon-toned **11** is slightly sweet but maintains balance & appeal.

Golden Vine

Shiraz ★★ Red-fruited **09** changes from off-dry to dry; clean leathery, meaty complexity. Stellenbosch WO.

Moja Tetra Pack range

Now discontinued.

Opener's range

Cabernet Sauvignon 🔲 **★★★ 08** had cool black & red berries, fine tannin grip last year. Like all following, not revisited. **Merlot** 🔲 **★★★** Meat & mulberries, **08** fresh, gentle tannic hug. **Dry Red** 🔲 **★★★** Bordeaux mix with drop tinta, surprising fruit quality for this price point. **NV. Rosé** 🔲 **★★** Strawberry-sweet **09** had zesty freshness mid-2010. WO Stellenbosch, like next. **Chenin Blanc** 🔲 **★★ 09** was demure but zippy, slightly tropical.

Sonata range

> **Sauvignon Blanc** ☺ 🔲 **★★★** Nettles, fresh hay & pithy grip on cheerful **11** preview.

Cabernet Sauvignon 🍷 ★★ Different bottling of **07** is generous, gently spiced & slightly spirity (14.5% alc). **The Ludwig** NEW 🍷 ★★ **04** unusual Bordeaux blend with tinta; raisiny, dominated by merlot, gruff tannins need time. **Chenin Blanc** 🍷 ★★★ Honeyed bottle-age noted last year, so best to enjoy **08** soon. — CvZ

Waverley Hills Organic Wines & Olives　🍴🍵🎋📷🐾♿

Location/map/WO: Tulbagh ▪ Est 2006 ▪ 1stB 2004 ▪ Tasting, sales & cellar tours Mon-Fri 8-5 Sat 10-4 Sun 11-3 ▪ Closed Easter Fri/Mon & Dec 25 ▪ Restaurant Tue-Fri 9-4 Sat 10-4 Sun 11-3 & Wed evenings ▪ Picnic baskets by appt; or BYO picnic ▪ Facilities for children ▪ Tour groups ▪ Farm produce ▪ Conferences ▪ Wedding venue & chapel ▪ Walks/hikes ▪ Mountain biking ▪ Conservation area ▪ Fynbos nursery & eco-centre ▪ Owner(s) Bremo-en-Kem (Pty) Ltd ▪ Cellarmaster(s) Johan Delport (Oct 2008) ▪ Winemaker(s) Albert Viljoen, with Andre Ewerts (Dec 2006/Jul 2008) ▪ Viticulturist(s) Magnus Joubert (Aug 2007) ▪ 80ha/27ha (cab, grenache, merlot, mourv, shiraz, chard, pinot grigio, sauv, sem, viog) ▪ 200t/10,000cs own label 75% red 15% white 5% rosé 5% MCC ▪ Other export brand: Dixon's Peak ▪ BWI champion, WIETA ▪ PO Box 71 Wolseley 6830 ▪ info@waverleyhills.co.za ▪ www.waverleyhills.co.za ▪ S 33° 24′ 21.2″ E 019° 14′ 19.6″ ▪ **T +27 (0)23-231-0002** ▪ F +27 (0)23-231-0004

Here the wines do the talking. As leading organic producers, Waverley Hills continue to innovate (witness experiments on weed control), for wines that are healthy, enjoyable and eco-friendly. The 'Best organic wine southern hemisphere' title for their SMV at the International Challenge du Vin seems a just reward.

Cabernet Sauvignon-Shiraz ☺🌿🔖 ★★★ Previewed **10**, with a drop of merlot. Fresh & juicy with spicy aromas, followed by a herbal lift to the end. **Semillon-Sauvignon Blanc** ☺🍷🔖 ★★★ Equal blend **10**, with a dash of oaked chardonnay for rounded complexity; peachy fruit & vibrant dry finish.

Cabernet Sauvignon 🌿🔖 ★★★ Modern, dark-fruited, plush **10** (with a dollop of merlot) has a toffee-sweet impression derived from oak, & a medium finish. **Shiraz** ✓ 🌿 ★★★★ **09** exudes attractive oak spice; brooding dark fruit on a soft & rounded palate. Shows variety's affinity for the region. **Cabernet Sauvignon-Merlot** 🌿 ★★★ **09** a 50/50 blend in sweetish style, with warming alcohol showing on finish. **Shiraz-Mourvèdre-Viognier** 🌿 ★★★★ Previewed last year, **09** (77% shiraz) has bright, expressive fruit, its richness cut by pepper spice, but ending a tad sweet. **Rosé** 🍷🌿 ★★ Await next. **Méthode Cap Classique** ★★ **09** from chardonnay; fresh & bone-dry, but lacks complexity. Discontinued: **Semillon-Chardonnay.** — JP

▪ **WaverleyTBS** *see* Cape Promise
▪ **Weathered Hands** *see* Dewaldt Heyns Family Wines

Webersburg Wines　🍵🏛📷♿

Location/map/WO: Stellenbosch ▪ Est 1995 ▪ 1stB 1996 ▪ Tasting, sales & cellar tours Mon-Fri 10-5 Sat 10-4 ▪ Fee R5/wine ▪ Closed Ash Wed, Easter Fri-Mon, Dec 25/26 & Jan 1 ▪ Seasonal menu's ▪ Tour groups ▪ Historic buildings: Manor House 1786; cellar & Jonkershuis 1796 ▪ 5-star Cape Dutch Guesthouse ▪ Conference facilities ▪ Weddings/functions ▪ Owner(s) Fred Weber ▪ Winemaker(s) Giorgio Dalla Cia & Matthew van Heerden (both consultants) ▪ Viticulturist(s) Johan Pienaar (consultant) ▪ 20ha/5ha (cab) ▪ 30t/2,000cs own label 80% red 20% white ▪ PO Box 3428 Somerset West 7129 ▪ info@webersburg.co.za ▪ www.webersburg.co.za ▪ S 34° 0′ 22.1″ E 018° 50′ 34.5″ ▪ **T +27 (0)21-881-3636** ▪ F +27 (0)21-881-3217

Considering this is a historic Cape property with the Manor House dating back to 1786 (now a luxury guest house), and cellar and Jonkershuis to 1796, the homes fully preserved and filled with antiques, one can understand Fred Weber's impatience with passing fads. The belief that 'all great wines take time' has been translated into 22-34 months barrel-ageing and a further 2 years bottle-ageing of the reds before release. A sauvignon joins the range, and available cellardoor only are two méthode cap classique sparklings, a Brut and Brut Rosé.

★★★★ **Cabernet Sauvignon** ✓ Everything in harmony, **06** is a delight, blackcurrant & cigarbox, elegant polished tannins. At perfect drinking age, but built to last 5+ years more. 18 months in oak, 70% new, as next.

★★★★ **Webersburg** Previously tasted **05**, a well-structured, cab-driven Bordeaux blend, was elegant, showed blackcurrant & dark chocolate, velvety tannins.

★★★★ **Sauvignon Blanc** NEW ✓ Minerality is key ingredient in **10**, with additional lime & passionfruit nuances. Finishes tangy, crisp. Cool climate indeed, but there's ripeness here too, & a lot of pleasure. — CR

Wedderwill Wine Estate

Location: Somerset West ▪ Map: Helderberg ▪ WO: Stellenbosch/Coastal ▪ Est 1992 ▪ 1stB 1997 ▪ Tasting, sales & tours by appt Mon-Fri 9-5 Sat 9-12 ▪ R200 for the first 6 people, R30pp for over 6 people ▪ Closed all pub hols ▪ Farm produce ▪ BYO picnic ▪ Guided walks/mountain bike tours T +27 (0)82-462-3624 Di Marais ▪ Game reserve ▪ Conservation area ▪ Conference/function facilities ▪ Lalapanzi Lodge T +27 (0)21-858-1982 & Cape Country Living T +27 (0)21-858-1607 ▪ Owner(s) Neil Ian Jowell & Cecil Jowell ▪ Cellarmaster(s) Nico Vermeulen ▪ Winemaker(s) Nico Vermeulen (Jun 2004) ▪ Viticulturist(s) Wolfgang von Loeper (Apr 2004) ▪ 400ha/41ha (cab, merlot, shiraz, sauv) ▪ 100-200t/15,000cs own label 60% red 40% white ▪ BWI champion, Carbon Neutral, Control Union Organic, Demeter Biodynamic, IPW ▪ PO Box 75 Sir Lowry's Pass 7133 ▪ sales@wedderwill.co.za ▪ www.wedderwill.co.za ▪ S 34° 5'55.0" E 018° 56'42.0" ▪ **T +27 (0)21-858-1558** ▪ F +27 (0)21-858-1461

With the Helderberg family farm now certified organic and biodynamic, the wine team has developed a unique spray programme to combat fungal disease in the vineyards, using the farm's own resources. Stellenbosch University is working on a better extraction method for one of the ingredients, another is seawater from False Bay! New to the wine range are a value-for-money white and red named for the temperatures at which to serve them.

★★★★☆ **Sauvignon Blanc** ✓ Elegant (under 13% alc), with taut minerality & proven ageing ability, usually released few vintages after rest of market. Three bottlings tasted: **10** ex-tank has gunflint as a central theme, with lemongrass & fennel. **09** (★★★★) shows an added honeyed tone, some delicate passionfruit; a bit subdued. **08** combines gooseberries & lime with the flintiness, intensifies the appeal & pleasure. Still in perfect condition, many years of life left.

17degreeC NEW ☺ 🍴 ★★★ Bordeaux varieties plus 21% shiraz, dash pinotage, **08** has appealing plums & blackcurrant, is elegant, harmonious. Drink soon. WO Coastal, as for 12degreeC.

Shiraz ★★★★ Cherries/red berries, **06**'s succulence partners the firm oak tannins, finishes dry, savoury. Lacks perfect balance of **05** (★★★★). **Wedderwill** ★★★★ Last was **04** cab, merlot, cab franc combo, showed maturing meat notes, firm, rounded tannins, good savoury length. **12degreeC** NEW 🍴 ★★ Mainly sauvignon in **10**, melon/pear flavours, lightish (12.7% alc) & crisp. — CR

Wederom Boutique Winery

Location: map/WO: Robertson ▪ Est 2002 ▪ 1stB 2003 ▪ Tasting, sales & cellar tours by appt ▪ Fee R20pp tasting/tour ▪ Closed Easter Fri & Dec 25 ▪ Meals by appt ▪ Tour groups ▪ Gifts ▪ Farm produce ▪ Conferences ▪ Weddings/functions ▪ Hikes ▪ Conservation area ▪ Italian prisoner of war museum ▪ Hanepoot Huisies guesthouse ▪ Owner(s) Philip & Almien du Toit ▪ Cellarmaster(s)/winemaker(s)/viticulturist(s) Philip du Toit ▪ 139ha/±17ha (cinsaut, merlot, shiraz) ▪ ±120t/419cs own label 100% red ▪ IPW ▪ PO Box 60 Robertson 6705 ▪ wederom@myisp.co.za ▪ www.wederom.co.za ▪ S 33° 49'5.5" E 019° 47'15.8" ▪ **T +27 (0)23-626-4139** ▪ F +27 (0)23-626-3306

'By making wine at Wederom,' say small-scale vintners Philip and Almien du Toit, 'we can bottle our love for the farm and share it with people around the world.' They plan to raise exports while lowering their carbon footprint and protecting the environment as members of the Rooiberg-Breede River Conservancy.

Shiraz ★★★ Mocha & dark choc-toned **09** still selling, not revisited. **Salvadori Vino Rosso Shiraz** ★★★ Savoury **08** laid-back & easy-drinking with luscious fruit, medium body. — Panel

Wedgewood Wines

Location: Malmesbury ▪ Map: Swartland ▪ WO: Swartland/Stellenbosch ▪ Est 2007 ▪ 1stB 2010 ▪ Wine sales Mon-Sat 9-5 from export offices: Nordic Wines 42 Paul Kruger Street Robertson ▪ Owner(s) Wiggo Andersen & Peter Tillman ▪ Winemaker(s)/viticulturist(s) Marius Malan (Nov 2010, consultant) ▪ 40ha/23ha (malbec, ptage, chenin, sem) ▪ 880cs own label 40% red 60% white ▪ Other export brand: Selma ▪ PO Box 896 Robertson 6705 ▪ nordicwines@xpoint.co.za, wedgewoodwines@xpoint.co.za ▪ www.nordicwines.co.za ▪ S 33° 32'19.6" E 018° 49'56.5" ▪ **T +27 (0)23-626-1413/+27 (0)83-283-5354** ▪ F +27 (0)23-626-1031

This main brand and Swartland base of Nordic Wines (the name signifying primary export markets) is now home to winemaking consultant Marius Malan. 'The focus has changed to his style of winemaking,' says CEO Peter Tillman. 'Wine is exciting because it is constantly evolving and reinventing itself. It is an expression of personality.'

Director's Choice range
Cabernet Sauvignon-Merlot 🔲 ★★★ Understated **09** follows style of **08** with appealing combo of cedar & savoury ripe berry. **Malbec-Pinotage** NEW 🔲 ★★★ Unusual but tasty blend, fruit-driven, **10** ripe plums & firm dry finish. Try with bobotie & pepper steak, suggests Peter T. **Chenin Blanc** 🔲 ★★★ Thatch & peach nuances last year on juicy **10**, from old Malmesbury vines, limy apricot tang in the aftertaste. — DB

■ **Welbedacht** *see* Schalk Burger & Sons Wine Cellar

Welgegund Wines

Location: Wellington ▪ Map: Paarl & Wellington ▪ WO: Wellington/Paarl/Western Cape ▪ Est 1800 ▪ 1stB 1997 ▪ Tasting & sales by appt ▪ B&B Cottage with pool & tennis court ▪ Walks ▪ Owner(s) Alex & Sheila Camerer ▪ Cellarmaster(s)/winemaker(s)/viticulturist(s) Daniël Langenhoven (Jun 2008) ▪ 35ha/15ha (carignan, cinsaut, ptage, chenin) ▪ 84t/320cs own label 60% red 38% white 2% rosé ▪ PO Box 683 Wellington 7654 ▪ sales@welgegund. co.za ▪ www.welgegund.co.za ▪ S 33° 39′ 38.3″ E 019° 2′ 13.6″ ▪ **T +27 (0)21-873-2123** ▪ F +27 (0)21-873-2683

Amongst Wellington's earliest private producers, the Camerers also pioneered carignan as a varietal wine. Now winemaker Daniël Langenhoven hopes his two red wines and white blend will help raise the area's image for quality, 'rather than being just another wine region'. Results suggest he's heading in the right direction.

★★★★ **Pinotage** Was 'Fiero' last edition. Bright hue, buchu & cherry aromas mark **10**. Silkiness clipped by fine, freshening tannins; long savoury, liquorice tail. Mostly new oak a subtle enrichment.

★★★★☆ **Chiara** ✓ 🔲 Grenache blanc joins chenin, chardonnay, sauvignon & viognier in **10**. Haunting, clean & complex aromas mirrored on suave, smooth-textured palate. Small portion oaked to highlight pure vinosity. Impressive, if not so long-lived as **09**. WO Paarl.

Ricco ★★★☆ Shiraz-led, Rhone-style blend with splash barbera. **09** ripe & smooth with rich earthy tones; not overly heavy. Older oak. WO W Cape. **Divina Carignan-Pinotage Rosé** 🔲 ★★☆ Uncomplicated plum, straw hints were noted on still available **09**. — AL

Welgeleë Boutique Wedding & Wine Farm

Location: Paarl ▪ Map: Paarl & Wellington ▪ Est 1999 ▪ 1stB 2003 ▪ Tasting & sales daily 9–5 ▪ Picnics by appt ▪ Function venues (±45 & 160 pax) ▪ Owner(s) Liris Trust (Chris & Lidea Meyer) ▪ Winemaker(s) Chris Meyer ▪ Viticulturist(s) Chris & Lidea Meyer ▪ 26ha/3ha (shiraz) ▪ 300cs 100% red ▪ PO Box 439 Klapmuts 7625 ▪ chris@welgelee.com ▪ www.welgelee.com ▪ S 33° 47′ 45.3″ E 018° 53′ 35.4″ ▪ **T +27 (0)21-875-5726** ▪ F +27 (0)21-875-5726

On Chris and Lidea Meyer's farm Welgeleë, the sound of popping corks could emanate equally from the cellar area, where their handmade shiraz is available for tasting and sale, or one of two lawn-fringed function rooms. These are popular as wedding venues, their attractiveness no doubt increased by the presence of a meadow with horses, rescued from neglect and abuse, and the Meyers' other 'children', a pack of Boerboel mastiffs.

Welgemeend Estate

Location/WO: Paarl ▪ Map: Paarl & Wellington ▪ Est 1974 ▪ 1stB 1979 ▪ Tasting, sales & cellar tours Mon-Fri 10–4 Sat 10–2 ▪ Closed all pub hols ▪ Owner(s) Welgemeend Estate (Pty) Ltd ▪ Winemaker(s) Lizette Steyn-James (Mar 2007), with Abraham Suse (Jan 2008) ▪ Viticulturist(s) Lizette Steyn-James (Mar 2007) ▪ 16ha/11ha (cabs s/f, malbec, merlot, shiraz) ▪ 11t/600cs own label 100% red ▪ PO Box 1408 Suider-Paarl 7624 ▪ welgemeend@worldonline.co.za ▪ www.welgemeend.co.za ▪ S 33° 47′ 50.8″ E 018° 53′ 8.5″ ▪ **T +27 (0)21-875-5210** ▪ F +27 (0)86-654-3806

Winemaker Lizette Steyn-James might say: 'Nothing grand about Welgemeend, we remain the same humble farm', but that doesn't quite cover it. Boasting more mature dryland vineyards for its five red varieties than most small properties, malbec the youngest at 23 years, cab oldest at 35 years, gives the farm lower yields and lower alcohols. The goal of getting back to Billy Hofmeyr's classic style of elegant, younger wines is still there. Hofmeyr produced SA's first Bordeaux blend here in the 1970s - and it was grand.

Estate Reserve ★★★★ First commercial Cape Bordeaux blend. 2 years oaking for **05** but 73% merlot gives succulence, red berry focus, touch of mint. **Douelle ★★★★** Malbec with cab, dark-toned **05** still sturdy, tannins dry; perfume attractive, smoky, creamy liquorice, hints of fynbos. **Soopjeshoogte** Await next. **Amadé ★★★** Individual blend, shiraz with grenache, pinotage, gives **05** enough brambleberry fruit to balance the sturdy tannins. — CR

◼ **Welgevallen Cellar-Stellenbosch University** *see* Stellenbosch University Welgevallen Vineyards & Cellar

Welgevallen Wines

Location/map/WO: Stellenbosch ▪ Est/1stB 2000 ▪ Visits Mon-Fri 10-2 ▪ Closed pub & school hols ▪ Owner(s) Paul Roos Gymnasium Old Boys Union ▪ Winemaker(s)/viticulturist(s) Wouter Pienaar & Tinnie Momberg (consultants) ▪ 400cs 75% red 25% white ▪ c/o Paul Roos Gymnasium Old Boys Union Suidwal Stellenbosch 7600 ▪ oldboys@prg.wcape.school.za ▪ www.paulroos.co.za ▪ S 33° 56′ 31.2″ E 018° 51′ 41.1″ ▪ **T +27 (0)21-883-8627** ▪ F +27 (0)21-883-8627

Largesse can run deep in the wine industry. This venture, coordinated by Wouter Pienaar, generates funds for 'talented boys from economically disadvantaged families' to attend Paul Roos Gymnasium. Wines are donated by winemakers and estate owners who are old boys of the prestigious Stellenbosch school.

Pinotage ✓ ★★★★ 09 succulent & smooth, worth seeking out as much for palate appeal as for noble (fundraising) intentions. Revisited, as for next. **Cabernet Sauvignon-Merlot ★★★ 09** good expression of the varieties: plum/violet merlot aromas, firm cab tannins, zesty acidity. **Sauvignon Blanc 🗎 ★★★ 11** delivers gravelly texture & weight absent in previous, though still tad closed mid-2011, may show better given time. — CvZ

◼ **Wellington Cooperative Cellar** *see* Wellington Wines

Wellington Wines

Location/WO: Wellington ▪ Map: Paarl & Wellington ▪ Est/1stB 2011 ▪ Tasting & sales Mon-Fri 8-5 Sat 8.30-12.30 ▪ Closed all pub hols ▪ Cellar tours by appt ▪ Owner(s) 79 members ▪ Production Manager Gert Boerssen (Oct 1980) ▪ Winemaker(s) Chris Smit & Pieter-Niel Rossouw (reds, Nov 2005/Jun 2009); Hugo Truter & Fritz Smit (whites, Oct 2005/Jan 2009) ▪ Viticulturist(s) Marko Roux (Nov 2008) ▪ 2,400ha (cab, ptage, shiraz, chenin) ▪ 25,000t/2,875cs own label 70% red 30% white ▪ BWI, BRC, Fairtrade, IPW, WIETA ▪ PO Box 509 Wellington 7654 ▪ info@wellingtonwines.com ▪ www.wellingtonwines.com ▪ S 33° 38′ 17.7″ E 018° 59′ 20.6″ ▪ **T +27 (0)21-873-1582** ▪ F +27 (0)21-873-3194

'It's been on the cards since 1939,' quips MD Johan Truter about the merger of Wamakersvallei and Wellington Cooperative cellars. It's more than just dropping the fences between these neighbours though. Shareholders gave their approval to a deal that's been bubbling under for a few years. But the integration has gone smoothly, with the two wineries each contributing something different, Truter says. The range has been streamlined and there's refreshing new energy and exciting plans afoot. Red tape and administrative backlogs involving company name registration stalled the rebranding significantly. So no labels, stationery or corporate ID until the new company's officially registered.

La Cave range

★★★★ Pinotage Concentrated, rich **09**'s raspberry chocolate charm countered by brooding earthy note. Ripe & accessible but textured, like **08**. Oak regime toned down, as for cab, to good effect.

Cabernet Sauvignon ★★★★ Lighter-styled cab with just 50% new oak. **09** maintains standard set by **08** & **07**. Savoury blackcurrant appeal. **Shiraz ★★★★ 09** offers plush plum spice & pepper twist, like previous. Earthy char note, very ripe. Oak as for Cab. **VCC 🗎 ★★★★** Barrel-fermented viognier, chenin & chardonnay. Debut **08** tangy & fresh previously, richer peach, pineapple & lemon overlay. Oak restrained: yr new French.

Wellington Wines range

Pinotage [NEW] ☺ 🗎 ▨ ★★★ Unpretentious berry spice & vanilla, **10** soft consistency with chocolate richness. Previewed, as for all reds. **Shiraz [NEW] ☺ 🗎 ▨ ★★★ 10** displays black cherry spice & some smoky meat. Light, chalky tannin grip. High 15.4% alc but still accessible. **Chardonnay** NEW ☺ 🍷 📖 ★★★ Unwooded **11** light citrus & bruised apple, fresh, simple & delicious. **Chenin Blanc** NEW ☺ 🍷 📖 ★★★ **11** offers straightforward tangy apricot & pear enjoyment.

Cabernet Sauvignon NEW ★★★ Spice & red fruit on maiden **10**, bit short & light bodied.

Fortified dessert range
Fishermans Jerepigo Await next. **Jagters Port** New vintage unready for tasting. —FM

Welmoed

Owned nowadays by The Company of Wine People, the Welmoed farm dates back to 1690, with a history to match. The well-priced Welmoed range commemorates, for example, Jacobus van der Heyden, sometime owner imprisoned for defying the Dutch East India Company's hegemony, with its Heyden's Courage bottlings.

Heyden's Courage White ☺ 🍷 ★★★ Sampled from tank, **10** fruit salad perfumes & tastes, plump but still lively lunch partner. Unusual blend includes verdelho & gewürztraminer. Coastal vines, as for Red.

Cabernet Sauvignon 🍷 📖 ★★★ Medium-bodied **10**, pure berry fruit but also some of the variety's firmness, inviting time or food to soften. Stellenbosch grapes, as for all unless mentioned. **Merlot** 🍷 📖 ★★★ Friendly **10** offers red berries, freshness & balance. **Pinotage** 🍷 📖 ★★ Berry fruit cushions the firmness but **10**'s probably better with a meal. **Shiraz** 🍷 📖 ★★ **10** smoky, rustic & brooding, needs bit of time to mellow. **Heyden's Courage Red** ✓ 🍷 ★★★★ The pick of these reds. **09** characterful, bold & packed with alluring berries & spice. Supple & silky Bordeaux blend. **Rosé** 🍷 📖 ★★ Light & smoky **11**, cranberry flavour from shiraz with tart & tangy bite. **Chardonnay** 🍷 📖 ★★★ Appealing oak-brushed **11**, crisp & vibrant varietal fruit, rounded & balanced for easy drinking. WO Western Cape, as for Sparkling. **Chenin Blanc** 🍷 📖 ★★ Crunchy apple freshness on **11**, light & zingy. **Sauvignon Blanc** 🍷 📖 ★★★ **11** crisp & lively green-fruit nuances, perfect summer white. **Sparkling** ★★ NV carbonated bubbly last listed as 'Charmat Brut'. Crisp & light appley freshness. —MW

Weltevrede Estate

Location: Bonnievale ▪ Map/WO: Robertson ▪ Est 1912 ▪ 1stB 1945 ▪ Tasting & sales Mon-Fri 8–5 Sat 9–3.30 ▪ Closed Easter Fri/Sun, Dec 25/26 & Jan 1 ▪ Cellar tours by appt ▪ Weltevrede Bistro Tue-Sat 9–3.30 ▪ Walks/hikes ▪ Conservation area ▪ Conferences ▪ Weddings/functions ▪ 4 self-catering guest cottages ▪ Owner(s) Lourens Jonker ▪ Cellarmaster(s) Philip Jonker (Jan 1997) ▪ Winemaker(s) Neil Strydom (2009) ▪ Viticulturist(s) Francois Viljoen (consultant) ▪ 360ha/106ha (cab, merlot, pinot, shiraz, chard, cbard, gewürtz, sauv) ▪ 1,300t/25,000cs own label 15% red 75% white 10% other ▪ Brands for clients: Woolworths ▪ BWI ▪ PO Box 6 Bonnievale 6730 ▪ info@weltevrede.com ▪ www.weltevrede.com ▪ S 33° 56' 30.9" E 020° 3' 4.4" ▪ **T +27 (0)23-616-2141** ▪ F +27 (0)23-616-2460

Making memories by continuing 100 years of winemaking on this family farm is what philosophical Philip Jonker is all about. Celebrating 'a century of blessings' this year will include the opening of several special wines, including magnums of the Brut sparkling (after 6 years on lees), the new Vanilla Chardonnay (which brings to 6 the number of terroir-based varietal expressions) and a Bourgogne Blanc made during a 2010 harvest in Burgundy. Philip and his family delighted in their lodgings in Flavigny-sur-Ozerain, the medieval village setting for the movie Chocolat. Weltevrede offers visitors a touch of the Old World in the excavations, completed after 15 years, of old tanks beneath the current winery. Tastings are by candlelight: it's all about the magic of wine here, not technical evaluation.

Estate range
★★★★☆ **Poet's Prayer Chardonnay** Developed **07** (★★★★), like oak-rich **06**, ex limestone/shale soils. rich texture, cleansing mineral core & warming alc. Range not revisited except Syrah & Place of Rocks Chard.
★★★★ **Rusted Soil Chardonnay** Last edition, we liked lime & tropical **07** (★★★★) as juicy, smooth & straightforward but needing drinking soon. Higher new oak component than **06**.
★★★★ **Place of Rocks Chardonnay 08** (★★★) flavoursome in oxidative style, bruised apple & sherry tones probably best enjoyed soon. Similar character last noted on **07** but more mineral freshness to balance.
★★★★ **The Travelling Stone Sauvignon Blanc** Bone-dry & grassy **10** (★★★★) first reviewed since racy **07**, lively, tasty, moderate 13% alc.

Bedrock Black Syrah ⭐⭐⭐ **10** a modern take on shiraz: plush blackcurrant fruit, hedonistic vanilla/coconut from new oak & fruit-sweet finish. **Gewürztraminer** ⭐⭐⭐⭐ Unshowy but typical rosepetal fragrance in **10**, fruity sweetness cleansed by brisk acidity.

Philip Jonker Brut Cap Classique Collection

⭐⭐⭐⭐ **Entheos** Engaging & serious champagne-method sparkling (even if name translates as 'energy of spontaneous laughter'). Chardonnay (60%) & pinot noir; brioche nuance, lingering appley refreshment. **NV**. **The Ring** ⭐⭐⭐ Oysters obvious choice with **07**, from chardonnay. Fresh mineral 'rockpool' highlights, invigorating bubble, bone-dry. Not revisited. **Aletheia** ⭐⭐⭐ **07** richer & sweeter than stablemate sparklings. Pinot noir, chardonnay combo, oak influenced. **Lindelize** ⭐⭐⭐ Rosé bottle-fermented bubbly named after Philip J's wife; latest **NV** is 100% pinot noir, hence the meaty/savoury, raspberry, toffee complexity, fine firm structure.

Vanilla range NEW

Chardonnay ☺ ⭐⭐⭐ **10** vanilla by name & by nature, yet with an engaging savoury thread.

River's Edge range

Tricolore Red ☺ ⭐⭐⭐ Easy-drinking cab, shiraz & merlot trio, **10** sweet-savoury character, bit of grip, nice supper red.

Shiraz Await new. **Unoaked Chardonnay** ⭐⭐ Ripe tangerine flavours on uncomplicated & plump **10** make for easy solo sipping. **Sauvignon Blanc** ⭐⭐ Hint green fruit on understated **11**. **Tricolore White** ⭐⭐⭐ Citrus-toned **09** from sauvignon, semillon & chardonnay tasted previously.

Heritage range

Oupa se Wyn ⭐⭐⭐⭐ Fortified dessert, **08** from red muscadel. Smooth, gently warming, not too alcoholic (15.5%) mid-2010. **Ouma se Wyn** ⭐⭐⭐ **07** fortified white muscadel delivered fiery, silky ease previously. —Panel

Welvanpas

Location/WO: Wellington ▪ Map: Paarl & Wellington ▪ Est 1704 ▪ 1stB 1994 ▪ Tasting & sales Tue-Fri 8–5 Sat/Sun 8–3 ▪ Fee R15pp ▪ Closed Easter Fri-Mon, Dec 16-Jan 2 ▪ Die Ou Meul Coffee Shop open daily ▪ Facilities for children ▪ Tour groups ▪ History package incl lunch & talk on Piet Retief family ▪ Farm produce ▪ BYO picnic (day permit R20pp) ▪ Walks/hikes ▪ Bains mountain bike trails ▪ Owner(s)/viticulturist(s) Dan Retief ▪ Cellarmaster(s) Dan Retief (Jan 1993) ▪ Winemaker(s) Dan Retief (Jan 1990), with Neels Kruger (Jan 1999) ▪ 260ha/50ha (11 varieties r/w) ▪ 25t own label 80% red 15% white 5% rosé ▪ PO Box 75 Wellington 7654 ▪ welvanpas@gmail.com ▪ S 33° 37'59.9" E 019° 4'12.5" ▪ **T +27 (0)21-864-1239** ▪ F +27 (0)21-864-1239

The wagons of the Great Trek have been replaced by roaring mountain bikes at the Retief family farm, where you can still view the ancient Bible that Piet Retief took on the trek, and his father's grandfather clock. A 'history package' includes a traditional lunch and wine-tasting with a short talk on the rich family history at Welvanpas. As well as wine, they bottle chutneys, preserves, dried fruit, peppadews and olives, and you can take your own picnic down to the river.

Cabernet Sauvignon NEW ⭐⭐ Savoury **10**, cranberry notes with overlay of dark cherries. **Shiraz** ⭐⭐ Now bottled, **09** toasty tobacco & liquorice aromas. Still bold & robust, needs more time to knit. **Revival Red** Await next. **De Krakeelhoek Rood** NEW ⭐⭐⭐⭐ Attractive dry red from merlot & shiraz, **NV**; smoky, savoury 'warm fireside' character, easy everyday drinking. **Suzanne Rosé** NEW ⭐⭐⭐ Crisp **10** from pinotage, cranberry fruitiness takes edge off dry palate. **Chardonnay** Not tasted. **Sauvignon Blanc** Await new vintage. **Amity** NEW ⭐⭐⭐ Unwooded chardonnay/chenin combo, **10** earthy & herbal, balanced by green-apple crispness. — DB

▪ **Weskus** see Winkelshoek Wine Cellar

Westbridge Vineyards

Location/map: Stellenbosch ▪ Est 1998 ▪ 1stB 1999 ▪ Tasting & sales by appt only (T 083-631-2229) ▪ Muldersvlei Stables B&B ▪ Chapel/wedding/conference venue ▪ Sunday lunch (booking required) ▪ Owner(s) JC Starke & Muldersvlei Estates ▪ Winemaker(s) Ian Starke ▪ Viticulturist(s) Julian Starke ▪ 3ha cab (chenin & sauv bought in) ▪ 40t/3,000cs own label 50% red 50% white ▪ PO Box 66 Muldersvlei 7607 ▪ wine@muldersvlei.co.za ▪ www.muldersvlei.com ▪ S 33° 49'30.2" E 018° 50'17.6" ▪ **T +27 (0)21-884-4433** ▪ F +27 (0)86-624-7446

Winemaker Ian Starke has a ready-made market for his Westbridge brand, namely Muldersvlei, the family farm, complete with conference and wedding venue (open for Sunday lunches, booking required) and accommodation. The wines, available exclusively on the estate, were again sold out at press time but Ian planned to release a sauvignon and a red blend in time for the summer season.

■ **Westerdale** *see* Kronendal Boutique Winery
■ **Westerkaap** *see* Linton Park Wines

Whalehaven Wines

Location: Hermanus ▪ Map: Elgin, Walker Bay & Bot River ▪ WO: Coastal/Elgin ▪ Est/1stB 1995 ▪ Tasting & sales Mon-Fri 9.30-5 Sat/Sun 10.30-4.30 ▪ Fee R10pp for groups of 5+ ▪ Tours by appt ▪ Owner(s) Bottega Family Wines ▪ Winemaker(s) Reino Thiart ▪ Vineyard manager(s) Tim Clark ▪ 120t capacity ▪ Private Bag X14 Hermanus 7200 ▪ wine@whalehaven.co.za, info@bottegafamilywine.co.za ▪ www.whalehaven.co.za, www.bottegafamilywine.co.za ▪ S 34° 24'36.9" E 019° 11'60.0" ▪ **T +27 (0)28-316-1633** ▪ F +27 (0)28-316-1640

Whalehaven is owned by Bottega Family Wines, and is the sibling brand to Idiom Wines. While Whalehaven might have been less in the spotlight due to the focus on Idiom, it deserves to 'stand on its own', offering great quality relative to price, according to the family owners. Pinot noir and chardonnay continue to be sourced from the Hemel-en-Aarde area or cooler-climate vineyards as close by as possible; other varieties are grown on family farm Da Capo Vineyards in the hills near Somerset West. Look out for the striking new labels featuring a mother and baby whale, linking the brand back to its name and the cellar's location in Hermanus.

Whalehaven Wines range
★★★★ **Pinot Noir 09** (★★★) from Elgin fruit. Raspberry, strawberry flavour, medium body with fresh acidity, fine tannins but lacks complexity, concentration of **08**.
Cabernet Franc ★★★ 08 shows dark fruit, some herbal character & toasty oak; rich & full bodied. **Merlot ★★★ 09** shows dark fruit, resinous oak. Good fruit concentration but very dry on finish. **Pinotage** NEW **★★★★ 09** red & black fruit, prominent but not unattractive oak, nicely tart acidity. **Chardonnay ★★★ 08** Evolved **08** shows sherry-like notes as well as some citrus. **Sauvignon Blanc** 🍸 Untasted. **Viognier-Chardonnay** 🍸 **★★ 09** juicy fruit, bright acidity, no great complexity when last tasted.

W range
Old Harbour Red 🍸 **★★ 09** is uncomplicated & rustic. **Crushed Velvet ★★★** Merlot-led blend **06** tad more angular than name suggests when last tasted, may since have mellowed. **Pinotage Rosé** NEW 🍸 📖 **★★ 10** some strawberry but generally simple, doesn't linger. — CE

■ **What? Wines** *see* Woolworths
■ **White River** *see* Bergsig Estate

Wildehurst Wines

Location: Koringberg ▪ Map/WO: Swartland ▪ Est 2006 ▪ 1stB 2009 ▪ Tasting & sales daily at The Wine Kollective & Bar Bar Black Sheep Restaurant, Riebeek-Kasteel; also at Cornberg Café, Koringberg ▪ Fee R50 ▪ Closed Dec 25 & Jan 1 ▪ Cellar tours by appt ▪ Cornberg Cottages (www.cornberg.co.za) ▪ Owner(s) Chris & Joanne Hurst ▪ Winemaker(s) Marais de Villiers (Nov 2008, consultant), with Raimond Maarman (Mar 2010) ▪ Viticulturist(s) John Loxton (2006, consultant) ▪ 0.5ha/±0.3ha (shiraz, viog) ▪ 1.8t/211cs own label 35% red 53% white 12% rosé ▪ PO Box 103 Koringberg 7312 ▪ joanne@wildehurst.co.za ▪ www.wildehurst.co.za ▪ S 33° 01'10.10" E 018° 40'26.42" ▪ **T +27 (0)22-423-8688** ▪ F +27 (0)86-657-8251

'If I had to choose between eating olives and drinking wine, then pfft to the olives!' This was owner Joanne Hurst's view when deciding what to plant on her tiny patch of garden in the heart of the Swartland. Proud members of the Swartland Independent group of winemakers, she and husband Chris have been working diligently with consultant Marais de Villiers to create the handcrafted, natural wines of their dreams, wines made to truly reflect their terroir.

★★★★ **Red** Commendably pure & unforced, **09** fresh, savoury blend shiraz, mourvèdre, hint viognier. Lovely lavender scent, generous toasted herb/wild fruit flavour, mere suggestion of (3rd fill) oak. Truly special.

Blush ★★★★ Serious rosé (& priced accordingly), mainly grenache, shiraz, chenin. **11** preview hardwired for food: savoury plum/cherry combo, delicious grip, lipsmacking dryness. **White** ★★★★ Another fine addition to burgeoning 'blanc de Swartland' category: ex-barrel **11** is 100% Perdeberg chenin proffering creamy pear flavours, peach kernel nuttiness & a savoury peach melba conclusion. Delectable - now & for several years. —Panel

Wildekrans Wine Estate

Location/WO: Bot River ▪ Map: Elgin, Walker Bay & Bot River ▪ Est/1stB 1993 ▪ Tasting, sales & cellar tours Mon-Fri 8.30–5 Sat/Sun 11-3 ▪ Fee R15 ▪ Closed Dec 25 ▪ Tour groups ▪ BYO picnic ▪ Conferences ▪ Walks/hikes ▪ Mountain biking ▪ Conservation area ▪ Self-catering Cottages ▪ Owner(s) Wildekrans Trust ▪ Cellarmaster(s)/winemaker(s) William Wilkinson (2006) ▪ Viticulturist(s) Braam Gericke (2008) ▪ 1,015ha/59ha (ptage, pinot, chard, chenin) ▪ 230t/±15,300cs own label 55% red 40% white 5% rosé; ±6,600cs for clients ▪ WIETA ▪ PO Box 31 Botrivier 7185 ▪ wines@wildekrans.com ▪ www.wildekrans.com ▪ S 34° 9' 42.6" E 019° 0' 36.0" ▪ **T +27 (0)28-284-9902** ▪ F +27 (0)21-413-0967

Although this Bot River farm dates back to 1924, own-label wines were only introduced in 1993 after some years of delivering fruit to a nearby co-operative cellar. Then the farm was spoken of by an international journalists as having the potential to be up with South Africa's best. That hasn't yet come to pass; there is potential, but perhaps too large a range of wines delays the achievement.

Osiris range

★★★★ **Pinotage Barrel Selection** High-toned raspberries, new oak vanillins happy partners in **09**. Sleek with sweet, fresh fruit cradled by polished tannins. 15% alc cleverly hidden.

★★★★ **Shiraz Barrel Selection** NEW Modern **09** shows nice lightness of touch, with hint of mint in its red fruit & spicy concentration. Overall balance dented by sweetish finish.

Chenin Blanc Barrel Selection ⊠ ★★★★ Big & bold in structure, honeyed, floral fruit somewhat lighter on **10**; alc glow & few grams sugar has sweet effect. **Sauvignon Blanc Barrel Selection** NEW ⊠ ★★★ Light oaking spices up quieter tropical tones on sampled **11**. Medium bodied, as is most of white range, may grow once bottled. **Méthode Cap Classique** ★★★ Light-textured, creamy **08** showed delicate biscuity tones last year. From chenin.

Wildekrans Estate range

Cabernet Sauvignon ★★★★ Fynbos & berry tones noted previously on smoke-infused **08**; firm tannin, 13.5% alc. **Merlot** ★★★ Simple herbal-edged plum fruit outpaced by dry tannin, sweet effect of 15% alc on **09**. **Pinotage** ★★★ **09** smells like pinot noir on steroids, explosive ripe dark cherries. Smooth & soft-centred, with sweet fruity tail. **Shiraz** ★★★★ Fruit-forward **09**. Gently juicy milk choc tones & kick of spice & tannin on finish. Like most of these reds, with a few grams of sugar. **Cabernet Franc-Merlot** ★★★ **09**'s light plummy fruit dominated by fiery tannins & 14.8% alc. **Merlot-Shiraz** Await next. **Pinotage Rosé** ☐ Await next. **Rosé** NEW ☐ ⊠ ★★ Strawberries & cream flavours on off-dry **11** sample. **Chenin Blanc** ☐ ⊠ ★★★ Striking ripe aromas introduce previewed **11**; well-sustained flavours too, though lacking youthful zest. **Sauvignon Blanc** ☐ ⊠ ★★★ Quiet grassy snatches on previewed **11**; tiny oak influence. **Director's Blend** NEW ☐ ⊠ ★★★ Chenin-led blend with sauvignon & oaked chardonnay. Appealing floral, melon fragrance on **11** (pre-bottling); juicy, persistent & bone dry. Discontinued: **Sauvignon Blanc Lot 1982**.

Jake White Selection

★★★★ **Jake White Selection** Lightly oaked, sweet-tannined red blend tasted few years back. **07** once off.

Caresse Marine range NEW

Cape Blend ☐ ★★ Sweetly ripe, smooth **09** tank sample. Unoaked. **Sauvignon Blanc** ☐ ★★ **11** ex tank, lightish, juicy, sweet 'n sour finish. —AL

■ **Wild Rush** see Rietvallei Wine Estate

Wilgenhof Wyne

Location: Vredendal ▪ Map: Olifants River ▪ Tasting & sales by appt only ▪ Owner(s)/winemaker(s) Gideon & Vere van Zyl ▪ (cabs s/f, merlot, p verdot, shiraz) ▪ BWI member ▪ PO Box 288 Vredendal 8160 ▪ wilgenhof@mylan.co.za ▪ www.wilgenhof.co.za ▪ **T +27 (0)27-213-2518** ▪ F +27 (0)27-213-2518

Steeped in Old Cape history, Wilgenhof was the first grazing farm on the Olifants River, established in 1732, and has been in the Van Zyl family ever since. Current scion Gideon van Zyl's cellar is in the old stables where casks of this specialist red-wine operation lie ageing on the old feeding troughs. The boutique winery's Bordeaux blend, Stalwyn (stable wine), reflects this heritage.

William Everson Wines

Location: Grabouw ▪ Map: Elgin, Walker Bay & Bot River ▪ WO: Elgin/Stellenbosch/Paarl ▪ Est/1stB 2001 ▪ Tasting, sales & tours by appt ▪ Self-catering accommodation (www.mentmor.co.za) ▪ Owner(s)/winemaker(s) William Everson ▪ 4t/400cs own label 60% red 40% white ▪ 2281 Essenhout Avenue Klipkop Grabouw 7160 ▪ william@eversonwine.co.za, william@eversonscider.com ▪ www.eversonwine.co.za, www.eversonscider.com ▪ S 34° 8'44.01" E 019° 1'1.21" ▪ **T +27 (0)82-554-6357** ▪ F +27 (0)86-662-4045

Using grapes from three Overberg farms, Grabouw winemaker William Everson produces 'numbered bottles of handcrafted wines', in time-honoured garagiste style. Last year was one of diversion and diversity, as he laboured over a handmade cider, made with wine yeast and aged on oak staves, and - a first - vinified a pinot noir for a private client.

William Everson Wines range

Stellenbosch Cabernet Sauvignon NEW ★★★ 09 earthy tones mixed with sour cherry flavours, needs more time to fill out. **Stone's End Pinot Noir** NEW ★★★ Textured 10, lovely balance between earthy notes & mulberry fruit, crisp dry finish. **Paarl Shiraz** ★★★★ Listed as 'Shiraz' last year. Fruity & rounded 08 abounds with dark ripe berries & warm plums. **Elgin Shiraz** ★★★ 'Shiraz-Mourvèdre' last time. Smoky/leathery 09 from Elgin grapes, more elegant, subtle & crisp than previous. **Chardonnay** ★★★★ Cedar scented with generous vanilla from barrel fermentation, fig & lime flavours. Crisp & balanced 10 preview a step up on understated 09 (★★★). **Sauvignon Blanc** Await next. **Sauvignon Blanc-Chardonnay** NEW ★★★ Early picked freshness on 10, light bodied, leafy, hints of greenpepper & lime. — DB

■ **Willowbrook** see Wine-of-the-Month Club

Windfall Wine Farm

Location/map/WO: Robertson ▪ Est 1998 ▪ 1stB 2006 ▪ Tasting, sales & tours by appt ▪ Closed all pub hols ▪ BYO picnic ▪ Owner(s) Bianca Weingartz, Sarah Alexander & Jaco de Wet ▪ Cellarmaster(s) Kobus van der Merwe (Jan 2006, consultant) & Jaco de Wet ▪ Winemaker(s) Kobus van der Merwe (Jan 2006, consultant), with Van Zyl de Wet (Jan 2009, consultant) ▪ Viticulturist(s) Jaco de Wet (Jan 2003) ▪ ±288ha/30ha (cab, merlot, pinot, ruby cab, chard, chenin, sauv) ▪ 534t/275cs own label 75% red 25% white ▪ PO Box 22 Robertson 6705 ▪ bee@windfallwine.com ▪ www.windfallwine.com ▪ S 33° 56' 33.37" E 019° 38' 42.98" ▪ **T +27 (0)21-685-4540** ▪ F +27 (0)86-743-4162

The family-owned farm and boutique winery in the Agterkliphoogte Valley formerly owned by cricketing legend Eddie Barlow was 'pretty much like a building site' mid-2010, but marketer Bianca Weingartz was optimistic that the tasting room and cellar would be ready come season. Also under construction is their range: a maiden pinot noir and blend have been unveiled, and their first brandy and méthode cap classique sparkling will follow 'once they are perfect'.

Cabernet Sauvignon ★★ 08 infused with mint & vanilla, tad green & leafy. **Pinot Noir** NEW ★★★ 10 super effort! Ripe berry flavours, plush centre & elegant conclusion. Very youthful still, promises well, deserves time. **Shiraz** ★★★ Retasted, 08 herbaceous tones to ripe fruit, firm tannic grip & spicy-sweet tail. **Barrel 41** NEW ★★ Sweet-sour fruit on 09 shiraz/cabernet (50/50) quick-sip. **Sauvignon Blanc** 🗐 ★★★ Elegant 11 very easy to drink thanks to mouthfilling fruit & gentle acidity. — Panel

Windmeul Cooperative Cellar

Location: Paarl ▪ Map: Paarl & Wellington ▪ WO: Paarl/Coastal ▪ Est 1944 ▪ 1stB 1945 ▪ Tasting & sales Mon-Fri 8-5 Sat 9-3 ▪ Closed all pub hols ▪ Cellar tours by appt ▪ Farmers' market every 1st Sat of each month, with fresh produce & meals ▪ Owner(s) 42 members ▪ Cellarmaster(s) Danie Marais (Oct 1999) ▪ Winemaker(s) Francois van Niekerk (Dec 2004), with Liani Theunissen & Pieter Rossouw (Dec 2010/Jan 2011) ▪ Viticulturist(s) Anton Laas (Oct 2007) ▪ 1,700ha ▪ 13,500t/6,000cs own label 54% red 44% white 1% rosé 1% fortified + 400cs for clients ▪ Brands for clients: Ses'Fikile ▪ PO Box 2013 Windmeul 7630 ▪ windmeul@iafrica.com ▪ www.windmeulwinery.co.za ▪ S 33° 40' 18.1" E 018° 54' 30.6" ▪ **T +27 (0)21-869-8100/8043** ▪ F +27 (0)21-869-8614

This cellar's success at wine competitions becomes clear when you realise how little is bottled under its own label: the wine team has the pick of extensive vineyards. 2010 boasts two Pinotage Reserve vintages at ABSA Top Ten, both listed below, and three Diamond Awards at Winemaker's Choice, where they were also nominated Producer of the Year. To honour 'Theuns' Briers, ex-Springbok, longtime supplier and until ill health forced his retirement, a director at Windmeul, The Legend was launched. Most of the grapes came from his farm.

Reserve range

★★★★ **Pinotage** ✓ Trademark succulent blueberries in these. Cocoa dusting on **10**, polished tannins. 18 months new French barrels, as for other reds. Bemedalled **09** (★★★★☆) more complex, fynbos & prosciutto layers, tannins firmer, built for 8+ years. No barrier to current enjoyment.

★★★★ **Shiraz** A serious wine, **10** needs time. Ripe (15% alc) but masked by fruit & oak (American & French here). Organic notes in bemedalled **09** add to the complexity, supple tannins supply definition. Both improve on **08** (★★★☆).

★★★★☆ **The Legend** NEW Top of the range doesn't always mean more of everything & OTT, as proven by Bordeaux red blend **10**. Complex spice, herb & fruit interweaving, some mocha shading, all backed by harmonious tannins. A handsome fellow, with winning ways. WO Coastal.

★★★★ **Cape Blend** ✓ Ripeness seen in black plums, fleshy body, **10** is mainly pinotage (60%) & it shows; cab's role is to aid structure, which it does with style & serious intent. Enjoy now till ±2018. No **09**.

★★★★ **Chardonnay** ✓ A savoury seam to **10** makes it food compatible but there's more to admire: tangerine & almond flavours, a limy freshness that has you pouring a second glass.

Cabernet Sauvignon ★★★★ Heaps of potential in **10**, ups the ante, molten berries counter the tannins, give a smoothly textured effect. Drink now till ±2018. Meatier **09** (★★★☆) has similar palate appeal. **Chenin Blanc** ✓ ★★★★ Smart winemaking retains chenin fruit in improved barrel fermented/matured **10**. Citrus & tropical tones refreshed by good acidity, lengthens the finish. More focus than **09** (★★★☆).

Windmeul range

Shiraz ☺ ★★★ Plumply smooth & liberally spiced, **09**'s lush fruit gives it tasty drinkability. **Sauvignon Blanc** ☺ ★★★ Mineral & leafy notes, zesty light **11** epitomises summer.

Cabernet Sauvignon ★★ Plums & dusty pepper, last **08** was sturdy, could age 3+ years. **Merlot** ★★★ **09** fleshy plums with year oak dollop for spice & ageing. **Pinotage** ★★★ Blueberries & cream, **09** has variety's trademark vibrancy, firm enough body to keep ±3 years. **Cabernet Sauvignon-Merlot** ★★ Smoked meat flavours, toasty oak give **09** a savoury slant. **Chardonnay** ★★ Soft, easy-drinking **10** has delicate tropical tones. Lightly oaked. **Chenin Blanc** ★★★ Red apples & thatch in **11**, a crisply dry quaffer. **Port** ★★★ Last was **07**, from ruby cab, paraded piquant berries, juicy sweetness. WO Coastal. — CR

■ **Winds of Change** see African Terroir

Wine4Us

Est 2010 ▪ 1stB 2009 ▪ All wine sales via website ▪ Owner(s) Mike Carter, Patrick le Roux & Edwin Blatt ▪ 6,000cs own label 50% red 50% white ▪ PO Box 5033 Helderberg 7135 ▪ mike@wine4us.co.za ▪ www.wine4us.co.za ▪ **T** +27 (0)82-706-5599 ▪ F +27 (0)86-510-4548

This self-proclaimed 'world first crowd-sourced, social wine brand' did good business last year; good enough to sell out of the four wines it bottled. This year, MD Mike Carter has tweaked his business model to cut costs: he'll source from an established winery and offer that under the Wine4Us brand through the web site.

Wine Concepts

Location: Cape Town ▪ Tasting & sales Mon-Fri 9–7 Sat 9–5 ▪ Owner(s) Michael Bampfield-Duggan, Murray Giggins, Derick Henstra, Peter Fehrson, Neil & Sue Proudfoot, Corlien Morris ▪ Winemaker(s) Murray Giggins ▪ Cardiff Castle cnr Kildare & Main St Newlands 7700 ▪ newlandshop@wineconcepts.co.za ▪ www.wineconcepts.co.za ▪ **T** +27 (0)21-671-9030 (Newlands), +27 (0)21-426-4401 (Gardens) ▪ F +27 (0)21-671-9031, +27 (0)88-021-426-4401

Partner-in-this-speciality-wine-store-business Michael Bampfield-Duggan's cryptic comment: 'Nothing in the pipeline at the moment but there'll be something soon...'

should keep fans of their house label, Lollopalooza, on their toes. The Shiraz 2009 was snapped up off the shelves by patrons of their outlets, and no wines were made in 2010 and 2011.

Winegro Marketing

Location: Bellville ▪ Est/1stB 2004 ▪ Closed to public ▪ Winemaker(s) Johan Pietersen ▪ Barinor's Vineyard South Building A Ground Floor The Vineyards 99 Jip de Jager Drive Bellville 7530 ▪ matubawine@gmail.com ▪ www. matuba.co.za ▪ **T +27 (0)21-913-8950** ▪ F +27 (0)21-913-8954

Winegro Marketing owns the well-established Matuba and Kleinbosch value brands, blended for easy, early enjoyment. See separate entries.

Wine-of-the-Month Club

Location: Cape Town ▪ Est 1986 ▪ Founder Colin Collard ▪ MD Tai Collard ▪ Private Bag X2 Glosderry 7702 ▪ wineclub@wineofthemonth.co.za ▪ www.wineofthemonth.co.za ▪ **T +27 (0)21-709-6300** ▪ F +27 (0)86-674-4690

Wine-of-the-Month Club, South Africa's original and still leading wine mail-order business, distributes third-party wines selected by its expert panel as well as own-label brands such as Montebello, Willowbrook, Giant's Peak, Steenhuis, Semara and Berg en Dal.

▪ **Winery of Good Hope** *see* The Winery of Good Hope

Wines of Cape Town

Location: Paarl ▪ Map: Durbanville, Philadelphia & Darling ▪ WO: Western Cape ▪ Est 2007 ▪ Tasting by appt ▪ Sales Mon-Fri 8-4.30 ▪ Owner(s) DS Sarnia (Pty) Ltd ▪ 50% red 50% white ▪ Export brands: Alphen Hill, Bushman's Creek, Dolphin Bay ▪ Brands for clients: Diamond Creek, Radisson Blu ▪ 11 La Med Crescent Elishua Villas Langeberg Rd Sonstraal Heights 7550 ▪ sales@winesofcapetown.com ▪ www.winesofcapetown.com ▪ **T +27 (0)21-987-0079** ▪ F +27 (0)86-272-0415

Christine Brand's one-woman show has doubled in size as Lana Greeff comes on board, primarily to help with design work, but increasingly to lend a hand in all aspects of this growing business. Exports continue to thrive and the local market is also prospering with own-label and sparkling wines proving popular.

Bushman's Creek range

Cabernet Sauvignon ▤ ★★★ Previewed **10** medium-bodied, red-fruited & juicy everyday red. **Merlot** ▤ ★★★★ Step-up **09**, appealing bright berry freshness with mocha dusting. **Shiraz** ✓ ▤ ★★★★ **10** smooth & ripe, showing good density & weight, typical leathery, savoury aromas. **Cabernet Sauvignon-Merlot** Await new release. **Chardonnay** ▤ ★★★★ Sampled pre-bottling, tropical **10** ripe pineapple & litchi on a mineral base, attractive hint of oxidative white nuts. **Chenin Blanc** ▤ New bottling not ready. **Sauvignon Blanc** ▤ ★★★★ **10** sweet floral & spice scents, elegant, ripe yet restrained & well-judged.

Dolphin Bay range

Cabernet Sauvignon ★★★ Dark & spicy cherries, cranberry notes on **08**, firm tannins noted last year. Still available, as for all these. **Chenin Blanc** ▤ ★★ Plumpish **08** with hints of quince & apple. **Semi-Sweet** ▤ ★★★ **09** lightish peachy summer sipper from chenin, with semi-sweet finish. **Sparkling Brut** ★★ **08** frothy & dry brunch bubbly. From chenin, like next. **Sparkling Vin Doux** ★★ **09** undemanding sweet melon-toned party pleaser. — DB

▪ **Wines of Charles Back** *see* Fairview

Wine Village-Hermanus

Location: Hermanus ▪ Map: Elgin, Walker Bay & Bot River ▪ Est 1998 ▪ 1stB 2004 ▪ Open Mon–Fri 9–6 Sat 9–5 Sun 10–3 ▪ Closed Easter Fri & Dec 25 ▪ Owner(s) Paul & Cathy du Toit ▪ ±1,000cs 50% red 50% white ▪ PO Box 465 Hermanus 7200 ▪ wine@hermanus.co.za ▪ www.wine-village.co.za ▪ S 34° 24′ 40.7″ E 019° 12′ 1.9″ ▪ **T +27 (0)28-316-3988** ▪ F +27 (0)86-509-4931

Paul du Toit's passion for fine food and wine started in the 1970s when he opened KWV's Kleinplasie Wynhuis in Worcester. In 1998 he and Cathy made a life-changing decision to create a wine shop at the entrance to the Hemel en Aarde Valley. A logical further step was their own range.

Are We Having Fun Yet range

Merlot 🖥 ★★ Piquant red fruit, dusty tannins on **09**. This, rest of range not re-visited. **Shiraz** 🖥 ★★★ Delicate fruit, brush of spicy oak & warm afterglow on **07**. **Shiraz-Cabernet Sauvignon-Merlot** 🖥 ★★★ Ripe & juicy **09**, tad rustic but characterful. **Chardonnay** 🖥 ★★★ **09** summer quaffer with lemon & toasty notes appeal. **Sauvignon Blanc** 🖥 ★★ Zesty tail to gently tropical, ripe **09**. **Viognier** 🖥 ★★ Soft, rounded **09** with 14.5% alc glow in tail. — AL

Wineways Marketing

Location: Cape Town ▪ WO: Western Cape ▪ Est 2000 ▪ Closed to public ▪ Owner(s) Carl Schmidt, Stephen Vermeulen & Fanie Marais ▪ Winemaker(s) Andries Blake (Swarland) & Morné van Rooyen (The Company of Wine People) ▪ 200,000cs own label 60% red 40% white ▪ Plot 689 Zinfandal Street Saxenburg Park 2 Blackheath 7580 ▪ info@wine-ways.co.za ▪ www.wineways.net ▪ **T** +27 (0)21-905-7713/6/9 ▪ F +27 (0)86-509-9587

'Think outside the box' is this negociant business' mantra, a literal example of which is the addition of a Black Tie range in 750ml bottles to complement the established Black Box offering in 5L casks. Carl Schmidt and the team have also added three more African countries and China to the markets for their 'affordable, easy-drinking wines for all occasions'.

Mountain Shadows range

Cabernet Sauvignon 🖼 ★★ **10** juicy drinkability with dark chocolate & red berry aromas. Unwooded, as for all wines/ranges. **Merlot** 🖼 ★★ Mocha/chocolate & raspberry on **10** party quaffer. **Merlot** ★★ 3L NV, fruit-driven red with crisp dry finish. **Pinotage** 🖼 ★★ Dusty plum wafts on outgoing & eager-to-please **10**. **Shiraz** ★★ Crisp & dry red-berried **09**. **Merlot-Cabernet Sauvignon** ★★★ NV 3L box. A step-up, easy appeal with ripe mulberry tones. **Chenin Blanc** 🖼 ★★ **11** fresh & fruity, with lime & green apple notes. **Sauvignon Blanc** 🖼 ★★ Light-bodied **11**, grassy & herbal, easy-drinking style. Discontinued: **Rosé Blush, Muscat du Cap.**

Coral Reef range

Cabernet Sauvignon ★★★ Dark berries, ripe plums on **10**; like all reds in range, unoaked for early enjoyment. **Merlot** ★★ **10** chocolate & raspberry quick-quaff. **Merlot-Cabernet Sauvignon** NEW 🖼 ★★ **10** commendably dry, black-berried mealtime companion. These all for export only. **Sauvignon Blanc** 🖼 ★ Zesty **11** lightly flavoured. **Shiraz Natural Sweet** ★★ Just 'Shiraz' last time. **10** dusty & fruit-filled glugger. Discontinued: **Muscat du Cap.**

South Africa range

Cabernet Sauvignon 🖥 ★★★ Amicable & ripe **10** for easy sipping; unfettered by oak, like other reds. All for export only. **Merlot** NEW 🖼 ★★ Chocolate & berry flavours on party-starting **10**. **Merlot-Cabernet Sauvignon** NEW 🖼 ★★ **10** dark fruit flavours, supple & dry. **Shiraz Natural Sweet** NEW 🖼 ★★ Gently sweet **10**, chill well for summer.

Black Box range

Merlot ★★ Prune & plum-fruited **NV** with spicy finish. 5L bag-in-a-box, as all these. **Pinotage** NEW ★ Shy & easy drinker, **NV** plumped by tad sugar. **Shiraz** NEW ★★ Juicy **NV** easy-drinker with fresh blackberry tones. **Merlot-Cabernet Sauvignon** ★★ Crisp & clean **NV** thirst quencher. **Johannisberger Red** NEW ★★ Sweet & juicy **NV** quaffer with smoky hints, black berries & plum notes. **Grand Cru Chenin Blanc-Sauvignon Blanc** ★ Crisp **NV** poolside quaffer.

Black Tie range NEW

Cabernet Sauvignon 🖼 ★★★ Leading this range, **10** pleasant drinking with dark berried-fruit & ripe plums. **Merlot** 🖼 ★★ **10** chocolate & raspberry scented picnic partner. **Merlot-Cabernet Sauvignon** 🖼 ★★ **10** easy-drinker with dark-berried fruit, ends dry. **Sauvignon Blanc** 🖥 🖼 ★ Crisp & fresh **11**, serve chilled. **Shiraz Natural Sweet** ★★ 'Shiraz' last edition. Dusty-sweet **10** complements mild curries. — DB

Winkelshoek Wine Cellar

Location: Piketberg ▪ Map: Swartland ▪ Tasting & sales Mon-Fri 9-4 Sat 9-12 ▪ Gifts ▪ Owner(s) Hennie Hanekom & Jurgens Brand ▪ Cellarmaster(s) Hennie Hanekom ▪ Winemaker(s) Hennie Hanekom (1984) ▪ PO Box 395

Piketberg 7320 ▪ info@winkelshoek.co.za ▪ S 32° 54'22.4" E 018° 46'2.0" ▪ **T +27 (0)22-913-1092** ▪ F +27 (0)22-913-1095

This cellar's easy-drinkers are available for tasting and sale from the visitor centre near the intersection of the N7 and R44 roads outside Piketberg. The wines, untasted this edition, include Weskus Dry Red, (new) Sweet Rosé, Grand Cru, Blanc de Blanc and Late Harvest; and the Cap Vino Red (unwooded) and White (chenin).

Winters Drift NEW

Location/WO: Elgin ▪ Est 2004 ▪ 1stB 2010 ▪ Tasting by appt ▪ Restaurant/deli ▪ Conservation area ▪ Owner(s) Molteno Brothers (Pty) Ltd ▪ Cellarmaster(s) Kobie Viljoen (Gabriëlskloof) ▪ Viticulturist(s) Christiaan Cloete (Jan 2011) & Francois Viljoen (Vinpro) ▪ 1,600ha/±54ha (merlot, pinot, shiraz, chard, sauv) ▪ 206t/3,000cs own label 17% red 66% white 17% rosé ▪ PO Box 128 Elgin 7180 ▪ gerhard@wintersdrift.com ▪ www.wintersdrift.com ▪ S 34° 08'59.42" E 019° 02'22.61" ▪ **T +27 (0)21-859-2527** ▪ F +27 (0)21-859-4893

Winters Drift is the wine brand of Molteno Brothers, a farming business situated in Elgin. Apples and pears remain the main focus but the first vines were planted in 2004, the total area under vineyard now 54ha. The first own-label wines were from the 2010 vintage and the goal is to increase production to 20,000 cases in the next 10 to 15 years. As owners of about 500ha of uncultivated veld, the company is also a founder member of the Groenberg Conservancy.

Rosé 🗎 📖 ★★★ 2 vintages reviewed: both dry, from merlot. **10** easy & light bodied; previewed **11** (★★★) step up, plummy red fruit, bit of complexity, nice summery aura. **Chardonnay** 🗎 ★★★ Serious intent evident in use of 100% new oak (for 50%, other half unwooded) yet – commendably – fruit remains the focus of fresh, rounded **10**. **Sauvignon Blanc** 🗎 📖 ★★★ Previewed **11** classic Elgin sauvignon profile: fresh apple, grapefruit & a lovely minerality from nose to tail. — Panel

Withington

Location: Darling ▪ Map: Durbanville, Philadelphia & Darling ▪ WO: Darling/Coastal/Western Cape/Paarl ▪ Est 2001 ▪ 1stB 2003 ▪ Tasting & sales at Darling Wine Shop Mon-Sat 10-6 (10-7 in summer) Sun 11-2 ▪ Closed Mar 21, Easter Fri/Sun & Dec 25/26 ▪ Fresh West Coast oysters served when available ▪ Owner(s) Withington family ▪ 3,000cs own label 70% red 30% white ▪ 4,000cs for clients ▪ Other brand for clients: Cape Diversity ▪ PO Box 236 Darling 7345 ▪ mail@withington.co.za ▪ www.withington.co.za ▪ S 33° 22'28" E 018° 22'38" ▪ **T +27 (0)22-492-3971/+27 (0)74-194-1711** ▪ F +27 (0)86-516-4010

Negociant Charles Withington sources wine for his own and customer labels across the winelands, but preferably around home base, Darling, where he's opening his 'cellardoor' retail outlet at the Darling Wine Shop. He reports burgeoning sales in China and Nigeria for his Greendale and Darlington export labels.

Withington range

Carignan ☺ 🗎 ★★★ Overtly plummy, ripe **10** similar to previous. Cheerful, sunny & appealing take on variety. WO Coastal.

Merlot 🗎 ★★ Juicy-fruity **09** has spicy turmeric notes with gentle texture. **Shiraz-Cabernet Sauvignon** 🗎 ★★★ **09** from Paarl shows vintage's ripeness, with sweet cherry & plum fruit, soft tannins. Likeable, easy-drinking. **Chardonnay** 📖 ★★★ Light, crisply acidic **10** begs food. Unpretentious quaffer. WO Coastal. **Semillon** ★★★ Unwooded **10** follows form, with striking nettle & greenpepper notes, backed by fullish, lanolin-oily body.

Darlington range NEW

Pinotage ☺ 🗎 ★★★ Fresh & zesty wild berry fruit on **09** lends quaffing appeal. Light, undemanding & refreshing.

Greendale range

Pinotage 🗎 ★★ **09** had some metallic notes last edition, stewy texture to ripe berry fruit core. **Chenin Blanc-Chardonnay** 🗎 ★★ **09** noted last time as past its best. WO W Cape.

Living Rock range

Cinsaut-Ruby Cabernet 🗎 ★★ Drink-now soft & juicy **10** shows vibrant berries, unfettered by oak. **Chenin Blanc-Chardonnay** 🗎 ★★ Previously, **10** 60:40 blend was slender & fresh, with ripe melon fruit. — GdB

Withoek

Location: Calitzdorp • Map: Klein Karoo & Garden Route • WO: Calitzdorp/Western Cape • Est/1stB 1996 • Tasting, sales & tours by appt • Self-catering cottages • Farm produce • Walks • Conservation area • Owner(s) Geyser Family • Winemaker(s) Fanie Geyser • Viticulturist(s) Johannes Mellet • 454ha/28ha (cab, p verdot, ruby cab, shiraz, tinta, touriga, chenin, cbard, hanepoot, muscadel) • ±300t/400cs own label 50% red 50% fortified • PO Box 181 Calitzdorp 6660 • withoek@telkomsa.net • www.withoek.blogspot.com • S 33° 32′ 24.1″ E 021° 40′ 59.8″ • **T +27 (0)44-213-3639** • F +27 (0)86-628-7853

Amiable Fanie Geyser felt blessed with a fortuitous balance of a cool summer followed by good rains that made for an excellent 2010 season - this after water in the drought-stricken region had dipped to worryingly low levels. Tasting facilities at the family's Calitzdorp farm were revamped before the town's annual port festival.

Cabernet Sauvignon NEW **10** artisinal, slightly spritzy. **Shiraz** ★★ Tasted mid-2010, **09** had beefy alc & dry tannin from 11 months oak. **Sauvignon Blanc** ★★ Amiable **11** grassy & fresh, satisfying vinosity. WO W Cape, as for Cab. **Kairos Muscadel** ★★★ Fortified dessert from mainly white muscadel, dash red for pinkish hue. Now bottled, **10** doesn't quite live up to preview rating. Appealing watermelon & honeyed notes fade fast. **Fick's Ruby Port** ★★ Raisin & dusty spices on uncomplex NV. **Geyser Cape Ruby** NEW ★★ Rustic NV port-style fortified fireside sipper with malty tones. **Geyser Cape Vintage** NEW ★★★ House's 3rd port-style offering; cranberry & tealeaf **10** makes up for lack of tannin grip with fiery tail. Discontinued: **Cabernet Franc-Shiraz, Muscadel, Geyser Tawny Port, Ruby Port.** — Panel

■ **Witklip** *see Eerste Hoop Wine Cellar*

Wolfkloof

Location/map/WO: Robertson • Est 1880 • 1stB 2004 • Tasting, sales & tours by appt • Tour groups • Facilities for children • Meals by appt; or BYO picnic • Conference facilities • Wedding & function venue • Hiking trail • Owner(s) JC Kannemeyer • Cellarmaster(s)/winemaker(s)/viticulturist(s) JC Kannemeyer • 60t/270cs own label 100% red • PO Box 40 Robertson 6705 • info@wolfkloof.co.za, leo@ripplesoft.co.za • www.wolfkloof.co.za • S 33° 47′28.1″ E 019° 52′ 1.4″ • **T +27 (0)23-626-3911/+27 (0)23-626-1555** • F +27 (0)23-626-3911/+27 (0)23-626-1555

In a secluded valley near Robertson, where the Dassieshoek Hiking Trail starts and ends, visitors can literally reach out and touch vines from a wooden deck. Here the Kannemeyers continue living their own 'child's dream' to make wine (they still proudly use the label little Frederick designed for his first bottling – of tea!).

JC Kannemeyer range
Child's Dream Merlot 08 available but not tasted by us. **Child's Dream Private Blend** Not ready. **Wolfkloof Merlot Rosé** 🍽 ★★ Charming **10** was fragrant, dry & brisk last year; is still selling. **Wolfkloof Tribute Chardonnay** Currently available **10** not reviewed. — Panel

■ **Wolvenbosch** *see Jason's Hill Private Cellar*

Wolvendrift Private Cellar

Location/map/WO: Robertson • Est 1903 • Tasting & sales Mon-Fri 8.30-4.30 Sat 10-1 • Closed Easter Fri-Mon, May 1, Dec 25/26 & Jan 1 • Cellar tours by appt • Refreshments/meals by pre-booking • Facilities for children • Tour groups • Walking/hiking trails • Conservation area • Weddings & functions • Owner(s) Michael Klue • Winemaker(s) Jan Klue (Jan 2003) • Viticulturist(s) Jan Swart (Jan 2000) • 120ha (cab, merlot, chard, chenin, cbard, sauv) • 45% red 45% white 10% fortified • PO Box 24 Robertson 6705 • info@wolvendriftwines.co.za • www.wolvendriftwines.co.za • S 33° 55′0.1″ E 020° 0′9.0″ • **T +27 (0)23-616-2890** • F +27 (0)23-616-2396

The function venue at this Robertson family farm on the banks of the Breede River overlooks viness, pecan trees and a lush lawn. They're hoping to attract more functions and weddings, a ready market for their wines, which fourth-generation winemaker Jan Klue describes as 'easy drinking but complex with diverse flavours'.

Cabernet Sauvignon-Merlot 🍽 ★★★ Last year **08** 60/40 mix had juicy blackberry & chocolate notes, smooth tannins. **Sauvignon Blanc** 🍽 ▨ ★★★ Crisp & lightish **10** offered crushed nettles & herbs. **Red Muscadel** ★★★ Warming 17% alc tail on honeyed **09** fortified dessert. Discontinued: **Chardonnay.** — DB

■ **Wolverine Creek** *see Van Loveren Private Cellar*

Women in Wine

Location: Stellenbosch ▪ Closed to public ▪ Fairtrade accredited ▪ PO Box 12869 Die Boord Stellenbosch 7613 ▪ info@womeninwine.co.za ▪ www.womeninwine.co.za ▪ **T +27 (0)21-872-8967** ▪ F +27 (0)21-872-8967

A feather in the cap of this export brand was its contribution to the Swedish drinks monopoly's first certified WIETA (Agricultural Ethical Trade Initiative of SA) product, as well as recognition from Drinks Business magazine for ethical trading. Creating business opportunities for women farmworkers is their prime motivation, says CEO Beverly Farmer. Available but not tasted this edition: Premium range Cabernet Sauvignon, Chardonnay and Sauvignon Blanc; and Eden's Vineyards range Cabernet Sauvignon-Shiraz, Pinotage Rosé and Chardonnay-Chenin Blanc.

Wonderfontein

Location/map/WO: Robertson ▪ Est ca 1884 ▪ Tasting & sales Mon-Fri 8.30-6 Sat 8.30-1 ▪ Tour groups ▪ Conferences/events (40-80 guests) & picnic facilities, 4×4 trail & other attractions ▪ Owner(s) Paul René Marais ▪ Winemaker(s) Stefan Bruwer (2002) ▪ Viticulturist(s) Gert Visser, Gerald Stemmet & Bennie Stemmet, advised by Brian Stipp ▪ 240ha (cab, merlot, ptage, ruby cab, shiraz, chard, chenin, sauv, viog) ▪ 5,500t/3,000cs own label 10% red 80% white 1% rosé 9% fortified ▪ PO Box 4 Robertson 6705 ▪ info@wonderfonteinestate.co.za ▪ www.wonderfonteinestate.co.za ▪ S 33° 49'3.5" E 019° 52'2.1" ▪ **T +27 (0)23-626-2212** ▪ F +27 (0)23-626-2669

The real wonder of pretty Wonderfontein is how few people know it was the birthplace of Klipdrift brandy, one of South Africa's top drinks brands. But while the historic Robertson estate holds one of the oldest agricultural distilling licences, granted in 1884, focus has shifted to handcrafted wines under current owner Paul René Marais – an upcoming champagne-method sparkling named in his honour.

The Marais Family Merlot ☺ 🍷 ★★★ Spice-dusted **10** perfect for early drinking: juicy plum & mulberry centre, gently wrapped with tannin.

La Bonne Vigne Merlot ★★★ Previously, soft & voluptuous **09** had expressive fruit, vanilla charm. This, Shiraz, Rosé & Red Muscadel still selling & not revisited. **La Bonne Vigne Shiraz** 🍷 ★★★ Smoky **09** earthy notes, rich & full, ended slightly sweet. **La Bonne Vigne Rosé** 🍷 ★★★ Mainly colombard with merlot's cherry tones, splash white muscadel. **NV** offers lightish semi-sweet enjoyment. **La Bonne Vigne Sauvignon Blanc** ✓ 🍷 ★★★★ Passionfruit & ruby grapefruit on fresh, well-balanced **11**. Less zingy, slightly fatter than most, makes for comfortable solo sipping. **Wonderfontein Red Muscadel** ★★★★ Still-available **06** all sunny raisined allure, well-contained sweetness, rich caramel & layered complexity. Rung above **05** (★★★). — Panel

Woolworths

WO: Various ▪ Category manager Danielle Croza ▪ Technologist Leoni Siebrits ▪ Selection manager Allan Mullins T +27 (0)21-407-2777 AllanMullins@woolworths.co.za ▪ Buying manager Ivan Oertle T +27 (0)21-407-2762 IvanOertle@woolworths.co.za ▪ Owner(s) Woolworths Holdings ▪ Woolworths House 93 Longmarket Street Cape Town 8000 ▪ www.woolworths.co.za ▪ **T +27 (0)21-407-9111** ▪ F +27 (0)21-407-3958

'Ivan and I have been working together for twenty-one years – that's longer than most marriages!' chortles Allan Mullins, selection manager for upmarket national retail chain Woolworths, of Ivan Oertle, buying manager and now co-taster since passing his Cape Wine Academy Diploma with distinction. A special blend made by Frans Smit from Spier honouring Allan's vast contribution to Cape wine over the years was released, but as always, this dynamic retailer prefers to look forward, predicting future trends. Organic and no-added-sulphur wines are the hottest picks at the moment, the latter in particular 'flying off the shelves', while sales of bag-in-box wines and méthode cap classique bubbly continue to grow. The Woolworths 'Good Food Journey' continues to be applied to wine suppliers too, with ever-increasing numbers improving their sustainability levels and farming for the future.

Cabernet Sauvignon range

★★★★☆ **Limited Release Cabernet Sauvignon 07** echoes scrub, fennel notes of Grangehurst's **06** plus new-oak cigarbox aromas. Classically styled: taut, sleek, dry with light-textured yet concentrated fruit filling. Deserves a fine steak & 6-7 years.

★★★★ **Founder's Reserve Cabernet Sauvignon** ✓ Elegant **09** from Diemersfontein, understated, with cassis, tobacco & herbal notes. Ripe dark berry fruit, mouthfilling with a firm grip. Cellar 6+ years.

★★★★ **Cabernet Sauvignon Reserve** With its dense fruit centre & firm oak structure, **09** from Spier needs cellaring 3+ years while tannins mellow. Mocha, cocoa, other oak aromas override dark fruit mid-2011.

Cabernet Sauvignon ☺ ★★★ Accessible, herbal **09** shows good varietal typicity with brisk savoury finish; from Villiera.

The Hutton Cabernet Sauvignon ★★★☆ Named for dominant soil type from which grapes sourced. Cassis mingles with milk chocolate & vanilla courtesy Spier's oaking on **09**. **NSA Organic Running Duck Cabernet Sauvignon** 🗐 ♨ ★★ Baked prunes & tobacco on **11** from Stellar Winery, earthy finish; for early drinking. **Longmarket Cabernet Sauvignon** 🖉 ★★★ **10** cherry nougat nuances, coffee highlights to almost jammy palate. Short end. From Bergsig, as is following. **Tell It Like It Is Cabernet Sauvignon** 🗐 🖉 ★★★ Slight spritz on **10** lifts raspberry mouthful, adds to uncomplicated fun.

Merlot range

★★★★ **Reserve Merlot** Appealing depth, plummy ripeness & flesh in last-tasted Morgenhof's **07**.

★★★★ **Limited Release Merlot** Serious, structured merlot from Jordan. Plums & dark berries with a savoury seam, **09** shows its 18 months French oaking (80% new) in firm dry finish, best matched to rich dishes. **Koffie Klip Merlot** ★★★★ Prunes, plums, Indian spices on exotic **09** from Spier. Intense woody flavours, very firm oak tannins on palate provide long, gripping finish. Named for dominant soil type in vineyard. **NSA Organic Swooping Falcon Merlot** 🗐 ♨ ★★★ Very sippable **11** has dark berries, smoke; bright & dense plum fruit centre. By Stellar Winery. **Merlot** ✓ ★★★★ Cedar, tar & black plum imprints on La Motte's **10**; very juicy, but enough grip for food. **Merlot** ★★★★ Lively 2009's plummy flavours restrained by pliable tannins & fresh acidity for enjoyable early drinking, not as complex as **07** (★★★★). From Villiera. **What Merlot** 🗐 ★★★ Wellington Wines' **10** bold plum & mulberry chocolate styling. Soft grip with depth & breadth. Year in old oak, but emerges with juiciness intact. **Longmarket Merlot** ★★★ Ripe, vibrant berry fruit, nicely rounded on **10**, ex Simonsvlei. **Tell It Like It Is Merlot** 🗐 🖉 ★★★ Translucent, faint plum nose & medium body, **10** from Bergsig slips down easily. **Organic Merlot** NEW ♨ ★★★★ **10** by Laibach shows earthy plum & cocoa intensity. Rich & full, with dry tannin from oak, just 25% new, long stylish finish. **Light Merlot** NEW ★★ Plummy **11** has decent grip & fruit, slight metallic edge; ex Spier.

Pinot Noir range

★★★★ **Reserve Pinot Noir** 🖉 **10**'s red berries give flesh to underbrush & farmyard features, elegant but a smidgen light. 20% new oak for 11 months, from Paul Cluver.

★★★★☆ **Limited Release CM Pinot Noir** Charming **10** from Catherine Marshall limpid, almost rosé-hued. Entices with its complex dark fruits, forest floor scents, shimmering silky feel & savoury length. Lovely drinking now, further 2-3 years.

★★★★☆ **Limited Release Pinot Noir** From Cape Chamonix, last edition **09** sweet ripe-fruited, well crafted & harmonious with oak giving structure & savoury-seaming the flavours.

Cabrière Pinot Noir NEW ★★★☆ **08**'s softly savoury, fresh cherry flavours underlined by pliable tannins & firm thread of acidity. From Haute Cabrière.

Pinotage range

★★★★ **Reserve Pinotage** **09** (★★★) by Bellevue has core of dark fruit but oak currently dominates, very drying on finish. Not as accessible as **08**.

★★★★ **Simonsig Pinotage** Prunes & black plums - **08**'s ripeness is a pleasure. Long-limbed smooth drinkability, juicy & alive. Despite its ready appeal, showed good ageing potential. Tasted last year.

What Pinotage ☺ 🗐 🖉 ★★★ No oak or tannin to hold back bright fruit of nearly-dry **10**. Ex Ken Forrester.

NSA Organic Glowing Firefly Pinotage NEW ★★★ Juicy yet savoury toned **11** has firm backbone, still charms; ex Stellar Winery. **Limited Release Pinotage** ★★★ **10** from Diemersfontein, has distinctive espresso, dark plum character. Smoothly rounded, for early enjoyment. **Pinotage** ★★★★ Rich, plummy **09** from M'hudi generously flavoursome & plush, balanced by pleasing savouriness. **Longmarket Pinotage** 🖉 ★★★ From Rooiberg, **10** smooth & supple, mulberry toned early-drinker.

Shiraz range

★★★★ **Reserve Shiraz** Distinctive & forceful **09** ex Groenekloof vines has delightful cocoa & pepper fragrance, coupled to silky black cherry fruit. Finely balanced offering from Darling Cellars.

Limited Release Shiraz ✓ 🍴 ★★★★ Brimming with bonhomie & likeability, Diemersfontein's **10** has concentrated mulberry, rich mocha choc flavours; food friendly & step up from previous. For early enjoyment. **Organic Hunting Owl Shiraz** 🌿🍷 ★★★ Sufficient succulent red berry fruit to pad out slightly stalky grape tannins on unoaked **11**. For early quaffing, ex African Terroir. **Hercules Paragon Shiraz** ★★★★ Smoky, intense **08** from Simonsvlei brims with black cherry fruit cloaked in chalky tannins. Pleasing spicy aromas. **Pumphouse Shiraz** ★★★ Last edition **07** took step up, offered blackberries, spice & herbs, friendly tannins. **Longmarket Redstone Shiraz** 🍷 ★★★ Honest & upfront, **10** charms with dusty oak, juicy red fruit & floral highlights. Ex Rooiberg. **Longmarket Shiraz** 🍴 ★★★ **09**, from Swartland, tasted last year had smoky dark fruit & coffee plumpness. **Light Shiraz** 🍴 ★ Low alc & sweetness on Spier's dilute **11**. Discontinued: **Syrah**.

Niche Red Cultivars range

★★★★ **Reserve Cabernet Franc** ✓ **09** in variety's sappy mode, but with super succulence of plump red berry fruit, it eschews austerity & drinks beautifully. 15 months in barrel, 20% new. Elgin wine by Paul Cluver.

★★★★ **Limited Release Malbec** Straightforward **09** (★★★) from Bellevue: shows red fruit, vanilla, noticeable herbal character. Not nearly as accomplished as juicy, vivacious **08**.

Discontinued: **Limited Release Cabernet Franc**.

Red Blends range

★★★★ **Reserve Cabernet Sauvignon-Merlot** Fine vintage & Elgin grapes yield a balanced, elegant & fruit-rich **09** blend by Neil Ellis. Ripe plum, cedar & leather with supple structure; deserves 3-5 years ageing.

★★★★☆ **Cobblers Hill** Bordeaux blend, best barrel selection from Jordan. Attractive underbrush & meaty notes in the plush fruit, excellent oak balance. **07** poised & seamless, already giving drinking pleasure, will do so till ±2018. 26 months new French barriques.

★★★★ **The Ladybird Red** ✓ 🌿 **10** from Laibach follows in **09**'s footsteps. 5-way Bordeaux combo. Ripe but still refreshing, tobacco leaf & earth nuances to firm body & slight chunky texture.

★★★★☆ **The W (Syrah-Mourvèdre)** 🌿 'W' recognises sustainability. Last tasted **07** ex TMV was mainly shiraz, some mourvèdre, tightly held & complete, but all in fine moderation.

★★★★ **Limited Release Shiraz-Grenache** **07** offered southern Rhône generosity last edition, pepper-&-spice with plump red berried succulence. By Ken Forrester.

★★★★ **Shiraz-Cabernet Sauvignon** Coffee-perfumed **08** is complex, with cloves & black pepper, juicy dark fruit that partners the firm but ripe tannin. From Diemersfontein. Not retasted.

★★★★ **Reserve Cabernet Sauvignon-Shiraz** ✓ 'Reserve' moniker added to La Motte stalwart. Taut **09** smoothed with requisite flesh by near-half shiraz, sufficient tannins for food or 2-3 years ageing.

House Red 😊 ★★★ **09** ripe cherry berry spice with light body. **One Off Cape Red** 😊 ★★☆ Ripe cherry-toned **NV** brushed with oak, up on previous. These both ex Wellington Wines.

Limited Release Cabernet Sauvignon-Merlot ★★★ Last was vanilla/chocolate **06**, offering streamlined drinkability; ex De Wetshof. **Grand Rouge** ✓ ★★★★ Tobacco-toned, La Motte's **09** punches above its weight with ample fruit in oh-so-soft tannins. Cab-led Bordeaux blend. **Cabernet Sauvignon-Merlot** ✓ ★★★★ Cooler vintage affords elegant restraint to Delheim's **09** 4-way blend, with good depth of dark fruit. Tablemate now & over next few years. Improves on oaky **08** (★★★★). **Longmarket Merlot-Cabernet Franc** ★★★ Herbaceous & characterful **09** from Simonsvlei middleweight with attitude. **Capstone Shiraz-Cabernet Sauvignon** 🌿 ★★★ Smoky overlay on vibrant **08** from biodynamic producer Reyneke. Spicy black pepper notes with brooding ripe fruit & a firm end. **Longmarket Shiraz-Pinotage** 🍴🍷 ★★★ Tarry, earthy **10** ex Spier medium bodied, supple for immediate enjoyment. **Goshawk's Chant** ✓ 🍷 ★★★★ Bordeaux base with roobernet, in **10** preview from Diemersfontein shows nice black fruit purity, herby overlay; smooth, with lingering oaky grip. Drink till ±2015. **Portuguese Connection** ★★★ From Boplaas, **10** commendably dry with sour plum/cherry flavours; balanced & integrated. No rough edges. **Juicy Red** ★★ **09** plummy quaffer with some dark char notes. Ex-Wellington Wines, as is next. **Racy Red** ★★ **09** all red berry. Soft, simple. Previously 'Reckless Red'. **Natural Sweet Red** 🍴 ★★ Spier's **11** low alc quaffer from shiraz. **Bel Rosso Sweet Red** ★★ Ex Bergsig, a gently sweet, lowish 11% alc **NV**. Discontinued: **Petit Rouge**, **The Boss**, **Secateurs Shiraz-Mourvèdre-Viognier**.

Rosé Wines range

Pinotage-Shiraz Rosé 😊🍷 ★★★ **11** light, vivaciously juicy. Drier style with appealing savoury nuance. This quaffer from Delheim steals the al fresco show.

Longmarket Blanc de Noir 🏺 ▥ ★★★ Pretty off-dry **11** from Swartland; bright berry & pot-pourri perfume. **NSA Organic Diving Hawk Rosé** 🏺 ✿ ★★★ Strawberry-toned, characterful & fruity **11** from Stellar **Longmarket Rosé** ▥ ★★★ Muscat adds fun to dry **11** pinotage-led blend ex Villiera. **Chenin Blanc-Pinotage** 🏺 ★★★ A tinge of pink in the gold, a little pinotage berry flavour in fruity, easy & charming, nearly-dry **11**. Ex Simonsig. **Perky Pink** 🏺 ★★From Bergsig, semi-sweet & fruity NV. **Pierre Jourdan Tranquille Blush** ★★★ NV still version of bubbly, light & berry-toned from Haute Cabrière tasted last year. **Natural Sweet Rosé** 🏺 ★★ By Spier, cherry-flavoured **10**.

Chardonnay range

★★★★☆ **Chardonnay Reserve** Well-judged oak the star of this timeless version by De Wetshof. Buttered toast & citrus peel nuances, crisp acidity giving **09** focus & freshness. Not revisited.

★★★★ **The Abacus Chardonnay** Lemon-toned **10** composed & considered with 60% new oak playing supporting, not dominant role. Taut & dry, wet clay & 'oyster shell' notes, enjoyable now or year/2. From Spier.

★★★★ **Chardonnay Lightly Wooded** ▥ Buttered toast with grapefruit, Jordan's **10** has a zinging freshness that awakens the tastebuds, has you reaching for a second glass.

★★★★ **Neil Ellis Elgin Chardonnay** NEW 🏺 ▥ **10** rich yet understated, layers of citrus peel, hazelnut & brioche flavours interwoven into subtle oak & waxy texture. Lovely balancing acidity & food pairing length.

★★★★ **Limited Release Chardonnay Sur Lie** ▥ Tropical fruit is part of Jordan's **11** (★★★★) appeal, rounded body, fresh drinkability the rest. Simpler than **09**.

★★★★ **Wild Yeast Chardonnay** Earthy & oatmeal touches to ripe, flavourful **09** from Springfield. Sweet, delicious fruit untrammelled by oak, with weight balanced by good acidity. To seriously enjoy.

Limited Release Chardonnay ★★★★ Oaked **07** ex Weltevrede tasted mid-2010; rich but shot through with zesty acidity; endless lemon finish. Drink up. **Organic Feeding Duck Chardonnay** 🏺 ✿ ★★★ By Stellar Winery & tasted previously, lightly oaked **10** & nicely rounded, lively fresh finish. **Chardonnay** ★★★ Butterscotch-scented & voluptuously padded **10** from Arendsig, boldly flavoured with grapefruit & marmalade. **Longmarket Chardonnay** ★★★ **10** by Robertson Winery. Just off-dry, full-flavoured; like a lemon pie in liquid form. **Limestone Hill Chardonnay** ★★★★ Unoaked De Wetshof **10** is fresh, vibrant & fruity with lees fatness & appealing lemongrass notes. **What Chardonnay** 🏺 ★★ Unoaked **10** from Weltevrede is ripe & curvy. **Tell It Like It Is Chardonnay** 🏺 ▥ ★★ Lemon-infused **10** mouthfilling but brief. From Bergsig. **Light Chardonnay** NEW ★ **11** faintly lemon toned; ex Spier. **The Ladybird Chardonnay** ✓ 🏺 ✿ ★★★★ From Laibach, previously 'Ladybird White'. Very lightly oaked **10**'s zesty citrus, peach richness balanced by fresh acid.

Chenin Blanc range

★★★★☆ **The W (Chenin Blanc)** Last year, **09** from biodynamic producer Reyneke had broad fruit appeal & savoury line, with gentle oak influence.

★★★★ **Limited Release Chenin Blanc** From Simonsig, with 40+ years chenin experience. Tasted last year, apple & thatch in classically styled **09**, oak perfectly attuned to fruit, restrained yet complete.

★★★★☆ **Chenin Blanc** 🏺 ▥ **10** mirrors hedonistic **09** with old-vine concentration. Pineapple, melon & bruised apple complexity complemented by supple oak, variety's characteristic firm acidity softened by touch sugar. From Spier.

★★★★ **Reserve Chenin Blanc** ✓ 🏺 Peachy **10** (★★★★) has integrated firm oak & balanced not-quite-dry fullness; less vibrant than **09**. This, 'NLH' & 'What' below from Ken Forrester.

★★★★ **Noble Late Harvest Chenin Blanc** Barrel fermented/aged **08** tasted previously; tangerine & pinenuts, mouthwatering tangy-sweetness packed with lingering botrytis flavours.

M'hudi Chenin Blanc NEW ☺ 🏺 ▥ ★★★ Full flavoured **11** blends tropical & light herbaceousness in engagingly rich fruitiness, balanced by zesty acidity.

What Chenin Blanc 🏺 ▥ ★★★ **10** thatchy veneer over sweetish tropical fruit, very brisk tail. **Longmarket Chenin Blanc** ▥ ★★★ Uncomplicated sipping from quiet, bubblegum-toned **11** from Rooiberg. **Light Chenin Blanc** 🏺 ★ Reticent **11** from Spier lacks varietal character.

Sauvignon Blanc range

★★★★☆ **Limited Release Sauvignon Blanc** ▥ Focused & vibrant Cape Point fruit, with added 'X' factor in **10** from special parcels in other areas. Higher acidity accentuates racy lemongrass flavours, balanced & elegant, lingering finish. Perfect with oysters, as was exceptional **09** (★★★★★), also from Cape Point Vineyards.

★★★★ **Limited Release Sauvignon Blanc** 🏺 ▥ Consistently delicious example from Nitida Cellars. Some Darling fruit in **11**, passionfruit with a leafy thread, & crisp minerality at the end making it food friendly.

★★★★ **Elgin Sauvignon Blanc** 🍸 ⊠ Riper **11** (★★★) vintage shows melon & grenadilla flavours, in earlier drinking, plump & succulent style. Shade off minerally, focused **10**. By Neil Ellis.

★★★★ **La Motte Sauvignon Blanc Organically Grown** NEW ✓ 🍸 ⚘ ⊠ Fuller than many of its peers, **11** nicely weighted gooseberry character tightened by lingering minerality. WO Walker Bay.

> **What Sauvignon Blanc** ☺ 🍸 ⊠ ★★★ Great varietal expression on **11** from Bergsig: grass & cat's pee, slightly sweaty flavours, brisk acidity.

Sauvignon Blanc Usually from Groote Post. Await new. **Lonely Blue Gum Sauvignon Blanc** 🍸 ⊠ ★★★★ Step-up for elegant **11** by Spier; initially shy, opens to cat's pee & grassy notes; extended lees-ageing adds weight & texture in a less than stellar year. **Organic Swooping Swallow Sauvignon Blanc** ⚘ ★★★ From Stellar Winery, ripe **11** bursts with tropical fruit & gooseberries. **Sauvignon Blanc Bush Vine** ★★★ Typical Swartland dusty-grassy aromas on **11** follow to bracingly fresh crispness & lean, minerally fynbos. From Darling Cellars. **Longmarket Sauvignon Blanc** ★★★ **11** easy-drinking & generous off-dry style from Robertson Winery. **Wet Rocks Sauvignon Blanc** ⊠ ★★★ Name says it all: **11** crisp & moderately flavoured, 12% alc; perfect lunchtime companion. This, Tell It Like It Is, from Bergsig. **Light Sauvignon Blanc** 🍸 ★★ Grassy toned **11**, by Spier, pleasant mouthful. **Tell It Like It Is Sauvignon Blanc** 🍸 ⊠ ★★★ Dried grass, hay aromas/flavours on **11**; lovely pithy grip.

Niche White Cultivars range

★★★★☆ **Limited Release Gewürztraminer** ✓ 🍸 Semi-dry **11** (★★★★) has pungent rose perfume with tropical/litchi notes, good sugar/acid balance & grip for food; but less riveting than **10**. 11% alc, ex Paul Cluver, like next.

★★★★ **Ferricrete Riesling** NEW Named for ironstone soils yielding low alcl (10%), semi-sweet (19g/l sugar) **11** with Germanic touch. Waxy gloss to river-stone minerality, lime & ginger in tingling finish.

★★★★ **Limited Release Semillon** Last edition **09**'s intense cut-grass & fynbos perfume reflected Nitida's terroir, but greenness was absorbed into the body's waxy smoothness. Great example of variety.

Pinot Grigio 🍸 ⊠ ★★ **11** aridly dry; will perk up seafood. One of a few in South Africa, from Van Loveren. **NSA Rhine Riesling** ⊠ **10** ex Villiera not ready at press time. Discontinued: **Limited Release Viognier**.

White Blends range

★★★★ **Garden Vineyards White** ✓ 🍸 **10** (★★★★☆) same generous, attractive chenin, viognier, roussanne blend as **09**. Aromatic posy of white flowers, honeysuckle; rich, flavoursome with tangy, mineral tail. Oak matured. From DeMorgenzon.

★★★★★ **Spectrum White** 🍸 From TMV, chenin with chardonnay, 3 Rhône varieties. A mellow earthiness to **09** (★★★★★) distinguished it last year. Good ageing potential, as for standout **08**.

> **One Off Cape White** ☺ ★★★ Full tangy apricot, peach appeal on **NV** simple chenin quaffer. **Wild White** ☺ ★★★ **10** all chenin pear & melon. Light, with fresh drinkability. **House White** ☺ ★★★ **10**'s lemon & grass unoaked 3-way blend a step up. These three easy-sippers from Wellington Wines.

Chardonnay-Semillon ⊠ ★★★ **10** is a plump & succulent tablemate by Delheim, waxy pear flavours lifted by zesty grapefruit. **Longmarket Chardonnay-Viognier** ★★★ Lemon-toned, freshly-fruity **10** from Spier previewed last edition. **Chardonnay-Pinot Noir** ★★★ A hint of colour & red berry overlay to Haute Cabrière's **10** tasted last year; friendly & light, slight sweetness. **Longmarket Sauvignon Blanc-Semillon** ★★★ Zesty passionfruit flavours, satisfying weight & vinosity on **11** from Spier. **Longmarket Sauvignon Blanc Chenin Blanc** ⊠ ★★★ **11** delightfully crisp tropical quaffer ex Villiera. **Zesty White** ★★ Simple **NV** pear & melon quaffer from Wellington Wines. **House Sweet** ★★ From Simonsvlei, juicy-fruity **10**. **Bianca Light** 🍸 ⊠ ★★ **11** off-dry, low-alc blend from Delheim. **Sassy Sweet** ★★ Ginger spice on Bergsig's gently sweet **NV**. **NSA Organic Fluttering Butterfly White** NEW ★★ From Stellar Winery, shy lunchtime sipper (12.4%) **11** lacks verve & charm. **Natural Sweet White** ⊠ ★★ From Spier, pineapple tang, grape succulence ex viognier in **11**. Discontinued: **Sauvignon Blanc-Semillon, Alexa**.

Méthode Cap Classique range

★★★★ **Blanc de Blancs Brut** Complexity & depth in graceful, mouthfilling **NV** chardonnay sparkling. Gorgeously rich, fresh & balanced. Ex Villiera.

★★★★ **Brut Natural** Villiera's all-chardonnay, bone-dry **08** has neither sulphur or dosage but plenty of creamy texture for pleasing appeal. Refined but not as complex as **07** (★★★★★).

★★★★☆ **Vintage Reserve Brut** Villiera's classy, rich & complex **06** limpid gold MCC an equal blend chardonnay-pinot noir, layered & luxuriously enriched by oak & 5 years spent on lees. Fresh & refined.

★★★★ **Krone Borealis Brut** From sparkling specialist The House of Krone. **08** bruised apple features; creamy mousse, very fresh, 'brut' conclusion. 50/50 chardonnay, pinot blend. Follows delicious **07** (★★★★★).

★★★★☆ **Limited Release Pinot Noir Rosé NSA** ✓ Pale onionskin **NV** (**10**) méthode cap classique from Simonsig - a fine advertisement for no added sulphur. Genuinely dry, with the savoury benefits of development & the quietly fruity-earthiness ones of good pinot grapes. Tasty but subtle. Lingers happily.

Brut ★★★★ Exceedingly popular chardonnay-based **NV** bubbly from Villiera, perfect for everyday celebration. Candied richness balanced for easy enjoyment. **Brut Rosé** ★★★★ Firm pinotage structure & earthiness in mouthfillingly fruity, crisp **NV**, also with pinot & chardonnay, from Villiera. Discontinued: **Cuvée Ten Millenium Brut Rosé**.

Sparkling Wines range

Spumante Brut ★★ Fizzy & appley. These from Rooiberg, **NV** unless stated. **Organic Sauvignon Blanc Brut** 🌿 🍃 ★★ Little varietal character, short finish on **10**. **Spumante Doux** ★★ Turkish Delight & explosive mousse; from white muscadel. **Spumante Rosé** ★★ Bubbly pink, gentle berries from red muscadel.

1L Box range

Dry Red ★★ Quaffable everything-blend. **Off Dry Rosé** ★★ Sunny strawberry-fruity quick-sip from pinotage. **Crisp White** ★★ From chenin/colombard, true to name. **Semi Sweet** ★★ Picnic companion ex chenin/colombard. Unless noted, all these box ranges by Simonsvlei, all **NV**.

2L Box range

Longmarket Cabernet Sauvignon-Merlot ★★ Fullish berry fruit, bit rough at edges. **Longmarket Merlot** ★★ Lightish with primary mulberry fruit. **Longmarket Chardonnay** NEW ★★★ Attractive lime/lemon notes on **10** brushed with butter; fresh & generously proportioned with touch sweetness on finish. Ex Robertson, as is next. **Longmarket Sauvignon Blanc** NEW ★★★ **11** appealing hay & white flower bouquet, zingy acidity & ruby grapefruit flavours. Discontinued: **Longmarket Shiraz**.

3L Box range

Dry Red ★★ Multi-varietal easy-sipper. **Light Rosé** ★★ Sweet low-alc party-starter ex pinotage. **Crisp White** ★★ Brisk chenin, colombard combo. **Light White** ★ Lean, thin low-alc tipple.

5L Box range

Dry Red ★★ Undemanding mix multitude varieties. **Blanc de Blanc** ★★ Easy-going & dry; chenin/colombard. **Stein** ★★ Off-dry version of Blanc de Blanc. — Panel

■ **Workhorse (Marks & Spencer)** see Ken Forrester Wines
■ **Wyma Vineyards** see Cape Hutton
■ **Y** see Yonder Hill

Yardstick Wines   NEW

Location: Cape Town ▪ WO: Western Cape ▪ Est/1stB 2009 ▪ Closed to public ▪ Owner(s) Peter Tempelhoff & Adam Mason ▪ Winemaker(s) Adam Mason ▪ 171cs own label 50% red 50% white ▪ adam@kleinconstantia.com, peter@collectionmcgrath.com ▪ www.yardstickwines.com ▪ **T +27 (0)82-924-3286 (Adam)/+27 (0)82-578-5320 (Peter)** ▪ F +27 (0)86-528-6463 (Adam)/+27 (0)86-216-7271 (Peter)

Klein Constantia winemaker Adam Mason and Cellars-Hohenort chef Peter Tempelhoff both have 'day jobs' but this collaboration is a way for them to 'have fun' while specifically making wines with food pairing in mind. 'I am continually amazed at how seldom the choice of wine does justice to a dish,' says Peter. Educating consumers that fresher, lighter wines are a better bet with food than showy blockbusters will happen via their website, blog and food demonstrations.

Yardstick range

★★★★ **Pinot Noir** As per house's spec, **10** is light & food-amenable in every way, with a really attractive spread of fruity & savoury flavours, ending dry. Friendly, with a touch of seriousness. Outeniqua vines.

Marvellous range

Kaboom! ✓ ★★★★ Well-named **09** Bordeaux red blend is quite explosive in the mouth but also spicy, savoury & fresh, & thus inherently food cordial. Hemel-en-Aarde & Elgin cab, merlot & cab franc. — Panel

Yonder Hill

Location: Somerset West ▪ Map: Helderberg ▪ WO: Stellenbosch/Western Cape ▪ Est 1989 ▪ 1stB 1993 ▪ Tasting & sales Mon-Fri 9-4 Sat (Oct-Mar) 10-2 ▪ Closed on pub hols ▪ Tour groups ▪ Gift shop ▪ Olives & olive oil tasting ▪ Owner(s) Naudé family ▪ Cellarmaster(s) Bennie Avenant (2008) ▪ Winemaker(s)/viticulturist(s) Bennie Avenant ▪ 14ha/10ha (cabs s/f, merlot, p verdot) ▪ 80t/10,000cs own label 95% red 5% white ▪ PO Box 914 Stellenbosch 7599 ▪ wines@yonderhill.co.za ▪ www.yonderhill.co.za ▪ S 34° 2' 22.5" E 018° 49' 40.2" ▪ **T +27 (0)21-855-1008** ▪ F +27 (0)21-855-1006

Ever-enthusiastic winemaker and viticulturist Bennie Avenant is resolutely replanting the lower Helderberg estate's vineyards a few at a time, and expects the first new blocks to come onstream this vintage. The labels have all had a facelift – gentle tweaking only – to bring them up to date, and he's fairly gushing about the new Nicola flagship red, in its innovative art-tissue wrapping (by a different artist each year, à la Château Mouton), set for launch as we went to press.

Yonder Hill range

★★★★☆ **Merlot** ✓ Statuesque, aristocratic bearing of 09 enhanced by opulent ripeness. Great concentration & complexity. Deep, dry, focussed black fruit in classic Bordeaux style. Routinely one of Stellenbosch's finest.

★★★★☆ **Inanda** Screwcapped since 08 (★★★★), Bordeaux-style red retained appeal last year with bright, accessible fruitiness. 07 was finely balanced & concentrated.

★★★★☆ **Estate** 08 Bordeaux-style blend was still in infancy last edition, but showed enticing herbaceous notes, ripe blackcurrant fruit. Real thoroughbred focus & agility.

Cabernet Sauvignon Await new vintage. **Shiraz-Merlot** ★★★★ Fruit-driven 73:27 blend, 04 still vibrant & cheerful mid-2010. Dark berries, hints of pepper & wild scrub.

Y range

Sauvignon Blanc ☺ 🍷 ★★★ Very youthful, crisp & youthfully bashful, 11 from Durbanville fruit should open up given time. Light, easy-going sipper.

Merlot 🍷 ★★★ Enticing juicy fruit on 09 in last guide continued tradition of easy-drinking value. **Shiraz** 🍷 ★★★ Loud & spicy 09 on review showed strong varietal character, leathery finish. WO W Cape for these. —GdB

▪ **Yvonne** see Almenkerk Wine Estate
▪ **Zalze** see Kleine Zalze Wines

Zandberg

Location: Somerset West ▪ Map: Helderberg ▪ WO: Stellenbosch ▪ 1stB 2001 ▪ Tasting & sales Mon-Sun 10-5 ▪ 96 Winery Road Restaurant (see Restaurants section) ▪ 4-star guesthouse & other amenities ▪ Owner(s) Chesterfield Group Holdings ▪ Winemaker(s) Anton & Pieter Bredell ▪ Viticulturist(s) Francois Hannekom ▪ 35ha (cab, merlot) ▪ PO Box 5337 Helderberg 7135 ▪ info@zandberg.co.za, wine@zandberg.co.za ▪ www.zandberg.co.za ▪ S 34° 1' 36.2" E 018° 48' 32.3" ▪ **T +27 (0)21-842-2945** ▪ F +27 (0)21-842-2085

'Our White Merlot has been a work in progress and continues to be very popular amoungst wine consumers - our Gauteng Distributor has requests for it every day' says Nick Ridley, marketing and operations chief. Exports to The Netherlands join established markets in Germany, Switzerland, Nigeria with exports to China on the rise.

Cabernet Sauvignon ✓ ★★★★ Ever-pleasant version; previewed 08 is mouthfilling, with sweet dark berry fruit, vanilla oak & lingering savoury aftertaste. **White Merlot** 🍷 ★★★ Preview back to form in 11, faintest pink hue, fresh & fun, spicy raspberry & cranberry flavours. Discontinued: **Dry Rosé.** —WB

Zanddrift Vineyards

Location/WO: Paarl ▪ Map: Paarl & Wellington ▪ Est 1995 ▪ 1stB 2006 ▪ Sales Mon-Fri 9-1 & 2-5 ▪ Tasting during restaurant hours ▪ Owner(s) Windsharp Trading 23 (Singapore) ▪ Winemaker(s)/vineyard manager(s) Christo Jacobs ▪ 48ha/6.6ha (cab, shiraz) ▪ PO Box 1302 Suider-Paarl 7624 ▪ zanddrift@telkomsa.net ▪ http://zanddrift.webs.com/ ▪ S 33° 45' 39.20" E 018° 59' 11.41" ▪ **T +27 (0)21-863-2076** ▪ F +27 (0)86-530-1892

It's all quiet at this Singapore-owned Paarl farm where the decision has been made, given the economic climate, to sell off the crop in bulk. Not that bottling under the own label isn't still on the agenda, it's simply the time frame that's shifted.

Chapel Cellar range

Cabernet Sauvignon ▤ ★★★ With supple tannins & chalky fruit, **07** last year slipped down easily despite 14.7% alc. **Shiraz** ▤ ★★★ Step up **07** previously had high-toned red fruit, zesty acidity. — CvZ

Zandfontein

Location: Napier ▪ Map: Southern Cape ▪ WO: Cape Agulhas/Western Cape ▪ Tasting & sales by appt ▪ Accommodation in two self-catering guesthouses ▪ Walking/hiking/fynbos trails ▪ Owner(s) Hennie & Annatjie Andrews ▪ Cellarmaster(s)/winemaker(s)/viticulturist(s) Hennie Andrews ▪ 800ha/6ha (shiraz, sauv) ▪ 3t sauv + bought in shiraz/±750cs own label 67% red 33% white ▪ PO Box 1080 Bredasdorp 7280 ▪ hennie@fijnboschfoods.co.za ▪ www.fijnboschfoods.co.za ▪ **T +27 (0)28-423-3468** ▪ F +27 (0)28-423-3468

You'll never want for wine on this guest farm near Napier, where 'retired' restaurateur and baker Hennie Andrews offers a sauvignon from home-grapes, and a shiraz from bought-in fruit until their own vines come on-stream. Nor get cold on chilly nights: wife Annatjie makes goose-down eiderdowns, duvets and quilts. A mixed-farming system includes olives and tobacco too.

Henry Shiraz ★★★ Now from Cape Agulhas grapes (previous from Wellington), previewed **10** a more modern take than most from this area: very ripe fruit, high but well-disguised alc (15%), berry compote & lashings oak. **Fijnbosch Sauvignon Blanc** ▤ ★★★ Lemongrass & herbaceous notes on early-picked **11** preview from Napier vines, crisp summer refresher. Vinified by Jean Daneel (Jean Daneel Wines). WO W Cape. — Panel

Zandvliet Wine Estate & Thoroughbred Stud

Location: Ashton ▪ Map/WO: Robertson ▪ Est 1867 ▪ 1stB 1975 ▪ Tasting & sales Mon-Fri 9–5 Sat 10–2 ▪ Closed Easter Fri/Sun, Dec 25/26 & Jan 1 ▪ Tour groups ▪ Private tastings presented by cellarmaster/winemaker in Zandvliet House by appt only - fee R55pp ▪ BYO picnic ▪ Owner(s) Paul & Dan de Wet ▪ Cellarmaster(s) Paul de Wet (1971) ▪ Winemaker(s) Ettienne Malan (Jul 2010) ▪ Viticulturist(s) Dan de Wet (1993) ▪ 830ha/148ha (cab, shiraz, chard, cbard, sauv) ▪ 1,134t/45,000cs own label 47% red 49% white 5% rosé + 2,000cs for clients ▪ Export brands: Enon, Cogmanskloof ▪ Ranges for clients: Cogmanskloof Cape Muscat, Rijckholt (Netherlands); Villa San Giovanni ▪ PO Box 36 Ashton 6715 ▪ info@zandvliet.co.za ▪ www.zandvliet.co.za ▪ S 33° 50'50.7" E 020° 2'13.7" ▪ **T +27 (0)23-615-1146** ▪ F +27 (0)23-615-1327

Established in 1867 and bottling under its own label since 1975, this 830ha Robertson Valley property has 148ha under vines and a famous thoroughbred stud besides. Joining cellarmaster and viticulturist Paul and Dan de Wet in July 2010, winemaker Ettienne Malan settled in time for the 2011 harvest, and most of the current Zandvliet whites and rosé bear his stamp. A large producer (47,000 cases per annum, split fairly evenly between red and white), Zandvliet also exports world-wide. According to Zandvliet managing director Judi Dyer, opening channels into China's growing wine market recently has been a fascinating business, with a five-year sales and distribution deal to show for it.

Zandvliet Estate range

★★★★ **Kalkveld Shiraz** New-French-oaked version. **07** (★★★★) drinks well: very ripe yet not overly sweet. As with perfumed **06**, oak is supportive, structural, adds savoury nuance; 15% alc tad warming. ★★★★ **Chardonnay** ✓ ▤ Lightly oaked offering; two vintages reviewed: **10** gets its breadth & generosity from fruit, not sugar. Limy **11** (★★★★) understated, less rich, but drinks as well as many dearer versions. ★★★★ **Kalkveld Chardonnay** NEW Restrained & savoury **10**, oak (100% new French) adds structure, weight & judicious seasoning; more earthy than sibling, better ageing potential, too. **Kalkveld 'Hill of Enon' Shiraz** Await new. **Shiraz** ★★★ Stalwart everyday shiraz, well-knit **08** is ready now.

Le Bistro range

Cabernet Sauvignon ▤ ★★ **09** appealing choc tones, slightly pruney fruit. **Chardonnay Unwooded** ▤ ★★ **11** smoky white peach & fresh acidity for uncomplex summer sipping. **Sauvignon Blanc** ▤ ★★ Departure from usual capsicum styling, **11** more oxidative. **Crème** ▤ ★★ Bone-dry mix colombard (80%) & sauvignon strangely quiet this year; faint creamy nut note on drink-soon **11**.

My Best Friend range

Shiraz Rosé ☺ 🍷 ★★★ Appealing just-baked butter biscuit & jam character on slightly sweet **11**.

Red 🍷 ★★ Strawberry compote, slightly sweet **09** easy everyday red. **Semi-Sweet** 🍷 ★★ Muted lemon & barley sugar notes on quaffing-style **11**. **White** 🍷 ★★ **11** straightforward, with food-inviting acidity. —Panel

■ **Zandwijk** *see* Kleine Draken
■ **Zantsi** *see* Darling Cellars
■ **Zaràfa** *see* Mountain River Wines
■ **Zebra Collection** *see* Rooiberg Winery
■ **Zee** *see* Anura Vineyards
■ **Zellerhof** *see* Huguenot Wine Farmers
■ **Zenith** *see* Kumala

Zevenwacht

Location/map/WO: Stellenbosch ▪ Est 1980 ▪ 1stB 1983 ▪ Tasting, sales & cellar tours Mon-Fri 8.30–5 Sat/Sun 9. 30–5 ▪ Fee R32 incl glass ▪ Closed Dec 25 ▪ Restaurant open daily (see Restaurants section) ▪ Picnics in summer ▪ Facilities for children ▪ Tour groups ▪ Gift shop ▪ Farm produce ▪ Conferences ▪ Weddings/banqueting ▪ Walking/ hiking & mountain biking trails ▪ 4x4 trail by appt ▪ Conservation area ▪ Mangwanani Spa ▪ 4-star Country Inn, vineyard cottages & self-catering chalet (see Accommodation section) ▪ Owner(s) Harold Johnson ▪ Cellarmaster(s) Jacques Viljoen (May 2005) ▪ Winemaker(s) Jacques Viljoen (May 2005), with Hagen Viljoen (Sep 2010) ▪ Viticulturist(s) Eduard van den Berg (Jan 2001) ▪ 473ha/150ha (cabs s/f, grenache, merlot, mourv, ptage, primitivo, shiraz, chard, chenin, gewürtz, Muscat de F, rouss, sauv, sem, viog) ▪ 657t/50,000cs own label 48% red 48% white 4% rosé & ±4,000cs for clients ▪ Brands for clients: Chevalier (Belgium), Indaba Hotel, Mangwanani Spa, Mooiberg (Belgium) ▪ BWI, IPW ▪ PO Box 387 Kuils River 7579 ▪ info@zevenwacht.co.za ▪ www.zevenwacht. co.za ▪ S 33° 55' 46.0" E 018° 43' 38.2" ▪ **T +27 (0)21-903-5123** ▪ F +27 (0)21-903-3373

Zevenwacht has such an extended tourism-related offering including a country inn, restaurant, cheesery, banqueting and conferencing facilities, spa as well as mountain bike and hiking trails that it's easy to overlook the wine. That would be unfortunate as this property is starting to make some smart stuff after a bit of a dip in quality in the late 1990s. Winemaker Jacques Viljoen began here as assistant to Karl Lambour (now of Constantia Glen) in 2002 and took full charge of the cellar in 2005. A recent innovation is the use of aerial photography, both normal and infra-red , to inform when to harvest.

Flagship range

Cabernet Sauvignon ★★★ **08** still selling mid-2011. Red fruit, bright acidity & well-judged oak, pleasingly dry finish. **Merlot** ★★★★ Delicate **08** has red & black fruit, 'oystershell' on the nose, medium body & smooth texture before a saline finish. **Syrah** ★★★★ Unpretentious **08** shows red & black fruit, hint of pepper; medium body with fresh acidity, well-judged oak. **Chenin Blanc** 🍷 📷 ★★★ **10** yellow fruit, clean & fresh, well balanced if not as complex as **09** (★★★★). **Sauvignon Blanc** ✓ 🍷 📷 ★★★★ Deftly handled **11** shows juicy lime fruit, hint of paprika, tangy acidity; well balanced & elegant, includes 2% barrel-fermented portion for extra palate weight. Improves on overtly herbaceous **09** (★★★☆). **10** untasted. **Semillon Straw Wine** 🍷 📷 ★★★ **10** from air-dried grapes. Very rich & concentrated but lacking verve when last tasted.

Z-Collection

★★★★ **CMC** Classically styled **08** Bordeaux red from 55% cab, 40% merlot, 5% cab franc, year in French oak, 50% new. Cassis, some 'oystershell' & vanilla; good concentration, fresh acidity, relatively soft tannins.

★★★★ **SMVG 08** (★★★★) 50% shiraz, 44% mourvèdre, rest viognier, grenache. Red & fruit, some spice, but generally closed, tight. Full bodied, lacks a little freshness, finishes very dry. Not as well delineated as **07**.

★★★★ **Gewürztraminer** 🍷 📷 Poised **11** (★★★★★) subtle lime & pot-pourri; juicy fruit, some spice, thick but not unctuous texture thanks partly to 5 months in 2nd fill 500L barrels, gentle but sufficient acidity. Also-reviewed **10** almost unbearably rich & heady with plenty of Turkish Delight character.

Limited Release range

★★★★ **Primitivo** Variety also known as zinfandel. Heady but delicious **09** (★★★★☆) is very aromatic with red & black fruit, herbs & spice. Rich & full but zesty acidity lends balance. Not quite as complete as **08**.

★★★★ **360° Sauvignon Blanc** 🍷 📷 Extravagant **10** shows asparagus, granadilla & gunpowder aromas; rich & ripe with tangy acidity, lacks focus of stellar **09** (★★★★★).

The Tin Mine Collection

★★★★ **White** 🍷 🌿 Elegant **10** (★★★★★) 46% chardonnay, 40% viognier, 14% chenin (**09** also included smidgen roussanne). Flavours of yellow peach, apricot & subtle spice; medium bodied with moderate acidity; understated but complex, you'll be constantly drawn back to the glass.

Red ✓ 🍷 ★★★★ Winning **09** is 72% shiraz but includes grenache, mourvèdre, primitivo. Red fruit, fynbos on nose; medium bodied with good flavour concentration, fresh acidity and fine, spicy tannins. Much better executed, more distinctive than **08** (★★★). Bit of a bargain, too.

Lifestyle range NEW

Pinotage 🍷 ★★ **09** sweet red fruit, pronounced coffee & chocolate notes. **Zevenrood** 🍷 ★★★ Merlot-driven **08** is fruity but not unduly sweet, medium bodied, balanced. **Rosé** 🍷 🌿 ★★★ From merlot, **11** is juicy & fresh, carries generous 12g/l sugar well. **Zevenblanc** 🍷 🌿 ★★ Sauvignon-led **11** is lean, neutral, acidic. **Bouquet Blanc** 🍷 🌿 ★★★ Viognier-led off-dry **11** has floral aromas, before juicy & flavourful palate; relatively thick textured, broad in structure. — CE

Zidela Wines

Location: Stellenbosch ▪ WO: Western Cape ▪ Est 2001 ▪ 1stB 2002 ▪ Closed to public ▪ Owner(s) Danie Kritzinger, Herman Nell & Jaco Kritzinger ▪ 70% red 25% white 5% rosé ▪ 5,000,000 litres for clients ▪ PO Box 3021 Matieland 7602 ▪ info@zidelawines.co.za ▪ www.zidelawines.co.za ▪ **T +27 (0)21-880-2936** ▪ F +27 (0)21-880-2937

The English poet and writer John Masefield's quote 'Oh some are fond of Spanish wine, and some are fond of French' on Zidela's website would be altered to continue 'but even more of South African' if the Stellenbosch negociant house has its way. With a new brand, Oranjeland, specifically for the Dutch market and inroads into Africa, Zidela clearly is intent on winning converts wherever it can.

Zidela Wines range

Cabernet Sauvignon ☺ ★★★ **10** appealing berry-toned sipper. Like all reds, with gentle tanninc nip thanks to brief sojourn oak.

Merlot ★★ Leafy **10** has some mulberry whiffs, good grip. **Pinotage** ★★ Still selling, not revisited **08** zippy & fruit-filled. **Shiraz** ★★★ No florals from viognier this edition; just smoke & leather, **09** dash sugar for crowd appeal. **Cabernet Sauvignon-Merlot-Petit Verdot** ★★★ **07** still available, easy red-fruit appeal should be enjoyed soon. **Chenin Blanc** 🍷 🌿 ★★ **11** thatch & floral quick-quaff with discernible sweetness. **Bouquet Blanc** NEW 🌿 ★★ **11** honest, softly sweet & grapey sipper from muscat ottonel. **Sauvignon Blanc** ★★ Last year we noted slimmer-friendly lowish alc but also waist-expanding 15g/l sugar on **10**.

Oranjeland range NEW

Shiraz Merlot 🍷 🌿 ★★ **10** packed with plums & mulberry, slightly malty but lots of unoaked appeal. **Rosé** 🍷 ★ Semi-sweet **11** has grassy aroma, no expected berry notes. **Chenin Blanc** 🍷 ★★ **11** uncomplicated, peachy anytime sipper with modest 12.5% alc. WO W Cape for all ranges.

Suikerbosch range

Reserve Shiraz ★★★ Last edition, **08** offered juicy fruit centre, taut tannin structure & unusual orange rind highlight. **Shiraz-Merlot** 🍷 ★★ **09** red berried & tad foursquare. Not revisited. **Rosé** 🍷 🌿 ★★ **11** authentic coral hue but lacks true rosé aromas/flavours. **Reserve Chardonnay** ★★★ Previously tasted **10** creamy & toasty courtesy brief visit French barrels, tangy lemon finish. **Chenin Blanc** 🍷 ★★ **11**'s pineapple & lemon fruit promises plenty uncomplicated summertime fun. **Golden Muscat** NEW 🍷 🌿 ★★ Ginger beer highlights on Natural Sweet **11** from muscat d'Alexandrie. Discontinued: **Golden Nectar**. — CvZ

Zoetendal Wines

Location/WO: Elim ▪ Map: Southern Cape ▪ Est 2002 ▪ 1stB 2004 ▪ Tasting, sales & cellar tours Mon-Fri 9–5; Sat 9–1 Sep-Apr & by appt May-Aug ▪ Closed Easter Fri/Sun, Dec 25 & Jan 1 ▪ Conservation area ▪ Draaihoek self-catering guesthouse ▪ Owner(s) Johan & Elizan de Kock ▪ Cellarmaster(s)/winemaker(s)/viticulturist(s) Johan de Kock ▪ 790ha/8.5ha (shiraz, sauv) ▪ 39t/2,000cs own label 15% red 85% white ▪ Other export brand: Last Chance ▪ BWI, IPW ▪ PO Box 22 Elim 7284 ▪ info@zoetendalwines.co.za ▪ www.zoetendalwines.co.za ▪ S 34° 36'1.0" E 019° 47' 20.9" ▪ **T +27 (0)28-482-1717** ▪ F +27 (0)28-482-1720

Elim-based sheep, grain and wine farmer Johan de Kock continues to nurture his patch of vines on the banks of the Nuwejaars River, including shiraz now registered as a single-vineyard. The small range will soon sport a new-look label, while retaining the 'Zoetendal' pincushion. Aptly so, as he is a prime mover behind the Nuwejaars Wetland Special Management Area, a government-approved (finally!), groundbreaking private initiative among 20-plus local landowners to develop a sustainable ecology in harmony with commercially viable farming.

★★★★ Milè Still-selling **08** cab-led blend with merlot, shiraz, petit verdot. Last edition was harmonious, elegant, worth seeking out.

★★★★ Sauvignon Blanc 🗒 🎐 **10** (★★★) needs time in glass to reveal cut-grass charm. Lighter (12. 5%), shade less flavoursome than vibrant **09**. Might reveal more with time in bottle.

Shiraz ★★★★ Sweet fruit, hint char on firm **09**. Commendably dry & savoury, holds head high in area recognised for the variety, just needs year/2 to settle & possibly gain stature of **08** (★★★★). — Panel

■ **Zondernaam** see Tokara

Zonnebloem

WO: Stellenbosch/Western Cape/Coastal ▪ Est 1893 ▪ Wine sales at Die Bergkelder Wine Centre ▪ Owner(s) Distell ▪ Cellarmaster(s) Deon Boshoff (Feb 2010) ▪ Winemaker(s) Bonny van Niekerk (reds, Oct 2007) & Elize Coetzee (whites, Jun 2010), with Gerhard Viljoen (reds, Aug 2007), Melissa Williams (reds, Dec 2009), Bradley van Niekerk (whites) & Natasha Williams (whites, Aug 2008) ▪ Viticulturist(s) Annelie Viljoen (Jun 2008) ▪ (cab, merlot, shiraz, chard, sauv, sem) ▪ 9,000t/±220,000cs own label 59% red 41% white ▪ ISO 9002, Fairtrade ▪ PO Box 184 Stellenbosch 7599 ▪ info@zonnebloem.co.za ▪ www.zonnebloem.co.za ▪ **T +27 (0)21-809-7000** ▪ F +27 (0)21-886-4879

They make around a quarter of a million cases of mostly modest, easygoing wine under this label in Distell's Adam Tas facility in Stellenbosch. A 'new label design for the range', and the possibility of a special Zonnebloem tasting room, might perhaps signal a revived ambition for what was a great name in Cape wine.

Limited Editions

Sauvignon Blanc 🎐 **★★★ 10** less complex than last-tasted **09** (★★★★), but its green notes have intensity & there's a nice crisp tail. WO Coastal. All others in range sold out, awaiting next release.

Zonnebloem range

★★★★ Cabernet Sauvignon Classically styled **09** (★★★★) first tasted since '07, has typical cab character plus a green hint. Lightly rustic, the finish fading fast.

Merlot ★★★ Podgy **09** tasted last year showed noticeable oaky tones. **Pinotage ★★★★ 09** revels in dark fruit, Asian spice with coffee overtones; not intense, but fine tannins help make it a good food wine. **Shiraz** 🎐 **★★★★** Rich, dark **10** packed with ripe, spicy fruit dusted with black pepper. Nice weight, but flavours don't linger. Lower acidity & alcohol on **09** add to its attractiveness. **Lauréat ★★★★ 09** adds malbec & petit verdot to **08**'s cab & merlot. Robust, with oak showing alongside the blackcurrant notes, but simple, with a finish marked by acidity. **Shiraz-Mourvèdre-Viognier ★★★★** Just 15% of latter grapes in **09**. Ripe, with attractive aromas & flavours, moderate weight & well integrated oak. **Chardonnay** 🗒 🎐 **★★★** Lightly oaked **10** with moderate alcohol adding to its easy-drinking appeal. WO W Cape. **Sauvignon Blanc** 🗒 🎐 **★★★ 11** in established mode: grassy, fresh & easy-going. WO W Cape. **Viognier ★★★** Last tasted was light-footed, apricotty **09**. **Blanc de Blanc** 🗒 🎐 **★★★** Reliably light-hearted, crisp **11** from chenin & sauvignon. WO W Cape. — JPf

■ **Zonneweelde** see Slanghoek Winery

Zorgvliet Wines

Location/map: Stellenbosch ▪ WO: Banghoek ▪ Est/1stB 2000 ▪ Tasting & sales Mon-Fri 9–5 Sat/Sun 10–5 pub hols 10–4 ▪ Closed Easter Fri & Dec 25 ▪ Fee R20pp, waived on purchase ▪ Cellar tours by appt ▪ Café Dijon @ Zorgvliet ▪ Zorgvliet Picnic Sep-Apr ▪ Facilities for children ▪ Tour groups ▪ Gifts ▪ Conferences ▪ Walks/hikes ▪ Zorgvliet Country Hotel (12 rooms) ▪ Owner(s) Van der Merwe family ▪ Winemaker(s) Neil Moorhouse (Jan 2003) ▪ Viticulturist(s) Hannes Jansen van Vuuren (Zorgvliet Farm) & Rudolf Jansen van Vuuren (Summer Court Farm) ▪ 58ha/24ha (cabs s/f, merlot, p verdot, pinot, shiraz, tannat, chard, chenin, sauv, sem, viog) ▪ 200t/10,000cs own label 50% red 40% white 7% rosé 3% MCC + 200t for clients ▪ PO Box 1595 Stellenbosch 7599 ▪ winecellar@

zorgvliet.com ▪ www.zorgvlietwines.com ▪ S 33° 54′41.7″ E 018° 56′32.0″ ▪ **T +27 (0)21-885-1399** ▪ F +27 (0)21-885-1318

Ebullient winemaker at self-made businessman Mac van der Merwe's winery, Neil Moorhouse was kept busy by many things this year, from switching closures to Stelvin Lux (from hi-teck WAK) screwcaps, the introduction of his own bottling line – giving total control from vineyard to ready-for-market cases – to the relocation of the tasting centre to the farm's original 1692 manor house and the opening of the Zorgvliet Country Hotel and Café Dijon @ Zorgvliet. Wines continue to be promoted to the flagship range as the vineyards mature: the MCC and Cabernet Franc joined the Tannat for this edition.

Zorgvliet range

★★★★ **Cabernet Sauvignon** ✓ Seriously styled mint-choc **08** has dabs cab franc & merlot, & plenty fruit to stay the distance, while assertive tannins from oaking & skins soften & integrate.

★★★★ **Cabernet Franc** ✓ ▣ Sample **09** shows variety's typically herbal aromas which belie succulent red fruit flavours underpinned by structured tannins & fine acid thread ensuring elegance. **08** was under Silver Myn.

★★★★ **Petit Verdot** Last tasted was dark-coloured **07** with savouriness added to fruit flavours.

★★★★☆ **Richelle** Flagship **07** cab-led blend all Bordeaux varieties, plus splash tannat. Youthfully opaque. Needs time in bottle but ample rich fruit, firm tannin & vibrant acidity superbly balanced & integrated. **06** (★★★★) less complex.

★★★★☆ **Five-Thirty-Five** ▣ From 15 rows of a high-altitude (535m) single vineyard. **10** sauvignon filled just 2 500L barrels. Non-interventionist approach from natural fermentation through to bottling. Intriguing, complex nuttiness, impressive depth & long, pithy finish (from extended skin contact) ensure satisfaction.

★★★★ **Sauvignon Blanc** ▣ Full-flavoured sample **11** with dash semillon exhibits both green & tropical flavour spectrums. Rich fruit gathered by fine acid & mineral backbone. Always needs time to show best.

★★★★ **Simoné** ▣ Enticingly smoky **10** (★★★★★) semillon, sauvignon blend in convincing style. Even more impressive on **09**, with super-long, savoury acidity & precise minerality to finish.

Tannat ▣ ★★★★ **08** was bold & assertive, earthy fruit underpinned by oak; needed time to soften, as did **07** (★★★★), when tasted last year. **Blanc de Blancs** ★★★★ Clean, crisp **08** chardonnay MCC is biscuity, bone dry & focused, with pleasurable elegance & creaminess. Replaces Silver Myn MCC noted last year (slightly different version of this).

Silver Myn range

★★★★ **Argentum** ▣ Merlot-led Bordeaux quartet **08** ex-barrel, invitingly juicy & harmoniously integrated. Dense plummy richness checked by grippy tannins & firm acidity.

Cabernet Sauvignon ▣ ★★★★ Leafy herbal edge to **08**'s supple blackcurrant fruit last year; firm acidity lent further elegance to classic style. **Merlot** NEW ★★★ Considerable tannins challenge baked plum fruit flavours in seriously structured **09**, giving overly stern finish. **Cabernet Franc Rosé** ★★★ Bone-dry **11** sample delivers plenty fruit but finishes hard. **Sauvignon Blanc** ▣ ★★★★ Mouthwatering **11** ex-tank has dash semillon for breadth & texture; ripeness balanced by zesty acidity & mineral appeal. — IM

On the nose!

Intimidated or just uninitiated?
Help is now in the palm of your hand.
Navigate any South African wine moment
with Platter's iPhone® App.

Search Platter's vintages & producers. Save favorites and
share discoveries. See for yourself - the GPS enabled map will
lead you to producers and wine experiences that make South
Africa one of the 8 Great Wine Capitals of the World.
visit us at www.wine-oh.info